DATE DUE

			PRINTED IN U.S.A.

Literature Criticism from 1400 to 1800

Guide to Gale Literary Criticism Series

For criticism on	Consult these Gale series
Authors now living or who died after December 31, 1959	*CONTEMPORARY LITERARY CRITICISM (CLC)*
Authors who died between 1900 and 1959	*TWENTIETH-CENTURY LITERARY CRITICISM (TCLC)*
Authors who died between 1800 and 1899	*NINETEENTH-CENTURY LITERATURE CRITICISM (NCLC)*
Authors who died between 1400 and 1799	*LITERATURE CRITICISM FROM 1400 TO 1800 (LC)* *SHAKESPEAREAN CRITICISM (SC)*
Authors who died before 1400	*CLASSICAL AND MEDIEVAL LITERATURE CRITICISM (CMLC)*
Black writers of the past two hundred years	*BLACK LITERATURE CRITICISM (BLC)*
Authors of books for children and young adults	*CHILDREN'S LITERATURE REVIEW (CLR)*
Dramatists	*DRAMA CRITICISM (DC)*
Hispanic writers of the late nineteenth and twentieth centuries	*HISPANIC LITERATURE CRITICISM (HLC)*
Native North American writers and orators of the eighteenth, nineteenth, and twentieth centuries	*NATIVE NORTH AMERICAN LITERATURE (NNAL)*
Poets	*POETRY CRITICISM (PC)*
Short story writers	*SHORT STORY CRITICISM (SSC)*
Major authors from the Renaissance to the present	*WORLD LITERATURE CRITICISM, 1500 TO THE PRESENT (WLC)*

ISSN 0740-2880

Volume 42

Literature Criticism from 1400 to 1800

Critical Discussion of the Works
of Fifteenth-, Sixteenth-, Seventeenth-, and
Eighteenth-Century Novelists, Poets, Playwrights,
Philosophers, and Other Creative Writers

Jelena O. Krstović, Editor

GALE

DETROIT · LONDON

STAFF

Jelena O. Krstović, *Editor*

Dana Barnes, Marie Lazzari, Daniel G. Marowski, *Contributing Editors*
Michelle Lee, Suzanne Dewsbury, *Associate Editors*
Ira Mark Milne, *Assistant Editor*
Aarti Stephens, *Managing Editor*

Susan M. Trosky, *Permissions Manager*
Kimberly F. Smilay, *Permissions Specialist*
Sarah Chesney, Steve Cusack, Kelly A. Quinn, *Permissions Associates*

Victoria B. Cariappa, *Research Manager*
Julia C. Daniel, Tamara C. Nott, Tracie A. Richardson, Cheryl L. Warnock, *Research Associates*

Mary Beth Trimper, *Production Director*
Deborah Milliken, *Production Assistant*

Pamela A. Reed, *Photography Coordinator*
Randy Bassett, *Image Database Supervisor*
Mike Logusz, Robert Duncan, *Imaging Specialists*

Library of Congress Catalog Card Number 94-29718
ISBN 0-7876-2411-X
ISSN 0740-2880
Printed in the United States of America

10 9 8 7 6 5 4 3 2 1

Contents

Preface vii

Acknowledgments xi

The Rise of the English Novel

Preface

*L*iterature Criticism from 1400 to 1800 (LC) presents critical discussion of world authors of the fifteenth through eighteenth centuries. The literature of this period reflects a turbulent time of radical change that saw the rise of modern European drama, the birth of the novel and personal essay forms, the emergence of newspapers and periodicals, and major achievements in poetry and philosophy. Many of these historical forces continue to influence modern art and society. *LC*, therefore, provides valuable insight into the art, life, thought, and cultural transformations that took place during these centuries.

Scope of the Series

LC provides an introduction to the great poets, dramatists, novelists, essayists, and philosophers of the fifteenth through eighteenth centuries, and to the most significant interpretations of these authors' works. Because criticism of this literature spans nearly six hundred years, an overwhelming amount of scholarship confronts the student. *LC* organizes this material into volumes addressing specific historical and cultural topics, for example, "Literature of the Spanish Golden Age," or "Literature and the New World." Every attempt is made to reprint the most noteworthy, relevant, and educationally valuable essays available.

Readers should note that there is a separate Gale reference series devoted exclusively to Shakespearean studies. Although belonging properly to the period covered in *LC,* William Shakespeare has inspired such a tremendous and ever-growing corpus of secondary material that the editors have deemed it best to give his works extensive coverage in a separate series, *Shakespearean Criticism.*

Each author entry in *LC* presents a survey of critical response to a topic or an author's oeuvre. Early criticism is offered to indicate initial responses, later selections document any rise or decline in literary reputations, and retrospective analyses provide students with modern views. The size of each author entry is a relative reflection of the scope of criticism available in English. Every attempt has been made to identify and include the seminal essays on each author's work and to include recent commentary providing modern perspectives.

The need for *LC* among students and teachers of literature and history was suggested by the proven usefulness of Gale's *Contemporary Literary Criticism (CLC), Twentieth-Century Literary Criticism (TCLC),* and *Nineteenth-Century Literature Criticism (NCLC),* which excerpt criticism of works by nineteenth- and twentieth-century authors. There is no duplication of critical material in any of these literary criticism series. Major authors may appear more than once in one or more of the series because of the great quantity of critical material available and because of their relevance to a variety of thematic topics.

Thematic Approach

Beginning with Volume 12, the authors in each volume of *LC* are organized around such themes as specific literary or philosophical movements, writings surrounding important political and historical events, the philosophy and art associated with eras of cultural transformation, and the literature of specific social or ethnic groups. Each volume contains a topic entry providing a historical and literary overview, and several author entries which examine major representatives of the featured period.

Organization of the Book

Each entry consists of the following elements: author or thematic heading, introduction, list of principal works, annotated works of criticism (each preceded by a bibliographical citation), and a bibliography of further reading. Also, most author entries contain author portraits and other illustrations.

- The **Author Heading** consists of the author's name (the most commonly used form), followed by birth and death dates. (If an author wrote consistently under a pseudonym, the pseudonym is used in the author heading, with the real name given in parentheses on the first line of the biographical and critical introduction.) Also located here are any name variations under which an author wrote, including transliterated forms for authors whose native languages use nonroman alphabets. Uncertain birth or death dates are indicated by question marks. Topic entries are preceded by a **Thematic Heading,** which simply states the subject of the entry.

- The **Biographical and Critical Introduction** contains background information that concisely introduces the reader to the author or topic.

- Most *LC* author entries include **Portraits** of the author. Many entries also contain illustrations of materials pertinent to an author's career, including author holographs, title pages, letters, or representations of important people, places, and events in an author's life.

- The **List of Principal Works** is ordered chronologically, by date of first book publication, identifying the genre of each work. In the case of foreign authors whose works have been translated into English, the title and date (if available) of the first English-language edition are given in brackets following the foreign-language listing. Unless otherwise indicated, dramas are dated by first performance, not first publication.

- **Criticism** is arranged chronologically in each author entry to provide a useful perspective on changes in critical evaluation over time. For the purpose of easy identification, the critic's name and the date of first composition or publication of the critical work are given at the beginning of each piece of criticism. Unsigned criticism is preceded by the title of the source in which it appeared. All titles by the author featured in the critical entry are printed in boldface type. Publication information (such as publisher names and book prices) and some parenthetical numerical references (such as footnotes or page and line references to specific editions of works) have been occasionally deleted to provide smoother reading of the text. Footnotes that appear with previously published pieces of criticism are reprinted at the end of each essay or excerpt. In the case of excerpted criticism, only those footnotes that pertain to the excerpted text are included.

- Critical essays are prefaced by **Annotations** as an additional aid to students using *LC.* These explanatory notes provide information such as the importance of a work of criticism, the commentator's individual approach to literary criticism, and a brief summary of the reprinted essay. In some cases, these notes cross-reference the work of critics within the entry who agree or disagree with each other.

- A complete **Bibliographical Citation** of the original essay or book precedes each piece of criticism.

- An annotated bibliography of **Further Reading** appears at the end of each entry and suggests resources for additional study. In some cases, significant essays for which the editors could not obtain reprint rights are included here.

Cumulative Indexes

Each volume of *LC* includes a cumulative **Author Index** listing all the authors that have appeared in the following sources published by Gale: *Contemporary Literary Criticism, Twentieth-Century Literary Criticism, Nineteenth-Century Literature Criticism, Literature Criticism from 1400 to 1800,* and *Classical and Medieval Literature Criticism,* along with cross-references to the Gale series *Short Story Criticism, Poetry Criticism, Children's Literature Review, Authors in the News, Contemporary Authors, Contemporary Authors Autobiography Series, Contemporary Authors Bibliographical Series, Dictionary of Literary Biography, Concise Dictionary of Literary Biography, Something about the Author, Something about the Author Autobiography Series,* and *Yesterday's Authors of Books for Children.* Readers will welcome this cumulative author index as a useful tool for locating an author within the various series. The index, which includes authors' birth and death dates, is particularly valuable for those authors who are identified with a certain period but whose death dates cause them to be placed in another, or for those authors whose careers span two periods. For example, F. Scott Fitzgerald is found in *TCLC,* yet a writer often associated with him, Ernest Hemingway, is found in *CLC.*

Beginning with Volume 12, *LC* includes a cumulative **Topic Index** that lists all literary themes and topics treated in *LC, NCLC, TCLC,* and the *CLC* Yearbook. Each volume of *LC* also includes a cumulative **Nationality Index** in which authors' names are arranged alphabetically under their respective nationalities and followed by the numbers of the volumes in which they appear.

Each volume of *LC* also includes a cumulative **Title Index,** an alphabetical listing of all literary works discussed in the series. Each title listing includes the corresponding volume and page numbers where criticism may be located. Foreign-language titles that have been translated followed by the tiles of the translation—for example, *El ingenioso hidalgo Don Quixote de la Mancha (Don Quixote).* Page numbers following these translated titles refer to all pages on which any form of the titles, either foreign-language or translated, appear. Titles of novels, dramas, nonfiction books, and poetry, short story, or essay collections are printed in italics, while individual poems, short stories, and essays are printed in roman type within quotation marks.

A Note to the Reader

When writing papers, students who quote directly from any volume in the Literary Criticism Series may use the following general format to footnote reprinted criticism. The first example pertains to material drawn from periodicals, the second to material reprinted from books.

> T. S. Eliot, "John Donne," *The Nation and the Athenaeum,* 33 (9 June 1923), 321-32; excerpted and reprinted in *Literature Criticism from 1400 to 1800,* Vol. 10, ed. James E. Person, Jr. (Detroit: Gale Research, 1989), pp. 28-9.

> Clara G. Stillman, *Samuel Butler: A Mid-Victorian Modern* (Viking Press, 1932); excerpted and reprinted in *Twentieth-Century Literary Criticism,* Vol. 33, ed. Paula Kepos (Detroit: Gale Research, 1989), pp. 43-5.

Suggestions Are Welcome

Since the series began, features have been added to *LC* in response to various suggestions, including a nationality index, a Literary Criticism Series topic index, and thematic organization of entries.

Readers who wish to suggest new features, themes or authors to appear in future volumes, or who have other suggestions or comments are cordially invited to write to the editor (fax: 313 961-6599).

Acknowledgments

The editors wish to thank the copyright holders of the excerpted criticism included in this volume and the permissions managers of many book and magazine publishing companies for assisting us in securing reproduction rights. We are also grateful to the staffs of the Detroit Public Library, the Library of Congress, the University of Detroit Mercy Library, Wayne State University Purdy/Kresge Library Complex, and the University of Michigan Libraries for making their resources available to us. Following is a list of the copyright holders who have granted us permission to reproduce material in this volume of *LC*. Every effort has been made to trace copyright, but if omissions have been made, please let us know.

COPYRIGHTED MATERIAL IN *LC*, VOLUME 42, WAS REPRODUCED FROM THE FOLLOWING PERIODICALS:

Bulletin of the New York Public Library, v. 74, January-December, 1970. Reproduced by permission.—*Eighteenth-Century Fiction*, v. 7, April, 1995. Reproduced by permission.—*Eighteenth-Century Studies*, v. 23, Summer, 1990. Copyright © 1990. Reproduced by permission of The Johns Hopkins University Press.—*ELH*, v. 61, Fall, 1994. Copyright © 1994. Reproduced by permission of The Johns Hopkins University Press.—*Genre*, v. X, Winter, 1977 for "Deserts, Ruins and Troubled Waters: Female Dreams in Fiction and the Development of the Gothic Novel" by Margaret Anne Doody. Reproduced by permission of the publisher and the author.—*Journal of English and Germanic Philology*, v. 91, April, 1992. Reproduced by permission.—*Journal of the History of Ideas*, v. XV, April, 1954. © 1954. Reproduced by permission of The Johns Hopkins University Press. —*Literature and Psychology*, v. XXXII, 1986. Copyright © Editor 1986. Reproduced by permission.—*Nineteenth-Century Fiction*, v. 38, March, 1984. Copyright © 1984 by The Regents of the University of California. Reproduced by permission —*PMLA*, v. 96, May, 1981. Reproduced by permission.—*Studies in Eighteenth Century Culture*, v. 19, 1989. Copyright © 1989. Reproduced by permission of The Johns Hopkins University Press.—*Studies in the Novel*, v. XI, Spring, 1979; v. 20, Spring, 1988; v. 19, Fall, 1987. Copyright © 1979, 1987, 1988 by North Texas State University. All reproduced by permission.—*The Eighteenth Century: Theory and Interpretation*, v. 35, Summer, 1994 for "The Unaccountable Wife and Other Tales of Female Desire in Jane Barker's 'A Patch-Work Screen for the Ladies'" by Kathryn R. King. Reproduced by permission of the author.—*The Southern Review*, Louisiana State University, v. 32, Winter, 1996, for "The Brainwashing of Lemuel Gulliver" by Denis Donoghue. Copyright © 1996 by Denis Donoghue. Reproduced by permission of Georges Borchardt for the author.—*University of Toronto Quarterly*, v. 53, Winter 1983/84 for "'Trompe l'Oeil': Gulliver and the Distortions of the Observing Eye" by David Oakleaf. Reproduced by permission of the University of Toronto Press, Inc., and the author.

COPYRIGHTED MATERIAL IN *LC*, VOLUME 42, WAS REPRODUCED FROM THE FOLLOWING BOOKS:

Beasley, Jerry C. From *Novels of the 1740s*. University of Georgia Press, 1982. Copyright © 1982 by the University of Georgia Press. All rights reserved. Reproduced by permission.—Birdsall, Virginia Ogden. From *Defoe's Perpetual Seekers: A Study of Major Fiction*. Bucknell University Press, 1985. Copyright © 1985 by Associated University Presses, Inc. Reproduced by permission.—Boardman, Michael M. From *Defoe and the Uses of Narrative*. Rutgers University Press, 1983. Copyright © 1983 by Rutgers, the State University of New Jersey. All rights reserved. Reproduced by permission of the author.—Bosse, Malcolm J. From an introduction to *Secret Memoirs from the New Atlantis* by Mary de la Rivière Manley. Garland Publishing, Inc., 1972. Reproduced by permission.—Bosse, Malcolm J. From an introduction to *The Adventures of Revella* by Mary de la Rivière Manley. Garland Publishing, Inc., 1972. Reproduced by permission.—Brown, Homer Obed. From *Institutions of the English Novel: From Defoe to Scott*.

The Rise of the English Novel

INTRODUCTION

The dominant genre in world literature, the novel is actually a relatively young form of imaginative writing. Only about 250 years old in England—and embattled from the start—its rise to preeminence has been striking. After sparse beginnings in seventeenth-century England, novels grew exponentially in production by the eighteenth century and in the nineteenth century became the primary form of popular entertainment.

Elizabethan literature provides a starting point for identifying prototypes of the novel in England. Although not widespread, works of prose fiction were not uncommon duirng this period. Possibly the best known was Sir Philip Sidney's *Arcadia,* a romance published posthumously in 1590. The novel also owes a debt to Elizabethan drama, which was the leading form of popular entertainment in the age of Shakespeare. The first professional novelist—that is, the first person to earn a living from publishing novels—was probably the dramatist Aphra Behn. Her 1688 *Oronooko, or The Royal Slave* typified the early English novel: it features a sensationalistic plot that borrowed freely from continental literature, especially from the imported French romance.Concurrent with Behn's career was that of another important early English novelist: John Bunyan. This religious author's *Pilgrim's Progress,* first published in 1678, became one of the books found in nearly every English household.

In the second half of the seventeenthcentury, the novel genre developed many of the traits that characterize it in modern form. Rejecting the sensationalism of Behn and other early popular novelists, novelists built on the realism of Bunyan's work. Three of the foremost novelists of this era are Daniel Defoe, Henry Fielding, and Samuel Richardson. Defoe's name, more than that of any other English writer, is credited with the emergence of the "true" English novel by virtue of the 1719 publication of *The Adventures of Robinson Crusoe.* In the work of these three writers, the realism and drama of individual consciousness that we most associate with the novel took precedence over external drama and other motifs of continental romance. Contemporary critics approved of these elements as supposedly native to England in other genres, especially in history, biography, and religious prose works.

A number of profound social and economic changes affecting British culture from the Renaissance through the eighteenth century brought the novel quickly into popular prominence.The broadest of these were probably the advances in the technology of printing in the sixteenth and seventeenth centuries which made written texts—once the province of the elite—available to a growing population of readers. Concurrent changes in modes of distribution and in literacy rates brought ever increasing numbers of books and pamphlets to populations traditionally excluded from all but the most rudimentary education, especially working-class men and women of all classes. As the circulation of printed material transformed, so did its economics, shifting away from the patronage system characteristic of the Renaissance, during which a nation's nobility supported authors whose works reinforced the values of the ruling classes. As the patronage system broke down through the seventeenth and eighteenth centuries, authors became free agents in the literary marketplace, dependent on popular sales for their success and sustenance, and thus reflecting more and more the values of a predominantly middle-class readership. The demand for reading material allowed a greatly expanded pool of writers to make a living from largely ephemeral poetry and fiction.

These monumental changes in how literature was produced and consumed sent shockwaves of alarm through more conservative sectors of English culture at the beginning of the eighteenth century. A largely upper-class male contingent, reluctant to see any change in the literary status quo, mounted an aggressive "anti-novel campaign." Attacks on the new genre tended to identify it with its roots in French romance, derided as a sensationalistic import antithetical to English values. The early targets of these attacks were those writers, including Behn, Eliza Haywood, and Delarivier Manley, who had produced original English prose "romances" based on the conventions of the French style. At the same time, however, more women in particular were writing novels that made a display of decorum and piety, often reacting to detractors who charged that sensationalistic tales of adventure and sexual endangerment had the potential to corrupt adult female readers and the youth of both sexes. The outcome of this campaign was not the demise of the novel, but the selective legitimation of novels that displayed certain, distinctly non-romantic traits. These traits became the guidelines according to which the novel as a genre developed and was valued. Most venerated by this tradition are the three leading eighteenth-century male novelists: Defoe, Richardson, and Fielding. Modern students of the novel are often unaware of the tumultuous controversy that attended its first steps at the end of the seventeenth century. For the most part, feminist scholars have been responsible for generating the recovery of the novel's earliest roots and for opening up discussion of its cultural value in its many different forms.

OVERVIEWS

Wilbur L. Cross (essay date 1899)

SOURCE: "From Arthurian Romance to Richardson," in *The Development of The English Novel*, The Macmillan Company, 1923, pp. 22-5.

[*In the following excerpt, first published in 1899 and reprinted in 1923, Cross summarizes the course of the English novel from its roots in the seventeenth century—in the French romance, religious and social commentary, diary, biography, and character sketch—to the characteristically "realist" English novel that emerged in the mid-eighteenth century.*]

The Elizabethans

. . . Elizabethan England inherited much that was best in English mediæval fiction: the Arthurian romances, the moralized stories of Gower, and the highly finished tales of Chaucer. From Italy came the pastoral romance in its most dreamy and attenuated form, the gorgeous poetic romances of Tasso and Ariosto, and many collections of *novelle*. Some of these *novelle* had as subject the interesting events of everyday life; others were of fierce incident and color, and furnished Elizabethan tragedy with tremendous scenes. From Germany came jest-books and tales of necromancy; from France, the Greek story of adventure with its shipwrecks and pirates; from Spain came 'Amadis,' the 'Diana' of Montemayor, and the picaresque novel. And what the noble printers of the Renaissance gave her, England worked over into fictions of her own.

The most characteristic of her adaptations, the one that most fully expressed her restless spirit of adventure and æsthetic restoration of the age of chivalry, was a romance midway between the knightly quest and the pastoral. Of this species, a conspicuous example is Sir Philip Sidney's 'Arcadia' (1590). This romance has in places as background to its pretty wooing adventures the loveliness of the summer scenery about Wilton House, where it was planned,—violets and roses, meadows and wide-sweeping downs 'garnished with stately trees,'—and into it was infused the noble courtesy, the high sense of honor, and the delicate feeling of the first gentleman of the age. Though touching at points the real in its reflection of English scenes and the

princely virtues of Sidney and his friends, the 'Arcadia' is mainly an ideal creation. The country it describes is the land of dream and enchantment, of brave exploit, unblemished chastity, constant love, and undying friendship. Villany and profane passion darken these imaginary realms, but they, too, like the virtues, are all ideal. In structure the 'Arcadia' is epic, having attached to the main narrative numerous episodes, one of which—the story of Argalus and Parthenia, faithful unto death—is among the most lovely situations romance has ever conceived and elaborated.

In direct antithesis to its Arcadias, Elizabethan England made hasty studies of robbers and highwaymen; out of which, under the artistic impulse of 'Lazarillo de Tormes' (translated into English in 1576), were developed several rogue stories of considerable pretension, such as 'Jack Wilton,' by Thomas Nash, and 'Piers Plain,' by Henry Chettle. To the same class of writings belong Greene's autobiographies, his 'Repentance,' and 'Groat's Worth of Wit,' in which the point of view is shifted from the comic to the tragic. Occasionally the Elizabethan romancers drew their subjects from the bourgeoisie. An amusing instance of this is 'Thomas of Reading,' by Thomas Deloney, which contains from the picaresque point of view a graphic picture of the family life of the clothiers of the West, and of their mad pranks in London. Its scene is laid in the time of Henry the First, and it thus becomes historically interesting as one of the earliest attempts of the modern story-teller to invade the province of history.

The most immediately popular Elizabethan fiction, whether romantic or realistic, was John Lyly's 'Euphues' (1579-80). In this romance of high life there are no enchantments and exciting incidents such as had furnished the stock in trade of Montalvo and his followers. Lyly sought to interest by his style: alliteration, play upon words, antithesis, and a revival of the pseudo-natural history of mediæval fable books. His characters are Elizabethan fops and fine ladies, who sit all night at Lady Flavia's supper-table, discussing in pretty phrases such questions as, why women love men, whether constancy or secrecy is most commendable in a mistress, whether love in the first instance proceeds from the man or from the woman—a dainty warfare in which are gained no victories. Lyly moralizes like a Gower on the profane passion; he steps into the pulpit and preaches, telling mothers to suckle their children, and husbands to treat their wives mildly, for 'instruments sound sweetest when they be touched softest;' and for young men he constructs a moral code in minute detail, such as Shakespeare parodies in Polonius' advice to Laertes. Weak, puerile, and affected as he was, Lyly wrote with the best intentions; he was a Puritan educated in the casuistry of Rome.

Lyly was the founder of a school of romancers, who, from their following the affectations of 'Euphues,' are known as Euphuists. With them all, language was first and matter secondary: 'A golden sentence is worth a world of treasure' was one of their sayings. Of these Euphuists, Robert Greene and Thomas Lodge excelled their master in the poetic qualities of their work; witness 'Menaphon' (1589) by the former, and 'Rosalind' (1590) by the latter. In fact 'Rosalind,' a pastoral composed in the ornate language of 'Euphues,' is the flower of Elizabethan romance. It satisfies some of the usual terms in the modern definition of the novel. For it is of reasonable length; it possesses a kind of structure, and closes with an elaborate moral.

The Historical Allegory and the French Influence

From Elizabeth to the Restoration, romancing and story-telling gradually became a lost art in England. An imitation of Sidney's 'Arcadia' now and then appeared, a sketch of a highwayman, and a few straggling imitations of contemporary French romance. That was about all. There was for a time a steady demand for Elizabethan favorites: 'Euphues,' 'Rosalind,' and especially the 'Groat's Worth of Wit,' and the 'Arcadia.' With the excitement that sounded the note of the oncoming civil war—the trial of Hampden and the uprising of the Scots—the English suddenly stopped reading fiction as well as writing it. . . .

The Restoration

After the battle of Worcester, the English began once more to read fiction. Lyly, Greene, and Sidney all survived the literary wreckage of the civil wars. From now on the French romances were translated as fast as they were published in France. And for reading them and discussing love, friendship, and statecraft, little coteries were formed, the members of which addressed one another as 'the matchless Orinda,' 'the adored Valeria,' and 'the noble Antenor.' Best known in their own time were the groups of platonic lovers, professing an immaculate chastity, who hovered about Katherine Philips and Margaret Duchess of Newcastle. The literary efforts of these romantic ladies and gentlemen were directed to poetry and letter-writing rather than to fiction. There proceeded from them only one romance, 'Parthenissa' (1664, 1665, 1677), by Roger Boyle, an admirer of Katherine Philips. The most noticeable thing about this inexpressibly dull imitation of Scudéri, is its mixing up in much confusion several great Roman wars. For this, particularly for bringing on the scene together Hannibal and Spartacus, Boyle defended himself in his preface by an appeal to Vergil, who neglected two centuries in his story of Æneas and Dido. For making the same character stand now for one person and now for another in his historical allegory, he gracefully apologized, but he might have cited Barclay as his precedent. Other similar romances were: 'Bentivolio and Urania' (1660), by Nathaniel Ingelo; 'Aretina' (1661), by George Mackenzie; and

'Pandion and Amphigenia' (1665), by John Crowne. The first is a religious fiction; the second, made up of adventures, moral essays, and disquisitions on English and Scotch politics, was an attempt to revive the conceits of Lyly; the third is an appropriation of Sidney's 'Arcadia.' Like Crowne, the Restoration romancers were generally satisfied to remodel and dress up old material. And what is true of them, is also true of the realists. An odd and wretchedly written production of this period is 'The English Rogue' (1665-71), by Richard Head, and in part by Francis Kirkman. For tricks and intrigues they pillaged Spanish and French rogue stories, Elizabethan sketches of vagabonds, and German and English jest-books; and seasoned their medley with what probably then passed for humor. On the other hand, they wrote much from observation. In their graphic pictures of the haunts of apprentices, pickpockets, and highwaymen, they discovered the London slums. Furthermore, unlike their brother picaresque writers, they sent their hero on a voyage to the East, and thus began the transformation of the rogue story into the story of adventure as it was soon to appear in Defoe.

More original work than this was done by Mrs. Aphra Behn, who wrote besides many comedies several short tales, the most noteworthy of which is 'Oroonoko' (1688). In this story, which is a realistic account of a royal slave kidnapped in Africa and barbarously put to death at Surinam, she contrasts the state of nature with that of civilization, severely reprimanding the latter. 'Oroonoko' is the first humanitarian novel in English. Though its spirit cannot for a moment be compared, in moral earnestness, with 'Uncle Tom's Cabin,' yet its purpose was to awaken Christendom to the horrors of slavery. The time being not yet ripe for it, the romance was for the public merely an interesting story to be dramatized. The novels of Mrs. Behn that bore fruit were her short tales of intrigue—versions in part of her own tender experiences. One of her successors was Mrs. Mary Manley, who wrote 'The Secret History of Queen Zarah and the Zarazians' (1705), 'The New Atlantis' (1709), and 'The Power of Love, in Seven Novels' (1720). Mrs. Manley was in turn followed by Mrs. Eliza Haywood, the author of 'Memoirs of a Certain Island Adjacent to Utopia' (1725), and 'The Secret Intrigues of the Count of Caramania' (1727). These productions taken together purport to relate the inside history of the court from the restoration of Charles the Second to the death of George the First. To their contemporaries, they were piquantly immoral; to later times, they are not so amusing. Nevertheless, in the development of the novel, they have a place. They represent a conscious effort to attain to the real, in reaction from French romance. They are specimens, too, of precisely what was meant in England by the novel in distinction from the romance, just before Richardson: a short story of from one hundred to two hundred pages, assumed to be founded on fact, and published in a duodecimo volume.

To John Bunyan the English novel owes a very great debt. What fiction needed, if it was ever to come near a portrayal of real life, was first of all to rid itself of the extravagances of the romancer and the cynicism of the picaresque story-teller. Though Bunyan was despised by his contemporary men of letters, it surely could be but a little time before the precision of his imagination and the force and charm of his simple and idiomatic English would be felt and then imitated. As no writer preceding him, Bunyan knew the artistic effect of minute detail in giving reasonableness to an impossible story. In the 'Pilgrim's Progress' (1678-84) he so mingled with those imaginative scenes of his own the familiar Scripture imagery and the still more familiar incidents of English village life, that the illusion of reality must have been to the readers for whom he wrote well-nigh perfect. The allegories of Barclay and Scudéri could not be understood without keys; Bunyan's 'Palace Beautiful' needed none.

Literary Forms that contributed to the Novel

Outside the sphere proper of fiction, there was slowly collecting in the seventeenth century material for the future novelist. It was quite the fashion for public and literary men—witness Pepys and Evelyn—to keep diaries and journals of family occurrences and of interesting social and political events. These diaries and journals suggested the novel of family life, and indicated a form of narrative that would lend to fiction the appearance of fact. In 'Robinson Crusoe' and 'Pamela' and hundreds of other novels down to the present, the journal has played a not inconsiderable part. At this time, too, men were becoming sufficiently interested in their friends and some of the great men of the past to write their biographies. In 1640 Izaak Walton published the first of his charming 'Lives.' A quick offshoot of the biography was the autobiography, which, as a man in giving a sympathetic account of himself is likely to run into poetry, came very close to being a novel. Margaret Duchess of Newcastle's 'Autobiography,' published in 1656 in a volume of tales, is a famous account of a family in which 'all the brothers were brave, and all the sisters virtuous.' Bunyan's 'Grace Abounding' is a story of the fierce struggles between the spirit and the flesh, and of the final triumph of the spirit. This autobiographic method of dealing with events, partly or wholly fictitious, has been a favorite with all our novelists, except with the very greatest; and it is employed more to-day than ever before.

It also occurred to several writers after the Restoration that London life might be depicted by a series of imaginary letters to a friend. A most amusing bundle of two hundred and eleven such letters was published in 1664 by Margaret Duchess of Newcastle. Her object was to transfer to letters, scenes and incidents that had hitherto been the material of the comedy of humor. In 1678 a new direction to this letter-writing was given by a translation from the French of the 'Portuguese Letters.' These letters of a Portuguese nun to a French cavalier revealed to our writers how a correspondence might be managed for unfolding a simple story, and for studying the heart of a betrayed and deserted woman. Edition after edition of the 'Portuguese Letters' followed, and fictitious replies and counter-replies. In the wake of these continuations, were translated into English the letters of Eloisa and Abelard, containing a similar but more pathetic tale of man's selfishness and woman's devotion. They, too, went through many editions and were imitated, mutilated, and trivialized. As a result of this fashion for letter-writing, there existed early in the eighteenth century a considerable body of short stories in letter form. Hardly any of them are readable; but one of them is of considerable historical interest, 'The Letters of Lindamira, a Lady of Quality, written to her Friend in the Country' (second edition, 1713). The author, who may have been Tom Brown 'of facetious memory,' states that, unlike his predecessors, his aim is 'to expose vice, disappoint vanity, to reward virtue, and crown constancy with success.' He accomplishes this 'by carrying Lindamira through a sea of misfortunes, and at last marrying her up to her wishes.' It was in this weak school of fiction, aiming at something it hardly knew what, that Richardson must in some degree have learned how to manage a correspondence.

Moreover, the character-sketch, which was the most prolific literary form in England and France during the seventeenth century, has a direct bearing on the novel. As conceived by Ben Jonson and Thomas Overbury, who had before them a contemporary translation of Theophrastus, it was the sketch of some person, real or imaginary, who embodied a virtue or a vice, or some idiosyncrasy obnoxious to ridicule. One character was set over against another; and the sentences descriptive of each were placed in the antithesis which the style of Lyly had made fashionable. Surely from this species of literature, the novelist took a lesson in the fine art of contrast. The type of sketch set by Jonson and Overbury was a good deal modified by the fifty and more character-writers who succeeded them. Not infrequently as a frame to the portrait was added a little piece of biography or adventure; and there are a few examples of massing sketches in a loose fiction, as in the continuations of 'The English Rogue,' and in the second part of the 'Roman Bourgeois.' The treatment of the character-sketch by Steele and Addison in the 'Spectator' (1711-12) was highly original. They drew portraits of representative Englishmen, and brought them together in conversation in a London club. They conducted Sir Roger de Coverley through Westminster Abbey, to the playhouse, to Vauxhall, into the country to Coverley church and the assizes; they incidentally took a retrospective view of his life, and finally told the story of his death. When they had done this, they had not only created one of the best defined characters in our prose literature, but they had almost transformed the character-sketch into a novel of London and provincial life. From the 'Spectator' the character-sketch, with its types and minute observation and urbane ridicule, passed into the novel, and became a part of it.

The Passing of the Old Romance

At the dawn of the Renaissance, verse was usually an embellishment of fiction, and the perfect workman was Chaucer, whose 'Troilus and Cressida' and 'Canterbury Tales' are differentiated from the modern novel mainly by the accident of rhyme. Of the later romances in prose, the two that have gained among all classes a world-wide fame are 'Don Quixote' and the 'Pilgrim's Progress'; and second to them is the 'Princess of Clèves.' Nearly everything else that has been mentioned is to the modern as if it had never been written. That such a fate should have overcome the old romances must be lamented by every one acquainted with their lovely imagery and inspiring ideals of conduct. But it was inevitable, for they almost invariably failed in their art. The great novelists since Fielding have taught the public that a novel must have a beginning and an end. A reader of contemporary fiction, after turning a few pages of Sidney's 'Arcadia,' becomes aware that he is not at the beginning of the story at all, but is having described to him an event midway in the plot. From this point on, the narrative, instead of moving forward untrammelled, except for the pause of an easy retrospect, becomes more and more perplexed by episodes, which are introduced, suspended, resumed, and twisted within one another, according to a plan not easily understood. The picaresque writers, the first of them, adopted the straightforward manner of autobiography; but under the influence of romance, they, too, soon began to indulge in episodes. If at their best the picaresque stories had a beginning, they had no end. They were published in parts; each part was brought to a close with the recurring paragraph that a continuation will be written if the reader desires; and so adventure follows adventure, to be terminated only by the death of the author. It is thus obvious that the romancers and story-tellers had no clearly defined conception of what a novel should be as an independent literary species. They took as their model the epic, not the well-ordered epic of Homer or Vergil, but the prose epic as perverted by the rhetoricians in the decadent period of Greek art.[1]

Moreover, it has come to be demanded not only that a novel must possess an orderly structure, but that it shall be a careful study of some phase of real life, or of conduct in a situation which, however impossible in itself, the imagination is willing to accept for the time being as possible. Accordingly, those who wish to shun the word 'romance' are accustomed to speak of the novel of character and the novel of incident. In the novel of character the interest is directed to the portrayal of men and women, and the fable is a subordinate consideration; in the novel of incident the interest is directed to what happens, and the characters come more by the way. To the former class no one would hesitate to assign 'The Mill on the Floss.' To the same class might very properly be assigned 'The House of the Seven Gables,' which, though Hawthorne called it a romance, is, as he intended it, 'true to the human heart.' To the latter class belong the Waverley novels, and to mention an extreme example, 'The Prisoner of Zenda.' Before Defoe, writers of fiction did in some degree fulfil the conditions necessary to a novel in the modern view; but to concoct fantastic adventures in high or low life, in accord neither with the truth of fact, nor with the laws of a sane imagination, nor with the permanent motives that sway our acts—that was the main business of the romancer and the story-teller. From them to Defoe and Richardson the transition is analogous to that from the first Elizabethan plays to Shakespeare and his contemporaries; it is the passing from a struggling and misdirected literary form to a well-defined species. Nevertheless, a study of European fiction before Defoe has intellectual, if not æsthetic, compensations, and to the student it is imperative. It gives one a large historical perspective. From Arthurian romance and the *fabliau* downward, in the eternal swing between idealism and realism, there is a continuous growth—an accumulation of incidents, situations, characters, and experiments in structure, much of which was a legacy to the eighteenth century.

8. Daniel Defoe

'Robinson Crusoe' (1719) is the earliest English novel of incident. It was at once recognized in England and throughout literary Europe as something different from the picaresque story to which it is akin. In what does this difference consist? The situations and jests of Head and Chettle were in some cases as old as Latin comedy; 'Robinson Crusoe' was an elaboration of a contemporary incident[2] that made a fascinating appeal to the imagination. The writer of the rogue story did not expect to be believed. The aim of Defoe was to invest his narrative with a sense of reality; to this end he made use of every device at his command to deceive the reader. He took as a model for his narrative the form that best produces the illusion of truth—that of current memoirs with the accompaniment of a diary. He adroitly remarks in his preface that he is only the editor of a private man's adventures, and adds confidentially that he believes 'the thing to be a just history of fact,' at least, that 'there is no appearance of fiction in it.' He begins his story very modestly by briefly sketching the boyhood of a rogue who runs away to sea—one of thousands—and thus gradually prepares the reader for those experiences which are to culminate in the shipwreck on the Island of Despair. When he gets his Crusoe there, he does not send him on a quest for exciting adventures, but surprises us by a matter-of-fact account of Crusoe's expedients for feeding and clothing himself and making himself comfortable. He brings the story home to the Englishmen of the middle-class, for whom he principally writes, by telling them that their condition in life is most conducive to happiness, and by giving expression to their peculiar tenets: their trust in dreams, their recognition of Providence in the fortuitous concurrence of events, and their dogmas of conviction of sin, of repentance, and of conversion. And finally, 'Robinson Crusoe' has its message. Undoubtedly its message is too apparent for the highest art, but it is a worthy one: Be patient, be industrious, be honest, and you will at last be rewarded for your labor. 'Robinson Crusoe' must have seemed to the thousands of hard-laboring Englishmen a symbol of their own lives, their struggles, their failures, and their final rest in a faith that there will sometime be a settling of things justly in the presence of Him 'who will allow no shuffling.' To put it briefly, Defoe humanized adventure.

'Robinson Crusoe' was the most immediately popular fiction that had yet been written. At once it became a part of the world's literature, and it remains such to this day. Defoe took advantage of its vogue to write many other adventures on land and sea. Captain Singleton's tour across Africa is as good reading as Stanley; and to the uninitiated, it seems quite as true to fact. In 'Moll Flanders' is gathered together a mass of material concerning the dregs of London—thieves and courtesans—that remains unequalled even among the modern naturalists. The 'Memoirs of a Cavalier,' once regarded as an actual autobiography, so realistic is the treatment, is the relation of the adventures of a cavalier in the army of Gustavus Adolphus, and later at Marston Moor and Naseby. It is a masterly piece of historical semblance, and it is thus significant. The 'Journal of the Plague Year' is so documentary in appearance that public libraries still class it as a history, though it is fictitious throughout. This verisimilitude which was attained through detail and the unadorned language of everyday life is Defoe's great distinction. Bunyan was in a measure his forerunner, and his immediate successor was Swift, who, under the guise of his delightful voyages among the Lilliputians and Brobdingnagians (1726), ridiculed in savage irony his king, 'his own dear country,' and 'the animal called man.' These three writers who usher in a new era for the novel are the source to which romance has returned again and again for instruction, from Scott to Stevenson.

Notes

[1] See the Greek romance, 'Theagenes and Chariclea,' translated, T. Underdown, 1577.

[2] See Steele's account of Alexander Selkirk in the 'Englishman,' No. 26.

Francis Hovey Stoddard (essay date 1900)

SOURCE: "The Evolution of the Novel," in *The Evolution of the English Novel*, in The Macmillan Company, 1902, pp. 1-42.

[*In the following excerpt, first published in 1900 and reprinted in 1902, Stoddard proposes a law of development that he believes is applicable to any literary form: "the depiction of the external, objective, carnal, precedes, in every form of expression of which we can have records, the consideration of the internal, the subjective, the spiritual."*]

I do not undertake to show that the novel has grown out of any preceding form of literature with such preciseness that the traces of its growth can be shown. It is extremely doubtful if we can yet work out a perfect statement of the development of the novel out of any other form of literature; it is doubtful if we can work out any chronological sequence even within the period—the one hundred and fifty years—of the novel's life in English literature to the present day. We cannot say that the novels of 1740 legitimately developed into the novels of 1780; that the novels of 1780 logically developed into the novels of 1820; that the novels of 1820 legitimately and regularly developed into the novels of 1850. As with poetry, with literature, with the drama, with the epic, we find ourselves confronted with the operation of the human mind expressing itself in forms antedating, or postdating the theoretical stages; expressing itself often in forms greater, expressing itself sometimes in forms much less, in importance than any theory would demand.

Nevertheless, we have to do in the English novel with a kind of literature separate in method and in extent from other sorts. It belongs to the eighteenth and nineteenth centuries. It has a character of its own; it is limited in extent; it is specific in its selection of subject and in its method of treatment. In such a limited field the study of a development, if possible anywhere, may be carried on with reasonable prospects of success. Granting the difficulty, it is yet more than probable that we can find, if we take up this limited division of literary expression, and if we study it with something of regularity and system, that certain indications of what may be properly, though not too technically, called a development may be shown; and that the examination of these indications, of these apparent stages of growth, may be useful. In this work I undertake the study of five specific kinds of expression in fiction: the novel of personality, the novel of history, the novel of romance, the novel of purpose, and the novel of problem. I take these five divisions in the order in which I have named them, for the reason that it is somewhat the order in which these specific kinds of expression in novel form appeared. The novel of personal life, of individual, separate, domestic life, is the basal form. A novel is a record of emotion; the story of a human life touched with emotion; the story of two human lives under stress of emotional arousement; the story of domestic life with emotion pervading it; the story of a great historical character in his day of aroused emotional activity; or the story of the romantic adventures of some person seeking strange regions under stress of emotional desire. So that the novel of personal life is really the basal form of the novel, and one may say that all novels become novels only when each is the story of some life stirred by some emotion. The earliest and the latest novel will come under this main division, to the discussion of whose characteristics the second chapter is given. The historical and the romantic novel, which are the subjects of the third and fourth chapters, developed later as a special form; and the novel of purpose later than either. In treating these in successive chapters I am, then, following somewhat a law of chronological appearance; but I by no means suggest that the novel of the domestic life, of the individual life, developed into the historical novel, and that again into the romantic novel, and that again into the novel of purpose, and that again into the problem novel. One must look farther than to this rough and general classification if he seeks to frame a law of the development of fiction.

We have seen that it is not easy to set forth in detail any order of succession of literary forms of expression. Yet I think he is but a superficial student of the literature of recorded time who does not note one tendency of later work, of later method, of later procedure, of later life, as compared with earlier work, earlier method, earlier procedure, and earlier life which seems to imply an underlying law. If there be such an underlying law, it is the purpose of this chapter to suggest it and to apply it with some exactness to the history of the novel form. This law of tendency is, in general, that the depiction of the external, objective, carnal, precedes, in every form of expression of which we can have records, the consideration of the internal, the subjective, the spiritual. We go from shapes, and forms, and bulk, and externals, to the presentation of the life within. To illustrate this law, I may call attention to a step in the development of art significant of the evolution of the idea of inner personality as opposed to outward symbol, which seemed to show itself in the last years of the Mediæval Ages, and the first years of the Reformation era. In the fourteenth and fifteenth centuries, in the day of Cimabue, of Quintin Massys, of Van Eyck, the typical presentation of the Madonna was that of a vague face, without expression, shone upon by a light from without, illumined and dignified by an external halo. The Madonna of the later time, of the greater time, was a human face, with human expression, illumined and glorified by a light from within. The halo, the external sign, had gone; the inner life, the expression of the divinely aroused human emotion, had come in its place. This seems to be

in accordance with a law that the progress of evolution is from external embellishment to inner life. It is this law that I propose in this work to apply to the novel.

The theory of development that I set forth is that progress, in speech, in literature, in methods religious, educational, and political, in theories of the relation of the individual to his life work and life duty, has always been from the expression of the external form, from the consideration of the external characteristics, from the suggestion of the external remedies for evils and rewards for endeavor, to the expression of the abstract thought beneath the external form, to the consideration of the internal character which finds embodiment in the external characteristics, to study into the causes of evils, and to the satisfaction of the soul with duty done in place of external reward of endeavor. It is a progress that advances from the physical to the intellectual, from the carnal to the spiritual. I shall endeavor to apply this theory to the novel with intent to suggest that such development of expression as we find in form of novels advances from the depiction of far-off occurrences and adventures to the narration and representation of contemporaneous, immediate, domestic occurrences; and, finally, to the presentation of conflicts of the mind and soul beneath the external manifestations. If the theory is true, we may expect to find at the beginning of novel-expression a wild romance, and at its end an introspective study into motive.

First, then, for the theory. The earliest speech of any people, the earliest speech of the Indian, of the savage, is a picture story. It is hardly probable that the Indian speeches familiar to our boyhood's days from the records of the "Boy's Own Speaker," are exact transcripts of the utterances of the chiefs around the war-party camp-fire two hundred years ago; but they are veracious in one respect,—the voice of the utterance is external. An Indian's speech is a series of pictures, of illustrations, of external representations of his ideas. He sees a happy hunting-ground, a great spirit. He lays the implements of the dead warrior by him in the grave; he makes visible images which he can touch, feel, handle, for the embodiment of his ideas. So the early primitive nation worships a visible God,—a sun, a totem, a joss, an idol. So primitive peoples personify phases of nature into nymphs, spirits, and fairies. It is the later day which gives the power to see, to speak, to think directly without the visible image, without the symbol, without the external form. It is an indication of progress in intellectual as well as mathematical excellence, when the boy ceases visibly to touch his actual fingers as he counts. And as in spoken speech, so also in recorded speech. It is no accident that the epic stands at the beginning of poetic life and that in modern days the epic has passed away; for the epic is the most objective, the most external, the most physical of all forms of poetic expression. With the complexity of modern life, if this theory of progress from the outward to the inward, from the external to the internal, from the objective to the subjective, is true, we might expect the passing of the epic, as it has passed. Or, again, if we interrogate folklore, one may note one characteristic of the tales of folklore which are dearest to the hearts of all peoples, and this characteristic is that the stories most loved are stories of the physically largest and most perfect, overthrown and defeated by the weaker, by the less physically great, by the more intellectually potent. The folklore story is always of the one physically strong overthrown by the one weak in body but strong in intellect and spirit. It is always the giant killed by the insignificant Jack; it is always the fire-breathing dragon killed by the saintly knight; it is always Grendel destroyed by Beówulf; it is always Brer Fox outwitted by Brer Rabbit. The external, the forceful, the physically massive, is overcome, defeated, by the physically weak, but the more intellectual, the more spiritual. If this be a law, we may look to find, as we study the novel, that it begins with the presentation of the external phases of life; finds the impulse of its action in compulsions from without, in accidents, incidents, catastrophes; takes its motive from the external. And we may find, if the theory is a true one, that the study of the romantic novel, or the historical novel, or the novel of domestic life, becomes a study of progress toward the depiction of the relation of man to man, taking the impulse of its action and its motive from the aroused desire in the mind or heart of its hero. Fiction begins with the objective novel; it progresses into the introspective and the subjective novel.

All this will follow if the theory is true. But it is worth while, in enunciating so far-reaching and apparently so arbitrary a proposition, to illustrate it still farther. I may, no doubt, find suggestion of it in very trifling matters close at hand even better than in more serious ones. It was but a few years ago that the engines on our railroads glittered in brass adornments; the bell, the water tank, the signal light, and the rails, shone like gold. There was a great outcry when the late Commodore Vanderbilt ordered all these engines to appear in plain black paint. It was argued that the love of the engineer for his engine, the pride in it, would pass with the passing of the glittering external. It did not. The excellence was inside, and the removal of the halo did not diminish the admiration of the driver for his engine. Or I may name the passing of certain details of the external on the stage. In one of the Miracle Plays, Adam is represented crossing the stage, going to be created. The imagination needed its visible symbol. Similarly there are ghosts in the Elizabethan plays. In Shakespeare's time there was a visible physical ghost, possibly with the "invisible" coat of the Middle Ages,—a remarkable garment through the donning of which an actor could become, as it were, conspicuously invisible,—more likely a visible ghost, boldly expressed, with no disguise. But since Shakespeare's day

we have progressed beyond the need of this physical symbol of the vanished spirit hovering for an instant on the confines betwixt life and death, and to us the externally manifested ghost has come to seem too close a personation. The later stage managers have tried various devices to spiritualize, to decarnalize, this ghost presentation; they have tried mirror reflections, illusions. But it was Henry Irving in the presentation of Macbeth who gave the modern thought. The ghost of Banquo is present in Shakespeare's play; but on the stage, as Henry Irving presents Macbeth, there is no ghost of Banquo; there is merely the empty chair and a light on the empty chair of Banquo. So we have come from the exhibition of an external form to the suggestion of the subtler thought beneath. For though no modern dramatist would ever introduce a ghost in writing a drama, and no modern novelist would ever make a ghost a real character in a serious novel, yet we think of these unthinkable things, we ponder on these spiritual problems in our plays and in our novels no less intently than did our anthropomorphic ancestors. We think and ponder only the more intently because unhampered by the external symbol. The visible ghost no longer walks the boards of our stage, nor stalks through the reveries of our imaginations; but the mystery of death, of life, of life extending beyond the visible death, is none the less a problem in our plays, in our novels, and in our meditations. It is but the external manifestation which has passed.

It has passed, too, in things very much greater than the speech of Indian, or the method of poetic expression, or the decoration of engines, or the portrayal of Madonnas, or the exhibition of incorporeal visions on the stage. The thought of sin cannot be said to be a modern thought; but it is only since the Reformation that repentance for sin has come to be a matter of spiritual exercise. We need go back only one thousand years to find that the religious exercise of repentance for sin committed demanded external observance as its essential. It was not alone the king who did penance for his people's sin in public, or led a Crusade as a religious rite; it was a universal proposition of religious procedure that penitence was a public function which involved penitential observances, external fastings, mortifications of the external flesh, removal from the shows of external social life, departure from the occupations of the external world, pilgrimages to shrines, to Meccas, to that Canterbury Cathedral in which lay the bones of the martyred Thomas à Becket. Penitence was to be expressed by some external observance, visible to the eye, painful to the flesh. It is a modern thought that penitence is a private duty; it is a modern thought that it demands contrition instead of external observance as its essential; that it concerns the sinner and is, perhaps, most sincere when least visibly manifested. The progress is from the requirement of objective external forms of atonement, of repentance, to the exercises of the individual soul. So far as this indicates a law, it would indicate that in the earlier method of the romantic novel, of the historical novel, of the novel of life, we should have the external phases of the historical day, of the romantic adventure, of the life procedure; and that in later stages we should have the relations of man to the historical day, we should have the subtler, the less physical, aspects of the romantic life, of the domestic life, portrayed.

But not alone is such a tendency as I have indicated evidenced in religious observances. It is even more easily recognized in educational and in political methods. Students of the educational tendencies of the last one hundred years have no doubt noted that the motive force upon the student has shifted in the last seventy years from an external to an internal compulsion. The college of seventy years ago was an absolute monarchy; the student was intellectually handled, mastered, disciplined, prepared, by an educational force, in the selection of which, toward the influencing of which, in the modelling of which, he had absolutely no choice. A faculty set for him certain required studies, to be pursued at certain stated times, to be evidenced by recitations, to be guaranteed by examinations at certain fixed periods under unchangeable rules and regulations. There was no election, no option, no opportunity of individual choice given the student. It was a compulsion from an external. Such was the system in our colleges—even in Harvard College—seventy years ago. Under such a system as this most excellent men were trained, and trained most excellently. There may be some who will maintain that we have not wholly gone toward perfection in education, as we have in modern times given, more and more, the voice of the determination of his college career to the student. I do not argue this point; I merely point out that the college of to-day has gone from a method of education by which the student was dominated from beginning to close by a force external to himself, to a system in which the student's own desire, the student's own choice, the student's own private notion, is in his case the keynote of procedure. And I am sure that this change from the external power modelling the boy, to the boy's own desire controlling his development, is a change in accordance with the theory I have been presenting—that evolution proceeds from the dominance of the external toward the preëminence and the potency of the immanent idea.

And in like manner, our days have seen a similar progress of the notion of political headship from the external, objective symbol to the dominance of the invisible idea. The earliest kings were kings by virtue of force. The largest man, the man with the strongest arm, with the muscle of iron, with the nerves of steel—was the first king. He was an objective manifestation of physical power. That is the first stage in the king-notion. The second stage is of to-day, in England let us say, where the king or queen is but the symbol of a power—without force, almost without influence—the inactive physical symbol of the power of the state. In more modern community systems men will not admit that they have a king at all. If a Democratic leader or a Republican leader rules the politics of a State, he rules it, not by displaying, but by concealing, the fact that he is a king—a political king—a "boss." In our government of the United States can it least of all be said that he who stands as President stands as king. The real ruler of these seventy millions of people is an intangible, immaterial, invisible force called "public opinion." Before the breath of that unembodied idea the physical force of a political boss, of a Congress, of a President, bows. The external yields to the internal, the physical to the mental and the spiritual.

If such examples as I have given are not sufficient, I can easily add to their number. I can, for example, suggest how the notion of individual personal liberty, in religious matters, in political matters—of liberty untrammelled by any external force, of liberty dominated only by the mind, the heart, the conscience—is a modern, an evolved, a developed idea. Or I can point out that a hint of all the suggestions that I have been making has been given in revelation, in the fire, the thunder, the lightnings, the tablets of stone when the first Commandments came; in the voice saying that "a little child shall lead them," that "except ye become as little children," and that "ye must be born again," uttered when came the New Commandments. The fire, the thunder, the lightnings passed, but God was in the still, small voice. And I may finally claim that a further suggestion can be found in the prophecy that in the world to come the body shall cease, and the spirit be alone the living force. I do not give these examples as proofs. I desire only to use such illustrations as are near at hand in making clear this suggestion of a general habit of progress in evolution. If true as respects the novel, we may expect to find a tendency away from external manifestations and toward the presentation of the motive beneath such manifestations,—away from the manifestation of the objective, the physical, from the picturing of a thoughtless hero dashing about through forests and over streams to rescue or to kill other individuals as unspiritual, as unintellectual as himself,—toward the study and the depiction of the internal relations of men and women in daily life. It is with illustrations such as these that I formulate a proposition concerning the novel in its growth to completeness: that, earlier than its appearance in the works of Richardson, Fielding, Smollett, and Sterne, in the decade of 1740 to 1750, we may find romances and chivalric tales of men on horseback ranging through strange countries; we may find romances of adventures, stories of wanderings and seekings through far lands; and that at a much later date, as typical of the most advanced thought of a later day, we may find novels of the soul, of the mind, introspective studies into the motives which move hearts and influence lives.

Let us then turn from theory to history and study the fact. When we interrogate the history of the true novel we find it a most recent literary form. A novel is a narrative of human life under stress of emotion. It differs from the epic in that it is a narration of human rather than superhuman life, under stress of ordinary rather than of excessive or heroic emotion. It differs from the drama in that the latter represents clashes and conflicts of emotion rather than a life procedure under influence of emotion, and represents in action rather than in narrative. In English speech, though not in German and French usage, the term novel is used as a general expression to include all prose fiction; the romance and the story being thus names of types and classes of novels; the term novel being the generic, the term romance and story being the especial, designation. In German usage a sharp distinction is drawn between the term *Novelle* and *Roman,* the latter being, as in the French, the general term corresponding to novel in English. In English usage the "story" is that form of novel which gives an action of life or a sequence of events of life with least possible complexity of emotion; and the "romance" is that form of novel which portrays a life when influenced by emotion to undertake material, spiritual, or physical exploration into regions unfamiliar. In English fiction the type form is the novel, and the novel in English literature was born in 1740 when appeared the "Pamela" of Richardson. It had predecessors rather than ancestors in English writings. Before it, had appeared Defoe's "Robinson Crusoe," which was a story of adventure arousing emotional interest, though itself but slightly touched with emotion. And earlier had appeared four works commonly cited by chroniclers as having in them enough of the quality of the English novel to warrant their position in a list of its predecessors. These four works were: Nash's fantastic narration of adventure called "The Unfortunate Traveller," which was printed in 1594; Lyly's "Euphues," which was really a handbook of court etiquette rather than a novel; and the altogether charming pastoral romances,—too delicate in tone, too vague in method, to be called novels,—the "Rosalind" of Thomas Lodge and the "Arcadia" of Philip Sidney. In these works I have given all the important predecessors of the novel in English literature. They can, I think, with but slight justice be termed its ancestors. In German literature for the same period I should name but three:—the German translation, published in 1569, of the "Amadis of Gaul"; *Der Abenteuerliche Simplicius Simplicissimus* of Grimmelshausen, 1668; and the Robinson Tales of 1720. In French literature for the same period I should name: *La Princesse de Clèves* of Madame de la Fayette, 1677, the *Gil Blas* of Lesage, 1715-1735, the *Marianne* of Marivaux, 1731-1736, which antedated "Pamela" half a dozen years and, perhaps, suggested it, and the *Manon Lescaut* of the Abbé Prévost, 1729-1733. One may note that the *Manon Lescaut,* the *Marianne,* and the completed form of *Gil Blas* are not only of the same gen-

eration but within the same decade as the earliest English novel. The true novel, therefore, appeared almost simultaneously in France and in England, though coming as most literary forms have apparently come, from the more eastern to the more western land.

And yet, while it is true that the decade 1735 to 1745 saw the birth of the novel in both France and England, and while it is true that only three or four predecessors can be found in either German, English, or French literature, it is not true that we can find no works of fiction in literary history to which the novel may be said to stand in the direct relation of descendant. The novel had its predecessors in at least three groups of works. The short tales found in Greek manuscripts, the composition of which dates from the second to the sixth centuries, and which, collectively, are known as the "Greek Romances," form the first group. The Italian and the Spanish romances of the fourteenth and fifteenth centuries form the second group. The prose romances of chivalry, themselves the descendants of the poetic romances of adventure, form the third group. First in time is the Greek romance group. It has come down to us in most fragmentary condition. All that we have of it is evidence, more or less complete, of the existence of eight tales. The first of these is a brief fragment of the first or second century, telling the story of the grief of one Nimrod at parting from a loved one, Derkeia, and telling the efforts of Nimrod to deserve her by valiant conduct in a campaign. The scene is laid in Nineveh, the language is Greek, the material seems to be Oriental, and the fragment is written on a roll of Egyptian papyrus, proving that even at that early date literature passed the bounds of nationality. The second of these Greek tales is known to us only in the report made six centuries after the tale itself was written, by one Photius of Constantinople. The book itself is called "The Marvellous Things beyond Thule." It is the story of the adventures of one Dinias who met a maiden Dercyllis, and with her and for her underwent marvellous adventures, which included, on his part, an expedition to the North Pole and to the moon, till, finally, they happily returned to Tyre. The third one, which is, like the one just mentioned, of the second century, is known to us also from the account of Photius, and is the *Babylonica* of Jamblichus. It is the story of Sinonis, who, with her husband Rhodanes, flies from the unwelcome suit of Garmus, the king of Babylonia. In their flight they meet with adventures in which they elude their enemies by feigning death, by occupying a new-made tomb, and by claiming to be ghosts. They exterminate their enemies by prowess impossible here fully to set forth. Misfortunes come upon them; Sinonis is carried off by a Syrian king, but finally Rhodanes defeats the Syrian king and conquers the Babylonian king, and the book ends, as a fiction should, with Rhodanes possessor of Sinonis, and firmly seated on the Babylonian throne. The next of these fictions, by one Xenophon, is of the third century, and is the first of those we have mentioned that has come down to us in the original text. It is the *Ephesiaca* of Xenophon (so called after the author's native town), and is the story of Anthia and Habrocomas, who, having been wont to scoff at love, meet one day by chance in the temple of Diana at Ephesus. They fall in love, but are doomed by Apollo to suffer and endure till the God of Love shall be appeased. The tale is the story of their travels. It is a narration of remarkable adventures. Of course they lose each other and spend weary years in search, and of course, also, great wonders are wrought; but in the end, as a story should, the tale brings them together at Ephesus, where, having been faithful to each other through their perils, they live happily ever after. This pleasing fiction is worthy of note, not alone because of its excellence, but because from it was drafted one of the famous mediæval stories,—"Apollonius of Tyre,"—which has come down to us through Gower in his *Confessio Amantis,* and through the Elizabethan play,—sometimes called Shakespearian,—of "Pericles, Prince of Tyre." The next of these is the most celebrated, with perhaps one exception, of the whole number. It is the *Ethiopica* by one Heliodorus. It is the story of Theagenes and Chariclea, and is really a good tale of adventure. The hero and heroine are shipwrecked, saved by a band of robbers, and carried away. They are separated, and the story of the work is the story of the adventures of these two, till, at last, in Ethiopia, they come happily to safe union, having not only passed through incredible dangers with marvellous feats of prowess, but having also accomplished a great moral reform in abolishing human sacrifices throughout all Ethiopia. The next story brings us to the fifth century. It is the story of "Clitophon and Leucippe," and is not unlike the others. It is a tale of two lovers who fly from enraged parents by eloping over the sea. They suffer shipwreck, are captured by pirates, and are separated. Then the adventures begin. Clitophon learns of the death of Leucippe and marries a widow; the widow's husband comes back; Leucippe is found, and out of it all comes the most unlikely thing in the world of fact, but the most sensible thing in the world of fiction, the reconciliation of the original lovers. The next of these fictions of adventure is, perhaps, of the sixth century. It is entitled "Chæreas and Callirhoe," and was written by one Chariton. In it the lovers have married, but the husband becomes jealous and kills his wife, as he supposes, and flies, leaving her for dead. The wife is carried to a tomb which robbers break into, and from which, finding her alive, they sell her into slavery. The husband learns this, and the tale records the search for her by this repentant husband. The last one of these Greek tales that has come down to us is the well-known "Daphnis and Chloe." It is in its form rather a pastoral than a fiction of adventure, and is the simple story of the lovers Daphnis and Chloe and their trials with their rivals and enemies, ending most happily in a joyous wedding festival. Such in briefest form is a

description of the eight prose tales which have come down to us from the Greek. They are charming tales, and I trust the brevity of my allusions to them gives no unfavorable impression. But I think any one will note, as he runs through the statement of the plots, that the emotional bond, the thread of love, running through them, is of the slightest possible description. They are stories of external adventure, with a motive of desire, but with detail of fighting, pirates, war, shipwreck, and strategies. If I had been manufacturing evidence to establish a proposition that the ancestor of the modern novel had been a story wholly external, depicting only adventures of the body, of the physical senses, I could have created no better example of such a theory than the Greek fictions; and they are in truth the earliest predecessors of our modern novel.

The second group of works of fiction, earlier in time than the novel, and in a certain sense related to it, is the group of Italian and Spanish pastorals. The direct connection of the pastoral with the novel is clear though slight; and its history is worth considering here, because the pastoral forms a link between the literature before the revival of learning, and that of the centuries immediately preceding the one that saw the birth of the English novel. The order of descent is from the Eclogues of Vergil and the Latin pastoral, to the Italian pastoral, to the Spanish pastoral, to the English pastoral tale of Sidney. The names one might mention would be Vergil in the first century, Boccaccio in the fourteenth, Sannazaro in the early sixteenth, Montemayor and Sidney in the middle years of the sixteenth century, Honoré D'Urfé in the early seventeenth century. The prose Italian tale of Boccaccio, *L'Ameto* (1341-1342), is a tale of the rural diversions of the hunter Ameto and the nymph Lia, and of the stories told at the midsummer festival of Venus. It antedates by one hundred and sixty-two years the poetic *Arcadia* of Sannazaro, which is the tale of the wanderings of Ergasto through the Arcadian groves. These two tales sum up the contributions of Italy, in complete form, to the pastoral romances. From Spain we get two works, at least, which deserve mention: Ribeiro's *Menina e Moça* (Girl and Maiden), 1554, and Montemayor's *Diana,* the latter the most famous of all the late mediæval pastoral romances. Ribeiro's work is in prose, and is the story of the loves and misfortunes of the knights Lamentor and Narbindel. It is a story of pastoral life, with a suggestion of grief, affection and melancholy, and with machinery of adventures, misfortunes, romantic episodes, and knight errantry. Montemayor's *Diana* is also a story of unrequited love. Two swains, Sireno, who had loved and lost, and Sylvano, who had loved and never gained, meet Selvagia, who had loved and thrown away, by a brookside; and forthwith set themselves to tell the story of their loves and sorrows. To them enter a group of nymphs and a shepherdess, with new tales of disguises, distresses, and adventures; and all together they set forth on a pilgrimage to the temple of the goddess Diana. On the way they rescue another shepherdess, likewise in grief for the loss of a loved one. Arrived at the temple, the priestess despatches the new shepherd-ess on a mission of mercy to find her own love and the loved ones of the others. She fills three cups from an enchanted stream and gives to Sireno, Sylvano, and Selvagia, who fall into a sleep from which they awake to happiness, gained through the forgetting, in sleep, of their former affections and the occurrence of new ones, means of gratifying which have been provided by the thoughtful priestess through the mission of the travelling shepherdess. Happiness does not come to all, but rather the atmosphere of melancholy pervades the end of the work; for although the loved one of Sireno is returned, the potion of the priestess has taken away from Sireno the power of loving, and the book in its ending is a prophecy of the romanticism of a later day.

It may be that the direct connection of these pastoral tales with the English novel is slight. But they vastly influenced the literature of Europe. Sidney's "Arca-dia" in English literature looks back to them directly, and itself influenced the later fiction; D'Urfé's *Astrée* in French literature looks back to them, and itself has greatly influenced later fictions. The tearfulness of Richardson's "Pamela," the pathetic emotion of Marivaux's *Marianne,* are akin to the sentimentality of the *Diana* of Montemayor; the *Nouvelle Héloïse* of Rousseau is saturated with this same romantic emo-tion; and the melancholy of Sireno, whose loved one was another's wife, is again with us in the despair of Werther. The relation of the pastorals of the fifteenth century to the novels of the seventeenth is indirect; it affects the spirit rather than the method; but the mel-ancholy sentimentality of the pastoral tale is the mel-ancholy sentimentality of the early novel. We must certainly consider these tales well when searching for the predecessors of the modern novel.

It is from Spain that we get the pastoral romance in its finished form; it is from Spain that we get the mediæval romance of chivalry in its finished form. In one sense the romance of chivalry has always been with us, for the Odyssey of Homer must be termed a romance of chivalry. The Greek tales are romances of adventure undertaken in chivalrous devotion to an ideal love; the prose tales of Arthur and the poetic songs and lays of the minstrels have as a basis ideal action, and as material romantic adventure. But in coherent form these stories come to us for almost the first time in the Spanish romances—themselves the descendants of Arthurian legends and the minstrel lays—the Spanish romances of the early sixteenth century, notably the *Amadis de Gaula* (1470-1510). I need not tell the story of this romance. It is a heroic tale of the loves, the adventures, the sorrows, the successes, of the knights who are its heroes. It is even now a charming tale, for

the recital of the exploits, and the wanderings, and the desperate deeds throws about it the magic atmosphere of the twilight days of the later Middle Ages. Its noble deeds, its noble thoughts, its magical assistances, which had a charm for man in earlier ages, which had a charm for us in our boyhood years, have a charm for us to-day. All these things had tremendous influence on the novel. Such stories, wrought into form by the artists of a later day, are with us still; such tales we find in Scott, in Dumas, in Stevenson. As with the pastoral, the tracing of a direct line of descent is difficult, but the spirit of these romances of the chivalric deeds of heroes in the past is the spirit of the historical romance of to-day. They are not the novel; but without their influence the true novel might never have come.

They are not the novel. For there came a day when wild stories of the adventures of knights, and kings, and princes; when tales of unreal character, unreal scenes, unreal emotions; when tales of adventure, in lands far away, under circumstances impossible, and with help of enchantment, and magic, and super-human assistance,—there came a day when the tale of all these external, far-off, glorious unrealities passed away, and in its place came the simple story of a humble life, in scenes real, at hand; the story of the emotion of a simple, homely, struggling soul; the story of a Pamela, of a Marianne, of a Manon Lescaut, of a Joseph Andrews, of a Clarissa Harlowe. In the mid-dle years of the eighteenth century there came such a day. When that day came, it was the birthday of the English novel.

William Warner (essay date 1994)

SOURCE: "Licensing Pleasure: Literary History and the Novel in Early Modern Britain," in *The Columbia History of the British Novel*, edited by John Richetti, Columbia University Press, 1994, pp. 1-24.

[*In the following essay, Warner charts the novel's progress from "scandalous" newcomer on the literary landscape to a serious, legitimate form sanctioned by the efforts of such key figures as Samuel Richardson, Henry Fielding, Samuel Johnson, and Clara Reeve.*]

The Scandal of Novel Reading

Novels have been a respectable component of culture for so long that it is difficult for twentieth-century observers to grasp the unease produced by novel read-ing in the eighteenth century. Long before it became an issue for debate in literary studies, a quantum leap in the number, variety, and popularity of novels pro-voked cultural alarm in England during the decades following 1700. The flood of novels on the market, and the pleasures they incited, led many to see novels as a catastrophe for book-centered culture. While the novel was not clearly defined or conceptualized, the targets of the anti-novel campaign were quite precise: seventeenth-century romances, novellas of Continental origin, and those "novels" and "secret histories" written by Behn, Manley, and Haywood in the decades following 1680. The central themes of this debate may be culled from several texts: Samuel Johnson's 1750 *Rambler No. 4* essay on the new fiction of Richardson, Fielding, and Smollett; Francis Coventry's enthusiastic pamphlet in support of Fielding, "An Essay on the New Species of Writing Founded by Mr. Fielding: With a Word or Two upon the Modern State of Criticism" (1751); and in *The Progress of Romance,* a literary history in dialogue form by Clara Reeve published in 1785.

These texts mobilize criticism and alarm, praise and prescription in an attempt to modulate the comparatively new vogue for novel reading. Francis Coventry mocks the unreflected "emulation" produced in readers by the French romances of an earlier day: "This [vogue] obtain'd a long Time. Every Beau was an *Orondates,* and all the Belles were *Stariras.*" Though Samuel Johnson could not account for the fashion for romance, his *Rambler No. 4* essay describes the more powerful identification that recent "familiar histories" like *Clarissa* and *Tom Jones* induce in their readers: "If the power of example is so great, as to take possession of the memory by a kind of violence, and produce effects almost without the intervention of the will, care ought to be taken that . . . the best examples only should be exhibited." If novels produce effects "almost without the intervention of the [reader's] will," then readers are at risk of becoming automatons, and the author must assume responsibility for the novel's moral effects.

The power and danger of novels, especially to young women not exposed to classical education, arose from the pleasures they induced. In *The Progress of Romance,* Clara Reeve's leading character, Euphrasia, remembers "my mother and aunts being shut up in the parlour reading *Pamela,* and I took it very hard that I was excluded." Closeted with a novel, some are included, and others excluded, from the circle of pleasure. Coventry remarks upon the tenacity with which readers clung to their pleasures: "For tho' it was a folly, it was a pleasing one: and if sense could not yield the pretty creatures greater pleasure, dear nonsense must be ador'd." Opposing this pleasure "lecture would lose it's force; and ridicule would strive in vain to remove it."

But what is so pernicious about reading novels? *The Progress of Romance* ends with a staged debate between the woman scholar Euphrasia and a high-culture snob named Hortensius. Hortensius develops a wideranging indictment of novel reading. First, novels turn the reader's taste against serious reading: "A person used to this kind of reading will be disgusted with every thing serious or solid, as a weakened and depraved stomach rejects plain and wholesome food." Second, novels incite the heart with false emotions: "The seeds of vice and folly are sown in the heart,—the passions are awakened,—false expectations are raised.—A young woman is taught to expect adventures and intrigues. . . . If a plain man addresses her in rational terms and pays her the greatest of compliments,—that of desiring to spend his life with her,—that is not sufficient, her vanity is disappointed, she expects to meet a Hero in Romance." Finally, novels induce a dangerous autonomy from parents and guardians: "From this kind of reading, young people fancy themselves capable of judging of men and manners, and . . . believe themselves wiser than their parents and guardians, whom they treat with contempt and ridicule." Hortensius indicts novels for transforming the cultural function of reading from providing solid moral nourishment to catering to exotic tastes; from preparing a woman for the ordinary rational address of a plain good man to leading her to expect a proposal from a hero out of romance; and from reinforcing reliance upon parents and guardians to promoting a belief in the subject's autonomy. Taken together, novels have disfigured the reader's body: the taste, passions, and judgment of stomach, heart, and mind. Here, as so often in the polemics that surround novels, the reader is characterized as a susceptible female whose moral life is at risk. By strong implication, she is most responsible for transmitting the virus of novel reading.

From the vantage point of the late twentieth century, and after nearly nine decades of film and five of television, the alarm provoked by novel reading may seem hyperbolic or even quaint. But a condescendingly modernist "pro-pleasure" position renders the alarm with novel reading, and its effects on early modern culture, unintelligible. Though it is difficult to credit the specific object of the alarm of the eighteenth-century critics of novels—after all, we recommend to students some of the very novels these early modern critics inveighed against—given our current anxieties about the cultural effects of slasher films, rap music, MTV, and soap operas, it seems contradictory to dismiss those who worried about the effects of novels when they were new. But there are fundamental obstacles to deciphering the eighteenth century's anxious discourse on the pleasures of novels. After psychoanalysis, most concede the difficulty of knowing why one experiences pleasure; it is even more difficult to define the content or cause of the pleasure of eighteenth-century novel readers. However, we can trace certain clear effects of the campaign against these unlicensed pleasures. First, cultural critics sketched the profile of the culture-destroying pleasure seeker who haunts the modern era: the obsessive, unrestrained, closeted consumer of fantasy. Then, novelists like Richardson and Fielding, accepting the cogency of this critique, developed replacement fictions as a cure for the novel-addicted reader. In doing so, they aimed to deflect and reform, improve and justify the pleasures of a new species of elevated novel.

Since Plato's attack on the poets, philosophers and cultural critics had worried the effects of an audience's absorption in fictional entertainment. During the early eighteenth century the market gave this old cultural issue new urgency. Although there had been a trade in books for centuries, several developments gave the circulation of novels unprecedented cultural force. At a time when state censorship in England was subsiding and technological advances were making all printed matter more affordable, the market in printed books offered a site for the production and consumption of a very broad spectrum of entertainment. Published anonymously, or by parvenu authors supported by no patron of rank, novels appeared as anonymous and irresponsible creations, conceived with only one guiding intention: to pander to any desire that would produce a sale. Novels not only violated the spirit of seriousness expected of readers of books like *The Pilgrim's Progress* or *Paradise Lost;* they made no pretense to making any lasting contribution to culture. Novels were the first "disposable" books, written in anticipation of their own obsolescence and in acceptance of their own transient function as part of a culture of serial entertainments. Although only a small part of print culture in the early decades of the eighteenth century, novels appear to have been the most high-profile, fashionable, and fast-moving segment of the market. The vogue for novels helped to constitute a market culture—in the modern sense of commodities for purchase by the individual. In short, novels desanctified the book. Little wonder that novels were figured as an uncontrollable menace to culture.

Many of the vices attributed to the novel are also characteristics of the market: both breed imitation, gratify desire, and are oblivious to their moral effects. The market appears as a machine evidencing an uncanny automatism. Once they had become "the thing," nothing could stop novels on the market. In critiquing novels, cultural critics deplored the market's powerful, autonomous effect upon culture. Coventry's description of the imitations provoked by the success of Fielding's novels develops a general rule about success and emulation in a market-driven culture: "It is very certain, that whenever any thing new, of what kind soever, is started by one man, and appears with great success in the world, it quickly produces several in the same taste." Producers for the market have become mere factors of the market. Using the by now clichéd terms for describing the Grub Street hacks, Clara Reeve emphasizes how the accelerating multiplicity of novels complicates her own efforts at the classification and criticism of romances and novels. Rampant production also allows bad imitations to proliferate and engenders

new institutions to deliver novels indiscriminately into the hands of every reader: "The press groaned under the weight of Novels, which sprung up like mushrooms every year. . . . [Novels] did but now begin to increase upon us, but ten years more multiplied them tenfold. Every work of merit produced a swarm of imitators, till they became a public evil, and the institution of Circulating libraries, conveyed them in the cheapest manner to every bodies hand." An uncontrolled multiplicity threatens to metastasize culture. For the scholar surveying the production of many ages, the market has the effect of blurring the distinctness and expressive readability of culture. Thus in his *History of Fiction* (1814) John Dunlop complains that while earlier epochs developed "only one species of fiction," which could then be read as "characteristic" of the age, more recently "different kinds have sprung up at once; and thus they were no longer expressive of the taste and feelings of the period of their composition." The critical histories of the novel by Reeve and Dunlop aim to restore the character to culture.

If, according to a formula developed in the writings of the French cultural critic Michel Foucault, power operates less by repressing or censoring than by producing new "reality," new "domains of objects and rituals of truth," then the success of novels on the market changed culture by producing a need to read. Clara Reeve describes this newly incited desire: "People must read something, they cannot always be engaged by dry disquisitions, the mind requires some amusement." Between uncritical surrender to novel reading and a wholesale rejection of novels in favor of "serious" reading, Richardson and Fielding traced a third pathway for the novel. In Reeve's words, the strategy was to "write an antidote to the bad effects" of novels "under the disguise" of being novels. This requires a cunning pharmacology. When Lady Echlin, Richardson's most morally exacting correspondent, warns that "the best instruction you can give, blended with love intrigue, will never answer your good intention," Richardson replies with a celebrated reformulation of the old demand that art should both amuse and instruct: "Instruction, Madam, is the Pill; Amusement is the Gilding. Writings that do not touch the Passions of the Light and Airy, will hardly ever reach the heart." Coventry describes the manner in which Fielding, "who sees all the little movements by which human nature is actuated," intervenes in the market for novels. "The disease became epidemical, but there were no hopes of a cure, 'till Mr. Fielding endeavour'd to show the World, that pure Nature could furnish out as agreeable entertainment, as those airy non-entical forms they had long ador'd, and persuaded the ladies to leave this extravagance to their Abigails with their cast cloaths." Thus the "disease" of romance, associated with the craze for new fashions, can be "cured" only by cutting new paths toward pleasure. Then the old novels, with their corrupting pleasures, can be passed on, along with old dresses, to the lady's servant.

It is beyond the scope of this chapter to give a detailed account of how the popularity of the "histories" published by Richardson and Fielding in the 1740s effected an upward revaluation of the novel in Britain. However, the key elements of their successful strategy are implicit in the metaphors of the antidote, the vaccine, and the gilded pill. First, a broad spectrum of earlier writings—romances, novellas, and secret histories written on the Continent and in Britain—are characterized as essentially equivalent. Deemed licentious, fantasy-ridden, and debased, they are decried as a cultural disease. Next, Richardson and Fielding produce substitute fictions to absorb the reader. Although Richardson and Fielding wrote antinovels, they didn't write nonnovels. Just as a vaccine can achieve its antidotal function only by introducing a mild form of a disease into the body of the patient, their novels incorporated many elements of the dangerous old novels of Behn, Manley, and Haywood into this "new species" of fiction. By including improving discourse familiar from conduct books, spiritual autobiography, and the periodical essay, the "histories" of Richardson and Fielding could appear radically "new."

Cervantes' *Don Quixote* (1605/1615) and Lafayette's *Princess de Cleves* (1678) had demonstrated the power of a modern fiction composed on the textual "grounds" of the earlier romance. Those who elevated the novel in England pursued a similar strategy by appropriating elements from the earlier novel—such as the female libertine, or the intricate seduction scheme—and articulating (by connecting together, and thus "speaking") them in a new way, with a new meaning, as part of a new form of novel. Thus, within Richardson's *Clarissa,* the rake Lovelace, by using disguise and manipulation to pursue seduction, upholds the old novel's ethos of amorous intrigue within the plot lines of the new. The bad old obsession with sex and passion is still there, but through Clarissa's resistance and its attendant critical discourse, sex is sublimated to the virtuous sentiments of the new and improving novel. Incorporated into a new species of novel, the old novel gilds the pill from within, helping to insure the popularity of the new novel. To secure the enlightening cultural address of their novels, Richardson and Fielding disavowed rather than assumed their debt to those popular novels whose narrative resources they incorporated and whose cultural space they sought to occupy. They simultaneously absorbed and erased the novels they would supplant.

The new novel reorients rather than banishes spontaneous reader identification; now a morally improving emulation is promoted. When, in *The Progress of Romance,* Hortensius complains that Richardson's epistolary novels "have taught many young girls to wire-draw their language, and to spin always long letters out of nothing," Euphrasia defends the cultural value of studying and imitating Richardson over the "stud-

ies" of an earlier generation: "Let the young girls . . . copy Richardson, as often as they please, and it will be owing to the defects of their understandings, or judgments, if they do not improve by him. We could not say as much of the reading Ladies of the last age. . . . No truly, for their studies were the French and Spanish Romances, and the writings of Mrs. Behn, Mrs. Manly, and Mrs. Heywood [*sic*]." In order to serve as an antidotal substitute for the poison of novels, the elevated novels of Richardson and Fielding had to be founded in an antagonistic critique and overwriting of the earlier novels of Behn, Manley, and Haywood. This elevating novel brought a new disposition of pleasure and value to its readers. But the novel's rise is not a spontaneous or organic development. On the contested cultural site of novel reading at mid-century, it is, as the Marxist critic John Frow suggests in a different context, not so much the old that has died, but the new that has killed.

Sublimating the Novel by Telling Its History

The successes of *Pamela* (1740), *Joseph Andrews* (1742), *Clarissa* (1747-1748), and *Tom Jones* (1749), as well as the many imitations they provoked on the market, helped to countersign the elevated novel as a significant new cultural formation. But such validation also depended upon those critics who grasped the possibilities of this new kind of fiction and sought to describe its signal features, cultural virtues, and history. This project often required inventive critical strategies. By rescuing the elevated novel from the general cultural indictment of novels, the early literary critics and historians I have cited—Samuel Johnson, Francis Coventry, Clara Reeve, and John Dunlop—made their texts supplements to the project of elevating the novel.

For Johnson, a critical intervention on behalf of the new novel meant arguing, by way of response to the recent popularity of *Tom Jones* and *Roderick Random,* in favor of the "exemplary" characters of Richardson over the more true-to-life "mixed" characters of Fielding and Smollett. In a pamphlet published anonymously, "An Essay on the New Species of Writing Founded by Mr. Fielding" (1751), Coventry follows the basic procedure Fielding had devised in the many interpolated prefaces to *Joseph Andrews* and *Tom Jones:* he transports critical terms and ideas developed earlier for poetry, epic, and drama to the novel. But Coventry goes farther. Just as Aristotle modeled the "rules" of tragedy upon Sophocles, and early modern French and English critics defined the rules for epic through criticism of Homer, Coventry made Fielding's work the template for the "species" of writing he had "founded." As the "great Example" and "great original" for "future historians of this kind," Fielding's work provides the terms for a new inventory of neoclassical "laws": "As Mr. Fielding first introduc'd this new kind of Biography, he restrain'd it with Laws which should ever after be deem'd sacred by all that attempted his Manner; which I here propose to give a brief account of." In his "word or two on the modern state of criticism," Coventry bewails the decline of criticism from earlier epochs (from Horace to Pope), quotes and corrects the modern scorn for critics, and inveighs against the partisanship discernible in the reception of new plays. Coventry's way of posturing as a critic—he is unctuous, defensive, and yet arrogant—is the very antithesis of the imperious law-givings and definitive pronouncements characteristic of Fielding's narrators. But both styles of address suggest there is as yet no preestablished cultural vantage point or institutionalized discourse for the criticism of novels.

But such an anchor for the articulation of the novel was developing. Written thirty-five years later than Johnson's or Coventry's criticism, Reeve's *Progress of Romance* (1785) composes what seems to be the first scholarly literary history of novels in English. Within the term *romance* Reeve comprehends not only the Greek romance, the medieval romances (in both verse and prose), and the seventeenth-century heroic romance; she also goes backward to the epics of Homer and forward to the "modern novels" of France and England. The inclusion of Homeric epic in the category of romance is a classification dubious enough to have been rejected by virtually every subsequent literary historian of the novel; but it gives Reeve's protagonist, Euphrasia, a way to refute the high-culture bias of her polemical antagonist, Hortensius. In addition, by developing the term *romance* into a global category inclusive of fictional entertainments produced over a vast expanse of "times, countries, and manners," she uses the historicist horizon of her study to develop an indulgence that protects the now unfashionable romances as well as the modern novels under contemporary attack. The literary history and criticism of the English novel that has developed over the two hundred years since Reeve's text—from John Dunlop and Hippolyte Taine to Ian Watt and Michael McKeon—inevitably comes to be implicated in the task Richardson and Fielding seemed to set going in England: that of securing an elevated cultural address for the novel.

We can begin to grasp the broader cultural uses of literary history by attending to the way John Dunlop introduces his ambitious three-volume *History of Fiction: Being a Critical Account of the Most Celebrated Prose Works of Fiction, from the Earliest Greek Romances to the Novels of the Present Age* (1815). In order to articulate the general cultural value of fiction over history Dunlop quotes Lord Bacon:

> Fiction gives to mankind what history denies, and, in some measure, satisfies the mind with shadows when it cannot enjoy the substance: . . . Fiction strongly shows that a greater variety of things, a more perfect order, a more beautiful variety, than

can any where be found in nature, is pleasing to the mind. And as real history gives us not the success of things according to the deserts of vice and virtue, Fiction corrects it, and presents us with the fates and fortunes of persons rewarded or punished according to merit. And as real history disgusts us with a familiar and constant similitude of things, Fiction relieves us by unexpected turns and changes, and thus not only delights, but inculcates morality and nobleness of soul. It raises the mind by accommodating the images of things to our desires, and not like history and reason, subjecting the mind to things.

By appealing to Bacon on the value of fiction, Dunlop not only invokes the authority of a major British thinker but also neatly hurdles almost two hundred years of wrangling over the morally dubious effects of taking pleasure from fiction. By using the general term *fiction* for his history of romances and novels, Dunlop encompasses the polemical terms of the debate he would nonetheless inflect and recast. Eighteenth-century defenses of the novel (from Congreve and Richardson to Fielding and Reeve) usually engage a set of polar oppositions still familiar to us: the novel is to the romance as the "real" is to the "ideal," as fact is to fantasy, as the probable is to the amazing, as the commonplace is to the exotic, and so on. Fiction is developed by Dunlop as a third term that can at once finesse and reconcile these polar oppositions. Fiction does this by becoming art, delivering "a more perfect order, a more beautiful variety" than "nature."

Through Dunlop's use of Bacon, Renaissance and Romantic aesthetics meet in a justification of fiction that is, finally, psychological. Through fiction, the reader is no longer "subject" to things, nor disgusted with "a familiar and constant similitude of things." Instead, fiction "relieves" and "delights," and "raises the mind by accommodating the images of things to our desires." The cultural efficacy of fiction comes from its successful gratification of the reader's pleasure. Dunlop's translation of Bacon assumes yet reverses the anxiety about the reader's pleasure that had motivated earlier condemnations of the novel. When Dunlop glosses Bacon's emphasis upon "delight," it becomes apparent that the pleasure Dunlop promotes is quite different from the pleasure that novel readers had been accused of indulging. Instead of obsessive, personal, deluded, erotic pleasures, we are called to soft and social ones: "How much are we indebted to [fiction] for pleasure and enjoyment! it sweetens solitude and charms sorrow. . . ." These pleasures improve and uplift the reader, by taking him or her into an elevated social and emotive space: "The rude are refined by an introduction, as it were, to the higher orders of mankind, and even the dissipated and selfish are, in some degree, corrected by those paintings of virtue and simple nature, which must ever be employed by the novelist if he wish to awaken emotion or delight." Having confirmed its beneficial effect, Dunlop can confirm the novel's rise from its earlier disreputable cultural position:

> This powerful instrument of virtue and happiness, after having been long despised, on account of the purposes to which it had been made subservient, has gradually become more justly appreciated, and more highly valued. Works of Fiction have been produced, abounding at once with the most interesting details, and the most sagacious reflections, and which differ from treatises of abstract philosophy only by the greater justness of their views, and the higher interest which they excite.

Dunlop's description of his project helps us to apprehend the broader purpose of his literary history: to sublimate the novel so as to produce a new disposition, or arrangement, of the pleasure of novel reading. With his title, which neither exiles all novels from culture in favor of drama, epic, sermons, or conduct books, nor favors the simple, uncritical acceptance of all novels into his narrative of the history of fiction, Dunlop announces that his history is to be "critical"—that is, it will judge works according to their quality so as to focus upon only "the most celebrated" prose fiction. What results, in both Reeve and Dunlop as well as in every subsequent literary history, is a chronological panorama, a certain spectacular sequential cinematography of culture in which selected cultural practices and productions are narrated as significant and valuable. By this means literary history (selectively) licenses (sublimated) pleasures. Through this literary history, novels produced in the market can be inserted into a (more or less) continuous narrative and turned toward higher cultural purposes: for example, serving as an expression of "the voice of the people" (Taine) or being part of "the Great Tradition" (Leavis).

Dunlop writes as though the culturally elevating role for fiction were already achieved. In fact, his own literary history is designed to promote that end. To argue the centrality of fiction to culture, Dunlop begins his introduction with an elaborate analogy between gardening and fiction making, which quickly implicates his own literary history. The analogy also indexes what we might call the necessary violence of literary history. Just as the "savage" has gathered, and placed around his dwelling, plants that please him, so too have men lived events "which are peculiarly grateful, and of which the narrative at once pleases himself, and excites in the minds of his hearers a kindred emotion." What are gathered are "unlooked-for occurrences, successful enterprise, or great and unexpected deliverance from signal danger and distress." A gardener learns that one must not just collect but also weed out the

> useless or noxious, and [those] which weaken or impair the pure delight which he derives from others

> . . . the rose should no longer be placed beside the thistle, as in the wild, but that it should flourish in a clear, and sheltered, and romantic situation, where its sweets may be undiminished, and where its form can be contemplated without any attending circumstances of uneasiness or disgust. The collector of agreeable facts finds, in like manner, that the sympathy which they excite can be heightened by removing from their detail every thing that is not interesting, or which tends to weaken the principal emotion, which it is his intention to raise. He renders, in this way, the occurrences more unexpected, the enterprises more successful, the deliverance from danger and distress more wonderful.

The same process that describes the "fine arts" of gardening and fiction making—selecting, weeding, and intensifying with an eye toward pleasure—applies also to the literary history Dunlop composes. Dunlop's "critical" history of fiction becomes an improving and enlightening cultivation of fiction for culture. By using the fiction of widely different epochs to survey the variety of cultural achievements, literary history makes novels more than instruments of private (kinky, obsessive) gratification. They are drawn into the larger tableau of cultural accomplishment—which Dunlop calls "the advance of the human mind"—until a certain disinterested moral and aesthetic pleasure appears to be the telos of all fiction making.

But the gardening metaphor insinuates certain assumptions into the project of this literary history. Literary history as cultivation spatializes time, so that the successive conflicts between the often antagonistic types of fiction written in England over the course of a century by, for example, Behn, Richardson, Fielding, and Radcliffe, are arranged to appear as one harmoniously balanced array of species that can be surveyed in one leisurely stroll, as one wanders through a garden. However, it proves as implausible to have a literary history without a literary historian as it is to have a garden without a gardener. It is the valuative role of the literary historian—the critic holding the scales over each text read—that produces the synchronic moment of judgment through which a narrative of the progress or history of romance, novel, and fiction can be grasped and told. Then, the way in which that story is told has a feedback effect: which writers are included and excluded, which are brought into the foreground, cast into the shade, or weeded away, determines what kinds of writing and authorship will come to count as "tradition" that grounds subsequent value judgments. This is the ironic terminus of a hegemonic literary history. Literary history can easily become tautological and self-confirming, a garden wall to protect specimens collected against the very factors it might have interpreted: history, change, difference.

A Vortex Mis-seen as an Origin

Once Dunlop's literary history gets under way, it becomes apparent that civilizing the novel requires a certain calculated violence. In a chapter entitled "Sketch of the Origin and Progress of the English Novel," Dunlop offers a typology of the elevated novel: novels are divided into the "serious" (Richardson, Sheridan, Godwin), the "comic" (Fielding, Smollett), and the "romantic" (Walpole, Reeve, Radcliffe). But before offering this schematic overview of what we would now call the eighteenth-century novel, Dunlop does some weeding by giving cursory negative treatment to the novels of Behn, Manley, and the early Haywood. Behn's novels, we are informed, "have not escaped the moral contagion which infected the literature of that age." Though Dunlop merely alludes to "the objections which may be charged against many" of Behn's novels, he ends the passage describing the "faults in points of morals" of Behn's "imitator," Eliza Haywood, in this fashion: "Her male characters are in the highest degree licentious, and her females are as impassioned as the Saracen princesses in the Spanish romances of chivalry."

By orientalizing these early novels and by characterizing them as inappropriately erotic—too feminine, too European, and too immoral—Dunlop relegates to the margins of *The History of Fiction* some of the most popular novels published in England between 1683 and 1730. How is the eclipse of an influential strain of popular fiction to be understood? Dunlop's dismissal of Behn, Manley, and Haywood from his history confirms a judgment that critics of the early amorous novel had been making since the 1730s. This negative judgment might be attributed to changes in sensibility, taste, or style, or to the idea that a certain formula has exhausted its appeal. But these words merely relabel rather than explain the cultural change we are trying to interpret. It is, no doubt, correct to argue that the novels of amorous intrigue are an integral expression of the culture of the Restoration, with the zeal of Charles II's court for sexual license, its eschewal of the dour asceticism of the Commonwealth, and its enthusiastic translation of French cultural forms. Such a historical placement of the early novel allows one to align its passing with the reaction, after 1688, against the excesses of the Restoration. Pleasures disowned become discomforting, and through embarrassment, a kind of unpleasure.

Some feminist literary historians have attributed the devaluation of Behn, Manley, and Haywood to their gender. However, even before Richardson and Fielding won ascent from the market for their novels of the 1740s, the moral improvement of the novel of amorous intrigue was undertaken by Elizabeth Rowe, Jane Barker, and Penelope Aubin. Explanations based upon taste, political history, and gender fail to come to terms with the particular way in which the novels of Behn, Manley, and Haywood were devalued and overwritten in the 1740s.

The erasure or forgetting of earlier cultural formations is an obscure process. Unlike material objects, cultural ideas and forms do not become used up or out of date. Cultural forms—from letters and love stories to national constitutions—can be rejuvenated by new technology, foreign transplants, and political strife. In other words, recycling seems to be the rule rather than the exception in culture. Thus, for example, the novel of amorous intrigue, developed in the late Restoration by Behn under strong influence from the Continental novella and the aristocratic literature of love, was exploited for politically motivated scandal and satire by Delariviere Manley in the *New Atalantis* (1709). Then, following the spectacular success of *Love in Excess* (1719-1720), this species of novel was turned into repeatable "formula fiction" on the market by Eliza Haywood in the 1720s. To remove elements from culture one must understand "forgetting" as, in Nietzsche's words, "an active and in the strictest sense positive faculty of repression." The incorporation of the novel of amorous intrigue within the elevated novel of the 1740s is one of the means by which old pleasures are disowned and effaced. As I have noted above, novelists like Richardson and Fielding promote this forgetting, first by defacing the novel of amorous intrigue and then by providing their own novels as replacements for the novels they characterize as degraded and immoral. These new novels overwrite—disavow but appropriate, waste but recycle—the novels they spurn.

Reeve and Dunlop do not commit their literary histories to exercising a "good memory." Unlike certain late-twentieth-century counter-hegemonic literary histories—whether feminist, African-American, or gay and lesbian—the works of Reeve and Dunlop do not set out to counteract a biased cultural memory. Instead they are constrained by the protocols of a culturally elevating literary history to be critical and selective, and thus forgetful. In the introduction to *The Progress of Romance,* Reeve tells her readers that she seeks "to assist according to my best judgment, the reader's choice, amidst the almost infinite variety it affords, in a selection of such as are most worthy of a place in the libraries of readers of every class, who seek either for information or entertainment." The effacement of Behn's novels from those literary histories written in the wake of the novel's elevation does not depend upon the good will of the literary historian. Thus, while Reeve is generous with Behn—"let us cast a veil of compassion over her faults"—and Dunlop is severe, both ignore all her novels except *Oroonoko.* By contrast, the novels of Richardson and Fielding are given positions of special priority in both accounts of the novel's rise. The success of the elevated novel in the 1740s—its appearance in culture as the only novel worthy of reading, cultural attention, and detailed literary history—means the early novels of Behn, Manley, and Haywood will be pushed into the margins of literary histories, where they nonetheless never quite disappear but serve—as they do in Richardson and Fielding's texts—as an abject trace or degraded "other" needed to secure the identity of the "real" (i.e., legitimate) novel.

From Reeve forward, scholarly literary history develops a paradoxical relationship to the forgotten texts of the past. It retrieves from the archival memory of culture and reads again what its contemporary culture has almost completely forgotten. This activity pushes Reeve toward a certain regret about the shifts in cultural value that can look quite arbitrary to one who has looked long enough down the "stream of time."

> Romances have for many ages past been read and admired, lately it has been the fashion to decry and ridicule them; but to an unprejudiced person, this will prove nothing but the variations of times, manners, and opinions.—Writers of all denominations,—Princes and Priests,—Bishops and Heroes,—have their day, and then are out of date.—Sometimes indeed a work of intrinsic merit will revive, and renew its claim to immortality: but this happiness falls to the lot of few, in comparison of those who roll down the stream of time, and fall into the gulph of oblivion.

This passage naturalizes the process of disappearance and forgetting—by its reference to the wheel of fortune that gives "princes and priests, bishops and heroes . . . their day" and then takes it away, as well as by its metaphorical characterization of the movement of a "work of . . . merit" down "the stream of time" into "the gulph of oblivion." These analogies obscure the particular cultural strife at work within shifts in cultural memory. Thus the differences of gender, politics, and class that separate Behn and Richardson, casting the first down into "oblivion" while the second is raised up into prominence, are conducted through the literary histories that translate them for a later age. Though literary historians attempt to be "unprejudiced" (Reeve) and embrace an ethos of "judgment, candour, and impartiality" (Coventry), and though their histories aspire to secure general moral or universal aesthetic grounds for critical judgment, the actual practice of literary history does not occlude but instead reflects cultural division.

Since one of the meanings of *gulf* is a "whirlpool, or absorbing eddy," I can accommodate my thesis about the novel's rise to Reeve's metaphor. The elevation of the new novel over the old novel of amorous intrigue produces a vortex or whirlpool within the land/seascape of eighteenth-century British culture. Where one kind of reading is thrown up, another is thrown down; where one kind of pleasure is licensed, another is dis-

credited. This turbulent vortex of reciprocal appearance and disappearance is mis-seen as the origin of the novel. But in order for the elevated novel to appear, the novel of amorous intrigue must be made to disappear into a gulf of oblivion. Thus birth requires a burial, but only after the murder of the other novel. While this vortex first appears in the cultural strife of the 1740s, it is also readable in every subsequent literary history devised to tell of the novel's rise.

To apprehend "the rise of the novel" as a vortex of cultural conflict helps to refocus the way gender difference and strife crosscut the expansion of novel reading in early modern culture. In aligning romances with French fashions and insisting that both are distinctly female addictions, Coventry was repeating one of the clichés of his age. The romance was associated with women because of its popularity with women readers. Reeve, by casting *The Progress of Romance* in the form of a series of salon-like lectures and debates between Hortensius and Euphrasia (with Sophronia acting the role of a nonpartisan judge), inscribes the debate about romance and its value within a battle of the sexes. Euphrasia rejects Hortensius's sweeping critique of romances, first by asking how Hortensius can banish all "fiction" of questionable moral standards—for this would mean indicting the classical authors boys study in their youth—and then by rejecting any double standard by which novels might receive sweeping censure because they are the favorite reading of women. By exfoliating her account of the novel's progress in a series of lessons that finally wins the willing conversion of a skeptical male, Reeve's text acquires the shape and feel of a seduction. Hortensius seems to relent in his opposition to romance because of his high regard for Euphrasia. But the resolution of this staged debate does not overcome the deeper resonances of the gendered contest around romances and novels. The pejorative terms applied to romance (*fanciful, wishful, out of touch with reality,* etc.) are also applied to women. The favorable terms applied to novels (*realistic, rational, improving*) are congruent with those that describe the male as a politically responsible member of the public sphere.

Within the context of the debate about novels, it is not surprising that male and female critics offer different pathways toward the novel's elevation. In elevating the novel, Coventry follows Fielding's attempt to splice classical knowledge and criticism into the reading of the novel. Although John Dunlop, like Reeve, applies a modern, historicist, more or less tolerant horizon of scholarship to the novel, his appeal to philosophical grounds for evaluating fiction helps push the novel toward a monumental cultural role. In elevating the novel, Clara Reeve (like Mary Wollstonecraft and Laetitia Barbauld later) turns the novel into a form for transmitting social knowledge. Reeve ends her literary history by offering two lists to parents, guardians, and tutors, "intended chiefly for the female sex": "Books for Children" and "Books for Young Ladies." This two-stage course of reading includes fables, spellers, conduct books, periodical essays, and only one item on the second list we would describe as a novel— "Richardson's Works." Following this curriculum prepares young female minds for an informed and critical reading of the romances and novels Reeve has described in *The Progress of Romance.* Literary history acquires the pedagogical function it still serves in literary studies: it becomes a reading list with its entries contextualized by narrative.

The gendered divide that expresses itself throughout the course of the institutionalization of the novel in England and in the various accounts of its "rise" is only one instance, though perhaps the most pervasive and important one, of the partisanship David Perkins has detected in much literary history. Given the way literary history is used to shape pleasure and define value, how could it be different? Thus the various positions upon what constitutes the first novel, and implicitly, what is the most valuable paradigm of novelistic authorship, work within the earliest literary histories of the elevated novel, and are reflected in the divergent critical valuations of Richardson and Fielding. In this way, the rivalry of Richardson and Fielding on the market during the 1740s was reproduced in the earliest literary criticism and history of the novel. Coventry ignores Richardson in proclaiming Fielding's unheralded achievements, while Johnson's prescription for the novel's cultural role is rigged to favor Richardson's fictional practice. The antagonism of Richardson and Fielding expresses itself through the writings of Hazlitt, Coleridge, Scott, and every subsequent literary historian of their differences. This antagonism shows little sign of dissipating in our own day. It is not just that different values reflect themselves in divergent accounts of our cultural repertoire. There are also always different agendas for the future dispositions of pleasure and value. Thus recent feminist critics have found Richardson most useful in their critical work, but Fielding *not.*

The elevation of the novel and its countersigning by literary history is neither simply right nor wrong, good nor bad. New discursive formations—like the elevated novel—incite new and valuable cultural production. Thus, howeverunfair or tendentious its judgments about the early novels of Behn, Manley, and Haywood, literary history's sublimation of "the novel" enables the ambitious novelistic projects of the nineteenth and twentieth centuries. One example is the quixotic ambition to write "the Great American Novel." Literary history does not have to be fair, or oriented toward the categories we would now credit, in order for it to bear its effects into culture. Yet its judgments are also always—and interminably—open to revision. The appeals court of culture is always in session. The recent feminist revaluation of the women novelists of the early eighteenth century seems to depend upon a contemporary reinterpretation of what is happening in the novels of Behn, Manley, and Haywood: explicit treatments of gender, sexuality, and power that have critical currency in our own time.

The Rise of Debate about the Rise of the English Novel

This chapter's account of the cultural scandal of novel reading, and of the inventive responses of novelists and literary historians to that scandal, suggests a signal tendency of most literary histories of the novel. Like a museum, literary history turns the strife of history into a repertoire of forms. It does so by taking differences that may have motivated the writing or reading of novels within specific historical contexts—differences of religion, politics, class, social propriety, or ethical design, to name a few—and converts them into differences of kind. Thus, for example, the polemic between Richardson and Fielding about the sorts of narrative and character fiction should possess comes to represent, within literary history, two species of novel: the Richardson novel of psychology and sentiment, and the Fielding novel of social panorama and critique. The novels of amorous intrigue written by Behn and the early Haywood have a bad difference that puts them entirely outside the frame of literary history of the elevated novel.

Notice the reversal of vision that literary history effects. If we interpret the writings of Behn, Richardson, and Fielding as part of the cultural history of Britain, we can find complex patterns of antagonism and detect the conscious and unconscious efforts of each author to distinguish his or her writing from its antecedents. By differentiating his novels from Behn's, Richardson engenders many of the differences evident between their novels. By contrast, literary history "finds," upon the archival table of its investigations, different novels, which it then attempts to distinguish and classify. Differences among novels are no longer effects of history, but the initial data for literary classification. Thus the category "novel" acquires a paradoxical role: pregiven and yet belated in its arrival, "the novel" is made to appear ready at hand, but it is actually that which the literary history of the novel defines. Often presented as the humble, minimal, and preliminary axiom of a literary history, the idea of the novel operates within the literary history of canonical texts as a kind of law. Changes in the idea of the novel during the nineteenth century were a necessary precondition for the belated emergence of the novel's origins as a compelling enigma.

Through the nineteenth and twentieth centuries, the novel keeps rising, and *The Columbia History of the British Novel* is one more symptom of that movement. Space does not permit a full genealogy of the evolution of the question of the novel's origins. But I can offer a brief sketch of those changes whereby the question becomes one of the Gordian knots of literary studies. Over the course of the nineteenth and twentieth centuries, novels are collected, edited, reviewed, and taught in schools and universities. Three basic shifts in the category of "the novel" are concomitants of this modern institutionalization of the novel as an object of knowledge in literary studies. First the novel is nationalized. Novels were once considered the type of writing most likely to move easily across linguistic and national boundaries. The critics and literary historians I have quoted in this chapter found the romances and novels of different nations on the same shelves. Reeve and Dunlop discuss the novels of Cervantes, Marivaux, and Rousseau within the same conceptual coordinates as the novels of Richardson and Fielding. But in the nineteenth century, novels come to be understood as a type of writing particularly suited to representing the character, mores, landscape, and spirit of the nation. At its most significant, a novel is, in the phrase of the French literary historian Hippolyte Taine, an expression of "the voice of the people."

In the wake of this idea, a thesis develops that would never have occurred to Reeve or Dunlop: that the modern English novel has little or nothing to do with earlier novellas and romances, and thus it does not develop out of Italian, Spanish, or French precursors. Instead the novel is said to derive from distinctly English discourses: the journalism of Addison and Steele, the party writers of the reign of Queen Anne, the new Science, religious autobiography like Bunyan's, writers of travel and adventure, and so on. This position was first clearly enunciated by the nineteenth-century professor of English at Glasgow, Walter Raleigh, in his book *The English Novel* (1894). It has been developed much more fully in recent books by Michael McKeon and J. Paul Hunter. While Reeve's "progress of romance" and Dunlop's "history of fiction" are inclusively multinational, extending backward to ancient and medieval times and across the channel to include Continental romance and novella, national literary histories cut these temporal and spatial links. Traits of the British culture—empiricism, protestant individualism, moral seriousness, and a fondness for eccentric character—are promoted from secondary characteristics of novels which happened to have been written in England to primary radicals of the novel's generic identity.

By narrowing the vortex of the novel's formation, a nationalist British literary history produces a new object of cultural value now dubbed "the English novel." The English novel becomes the subject and eponymous protagonist in a series of literary histories written by Walter Raleigh (1894), George Saintsbury (1913), and Walter Allen (1954). The phrase appears again in the titles of William Lyon Phelps's *Advance of the English Novel* (1916), Ernest Baker's *History of the English Novel* (1924-1936), and Arnold Kettle's *Introduction to the English Novel* (1951). Within these literary histories, Richardson and Fielding and Smollett and Sterne become the "dream team" of eighteenth-century fiction, and, in Saintsbury's famous metaphor, they are the four wheels of that carriage of English fiction that, with its full modern development into a repeatable "formula" by Austen and Scott, is "set agoing to travel through the centuries." After Saintsbury, Defoe is added as a fifth early master of the English novel. With Ian Watt's *Rise of the Novel* (1957), the modifier "English" is implied but erased. Now the rise of "the English novel" marks the rise of "the" novel, that is, *all* novels. A synecdoche wags the dog. In this way a national literary history overcomes what has always worried the earliest promoters and elevators of the novel in Britain: the belatedness and indebtedness of English fiction.

The claim for the priority of the English novel made by this group of literary historians involves a shift in the novel's distinct identity: instead of consisting in its moral coherence, the novel's identity comes to derive from its adherence to some sort of realism. Although the kernel of this thesis is at least as old as the distinction between romance and novella defined by Congreve, Reeve, and others, the nineteenth century contributes an arduous and subtle development to the idea of what constitutes realism. With the development of the idea of society as an organic totality, the novel becomes—for Balzac, Dickens, and Eliot—uniquely appropriate for its study and analysis. Novelistic realism is complicated and enriched by those novelists—especially Flaubert and James—who undertake to aestheticize the novel. As art, the novel realizes its equality with poetry, and prepares itself for entrance into the "Great Tradition" (Leavis's 1948 title) of Western literature. The idea of the novel as art means that novel studies, and literary histories of the novel, come to privilege the novel's "form." Claims for the novel's formal coherence are not fatal to the idea of the novel's realistic imitation of social or psychic life. Instead the two ideas work together in literary histories from Ernest Baker's ten-volume *History of the English Novel* to Ian Watt's *Rise of the Novel* (1957). For Ian Watt "formal realism" becomes the distinctive characteristic of the novel and the crucial invention necessary for its "rise" to being the most influential linguistic vehicle of subjective experience.

With the idea of the novel's nationalism, its realism, and its power to express a personal interiority emerge three questions that have preoccupied scholarly study of the early British novel for at least one hundred years. Out of the concept of the novel's Englishness emerges a new question: how, where, and why does the *English* novel begin, originate, arise? This question is framed so as to assure that its answer will come from within the study of British culture. Once the novel is given a modern, relatively scientific epistemological mission—to be realistic in its representation of social and psychological life—one must ask, what constitutes realism? What form of writing should serve as the paradigm for novelistic mimesis? These are not so much questions that can be answered as a terrain for interminable negotiation and invention. Finally, how is the Englishness and realism of the novel implicated in the invention of the modern subject? With Watt, and those many critics and literary historians who have followed in his wake, the notion that the novel is a fully actualized form of a nation's literature, characterized by realism, is brought into alignment with two relatively new ideas about the novel's beginnings: its sudden birth and its distinctive modernity. Recently, new work on the novel's rise, influenced by Marxism, feminism, and poststructuralism, has sought to contest and complicate this classic interpretation of the rise of the novel. Instead of trying to summarize this rich vein of work, I will close with an observation. The themes of the novel's modernity and sudden birth, its realism and aesthetic greatness, its expression of nationhood or moral guidance to the reader—whether formulated early or late in the novel's "progress"—all these themes serve to update the cultural project that unfolded in the eight decades after 1740, and that this essay has explored: the impulse to elevate the novel and to sublimate the pleasures it incites.

Works Cited

Baker, Ernest. *The History of the English Novel.* New York: Barnes and Noble, 1924.

Coventry, Francis. "An Essay on the New Species of Writing Founded by Mr. Fielding." London, 1751. Los Angeles: Augustan Reprint No. 95, 1962.

Dunlop, John Colin. *The History of Fiction.* 3 vols. London, 1814.

Frow, John. *Marxism and Literary History.* Cambridge: Harvard University Press, 1986.

Perkins, David. *Is Literary History Possible?* Baltimore: Johns Hopkins University Press, 1992.

Raleigh, Sir Walter. *The English Novel: A Short Sketch of Its History from the Earliest Times to the Appearance of "Waverley."* London: John Murray, 1894.

Reeve, Clara. *The Progress of Romance.* Colchester, 1785.

Saintsbury, George. *The English Novel.* London: Dent, 1913.

Taine, Hippolyte A. *History of English Literature.* 1863. Trans. H. Van Laun. New York: Frederick Ungar, 1965.

Watt, Ian. *The Rise of the Novel.* Berkeley: University of California Press, 1957.

WOMEN AND THE NOVEL

Paula R. Backscheider (essay date 1979)

SOURCE: "Woman's Influence," in *Studies in the Novel*, Vol. XI, No. 1, Spring, 1979, pp. 3-22.

[*In the essay that follows, Backscheider examines some methods of influencing other people, particularly men, and bringing about change that female authors of early novels gave to their female characters.*]

The meaning and attainment of influence, power, and success frequently provide conflicts and themes for fiction. In spite of the fact that female writers were necessarily concerned with these concepts, that readers of novels were predominantly women, and that the issues of the Feminist Controversy remained alive throughout the eighteenth century, critics have paid little attention to a central problem for the heroine of many early English novels by women: discovering appropriate and effective ways to influence the men around her.

In Jane Barker's *Love Intrigues,* the heroine Galesia describes her girlhood experiences in order to divert a friend from the melancholy news of the War of the Spanish Succession:

> I shall delight myself to see the Blood pour out of his false Heart; In order to accomplish this detestable Freak, I went towards the place of his Abode, supposing a Rapier in my hand, and saying to my self; the false *Bosvil* shou'd now disquiet me no more, nor any other of our Sex; in him I will end his Race, no more of them shall come to disturb, or affront Woman-kind; this only Son, shall die by the hands of me an only Daughter; and however the World may call it Cruelty, or barbarous; I am sure our Sex will have reason to thank me, and keep an Annual Festival, on which a Criminal like him is executed. . . . [1]

Although this passage is somewhat unusual because it is so explicit in its fantasy of the planned act of violence and in its fantasy of the meaning of the event, it is representative of a common strain in many novels written by women in the Restoration and eighteenth century.[2] First, the heroine must find the means to exert influence in a male-dominated world. Second, violence, especially planned violence, is by no means unusual. Third, the female character sees herself as a representative of her sex, a victim of the "wrongs of woman" which are fairly consistent, and likely to be understood by women. The quotation says that the "world will call it barbarous"; the judging world is male. Women, however, will understand and appoint a festival day. Finally, the man has commited a "crime" which women recognize as being analogous to a legally punishable offense. This crime forces the woman into a position in which she becomes a "freak" or perpetuates a "freakish" action.

Mrs. Barker's story outlines the formulaic treatment[3] of the problem of influence in the early novels by women. Such tales operate as escape literature does: they engage the reader immediately in a story full of action and accessible emotion which usually requires little interpretation of character or meaning. The story, however, especially when seen as a set of conventions, reveals the anxieties, conflicts, and daydreams of a definable group of people. More significantly for our purposes, escape literature shows characters in rebellion and, ultimately, in compliance with realistic social situations and conventional opinions. The heroine must pit herself not only against the men she needs to influence, but also against opinion that does not label the male's behavior as criminal but judges her as "freakish." The reader is asked to understand her action, but also is expected to recognize that the action will determine the woman's limitations and the story's resolution.[4]

My purpose is to delineate the means and limits of influence in novels by women, to examine some of the conventions, and to conclude with some observations and speculations about the implications of the conventions used in the novels by women. Although I found few differences between the means of influence and formulae in novels by men and those by women, I shall focus exclusively on the novels by women except to point out particularly intriguing contrasts. I do not pretend to offer an exhaustive treatment of the implications of this theme, but rather to suggest some problems and lines of inquiry for future investigation.

I

In many early novels, the situation of the heroine follows a familiar pattern. Her beauty or wealth makes her desirable;[5] her family (if she has one) has plans for her which seldom take into account her future happiness; an undesirable man wants to possess her. She is confined to a house, often to a single room; her privacy, her self are under siege. Paradoxically, her cocoon-like situation forces her to assert herself and influence others. Her position and training instruct her in one role and her "heart" in another. Her education and her role have taught her to submit, to dissemble, and to flirt. Her new situation necessitates resistance to fathers, brothers, and lovers.

The most common means of influence to which the heroines resort are outgrowths of prescribed feminine and, therefore, "normal" behavior: appeals to an "indulgent" father or a favorite uncle, insistence on the rights of beauty, virtue, or social class, compromise, and feigned modesty. A typical example, Eliza Haywood's *Philidore and Placentia* (1727), shows Placentia falling in love with Philidore during the time he is impersonating a servant in order to be near her. Because of her beauty and social class, she insists on her right to marry him. When he refuses, she is enraged and sends him away. Almost immediately, Placentia regrets her rash act and follows him to sea. When the captain of the ship insists that he will marry her or rape her, she again acts in a manner that extends her feminine role. First, she reverts to an appeal to her rank and hopes that her superiority will keep him at bay. Frightened by his persistence, she begs for three days to consider his proposal. By pretending to compromise, she gains a little time, but an outsider is required to rescue her.[6]

When the methods that extend normal female patterns of influence fail, the heroine may begin to nag, to show contempt, or to demand the "right" of refusal of a suitor. At this point, the heroine displays little awareness of the seriousness of the threat to her, but shows a growing understanding of her helplessness. All of these means of influence in the novels I have examined are completely ineffectual. Such methods are unacceptable patterns of behavior in male society, but they are not violent enough to have any effect. In fact, the authority figure exerts extra effort in order to maintain or restore the balance of influence which he sees as correct.[7] Clementia, for example, in Haywood's *Agreeable Caledonian* (1729), dismisses with contempt the cardinal whom her father intends her to marry and is confined to a very strict convent as punishment. Yxmilla in *The Adventures of Eovaai* (1736) is rewarded for her contempt of Broscomin with a forced marriage and a brutal wedding night.

Immediacy of danger elicits extreme behavior from the heroines of the books. The more rigid the constraints, the more threatening the situation, the more violent the behavior of the heroine. In some cases, the behavior is the most extreme example of feminine despair: helpless, desperate weeping. The last stages of desperation call forth a weeping marked by violence. Women "tear their ruffles," roll on the floor, fling themselves against bedposts, even claw their faces. They have no plans to influence at this point. The girlish tears, the artfully moist eyes and trembling lip have no part in these scenes. The more strong-willed the heroine, the more violent the weeping. Clementia, who will eventually escape the convent with her best friend's fiancé, is described in a typical passage: "In the Anguish of her Soul, she tore not only her Hair and Garments, but her very Face. And her Woman, who alone was Witness of her Disorders, fearing she would commit some Violence against her own Life, endeavor'd all she could to pacify her, but in vain; the stormy Passions rolling in her Mind, grew stronger by Opposition. . . . "[8] Only a single confidante, one helpless to relieve the heroine and without influence with the authority figure, witnesses such weeping.

Such weeping expresses helplessness and rage. The impulse is self-destructive rather than charming. Compare, for example, the stock description of the weeping beauty in distress from Sarah Scott and Barbara Montagu's *Millenium Hall* (1762): "Tears insensibly stole down her face, and bestowed on it still greater charms than it had ever yet worn, by giving her an air of tenderness, which led him to hope that she did not behold his passion with indifference."[9] Tears like these express strong emotion, pity, sentiment, weakness, disappointment, distress—feminine frailty and tenderness. Violent weeping, accompanied by frenzied movement and disordered clothing, becomes an expression of frustration and anger turned upon the woman herself.

Tears are one of the most important means of influence and of the expression of emotion in novels by male writers in the century. Because they went to considerable pains to separate themselves and their books from the formula novels,[10] their treatment of conventional elements holds considerable interest. Henry Fielding's women influence because of their beauty and virtue.[11] Their eyes are especially expressive: when Tom rescues Sophia after her horse rears, her looks tell her passionate feelings; later she sinks trembling in a chair after her father insists that she must marry Blifil and "had not a Flood of Tears come immediately to her Relief, perhaps worse had followed." These tears lack the substance of real grief and despair; they provide the release for strong but brief emotion over the thwarting of desire. The diction is decidedly light. Sophia Western often takes direct action, as she does when she escapes from her house and sets out for London. She appears both resourceful and naive, and her undertaking is more dramatic than desperate. Again Fielding's tone and diction determine the reader's reaction.

Richardson shares much of women's sense of limitations, their understanding of what means of influence are at their disposal, and their perception of men as looming figures in their world. Because he shares some of their sensibility, the novels by women provide new contextual reasons for Richardson's achievement. His characters are physically threatened in a way that Defoe's, Fielding's, and Smollett's are not. Beauty is a trap, not power for Richardson's female characters. They realize their helplessness and contemplate violence against themselves or descend into madness.[12] Rather than seeking to gain security in marriage, they hope to retain enough influence to protect themselves. This contrast between Richardson's and the other male

novelists' perception of the conflict may explain some of the harsh criticism and ridicule directed at Pamela's behavior. A number of satires turn upon their authors' inabilities to conceive of Pamela in terms other than scheming with marriage as the goal. *Anti-Pamela: or, Feign'd Innocence detected* (1742) exposes Syrena Tricksy's attempts to snare a husband and a fortune. Not only does she have her mother's help, but she takes advantage of anyone showing her kindness.[13]

Clarissa's streaming eyes are among the "assemblage of beauties" which Lovelace catalogues, but Lovelace's finding them attractive adds to the picture of Lovelace the perverted villain. Clarissa's feelings are diametrically opposed to Lovelace's reaction. She is not trying to influence; in fact, she feels that all is lost. She is despairing because she is in Lovelace's power and for a moment has not even kept her feelings within her own control; her consciousness, not her beauty, is what Richardson focuses on, but he adds the dimension of revelation about Lovelace. That Lovelace enjoys being moved by Clarissa's grief increases our revulsion at his misuse of power. Similarly, Pamela is told by B. that she is "most beautiful" in her tears. Pamela is cowering in the corner of the room; the last thing she wants at that moment is to be attractive. Once again, Richardson has shown the coincidence of the woman's helpless, trapped feelings with the man's desire and sense of power. Richardson, however, moves toward the domestic and conventional novels in *Grandison*. Clementina is not allowed the religious withdrawal of Clarissa.[14] Worse, the tears and physical expressions of emotions are not the overflow of recognized internal conflict; they seem to be the whole of the feelings conventionally expressed. And they are the only signs of sympathy or disappointment except in the sections in which Clementina's situation parallels Clarissa's. Clarissa seems to seethe with emotions too great to be confined; her tears imply passion within. Clarissa and many of the heroines of the early novels by women weep because words and actions are inadequate and futile. Harriet Byron, on the other hand, seems to express all of the emotion she feels.

A second response to immediate threat is the most extreme example of behavior foreign to the perceived character of women; physical violence. The last resort of the threatened woman who wants to control her own destiny, the violence often begins directed at another, then is turned on the woman herself. Such fantasy scenes as the one quoted from Jane Barker's *Love Intrigues* (1727) end with the woman considering suicide. Placentia in Haywood's *Philidore and Placentia* (1727) threatens to kill herself with a penknife some twenty years before Clarissa Harlowe intimidates Lovelace with the same weapon.[15] Sophia, a character in Haywood's *History of Jemmy and Jenny Jessamy* (1753), defends her virtue from her fiancé by placing herself in front of an open upstairs window while she holds him at bay with his sword. She seems to be poised between throwing herself out of the window and stabbing him. The gesture which began aimed at the male could in an instant be turned on the woman against herself.

Other women turn infatuated men into weapons. Miranda in Aphra Behn's *Fair Jilt* (1688) is able to send a page and her husband to kill Alcidiana, her sister. Just as deadly is a traditional feminine weapon, gossip. Elvira enlists Don Alvaro in her jealous cause and directs a rumor which kills Constantia in Behn's *Agnes de Castro* (1688). Miranda ruins Father Francisco by crying "rape" in *The Fair Jilt.* Dorimene brings about Dumont's death by threatening Isabelle in *David Simple* (1744). The tongue is often intended to be and is a murderous weapon.

A few female characters use weapons or unusual force on men. Isabella in Aphra Behn's *Fair Vowbreaker* (1688) kills both her husbands. She smothers the first husband, who has come home from the war after she presumed him dead, packs him in an oat sack, stitches that to her second husband's collar when he offers to dispose of the body, and both go over the waterfall. Atlante, in Behn's *Lucky Mistake* (1688), threatens Vernole with a pistol to preserve her privacy. Eovaai frees herself from Ochihatou, the magician, by physical strength and breaks his wand, symbol of masculine power.

Some heroines, however, are able to exert influence even in situations that seem hopeless. Miranda in *The Mercenary Lover* (1726) controls one of the most cruel characters in any of the novels with her knowledge of her husband's incestuous affair. Rivella exerts influence solely because she "knows how to live." D'Aumont, having heard the story of Rivella's life, says, "let us not lose a Moment before we are acquainted with the only Person of her Sex that knows how to *Live,* and of whom we may say, in relation to Love, since she has so peculiar a Genius for, and has made such noble Discoveries in that Passion, that it would have been a *Fault in her, not to have been Faulty.*"[16] Delariviere Manley's description affirms that Rivella is unusual, "the only one of her Sex," and that she is "faulty," but affirms Rivella's freedom and lifestyle.

Fainting, another conventional means of influence, provides a key to understanding the courage and quality of the heroine in some novels. Female characters who receive catastrophically bad news or are about to be raped often faint. The heroine who faints is overwhelmed; she surrenders the capacity to see the issues, the will to resist, and the rational capacity to know. Eliza Haywood's very popular novel *Love in Excess* (1719) includes a number of illustrations of common incidents of fainting. The heroine of Part I, Alovisa, is

an immodest schemer. Motivated by lust and ambition, she sends letters to D'Elmont and engineers the rival's removal to a convent. Alovisa faints twice: once when her letter to D'Elmont is misunderstood and he dances with the rival, Amena, and once when she discovers D'Elmont in bed with another woman. In each case, her fainting symbolizes despair. Amena, the rival, faints when she finds out that she can never go back home. Their fainting broadcasts their weakness.

The most noble heroines never faint but face any situation relentlessly. Haywood's Althea in *The Mercenary Lover* (1726) has something of the tragic vision. She struggles in hopeless situations and recognizes her share of the responsibility for her predicament and helplessness, therefore suffering more intensely. Althea has been the epitome of feminine prudence and virtue. Living a retired life with her beloved sister and brother-in-law, she falls under the brother-in-law's influence. He finally overwhelms her, rapes her, then poisons her. Her understanding of her actions makes the last months of her life a prolonged hell, suitably ended by an agonizing death from the poison. Yxmilla in *The Adventures of Eovaai* (1736) resists marriage to Broscomin courageously. When she does faint, Broscomin seizes the opportunity, has the priests wave the sacred bough over her head, and marries her. Eovaai, in contrast to Yxmilla, never faints, although Ochihatou threatens her in more frightening ways.

By midcentury, domestic intrigue and social humiliations replace rapes, poisonings, sorcerers, and convents in escape literature.[17] Changes in the conventions found in such novels often provide imaginative constructs for new anxieties and daydreams. Some values appear to be assimilated, certain causes for rebellion evaporate, and new mores and dissatisfactions surface. The threat of an unfulfilling marriage based on the male's desire to possess the heroine gives way to greater emphasis on courtship designed to establish mutual respect. The novelists expand their investigations of influence, and the problem of legitimate and illegitimate forms of influence provide the themes for some of the best women writers of the second half of the century.

Elizabeth Inchbald's *Simple Story* (1791) seems to say that "love is the desire to dominate." Miss Milner and Matilda, heroines of the novel, represent a contrast; Matilda's means of influence are legitimate and "feminine," while Miss Milner's are not. Both women try to influence the same men, Dorriforth, the guardian who marries Miss Milner and fathers Matilda, and Sandford, Dorriforth's tutor. Miss Milner has obeyed Dorriforth as long as he is her guardian because of his inflexible good manners. Once they are engaged, she insists on the rights of a beautiful woman and of a fiancée. She will dominate and control, she says, and force him to forgive the unforgivable. She admits that she wants to test her power over his affections. The result is a broken engagement. Matilda must try to win the affection of Dorriforth and does so with complete obedience, prudent behavior, and blind affection. Miss Milner has submitted to her social role with poor grace and used it as an excuse when convenient. Matilda is completely submissive. Even the minor characters, like the meek, exemplary Miss Woodley, maneuver to exert influence. She interests herself for Miss Milner repeatedly, but when she is afraid that Miss Milner will corrupt Dorriforth the priest, she sends her away. In telling Dorriforth that Miss Milner loves him and in refusing to exile herself from his table, she controls. Like her predecessors in the romances, however, all of the women weep in helpless agony when they cannot influence Dorriforth.

Fanny Burney's Evelina (1778) must learn the legitimate methods of feminine influence. Her humiliations and disappointments result from inappropriate maneuvering. Evelina tries to keep herself free to dance with Lord Orville at a ridotto, is exposed in the attempt, and bursts into tears. She cannot manage Sir Clement Willoughby or her relatives and is disappointed time after time in her desire to be with Lord Orville. Lord Orville himself has defined feminine influence as informed, sensible, and modest behavior which does not "seize the soul by surprise, but, with more dangerous fascination, she steals it almost imperceptibly." At a performance of *Love for Love,* Orville remarks that "Angelica bestows her hand rather with the air of a benefactress, than with the tenderness of a mistress. . . . The uncertainty in which she keeps Valentine, and her manner of trifling with his temper, give no very favourable idea of her own."[18] Evelina learns social grace and effective means of influence. At one point, she demonstrates the use of the social code for influence. Orville asks her to go to Bath with him to "convince the world you encourage no mere *danglers.*" "You teach me, then, my Lord, the inference I might expect, if I complied," she answers and has her way. Her honesty, good sense, and benevolence win both her father and husband. She trifles with no one.

Burney does, however, explore the effects and the social and personal meaning of means of influence in considerable depth just as other women writers do. Evelina would like to have things her own way and often agrees with Mrs. Selwyn, but she knows the image others have of the older woman.[19] Madame Duval is punished repeatedly for her inappropriate attempts to control. Evelina explores the meaning of forms of influence and learns to reconcile her internal needs and values with external opinions. Success is often measured in unexpected ways.[20] In the novels by men, influence leads to the woman's being crowned with an appropriate marriage; in many of the novels by women, influence becomes confined to an appropriate sphere and to appropriate methods that protect the heroine from future humiliation and disquiet. In both sexes' novels with happy endings, the heroine earns the respect of her husband and, thereby, assures herself of future influence.

The means of feminine influence have subtle variations in the domestic, sentimental novels of the second half of the century. *The History of Emily Montague* (1769) by Frances Brooke has almost no action, but presents four different women, each intent on marrying. Emily Montague is a paragon, and like Rivella, knows how to live (but Frances Brooke means something completely different by "live" from Delariviere Manley). Emily Montague influences by her virtue and her straightforward behavior. At a costume ball, she dresses as a French peasant, a representation of her simplicity and artlessness. Arabella Fermor, the familiar lively foil, named with some justification after Pope's heroine,[21] is a coquette who ensnares her intended with feminine tricks, and so it goes. Only one of the women comes to a bad end: she dies in a hovel with her illegitimate child. The obstacles to marriage are minor; the concern is manipulation of men by women. The more honorable the methods, the greater the reward for the women.

John Richetti has argued that the scandalous memoirs of the eighteenth century provided an important release for liberating fantasies for women in a time of great social limitation.[22] Perhaps the extremes of behavior in female characters created by women indicate deep feelings of helplessness and hostility, a complex blend of the futility of action and of wish fulfillment. Insistence on the rights of beauty and birth, compromise, nagging, showing contempt, weeping, and physical violence are all attempts to influence men, but they carry an underlying fear of female helplessness. Modifications in the presentations of means of influence suggest that women writers were well aware of the problems of credibility and effectiveness.

II

The recognition of external and internal limits circumscribing women's lives and the demands for more realistic fiction may have reduced the kinds of influence women writers assign to their heroines, but this consciousness of barriers provides the impetus for the establishment of conventions in plotting, for some of the best burlesques of formula novels, and, most significantly for the development of the novel, for the exploration of the psyche under the stress of bringing the inner self into harmony with the social self.[23]

In the novels by women, the female characters are largely responsible for advancing the plot up to a point. Circumstances and the actions of male characters become increasingly decisive, but the focus remains upon the female character. For example, Isabella in *The Fair*

Vowbreaker (1688) decides to leave the convent and marry. The decision is her own. Throughout the marriage, their problems are explained through her emotions. Henault joins the army to repair his fortune, but only after Isabella has released him. She assumes him dead after a time, remarries, but he returns. She kills him, then kills her second husband. At each point, she acts alone. Such independent action in the early part of the novels by women is typical. Even the most lady-like heroine, Emily Montague, is chiefly responsible for the plot's progress. She breaks her engagement with Sir George, she makes her love for Ed Rivers obvious, she leaves Canada forcing him to follow her, and it is her guardian who makes them a wealthy couple.

Several decisions seem to be the prerogative of the female character: she decides which man is acceptable, she selects the man she wants to marry, she writes to someone, she devises a plan, she confides in someone, she runs away, she selects the moment to "submit" to the chosen object of her affection if there is a happy ending. At each of these stages, the woman usually advances the plot.

At some point, however, the heroine's influence ends. Her ability to awe the man by beauty, by position, or by virtue is at an end. Her tactics to delay the settlement have been exhausted. Then the heroine casts about her, sees she is trapped, and may behave in extreme ways. Isabella in *The Fair Vowbreaker* (1688) kills her husband only when she feels that discovery and ruin are inevitable. Significantly, she runs about her apartments like a trapped mouse in a maze before and after the murder. The novels end with the death of the heroine, with a miraculous rescue brought about by coincidences, or by the appearance of the real lover. In any case, influence is out of the heroine's hands. Eovaai, who has delayed so long, fought so valiantly, escaped and broken Ochihatou's wand, ends her struggle tied naked to a tree. Ochihatou intends to beat her with nettles. Dorriforth relents and marries Miss Milner. Coincidence, common in the eighteenth-century novel, is especially strong in the formula novel's ending—a lost father or uncle appears, a brother has been castrated by a sultan leaving his sister the only heir to the family fortune.

The women writers seem to know the limits of credibility of their heroine's power. No matter how prudent, beautiful, virtuous, and deserving the woman is, her influence is limited. At some point, usually marked by extreme behavior, power shifts to the male characters. The recognition of feminine helplessness results in more than violent behavior: it determines stock endings. If there is a happy ending, it is because the male character has taken over or a rich benefactor has appeared.[24] Clementia, for example, seduces Broscomin away from her only friend and plants the idea of their running away as a test of their ingenuity which suits

them for each other, but it is he who devises the means for her escape. Rivers arranges property settlements so that he and Emily Montague can marry, and her wealthy male guardian appears to solve her difficulties.

Unhappy endings are more frequent in the early half of the century. The faithful woman dies. Constantia grieves to death. Camilla dies and leaves David Simple prostrated with sorrow. The evil woman is caught; then she can be beheaded as Isabella is or she can repent as Miranda does. Jane Barker's characters come to the most provocative ends: Galesia in *Love Intrigues* (1713) decides to become a poet and affects eccentric dress; another is married to a fish in *Exilius* (1715).

A few perceptive female novelists burlesque the means of influence. Charlotte Lennox's *Female Quixote* catalogues the conventions of earlier novels. Arabella, steeped in French romances, believes in the absolute power of woman before marriage. She is certain that everyone from Edward the gardener, a casual passer-by, and serious suitors intend to commit verbal outrages (declaring their passions), kidnap and "ravish" her, or kill themselves in despair. In the midst of her sense of power she lives in constant insecurity. Her rightful powers, she believes, include banishing men, making them wait for her for years, insisting upon heroic deeds, and having absolute control over whether they live or die.

By 1752, Lennox can both ridicule and rework the conventions. She exposes the impracticality and absurdity of the conventions in nearly every assumption and speech by Arabella, but she also makes Glanville conform to them in ironic ways. Glanville loves Arabella. This fact puts him as much in Arabella's power as if he were the hero of one of Haywood's novels. He loves her enough to abide by her conventions and wait most of the time. Comic scenes result when he tries to deceive her and pretend knowledge of romances and when he gets sick and will not recover on command. The hero, Arabella says, must undergo many trials to earn his beloved. Paradoxically, he does. Day after day, he tries to keep Arabella from making a fool of herself and suffers the embarrassment of loving a woman who almost everyone has concluded "has her head turned." Eventually Arabella jumps in the Thames in imitation of Clelia's swimming the Tiber. Arabella's doctor persuades her that romances are not histories, and she blushes for her folly and marries Glanville.

These few novelists see the absurdity of the conventions clearly. Lennox has Arabella explain that threatened ladies "are terrify'd into a fainting Fit, and seldom recover till they are conveniently carried away; and when they awake, find themselves many Miles off in the Power of their Ravisher."[25] Jane Austen writes in *Love and Freindship:* "I die a Martyr to my greif *(sic)* for the loss of Augustus. . One fatal swoon has cost me my Life. . . Beware of swoons Dear Laura . . . . A frenzy fit is not one quarter so pernicious; it is an exercise to the Body and if not too violent, is I dare say conducive to Health in its consequences—Run mad as often as you chuse; but do not faint—"[26]

The conventions of escape literature provide subject matter and form for novelists from mid-eighteenth century to the present. The relationship between so-called escape or "entertainment" literature and "serious" literature is complex, the influences tangled inextricably, yet each vitalizes the other and each reveals much about the other. Although escape literature never departs far from its conventions, it can feed upon different kinds of novels and gradually assimilate their characters, forms, and opinions. Such conventions provide an immediately accessible imaginary world and a set of characters and situations which may be used as a kind of shorthand or as an interlude or, as Lennox, Austen, and Agnes Bennet (*Countess of Castle Howel,* 1794) did, as the subject of ridicule.

Fielding, for example, often parodies conventional scenes and emotional displays. *Joseph Andrews* includes the mock romance of Leonora told by the "well-bred lady" in the coach. Although the plot follows the pattern of the vain woman's downfall, the heroine's emotional outbursts are exaggerated. Fielding selects four points in the plot, describes them, and exposes the predictability of the emotional outcome. Leonora's love is obvious to everyone, for example, but when Horatio "declares" it, she pretends to be overcome, blushes, trembles, and has to be helped back inside. Drawing upon the common accusation that women fall in love with coaches rather than with men, Fielding next shows Leonora exclaiming, "O, I am in love with that equipage!" as Bellarmine passes. Her thoughts and postures make her ridiculous, but she soon ensnares the fortune hunter, Bellarmine. Bellarmine and Horatio duel, Bellarmine is wounded, and Leonora receives the news with extravagant despair; she "danced about the room in a frantic manner, tore her hair and beat her breast in all the agonies of despair." Finally, Leonora learns that Bellarmine's interest in her was as shallow and materialistic as her own, and she finds herself abandoned. She retires to a country-house and lives a "disconsolate life." The well-bred lady is well aware of the reaction to such romances, and she reminds her listeners that they feel both pity and censure toward Leonora. Fielding further satirizes the conventional story by having it told by women and especially by giving the women many of the uncharitable, frivolous, and affected characteristics of Leonora and Lindamira.

The romance as interlude became commonplace. Isabelle's story in *David Simple,* Matilda's in *The Vicar of Wakefield,* and many others carry the convention into the nineteenth century. Dorothea's story in Mary Collyer's *Felicia to Charlotte* (1749) supplies the tyrannical father, the complication of the heroine's Catholic faith, and a suspicion of theft to a more realistic interlude. These interpolations became increasingly fantastic and novel in the hands of the late eighteenth-century novelists.

A third response to the limitations experienced by eighteenth-century women was the emphasis on woman's interior world. As Patricia Meyer Spacks perceptively argues,

> The nature of public and private selves, these eighteenth-century texts suggest, is for women, in some ways, the reverse of what it is for men. . . . For women . . . the public self often stresses weakness. Passivity and compliance comprise the acceptable poses that fictional and factual heroines alike employ.

> Anger, aggression, forcefulness belong to the inner self.[27]

The novels provide the means to express anger, the grounds to test the boundaries of acceptable behavior, and, in their conclusions, material for self-pity or the affirmation of compliance with social demands.

Some of the more fantastic novels express the themes of rebellion and compliance through extreme episodes. Isabella in *The Fair Vowbreaker* seems to act almost entirely from her heart. She falls in love and leaves the convent, wants to preserve her marriage and kills her first husband, then kills the second out of fear of reproach. She rebels against all the traditional vows—religious, marital, and legal—which exist to restrict her actions. "Nature was frail, and the Tempter strong," Mrs. Behn records. Although Isabella asserts her innocence, the narrator frequently calls attention to her broken vows and to the number of times Isabella "dissembles." Both of her marriages have given her a great deal of freedom. Since she is childless, she is free to do as she pleases, and the wealth of her second husband increases her liberty. Henault's return means that she will lose the wealth and tranquillity of her second marriage, and she kills Henault. Villenoys's knowledge of the death puts her in his power, and she imagines his reproaching her and kills him. These two murders bring the wrath of heaven down on her. She imagines herself pursued by her dead lover, she suffers from insomnia and nightmares alternately, and finally confesses. She "joyfully" receives the death sentence and dies a penitent. Her passion for her husbands, her frail reasoning ability, her suffering and finally her full repentance allow the readers to pity her while they condemn her actions. The story provides satisfying fantasies about romantic love and emotional behavior and ends with the lesson that such freedom of choice and self-gratification are impossible and certain to end in ruin. The desire for such liberty can be lamented while conventional morality asserts itself fully at the end. The reader can partake of the forbidden and then reject the course of action and affirm her own experience of the world and woman's options in it.[28]

While such novels testify to the helplessness of women, they are also powerful expressions of frustration and of the violence which seems to lie dormant in women.[29] Jane Barker writes in *Love Intrigues* that "if the Feebleness of our Hands did not moderate the Fury of our Heads, Woman sometimes wou'd exceed the fiercest Savages."[30] Inchbald's *Simple Story* follows the pattern of rebellion and punishment. Miss Milner insists upon the brief freedom and power of the beloved fiancée: "If he will not submit to be my lover, I will not submit to be his wife—nor has he the affection I require in a husband," she says. She tests this love by dressing in an immodest costume and going to a forbidden masquerade. The warring desires to assert and comply appear in all three parts of the episode. The invitation has appealed to her vanity and curiosity, but she is depressed by Dorriforth's contempt for the event. Dorriforth's attitude toward the amusement turns on her, and by the end of the discussion, he has sneered at the ball, her reading, and her judgment. Her response is to defy his anger and his love. The ball itself clarifies her true feelings. She goes as "Chastity" although her costume suggests the opposite; she wants Dorriforth to admire her, but she is ashamed for him to see her dressed as she is. Her rebellion is grim, but she is determined to carry the action through. In the final part, Dorriforth confronts her. Her first reaction is shame and regret, but his tyrannical behavior and the presence of Sandford leave her torn between grief and anger, and she expresses both, "you think to frighten me by your menaces, but I can part with you; heaven knows I can—your late behaviour has reconciled me to a separation."[31] Here she recognizes the characteristics in both of their natures which argue against eventual happiness. The entire episode outlines her growing awareness both of Dorriforth's importance to her happiness and the extent of the renunciation required for marriage to him. Although he finally marries her, she continues to disobey him out of revenge and desire for pleasure and admiration. Part II begins with a description of her death in a lonely retreat, exiled for adultery. Here again, the heroine has gone beyond the limits of allowed behavior, and her death allows the sympathetic reader to pity her while assenting to her punishment.

Whenever we examine these heroines, we cannot help noticing their painful impotence. What brief power they gain is often an illusion, even the instrument of the woman's downfall. The only freedom a woman can have comes from the brief indulgence of father and lover tolerated because of her coming total submis-

sion, marked appropriately by the loss of her name and many of her legal rights. Men and women acknowledge this freedom as a whim and an anomaly. Yet the insistence upon freedom and the exertion of power immediately before marriage express something profoundly aggressive. Character after character comments on or exults in her influence over her intended. Arabella in *The History of Emily Montague* (1769) writes, "Fitzgerald takes such amazing pains to please me, that I begin to think it is a pity so much attention should be thrown away. . . ."[32] The more rakish or tyrannical the male, the more the relish of the female. Dorriforth's iron self-control, faultless character, and latent tyranny add danger to Miss Milner's testing of his love. He has controlled her as no other man ever had when she was his ward; she knows he will be the stern master of his household after marriage. Her desire for power and total influence is a reflection of Dorriforth's personality, and a final, last act of rebellion.

Quite often the education of the young woman involves the discovery of perimeters. The heroine has goals and a sense of her own worth but must learn to confine them and express them acceptably. Althea in *The Mercenary Lover* suffers more because she betrays herself. Heroines in *The Auction* (1760), *Betsy Thoughtless* (1751), and *The Exemplary Mother* (1769) reluctantly decide they must leave husbands regardless of the world's opinion. Self-discovery, self-respect, and harmony within replace the overcoming of external obstacles to marriage as the subject of many novels by women. Austen's protagonists illustrate the emphasis on these themes. Emma, "handsome, clever, and rich," learns lessons in behavior as Burney's Evelina does,[33] but, more important, she comes to know what will make her happy. She speaks of avoiding having her affections "entangled," insists that she will never marry, and enjoys thinking that she knows what is best for Miss Taylor, Mr. Elton, Frank Churchill, Jane Fairfax, and Harriet. Only after she has been hurt by the Eltons, accepted comfort from Knightley, and admitted her mistakes can she marry. She says, "I was very foolishly tempted to say and do many things which may well lay me open to unpleasant conjectures, but I have no other reason to regret that I was not in the secret earlier." Here she brings together a just appraisal of herself and what she has no reason to know and an awareness of the appearance she gives. Her good sense now promises her suitable influence over Knightley and more tranquillity because she is not entangling herself in others' affairs.

Harmony and self-respect often come from self-control. "Vivacity" usually arouses suspicion, and modesty and prudence replace this youthful quality. Manley's Rivella, Behn's Isabella, and Haywood's Alovisa succumb to their desires for pleasure and freedom. Later Inchbald's Miss Milner comes in from an indiscreet meeting, eyes dancing michievously. She thinks she is attractive and desirable; her actions bring nothing but trouble. Frances Brooke records the general opinion in *Emily Montague:*

> *À propos* to women, the estimable part of us are divided into two classes only, the tender and the lively.

> The former, at the head of which I place Emily, are infinitely more capable of happiness. . . . [34]

Vivacious women often flirt, and Charlotte Lennox's Harriot Stuart insists, "I was born a coquet and what would have been art in others, in me was pure nature."[35] When the heroine insists that her behavior expresses temperament or nature, she usually offers a transparent excuse for lack of self-control. Such lack of restraint is rebellion and may even express self-destructive tendencies. In most cases, however, the behavior concludes with a lesson. Charlotte, the witty city correspondent, joins Felicia in the country and finds happiness in sober conversation after the death of her husband.[36]

J. Dollard argues in *Frustration and Aggression* that "the occurrence of aggressive behavior always presupposes the existence of frustration."[37] The last step in human destructiveness is aggression turned against the self. Such an act expresses ultimate helplessness, self-loathing,[38] and emphasizes the perceived threatening nature of the real object of hostility. In the final analysis, the heroine most often turns the violence against herself. Ciamara in *Love in Excess* (1719) poisons herself. Galesia gives up her plan to kill Broscomin and plans her own suicide. Constantia lies down and dies. Evelina sobs in humiliation over faults not her own. Miss Milner accepts full responsibility for her unfaithfulness and dies in misery.

Escape literature expresses, explores, and finally rejects opinions and behavior incompatible with the cultural norms of the group. Yet escape literature does more than affirm opinion and allay anxiety; it also reveals aspirations and, many of its readers believe, suggests ways for women to cope.[39] The heroine must sometimes overcome obstacles and succeed. Patricia Meyer Spacks points out that "Written largely for female readers, these books exploit contradictory appeals, suggesting that a woman may differ from her kind without penalty but also assuring the reader that, even in the remote country of romance, orthodox definitions of virtue apply and compliance will be rewarded. The hints of strain and resentment that such should be the case rumble just beneath the surface."[40] Many a heroine "dwindles into a wife." Women writers, faced with the ineluctable social world, turn to the analysis of influence over the self. Burney, Manley, Inchbald, and the best of the women writers had seen the necessity

for harmony between the inner and the social selves; a few of them and especially Jane Austen and the nineteenth-century novelists probe woman's inner conflicts.

Success for the heroine, perhaps, should be measured in terms of self-mastery and renunciation. Even so gentle and happy a heroine as Felicia can feel depressed over her coming marriage and single out "honour and obey" as the most formidable words in the marriage ceremony.[41] The number of heroines who become contented wives or widows testifies to the possibilities of happiness measured in somewhat unexpected ways. David Simple's wife carries on in the face of stupefying hardships drawing pleasure from her family and her ability to help others. *The Exemplary Mother* describes a useful and satisfying widowhood. Felicia accepts her husband's illegitimate daughter. The cost of conforming and the struggle for what one critic calls "private tranquility" becomes a convention in its own right.[42]

The question remains, however, whether we are defining success and happiness adequately. The significance of many conventions remains to be explored; in fact, the amount of violence in novels by women needs to be recognized and analyzed objectively. Education has been a common excuse for the perceived deficiencies in the novels by women too long; it is time to look for more reasons for the nature of these novels. Perhaps modern critics underestimate the impact of the social restrictions and of woman's frustration and emotional outrage; perhaps we fail to recognize forms of rebellion, means of coping, and success more difficult to achieve than that of the familiar eighteenth-century hero's.*

Notes

[1] Jane Barker, *Love Intrigues* (New York: Garland, 1973), pp. 43-44, originally published 1713.

[2] My study includes novels from Aphra Behn to Jane Austen. Behn's novels clearly influence many later women novelists; by Jane Austen's time, the novel for women is a mature form. Although more than 100 novels were considered, I have selected novels for discussion according to how representative they are, to their quality, and to their contribution to the understanding of the topic. I have tried to include the dreadful and the delightful. Other studies which define the feminine perspective in the novel include Joyce Horner, *The English Women Novelists and Their Connection with the Feminist Movement (1688-1797)* (Northampton, Mass.: Smith College, 1929-1930); Hazel Mews, *Frail Vessels* (London: Athlone Press, 1969); Jo Ellen Rudolf, "The Novels that Taught the Ladies" (Diss. Univ. of California, San Diego, 1972); O. P. Sharma, "The Emergence of Feminist Impulse as Aesthetic Vision in the English Novel," *Panjab Univ.*

Research Bulletin (Arts), 2 (1971), 1-28; Ellen Moers, *Literary Women* (Garden City: Doubleday, 1976); Virginia Woolf, "Women and Fiction" in *Granite and Rainbow* (London: Hogarth Press, 1958), pp. 76-84; Nancy K. Miller, "The Exquisite Cadavers: Women in Eighteenth-Century Fiction," *Diacritics,* 5 (1975), esp. p. 39: "It is not surprising that the archetypal eighteenth-century novel of the feminine destiny should focus on defloration"; Ian Watt, *The Rise of the Novel* (Berkeley: Univ. of California Press, 1967), pp. 298-99. Sir Walter Scott's review of *Emma* in *The Quarterly Review,* 14 (1816), 188-201, makes many of the same points.

[3] John G. Cawelti defines formula literature as "a means of generalizing the characteristics of large groups of individual works from certain combinations of cultural materials and archetypal story patterns" and explains its goals as escape and entertainment in *Adventure, Mystery, and Romance* (Chicago: Univ. of Chicago Press, 1976), pp. 7 and 13.

[4] A number of critics have noticed the possibilities of identification with forbidden modes of behavior while denying participation in it because of the fictional form and of the certain punishment of the transgressor. See, for example, Cawelti, pp. 35-36; Simon O. Lesser, *Fiction and the Unconscious* (Boston: Beacon, 1957), pp. 42 and 104.

[5] Patricia Meyer Spacks writes

> When men write of their own lives, they write of feminine sexuality usually as attraction but also threat. Women exist, sexually, to be conquered by men; but before the conquest takes place, they can cause masculine suffering and even certain forms of masculine capitulation. Women writing of themselves, on the other hand, see their own sexuality often as a trap, an agent of self-defeat, or at best an inadequate fulfillment.

"Reflecting Women," *Yale Review,* 63 (1973), 32. The point is also made in Professor Spacks's *Female Imagination* (1972; New York: Avon, 1976), pp. 162-64; and in Elizabeth Hardwick's *Seduction and Betrayal* (New York: Random House, 1974), pp. 189, 206-7.

[6] Eliza Haywood, *Philidore and Placentia* (London: Greene, 1727).

[7] Joan Kelly-Gadol reports the same effect in life in "The Social Relation of the Sexes: Methodological Implications of Women's History," *Signs,* 1 (1976), 816.

[8] Eliza Haywood, *The Agreeable Caledonian* (New York: Garland, 1973), p. 12; originally published in 1728.

[9] Sarah Scott and Barbara Montagu, *A Description of Millenium Hall, and the Country Adjacent,* 2nd ed. corr. (London: Newbery, 1764), p. 119.

[10] See Defoe's prefaces to *Moll Flanders* (1722) and to *Roxana* (1724) chapter 1, Book IX, and chapter 1, Book XIV of Fielding's *Tom Jones* (1749), and the preface to Smollett's *Roderick Random* (1748).

[11] Helen C. Sarchet discusses the "impregnable virtue" of the eighteenth-century heroine in "Women in English Fiction of the Mid-Eighteenth Century from 1740-1771," Diss. Univ. of Minnesota, 1939.

[12] Both Clarissa and Clementina have periods of madness. Again, modern psychologists find madness in women a form of self-destruction. *Cf.* Walter R. Gove and Jeannette F. Tudor, "Adult Sex Roles and Mental Illness," *Changing Women in a Changing Society,* Joan Huber, ed. (Chicago: Univ. of Chicago Press, 1973), pp. 53-54 and 65-66; Walter R. Gove, "Sex, Marital Status, and Suicide," *Journal of Health and Social Behavior,* 13 (1972), 204, 206, 210-11. Claudeen Cline-Naffziger, "Women's Lives and Frustration, Oppression, and Anger: Some Alternatives," *Journal of Counseling Psychology,* 21 (1974), 51-52, 55: "They [angry women] are self-destructive since it's not good to express anger, and therefore it must turn inward and be used to deenergize."

Literary studies which discuss this point include Leo Braudy, "Penetration and Impenetrability in *Clarissa,*" in *New Approaches to Eighteenth-Century Literature,* Phillip Harth, ed., (New York: Columbia Univ. Press, 1974), pp. 192-93 and Naney K. Miller, "Female Sexuality and Narrative Structure in *La Nouvelle Héloise* and *Les Liaisons dangereuses,*" *Signs,* 1 (1976), 628-29 and 632-33.

[13] *Anti-Pamela: or, Feign'd Innocence Detected* (New York: Garland, 1975), reprint of the second edition, 1742. See also *Pamela Censured, Augustan Reprint Society* (Los Angeles: Clark Library, 1976), pp. 21-34, and Fielding's *Shamela.*

[14] Interestingly enough, women appeal to God for help in novels by men while they rarely do in novels by women. Cynthia Griffin Wolff in "The Problem of Eighteenth-Century Secular Heroism," *Modern Language Studies,* 4 (1974), explores the effect of the end of portrayal of religious roles for women, pp. 35-42.

[15] Syrena Tricksy threatens to kill herself with a penknife as part of her ploy to force Mr. L. to marry her, p. 96, *Anti-Pamela.*

[16] Delariviere Manley, *The Adventures of Rivella* (New York: Garland, 1972), p. 120; originally published in 1714.

[17] The novel was affected by the age's desire to refine literature and to shape manners and morals. Leonard Welsted's prologue to Steele's *Conscious Lovers* (1722) insisted, "'Tis yours with breeding to refine the age." *Spectator* #51 wanted "Wit, Humour, Mirth, good Breeding, and Gallantry" taught to the public. The movement from aristocratic to middle-class literature, its stimuli, and results are detailed in Vineta Colby's *Yesterday's Woman. Domestic Realism in the English Novel* (Princeton: Princeton Univ. Press, 1974), pp. 4, 8, 12, 30; and Mews's *Frail Vessels,* pp. vii and 7. Cawelti demonstrates that "formulas become collective cultural products because they successfully articulate a pattern of fantasy that is at least acceptable to if not preferred by the cultural groups who enjoy them" and "When a group's attitudes undergo some change, new formulas arise and existing formulas develop new themes and symbols . . ." (p. 34).

[18] Fanny Burney, *Evelina* (New York: Norton, 1965), pp. 329 and 71; originally published 1778.

[19] Rose Marie Cutting discusses Burney's women in some detail in "Defiant Women: the Growth of Feminism in Fanny Burney's Novels," *Studies in English Literature,* 17 (1977), see esp. pp. 521-23.

[20] "The idea of success has failed to engage the female imagination," Professor Spacks writes in *Imagination,* p. 409; also pp. 411, 413-14. In *Imagining a Self* (Cambridge: Harvard, 1976), she suggests that "female self-fulfillment may demand the pursuit of other goals than happiness," p. 69. The question is whether the novels are limited as Watt (pp. 298-99) and Joyce and numerous others have argued or whether we are falling into the seductive trap of demanding that a writer imagine what never was (see Ruth Yeazell's "Fictional Heroines and Feminist Critics," *Novel,* 8 [1974], 35; and Cynthia Griffin Wolff, "A Mirror for Men: Stereotypes of Women in Literature," *Massachusetts Review,* 13 [1972], 206-7). Cline-Naffziger's discussion of frustration suggests another reason: "Angry women have lost the ability to fantasize. They are unable to share their dreams because they have given up dreaming," p. 55.

[21] Frances Brooke is probably indulging in the eighteenth-century's delight in knowing the "key" to *The Rape of the Lock.* Arabella Fermor, daughter of a prominent Catholic landowner, was familiar to London society and celebrated for her beauty. She seems to have been modest rather than ostentatious. The verses from *The Celebrated Beauties* describing her fit Mrs. Brooke's character well:

F-rm-r's a Pattern for the Beauteous Kind,
Compos'd to please, and ev'ry Way refin'd;
Obliging with Reserve, and Humbly Great,
Tho' Gay, yet Modest, tho' Sublime, yet
   Sweet;

Fair without Art, and graceful without Pride,
By Merit and Descent to deathless Fame
   ally'd.

The character in *The History of Emily Montague* engages in the somewhat outworn coquetry of Pope's Belinda. For a discussion of Arabella Fermor, see *Alexander Pope: The Rape of the Lock and other Poems,* Geoffrey Tillotson, ed. (London: Methuen, 1940), pp. 83-105 and 349-53.

[22] John Richetti, *Popular Fiction before Richardson, 1700-1739* (Oxford: Clarendon, 1969), pp. 123-26. See also J. M. S. Tompkins, *The Popular Novel in England, 1770-1800* 2nd ed. (1932; Lincoln: Univ. of Nebraska, 1967), pp. 129-32; Spacks, *Imagination,* p. 402.

[23] Professor Spacks considers the nineteenth-century novel in *Imagination,* pp. 57, 66, 73, 77, 151, 295, and 380; she also notes the growing power of passivity.

[24] A major subject of Pierre Fauchery's *La Destinée Féminine dans le roman européen du dix-huitième siècle, 1713-1807* is conventional endings and the literary and social factors which determined them (Paris: Colin, 1972). See also Miller, p. 43.

[25] Charlotte Lennox, *The Female Quixote* (London: Oxford, 1970), p. 300; originally published 1752. For a discussion of the convention of fainting heroines, see Elizabeth MacAndrew and Susan Gorsky, "Why Do They Faint and Die?—The Birth of the Delicate Heroine," *Journal of Popular Culture,* 8 (1975), 735-43; Ilza Veith's *Hysteria. The History of a Disease* (Chicago: Univ. of Chicago Press, 1965) discusses fainting as a symptom of hysteria, pp. 121, 163-64.

[26] Jane Austen, *Love and Freindship* in *The Works of Jane Austen,* R. W. Chapman, ed. (London: Oxford Univ. Press, 1954), pp. vi, 102; see also pp. 86, 89 and 99-100 for incidents of fainting.

[27] Spacks, *Imagining,* p. 88; see also pp. 63-65.

[28] Ibid., pp. 57-58. Again, these are qualities associated with escape literature; see Cawelti, p. 36; Lesser, pp. 42-46, 104, and 115.

[29] This is not to say that some of the acts of violence in the novels by women are not simply conventional or the stuff of masochistic fancy. Within the escape literature of their day and within the conventions, the women novelists underscore feminine helplessness and dramatize feminine frustration over and over again. Were female violence simply convention, the outcome and the responses to situations would be less significant in the context of the books.

[30] Barker, *Love Intrigues,* p. 44.

[31] Elizabeth Inchbald, *A Simple Story* (London: Oxford Univ. Press, 1967), originally published in 1791, p. 164. Lloyd W. Brown argues that Jane Austen described similar illusory power in *Lady Susan* in "Jane Austen and the Feminist Tradition," *Nineteenth-Century Fiction,* 28 (1973), 321-38.

[32] Frances Brooke, *The History of Emily Montague* (Ottawa: Graphic Publishers Limited, 1931), p. 198; originally published 1769.

[33] Moers argues that Emma's influence is her status as an heiress, p. 158. Austen condemns the scheming Susan with irony, p. 274, with satire, p. 282, and by her complete exclusion from society at the end of the story (*Works,* vi).

[34] Brooks, p. 160.

[35] Charlotte Lennox, *The Life of Harriot Stuart* (London: Payne and Bouquet, 1751), p. 8.

[36] Mary Collyer, *Felicia to Charlotte* (New York: Garland, 1974), Part I originally published in 1744 and Part II in 1749.

[37] John Dollard, et al., *Frustration and Aggression* (New Haven: Yale Univ. Press, 1939), p. 1.

[38] Spacks in "Ev'ry Woman is at Heart a Rake," *Eighteenth-Century Studies,* 8 (1974), 36, points out that "Passion lies within, the self is the ultimate enemy, the struggle is endless." Compare Braudy, "But Clarissa knows the truth of her frailty: *weakness comes from within,*" p. 195.

[39] Lesser, pp. 265-66.

[40] Spacks, *Imagining,* pp. 59-60.

[41] Collyer, pp. ii and 12.

[42] The term appears in Valerie Shaw's "Jane Austen's Subdued Heroines," *Nineteenth-Century Fiction,* 30 (1975), 284-85.

* I am grateful to the William Andrews Clark Library, UCLA, and to the American Philosophical Society for grants which made this research possible.

Paula R. Backscheider (essay date 1987)

SOURCE: "Women Writers and the Chains of Identification," in *Studies in the Novel,* Vol. 19, No. 3, Fall, 1987, pp. 245-62.

[*In the essay below, Backscheider examines ways in which women novelists responded to popular conceptions about their sex, some choosing to rebel against the demand for well-mannered, sentimental works, others choosing to meet common expectations in return for sales and approval.*]

The great female characters of the eighteenth century—Moll Flanders, Roxana, Clarissa Harlowe, Sophia Western, Amelia Booth—were created by men; those of the nineteenth century—Elizabeth Bennet, Emma Woodhouse, Jane Eyre, Gwendolyn Harleth, Catherine Morland, Dorothea Brooke—by women. It is no coincidence, I believe, that, with the exception of Jane Austen, the women who created these great characters published under pseudonyms. Ironically, as more and more women became writers, the range allowed their work became more and more constrained. Above all, the tendency to identify women writers with their work confined their creativity. Seen as committing not just outrageous acts but outrageous *autobiographical* acts, women writers found protest futile.

With considerable passion, Hannah Cowley, author of thirteen plays, wrote in 1786,

> They will allow me, indeed, to draw strong character, but it must be without speaking its language. I may give vulgar or low bred persons, but they must converse in a stile of elegance. I may design the coarsest manners, or the most disgusting folly, but its expressions must not deviate from the line of politeness. Surely it would be as just to exact from the Artists who are painting the Gallery of Shakespeare, that they should compleat their designs without the use of light and shade.
>
> It cannot be the *Poet's* mind, which the public desire to trace, in dramatic representation; but the mind of the *characters,* and the truth of their colouring. Yet in my case it seems resolved that the point to be considered, is not whether that *dotard,* or that *pretender,* or that *coquet,* would so have given their feelings, but whether Mrs. *Cowley* ought so to have expressed herself.[1]

Cowley went on to say that novelists were not so treated, but that was not so. In a far from unusual gesture, the *Monthly Review* chastised Sophia Lee for *The Life of a Lover* (1804):

> We do not mean to assert that no vicious characters should make their appearance in a lady's novel: but we expect that the natural modesty of her sex should contrive to cast a veil over such images as would bespeak, if exposed, loose and irregular ideas in the writer's mind, and are calculated for other purposes than the *moral improvement* of the reader ... we lament that the fair author should have ever heard such *arguments,* or should

have suffered her mind to contemplate their force and efficacy.[2]

By the end of the eighteenth century, men and women held strong opinions about the appropriate subjects, themes, characters, and purposes of novels by women, and female dramatists faced equally strong, though somewhat different, demands. The woman and her material had become inseparable, and the *writer* became self-conscious, afraid lest she be mistaken for her heroines and nervous about her minor characters and conclusions. Such writers stripped their heroines of the ability to fantasize, scheme, and engage in immorality. The heroes had correctable faults, but the heroines were paragons.[3] Plots became increasingly domestic and centered on reactions and feelings rather than events, and endings conformed rigidly to virtue rewarded and evil punished. The narrow scope that Ian Watt found characteristic of most novels after Fielding seemed institutionalized.[4] The Aphra Behn who could present her first play with a prologue identifying herself as a woman, a "scout," and a person willing to "face you down 'twas full of Wit" became an embarrassment waiting for Virginia Woolf to say that every woman should let flowers fall on her tomb.[5]

A full study of the years between Behn's *The Forced Marriage* in 1670 and the great novels of the nineteenth century would surely begin with the poets who were more numerous at first than the novelists and playwrights. It would include careful analyses of women's writings and their careers both in isolation and in comparison to those of men; it would consider changes in individual writers' work and in the statements they made about their work; and finally, it would examine plots, heroines, and these heroines' foils. Such a study would lead to conclusions about the evolving psychological identity of "the woman writer" and the ways actual women saw themselves in relation to their work, their readers, and their society.[6] Here, however, I shall focus only upon how some of the ways existing conventions in drama and fiction heightened the tendency to identify women with their material.

Convention

In many ways, the submission of *The Forced Marriage* to the Duke's Men is one of the most audacious acts in history. Here was a woman presenting a play for public performance to a company which had only recently begun to put actresses on the stage.[7] Moreover, although the work has many characteristics of the Restoration love/duty plays, it includes the first of Behn's outspoken condemnations of arranged marriages. In another early play, *The Rover* (1677), one of her characters strips to his underwear on stage. Yet despite such gestures of apparent defiance, Behn provided the first links in the chains that would restrict women's

authorial freedom. In the prologue to *The Forced Marriage,* she allied herself with women, then said, "To day one of their Party ventures out,/Not with design to conquer, but to scout./Discourage but this first attempt, and then/They'll hardly dare to sally out again." Behn is careful to define her action in non-threatening terms, to present herself as timorous, and to appeal to male chivalry and female sympathy.

Behn's appeals and apologies are in certain respects completely conventional. The prologue for the revival of John Dryden's first play, *The Wild Gallant,* concludes in almost exactly the same way: "But, if once more you slight his weak indeavour;/For ought I know, he may turn taile for ever."[8] It was common practice to plead youth, inexperience, or any number of other circumstances to gain the audience's sympathy, and prologues often made specific appeals to men and to women. A few bold playwrights confessed an ambition to "conquer" the audience or the stage of Jonson and Shakespeare, but Behn's tone is far more typical of the prologues for her time. Accustomed to the conventions in prologues for men's work, audiences paid attention to delivery and content; but when the prologue confessed that the playwright was female, the audience could not help but be struck by the novelty of a *woman* playwright, especially in a time when actresses were still unfamiliar. The awareness that a woman was the author acted like background music: at least periodically, it interfered with the act of watching (or reading) from beginning to end.

Early women novelists sometimes made the same appeals for women's sympathy and loyalty that the dramatists did. Mary Davys, for example, addressed the preface of *The Reform'd Coquet* (1724) to the "Ladies of Great Britain": "whatever my Faults may be, my Design is good, and I hope you *British* Ladies will accordingly encourage it" (p. iv). By mentioning personal details, women writers suggested additional bonds with their female readers. Penelope Aubin occasionally mentioned her husband in the novels she wrote about married life; others referred to their children's needs, and Sarah Spencer depicted herself writing beside her husband's sickbed.[9]

Aphra Behn wrote fiction as well as drama, and, throughout the Restoration and eighteenth century, many of the women who wrote plays wrote novels. Especially after the two theater companies united in 1682, fiction paid far better than drama. Unfortunately, just as some dramatic conventions tended to underscore the sex of the playwright, so did certain novelistic features. From its beginning and throughout the century, the English novel was overwhelmingly first-person; it appeared in any number of pseudo-autobiographical forms. The discovered manuscript, the set of letters, the "lives," and "memoirs" identified the writer with the text—or pretended to do so. The earliest women writers innocently participated in the convention. In her novels, Behn, whose past was fairly well known, mentioned meeting real people and having been in Antwerp. Occasionally she reminded her reader that she used the same material in her plays and her novels, as she did with Colonel Martin in *Oroonoko* (1688) and *The Younger Brother* (1696; spelled "Marteen" in the play). Catharine Trotter created a heroine who lived with her poor-but-respectable widowed mother in *Olinda's Adventures* (1693), just as the author did. The autobiographical nature of Delarivière Manley's *The Adventures of Rivella* (1714) has been notorious since its publication, and giving to another of her heroines whose adventures obviously followed her own name of "Delia" (*The New Atalantis,* 1709) assured at least some identification. Jane Barker claimed that some of the "Levities and Misfortunes" described in her *Love Intrigues* were hers.

Moreover, from prefaces and from non-fictional prose, these writers carried over the conventions of familiar address and distinctive voices. To include sentences beginning, "Reader," and even to establish the narrative voice of a concerned citizen, an elderly Whig, or the Spectator, no matter how unobtrusive, was to suggest identification of writer with text. These conventions not only emphasized the writer's sex and, therefore, the novelty of it; they also implied that firsthand experience made the story useful as example in the ways sermons were.

Like all neophytes, early women writers drew upon existing conventions. Unfortunately the presentation of dramatic works came with self-conscious and obsequious introductions and fictional works with self-conscious and apologetic ones. Men could assume these stances until free to reveal their manly, forthright, daring, ambitious selves; the same stances, however, were so close to perceived or demanded characteristics of the female that the conventions reinforced gender expectations. From men, they appeared to be what they were—conventions; from women, they appeared to be, at least in part, proper extensions of sex roles. From men, the appeal was for fair play; from women, for chivalry. Behn's appeals to sympathy, her coyness, and her carefully designed non-threatening, even feminine stance, recur repeatedly, as when Susannah Centlivre had the actress Mrs. Oldfield admonish the audience at her first play (1700), "'tis not for your Glory/t' insult a Lady." This prologue concludes, "she's sure to gain the Field,/For Women always Conquer when they yeild" [*sic*]. Centlivre here is mundanely conventional, but the problem she created for herself might best be illustrated by the fact that years later Fordyce would end one of his sermons, "It is thine, thou fair form, to command by obeying, and by yielding to conquer."[10]

Criticism

The most frequent contemporary criticisms of eighteenth-century mass literature were that it was immoral and was the work of a horde of illiterate, ignorant scribblers. These repetitious complaints did nothing to reduce the number of aspiring authors, but they gradually influenced themes, plots, and characters, and they did foster a new set of conventions. Men and women shared these new conventions developed to override familiar critical prejudices, but the conventions, when adapted by women, further emphasized gender.

Both novels and plays in the eighteenth century came under vigorous attack for being "immoral" and dangerous corrupters of morals, especially the morals of the young. By charging women writers with immodesty, critics and moralists intensified the idea of immorality—a work produced by an immodest woman became doubly immoral, for both its content and its composition could be condemned. In a time when many believed that evil men could not produce good books, and even so great a critic as Samuel Johnson habitually discussed the character of the author of a work as an essential part of his evaluation of worth and achievement, this kind of judgment of women's work was to be expected. The ways in which the very act of publication violated the nearly universal opinion of women's modest nature and unobtrusive place require no explication.[11] Ludicrous as it now seems to us, the Spectator's preference for tapestry weaving over writing as an occupation for women perfectly captures the atmosphere in which women wrote: "I cannot forbear wishing, that several Writers of that Sex had chosen to apply themselves rather to Tapestry than Rhime," the Spectator explained and went on to say that it was "the most proper way wherein a Lady can shew a fine Genius" and would divert her from scandal and politics (no. 606 for 13 October 1714).

A woman like Aphra Behn or Delarivière Manley might realize that she had no reputation to lose and capitalize on this fact by appearing as a dashing political character or by publishing a sensational autobiography.[12] Most women, however, were at pains to remain respectable. Catharine Trotter, for instance, dedicated her first play, *Agnes de Castro* (1696), to the well-known patron, the Earl of Dorset, and explained, "she Conceals her Name, to shun that of Poetress [*sic*]" and "I wish I cou'd separate them here, for then I shou'd be proud to own my self to the World." Mary Brunton said that she "would sooner exhibit as a rope-dancer" than be known as a writer.[13]

For men and women alike, the obvious answer to the objections of the moralists was to invoke Horace and to emphasize the instructive nature of their work. In addition to pleading the necessity of "sugar-coating" pills, these writers increasingly included the kinds of examples and stories found in conduct books and sermons. Prefatory material (if not the stories and plays themselves) quickly began to reflect the alleged wishes of society. In contrast to her 1713 *Love Intrigues,* for instance, Barker characterized her 1715 *Exilius* as a work "After the Manner of Telemachus, For the Instruction of Some Young LADIES of Quality;"[14] and she called her *Patch-Work Screen* (1723) a "Collection of Instructive Novels." In 1722, Penelope Aubin wrote that "Religious Treatises grow mouldy on the Booksellers Shelves in Back-Shops" and hailed *Robinson Crusoe* as a new way to teach morality.[15]

Dedicated to morality, respectability, and education, Penelope Aubin, Jane Barker, and a few other writers like them pioneered what would be the dominant type of women's writing for over 200 years.[16] Mary Davys, for instance, said she would "bless my Labour" if her book "but Make some impression upon the young unthinking Minds of some of my own sex" (p. ix-x). These women could tap into a rich tradition of didactic prose, take heart from the continued popularity of conduct books, and even cite examples of women who had written religious and philosophical treatises. For example, Hannah Wolley wrote in the preface to *The Gentlewoman's Companion* (1675), "It is no ambitious design of gaining a name in print . . . that put me on this bold undertaking . . . To be useful in our generation is partly the intent of our creation; I shall [be content] if any shall profit by this following discourse."[17] By mid-century, the expectation of educational benefits presented in delicate, graceful language had been nearly universally absorbed by women writers. Sarah Scott, for instance, wrote an "Advertisement" for *The History of Cornelia* (1750) expressing the hope that "any inaccuracies will be overlooked for the sake of the intention [to exemplify morality], which appears throughout the whole performance." In 1793, Clara Reeve wrote in *Memoirs of Sir Roger de Clarendon* that she had "been careful to avoid any noxious ingredient" that might "mislead the reader, or . . . give pain to herself in the awful hour of her dissolution." Novel after novel allied itself with the older tradition of the conduct book; Fanny Burney captured the approved aim of these novels in *The Wanderer* when she explained that the purpose of novels was to give "knowledge of the world, without ruin or repentence; and the lessons of experience, without its tears" (l:xvi). Books like Sarah Fielding's *The Governess* (1749), a girls-at-school children's collection intended to teach benevolence and virtue, and the later Sunday School literature for children by Sarah Trimmer and Hannah More, illustrate the off-shoots of didactic fiction as well as the continued growth and definition of special audiences of readers.

Men instructed their readers in the ways of the world, human nature, and the means of achieving success. They took such roles as that of sage, experienced traveller, and retired man of business. Women adapted the role of mother and offered woman's knowledge as an alternative to man's education. By doing so, they gained real authority, while their gentle guidance often had tones of affection, concern, and even mild pathos. They told the stories of disappointed love, missed opportunities, renounced dreams, and endured marriages. Their "lessons of experience" taught girls how to please men, whom to marry, how to deal with the problems of marriage, and by what means they might find contentment or even fulfillment as women. Narrative mothers could illustrate and urge; they could even speak out judgmentally, but they were never allowed to be pedantic, dictatorial, or openly irreverent. In a century when Addison, Fielding, Johnson, and most other critics agreed that learning alone was not enough for a writer, the experience of women gave validity to their books. They extended their role as mothers (or older female friends) into a distinctive narrative voice and, incidentally, circumvented objections to their lack of learning and worldly knowledge.

The concern for the younger members of their sex, the allusions to the hard lessons of experience, and personal references in the prefaces of women's books developed their role as mother. Characters admonished others to consult older women, and conclusions such as Lucasia's at the end of Galesia's story in *Love Intrigues* were common: "The only thing . . . I blame you for is, that you did not consult your Mother, whose Wisdom might have found out a way to have accommodated things to all your Satisfactions" (p. 70). In some cases, both the narrative voice and the stories of the characters draw upon motherhood, as they do in Clara Reeve's *School for Widows* (1791). Mary Wollstonecraft used the fiction of a mother writing to her child in *The Wrongs of Woman*. Because Maria's own child is dead and because she incorporates the experiences and advice of Jemima, the lower-class madhouse attendant, Maria becomes a kind of universal mother figure weeping for erring and victimized womankind.

The second common attack on eighteenth-century popular literature was that an invasion of scribblers and hacks had ruined it. Johnson summarized, "The province of writing was formerly left to those, who by study, or appearance of study, were supposed to have gained knowledge unattainable by the busy part of mankind."[18] Women, of course, fit Johnson's description of these interlopers in the "province of writing" even better than most men, for women could not study, and those women willing to publish almost invariably wrote for money and, therefore, had little choice but to "hack," to write for demand. Just as women were doubly vulnerable to complaints about immorality, so they were doubly susceptible to charges of presumption and ignorance.

Presumption, like immodesty, carried serious moral overtones. After all, Clarissa's sin was presumption; she dared to trust in her own strength and judgment. Often described as "monstrous," women writers felt sharply the reaction that Bathsua Makin described in *An Essay to Revive the Antient Education of Gentlewomen* (1673): "A Learned Woman is thought to be a Comet, that bodes Mischief, when ever it appears. To offer to the World the liberal Education of Woman is to deface the Image of God in Man."[19] To be presumptuous implied a rebellion against nature and Providence. Aphra Behn had recognized the conception of women's place that lay behind growing resistance to her work. When her third play, *The Dutch Lover* (1673), failed, she blamed those who believed that her sex incapacitated her art. In the preface she wrote for the printed version of the play, she included a striking description of the first performance: "that day 'twas Acted first . . . a phlegmatick, white, ill-favour'd, wretched Fop . . . opening that which serves it for a mouth, out issued . . . that they were to expect a woful Play . . . for it was a woman's."[20] Behn's epilogue for *Sir Patient Fancy* (1678) gives Nell Gwyn a scathing speech dramatizing this very incident and reworking each of her resentments:

> I here and there o'erheard a Coxcomb cry,
> Ah, Rot it—'tis a Woman's Comedy,
> One, who because she lately chanc'd to please us,
> With her damn'd Stuff, will never cease to teeze us.
> What has poor Woman done, that she must be
> Debar'd from Sense, and sacred Poetry?
>
> . . . . .
>
> For who but we cou'd your dull Fopperies bear,
> Your saucy Love, and your brisk Nonsense hear,
>
> . . . . .
>
> Both striving who shall most ingenious grow
> In Leudness, Foppery, Nonsense, Noise and Show.
> And yet to these fine things we must submit
> Our Reason, Arms, our Laurels, and our Wit.
>
> . . . . .
>
> Your way of Writing's out of fashion grown.
> Method, and Rule—you only understand;
> Pursue that way of Fooling, and be damn'd.
>
> . . . . .
>
>   pray tell me then,
> Why Women should not write as well as Men.

Women quickly learned that, if sex could incapacitate art, then art could confound sex. As Anne Finch wrote in the Prologue to *Aristomenes* (1713), "in spite of all editing, / A woman's way to charm is not by writing" (lines 31-32). In what may be the earliest English fictional portrayal of a woman writer, Jane Barker has her Galesia conclude that learning is "neither of Use nor Ornament in our Sex" (p. 53). The central event in *Love Intrigues* is a horrifying dream that Galesia has at the very moment her happy marriage seems assured. A specter appears to her and says, "Unlucky Maid! / Since, since thou has the Muses chose / *Hymen,* and Fortune are thy Foes." This specter puts the "curse of Cassandra"—she will always be misunderstood—on her and says, "A thousand other Ills beside / Fortune does still for them provide, / Who to the Muses are ally'd" (pp. 33-34). Galesia has turned to poetry as refuge from turmoil and disappointment, but it leads her to eccentric dress and behavior and to vanity. She and her lover remain at cross purposes, and Galesia begins to learn Latin, read her brother's medical books, and become proud. Her writing—like her skills as a farmer and her silence about her feelings—are above the proper reach of women, and she suffers spinsterhood as punishment.

One of the most obvious ways for women to defend themselves against the charge of presumption was to deny serious intent; in other words, to deny that they were competing with men or doing the same things. Novelists called their books "this Trifle," "this Woman's-Toy," the work of a few or of "leisure" hours. The prologue described Susannah Centlivre's first play, *The Perjur'd Husband* (1700), as "a Ladys Treat." Sometimes women openly depreciated their work. Jane Barker declared that she only hoped to provide "Half an Hours [*sic*] Amusement" (dedication, *Love Intrigues*); Eliza Haywood protested that she "pretend[ed] no farther Merit, than to please" (dedication, *Fatal Secret*, p. viii). Even some of the playwrights labeled their work "trifles."[21]

Indisputably unlearned, women also lacked experience with the public world and "conversation," two qualities that Fielding listed as essential for novelists. No matter that they could translate Boccaccio, Epictetus, Fontenelle, Xenophon, Marivaux, and Kotzebue.[22] They still slipped into egregious errors in geography, history, and commerce. No matter that prose fiction by men was also shot through with improbabilities.

Women could not deny their lack of learning; their apologies were ubiquitous, ranging from complaints such as Haywood's "Custom has allow'd Millions of Advantages [to men], denied to us," to the simple, unadorned (and disingenuous) statement of Hannah More: "To what is called learning I have never had any pretension."[23] Aphra Behn's forthright statement contrasts more and more starkly with women's disclaimers as the years pass:

Plays have no great room for that which is men's great advantage over women, that is Learning; We all well know that the immortal Shakespeare's Plays (who was not guilty of much more of this than often falls to women's share) have better pleas'd the World than Johnson' works, though by the way 'tis said that Benjamin was no such Rabbi neither. (1:224, Epistle to the Reader, *Dutch Lover*)

Self-conscious to the utmost, Mary Pix apologized abjectly for mistakenly calling her play *"Ibrahim, the Thirteenth Emperour of the Turks"* when the hero was the twelfth emperor.[24] Mary Davys asked to be forgiven for just one improbability and reminded readers of *The Reform'd Coquet* that "such are to be met with in most Novels, many Plays, and even in Travels" (p. xii).

Critics busily told women what they ought to be doing. Some were quite direct, as Hodgson was in his prologue for Mary Pix's *The False Friend* (1699):

Amongst Reformers of this Virtuous Age,
Who think it Duty to Refine the Stage:
A Woman, to Contribute, does Intend
In Hopes a Moral Play your Lives will Mend.
Matters of State, she'l not pretend to Teach;
Or Treat of War, or things above her Reach:
Nor Scourge your Folly's, with keen *Satyrs*
  Rage.

—That part then of Reformation,
Which she believes the fittest for her Station;
Is to shew *Man* the surest way to Charm.

Richard Steele expressed a common opinion when he praised the plot and "incidents" in Centlivre's *The Busie Body* (1709) for "that subtilty of spirit" which is "very seldom" achieved by men, "in whom craft in love is an act of invention, and not, as with women, the effect of nature and instinct" (*Tatler*, no. 19). Women, then, were to reform morals and their field of play was to be love. Joseph Gay praised Mary Hearne in the same terms: "That best a *Woman* knows to write of Love/Nature instructs Her with expressive Powers . . . / [To] well describe, what she concerts so well" (prefatory poem, *The Lover's Week*). George Colman's prologue for Inchbald's *I'll Tell You What* (1785) presented a woman nearly smug in her choice of love over learning:

Men, 'tis true, in their Noodles huge Treasures
  may hoard,
But the *Heart* of a Woman with Passions is
  stor'd.
With Passions not copied from Latin or Greek,
Which the Language of Nature in plain
  English speak.
Girls who grieve, or rejoice, from true
  Feelings, as I do,
Never dream of Calypso, or Helen, or Dido.

Women accepted this compliment, and their work is full of such statements as Haywood's observation in the dedication to *The Fatal Secret* that no one knows the "Graces which compleat the Fine Gentleman" as well as a woman. Men were quick to ridicule women's mistakes about history, geography, and social customs and willing to praise writers like Charlotte Smith: "Mrs. S. writes like a gentlewoman. . . . She faithfully follows nature as far as she can see . . . when she attempts to combine without a model, she is lost."[25]

One of the great subjects of plays and fiction was love, and it was easy for women to claim to have made men and love the studies of their lives. By concentrating upon personal relationships, moral examples, women's feelings and thoughts, and what Gilbert and Gubar call the woman's *Bildungsroman,* they avoided censure. Delarivière Manley, Eliza Haywood, and even Jane Barker set themselves up as experts in love. By narrating tales of courtship and marriage, they established themselves as authorities in a field men were willing to grant them. Just how conscious women were of what they were choosing, and why, appears in statements such as one by Eliza Haywood in her dedication to the third edition of *The Fatal Secret* (1725):

LOVE . . . requires no Aids of Learning, no general Conversation, no Application; a shady Grove and purling Stream are all Things that's necessary to give us an Idea of the tender Passion. This is a Theme . . . frees me from the Imputation of vain or self-sufficient:—None can tax me with having too great an Opinion of my own *Genius,* when I aim at nothing but what the meanest may perform.

Their acceptance of this role contributed to the idea that, while men might be artists, creators, and thinkers, women were usually merely repeaters of their own or other women's autobiographical stories.[26]

Success

The phenomenal rise of the woman reader accompanied the establishment of the woman writer, and women novelists began to write for this rapidly growing female audience. The reciprocal relationship continued to increase the numbers of readers even as it encouraged and supported more women writers. As early as 1696, Mary Pix could sign *The Inhuman Cardinal,* "A Novel written by a Gentlewoman for the Entertainment of the Sex." In combination with the theater's insatiable appetite for new material and the rise of literacy and leisure time, this special market for "women's novels" made writing one of the most lucrative of all occupations for women. The early novelists who were also playwrights generally attempted to appeal to both sexes, depended on incident and dialogue, and often integrated undisguised, even radical, topical material. Aphra Behn's *Oroonoko* (1688),

Delarivière Manley's romans à clef, and Eliza Haywood's political allegory, *The Adventures of Eovaai* (1736), attracted the same audience as their plays.

Some of the very earliest women novelists, however, had no theatrical or other publication experience. Since the audience for novels had not yet been defined, writers had to develop a sense of audience. At a time when periodicals such as Dunton's *Athenian Gazette* and even *The Tatler* were openly courting female readers, booksellers could hardly be oblivious to the commercial value of novels for women. They encouraged new writers, including inexperienced women, and necessity and profit opened doors that merit could not. Some booksellers kept "stables" of women writers,[27] and both the dramatists and the new novelists began to write for the rapidly growing female audience. Haywood's titillating *Idalia* (1723), *Fantomina* (1725), *The Mercenary Lover* (1726), and many other similar books were published alongside Aubin's pious *Life of Madame de Beaumont* (1721) and Barker's realistic *A Patch-Work Screen for the Ladies*. Novels advertised as "By a Young Lady," or located with other novels by women through descriptive words emphasizing the "Misfortunes of . . . Fair-ones . . . represented with so forcible, so natural a Delicacy," incidentally narrowed their scope as they appealed to a defined audience.

Some novels, such as Haywood's *The British Recluse* (1722), Mary Collyer's *Felicia to Charlotte* (1744-1749), Sarah Scott's *Millenium Hall* (1762), Elizabeth Griffith's *The History of Lady Barton* (1771), and Charlotte Lennox's *Euphemia* (1790) almost exclusively depict women together. The number of male characters is drastically reduced, and women talk about men far more often than they talk to them. Novels like Maria Edgeworth's *Belinda* (1801) continued the common practice of invoking earlier women writers (here Burney) and allying themselves with these earlier writers' readers. The problems of etiquette, of maintaining a happy marriage, and of discovering ways to occupy oneself productively replace adventure, travel, and even courtship. Modern Europe, ancient Rome, the Royal Exchange, and the New World port disappeared from the novels and were replaced by the closed coach, the garden seat, and the drawing room.

Not only did women surrender adventurous settings, plots, and themes, but most gave up engagement with important, immediate events. Sheridan once said that the purpose of plays was to provide "abstract and brief chronicles of the time," and, with *The Critic* (1779), he returned the stage to political satire.[28] Women, however, fell in with Hannah Cowley, who denied that her *A Day in Turkey* had political relevance: "I protest I know nothing about politics;—will Miss Wollstonecraft forgive me—whose book contains such a body of mind as I hardly ever met with—if I say that politics are *unfeminine?*" (Advertisement)

Again, the departure from the work of Aphra Behn and other earlier women is striking. Certainly Behn, a loyal Stuart partisan, believed in political commentary. The joke of her *False Count* (1681) turns on Behn's avowed "conversion" to the Whig party. The prologue to *The Round-Heads* (1681) extends the attack on the Whigs of her day by linking their present behavior to "the spirit of '41,"[29] thereby labeling them a rebellious, lawless faction. Catharine Trotter's *The Unhappy Penitent* (1701) includes a blatantly political prologue; Delarivière Manley wrote political propaganda for, among others, no less a periodical than the *Examiner,* and Eliza Haywood wrote a political allegory and included partisan politics in her plays.[30] Susannah Centlivre defended her work by reminding her countrymen, "What cannot *England* boast from Women? The mighty *Romans* felt the Power of *Boadicea's* Arm; *Eliza* made *Spain* tremble; but ANN, the greatest of the Three, has shook the Man that aim'd at Universal Sway" (dedication to *Platonick Lady,* 1707). Centlivre later wrote *The Gotham Election,* a dramatic satire of election abuses and Jacobite sentiments, that was denied a license by the Master of Revels. Even though she had offered the play at the time widespread rioting greeted the accession of King George I, she dared to attack the Tories anew in the preface to the printed edition.

Convention

By the end of the eighteenth century, the identification of the woman writer with her material had become fixed. Comment upon content—and even style—became indiscriminately mingled with comment on the woman. Sometimes it is not immediately clear whether woman or book is being described. For instance, critics had made Charlotte Smith's style, lauded for "gentleness, that lovely simplicity, that nice sensibility, that true feminine beauty," the ideal.[31] The reviewer of Hannah Cowley's *The Runaway* (1776) wrote: "After so frank and candid a confession of weakness, we wish to shew the comedy as much indulgence in the closet as the Lady tells us it has met with in the theatre. She might with equal justise ascribe its excellencies and imperfections, as well as the applause it has received, to her sex. It bears every mark of a female production." In another review of her work, Cowley is introduced with metaphors of breeding: "The genius of Mrs. Cowley is so prolific. . . . The Lady never loses her teeming time, but breeds regularly every year."[32] Even when the conventions of avowed reticence were ludicrous, critics praised the women who conformed to them. They applauded Elizabeth Inchbald for a "Preface [to *A Simple Story,* 1791], so ingenuous, so modest, and so pathetic, that, while she seems willing to depress her own consequence, every line of the Introduction gives new value to her character." And this after ten plays that had brought "the fair writer" "often at the tribunal of our Review." Blinded by bias, other critics ludicrously praised works they found deplorable in every way but for their morality. For instance, a review of Sophia Lee's *Canterbury Tales* acknowledges the improbable, "wild and romantic" fable, the inconsistent and unrealistic characters, the "florid," incorrect language, and the "artificial" and even "absurd" events. Yet the reviewer concludes with "a favourable opinion of the inventive powers of the fair writer" because "no objection can be made to the moral tendency of her work," for "the prevailing sentiments are virtuous and pious," and "bright examples of excellence in domestic life" are appropriately rewarded.[33] This praise seems based upon expectations for the work of women writers.

By using the conventions that existed when they first became writers and by accepting others as they were created, women contributed to the identification of themselves with their material. And, just as women writers do today, some exploited the identification, some resisted it, some raged against it, and some transformed old conventions into new. As dozens of feminist critics have shown, however, women's writing in the eighteenth century was never as narrow as the generation before ours believed. Regardless of their apparent domestication, later women writers continued to say many of the same irreverent things that the earliest women had said: Men's values may be wrong; men are often vain, proud, and, therefore, likely to make fools of themselves. Women are clever enough to "manage" them. Jane Austen's ironic observer, so suited to serious social criticism, appeared earlier in Sarah Fielding's novels, in Charlotte Lennox's *Female Quixote* (1752), and in the work of the Fanny Burney who could expose male arrogance in characters as diverse as Mr. Smith, Sir Clement Willoughby, and Delvile.

A close look at women's novels and plays reveals the encoding of resistance and endurance. Fanny Burney's Cecilia may lose her fortune, but she is certainly not only morally superior to any other character in the novel but also more emotionally stable. In spite of her breakdown at the end, it is she and not Delvile who resists passion, and he who is rash, uncharitable, and even murderous. As many critics have remarked, Delvile's pride, like that of Darcy in *Pride and Prejudice,* is the major obstacle to the couple's happiness. When a Burney character contemplates or commits suicide, that character is male, not female. Strengths similar to those of Burney's women can be found in Jane Barker's Galesia, in Charlotte Smith's Emmeline and Monimia, in Frances Sheridan's Sidney Bidulph, and many other characters. Behn's women may use the stage's clever tricks, but Felicia in Mary Collyer's *Felicia to Charlotte* and Mrs. Hearne in Jane West's *Advantages of Education* (1792) are no less adept at manipulating men into becoming reformed, good husbands.

The publication of William Godwin's *Memoirs of the Author of a Vindication of the Rights of Woman* (1798) increased the number of women who avoided the appearance of engagement with public issues. Women writers saw Mary Wollstonecraft denounced as a whore and her work, especially her novels, transformed into the immoral wishes of a depraved libertine. Even so able a woman as Maria Edgeworth wrote that women "cannot always have recourse to what *ought to be,* they must adapt themselves to what is."[34] Fanny Burney's *The Wanderer* (1814) and Jane Austen's *Emma* (1816) reflect the subdued spirits of women writers. Both, however, also reflect renewed brooding over women's fate.

Emma, for instance, that novel still so often described as "the life Jane Austen was leading,"[35] revises *Pride and Prejudice's* "light and bright" romance of a young lady without fortune but with embarrassing relatives and a young man of superior fortune, giving us somber Jane Fairfax and trivial Frank Churchill instead.[36] Like Burney's Cecilia, Jane suffers because of a secret engagement. Once the circumstances are known and the principals roundly criticized for their sneakiness, Emma concludes, "If a woman can ever be excused for thinking only of herself, it is in a situation like Jane Fairfax's.—Of such, one may almost say, that 'the world is not their's, nor the world's law'" (3:10). This quotation, modified from "The world is not thy friend nor the world's law" in *Romeo and Juliet* (5.1.72), comes strangely from Emma's lips. In the past, she has avoided and disliked Jane, and, moreover, has never kept any of her many plans for reading; nowhere else does she show a literary temper. This quotation, however, could gloss Wollstonecraft's *Maria,* and it partakes of the same theme. The world condemns—and kills—the Romeos and Juliets, the Marias, and the Janes if it can. They must, then, take their chances outside the law. Unlike Romeo and Juliet, Frank and Jane are allowed their unrealistic ending, allowed to remain "outside the law." As Knightley says of Frank in summarizing their improbable history, "He has used everybody ill—and they are all delighted to forgive him.—He is a fortunate man indeed!" (3:13).

But Emma is not outside the world and the law. Like Maria, she has been educated to see woman's lot and to see it whole. By the end of the novel, she understands the sufferings of the rich and poor and of the young and old. Just as Emma comes to understand what could lead a woman as admirable, moral, and able as Jane to deceit, she sees what Miss Bates's old age promises and comes to exclaim "Poor child" when she speaks of Mrs. Weston's infant daughter.

Emma is captivating and admirable because she has done the best that can be done with her world of trivia, repetition, and banality. Yet surely Avrom Fleishman, who sees Emma as a driven neurotic, is as close to the truth as Gilbert and Gubar are when they make *Emma* into an "avatar of Austen the artist."[37] Austen no doubt meant to assure that Knightley, faced with giving up Donwell as Burney's Delvile had had to surrender his name, would remain Emma's equal, not be her superior.

Generations of critics may confine Jane Austen to Emma's Highbury, and the chains of identity may never lose their power, but Austen—and hundreds of other women writers—learned to make the chains themselves speak. Ironically, the heroines are like their creators: resourceful, ingenious, resilient, and tough. Women writers and their characters seek respect and fulfillment. Increasingly, women writers expanded women's options even as they began to experiment with the novel's range. And most of them remained true to themselves as they lived out the truth that adaptation is strength and survival.

Notes

[1] Hannah Cowley, "An Address," *A School for Greybeards,* p. vi, in *The Plays of Hannah Cowley,* 2 vols., ed. Frederick M. Link (New York: Garland, 1979), Volume 2.

[2] Review of *The Life of a Lover, Monthly Review,* 2d ser., 45 (1804), 360.

[3] Women writers observe this convention throughout the period. Delarivière Manley's "To the Reader" in *The Secret History of Queen Zarah* complains that heroes may have faults but heroines are "exempted from all the Weakness of Humane Nature, and much above the Infirmities of their Sex." Nearly a hundred year later, Mary Wollstonecraft resented the fact that "the hero is allowed to be mortal" while the heroines "are to be born immaculate," "Author's Preface" to *The Wrongs of Women.*

[4] Ian Watt, Introduction, *Jane Austen. A Collection of Critical Essays* (Englewood Cliffs, NJ: Prentice Hall, 1963), pp. 2-5. In this essay, Watt complains of the tendency in novels toward "social and spiritual narrowness of the content" (p. 4). See also *The Rise of the Novel* (1957; rptd. Berkeley: Univ. of California Press, 1967), in which Watt finds that "the advantages of the feminine point of view outweigh the restrictions of social horizon" in the works of Burney, Austen, and Eliot (p. 299).

[5] Behn's play was produced in 1670 at Lincoln's Inn Fields and printed in 1671; quotations from Behn's plays are from *The works of Aphra Behn,* 5 vols., ed. Montague Summers (London: Heinemann, 1915), 3:286. Virginia Woolf, *A Room of One's Own* (1929; rptd. New York: Harcourt Brace, 1959), p. 69.

[6] Most of the best studies of women writers, such as Sandra Gilbert and Susan Gubar's *Madwoman in the Attic,* Elaine Showalter's *A Literature of Their Own,* and Ellen Moers's *Literary Women,* begin with the nineteenth century. A central argument of *Madwoman,* however, is that women see their gender as an obstacle to writing; see also Christiane Rochefort, "Are Women Writers Still Monsters" in *New French Feminisms,* eds. Elaine Marks and Isabelle de Courtivron (New York: Schocken Books, 1981), pp. 185-86. Books and articles on single authors such as Behn, Burney, and Austen do consider some of these issues; Margaret Anne Doody's forthcoming biography of Fanny Burney is a notable example. A recent book which discusses some of these points admirably is Jane Spencer's *The Rise of the Woman Novelist* (Oxford and New York: Basil Blackwell, 1986). This book came to my attention after I had nearly completed my paper, and I have not cited all agreements and differences. Spencer's discussion of the autobiographical nature of the earliest novels by women is particularly useful.

[7] Angeline Goreau points out that Behn was not quite the first woman to be so bold; see *Reconstructing Aphra* (New York: Dial, 1980), pp. 115-16.

[8] John Dryden, "Prologue to the *Wild Gallant* Reviv'd," *The Works of John Dryden,* eds. John H. Smith, Dougald MacMillan, Vinton A. Deering, et al. (Berkeley: Univ. of California Press, 1960), 8:6. The play was acted in 1663 and published in 1669.

[9] See Aubin's *The Life and Adventures of Lady Lucy* (London, 1726) and Sarah Spencer's *Memoirs of the Miss Holmsbys* (London, 1788). Unless otherwise noted, I have used the first editions of all novels cited.

[10] *The Plays of Susannah Centlivre,* ed. Richard Frushell. 3 vols. (New York: Garland, 1982); her first play was *The Perjur'd Husband* and is in Volume 1. Fordyce's sermon is quoted in Spencer, *The Rise of the Woman Novelist,* p. 18.

[11] This has been a frequent subject for study. Virginia Woolf notes a "convention" that "publicity in women is detestable." Ellen Moers quotes Stendhal as saying that the first thing a woman writer will lose will be her lover "if she has the good fortune to have" one, *Literary Women* (Garden City, NY: Doubleday, 1985), p. 178. See also Gilbert and Gubar, *The Madwoman in the Attic* (New Haven: Yale Univ. Press, 1979), pp. 49-72 et passim; Angeline Goreau, *Reconstructing Aphra,* pp. 144-55; and Goreau, ed. *The Whole Duty of a Woman* (Garden City, NY: Dial, 1984), pp. 13-17.

[12] Behn has such a character in her prologue to *The False Count;* Manley's *Adventures of Rivella* is a sensational autobiography.

[13] Trotter adapted Aphra Behn's novel by the same title (1688) for her first play. Mary Brunton's words are quoted by Showalter, *A Literature of Their* Own (Princeton: Princeton Univ. Press, 1977), p. 18.

[14] The reference is to Fénelon's popular didactic romance, *Télémaque* (1699).

[15] See John J. Richetti, *Popular Fiction before Richardson* (Oxford: Clarendon, 1969), pp. 216-30, and my *Daniel Defoe: Ambition and Innovation* (Lexington, KY: Univ. Press of Kentucky, 1986), pp. 225-28.

[16] See Spencer's chapter, "The Terms of Acceptance."

[17] Quoted in Goreau, *Whole Duty,* p. 233. This kind of publishing seems to have been generally well accepted. Advertisements as early as 1646 praised books by women even as they called attention to the sex of the author; see Roger P. McCutcheon, "The Beginnings of Book-Reviewing in English Periodicals," *PMLA* 37 (1922), 699-701.

[18] Samuel Johnson, *Adventurer,* no. 115 (11 December 1753), in *The Idler and The Adventurer,* Vol. 2, eds. Walter Jackson Bate, John M. Bullitt, and L. F. Powell (New Haven: Yale Univ. Press, 1963).

[19] [Bathsua Makin], *An Essay to Revive the Antient Education of Gentlewomen* (1673), Augustan Reprint No. 202 (Los Angeles: Clark Library, 1980), p. 3.

[20] Behn, 1:223-24. Goreau, *Reconstructing Aphra,* analyzes this episode at length, pp. 132-37. Susannah Centivre's preface to *The Platonick Lady* (1707) describes a similar incident.

[21] Respectively, Jane Barker, *Love Intrigues* (London, 1713), Mary Hearne, *The Lover's Week* (London, 1718), Ma[dame] A, *The Prude* (London, 1724), Penelope Aubin, *The Strange Adventures of the Count de Vinevil* (London, 1721), Eliza Haywood, *The Rash Resolve, The Fatal Secret, The Injur'd Husband* (all London, 1724), Mary Hearne, *The Female Deserters* (London, 1719), and Aubin's *The Life and Adventures of Lady Lucy* (London, 1726), dedication to *Love Intrigues* and dedication to *Fatal Secret,* p. viii.

[22] Mary Pix translated Book 8, Day 2 of the *Decameron* (*Violenta,* 1704); Elizabeth Carter, Epictetus (1758); Aphra Behn, Fontenelle (1688); Sarah Fielding, Xenophon (1762); Mary Collyer, Marivaux (1743); Inchbald translated and adapted several of Kotzebue's plays.

[23] Eliza Haywood, dedication to *Masqueraders* (London, 1724); More, *Works* (Philadelphia: Woodward, 1830), preface, p. x. See also Haywood's dedications to her *Rash Resolve,* p. viii, and her *Fatal Secret.*

[24] Mary Pix, preface, *Ibrahim, The Thirteenth Emperour of the Turks* (London, 1696).

[25] Review of *Ethelinde, Analytic Review* 5 (1789), 484.

[26] For feminist critics' responses to the tendency to call women's novels autobiographical or even gossip, see Judith Kegan Gardiner, "On Female Identity and Writing by Women," *Writing and Sexual Difference,* ed. Elizabeth Abel (Chicago: Univ. of Chicago Press, 1982), p. 185; and see Moers, *Literary Women,* pp. 94, 144-45, and 176.

[27] William H. McBurney describes this form of employment in "Mrs. Penelope Aubin and the Early Eighteenth-Century Novel," *HLQ* 20 (1957), 249-52.

[28] Richard B. Sheridan, *The Critic,* 2.1.1-4; the character is quoting *Hamlet,* 2.2.512, but changes "players" to "plays."

[29] The play itself is Behn's most political. It offers the conduct of powerful men after Oliver Cromwell's death as an allegory for her own time.

[30] Jerry C. Beasley discusses political themes in novels by women in "Politics and Moral Idealism: The Achievement of Some Early Women Novelists" in *Fetter'd or Free?,* eds. Mary Anne Schofield and Cecilia Macheski (Athens, OH: Ohio Univ. Press, 1986), pp. 221-34; he is especially helpful with Eliza Haywood's political allegory, *The Adventures of Eovaai.*

[31] Review of *Ethelinde, Monthly Review,* n.s., 2 (1790), 162.

[32] Review of *Runaway, Monthly Review,* 1st ser., 54 (1776), 216-17, and of *Which is the Man?, Monthly Review,* 1st ser., 67 (1782), 249-50, respectively. Such comments as those from the *Monthly* on Cowley's *Which is the Man?* were not new. William Wycherley's prologue for Trotter's *Agnes de Castro* (1696) includes the lines, "And like the Pregnant of her Sex, to gain,/But for your pleasure, more Disgrace, and Pain."

[33] Review of A *Simple Story, Monthly Review,* n.s., 4 (1791), 434-35, and review of *Canterbury Tales, Monthly Review,* n.s., 27 (1798), 416-19.

[34] Maria Edgeworth, *Practical Education* (London, 1798), p. 699.

[35] Preface to the Norton Critical Edition of *Emma,* ed. Stephen M. Parrish (New York: Norton, 1972), p. viii.

[36] Emma calls Frank a "child of fortune" and Knightley summarizes the lovers' story as a romance in volume 3, chapter 13; all references to *Emma* are given by volume and chapter.

[37] Avrom Fleishman, "Two Faces of Emma," in *Jane Austen: New Perspectives,* ed. Janet Todd (New York: Holmes & Meier, 1983), pp. 248-56; Gilbert and Gubar, *Madwoman in the Attic,* p. 189.

Janet Todd (essay date 1989)

SOURCE: "The Female Wits: Women Writers of the Restoration and the Early Eighteenth Century," in *The Sign of Angellica: Women, Writing and Fiction, 1660-1800,* Columbia University Press, 1989, pp. 36-51.

[*In the following excerpt, Todd surveys the primary female novelists of the genre's early development, as well as the major styles adopted by those pioneers.*]

Ever since Caxton founded his printing press in the fifteenth century fiction had been printed in England—and condemned as escapist and vulgar by the guardians of high culture. Its vulgarity was due to its association with the vernacular but also perhaps to its connection with women. From the Middle Ages onwards, the association of romance with women and idleness was expressed in the constant male fear that a perusal of fiction would corrupt female morals.

In Elizabethan England, Lyly, Sidney and Greene assumed women among the readership for their courtly romances. Greene was described as the 'Homer of women', while Lyly announced in his *Euphues* (1579) that 'It resteth Ladies, that you take the paines to read it'.[11]

Lyly seems to have gauged his market well, for, although the complete gentleman would certainly be helped by a knowledge of romance, it was soon reported that success for ladies at court absolutely required them to use the mannered, antithetical style of Lyly's romance in much the way it required them to dress in elaborate court fashion. The use of language as a seductive screen or mask would be a feature of women's writing when they themselves entered fiction in the next century.[12]

Sir Philip Sidney declared that he wrote his prose romance *Arcadia* for his sister's entertainment and, like Lyly, he addressed 'fair ladies'. The work, which delivered exemplary figures and pathetic stories, was immensely popular throughout the seventeenth and the first part of the eighteenth centuries and was imitated and continued by many, including, most significantly, his niece.

Lady Mary Wroth published *The Countesse of Montgomeries Urania* in 1621 and it was thus the first known fictional work of a woman to be printed in English—despite the Duchess of Newcastle's claims to preeminence several decades later. In many ways Lady Mary is closer to the later women writers than is the privileged Duchess for, despite her aristocratic status, she may well have been writing for money, thereby anticipating scores of eighteenth-century spinsters, wives and mothers in embarrassed circumstances.

Using her relationship to the popular hero Sidney and his romance, she insisted on situating herself and her work in her uncle's shadow. But in fact the *Urania* is distinct in its foreshadowing of the later female fictional plot of what Eliza Haywood would call 'faithless Men, and ruin'd Maids'. Her emphasis is on female experience of marriage, as well as on the courtship of male romance, and, along with idealised pictures, she displays women destroyed by jealousy, rejection and lust, trapped in the code of constancy while men travel off to love again. The tone is caught in the request of one character for stories of female misfortune—a request that the later Aphra Behn or Delarivier Manley might be seen fulfilling:

> Let me but understand the choise varieties of Loue,
> and the mistakings, the changes, the crosses; if none
> of these you know, yet tell me some such fiction, it
> may be I shall be as luckless as the most unfortunate;
> shew me examples.[13]

Lady Mary Wroth's *Urania* is also distinct from the *Arcadia* in probably being a *roman à clef,* or secret history, as Sidney's work was not. It uses the romance form to comment on contemporary figures and their scandalous activities in a manner that would become common in cavalier circles in the Civil War. It would recur in the early eighteenth-century novels of women like Manley and Haywood.

Naturally such a use of romance created a furore at the court of James I and one of the victims furiously attacked Lady Mary as an 'Hermaphodite in show, in deed a monster', a form of gendered—or rather ungendering—abuse that would commonly be hurled at women writers entering the male preserve of political or social satire. Despite denying some of the apparent identifications, she had in the end to withdraw her work from sale—possibly it had originally been published without her consent.[14] The continuation she had written was not printed.

Perhaps it was her experience with the first part that caused her to create in the second a weird character called Antissia, who seems to hint at her own self-hatred as an author. Antissia is a mad writer who understands her literary activities as part of her madness: 'I was possest with poettical raptures, and fixions able to turn a world of such like womens heads into the mist of noe sense,' she declares. Her dress of veils, feathers and ruffs makes her the very image of eccentricity—as well as a precursor of the 'mad' Duchess of Newcastle who scandalised England by publishing her poetic raptures and wearing outlandish clothes.

Despite the unhappy experience, Lady Mary was not the only female imitator of Sidney. In 1651 Anne Weamys, a 'young Gentlewoman', wrote *A Continuation of Sir Philip Sidney's Arcadia* in a style far plainer than Sidney's, with the conceit that 'no other than the lively Ghost of Sydney, by a happie transmigration, speaks through the organism of this inspired Minerva', and in 1725 appeared *Sir Philip Sidney's Arcadia, Moderniz'd by Mrs Stanley,* presenting Sidney in more decorous, less exuberant language.[15]

Lady Mary Wroth and the imitators of Sidney represent a newer kind of romance, with psychological and down-to-earth elements. But, while they were writing, another heroic type from France was gaining ground, avidly read by the young gentlewoman Dorothy Osborne, who admitted she 'cryed' for a heroine 'though shee were but an imaginary person'.[16] Throughout the Civil War years and on into the eighteenth century French romance was consumed by the ladies of the court of Charles I's queen, Henrietta Maria, and by the exiled court which included the Duchess of Newcastle, although she herself was not a great reader of romance. By the time of the Restoration it was widely diffused throughout England.

French romance was leisurely, the introduction of a character always heralding a new digressive story. It was associated with, among others, Madeleine de Scudéry, whose *Clelia* ran to ten volumes, published between 1654 and 1661. She and her genre were still somewhat current in the mid-eighteenth century when Charlotte Lennox created her romance-maddened heroine in *The Female Quixote* and when the learned Bluestocking Elizabeth Carter could be taken to task for her romance-addiction.

In the seventeenth century, however, Scudéry was entirely the vogue and so sensible a girl as Dorothy Osborne, scathing about the eccentricities of the publishing Duchess of Newcastle, can sound remarkably like Lennox's satirised heroine in response, although it should be noted that Osborne swallowed the myth of the day, encouraged by Scudéry, that her brother rather than she herself was the main author of the fiction. 'Have you read Cleopatra?' Osborne excitedly asked her future husband in 1653, 'I have six Tomes on't heer . . . 'The idea of six tomes of French romance would sink the heart of Charlotte Lennox's hero when he realised that the reading of them was to test his worthiness; he failed the test.

The heroic French romance was primarily concerned with love and with women as writers and readers. It was connected with the salons of the *précieuses* who aimed to speak in a refined intellectual way and to cultivate good social manners—inevitably such women were much mocked as pretentious and ignorant by men, most famously by Molière in *Les Précieuses ridicules.*[17] Through their endeavours and the fiction that grew from them, a kind of fantasy world was established in which the problems of love became the most important concerns; politics turned on private passion, and male public history became feminine romance.[18] Love was endlessly analysed and interrogated. But it was emphatically pure love not lust, love which could as well be expressed in female friendship as in heterosexual passion; it is not surprising then that these translated romances should share diction and platonic conceits with the poetry of Katherine Philips and her circle. The romances came out serially and their characters and problems were minutely discussed in England and France in much the same way that the serial *Clarissa* would be scrutinised over a century later.

Since Scudéry's famous portraits were based on figures she knew, the novels, like Wroth's *Urania,* were *romans à clef,* although women readers of England would not have responded to this element. But there the resemblance between the French romancer and the main English novelists of the Restoration ceases. For all her success and her need for money, Madeleine de Scudéry did not openly embrace professional authorship, and her sense of literature remained aristocratic. In many ways she sounds more like the ladies of the Bluestocking salons in the mid-eighteenth century, desiring authorship but needing to show reluctance. This was not the stance of the first major female novelists in England: Behn, Manley and Haywood.

By the time these women were writing, many sorts of fiction were current besides the romance, such as marvellous tales, tall tales, fantastic voyages, saints' lives and rogue biographies; all refuse the modern dichotomy of history and fiction and several make claims of historical validity buttressed by documents and records while still implying the pattern typical of romance. These different fictional varieties join romance in influencing women writers, who produced fast-paced, often political short stories and long episodic tales, opposing the huge French romances with their epic pretensions and elaborate constructions. In 1692 Congreve distinguished between romances and shorter novels 'of more familiar nature', mocking the former, while the preface to the anonymous *Adventures of Lindamira* (1702) declared that the author was turning from 'the histories of foreign amours and scenes laid beyond the seas' to 'domestic intrigues', aiming not at fabulous knight errantry but at 'real matter of fact'.[19] Manley insisted that the new bustling public was impatient with the aristocratic romance and that 'Little Histories' must be created, 'much more agreeable to the Brisk and Impetuous Humour' of the times; her own stories would not be romantic allegories, nor yet reportage, but they would be psychologically probable.[20] Yet to hide (mockingly) their connection with contemporary scandal, they too claimed to derive from manuscript sources, described as so ancient that they were written in the Land of Nod.

Behn, Manley and Haywood differed from Scudéry not only in form but in content, their roguish acceptance of sexuality. Love changes from the ceremonious code of French romance into lust with all its physical pleasures and social disadvantages for women. So it functions as disruptive desire even within the female characters, not simply as a masculine threat from without. The heroines sometimes retain the noble legitimacy of romance but gain something of the thrusting quality of the younger son who is forced to make his own fortune in the world. In women's case, however, there was only one way to do this.

But as drama was changing with the times, so was fiction. Other women writers wanted to harness its seemingly amoral power for more immediately moral ends. The secret history was called a 'growing evil' and attacked as French by Richard Steele in *The Tatler,* a form of abuse that would be used a hundred years later when women again tried to comment on the political and social scene. Jane Barker in *Exilius* (1715) firmly dissociated herself from Aphra Behn and took Orinda as her model. She opposed the 'Deluge of Libertinism which has overflow'd the Age' and saw herself reverting to the expression of virtue and honour characteristic of earlier heroic romance; in *Exilius* characters give such Scudéry-like commands as 'Go . . . conquer Lybia.' Much later Elizabeth Rowe eschewed the directly erotic by combining romantic and religious sentiment in her popular elegiac series of letters, *Friend-ship in Death* (1728); in time she would become the heir of Orinda as the lady writer whose example it was decorous to follow. Penelope Aubin added absolute morality and providence to her breathless romance plots, while the brisk, often satiric Mary Davys in *The Reform'd Coquet* (1724) rescued the sensational story of innocence in a villainous world, so typical of Manley and Haywood, by making it didactic. Through the figure of a male guardian the coquettish heroine is defended from the consequences of her 'head-strong' ways.

Yet, although these women differ in tone from the naughty triumvirate of Behn, Manley and Haywood, there are resemblances between the two groups. The decorous Barker's later magazine-like novel, *A Patch-Work Screen* of 1723, has an uneasy, unsettling nature reminiscent of the short tales of Aphra Behn. Each of the writers in both groups sees women constructing themselves and playing different roles; each talks self-consciously of the influence of fiction on the mind and each tries to come to terms not with some abstract humanity but with people living, in Barker's words, 'as the World now rolls'. The concern in this age is survival and existence in society, and the realisation that manners and morals are very often at odds.

Despite the romantic names and rushed schematic plots, several stories have a psychological probability that the sentimental novel will eschew. Mary Davys and Eliza Haywood show the slow ripening into love, the unromantic insistence on a basis of esteem and respect in marriage. Most of the fiction writers depict the social and psychological misery of sexual passion, the painful loss of simplicity and the self-hatred that ensues, and many display the unexplained dislike of marriage, so common though obliquely expressed in poetry. An Aphra Behn heroine runs away into great hardship from a suitor she should marry and is only brought to matrimony just before her baby is born; Jane Barker's heroine Galesia retreats from marriage, hardly knowing why she does so. Motherhood is rarely glorified as it would be in later sentimental novels; the childless Duchess of Newcastle denigrates it, while both Haywood and Manley mention the agonies of childbirth, 'the Rack of Nature'.

Like the scandalous writers, the early moral novelists tend to muddy the line of fiction and nonfiction, fantasy and autobiography, making the narrator a sincere observer, moral placer, and skilled romancist. In Manley and Haywood facts become fables and fables turn into facts with a key; the Duchess of Newcastle moves in and out of her own fantasy. In Barker the fictional patchwork screen is made of colourful scraps from her own life which are fitted into a literary artistic pattern or discarded as unsuitable. She is as likely to put herself forward in her character Galesia as the naughty Manley is to display herself as Rivella. What we might now call new journalism seems, then, to be a common form, a confronting of facts with mental constructions. The writers attempt to make meaningful patterned versions of a world that would otherwise threaten chaotically.

In all the women the didactic impulse tends to be accepted, but it is not scientific and historical fact, largely deemed unsuitable for the female pen, that is taught but worldly commonsense or morality. The ritual claims to authenticity can be mingled with romance, allowing the reader to be sceptical of both, but little scepticism is brought to bear on the message—the need for understanding the feminine predicament in the early writers and of compensating for it in the later. In spite of enormous differences among women and ages, this last characteristic will be a constant in female writing throughout the century, from Aphra Behn at the beginning to Fanny Burney at the end.

Notes

[11] For a description of Elizabethan prose fiction see Paul Salzman, *English Prose Fiction* 1558-1700 (Oxford: Oxford University Press, 1985).

[12] See Madelon Gohlke, 'Reading "Euphues" in *Criticism,* 19, 1977, for the idea that deceit is central to *Euphues.*

[13] Salzman, *English Prose Fiction,* p. 142.

[14] Salzman, *English Prose Fiction,* pp. 139 and 144. See also G. F. Waller, introduction to Lady Mary Wroth's *Pamphilia to Amphilanthus* (Salzburg: Studies in English Literature, 1977).

[15] For accounts of this work, see Salzman, *English Prose Fiction,* pp. 130-31, and B. G. MacCarthy, *Women Writers: Their Contribution to the English Novel 1621-1744* (Cork: Cork University Press, 1944).

[16] *The Letters of Dorothy Osborne to Sir William Temple,* ed. Kingsley Hart (London: Folio Society, 1968).

[17] Ian Maclean, *Woman Triumphant: Feminism in French Literature 1610-1652* (Oxford: Oxford University Press, 1977); Domna Stanton, 'The Fiction of *Preciosity* and the fear of women' in *Yale French Studies,* 62, 1981, pp. 107-34.

[18] For an account of this process see Rosalind Ballaster's unpublished dissertation 'Seductive Forms: Women's Amatory Fiction 1680-1740.'

[19] William Congreve, preface to *Incognita* (1692; Menston: Scolar Press, 1971). See Lennard J. Davis, *Factual Fictions* (New York: Columbia University Press, 1983) for a discussion of various real-life genres.

[20] Preface to *Queen Zarah, Novels of Mary Delariviere Manley,* ed. Patricia Koster (Gainesville: Scholars' Facsimiles & Reprints, 1971).

CONTEMPORARY COMMENTARY ON THE NOVEL

Lennard J. Davis (essay date 1983)

SOURCE: "Theories of Fiction in Early English Novels," in *Factual Fictions: The Origins of the English Novel,* Columbia University Press, 1983, p. 102-22.

[*In the following essay, Davis argues that early novelists put forth concepts of fiction that implicitly sought to disarm a public that paradoxically both demanded fiction and looked down upon "untruthful" tales.*]

If Robinson Crusoe wound up on an island, historians of the novel were partially responsible for putting him there. Until fairly recently, it had generally been the practice of literary histories of the novel, to regard Defoe as the first English novelist, and most treatments of the novel tend to move quickly from *Don Quixote* to English *Robinson Crusoe,* from one gaunt touchstone to the other, with the assumption that this was the most direct way along the road to the great tradition. *Crusoe,* however, was far from being an isolated novel in a sea of romances. Quite a few other English writers had been creating what we might call, without fear of abusing the term, novels.[1] These early novels have been relegated to the category of "popular fiction" and allowed to moulder there. Charlotte Morgan noted, for example, that "popular fiction, generally speaking, had no literary merit; and as it had no other aim than immediate success, it rarely possessed more than ephemeral interest, so that on the whole it may be regarded as a negligible factor."[2] Even Ian Watt, whose *Rise of the Novel* had done much to place novels in their proper class perspective, begins his book with *Robinson Crusoe* and dismisses the earlier forms of popular fiction as irrelevant. Watt glides over serialized fiction, which, as we will see, was the predominant reading material for a good deal of the literate public, saying that "the poorer public is not very important; the novelists with whom we are concerned did not have this [serial] form of publication in mind. . . . ,"[3] Watt is wrong on this score, and his decision to begin at the moment when novels began to be more widely accepted by the middle-class reader creates the impression that before Defoe there was not much in the way of prose fiction. Watt barely mentions the novels of Aphra Behn, Mrs. Manley, Mary Davys, Ned Ward, Eliza Haywood, and others.

While it may be true that many of these works are inferior to those of Defoe, Richardson, or Fielding, there is much in them that is essential to understanding the history of the novel. Certainly, Defoe at his worst is not as good as Manley at her best, and the *History of Rivella* is as inventive and creative as two-thirds of Defoe's hack exercises.

These early English writers, like some of their French counterparts, took particular pains to distinguish their works from the romance. Even such a remote viewer as Samuel Johnson, writing well after the formative period of the novel, said of romance, "Why this wild strain of imagination found reception so long, in polite and learned ages, it is not easy to conceive."[4] Johnson sounds the characteristic English call against the French romance. Although most British novelists took pains, as we will see, to divorce themselves from heroic romance, there was a vogue in certain English social circles for the French romances. These were translated into English during the mid-seventeenth century. However, quite quickly the antiromances of Furetière, Sorel, Scarron, Le Sage, and Subligny were also translated between 1654 and 1678, a fact which indicates the strength of antiromance sentiments in England as well. The appeal for romances came mainly from the English upper classes who frequently assumed classical names and read these works in groups.[5] English romances tended to be pale imitations of French works— see, for example, Roger Boyle's *Parthenissa* (1654) and Sir George MacKenzie's *Aretina or the Serious Romano* (1660).

While there was no doubt interest in romance, that interest came from a small, elite part of the potential reading public. Congreve, in 1692, clearly reveals the taste of the majority of readers in his definition of the novel and the romance. In contrast to the "lofty language, miraculous contingencies and impossible performances" of the romance, "novels are of a more familiar nature" and "delight us with accidents and odd events, such which not being so distant from our belief bring also the pleasure nearer us."[6] This distinction was also obvious to Lord Chesterfield in the mid-eighteenth century who wrote that a romance was "twelve volumes, all filled with insipid love, nonsense, and the most incredible adventures."[7] And thirty years later, Clara Reeve could again make the same division between lofty, heroic romances which were remote and cold, and the novel which "gives a familiar relation of such things, as pass everyday before our eyes, such as may happen to our friend, or to ourselves and we are affected by the joys or distresses of the person in the story, as if they were our own."[8]

Early English novelists developed, to a far lesser degree than their French counterparts, a theory of fiction that makes clear that English writing is meant to be seen as distinctly English, as opposed to the French romance. Like French novelists, the English distinguished between novel and romance by noting that novels were not made up or based on remote history, but were true. Thus, the English novel begins on an inherently framed assumption. There seems to have been in England a far greater sanction against fictions than there was in France, and this state of affairs was no doubt due in part to the Puritan condemnation of fiction as being only lies.

Puritan writers like John Bunyan had to take great care to avoid writing lies when they had recourse to narrative. Bunyan manages to steer his way around the problem of fictionality in his work by falling back on the older tradition that poetical truths might be truer than real ones. In his introduction to *Pilgrim's Progress* (1678), Bunyan defends himself against the charge that his work is "feigned" by saying

> . . . What of that? I trow
> Some men, by feigned words, as dark as
> mine,
> Make truth to spangle and its rays to shine.[9]

Of course, Bunyan can refer to the biblical example of Christ who spoke in parables "by types, shadows, and metaphors,"[10] and in fact the epigraph on the title page of *Pilgrim's Progress* is taken from *Hosea* 12:10 "I have used similitudes." So armed with biblical justification, Bunyan journeys through the thickets of the fact-and-fiction controversy, and camouflages his backsliding into invention by claiming that his story is really "delivered under the similitude of a dream." Thus the work is framed doubly by its open demand for interpretation and yet its deliberate inclusion into the shadowy world of sleep and dreams.

Though *Pilgrim's Progress* is caught between its existence as a "feigned" work and its aim to make truth "spangle and shine," its story is about the quest for the ultimate truth. Novels, it would seem, have taken on the burden of trying to give us reports on the world, and this virtue seems to have been conferred paradoxically by the fact that the very existence of novels is bound up in the illusory creation of the appearance of truth. Bunyan's *Life and Death of Mr. Badman* (1680) is also an allegory, but this time instead of being a dream, it is structured as a dialogue between Mr. Wiseman and Mr. Attentive. The dramatic form permits an air of credibility to enter the story, and of course frames the work. Bunyan claims this time that "all things that I here discourse of, I mean as to matter of fact, have been acted upon the state of this world, even many times before mine eyes."[11] By this we can presume that Bunyan means that Badman, while not a real person, is a composite character and the particulars of his life are "true" in the sense that they have happened to other people at other times. However, Bunyan takes this notion one step further and says that he will include in the work true stories "which are things known by me, as being eye and earwitness thereto, or that I have received from such hands, whose relations as to this, I am bound to believe."[12] He will indicate these true stories by inserting in the margins a small printed hand to point to the special paragraphs that are in fact interpolated tales not all unlike the brief lives of criminals newspapers usually carried. For example:

> I know one that dwelt not far off from our town, that got himself a wife as Mr. Badman got his, but he did not enjoy her long: for one night as he was riding home . . . his horse threw him to the ground, where he was found dead at break of day; frightfully and lamentably mangled with his fall, and besmeared with his own blood.[13]

One does not have to read many of these specially marked stories to realize that their "truth" is based on the same criteria as the truths of the early newsbooks. Such stories are plentiful. For example, there is the one about a woman who used to swear by using the expression "I would I might sink into the earth if it be not so," and who met a strange but not at all unpredictable end.

Bunyan's crude method of segregating fact and fiction by confining the former to a semiologically identifiable section of the page is an attempt to resolve the troublesome intermixing of fact and fiction which seems to be characteristic of these early prose narratives. Bunyan's solution lacks subtlety, however, because it fails to see how deeply enmeshed in the dialectic of fact and fiction is the very structure of such works as his. Perhaps Bunyan realized intuitively his complicity in the sin of fictionalizing when he stressed that Mr. Badman's worst trait was in fact the telling of lies: "When he was but a child, he was so addicted to lying that his parents scarce knew when to believe he spake true, yea, he would invent, tell, and stand to the lies that he invented and told. . . . "[14]

Badman's parents might be likened, allegorically speaking, to the reader of prose narrative of his time. In fact, Bunyan seems to make a specific reference to the news/novels discourse when he says that people tell lies in "their news, their jests, and their tales must needs be adorned with lies; or else they seem to bear no good sound to the ear, nor shew much fancy to him to whom they are told."[15] The linking of news, tales, and jests here seems to be far from fortuitous, and the implication that such modes of narrative are necessarily contaminated with fictions is also worth noting. It was Bunyan's accomplishment to step lightly around this contamination of fiction and carry forth his message to the world.

Aphra Behn was among the first novelists in England to claim her work was true. Of course, ballads, newsbooks, and criminal tales had made such claims, so it does not seem unusual to have Behn make the same assertion. As early as 1688, when *Oroonoko* was written, Behn inaugurated, it would seem, the now familiar disclaimer:

> I do not pretend, in giving you the history of this royal slave, to entertain my reader with adventures of a feigned hero, whose life and fortunes Fancy may manage at the poet's pleasure; nor in relating the truth, design to adorn it with any accidents, but such as arrived in earnest to him: And it shall come simply into the world, recommended by its own proper merits, and natural intrigues; there being enough of reality to support it, and to render it diverting, without the addition of invention.[16]

The tone one instantly perceives is a sort of general scorn for invention, entertainment, and feigned heroes. Works of imagination, which may be manipulated at the writer's discretion, are not really worth one's time. The hidden reference seems to be against the French romance's predeliction to add to history, to invent upon historical foundations. Behn has discarded Bishop Huet's justification of fiction by its elegance of style or by its moral instruction. She can do this because,

according to the framing device she has established, she is not writing fiction. That there is "enough reality to support" the novel and that such facts as there are will divert the reader are sufficient justifications for the work.

Behn instinctively places herself in the news/novels discourse by inaugurating an inherently reflexive or double discourse based on contradictory assertions. For example, she places a sanction on the use of "accidents" and "intrigues." An "accident," as the word was used in the seventeenth century according to the *Oxford English Dictionary,* was "anything that happens without foresight or expectation, an unusual event, which proceeds from some unknown cause"; an intrigue was "a complicated state of affairs . . . plotting or scheming." In other words, Behn is saying that novelists should avoid coincidences, unexpected turns of event, plotting, scheming, reversals of plot—in short, a novel should avoid being a novel.

Behn is here practicing the essence of reflexive discourse—affirmation by denial. When she says her work is truth, she means that it must shun fictional devices such as coincidence. However, coincidence in a novel is a structuring device that aligns parallel plots, unites formally disparate elements, and allows metaphoric and moral meaning to be drawn from the work. Outside of the realm of literature, however, coincidence was seen during the seventeenth century as an act of Providence, the hand of God at work in the world. So if a novelist denied writing a fiction, thus attributing all coincidences to the hand of Providence, then that novelist would put him or herself in the bad faith position of claiming to know how Providence *would have* acted in a particular situation. The author pretends, in effect, to be God—an action not generally smiled upon in religious circles.

Aphra Behn is very clear in claiming not to be writing a fiction: "I was myself an eye-witness to a great part of what you will find here set down; and what I could not be witness of I received from the mouth of the chief actor in this history, the hero himself, who gave us the whole transaction of his youth."[17] This proof by physical contiguity is typical of the news/novels discourse, as we have seen in ballads and newsbooks, and we should recall that such personal testimonial is impossible given the limits of romance. In another work by Behn, *The Fair Jilt* (1688), the dedication is to one Henry Pain, Esq. However, we are not simply presented with a laudatory puff; Behn takes the occasion to ask Pain to authenticate the truthfulness of the text, a ploy which ballad writers had used as well. The work, writes Behn, is recommended by the fact that "it is truth: truth, which you so much admire. But 'tis a truth that entertains you with so many accidents diverting and moving, that they will need both a patron, and an assertor in this incredulous world."[18] With a little help from her legal friend, Behn can claim to have backing for the assertion that her work is true. In this sense, patronage becomes attestation as well.

It seems fitting, in view of Behn's attitude toward fact and fiction that so much of *Oroonoko* should have to do with fabrications, deceit, and lying in one form or another. In Oroonoko's tribe, lies are unknown. Lying is seen by Behn as a natural consequence of civilization and does not exist in a natural state. She writes of Oroonoko's tribe that "these people represented to me an absolute idea of the first state of innocence, before man knew how to sin."[19] The tribe is so oblivious to false statements that, for example, they begin to mourn an English governor who had sworn to come on a certain day and failed to show up or to send word that he could not come. The tribe believed that "when a man's word was past, nothing but death could or should prevent his keeping it." When the governor actually did arrive, " . . . they asked him what name they had for a man who promised a thing he did not do? The governor told them, such a man was a liar, which was a word of infamy to a gentleman. Then one of them replied *Governor, you are a liar, and guilty of that infamy.*"[20] The joke here is that the black men are so innocent that they cannot even perceive that their response is an insult. This innocence constitutes an inability to perceive framings and fabrications—the tribe cannot make out the context, the series of frames, in which the "civilized" world is wrapped.

Aphra Behn's own narrative fares no better than the words of other whites. We doubt her from the opening "authentication" to the numerous lies and tall tales included in the exotica of the novel. She tells us, for example, that even the most severe wounds heal rapidly in the tropical zone—except, inexplicably, those sustained by the leg.[21] Medical wonders are compounded by zoological anomalies such as the fact that a lion may live with several bullets in his heart—a fact which even the author has the good sense to note "will find no credit among men."[22] Another wonder is the "numb-eel" which will paralyze the fisherman who holds the rod at the moment the eel touches the bait. Aphra Behn's "truthful" account of Oroonoko's life ends with his execution during which he is castrated, has his nose and ears cut off, and his arms severed while he remains in an unlikely state of calm, continuing to smoke his pipe.

In the jungle, Behn even manages to meet Colonel Martin who, as it just happens, is to be the protagonist of a new play appearing in London called *The Younger Brother or the Amorous Jilt* surprisingly written by none other than Aphra Behn herself. Such a meeting is a shrewd bit of public relations work to encourage some financial success, but also intermixes fact and fiction a bit. One wonders if Behn is consciously testing the credulity of the reader as Oroonoko's own credulity had been tested.

From the prestructure, to the presentation, through the content and even the digressions of *Oroonoko,* fiction-making and lying are central to the work. Fabrications build up into frames within frames doubling back upon themselves until every turn reveals fact warped into fiction which turns back upon itself to become fact. This novel, as others, seems to be steeped in an insecurity resulting from bad faith, criminality, lying, and fabrication.

The prefaces to the works of Mary de la Rivière Manley reveal English attitudes toward the novel and the romance, as well as toward fact and fiction. In the *Secret History of Queen Zarah* (1705), Manley writes about the differences between the English "humour" and that of the French in regard to narrative:

> The romances in France have for a long time been the diversion and amusement of the whole world; people both in the city and the court have given themselves over to this vice, and all sorts of people have read these works with a most surprising greediness; but that fury is very much abated, and they are all fallen off from this distraction.[23]

What has replaced these romances are "little histories," which Manley points out are much more agreeable to "the brisk and impetuous humour of the English, who have naturally no taste for long-winded performances. . . . " She also finds fault with the exaggerated language of romance which might refer to water as "the liquid element" or a mirror as the "council of the graces," and advocates in its place the plain style saying that conversation

> ought to be writ after an easy and free manner: fine expressions and elegant turns agree little to the style of conversation, whose principal orna-ment consists in the plainness, simplicity, free and sincere air . . . for 'tis not natural for man to entertain himself, for we only speak that we may communicate our thoughts to others. . . . [24]

This literary fundamentalism echoes the Puritans, but also places Manley's discourse squarely in the "plain" language of news/novels.

If fiction cannot be justified by elegant language, then moral instruction seems to have been the agent to wash away the sins of fiction-making. Manley writes: " . . . the chief end of history is to instruct and inspire into men the love of virtue and the abhorrence of vice, by the examples proposed to them; therefore the conclusion of a story ought to have some tract of morality which may engage virtue. . . . "[25] Manley presents other literary dicta veiled in moral terms. She discusses verisimilitude and agrees that a writer "ought with great care to observe the probability of truth, which consists in saying nothing but what may morally be believed." One notices immediately a paradox here: if one is to write a probable work, one needs to write about the world as it is, yet such a world is not necessarily morally probable. The problem is quite similar to the conflict between *bienseance* and *vraisemblance* that we have seen among the French romancers. As Manley elaborates: " . . . there are truths that are not always probable; as for example, 'tis an allowed truth in the Roman history that Nero put his mother to death, but 'tis a thing against all reason and probability that a son should embrue his hand in the blood of his own mother."[26] Manley is saying, in effect, that there are two kinds of verisimilitude—actual and moral. It seems clear that these are contradictory types of verisimilitude. A work that shows the world as it is will run into the problem of allowing vice to triumph over virtue, as it does sometimes. But a work that is morally verisimilar will always show virtue triumphing over vice.

We are dealing with types or varieties of truth. The paradox is that for a work to be morally verisimilar it has to be actually *un*verisimilar. When one throws in the conception of providence, things get even more complex. According to Christian thought, God acts in the world to effect the punishing of vice and the rewarding of virtue, so that all outcomes other than these, while novelistic perhaps, would be seen as improbable—hence unverisimilar. John Dennis comments:

> . . . 'tis observable, that both in a poetical fiction and an historical relation, those events are the most entertaining, and the most wonderful, in which providence most plainly appears. And 'tis for this reason that the author of a just fable, must please more than the writer of an historical relation.[27]

Thus the fable writer must be more accurate than the historian because human actions are more "liable to be imputed rather to chance than Almighty conduct and sovereign justice."[28] If actual verisimilitude is then opposed to providence, and moral verisimilitude as antinovelistic in presenting the world as it should be and not as it is, then can we not say that the theory of the novel at this time was a reflexive or double one since it maintained two contradictory imperatives at once? Like the newsbooks and ballads, which maintained their reflexivity through an insistence on their verity, these novels reclothed this fundamental reflexivity in moral terms. Ballads maintained they were true while insuring such assertions were actually a kind of guarantee of the opposite; novels, by clinging—in theory—to moral verisimilitude, insured that their predisposition—in practice—to verisimilitude was contradicted. The important point to remember here is that novelists were not developing a new theory of the novel so much as they were using new terms to argue against the old inherent contradictions of the news/novels discourse that they had inherited. It is as if the limits and constraints of the news/novels discourse were uncon-

scious ones in the minds of novelists, and so these writers had to justify, as it were, intuitively these limits in a variety of ways without ever recognizing them overtly.

If the writer of fiction had to take more care to be morally probable than the writer of history, who had only to write what had happened, then it seems logical for novelists to claim that their works were not fictional but true. This way novelists could avoid the necessity for depicting only probable events. In other words, the theory of the novel as it developed stood in contradiction to the actual content of novels since that content tended to be filled with improbabilities, coincidences, sensational material, exotic situations, chance events, and so on. In this sense, the theory of the novel during the late seventeenth century was a false theory or, as I shall call it, a *simulacrum* theory, that if followed in practice could never result in a novel being written. Thus, to negate the effect of the theory, authors would claim that the work was true, hence not a novel. The initial frame of fabrication ("this work is true") permits the ensuing plot-events to be improbable, fanciful, illogical—in short, novelistic. However, in this context it is important to see that there are two levels to this fact/fiction problem. First, the novel is based on a theory which is inherently reflexive in its simultaneous call for overt moral verisimilitude and covert actual verisimilitude—and on the contradiction between these two varieties of truth. At the same time, on the second level, an entirely other assertion of truth is taking place that in effect frames the first contradiction. This second contradictory assertion falsely maintains that the work is not a fiction at all.

Mary de la Rivière Manley's works themselves do not look or feel like novels, at least like the novels of Defoe, Richardson, or Fielding. The assertion has been made with works like hers that one is observing romance and not the novel. There are in Manley's works swooning lovers, aristocratic intrigues, and adventures performed by characters with classical or oriental-sounding names—Zarah, Zelinda Rivella. But since Manley insists so strongly in her introductions that she is not writing romances, we need to consider the nature of her difference.

First, of course, is the insistence that her work is true. The subtitle to *Queen Zarah* reads *Faithfully Translated From the Italian Copy Now Lodged in the Vatican at Rome, and Never Before Printed in Any Language*. This ploy echoes Mlle. Scudéry's joke about her work being taken from a manuscript in the Vatican Library, but here it seems to be proposed more seriously. Manley seems to be saying that though her work might be taken for a falsehood, the manuscript, at least, is genuine. Yet, from her introductory discussion of the theory of her novel, it is clear that this is a work with an author, and Manley suggests this when she talks about the rules that apply to the writing of fictional works. In reality though, her work is, among other things, a *roman à clef* like the works of Mme. de Lafayette. It not only tells a story of love and passion, but is also a commentary on most of the major political and aristocratic figures of the age. In this sense, it is a work that is at once true and false—as any allegory would be. The level of the allegorical can be very *outré* in Manley's work, as when Zarah attempts to ride various horses that are also representations of various politicians:

> What though Danterius [Daniel Finch, Earl of Nottingham] was made a stalking horse to the state . . . they were forward to part with him before they could catch the game Volpone [Godolphin] was hunting for; and though the Cambrian [Harley] be a tamer beast, he's but an ass at best, whose ears will scare the the partridge before they can drive them to their nets.[29]

Even the more obtuse readers could easily penetrate the metaphoric level with a key to the work that was usually printed at the end of the novel or appeared separately and could be bound into the work. In this metaphoric way, *Queen Zarah* and other works by Manley such as *The History of Rivella* and *The New Atlantis* were fictional stories and at the same time factual reports on the world. As such these works participated in both the factual and fictional components of the news/novels discourse.

Further, these works claimed to be "secret histories," that is, they were the histories of private citizens as well as public officials, laminated with a veneer of exotic names and settings, as is the case of *Queen Zarah,* set in that mysterious country of Albignion. Such works inaugurate an interest in the private life—an interest that had been more or less the exclusive province of nontypographic spiritual autobiographies and private diaries of the seventeenth century. They also sound the familiar notes of recentness and reduction of cognitive space between reader and text by allowing history to enter the nonpublic realm.

In the introduction to the second part of *Queen Zarah,* Manley counters those critics who had claimed her work was not fiction:

> . . . some have conceived [that *Queen Zarah*] . . . was a modern history, and related to several affairs at home . . . [that] the whole story is a fiction, that there is no such country in the world as Albignion, nor any such person living, or ever was, as Zarah. . . . The manuscript is so ancient that 'tis supposed to be writ by Cain in the land of Nod.[30]

Manley's assertion of antiquity may place her in a preliterate culture, but that is of little concern to her. One

of the virtues of the news/novels discourse at this point is that it could go both ways in terms of its assertion of fact or fiction. Manley, in writing a political commentary on English government and society must claim that her work is fictional, if only to protect herself from the punishment of the libel laws. As it was, Lord Sunderland swore out a warrant for her arrest after the publication of her *New Atlantis,* although charges were eventually dropped. The fact remains, though, that at this juncture, for a work of literature to be part of the news/novels discourse and to claim to comment on the real world, it had to adjure that it was a fiction, while for a pure fiction to appear in print it had to claim to be true. Such was the built-in reflexivity of the rules of the news/novels discourse.

Of course, we should not overlook the fact that Manley's novels were reviled not only for daring to comment on the world, but because they were perceived as sexually scandalous. Indeed, Manley continues the tradition we have seen in the ballads which involves the reader as voyeur to sexual encounters. Ballads were in fact, along with operas and books of love, designed as devices for "heightening the passions."[31] Eliza Haywood writes that the function of such works was to be "preparatives to love and by their softening influence, melted the soul and made it fit for amourous impressions. . . . "[32] In Manley's work sexual scenes such as the following are not unusual: " . . . without further dallying he made his last efforts, and rendered those of Zarah so useless that she lay at his mercy. But it was not long e'er this transported lover had allayed his passion, when he would have withdrawn without saying a word."[33] In *New Atlantis,* Polydore and Urania, brother and sister, fall in love and consummate an incestuous passion. With such forays into erotica, it is no wonder that the *Tatler* criticized Manley, saying "where crimes are enormous, the delinquent deserves little pity, but the reporter less."[34] But Manley replied to this charge saying that without proper reportage "vice may stalk at noon secure from reproach."[34] Her defense is consonant with the simulacrum theory which seeks to deny the essential ingredients of the novel—in this case voyeurism. Given the news/novels discourse, the reader is usually in voyeuristic relation to the text since here too the reader is both subject and observer. This was so not only because these books were meant to be training devices for the passions, self-help manuals for the erotically undereducated, but because the readers would only have to lift the veil of allegorization to realize that these erotic stories were about people the reader might know personally either directly or indirectly. By virtue of the omnipresent key, these texts were brought into the lives of readers in a way new to the history of narrative.

The reading process itself was becoming eroticized through the identification of observer with subject in a way quite new to society. To be sure, pornography had existed since the Greeks and Romans if not before, and during the seventeenth century there were numerous pornographic works,[36] but there was no regularly accepted, written genre which was identified with sexual arousal.[37] It seems probable, if one looks at descriptions of the process of reading novels during the Early Modern period, there is a definite sense of the reading process becoming eroticized in a way quite new to the culture. Take, for example, a description by Manley:

> . . . the reader is filled with a curiosity and a certain impatient desire to see the end of the accidents, the reading of which causes an exquisite pleasure when they are nicely handled; the motion of the heart gives yet more, but the author ought to have an extraordinary penetration to distinguish them well, and not to lose himself in the labyrinth.[38]

The language here must strike the modern reader as suggestive. The "desire" to come to the end causes "an exquisite pleasure" when things are "nicely handled," and all this is added to by the "motion of the heart." All this stimulation presumes that the author has "an extraordinary penetration" (the word had both meanings at the time) and does not "lose himself" in this "labyrinth." What unconscious material Manley was working through will be bereft of analysis for our purposes, but the visceral and affective aspects of this description, even without a modern reading of the unconscious connections, is striking. Both consciously and unconsciously, the message of this statement is that reading a book is analogous in some way to being sexually aroused by the author. Although the reader is involved, his or her role is distinctly passive.

This language of sexual stimulation can also be found in some writings of John Dennis on reading:

> . . . authors excite our curiosities, and cause those eager longings in their readers to know the events of things, those longings, which by their pleasing agitations, at once disturb and delight the mind, and cause the prime satisfaction of all those readers who read only to be delighted.[39]

These excitations, longings, curiosities, and pleasing agitations which cause the prime satisfaction seem to be tokens of an eroticized reading process. The effects of such an eroticization are difficult to pinpoint, but Lawrence Stone suggests that the eros-laden novel as a social formation profoundly affected people's conceptions of love, family, and marriage. Stone partially attributes the growth of "affective individualism" to the reading of erotically inclined novels, and even suggests that ideas of romantic love were fostered in the culture through the widespread reading of novels.[40] As readers became more intimately associated with their narratives, voyeurism combined with action in a new way.

Manley's *The History of Rivella* (1714) is a book which combines many of the characteristics I have been discussing. Not only is the reader of this novel drawn into the eroticism of the work, but the author herself is the book's central subject. The novel serves as a kind of literary pimp soliciting the reader on behalf of the author. Rivella is unambiguously meant to be Manley, and the book begins with a conversation between an older English gentleman, Sir Charles Lovemore, and a young, handsome French visitor, Chevalier D'Aumont, on the subject of the history, charms, and sexual intrigues of Mrs. Manley *cum* Rivella. As D'Aumont is made to say: "I have not known any of the moderns in that point come up to your famous author of *Atlantis*. She has carried the passion farther than could be readily conceived."[41] Lovemore's description of Rivella takes up the rest of the book as D'Aumont listens in rapture. Manley's modesty is certainly not one of her distinguishing features, and descriptions of herself through the smoking-room vision of these two men abound in the work.

> Her person is neither tall nor short; from her youth she was inclined to fat; whence I have often heard her flatterers liken her to the Greecian Venus. . . . I have heard her friends lament the disaster of her having had the smallpox in such an injurious manner, being a beautiful child before that distemper; but as that disease has now left her face, she has scarce any pretence to it. Few, who have only beheld her in public, could be brought to like her; whereas none that became acquainted with her, could refrain from loving her.[42]

Manley's placing of herself so directly in the novel, of placing her physical body so centrally in the work, is unique in the history of narrative. Each of her virtues, as well as some of her defects, are enumerated as part of the catalogue. Her eyes: "Nothing can be more tender, ingenious and brilliant with a mixture so languishing and sweet when love is the subject of the discourse, that without being severe, we may well conclude, the softer passions have their predominancy in her soul." Her hands and arms " . . . have been publicly celebrated . . . her neck and breasts have an established reputation for beauty and colour."[43] Manley has done much here for her ego, but also for narrative by greatly extending the capacity of print to embody a life. Her every detail, every characteristic is preserved in print.

In the same way that we saw the intersection of the real and the fictional in *Don Quixote* and *Roxana,* here too Manley transforms her narrative by intersecting the literary creation with the real and sexual politics of her time. The eroticization of the text by this means intensifies the respective roles of author, character, and reader. The process of reading this novel is the process of approaching Rivella, having her body revealed, her sexual habits displayed, and her being made immanent. Likewise, the eighteenth-century reader was given the actual possibility of approaching Manley—voyeuristically, of course—but always with the real possibility of knowing her, meeting her, or seeing her in London. Given the intimacy of literary circles in London, it is not inconceivable that most of Manley's readers had either seen her or knew someone who knew her. The novel then closes even more the perceptual distance between reader and text. In fact, the whole movement of the novel is structured to bring us closer and closer to Manley and her boudoir. At the end of the discussion between Lovemore and D'Aumont, the Englishman offers to bring the admiring Frenchman to Rivella:

> I should have brought you to her table, well furnished and well served. . . . From thence carried you (in the heat of the summer after dinner) within the Nymph's alcove to a bed nicely sheeted and strowed with roses, jasmines, or orange flowers, suited to the variety of the season; her pillows neatly trimmed with lace or muslin, struck round with jonquils, or other natural garden sweets, for she uses no perfumes and there have given you leave to fancy yourself the happy man, with whom she chose to repose herself during the heat of the day in a state of sweetness and tranquility.[44]

This description is at once a proposition on behalf of Manley to D'Aumont (and to the reader) and at the same time a fantasy of Manley's in which she offers herself to her collective readership. The incredible detail, the superabundance of flowers, the oriental suggestions all strike the reader as part of colossal autoerotic reverie the likes of which had probably never occurred so directly between author and reader in the history of narrative up to this point. While I am not claiming that Manley would actually have welcomed all who paid the price of the book, it is worth noting the closing of the distance between reader and text and the eroticization of the reading process which partially helps accomplish this change. The reader is made to agree with D'Aumont who finally bursts out of the confines of the book crying:

> *Allons,* let us go . . . let us not lose a moment before we are acquainted with the only person of her sex who knows how to *live,* and of whom we may say, in relation to love, since she has so peculiar a genius for, and has made such noble discoveries in that passion, that it would have been a fault in her, not to have been faulty.[45]

The book ends with a hypothetical, off-stage consummation, one presumes, as author, reader, and D'Aumont are left the possibility of fulfilling their fantasy. The notion offered here, even only hypothetically, that the ending of the novel represents an entrance into the real world of Rivella/Manley—a continuum between fact and fiction—is an innovation that we would have to

speculate was made possible by the terms of the news/novels discourse which always permits the reader to put down the newspaper and witness the printed account as it continues in the real world.

The frame surrounding *Rivella* is worth noting for what it reveals about fact and fiction. The work is supposed to be a translation of a French edition written presumably by D'Aumont himself about Lovemore's account of Rivella's life. Here the reader is at least three removes from reality. But another remove can be added since Rivella is not presented immediately as Manley but as the character of Delia in *New Atlantis.* Lovemore underlines this when he says: "I must refer you to her [Rivella's] own story, under the name of Delia, in the Atlantis, for the next four miserable years of her life."[46] In this case, the reader would have had to consult the *fictional* novel to get the *true* story of the *disguised* character discussed in *The History of Rivella.* The framing at this moment is complex enough to baffle the observer at first glance.

It was this interpenetration of fact and fiction that got Manley in trouble and provoked Lord Sunderland to bring her to court claiming that Manley's work had "the barbarous design of exposing people that had never done her injury." Manley, however, denied this intention by saying that she did not intend to reflect on any person and only wrote her book by "inspiration," not by receiving special "facts" from other sources. Indeed, Manley's book would be one of the great homages to imagination if it could have satirized so many people by mere chance. Actually, according to Manley, she was convinced after this legal trouble to avoid politics and write mainly for the theater. As Lovemore is made to say: "She now agrees with me that politics is not the business of a woman, especially one that can so well delight and entertain her readers with more gentle pleasing themes. . . . "[47] It is interesting that Lovemore concentrates on the inherently political cast to the news/novels discourse as he strikes this blow against feminism. Although we are supposed to believe that Rivella renounces her political designs in also renouncing narrative, this *History of Rivella* is clearly very much part of the news/novels discourse with its commentary on the political and social lives of the English gentry; the predisposition of novels to comment on, expose, and satirize the world is not so easily disbanded. Manley's solution is to disguise sufficiently the political content of her novel by elaborately framing it and so attempt to avoid further prosecutions. In other words, she had to make her work more overtly fictional.

In general, then, it can be said that these early novelists saw themselves as quite clearly separated from the discourse of romance, that their works tended to exhibit the type of ambivalence toward fact and fiction that has been characteristic of the news/novels discourse, as well as displaying a reduction of cognitive distance between author and reader, the development of a simulacrum theory, and the tendency to report on the events of the world. This argument is more difficult to make with writers like Elizabeth Haywood and Mary Davys whose works tend to look much more like the romance with its upper-class characters, affairs of love and passion, intrigues, and so on. Such works seem to lack ambivalence and a special attitude toward fact and fiction—even though their authors may occasionally claim to be writing true accounts, as does Haywood in *The Injured Husband or the Mistaken Resentment: A Novel:* " . . . as I have only related a story, which a particular friend of mine assures me is matter of fact, and happened at the time when he was in Paris, I would not have it made use of as an umbrage for the tongue of scandal to blast the character of anyone."[48] However, in the case of Davys and Haywood, both authors specifically refer to their works as novels. Davys, though, is using the word "novel" to refer to the French heroic romances, as is clear when she says that novels "have been a great deal out of use and fashion."[49] Given the date of this statement, 1727, it would be impossible for Davys to be referring to the novel in our sense of the word. Also her description of such works as "tedious and dry . . . four hundred pages without the least variety of events," leads me to suspect that she is talking about the long heroic romances. She is against the idea of "probable feigned stories" such as the French have written, and so opts to write a novel with only "one entire scheme or plot, and the other adventures are only incidental or collateral to it . . ." in a shorter work.[50] Davys does not claim her work to be true, and in her rejection of romance as overly complex, she seems to be setting out on her own course. She actually seems to be writing something closer to a tale or short story.

With such ambiguous works as these, one cannot finally say what kind of a genre is being described. To attempt to include all narrative in a system would constitute a kind of closure that would be, by definition, falsifying. The inability, in formal terms, of such works to create or belong to a genre points to their unique and experimental value. It is worth recalling, though, that while Haywood's and Davy's works are difficult to categorize, their prefatory material seems to take into account the complexities of the transformations of narrative that were occurring at the time. In this sense, they can be said to be part of the ongoing definition of news and novel, although each work might not conform to recognizable patterns.

Notes

[1] See John Richetti, *Popular Fiction Before Richardson* (New York: Oxford University Press, 1969), one of the few books on the subject.

[2] Charlotte Morgan, *The Rise of the Novel of Manners: A Study of English Prose Fiction Between 1600 and 1740* (New York: Columbia University Press, 1911), p. 2.

[3] Ian Watt, *The Rise of the Novel* (Berkeley: University of California Press, 1964), p. 42.

[4] Samuel Johnson, *Works,* ed. W. J. Bate and Albrecht B. Strauss (New Haven: Yale University Press, 1969), 3:19.

[5] Morgan, *Rise of the Novel of Manners,* p. 35.

[6] William Congreve, *Incognita: or Love and Duty Reconciled. A Novel,* ed. H. F. B. Brett-Smith (Oxford: Basil Blackwell, 1922), pp. 5-6.

[7] Lord Chesterfield, *Letters* (London, 1800), 1:197-98.

[8] Clara Reeve, *The Progress of Romance* (London, 1785), 1:iii.

[9] John Bunyan, *The Pilgrim's Progress From This World to That Which Is to Come* (New York: Grosset and Dunlap, n.d.), p. 12.

[10] *Ibid.*

[11] John Bunyan, *The Life and Death of Mr. Badman and The Holy War,* ed. John Brown (Cambridge: Cambridge University Press, 1905), p. 3.

[12] *Ibid.,* p. 6.

[13] *Ibid.,* p. 74.

[14] *Ibid.,* p. 21.

[15] *Ibid.,* p. 23.

[16] Aphra Behn, *The Works of Aphra Behn,* ed. Montague Summers (1915; rpt. New York: Phaeton Press, 1967), p. 129. Ernest Bernbaum has proven that Behn is indeed lying about the truth of her encounters with Oroonoko in an article entitled "Mrs. Behn's Biography a Fiction," *PMLA* (1913), 28:432-53.

[17] Behn, *Works,* p. 129.

[18] *Ibid.,* p. 70.

[19] *Ibid.,* p. 131.

[20] *Ibid.,* p. 132.

[21] *Ibid.,* p. 206.

[22] *Ibid.,* p. 182.

[23] Mary de la Rivière Manley, *The Novels of Mary de la Rivière Manley,* ed. Patricia Koster (Gainesville: Scholar's Facsimile and Reprint, 1971), unnumbered preface to *The Secret History of Queen Zarah.*

[24] *Ibid.*

[25] *Ibid.*

[26] *Ibid.*

[27] John Dennis, *The Critical Works of John Dennis,* ed. Edward N. Hooker (Baltimore, Md.: Johns Hopkins University Press, 1943), 2:6.

[28] *Ibid.*

[29] Manley, *Novels,* p. 109. The identification key is on p. 263.

[30] *Ibid.,* pp. 123-24.

[31] *Ibid.,* p. 568.

[32] Eliza Haywood, *Love in Excess: or the Fatal Inquiry,* in *Secret Histories* (London: R. Ware, 1742), 1:84.

[33] Manley, *Novels,* p. 89.

[34] Criticisms of Manley appear in *Tatler,* nos. 6, 35, 63, 92, 177, 229, and 243.

[35] Manley, *Novels,* 529.

[36] See David Foxon, *Libertine Literature in England 1660-1745* (New Hyde Park, N.Y.: University Books, 1966).

[37] See John Berger, *Ways of Seeing* (Harmondsworth, England: Penquin, 1972), for an excellent description of the pornographization of art.

[38] Manley, *Novels,* unnumbered preface to *Queen Zarah.*

[39] Dennis, *Works,* 2:49.

[40] See Lawrence Stone, *The Family, Sex, and Marriage in England 1500-1800* (New York: Harper and Row, 1977), chapter 7.

[41] Manley, *Novels,* 2:740.

[42] *Ibid.,* p. 744.

[43] *Ibid.,* pp. 745, 746.

[44] *Ibid.,* p. 855.

[45] *Ibid.,* p. 856.

[46] *Ibid.,* p. 765.

[47] *Ibid.,* pp. 845, 849, 853.

[48] Eliza Haywood, *The Injured Husband or the Mistaken Resentment: A Novel* in *Secret Histories,* 1:2.

[49] Mary Davys, *The Accomplished Rake or Modern Fine Gentleman* in *Four Before Richardson: Selected English Novels 1720-1727,* ed. W. H. McBurney (Lincoln: University of Nebraska Press, 1963), p. 235.

[50] *Ibid.*

FURTHER READING

Allen, Walter. *The English Novel: A Short Critical History.* New York: E.P. Dutton & Co., Inc, 1951, 454.

Devotes a prefatory chapter to considering which pre-eighteenth-century literary forms precipitated the emergence of the novel. The critic focuses primarily on the divergent threads of realism, exemplified by John Bunyan, and romance, exemplified by Aphra Behn, in the development of the novel genre..

Armstrong, Nancy. *Desire and Domestic Fiction: A Political History of the Novel.* New York and Oxford: Oxford University Press, 1987, 300 p.

Treats the development of the novel—both as concrete literary genre and as cultural force—as inseparable from the social, economic, and political status of women.

Baker, Ernest A. *The History of the English Novel, vol. III: The Later Romances and the Establishment of Realism.* New York: Barnes & Noble, Inc., 1929, 278 p.

The third volume in this series, a very thorough and comprehensive view that tends to present the novel as progressing inevitably from fabulous romance to "a truthful and cogent study of realities."

Brown, Homer Obed. *Institutions of the English Novel: From Defoe to Scott.* Philadelphia: University of Pennsylvania Press, 1997, 228 p.

Examines the growth of thought about the novel alongside the growth of the novel itself, emphasizing the strategies that certain advocates used to sanction those novels that first displayed the qualities we now think of as characteristic of the novel.

Crawford, Patricia. "Women's Published Writings 1600-1700." In *Women in English Society 1500-1800,* edited by Mary Prior, pp. 211-81. London and New York: Methuen, 1985.

Documents works published by women in the seventeenth century. The critic also investigates ways that these authors responded to contemporary prejudices about women, specifically against female assumption of authority.

Hunter, J. Paul. *Before Novels: The Cultural Contexts of Eighteenth-Century English Fiction.* New York and London: W.W. Norton & Company, 1990, 421 p.

Explores the forms in which the novel eventually emerged and grew by tracing its roots in British literature—across all genres—and culture. Written to be accessible to a non-specialist audience.

Lovett, Robert Morss and Helen Sard Hughes. *The History of the Novel in England.* Boston: Houghton Mifflin Company, 1932, 495 p.

Devotes several chapters to a broad survey of the novel's beginnings. Lovett and Hughes examine the efforts of many minor and experimental writers, and provide extensive coverage of the major male authors of the eighteenth century.

MacCarthy, B. G. *Women Writers: Their Contribution to the English Novel 1621-1744.* Oxford: Cork University Press and B .H. Blackwell, 1946, 288 p.

Early and distinctly feminist argument that women contributed substantially to the novel's development. The critic associates women's success as novel-writers with the gradual loosening of social, political, and economic restrictions.

McKeon, Michael. *The Origins of the English Novel, 1600-1740.* Baltimore and London: The Johns Hopkins University Press, 1987, 529 p.

Emphasizes a broad chronological scope and stresses the importance of critical method. The critic pursues a "genre study" of the novel as "an early modern cultural instrument" deployed specifically for social and political purposes.

Perry, Ruth. *Women, Letters, and the Novel.* New York: AMS Press, 1980, 218p.

Focusing specifically on epistlary fictions—novels presented in the form of letters—delineates the major cultural shifts that facilitated the novel's emergence, especially as these shifts altered women's social status.

Richetti, John J. *Popular Fiction Before Richardson: Narrative Patterns, 1700-1739.* Oxford: The Clarendon Press, 1969, 274 p.

Examines the dominant forms of prose fiction in the half-century preceeding Samuel Richardson, paying particularattention to the popular, usually romantic forms embraced by the broad reading public.

Tompkins, J .M .S. *The Popular Novel in England, 1770-1800.* Westport, CT: Greenwood Press, 1961, 388 p.

Approaches the novel "rather as a popular amusement than a literary form" in order to study the audience and the market as much as the books and their authors.

Jane Barker

1652-1732

British novelist and poet.

INTRODUCTION

Barker's chief contribution to literature is her "Galesia Trilogy," consisting of *Love Intrigues; or, The History of the Amours of Bosvil and Galesia* (1713); *A Patch-Work Screen for the Ladies; or, Love and Virtue Recommended* (1723); and *The Lining of the Patch-Work Screen: Design'd for the Farther Entertainment of the Ladies* (1726). Although *Love Intrigues* was originally credited as being authored only by "A Young Lady," by the time of *A Patch-Work Screen*, Barker had decided to take credit for the work using her own name; historians of women's literature take interest in Barker's unabashed authorship. Barker wrote during a period of transition spanning the time when literature was written for the elite few and circulated privately to the time when novels were written expressly with the buying public's taste in mind. During this time of change, histories, romances, and novels overlapped and commingled, with no clear lines separating and defining the genres. Literature historians give credit to Barker for her influence on making the novel more socially acceptable by making it morally instructive, particularly on sexual matters. Additionally, Barker is praised for her realism, subtlety, irony, experimentation in form, and modernistic conclusions in which not all problems are neatly resolved.

Biographical Information

Barker was born in Northamptonshire in 1652 to Thomas Barker, a Royalist who served in the court of Charles I, and to Anne Connock, whose prestigious family supported the Stuart monarchs. Sometime in the 1660s Barker attended a girls school near London and also learned farm management—unusual for a female—firsthand at her family's extensive agricultural property in Lincolnshire. This rural life and activity became the subject of many of Barker's poems. Barker shared her poetry with family and educated friends, many of whom were male. It is also believed that at this time—under the working title "Scipiana"—she began her first novel, *Exilius, or, The Banish'd Roman: A New Romance: In Two Parts, Written after the Manner of Telemachus*, which would not be published until 1715. Barker's association with students of Cambridge eventually yielded a two-volume collection entitled *Poetical Recreations: Consisting of Original Poems, Songs, Odes &c. With Several New Translations. In Two Parts, Part I. Occasionally Written by Mrs. Jane Barker. Part II. By Several Gentlemen of the Universities, and Others*, published in 1688. In approximately 1685 Barker moved to London. James II succeeded Charles II to the throne upon the latter's death, and granted Catholics rights previously denied to them; Barker is believed to have converted to Roman Catholicism during this time. Many powerful Protestants opposed James and in 1688 he fled to France, yielding to William of Orange. Tens of thousands of James's supporters left England for France, and their number included Barker. As a Connock and royalist, Barker enjoyed respect in her new setting, and continued to write poetry, much of it in praise of James. In 1704 Barker returned to England. It was here that *Love Intrigues* was published by the notorious bookseller Edmund Curll. Curll, who advertised heavily his publications, found that the public was fond of Barker's writings, encouraged Barker to satisfy her readers, and continued to publish her books. Critics note that Barker first saw her writing in print at a relatively late age and that she continued working into her seventies. She persevered even after becoming blind in her last years by hiring someone to take down her dictated words. Barker died in France in 1732.

Major Works

Poetical Recreations saw the first appearance of Barker's Galesia, a poet character considered by critics to be the alter-ego of the author. The poetry that constitutes this volume reflects Barker's rural upbringing, explores female-female relationships, and stresses the importance of keeping control of one's emotions and maintaining faith. In certain poems Barker, never married, celebrates life as a spinster. *Love Intrigues* was originally released with the author credit of "A Young Lady," although in reality Barker was already over sixty years old. *Love Intrigues* was very successful and went through four editions by the middle of the century. The two-volume set *The Entertaining Novels of Mrs. Jane Barker* (1719) includes revised versions of *Love Intrigues* and *Exilius* and several previously unpublished short stories. *Exilius* mixes various romances in an ambiguous moral fable centering on the heroine Scipiana. In *Exilius*, Scipiana extolls the value of learning for women. *Love Intrigues* was Barker's first semi-autobiographical novel. In it, Galesia recalls her younger days when she was romantically pursued by Bosvil, her cousin. This tale of an on-and-off, on-and-off, unrequired-love relationship has a deliberately inconclusive ending. The sequel, *A Patch-Work Screen for the Ladies,* finds Galesia embittered toward the idea of marriage after having suffered from Bosvil's baseness. The title refers both to the experimental nature of having the story seen through various characters, with their narratives of differing tones, and the nature of the stories themselves, which range from love stories to murder tales. Murders are even more prominent in the last work of the Galesia trilogy: *The Lining of the Patch-Work Screen.* Galesia, now older, reflects on the follies she has witnessed in the world. The tone is grim as Galesia details the difficulties women face in society.

Critical Reception

Feminist critics find Barker's work an excellent source for the history of women's roles in society and personal relationships. Kathryn R. King (1994) finds noteworthy the fact that Barker freely associated with educated men, a practice that runs counter to some commonly-held conceptions about early women writers. Critics agree that Barker did not simply cater to the public's demand and write whatever she thought they would buy; on the contrary, critics find her work to be of considerable depth, with psychological insights that would not be out of place in twentieth-century novels. Margaret Anne Doody writers: "In her mingling of tones and impressions, in her representation of fancy, memory, and desire, Barker was an influence upon the Richardsonian novel. She also announces themes and techniques found in twentieth-century novelists, particularly women writers such as Dorothy Richardson, Katherine Mansfield, Virginia Woolf, and Barbara Pym. Like these writers, she draws upon and fictionalizes her own experience, often with considerable humor."

PRINCIPAL WORKS

Poetical Recreations: Consisting of Original Poems, Songs, Odes &c. With Several New Translations. In Two Parts, Part I. Occasionally Written by Mrs. Jane Barker. Part II. By Several Gentlemen of the Universities, and Others. [editor and contributor] (poetry) 1688
Love Intrigues; or, The History of the Amours of Bosvil and Galesia, As Related to Lucasia, in St. Germains Garden [as A Young Lady] (novel) 1713
Exilius, or, The Banish'd Roman: A New Romance: In Two Parts, Written after the Manner of Telemachus (novel) 1715
*The Entertaining Novels of Mrs. Jane Barker. 2 vols. (novels) 1719

A Patch-Work Screen for the Ladies; or, Love and Virtue Recommended: In a Collection of Instructive Novels. Related After a Manner intirely New, and interspersed with Rural Poems, describing the Innocence of a Country-Life (novel) 1723
The Lining of the Patch-Work Screen: Design'd for the Farther Entertainment of the Ladies (novel) 1726

*Contains the revised versions of *Exilius; or, The Banish'd Roman: A New Romance: In Two Parts, Written after the Manner of Telemachus* and *The Amours of Bosvil and Galesia, As related to Lucasia in St. Germain's Garden.*

CRITICISM

Myra Reynolds (essay date 1920)

SOURCE: "General Learning and Literary Work," in *The Learned Lady in England, 1650-1760,* Peter Smith, 1964, pp. 137-257.

[*In the following excerpt, first published in 1920 and reprinted in 1964, Reynolds contends that Barker's novels explore the same material covered earlier in her verse. Reynolds also considers some of the circumstances of Barker's life that are revealed through her character Galesia.*]

. . . Miss Jane Barker is a literary lady whose productions belong in two epochs. Her collected poems appeared in 1688 under the title *Poetical Recreations: Consisting of Original Poems, Songs, Odes, etc. With Several New Translations. In Two Parts, Part I. Occasionally Written by Mrs. Jane Barker. Part II. By Several Gentlemen of the Universities, and Others.* Twenty-seven years after the publication of this verse Miss Barker again came before the public, this time as a writer of romances which proved very popular. They were collected under the title *The Entertaining Novels of Mrs. Jane Barker,* and a second edition had appeared by 1719. In 1723 she brought out *A Patch-Work Screen for the Ladies; or Love and Virtue Recommended: In a Collection of Instructive Novels. Related after a Manner intirely New, and interspersed with Rural Poems, describing the Innocence of a Country Life. By Mrs. Jane Barker, of Wilsthorp, near Stamford, in Lincolnshire.*[1]

The long silence between the verse of 1688 and the romances of 1715-26 is unbroken by any explanatory hint or reference. Yet Miss Barker had but one story to tell and that was told in her youth. In her novels she uses the characters, events, and emotions recorded in her early verse. Under the form of a sustained narration, with the addition of much in the way of romantic adventure, they make more entertaining reading, but offer no essentially new elements. The fifth novel, *Clodius and Scipiana,* is perhaps but an enlargement of a romance entitled *Scipina,* which had been published and concerning which she had received several congratulatory poems, before 1688.[2]

One persistent element in Miss Barker's verse and prose is autobiographic reference. Especially is this true of the poems, *The Amours of Bosvil and Galesia* and *A Patch-Work Screen.* From these sources various facts emerge concerning Miss Barker's life and personality.

She says that she was sent at first to the "Putney School," but that she was taken home at about ten by her mother who had come to consider such schools as "Academies of Vanity and Expense, no Way instructive in the Rudiments of a Country Gentlewoman's Life." At fifteen she was sent to London under the care of an aunt to learn "Town Politeness."[3] Her father lived near Cambridge,[4] and through her brother, a Cambridge man, she was well known in the younger literary set at the University. The praise accorded her verse was excessive. "Philaster" of St. John's hails her as the true heiress of the great Orinda. To "C. G." she is the Elijah for whose mantle meaner poets wait. "Exilius," also of St. John's, celebrates the miracles of her Almighty Pen. "S. C." wonders to see men "tug at Classic Oars" and "sweat over Horace" when along comes a lady who without effort utters "well-shapt Fancy and true Digested Thought." "Fidelius" rejoices to see "Physick and Anatomie done into purest Verse." And "J. N.," Fellow of St. John's, praises her Scipina as writ in lines,

> More than Astrea's soft, more than Orinda's
> Chaste.

Another gentleman from St. John's said that she surpassed "the Scaroons and Scudderies of France" and showed that England could originate as well as translate.[5] Miss Barker was evidently in the stimulating and unusual position of being the temporary literary idol of an academic coterie.

There was a false lover in Miss Barker's early life who, as "Strephon" in verse[6] and as "Bosvil" in prose,[7] is copiously written up along with her own emotional experiences as "Galesia." The most interesting portion of the affair has to do with Galesia's original ways of reëstablishing her happiness. She found comfort in contemplating the wonderful works of Creation.[8] She wandered along shady paths, by little streams, and through the meadows. She loved the early morning, the evening dews, the starry night sky. There is no felicitous phrasing in the references to nature, but the fact remains that Galesia found in nature a satisfaction and sometimes an exaltation quite foreign to the heroines of her time.

Galesia's second resource is study. She says of this new occupation:

> Finding myself abandon'd by *Bosvil* and thinking it impossible ever to love any Mortal more, resolv'd to espouse a Book, and spend my Days in Study . . . I imagin'd my self the *Orinda* or *Sapho* of my Time. In order to this, I got my brother, who was not yet return'd to Oxford,[9] to set me in the way to learn my Grammar, which he really did, thinking it . . . a Freak without Foundation to be overthrown by the first Difficulty I shou'd meet with in the Syntax, knowing it to be less easy to make Substantive and Adjective agree, than to place a Patch or Curl.[10]

Her indulgent brother, when he came back from his studies abroad, also taught her medicine. With him she went on long "simpling" excursions to gather flowers for the "large natural Herbal" they were making. With him she read "Bartholine, Walæus, Harvey, his Circulatio Sanguinis, and Lower's Motion of the Heart."[11] She learned to write prescriptions, or "bills" as she called them, in Latin, with the same "Cyphers and Directions as Doctors do," so that even the apothecaries were misled and filled her "bills" with those of the regular physicians.[12] She also ventured on something in the way of practice and gained some repute for curing cases of gout given up by the doctors.[13] She began to abandon the Muses for Paracelsus. Or if she wrote poems the processes of digestion and the circulation of the blood were her themes.[14] If the shackles of rhyme hindered scientific accuracy of statement, she squared herself with facts by abundant footnotes in which the proper Latin terminology was given full scope. Her interest in medicine was a vital one. She even thanks Strephon, through whose falsity she had been driven to study, and had so gained a joy beyond "the sottish ease" that waits on love. In her new love of learning she even took a vow of virginity:

> In this happy life let me remain,
> Fearless of twenty-five and all its train
> Of slights or scorns, or being call'd Old Maid,
> Those Goblings which so many have
> betray'd[15]

Somewhat later Galesia gained a complete victory over her lovelorn self by a most original and sensible method. She took entire charge of her father's farm. She planned the work, hired the laborers, superintended in person the occupations of each day, paid the wages, and kept the accounts. The wholesome interests of each day and equally wholesome fatigue at night left no intervals in which to regret her lost lover.[16]

Galesia's recourse to hard study and responsible farm management as a cure for a wounded heart sets her as a heroine in a class by herself. She is so sensible and reasonable as to seem out of place in a romance. It is therefore something of a surprise to find her out-distancing the most sentimental in sighs and sobs and tears. Her utterance in recounting the baseness of Bosvil, "It is fitting that I should weep on all occasions," might serve as her permanent order of business. "My sighs alternately blew up my Tears and my Tears allay'd my Sighs" till "fresh Reflections rais'd new Gusts of Sorrow," describes her stormy woes. Sometimes she is able to restrain "the briny Ebullition," but usually "a new Flux of Tears" breaks down all barriers.

With the death of her brother the joy of Galesia's life went out. Books and medicine lost their charm. Without his inspiring presence all her occupations became insipid. Her view of learned women also changed. She says a learned woman is as ridiculous as a spinning Hercules; that books are as unfit for women as paint, washes, and patches are for a man; that a studious woman and an effeminate man may be classed together as out of their sphere. A learned woman is "like a Forc'd Plant that never has its due or proper Relish but is wither'd by the first Blast," or "like the Toad in the Fable, that affected to swell itself as big as the Ox," and burst in the enterprise.[17] This bitter view of learning comes only in the novels, and probably indicates some unhappy experiences on Miss Barker's part since the days when her muse was honored by the University wits. . . .

Notes

[1] The most complete account of Miss Barker is in an inaugural dissertation by Karl Stanglmaier, Berlin, 1906, entitled *Mrs. Jane Barker. Ein Beitrag zur Englischen Literaturgeschichte.*

[2] "To Mrs. Jane Barker on her most Delightful and Excellent Romance of Scipina, now in the Press."

"To my Ingenius Friend Mrs. Jane Barker, on my Publishing her Romance of Scipina."

Both of these poems are in Part II of *Poetical Recreations* (1688). The second one is by Benjamin Crayle.

[3] *Amours of Bosvil and Galesia,* pp. 3-4.

[4] In the second edition of the *Entertaining Novels* (1719), in a dedication to the Countess of Exeter, Miss Barker says, "Was it not Burleigh House with its Park, &c., that formed in me the first idea of my Scipio's country retreat? Most sure it was, for when I composed my Romance I knew nothing further from home than Burleigh and Warthorp." These two seats of the Exeter family are about seven miles from Wilsthorp. (*Notes and Queries,* Series IX, no. 10, p. 171.) Miss Baker lived at Wilsthorp which is near Stamford and only about forty miles from Cambridge.

[5] Barker, Jane: *Poems, passim.*

[6] *Poems:* "To my Unkind Strephon."

[7] In *Amours of Bosvil and Galesia* and *A Patch-Work Screen.*

[8] *Amours,* p. 11.

[9] Mr. Barker studied at both Universities.

[10] *Amours,* p. 13.

[11] *A Patch-Work Screen,* p. 10.

[12] *Ibid.,* p. 56.

[13] *Poems,* "On the Apothecary's Filing my Bills amongst the Doctors."

[14] *Poems:* "A Farewell to Poetry with a Long Digression on Anatomy."

[15] *Poems:* "A Virgin Life."

[16] *Amours,* pp. 44-46.

[17] *Amours,* p. 47.

William H. McBurney (essay date 1958)

SOURCE: "Edmund Curll, Mrs. Jane Barker, and the English Novel," in *Philological Quarterly,* Vol. 37, No. 4, October, 1958, pp. 385-99.

[*Below, McBurney discusses the effect the infamous publisher Edmund Curll had upon the popularity of Barker's romance novels.*]

In his *Characteristics of Men, Manners, Opinions, Times,* published in 1711, the Earl of Shaftesbury declared that "our modern authors . . . are turned and modelled (as themselves confess) by the publick relish and current humour of the times. . . . In our day the audience makes the poet, and the bookseller the author."[1] Of no literary or sub-literary field was this statement more true than of the novel. Because of a combination of economic, social, and political circumstances, the sale of copy to booksellers, rather than subscription, patronage or governmental subsidization, was the most likely resource of the writer of prose fiction.[2] The business arrangements of the London publishing world, therefore, had considerable influence, through the focal figure of the bookseller, upon the form, content, and aims of the emerging genre.

Unfortunately this influence was seldom directed toward cultivation of higher literary standards. In the early eighteenth century the novel was still a matter of financial speculation rather than a product with predictable sales value as, for example, were religious treatises.[3] As a result, any pressure exerted by the bookseller upon the novelist was usually toward increased marketability. Study of this intangible but real formative influence on the English novel is complicated by the lack of extensive publishers' records and by the general obscurity of the more than 250 booksellers and printers who by 1700 crowded Grubstreet and controlled its large body of professional translators, compilers, hack-writers, and aspiring authors from the universities and the provinces.[4]

From this noisy multitude few figures emerge so clearly, and none in such an unfavorable light, as the bookseller Edmund Curll. Pope assured him a degree of immortality by a place of unsavory prominence in the *Dunciad,* but as early as 1710 Curll's shop at the Sign of the Dial and Bible was well known for its scurrilous and sensational publications. And, though Defoe had not yet coined the term "Curlicism,"[5] the bookseller's name was already synonymous with unethical publishing methods. Whether or not his hackney authors actually starved to death or "his translators in pay lay three in a bed at the Pewter Platter in Holborn,"[6] is debatable. There can be no doubt, however, that his "poetical Garret"[7] was filled with versatile writers who produced a variety of wares designed to please any and all tastes of the Town.

Curll's career followed with only slight exaggeration the general practices of the Trade, and his publications reflected, with equal accuracy, the reading tastes of the times. As James Bramston later pointed out in ironic tribute,

> How oft has he a Publick Spirit shown
> And pleas'd our Ears regardless of his own?
> But to give Merit due, though *Curll's* the
>   Fame,
> Are not his Brother-Booksellers the same?[8]

Certainly, any publishing venture by Curll was a strong indication that a lucrative market for such a product existed. Since his flamboyant career is more easily traced than those of most of his fellow-inhabitants of Grubstreet,[9] his expeditions into the field of the novel are especially valuable in illuminating its obscure but important pre-Richardsonian phase.

Generally speaking, the time of Curll's first novelistic publication in 1713 was not auspicious. It was axiomatic among the Trade that "the best time for bookselling is when there is no kind of news stirring."[10] This condition was definitely lacking in the days of intense political and religious controversies which disturbed the reign of Queen Anne and were intensified by the Hanoverian succession. For a time, Mrs. Mary Manley

had capitalized on the unfavorable situation by astutely adapting the French *chronique scandaleuse* to the English political scene in such works as *The Secret History of Queen Zarah* (1705) and the *New Atalantis* (1709). She had delighted such polite readers as the future Lady Mary Wortley Montagu with her lush anti-Whig confections, but the years which immediately followed her successes were marked by a considerable decline in fictional publication.

If the time was inappropriate, Curll's choice of copy would also seem to have been unwise or highly uncharacteristic. Certainly **Love's Intrigues; or, the History of the Amours of Bosvil and Galesia** (1713), a very moral semi-autobiographical work, and **Exilius; or, The Banish'd Roman** (1715), a belated seventeenth century romance, both by Mrs. Jane Barker, were unlikely company for his more typical publications such as *The Cases of Unnatural Lewdness* and *The Case of Insufficiency Discuss'd,* which were already on his shelves, or under his counter. Nor was the presence of Mrs. Barker, a provincial Catholic maiden lady, in the Dial and Bible which was frequented by "all the high whores in town" who came "to buy his dialogues and other lively books"[11] any less incongruous. It must be remembered, however, that Curll pleased all publics, and that Sir Thomas Browne and the Bishop of Winchester were as welcome as Ovid and the Earl of Rochester, if they sold as well—and, with Curll's expert advertising, they undoubtedly did.

Perhaps the reason for these strange ventures in fiction was a new shop which he had just opened in 1712 in fashionable Tunbridge Wells. Mrs. Barker's works could hardly be classified as "lively books" but were probably intended as suitable summer reading for ladies such as Addison's Leonora, whose library included six heroic romances and "a Book of Novels." In any case, Mrs. Barker was the first of a number of minor women novelists to find a market at the Dial and Bible, and her novels, curiously enough, set a pattern for the fiction which Curll was to issue during the next thirty years. Thus, he must be given credit not only for a willingness to experiment with non-political types of fiction,[12] but also, in a sense, for the continuation of the short seventeenth-century "novel" during the second and third decades of the eighteenth century, as opposed to the longer "histories" then coming into vogue.

Whatever his motives (and they were certainly not the same that led him to blackmail the notorious Mrs. Manley into writing her fictionalized autobiography, *The Adventures of Rivella,* which he published in 1714), the bookseller reduced the risks involved in accepting Mrs. Barker's anachronistic **Exilius** by a title-page of excellent "Curlicism":

> Exilius: or, The Banish'd Roman, a new Romance
> in Two Parts. Written after the Manner of

Telemachus, for the Instruction of some Young Ladies of Quality.

In addition to emphasizing the instructive and genteel elements of the work, he also managed to trade upon the popularity of Archbishop Fénelon's *Adventures of Telemachus,* which by 1715 had had at least seven English editions and, by showing the possibilities of the romance as an educational vehicle, had revived to some extent the popularity of that waning literary form.[13]

Actually, Mrs. Barker had begun her romance a decade before the publication of Fénelon's work in 1699, and the form, content, and tone of *Exilius* were natural outgrowths of her life.[14] Born of a staunchly Royalist family about 1660, she spent most of her youth in the village of Wilsthorp, near Stamford in Lincolnshire, where she received her education from a country clergyman. Her first poetic and prose works were written for a rural literary circle, which continued the tradition of the "Society of Friendship" over which Mrs. Katherine Philips had presided in Cardigan earlier in the century.[15] Upon reading the verses of "the matchless Orinda," Mrs. Barker "began to emulate her Wit, and aspired to imitate her Writings."[16] She adopted the name of Galesia and was addressed as such in laudatory verses by the "several Gentlemen of the Universities and others" with whom she shared the authorship of *Poetical Recreations,* published in 1688. In addition to occasional versifying, she began a prose work, "the excellent Romance of Scipina," which an admirer urged her to continue:

On then, brave Maid, secure of Fame advance,
Gainst the Scaroons & Scudderies of France.
Shew them your claim, let nought your Merit
    awe,
Your Title's good spight of the Salique Law.
Safe in the Triumphs of your Wit remain:
Our English Laws admit a Woman's Begin.[17]

Praising the same work, another friend declared that Mrs. Barker's Muse "out-strips the Dedalean Scuddery,"[18] thereby describing with almost embarrassing accuracy the style and model of her fictional work which Curll published twenty-seven years later in an expanded form as *Exilius.*

Mrs. Barker's gift for imitating the Scudéry romances was doubtless strengthened by her residence in France, to which she went as a Stuart sympathizer and Roman Catholic after the flight of James II.[19] There, despite increasing blindness, she continued her versifying, often with a strong political tinge,[20] and worked on her prose romance. During the reign of Queen Anne, she returned to Lincolnshire, and in 1715 was described in a list of Catholic Non-Jurors as "Jane Barker of Wilsthorp, spinster," possessor of a small annual income which had been granted to her father, Thomas Barker, for eighty years by Charles I.[21] Her continued pro-Stuart sympathies brought her to London in 1718, where she engaged in clandestine correspondence with the exiled Jacobite peer, James Butler, Duke of Ormond. Of this phase of her activities, however, we are as ignorant as, apparently, her French correspondents were of her identity.[22] It is tempting to picture her as a bizarre figure using Curll's shop as a cover for international political intrigue, but her fictional works reflect none of the Pretender's troubles and seem to indicate a placid if impecunious rural existence, under the patronage of the Countess of Exeter, whose country seats were at Burleigh and Worthorp near Mrs. Barker's native Wilsthorp. To her in 1715 Mrs. Barker dedicated *Exilius.*

In this dedication Mrs. Barker stated that her aim was "to reform the World & restore Heroic Love to its ancient Jurisdiction." Her pointed defense of romances showed an awareness of the diminished appeal of that type of fiction, and she attempted to justify its composition with arguments very similar to those of Bishop Huet, whose *Essai sur l'origine des romans* appeared in a new English translation that same year:

The Study of these Books helps to open the Understanding of young Readers, to distinguish between real Worth and superficial Appearance. . . . But beside these Love Lectures the young Readers may also reap Handfulls of good Morality, and likewise gather some Gleanings of History, and Acquaintance with the Ancient Poets. In short, I think I may say of Romances as Mr. *Herbert* says of *Poetry,* and hope, that a pleasant Story may find him, who flies a serious Lecture.

To these familiar arguments of the moral, educational, and social benefits to be derived from the reading of fiction, Mrs. Barker added the prestige of Sir Philip Sidney, "whose Steps, with awful Distance, I now take Leave to trace," of Fénelon, and of Dryden,

whose Writings have pleas'd all the World; tho' I think I may say, None have found better Reception than their Romances, *Telemachus* for the one part, and *Chaucer's* Tales reviv'd on the other.

The structural outline of *Exilius* is negligible. Seven short novels are woven into the title-story in imitation of the earlier Arcadian and heroic romances, but with much less skill. The artificiality of construction is so marked that there can be little doubt that Mrs. Barker wrote the individual "novels" separately—a conjecture which is supported by a reference (probably to the story of Scipiana) in the dedication:

As I was extreamly confused to find my little Novel presenting itself to your Ladyship without your

Leave or Knowledge, so I am as delighted in having permission to lay this large Composure at your Ladyship's Feet.

The romance, which Bridget MacCarthy describes as a "deplorable medley of hair-raising adventures in which female paragons incredibly become entangled,"[23] tells of two groups of noble Roman lords and ladies who, led by the banished Exilius and his beloved Scipiana respectively, wander about on different parts of the great. Sardinian estate of Publius Scipio. They recount their adventures and decide to end their lives in pious sorrow and solitude. Finally, through the aid of the goddess Aurora, the two bands meet, and after more story-telling the reunited lovers are married.

In addition to the romantic narrative method, a number of close parallels between Mrs. Barker's characters, action, and description and those of Mlle de Scudéry's *Clélie* have been pointed out, especially in the story of "Clelia and Marcellus, or, the Constant Lovers."[24] The French romances of *Cléopatre* and *Cassandre* may also have furnished hints for the Egyptian background occasionally depicted,[25] and the short inserted novels suggest familiarity with the works of Mme de Villedieu, such as *Cléonice, ou le roman galant* (1699) and *Les Exiles* (1672).

In some minor respects *Exilius* is not merely a composite of material borrowed from the *romans de longue haleine.* Stanglmaier speculates on political and autobiographical identifications for many of the characters, and the romance is, or was intended by the author to be, short and "free from long Speeches, and tedious Descriptions of Towns, Places, Sieges, Battles, Horses, & their Trappings." Mrs. Barker's digressions are often tinged with highly unromantic and practical sentiments,[26] and she departed from precedent by attempting to write in "the familiar Stile of the Age, neither so obsolete nor so refin'd, as to render it obstruse." In practice, however, *Exilius* resembles earlier romances and one may apply to it with equal validity Dorothy Osborne's criticism of the Earl of Orrery's *Parthenissa:*

'Tis handsome language: you would know it to be writ by a person of good quality though you were not told it; but, in the whole I am not much taken with it. All the stories have too near a resemblance with those of other romances, there is nothing new or *surprenant* in them.[27]

In contrast to *Exilius* Mrs. Barker's second composition in the form, *Love's Intrigues; or, the History of the Amours of Bosvil and Galesia,* shows clearly the change in fiction which came about during the reigns of William III and Queen Anne. Since Curll provided a panegyrist for the novel from among his hack-writers, the prefatory poem by Dr. George Sewell reflects the advertising aims of the publisher:

Condemn me not, Galesia, fair unknown,
If I, to praise Thee first my error own;
A partial View & Prejudice of Fame
Slighted thy Pages for the Novel's Name.
Methought I scorn'd of Nymphs & Knights to
  dream,
And all the Trifles of a tortur'd Brain,
Where we see none but the Composer's Pain.
Thus, I, by former Rules of Judgment led,
But soon my Fault recanted as I read.

Instead, he finds that her novel presents "the Charms of Nature, & those painted True":

All this, so well, so naturally dress'd,
At once with Wit and Innocence express'd,
So true appears, so just, & yet so plain,
We mourn thy Sorrows, & we feel thy Pain.

However unspontaneous, this praise serves to underscore the new and more "natural" tone which was becoming increasingly current. *Love's Intrigues* is placed in a conversational framework and has a very briefly suggested historical background. Galesia, who is awaiting news of the outcome of "King James' Affair," meets a friend, Lucasia, in the gardens of St. Germain and tells the story of her unrequited love for her cousin Bosvil. For him she rejected Mr. Brafort, and through his machinations she lost a second suitor. Finally she was left to the consolations of piety and study when he married someone else.

The first awakening of Galesia's emotions, her struggles against recurring love for the villain, and Bosvil's mixture of fickleness and jealousy are depicted with considerable skill reminiscent of the short novels of Mrs. Aphra Behn. At the same time, the middle-class material and the didacticism of Lucasia's critique which concludes the novel show the influence of the early eighteenth-century periodical essay. *Love's Intrigues* thus fits naturally into the progressive development of English prose fiction, its introspective analysis both reflecting the seventeenth-century romances and looking forward to the translations of works by Prévost and Marivaux. Mrs. Manley's characteristic salaciousness was lacking, but the remaining popular fictional elements gave *Love's Intrigues* sufficient sale to justify a second edition in 1719, inclusion in the first edition of Mrs. Barker's collected works in the same year, and, presumably, a contract from Curll for any future productions.

In the preface of her next novel, *A Patch-Work Screen for the Ladies, or Love & Virtue Recommended in a Collection of Instructive Novels* (1723), she wrote:

My Two former Volumes of Novels having met with a favorable Reception (much beyond their Desert) encourages me to perform my Promise in pursuing the Sequel of Galesia's Story.

The volume is not actually a sequel to *Love's Intrigues,* but a slight autobiographical element provides what general unity it possesses. Galesia leaves London and travels northward by stage coach. The coach overturns and she is befriended by a lady with whom she spends the summer making a patchwork screen out of pieces of "Romances, Poems, and Letters." The novel ends as Galesia and her hostess abandon their work to participate in rural festivities.

Mrs. Barker's fourth and final novel, *The Lining for the Patch-work Screen: Design'd for the Farther Entertainment of the Ladies,* was published by Curll in 1726. Her idea was apparently to write a companion volume to *A Patch-Work Screen* recounting Galesia's activities during the fashionable London winter season. Once again, however, autobiography provides only minimal unity and the secondary framework of the "lining" is so poorly contrived that the only merit of the book must be found in the fifteen short novels which are unusually vivid and well-written.

In *A Patch-Work Screen* she begins with five stories told in the stage coach after the passengers have been alarmed by the appearance of a band of horsemen. Four of these are exempla for homely proverbs, and the detailed backgrounds of isolated farmhouses, inns, and barns seem to have as their source rural story-telling under very similar circumstances. A second group of five novels placed on the screen deal with urban characters and also have a realistic tone which shows that Mrs. Barker had profitably studied Defoe's novels, which she mentions in the preface.[28]

The Lining for the Patch-Work Screen also shows considerable skill in utilizing contemporary material. For instance, in the story of Mrs. Goodwife the reader is given a well-sketched vignette of an impoverished but worthy Irish couple in London. The wife is forced by the hunger of her children to sell boiled wheat from door to door. By running errands for servants of great households and by virtuously avoiding the advances of London rakes, she manages to set up a barter exchange and restores the family to middle-class respectability. Of special interest is the sentimental portrayal of Mrs. Goodwife's children and an early attempt to reproduce childish speech.

The best of this group of realistic stories dealing with English material is that of Dorinda, a young lady of quality who reads plays, novels, and romances "till I began to think myself a Heroine of the first rate." She embarks upon a series of innocent but dangerous escapades in London playhouses, parks, and taverns, which culminates in a quixotic proposal of marriage to her footman. His unexpected presumption and the conflict of desire, shame, and anger at the attempted interference of other servants which lead her into the unfortunate alliance are recounted briefly but with a clarity

and psychological insight foreshadowing later treatments of similar situations in *Pamela* and *Joseph Andrews.*

In many of these stories Mrs. Barker showed a genuine but rarely exercised gift for realistic description. Outstanding is her picture of the ale house to which Galesia is taken after her coach overturns in a stream:

> All wet and dropping she got to this House, which was a poor Village-Alo-house; and a poor one indeed it was; it being Evening, the Woman of the House was gone out a Milking, so that the Good Man could come at no Sheets, so that she might have got rid of her Wet Cloaths, by going to Bed; However, he laid on a large Country Faggot; so she sat smoaking in her wet Cloaths, 'till the good Woman came; who hasten'd and got the Bed sheeted, into which she gladly laid herself; but the poorest that her Bones ever felt, there being a few Flocks that stank; and so thin of the same, that she felt the Cords cut through. The Blankets were of Thread-bare Home-spun Stuff, which felt and smelt like a Pancake fry'd in Grease; There were four Curtains at the Four Corners, from whence they could no more stir than Curtains in a Picture; for there were neither Rods nor Ropes for them to run upon; no Testern, but the Thatch of the House; a Chair with a Piece of a Bottom, and a brown Chamberpot, furr'd as thick as a Crown Piece.[29]

Despite this Defoesque verisimilitude, Mrs. Barker's fictional techniques remained reminiscent of the seventeenth-century novelle, and her two final publications provide confirmation of a probable but unacknowledged debt to Mrs. Aphra Behn. In the second story told by Philinda in *The Lining for the Patch-Work Screen* an erring wife drowns her husband as he disposes of the body of a lover whom she has murdered. According to Mrs. Barker, the story was taken from "an Old Book." Actually it is an abbreviated version of Mrs. Behn's *History of the Nun; or, The Fair Vow-Breaker* (1689) with a slightly altered ending.[30] Several religious characters and such stock situations as escapes from and unexpected reunions in convents may also have been derived from the same source. These borrowings from her predecessor become even more interesting when a scene in *A Patch-Work Screen* is noted: Galesia, when questioned by a city lady upon the relative literary merits of Mrs. Behn and Mrs. Katherine Philips, replies "with blunt Indignation that *they ought not to be nam'd together.*"[31]

The influence of Mrs. Behn, however, should not be over-emphasized, for Mrs. Barker was equally familiar with Continental prose fiction. The story of the Portuguese nun in *The Lining for the Patch-Work Screen* is an attempted continuation of the famous French letter-sequence, just as the story of the chevalier and the nun in *A Patch-Work Screen* is a non-tragic rework-ing of the same basic plot. The histories of "the Lady Gypsie" and of "the Gentleman Gypsie" have elements of the Spanish picaresque tradition, and some acquain-tance with Cervantes' works is shown by several ref-erences to *Don Quixote.*

Less evident are the influences of contemporary En-glish writers, an independence which may be explained by her residence in Lincolnshire. There are occasional resemblances to the periodical essays of Addison and Steele,[32] to the key device of Mrs. Manley, and to the moralizing of Mrs. Penelope Aubin's Defoe-like nov-els. Actually, she did not wish to compete with her fellow novelists, for "the Stories of our Times are so black, that the Authors can hardly escape being smut-ted, or defil'd in touching such Pitch."[33] She doubted that any character in *Exilius* "will hit the Humour of the Age" and in the preface of *The Lining for the Patch-Work Screen* she pictured herself as trying to divert her feminine readers "with a Dance at your Closet-Doors, whilst my Crowdero-Pen scrapes an old Tune, in fashion about threescore and six years ago." The metaphor was particularly apt, and the book ended with a dream vision fantasy in which Mrs. Katherine Philips is crowned "Queen of Female Writers." With this continued devotion to the literary modes of the Restoration period it is strange that she did not contin-ue to write romances modelled on Mlle de Scudéry or Sir Philip Sidney. That she did advance from *Exilius* to the realism of her short stories makes her of interest in tracing the varied influences upon the evolving novel in the early eighteenth century.

Especially significant, and strange, when one consid-ers her publisher, was Mrs. Barker's avoidance of the moral license which was still prevalent in English fic-tion during the 1720's. In this respect she may repre-sent the delayed appearance in the novel of the influ-ences of the reign of William and Mary which pro-duced the most important writing of Mary Astell, whom Mrs. Barker resembled in background, education, and general morality. Unquestionably she is one of the first of the new school of "lady" novelists who, shunning the tradition of the earlier "female gallants," were beginning to emphasize the instructive and edifying potentialities of the novel. Like her successor in this movement, Sarah Fielding, she missed no opportunity to advance the cause of feminine education by a dis-play of learning, and her attempts to elevate the novel as a genre led her to embellish it with her own verse and that of better-known poets.

In her inability or unwillingness to attempt "Histories at Large" she was probably encouraged by Edmund Curll, whose fictional publications between 1713 and 1745 show a definite predilection for short "novels" which he could issue either separately or in groups. In general, the popularity of native collections of short anecdotes and jests had declined after 1700, and such publications had descended to a lower level of readers along with abbreviated versions of the chivalric, Arca-dian, and heroic romances. The fictional trend of which the bookseller was aware doubtless came from France, where numerous collections of Arabian, Persian, Turk-ish, Tartarian, Chinese, and Indian tales were being produced in imitation of Galland's great success, *Les Mille et une nuits* (1704-1711).

Charles Gildon, one of Curll's hacks, in the dedication of a novel (or collection of tales) published by his employer in 1718, attempted to give such publications classical sanction:

> This *Prosaic Poetry* is of as ancient a Date as the *Milesian Tales,* which so charm'd Antiquity it self. The Moderns since the time of Heliodorus have often vary'd their Form; some Years ago they swell'd them into large Volumes, but of late the general Taste runs for such as are compriz'd in a much narrower Compass; from whence, we derive so many Books of *Tales,* which have not yet fail'd of Success.[34]

Although Gildon had some reputation as a classical scholar and critic, his remarks bear the stamp of Curll's familiar method of prefatory advertisement rather than of serious study of literary origins. Nor was Gildon himself entirely disinterested, for he had published a miscellany of fictional letters entitled *The Post-Boy Robb'd of his Mail* in 1692 and in 1718 was writing *The Post-Man Robb'd of his Mail,* which appeared in the following year.

The "Prosaic Poetry" mentioned by Gildon was Mrs. Sarah Butler's *Milesian Tales,* which followed and was perhaps identical with her *Irish Tales,* advertised by Curll in 1716.[35] The latter title was designed to utilize the publicity provided by a two-volume edition, pub-lished by Curll and William Taylor in 1717, of *The Adventures of Theagenes and Clariclea,* translated from the Greek of Heliodorus or an intermediate French version. In reality, Mrs. Butler's tales had as little connection with their alleged classical predecessor as Mrs. Barker's *Exilius* had with Fénelon's *Télémaque,* In a separate preface the "Fair Authress" asserted the historical basis of the stories in the Danish invasions of Ireland and by a series of quotations from ancient and modern authorities defended her method of "dress-ing" the words of her characters in "as becoming a Phrase as my weak Capacity could frame or the time I did it in would allow." Despite the impressive intro-ductions and the unusual setting, the action of *Mile-sian Tales* is a series of romantic commonplaces re-counted in an inflated style. Disregarding both content and structure Curll typically declared it to be a collec-tion of *Instructive Novels for the Proper Conduct of Life.*

His evident belief in the unfailing success of "Books of Tales" led to the publication of a number of such works by a succession of authoresses even more shadowy than Mrs. Jane Barker and probably as pseudonymous as Mrs. Sarah Butler. Among them were *The German Atalantis . . . Written by a Lady* (1715) and *The Lover's Week; or, the Six Days Adventure of Philander and Amaryllis* (1718) by Mrs. Mary Hearne, who admittedly followed in the steps of Mrs. Manley with this tale of a willing seduction and happy liaison. The latter publication, which went into three editions in two years, was followed promptly by a sequel entitled *The Female Deserters* (1719) and this in turn, by "Curlicized" combination with *The Lover's Week,* became *Honour the Victory and Love the Prize. Illustrated in Ten Diverting Novels* (1720). Mrs. Martha Fowke's epistolary effusions of *Clio and Strephon* (1720; Part II, 1728) likewise reappeared as a "new" work, *The Platonic Lovers,* in 1732 and Mrs. Elizabeth Thomas, like Mrs. Barker, offered the public an account of her amours under the title of *Pylades and Corinna.* Still more to Curll's taste were Mrs. Lydia Grainger's *Modern Amours* (1733) containing ten contemporary scandals "with a Key prefixed," and the short *romans à clef* of "Lady Margaret Pennyman." In addition to these native products, Curll also issued, usually in heated competition with rival booksellers, translations of such Continental collections as *Chinese Tales* (1725) and *Peruvian Tales* (1734) by Thomas-Simon Gueulette, and among his last six publications was *Iberian Tales and Novels. Translated from the Spanish Originals* (1745).

Thus, for twenty years after the death of Mrs. Jane Barker Curll did not advance beyond the standards for prose fiction set by her **Exilius** and **A Patch-Work Screen for the Ladies.** This taste for short romances, often advertised as a series of novels, and for collections of short stories characterized much of the fiction published between 1700 and 1740 and was not greatly altered even by the works of Richardson and Fielding. The effect of this continued emphasis of variety upon the structure of the new literary genre was considerable. For this, Edmund Curll, Mrs. Barker, and his other "ladies" must be given much of the dubious credit.

Notes

1 Ed. John M. Robertson (London, 1900), 1, 172-173.

2 James Ralph in *The Case of Authors* (1758) could suggest as alternatives to dependence upon booksellers only writing for the stage or "for a faction in the Name of the Community." The early eighteenth century, however, had seen a serious decline in the theater (and in particular there was a strong prejudice against the works of "female wits"). At the same time the corruption of the Walpole administration and the anti-cultural attitude of the first Hanoverian court had resulted in a decline in political and social patronage.

3 Between 1668 and 1709 religious publications listed in *The Term Catalogues* (ed. Arber, I, xv) outnumbered all other kinds of books. The largest single payment in the surviving records of the publisher Bernard Lintot was one of £ 252 to the Rev. Mr. Fiddes for his *Body of Divinity.* See Nichols, *Literary Anecdotes of the Eighteenth Century,* VIII (1814), 296.

4 Marjorie Plant, *The English Book Trade: An Economic History of the Making and Sale of Books* (London, 1939), p. 64.

5 *Weekly Journal,* ed. Nathaniel Mist, April 5, 1719 (William Lee, *Daniel Defoe: His Life and Recently Discovered Writings: Extending from 1716 to 1729* [London, 1869], II, 30-33).

6 Thomas Amory, *The Life and Opinions of John Buncle, Esq.* (London: Routledge, 1904), p. 392.

7 "I comforted myself that Mr. *Curll* had not made a Fool of me, as he has done of many a better Writer and secured me a Prisoner in his poetical Garret."—Mrs. Laetitia Pilkington, *Memoirs* (London: Routledge, 1928), p. 260.

8 *The Man of Taste* (Printed for Lawton Gilliver, 1738), p. 8.

9 The most thorough study of Curll's career, and one to which I am indebted for many details, is the sympathetic portrait by Ralph Straus, *The Unspeakable Curll* (London, 1927).

10 James Lackington, *Memoirs,* 10th ed. (London, 1792), p. 386.

11 Amory, *John Buncle,* p. 393.

12 In the fictional field he had previously published only translations from the French and two imitations of Mrs. Manley's *New Atalantis* by John Old-mixon and by Captain Bland in 1712 and 1713.

13 Still more to the point is the fact that John Ozell, the chief of Curll's hackney translators, was then at work on a new version of *Télémaque* which was published in July 1715.

14 *Exilius* was the first piece of prose fiction written by Mrs. Barker, although not the first published. A detailed study of Mrs. Barker's writings, with special reference to her poetry, was made by Karl Stanglmaier in *Mrs. Jane Barker: Ein Beitrag zur Englischen Literaturgeschichte* (Berlin, 1906). For detailed biographical information see G. S. Gibbons, "Mrs. Jane

Barker," *Notes and Queries,* 12th ser., XI (1922), 278-279.

[15] There is no evidence that Mrs. Barker's circle actually included "younger members of that circle . . . which had formerly surrounded Mrs. Katherine Philips," as Charlotte Morgan suggests in her *Rise of the Novel of Manners* (New York, 1911), p. 103. Mrs. Barker's use of "Lucasia" as auditor in *Love's Intrigues* seems imitative rather than indicative of any connection with Mrs. Anne Owen, the Lucasia of the Philips coterie.

[16] Barker, *A Patch-Work Screen for the Ladies* (1723), p. 3.

[17] "On the Most Charming Galecia's Picture," *Poetical Recreations,* Part II, p. 36.

[18] *Ibid.,* p. 196.

[19] In the preface to her translation of *The Christian Pilgrimage* (1718) she wrote: "I shall not regret the Time I pass'd in a foreign Country, where I learn'd so much of the Language, as to bring Home this valuable Book in English for Use of those who have not taken the Trouble to learn French."

[20] A manuscript volume of Mrs. Barker's verse, preserved in the British Museum, is entitled *A Collection of Poems Refering to the Times.* It is stamped with the arms of Armand Louis du Plessis Richelieu, Duc d'Aiguillon, and dedicated to the Prince of Wales (James Francis Edward, then twelve years old) whom she prays to "disperse all vapor of Rebellion" and to whom she wishes "not only a happy new year, but a happy new Century." This remark seems to date the collection in 1700, and the poems show Mrs. Barker (in the guise of Fidelia) in a French convent garden lamenting various political events in England which have been occasioned by "that monster Orange and his crew/Who never honor, nor yet conscience knew."

[21] Gibbons, *op. cit.,* p. 278.

[22] In Stowe MS 232, British Museum (*Hanover State Papers, 1692-1719,* Vol. XI, "Jacobite Correspondence, 1717-1719"), Mrs. Barker writes to the Duke of Ormond from London on March 19, 1718, telling him that the number of his adherents increases daily and that they hope to see him soon with "vostre jeune amy et qu'il puisse deposseder eux qui luy retiennent injustment son bien." She warns him cryptically that "si vous voulez touver icy des maisons à bon marché, il y faut venir apres la fin de la session du Parlemt, lorsque chacun va à la campagne. Je ne vous conseillerai jamais de venir pendant la session tout estant alors trop cher." A marginal note remarks, "On ignore qui est Barker."

[23] *Women Writers: Their Contribution to the English Novel, 1621-1744* (Cork University Press, 1945), p. 252.

[24] Stanglmaier, *op. cit.,* pp. 48-50.

[25] *Ibid.,* p. 50.

[26] Morgan, *Rise of the Novel of Manners,* pp. 104-105.

[27] *Letters,* ed. E. A. Parry (London, 1903), p. 220.

[28] "My *Reader* will say . . . why a History reduc'd to Patches? especially *Histories* at *Large* are so *Fashionable* in this Age; viz. *Robinson Crusoe,* and *Moll Flanders; Colonel Jack,* and *Sally Salisbury;* with many other Heroes and Heroines."—"Address to the Reader," *A Patch-Work Screen.*

[29] *Patch-Work Screen,* Introduction, n.p.

[30] In Mrs. Behn's novel Isabella kills Henaut and persuades Villenoys to throw the body into a river. They place the corpse in a sack, which she sews to Villenoys' collar so that he is pulled into the water and drowned. Mrs. Barker makes her heroine's second murder accidental.

[31] *Patch-Work Screen,* p. 44.

[32] The story of Captain Manley in *A Patch-Work Screen* includes the desscription of a fop's day much in the manner of *The Spectator.*

[33] *Lining,* pp. 128-129.

[34] "The Epistle Dedicatory," *Milesian Tales,* pp. ix-x. Gildon also declared that "the following Sheets . . . are allow'd by the Learned to be a useful sort of *Poetry,* tho' without the advantageous Harmony of Verse. For as all *Poetry* is an *Imitation,* as *Aristotle* justly observes, it is plain that all *Fables* are *Imitations of Actions,* which is the essence of both the *Dramatic* and *Epic Poesie*" (p. ix).

[35] Curll advertised the publication of *Irish Tales* by Mrs. Sarah Butler is *The Post-Man,* June 30, 1716. Advertisement by Curll did not invariably mean publication, and although his announcement has been noted by several bibliographers of the period, I can find no mention of an actual copy. Since *Milesian Tales* advertised two years later deals with ancient Irish history, it is not unlikely that this second work by Mrs. Butler was a second edition (or a reissue) of *Irish Tales* with a new title page. For that matter, the "Fair Authress" who, according to Gildon, is dead may be a fiction herself like Curll's "Joseph Gay" and "Lady Margaret Pennyman." Certainly Gildon's dedication and Mrs. Butler's preface might have come from the same pen.

Josephine Grieder (essay date 1973)

SOURCE: Introduction to *Exilius, or the Banish'd Roman*, by Jane Barker, Garland Publishing, 1973, p. 142.

[*In the following essay, Grieder divides early-eighteenth-century women's writings into two categories: one type salacious and gossipy, the other moralistic and didactic. The critic contends that* Exilius, *which fits into the latter group, stresses that conforming to societal expectations must supersede one's personal passion.*]

Female writers of fiction during the early eighteenth century may generally be divided into two groups, according to their conception of the novel's intent and function. On one hand are Mrs. Manley and Mrs. Haywood, whose scandal chronicles were designed to titillate their readers with gossip and eroticism. On the other are ladies who viewed the novel as a vehicle for moral instruction: Elizabeth Singer Rowe, Penelope Aubin, and the authoress of the present volume, Mrs. Jane Barker.

Mrs. Barker makes her intentions concerning *Exilius: or, The Banish'd Roman* very plain, both on the title page and in the preface. It is "Written After the Manner of Telemachus," Fénélon's celebrated didactic romance, "For the Instruction of Some Young Ladies of Quality." Convinced as she is that "a happy Marriage, by the way of Virtue and Honour . . . lyes through, or borders upon, Heroick Love," she finds that "Romances (which commonly treat of this virtuous Affection) are not to be discarded as wholly useless." Such novels offer examples of what is, and is not, to be esteemed; they also "help to open the Understandings of young Readers, to distinguish between real Worth and superficial Appearances" and contain "many Handfulls of good Morality." She cites with pleasure a reader's opinion that she has successfully rendered "such an idle subject [as Love] both pure and useful; so 'tis to be hop'd there is nothing opposite to real Virtue; I am sure, if I knew or thought there were, I would burn both the Copy and my Fingers, rather than employ them towards its Publication."

Mrs. Barker keeps her promise: *Exilius* is an impeccably high-minded work which contains a multitude of examples of heroic and virtuous love suitably recompensed by Heaven, augmented by the characters' own reflections concerning the folly or wisdom of their behavior. Structure (and plausibility) is sacrificed to purpose, for there is little plot per se; each character relates his own story, and each story meshes intricately with those of his fellow narrators, until at the end Mrs. Barker has succeeded in unraveling all mysteries and uniting all possible pairs of lovers.

Since she speaks to a female audience, the authoress is concerned less with masculine behavior—the male characters belong in general to the heroic mode, fiery and passionate, but respectful, courageous, and loyal—than with the responsibilities and obligations of her virtuous heroines.[1] And she reveals herself to be an extremely strict moral disciplinarian. A girl's duty to her parents supersedes everything in her life. Though she may burn with passion for a worthy suitor, she must not reply to his advances until he has solicited parental consent. If her father has betrothed her to one she views with indifference or aversion—as is the case with Marcellus and Jemella and Fabius and Scipiana—she has no alternative but to accept his arrangement and hope that her lamentations may soften his heart. No matter what a father may do, his daughter never loses her sense of obligation to him. Thus, Clarinthia discovers to her dismay that "contrary to all Morality, and the Laws of Heaven, my wretched Father became inamoured of me" (I, 28); when he attempts to rape her and is killed, she tries to fly from her gallant rescuer, for "his Hands [were] still wreeking with my Father's Blood (for wicked as he was he was still my Father)" (I, 32).

A girl also has the duty to conform to the dignity and honor expected of her sex. She must not be forward: "'tis certain nothing so charms the Heart of Man as Modesty in Woman; this being the Beauty of the Mind, exceeds that of the Body, and remains when the other perishes" (II, 95).[2] Though passionately in love, she must conceal it; and if insuperable obstacles like rank or parental opposition stand in the way of marriage—as in the case of Cordiala and Scipio—she must lecture her lover firmly about respecting their importance. The conflict between the necessity to conform to public expectations and the strength of the individual's passion provides, of course, the tension in most of the heroines' stories; but Mrs. Barker never wavers in her advocacy of submitting to conformity.

But, as all the tales prove, Heaven justly recompenses one's behavior. So each heroine who, while doing violence to her own feelings, has obeyed parental commands and public obligations, is suitably matched up with a properly noble hero. Clelia is united with Marcellus, Clarinthia with her childhood sweetheart Asiaticus, Scipiana with the dashing Exilius. Those whose behavior has been less honorable are also carefully paired according to their deserts. The perfidious but finally repentant Libidinia falls to the libertine Clodius; Artemisia and Valerius suit one another since the mothers of each were notoriously dissolute, and even debauched by the same man.

Amidst this harmonious matrimonial manipulation, two incidents call attention to the severity with which Mrs. Barker can mete out justice to the vicious. The shipwrecked Jemella is rescued by a siren, half-man, half-fish, and makes the acquaintance of the siren's human wife. The woman recounts her story: defying her father's choice of a husband, she was debauched and deserted by a rake, cast out by her family, delivered of an illegitimate child, and finally taken in by the siren. "In this I could not but again admire the exact Justice of Heaven, in thus punishing her Lewdness and Disobedience to her Parents," observes Jemella; "She that refus'd the honest Espousals provided by her Father, became Wife to a Monster; she that disgrac'd herself and her Friends by unlawful Lust, was a Prostitute to a Fish" (II, 72). The wife identifies Clodius, also saved by the siren, as her seducer, but he has no sympathy whatsoever for her. Dissolute women deserve nothing "but to become the broken Meat for lost Vertue to feed upon, and be the miserable Support of a ruin'd Reputation," he says contemptuously, "therefore it is your self you are to reproach for all your Misfortunes" (II, 76). The most vicious female character of all, Asbella, former mistress to Turpius and mother of his bastard Valerius, tries to poison Turpius. But he throws the potion on her, and she is instantly—and appropriately—disfigured: "*Asbella*'s Eyes, that gave way to loose Glances and alluring Looks, are now only Blindness and Deformity; and her Ears, that were open to the soft Whispers of unlawful Love, are now shut from all Conversation" (II, 103).

One must admit that as a formal novel, *Exilius* is very weak: an implausible tangle of plots with scarcely any characterization. As a moral romance, however, it has its points: exciting adventures, elevated sentiments, and impeccable propriety. That it was intended to define the standards set for the female sex offers an interesting commentary on the status of Englishwomen in the early eighteenth century.

Notes

[1] John J. Richetti, who discusses Exilius in his Popular Fiction before Richardson: Narrative Patterns, 1700-1739 (Oxford: Clarendon Press, 1969), pp. 230-236, points out that to the male hero, the woman is "a divine messenger whose beauty and saintly presence both prove and prefigure the truths and joys of religion in this life and the next" (p. 235). There are indeed occasional hints of Platonism in the novel, like Scipiana's remark, as she laments to the "importal Powers," "why Oh why have you given me an Interior bearing so great Resemblance to your own Divine Purities, and not given me the Power to act accordingly" (I, 165).

[2] Occasional remarks indicate that she should not even be particularly well educated. Scipiana has studied philosophy and languages; but "How far this is suitable to our Sex I dare not pretend to determine, the Men having taken Learning for their Province, we must not touch upon its Borders without being suppos'd Usurpers" (I, 76).

Josephine Grieder (essay date 1973)

SOURCE: Introduction to *The Prude: A Novel by a Young Lady*, by Ma A., and *A Patch-Work Screen for Ladies*, by Jane Barker, Garland Publishing, 1973, p. 143.

[*In the excerpt below, Grieder praises* A Patch-Work Screen for the Ladies *for the historical importance of its authentic descriptions of ordinary life; its atypical heroine, Galesia; and its modernistic conclusion, which leaves some narrative conflicts unresolved.*]

. . . [*A Patch-Work Screen for the Ladies*] hangs together by that most fragile of threads, a central narrator who discusses her observations and recounts her own and others' adventures. The numerous poetic epistles, though composed by Galesia and appropriate where inserted, do little to unify the narrative. And since, as Galesia herself confesses, her own existence has been either solitary or confined to extremely modest social circles, her anecdotes have little drama and almost never a climax. The book tails away, in fact, into a conversation with her noble hostess about historical events, the evils of ambition, and more poetry.

At the same time, this very mundaneness has its own interest. The anecdotes of robbers and robberies with which her fellow coach riders amuse themselves in the introduction bear witness, no doubt, to contemporary interest in criminal fiction, but they are also so ordinary and plausible that they suggest newspaper reporting.[1] When Galesia's coach unceremoniously dumps her in the river, she is given shelter by a peasant couple whose meager but well-meant hospitality is observantly and realistically described. The details of her acquaintances and her mode of life in London are trivial; but as in the previous cases, the simplicity and the commonplaceness of event and character partake more of non-fiction than of fiction, and one is inclined to accept Mrs. Barker's observations as an authentic and undramatized view of life at the time.

Just as *A Patch-Work Screen* is an atypical novel, Galesia is an atypical fictional heroine. John J. Richetti calls her "a combination of the female moral censor and the learned and pious semi-recluse lady who is a familiar moral character of the age" and further notes that "Mrs. Barker's 'development' records the clear emergence of the heroic 'she-saint' from the erotic turbulence of popular female fiction."[2] Certainly she differs from, for example, the lustful Elisinda and the anodine Bellamira. But one wonders whether Mrs. Barker indeed intended to hold Galesia up to her readers as a "she-saint," for her validity as a character comes precisely from the sense of confusion and stress she experiences at finding her inclinations contrary to those duties society imposes on her and yet being unable to rebel with confidence against its dictates.

The question of love and marriage presents to her, for example, never-ending difficulties. The off-again-on-again relationship with Bosvil, to whom she proudly refused to reveal her affection because he did not properly declare his intentions to her parents, has already been described in *Love Intrigues.*[3] The post-Bosvil Galesia is, if anything, more cautious about propriety and, unfortunately perhaps for her, more percipient about her suitors. Bellair does observe the necessary ceremonies in informing both his and her parents of his intent, thereby delighting his father, who believes that marriage will reform his wayward son. Nevertheless, Galesia hesitates: "I was not so ignorant of the World, but to know or believe, that often those Beau Rakes, have the Cunning and Assurance to make Parents on both sides, Steps to their Childrens Disgrace, if not Ruin" (p. 37). Her caution is more than justified by Bellair's being hanged for a frolicsome robbery. Lysander, another suitor proposed to Galesia by her mother, is known to keep a mistress; when he declares to his inamorata that he wishes his freedom, she taunts him so mercilessly that he shoots himself—"A very fatal Warning to all unwary Gentlemen" (p. 88), Galesia reflects. She never does succeed in resolving her situation. She regrets Lysander's death, but "I had found so many Disappointments, that I began to be displeas'd at my-self, for hoping or expecting any thing that tended to Happiness" (p. 89). Certainly Galesia is an unrewarded heroine—but not one who is dishonest enough to pretend that all goes well with her.

The other great source of internal confusion and stress involves education—that is, the suitability of the intellectual life as a feminine pursuit. For poor Galesia, learning has been her only comfort. Studying medicine and anatomy comforted her when her beloved brother died and she felt herself "a useless Wretch; useless to the World; useless to my Friends, and a Burden to myself" (p. 14). She maintains a lively and harmless friendship with university students through an exchange of poetry. Obliged to reside in London, she sees that her country manners and discourse are considered ridiculous; "I was like a *Wild Ass* in a Forest, and liv'd alone in the midst of this great Multitude" (p. 45). Once again, study comes to her aid: "it furnish'd me with Notions above the Trifles of my Sex, wherewith to entertain my self in Solitude" (p. 47).

Society's views are, however, pitilessly exposed to her by her reproachful mother, who urges her to leave off "idle Dreams on *Parnassus,* and foolish Romantick Flights, with *Icarus*" (p. 79). The lesson she reads her daughter is straightforward but grim for an intelligent woman: "[become] a good Mistress of a Family; and imploy your Parts in being an obedient Wife, a discreet Governess of your Children and Servants; a friendly Assistant to your Neighbours, Friends, and Acquaintance: This being the Business for which you came into the World, and for Neglect of this, you must give an Account when you go out of it" (p. 80).

Galesia is never able to come to terms with society's definition of a woman's function, as expressed by her mother, and her own inclination to study and to write. She believes that her studies "serv'd to make me unfit Company for every body; for the Unlearned fear'd, and the Learned scorn'd my Conversation; at least I fancy'd so: A Learned Woman, being at best but like a Forc'd-Plant, that never has its due or proper Relish, but is wither'd by the first Blast that Envy or Tribulation blows over her Endeavours" (p. 11).[4] Nor can she help reiterating society's views: "how useless, or rather pernicious, Books and Learning are to our Sex. . . . for by their Means we relish not the Diversions or Imbellishments of our Sex and Station; which render us agreeable to the World, and the World to us; but live in a Stoical Dulness or humersome Stupidity" (p. 79). Yet it is equally clear that she can neither accept nor adhere to these views.

In the popular romances a heroine may be torn by conflict, but eventually the conflict is solved and she lives happily ever after. Galesia, incapable of decisiveness or of having decisiveness thrust upon her, does not live happily ever after; she remains in the limbo of the unconcluded *Patch-Work Screen.* Yet it is this uncertainty, this equivocation of character that makes of her a heroine in the modern sense of the term. If the reader, upon finishing the novel, cannot help but wish that somehow she might come to terms with herself and with society, that somehow she might be rewarded for her lucidity, he feels at least that he has encountered real life, even if dull and undramatic, and a real person—not a common occurrence in the fiction of the period.

Notes

[1] Michael F. Shugrue shows how Mrs. Barker capitalizes here on criminal fiction in "The Sincerest Form of Flattery: Imitation in the Early Eighteenth-Century Novel," *The South Atlantic Quarterly,* 70 (Spring 1971), 248-255.

[2] *Popular Fiction before Richardson* (Oxford, 1969), p. 237.

[3] Reprint ed., New York: Garland Publishing, 1973.

[4] She expresses similar sentiments in poetry, lamenting the tree of knowledge:

> Though in its Culture I have spent some
> Time,
> Yet it disdains to grow in *our* cold Clime,*

Where it can neither Fruit nor Leaves
   produce,
Good for its Owner, or the publick Use.

                        (p. 25)

The * is identified in a footnote as "A Female Capacity."

Margaret Anne Doody (essay date 1977)

SOURCE: "Deserts, Ruins, and Troubled Waters: Female Dreams in Fiction and the Development of the Gothic Novel," in *Genre*, Vol. X, No. 4, Winter, 1977, pp. 529-72.

[*In the following excerpt, Doody elaborates on ways that Barker's descriptions of the dreams of her female characters emphasize the women's unheroic and subjective lives.*]

   My Harriet has been telling me how much she suffered lately from a dream, which she permitted to give strength and terror to her apprehensions from Mr. Greville. Guard, my dear Ladies, against these imbecillities of tender minds. In these instances, if no other, will you give a superiority to our Sex. . . .[1]

So says Richardson's Sir Charles Grandison, airily dismissing Harriet's disturbing sequence of nightmares. Sir Charles voices the accepted rational and masculine view. In eighteenth-century English fiction, until the appearance of the Gothic novel, it is women, not men, who have dreams. Masculine characters rarely dream; those who do are usually simpletons whose dreams can be jocosely interpreted. Heroes are not dreamers.

This certainly marks a change from earlier literature. In Elizabethan and Jacobean drama, for instance, men have very vivid dreams. In the seventeenth century all sorts of men regarded dreams as significant, bearing a message from God. Men with diverse religious views, such as Laud and Bunyan, thought their dreams worth recording. The credit given to dreams became associated with religious wars, fanaticism, and all kinds of irrational and useless behavior. In the eyes of later generations, reality is the thing. Defoe alone among the novelists maintains an old tradition, believing in the spiritual import of dreams and prophetic apparitions. His central characters, male and female, have revelatory dreams. But Defoe was considered a writer for the low, the unenlightened. In polite eighteenth-century fiction, men—if they are admirable, if they are strong—must be shown to be in touch with reality; they exert rational control without idiosyncratic private assistance from the Voice of God and without any awkward manifestations of the unconscious self. Men belong to the scientific world rather than to that of superstition; hence, they do not have prophetic dreams or premonitions. They exercise masculine authority in

a world whose ways, even if sometimes distasteful, are comprehensible. They are either essentially in control, or they are failures, deserving of pity or contempt. The strong man does not have the dreams or nightmares which reveal self-division or perturbation. The only real exception is Lovelace, whose remarkable dream is a sign of (deserved) disintegration and dereliction, and who appears in a novel which has its roots in seventeenth-century comprehension of experience. Even there, the dream is connected with, and serves as a punishment for, Lovelace's moral madness. As Michael DePorte has shown, eighteenth-century psychology saw dreaming and madness as closely connected, and was frightened of both.

The mystical view of dreams implies a high correlation between subjective and objective: it insists that the universal can be manifested in the most personal experience; it validates idiosyncratic insight. The view of dreams as temporary madness, on the other hand, reflects a profound distrust of subjectivity. Again and again Augustan writers identify the tendency toward insanity with the tendency toward the subjective. . . . The lunatic is typically represented as . . . a person with no sense of limit. In this respect the eighteenth century's attitude toward madness is almost exactly the reverse of that of modern psychiatry, with its growing stress on the connection between insanity and an underdeveloped sense of self.[2]

Masculine novelists must show the world of men as objective, not subjective. The same considerations do not apply, or not quite in the same way, to the presentation of women. Richardson, whose guiding interest was in the subjective, necessarily wrote about women. Clarissa, in her dreams and madness, is not morally reprehensible. *Grandison*, more completely a novel of its time than *Clarissa*, has a hero who is supposed to epitomize all the current conceptions of good masculinity; it is the women around the hero who have weaknesses and perturbation. It is the women who have dreams. Sir Charles teases Harriet about having allowed herself to be affected by "a dream, a resverie," and the embarrassed heroine confesses apologetically, "I own I should have made a very silly, a very pusilanimous [*sic*] man" (III, 248). Dreaming is feminine; men are not to be subjected to inner terrors.

Women, weaker than men, not in control of their environment, are permitted to have dreams. The censorship of dreaming doesn't quite apply to them. Officially, in the eighteenth century, women are thought of as weak and superstitious; they have something of an archaic consciousness, not enjoying the full benefits of masculine reason and masculine knowledge of reality. Their dreaming is not necessarily insanity, nor is it the sign of an unbecoming and ignoble weakness. A female character can be shown as dreaming—or having nightmares or delusions—without forfeiting the reader's respect. The "imbecillities of tender minds" are not unattractive. A female dreamer does not seem comic, nor need the fact that she dreams be interpreted as a distasteful psychic dereliction. Women are often seen as living an inward life rather different from that of men, whose consciousness is more definitely related to the objective world and to action within it. Women, less able to plan and execute actions, are seen as living a life closer to the dream-like, and closer to the dream-life.

That this is so can be seen in Pope's presentations of both Belinda and Eloisa. The dreams of both are related to their sexual natures, and to disturbances about their sexual nature. It has often been pointed out that the imagery in *Eloisa to Abelard* prefigures the Gothic manner:

> methinks we wandring go
> Thro' dreary wastes, and weep each other's
> woe;
> Where round some mould'ring tow'r pale ivy
> creeps,
> And low-brow'd rocks hang nodding o'er the
> deeps.
>
> (ll. 241-44)

This imagery—the imagery of the sublime—is certainly present in the national consciousness, but can be used freely here precisely because the poet is dealing with a woman's experience. When we read *The Dunciad* we may wonder if the sublime and the dream-like are not both thought of as dangerously associated with the feminine; it is the "mighty Mother" who threatens masculine rational objectivity. In *Eloisa* Pope treats his subject sympathetically. There is no need to ask about meaning or sense aside from the psychological. Eloisa need not be asked to do anything in the objective world because she cannot. There is no event in the poem; the poem is Eloisa, that passive victim and active dreamer whose sexual nature is inseparably associated with pain, dread and guilt. When the feminine is feminine, there is no need for hostility. We do not need to ask, while reading about Eloisa's dream, if the character is evincing the inferiority of her sex and the superiority of the other—ultimately, she is, perhaps, but we need take her only as she is, attending to her experience. The poem was popular with women, especially with the ladies of the town, who must have taken the work as a vindication of feminine passion.

When women writers themselves describe feminine dreams, the effects are both similar to and different from those in Pope's poems. In writing novels the women writers, although dealing with the objective everyday world, felt free to include dream experience as part of the heroine's life. Unlike Defoe, they do not follow the old tradition which relates the dream to the promptings of God or the Devil. Female novelists interest themselves in the psychology of the heroine; her subjective life has meaning, and her dreams cry out for interpretation, but not the old religious meaning or spiritual interpretation. The reader's sympathetic understanding of the dream rises from an understanding of the character in her situation. The dreams delineated by women writers are much lonelier and more complex than those which Pope describes. What gives rise to the dream may not be quite what we expect, and the dream-content is powerfully related to the sense of individuality under attack. Women's heroines usually are not as simply hopeful as Belinda or as simply grief-sticken as Eloisa. In an apparently placid situation the heroine's relationship to a lover or to marriage may be fraught with anxiety amounting to dread. The heroine has a strong but divided sense of self, and the self is usually suffering from something more complicated than simple desire or simple grief. Some sort of good self-realization is being thwarted, and tension and terror arise from a sense of incomplete and unsatisfactory alternatives. The pain is related to the woman's sexual nature; the sexual nature and the whole sense of identity do not coincide satisfactorily, and the individual is threatened with severe loss.

One of the most interesting examples of the disturbing feminine dream occurs in Jane Barker's ***Love Intrigues: The History of the Amours of Bosvil and Galesia*** (1713). The heroine is in a constant state of uneasy suspense about her relationship to Bosvil and his on-again-off-again courtship (if that is what it is). When Bosvil appears to have abandoned her, the heroine goes for solitary rambles and begins to write poetry. Deciding to dedicate herself to her work, she writes verses on an ash tree in a grove:

> *Methinks these Shades, strange Thoughts*
> *suggest,*
> *Which heat my Head, and cool my Breast;*
> *And mind me of a Laurel Crest.*
>
> *Methinks I hear the Muses sing,*
> *And see 'em all dance in a Ring;*
> *And call upon me to take wing.*
>
> *We will (say they) assist thy Flight,*
> *Till thou reach fair ORINDA's Height,*
> *If thou can'st this World's Follies slight.*
>
> . . . . .
>
> *Then gentle Maid cast off they Chain,*
> *Which links thee to thy faithless Swain,*
> *And vow a Virgin to remain.*

After this self-dedication, Galesia devotes herself to poetry and study: "Thus I thought to become *Apollo*'s Darling Daughter, and Maid of Honour to the

Muses."[3] Her activities become important in themselves, but when Bosvil returns and appears to be on the point of a declaration she drops her studies. Things are apparently going prosperously, but she is still in a state of suspense about herself and her future. While in this state of suspense, she has an important dream:

> I thought my self safe landed on Love's Shore, where no cross Wind, unseen Accident, cou'd oppose my Passage to *Hymen*'s Palace, or wrack me in this Harbour of true Satisfaction. . . . Now my Thoughts swam in a Sea of Joy, which meeting with the Torrent of the foresaid Vexations, made a kind of dangerous Rencounter, ready to overset my Reason. I pass'd some Nights without Sleep, and Days without Food, by reason of this secret Satisfaction. At last, being overcome with a little Drowsiness, I fell asleep in a Corner of our Garden, and dream'd, that on a suddain, an angry Power carried me away, and made me climb a high mountain: at last brought me to that Shade where I had heretofore writ those Verses on the Bark of an Ash, as I told you, in which I seem'd to prefer the Muses, and a studious Life, before that of Marriage, and Business. Whereupon,
>
> —*My uncouth Guardian said,*
> —*Unlucky Maid!*
> *Since, since thou has the Muses chose,*
> Hymen *and Fortune are thy Foes.* (pp. 32-33)

In a later edition of this novel (1719) the dream is more surprisingly revealing:

> . . . a mountain where I met *Bosvil,* who endeavour'd to tumble me down, but I thought the aforesaid Power snatch'd me away, and brought me to that Shade. . . . [4]

The dream is not related only to Galesia's lover, or even primarily to her repressed passion for him. The dream is related to her own sense of an enforced choice, and to a decision she must make about her own nature. If she is "Apollo's Daughter," she must give over the desire for marriage, for sexual fulfillment. She recognizes and fears the penalty of sexual frustration even while her own sense of herself makes her unhappily reject the man she loves. Her own will does not govern the nature of the alternatives. In the second (and unexpurgated?) version of the dream, the high mountain represents a freedom from anxiety, a sexual aspiration fulfilled—but it cannot be obtained after all; she is transported back to the "Shade" of her intellect. In some fashion she knows that the affair with Bosvil will never mature (as it does not—the subtitle of the story is ironic). What makes the dream terrifying is the helplessness, the sense of being "snatch'd away" from fulfillment and being compelled to confront the truth about herself. A modern psychological allegorist must inevitably

see the "power" as representing not just Fate (though external conditions make this division inevitable), nor the irresistible power of Apollo, but Galesia's inner nature which makes a bitter choice her will does not know how to make. She had made a life for herself without Bosvil, and this has been more than a substitute for him. She had decided on a single life (in which she could use her intellect)—although she didn't expect herself to take her at her word. Her dream-journey travels over the landscape of her divided self—and the dream vision powerfully intimates anxiety and loss.

In the sequel, *A Patch-Work Screen for the Ladies* (1723), loss and perturbation are repeated. Here the heroine is living her single life, in fulfillment of the prophecy. The kind brother with whom she studied medicine, her only intellectual companion, dies. The heroine is disdainful about the superstitions of other girls, which include "Our little Follies of telling our Dreams; laying Things under each other's Heads to dream of our Amours . . . drawing Husbands in the Ashes; St. *Agnes*'s Fast; and all such childish Auguries,"[5] but she is impressed by her own dreams of the lost brother, remembering "that I even wish'd for that which is *the Horror of Nature,* that I might see his *Ghost*" (p. 13). Telling dreams is a silly feminine pastime, the mature Galesia indicates—but what about the force of experience in some dreams? The life Galesia knew seems lost. She has to go with her widowed mother to London, where she spends most of her time working in the garret, or on the roof of their humble lodging, gazing over the city:

> Out of this Garret, there was a Door went out to the Leads; on which I us'd frequently to walk to take the Air, or rather the Smoke. . . . Here it was that I wish'd sometimes to be of *Don Quixote*'s Sentiments, that I might take the *Tops* of *Chimneys,* for *Bodies* of *Trees;* and the *rising Smoke* for *Branches;* the *Gutters* of *Houses,* for *Tarras-Walks;* and the *Roofs* for stupendous *Rocks* and *Mountains.* However, though I could not beguile my Fancy thus, yet here I was alone, or, as the Philosopher says, never *less alone.* Here I entertain'd my Thoughts, and indulg'd my solitary Fancy. (p. 67)

Such reverie is not like that of Eloisa, simply and strongly connected with erotic passion; rather, it is connected with a sense of solitary identity, both losing and finding itself. Galesia contemplates London rather as Mrs. Radcliffe's Ellena will contemplate the mountains and valleys from her turret in the convent; imprisoned, the self can create meaning from inner impressions. Galesia's mountaintop in her dream has now become the rooftop where she finds herself, and, in looking down from her height, she can transcend reality for a while, although not without a fear of that outer world which would be too powerful for her if she were to descend to it. . . .

Notes

[1] Samuel Richardson, *Sir Charles Grandison* (Oxford English Novels Edition, London, 1972), Part III, p. 242.

[2] Michael V. DePorte, *Nightmares and Hobbyhorses: Swift, Sterne, and Augustan Ideas of Madness* (San Marino: The Huntington Library, 1974), p. 31.

[3] Jane Barker, *Love Intrigues* (New York: Garland Press Reprint, Foundation of the Novel series), pp. 14-15.

[4] Barker, *The Entertaining Novels of Mrs. Jane Barker* (2 vols., London: 1719), II, 29.

Marilyn L. Williamson (essay date 1990)

SOURCE: "Jane Barker (1652-1727)," in *Raising Their Voices: British Women Writers, 1650-1750*, Wayne State University Press, 1990, pp. 102-6.

[*In the following excerpt, Williamson examines some of the ironies of Barker's poetry, as well as the patterns found in Barker's novels which give advice for women regarding courting.*]

Jane Barker was one of the most self-conscious daughters of Orinda, and her career began in a way that would have made the identification logical. Early in her career, Barker enjoyed the encouragement of men: *Poetical Recreations: Consisting of Original Poems, Songs, Odes* (1688) was jointly created by Barker with "several gentlemen of the universities," who, we learn from the book, were friends of Barker's brother, a physician who shared his learning with her.[37] She was also apparently educated by a clergyman in Lincolnshire after her father had lost his court position and the family lived on his pension from the king after 1675.[1] We learn from the volume that, although her mother had reservations about educating her, Barker seems to have learned a good deal from her brother and his friends at Cambridge. Yet the approach her publisher took to her share of *Poetical Recreations* also used the familiar technique of undoing as he compared her poetry to that of men:

> The *First Part* of the *Miscellanies* are the effects of a Ladies Wit, and I hope all the Courtly will (though out of a complement) allow them for valuable: But however, not to say much more of her Verses, I doubt not but they will commend themselves for better than I can pretend to; for all good things carry with them a certain irresistable Authority, not to be oppos'd.

> The *Second Part* flows from the *Pens* of those whose Educations gave them the opportunity of improving their natural Endowments at the *Universities,* and

some others who wanted those advantages; and by reading you may find the difference of Parts improv'd, and Parts as barely natural. (Sigs. A3ᵛ-A4)

The male authors of the dedicatory poems in *Poetical Recreations* represent men as monopolizing wit, as triumphant after Orinda's death until Barker's appearance:

> But, lo, the Heiress of that Ladies *Muse,*
> Rivals their Merits [male poets] and their
>   Sence out-do's;
> With swifter flights of fancy wings her *Verse,*
> And nobler Greatness valient acts reherse.
>
>   (Sig. A4)

Another poem repeats the idea that since Adam named the beasts, men have exclusively claimed power over words, but "How grossly we mistook, *Orinda* knew, / We are convinc'd too by your *Verse* and *You*" (Sig. a). Although a poem in part 2 praising Barker's romance *Scripina* also alludes to Behn ("Thy *Lines* may pass severest *Virtue's Test,* / More than Astrea's soft, more than Orinda's chast" [11, 32], the primary identification Barker's circle made was with Orinda, one that Barker assiduously cultivated in her fiction and her poetry. Barker is one of the creators of the Orinda tradition. Barker's art is a complex mixture of autobiography, fictional self-representation, and fantasy, much of it dedicated to the development of the image of a woman writer, Galesia, who has much in common with Barker and who dreams of Orinda's apotheosis in one of her latest novels *The Lining of the Patch-work Screen* (1726). . . . [The] autobiographical details [of Barker's fiction] are helpful in dealing with her poetry here.

Barker's poetry records that her brother's death was a blow to her, but it seems not to have crippled her life in the way Elizabeth Elstob's brother's death transformed hers. Barker and her mother seem to have moved to London after the death of her father around 1675, and her mother died in London in 1685. There is evidence that after James II fled England in 1688, the year of *Poetical Recreations,* Barker fled to France, where she became an ardent Roman Catholic and retired to the court of Saint Germain. She returned to Lincolnshire by 1715, where she lived on her father's royal grant. These transitions may account the division in her career between 1688 and 1713, with her published poetry identified with the earlier era and her fiction published after her return to England.[2] A Magdalen College manuscript reveals that Barker was revising her poems at the end of the century, and her fiction contains a number of poems, several from *Poetical Recreations.*

Although in later life Barker represents her persona as ambivalent about women's learning, in *Poetical Rec-*

reations she is deeply envious of her friends at Cambridge, a place that should be Paradise, but only certain people—males—are allowed to eat of the tree of knowledge. Women are excluded by their original transgression:

> For in our maker's Laws we've made a
>   breach,
> And gather'd all that was within our reach,
> Which since we ne're could touch; Altho' our
>   Eyes
> Do serve our longing Souls to tantalize
> Whilst kinder fate for you do's constitute
> Luxurious Banquets of this dainty Fruit.
>
>   (P. 4)

Barker therefore invites her Cambridge friends to join her in a retreat where in solitude one can maintain innocence and avoid pride, avarice, ambition, luxury, and wantonness—all the temptations of the world.

In a fascinating poem about a minor incident—an apothecary putting *her* recipes for cures under the name of her physician brother—she fantasizes about women's being educated enough to find cures for men's ills, which are, of course, not imaginary as women's are. (She confesses that if Strephon had not jilted her, she would never have learned medical arts.) At the end of the poem, she resolves to write all her cures in verse ("The Gout and Rickets too shall run on feet"): "For since the Learn'd exalt and own our Fame. / It is no Arrogance to do the same, / But due respects and complaisance to them" (p. 34). Barker's irony ill conceals her envy of male learning and status or even her bitterness at conventional female roles that preclude women's education. Yet the irony and the shifts in tone also suggest Barker's continuous ambivalence about her own goals and her place in society. This poem is one included in *A Patch-work Screen for the Ladies* (1723). Characteristically, she excused her writing poetry because she was compelled to do it by "necessity of fate." She has forsaken, she says, honors, pleasure, riches,

> All for the *Muses* Melancholy Tree,
> E're I knew ought of its great Mystery.
> Ah gentle Fate, since thou wilt have it so,
> Let thy kind hand exalt it to my brow.
>
>   (P. 40)

Making fate responsible absolved Barker from any violation of social norms in the privilege of writing.

Like others of Orinda's daughters, Barker idealized a retreat from the world, which she viewed as having become hopelessly corrupt. In fact, she was one of the poets who genuinely enjoyed the country, and lived in her later years as a spinster on her father's tenancy. In these early poems, she urged others to escape in order to preserve virtue and integrity:

> 'Tis hard we must (the World's so wicked
>   grown)
> Be complaisant in Sin, or live alone:
> For those who now with Verture are endu'd,
> Do live alone, though in a multitude.
>
>   . . . . .
>
> 'Tis not ignoble an escape to make:
> But where no Conquest can be hop'd by fight,
> 'Tis honourable, sure, to 'scape by flight.
>
>   (P. 22)

Retreat, then, is as much a moral decision about contemporary society as an attraction to country life. Barker's grim feelings about the state of things were no doubt intensified by her royalist and Roman Catholic perspective on the events leading to the Glorious Revolution. She left for France in 1688.

Barker's Roman Catholicism also gave a distinctive cast to her formulations of the personal integrity so much valued in the Orinda tradition. For Barker the celibate life of single blessedness was a realistic alternative for women. In one of her best-known poems, which repeats Orinda's in the title, "A Virgin Life," the speaker prays that she will be able to withstand "Men's almost Omnipotent Amours," even as the dreadful age of twenty-five approaches with the prospect of scornfully being called an old maid. A virgin has equanimity: she is a true friend, a charitable neighbor, an obedient subject. Alone, she enjoys the society of God: "She drives her whole Life's business to these ends, / To serve her God, enjoy her Books and Friends" (p. 13; *WD,* 227).

In a song from the romance *Scipina,* Barker went even further in presenting Anchorites as the essence of personal integrity:

> Ah, happy are we Anchorites that know
> Not Women's Ebbs, nor when their love will
>   Flow
> We know no storms that rage in women's
>   Breasts,
> But here in quiet build our Halcyon Nests;
> Where we deceitfull Calm our Faith beguiles,
> No cruel frowns, nor yet more cruel smiles;
> No rising Wave of Fate our hopes advance;
> Nor fear we fathomless despair of Chance;
> But our strong Minds, like rocks, their
>   Firmness prove,
> Defying both the Storms of Fate and Love.
>
>   (P. 91; *FF,* 173)

Here we see that Barker was not, like Chudleigh, rejecting marriage because it was demeaning and oppressive for women, but celebrating a version of the ideal female integrity that many of Orinda's followers extolled. For Barker the ideal extended to virginity and monastic peace because her faith still supported that vision.

Paradoxically, however, Barker was one of the few of Orinda's progeny who wrote of sexual love; and this, I believe, is a function of time and temperament. Her sensibility was formed after the Restoration and its freer mores took hold, and her temperament as an artist positively relished irony and ambivalence. So, although she wrote about Strephon, Exillius, and other lovers, Barker's speakers do not trust men, who invariably represent "interest" in relationships, abandon women, or seek only their fortunes. In **"To Dr. R. S. my indifferent Lover, who complain'd of my Indifferency,"** the speaker tells R. S. that he has little reason to complain of her "since I by many a circumstance can prove, / That int'rest was the motive of your love." Such courtship may be suitable for cunning baggages in town, but not for honest country maids. The speaker was saved by her temperament—her ill nature—from taking Dr. R. S. seriously, but she hates to think what might have happened to another woman because "Your Flames and Sighs only for Money were. / As Beggars for their gain turn Blind and Lame." This experience has taught the speaker "ne'er to be *Mistress* more" (pp. 16-17). In another poem, **"To my Unkind Strephon,"** the speaker speculates about how to react to Strephon's withdrawal of love; she decides that "like good old Romans, although banish'd I / Shall still retain my first integrity" (p. 35). As she explores the probable causes for his waning feeling, the speaker concludes that Strephon, like Dr. R. S., is driven by interest: "But now, alas, Love's Powers are all deprest, / By th' pow'rfull Anarchy of Interest" (p. 36).

On her side a woman must have the favor of fortune if she is to be loved by most men, as in **"A Song of Scipina":**

> In Vain do's *Nature* her free gifts bestow,
>   To make us wise or fair;
> If *Fortune* don't her Favours show,
>   Scorn'd or neglected we may go,
> Not worth a Look, much less a Lover's care.
> (P. 79)

This cynical thinking becomes an assumption of Barker's thought as in these lines about why she is forsaking poetry, written presumably in her own voice: "No more than Beauty, without Wealth, can move / A Gallant's heart to strokes of Love / . . . No more can verse in London grow' (p. 108).

The representation of men that emerges here is the one we find in seventeenth-century fiction written by Aphra Behn and her followers: males are predatory and motivated by the worst values of a commercial economy that will destroy women if they do not learn how to cope with it. In another context Barker meditates about the mistakes made by classical ladies in **"To Ovid's Heroines in his Epistles"** (pp. 28-29). Women, Barker's poems suggest, have in their capacity to control their lives if they are willing to accept the consequences of independence and possibly live out their destinies unconventionally on the margins of society. Her religion, moreover, did not lead her to balk at such alternatives.

Although she helped create and perpetuate the tradition of Orinda. Barker is full of ironic complexity, more of which will be apparent in analysis of her fiction in chapter 4. She continued the identification of her self-representation (Galesia) with Orinda in the later fiction, although it represents the artist not in rural retirement but coping with the oppression of women in London. She was constantly ambivalent about the value of learning for women. She was a committed celibate who wrote eloquently of women's problems in courtship and marriage. She was an ardent Jacobite whose sympathy for the suffering of marginal people of London is palpable in her fiction. She was the most complex of Orinda's daughters, much resembling Margaret Cavendish in her swings of attitude, but she is an almost perfect example of Lipking's paradigm: "Poetry is the expression of a life, personal and incomplete, and proportioned to the self; employing whatever language and conventions one has been allowed to acquire; presented in fragments; and achieving, through sharing the emotions of loneliness and abandonment, a momentary sense of not being alone."[3]

. . . . .

Three writers of fiction may accurately be described as Orinda's daughters: Jane Barker, Penelope Aubin, and Elizabeth Singer Rowe. They put the amatory structures we have been investigating to a different use, for through romance they show the reader not only moral patterns in human life but a larger providential design as well. These writers translate the predatory world of the romances into a moral and spiritual obstacle course in which their persecuted heroines struggle to fulfill a destiny that may be a commitment to married love or to a single life lived according to personal values. These writers' fantasies are not tragic but melodramatic, in that forces of good eventually triumph. Men are sometimes allies and sometimes the enemy, for the threat represented by the corrupting rake has now been subsumed by larger forces within the heroine's world. Barker, Aubin, and Rowe are definitely, but subtly, concerned about children obeying parents and parental authority about marriage choices. Although their fictions ostensibly endorse filial obedience, the larger patterns they represent, as we shall see, cause the reader to question parental wisdom in choosing suitable mates for their children. These fictions illustrate the waning of parental authority in the work of writers who overtly wish to sustain it, but the same works do not, except occasionally in Barker, mediate marriage choices because they have larger spiritual work to do.

Jane Barker . . . contributed four major pieces to this fiction: *Love Intrigues* (1713), *Exilius* (1715), *A Patch-Work Screen for the Ladies* (1723), and *Lining for the Patch-Work Screen* (1726). *Love Intrigues* is the closest of her works—or any of the fiction by this group—to the Behn tradition. It is clearly written to represent a young woman's predicament as she is courted by a man who toys with her emotions, attempts to get her to agree to a hasty marriage, swears everlasting devotion and urgent desire, but then leaves her for long periods and finally never asks her parents for her hand in marriage. The writer of a poem of praise for the novel suggests its monitory function; the novel describes,

> The Charms of Nature, and those painted true.
> By what strange Springs our real Passions
>   move,
> How vain are all Disguises when we Love;
> What Wiles and Stratagems the Men secure,
> And what the tortur'd Female Hearts endure;
> Compell'd to stifle what they feign would tell,
> While Truth commands, but Honour must
>   rebel.[4]

Galesia is indeed constrained by her sense of propriety in not revealing her passion for Bosvil, either to him or to her mother, but the reader has a sense that the revelation would have made little difference to the inconstant Bosvil. When he presses Galesia for a "speedy Marriage," she rebukes him for treating her like a mistress, and he responds passionately but with patent hypocrisy:

> Sure, dear Cousin, said I, (with a Tone wholly confus'd) you forget in whose Company you are, and believe your self with fair Mrs. *Lowland:* if such an amorous Slumber has cast you into this *Delerium,* pray awake, and behold before you, your Cousin *Galesia* with whom I converse at present: her reserv'd Behaviour, with which she treats me her faithful Lover, is a sufficient Demonstration, that it is the prudent, vertuous, chast *Galesia!* It is this reserved Mein, Madam, which has often deter'd me, and commanded my Tongue to a respectful Silence; whilst my poor Heart, over-charg'd with Passion, only eas'd with Sighs, and my Looks were the only Language whereby to express my interiour Thoughts. (P. 28)

Here Barker anticipates Haywood in demonstrating the ways men blame their perfidy on women. Although Galesia is the stereotypically innocent young woman, she is responsible for her involvement with Bosvil and her survival after the relationship: both occur because of

Orinda. As Margaret Doody has said and as we noticed in chapter 2, modeling on Orinda went on throughout Jane Barker's fiction: *Love Intrigues* is "related to Lucasia," for example (Sig. B).[5] As the story opens, the reader is aware that Galesia has been made very vulnerable to fantasies of love by her reading, which also has made her equally eager to imitate Orinda in writing poetry and to write her commitment to single life upon a tree, the old pastoral lover's gesture:

> Then gentle Maid cast off thy Chain,
> Which links thee to thy faithless Swain,
> And vow a Virgin to remain.
>
> Write, write thy Vow upon this Tree,
> By us it shall recorded be;
> And thou enjoy Eternity.
>
>   (P. 14)

When she is actually abandoned by Bosvil, Galesia

> resolved to espouse a Book, and spend my Days in Study: This Fancy having once taken Root, grew apace, and branch'd it self forth in a thousand vain conceits. I imagined my self the *Orinda,* or *Sapho* of my Time, and amongst my little Reading, the Character of the Faithful Shepperdess in the Play pleas'd me extreamly; I resolved to imitate her, not only in perpetual Chastity, but in learning the Use of Simples for the Good of my Country Neighbors. Thus I thought to become *Apollo's* Darling Daughter, and Maid of Honour to the Muses. In order to do this I got my Brother (who was not yet return'd to *Oxford*) to set me in the way to learn my Grammar, which he willingly did, thinking it only a Vapour of Fancy. (P. 15)

Literature has a double meaning for Galesia: it feeds her fantasies of love and models her behavior in life, but it also changes the meaning of Bosvil's desertion. Writing gives Galesia a means of surviving her abandonment: like the Portuguese nun, Galesia has a voice, in part, because her relationship to Bosvil does not culminate in marriage. The relationship has ended, but the emotions remain to be explored and analyzed.

Throughout the process of the novel, which is, of course, narrated by Galesia, both she and Bosvil appear to be imitating romances, largely because of Galesia's innocence of the world. Thus the text is a mirror of the social transaction of amatory fiction: a female reader, largely without access to the world, learns about it and models her behavior through reading. We feel for Galesia as she tries to cope with Bosvil's actions, in this case, informing a friend that he will not introduce him to Galesia because "he design'd his Cousin *Galesia* for himself":

> This Transaction, tho' coming to me by a third hand, gave me a strong Belief of *Bosvil's* Sincerity; and

made me interpret every little dubious Word, which he sometimes mix'd with his fond Actions, to be Demontrations of a real Passion; not doubting but a little time wou'd ripen the same into an open Declaration to my Parents, as well as formerly to me, and now lately to young *Brafort.* In the mean time attributing this Delay to his Prudence, in acquainting himself with my Humour, and Inclinations, before he gave himself irrevocably to me; which made me regulate my Behaviour with discreetest Precautions my poor inexperienced Thoughts cou'd dictate. My Grammar Rules now became harsh Impertinences, for I thought I had learnt *Amo* and *Amor,* by a shorter and surer Method; and the only Syntax I studied, was how to make suitable Answers to my Father, and him, when the long'd-for Question shou'd be propos'd; that I might not betray my Weakness. (P. 21)

Here Barker clearly presents the central function of amatory fiction: to teach its readers the complex codes of the grammar of love, to provide in Foucault's terms, a discourse of sexuality in which any subject may find a syntax. Although the narrative frequently implies that Galesia's prudence with Bosvil is a cause of his cooling toward her, the reader can only conclude that her reserve has saved Galesia from being ruined and that she is blaming herself as a victim. The novel is a fascinating and complex representation of a woman's predicament, in which she escapes the fate of a Haywood heroine because of the particular literary models she has chosen. Barker is simply more explicit than her contemporaries in showing how her characters model their behavior on what they read.

Exilius or, the Banish'd Roman (1715) was Jane Barker's reply to tales of gallantry. As her subtitle informs the reader, Barker wrote "for the Instruction of Some Young *Ladies* of Quality," to stem the tide of libertinism with a concept of heroic love that would fulfill itself in marriage:

> Thus it has far'd with this kind of Heroick Love of late; it has been as it were rallied out of Practice, and its Professors laughed out of Countenance, whilst Interest and loose Gallantry have been set up in its Place, and monopolized all its Business and Effects. How far this has been an Inlet to that Deluge of Libertinism which has overflow'd the Age, the many unhappy Marriages and unkind Separations may inform us, and at the same time show how proper an Ingredient Love is, towards the making of a happy Marriage: for where Love is not the Cement, as well as Interest the Foundation, the Superstructure of Conjugal Faith, seldom stands long, the first Wind that blows . . . will go near to shake, if not quite overthrow the Fabrick.[6]

Romances, Barker tells her reader, are therefore justified in demonstrating how heroic love is to be achieved. To represent the value of heroic love, four sets of Roman mates—Cordiala and Scipio, Clelia and Marcellus, Clarinthia and Asiaticus, and Scipiana and Exilius—have complicated and farflung adventures that culminate in their unions. *Exilius* is written "after the Manner of Telemachus," which implies that it celebrates the manly virtues Odysseus's son defended in his scenes with Penelope. Thus, drawing on the epic sources of romance, Barker makes marriage of the four couples into their destinies, like the founding of Rome or the conquest of Jerusalem. For example, Clelia has the approval of Jupiter's oracle for her love of Marcellus. In these stories men and women are allies as they struggle against obstacles to their destined mates. Their commitment to one another does not begin with marriage, for it has already been amply demonstrated. Interest and marriage bonds are no longer the enemies of love but, with it, support the ideal relationship.

Another important theme in *Exilius* is obedience to parental authority and its relation to heroic love. *Exilius* overtly and repeatedly condemns filial disobedience. Daughters who defy their fathers end up married to monsters or fish: "In this I could not but again admire the exact justice of Heaven, in thus punishing her Lewdness and Disobedience to her Parents. She that refus'd the honest Esposals provided by her Father, became Wife to a monster; she that disgrac'd herself and her Friends by unlawful Lust, was a Prostitute to a Fish" (2:72). Still, as Doody points out, the woman's predicament as a fish's spouse is not as bleak as one might expect: "There are delicate ambiguities to the moral fable; although the author seems officially to present the undersea world as the domain of the inhumane and lustful, the world under water has its attractions and advantages. The comic, the grotesque, and the beautiful combine in a manner that complicates interpretation and resists simple moral exemplification."[7] And, paradoxically, *Exilius* leaves the reader skeptical of parental authority in relation to genuine heroic love of the sort experienced by the four central couples. If parents become tyrannical in opposing a destined heroic love, as they invariably do, then children are justified by the romance in opposing them. Parents do not come off very well in this novel: at least they are blind to the destined loves of their children, and at worst they oppose them because of incestuous longings. The children's relationships are only unsuitable, but never adulterous or lustful; and so the effect on the reader is to inspire skepticism about parental authority in filial marriage choices, which should be left to providential design, sensed and understood only by the children. Just as Barker's fantasies support and interrogate social structures, so the narrative is more subtle than first appears about both supporting and subverting parental authority.

A Patch-Work Screen for the Ladies (1723) continues Galesia's story from *Love Intrigues.* Barker proves herself a true daughter of Orinda by using undoing generously in the address to the reader. She has chosen a patchwork screen as a metaphor for her narratives, she says, "the better to recommend it to my Female Readers, as well in their Discourse, as in their Needle-Work," for "whenever one sees a Set of Ladies together, their Sentiments are as differently mix'd as the Patches in their Work."[8] Then she exclaims, characteristically, "Forgive me, kind Reader, for carrying the Metaphor too high; by which means I am out of my Sphere, and so can say nothing of the *Male Patch-Workers*" (p. vi). Barker's fiction is that Galesia has become a virgin recluse who passes her time in retreat, reading, writing poetry, telling stories, and rescuing women in distress. Barker records the stories in a work that gives the appearance of fragmentation, "but in a **Patch-Work** there is no Harm done" (p. viii).

The patches present Galesia's story as well as those she tells the narrator. Both Galesia and the narrator are personae for Barker. We learn that Galesia has been engaged to a young man whom she did not greatly fancy but who was much favored by her parents. At the last minute, he was arrested for robbery, and so she escaped that union. Galesia and her mother move to the city, and a friend tries to persuade Galesia to marry an old man; but she is now too wise for that (p. 54). Her mother also urges Galesia to marry, but her "Reflections on Bosvil's Baseness, gave me a secret Disgust against Matrimony" (p. 79). Later, when another suitor has committed suicide after a violent argument with his mistress, Galesia wonders if fate is persecuting her; but at this time, as at all other moments of despair, she is comforted by thoughts of Katherine Philips and her poem, "A Virgin Life." Galesia concludes that fate has designed her for a single life (p. 89).

Orinda, then, is the inspiration for Galesia, as she writes poetry in her garret, eschewing ambition or wealth for the sake of virtue:

> The Pleasure of [retreat] was greatly improv'd by reading Mrs. *Phillips.* I began to emulate her Wit, and aspir'd to imitate her Writings; in doing of which, I think, I deserv'd *Arachne's* Fate, or at least to be transform'd into one of the lowest of Mack-Fleckno's Followers: Her noble Genius being inimitable; especially in Praise of a Country-Life, and Contempt of human Greatness . . . Her Poetry I found so interwoven with Vertue and Honour, that each Line was like a Ladder to climb, not only to Parnassus, but to Heaven. (P. 3)

Galesia becomes a learned woman (she is interested in Harvey's theories of circulation of the blood, for example). Although her brother, like Barker's, humors Galesia's interests, the rest of the world finds her unfit company, "for the Unlearned fear'd and the Learned scorn'd my Conversation; at least, I fancy'd so: a Learned Woman, being at best but like a Forc'd Plant,

that never has its due or proper Relish, but is wither'd by the first Blast that Envy or Tribulation blows over her Endeavours" (p. 11). Barker portrayed Galesia and her mother as further internalizing this view of learned women, who are not made attractive by learning, "but live in a Stoical Dulness or humersome Stupidity" (p. 79). Again there is tension between the values Barker herself held and those she represented in her fiction. In the early eighteenth century, to be sure, a learned woman was often regarded as an oddity, but Orinda was certainly not rejected by society because of her achievements.

A Patch-Work exhibits parents in very much the way they appeared in **Exilius:** lacking in understanding of their children's welfare. Galesia's parents favored her marriage to the robber, for example, and her mother favored her marriage to the suicide. In a telling example of Galesia's stories, a father forces his daughter to marry a man other than the lawyer she desires. The husband goes bankrupt, whereas the lawyer grows to fame. Wherever parents set their judgment ahead of the inclination of their children, the outcome in both the short and long run is bad for the children.

Another important pattern in Barker's fiction is the woman rescuer. One of Galesia's stories tells of a goldsmith who seduces an innocent girl and then denies her. Galesia gets her into a hospital and thence to a plantation (p. 54). Belinda is a similar example. A married man preaches to her of platonic love, but she soon finds herself pregnant; and when he deserts her, Galesia and her landlady come to her rescue. The culmination of this theme is the story of "The Unaccountable Wife," which paradoxically conforms to and violates all contemporary codes for female behavior. It begins with a wife's toleration of her husband's open affair with their servant. When the husband tries to get rid of the servant, however, the wife does the servant's work, much to the disapproval of their friends. Both wife and servant finally leave for the servant's hovel in the country. There the neighbors try to get rid of them "to prevent a Parish charge" (p. 103). A lady of quality sees them being driven from town and shelters them in her house. They return to the husband because he is ill, and he soon dies. The queen eventually offers the wife a pension, but she refuses it and ends her life a beggar. The narrator attributes the "unaccountable" actions to infatuation, yet to a reader familiar with women's discourses, the story is full of resonances about women's predicament, and one of its points is the lack of social understanding of contradictions in codes of behavior. For example, the women live out the opening line of Mary Chudleigh's famous poem "Wife and Servant are the same." One also recalls the many pleas in advice books for wives to tolerate their husbands' extramarital affairs, rather than disturb their marriages. The problem with social acceptance of these terms is that the women, as in a comedy, have followed them to their logical extreme and thereby expose the social system. The husband wanted to cast off only the awkward member of the triangle, not both women. The social system (i.e., the Poor Law) will not tolerate two unattached, unemployed women in the servant's former village. The wife's refusal of the pension is a rejection of her social station and illuminates the condition of all less fortunate women. Unaccountable in contemporary terms is the fact that the wife calls the servant the only friend she has. Women wooed by the same man and bonding across class lines are simply not to be understood. The story is a powerful indictment of the status of women in Barker's society, but it is presented without rancor: rather, its effect is to interrogate the social structure through irony, not anger.

The Lining of the Patch-Work Screen: Designed for the Farther Entertainment of the Ladies (1726) extends the reader's sense that women help women. Barker creates this impression partly by having a group of women who listen to Galesia and contribute stories to the text, but her most effective device is to use several stories of the Behn tradition for new purposes. The Portuguese nun reappears, as does Behn's fair vow-breaker, but she now accidentally sews her first husband's shroud to the second husband's coat. The old stories from the libertine tradition refined and set in a moral framework impress the reader with the scope of the female community and its strong internal bonds. . . .

Notes

[1] See *First Feminists: British Women Writers, 1578-1799*, ed. Moira Ferguson (Bloomington: Indiana University Press; Old Westbury, N.Y.: Feminist Press, 1985), pp. 171-72. See also Margaret Doody, "Jane Barker," *British Novelists, 1660-1800*, ed. Martin C. Battestin (Detroit, Mich.: Gale, 1985), 39:24-30.

[2] See *First Feminists*, pp. 171-72, and Doody, "Jane Barker," *British Novelists*, 39:24-30.

[3] Lipking, "Aristotle's Sister, p. 77.

[4] S. G., "To the Author," *Love Intrigues: Or, The History of the Amours of Bosvil and Galesia* (London: E. Curll and C. Crownfield, 1713; facsimile, ed. Josephine Grieder [New York: Garland, 1973]), Sig. A[v].

[5] Margaret A. Doody, "Jane Barker," *British Novelists, 1660-1800*, ed. Martin C. Battestin (Detroit, Mich.: Gale, 1985), pp. 27-28. For analysis of the dreams in *Love Intrigues*, see also Doody's "Deserts, Ruins and Troubled Waters: Female Dreams in Fiction and the Development of the Gothic Novel," *Genre* 10 (Winter 1977): 529-72.

[6] Jane Barker, *Exilius or, the Banished Roman* (London: E. Curll, 1715; facsimile, ed. Josephine Grieder [New York: Garland, 1973]), Sig. A2-A2[v].

[7] Doody, "Barker," p. 26.

[8] Jane Barker, *A Patch-Work Screen for the Ladies; or, Love and Virtue Recommended: In a Collection of Instructive Novels* (London: E. Curll, 1723; facsimile, ed. Josephine Grieder [New York: Garland, 1973]), pp. iv-v.

Kathryn R. King (essay date 1993)

SOURCE: "Galesia, Jane Barker, and a Coming to Authorship," in *Anxious Power: Reading, Writing, and Ambivalence in Narrative by Women*, edited by Carol J. Singley and Susan Elizabeth Sweeney, State University of New York Press, 1993, pp. 91-106.

[*In the following essay, King examines what* A Patch-Work Screen for the Ladies *reveals concerning Barker's anxieties about the public's reception of her writing.*]

I

The story told by the poet and novelist Jane Barker, in three autobiographical narratives about her struggle to fashion an identity as a writing woman, is inevitably a study in ambivalence. It is impossible that a woman coming to writing in England in the 1670s and 1680s would not be anxious about her own acts of authorship. But it is hardly surprising that such a woman, talented and stubbornly intelligent, living in relative isolation in rural Lincolnshire, would turn to writing as a way of maintaining, perhaps inventing, a sense of self. Nor is it surprising that she would fantasize about achieving the kind of acclaim enjoyed by a small but visible number of female poets in the generation before her, most conspicuously Katherine Philips ("Orinda"), whose verse seems to have aroused in the teenaged Barker her first desire for literary fame.[1] What *is* surprising is that the three autobiographical novels in which Jane Barker recounts her early history as a writing woman should remain so little known.[2]

The anxieties of authorship exposed in the Galesia trilogy—*Love Intrigues* (1713), *A Patch-work Screen for the Ladies* (1723), and *A Lining for the Patch-Work Screen* (1726)—belong to a cultural moment when, for the first time, the work of an appreciable number of English women began to be published. It is estimated that between 1640 and 1700 the writings of as many as four hundred women found their way into print.[3] These included devotional works, educational theories, religious polemics, lives and letters, household advice, plays, poetry, prose fiction. By the early decades of

EXILIUS:

OR,

The Banish'd ROMAN.

A NEW

ROMANCE.

In Two Parts:

Written

After the Manner of TELEMACHUS,

For the Instruction of

Some Young LADIES of Quality.

By Mrs. JANE BARKER.

LONDON

Printed for E. CURLL at the D l and B b't
againſt St. Dun an's Church in Fleetſtreet.

M DCC XV

Frontispiece and title page of Barker's novel Exilius: or, the Banish'd Roman, A New Romance.

the eighteenth century, growing numbers of women were adding to the increasingly busy traffic in novels and, in ways which we are only now beginning to recognize, shaping the emerging novelistic discourse. Eliza Haywood, Mary Davys, Penelope Aubin, and Mary Hearne (and before them Aphra Behn and Delariviere Manley) were just a few of the women who, spurred by the expansion of the print trade and the new moneymaking possibilities of authorship, lived (at least in part) by the proceeds of novel writing.

Though Barker was herself an innovator in the novel, she came to writing in a less print-aggressive age. She appears to have begun composing verse for her own pleasure while living with her family in rural Lincolnshire, perhaps as early as the late 1660s, and then circulating her work in manuscript among a circle of friends. In 1688, in her mid-thirties, a collection of her verse was published as the first part of **Poetical Recreations.** Not until 1713, a quarter of a century later, would Barker's writing again see print. By then relations among writers, readers, and texts had altered dramatically. In the previous century women rarely wrote for print or for money. (Barker later claimed that the poems in **Poetical Recreations** were published without her consent.)[4] In the manuscript culture to which Barker and other seventeenth-century writers belonged, verse writing was a genteel accomplishment and a sociable act, the products of which were to be shared with friends, in Barker's case a group of Cambridge students. But by 1713, when Barker published her first prose narrative, **Love Intrigues,** professional writers, male and female, sought unknown readers through the impersonal mechanisms of the commercial book trade. The discomforts attendant upon this entry into the marketplace are one source of Barker's ambivalence, which makes her autobiographical Galesia fictions unusually rich texts for the study of anxieties of authorship in an early professional female writer.

The pages which follow focus on the problem of audience in one of these fictions, **A Patch-work Screen for the Ladies** (1723), as a way of charting some of these anxieties. The discussion draws upon Nancy K. Miller's practice of reading narrative as figurative of the "symbolic and material process entailed in becoming a (woman) writer" (129); it argues that *A Patch-work Screen* encodes within itself the story of its own creation and, by implication, the story of how one early eighteenth-century professional writer managed to construct for herself the conditions, psychological and discursive, that made addressing an impersonal readership possible. More specifically, it argues that the complex layerings of female auditors built into the framing fictions of *A Patch-work Screen for the Ladies* attempt to ease the anxieties of authorship thematized in its core narrative.

II

In a brilliant series of essays, Miller demonstrates that the process of coming to writing is usefully understood as a problem of location. Constructing an authorial identity entails locating a place from which to "imagine and image a writing self" (109); it entails also finding a place within the range of public discourses from which to speak and be heard. For women, the process is complicated by two familiar conditions: discourses are gendered, and gender matters for women in ways that it often does not for men. A woman of Barker's generation knew that she could gain approval by confining herself to female discourses—to "lofty Themes of useful Houswifery, / Transcribing old Receipts of Cookery," as in 1703 Sarah Fyge mockingly put it—but she also knew that such approval carries its own dismissal. The dynamic is hilariously invoked in the late eighteenth century by Elizabeth Moody, whose "Sappho," having burnt her books and replaced poetry with cultivation of the culinary arts, discovers that "none but cooks applaud her name [and] naught but recipes her fame."[5] But departures from recipes and the like might arouse contempt, ridicule, or hostility—dismissal of a ruder sort.

In *A Patch-work Screen* the perplexities of location haunt the narrator, Galesia, who looks back on her younger versifying self with the ambiguous feelings of one who grounds her identity in acts of writing but questions the legitimacy of literary activities for women in general. Barker's preoccupation with the female writer's uncertain and contradictory relation to male culture is adumbrated in *Love Intrigues,* the first of the Galesia trilogy. The story, which recounts Galesia's entanglement in a strange and finally unreadable courtship, is centrally concerned with relations between language and interiority as well as with issues of female self-identity. Galesia is forced to mask "with an outside Indifference" (*Love* 19) the realities of her inner life; her speech is broken, false, guarded, faltering. And thus the importance for her of poetry. Poetry offers a space in which to exercise control over the linguistic forms which break apart under the pressure of a code of propriety that requires her words be kept "close Prisoners" (34). In poetry—a private space—she can articulate the desires she must guard against revealing to the world and her unaccountable lover. The privateness of poetry offers momentary release from the bleak disciplines of duplicity, but its separation from public discourses means that Galesia ends up colluding in her own silencing.

The condition of being at once present in, and split off from, one's own acts of writing is more fully developed in *A Patch-work Screen,* especially in those moments when Galesia brings a text before a reader or group of readers. An exemplary instance is the episode concerning her literary correspondence with the group of Cambridge students who offer the intellectual companionship missing in her immediate environs. The scene evoked in a letter from one of these students hints, however, at the problematics of using writing to supply a lack:

> We all return you Thanks for your *Ballad;* to which our Friend *Sam. Setwell,* put a Tune, and we sung it in a Booth merrily, 'till the *Proctor* had like to have Spoil'd the Harmony. But he finding no Female amongst us, drank the innocent Author's Health, and departed. (31)[6]

In this assemblage, Galesia's text is present ("put [to] a Tune") and its author noisily toasted. But the woman herself is not only absent from the scene but firmly excluded; indeed, only upon condition of her continuing exclusion ("he finding no Female amongst us") does authority, in the person of the Proctor, permit the merriment to continue. To the extent that a Cambridge songfest can be thought of as standing for the male-constituted cultural establishment, this scene of collegiate roistering figures the (familiar) relegation of the writing woman to the cultural margins, as well as her split relation to a dominant male culture that celebrates her work but excludes *her* from its precincts.[7]

Another instance of such exclusion is found in Galesia's account of her experience writing within male medical discourses. Her pride in her knowledge of botany, anatomy, physiology, and Latin (still used to encode medical knowledge) reaches a pitch when she discovers that she can pass off as the texts of university-trained doctors prescriptions she has written herself in the male-specialized Latin code—"this being," she notes with satisfaction, "particular in one of my Sex" (4).[8] But she longs, understandably enough, to enjoy recognition for this and other medical accomplishments, as shown in her remarkable poem, "*On the* Apothecaries *Filing my* Recipes *amongst the* Doctors":

> The *Sturdy Gout,* which all Male-Power
>   withstands,
> Is overcome by my soft Female Hands.
> Not *Deb'rah Judith,* or *Semiramis,*

Cou'd boast of Conquest half so great as this;
More than they slew, I save, in this Disease.

(57)

That Galesia's boast of the triumph of her "soft Female Hands" over "all Male-Power" is, at best, a fantasy of female power becomes clear from the narrator's ironic comment:

> Thus, Madam, as People before a Looking-glass, please themselves with their own Shapes and Features, though, perhaps, such as please no body else; just so I *celebrated my own Praise,* according to the Proverb, *for want of good Neighbours to do it for me.* (59)

Galesia's invisibility (except within the self-regarding mirror of her own verse) reproduces in another key her absent presence vis-à-vis the Cambridge students. If literary authority involves the ability to be seen and to be heard in the realm of public discourse, then Galesia's authority is strictly limited: it enacts itself "before a Looking-glass."

Whether Galesia writes *as if male,* using the language and discourses of university-trained men, or *as female,* disengaged from public modes of discourse, the effect is much the same: the female subject is herself invisible, absent, or excluded. Positioned in the contradiction between her inner needs for personal expression and external recognition and a discursive realm that renders her invisible, Galesia experiences divisions that amount at times almost to self-cancellation. Her story is shot through with images of exile, loneliness, alienation, and even dismemberment (most memorably in her tale of a murdered man whose body is hauled up "Piece-meal" from a ditch [sig. A9r]); and her consciousness of herself as a writer oscillates between fantasies of literary achievement and the recognition, by turns sardonic, wistful, resentful, self-mocking, and bemused, of the real slenderness of what she has achieved. Toward the end of *The Lining of the Patch-Work Screen,* the final novel in the trilogy, Galesia relates a bizarre dream. She is led up to the summit of Parnassus to see her poetic idol Orinda (Katherine Philips) crowned "Queen of Female Writers" (174). But Galesia, who had earlier yearned to rise to "fair ORINDA's Height" (*Love* 14), arrives too late to witness the ceremony, and after hiding awhile in the corner is discovered and sent away. Belatedness, banishment, failed aspiration: the vision is a fitting image of an abortive struggle to come fully into authorship.

III

But this is only part of the story. If the story Galesia tells of herself as a writing woman exposes the split between language and interiority, between desire for power and actual powerlessness, the larger narrative in which it is embedded, *A Patch-work Screen for the Ladies,* declares the possibility of patching together the pieces. Crucial to my reading of the narrative as a whole is the framing fiction which comes toward the end of the preface. It stages a reunion between an exiled poet named "Jane Barker" and her old friend Galesia. This meeting of two poets, each an alter ego of the historical Jane Barker (or more precisely, that part of Barker which defined itself as a woman writing), is at once a meeting of two versions of the writing self and of two styles of authorship. Galesia, now a seasoned, wry commentator on her earlier self, represents a style of authorship with its roots in the manuscript culture of the seventeenth century when young women wrote verse for themselves and a circle of friends. The "Jane Barker" who appears in the preface is very much a woman of 1723—urban, briskly ironic, disinclined to indulge in "Romantick" fancies about the poetic vocation. She belongs, indeed, to the new breed of writer, the novel-writing woman who casts a commercial eye on that new breed of reader, the novel-buying public. Galesia emerges as "Jane Barker" 's precursor; and the *other* Jane Barker, the historical author who stages this meeting between two fictionalized alter egos, stands screened somewhere behind it all, simultaneously rehearsing and rewriting her own history as a woman coming to authorship.[9] The conception is dazzling, and as I will now show, contains within itself a radical reimagining of the conditions in which a coming to authorship takes place.

The image of writer-as-Icarus which appears both in Galesia's story and in the framing fiction of the Preface provides an entry into this act of reimagining. In the cautionary tale offered by Galesia's mother in the core narrative, Icarus is a figure for the folly of literary aspirations ("idle Dreams on *Parnassus,* and foolish *Romantick* Flights") as well as their dangers (his "waxen Wings fail'd him so as to let him fall into the Sea" [79-80]). The Preface invokes just such folly when "Jane Barker" concedes (with considerable irony) that her own "high Flight in Favour of the Ladies" has made a "mere *Icarus* of me, melted my Wings, and tumbled me Headlong down, I know not where" (vi). The episode of banishment which now follows strongly resembles—but only up to a point—the scenes of alienation and isolation reiterated within Galesia's narrative. Discovered to have manuscripts of verse in her pockets, "Jane Barker" is thrust out of the "joyful Throng" into which she had tumbled, "every one hunching and pushing me, with Scorn and Derision" (vii). But what comes next brings an end to exile, isolation and freakishness. The banished poet, fleeing this jeering crowd, now comes upon Galesia, who again takes up the life story she began in *Love Intrigues.* And *that* story contains yet another: the story of how Galesia told her story to a kindly aristocratic lady. Working outwards, what we have, finally, is this: Galesia's life story, as told to a fictive Lady, as told to a fictionalized "Jane Barker," as fashioned by a professional author named Jane Barker into a patchwork narrative published under the title *A Patch-work Screen for the Ladies*—a recursive layering of sympathetic listeners which, by framing a space in which tale, teller, and told are at last brought together, revises the plot of female exclusion and isolation in which young Galesia remains confined.

That the release from isolation is linked to a new conception of female authorship is strongly implied by the patchwork analogies which introduce a pattern of needlework symbolism common to women's writing at this time. Similar text/textile equivalences can be traced back at least to 1599, when Mary Sidney, in "To the Thrice-Sacred Queen Elizabeth," described her collaboration with her brother on a translation of the Psalms as a shared textile production: "he did warpe, I weav'd this webbe to end" (89). A half century later another aristocratic writer, Margaret Cavendish, likened the writing of poetry to a "*Spinning* with the *braine*"; while at roughly the same time, on the other side of the Atlantic, Anne Bradstreet sent forth her poems trimmed in "home-spun Cloth." Metaphors such as these, which assimilate an emerging form of female work (authorship) to a familiar domestic one, assert continuities between writing and traditional forms of women's work. By associating the work of the pen with that of the distaff and needle, these early writers found a way to authorize their own acts of authorship.

Read within this intertextual field, the patchwork analogies situate the Galesia/Jane Barker story within the larger story of emergent female authorship. Such, at any rate, is the implication of the preface's enigmatic final paragraph, in which Galesia walks into the text (and perhaps literary history) with legs cramped from "long sitting at her Work." The paragraph, which appears to develop an allegory about a collective female coming to authorship, deserves full quotation:

> When I was got out of this Throng into the open Field, I met with the poor *Galesia,* walking to stretch her Legs, having been long sitting at her Work. With her I renew'd my Old Acquaintance; and so came to know all this Story of her *Patch-Work:* Which if you like, I will get the remaining Part of the *SCREEN;* for they are still at Work: And, upon my Word, I am glad to find the Ladies of *This Age,* wiser than *Those* of the *Former;* when the working of *Point* and curious *Embroidery,* was so troublesome, that they cou'd not take *Snuff* in Repose, for fear of soiling their Work: But in *Patch-Work* there is no Harm done; a smear'd Finger does but add a *Spot* to a *Patch,* or a *Shade* to a *Light-Colour:* Besides, those curious Works were pernicious to the Eyes; they cou'd not see the *Danger themselves* and *their Posterity might be in, a Thousand Years hence, about I know not what.* (viii)

The passage develops a contrast between the work performed by Barker's own generation (patchwork/novel-work) and women's work of the generations before her. (Until our own century, it should be recalled, the word *work* in a female context meant needlework.) The work of these earlier women—"*Point* and curious *Embroidery*"—was elegant but also finicky, anxious, and "pernicious to the Eyes," as opposed to the sloppy but on the whole agreeable work undertaken by Barker's contemporaries, which admits of a smudge (of ink?) here and there: "a smear'd Finger does but add a Spot to a Patch."[10] The allegory remains perplexing in places—I would like to know what is meant by the final assertion that these earlier women "cou'd not see the *Danger themselves* and *their Posterity might be in,*" for example—but it seems evident that its implicit conception of authorship moves beyond a preoccupation with the isolated writing self to assert a larger unity with other writing women and to affirm connections between authorship and shared female experience.

The patchwork frame may also imply new relations between the female author and her reading public. Barker's technical and thematic concern with relations between teller and told—and, by implication, writer and readership—is discernible in the framing device she used ten years earlier in *Love Intrigues.* Galesia tells her story to a companion, Lucasia, who projects the character Galesia's need for an auditor, but in a broader sense the text's need for a sympathetic readership. In choosing to call her by the name used by Katherine Philips to address her best-known female friend, Barker places her narrative within the tradition of chaste female authorship. The choice of name may also point toward Barker's desire to imagine for her work a readership of literary women. The multilayered astold-to structure of *A Patch-work Screen* suggests that the writer is reaching beyond a single listener (Lucasia) to an entire community of auditors—a public comprised in large part of a distinct female readership.

The patchwork screen, arranged by a group of women out of the patches derived from the shared materials of female life, may thus inscribe a distinctively female set of conditions for coming to authorship. Certainly the layering of teller-told relationships constructed in the framing fiction affords the narratorial Galesia the kind of sympathetic audience that proved unavailable or problematic in the context of the life story she now rehearses. If coming to authorship involves a double process of imagining a writing self and finding a discursive place from which that self can speak and be heard, then *A Patch-work Screen for the Ladies* symbolically reenacts such a process, as Galesia finds within an imagined community of patchworking women an end to ostracism, exclusion, loneliness, and self-division, and then goes on to tell her story to her literary successor, "Jane Barker." *A Patch-work Screen* is finally a story of empowerment, of becoming present, of patching together the pieces.

IV

That said, I begin to wonder if my own high flight in favor of *A Patch-work Screen for the Ladies* has made a "mere Icarus" of me. Am I burdening a simple framing device with more than is "really" there? Constructing out of what amounts to a narrative convention a Utopian vision of gynocentric creativity? Sentimentalizing women and professional authorship in ways that Barker herself would fail to comprehend or appreciate? Possibly. The view of women she presents is in fact anything but sentimental: Galesia is sharply critical of female frivolity, vanity, shallowness, indifference to the life of the mind, and is happy enough to dissociate herself whenever possible from the general run of womankind. And my impulse to celebrate Barker's coming to authorship is tempered by the reflection that Barker herself may have felt something less than rapture at finding herself late in life (she was at least seventy when she published *A Patch-work Screen*) required to face the indignities of the London book trade, especially as carried on by her publisher, the notorious Edmund Curll, already known for his "scurrilous and sensational publications" (McBurney 386). Barker may have derived considerably less satisfaction from the patched-together screen she placed between herself and possible economic distress than we take in her accomplishment.

Jane Barker's feelings about her role as a professional writer remain finally unknown, but from her texts we have much to learn about what it has meant historically for women to come to writing. I would suggest by way of concluding that Myra Jehlen's understanding of the process by which women writers "create their creativity" accounts for some of the resonance of the Galesia fictions. Jehlen argues that the female coming to writing, often thought of in largely psychological terms, is "also a conceptual and linguistic act: the construction of an enabling relationship with a language that of itself would deny [women] the ability to use it creatively" (583). We might, following Jehlen, think of *A Patch-work Screen* as a text revelatory of the activities undertaken prior to its creation, a record of the process by which its author imagined a network of enabling relationships—with language, but also with traditions of female culture as they authorize writing, and with female audiences as they offer a place in which to speak and be heard. It would be too simple to say that Barker argues for sexual separatism or valorizes a distinct female subculture—though it seems clear that literary empowerment is for her unimaginable outside of female contexts and the connectedness they provide. Rather, in *A Patch-work Screen* she claims her own creativity by imagining the conditions under which her work is to be produced and read. This

too is a revisionary project, and perhaps a collaborative one as well: the screen, as Barker says in her preface, is not yet finished, the patchworkers are "still at Work."[11]

Notes

[1] For a valuable discussion of Philips and the literary contexts of seventeenth-century poetry by women, see Mermin.

[2] Jeslyn Medoff discovered that Barker was baptized in 1652; she was thus in her sixties and seventies when the Galesia fictions were published (Greer et al. 354). For introductory discussions of the fictions, see Spencer 62-70 and Williamson 244-51. The perception that Barker is a key figure for the study of women's entry into the literary culture is beginning to gain currency; see Donovan for an important account of the role of *A Patch-work Screen* in the emergence of the novel.

[3] Wilson and Warnke xi. For an account of female publication in the seventeenth century, see Crawford.

[4] See Medoff's note in Greer et al. 361. *Poetical Recreations* is briefly discussed in Hobby 159-62 and Williamson 102-07.

[5] The Fyge citation is from "The Liberty" (Greer et al. 347). Moody's 1798 poem, "Sappho Burns her Books and Cultivates the Culinary Arts," includes this invocation to the "Goddess of Culinary Art": "Teach me more winning arts to try, / To salt the ham, to mix the pie" (Lonsdale 406). The versified recipe is one of many poetic genres represented in *A Patch-work Screen.* My favorite of these "Receipts," one for French soup, begins with this splendid line: "Take a large Barn-door Cock, and all his Bones break" (109).

[6] Here and in a few other passages, I silently reverse italics for ease of reading.

[7] The Proctor suggestively prefigures the Beadle in Woolf's *A Room of One's Own.* I owe the notion of duality developed here to Jacobus's discussion of Woolf 59-61.

[8] The original erroneously reads "being in particular."

[9] This pattern, Mason argues, is fundamental to female autobiographies: such splitting and doubling appears to construct the audience which disclosure of female self-identity depends upon. Recent studies have arrived at similar conclusions. See the essays collected by Brodzki and Schenck, and Benstock (especially Friedman).

[10] This detail may also point toward ambivalence about the sullying effects of writing for the marketplace. It is

perhaps pertinent that when Galesia is banished from Parnassus in her dream, she is given a bag of gold.

[11] I thank Ruth Looper, Jes Medoff, Sarah Palmer, and Ellen Wright-Vance for their very useful responses to this essay.

Works Cited

Barker, Jane. *The Lining of the Patch-Work Screen: Design'd for the Farther Entertainment of the Ladies.* London: Printed for A. Bettesworth, 1726.

———. *Love Intrigues.* Ed. Josephine Grieder. New York: Garland, 1973.

———. *A Patch-work Screen for the Ladies.* Ed. Josephine Grieder. New York: Garland, 1973.

Benstock, Shari, ed. *The Private Self: Theory and Practice of Women's Autobiographical Writings.* Chapel Hill: U of North Carolina P, 1988.

Brodzki, Bella, and Celeste Schenck, eds. *Life/Lines: Theorizing Women's Autobiography.* Ithaca: Cornell UP, 1988.

Cavendish, Margaret. *Poems and Fancies.* Menton, Yorkshire: Scolar P, 1972.

Crawford, Patricia. "Women's Published Writings 1600-1700." *Women in English Society 1500-1800.* Ed. Mary Prior. New York: Methuen, 1985. 211-82.

Donovan, Josephine. "Women and the Rise of the Novel: A Feminist-Marxist Theory." *Signs* 16 (1991): 441-62.

Friedman, Susan Stanford. "Women's Autobiographical Selves: Theory and Practice." Benstock 34-62.

Greer, Germaine, et al., eds. *Kissing the Rod: An Anthology of Seventeenth-Century Women's Verse.* New York: Noonday-Farrar Straus Giroux, 1988.

Hobby, Elaine. *Virtue of Necessity: English Women's Writing 1649-88.* Ann Arbor: U of Michigan P, 1989.

Jacobus, Mary. "The Difference of View." *The Feminist Reader: Essays in Gender and the Politics of Literary Criticism.* Ed. Catherine Belsey and Jane Moore. New York: Basil Blackwell, 1989. 49-62.

Jehlen, Myra. "Archimedes and the Paradox of Feminist Criticism." *Signs* 6 (1981): 575-601.

Lonsdale, Roger, ed. *Eighteenth-Century Women Poets: An Oxford Anthology.* Oxford: Oxford UP, 1989.

Mason, Mary G. "The Other Voice: Autobiographies of Women Writers." Brodzki and Schenck 19-44.

McBurney, William H. "Edmund Curll, Mrs. Jane Barker, and the English Novel." *Philological Quarterly* 37 (1958): 385-99.

Mermin, Dorothy. "Women Becoming Poets: Katherine Philips, Aphra Behn, Anne Finch." *ELH* 57 (1990): 335-55.

Miller, Nancy K. *Subject to Change: Reading Feminist Writing.* New York: Columbia UP, 1988.

Sidney, Mary. *The Triumph of Death and Other Unpublished and Uncollected Poems.* Ed. Gary Waller. Salzburg: Universität Salzburg, 1977.

Spencer, Jane. "Creating the Woman Writer: The Autobiographical Works of Jane Barker." *Tulsa Studies in Women's Literature* 2 (1983): 165-81.

———. *The Rise of the Woman Novelist: From Aphra Behn to Jane Austen.* New York: Basil Blackwell, 1986.

Williamson, Marilyn L. *Raising Their Voices: British Women Writers, 1650-1750.* Detroit: Wayne State UP, 1990.

Wilson, Katharina M. and Frank J. Warnke. Introduction. *Women Writers of the Seventeenth Century.* Ed. Katharina M. Wilson and Frank J. Warnke. Athens: U Georgia P, 1989. xi-xxiii.

Kathryn R. King (essay date 1994)

SOURCE: "The Unaccountable Wife and Other Tales of Female Desire in Jane Barker's *A Patch-Work Screen for the Ladies,*" in *The Eighteenth Century: Theory and Interpretation*, Vol. 35, No. 2, Summer, 1994, pp. 155-72.

[*In the following essay, King discusses female-female relationships depicted in* A Patch-Work Screen for the Ladies. *She notes that what may have been intended by Barker as a warning to women who experience same-sex desires can instead be interpreted as criticism of a patriarchal society.*]

> —and she said, We all join'd with her Husband to make her miserable, by removing from her, the only Friend she had in the World; and passionately swore by Him that made her, that if we combin'd to send the Woman away, she would go with her.
>
> *A Patch-work Screen for the Ladies,* 101

1

The episode of female homoerotic desire which is the subject of this essay is a valuable text for study of the making of modern sexualities. The story of The Unaccountable Wife, one of several inset-tales in Jane Barker's 1723 novel *A Patch-work Screen for the Ladies,* tells of a woman who defies the authority of her husband, the importunities of her family, and the claims of her class to elope with the person she calls her "only Friend," a female servant; the two women disappear into an unnarrated (and unnarratable) space. In pursuing a desire that takes her outside the heterosexual social order, the Unaccountable Wife chooses a destiny that can be enacted only outside the borders of Barker's text: in 1723 a story of lesbian desire could scarcely be narrated. But readers today can find in the oblique and ambiguous story of an Unaccountable Wife a representation of a lesbian relationship before a lesbian identity "officially" existed or before woman's desire for woman had a name.[1]

The inset-tale is one of very few accounts of female same-sex desire authored by an early modern woman—though not, apparently, a woman who would today identify herself as a lesbian.[2] As such it has much to tell us about how female same-sex desire was perceived and (probably) misrecognized in the early eighteenth century. The tale also brings into view an early moment in the process of broad cultural change which, over the course of the eighteenth century, resulted in the emergence of the modern sex/gender system. The perception that the human being is "most essentially a sexual subject"[3] is, as Nancy Armstrong and others have argued, relatively recent, the product of what Armstrong analyzes as the displacement of hierarchies of class and status onto an emerging binary system for sex and gender. My discussion of the representation of lesbian desire in The Unaccountable Wife reads this desire in relation to the process by which sexuality came to be understood as—and I quote Thomas Laqueur drawing upon Foucault—"a singular and all-important attribute with a specific object—the *opposite* sex."[4] By the close of the century, a class-structured world which thought sexuality in terms of social hierarchies had given way to a gender-structured world in which sexuality was thought in terms of asymmetrical sex and gender binaries (hetero/homosexual, male/female). Heirs to this gender-structured world, we take it as given that sexuality and particularly sexual object-choice organize a great, if not the greatest, part of who we are, what we feel, and how we act with others—organize, that is to say, the "natural" core of personal identity.

But the story of The Unaccountable Wife reminds us that it was not always so. In 1723, in a world still understood more in terms of class hierarchies than gender opposition, Jane Barker could recount the story of a woman whom many today would call a lesbian without, it seems, being especially alarmed by its (homo) sexual implications.[5] Not that she was unmindful of them: I am persuaded that Barker recognized the

homoerotic nature of her material, though she certainly attached to it meanings other than those a modern reader would. As products of the reconfigurations of class, gender, and sexuality summarized above, we attach to sexuality and sexual object-choice a primacy absent in Barker's text, where what I would call the tale's lesbian content is filtered through a class-based, hierarchical mode of viewing the world. Form the gendered perspective of Now, the tale's homoeroticism is the vivid figure in the carpet; but viewed through the eyes of Barker's narrator—the perspective of Then—figure and ground begin to reverse and the lesbian aspect comes to seem at once there and not there: the result, one might say, of trying to read a pre-gendered figure through a post-gendered lens.[6]

This essay considers some ambiguities of one early modern representation of female sexuality. It aims to unsettle faith in the inevitability of our present sex/gender arrangements and in this way contribute to the feminist assault on what Armstrong has called the "reigning metaphysics of sexuality"[7]—the notion that gender and sexuality are natural, prior, essential, "already-there." The discussion will also, I hope, contribute to a more exact appreciation of Barker's role in the "rise" of the novel.[8] My method is to play off one another the differing meanings generated by the story when the transgressive desire that drives its plot is variously framed. The essay begins by situating the story in the context of the novel as a whole and in the still larger context of Jane Barker's project as a novelist. It then considers the tale's homoerotic content.[9] Drawing on the findings of gay and lesbian historians, I attempt to reconstruct what Barker and her first readers would have made of the "unaccountable" attachment of one woman to another. I then read for the gendered power struggles which presently command intense attention in feminist literary and cultural studies; the tale emerges as a site of resistance to the ideology of compulsory heterosexuality as well as to the masculinist culture's powers of representation. Finally, I consider ways in which the tale resists my feminist/lesbian reading. What does it mean, I ask, that the text does not share my fascination with its homoerotic content?

2

A Patch-work Screen for the Ladies is Barker's fullest articulation of a preoccupation that I see as central to her project as a novelist: an attempt to renarrate the exemplary female life around the idea of celibacy and the single life. Preference for the single life is something of a convention in fiction of the period; but unlike novels in which this preference functions as shorthand for the moral excellence of a woman destined either for marriage, seduction, or rape (*Clarissa* most famously), *A Patch-work Screen* is a serious inquiry into the possibilities of the single life for a woman.[10] Barker began working with this theme as early as *Love Intrigues* (1713), the first of three narratives comprising her autobiographical Galesia trilogy.[11] The courtship plot put into play in *Love Intrigues* is dismantled over the course of the novella, thus clearing the way for the more radical renarrativizing of the female life she would undertake a decade later in its sequel, *A Patch-work Screen.* In this 1723 novel she structures out of the materials of her own life and writings (the patches of the title) a new pattern (a "patch-work") for the exemplary female life. Barker uses two linked strategies. First, she displaces onto a series of inset tales elements of the (discredited) courtship plot. Then, in the space thus freed in the center of the narrative she places a single woman, Galesia, whose life-story exemplifies successful disengagement from the courtship plot and the (hetero) sexual ideology whose paradigms of female vulnerability it encodes.[12] (Hence its crucial opening gesture: "Having disingag'd my Thoughts from Bosvil," Galesia says.[13]) The elements of this life—solitude, study, contemplation, writing, and celibacy—are drawn from a classical retirement ideal which also supplied paradigms for exemplary female lives in the verse of women poets of the time.[14] Based upon a conservative social ideal, deriving authority from its classical roots and more recent royalist uses, the retirement ideal offered women what appears to have been an empowering alternative to the models of amatory destiny inscribed in courtship plots.

Amatory writers such as Aphra Behn, Delariviere Manley, and Mary Hearne develop plots around an ideal of marriage for love and, as Marilyn Williamson has observed, create within their narratives a separate erotic space for privileged male-female couples.[15] Barker, in contrast, creates in her work a kind of counter-courtship plot in which the narrator-heroine (Galesia) undergoes initiation into the perils of the heterosexual world while simultaneously removing herself (or being removed) from its networks of sexual exchange as one by one male relations—first brother, then father—and prospective suitors die off (one is executed for highway robbery; another commits suicide). By the end Galesia-the-heroine has successfully established a personal identity independent of patriarchal lineage bonds (marriage, family, children) and has disentangled herself from the diffusive psychosexual bonds that go by the name of love and romance. In *A Patch-work Screen* the exemplary celibate heroine ends her story neither wed, raped, seduced, abandoned, or desperately unhappy.

In Barker's representation of the single life the inset-tales play an important role. Taken as a group these insets—with the crucial exception of the tale of The Unaccountable Wife, to which I will soon turn—serve as reminders of the courtship plot which Galesia's core narrative rewrites. Many tell of female sexual vulner-abilities, of women who fall victim to an incursive

male sexuality that is always darkly present at the edge of Galesia's life story and that breaks into the text in the form of tales told by (or about) other women—tales concerned with pregnancy, venereal disease, bigamy, debauched innocence, untrustworthy father figures. Turning on scenarios of seduction, abandonment, and conjugal disappointment, they represent the more familiar trajectories of the heroine's destiny, textualized maps of the heterosexual road not taken.

These tales of female desire and female discontent act as moral warnings, as one might expect; but despite the strong monitory tone, they are by no means simply or straightforwardly didactic. They stand, in fact, in complex relation to the core narrative and appear to speak the ambivalence which (perhaps inevitably) attended Barker's novelistic project. Though critical of patriarchal sexual mores, Barker shared with a number of other women writers of her generation a rooted conservativism on social as well as religious and political matters. However searching her scrutiny of woman's condition in male-dominated society, however dim her view of the possibilities for female happiness under patriarchy, she does not contest the legitimacy of male authority or question the presumption of women's natural inferiority. Instead she devises strategies of accommodation which enable a woman to wrest for herself a modicum of autonomy while leaving the system of male domination in place. Like Mary Astell, another philosophically conservative but temperamentally independent woman of her generation,[16] Barker found that the single life enabled her to remove herself from the complex demands of male control, as well as offering (to her stand-in Galesia anyway) freedom from the endless distractions of (hetero) sexual obsession.

In *A Patch-work Screen* Barker was, then, in the difficult position of endorsing as exemplary the single life while continuing to affirm a conservative value system which placed matrimony, procreation, and female subordination at the center of the well-ordered society. To the extent that the single life shares in the virtue and moral excellence conventionally associated with female celibacy, it is unproblematic; but in *A Patch-work Screen* celibacy is tied as well to unquestionably suspect inclinations on the part of the heroine, among them desire for sexual autonomy, social independence, private space, and a life of the mind—desires that point in the direction of the self-seeking individualism that Barker elsewhere condemns. The parade of heterosexual disasters set before the reader in the insets functions in part then to shore up Barker's brief against the courtship plot and the view of female destiny it inscribes, and thus legitimate Galesia's (and Barker's) own faintly dubious life choice.

Which brings us to The Unaccountable Wife. Among the several inset-tales, this one stands alone in its emphatic rejection of the heterosexual order. It concerns a woman—possibly an allegorical version of Galesia herself—who fashions her own destiny in determined opposition to her culture's codes of compulsory heterosexuality, choosing penury, derision, and exile in order to live out her desire for a woman. In telling the story of a wife who rejects submission to her husband's authority, Galesia-the-narrator is thus rehearsing a version of her own dilemma: that of a marriageable young woman who, by her own admission, had conceived a "secret Disgust against Matrimony" (80). But Galesia's "secret Disgust" is recast in the form of a far more transgressive refusal. For the Unaccountable Wife not only refuses her husband; not only defies kin, community, and ultimately the Crown; not only chooses what amounts to social nonbeing rather than continue in her marriage: she chooses for her partner another woman. The wife's refusal of the heterosexual social order stages, then, an extreme version of the more hesitant sexual withdrawal enacted by Galesia in the core narrative. The plot of this inset-tale, which I shall now take up, may be said to figure the ambivalences of a single woman who chooses to live—and represent—her life in opposition to the class-gender codes of her time.

3

The story concerns a curious *ménage à trois* which turns out to be less, or more—at any rate other—than it appears. For years husband, wife, and female servant share a bed; both women bear him children.[17] Community gossip casts the wife in the role of victim who acquiesces in what amounts to an at-home extramarital sexual affair instigated and sustained by the husband. The narrative begins at the point where the husband, tired of this arrangement and increasingly unwilling to bear the expense of his illegitimate children, asks the narrator's mother to help him send servant and brood back to her parish. To the astonishment of everyone, the wife proclaims the banished servant her "only Friend" and then, to even greater astonishment, follows the servant into the country, refusing to return even when offered a pension by the queen. For the remainder of her life, we are told, she supports the servant and her children by begging in the streets.

Questions abound. What took place in the conjugal bed when the threesome bedded down each night? Were the two women sexually active with one another during the triangulated phase of their relationship? Did they later become lovers? Did the servant (a muted presence in the story) return the Wife's passion? What kind of passion are we talking about anyway? Was one or both of these women a "lesbian"? On these points the text is frustratingly silent. The narrator, perplexed by the strange story she tells, makes no attempt to specify the nature of its enigmatic female relation. Her discourse is permeated instead by the question *how*. *How* could the wife willingly leave behind dignity,

honor, wealth, status, privilege—not to mention husband and home? *How* could she, in effect, choose social nonbeing? The question *why* anyone would behave in so puzzling a fashion is not pursued by the narrator, who apparently regards the wife's actions as proceeding from a species of desire so bizarre as to baffle understanding. She calls the wife an "infatuated Creature" whose "unaccountable" behavior inspires "amazement." The narrator returns again and again to her sense of bewildered amazement: the wife inspires "great amazement," "the greatest amazement possible"; her behavior is "unheard-of," "impossible," "unaccountable," "strange," "extraordinary," "incredible," "amazing." Nor is the Lady who listens to the story and provides the final comment any more precise. She concludes merely that the Unaccountable Wife must have been "under some Spell or Inchantment" to have behaved "in so strange a manner" (105).

If the discourse of the narrator assigns the behavior of the strangely besotted Wife to the realm of the "unheard-of" and "unaccountable," a host of modern readers, myself among them, would be quick to venture an explanation. Surely we are looking here at the action of sexual desire: what else could explain behavior otherwise so bizarre? In our complacent faith in modern sexual enlightenment we might even assume that neither Barker nor her narrator could recognize the homoeroticism which strikes us as powerfully explanatory. Since, as will be seen in the next section, (mis)recognition is an important element in the range of meanings generated by the tale, we should now consider more closely the question of how Barker and her contemporaries might have read the sexual dimension of this female relation.

Historians of lesbianism agree that there existed in the early eighteenth century no public identity or social role for a woman who chooses to be in erotic or sexual relationships with other women;[18] there is evidence for the beginnings of such a public identity starting around mid-century,[19] but in 1723 the codes for thinking a woman we would now call a lesbian did not exist, any more than the name did. This does not mean there occurred no behavior that would now be regarded as expressing female same-sex desire—though, as Martha Vicinus has observed, such desire might have been differently interpreted at the time. Vicinus has identified four main paradigms by which visible female same-sex desire was constructed in the late seventeenth and early eighteenth century; each, as she points out, is tied to the social class of the women involved: 1) "passing" or cross-dressed women, often of the working classes;[20] 2) "mannish" women, also usually working-class; 3) bisexual or "occasional lover of women" of the aristocracy; and 4) romantic friends, usually of the middle classes.[21]

As a cross-class relationship, the wife-servant relation fits none of these categories; yet class difference may have disposed Barker's contemporaries to imagine (or assume) sexual involvement on the part of the two women. Work on male-male relations in the early modern period suggests, first, that sexual desire was often entangled in class difference and, second, that what we call sexual identity was constructed largely in terms of class rather than sexual-object choice.[22] It is possible that research on female same-sex relations will yield similar conclusions. We should also keep in mind the tendency among members of the upper and middling classes to regard servants (potentially at least) as sexual commodities. Fiction of the time abounds with (heterosexual) examples of servants figuring as objects of desire for upper-class women, coachmen and footmen recurring with especial frequency.[23] One recalls, for example, the Laputan Court Lady whose tale of desire in Book III of *Gulliver's Travels* (1726) duplicates in certain respects that of Barker's Unaccountable Wife when she steals off to live in penurious but presumably robust sexual happiness with an "old deformed Footman." Given the well-established convention of the servant as willing (and often opportunistic) instrument of upper-class sexual pleasure,[24] Barker's readers may have expected sexual desire on the part of the wife and mistress. And it would have required little imagination to see the servant—because she is, after all, a servant—as a sexual opportunist willing to trade her body for material security, for the clothes, fuel, money the wife is in fact shown to provide. That the text is never explicit on this matter may be evidence that it did not need to be.

In other ways the text hints at the nature of the wife's transgressive desire. The narrator's characterization of the wife as given to emotional excess (her declarations of loyalty to the servant are outbursts of "Passion," "violent oaths"; have an "Air of Vehemency") suggests the lustfulness with which female same-sex desire is often associated in contemporary accounts.[25] It also seems likely that early readers would have seen in the obsessive behavior of the wife something not unlike what Lawrence Stone has identified as the condition of mental derangement which in the eighteenth century went by the name of being "cunt-struck": "this was assumed," Stone writes, "to be a force operating outside the bounds of marriage, something for which the man in its grip was prepared to abandon all other obligations, responsibilities and interests—work, home, wife, children, friends, reputation, everything."[26] Substitute *woman* for *man,* and *husband* for *wife,* and you have a startlingly close synopsis of the main action of the inset.

Moreover, in the physical description of the wife there are some faint hints of hermaphroditism, a biological condition which in the early eighteenth century was often associated with both same-sex desire and strong sexual appetite: hermaphroditism in a person predominantly female was thought to be accompanied by both active sexuality and a predilection for other women.[27] I am thinking of the description of the Wife as ill-

favored—"her Person was not at all agreeable" (97)—and, more tellingly, as possessed of "Imperfections, and Deformity" (98). The language may imply a somewhat mannish appearance and may even hint that, genitally speaking, the Wife occupies a kind of anatomical middle ground. If her "Imperfections" and "Deformity" are intended to hint at the physical irregularities (masculine appearance, enlarged clitoris, or both) thought to constitute female-hermaphroditism, then they would have coded her as the kind of woman in whom one expects to find desire for her own sex. Admittedly evidence of such deliberate coding is slight and ambiguous, at best;[28] and the text contains none of the markers of same-sex desire that in sensation-seeking texts flag a woman as possessing "unnatural" or transgressive sexual proclivities: no "leathern cylinders" or "Signor Dildoes," not so much as a hint of the apparition of male-impersonative sex that both amused and horrified the early eighteenth-century.[29] But such markers are hardly to be expected in an account of transgressive sexual desire which seeks neither to sensationalize nor to trivialize its subject.

4

Read for its protolesbian content, as I now propose to do, the story of the Unaccountable Wife emerges as a refusal of heterosexuality compelling in its insistence upon female same-sex desire and in its exposure of the workings of heterosexist power regimes. Read as a scene of misrecognition, the tale becomes a striking example of the way, in Judith Butler's words, the "ambiguities and incoherences" within a multiplicity of sexual practices—heterosexual, homosexual, bisexual—are "suppressed and redescribed within the reified framework of the disjunctive and asymmetrical binary of masculine/feminine."[30]

A feminist/lesbian reading might begin by observing that the text is careful to distinguish the female relation at its core—enigmatic, undecidable, but unquestionably "there"—from the heterosexist misrepresentations that various onlookers impose upon it. (These onlookers are kin and members of the community whose commentaries upon the *ménage à trois* constitute an important layer of the complex narrative structure.) The action of the story lays bare the distance between the interpretations of the patriarchal community and the actual (if occluded) text of female desire which the community persistently misreads. The inevitable gap between representation and reality, between "seeing-as and seeing" as Laqueur has put it, functions here to make visible the discrepancy between dominant phallocentric assumptions about female sexuality and the muted realities of female homoerotic desire.

When the wife elopes with the servant, she makes ludicrous the readings produced by the "Friends, Neighbours, and Acquaintance" who refuse to believe that a woman would forsake wealth, home, husband, family, and community to live with another woman. Governed by phallocentric logic, they insist upon reading the *ménage à trois* in terms of male domination and desire: "All this [the *ménage*, including its unusual sleeping arrangement] her Friends knew, or at least suspected; but thought it Complaisance, not Choice in her; and that she consider'd her own Imperfections, and Deformity; and therefore, was willing to take no Notice of her Husband's Fancy in the Embraces of this Woman her Servant" (98). The *husband* must have coerced his wife to put up with so outlandish a relation. *He* must have compelled her to put up with the woman whose body he fancied. The entire arrangement must be "Complaisance, not Choice" in her. When the husband attempts to convince the narrator's mother of his wife's vehement attachment to the woman widely assumed to be his mistress, even he meets with incredulity: "Can you imagine me so stupid," the mother bursts out, "as to believe your Wife can persist in such a Contradiction of Nature? It is impossible a Wife should oppose her Husband's Desire in parting with such a Woman" (99). Even when the wife elopes with the servant—an act which one might have thought would unsettle even the most entrenched phallocentric assumptions—the community continues to believe that the husband is somehow behind it all: "there arose a Murmuring," reports the narrator, "as if he had made his Wife away; and when he told them the manner of her Departure, they would not believe him, the thing in itself being so incredible" (102). When after the husband's death the wife still clings to the servant, the community's capacity for interpretation collapses. Deprived of the explanatory fiction of male desire and female "Complaisance," the wife's behavior—perplexing, singular, baffling, perverse as it had been all along—becomes "unaccountable."

The tale, then, exposes simultaneously the fiction of the enchanting phallus and the inadequacy of what Joan deJean calls a culture's "fictions of the feminine"—its "received ideas about female desire, its expression, its plot, and its fate."[31] It shows most emphatically how various "readers" within the boundaries of the tale struggle to make what they see fit what they believe to be true about female nature and desire, about the inevitability of male sexual dominance and female submission. Yet events expose a slippage between their assumptions and the actualities of female desire. What had been read as *his* desires turn out to have been *the wife's;* and when the doubled male-female bond is replaced by a single female-female one (with the husband left out altogether) the fiction that a man is the centrally meaningful fact in the women's lives explodes, and what remains is a discourse subversive of those cultural "fictions of the feminine."

Just how subversive can be gauged by comparing the relationship between the two women with that typically presented in pornography of the period. In male pornographic fantasies women's desire for women flourishes in environments from which men are absent—convents, brothels, girl's schools, seraglios, and the like, the assumption being that sex between women is a weak substitute for the "real" thing. The same assumption lies behind the pornographic convention by which female lovemaking is presented as prologue to "proper" sexual congress,[32] implying once again that woman's desire for woman occurs in the space created by masculine absence and that such desire will—upon happy discovery of the penis or renewed acquaintance with it—resolve itself into a dear girlish memory. Such is the case, for example, in *Fanny Hill:* Fanny's interest in lesbian sex wilts at first sight of a penis.[33] From such phallocentric assumptions The Unaccountable Wife departs fully and conspicuously. Husband and penis could scarcely be more present: after all, he shares a bed with the two women, and we learn early in the text that each has had children by him. It is all the more striking, then, that the phallic nexus—imagined to be primary, compelling, and all-explanatory—gives way to the female bond. The relationship between the two women, unaccountable though it might be, must be read as a rejection of—not a prelude to—the "real" thing.

5

My feminist/lesbian reading ignores, unfortunately, a crucial element of the inset-tale: the narrator. If instead of homoeroticism one foregrounds the narrator and *her* reading of events, then the lesbianism—at first so sharp and self-evident, so very much *there*—begins to fade and blur, to seem at once there and not there. This odd "there-not-there" quality is registered by the rhetoric of disapprobation employed by the narrator. Her language seems at first charged with the kind of condemnatory energy often generated by instances of what is deemed female sexual misconduct (Fielding's *The Female Husband,* written only two decades later, offers many examples).[34] The Unaccountable Wife is "a Shame to Woman-kind" who has "offended God, disgrac'd her Family, scandaliz'd her Neighbours" (100); she possesses "an Interiour thoroughly degenerated" (100); her behavior is a "Contradiction of Nature" (99). To the modern ear a rhetoric turning on references to shame, offence, disgrace, scandal, degeneration, and the unnatural resonates with specifically sexual disapproval. Yet returned to the context of the story, the disapproval is seen to belong to an earlier understanding of what is and is not "natural," and one begins to realize that the narrator's oft-proclaimed amazement is much more than a response to sexual improprieties: what is unaccountable about the wife, what makes her at once a puzzle and a "Shame to Woman-kind" is not only, as it turns out, her fierce and even obsessive attachment to another woman. It is the fact that the other woman is a servant.

My own fascination with what I regard as the story's protolesbian content is simply not shared by the narrator. Where I see resistance to an oppressive masculinist order, the narrator sees a dangerous threat to a social system that depends upon continued subordination of the "lower orders"; where I see (and want to celebrate) homoerotic desire, the narrator sees (and roundly condemns) a confusion of mistress-servant roles. In the description which follows the attention of the disgusted narrator is fixed on the spectacle of role inversions—on the mistress cleaning, washing, and scouring while the "vile Wretch" (97) who should be doing the common household work dawdles about at her pleasure:

> [the mistress] was extremely kind to this Woman, to a Degree unheard-of; became a perfect Slave to her, and, as if she the Servant, instead of the Mistress, did all the Household-Work, made the Bed, clean'd the House, wash'd the Dishes; nay, farther than so, got up in the Morning, scour'd the Irons, made the Fire, &c. leaving this vile Strumpet in Bed with her Husband; for they lay all Three together every Night. (98)

Notice that the (presumed) sexual improprieties of the threesome ("for they lay all Three together every Night") amount to little more than an afterthought.

Given the way dress "speaks" the symbolic relations among class, power, and the social order in the early eighteenth century,[35] it is scarcely surprising that abhorrence of the "vile" servant would emerge most powerfully in the moment in which, decked out in the mistress's clothes ("very good lac'd Linnen, having clean Gloves on her Hands"), she is found perched on "a handsome Velvet Chair" while the wife washes dishes. The "violent Passion" (99) that the sight of this affront to the social order provokes in the mother testifies to the alarmed tenacity with which the tale as a whole thinks itself in terms of class distinctions. The events which in my reading expose and disrupt masculine hegemony come out, when filtered through the narrator's class-based conceptual lens, as the story of an uppity, usurping servant and her strangely irresponsible mistress. The wife's refusal of heterosexuality (to return to my idiom) is thus cast primarily in terms of a transgression against class hierarchies, and whatever liberatory energies might have been set into play get lost in a haze of narratorial amazement. For all its potentially subversive implications, the inset-tale must be seen, finally, as affirming a fundamentally conservative, if somewhat restive, commitment to the existing social order.

6

What, we might now speculate, did Jane Barker think she was doing when she included in *A Patch-work Screen for the Ladies* this tale of The Unaccountable

Wife? My sense is that she set out more or less consciously to demonstrate in cautionary-tale fashion the dangerous consequences of following one's own will; but in the process of telling the story of a woman who, in pursuit of her own desires, slips free of the "natural" submission of wife to husband, she created, probably unwittingly, a tale which can be read without strain as a fable of resistance to compulsory heterosexuality. There is no way of knowing, of course, whether the story of a woman's attachment to her servant offers a glimpse of lesbian desire—though I believe that it does, and that the inset is a fragment from lesbian prehistory—but whatever the nature of their relation, the layers of suppression and redescription (to use Judith Butler's terms) which surround it suggest an allegory for the way misrecognition has rendered lesbian existence invisible over the centuries. Within the inset, as within the story told by early modern culture about itself, woman's desire for woman could appear only in oblique, ambiguous, and fragmentary forms. With no place in the received narratives of female deshe and behavior, the "lesbian" would have been, culturally speaking, unaccountable.[36] Her story could enact itself—unspoken, unrepresented—only outside the borders of the cultural text.

The relative indifference of the text to its protolesbian elements belongs in part to the failure of early eighteenth-century culture to imagine non-phallic forms of sexual pleasure.[37] Barker's care to expose as dead wrong the community's phallocentric readings of the menage-à-trois contains the beginnings of a critique of patriarchal culture's blindness to forms of female desire which exist apart from procreation or the desiring male. She seems almost to suggest that so long as the phallus is allowed to determine and define what counts as sexual desire, many of women's sexual energies—including desire for women—will remain disregarded and unnarratable. But it would be wrong to think of the tale as sexually liberatory in any modern sense or as celebratory of transgressive desires. Indeed, in showing the cost of the wife's choice of an existence so far removed from anything recognizably suitable for someone of her gender and class, the inset operates in some ways as a cautionary tale warning of the perils of self-seeking individualism and defiance of the rules of patriarchy.

The fact that the tale can generate so many contradictory readings may express, finally, divisions inherent in Barker's desire to maintain the social status quo with its conservative view of woman's properly subordinate role and at the same time construct less oppressive narratives of selfhood for women. These divisions are figured in the simultaneously compelling and frightening behavior of the wife. We have already seen that on one level the wife's flight from the heterosexual order projects Galesia-the-narrator's ambivalence toward the single life she has chosen, at once expressing and disowning her dissatisfactions with men, their sexual demands, and the marriage market they control.[38] On another level the wife figures the anxieties generated by Barker's novelistic commitment to narrativizing a female life which achieves meaning outside the customary heterosexual contexts organized around men, marriage, and procreation. The wife emerges on this level as an allegorical version of Jane Barker the novelist: in choosing to do what she will with her own body and desires, in choosing to live outside the bounds of cultural convention and patriarchal authority, she figures at once Barker's novelistic departures from the standard plots of female selfhood and the cost of departure. Thus the deformities and imperfections of the wife, the censure and ostracism into which her transgressive desires take her: a fable, if you will, for the perils awaiting the woman novelist who tries to narrate the female life against the grain of the heterosexual plot and the conception of female destiny it encodes.

Notes

Portions of an earlier version of this essay were presented in a session organized by Kristina Straub at the ASECS meeting in Pittsburgh in 1991. The present version has profited by suggestions from Straub and Robert Markley. I would like to thank also Paul Hunter, Sue Lanser, Jeslyn Medoff, and John Sitter.

[1] The anachronistic but seemingly unavoidable term "lesbian" (like "homo-" and "heterosexual") has the unfortunate effect of suggesting as fixed and immutable categories that came into place only in the late nineteenth century. This essay understands these categories to belong to what Judith Butler calls "regulatory fictions that consolidate and naturalize the convergent power regimes of masculine and heterosexist oppression"; Butler, *Gender Trouble: Feminism and the Subversion of Identity* (New York, 1990), 33.

[2] The earliest known instance of female writing of same-sex desire in English is found in the journals of Anne Lister. Helena Whitbread, *I Know My Own Heart: The Diaries of Anne Lister (1791-1840)* (London, 1988). Carolyn Woodward, however, has discovered a "lesbian love story" interwoven in the 1744 travel narrative *The Travels and Adventures of Mademoiselle de Richelieu*. It is possible, although Woodward does not press the point, that the unknown author is lesbian. Woodward, "Loving Her 'As Never Woman Loved Another': Longing and Disruption in 18th-Century British Fiction," *Signs: Journal of Women in Culture and Society* (forthcoming). Earlier still is Delariviere Manley's depiction in *The New Atalantis* (1709) of a sensuous female "new *Cabal*" which has been read as a lesbian community; however, as Harriette Andreadis points out in "The Sapphic-Platonics of Katherine

Philips, 1632-1664," *Signs: Journal of Women in Culture and Society* 15 (1989):n.56, Manley may have been playing to the libertinism of her audience.

[3] Armstrong, *Desire and Domestic Fiction: A Political History of the Novel* (Oxford, 1987), 11.

[4] Laqueur, *Making Sex: Body and Gender from the Greeks from the Greeks to Freud* (Cambridge, 1990), 13.

[5] It is doubtful that a woman could have unselfconsciously recorded this story in the latter decades of the century. cf. Mrs. Thrale's anxious preoccupation with sapphism (as she called it): in 1795 she observed that "'tis now grown common to suspect Impossibilities—(such I think 'em)—whenever two Ladies live too much together." Katharine C. Balderston, ed. *Thraliana: The Diary of Mrs. Hester Lynch Thrale (Later Mrs. Piozzi) 1776-1809* (Oxford, 1942), 2:949. For the emergence of the sapphist role in the late eighteenth century, see Randolph Trumbach, "London's Sapphists: From Three Sexes to Four Genders in the Making of Modern Culture," *Body Guards: The Cultural Politics of Gender Ambiguity,* ed. Julia Epstein and Kristina Straub (New York, 1991), 130-34.

[6] Lesbian theorists point out that we lack a language for registering undifferentiated desire. Kendall, "Finding the Good Parts: Sexuality in Women's Tragedies in the Time of Queen Anne," *Curtain Calls: British and American Women and the Theatre, 1660-1820,* ed. Mary Anne Schofield and Cecilia Macheski (Athens, Ga., 1991), 168, says of the early eighteenth-century "sexual universe" that it was one "in which lines were not clearly drawn; in which sexual identity was blurred; in which eroticism was a language transcending the naming of parts or the claiming of identity." See also Eve Kosofsky Sedgwick, "Jane Austen and the Masturbating Girl," *Critical Inquiry* 17 (Summer 1991):826, on the "rich, conflictual erotic complication of a homoerotic matrix not yet crystalized in terms of 'sexual identity.'"

[7] Armstrong, 25.

[8] The perception that Barker is a key figure for study of relations between the emergence of the professional woman writer and the novel is beginning to gain currency. Josephine Donovan, "Women and the Rise of the Novel: A Feminist-Marxist Theory," *Signs: Journal of Women in Culture and Society* 16 (1991):452, calls *A Patch-work Screen* "one of the most important, if ignored, works in women's literary history." Donovan's analysis of women's contribution to the "rise" of the novel includes a valuable discussion of the novel. For introductions to Barker's narratives, see Jane Spencer, *The Rise of the Woman Novelist: From Alphra Behn to Jane Austen* (Oxford, 1986), 62-70, and Mari-

lyn L. Williamson, *Raising Their Voices: British Women Writers, 1650-1750* (Detroit, 1990), 244-51.

[9] Incredibly enough, with the exception of Janet Todd, *Women's Friendship in Literature* (New York, 1980), 326, all commentary on this tale has ignored its lesbian implications. See, for example, Patricia Meyer Spacks, *Imagining A Self: Autobiography and Novel in Eighteenth-Century England* (Cambridge, 1976), 67-68. For an alternative to my reading, see Williamson, 250-51; I find problematic Williamson's stress on shared gender oppressions, which suppresses the narrator's insistence upon class difference.

[10] This preoccupation reflected the social and economic realities of many of Barker's female contemporaries. The number of upper-class women who never married rose from 5% in the sixteenth century to as much as 25% in the eighteenth; in London at the end of the seventeenth century women outnumbered men by thirteen to ten. See Lawrence Stone, *The Family, Sex and Marriage in England 1500-1800* (New York, 1977), 380-81. For the social and economic dimensions of spinsterhood in the eighteenth century, see Bridget Hill, *Women, Work, and Sexual Politics in Eighteenth-Century England* (Oxford, 1989), 221-39. According to Ruth Perry, Mary Astell's *A Serious Proposal* responds to these demographics; Peny, *The Celebrated Mary Astell: An Early English Feminist* (Chicago, 1986), 105-06.

[11] The third is *The Lining of the Patch-work Screen,* publishedin in 1726. Barker's interest in rewriting the cultural meaning of the single life predates by several decades her prose fictions; her poem "A Virgin Life" was printed in her *Poetic Recreations* in 1688.

[12] The discussion is indebted to Nancy K. Miller's influential formulation of "the heroine's text" of the eighteenth century as "the text of an ideology that codes femininity in paradigms of sexual vulnerability." Miller, *The Heroine's Text: Readings in the French and English Novel, 1722-1782* (New York, 1980), xi. It should be noted that Galesia's life-story fits neither the "euphoric" nor the "dysphoric" plots identified by Miller.

[13] Jane Barker, *A Patch-work Screen for the Ladies; Or, Love and Virtue Recommended* (1723; New York, 1973), 2. Future references are cited in the text.

[14] For the retirement ideal in seventeenth- and early eighteenth-century verse by women, see Perry 121-29, Williamson 68-78, and Elaine Hobby, *Virtue of Necessity: English Women's Writing 1649-88* (Ann Arbor, 1989), 134-35. The standard treatment of the retirement ideal is Maren-Sofie Rostvig, *The Happy Man: Studies in the Metamorphoses of a Classical Ideal 1600-1700* (Oxford, 1954).

[15] Williamson, 212-28.

[16] See Ruth Perry, "Mary Astell and the Feminist Critique of Possessive Individualism," *Eighteenth-Century Studies* 23 (Summer 1990):444-57.

[17] One would like to know what went on in the conjugal bed. For the (in some ways) analogous libertine practice of one man taking to bed two prostitutes (known as "lying in state"), see Trumbach, "London's Sapphists," 31.

[18] Which is not to say that the idea of sex between women lay outside the early eighteenth-century imagination. Pornographic and semipornographic works like Delariviere Manley's *The New Atalantis* (1709) demonstrate the contemporary awareness that women might experience sexual pleasure with women; see Manley, *Secret Memoirs and Manners of Several Persons of Quality, of Both Sexes from the New Atalantis, an Island in the Mediterranean* (London, 1709), 2:43-56.

[19] See Trumbach, "London's Sapphists."

[20] For a full account of working-class "female warriors" in balladry and history, see Diane Dugaw, *Warrior Women and Popular Balladry, 1650-1850* (Cambridge, 1989). For cross-dressed women, see Lynne Friedli, "'Passing women': A Study of Gender Boundaries in the Eighteenth Century," *Sexual Underworlds of the Enlightenment*, ed. G. S. Rousseau and Roy Porter (Chapel Hill, 1988):234-60; and Kristina Straub, "The Guilty Pleasures of Female Theatrical Cross-Dressing and the Autobiography of Charlotte Charke," *Body Guards: The Cultural Politics of Gender Ambiguity*, ed. Julia Epstein and Kristina Straub (New York & London, 1991), 142-166.

[21] Martha Vicinus, "'They Wonder to Which Sex I Belong': The Historical Roots of the Modern Lesbian Identity," *Feminist Studies* 18 (Fall 1992):473-79. Vicinus, 473, concludes that the "correlation between class, public appearance and sexual behavior" observable in these categories "suggests an effort to categorize women's deviancy in a satisfactory manner that did not threaten the dominant heterosexual and social paradigms of the age." For a compact account of what is known of late seventeenth-century attitudes toward and understanding of female same sex desire, see Andreadis, esp. 53-56.

[22] See Kristina Straub, "Colley Cibber's Butt: Class, Race, Gender, and the Construction of Sexual Identity," *Genre* 23 (Summer/Fall 1990):135-59, and Randolph Trumbach, "Sodomy Transformed: Aristocratic Libertinage, Public Reputation and the Gender Revolution of the 18th Century," *Journal of Homosexuality* 19 (Summer 1990):105-24.

[23] The unredeemable sexual lewdness of the Princess in Aphra Behn's "The Fair Jilt," *Selected Writings of the Ingenious Mrs. Aphra Behn* (New York, 1950), 110, is manifested in "her lusts with people that served her, and others in mean capacity." Ma. A., *The Prude* ([Part I, 1724] New York, 1973), 16, 22, offers an interesting example of cross-class sex initiated by two female companions who take their pleasure of a footman who "faithfully divided himself between them." Female-initiated cross-class sex seems to have been an especially strong marker of female lewdness; Elisinda, the eponymous prude, is a woman of wide-ranging sexual appetite whose liaison with the footman is called "the grossest part of Love."

[24] Daniel Defoe, *Conjugal Lewdness; or, Matrimonial Whoredom* (1727; Gainesville: 1967), 232, 237, uses the term *servant* to denote a man willing to exchange his body for material gain. Of an older woman whose lust has as its object a younger and "meaner" man Defoe asks, "Now what was all this but Matrimonial Whoredom? she married him for nothing more or less but the meer Thing called a Bedfellow; and he took her to be her Servant, to give it no worse a name."

[25] For the link between strong feeling and transgressive desire, see Henry Fielding, *The Female Husband and Other Writings,* ed. Claude E. Jones (1746; Liverpool, 1960), 31: "As *Molly Hamilton* was extremely warm in her inclinations, and as those inclinations were so violently attached to Mrs. *Johnson,* it would not have been difficult for a less artful woman, in the most private hours, to turn the ardour of enthusiastic devotion into a different kind of flame."

[26] Stone, 272.

[27] For the associations between hermaphroditism and female same-sex desire, see Trumbach, "London's Sapphists," esp. 7-20. He finds that a woman who desired women and had "overt masculine characteristics" was often supposed to be biologically hermaphroditic, while hermaphroditic females were supposed to seek sexual pleasures with women. The anonymous author of *The Treatise of Hermaphrodites* published by Edmund Curll in 1781 is quoted by Trumbach, 12, as saying that "the intrigues of my hermaphrodites [presumed to be mostly female] are indeed very amazing and monstrous as their natures; but that many lascivious females divert themselves one with another at this time in this city, is not to be disputed." Friedli, 247-48, argues that the enlarged clitoris associated with female homosexuality "provided a metaphor for confronting the excess of female sexuality, which found its most threatening expression in the appropriation of the male role—'women's abuse of them with each other.'" The quote is from James Parsons, *A Mechanical and Critical Enquiry into the Nature of Hermaphrodites* (London, 1741), 10. For a fascinating account of hermaphrodit-

ism and the premodern understanding of the relations between sex and gender, see Laqueur, 135-42.

[28] And is partially countered by evidence at the beginning of the tale of the wife's heterosexual attraction to the "truly handsome" husband whom she married in opposition to her family's wishes. Her willfulness may hint at sexual appetitiveness. Taken together the evidence offers some corroboration of Trumbach's conclusion that female same-sex desire at this time was understood according to a bisexual model; see "London Sapphists," esp. 125-28.

[29] For an amusing account of the dildo in contemporary writings, see Peter Wanger, "The Discourse on Sex—Or Sex as Discourse: Eighteenth-Century Medical and Paramedical Erotica," *Sexual Underworlds of the Enlightenment,* ed. G. S. Rousseau and Roy Porter (Chapel Hill, 1988), 52-54.

[30] Butler, 31.

[31] Joan DeJean, *Fictions of Sappho 1546-1937* (Chicago, 1989), 22.

[32] See Todd, 322; Lillian Faderman, *Surpassing the Love of Men* (New York, 1981), 23-27.

[33] John Cleland, *Memoirs of a Woman of Pleasure* (New York, 1963), 64-67.

[34] In *The Female Husband* lesbian acts are "monstrous and unnatural," "brutal and shocking"; "abominable and unnatural pollutions" (29, 30). Similar language can be found in the commentary on Bianchi's *Dissertation On the Case of Catherine Vizzani* attributed to John Cleland. The "English Editor" (Cleland) argues that her "Lewdness" comes from "some Disorder or Perversion in the Imagination": "the Source of so odious and so unnatural a Vice" is "her Mind" (where various "monstrous Productions" have their origins). See Roger Lonsdale, "New Attributions to John Cleland," *RES* NS 30 (1979):268-90. Friedli, 240, notes that *The Female Husband* "can be seen to preclude a reading that constitutes gender roles as a site of struggle; 'unnatural lusts' function not to make problematic concepts of 'natural' sexual expression, but to excite the reader." For a fine discussion of *The Female Husband,* see Terry Castle, "Matters not fit to be mentioned: Fielding's *The Female Husband,*" *ELH* 49 (1982):602-22.

[35] See Terry Castle, *Masquerade and Civilization: The Carnivalesque in Eighteenth-Century English Culture and Fiction* (Stanford, 1986), esp. 90-94.

[36] It is possible that the term "unaccountable" in the early eighteenth century is a coded word. Charlotte Charke, *A Narrative of the Life of Mrs. Charlotte*

Charke (2nd. ed., 1755; Gainesville, 1969), 13, proposes to "give some Account of my UNACCOUNTABLE LIFE." In Cleland, 45, Phoebe's same-sex desire is said to be "one of those arbitrary tastes, for which there is no accounting."

[37] Except in instances where male dominance is left unthreatened—as a form of sexual apprenticeship, for example. The close association of female sexuality with the reproductive process may also help explain why the early eighteenth century found it difficult to imagine "sex" between two women. The fact that female same-sex desire, even when imaginable, was seldom seen as challenging traditional gender hierarchies may account for the relative tolerance of female, as opposed to male, homosexuality in English history.

[38] It is significant that the inset comes at the point in the narrative when Galesia has finally decided to remove herself from the heterosexual marriage market and is most divided about the implications of this choice. Despite her "secret Disgust against Matrimony" (80), she shares in her mother's apprehension that the single life is an "uncouth kind of *Solitude*" whose effect is to "frustrate the End of our Creation" (79).

Kathryn R. King (essay date 1994)

SOURCE: "Jane Barker, *Political Recreations*, and the Sociable Text," in *ELH*, Vol. 61, No. 3, Fall, 1994, pp. 551-70.

[*In the essay that follows, King explores Barker's participation in a complex literary community that also included men.*]

In *Writing Women's Literary History* (1993), Margaret Ezell argues forcefully for a rethinking of the assumptions that govern feminist literary history.[1] Feminist historiography, she contends, derives its models of female authorship from nineteenth-century practices; these models distort our understanding of the circumstances and modes of production of women writers of earlier eras. In the narratives generated by such a historiography early modern women writers are constructed as isolated eccentrics at odds with themselves and their culture; their story is the recurring one of exclusion and absence, of female voices silenced and female talents repressed. Not only does such a story misread women's past; it also invites continued misreadings. To focus on exclusion is to encourage contemplation of the forces that have thwarted female literary production and to summon up yet more evidence of the silenced (alienated, isolated) woman writer—when what is needed is a great deal more in the way of basic information about the texts, contexts, and situations of early women writers.

The present essay seeks to characterize some features of the early verse and circumstances of Jane Barker (1652-1727?), focusing on poems written in the 1670s and 1680s and printed in *Poetical Recreations* (1688).[2] Barker, an important figure in the emergence of the novel in the early decades of the eighteenth century, is best known for the trilogy of autobiographical fictions she published between 1713 and 1726, the second of which, *A Patch-work Screen for the Ladies* (1723), attracts admiring notice from feminist critics and literary historians.[3] But long before Barker began fashioning her quirky narratives of the self, she composed occasional verse and, like other country gentlewomen, exchanged poems and other pieces of writing with relatives and friends. Late in 1687 (1688 is the date on the title page) more than fifty pieces of what appear to be largely coterie verse were printed without Barker's authorization as part 1 of the two-part *Poetical Recreations.* This body of verse makes available for study an obscure manuscript circle that included, in addition to Jane Barker, several Cambridge students.[4] My research into Barker and the young men who formed her circle, praised her poetry, and sponsored its passage into print calls into question the assumption of much feminist criticism that women writers of the early-modern era struggled into print against a tide of male hostility and derision; it also suggests that sociability is a more important feature of early women's verse than much feminist scholarship, preoccupied with themes of personal isolation and cultural exclusion, has permitted us to see.[5] My own focus on the sociable dimensions of Barker's verse aims to promote a richer and more exact understanding of the place of women writers in their immediate social setting and in relation to the larger culture.

I

Poetical Recreations appeared late in 1687 to little acclaim.[6] Roughly the first third of the volume—fifty-one poems on 109 octavo pages—consists of verse by Jane Barker. The remainder consists of poems written by "Gentlemen of the UNIVERSITIES, and Others," as the title page has it. Barker's contributions include Pindaric odes, ballads and songs, verse epistles, meditative lyrics, elegies. Of likely interest to readers today are those that directly engage gender issues ("**A VIRGIN LIFE**," "*An Invitation to my Friends at* **Cambridge**," "*To* Ovid's Heroines *in his Epistles*"), and those on the poetic vocation *("Necessity of Fate,"* "**To the Importunate ADDRESS OF POETRY**," *"Resolved never to Versifie more"*) and on medicine *(***"On the** Apothecary's *Filing my Bills amongst the* **Doctors**" and "**A Farewell to POETRY, WITH A Long Digression on ANATOMY.**")** Part 2 includes a scattering of poems to and about Jane Barker but consists mostly of unrelated verse by a number of men, many unidentified. Largely forgotten today—Charles Cotton and "Sir C. S." (Sir Charles Sedley) are the biggest names in the group—they appear to have been an uncelebrated lot even in their own time.[7]

Because many of Barker's poems bear traces of their coterie origins, it is easy to see that Barker wrote to and for friends and family rather than for a wider readership. Some of these poems are moralized meditations *("To my Dear Cousin Mrs.* **M. T.** *after the Death of her Husband and Son")*; some are playful moments in a friendship—("To my Friend *S. L.* ON HIS Receiving the Name of *Little Tom King")*; others commemorate small private occasions, much as today we might take a snapshot *("To Mr.* HILL, *on his Verses to the Dutchess of* YORK *when she was at* Cambridge"). In view of Barker's current reputation as a champion of female friendships it is striking how many of these verses are addressed to men: to "my Cousin Mr. E. F.," "Mr. G. P. my Adopted Brother," "Dr. R. S. my Indifferent Lover," "my Honoured Friend Mr. E. S.," "my Brother," "Sir F. W.," "my Honourable Unkle Colonel C———" and many more. Indeed, of the twenty-two poems addressed to someone specific, only one—unless one wishes to count an epistle to Ovid's Heroines—is written to a woman, the previously mentioned epistle to Mrs. M. T.

If verse writing afforded many seventeenth- and early eighteenth-century men an opportunity to display the linguistic talents that might lead to patronage or preferment, it seems to have offered Barker an entree—of sorts—into the centers of learning from which she as a woman was officially excluded. (It is surely significant that, if Barker's autobiographical writings are any guide, the friends she valued most highly were students at Cambridge, and the family member she adored above all others was her brother Edward, at various times a student at Merchant Taylors, Gray's Inn, and Oxford—an impressive roster of sites of masculine intellectual privilege.)[8] Barker may also have used verse exchange to create and sustain friendships more mentally challenging and linguistically sophisticated than those existing in the world she actually inhabited. Barker's writing-into-being a network of literary friendships might be read as a kind of Cavendish-like manuever intended to construct herself at the center of a textualized world—not blazing exactly, nor entirely new—but instinct with intellectual possibilities unavailable outside the domain of literary exchange.

The poems in which Barker self-consciously addresses a male reader as one poet to another provide some of the most telling moments in her printed verse, especially as they make visible the inadequacy of the forms of self-representation available to a (woman) poet at this time. **"To My Friends against POETRY,"** for example, is filled with odd, instructive, and (as I read them) unintentional ironies generated by the mismatch between the speaker's gender and the patriarchal code within which she represents the poetic self. The iro-

nies cluster around the figure of the sexualized muse hinted at in the poem's opening lines—

> Dear Friends, if you'll be rul'd by me,
> Beware o' th' Charms of *Poetry;*
> And meddle with no fawning *Muse,*
> They'll but your harmless Loves abuse.

—and then made explicit: the muses are "all grown *Prostitutes.*" The whorish muse is meant, of course, to stand for the increasing commercialism of the world of letters, the satiric attack on which is an expected feature of the "poem against poetry." Still, the figure sits oddly, as does the later troping of desire for literary fame as an *"itch"* as "hard to cure as Dice or Whore." The coarse language says something about the relative freedom from the burdens of propriety enjoyed by women in the late seventeenth century, and it reminds us, in Janet Todd's words, that before the "sentimental image of chaste, maternal, subordinate womanhood hardened into a prescription," even decorous writers like Barker could permit themselves to traffic in tropes that associate the impulse to write with disease, gaming, and phallic compulsion.[9] But we are also reminded of the insistently patriarchal cast of the conventions governing representations of the poetic vocation available to women writers at this time. It is not surprising, as Deborah Payne has said of Barker's contemporary Aphra Behn, "that the only words available to a seventeenth-century woman such as Behn to describe her writerly self were 'my Masculine Part the Poet in me.'"[10] Nor is it entirely surprising that Barker would draw upon a symbolism of sexual/textual commerce in circulation at the time to pass on, with no subversive or oppositional intent that I can detect, an image of poetry-making as fornication with a whore.

More satisfying to readers today, and more closely related to the lifelong fascination with ambivalence that makes Barker's later narratives such rich studies of female subjectivity, are poems in which inherited codes and conventions are reworked as part of a discourse expressive of a female poet-subject. Especially interesting are those in which the figure of the muse is removed from sexualized contexts and made to project divisions in the speaker's consciousness—her sense of herself as one who can neither wholly embrace nor wholly free herself of an urge to versify that borders at times on compulsion. The opening lines of **"A Second EPISTLE. To . . .** *Mr. E. S.,"* for instance, dramatize the poet-as-obsessive with engaging self-mockery:

> Oft has my *Muse* and I fall'n out,
>   And I as oft have banish'd her my Breast;
> But such, alas, still was her interest,
>   And still to bring her purposes about:
> So great her cunning in insinuation,
> That she soon gain'd her wish'd-for
>   restoration:

But when I found this wou'd not do,
  A Violent Death I put her to.
But see, my Friend, how your All-pow'rfull
  Pen
(O Miracle!) has rais'd her from the Dead
  again.

("A Second EPISTLE. *To my Honoured
  Friend Mr.* E. S.")

This epistle is primarily, of course, a graceful compliment to a friend in which Barker has fun playing with the convention of the muse. But it also instances something that will be explored far more seriously in the later narratives of self: a mind that knows itself in part through its conflicted experience of the desire to write.[11]

Although little is known about the people addressed in these poems, most of whom remain at this juncture initials only, I have been able to identify the Cambridge student whose coterie name was "Philaster" as John Newton of Uffington, Lincolnshire.[12] The biographical information on Newton is sparse, unfortunately. A student at St. John's from 1678 and a Fellow from 1685 to 1700, Newton, who was remembered at Cambridge as something of a wit, went on to enjoy an unremarkable career as rector of King's Cliffe, Northamptonshire, until his death in 1714.[13] Newton's poetic ambitions appear to have been modest: outside the pages of *Poetical Recreations* (to which as "J.N." and "Philaster" he contributed three poems to or about Jane Barker) he seems to have published only what amounts to literary exercises in official Cambridge commemorative volumes such as *Hymenaeus Cantabrigiensis* (1683) and *Moestissimae ac Laetissimae Academiae* (1685). During the years Newton was in residence at Cambridge, his family lived in Uffington, only a few miles from the small village of Wilsthorpe where Barker lived with her mother and father. Newton may have been related to the Barkers through his mother, Elizabeth, whose maiden name was Barker. The account given by Barker in *A Patch-work Screen* of the genesis of the Cambridge friendship is important for the rare glimpse it offers of the formation of a non-aristocratic literary circle. "It was at this Time," relates Galesia (Barker's fictional persona and poetic *nom de plume*), "that I had a Kinsman a Student at the University; who at certain Times, frequented our House; and now and then brought some of his young Companions with him; whose youthful and witty Conversation, greatly help'd to divert my Chagrin" (*PWS*, 22). Two of these young men in particular, the Kinsman and a "vertuous young Gentleman," would come to her home

  now and then, a little to relax their College
  Discipline, and unbend the Streightness of
    their
  Study; bringing with them little Books, new
  Pamphlets, and Songs; and in their Absence,

  convers'd with me by Writing; sometimes
    Verse,
  sometimes Prose, which ingaged my Replies
    in the same manner.

                                        (*PWS*, 23)

These young men—if John Newton's age they would have been roughly ten years younger than Barker—are doubtless the friends she addresses in **"To my Friends against POETRY,"** *"Resolved never to Versifie more,"* and *"An Invitation to my Friends at* **Cambridge."**[14]

The last of these poems is worth careful study. In *"An Invitation,"* which appropriately enough opens Barker's portion of the volume, Barker extends to her young friends an invitation to the countryside that also twits them for failing to appreciate the world of learning that her gender debars her from entering. Its ironic play on the symbolism of the Fall projects a distinctively female re-visioning of the expulsion from the garden: for their transgressions the daughters of Eve are denied the Tree of Knowledge, which is here literalized, in a droll and characteristically Barkerian way, as the classical learning reserved for men at the universities.[15] Her rural retirement would be a "Paradise," except that

  the *Tree* of *Knowledge* won't grow here:
  Though in its *culture* I have spent some time,
  Yet it disdains to grow in our cold *Clime,*
  Where it can neither Fruit nor Leaves produce
  Good for its owner, or the publick use.

The poem plays out in a small way the conflict between female desire and social actuality that provides a central tension in Barker's later fiction. The speaker makes no effort to conceal either her envy that men are granted "Luxurious Banquets of this dainty Fruit" or the fact that women's desires for knowledge ("our longing Souls") are far from extinguished by prohibitions against female learning:

        Altho' our Eyes
  Do serve our longing-Souls to tantalize,
  Whilst kinder fate for you do's constitute
  Luxurious Banquets of this dainty Fruit.
  Whose *Tree* most fresh and flourishing do's
    grow,
  E'er since it was transplanted amongst you.

While it would be going too far to call *"An Invitation"* an attack on male privilege, Barker's control of tone in this epistle permits her to affirm affection for her friends even as she complains, with delicate tact, of a masculine privilege so deep and so assured as to be unaware of its "transplanted" nature.

Her delighted affection for the Cambridge friends is the subject of an unprinted poem written sometime after the publication of *Poetical Recreations.*[16] Addressed "To my friends who prais'd my Poems, and at the begining of the little printed book placed this motto—pulcherrima virgo / Incedit, magna juvenum stipante caterva," it shows that Newton and the other Cambridge students played a role in preparing "the little printed book" for publication.[17] In addition, the poem provides one of very few known instances of an early woman poet responding to the support and encouragement of male friends—called by Barker the "gayest, sweetest, gentlest, youths on earth":

> I doubt not to come safe to glories port,
> Since I have such a troop for my escort,
> This band of gallant youths, bear me along,
> Who teach me how to sing, then praise my
>   song.
> Such wreaths and branches, they've bestow'd
>   on me,
> I look like Daphne turn'd into a tree,
> Whilst these young sons of Phoebus dance
>   around
> And sing the praise of her themselves have
>   crown'd.[18]

It is hard to know how to take Barker's claim that the *Poetical Recreations* verses were printed "without her consent," a matter to be taken up shortly; however, if the warmth of this tribute is any indication, there is little reason to imagine her distressed by their publication.[19] The whimsical portrait of the "young sons of Phoebus" dancing merrily around a tree of their own making doubtless contains an element of deliberate mockery, but the tone of the poem as a whole exhibits none of the sustained ironies of *"An Invitation"*: from first to last it speaks both lovingly and gratefully of the "band of gallant youths" who have taken it upon themselves to escort her "to glories port."[20]

With the help of verses to and by the Cambridge friends and the account in *A Patch-work Screen,* we can begin to piece together a picture of the role of the young men in the making of *Poetical Recreations.* It is probable that at some point no earlier than 1678 (when Newton matriculated at St. John's) Barker entered into a literary correspondence with Newton and an unspecified number of "young Companions" from the University, one of whom, "Exilius," was to become especially important.[21] This correspondence, begun in Wilsthorpe, continued after Barker moved to London sometime in the eighties, as shown by the final poem in part 1 of *Poetical Recreations* (**"Resolved never to Versifie more"**), in which she explains to the friends why "No more can Verse in *London* grow." It seems likely that a correspondence of many years duration would have furnished the Cambridge friends with a body of poetry sufficient to fill out a volume, although this must be a matter of speculation. We do know that they supplied the volume with its Virgilian motto and at

least three of its commendatory verses (signed "Philaster," "Exilius," and "Fidelius"), and it is conceivable that they supplied the bookseller with copies of the Barker poems as well. From the evidence thus far adduced one might reasonably conclude that the Cambridge circle—out of admiration for Barker, appreciation of her poems, or both—took it upon themselves to get a body of her verse into print, perhaps seeking out a cooperative bookseller for the purpose. Such a scenario, though attractive and tidy, leaves out an important player in the *Poetical Recreations* story: the publisher, Benjamin Crayle.

Crayle is a little known but intriguingly disreputable figure who until now has entered the historical record only in the soiled margins of the "lascivious and vitious" books he was fined for publishing in 1688 and then again in 1690, when he was briefly imprisoned.[22] Born into a well-to-do Newark-upon-Trent family with City connections, Crayle was sent to London in 1676 to learn the book trade; in June of 1683, the same month that he became free of the Stationers' Company, he advertised his first title in the *Term Catalogues.*[23] It is doubtful that Crayle would have known Barker or members of her Cambridge circle much before the mid-eighties. But as a young stationer ambitious to establish himself as a publisher as well as bookseller, Crayle would have sought contacts with aspiring literary talent, male or female, the more so, perhaps, in that he may have possessed literary pretensions of his own.[24] (Part 2 of *Poetical Recreations* includes twelve poems by Crayle, said to be "done by a Conceal'd Author for his private Recreation.") When Crayle and Barker met is not known, but evidence suggests they were acquainted by 1685.[25] By what chain of circumstances a Lincolnshire gentlewoman newly arrived in London might have come into contact with a City bookseller still in his mid-twenties and scrambling for a foothold in the trade remains a tantalizing puzzle.

Of their relationship Crayle provides an account of sorts in the group of poems he inserted in the second part of *Poetical Recreations.* It is hard to know how seriously to take his professions of love for the woman he calls variously Galaecia (a variant of her poetic name), Cosmelia (the name he gave her), and Jane Barker: such amorous professions may have been mere literary convention or dramatic impersonation. But that bookseller and poet were engaged in literary play of some kind seems certain. Three poems by Barker to "Her Young Lover" may have been written to Crayle, who was about eight years her junior.[26] Crayle's role in the exchange is more certain. In addition to declaring Barker his beloved, he wrote several poems answering hers, including "The Young Lover's ADVOCATE: Being An Answer to a Copy of Verses. *Written by* Galaecia *to her* Young Lover *on his* Vow."[27] (Barker had chided the "Sweet *Youth*" for knowing nothing of love; the "Young Lover" pronounces her

"Too rigid, too censorious and severe" and then produces a classical precedent for their amour in the "Famous *Sappho*" who found joy in "the Embrace of a *Sicilian* Boy.") The Crayle/Barker exchange is too conventionally literary to permit more than guesses about their real-life relations; we cannot even know whether Crayle was himself "the Young Lover" or simply his "advocate."

Nor can we know whether the idea of publishing a collection of Barker's verse originated with Crayle, although in some ways it is logical to assume so since as bookseller it was he who stood to gain financially from the venture. It is equally plausible, however, that the idea came from one or more members of the Cambridge circle. Once the project was underway we can be reasonably sure that at least three of the Cambridge friends collaborated with Crayle in the venture—the commendatory verse and the Virgilian motto they supplied would suggest as much. Assessing Barker's part in the project is more difficult. Her claim that the verses had been printed "without her consent" may of course be disingenuous, a merely formulaic defense against charges of presumption or imputations of commercial motives; but even if quite genuine, it could mean any of a number of things: that Barker knew of the venture and strenuously opposed it; knew and acquiesced with sadness; knew and concealed her boundless delight; did not know but was not greatly displeased in the event—the possibilities go on. We have only an ambiguous claim of their having been printed without her consent some twelve years or so after the fact and a manuscript poem brimming with affection for the literary allies who helped prepare "the little printed book."[28]

II

That friendships of various sorts are the primary matrix for Barker's early verse is less surprising than the fact that overwhelmingly the friendships recorded are with men. The image of Barker that has emerged in the spate of feminist handbooks and anthologies appearing over the last decade or so is that of a woman-preoccupied author inhabiting an imaginative world of female relationships. We learn, for example, in the headnote of a 1985 anthology that Barker's poems "attach emphatic significance to female friendship and the single life." An entry in the 1990 *Dictionary of Women Writers* asserts that Barker "formed close female friendships and was well aware of male dominance."[29] The impulse to honor Barker as a celebrant of female friendships is so powerful that Elaine Hobby, who provides one of the very few nuanced discussions of Barker's poetry, says of Barker's best-known poem, **"A Virgin Life,"** that it shows the spinster as "released to pursue female friendships."[30] In fact **"A Virgin Life"** says nothing specific about *female* friendships at all. The lines that come closest say only that

the exemplary single woman "drives her whole Lives business to these ends, / To serve her God, enjoy her Books and Friends." And when one searches the corpus of Barker's printed verse for other poems illustrative of the "emphatic significance" Barker attached to "female friendship," one finds precisely one: ***On the DEATH** of my Dear Friend and Play-fellow,* **Mrs. E. D.** *having Dream'd the night before I heard thereof, that I had lost a Pearl."*[31] One female friendship poem—and that more properly speaking an elegy—and that is it.

The contemporary attachment to the idea of Barker as poet of female friendships is understandable given the feminist project of demarginalization: women-centered stories are an important counter to the "master plots" that dominate traditional literary histories. Yet it would be a sad irony if, in our zeal to clear a space in the thick growths of patriarchal history, we should re-obscure the nature of women's aims and achievements. **"A Virgin Life"** is a case in point. To read the poem as a proto-feminist valorization of female friendships is to pass over those very features—features bound up in late-seventeenth century poetic themes and conventions—which make **"A Virgin Life"** such a remarkable moment in the history of female re-visioning.

An approach to the poem alert to its own cultural contexts might begin by noting that **"A Virgin Life"** belongs to a poetic kind quite popular with both men and women at that time, the poem of preference for the single life.[32] Two examples turn up, in fact, in part 2 of *Poetical Recreations,* one of which, *"A Batchelor's Life,"* is an explicit reworking from a male point of view of the Barker piece, and it is written, interestingly enough, by Benjamin Crayle. In the hands of women poets, the poem of preference for the single life becomes, almost inevitably, a vehicle for questioning society's expectations for women and for expressing doubts about the marriage ideal.[33] Barker's **"A Virgin Life"** shares with these female-authored poems a view of marriage as organized for the convenience of men and as entailing for women a loss of liberty and happiness, and like them it takes a critical look at forms of male power. But where this power is elsewhere often understood as a specifically legal subjugation of women within patriarchal marriage, Barker, attentive always to the psychological dimensions of power relations, brings out the ambiguities in relations of domination and submission: the virgin's prayer that she not "fall into the power, / Of mans allmost omnipotent amour" contains within it the hint that male power has, if not its sources then much of its continuance, in a woman's abrogation of her own powers of self-governance.

"A Virgin Life" also goes well beyond a questioning of courtship and marriage to do something quite bold: to propose the single life as a real alternative to marriage, not just a critique of it. Drawing upon the royalist retirement models, Barker shows the exemplary female life as a combination of study, happy solitude, and quiet service to God and country.[34]

> by Obedience testifies she can
> Be's good a Subject as the stoutest Man.
> She to her Church such filial duty pays,
> That one would think she'd liv'd i'th' pristine days.
> Her Closet, where she do's much time bestow,
> Is both her Library and Chappel too,
> Where she enjoys society alone,
> I'th' Great Three-One————
> She drives her whole Lives business to these Ends,
> To serve her God, enjoy her Books and Friends.

With these lines, which conclude the poem, Barker invents for the exemplary spinster a new lineage that transforms the meaning and value of the unmarried life. Notice, for example, the way the reference to the virgin's "filial duty" to the Church shifts the locus of a woman's obligations away from the patriarchal family and onto the Church, implicitly redefining the relationships that give a woman's life meaning. No longer primarily a daughter, wife, mother, the spinster finds her value not in the production of heirs and the transmission of property—the chief function of the married woman in the heterosexual economy—but in her own direct "filial" relation to God. And her service is not confined to the patriarchal family: she serves God, state, and the community.

But before arriving at the expanded conception of the unmarried life conveyed by these final lines, Barker must first demystify the supposed terrors of spinsterhood ("Ah lovely State how strange it is to see, / What mad conceptions some have made of thee.") Thus the poem opens by proclaiming the hollowness of those dire warnings against the dangers of foregoing male protection pronounced by, among others, men's seduction poems. In Barker's anti-carpe-diem, the ridicule and contempt heaped on unmarried women, indeed the very name "Old Maid," are exposed as "Goblings," illusions that prevent women from recognizing their own best interests; and male protection is declared a fiction:

> Since, O ye Pow'rs, ye have bestow'd on me
> So great a kindness for Virginity,
> Suffer me not to fall into the Pow'rs
> Of Mens almost Omnipotent Amours;
> But in this happy Life let me remain,
> Fearless of Twenty five and all its train,
> Of slights or scorns, or being call'd Old Maid,
> Those Goblings which so many have betray'd:
> Like harmless Kids, that are pursu'd by Men,
> For safety run into a Lyon's Den.

Properly demystified, even the celibate woman's failure to produce children—her supreme social demerit—is seen to belong to the new ideal: "Her Neighb'ring Poor she do's adopt her Heirs, / And less she cares for her own good than theirs." That the poem as a whole is cast in the form of a prayer of gratitude for the gift of virginity ("Since, O ye Pow'rs, ye have bestow'd on me / So great a kindness for Virginity") suggests that the woman who chooses to live outside holy matrimony enjoys a condition that is not only exemplary but, in its own way, sanctified. Returned to its own cultural contexts, **"A Virgin Life"** thus emerges as a striking example of Barker's commitment to reconceiving the exemplary female life in terms of socially responsible celibacy. We might say, employing the idiom of our own time, that the poem offers a compelling instance of the intervention of one early modern woman in her culture's modes of female representation.

III

Scrutiny of *Poetical Recreations* shows that, far from being alienated, eccentric, tormented, or—in another version of the romantic narrative—a lonely voice from the periphery, Barker was engaged in literary exchange with a number of fellow poets, including at least three Cambridge students and (probably) a London bookseller. Contrary to expectations (and perhaps to our wishes), the vast majority of Barker's occasional verse is addressed to men—to her brother; a clergyman; a London physician; a soldier uncle; a "Young Lover," an "Indifferent Lover" and an "unkind" one—although it is possible that, for any of a number of reasons, Barker exchanged verses with other women that were not preserved.[35] It appears that during the phase of her life recorded by these poems Barker sought connections with men in order to participate, if at a remove, in the world of learning and letters from whose institutional centers she was formally debarred. The picture that emerges of Jane Barker the poet of *Poetical Recreations* is that of a youngish unmarried woman for whom verse writing was a social as well as an intellectual act, an opportunity to exercise the mind, talents, and personality in acts of textual sociability.

These findings challenge the widespread perception of early women as excluded from literary communities such as the "loosely organized groups of male writers who supported and encouraged the works of artists like Marlowe, Shakespeare, and Jonson."[36] If Barker's experience is any indication—and the work of Margaret Ezell, Joanna Lipking, and others suggests that she is more representative than had been believed—we will need to conceptualize more inclusive models of early female authorship. The present emphasis upon the masculine jeers, opposition, and hostility that certainly did on occasion greet the literary efforts of early women will need to be shifted to a more complicated view that acknowledges the cheers as well. The aim of such a shift, I hasten to add, is more than the fairminded one of giving men their due. My main concern is that the recovery of women's past include the full, untidy, sometimes discomforting perplexities of women's experience of that past.

Scrutiny of *Poetical Recreations* also obliges us to think more closely about the implications of the name "Mrs. Jane Barker" placed on the title page. In the absence of a dedication, preface, or other forms of prefatory address, we should be wary of drawing conclusions about Barker's concept or presentation of herself as a writer—as Mulvihill does, for example, when she includes Barker in a list of women who "asserted their new literary identity" by publishing their names or initials.[37] The presence of Barker's name on the title page may in this instance say more about the bookseller's assessment of the literary marketplace than about Barker's concern for a public persona. With his eye on recently published volumes of verse by Ephelia, Aphra Behn, and Anne Killigrew—the appearance of which prompted Lady Masham late in 1685 to call women's verse "much the Fasion of late"—Crayle may have sensed that a woman's name on the title page would attract higher sales.[38] The fact that Crayle placed in the *London Gazette* an advertisement for *Poetical Recreations* that featured the name of Mrs. Jane Barker—the single instance I have found of Crayle promoting any of his titles in the newspapers—may suggest his hopes for its commercial success.

The case of a coterie poet like Jane Barker suggests that the sharply drawn distinction between private writing and public authorship needs rethinking. Ezell has called attention to other coterie poets of roughly this time, among them Mary Monck (author of the posthumous *Marinda* verses of 1716), Anne Killigrew, and most famously Katherine Philips. Their poetry is not "public"—that is, it was not written for the consumption of an impersonal public readership. But it cannot exactly be called "private" either, for in terms of the manuscript culture to which these women belonged their verse was clearly intended for an audience of friends and other poets. My work on Barker reinforces the idea that the line between so-called public and private modes of expression may have outlived its usefulness in feminist scholarship. The public/private dichotomy has been crucial to analysis of a host of concerns ranging from the politics of canon formation to female anxieties of authorship, but it is already being displaced by a more complex view. Female marginalization in early modern England, we are learning, is produced in part by our own modern habits of mind in combination with a romantic narrative that emphasizes the isolation of the exceptional (writing) woman—for whom poetic creation emerges as a demonic act of such anti-social presumption as to threaten the creator with ostracism and death. In one account the woman

poet "literally or figuratively risks a melodramatic death at the crossroads of tradition and genre, society and art."[39] In the narratives generated by a romantic ideology, actual historical women collapse into "the" female poet—a solitary figure, lonely and unread, at odds with patriarchal culture and masculinist literary traditions, a woman whose "voice," to use a favorite romantic metaphor, has been silenced or only barely heard.

The complex set of relationships, literary and personal, embedded in the verses of *Poetical Recreations* challenges an image that obscures understanding of how actual women went about producing actual texts in the early modern period. I would conclude by proposing that we set aside for a while some of our most cherished metaphors about how early women poets came to writing: instead of talking about the woman writer finding her voice or—to use an even more dubious critical cliche—inventing herself, it is time we talk more seriously about the social (and sociable) dimensions of authorship that the romantic ideology persistently effaces, especially when the author is female. It is time we begin taking seriously the fact (which no one would seriously deny) that female voices are raised within social environments and in response to other voices. In fact, it may be time to reconsider the implications of the metaphor of the female voice—a metaphor whose effect is often to disembody female poetic production and detach the poet from her social and cultural relationships, and thus contribute to the remarginalization of the women thus troped. I propose that we seek ways of reimagining an early modern writer as a gregarious being who exists, like the poems she produces, within a circle of human and textual relations.

Notes

I am grateful to those who responded to earlier versions of this essay: Paula Backscheider, Elizabeth Hageman, Jeslyn Medoff and members of the NEH summer seminar directed by Professor Backscheider in 1992.

[1] Margaret Ezell, *Writing Women's Literary History* (Baltimore: Johns Hopkins Univ. Press, 1993). For a compressed version of the argument, see "The Myth of Judith Shakespeare: Creating the Canon of Women's Literature," in *New Literary History* 21(1990): 579-92.

[2] The full title is *Poetical Recreations: Consisting of Original Poems, Songs, Odes, &c. With Several New Translations. In Two Parts. Part I. Occasionally Written by Mrs Jane Barker. Part II. By several Gentlemen of the Universities, and Others.* The volume, never reprinted, is available on microfilm in UMI's Early English Books 1641-1700 series, reel 52:3.

³ Comprising the trilogy are *Love Intrigues: Or, The History of the Amours of Bosvil and Galesia* (London: Curll and Crownfield, 1713), *A Patch-work Screen for the Ladies; Or, Love and Virtue Recommended: In a Collection of Instructive Novels* (London: Curll and Payne, 1723)—both of which are available in reprints from Garland Press—and *The Lining of the Patch-work Screen; Design'd for the Farther Entertainment of the Ladies* (London: Bettesworth, 1726). References to *A Patch-work Screen* are indicated parenthetically in the text and abbreviated *PWS.* Josephine Donovan, "Women and the Rise of the Novel: A Feminist-Marxist Theory," in *Signs: Journal of Women in Culture and Society* 16 (1991): 441-62, calls *A Patch-work Screen* "one of the most important, if ignored, works in women's literary history" (452). Useful discussions are also provided by Jane Spencer in *The Rise of the Woman Novelist: From Aphra Behn to Jane Austen* (New York: Basil Blackwell, 1986), 62-70 and Marilyn L. Williamson in *Raising Their Voices: British Women Writers, 1650-1750* (Detroit: Wayne State Univ. Press, 1990), 244-51. The most reliable biographical account is Jeslyn Medoff's headnote in *Kissing the Rod: An Anthology of Seventeenth-Century Women's Verse,* ed. Germaine Greer, Susan Hastings, Jeslyn Medoff, and Melinda Sansone (New York: Farrar Straus Giroux, 1988), 354-55.

⁴ Moria Ferguson speculates that Barker's "first literary efforts may have been for a small provincial coterie" in the tradition of the Society of Friendship associated with Katherine Philips; see *First Feminists: British Women Writers 1578-1799* (Bloomington: Indiana Univ. Press; New York: The Feminist Press, 1985), 171.

⁵ Maureen E. Mulvihill, "A Feminist Link in the Old Boy's Network: The Cosseting of Katherine Philips," in *Curtain Calls: British and American Women and the Theatre, 1660-1820,* ed. Mary Anne Schofield and Cecilia Macheski (Athens: Ohio Univ. Press, 1991), 71-104, criticizes the preoccupation of much recent criticism with an adversarial relationship between men and professional women writers, which she finds "disturbing and historically unsupportable" (74); for her critique of "the new feminist reconstructive criticism," see 74-78. Joanna Lipking comes to similar conclusions in her witty discussion of the generally supportive role of male writers in the literary careers of women poets in "Fair Originals: Women Poets in Male Commendatory Poems," in *Eighteenth-Century Life* n.s. 12 (1988): 58-72. She finds "hosts of male writers great and small who willingly heaped praise, acted as go-betweens with publishers, composed public endorsements, and often gave effectual help" (59). Dorothy Mermin discusses the "small private worlds" of the early poets and the sociable tone of their verse as part of an argument that the tradition of gentlemanly amateurism provided women with an enabling poetic mod-el; see "Women Becoming Poets: Katherine Philips, Aphra Behn, Anne Finch," *ELH* 57 (Summer 1990): 335-55. It is becoming evident that a major challenge facing feminist criticism today is to find ways to combine the ongoing deconstruction of inherited patriarchal codes with a historical narrative that more fully acknowledges women's participation in male-dominated culture—without re-encoding male domination.

⁶ The volume was never reprinted nor were individual Barker poems included in any later miscellanies that I have been able to discover. I have located no printed reference to Barker's poetry earlier than Robert Southey's entry in a commonplace book; see John Wood Warter, ed., *Southey's Common-Place Book,* 4th series, 4 vols. (London: Longman, Brown, Green, and Longmans, 1850), 4:296.

⁷ Other named contributors include Mr. [Sir William] Godolphin, Mr. B. Willie (identified in the Table of Contents as master of the Free-School of Newark-upon-Trent), J.[ohn?] Whitehall, Thomas Wright (who produced for Benjamin Crayle a commercially successful adaptation of Reynold's *God's Revenge against Murther and Adultery*), a Mr. Worsdell, Hovenden Walker (who translated *Elegies of Old Age* for publication by Crayle). For more on J. Whitehall, see note 15.

⁸ For biographical data on Edward Barker, see *Alumni Oxonienses: The Members of the University of Oxford, 1500-1714,* comp. Joseph Foster, 4 vols. (Nendeln/Liechtenstein: Kraus Rpt., 1968), 1:70. There is no factual basis for the frequently encountered claim that Jane's literary friends were members of her brother's circle.

⁹ Janet Todd, "Life after Sex: The Fictional Autobiography of Delariver Manley," *Women's Studies* 15 (1988): 44.

¹⁰ Deborah C. Payne, "'And Poets Shall by Patron-Princes Live': Aphra Behn and Patronage," in Schofield and Macheski (note 5), 117. The Behn quote is from the Preface to *The Lucky Chance.*

¹¹ See also Barker, *"Resolved never to Versifie more,"* "A Farewell to POETRY, with a Long Digression on ANATOMY," *"Necessity of Fate,"* and "To the Importunate ADDRESS of POETRY." The latter begins with an image of poetry as a "Kind Friend" infesting the "barren *Region* of my Breast," the almost grotesque contradictions of which express the speaker's complex relation to her own writing urges.

¹² He is further identified in *Poetical Recreations* as "J. N. *Fellow of St.* John's *Colledge,* Cambridge."

¹³ I am indebted to Alison M. Pearn, Biographical Assistant for St. John's College, Cambridge, for sharing

with me the Biographical Record Sheet on John Newton. Newton was admitted as a sizar 10 June 1678, received a B.A. in 1682, an M.A. in 1685; he was a Fellow from 1685 to 1700. See John Venn and J.A. Venn, *Alumni Cantabrigienses: A Biographical List of All Known Students, Graduates and Holders of Office at the University of Cambridge From the Earliest Times to 1900,* Part 1, 4 vols. (Cambridge: Cambridge Univ. Press, 1922-1927), 3:252.

[14] In *A Patch-work Screen* Galesia gives her age at this time as "but little more than Twenty" (*PWS,* 27). If I am correct that Newton, who matriculated in 1678, is one of the Cambridge friends, then Barker could have been no younger than twenty-six.

[15] A strikingly similar figure (but also strikingly different in its implications) occurs in *"To the University of Oxford"* by John Whitehall. The male speaker characterizes Oxford as a "sweet *Paradice*" where stands the "unforbidden Tree of *Knowledge,*" from which he for undisclosed reasons has three times been debarred. The source of his regret is that lack of a University degree thwarts his desire for preferment and wealth. The poem appears in *Miscellaneous Poems, With some Remarks on the Death of King Charles the II. And the Happy succession of King James II. To the Magistracy of England* (London: printed for T. Salusbury, 1685). Since part 2 of *Poetical Recreations* includes three poems by a Mr. J. Whitehall, including one to his "Much-esteemed Friend Mr. *J. N.*" (possibly John Newton), it is tempting to suppose that Barker and Whitehall were in poetic correspondence.

[16] Magdalen MS 343, part 2, f. 18. The poem, which has never been printed, is one of seventy-nine separate pieces copied (probably by Barker) into the three-part manuscript volume now deposited at Magdalen College, Oxford.

[17] The motto comes from *Aeneid* 1:496. The friends have substituted *virgo* for the original *Dido* and in so doing have fashioned a playful tribute: Barker becomes, loosely translated, the loveliest of virgins, attended by a crowd of young men.

[18] This punctures Joanna Lipking's (note 5) assertion that early women poets "never" recorded their responses to men's commendations (66). However, the general truth of her observations stands. Magdalen MS, part 2, f.18v, v.

[19] The quote comes from the headnote to part 3 of Magdalen MS 343: "These following poems, are taken out of a book of Miscellany poems, and writ by the same author as the former, But without her consent, were printed in the year 1688: now corrected by her own hand, which makes the third part of this Collection."

[20] For examples of the handling of the Daphne story in poems by Behn, "Philo-Philippa," and Anne Killigrew, see Dorothy Mermin (note 5), 349-50.

[21] "Exilius" is identified in *Poetical Recreations* only as "*a Gentleman of* St. John's *College,* Cambridge." Barker gives a brief account of their friendship in *A Patch-work Screen:* "There was one [of the "young Companions" who accompanied her kinsman to her home in Wilsthorpe], whose Merit ingaged my particular Esteem, and the Compassion he had for my Griefs, planted a Friendship, which I have ever since cultivated with my best Endeavours." The two young men "joyn'd to consolate me with repeated Proofs of their Friendship; all which my dear Parents approv'd; and promoted their Visits to our House by a generous and kind Reception at our Country Retreat; where they came now and then, a little to relax their College Discipline, and unbend the Streightness of their Study" (*PWS,* 22-23).

[22] In May of 1688 Crayle was fined twenty shillings at the Guildhall Sessions of the Peace for publishing *The school of Venus;* the bill of indictment in the Sessions Files at the Corporation of London Record Office (CLRO) charges him with publishing and selling a "scandalosum flagitosum lasciviosum et vitiosum librum [scandalous, shameful, lascivious and vicious book]" (CLRO, SF 356). In January of 1690 the same court imposed upon Crayle a fine of twenty pounds for publishing the play *Sodom: or, the quintessence of debauchery.* See D. S. Thomas, "Prosecutions of *Sodom: Or, The Quintessence of Debauchery,* and *Poems on Several Occasions by the E of R,* 1689-1690 and 1693," *Library* 5th ser., 24 (1969): 51-55. For the earlier prosecution, see David Foxon, *Libertine Literature in England 1660-1745* (rpt. with revisions, from *The Book Collector* (1964): 10-11.

[23] Born in 1660, Crayle was the youngest son but one in a family of nine children. His father, Richard (1600-1671), was a substantial London watchmaker who had retired to Newark by 1660; at his death he left to Benjamin and his brother James property in Acton with instructions that the two boys were to be put out as apprentices in "such Trades as hereafter they may bee inabled to get their Living" (Public Record Office, PROB 11/337/220v). On 4 June 1683 the brothers were admitted to the freedom of the Stationers' Company (*Stationers' Company Apprentices 1641-1700,* ed. D. F. MacKenzie [Oxford Oxford Bibliographical Society, 1974], 33, 49). A fifty-five page account of the Crayle family by Edmund Royds was published in 1927 by The Architectural & Archeological Society of the County of Lincoln; it is available in volume 9 of the collection of "Tracts" at the Society of Genealogists, London. Crayle's first publication was *Triumphant Chastity* by Jo. Quarles (or Jacob Catts). In his brief (1683-90) and mildly disreputable career as a bookseller, Crayle published a variety of titles; the only

ones to go into a second edition were two collections of racy narratives, Thomas Wright's *The Glory of God's Revenge* (1685) and *Delightful and Ingenious Novels* (1685), and a translation from Latin of *Elegies of Old Age* (1688), which he reissued the next year as *The Importent Lover*. *Poetical Recreations* was the only Crayle imprint to feature a woman writer and his only venture into contemporary poetry.

[24] Crayle is not one of the members of the booktrade profiled in *The Life and Errors of John Dunton* (1705), probably because he died in 1690 some fifteen years before Dunton composed his account. The only comment on Crayle's practices as bookseller I have located comes from John Twells, a Newark school-master who produced a number of Latin grammars and provided Crayle with the two essays published in 1686 as *Tentamina Elegantiarum bina: Or, Two Essays of Elegancies;* in a letter to Crayle inserted by way of preface Twells offers the essays in order "in some measure [to] satisfie your frequent importunities."

[25] In one of the twelve poems of his own that Crayle printed in part 2 of *Poetical Recreations,* Crayle claims to have known Barker for three years. Since the poem, "On his Secret Passion for Cosmelia," had to have been written by autumn of 1687 (the volume was entered in the Stationer's Register 25 October 1687 and was on sale by 5 December, when it was advertised in the *London Gazette*), the meeting, assuming the poem's chronology is to be trusted, would have occurred at some point during the second half of 1684. This time frame would square with Barker's account in *A Patch-work Screen* of her removal from Lincolnshire to Westminster at some point before the death of Charles II in 1685. Thus far I have located no documentary evidence firmly establishing Barker's residence in the London area in the 1680s. However, there does exist a tantalizing bit of evidence from 1685 of the Barker-Crayle connection: at the bottom of a list of recent Crayle publications is a notice announcing that at Crayle's shop could also be found *"Dr Barkers Famous Gout Plaister."* A footnote doubtless supplied by Barker in *A Patch-work Screen* informs us that Galesia, Barker's name for her younger self, possessed "a particular *Arcanum* for the Gout" (57). The advertisement for the gout plaster occurs at the end of *Delightful and Ingenious Novels* (1685).

[26] However, *A Patch-work Screen* (*PWS*, 26-28) has them addressed to one of the unnamed Cambridge friends. It is possible that Crayle for his own reasons concocted a romance for the pages of *Poetical Recreations.*

[27] "To COSMELIA, on her Departure into the COUNTREY" begins, for example. "Farewell, fair *Mistress* of my chief desires, / Whose charming *Beauties* kindleth pleasing fires."

[28] Barker's involvement with Crayle lends some support to Janet Todd's observation in *The Sign of Angellica: Women, Writing and Fiction, 1660-1800* (London: Virago, 1989), 18-19, that at this time women's political writings were more likely to be published when their author was personally involved with someone in the book trade. We know from Crayle's "To my Ingenious Friend Mrs. JANE BARKER on my Publishing her Romance of SCIPINA" that Crayle was also preparing to publish the royalist allegory (in the form of heroic romance) that did not come out until 1715, when it was published by Edmund Curll under the title *Exilius.* One has to wonder how the famously decorous Barker came to be published at two junctures by two different pornographers. The circumstance, while probably a coincidence, is intriguing.

[29] Moira Ferguson (note 4), 172; Maureen Bell, George Parfitt, and Simon Shepherd, *A Biographical Dictionary of English Women Writers 1580-1720* (Boston: G. K. Hall, 1990), 17.

[30] Elaine Hobby, *Virtue of Necessity: English Women's Writing 1649-88* (Ann Arbor: Univ. of Michigan Press, 1989), 160.

[31] One other poem, a meditation on death, is addressed to her "Dear Cousin Mrs. M. T."

[32] See, for example, Philips's "A marryd state affords but little Ease," Denham's "Friendship and Single Life Against Love and Marriage," Cowley's "On Solitude," and Cotton's "The Joys of Marriage."

[33] For examples see Margaret J. M. Ezell, *The Patriarch's Wife: Literary Evidence and the History of the Family* (Chapel Hill: Univ. of North Carolina Press, 1987), esp. 106-8. Ezell mistakenly attributes to Barker "The Preference of a Single Life before Marriage," which had appeared in part 2 of *Poetical Recreations.*

[34] The standard treatment of the retirement ideal is Maren-Sofie Rostvig, *The Happy Man: Studies in the Metamorphoses of a Classical Ideal 1600-1700* (Oxford: Basil Blackwell, 1954). For its application by women poets, see Williamson (note 3), 68-78, and Hobby (note 30), 134-35. Notice that the retired life Barker's poem promotes is not retirement from the demands and excitation of public life but from the demands and excitation of men, children, and sexuality.

[35] Magdalen MS offers some evidence for this.

[36] *The Norton Anthology of Literature by Women: The Tradition in English,* ed. Sandra M. Gilbert and Susan Gubar (New York: Norton, 1985), 3-4.

[37] Mulvihill (note 5), 74.

[38] Letter to John Locke from Lady Masham, 14 December 1685, in *The Correspondence of John Locke,* ed. E. S. De Beer, 8 vols. (Oxford: Clarendon, 1976), 2:762.

[39] Sandra M. Gilbert and Susan Gubar, "Introduction: Gender, Creativity, and the Woman Poet," in *Shakespeare's Sisters: Feminist Essays on Women Poets,* ed. Sandra M. Gilbert and Susan Gubar (Bloomington: Indiana Univ. Press, 1979), xx. I do not pretend that this essay speaks for feminist historiography today, but the romantic assumptions that it exposes continue to shape the way women's texts are presented and discussed. See, for example, the introduction to one of the most recent anthologies of early women's verse, Joyce Fullard's *British Women Poets 1660-1880: An Anthology* (Troy, New York: Whitston Publishing Co., 1990).

FURTHER READING

Donovan, Josephine. "Women and the Rise of the Novel: A Feminist-Marxist Theory." *Signs: Journal of Women in Culture and Society* 16, No. 31 (1991): 441-62.

Marxist study of how women novelists responded to their social and economic positions discusses Barker's rejection of the notion of brides as commodities.

Richetti, John J. *Popular Fiction Before Richardson: Narrative Patterns 1700-1739.* Oxford: Clarendon Press, 1969, pp. 230-39.

Argues that Barker's works invited a wider audience to the novel by maintaining scrupulously moral standards.

Spacks, Patricia Meyer. *Imagining a Self: Autobiography and Novel in Eighteenth-Century England.* Cambridge, Mass.: Harvard University Press, 1976, pp. 66-9.

Describes *A Patch-Work Screen for the Ladies* as a work of rage and anger at society's values, particularly in regards to relationships between the sexes.

Wilson, Carol Shiner. "Introduction." In *The Galesia Trilogy and Selected Manuscript Poems of Jane Barker,* edited by Carol Shiner Wilson, pp. xv-xliii. New York: Oxford University Press, 1997.

Includes excellent biographical sketch of Barker and critical overview of her works.

Aphra Behn: *Oroonoko*

1640?-1689

(Pseudonym of Aphra Johnson or Aphra Amis; also Aphara, Ayfara, and Afray; also wrote under pseudonyms of Astrea and Astraea.) English novelist, dramatist, poet, essayist, and translator.

The following entry presents criticism of Behn's novel *Oroonoko* (1688). For a discussion of Behn's complete career, see *LC*, Volumes 1 and 30.

INTRODUCTION

Oroonoko is Behn's best known work and critics consider it her best book—the novel which earns her a place among the most noted writers in English literature. The book is set in Surinam and chronicles the struggles and ultimate destruction of the title character, an African slave. Oroonoko represents the ideal man and is often regarded as the first "noble savage" character in English literature. Through her work in *Oroonoko* Behn is credited with adding realism to the novel genre and advancing its development.

Biographical Information

Behn is believed to have been the first woman to earn her living as an author. After the death of her husband, Behn was engaged by Charles II to spy on disaffected British citizens in Antwerp, Holland. She returned to England destitute and spent time in a debtor's prison. Looking for a means of making a living, Behn turned to writing, primarily plays. She soon developed a reputation for writing material as bawdy as that of her male counterparts. As a supporter of the Tories, Behn was prohibited to write for the stage from 1682 until 1688. During this period she wrote *Oroonoko*, which critics have considered far superior to her plays. Behn claimed that the book resulted from events which she experienced as a young woman in Surinam. According to Behn, her father was appointed to a junior position in the colonial government but while en route with his family to the colony he died. The family spent several months in Surinam before boarding a returning vessel. Behn filled her novel with remarkably detailed and realistic descriptions of the area, the people, and colonial life, supposedly based on her first-hand observations. However, at the turn of the century scholars refuted Behn's claim, arguing that she had never been to Surinam and that she based her novel on secondary sources. Despite these factual uncertainties, it is apparent that the novel reflects Behn's social and political philosophies, especially her pro-Royalist stance. She died in 1689 and was buried in Westminster Abbey.

Plot and Major Characters

Oroonoko is the tale of an African prince, himself engaged in the slave trade, until he is captured and sold into slavery in Surinam. When his West Indian lover, Imoinda, becomes pregnant, Oroonoko cannot face the idea of his child being born into slavery and he escapes. The eponymous protagonist is often considered the first example in English fiction of the "noble savage." Deriving from the philosophical ideas of Jean-Jacques Rousseau, this concept supposes that members of preliterate and so-called primitive cultures exist in a state of grace and possess innate virtue. The novel juxtaposes Oroonoko's views and concept of honor with those of the colonists who ultimately betray and kill him.

Critical Reception

Although Behn has attracted much critical attention as an early and very popular woman writer, critics have focused almost exclusively on *Oroonoko*, especially noting its realistic tone, unprecedented for romantic fiction in Behn's age. Myra Reyonlds has written: "At a time when French heroic romances, with their high-flown adventures, unreal characters, and stilted dialogue, were the only works of fiction, Mrs. Behn's short, simple, vigorous, and affecting story of real life comes with a startling sense of novelty." Until the twentieth century it was assumed that this realism sprung from Behn's personal experiences; however, in 1913 Ernest Bernboun argued that Behn had never been to Surinam and that the novel was based on secondary sources. The debate over its varacity continues in the late twentieth century. In 1988 Katherine Rogers placed the argument in new light, writing that Behn's true accomplishment was "imaginative creation building on a foundation of fact, which probably included personal experience." Recent scholarship has also revised the earlier assumption that *Oroonoko* is one of the first anti-slavery novels. Anita Pacheco has argued that the significance of the protagonist is not that he is a slave, but rather that he is a prince. Other critics agree that the book must be viewed as a political defence of pro-Royalist sentiment in Restoration England.

CRITICISM

Ernest A. Baker (essay date 1905)

SOURCE: Introduction, in *The Novels of Mrs. Aphra Behn*, George Routledge and Sons, Ltd., 1905, pp. vii-xxi.

[*In the excerpt below, Baker argues that* Oroonoko *represents the ideal man, and that through her novel Behn condemns European civilization.*]

It was the truth and power with which she recounted what she had herself witnessed in Surinam that has singled out for permanence the best of her novels, the story of the royal slave, Oroonoko. We need not give ear to the whispers of a liaison with the heroic black. A very different emotion inspires the tale, the same feeling of outraged humanity that in after days inflamed Mrs. Stowe. *Oroonoko* is the first emancipation novel. It is also the first glorification of the Natural Man. Mrs. Behn was, in a manner, the precursor of Bernardin de Saint-Pierre; and in her attempts to depict the splendour of tropical scenery she foreshadows, though feebly, the prose-epics of Chateaubriand. There is fierce satire in *Oroonoko.* Who would think that Astrea, who entertained the depraved pit at the Duke's Theatre, could have drawn those idyllic pictures of Oroonoko in his native Coromantien, of the truth and purity of the savage uncontaminated with the vices of Christian Europe, or have written such vehement invectives against the baseness and utter falsehood of the whites?

'These people represented to me,' she said, 'an absolute idea of the first state of innocence, before man knew how to sin: and 'tis most evident and plain that simple nature is the most harmless, inoffensive and virtuous mistress. 'Tis she alone, if she were permitted, that better instructs the world than all the inventions of man: religion would here but destroy that tranquillity they possess by ignorance; and laws would teach em to know offences of which now they have no notion. They once made mourning and fasting for the death of the English governor, who had given his hand to come on such a day to em, and neither came nor sent; believing when a man's word was past, nothing but death could or should prevent his keeping it: and when they saw he was not dead, they ask'd him what name they had for a man who promis'd a thing he did not do? The governor told them such a man was a lyar, which was a word of infamy to a gentleman. Then one of em replied, 'Governor, you are a lyar, and guilty of that infamy.'

It is said further on, 'Such ill morals are only practis'd in

Christian countries, where they prefer the bare name of religion; and, without virtue and morality, think that sufficient.'

Oroonoko is no savage, but the ideal man, as conceived by Mrs. Behn, the man out of Eden; and in him she has an absolute criterion by which to judge and condemn the object of her satire—European civilisation. His bravery, wisdom, chastity, his high sense of honour, are the idealisations of a sentimental young lady, carried away by her admiration for a truly heroic figure, and disgusted by the vicious manners of the colonists, whom she describes as 'rogues and runagades, that have abandoned their own countries for rapine, murder, theft and villainies.' 'Do you not hear,' says Oroonoko, 'how they upbraid each other with infamy of life, below the wildest savages? And shall we render obedience to such a degenerate race, who have no one human virtue left, to distinguish them from the vilest creatures?'

The story has the natural elements of drama. Southern wrote a very bad tragedy on the theme of Mrs. Behn's narrative, altering it slightly, and adding a great deal of foulness that is, happily, not in the original. Oroonoko loves the beautiful Imoinda, a maiden of his own race, not the child of a European who has adopted a savage life, as in Southern's play. But when they are on the brink of happiness, the old king, Oroonoko's grandfather, demands her for his harem. Imoinda acts the part of Abishag the Shunamite, and her lover that of Adonijah. The vengeful monarch discovers their attachment, and sells her into slavery. Oroonoko, soon afterwards, is kidnapped, and finds himself in Surinam, where Imoinda is already famous as the beautiful slave, as chaste as she is beautiful. They recognise each other in a touching scene, and are suffered to be re-united. Oroonoko distinguishes himself by his virtue and prowess. But he quickly finds that his tyrants promise freedom to himself and Imoinda merely to delude them into good behaviour. He flies into the wilderness at the head of a body of slaves. The planters follow, the blacks fling down their arms, and Oroonoko surrenders on the assurance that they shall not be chastised. The white governor is a scoundrel. The magnanimous negro is put in irons and tortured. Imoinda is set apart for a worse fate. But she prefers to die at his beloved hands, rather than bear dishonour. Oroonoko, with Roman fortitude, slays his wife, and with the stoicism of the Indian smokes a pipe of tobacco while his captors execute him piecemeal.

The Fair Jilt; or, the Amours of Prince Tarquin and Miranda, also purports to be a recital of incidents Astrea herself had witnessed. 'As Love,' it begins, 'is the most noble and divine passion of the soul, so it is that to which we may justly attribute all the real satisfactions of life; and without it man is unfinish'd and unhappy.' She hardly succeeds in proving the divinity of the passion she portrays. Miranda is only a false name for a Beguine at Antwerp, who had many lovers; Tarquin is the real name of a German prince, the most illustrious of her votaries. It is the story of a fair hypocrite, whose beauty drives men mad. Miranda, whose raging fever of desire reminds one of Phaedra, being repulsed by a handsome young friar, falls back on the device of Potiphar's wife, to secure revenge. This episode is full of force and vigour; but Tarquin's subjugation to the enchantress, his complaisant obedience to her criminal schemes, which is offered for our admiration as an example of the illimitable power of love, does not strike us so. Passion, Mrs. Behn maintains, condones everything. There is nothing too heinous, too flagitious, to attain a sort of dignity if done in the cause of love. Tarquin attempts to assassinate the Fair Jilt's sister, and is deservedly condemned to death. The novelist depicts him as a martyr, and has a tear to spare even for the more culpable Miranda.

> At last the bell toll'd, and he was to take leave of the princess, as his last work of life, and the most hard he had to accomplish. He threw himself at her feet, and gazing on her as she sat more dead than alive, overwhelm'd with silent grief, they both remained some moments speechless; and then, as if one rising tide of tears had supplied both their eyes, it burst out in tears at the same instant: and when his sighs gave way, he utter'd a thousand farewells, so soft, so passionate, and moving, that all who were by were extremely touch'd with it, and said, 'That nothing could be seen more deplorable and melancholy.'

All that can be said in comment is, that there have been novelists since Mrs. Behn who have written stuff that is quite as false, lurid, and depraved, and readers who have gushed over it. Only the sinners begotten of later romancers do not sin with such abandon. Astrea has never lacked successors, though the cut of her mantle has been altered to suit the changes of the mode.

The omnipotence of love is again the theme in another 'true novel,' ***The Nun; or, the Perjured Beauty,*** in which a similar heroine is also the villain of the plot. Astrea frankly accepted Charles the Second's well-known opinion as to the frailty of woman. 'Virtue,' she makes one of her characters say, 'is but a name kept from scandal, which the most base of women best preserve.' But Ardelia does not even trouble about appearances. She is one of those passionate, insatiable, capricious women who play a leading rôle in every one of Astrea's comedies, and are always drawn with energy and truth because their author's heart was in them. The plot is worked out with great ingenuity in this story, and also in a later one, ***The Lucky Mistake,*** in which the reader is kept in the titillations of suspense to the final page. In the last-named, also, there is some attempt at character-drawing.

Oroonoko was not the only novel in which Mrs. Behn tried to portray ideal feelings and elevated morality. ***Agnes de Castro*** is a sweet, sentimental tragedy, which at least has the merit of being free from errors of taste. Agnes is maid-of-honour to Donna Constantia, wife of the Prince of Portugal, and has the misfortune to be loved by her mistress's husband. But there is no foul intrigue in the story. Don Pedro struggles honourably against his passion: 'his fault was not voluntary': . . . 'a commanding power, a fatal star, had forc'd him to love in spite of himself.' The Princess is so high-minded—after the seventeenth-century pattern of high-mindedness—that she admits his innocence. 'I have no reproaches to make against you, knowing that 'tis inclination that disposes hearts, and not reason.' Her complaisance goes so far that she even conjures Agnes not to deprive him of her society, since it is necessary to his happiness. But the truce is brought to a fatal ending by the malice of an envious woman, who persuades Constantia that the lovers are guilty, and so breaks her heart. The novel is painfully stilted, and reads like the discarded sketch for a tragedy, which had been worked up to suit another style.

It must be confessed that, apart from ***Oroonoko,*** Mrs. Behn's fiction is of very little importance in the history of our literature. Her best work was put into her comedies, which contain, not only much diversion, but also strong, and perhaps too highly coloured, pictures of the manners and morals of the pleasure-seekers of her time, in all classes. Unfortunately, it would be difficult indeed to compile even a book of elegant extracts that would give the modern reader any adequate idea of their merits, without either emasculating them altogether or nauseating him with their coarseness.

Ernest Bernbaum (essay date 1913)

SOURCE: "Mrs. Behn's *Oroonoko*," in *Anniversary Papers by Colleagues and Pupils of George Lyman Kittredge*, Ginn and Company Publishers, 1913, pp. 419-34.

[*In the essay below, Bernbaum addresses the question of realism in* Oroonoko, *concluding that much of Behn's material came from secondhand sources.*]

Historians of the novel assign to Mrs. Behn's *Oroonoko* a place of distinct importance in the development of realism. They concede that those parts of the narrative which recount the adventures of Oroonoko in Coramantien are full of romance, but maintain that his subsequent slavery in Surinam, his reunion with his bride Imoinda, his insurrection, and his violent death, are on the whole delineated with fidelity to fact. "Imagination," says Professor Canby, "colored the heroic life of the slave as well as the romantic intrigue of the negro prince," but only, it seems, in a few negligible respects; the rest is considered "truthful, touching, and vivid."[1] If we ask why Mrs. Behn writes romantically about Coramantien, and realistically about Surinam, we are reminded that she had visited the latter country but not the former. "The localities considered in the second part of the story," explains Professor Siegel in his monograph on Mrs. Behn, "she knows from her own observation; in the events she has to some extent participated; her description is consequently far more credible and probable than in the first part."[2] And Mr. E. A. Baker, editor of Mrs. Behn's stories, concludes: "It was the truth and power with which she recounted what she herself had witnessed in Surinam that has singled out for permanence the best of her novels."[3]

If, remembering these opinions, we read *Oroonoko* itself, we come now and then upon incidents that surprise us. Mrs. Behn tells us of a monstrous tiger which had long infested Surinam, and had been repeatedly shot quite through the body, but without effect until the mighty hunter Oroonoko slew it; and "when the heart of this courageous animal was taken out, there were seven bullets of lead in it, the wound seamed up with great scars, and she lived with the bullets a great while, for it was long since they were shot."[4] Elsewhere she writes: "Sometimes we [four women and two men] would go surprising, and in search of young tigers in their dens, watching when the old ones went forth to forage for prey; and oftentimes we have been in great danger, and have fled apace for our lives, when surprised by the dams."[5] Those who know anything of the dreaded jaguar of South America can hardly believe that such visits of a pleasant afternoon were ever regarded by the colonists as suitable diversions for ladies and gentlemen.

Mrs. Behn's sensational description of her hero's attempted suicide likewise gives us pause. We are told that Oroonoko, after remaining beside the dead body of Imoinda, in agony of spirit and without food, for eight days, roused himself on the approach of his pursuers, defiantly "cut a piece of flesh from his own throat and threw it at them," "ripped up his own belly, and took his bowels and pulled them out," and still had strength enough to drive his knife into the heart of an onrushing opponent. Yet Oroonoko did not die. His captors carried him a long distance to the plantation, "laid him on a couch, and had the chirurgeon immediately to him, who dressed his wounds, and sewed up his belly, and used means to bring him to life, which they effected." "In six or seven days he recovered his senses; for you must know that wounds are almost to a miracle cured in the Indies, unless wounds in the legs, which they rarely ever cure."[6] In such instances we may surely suspect that Mrs. Behn is more desirous of magnifying the strength and bravery of her hero than of narrating experiences veraciously. The exaggeration or improbability we see in them is, however, insufficient to destroy, though it may impair, her reputation as a realist. In fact, incredible as seems the recovery of Oroonoko from such frightful wounds, we cannot disprove its possibility. Though similar cases are rare, medical literature records a sufficient number to compel reluctant belief.[7] At any rate, the dubious episodes which I have pointed out do not seem to have disconcerted the admirers of Mrs. Behn, and were presumably dismissed from their minds as inconsiderable deviations from the truth. They remark upon the significance of her calling *Oroonoko,* not a novel or tale, but a "history," and of her opening it with these words:

> I do not pretend, in giving you the history of this royal slave, to entertain my reader with the adventures of a feigned hero, whose life and fortunes fancy may manage at the poet's pleasure; nor, in relating the truth, design to adorn it with any accidents, but such as arrived in earnest to him: and it shall come simply into the world, recommended by its own proper merits and natural intrigues; there being enough of reality to support it, and to render it diverting, without the addition of invention. I was myself an eye-witness to a great part of what you will find here set down; and what I could not be witness of, I received from the mouth of the chief actor in this history, the hero himself.[8]

This statement of her intention is generally accepted as sincere. Oroonoko's history, says Professor Canby, "I can only believe after many readings, she wished to set forth with a reasonable degree of truth." The resulting vividness of her story he graphically describes as follows:

> The recital of Oroonoko's slavery is too circumstantial to be suspected, before Defoe, of being fictitious. His fortitude, his high spirit, the revolt which he inspired, the brutal tortures he suffered, his fidelity to Imoinda, whom he finds a

fellow slave, all bear the print of truth as well as the increase of a romantic fancy. His death is told not only with Flaubertian realism but with the passion of one seeking to expose unjust officials who had been cruel to a friend. Furthermore, it is a real South America, with gorgeous vegetation, Indian villages most anthropologically described, armadilloes, and even electric eels, with a "quality so cold" that the catcher's arm is benumbed. I have seen many early "voyages" to the "other world," as Aphra always calls it, whose descriptions are less specific than the setting of this story.[9]

The historical bearing of the realistic purpose and character of *Oroonoko* has not been overlooked. Our attention is called to the fact that when the work appeared, in 1688, romance was the predominant form of fiction. "Of the highest importance for the substance of narrative literature," says Professor Siegel, "is the appearance of Mrs. Behn; for the first time after a long interval, actuality is again emphasized."[10] "For making use of incidents of real life in the service of fiction at a time when the heroic romance was at the height of its vogue," says Professor Raleigh, "she deserves all credit."[11] These remarks indicate that if there is an error in the commonly accepted doctrine, it affects not merely our understanding of *Oroonoko,* but complicates one of the most puzzling and important problems of modern English scholarship—namely, the true origin of the realistic novel.

The nature of the foundation on which the prevailing doctrine rests may be revealed by asking some pertinent questions. Were the political and social conditions of Surinam, at the time when these events are supposed to have occurred, such as to render them possible? Can Mrs. Behn's descriptions of the countryside, the climate, the colonists, the slaves, and the natives, be shown to correspond to reality? Surely, until we have satisfactory answers on such points, we do not know the real character of the story. Yet, astonishing as it may seem, these questions, so far from having been answered, have hardly been raised. Mrs. Behn's assurance that she is faithfully recording fact is, as to the principal part of her story, passively accepted even though she is known to be romancing in other parts. Because the narrative is vivid, it is believed true. The fact that an imaginary experience may be as vividly told as an actual one, is ignored. In other words, what in this case passes as literary history rests on the author's assertion and on impressions produced by her artistic power.

Possibly the reason why no real effort has been made to discover whether *Oroonoko* is based upon actual observation may lie in the fact that there are unusual obstacles to such an inquiry. To determine what the appearance and condition of a small tropical colony really were two hundred and fifty years ago, is in no case easy; and respecting Surinam the ordinary diffi-

culties are magnified. In 1667 it was surrendered by the English to the Dutch; and consequently the English historians neglect the colony because it did not remain British, while the Dutch say little or nothing concerning its history before the time of their possession. Nevertheless, oblivion has not wholly obscured the character of the environment in which Oroonoko dwelt.

Though Mrs. Behn does not mention the date of Oroonoko's sojourn in Surinam, she chances to provide us with information that enables us to calculate it. "Immediately after his time," she says, the Dutch took the colony[12]—an event which occurred in March, 1667. Furthermore, she tells us that Oroonoko, because of the outrageous injustice of his enslavement, was promised his liberty as soon as the Lord Governor of Surinam, "who was every day expected," should revisit the colony.[13] The Lord Governor referred to must have been Francis Lord Willoughby of Parham, a distinguished administrator of several British dependencies in the West Indies, whose headquarters were in Barbadoes. He came to Surinam rarely, his last visit extending from about November, 1664, to May, 1665.[14] In July, 1666, he was lost at sea. These data serve to place the action of *Oroonoko* in the latter part of 1665 and the earlier part of 1666. It may be added that several allusions, in the course of the story, to the lapse of time make it evident that between the arrival of Oroonoko and his death a period of not much less than seven months, and hardly more than nine, must have passed.[15] Since all these chronological particulars agree with one another, the problem whether Mrs. Behn's narrative is true reduces itself to the question, Does her account of Surinam correspond with its actual state in 1665 and 1666?

Mrs. Behn's allusions to historical personages and political conditions prove in some respects quite correct. She calls the Deputy Governor, Byam; and William Byam was, as a matter of fact, "Lieutenant General of Guiana and Governor of Willoughby Land" from about 1662 to 1667.[16] The only other official whom she names is one Banister, according to her account a member of the Governor's Council.[17] The colonial state papers do not contain a list of the councilors, but it is not unlikely that Banister was one of them; for after Byam's departure in 1667 "Sergeant Major James Banister, the only remaining eminent person," became lieutenant governor.[18] It is noteworthy that the wars with the Dutch made each of these men known in England. It was Byam who headed the forces that vainly defended Surinam against the Dutch admiral Crynsens in 1667; and it was Banister who, in 1668, made the final surrender of the colony. The latter again became prominent when, in arranging the transportation of the English settlers from Surinam, he quarreled with the Dutch and was imprisoned by them; and in the British declaration of war in 1672 his imprisonment was stated as a *casus belli.* That

Mrs. Behn correctly names these officials is therefore but slender evidence of intimate familiarity with the local affairs of Surinam.

Mrs. Behn's statement that when Oroonoko, seeking freedom, put himself at the head of three hundred negroes, many of the leading colonists pitied him so much that they would not pursue him, is questionable. It seems strange that in a slave-owning community they should have failed to realize that mere self-preservation demanded the crushing of so formidable an insurrection. Another dubious passage is that describing the militia which, under Byam's leadership, set out after Oroonoko:

> Never did one see so comical an army march forth to war. . . . Most of their arms were of those sort of cruel whips they call cat with nine tails; some had rusty useless guns for show; others old basket-hilts, whose blades had never seen the light in this age; and others had long staffs and clubs.[19]

Shall we believe that Byam, who at this very time had sufficient military forces to carry the war against the Dutch and the French into the enemy's territories, and to capture posts from each of them,[20] commanded so ill-armed a rabble?

Likewise difficult to bring into accord with the historical situation is Mrs. Behn's scornful characterization of the Council:

> . . . who (not to disgrace them or burlesque the government there) consisted of such notorious villains as Newgate never transported; and, possibly, originally were such who understood neither the laws of God or man, and had no sort of principles to make them worthy the name of men; but at the very council table would contradict and fight with one another, and swear so bloodily, that it was terrible to hear and see them.[21]

If such was the real character of the government, we should expect to find that the British colonial office, whose correspondence of this period contains many complaints of maladministration in other dependencies, would have been frequently appealed to by the settlers in Surinam; but the only evidence of that kind appears in a letter of 1662, which charges Byam with an act of oppression—a charge which was apparently dismissed.[22] A year later one Renatus Enys writes from Surinam to the Secretary: "The colony is in good order, being nobly upheld by the power and prudence of those at the helm."[23] It seems unlikely that men as vicious and unrestrained as those described by Mrs. Behn could have guided Surinam, through all the difficulties of a new settlement in an unwholesome region, to that strength and prosperity which it had attained by 1666.

Our suspicions are increased by Mrs. Behn's parting shot at the Council: "Some of them were afterwards hanged, when the Dutch took possession of the place; others sent off in chains."[24] Whereas the other accusations are merely difficult to reconcile with our conception of the general state of affairs; the last one directly conflicts with known historical facts. Under the treaty of surrender, it was explicitly stipulated that the lives and property of every settler should be spared by the Dutch, and that the British should freely depart from Surinam with their possessions. When Major Banister, because of petty interferences with these rights, protested and was imprisoned, Great Britain raised protests which led to a renewal of the war. Had the Dutch treated members of the Council in the violent way alleged by Mrs. Behn, it would certainly have transpired in the diplomatic correspondence which the actual situation developed. In short, we find in the historical background of **Oroonoko** several improbabilities and one misstatement.

Of the climate of Surinam the characteristics that strike the European visitor are intense heat and great moisture. One effect of the latter is noted by Mrs. Behn in her derisive description of the rusty arms of the militia; but otherwise she seems, for a supposed realist, peculiarly insensible to the true nature of the climate. Though, according to her story, she must have been in the land not less than seven months, she never mentions the rainy seasons. She casually remarks that "the rays [of the sun] are very fierce here"; but the costumes which she and her friends wore on an eight-day river journey, and which excited the amazement of the Indians, may cause us wonder too. "We were dressed," she declares, "so as is most commode for the hot countries, very glittering and rich, so that we appeared extremely fine; my own hair was cut short, and I had a taffety cap with black feathers on my head; my brother was in a stuff suit, with silver loops and buttons, and an abundance of green ribbon."[25] The atmosphere in which her story is immersed is best expressed in her ardent words: "It is there eternal spring, always the very months of April, May, and June."[26] We are reminded thereby of "the sweet ayre" praised by Raleigh and his immediate followers in those rose-colored passages describing their explorations upon the Orinoco, wherein they mingle enthusiasm and inaccuracy.[27]

Some of the geographical allusions in **Oroonoko** are startling. Surinam, we are told, "reaches from east to west, one way as far as China, and another to Peru,"[28]—which suggests the geography of the sixteenth century rather than that of the seventeenth. Again, we are informed that the Governor commanded a guard to be set at the mouth of the Amazon to prohibit people ascending it—a wild scheme which is conceivable only if we accept Mrs. Behn's statement that the Amazon is "almost as broad as the river of Thames."[29] Yet, as the Amazon is over four hundred miles from Surinam, and as the interior regions of Guiana were still unexplored, we may perhaps consider such slips possible even in a visitor to the colony.

The immediate topography of the colony itself, however, we should expect to find fairly distinct and true. Mrs. Behn narrates several journeys on the Surinam, but seems to think the riverside occupied only by plantations. In silence she passes by outstanding features of its shores—the fort, the settlement of Jews, and the town of Tararica, with its hundred houses and a chapel.[30] She tells us that the colonists went aboard the slave ship bearing Oroonoko, at the mouth of the river.[31] This is possible; but it seems to have been customary for ships to proceed some fifty miles up the river to the good anchorage before Tararica, naturally the local center of the slave traffic. She implies that one of the plantations was near the mouth of the river;[32] but we know that the lowest was some thirty-five miles upstream. Indeed, it was because the fort (about fifteen miles from the mouth of the Surinam) was so distant from the settled region that Byam was handicapped in trying to hold it against the Dutch.[33] Ignoring apparently the site of the fort, Mrs. Behn says that Oroonoko proposed to lead his fellow slaves towards the sea, a plan that seems hardly in accord with his oft-praised intelligence. When negroes ran away in Surinam, they made for the interior, where their descendants, the "bush negroes," live to this day.

A striking landmark in the country, as she depicts it, is the site of Mrs. Behn's residence:

> As soon as I came into the country, the best house in it was presented me, called St. John's Hill. It stood on a vast rock of white marble, at the foot of which the river ran a vast depth down, and not to be descended on that side; the little waves, still dashing and washing the foot of this rock, made the softest murmurs and purlings in the world.[34]

As any one may observe who compares the geological chart of the Surinam basin in Karl Martin's *Niederländisch West Indien* with the map thereof in Hartsinck's *Beschryving van Guiana,* "vast rocks of white marble" have no place in this flat alluvial plain. The nearest approach to such an eminence is the "Parnassus of blauwe Berg," a hundred meters high. But this is composed of dark-colored diabase; and it is ten miles above Marshall's Creek, then the limit of the plantations. When Raleigh penetrated into the interior of what is now British Guiana, he saw afar off "a mountain of chrystal [really of sandstone] like a white church tower of an exceeding height," and other explorers in those parts reported many hills;[35] but none resembling Mrs. Behn's description rose in the inhabited district of Surinam. On the other hand, we miss an interesting natural feature of the region which, it seems, should have impressed Mrs. Behn on her journey to a distant

Indian village. Travel on the Surinam, soon after passing Sara Creek, about forty miles above Marshall's, becomes very difficult, if not impossible, owing to the falls, of which there are at least twenty-eight.[36] Yet though Mrs. Behn traveled by boat eight days to reach the village, she never mentions a waterfall.

It is noteworthy that some of the true characteristics of the country might have been serviceably employed by Mrs. Behn. Since Oroonoko was the leader in the expedition to the Indian village, the obstacles that falls would place in his way should have presented his admirer good opportunities for the further display of his intelligence and strength. She might likewise have intensified our sympathy for some of his hardships by making us realize the humid heat in which they were endured. And the hopelessness of Oroonoko's insurrection would have appeared more poignantly if she had shown him rising, not in a sparsely settled district, but against a well-established community and a respectable military force. Why should an author who had dwelt face to face with these circumstances, ignore and even contradict them?

But had the author of *Oroonoko* really been in Surinam? *The Life and Memoirs of Mrs. Behn,* her earliest biography of any length, says that she had been there; and no one has hitherto questioned the statement. How any one can read the *Life and Memoirs,* including its fantastic account of her meeting a marble platform floating on the English Channel, and place confidence in it, is to me incomprehensible; but this is not the place to expose its general worthlessness. What concerns us particularly is that it draws its account of Mrs. Behn's life from passages in her stories; and that its assertion of her visit to Surinam is not independent testimony but a repetition of the autobiographical statements in *Oroonoko* itself.[37] Of those statements, one—that her father was to have been "Lieutenant General of six-and-thirty islands, besides the continent of Surinam"—has been shown unreliable, Mr. Gosse having discovered that her father was a barber.[38] I may add that no hint of any appointment to replace Byam appears in the colonial papers of the period. Though this falsehood has been generally recognized, its full bearing on *Oroonoko* has apparently been overlooked; for it has not shaken belief in Mrs. Behn's journey. Yet if Mrs. Behn's father was not sent to Surinam, the only reason she gives for being there disappears. Furthermore, if she was not the daughter of the future governor, why was she assigned "the best house in the country"? (We recall that it stood on that remarkable "vast rock of white marble.") Those excursions which she and her friends enjoyed in the royal slave's company, and which constitute so large a portion of the narrative, depended largely upon the confidence placed in her promises by Oroonoko, whom, she says, she "had assured of liberty as soon as the governor arrived";[39] and that confidence, in turn, depended upon her being related to the great. It seems as if, when the fundamental allegation is revealed false, the very structure of her "history" crumbles; and as if such a downright statement as Professor Canby's "the royal slave she unquestionably knew, and knew well"[40] were made without scrutinizing the evidence.

If we nevertheless find it difficult to believe that Mrs. Behn was not in Surinam, let us tentatively surmise that she was in some way connected with a colonist; and that in *Oroonoko* she pretended to a more distinguished relationship in order, perhaps, to place herself more plausibly in the center of the events narrated. But that is, of course, an assumption. What we know is that at least one important statement of hers is a falsehood. Her unsupported word that she was in Surinam is therefore untrustworthy unless in our further examination of *Oroonoko* it shall appear that she reports veraciously facts which only an eye-witness could have observed.

Mrs. Behn speaks of a considerable number of the animals of Surinam. The buffalo and deer she merely mentions; but she gives correct though brief descriptions of the armadillo, the "cusharee," the marmoset, and some strange flies.[41] Of the "tigers," that is, jaguars, which Oroonoko delights to hunt, her accounts are exaggerated; one of them "was about the height of a heifer"[42]—hardly a realistic description. Oroonoko's adventure with a "numb eel" is sensational. He is angling on the shore, when the eel takes his hook and sends its electric current through the line and rod to his hand. He bravely grasps the rod harder, faints from the shock, falls into the water, and is carried a league down the river. As he floats past, some Indians seize his body, and from it receive a strong shock. "By that they knew the rod was in his hands which with a paddle they struck away, and snatched it into the boat, eel and all."[43] She adds that the eel was "a quarter of an ell about,"—some eleven inches. The size of the eel, the duration of its electric charge, and above all the circumstance that it does not shock by direct contact but sends its current through the fish line, are more than questionable. Yet the truth remains that with the exception of the cayman, the most interesting animals of Surinam are in a manner known to the author. We should revive our faith in her credibility, were personal observation the only means by which she could have learned the fauna of Surinam.

In 1667, George Warren, who had lived three years in that colony, published a little pamphlet, now rare, entitled *An Impartial Description of Surinam.* Herein its fauna is likewise described, and here too the cayman is the only important animal omitted. With the single exception of the marmoset,[44] every animal that Mrs. Behn describes is described by Warren. For example, the latter says of the armadilloes:

They are short legged, have three claws upon their feet, are headed like a hog, have no teeth and but very little mouths; they are defended all over, save the head and belly, with an armor as it were plated, scarce penetrable by a lance, unless it happen in a joint. They burrow in the ground, and had they not quite so strong a smell of musk, would be no contemptible meat.[45]

Compare Mrs. Behn:

The very meat we eat, when set on the table, if it be native, I mean of the country, perfumes the whole room; especially a little beast called an armadillo, a thing which I can liken to nothing so well as a rhinoceros. It is all in white armor, so jointed that it moves as well in it as if it had nothing on.[46]

The only animals in connection with which Mrs. Behn relates any incidents are the "tiger" and the electric eel; the same is true of Warren. The latter's story about the eel is worth comparing with the above adventure of Oroonoko:

The torpedo or numb eel, which, being alive, and touching any other living creature, strikes such a deadness into all the parts as for a while renders them wholly useless and insensible, which, is believed, has occasioned the drowning of several persons who have been unhappily so taken as they were swimming in the river. It produces the like effect if but touched with the end of a long pole, or one man immediately laying hold of another so benumbed. The truth of this was experienced, one of them being taken and thrown upon the bank, where a dog spying it stir, catches it in his mouth, and presently falls down, which the master observing, and going to pull him off, becomes motionless himself; another standing by, and endeavoring to remove him, follows the same fortune; the eel getting loose, they return quickly to themselves.[47]

Much of the vividness of the background of *Oroonoko* arises from the specific descriptions of the exotic and indigenous flora. In this respect, too, the particulars that are true are to be found in Warren.[48] When differences appear, they show Mrs. Behn not independently observing but inaccurately amplifying, as in the passage which for its *anschaulichkeit* is quoted entire by Professor Siegel, and which describes a lovely grove of orange and lemon trees crowning the "rock of white marble."[49] "Vast trees" they are indeed, "as big as English oaks"! The orchids of the forest, and the great palms that border the river banks, though conspicuous, are omitted by Warren—and by Mrs. Behn. Her landscape is uniformly flowery; we read of "the trees appearing all like nosegays," and that "the opposite bank was adorned with such vast quantities of different flowers eternally blowing, and every day and hour new."[50]

In this riot of color we see what has been called "the old tropical fallacy," which was exploded by A. R. Wallace in his *Tropical Nature.* The early European travelers reported especially the striking, gorgeous plants; and, though these are usually scattered amid great masses of green, gave the impression that everywhere the flowers grew in solid banks of bright color. "There is never there," says E. F. Im Thurn, "a growing carpet of flowers such as is made in England by primroses and anemones."[51] Here again Mrs. Behn's eye does not seem to have been upon the object.

It may be urged that accuracy in describing nature is hardly to be expected, even from a "realist," in Mrs. Behn's time, when the proper study of mankind was man. Do we find her powers of observation more reliable when directed on Oroonoko and his fellow slaves? That some important characteristics of the hero and the heroine are idealized, every one grants; but the description of slave life is in general assumed to be copied from grim reality. In Oroonoko's savage delight in slaughter, says Professor Siegel, Mrs. Behn followed truth; "the brutal murder of Imoinda, and the stoical endurance of torture," adds Miss Morgan, "is the conduct of a savage; and in those passages Mrs. Behn was depending upon her observations."[52] But turn to Warren's short chapter on the negroes, who, he notes,

are most brought out of Guiny in Africa to those parts, where they are sold like dogs, and no better esteemed but for their work sake, which they perform all the week with the severest usages for the slightest fault, till Saturday afternoon, when they are allowed to dress their own gardens. . . . Their lodging is a hard board, and their black skins their covering. These wretched miseries not seldom drive them to desperate attempts for the recovery of their liberty, endeavoring to escape, and if like to be retaken sometimes lay violent hands upon themselves. Or, if the hope of pardon bring them again alive into their masters' power, they'll manifest their fortitude, or rather obstinacy, in suffering the most exquisite tortures can be inflicted upon them, for a terror and example to others without shrinking. . . . Many of them over fondly woo their deaths, not otherwise hoping to be freed from that indeed unequalled slavery.[53]

Is it not significant that this little outline emphasizes the very traits that constitute the realistic elements on the larger canvas of Mrs. Behn?

Needless to say, she amplifies and adds; but, as we have already seen in the case of Oroonoko's horrible wounds, the elaborations do not of themselves inspire confidence. What a singularly lax plantation it is that permits the tasks of Imoinda to be daily done for her by "some sighing lover"![54] "Cæsar," we are told, was the plantation name of the negro prince; his native name was Oroonoko.[55] Of course "Oroonoko" is not African; but "Orinoco" is Indian for "coiled serpent," and was suitably applied to the winding river whose name Raleigh made famous. That such an obvious slip has not aroused remark seems singular, until we find the general inattention to such matters manifested in an even more fantastic confusion, namely in the suggestion that Oroonoko's home, Coramantien, may be the Coramandel Coast[56] (in East India!). Coramantien was a district of Guinea. It was well known to the English, who, about 1662, had a "castle" there, which was an important supply station for the African Company that monopolized the slave traffic of the British West Indies.[57] Though Mrs. Behn is therefore correct enough in assigning her royal slave to that country, she seems to ignore some particulars concerning it. The English ship which bore Oroonoko from Coramantien must, according to Mrs. Behn's narrative, have arrived in Surinam in May, 1665, at the very earliest.[58] But early in 1665 Coramantien was captured by the Dutch, under the famous De Ruyter, who thence sailed to attack Barbadoes.[59] It appears improbable that English slavers ventured from Coramantien to Surinam from the close of 1664 until the end of the Dutch war in 1667.

We may also question the description which Mrs. Behn gives of the Coramantien negro. Oroonoko, she says, was "carved with a little flower or bird at the sides of the temples," and Imoinda was "carved" "all over her body," "resembling our ancient Picts that are figured in the chronicles" (!). As a matter of fact, many tribes of negroes were thus "carved"; but those from Coramantien happened to be exceptional in this respect, and were noted for their "fine, smooth, black skin."[60] In short, the more one learns about Coramantien, the less true seem those strokes in her picture of negro life that are peculiarly her own.

About the Indians of Surinam, Mrs. Behn writes in tones of admiration, and with a vividness that has been especially commended.[61] The natives of that region were the Caribs, between whom and the English no serious trouble, such as is assumed in a part of *Oroonoko,* appears actually to have taken place in Surinam during the time in question.[62] They were more numerous than Mrs. Behn intimates, and their habitations were less remote.[63] They were not so handsome as she describes them, nor did they woo in so languishing a manner.[64] She recounts that her companions aroused their wonder by playing the flute, but the natives were quite familiar with that instrument.[65] They were so honorable, she declares, that they could not conceive of a "liar"; but the Jesuit missionary Pellepart, who in 1655 compiled a little dictionary of their language, gives no less than five Carib synonyms for "menteur."[67]

What Mrs. Behn tells us about Indian dress, adornments, weapons, and customs is often correct; but in no instance does she present a true fact that is not to be found in Warren's chapter on the Indians. Her omissions agree with his. Both authors, in discussing the "peaiman," omit the long fasts and solitary wanderings that were so interesting a part of the medicine man's training.[68] Both, in describing the appearance of the Caribs, omit the leg band which, tied above the ankle and below the knee of female infants and never thence removed, caused a gross distortion of the calf, which was most conspicuous.[69]

As we have seen to be the case in other parts of the story, circumstances accurately stated by Warren are by Mrs. Behn so elaborated as to become improbable or false. Warren deplores that the Indian girls are unacquainted with "that innocent and warm delight of kissing; but conversing so frequently with Christians, and being naturally docile and ingenious, we have reason to believe they will in time be taught it."[70] Instead of this speculative pleasantry, we have in Mrs. Behn an episode showing that it was her party that taught the Indians how to kiss. In her lively account of the occasion, we miss, however, an explanation of how the practice could have been so enjoyable to the Caribs, whose lips are pierced with holes, in which are inserted thorns or pins.[71] In describing the hospitality of the Indians, Mrs. Behn again provides some information like that in Warren; but with regard to the food and drink, the service, the "napery," etc., makes so many errors of omission and commission that they cannot be enumerated here.[72]

Her regular method may be illustrated by her transmutation of the following true statement by Warren concerning Indian captains,

> whose courage they first prove, by sharply whipping them with rods, which if they endure bravely without crying, or any considerable motion, they are acknowledged gallant fellows and honored by the less hardy.[7]

Mrs. Behn, on the other hand, tells us that Oroonoko marvelled at the frightful scars of the chiefs, who explained that competitors for a captaincy mutilated themselves in the following manner:

> Being brought before the old judges, now past labor, they are asked what they dare do to show they are worthy to lead an army. When he who is first asked, making no reply, cuts off his nose, and throws it contemptibly on the ground; and the other does something to himself that he thinks surpasses him, and perhaps deprives himself of lips and an eye. So they slash on till one gives out, and many have died in this debate,— . . . a sort of courage too brutal to be applauded by our black hero.[73]

Yet despite such monstrous perversions, Mrs. Behn, according to some, presents Indian life "most anthropologically"!

It was not a vivid imagination alone that furnished Mrs. Behn with her enlargements upon Warren. In her idealization of the moral character of the savages (the "impartial" Warren found them "cowardly and treacherous"), she shows the influence of a sentimental tradition in the European literature of the sixteenth and seventeenth centuries, which likewise manifests itself in the noble Indians of the heroic drama.[74] Some details in the appearance of Mrs. Behn's Indians are also traditional. She clothes them in "short habits" and "glorious wreaths" of feathers. "I had a set of these presented to me," she says, "and I gave them to the King's Theatre; it was the dress of the Indian Queen, infinitely admired by persons of quality, and was inimitable."[75] To think of Nell Gwynn in the true costume of a Carib belle is indeed ludicrous. Besides the apron, the principal Carib adornments were strings of beads or shells; the men might, on great occasions, wear some feathers on their heads and shoulders. In Surinam anything like the elaborate feather costume of Mrs. Behn's fancy was unknown.[76] But the first aborigines whom the Europeans learned about were the incomparably superior natives of Mexico, whose gorgeous featherwork garments were among the noble presents sent by Montezuma to Cortez, and by Cortez to the king of Spain. "No one of the American fabrics excited such admiration," says Prescott, who cites many passages of admiring description of them.[77] For literary purposes they thenceforth became the conventional garments of all Indians. Probably the quivers mentioned by Mrs. Behn are derived from the same tradition; the Carib arrows were very long, and their quivers were small cases to hold only the poisoned points.[78]

From an English point of view perhaps the most interesting tradition that may be recognized in *Oroonoko* appears in the episode of the gold-bearing savages. In his preface, Warren cautiously remarks: "The Indians will tell you of mighty princes upwards, and golden cities, how true I know not." The colonists of 1665 were not seeking gold: they were raising sugar. But Oroonoko and Mrs. Behn meet "Indians of strange aspects," who come from the mountains, speak an unknown tongue, and carry bags of gold-dust, "which, as well as they could give us to understand, came streaming in little small channels down the high mountains, when the rains fell." These are, I think, the echoes of the hopeful words that the brave Elizabethans sent home across the seas, when they were seeking El Dorado, which lay ever "on the other side of those great hills," where ran "streams of gold about the breadth of a goosequill."[79]

If these observations are approved, we must at last abandon the interesting assumption that it was personal acquaintance with an unfortunate slave, and actual observation of Surinam, that furnished Mrs. Behn with the materials for *Oroonoko.* The Dutch wars, which drew attention to that colony, provided her with the few correct touches in the historical background of the picture. For the rest, whatever was real in the local color was given her by Warren's description of the natural environment, the slaves, and the Indians. In thus employing a true account, she was using the method of Defoe and his predecessors, whose fiction is rooted in the literature of fact. Those writers, however, when rearranging and elaborating journalistic reports, managed to carry their Captain Singletons from Mozambique to Guinea without seriously blundering into the unreal; for they made it their controlling aim not to deviate from the probable. No such bounds confined the romantic, sensational, and hero-worshipping Mrs. Behn. Whatever in Warren's account might serve to make the scene of Oroonoko's actions interesting, or might be utilized in an episode displaying his noble qualities, was thus employed; but whatever did not please her fancy, she at will suppressed or modified. She exalted the loveliness of the climate and landscape of Surinam, the marvels of its flora and fauna, and the innocence of its inhabitants. She enhanced its charm with touches taken from the picturesque traditions of Cortez and of Raleigh. What she says of Miranda in **The Fair Jilt** seems applicable to herself: "She had a great deal of wit, read much, and retained all that served her purpose." If she ever sincerely intended to write anything like a true story, she abandoned that intention as soon as she had stated it, and gave her fancy free rein. The second-hand materials that form the realistic foundation of **Oroonoko** are so inconspicuous in comparison with the romantic superstructure that to emphasize their presence is to obscure the purpose and character of her art.

Notes

[1] H. S. Canby, *The Short Story in English,* New York, 1909, pp. 164, 167.

[2] P. Siegel, *Aphra Behns Gedichte und Prosawerke: Anglia,* XXV, 352.

[3] *The Novels of Mrs. Aphra Behn,* ed. E. A. Baker, London, 1905, p. xxiii.

[4] *Oroonoko,* ed. E. A. Baker, p. 55.

[5] *Oroonoko,* p. 52.

[6] *Oroonoko,* pp. 78-79.

[7] I am indebted for this comment on Oroonoko's cure to Roger Irving Lee, M. D., of Boston.

[8] *Oroonoko,* p. 1.

[9] Canby, pp. 164, 165.

[10] Siegel, p. 379.

[11] Walter Raleigh, *The English Novel,* 5th ed., New York, 1906, p. 107.

[12] *Oroonoko,* p. 42.

[13] Ibid., pp. 47, 50.

[14] *Calendar of State Papers, Colonial Series, America and West Indies, 1661-1668;* London, 1880, pp. 249, 297-298.

[15] *Oroonoko,* pp. 40, 42-44, 47, 57, 62, 67, 74, 76, 78-79.

[16] *State Papers,* pp. 104, 108, 449.

[17] *Oroonoko,* p. 80.

[18] *State Papers,* p. 599.

[19] *Oroonoko,* pp. 66-67.

[20] James Rodway, *Guiana: British, Dutch, and French;* London, 1912, p. 63.

[21] *Oroonoko,* pp. 72-73.

[22] *State Papers,* pp. 104, 108.

[23] Ibid., pp. 166-167.

[24] *Oroonoko,* p. 73.

[25] *Oroonoko,* pp. 57-58.

[26] Ibid., p. 51.

[27] For example, *Newes of Sr. Walter Rauleigh* (1618), in Peter Force's *Tracts,* Washington, III (1844), 23, and especially pp. 27-28. Cf. Harcourt's description of the lovely land Cooshebery, in *Purchas His Pilgrimes,* Glasgow, XVI (1906), 369.

[28] *Oroonoko,* p. 50.

[29] Ibid., p. 62.

[30] Jan Jacob Hartsinck, *Beschryving van Guiana,* 1770, II, 567-574; James Rodway, *Guiana,* 1912, pp. 51-53, 61-62. Some discrepancies between these two descriptions do not affect my argument.

[31] *Oroonoko,* p. 38.

[32] Cf. the three-day trip mentioned in *Oroonoko,* p. 40, with the corresponding distance noted on p. 80.

[33] Rodway, p. 64.

[34] *Oroonoko,* pp. 51-52.

[35] Raleigh, Sir Walter, *The Discovery of Guiana,* ed. Schomburgk, 1848, p. 101 and note; *Purchas His Pilgrimes,* XVI, 367, 370, 408.

[36] Hartsinck, II, 574.

[37] *The Life and Memoirs of Mrs. Behn,* in her *Works,* London, 1871, V, 2; *Oroonoko,* p. 50.

[38] *Dictionary of National Biography,* art. "Aphra Behn."

[39] *Oroonoko,* pp. 46-47.

[40] Canby, p. 163.

[41] *Oroonoko,* pp. 2, 5.

[42] Ibid., p. 53.

[43] Ibid., pp. 55-56.

[44] These appear to have been taken to Europe as pets. See *Purchas His Pilgrimes,* XVI, 313, 348, 379, 395.

[45] Warren, George, *An Impartial Description of Surinam,* London, 1667, p. 11.

[46] *Oroonoko,* p. 51.

[47] Warren, p. 2.

[48] Cf. *Oroonoko,* p. 51, with Warren, pp. 5, 1

[49] Siegel, pp. 88-89; *Oroonoko,* p. 52.

[50] *Oroonoko,* pp. 51-52.

[51] Im Thurn, E. F., *Among the Indians of Guiana,* 1883, pp. 87-91.

[52] Siegel, p. 346; Morgan, Charlotte E., *The Rise of the Novel of Manners,* New York, 1911, p. 81.

[53] Warren, pp. 19-20.

[54] *Oroonoko,* p. 44.

[55] Ibid., p. 41.—Warren, p. 23, spells Orinoco "Oronoque."

[56] Canby, p. 163.

[57] *State Papers,* pp. 113, 135, 146, 174, 194; C. P. Lucas, *Historical Geography of the British Colonies,* Oxford, 1905, II, 44, 64.

[58] See above, p. 422.

[59] *State Papers,* pp. 294-295.

[60] Hartsinck, II, 921-922; H. G. Dalton, *History of British Guiana,* London, 1855, I, 163.

[61] Siegel, p. 357 n. 1.

[62] *State Papers,* p. 598; Warren, p. 26.

[63] Warren, p. 23; Rodway, *Guiana,* p. 44.

[64] *Oroonoko,* p. 3; Im Thurn, pp. 188, 221; John Davies, *History of the Caribby Islands,* London, 1666, pp. 270, 334.

[65] *Oroonoko,* p. 59; Im Thurn, p. 309; Davies, p. 307.

[66] *Oroonoko,* p. 4; Pierre Pellepart, *Introduction à la langue des Galibis,* Paris, 1655, p. 25.

I have compared the Indian words given by Mrs. Behn (*Oroonoko,* p. 58) with old wordlists and with modern, both Carib and Arowak, and believe them not authentic; but in the confusion of Indian tongues, I feel it unsafe to declare them certainly fraudulent. Cf. *The Voyage of Robert Dudley to the West Indies,* ed. G. F. Warner, London, 1899, pp. 65, 78-79; Davies's Caribbean vocabulary in his *History of the Caribby Islands,* 1666, pp. 353 ff.; D. G. Brinton, *The Arawack Language of Guiana,* 1870; J. Crevaux, P. Sagot, L. Adam, *Grammaires et Vocabulaires roucouyenne, arrouague, piapoco et d'autres langues,* Paris, 1882.

[67] *Oroonoko,* p. 59; Warren, pp. 26-27; Im Thurn, p. 334.

[68] Im Thurn, p. 192.

[69] Warren, pp. 23-24.

[70] *Oroonoko,* p. 60; Im Thurn, p. 193.

[71] *Oroonoko,* pp. 58-59; Davies, chap. xviii ("Of the Entertainment which the Caribbians make those who come to visit them"); Im Thurn, chaps. xiii and xv ("Food" and "Feasts").

[72] Warren, pp. 24-25; Davies, pp. 314, 315.

[73] *Oroonoko,* pp. 60-61.

[74] Charlotte E. Morgan, *The Novel of Manners,* pp. 81-82; Gilbert Chinard, *L'Exotisme américain,* 1911.

[75] *Oroonoko,* p. 2.

[76] Im Thurn, p. 199.

[77] W. H. Prescott, *Conquest of Mexico,* Philadelphia, 1873, I, 147, 299, 356, 430; II, 68, 129.

[78] *Oroonoko,* p. 60; Im Thurn, p. 243; *Purchas His Pilgrimes,* XVI, 415.

[79] *Oroonoko,* p. 61; *Purchas His Pilgrimes,* XVI, 306, 340, 346, 386, 387, 396, 407, 409. Traces of the tradition in Hall, Donne, and Milton are mentioned in *Voyages of the Elizabethan Seamen to America,* ed. E. J. Payne, Second Series, 2d ed., Oxford, 1900, p. xlvii.

Victoria Sackville-West (essay date 1927)

SOURCE: *Aphra Behn: The Incomparable Astrea,* Gerald Howe Ltd., 1927, p. 92.

[*In the excerpt below, Sackville-West argues that Behn limited herself to exotic subjects instead of depicting life in her native Britain.*]

Some concluding estimate of Mrs Behn's work [is] inevitable. . . . Her work has been kept subordinate to her life and to her personality, yet neither life nor personality can be of much interest save in relation to her accomplishment. That she went to Surinam, and cut a figure as a wit in London, is very well, but what has she left behind her that is of any real value? That she opened the way for women as writers, is her principal claim on our gratitude, but still we ask what quality besides courage entitles her to a place in English literature? And instead of extolling her gifts in the management of the comedy of intrigue, we shall do much better to avow frankly that Mrs Behn, given her natural talent, prodigally wasted her opportunities.

For the pity is that Mrs Behn, as a novelist, thought her London experiences beneath the dignity of her pen. She had been granted that gift of God, a free, rapid, and colloquial style, and she neglected to turn it to its best advantage. She trifled with French and Spanish authors, she who might have had honest speech with her countrymen. Of what use to us are these Isabellas, Belvideeras, Rinaldos, and Gonzagos? They get into cupboards, they mistake one another's identity, they are shipwrecked in infancy, they fall in love with their sisters, but not one gleam of interest do they arouse. Ah, Mrs Behn, Mrs Behn! was it for nothing that you were cast into prison? made Grub Street welcome? knew old Downes and Mr Tonson? Was it for nothing that you hurried in and out of the green-rooms, bestowing here a word of advice and there a smile of encouragement? saw dear Tom Betterton, with his great stomach and short arms, rehearsing, and Mrs Barry without her make-up, striving to keep her crooked mouth straight? Oddly enough, all Mrs Behn's critics have referred to her as a forerunner of Defoe, which is what she ought to have been and just failed to be. Was it owing to some unanalysed intuition in the minds of the critics? or owing perhaps to some vague association between Oroonoko and Man Friday? Whichever it is, the critics are very nearly, but just not quite, right. We might have had the mother of Moll Flanders, and all we get is the bastard of Mademoiselle de Scudéry.

Stay, though: not quite all. The **Unfortunate Happy Lady** and the **Black Lady** are just enough to show us what we have missed. This is London, and rich, seventeenth-century humour. Mrs Behn could do it when she wanted. The pity is, that she wanted so seldom, and thought it more aristocratic to mince through Castile, than to bawl in Alsatia and loiter arms akimbo through Newgate and Covent Garden. That loose, expressive style of hers is wholly unsuitable to the romance of cloak-and-sword. It is not, as she imagined, cosmopolitan, daring, fashionable; it is simply the coster-girl dressed up as a lady. There, again, Swinburne with a stroke of intuitive perspicacity was right (for it is not to be assumed that he had given very special thought to Aphra Behn), when he calls her the 'plebeian poetess,' and speaks of her abused and wasted genius. For it was of the people that she should have written; of paupers huddled together on the debtors' bench, of link-boys, of landladies and ancient pandars. Then indeed, given her vigour and rapidity, her shameless candour and her knock-about experience, we should have had an earlier Defoe; we should have had a great realistic painter, own sister to Teniers and Hogarth; we should have had

> The young, the old, the witty, and the wise,
> The fair, the ugly, lavish, and precise,
> Cowards and braves, the modest and the loud
> Promiscuously blended in the crowd.

Mrs Behn, however, would not trust to her own native genius. The most original contribution made by her to English literature was certainly **Oroonoko,** but even in that story, drawn out of her own life, she allowed her readings of the heroic romances to colour her description of colonial existence and to flavour her interpretation of her hero with an air of classic chivalry. Oroonoko resembles those seventeenth-century paintings of negroes in plumes and satins, rather than an actual slave on a practical plantation. She dresses him, it is true, in a suit of brown hollands; but none the less the plumes continue to wave in the breeze and the satins to glisten in the sun. She could not wholly escape from *Le Grand Cyrus.* And naturally, she was in far worse case when she frankly adopted the French, Spanish, or Italian convention; her novels then descend to an intolerable artificiality, and are readable only thanks to their brevity and to the colloquial raciness which was never absent from her style. The brevity of the novels is much to be thankful for. The English novel at that period was undergoing a change; the story, popular in Elizabethan times in the form of the Italian novella, but smothered during the first half of the seventeenth century under the voluminous feather-bed of the 'heroic romance,' was now (even as the drama) blossoming for the second time. From the year 1670 onwards, there is an enormous crop of short stories, or long-short stories, scarcely to be called novels, but more properly novelettes, the natural reaction of a flippant and pleasure-loving age. 'Novels are of a more familiar nature [than romances]' wrote Congreve, himself trying his hand at the new genre in his *Incognita, or Love and Duty Reconciled:* 'Come near to us, and represent to us intrigues in practice, delight us with accidents and odd events, but not such as are wholly unusual or unprecedented, such which not being so distant from our belief bring also the pleasure nearer us. Romances give more of wonder, novels more delight.' The French and Spanish tradition of cloak and sword and intrigue is dominant. Criss-cross love, duels, stolen encounters, abductions, escaped nuns,—such was the paraphernalia of which these stories were made, and Mrs Behn adopted it wholesale.

The result is dishearteningly sterile. The English genius was not created for such artificialities; it seldom wears fetters with becoming grace. Something ruder and more barbarous is always trying to burst through. The Elizabethans by the miracle of a young and violent poetry twisted their Italian borrowings to a dark magnificence of their own, but their power had not descended to the hand of the Carolines. The Carolines still borrowed from abroad, but their transmutations produced no extravagant splendour such as Webster and Tourneur had produced; they turned, for one thing, more willingly to the gallant and amorous than to the tragic and sublime, an affectation of Latin frivolity which did not sit well upon them. The Goth was trying to frisk. The Elizabethans, in spite of their Spanish cloaks and Genoese palaces and sonorous diction, were speaking in the English language of things which they were well fitted to interpret: of ambition and adventure, of terror, superstition, passion, and death. The 'plot' was but the excuse for all their turbulence of poetry. The minor dramatists of the Restoration, Mrs Behn among them, fell between two stools. With the one hand they clung to the heroic tradition, while with the other they reached out instinctively towards a naturalness of speech and manner which their foreign reading still taught them to mistrust. Thus in the case of Mrs Behn, as of all those who lacked the genius of a Congreve or a Wycherley, we get the absurd spectacle of a right instinct struggling with the affectation of what was thought to be culture. These flames and charms, cruelties and languishments, with which Mrs Behn's pages are besprinkled, are not English speech. Her pen races; it writes good home-made English; then she recollects herself: this will never do, we must have some foreign spice to lighten this English bread. Let us be elegant at all costs. The cloaked figure in the sombrero is the only ghost which haunts the Caroline imagination.

The habit of borrowing, then, remained long after the power of naturalization had gone, and long after the glow of that fiery poetry had faded. It was perhaps inevitable that such a furnace should temporarily burn itself out. But there was that other side of the English genius to which Mrs Behn might have turned in her novels: the plain, broad, humorous, English realism that would so excellently have suited her temper. How briskly she begins, when she writes of the things she knows, and how all London rises out of her phrases: 'About the beginning of last June, as near as I can remember, Bellamora came to town from Hampshire, and was obliged to lodge the first night at the same inn where the stage-coach set up. The next day she took coach for Covent Garden . . . 'Here, it is no matter that the heroine is called Bellamora; she might much more appropriately have been called Lucy, but that her birthplace is Hampshire and that she is a stranger in London we never question. Or take the history of Philadelphia, an innocent and inconvenient sister placed by an unscrupulous brother in a brothel: 'You won't stay late, Mr Gracelove? said the mother of mischief. No, no, replied he, I will only show the lady a play and return to supper. What is played to-night? asked the old one. *The Cheats,* mother, *The Cheats,* answered Gracelove. Ha! said Beldam laughing, a very pretty comedy indeed. Ay, if well played, returned he. At these words they went down, where a coach was waiting . . . ' It lives, as the lovers on or under balconies can never live. It lives sufficiently to exasperate us into imagining what Mrs Behn could have made out of her London had she realised the unexploited treasure that lay at the command of her pen.

H. A. Hargreaves (essay date 1970)

SOURCE: "New Evidence of the Realism of Mrs. Behn's *Oroonoko*," in *Bulletin of the New York Public Library*, Vol. 74, January-December, 1970, pp. 437-44.

[In the following essay, Hargreaves addresses the question of Behn's claims of travel to Surinam, arguing that new evidence suggests she did travel there.]

In 1688 Mrs Aphra Behn, England's first professional woman writer, published a prose tale entitled *Oroonoko, or, The Royal Slave.* Her use of first-person narration provided an immediacy and verisimilitude which captured the fancy of the reading public, and the work has remained in print through centuries to the present day. It was a superior piece of writing, and scholars and critics eventually assigned it a position of importance as an early example of the use of realism in the developing forms of prose fiction. Realism has been defined in several ways, but in this case it is clear that much of the realistic effect was gained by Mrs Behn's claim, in many places through the piece, to have been eye-witness to events which she related. At one point, for example, she stated:

> My stay was to be short in that Country; because my Father dy'd at Sea, and never arriv'd to possess the Honour design'd him (which was Lieutenant General of six-and-thirty Islands, besides the Continent of Surinam) nor the advantages he hop'd to reap by them; So that though we were oblig'd to continue on our Voyage, we did not intend to stay upon the Place.[1]

Mrs Behn's claim to have been in Surinam, and thus to have based *Oroonoko* upon actual experience, was implied elsewhere as well—in her Dedication to a play called *The Young King* (1679) and in the compelling descriptions of colonial life informing one of her last plays, *The Widdow-Ranter, or, The History of Bacon in Virginia* (produced after her death in 1689). The claim seems to have been accepted in her own lifetime, and was offered as fact in the first two biographies to appear after her death. Said her "Female Biographer":

> She was a Gentlewoman by Birth, of a good Family in the City of *Canterbury* in *Kent:* her Father's name was *Johnson,* whose relation to the Lord *Willoughby,* drew him for the advantageous Post of Lieutenant General of many Isles, besides the Continent of *Surinam,* from his quiet retreat at *Canterbury,* to run the hazardous Voyage of the *West-Indies.* With him he took his chief Riches, his Wife and Children, and in that number *Afra,* his promising Darling, our future Heroine and admir'd *Astrea.*[2]

Mrs Behn came of age at the beginning of the Restoration, and was an independent, talented, and attractive woman. She had begun the unusual and rigorous task of competing in a world of male writers by 1670, but before that she had actually been commissioned to act as a spy for Charles II in Antwerp, during the Dutch wars.[3] It is not surprising that some parts of her life and less decorous qualities of her writing should have come under fire on moral grounds. Only late in the nineteenth century, however, were certain parts of her biography brought into question as either romanticised or fabricated. Then, one after another, her place of birth, her father's occupation, her maiden name, her social station, her marriage, and even the fact of her spying activities were made suspect. That most of these suspicions and allegations were eventually dispersed is an interesting story, but not of direct concern here.[4] What is of far greater significance is that they culminated, in 1913, in an attack upon the authenticity of *Oroonoko* as a work of realism based upon personal experience.

The attack was made by Ernest Bernbaum, in a piece written for a collection honouring G. L. Kittredge, and titled "Mrs. Behn's Oroonoko."[5] Here he set out to prove that Mrs Behn had never gone to Surinam, that her material was either borrowed, or imagined, and that the tale was therefore a stylistic variation on the standard romances of the period. First he accepted an apparent proof that Mrs Behn had been the daughter of a barber in Wye rather than of a gentleman in Canterbury. From this he deduced that the man could certainly not have been sent to Surinam in such a position, if at all, and so it was doubtful that Mrs Behn had gone. Second, he cited a group of "accuracies" and "errors" in *Oroonoko* itself, concerning the flora, fauna, topography, location of plantations, settlements, and fortifications, and the nature and habits of the Indians and slaves. Where Mrs Behn was correct, he asserted, she had made use of a contemporary work by George Warren, *An Impartial Description of Surinam.* Third, he established that names which had appeared in the tale were made prominent by the actions of 1667 during which the Dutch took Surinam. Last, from his own reconstruction of events, he concluded that Mrs Behn's implication of the time she was there conflicted with the time in which she was supposedly married, widowed, and sent on her mission to Antwerp.

The work as a whole was spirited and convincing, and Bernbaum seemed to have every right to take the literary historians to task for their uncritical acceptance of *Oroonoko* in order to develop a theory of generic evolution. There can be no doubt that the paper was influential, and that it has continued to sway historians of the novel since. Bernbaum himself, convinced of his argument, continued his assault upon Mrs Behn with an article published the same year—"Mrs. Behn's Biography a Fiction"—in which he stated that "the absolute untrustworthiness" of the tale "has recently been revealed . . . by the discovery that Mrs. Behn in Oroonoko deliberately and circumstantially lied."[6]

This was rather strong language, particularly since, had Bernbaum continued his research into Surinam materials, he might have come upon published items which lent support to Mrs Behn's claim. In 1912 James Rodway had produced a work called *Guiana: British, Dutch, and French,* in which this native of Guiana, explorer, naturalist, and historian, dealt with the history and geography of Surinam. He included a number of photographs of Indians in costumes which had changed so slightly that they exactly matched Mrs Behn's descriptions—descriptions which Bernbaum disparaged and which did not appear in Warren's work. Bernbaum had wondered, for example, why Mrs Behn never mentioned the prominent legband worn by the Indians. About half of those pictured wore none. Small wonder that Rodway, collaborating with Watt years earlier, in 1888, had made ample reference to Mrs Behn's *Oroonoko* in their *Chronological History of the Discovery and Settlement of Guiana: 1493-1668,*[7] finding her descriptions of Surinam so close to his own long and intimate knowledge of that country that he quoted some of them verbatim, and dated her trip to Surinam with a "foster-father" as 1658.

Still, the damage was done. Bernbaum's set of papers was subsequently attacked by a number of people, and found to have serious weaknesses. Montague Summers in 1915 showed that Bernbaum's dating was errone-ous.[8] H. D. Benjamins published three successive arti-cles, the last of which raised doubts about Bernbaum's scholarship.[9] Taking Bernbaum's four points, and us-ing a mass of archive material, he disarmed the argu-ment against Mrs Behn's having gone to Surinam. Nevertheless, he had to conclude that "I was unable to prove that she was in Surinam, but I believe I was able to show that Prof. Bernbaum did not prove she was *not* there."[10] This was a somewhat modest assessment, as he did bring to light a fair amount of circumstantial evidence from his sources, including the Harley Pa-pers, in which a number of other persons whom Mrs Behn named are found to have been in Surinam at the correct time, and an unspecified group of "ladeyes" was cited as there and living at St John's Hill, one of Lord Willoughby's plantations which had figured prom-inently in *Oroonoko.*

Not much more has been added to the evidence for Mrs Behn's veracity since that time. Successive biog-raphers have rehearsed with more or less accuracy the evidence already assembled and continued to attack Bernbaum's arguments.[11] H. G. Platt, using yet another letter from Surinam, has given a brilliant, if somewhat imaginative theory, based on the code names "Astrea and Celadon" used by Mrs Behn and her fellow agent William Scott in her letters sent from Antwerp to England during the Dutch Wars. Since the letter he discovered uses these same names to describe the ac-tivities of two people who have just left Surinam in 1664, Platt concludes that Mrs Behn was undoubtedly there, as the mistress of Scott.[12] W. J. Campbell has done an admirable reconstruction of the major conten-tions, but he concludes that while no clear case re-mains for disproving Mrs Behn's claim, no strong case has been made to prove it either.[13]

There remain other possibilities for investigation, how-ever, some of which have actually been touched upon by various writers. Mrs Behn had made some rather straightforward comments in *Oroonoko* which could have been challenged by her contemporaries, but though some of them accused her of things ranging from li-centiousness to French Pox none raised an objection to her claim to have gone to Surinam. She had remarked on "some rare Flies, of amazing Forms and Colours," which she had presented to the King's Antiquary, "some as big as my Fist, some less, and all of various Excel-lencies, such as Art cannot imitate," and which might still be seen there.[14] At another point she stated flatly, while describing the feathered costumes of the Indi-

ans, "I had a set of these presented to me, and I gave 'em to the King's Theatre, and it was the Dress of *The Indian Queen,* infinitely admir'd by Persons of Qual-ity; and was inimitable."[15] Bernbaum had been derisive of Nell Gwyn appearing in native South American costume, though it is important to note that she was the *first* Indian Queen and that the role became Mrs Bracegirdle's thereafter. Yet, as Helen McAfee retort-ed in 1916,

> . . . the matter, however, cannot be so briefly dismissed. It is improbable that Mrs. Behn would have gone out of her way to expose herself to contradiction upon so easily verifiable a statement. And we may infer from the play itself that there was some attempt at realism in the costume, however slight or "ludicrous" it might have been.[16]

Woodcock, too, noted:

> The Indian Queen was produced only twenty-five years before [*Oroonoko*], and one of its authors, Dryden, a friend of Mrs. Behn, was still alive in 1688, as well as many other people who would have known enough about this play to dispute such a statement if it were false.[17]

Ironically, it is a rather out-of-the-way comment that proves most interesting concerning this costumery. In 1920 George Odell, writing of the treatment of Shakes-peare's drama on the English stage, broached the fol-lowing:

> . . . that as a whole the actress did not occasionally alter her attire to suit the occasion could not be maintained in view of Smith's rare and interesting picture of the Indian Queen, reproduced on the page opposite. This plate is supposed to represent the famous Mrs. Bracegirdle, and in subject is as notable for fuss as for feathers. In connection with the latter one can quote with interest if not much belief Mrs. Behn's account of Surinam in *Oroonoko, or, the Royal Slave.* . . . This, of course, refers to the original representative of the part, Nell Gwyn, and not to Mrs. Bracegirdle, whose dress, indeed, displays considerable modification from the Behn description.[18]

Victoria Sackville-West remarked: "It is, indeed, a very curious curse that has been laid upon the legend of Aphra Behn," referring to the many errors and distor-tions which appeared in the biographical material, and one might well believe it. Over a decade ago I came upon the reference to this picture and to another of Mrs Bracegirdle as Semernia, the Indian Princess, in Mrs Behn's own play, *The Widdow-Ranter, or, the History of Bacon in Virginia* (1690). I wrote, in Jan-uary 1959, to secure photographs of these from the Enthoven Collection, in the Victoria and Albert Muse-um. After a lengthy wait, and several queries, I received the photographs in July. Unfortunately, the individual who sent them had been seriously ill and was attempting manfully to catch up his back correspondence. When I received them they were mislabelled, and I believed that the most promising was that of Mrs Bracegirdle in a role played nearly thirty years after Dryden and Howard's *Indian Queen* appeared. Moreover, it was painfully clear that this was an engraving taken from the original mezzotint. What authenticity might be found in the costume was made questionable by the license of the artist and lack of detail, and certainly, even given the frugality of theatre people, I felt that the use of such a costume thirty years later, though highly appropriate, was at best too fortuitous. Nevertheless, I requested the opinion of Dr Frederick J. Dockstader, of the Museum of the American Indian, who obliged me with an encouraging assessment, and there I rested my case.[19]

It was not until early in 1968 that I chanced upon the picture of Mrs Bracegirdle again, this time in the Lowe edition of Cibber's *Apology*,[20] where the original mezzotint was cited as being held in the Print Room of the British Museum. Once more intrigued, I secured another photograph, this time with assurances that *this* was indeed Dryden and Howard's Indian Queen, and found that there was a significant increase in the amount and quality of detail in the costumes shown, both for Bracegirdle and for her two little Negro attendants. I sent the photograph off again to Dr Dockstader, now Curator of the Museum. But the "curse" is not so easily avoided. Dr Dockstader was away on a prolonged leave, and in the interim my correspondence was lost in the Museum files. I persisted, however, and finally in December 1969 Dr Dockstader studied my second, and only remaining, photograph and provided his new assessment, with extraordinary courtesy going into painstaking detail. The results, here excerpted without bias, were well worth waiting for. He says, regarding the headdress of one attendant:

> . . . the artist either copied from a painting or sketch made in the Guiana region, had been there himself, or (and what is probably most likely) had a feathered diadem in front of him. . . . Had it been from a different area, the artist would have sketched to more common corona as shown in Plate 221 of the Indian Art Book; these are what most people are familiar with. On the contrary, he specifically introduced not only the corona effect around the rim, but also was careful to show the upstanding plumes in the rear (see the small illustration enclosed herein). It is this arrangement which makes me feel the original model was from the Guianas—together with the fact that the timing is right. These were brought over to England by some of the first colonial travellers, and so your artist could have seen them, either exhibited in some peer's "Cabinet of Curiosities," at the Museum—was it founded that early?—or on display in one of the many Oddity Halls which were so popular then.[21]

A parenthetical comment is in order at this point. The Harvean and Ashmolean Museums were at that time rebuilding their holdings rapidly, though what access might be had to them by "lesser folk" is unclear. The "Museum" was far from a reality yet, but its predecessor, the Royal Society Repository, was enjoying a huge response to its request for examples of natural phenomena. I have so far been unable to trace the "King's Antiquary" to whom Mrs Behn claims she gave her rare flies, but from the descriptions of the Royal Society Repository in the *Record* I suspect that he may have been either Robert Hooke, the Curator, or an underling. This collection, apparently, was open to public view, and there is also the possibility that the artist Smith had access to a peer's "Cabinet." Yet one must wonder that the occasion would have demanded such authenticity, if the actors were not using the costumes already. I will admit that they could have been borrowed, however, since we have proofs of costumes lent for particular performances of plays. But to return to Dr Docktader's assessment.

> The young lady, by the way, holds in her hand what may well be a fire fan; these are clusters of feathers, tied in a fan arrangement, used for blowing up a fire, etc.; there are also certain types of headdress which could possibly be represented by her fan.

> So, in summary, I would feel that the artist did have an original model in front of him, in one form or another, and worked from a known specimen or sketch; that his departure from precise accuracy (as represented by the little color card enclosed) was possibly due to wear and tear on the head-dress, or it may just have been ill-assembled . . . and the Negroid cast to the children's (or dwarf's, which seems more likely) features was a common practice when sketching or rendering Amerindian people.

Another parenthetical insert. Negroes were actually employed as supers in the theatre at this time, and would have been available for the portrait.

Dr Dockstader makes one last contribution, albeit somewhat reluctantly, and I would like to include it here.

> There is one more very minor point, which I almost hesitate to mention, for I dislike reading into an illustration something which may not be at all likely. The Indians of this region manufacture a great variety of bark cloth, beaten out of bark into long sheets which can [be], and are, used as garments, wrappers, and the like. In many areas, these are painted or stamped in geometric patterns. Your lovely lassie has an interesting train to her costume, and it is just possible, although I grant a very slim chance, that this was a bark-cloth sheeting. These are often made in width of about 2 feet, and sometimes 10 or 15 feet in length.

My main reason for quoting the last is that the train, as the fire fan, is part of the costume of the Indian Queen, while the headdress is part of the costume of the attendant. Mrs Behn mentioned specifically that she gave the theatre the costume of the Queen. The last material should be accepted as Dr Dockstader qualified it, however.

All of this is still not absolutely conclusive evidence that Mrs Behn went to Surinam and did all of the things she claims to have done there, as a child or a young girl. I submit, however, that the coincidence of authenticity in the costumery provided for a portrait of Mrs Bracegirdle, in the very role for which Mrs Behn claims to have donated the costume, ought to make her statement a good deal more credible. Taken with the series of attacks upon Bernbaum's article, with the information supplied by Benjamins, and with the neutral or more generous attitude of later biographers and scholars, it should help to restore faith in Mrs Behn's veracity. *Oroonoko,* then, may well deserve a position of importance in the history of realism in English prose fiction.

Notes

[1] *The Histories and Novels of the Late Ingenious Mrs. Behn* (London 1696) 64. All subsequent references to material in *Oroonoko* are from this edition, hereafter cited as *The Histories and Novels.*

[2] "Memoirs" *The Histories and Novels* n. p.

[3] See *The Calendar of State Papers, Domestic Series, of the Reign of Charles II: 1666-67* VI (London 1864) for seventeen letters containing a variety of information which Mrs Behn sent to England under code name Astrea.

[4] For a summary see my "Life and Plays of Mrs. Aphra Behn" unpublished PhD thesis (Duke University 1960.) Available as University Microfilms 60-6030 (Ann Arbor, Michigan).

[5] *Anniversary Papers by Colleagues and Pupils of George Lyman Kittredge* (London 1913) 419-435.

[6] *PMLA* 28 (1913) 433.

[7] (Georgetown, Demerara 1888).

[8] *The Works of Aphra Behn* (London 1915) I xvii-xxi.

[9] "Een Koninklijke slaav in Suriname" *De West-Indische Gids* I (Oct 1919) 474-476; "Nog Eens: Aphra Behn" *Gids* III (Feb 1921) 517-538; "Is Aphra Behn in Suriname Geweest?" *Gids* IX (Feb 1927) 451-462.

[10] "Is Aphra Behn in Suriname Geweest?" 459.

[11] Victoria Sackville-West *Aphra Behn: The Incomparable Astrea* (London 1927) 21-28; George Woodcock *The Incomparable Aphra* (London 1948) 18-26; Frederick M. Link *Aphra Behn* (New York 1968) 18-20.

[12] "Astrea and Celadon; an Untouched Portrait of Aphra Behn" *PMLA* 49 (1934) 544-559.

[13] *New Light on Aphra Behn* University of Auckland Monograph No 5 (Auckland 1961).

[14] *The Histories and Novels* 2-3.

[15] *The Histories and Novels* 3. Here Mrs Behn refers to the title role of Dryden and Howard's *The Indian Queen,* first performed in January 1663/64, at the Theatre Royal.

[16] *Pepys on the Restoration Stage* (New Haven 1916) 156.

[17] *The Incomparable Aphra* 19.

[18] *Shakespeare: From Betterton to Irving* (New York 1920) I 205.

[19] See 80-81 of my thesis, cited in footnote 4.

[20] Colley Cibber *An Apology for the Life of Colley Cibber* ed Robert W. Lowe (London 1886) I 188.

[21] Written communication December 26 1969.

William C. Spengemann (essay date 1984)

SOURCE: "The Earliest American Novel: Aphra Behn's *Oroonoko,*" in *Nineteenth-Century Fiction*, Vol. 38, No. 4, March, 1984, pp. 384-414.

[*In the following excerpt, Spengemann argues that Behn's efforts to create a novel popular with the public resulted in a noteworthy and remarkable work.*]

Reading *Oroonoko,* as we necessarily do, in the light of all the prose fiction produced over the last three centuries, we tend automatically to think of Behn's work as a novel and then, with *Clarissa* and *Moby-Dick* and *Ulysses* in mind, to dismiss it as a very imperfect example of the genre. Although perhaps unavoidable, this ahistorical view begs its own question: why should we so readily attach the name "novel" to a work written at a time when the various things we understand by that word—the form itself, the world it describes, its peculiar language, the readership to whom it speaks—did not yet exist, were only in the process, so to speak, of being invented? When, "never rest[ing] my Pen a Moment for Thought," Behn composed her history of the Royal Slave, she was not trying to write a novel and failing. As one of the newly emerging class of professional writers created by the decline of aristocratic patronage after the Civil War and the rise of a new audience of book buyers, she was simply trying to earn a living by composing, from the literary materials available to her, a story that this as yet ill-defined readership would buy and praise because it portrayed a world they recognized.

In one respect, Behn was unusually well equipped for her task. Her pen had supported her reasonably well for nearly twenty years, and she had worked successfully in virtually every important genre of her time except the epic. For the Restoration theatre she had composed heroic dramas, romantic tragicomedies, comedies of wit, of intrigue, and of manners, farces, pastorals, masques, operas, and a single tragedy. Forced by changes in the political, economic, and social climate to seek support in the popular marketplace, she had turned in recent years to writing those varieties of prose entertainment that her contemporaries lumped together under the name of "fiction"—epistolary romances, novellas, Italian romances, French Arcadian romances, romantic tales, and translations of moral maxims and popular scientific treatises from the French. Alert to sources of income in every level of her society, she had also produced celebratory odes for the royal family, lyrics and verse narratives dedicated to courtiers and to influential members of the professions, and anthologies of poetry for the commercial market. She was an accomplished professional who knew what would sell and how to write it.

In almost every other respect, however, she was singularly ill-prepared for her assault on the common reader. Although her own pedigree is obscure, she was apparently reared and educated among the landed gentry, and she identified herself always with the titled classes, professing an unswerving devotion to the Stuart monarchy in the very face of its imminent collapse. She was an unreconstructed Tory and an avowed Catholic in a society whose tolerance for such recherché attitudes was growing slimmer by the day. Worse yet, she was a social rebel whose undisguised hatred for the legal institution of marriage and allegiance to the authority of disinterested love were mistaken by her aristocratic friends and middle-class enemies alike for libertinism. It was a romantic ideal of natural love that she celebrated in her plays, not sexual license. But the attitude toward conventional morality and the behavior arising from that attitude were not always distinguishable from those routinely displayed in the Restoration theatre. And if the Court had called her plays salacious simply because they were written by a woman, what sort of reception could she expect in the City, whose denizens she had repeatedly portrayed as joyless, puritanical hypocrites undone by witty, amorous Cavaliers?

Behn's is the classic case of the modern professional writer, schooled in a lofty ideal of truth and art and forced by mundane circumstance to make her living in a world that she disdained and that held her ideals in contempt. That her personal vision of the good as a Tory Arcadia ruled by peaceful shepherd kings was a nostalgic fiction, hopelessly out of touch with modern history, is nothing to the point. Unless she simply abandoned that vision, she would have to find some way to bridge the gulf between her feudal paradise and the progressive "new England" of her intended audience. Had she been merely a hack, unhampered by allegiances of her own, she could have manufactured tales of honest apprentices, religious romances, or antiromantic burlesques as effortlessly as she had churned out satires on the Parliamentarians or congratulatory poems to the several monarchs who occupied the English throne in rapid succession during the 1680s. In that case, *Oroonoko* would have been a very different book, and we would not be scratching our heads over it today, for it would have disappeared from sight along with *The City Heiress, The Amours of Philander and Sylvia,* and *A Voyage to the Isle of Love.* Because she was motivated by personal conviction as well as by necessity, however, she sought to make a place for her antique ideals in the hated modern world. Out of that quixotic ambition, she produced a book so remarkable that it has rescued the rest of her oeuvre from oblivion and seems now, for all its stumbling oddity, to anticipate the whole subsequent history of English fiction.

The strategy Behn devised to reconcile the conflicting demands of personal inclination and public taste is, on the face of it, ingeniously simple. She merely fashioned a romantic tale of highborn lovers caught in the crosscurrents of desire and duty and then presented this old story in the very modern guise of a Brief True Relation of her own travels to America. This conflation of Old-World and New-World genres seems to have suited her purposes exactly. On the one hand, the prose romance was in every sense her métier. Not only was she thoroughly practiced in its conventions, having read romances all of her life and modeled most of her plays (to say nothing of her own behavior) upon them, but, like most persons of her class and education, she regarded them as accurate pictures of reality and as dramatizations of her own most cherished values. The Brief True Relation, on the other hand, simultaneously evaded her busy middle-class readers' distrust of idle fictions and met their demands for useful information about current affairs in brief compass. What is more, because the Brief True Relation rested the authority of its statements upon the writer's experiences rather than upon his or her social station or sex; the form allowed Behn to assume an authority that had been begrudged her in the masculine, courtly domains of drama and poetry. And because the experiences reported in these narratives of New-World travel were necessarily unverifiable, the form permitted her to call her tale a true history without fear of rebuttal. By enfolding her romance of the Royal Slave in a Brief True Relation, Behn could stick to her romantic last, proffer her fiction as news from the New World, and thus foist it upon the very audience whose members were busily dismantling the world that the romance had been devised to validate.

To say that Behn wished to make a place for romance in a new world is true in more than just a commercial sense. She was not simply trying to peddle an old product in a new market; she wished to discover in the prosaic and turbulent modern world that history was constructing about her a place where the vanishing ideals embodied in romance could survive the predations of change and even rise again to regulate human society. To Behn, as to many another European who lamented the passing of traditional ways and the decline of civil order in the seventeenth century, America seemed a place out of time, where man's original estate might be regained. Ever since the discovery, narratives of New-World travel had couched their actions in the tropes of chivalric romance and described America in images of the Earthly Paradise, the Garden of Eden, and the Golden Age.[4] If the discovery, exploration, and settlement of America formed an inextricable part of that historical change which had removed humankind from its primal condition, then by casting themselves upon this historical tide men might hope to complete the circular course of human history, arrive again at the beginning, and remain in that perfected state forever. For Behn, America embodied an ideal condition of feminine nature, the original kingdom of love from which men fell into history when they took up the masculine pursuits of war and commerce. Transported there by masculine desires for glory and wealth, the loving woman and bellicose male of romantic tradition might be reconciled in a perfect, eternal marriage. For such a redeeming expedition from the Old World to the New, the narrative form of the Brief True Relation, even though it was devised to take hold of the most world-shaking event in modern history, might well seem the speediest craft.

The vessel is fairly launched with the narrator's opening announcement that the story to follow is a true "History," rather than the "Adventures of a feign'd *Hero,* whose Life and Fortunes Fancy may manage at the Poet's Pleasure." Although it will prove as "diverting" as any fictional romance, like all such reports by plain-speaking voyagers, "it shall come simply into the World," without the adornments of artistic "Invention," recommended solely "by its own proper Merits, and natural Intrigues." The truth upon which its charm depends, moreover, will lie not in the familiarity of its details or its conformity with recognized conventions but in the narrator's own experience. "I was myself an Eye-witness to a great Part of what you will find here

set down," the narrator maintains, "and what I cou'd not be Witness of, I receiv'd from the Mouth of the chief Actor in this History, the *Hero* himself." Addressing her busy reader, who has not the leisure demanded by the conventional, multivolume romance, she then explains that she has omitted, "for Brevity's Sake, a thousand little Accidents of [the hero's] life, which . . . might prove tedious and heavy to my Reader, in a World where he finds Diversions for every Minute, new and strange" (v, 129). And to inspire the confidence of this apparently preoccupied and literalminded reader, she precedes the introduction of her hero with a circumstantial account of the slave economy, flora, fauna, and native inhabitants of Surinam, couching these data, all the while, in images of the Golden Age—of innocent, free Indians who live, like "Adam and Eve," without either shame or immodesty, codified laws or organized religion, "Curiosity" or "Fraud," "Vice, or Cunning" (v, 131-32)—those images which had recommended America to Behn as the ideal setting for a New-World romance.

That Behn regarded the Brief True Relation primarily as a vehicle for her romance is evident in the dispatch with which the narrator abandons that modern conveyance, after five pages, and turns her attention to its precious, Old-World cargo. The next thirty-odd pages, nearly half of the complete text, are devoted to Oroonoko's life in the court of Coramantien and his rivalry with the King, his grandfather, for the hand of Imoinda. Taken straight from the English heroic drama and the French Arcadian romance, and offered here as an account given to the narrator by Oroonoko after his arrival in Surinam, this familiar story of conflicting romantic principles employs none of the narrative techniques introduced in the opening relation. The narrator is now undramatized and omniscient, a teller of someone else's tale and, like her reader, an audience to that tale, rather than a particular person reporting her own observations in a particular place. Indeed, the narrator does not even take care to report only those things that Oroonoko, her supposed source of information, could have seen at the time or learned about subsequently. Romantic actions happen objectively, in the eternal order of things, and do not depend for their existence, as the recently discovered and ever-expanding New World did, upon the perceptions of individual human beings. The value of these actions lies not in their individual contributions to the accumulating store of human knowledge about the world, but in their coherent moral structure, which imitates the divinely instituted form of the world and of human history.

Unlike the structure of the Brief True Relation, which arises from a sequence of actions performed by an observing, reflecting individual on the ground, that of the romance precedes its action as an empty form, into which details of various sorts, from the most realistic to the most fantastic, can be poured and thus given a familiar valuation. In broad outline, this form comprises an initial situation, a conflict arising from (or introduced into) that situation, a series of complications that elucidate both the conflict and the particular virtues required to overcome it, and a resolution which serves to confirm those virtues and to create a final situation that demands no further action. Because these virtues are of the highest sort, the action is performed by noble characters; and because these noble actions have universal meaning, their physical setting in any particular instance remains a matter of virtual indifference, a mere backdrop against which the moral drama is played out. Nowhere in Oroonoko's African adventures do we find anything resembling the narrator's earlier interest in the topography, economy, botany, and zoology of Surinam and its closely related anthropology. Behn's readers have often observed that the African court of Coramantien bears a striking resemblance to the courts of Europe. The point is, rather, that the story of Oroonoko and Imoinda told thus far, being a romance, could happen anywhere without affecting its form one whit.

Since the romantic conflict of this story pits Oroonoko's love for Imoinda against his duty to the King, who wants her for his harem, it projects a resolution in the form of a wedding between the lovers and a reconciliation with their monarchical parent. Nothing irremediable appears to lie in the way of such a resolution. The King has violated the local taboo against a father's coveting his son's intended bride, and Oroonoko has retaliated by breaking the corresponding taboo against a son's meddling with one of his father's chosen wives. But these transgressions do not seem to be fatal. No one has been killed or cursed, and Imoinda has not been physically dishonored; so the way to sanity and bliss still lies open. To be sure, the King sells Imoinda into slavery after discovering her midnight tryst with Oroonoko. But Oroonoko himself is captured by a slaver very soon thereafter, and if the lovers do not know that they are bound for the same place, the experienced reader of romances certainly does. Apparently, the conflicts and divisions that have arisen in the Old World and, with the transportation of the two lovers, have become insoluble there, are to be repaired in that innocent, aboriginal America to which we were introduced in the opening description of Surinam. As Oroonoko says upon disembarking from the ship that has brought him to America, *"Come, my Fellow-Slaves, let us descend, and see if we can meet with more Honour and Honesty in the next World we shall touch upon"* (v, 166-67).

The reader's expectations of a happy resolution to the romantic conflict are seemingly vindicated in the events that follow quickly upon Oroonoko's landing in the colony. He is immediately recognized as a king, given the name of "Caesar," greeted by the loyal colonists as if "the King himself (God bless him) had come ashore,"

and "received more like a Governor than a Slave" (v, 169). In addition to the customary freight of heroic virtues, it appears, Oroonoko comes bearing his creator's loyalty to the beleaguered Stuarts and her fond if unsubstantiated hopes for their permanent restoration to power over an obedient, orderly realm. While the local slaves, many of whom are Oroonoko's own former captives, prostrate themselves before him, "crying out . . . *Long live, O King!*" and paying him "even Divine Homage," Trefry, his new owner, treats him "as his dearest Brother," lodges him in his own house, rather than amongst the common slaves, and promises "on his Word and Honour" as a gentleman to return the Prince to Africa (v, 170, 168). At a great feast staged in Oroonoko's honor by the slaves, Trefry tells him about a recently arrived beauty named Clemene, who turns out, of course, to be Imoinda; and within three pages the lovers are reunited, wed, and expecting a child. For the happy conclusion of the romance, only the rupture between these lovers and the old King of Coramantien remains to be healed; and, as anyone familiar with the genre would know, such problems are easily dispatched. Whether Oroonoko and his gravid spouse return to the welcome of a once tyrannical parent now softened by remorse, or the King conveniently dies during their absence, or they decide to remain in America and establish a peaceful dynasty of commingled love and honor in that regained paradise, the romantic action has virtually arrived at its projected conclusion.

At this point, however, the action takes an unexpected and decidedly unromantic turn. Oroonoko is still a slave and cannot be freed until a new Governor arrives from England to replace the previous one, the narrator's father, who has drowned at sea in a hurricane. True, Oroonoko suffers "no more of the Slave but the Name" (v, 169-70), and his aristocratic friends at Parham House have promised to secure his freedom. Nonetheless, "Caesar" is a slave name in fact and a royal title only in a fictional sense—in another world, as it were. Nor is the English colony populated solely by aristocrats of the sort who rule the world of romance. During this interregnum, the real power lies in the hands of ambitious upstarts and wealthy hoodlums like Byam and Banister, "such notorious Villains as *Newgate* never transported," who cannot be expected to assist the designs of a romantic action because they "understood neither the laws of God or Man, and had no sort of Principles . . ." (v, 200). These uncultivated renegades, Oroonoko fears, will never let him go, for his title and noble bearing only make them detest him the more, while his wife and expected child triple his value in the slave economy. As a slave, Oroonoko has neither love, since his wife and child do not belong to him, nor honor, since his present safety and eventual liberation depend on his lying low at Parham house, showing no signs of restiveness until the new Governor arrives. If he attempts to secure his love and regain his honor by inciting a slave rebellion, Imoinda will become Byam's hostage, and his friends among the aristocratic planters will be forced to side with the overseer class against him.

Oroonoko's entanglement in the intractable circumstances of colonial politics, economics, and class conflict markedly alters the tone and import of the narrative. We seem to have moved without warning from that morally translucent world where "Heaven was so kind to the Prince as to sweeten his Misfortunes by so lucky an Accident" as his reunion with Imoinda (v, 173-74) to an altogether different sort of world, one governed by untidy historical conditions rather than by universal principles of love and honor. These unlooked-for complications follow so closely upon Oroonoko's arrival in the New World that a devout Americanist might be tempted to ascribe them directly to the change of geographical venue from Africa to America, on the assumption that America is, after all, a very special sort of place. The fact is, however, that life in seventeenth-century Coramantien was obviously no less subject than Surinam to such historical conditions, while Surinam, as the opening pages of **Oroonoko** demonstrate, was no less susceptible than Coramantien to romantic treatment. The crucial change, in other words, is formal and stylistic. It occurs at the point where the action departs from the timeless circle of romance form and enters the historical form of the Brief True Relation for the first time. In the opening four or five pages of the text we heard the beginnings of Behn's Brief True Relation of life in Surinam, without Oroonoko. The succeeding forty pages gave us the romance of Oroonoko and Imoinda in Coramantien, outside both Surinam and the narrator's own immediate experience. Now, with only a third of the volume remaining in the reader's right hand and the action seemingly poised for its final sprint to a happy conclusion, Oroonoko finds himself in a strange new world, created by conflicting human desires rather than by divine intentions, where nothing is conclusive but death.

In calling her tale a "History," Behn appears to have intended only to imply that it actually happened and thus to lull the philistine prejudices of her middle-class reader. In adopting for this purpose the narrative form of the Brief True Relation, however, she was in effect subscribing, and subjecting her hero, to a radically modern idea of what "history" means. Because the Brief True Relation was devised specifically to report observed conditions in a new world that had first come to light as a direct result of present human enterprise, rather than through knowledge transmitted from the distant past, and because that world grew larger with each effort to encompass it, the form portrayed human action in terms of an unfolding geography and this expanding landscape in terms of a corresponding change in the character and attitudes of the traveler.[5] In the romance, as in medieval historiography, the chronology of events proceeds independent of geography, which serves merely as a backdrop for the exemplary actions of exemplary figures who, being motivated by universal moral principles, do not change significantly in the course of the action. In the Brief True Relation, on the other hand, human action and geographical situation are mutually conditioning elements in the historical evolution—the creation—of reality. Geography and chronology, Richard Hakluyt proclaimed, are "the right eye and the left eye of all history."[6] History without geography, John Smith agreed, "wandreth as a Vagrant without a certaine habitation"[7]—thus denying at a stroke the belief held by medieval historian and romancer alike that human history has its home in the divine mind, in the eternal plan of redemption, and locating that history squarely in the evolving individual soul.

Behn's investment of her romantic action in this narrative form generates a sequence of events and a level of discourse, somewhere between fiction and history, whose import can only be called novelistic. While Oroonoko continues to pursue the goals of love and honor set for him in the romance of Coramantien, he must do so through an ever-thickening jungle of bureaucratic delays, demeaning expediencies, political rivalries, and geographical circumstances. Born with "a Spirit all rough and fierce . . . that could not be tam'd to lazy Rest" (v, 176), he is yet obliged to spend his time entertaining the narrator with tales of his former exploits and listening to "all the pretty Works" in her repertoire but avoiding the sort of heroic action that might imperil his and Imoinda's safety and that would, in the best possible case, only send him into the wilderness to live like a savage with no hope of either returning to Coramantien or establishing his dynasty in Surinam. Whatever notions Behn may have held regarding the New World as a theatre for heroic actions and a haven for romantic ideals, these fond designs seem to be enmeshed now in a tightening coil of petty, vulgar constraints.

With Oroonoko trapped between unheroic docility and suicidal rebellion, the narrative takes an evasive turn, off the line of fatal action that seems headed for either dishonor or death, into a series of diverting adventures in the countryside. By means of this "Digression," which she admits "is a little from my Story" (v, 189), the narrator apparently means to provide her frustrated hero with some opportunities for action that will get him out of the house but will not require the colonists to crush him. In a succession of tall tales, recounted in the purest manner of the Brief True Relation, Oroonoko kills "Tygers," wrestles with an electric eel, and guides the narrator's party to an Indian village, behaving all the while with appropriate bravery and chivalrous concern for his female companions. "Diverting" as they are, however, these exploits merely forestall the inevitable decision Oroonoko must make regarding his dishonorable captivity. What is more, even though his companionship gives the narrator and her friends the heart to venture into the wilderness, his undignified role as a captive entertainer of idle aristocrats robs his heroism of any real consequence. The narrator herself appears to realize the falsity of Oroonoko's position, for he fades from view for long intervals, while she describes the local topography and inhabitants, supplanting his actions with her own reflections upon the exotic world that unfolds before her as she penetrates the unexplored wilderness beyond the settlement.

Digressive as it is, this interlude has a profound effect upon the main action. Not only does it demonstrate that Oroonoko's heroism depends on his making the fatal choice between love and honor, but, by reemphasizing the narrative methods of the Brief True Relation, it places the narrator at the very center of the action and involves her directly in that choice. Whereas the narrator of a romance stands outside the action, in the presence of the reader, the Brief True Relation places the narrator, who is both the principal actor and the reporter of that action, in the game and out of it at once. What is more, because it is the narrator's experiences that have made him who he is, someone with the authority to speak, he tends quite naturally to identify himself more closely with those experiences than with the untraveled reader. Throughout her first-person report, Behn's narrator has moved back and forth between the familiar English world of her readers and the exotic lands that only she knows—at one moment claiming that, since her return to England, she has placed certain entymological specimens on display at "his Majesty's *Antiquary's*" (v, 130), where the reader can presumably go and see them, or alluding to well-known historical events, like the Treaty of Breda and the death of Charles II, which have occurred since the putative year of her departure from Surinam; and at another moment referring to Oroonoko in the imperfect tense—"I have often heard him say . . ." (v, 159-160)—as if he were still alive and she were still with him in America. At one point in the narrative, in fact, she manages this temporal and geographical shift in the course of a single sentence, traveling by way of those uncertain pronominal references and unsteady verb tenses that make seventeenth-century English prose such a puzzle for modern readers. Upon first introducing her hero, the narrator addresses her audience on its own English ground: "But before I give you the Story of this *Gallant Slave,* 'tis fit I tell you the Manner of bringing them [i.e., slaves] to these new *Colonies. . . .*" As the sentence continues, however, it abruptly removes the narrator across the Atlantic to Surinam and into the midst of her own narrative: "those [slaves] they [the colonists] make Use of there [in Surinam], not being *Natives* of the Place: for those [natives] we [colonists] live with [here in Surinam] in perfect Amity" (v, 129). Drawn by the rhetorical gravity of the Brief

True Relation into the action of her tale, the narrator will eventually find herself not merely a witness to its outcome but a principal actor in it.

The final episode in the digressive interlude that lies between Oroonoko's happy marriage and his horrible death takes the narrator and her traveling party to an Indian village upriver, where she undergoes an experience that fixes her more firmly in the New World than anything, perhaps, except her assumption of responsibility for Oroonoko's safety and liberation. Meeting the Indians, who have never seen a white person before, she immediately becomes conscious of her own strange appearance, as if she were seeing herself through their wondering eyes, and describes herself for the first time. What she sees of herself and her companions from this outlandish point of view is reported in the Indians' words, which, although perfectly innocent, assume in context an ironic edge that is hardly flattering to European assumptions of cultural superiority. *"We shall know whether those Things can speak,"* the natives exclaim, whether they have "Sense and Wit" and can "talk of Affairs of Life and War," as Indians can (v, 185-86). Like so many New-World explorers before her and many more to come, the narrator has been given a new perspective on the world as a whole. Seen from this American coign of vantage, Europe is no longer the center of the circle of lands. It is merely one more place on the globe, as backward in its way as are the barbarous nations in theirs, a relative thing rather than the seat of absolute values by which the rest of the world may be judged. Noting the innocent credulity of the Indians, she quickly realizes that "it were not difficult to establish any unknown or extravagant Religion among them, and to impose any Notions or Fictions upon 'em" (v, 186), a realization that unavoidably includes in the category of "Fictions" the religion that she and her reader share.[8] It is a vision that, once entertained, can never be thrown off, and it severs the traveler irreparably from the untraveled reader, the very person upon whose sympathy and assent the authority of the narrator ultimately depends. If the effect of the romance is to unite narrator and reader in a world of shared beliefs, that of the Brief True Relation is inevitably to place the narrator in a new and distant land, one that readers can inhabit only by abandoning their own.

Having sought to evade the unpromising drift of her tale by means of the narrative form that caused all her difficulties in the first place, the narrator returns to her proper "Story" to find nothing changed, except that this story has now become her own—a tale of her increasing departure from the settled moral world of her English readers into the unexplored American wilderness of her own invention. When, weary of prudent inaction, Oroonoko finally rebels against his captors, the narrator finds herself swept up in his mounting hostility to her own kind. Throughout her narrative, she has taken an ambiguous attitude toward her fellow colonists, employing the pronoun "we" to distinguish the white settlers from the Indians and the African slaves but isolating herself by calling the English "they" whenever slavery, especially cruelty to Oroonoko, is the subject. There are, in addition, a number of passages in which the Indians, like Montaigne's cannibals, are depicted as more noble, even more essentially Christian, than their supposedly civilized oppressors. Now, however, all semblance of ambiguity and lofty satire vanishes as the narrator submerges her voice in Oroonoko's, first paraphrasing the harangue by which he stirs up his fellow captives and then modulating into direct quotation as he excoriates all white people for their faithlessness and inhumanity.

Depending on their politics, Behn's readers have taken this speech either as an expression of her own views on slavery or, noting the complaisance of the narrator's remarks on the subject elsewhere, as Oroonoko's opinions alone.[9] Both of these readings seem partly right. While Behn appears to have held no very advanced ideas about the evils of slavery itself, it is impossible to avoid the impression that Oroonoko's diatribe bespeaks her own suppressed rage against the betrayal of all those cherished things that her romantic hero has come to represent. Called "Caesar," he bears a name synonymous with "absolute monarch" in Behn's time, the one she gives to Charles II in her poem "A Farewell to Celladon on His Going Into Ireland" (1684) and to James II in her *Congratulatory Poem to Her Sacred Majesty Queen Mary, Upon Her Arrival in England* (1689). As a slave, he shares the plight of women, regarding whom the anonymous author of the *Defense of the Female Sex* (1696) observed, " . . . like our Negroes in our western plantations, [they] are born slaves, and live prisoners all their lives,"[10] and whom Hippolyta, the betrayed woman in Behn's play **The Dutch Lover** (1673), compares to "a poor, guilty slave" who "drags his loathed Fetters after him" (I, 273-74). If it seems strange to think of Behn's presenting her feminist indictment in a masculine voice, we should observe that her preface to **The Lucky Chance** (1686) proclaims, "I value Fame as much as if I had been a *Hero,*" that in the same speech she refers to "the Poet in me" as "her masculine Part" (111, 187), and that in all the other fictions she composed during the 1680s Oroonoko's role is taken by a woman. But, above all, Oroonoko personifies the ideals of cosmic order, social harmony, and individual nobility embodied in the romance, ideals that, Behn saw, were being ravaged by modern history in the world about her and subverted by some implacable fictive logic in her own narrative.

When, following Oroonoko's inflammatory speech, the narrator resumes her own voice, she adopts a sardonic tone of thinly disguised hostility that is notably absent from her previous discourse and can only be attributed to her preceding identification with the rebellious Oroonoko. At the same time, she seems eager to reestablish contact with her reader and to dissociate herself from Oroonoko, whose accelerating troubles she feels powerless to alleviate, even as she feels guilty for having failed him. If Oroonoko is responsible for the unprecedented passion of her tone in these concluding episodes, he is also the cause of her efforts to distance herself from him. The grievances aired in his harangue to the slaves include the complaint that "we are bought and sold like Apes or Monkeys, to be the Sport of Women," which seems to refer to the narrator herself and to those early days of his captivity when, she says, "we entertain'd him . . . , or rather he us" (v, 191, 177). Once the uprising has begun, moreover, she naturally identifies herself with the white colonists, using the pronoun "we" to denote the common targets of his revenge. In the next moment, however, Oroonoko's enemies become "they," as Byam's vigilantes pursue the fugitive, and the narrator stands by powerless to protect him. For the remainder of her story, the narrator shifts her position repeatedly, now aligning herself with Oroonoko's aristocratic friends against his low-life pursuers, then speaking familiarly to the reader as an English author, then dissociating herself from all the colonists and from the reader as well by referring sarcastically to one timid member of her party as "a bold *Englishman*" (v, 205), then implicitly condemning herself by quoting Oroonoko's charge that all whites are liars, and then ranging herself among the whites by begging Oroonoko's pardon on behalf of his tormentors. But, most of all, she vacillates between protestations of her own innocence and apologies for her faintheartedness, her absence during his capture and execution, her failure to assert her "Authority" on his behalf, and, finally, for the inadequacy of the tale itself as a fitting tribute to "this great Man" (v, 198, 208).

These rapid shifts in narrative attitude create an ambiguity of tone that enhances the novelistic effects already produced by the collision of Behn's romantic theme with her historical narrative form. Neither romance nor Brief True Relation, her narrative has become a rhetorical blending of heroic ideals and brute reality into a symbolic expression of the narrator's conflicting allegiances to her civilized audience and her savage art. When Oroonoko finally realizes that conditions in Surinam forbid the marriage of love and honor, nature and culture, that he hoped to discover in this "next World," he takes Imoinda into a nearby grove, love's own pastoral domain, and beheads her, thereby removing the impediment to honorable rebellion and, in destroying his wife and unborn child, removing at the same time his main reason to rebel. Unmanned by grief, he mourns over the half-buried body of Imoinda for eight days, until a searching party, attracted to the spot by an egregiously unromantic "Stink that almost struck them dead" (v, 204), discovers him. Thinking to take advantage of his weakness, "The *English*" move to recapture him, whereupon he repulses his enemies by hacking off a piece of his own flesh and throwing it in their faces. This barbarous gesture, learned from the Indian braves he visited during his expedition with the narrator, betrays a striking change in Oroonoko's character, an assimilation to his savage surroundings in preference to the putative civility of his faithless captors and feckless friends. He has gone native, thereby committing the one unpardonable sin available to the missionaries of Old-World culture; and insofar as the narrator follows him imaginatively, she must relinquish all claims to her reader's sympathy and trust.

How deeply Oroonoko penetrates into the heart of the savage wilderness and how closely the narrator follows him may be discerned in the powerfully affecting language of the tale's final episode. After some days spent recuperating at Parham House, Oroonoko is abducted by the parvenu rabble and executed. As they slowly dismember him, he stoically smokes an Indian pipe. Before he dies—or "gave up the Ghost," as the text has it—he blesses his executioners. And when he is dead, Byam sends to the plantations, by way of a warning to the other slaves, Oroonoko's quartered remains, the "frightful Spectacles of a mangled King" (v, 208). Amalgamated in this unforgettable tableau are images of all the hopes that the narrator has invested in her Royal Slave: the natural nobility of the American Indian, the divine right of the martyred Charles, and the redemptive sacrifice of Christ.[11] Having been brought down from the luminous spheres of romantic allegory to the opaque realities of bureaucratic delay, class jealousy, hopeless servitude, and decomposing flesh in the New World, Oroonoko is elevated by his debasement into a complex symbol of Old World hopes aesthetically vindicated in the very moment of their historical extinction.

The closing pages of *Oroonoko* reenact the psychic turmoil of all those European explorers who came to America armed with Old-World ideas about it, and then, having undergone experiences that utterly discredited these ideas, found themselves unable either to resume their previous lives at home or to remain isolated in the new world they had discovered. Oroonoko's death constitutes an indictment of everything that Behn's new reader represents— social ambition, commercial enterprise, the subjugation of "dusky tribes," the dismantling of ancient institutions. Insofar as she clings to her hero, acknowledging the savage metaphor of his rebellion and death as her own truest language, she forfeits the support of that audience upon whom all modern writers must depend not only for their livelihood but for their very sense of themselves as writers. Insofar as she distances herself from Oroonoko, however, and aligns herself with her English reader, her tale condemns her as a coward and a liar. The narrator's opening remarks located the value of her tale in its historical truth and the authority for that truth in her own experiences as an American. Later,

recognizing the failure of her account to do Oroonoko full justice, she ascribed its deficiencies to that same source: "But his Misfortune was, to fall in an obscure World, that afforded only a Female Pen to celebrate his Fame" (v, 169). Now, in closing, she blames its weaknesses on her lack of artistry, the very feature that she originally offered in evidence of its truth and had advertised in the prologue to *The Young King* (1679) as an American characteristic (II, 105). A "more sublime wit" might have succeeded in conveying Oroonoko from his "obscure World" to the new England. As it is, the survival of his "glorious Name . . . to all Ages" must depend not on the narrator's authority as an American but on the "Reputation of my Pen," the fame she has won in the London theatre since her return from the New World (v, 208).

Appearing to recognize that her very dubious reputation as a libertine author of scandalous aristocratic plays will hardly impress her middle-class reader, Behn turns her back upon this audience and, in a dedicatory epistle to Lord Maitland (v, 509-11), seeks the protection of a noble patron, a ghost of the old order that died with Oroonoko. Once again, she admits the shortcomings of her book, seemingly equating these with her hero's "Inglorious . . . end" and her own inability to prevent that catastrophe. It is a "true Story": "The Royal Slave I had the Honour to know in my Travels to the other World." Since this world is not further identified, the reader is permitted to think of it both as America and as an imagined country: "If there be anything [in the story, in the place] that seems Romantick [i.e., fictional, untrue] I beseech your Lordship to consider these Countries do, in all things, so far differ from ours that they produce unconceivable Wonders, at least, so they appear to us, because New and Strange." What happens in that "other World," it appears, is both fictional and true at once, according to a logic that nullifies the author-traveler's intentions. "Though I had none above me in that Country," Behn quite justly insists, "yet I wanted power to preserve this Great man." The problem, she concludes, is a formal one, evidenced in certain "Faults of Connexion" among the various elements of her tale. These faults, however, she now attributes not to her want of "sublime Wit" or to her "Female Pen" but to her headlong, unreflecting methods of composition. "I writ it in a few Hours," she explains, and "never rested my Pen a Moment for Thought" (v, 511). Having embodied her romantic hopes in Oroonoko and then cast him upon the narrative tide of the Brief True Relation, it seems, she could only sit and watch him perish. Recounting her early meetings with the Royal Slave, the narrator says, "He call'd [me] his *Great Mistress;* and indeed my Word would go a great Way with him" (v, 176). In the event, his words were to go even farther with her, to an "other World" where English fiction had never been before and from which there was no returning.

Notes

[4]For information that would permit an accurate plotting of Behn's location on the map of ideas about the Golden Age, see her poem "The Golden Age," in *The Works of Aphra Behn,* ed. Montague Summers, 6 vols. (London: William Heinemann, 1915), VI, 138-44. Subsequent references to *The Works of Aphra Behn* appear in parentheses in the text. See also Harry Levin, *The Myth of the Golden Age in the Renaissance* (Bloomington: Indiana Univ. Press, 1969).

[5] For detailed studies of the Brief True Relation, see Jarvis Means Morse, *American Beginnings* (Washington, D.C.: Public Affairs Press, 1952), ch. 2; and Wayne Franklin, *Discoverers, Explorers, Settlers: The Diligent Writers of Early America* (Chicago: Univ. of Chicago Press, 1979). Differences between this form and that of the romance are outlined in William C. Spengemann, *The Adventurous Muse: The Poetics of American Fiction, 1789-1900* (New Haven, Conn.: Yale Univ. Press, 1977), chs. 1 and 2.

[6] Richard Hakluyt, *Voyages* (London: J. M. Dent, 1907), I, 19.

[7] John Smith, *Travels and Works of Captain John Smith,* ed. Edward Arber and A. G. Bradley, 2 vols. (Edinburgh: John Grant, 1910), II, 625.

[8] For a full discussion of these cultural epiphanies in voyage narratives and their impact on literature, see Stephen Greenblatt, *Renaissance Self-Fashioning: From More to Shakespeare* (Chicago: Univ. of Chicago Press, 1980), pp. 222-29.

[9] See, for example, George Guffey, "Aphra Behn's *Oroonoko:* Occasion and Accomplishment," in *Two English Novelists,* by George Guffey and Andrew Wright (Los Angeles: Clark Memorial Library, 1975), pp. 3-41, esp. p. 37; and Angeline Goreau, *Reconstructing Aphra: A Social Biography of Aphra Behn* (New York: Dial Press, 1980), pp. 288-89. Although published years later, we note, Goreau's biography does not confront Guffey's arguments against the idea of Behn's radicalism.

[10] Quoted in Goreau, *Reconstructing Aphra,* p. 290.

[11] Behn explicitly identifies Charles II with Christ in her *Pindarick on the Death of Our Late Sovereign* (London: J. Playford for H. Playford, 1685) and her *Poem Humbly Dedicated to the Great Patern of Piety and Virtue Catherine Queen Dowager* (London: J. Playford for H. Playford, 1685). Charles, Caesar, and Christ, of course, are symbolically akin in having all been kings betrayed by their "sons"—Monmouth, Brutus, and mankind.

Beverle Houston (essay date 1986)

SOURCE: "Usurpation and Dismemberment: Oedipal Tyranny in *Oroonoko*," in *Literature and Psychology,* Vol. XXXII, No. 1, 1986, pp. 30-6.

[*In the following essay, Houston discusses the construction of the text and some thematic contradictions inherent within* Oroonoko.]

May we assume for the duration of this paper that texts are produced by a collaboration of the conscious, the unconscious, other texts, and the institutions that shape individual life. Perhaps we may also say that literary texts come into existence as verbal representations of ideas and images that are not fully accessible to consciousness. Thus texts will reveal, not only fully accessible material whose imaginative or fantastic nature has been mediated by generic conventions, rules of grammar and discourse, and secondary revision in a number of forms. These texts will also display traces of material that has barely sneaked by the censor, that by devious methods has insinuated itself into our perception, that signals its partiality by the peculiar characteristics of contradiction, reversal, doubling, and other a-rational techniques of representation.

A focus on this kind of work in the construction of imaginative texts seems to me particularly appropriate to **Oroonoko** for two reasons: the text is marked by extraordinary excess and by systematic contradictions, both of which emphasize the power of the unconscious and its fantasy fears and wishes as it puts pressure on both plot and strategies of enunciation. First of all, the matter of excess. **Oroonoko** has been subject to a number of illuminating readings, focusing on its potential political implications in terms of a victimized young King and the Dutch menace, the role of the narrator in bringing exotic culture to the English readers, and, above all, the question of its truth to the life of its author, an issue that hangs on with peculiar tenacity. Yet for me, the fore-grounded quality, the power of the Romance as fantasy, its inescapable quality, has always been in the lingering images of the unbelievably extreme punishments to which its noble hero is subjected—in other words, the extraordinary excess of what happens to Oroonoko, the Royal Slave. First, the woman he loves is taken from him by his own grandfather and is later sold into slavery. In the second major division of the work, the glorious hero-as-victim is dismembered, hacked limb from limb, and the physical remains of his existence are distributed among a number of friends and enemies. These elements give the work the character it has in memory for me, and for many other readers such as Vita Sackville-West, who, in granting Behn the experiential basis of her realistic detail, locates the work's power, its center and organizing principles, in the images of "Oroonoko and Imoinda, glistening ebony, tortured figures that they are, running with little rivulets of blood, crowned with their martyrdom." So it is for me, and from these central events and images of excess, and from the contradictions that mark the work so strongly, I will construct a reading.

The conception and construction of *Oroonoko* are largely determined by a number of contradictions. First of all, in its primary concept, we find the irreconcilable and perverse doubleness of "Royal" and "Slave." The man Oroonoko is the site of tremendous power and appeal, one who evokes adoration: "They all cast themselves at his feet, crying out, in their language, Live O King! Long live, O King! and kissing his Feet paid him even Divine Homage." Yet at the same time, he is utterly victimizable by every father figure/white man with whom he comes in contact and whom he is forced to trust—even Trefry is tricked by the Deputy Governor into giving Oroonoko advice that leads to his victimization. This central contradiction is carried out in smaller details as well. Oroonoko is "European" but "Savage," "Black" but "Roman." Thus we locate at the center of the work a figure, each of whose contradictory extremes seems to suggest the shadow of its own opposite. As in Christ himself, the beauty of the noble young god shimmers in a specially radiant way because his youthful glory itself conveys the suggestion of his ultimate victimization, his torturability, as it were.

As readers, we are taught to expect this contradiction once we have seen the usurpation of Imoinda and Oroonoko's entrapment by the English captain of the slave ship. After that, every time a white person, especially a male authority figure, tells Oroonoko how wonderful he is, or makes a promise of any kind, we are aware that these statements signal their own opposites; those who praise and support him are promising, by those very words, that sooner or later they will kill him. The full power of this contradiction (as hypocrisy) is displaced onto the figure of the Deputy Governor, who stands in for the narrator's father who died before he could assume office—one of the many fathers who is instrumental in Oroonoko's horrible fate. The narrator calls the Deputy Governor "the most fawning fair-tongued Fellow in the World . . . one that pretended the most Friendship to Caesar . . . now the only violent man against him . . . ," and says that he is "thirsting after Revenge of another sort, than that of depriving him of life. . . ." The revenge signalled by his fawning is apparently too horrible to describe at this point in the text. The slaves, too, who had bowed to his royal glories, now "by degrees . . . abandoned Caesar, and left him only Tuscan and his Heroick Imoinda." So, we often find that the tale of god-like glory [like Christ with Judas and Mary Magdelene, like Beowulf with his single remaining warrior,] seems to carry within itself its own reversal, its own contradiction of betrayal, victimization, and death.

We find the second major contradiction or combination of irreconcilable but interdependent opposites in the generic identity of *Oroonoko.* The mixed elements of Novel and Romance might be apporached in this way. The fate of Oroonoko and Imoinda themselves seems to lie at the center of the Romance/Fantasy element of the work, while the realism of its pre-Novel, travel-journal identity is carried by the commentary of the narrator, who is constructed as keeper of the real, supplier of details of the outside world, however exotic. She can be seen, as Martine Watson Brownley puts it, as mediator between the primitive and the European.

The doubleness that structures these contradictions can be seen, in a somewhat altered form, as structuring the work itself as a whole. We encounter essentially two Oroonoko stories: one of sexual usurpation and betrayal by his (grand)father, which puts him in the position of being trapped by the slave captain; and another, marked by his change of visual identity and name, is characterized by his betrayal and entrapment, not as a sexual rival, but as a social rebel. A page or two off the exact center of the text, Oroonoko is restored and reestablished as Caesar at a high point, with the adoration of all races at Surinam, so that he can be brought down *again,* but this time for having been incited to threaten authority more directly. These two stories can be read as a doubling of certain elements of the Oedipal drama, as I shall now try to show.

The Romance of Oroonoko and Imoinda and of Oroonoko as a Royal Slave can be read as a fantasy in which the young aspirant creates exaggerated images of personal power, glory, and sexuality which brings on the opposition of monstrous fathers who totally block the young man's trajectory. The gross transgression of the first usurpation is well signalled by the fact that the father figure is rendered as a grandfather who cannot consummate his piracy. The "old lover" is reported to be "troubled, for having been forced by an irresistible Passion, to rob his Son of a Treasure." Oroonoko is repositioned in the second half as a slave. The sexual usurpation is echoed in Trefry's noble restraint. He does not rape Imoinda: another near miss. Later, fear of this usurpation forces Oroonoko to kill Imoinda because he can no longer defend her against rape. (Let us note in passing that the threatened rape is narrativized in its significance for Oroonoko, the *man,* not for the woman herself; the woman functions as a token of power-exchange among the men.) In the second story, the moves of the young man to establish some sort of social power among the men who desire to control him utterly bring from the white rulers a completely annihilating image of retribution. The white Colonials are interchangeable as father doubles. At one point, the narrator tells us that Oroonoko had a great respect for Colonel Martin and took his advice like that of a parent. We are often told how Oroonoko wanted to love the captain or some other authority figure whom he trusted briefly. The attribution of the father role to the Colonials links his social identity as black threat to his earlier role as sexual aspirant: In both of these roles he will be crushed utterly in the name of racial and patriarchal hegemony.

This power struggle among a victimized god, all his fathers, and Imoinda, the foster-sister whom he desires, also involves a narrator constructed in contradiction as well. As the struggle of Behn's life revealed to her over and over, the society wishes to define the woman, like the slave, as utterly powerless, a token of exchange and helpless dependent in the world of men and property. In addition, as Patricia Meyer Spacks argues in "Ev'ry Woman Is at Heart a Rake," discourse at this time was beginning to define the woman as a non-sexual being as well. Yet in contradiction to those roles, it is the woman who manages the enunciation of this powerful Romance/fantasy called *Oroonoko,* mediating between two cultures but, more important for the text itself, acting like the lady in charge of secondary revision, trying to keep control of the fantasy through realism and other interventions, trying in vain to keep the lid on the excess into which the text is constantly erupting. (In fact, the realism itself is somewhat distressed, emerging out of the story in the form of numerous digressions.) Careful study of the positioning of the narrator reveals the contraries of intervention or absence at key moments of narrative pressure; indeed she flees at certain times. Not imbricated in the literal sexuality of the early phase between Oroonoko and his grandfather, she enters the scene right after the hero reencounters Imoinda in the new world. Early in this story, the narrator is called in to control a potential eruption: "I was obliged, by some Persons who fear'd a Mutiny . . . to discourse with Caesar. . . ." A little later, there is trouble with the Indians, "So that we could scarse trust ourselves, without great Numbers, to go to any Indian Towns or Place where they abode, for fear they should fall upon us, *as they did immediately after my coming away.* . . ." (Ital. mine.) No sooner does she leave the area than the Indians "cut in pieces all they could take, getting into Houses, and hanging up the Mother, and all her Children about her; and cut a Footman, I left behind me, all in Joints, and nail'd him to trees." During the abortive slave rebellion, while "Apprehension made all the Females of us fly down the River," the violence of the Romance erupts into images like the following: "When they thought they were sufficiently revenged on him, they unty'd him, almost fainting with loss of Blood, from a thousand Wounds all over his Body; from which they had rent his Clothes, and led him bleeding and naked as he was, and loaded him all over with Irons, and then rubb'd his Wounds, to compleat their Cruelty, with Indian Pepper, which had like to have made him raving mad; and in this Condition made him so fast to the Ground, that he could not stir, if his Pains

and Wounds would have given him leave." But when she returns to the area, the narrator is still able to exert control: "Begging us to give him our Hands, he took them, and protested never to lift up his, to do us any harm. He had a great Respect for Colonel Martin, and always took his Counsel like that of a Parent. . . ." The evocation of Colonel Martin's advice in this passage links the narrator's exercises of control with the authority of the parent and hence with that of the Colonials, with the superego, and with secondary revision in its functions of repression and rationalization. It betrays the narrator's fear of Oroonoko and foreshadows her final failure of control. Her last flight from the excesses of Oroonoko's fate comes after his decline following the killing of Imoinda and his attempt at disembowelment. The narrator tells us: "the earthy Smell about him so strong, that I was pursuaded to leave the place for some time. . . ." Again, "I was no sooner gone" when the Deputy Governor sets in motion the final barbarity against Oroonoko. The narrator does not witness the return of the repressed horror of torture and dismemberment, the vision of torment and bondage that Northrop Frye tells us in the nightmare reversal of the Romances of god-like glory.

However, the narrator's role in *Oroonoko* is not defined simply in her function as failed censor allied with the Colonial hegemony. Rather, it is a complex interweaving of distances and identifications. By entering the text right after Oroonoko's reunion with Imoinda in the new world, she is metonymically identified with his beloved to some extent. They are both absent from his final agony, and as Brownley says of the narrator: "She does not finally trust him." As well she might not. After all, he has just murdered his beloved and failed to kill himself afterwards. Like Hamlet, he seems morally looser than we had thought. Without the woman as sign of his power, he seems to dissolve, as he did when he thought his grandfather had had Imoinda killed. Now that she is truly dead, he lies near her corpse for eight days, feebly trying somehow to die. So the woman is the source, not only of his ego identity, but also of his life organization and energy; her death is necessarily an expression of his defeat and dissolution. No wonder the narrator "does not finally trust him." As it is the narrator's despised father substitute (the Deputy Governor) who leads the army against Oroonoko, so it is Imoinda who inflicts on the bad father the wound that almost kills him. Thus the narrator and Imoinda can also be seen as standing in for each other in their hatred of the man who kills their beloved.

But perhaps most interesting in these signals of the narrator's multiple identifications are those with the hero himself. A number of times, throughout the work, she makes an identification between the inadequacy of Oroonoko's fame and the social inadequacy of woman-as-author. The following is typical: "But his Misfortune was, to fall in an obscure World, that afforded only a Female Pen to celebrate his fame. . . ." The "soft" Oroonoko and the narrator are further identified in their social limitations, she as woman, he as slave: "He liked the company of us Women much above the Men, for he could not drink and he is but an ill Companion in that country that cannot." And the hero, like the woman who writes, is completely isolated. What Lore Metzger says of the hero in her Introduction might almost be said of the narrator, and certainly of Behn at various times in her extraordinary life: "Separate from his kingdom and reduced to . . . impotence . . . he pits his personal code of honesty, honor, loyalty, and fortitude against the social order that sanctions self-interest, arrogant power, and sadistic brutality." In the end, the narrator cannot tolerate Oroonoko's despair because it parallels her own: "I was persuaded to leave the place for some time, (being myself but sickly, and very apt to fall into Fits of dangerous Illness upon any extraordinary Melancholy)."

As Judith Gardiner argues, Behn's identification with the male hero is consistent with her beliefs and with her other work. She analyzes Behn's belief in "each sex's capacity for the traditional traits of both." She goes on to explain the way in which "Behn's identification with the role of hero" helps to explain her attitudes toward the rogues, rebels, and kings who populate her works and her own Royalist romanticism.

So, like all women in patriarchy who wish to contribute to the cultural production of language-as-text, the position of the narrator (and of Behn herself) is elusive. Her identifications are multiple, androgynous, and shifting. The woman-as-failed-controller-of-the-repressed-fantastic looks at the events of **Oroonoko.** Seeing there the fantasy of the androgynous self-as-destroyed-hero, she gazes until she can't look any more and then, abandoning all attempts to maintain the repression, fearing the price that she-as-Imoinda and all women must pay for inciting desire, she flees the scene of textual eruption, releasing the tenuous hold of Realism on Romance, of Law on Desire. In this way, the Colonial tyranny, the tyranny of the father against the emerging sexuality of youth, and the repression of the woman by patriarchal tyranny are condensed in the various events and figures, and especially in the narrator, of **Oroonoko.**

The last paragraph reads: "Thus died this great Man, worthy of a better Fate, and a more sublime Wit than mine to write his Praise: Yet, I hope the Reputation of my pen is considerable enough to make his glorious Name to survive all Ages, with that of the brave, the beautiful, and the constant Imoinda." In the end, in the tradition of Lyric and Romance (and not at all like that of the Novel), the fate of the hero is eternally bound to the powers of the individual poet, and in this case, the name of the woman is the last word.

Michael McKeon (essay date 1987)

SOURCE: "Histories of the Individual," in *The Origins of the English Novel, 1600-1740*, The Johns Hopkins University Press, 1987, pp. 90-128.

[*In the following excerpt, McKeon explores the issue of authenticity in* Oroonoko, *arguing that Behn idolizes Surinam.*]

No mode of discourse is more likely to avail itself of the "strange, therefore true" paradox than the travel narrative, one of whose cardinal conventions is to expect the unexpected.[47] And many of the travel narratives of this period have recourse to this most daring, and most dangerous, claim to historicity. Vairasse d'Allais has his publisher remark that

> the Histories of *Peru, Mexico, China,* &c. were at first taken for Romances by many, but time has shewed since that they are verities not to be doubted of.

> It is an idle humour in any of us to despise or reject strange Discoveries . . . If any thing is here related of this Country or People seemingly beyond all possibility, we must know, that as this People have the advantage of living in the earthly Paradise, they have knowledges of Nature and natural Effects, which look like Miracles.

As this argument implies, the relativizing effects of travel need not lead us to conclude that nature itself is relative to climate and custom. On the contrary (as another writer suggests), "Nature performs its operations in all parts of the World, according to its primitive Fundamental Laws . . . The Monsters of *Africa* or the *Indies,* are no more surprising to the Inhabitants of these parts, than the Beasts that are commonly seen and bred among us are to the Europeans." Rather, it is our own capacity for knowledge that is relative to our concrete physical circumstances and opportunities. "We have taken for Fables what the Poets or the Ancients have told us of the first Inhabitants of the World," remarks a third, yet the natives of America answer well to those descriptions. "They who never saw more than their own Village, never imagin that Steeples are of any other fashion than their own . . . For of those things which we do not see, we know nothing but by the Report of others. Now Men have not reported to us all things for want of having been upon the Places." But then to dismiss as "romance" what has not yet been seen or reported, or if reported, not yet read, is (says a fourth) beyond foolishness.[48]

These self-defensive efforts by authors of voyages both "real" and "imaginary" find persuasive parallels in the more exotic of Aphra Behn's imaginary "true histories." The well-known claim to historicity that opens

Oroonoko; or, The Royal Slave. A True History (1688) is echoed, more succinctly, at the beginning of ***The Fair Jilt*** . . . (1696): "I do not pretend here to entertain you with a feign'd story, or any thing piec'd together with *Romantick* Accidents; but every Circumstance, to a Tittle, is Truth. To a great part of the Main, I my self was an Eye witness; and what I did not see, I was confirm'd of by Actors in the Intrigue, holy Men, of the Order of St. *Francis*."[49] Frequent narrative intrusions of this sort occur throughout Behn's third-person Surinam histories, but no tension exists in her dual role as narrator and character, because both roles are dedicated to the single end of physically witnessing, and thereby authenticating, a central character whose personal history is distinct from her own. This authenticating end is also served by Behn's rendition of the "strange, therefore true" formula with reference to ***Oroonoko:*** "The *Royal Slave* I had the Honour to know in my Travels to the other World . . . If there be any thing that seems Romantick, I beseech your Lordship [Lord Maitland] to consider, these Countries do, in all things, so far differ from ours, that they produce inconceivable Wonders; at least, they appear so to us, New and Strange."[50]

The potential risks involved in this method of claiming historicity are fully actualized in Behn's travel narratives, whose naive empiricism betrays no parodic intent. If, in Vairasse d'Allais's "earthly paradise," natural effects are said at least to "look like miracles," Behn audaciously and unapologetically idealizes her Surinam as a prelapsarian Eden; the royal slave on whose historicity she elsewhere insists is made to fantasize about his beloved in the familiar figures and heightened language of romance; and the lovers, after a separation in the Old World, are reunited in the New with all the miraculousness of a romance discovery (see 2-3, 14, 43-44, 48-49). In the face of such incongruity, we might be tempted to suppose for writers like Behn an especially opportunistic "critical theory": only call your travel narrative a true history, and its historical truth will thereby be empowered to survive the most patent romance fictionalizing. The comparison with a highly self-conscious antiromance like *Incognita* is instructive, for Behn shares with Congreve the energizing antiromance impulse and the will to pursue questions of truth into the plot itself; yet the pursuit stops short of extreme skepticism even though the logic of that movement into self-parody feels at times quite implacable.

Behn values the Surinam Indians for their natural simplicity, and she derives from their example the precept "that simple Nature . . . better instructs the World, than all the Inventions of Man." (3). But she also knows that natural simplicity is an invitation to imposture, as one of her kinsmen discovers when the natives seek to deify him for the powers of his magnifying glass: "It were not difficult to establish any unknown or extrav-

agant Religion among them, and to impose any Notions or Fictions upon 'em" (56). In passages like these, Behn is torn between her admiration for the natural receptiveness of credulity and the artful protections of skepticism, and in Oroonoko she creates a hero who embodies these antithetical qualities in recognizably Restoration guise. Schooled in an aristocratic doctrine that enjoins implicit faith in the word of others, Oroonoko falls easy victim to the routine duplicity of the English captain by whom he is enslaved: "And ***Oroonoko,*** whose Honour was such as he never had violated a Word in his life himself, much less a solemn Asseveration, believ'd in an instant what this Man said" (34-35). But he can also play the freethinker and make a "Jest" of the gullible "Faith" that Christians have in "our Notions of the Trinity" (46). When Oroonoko learns definitively that "there was no Faith in the White Men, or the Gods they ador'd," he is even obliged to embrace the decadence of literacy and documentary objectivity, resolving "never to credit one Word they spoke" and requiring that all pledges henceforth "should be ratify'd by their Hands in Writing" (66). But something is lost in this rueful conversion to Western skepticism, and Oroonoko's history soon after comes to its violent close in an apotheosis of desperate revenge and self-sacrifice.

The unstable compound that Oroonoko's character exists to mediate is most suggestively expressed by an earlier episode, in which his "great Curiosity" is so piqued by the incredible phenomenon of the South American "Numb-eel" that "for Experiment-sake" he grasps one of them and almost drowns himself (53). Here the blend of skepticism and credulity is conveyed by an engaging, if momentary, glimpse of Oroonoko as gentleman virtuoso of the Royal Society, and it is this same cultural type that his creator enacts in her own epistemological instability. Naive empiricism and the claim to historicity partake both of the skeptical denunciation of "all the inventions of man" and of the credulous faith that human inventions may thus be replaced by immediate perception and experience. As the ready idolatry of the Indians seems to show, however, neither does the absence of skepticism guarantee the absence of invention, which will always intervene in whatever shapes are conditioned by the particular cultural tribe to which we belong. For Behn this is the point at which skepticism becomes self-defeating, for it denies her the capacity to tell the truth; and she never is moved, like Congreve, to disclose the manipulative power of the author "to impose any notions or fictions upon" the reader.[51] Because the parallel between credulous Indians and credulous readers never breaks the surface of narrative self-consciousness, Behn may perhaps be assured that our simple and receptive faith is rewarded not by imposture but by the truth of what really happened. The hope is that antiromance, the negation of the negation, will thus fulfill itself as the true history of travel narrative. The risk is that for skeptical readers it will simply seem the "new romance."

Notes

[47] E.g., see Spenser's defense of his "voyage" to "Faerie lond" in *The Faerie Queene* (1590), II, proem. On the paradox see above, chap. I, nn. 73, 100, and chap. 2, nn. 11, 41.

[48] Vairasse d'Allais, *History* (1675), sig. A4[r]; idem, *History* (1679), sig. A3[r-v]; Dellon, *Voyage to the East-Indies,* translator's "Preface to the Reader," sig. A6[v]; Heliogenes de L'Epy, *A Voyage into Tartary* . . . (1689), "The Preface," sig. A7[r]-A8[v], A9[v]; Father Louis Hennepin, *A New Discovery of a Vast Country in America* . . . (1698), 4.

[49] Aphra Behn, *The Fair Jilt; or, The History of Prince Tarquin, and Miranda,* in *The Histories and Novels Of the Late Ingenious Mrs Behn* . . . (1696), 4. Compare Behn's dedication to Henry Pain: "This little History . . . is Truth; Truth, which you so much admire . . . This is Reality, and Matter of Fact, and acted in this our latter Age . . . [Part of it] I had from the Mouth of this unhappy Great Man [Tarquin], and was an Eye-Witness to the rest" (sig. A2[v], A3[r]). For other claims to historicity see 19, 24, 35, 161. Cf. Behn, *Oroonoko,* ed. Lore Metzger (New York, Norton, 1973), 1; subsequent citations will be to this edition and will appear in the text. For a summary of the scholarship arguing the fictionality of Behn's experiences in Surinam as recounted in these writings, see George Guffey, "Aphra Behn's *Oroonoko:* Occasion and Accomplishment," in *Two English Novelists: Aphra Behn and Anthony Trollope,* William Andrews Clark Memorial Library (Berkeley and Los Angeles: University of California Press, 1975), 5-8.

[50] *Histories and Novels Of . . . Mrs Behn,* "Epistle Dedicatory," sig. A5[v]-A6[v].

[51] Contrast Congreve's teasing invitation that we discover a "force, or a whim of the author's"; see above, chap. 1, n. 124.

Katharine M. Rogers (essay date 1988)

SOURCE: "Fact and Fiction in Aphra Behn's *Oroonoko,*" in *Studies in the Novel,* Vol. 20, No. 1, Spring, 1988, pp. 1-15.

[*In the essay below, Rogers argues that* Oroonoko *is a creative treatment of facts derived from Behn's personal experiences.*]

In 1913 Ernest Bernbaum gleefully exposed borrowings and inaccuracies in Aphra Behn's **Oroonoko** so as to show that Behn could not have been an eyewitness to the events, as her first-person narrator claimed.[1] In accordance with the general tendency of male-dominated criticism at the time to sneer at pioneering women writers, he presented this as evidence of personal untruthfulness in the author. In reaction, Behn's two recent feminist biographers, Maureen Duffy (1977) and Angeline Goreau (1980), have accepted the tale as reliable autobiography. Both interpretations are too extreme, and both distract from Behn's actual artistic achievement: imaginative creation building on a foundation of fact, which probably included personal experience. This was, of course, no more dishonest in her than was Daniel Defoe's development of the real adventures of Alexander Selkirk into the fictionalized ones of Robinson Crusoe. The factual elements in Behn's romantic story are her use of a narrator much like herself and a wealth of local color detail from both Surinam and Africa.

Behn's first-person narrator claims that she went to Surinam[2] as the daughter of the Lieutenant-General-elect of the colony, along with her mother, sister, and brother. Her father died on the voyage, so the family arrived in Surinam with high social status but no political position, and remained there (presumably) until the next boat back to England. In the colony she met a remarkable slave, Oroonoko, a prince who had been kidnapped by a slaving captain. Oroonoko told her his adventures in his own country; she witnessed his reunion with his beloved Imoinda, his growing realization that the whites had no intention of freeing and returning them to their native land, his consequent organization of a slave rebellion, and his gruesome execution.

There is no documentary evidence that someone named Amis or Johnson (Aphra's possible maiden names) was sent as Lieutenant-General to Surinam, nor that the Governor, Lord Willoughby of Parham, had any intention of replacing the incumbent, William Byam. But none of her contemporaries—and there were many who seized every possible pretext for attacking her character—suggested that she had not been there. Harrison Platt has argued convincingly that a letter from Byam telling of the sudden departure of Astraea and Celadon from Surinam refers to Aphra and a male friend named William Scot: the two were known to have used these code names when they were engaged in secret service in the Low Countries in 1666,[3] and Astraea of course became Aphra's literary name. Platt cites further correspondence which refers to ladies living at St. John's Hill, precisely the plantation where the narrator of **Oroonoko** claims to have stayed, in January 1664. Perhaps Aphra's father had been coming to take a minor office (which she raised in accordance with the heightening usual in romance); perhaps she met Scot in Surinam and through him became involved in local politics. If these letters indeed refer to Aphra, she would have been in Surinam in January 1664 and left in March 1664. Oroonoko could have been brought on the Guinea slave ship which was known to have arrived at the Surinam River in January 1664.[4] In the story, his demands for freedom are put off until the Lord Governor should come; this pretext could have been based on fact, since Lord Willoughby was imminently expected from Barbados over a period of many months, but did not arrive until November 18, 1664;[5] that is, after the presumed departure of Aphra, which followed the execution of Oroonoko. (Her story also mentions Willoughby's subsequent death at sea.)[6]

Almost certainly, Behn did consult George Warren's *Impartial Description of Surinam* for *Oroonoko,* as Bernbaum pointed out; she used many of his details about the native animals and the Indians and elaborated his (heightened?) account of the powers of a "numb-eel" (electric eel) into an appropriate adventure for her hero.[7] The obvious explanation, however, is that, wanting a vivid and authentic background for her story, she consulted Warren to refresh twenty-five-year-old memories. Some of her details, such as some Indian words, are not found in Warren; nor are the larger Indians of a different tribe who come over the mountains carrying gold dust and knotted strings which record their journey, evidently Incan *quipus* (pp. 188-89). And her claim that she brought feather costumes home which were used in John Dryden and Robert Howard's *The Indian Queen* (p. 130) is substantiated by a picture of Anne Bracegirdle in the title role of that play.[8]

Even more convincing evidence of her having been on the spot is her detailed and partisan account of local politics: had she not actually been there, it is unlikely that she would have known so much or felt so passionately. William Byam, the villain of *Oroonoko,* was in fact the Deputy-Governor (and Lieutenant-General) of Surinam. He may have been an effective leader, but his enemies accused him of tyrannical high-handedness, cruelty, and disregard for law. He was also accused of cowardice in surrendering the colony to the Dutch in 1667 (though subsequently acquitted by a court martial). His defense argument that the colony was disunited and poorly armed substantiates Behn's caustic description of the militia.[9] Major James Banister was also a real man, an associate of Byam's who succeeded him as deputy governor and therefore might plausibly have been a member of the Governor's Council in Oroonoko's time.[10] John Treffry (Trefry in *Oroonoko*) was in fact the overseer of St. John's Hill. His three-day journey up the river to take Oroonoko to this plantation is consistent with the layout of the colony, since plantations lined the banks for many miles beyond the port where the slave ship would have docked.[11] Finally, "the great Oliverian" Harry Marten (p. 180, Martin in *Oroonoko*) was, historically, a zealous republican; and he had one brother, George. Captain George Marten (called Colonel in the story) was

naturally off stage during most of the action, since his plantation was located, as Behn says, about three days journey down river from the main scene.[12] George's character may be further corroborated by the fact that Behn did, as she claimed in *Oroonoko* (p. 198), represent him as George Marteen, a dashing young hero, in her comedy *The Widow Ranter.* Behn's more general references to the troubles of the colony after the main action of her story concludes with Oroonoko's death are also factually based: Surinam was taken by the Dutch, retaken by the English, and finally ceded to the Dutch, with consequent loss to the English planters; there was a disastrous epidemic in 1666 (in which George Marten died), and the previously friendly Indians took to raiding plantations and massacring their inhabitants.[13]

Even those who accept the (partial) authenticity of the Surinam scenes are likely to dismiss the African background and the character of the hero as far-fetched romance. Certainly the adventures at the court of Coramantien suspiciously resemble those of Restoration heroic drama. The love of Oroonoko and Imoinda is presented with an exaggerated sentimentality and a precious language totally remote from African culture. However, other details—such as the king's seraglio, Oroonoko's knowledge of European culture, his special treatment in Surinam, and his extreme fortitude under torture—are not so fantastic as they seem.

In its major outlines, Behn's representation of West African culture is accurate. (She could have got her information both from published accounts and from talking with slaves and owners in Surinam or traders and travelers in England.)[14] The kingdoms of West Africa waged war constantly, and the victors regularly sold their prisoners of war to European slavers. The trade was carried on by and for the benefit of the ruling class, though it was the king and his agents (not the general, as Behn says), who had "all the profit" (p. 134). Strongly marked class stratification, while not universal, was common. European observers particularly noticed the extreme deference paid to the king. An Englishman at the court of Benin in 1553 wished that Christians showed their Savior Christ "the great reverence" the subjects of the King of Benin showed him.[15] Since kings were regarded as divine, their subjects accepted an obligation to implicit obedience, "and the most oppressive mandates are submitted to without a murmur";[16] nevertheless, in practice, they might lie to their king or evade his commands, as happens in *Oroonoko.* In Whydah, a West African coastal kingdom, a person meeting a superior would drop to his or her knees and kiss the earth three times, remaining on the ground "till the other departs, or says it is enough." This deference was also shown by younger to older brothers, children to fathers, and wives to husbands. Such prostrations, however distasteful they seem to us, were seen by seventeenth century observers, presumably including Behn, as evidence of politeness; William Bosman, a captain of the time, contrasted these people with other groups who lived "together like Brutes, without any Distinction."[17]

Subjection of women was almost universal in black Africa. Wives might not eat with their husbands and never spoke to them "but on their Knees."[18] Polygamy was general in the upper classes, and kings might have hundreds (by some accounts, thousands) of wives and concubines. Adultery was punished by execution or sale into slavery overseas. On the other hand, when the king got tired of a favorite wife and sent her away, he would provide her with an allotment of land for her maintenance.[19] Behn makes a point of praising the Africans for not casting off women when they grew tired of them (p. 139).

Like the old king in **Oroonoko,** the King of Whydah spent most of his life in his seraglio. Behn's use of this word does not reveal confusion between black Africans and Moors; it was commonly, and accurately, used by African travelers to describe a king's household, in which a large number of women would be kept secluded. Palaces were quite elaborate. That of the King of Ardra, though built of clay, was spacious and enclosed by walls five feet thick. It consisted "of large Courts, surrounded with Porticos, over which lie the Apartments . . . The Gardens were spacious, laid out into long, strait Alleys," with trees for shade and fruit and beds of herbs and flowers. It had some European furnishings, including large Turkey carpets.[20] The Dahomean king's palace also covered many acres, consisted of several courtyards, was surrounded by substantial walls and well guarded by women and eunuchs. Men rarely entered the inner recesses, and the female apartments were "guarded from intrusion, with more than eastern jealousy."[21] A king had an unquestioned right to take any woman whom he wanted, regardless of her or her family's wishes.[22] Wives were subjected to "strict confinement," and the king's women were forbidden "to hold discourse with any man." However, the wives did occasionally dance in public, well guarded,[23] as they do in **Oroonoko.** Any man who barely touched one of them, even by accident, was liable to death or enslavement. Nevertheless, they did sometimes manage to have affairs, although one suspects rhetorical heightening in the claim that: "Notwithstanding the rigorous Punishments, the Women of the Seraglio, . . . chuse to run all Hazards, rather than want a Gallant. Whidah would furnish abundant Memoirs for a Negro Atalantis." An authentic experience of Captain William Snelgrave in 1730 bears a remarkable resemblance to what happened to Onahal and Imoinda. The King of Dahomey sent him two women, one past fifty and the other about twenty, and wanted him to buy them as a pair "and not let them be redeemed by anyone." The older woman had "highly offended the King, as he suspected, by assisting his Majesty's Women in their Intrigues."[24]

As Behn says, girls were given systematic sex education, including "love-language" and various positions for intercourse, by mature women; and they were expected to remain virgin until marriage. Her statement that "the Way to be great" was to court "She-favourites . . . the Persons that do all Affairs and Business at Court" (p. 147) also proves to be surprisingly accurate; for, in spite of the general subjection of women, certain of the king's wives constantly attended his conferences with his ministers and mediated between them.[25] Imoinda's martial exploits (p. 195) derive from the women warriors of Dahomey, who made a strong impression on European visitors. These women, called wives of the king (though, unlike Imoinda, they were not sexual partners), were given regular military training; they normally acted as bodyguards and occasionally followed him to war. Among them were young girls who were accomplished archers.[26]

Other accurate details of African life which appear in **Oroonoko** include the name of Oroonoko's best friend, Aboan (who was an actual coastal king) and his army's use of tents (so called by an eighteenth century observer, though they were actually simple huts).[27] It is appropriate that Oroonoko should sustain himself with a pipe during his final torture, since blacks were very fond of tobacco: in Africa they were "always smoking Tobacco" in nicely made pipes. They believed, as Imoinda does, "that when they die they return to their own Country and Friends again."[28]

The physical descriptions of Oroonoko and Imoinda, as black versions of standard romance heroes, obviously owe much to convention. However, the details are not entirely fantastic. Travelers constantly remarked that one tribe or another was better looking than others, meaning closer to the European standard. Like Oroonoko, the Issinese of the Gold Coast combed their hair out so that they could wear it in long ringlets on their shoulders. As Imoinda was "carved in fine Flowers and Birds all over her Body," noblemen of one Guinea kingdom "pounce and raise their Skins in divers Figures, like flowered Damask."[29]

Oroonoko is supposed to come from the kingdom of Coramantien; that is, he is a Cormantine (also known as Coromantee and Koromantin). This is one of Behn's few specific inaccuracies, but one which she shared with British colonials in general. Actually, Coramantien was not an African kingdom but a town on the Gold Coast, where the English had built their major trading station. "Cormantines" could be members of any tribe who had been shipped out from this port. For the planters in America, the immediate source of slaves was more evident than their tribal origins. Nevertheless, while the term "Cormantine" is not anthropologically accurate, it was in standard use in the colonies, and it denoted the group to which Oroonoko would appropriately belong. Cormantines were supposed to be the finest of all blacks—good-looking, daring, stoical, loyal, but implacably resentful of injustice.[30]

Oroonoko's familiarity with European manners and languages and his general sophistication are not improbable in view of the fact that coastal blacks had been dealing with Europeans for two centuries: the Portuguese arrived on the West African coast in the mid fifteenth century, the other Western European nations soon after. Moreover, in Oroonoko's time they dealt with the black ruling class on equal terms: traders would exchange hospitality, banter, and compliments with representatives of the local king; and then they would arrive at a mutually acceptable bargain. European visitors treated the rulers with respect, and kings' sons were educated in Europe. An agent of the French West India Company, in 1669, described the Prince of Ardra as a big, handsome man with "an Air of Grandeur and Dignity, tempered with a Sweetness, that at once gained him Love and Respect." Entertaining the Frenchman at dinner, the Prince proved a gracious host and kept "up the Conversation with Spirit." He was quite well "acquainted with the Situation and Affairs of Europe" and "asked several Questions . . . which discovered his Penetration, and the Delicacy of his Genius." After dinner, they washed from crystal bowls and drank "Palm-Wine, Sack, Port, and French Wines."[31] Already in the sixteenth century, the King of Benin spoke good Portuguese; and by Oroonoko's time many blacks spoke European languages. There were enough Europeans in the area that men of wit and learning, like Oroonoko's French tutor, might well be among them.

It was not evident in the seventeenth century that enslaving black people is an extreme expression of racism. Blacks themselves saw slavery as a matter of class rather than race, and so did Europeans. For example, the King of Ardra sent an ambassador to Louis XIV of France in 1670. This man went with a suitable entourage and was received with magnificence by King Louis, made much of by the French, and in general treated like any European ambassador. Under the hatches of the ship which carried him in style to France was a consignment of his fellow blacks, destined for slavery in the West Indies.[32] Just as there was a sharp distinction between blacks who were to be treated as business associates and blacks who were to be treated as slaves, there was a sharp distinction between "legitimate" traders, who dealt only in slaves bought from their legal owners, and lawless ones, like the captain who kidnapped Oroonoko. Legitimate traders, regular agents of the African Companies, often complained of those who antagonized the blacks by treating them rudely or by kidnapping free people.[33]

Once kidnapped, of course, it was difficult for a person to establish his rights. But such people might get special treatment, as Oroonoko does. In 1476, a Spanish slaving captain invited on board a black king who regularly sold his prisoners of war to the Portuguese. "After the feast was ended, the patron invited him to visit the interior of the ship," then promptly seized him, together with "140 nobles of splendid physique." The king, a royalist like Oroonoko (p. 163), asked the Spaniards "whether they obeyed any king, and, when he was told they obeyed a most noble one, he expressed his confidence that he would free him from such an iniquitous captivity." On arrival in Spain, they "wished to force him to walk in the crowd amongst the other slaves. But he resisted, and said that they should take him either dragging by a rope or on horseback, because his misfortune must be either terrible or dignified." The local commander was sufficiently impressed to have a horse brought; the king mounted and "began to march with a majestic air." Though King Ferdinand of Spain, hearing of this, ordered the black king to be released, some months passed before he was repatriated, and even so his relatives were sold as slaves. The friar who wrote this account (which was printed in 1490) sums up: "That savage maintained a certain regal authority during his captivity, and he displayed dignity in his countenance, gravity in speech, prudence in conduct, and courage in adversity."[34] Behn might actually have seen such a man in England in 1678, when a tall African king, kidnapped by an English interloper, sold as a slave in Jamaica, and redeemed by a London merchant, was on display there.[35]

Even hardened dealers were capable of recognizing, even in a way respecting, extraordinary quality in a slave. Looking over slaves in a holding pen in Africa, John Atkins noticed a particularly big, stern-looking man who "seemed to disdain his Fellow-Slaves for their Readiness to be examined, and as it were scorned looking at us, refusing to rise or stretch out his Limbs as the Master commanded." As a result, the master whipped him ferociously, "all which the Negro bore with Magnanimity, shrinking very little, and shedding a Tear or two, which he endeavoured to hide as tho' ashamed of." This man, called Captain Tomba, had led his people against the slavers and been captured by stratagem. Once on the slave ship, Tomba plotted with four of his countrymen and a woman slave to seize the deck and escape to the shore. They almost succeeded, killing most of the few men on deck, but were caught in the nick of time. The captain tortured three of the men and the woman to death, but contented himself with savagely whipping Tomba and the other leading slave.[36] Evidently the market value of a strong slave outweighed his potential dangerousness; this explains why Byam abstained from killing Oroonoko upon capturing him after his rebellion failed.

The grisly details of Oroonoko's execution and his preternatural stoicism under torture are authenticated by actual events. Whipping a slave raw and then rubbing his wounds with pepper was a regular punishment. In 1722, a condemned black in Martinique asked for tobacco and then sustained burning to death without saying a word; he kept on smoking even after his legs burst in the fire. A Cormantine slave in Jamaica, being slowly burned to death for rebellion, "uttered not a groan, and saw his legs reduced to ashes with the utmost firmness and composure"; at this point, he managed to free one of his arms, "snatched a brand from the fire that was consuming him, and flung it in the face of the executioner."[37] Slave rebellions were common in Surinam, according to Warren. Rebels were likely to commit suicide rather than be taken, and if they yielded alive on a fraudulent promise of pardon, as Oroonoko did (pp. 196-97), they would suffer "the most exquisite tortures can be inflicted upon them . . . without shrinking." Often the rebellions failed for the same reason Oroonoko's did, from disunion among the slaves because they came from competing nations.[38]

Oroonoko acts as a traditional African king when he sells his prisoners of war as slaves. That the involvement of Europeans in the slave trade greatly increased its destructiveness is obvious now, but could not have been to Africans in his time. It was assumed that the conqueror had proven himself a better man than the conquered and therefore had the right to dispose of their lives as he chose—to sacrifice them to his ancestors, to use their labor in his own country, or to sell them overseas. This is a key argument in Oroonoko's appeal to the slaves to revolt: had the white colonists proven themselves better men by conquering the blacks in battle, it would not be disgraceful to submit to them (p. 191). The same rationale was used by whites to make some sense of their attitude. Jean Barbot, a seventeenth century agent of the French African Company, called on Old Testament precedent: among the Israelites, victors had the right to kill their captives, but might decide it was better "to save their lives and make use of their service"; the conqueror rightly owned the children of slaves because "they could never have been born, had he not preserved the father."[39] Even the libertarian John Locke used a similar argument to rationalize slavery (and his own investment in the Royal African Company): slaves, "being Captives taken in a just War, are by the Right of Nature subjected to the Absolute Dominion and Arbitrary Power of their Masters." Somehow the same right extends to those who buy such legitimate captives. Having, by this theory, forfeited their lives, these people could not complain of injustice if they were enslaved rather than killed.[40]

But rationalizing slavery as moral did not necessarily entail hatred or contempt for black people. Thomas Phillips, a seventeenth century slave-ship captain, rejected with horror the proposal that he mutilate some of his slave cargo to terrify the rest, on the grounds that they were human beings like himself:

excepting their want of christianity and true religion (their misfortune and not their fault) [they] are as

much the work of God's hands, and no doubt as dear to him as ourselves; nor can I imagine why they should be despis'd for their colour . . . I can't think there is any intrinsick value in one colour more than another, nor that white is better than black, only we think so because we are so . . . as [do] . . . the blacks, who . . . say, the devil is white.[41]

It seems clear, then, that Behn made a serious effort to fortify her romance with realistic detail. She followed the outlines of what was known in her time and also did research to substantiate her portrayal of Oroonoko's situation in Africa and in Surinam. Of course, she went on to enhance the facts, in accordance with contemporary esthetic ideals. Like Dryden dealing with Mexican history in *The Indian Emperor,* she took "the liberty of a Poet, to adde, alter, or diminish, as I thought might best conduce to the beautifying of my work."[42] Oroonoko's natural nobility and incredible prowess in war align him with the heroes of the heroic plays, and her remarkable statement that the best lovers are great soldiers (p. 137) echoes a convention of that drama of "love and valor."[43] In the same way that she elevates herself as narrator to daughter of the Lieutenant-General of the colony, she makes Oroonoko entirely superior to physical pain and shows Imoinda's beauty overpowering every male, black or white, in her vicinity. Nevertheless, Behn showed far more genuine interest in foreign cultures and concern for probability than did the heroic dramatists. While they might take advantage of their exotic settings to make cross-cultural comparisons, these have none of the specificity of Behn's naked, guilt-free Indians or polygamous, status-conscious Africans. There are no recognizable features of Aztec culture in *The Indian Emperor.*

Though heroic play conventions weaken the realism of *Oroonoko,* they contribute to its symbolic power. Oroonoko is not just a petty African chief, but a natural king like Dryden's Almanzor, an embodiment of "natural"—actually ideal—honesty and nobility, outside of and immeasurably superior to the corrupt society of his story. Oroonoko is not a fetishist as superstitious as his Christian oppressors, but a spokesman for natural reason against sectarian dogma and hypocrisy. Like Dryden's Montezuma, he is given the opportunity to shine in contrast to self-righteous European Christians. In the very act of torturing Montezuma to reveal where his gold is, a priest cants: "Marke how this Impious Heathen Justifies/ His owne false Gods, and our true God denyes." Montezuma retorts that he will not betray "The light of Nature."[44] In the same way, Oroonoko rejects the doctrine of the Trinity as irrational (p. 175) and highlights the nauseating hypocrisy of Christians who, utterly lacking in honesty themselves, distrust a "heathen" because he cannot swear by the "true God" (pp. 163-64). In the best seventeenth-century Epicurean tradition, Oroonoko demonstrates that personal honor and concern for other people are more reliable supports for moral behavior than are religious professions and the hypothetical rewards of some future state. He also shares the Restoration true wit's values in his confidence that "A Man of Wit could not be a Knave or Villain" (p. 168).

An exposure of Christian hypocrisy is directly used to attack slavery in a work which appeared a few years before *Oroonoko,* Thomas Tryon's *Friendly Advice to the Gentlemen-Planters of the East and West Indies* (1684). Tryon also presents a slave who is highly moral but despises doctrinal argument and religious intolerance and rejects as illogical the concepts of the Resurrection and the Holy Trinity when his master tries to explain them. As Oroonoko charges that no one professed so much as the Christians and performed so little (p. 196), Tryon's slave says the world despises Christians since their lives belie their professed faith.[45]

Very few people in the seventeenth century would have agreed with Tryon's outright condemnation of slavery; Behn was not an abolitionist any more than her hero was. On the other hand, it is surely a distortion to deny her any serious concern with the subject, as when George Guffey sees Oroonoko, the maltreated prince, as a stand-in for James II, who was in imminent danger of deposition at the time Behn, an ardent royalist, was writing.[46] The abundant detail she provides about Africa, Surinam, and slavery emphasizes Oroonoko's identity as a black man. Her representation of this black man as clearly superior to every white person around him inescapably tells us that it is not right to enslave people because they are black. Once in chains, Oroonoko's race denies him the freedom to which his class and personal worth entitle him. Behn's exposure of Christian hypocrisy demolishes the rationalization that slavery brought to blacks the blessings of European culture. And Oroonoko's eloquent speech to his fellow slaves directly asserts that it is beneath human dignity to submit to slavery at all (p. 190). Certainly the following century thought Behn was serious about slavery: *Oroonoko* was among the English novels most widely read in eighteenth century France, because the French saw it as an abolitionist tract.[47] And even though Thomas Southerne's play *Oroonoko* softened and adulterated Behn's message, it aroused powerful anti-slavery feeling in eighteenth century audiences.

Behn used this romantic tale to prove a serious point—to attack the conventional "respectable" morality that professes Christianity at the same time that, on the one hand, it abandons a mistress "to Want, Shame, and Misery" (p. 139) and, on the other, it shamelessly cheats people who are not Christians. The significant theme of *Oroonoko* gives it an intellectual weight and a power to move which sets it above typical sixteenth and seventeenth century fiction. Behn's own other tales, for example, play endless variations on model courtships and contrived love difficulties.

A significant and deeply felt subject perhaps inspired Behn to unusual efforts toward making her story believable. Her use of realistic detail was not new, for predecessors such as Thomas Nashe and Thomas Deloney had used such details, typically seamy ones, in their realistic fiction. But while their aim was to reproduce common life vividly, hers was to ground extraordinary adventures in actuality. Here she anticipates the Defoe of *Robinson Crusoe,* as she does also in her use of a clearly defined narrator.[48] First person narration is used in earlier fiction, such as Nashe's *Unfortunate Traveler* and Joseph Kepple's *The Maiden-head Lost by Moon-light,* but the narrator is sketchily characterized (if at all) and soon disappears from the main plot. In contrast, Behn tells most of her stories through a narrator who is female, Tory, the same person who wrote her plays (mentioned in "The Dumb Virgin," p. 429, as well as *Oroonoko,* p. 198), and a forthright critic of self-righteous snooping (as in "The Adventure of the Black Lady," pp. 8-10).

Only in *Oroonoko,* however, does the narrator have a definite social position in the world of the story. She is placed as an intelligent upper class woman who is fascinated by the exotic cultures she encounters, sensitive enough to appreciate Oroonoko, able to relate to him and win his trust because of her isolation from the status and power structure of colonial society, and for the same reason powerless to influence events and thus avert the catastrophe.[49] Lacking the definition of Defoe's narrators, she can still comment consistently on the action and provide an intellectual context for it. Despite obvious weaknesses in structure and misjudgments of tone, *Oroonoko* brings together romance, authenticity, and moral vision in a way that presages the great fictional achievements of the eighteenth century.

Notes

[1] Ernest Bernbaum, "Mrs. Behn's *Oroonoko,*" in *Anniversary Papers by Colleagues and Pupils of George Lyman Kittredge* (Boston: Ginn and Co., 1913).

[2] Some say the colony involved is modern Guyana. However, since the narrator explicitly states that Oroonoko's slave ship "arriv'd at the Mouth of the River of Surinam" (p. 166), a look at the map indicates modern Surinam. It makes little difference in any case, since the area was not clearly defined in the seventeenth century.

[3] Harrison Gray Platt, "Astraea and Celadon: An Untouched Portrait of Aphra Behn," *PMLA* 49 (1934): 547-48.

[4] *Publications of the Hakluyt Society, Ser. 2, Vol. 56: Colonising Expeditions to the West Indies and Guiana* (London: Hakluyt Society, 1925), 190.

5 James A. Williamson, *English Colonies in Guiana and on the Amazon 1604-1668* (Oxford: Clarendon Press, 1923), p. 175.

6 Aphra Behn, *The Works,* ed. Montague Summers (New York: Benjamin Blom, 1967), 5:189. All subsequent references to *Oroonoko* and other novellas by Behn are to this edition and volume.

7 George Warren, *An Impartial Description of Surinam* (London: Nathaniel Brooke, 1667), p. 2; Behn, pp. 182-83.

8 For the Indian words, see B. Dhuicq, "Further Evidence on Aphra Behn's Stay in Surinam," *Notes and Queries* 26 (1979): 524-26. In "New Evidence of the Realism of Mrs. Behn's *Oroonoko,*" *Bulletin of the New York Public Library* 74 (1970), H. A. Hargreaves describes a picture of Anne Bracegirdle carrying a feather fan such as the Indians used to blow up fires, while her two attendants wear feather crowns ("glorious Wreaths") exactly like those worn by the Indians of Guyana (pp. 442-44). Since the feather costumes would have been quite old by the time Bracegirdle played this role, perhaps the crowns had become too shabby for the leading lady herself to wear.

9 *Colonising Expeditions,* pp. 184-85 N, 199; Behn, pp. 193-94.

10 Bernbaum, p. 422; Behn, p. 207.

11 Williamson, p. 160. There is some confusion in the story between St. John's Hill and Parham or Parham-House plantations. Treffry, as overseer of St. John's Hill, presumably bought Oroonoko to work there (p. 166); yet Oroonoko was "destin'd a Slave" at Parham-House (p. 169). Perhaps the two plantations were adjacent, or perhaps the two names referred to the same plantation: Parham-House "was on the same plantation" (p. 174). In any case, the area was somehow under the jurisdiction of the absent governor, Willoughby. Sir Robert Harley, the absentee owner of St. John's Hill, was a friend and subordinate of Willoughby's; and Treffry is referred to in a letter of Byam's as an agent of Willoughby's.

12 Behn, p. 207; Platt, p. 550.

13 Behn, pp. 183-84, 208; Platt, p. 550; Nassy, David, J. H. Barrios, et al., *Essai historique sur la colonie de Surinam* (Amsterdam: S. Emmering, 1968), p. 32.

14 From the beginning of the seventeenth century, first-hand reports from travellers in West Africa were available in every country in western Europe. Despite obvious difficulties in understanding an alien culture, these accounts are considered accurate enough to be accepted by scholars today. Hakluyt's collection of voyages was published in 1589-1600, Purchas's *Hakluytus Posthumus or Purchase His Pilgrimes* in 1625; both contain reports on Africa. I have supplemented these early accounts with more detailed ones from Astley's (1745), Churchill's (1746), and Pinkerton's (1816) collections, which include much seventeenth century material; it is likely that the information they provide would have been circulating orally long before it appeared in print. These further substantiate Behn's accuracy. Although Oroonoko came from the Gold Coast (modern Ghana), I have included details from the neighboring kingdoms of Whydah, Benin, and Dahomey, slightly east on the Guinea Coast (modern Benin), on the grounds that neither Behn nor any other European who had not been to Africa would have made fine distinctions among tribes in the same general area; moreover, the culture of West Africa was fairly uniform.

The only definite inaccuracy I have found in Behn's account of Africa is her statement that a son or grandson could not take a deceased father's wives (p. 142). Actually, the universal custom seems to have been to allot a dead man's wives to his sons, who would have conjugal relations with any except their own mother.

15 Richard Hakluyt, ed., *The Principal Navigations, Voyages, Traffiques, and Discoveries of the English Nation* (Glasgow: James MacLehose and Sons, 1904), 6:149. Cf. Behn, pp. 140, 170.

16 Archibald Dalzel, *The History of Dahomy, an Inland Kingdom of Africa* (London: T. Spilsbury, 1793), p. ix.

17 Thomas Astley, ed., *A New General Collection of Voyages and Travels* (London: Thomas Astley, 1745), 3:14-15, 21, 46-47.

18 Astley, 3:46-47. Cf. Behn, pp. 193, 202.

19 Astley, 2:285.

20 Astley, 3:46-47, 82.

21 Dalzel, pp. xiii-xiv.

22 Melville J. Herskovitz, *Dahomey: An Ancient West African Kingdom* (New York: J. J. Augustin, 1938), 1:338-39. Cf. Behn, p. 147.

23 Dalzel, pp. 96, 98, 131.

24 Astley, 2:500, 3:19, 48; cf. Behn, p. 150.

25 Behn, p. 147; Herskovitz, 1:110-11, 277-78, 281-82.

26 Dalzel, p. xi; Herskovitz, 2:89.

27 Astley, 1:167; Behn, p. 156; Dalzel, p. 31. Jamoan could also be a genuine Gold Coast name: *Tshi* names

include Abo, Boam; and Amoa. "Oroonoko" is not African and presumably derives from the Orinoco River (sometimes called Oroonoque); perhaps Behn wanted to separate him from African society and connect him with the golden age-noble savage associations of the New World. See Uwe Boker, "Namengebung in Aphra Behn's *Oroonoko*," *Anglia* 90:1/2 (1972): 95 ff.

[28] Astley, 2:265-66, 296; Behn, p. 202.

[29] Astley 1:148, 2:433, 435; Behn, pp. 136, 174.

[30] Wylie Sypher, "A Note on the Realism of Mrs. Behn's *Oroonoko*," *Modern Language Quarterly* 3 (1942): 402-03. The confusion among tribes was compounded by the regular practice, alluded to in *Oroonoko* (p. 166), of separating compatriots in the colonies.

[31] Astley, 3:67.

[32] Astley, 3:74 ff.

[33] John Pinkerton, ed., *A General Collection of the Best and Most Interesting Voyages and Travels in All Parts of the World* (London: Longman et al., 1814), 16:489; Churchill, ed., *A Collection of Voyages and Travels* (London: Lintot and Osborn, 1746), 5:110.

[34] *Publications of the Hakluyt Society, Ser. 2, Vol. 86: Europeans in West Africa 1450-1560,* trans. and ed. John William Blake (London: Hakluyt Society, 1941), 216-17.

[35] W. J. Cameron, *New Light on Aphra Behn* (Auckland, N.Z.: University of Auckland, 1961), p. 7. In another case, the King of Annamaboe sent his son with a companion to be educated in England. Instead, the slaving captain sold them in the West Indies. However, when the story became known in England, the two youths were ransomed by the British Government, brought to England, and suitably educated. Horace Walpole wrote in 1749: "There are two black princes of Annamaboe here, who are in fashion in all assemblies." See Basil Davidson, *Black Mother: The Years of the African Slave Trade* (Boston: Little, Brown, 1961), p. 274. The most famous eighteenth century case of a "wrongfully" enslaved black was that of Job ben Solomon, sent to the coast by his father, a prominent Moslem priest, to sell some slaves; on the way he was captured by members of a hostile tribe and himself sold to an English captain. Like Oroonoko, he offered to ransom himself in slaves (Behn p. 175—Job offered two for one; Oroonoko, "a vast Quantity" for himself and Imoinda); but they could not be obtained before the captain sailed for Maryland. There Job was sold, and only got his freedom because a letter he wrote to his father drew attention to him. He too spent time in England and was well treated there, even while he was still legally a slave. See Douglas Grant, *The For-tunate Slave: An Illustration of African Slavery in the Early Eighteenth Century* (London: Oxford Univ. Press, 1968).

[36] Elizabeth Donnan, ed., *Documents Illustrative of the History of the Slave Trade to America* (Washington, DC: Carnegie Institution of Washington, 1930), 2:265-66.

[37] Sypher, pp. 404-05.

[38] Warren, p. 19.

[39] Churchill, 5:272. Actually, even in Oroonoko's time, not all slaves had been conquered in war. Some people were enslaved for debt or crime (including adultery), and some unscrupulous kings raided peaceful villages to take slaves.

[40] Qtd. David Brion Davis, *The Problem of Slavery in Western Culture* (Ithaca: Cornell Univ. Press, 1966), pp. 118-21.

[41] Donnan, 1:403.

[42] Dedication, qtd. in Dryden, *Four Tragedies,* ed. Lester Beaurline (Chicago: Univ. of Chicago, 1967), p. 31.

[43] John Dryden, *Three Plays,* ed. George Saintsbury (New York: Hill and Wang, n.d.), p. 8.

[44] Dryden, *Four Tragedies,* pp. 90, 92. Though it is unlikely that a real-life Oroonoko would have been a freethinker, there are a few references in the literature on Africa that support Behn's interpretation. One writer says that some of the blacks have heard of Jesus and say he was a very good man, but "The Doctrine of the Incarnation is a great Rock of Offence to them." Europeans say much of the absurd superstitions of the Africans, but one claims that "The wiser Sort, and the Grandees" of Whidah are freethinkers who believe the priests to be impostors, "as they often own to the Whites, in whom they can confide," but that they cannot reveal their skepticism "lest the Priests should raise the Populace against them" (Astley 2:296,3:35).

[45] Ruthe T. Sheffey, "Some Evidence for a New Source of Aphra Behn's *Oroonoko*," *Studies in Philology* 59 (1962): 53-57.

[46] George Guffey, "Aphra Behn's *Oroonoko*: Occasion and Accomplishment," in *Two English Novelists: Aphra Behn and Anthony Trollope* (Los Angeles: William Andrews Clark Memorial Library, 1975). This interpretation of Oroonoko as James II in blackface seems to me remarkably far-fetched, although it is supported by Marten's reference to slaughtered Oroonoko as "a mangled King" (p. 208).

[47] Edward D. Seeber, "Oroonoko in France in the Eighteenth Century," PMLA 51 (1936): 954-55.

[48] The realist Defoe similarly enlivened his fiction with exaggeration and melodrama—consider, for example, the remarkable lasting powers of Moll's and Roxana's beauty, the amount of money that Roxana accumulates, and the series of coincidences that bring about Moll's incestuous marriage to her brother.

[49] The woman author of An Essay in Defence of the Female Sex (1696) explicitly compared the lot of women in Europe to that of black slaves on the West Indian plantations (p. 22).

Elaine Hobby (essay date 1988)

[In the following excerpt, Hobby analyzes Behn's portrayal of women in her writings.]

SOURCE: "Romantic Love-Prose Fiction," in Virtue of Necessity: English Women's Writing, 1646-1688, Virago Press Limited, 1988, pp. 85-101.

. . . Aphra Behn's stories map out a world of female possibilities and limits: a bleak world, since the options open to her heroines are shown to be few indeed.[24] It is rescued from despair only by the sparkling courage and daring of her women protagonists, who with great determination negotiate their way through a universe where men have all the power.

Her most well-known story, Oroonoko, sits uneasily in my account of female romance in other respects, but it nonetheless exhibits some central features of the genre. The tale's two main protagonists are startlingly beautiful, and they maintain an undying love despite opposition from a tyrannical parent. The heroine's bravery in battle and her subjection to the ever-present threat of rape also bear the hallmarks of Behn's special vision of femininity. Nonetheless, my attempt to reduce the novel to such factors distorts it. Its central characters, Oroonoko and Imoinda, are Black slaves, and Behn's presentation of a slave rebellion and white racism introduces a further set of issues which cannot be fitted into my argument. Both I and others need to rethink our work on white women's writing to take account of these concerns.[25]

Behn's novels show that male control of women has two main sources, economic and ideological: to begin with, men have money; in addition, they set the terms of sexual relationships, deeming female desire repellent while callously exploiting their own capacity to rape when it suits their purposes. In such circumstances, women repeatedly discover, although arranged property matches might be repulsive, a liaison based on love or passion is also no guarantee of happiness.

Nearly all the novels have as their central figures strong young women who are trying to make their way through the maze of male intrigue that surrounds them.[26] These female characters bear the names of romance: Philadelphia, Alcidiana and Belvideera are no more likely inhabitants of seventeenth-century England than of the twentieth century. It is sometimes argued that such romance figures are two-dimensional, lacking the character-development that typifies the novel. The use of this naming convention, however, does not prevent Behn's protagonists being vividly individual. Although the primary focus of each tale is the situation the heroine confronts, rather than her individual personality, the women are not at all interchangeable with one another. The accepted wisdom of dating the rise of the novel to the appearance of Daniel Defoe's Robinson Crusoe, 1719, some forty years after Behn was writing, and a full sixty-five years after Carleton, seems a singularly arbitrary act if we once pay serious attention to the romances that preceded it. Maureen Duffy's research on one of Behn's best-known stories, The Fair Jilt, has shown that the most 'unlikely' incident in this romance, the abortive execution of Prince Tarquin, in fact closely accords with contemporary newspaper accounts of the affair. Novel critics have been too quick to dismiss these romances as 'fantastic'.[27]

The opening paragraph of The Adventure of the Black Lady shows how Behn's writings reverberate with echoes from the timelessness of romance, while firmly particularising the story with details from the contemporary scene (a combination that is supposed only to characterise the novel). The heroine's name, and apparently her situation, are pure romance: her setting, however, is London, and her identity, it is claimed, personally known to the narrator.

> About the beginning of last June (as near as I can remember) Bellamora came to town from Hampshire, and was obliged to lodge the first night at the same inn where the stage coach set up. The next day she took coach for Covent Garden, where she thought to find Madam Brightly, a relation of hers. (p. 3)[28]

It quickly becomes apparent that the generality of this novel comes from elements of Bellamora's circumstances that are indeed timeless: she is unintentionally pregnant. The way in which a solution to this problem is worked out, however, is quite particular to Aphra Behn's society. Bellamora's pregnancy is due to Fondlove having 'urged his passion with such violence' that eventually she had been forced to give in to his desires (p. 6). This experience was quite sufficient to warn her that a man's love was not reliable, and she had run away to the city to bear her child alone, refusing Fondlove's proposal of marriage. Since the rape, she has 'abhorred the sight of him' (p. 7). She would rather risk the ignomy of raising her child alone, in the relative anonymity of London, than place her hopes in the chanciness of such a marriage.

In late seventeenth-century England, single parenthood was not supposed to be available to women. The bailiffs of the parish are alerted to Bellamora's presence, and rush to send her to a House of Correction and her child to a parish nurse. The Black Lady does the only thing she can: she marries the child's father in the nick of time. The bailiffs arrive to be directed mockingly to the only unmarried mother in the household: a black cat that had just had kittens.

> The landlady showed 'em all the rooms in her house but no such lady could be found. At last she bethought herself, and let 'em into her parlour, where she opened a little closet door, and showed 'em a black cat that had just kittened: assuring 'em, that she should never trouble the parish as long as she had rats or mice in the house; and so dismissed 'em like the loggerheads as they came. (p. 10)

As this quotation indicates, the novel portrays a spirited solidarity between its female characters: something also true, for instance, of *Agnes de Castro*. **The Black Lady** seems, indeed, to twist from its initial trajectory at the appearance of this theme. In the opening scene, the novel sets out as a tale about a country bumpkin who arrives in the big city only to lose her luggage. The landlady is initially implicated in a suspicion of theft. This narrative is swiftly abandoned in favour of another story altogether, and male characters are banished to its edges. Fondlove, though mentioned early in the story, never appears, and the landlady's husband is sent on his way with little ceremony.

> The gentleman, her husband, just saw her within doors, and ordered the coach to drive to some of his bottle-companions; which gave the women the better opportunity of entertaining one another. (p. 5)

Although the framework of the society is man-made, men are kept to this skeletal periphery. The question of interest is the shape of the spaces inhabited by women.

Whereas female friendship is shown as an enduring value in such stories, men's commitments to one another are seen as far more fitful. Time and again, central male characters perish having turned automatically to the sword on discovering that they love the same woman. In **The Nun; or, the Perjur'd Beauty,** for instance, Henrique and Antonio send the beauteous Ardelia off to a nunnery for a few hours, while they fight out their rival claims over her. By the end of the novel, all the major protagonists have been killed. There are comparable episodes of irrational male violence in **The Unfortunate Bride** and **The Dumb Virgin.**

Nunneries feature frequently in Behn's stories, and several of her heroines start out as nuns who, in their assertive expression of desire, become the viragos of

Restoration men's nightmares. (It is important to remember what we are only too inclined to forget in this post-Victorian age: before about 1700, women were seen as the more lustful sex, with a larger carnal appetite than men.) Perhaps the most interesting of Aphra Behn's nuns is Miranda, **The Fair Jilt,** the perfect romance heroine, a rich young orphan who retires to a nunnery to await the advent of a suitable husband. She is supremely desirable, unflawed in body, soul and mind. All the young men who pass through the city come to court her, and 'thousands of people were dying by her eyes' (p. 7).

She continues to play the game of the desired lady until she falls desperately in love with a young friar, Prince Henrick. The tables are turned, and she is forced into a traditional male role, courting him with promises of wealth if he will only agree to leave the church and marry her. When he refuses, she wreaks a male revenge on him. A man could rape his reluctant beloved, and force her to wed him. Miranda essays a female version of this by falsely charging Henrick with rape, and he is imprisoned.

The second man of her choice is Prince Tarquin, and this one she marries. Her delight in high living leads her to misappropriate her sister Alcidiana's trust fund, however, and she nearly loses her husband when he is arrested for attempting to murder the sister. At the end of the story, she is nevertheless triumphant. She and Tarquin flee the country and live happily till his death. All in all, Miranda has done the best she can.

> They say Miranda has been very penitent for her life past, and gives Heaven the glory for having given her these afflictions, that have reclaimed her, and brought her to as perfect a state of happiness as this troublesome world can afford. (p. 178)

Isabella of **The Fair Vow-Breaker,** by contrast, discovers that abandoning celibacy for reasons of passionate love (or to seek social advancement) is no recipe for fulfilment. Having been raised in a nunnery she decides aged thirteen to take a vow of chastity. When subsequently she falls in love with Henault, she immediately experiences her passion as oppressive and a loss of autonomy, but marries him nonetheless.

> He has done that in one fatal hour, that the persuasions of all my relations and friends, glory, honour, pleasure, and all that can tempt, could not perform in years; I resisted all but Henault's eyes, and they were ordained to make me truly wretched. (p. 42)

Her life with Henault indeed turns out to be miserable. The marriage is disapproved of by his family, and their only financial support comes from Isabella's aunt. In quick succession, the aunt dies and Henault is lost in battle. It happens that Villenoys, who comes to bring news of the tragedy, is an old suitor of Isabella's. She decides, pragmatically, to marry him for material security. When Henault returns some years later, she realises that both men have to be disposed of. She smothers Henault, and tells Villenoys that he has died a natural death. Persuading Villenoys to dispose of this friend's body by carrying it up to a nearby bridge and throwing it into the river, she sews together the coats of the two men once Villenoys has Henault on his back. In the light of Villenoys's consequent drowning by being pulled into the water after the corpse, her anxious directions to him to make a good job of it take on a macabre humour.

> When you come to the bridge, (said she) and that you are throwing him over the rail, (which is not above breast high) be sure you give him a good swing, lest the sack should hang on anything at the side of the bridge, and not fall into the stream. (p. 136)

Even when she goes to identify the corpses of her erstwhile lovers Isabella's nerve does not crack, and she does not confess until directly accused. The narrative voice nowhere suggests, however, that her murder of two unsatisfactory husbands was wrong. Her crime lies in not having stayed faithful to her initial vow, true to herself, as her closing scaffold speech explains (p. 147).

The fault lies not with her, but with a society which has given her such dire choices in life. Behn suggests the existence of a female subculture that has its own values, one superior to the dominant, male imperatives, but which gradually becomes sullied and eroded. It is important to note that these higher ethics, according to Behn, would cause women to be so faithful to their lovers that they 'like Indian wives, would leap alive into the graves of their deceased lovers, and be buried quick with 'em' (p. 3). This is not a liberating vision. Nonetheless, her consistent premise is that the world would be a more loving and supportive place if it were run according to these 'female' beliefs. Her grim conclusion is that such a revolutionary change is impossible. All women can do is to make the best they can out of the status quo.

> Since I cannot alter custom, nor shall ever be allowed to make new laws, or rectify the old ones, I must leave the young nuns enclosed to their best endeavours, of making a virtue of necessity; and the young wives, to make the best of a bad market. (p. 7)

This blunt assumption of female impotence in the public world of law-making contrasts sharply with the committed lobbying of the 1650s women. This new generation of women writers, who engage in far more 'literary' pursuits than their predecessors, are also more quietist or reactionary in their relation to national politics. Many of them were outspoken royalists: Behn even worked as a pamphleteer for the Tories. As women were beaten back into the home, moulded into companions for the Enlightenment man, they engaged in a detailed analysis of love which had been unnecessary in earlier decades, when women's lives had been filled with so many larger concerns. Once women are confined to a sphere of romantic love, they must, as Behn argues, turn their energies to designing strategies to win as much space as possible.

Since men, she demonstrates, are violent and dangerous to women, such an endeavour is far from easy. The most striking feature of Behn's novels, in fact, is a characteristic they share with her plays. She starkly portrays the connections between masculine desire and male violence, and makes it clear through the actions of her heroines that female choices were few and nasty. Love, romance and courtship as viewed by these female authors of prose fiction were not at all a stylised game. Living in a world where they were men's prized or despised possessions, women's explorations of these issues unfailingly involved an examination of the power relations between the sexes. The fictions they construct out of their female view of male conventions show plotting and daring as necessary to a woman if she is to escape domination and abuse from her 'lovers'. They might all say with Mary Carleton, in her vindication of her exploits,

> Let the world now judge, whether being prompted by such plain and public signs of a design upon me, to counterplot them, I have done any more than what the rule, and a received principle of justice directs. (Mary Carleton, *The Case*, p. 45)

Notes

[24] This idea is proposed by Goreau, op. cit., although developed by her along rather different lines. My discussion of Behn's prose fiction might properly be extended to include the semifictional *Loveletters from a Nobleman to his Sister*.

[25] Studies of the story include Charles Batten, 'The Source of Aphra Behn's *The Widow Ranter*', *Restoration and Eighteenth-Century Theatre Research*, 13, 1974; Martine Brownley, 'The Narrator in *Oroonoko*', *Essays in Literature*, 4, 1977; B. Dhuicq, 'Further Evidence on Aphra Behn's Stay in Surinam', *Notes and Queries*, 26, 1979; Edwin Johnson, 'Aphra Behn's *Oroonoko*', *Journal of Negro History*, 10, 1975; J. Ramsaran, '*Oroonoko*: A Study of the Factual Elements', *PMLA*, 205, 1960; Edward Seeber, '*Oroonoko* in France in the XVIII Century', *PMLA*, 51, 1936.

[26] In general, page references to Behn's works are to the first edition as a separate. References to *The Fair Jilt* (not issued separately) are to *Histories and Novels,* 1696. Quotations from *The Adventure of the Black Lady* are from Montague Summers's edition of her *Works,* 1915, volume 5.

[27] Ian Watt, *The Rise of the Novel,* 1957; Maureen Duffy, *The Passionate Shepherdess: Aphra Behn 1640-1689,* 1977.

[28] See also, for instance, *The Court of the King of Bantam.*

Rose A. Zimbardo (essay date 1989)

SOURCE: "Aphra Behn in Search of the Novel," in *Studies in Eighteenth Century Culture,* Vol. 19, 1989, pp. 277-87.

[*In the following essay, Zimbardo argues that Behn's skill in using established as well as newly developing styles of discourse is evident in* Oroonoko.]

In his brilliant book, *The Discourse of Modernism,* Timothy J. Reiss traces the development in Western discourse from what he calls "the discourse of patterning" to "analytico-referential discourse," the discourse of modernism that was born in the seventeenth century: "a passage from what we might call a discursive *exchange within* the world to the expressions of knowledge as reasoning *practice upon* the world."[1] A work of art rendered in the older "discourse of patterning" is what Paul de Man calls a "calligraphy" of emblems "rather than a mimesis."[2] That is to say, within the older system of discourse a work of art is the organization of a pattern of emblematic figures or abstract concepts "whose function is 'to guarantee ideal convertibility between the celestial and the terrestrial . . . the universal and the individual . . . nature and history.'"[3] This is the process that I described elsewhere as the "Imitation of Idea" which obtained in English dramatic art in the decades of the 1660s and early 1670s.[4]

The newer "analytico-referential discourse" creates distance between the eye of the perceiver and the objectified "reality" perceived. Reiss uses Galileo's invention of the telescope as a nexus of the change with which he is concerned. This newer discourse of modernism required the invention of the novel as its best artistic medium. Under the governance of the older discourse of patterning the function of a work of dramatic art was to show a closed system of ideational relationships to the spectator which would reveal to him or her the harmonious systematic interaction among ideas, a model of the whole cosmological reality. It is true that the larger aim of such dramatic discourse was to disclose a method by which human participation

within the metaphysical order occurs; that participation was of a kind by which we, as a species, are placed within the celestial-terrestrial system which the abstract discourse of patterning shows. For example, a character in one of Aphra Behn's early plays, *The Young King,* says:

> *Orisames:* I to my self could an *Idea* frame
> Of Man in much more excellence.
> Had I been *Nature,* I had varied still,
> And made such different *Characters* of Men
> They should have bow'd and made a God of me
> Ador'd and thank'd me for their great Creation.
>
> (act 2. sc. 1)[5]

Here "nature," or "reality," is a configuration of ideas; dramatic characters are concepts, and the function of dramatic discourse is to pattern a rhetorical design, a closed system analogous, as the human mind itself is analogous, to a metaphysical system of reality.

The new analytico-referential discourse created distance between subject and object, the human being and the world at which he looks; it also established a more intimate relationship between the human eye and the scaled down "reality" which the human eye could perceive and the human tongue describe. The older discourse erased the importance of the individual human being. Indeed, in English drama of the 1660s and early 1670s it is relatively unimportant which speaker declaims a set rhetorical speech; what is crucially important is the position of that set piece within the whole rhetorical design of the play. The newer discourse brought a manageable "outside" reality into the range of human perception, possession, and control. As Reiss puts it, "Its exemplary formal statement is *cogito-ergo-sum* (reason-semiotic mediating system-world). . . . Its principal metaphors will be those of the telescope (eye-instrument-world) and of the voyage of discovery (self-possessed point of departure—sea journey—country claimed as legitimate possession of the discoverer)."[6] It is interesting that Aphra Behn's late, best work, *Oroonoko,* not only employs the new analytico-referential discourse whose operation Reiss describes here, but also enacts what he considers one of its principal metaphors—the narrator "I" 's journey to Surinam, the reader's discovery of that colonial possession, and even the politico-economic consequences that such "possession" entails.

Aphra Behn is an important figure in seventeenth-century English literature because, had we no other remaining evidence than the works of Dryden and Behn upon which to judge, we could yet trace the course of one of the most important revolutions in aesthetics and consciousness that has occurred in the history of English thought. This is not to suggest that Behn was a great dramatist—she was not among the best of her time—nor to suggest that she was a theorist, as Dryden was. In part, her importance lies in the fact that she was an almost faultless barometer of popular taste and consciousness; she described herself as one "who is forced to write for Bread and not ashamed to owne it, and consequently ought to write to please (if she can) an Age which has given severall proofs it was by this way of writing to be oblig'd."[7] What makes Behn a crucially important figure, however, is that she was a pioneer in the invention of the novel; her **Oroonoko** is not only the first, but also one of the best, early English novels. This study therefore is entitled "Aphra Behn in Search of the Novel" because what I shall attempt to establish is the movement in Behn's practice that led her from using language in the service of an abstract design of discourse that patterns an ideational metaphysical "reality" to using an analytico-referential discourse that led her inevitably to the novel as her best medium of expression.

In Behn's first play, **The Forc'd Marriage,** or **The Jealous Bridegroom** (1670), the object of dramatic imitation is an ideal of heroic love and honor. Characters, as well as the speeches they declaim, are figures, or, to be more precise, placements within what Eric Rothstein called "a fixed grid of love and honor."[8] Discourse is declamation, set rhetorical pieces that are positioned within a dialectical progression that mounts toward a complex metaphysical concept, which it does not, indeed cannot, describe. Words are ideational counters; for example:

> Erminia: *Philander* never spoke but from a
>   Soul
> That all dishonest Passions can controul;
> With flames as chaste as Vestals that did
>   burn,
> From whence I borrow'd mine to make
>   return . . .
> Upon my life no other thing he spoke
> But those from dictates of his Honour took.
>   (act 1. sc. 4)

Words here are abstract counters for abstract concepts. They form a set rhetorical pattern, which, positioned in relation to a variety of other such set pieces, in turn, pattern the rhetorical design of the whole. So much is it the case that discourse figures a pattern here that at a climactic moment in the play language can be dispensed with altogether and the pattern achieved by mute, still figures positioned in significant gestural relation to one another. For example, act 2 of this first play begins with a *tableau vivant* called "The Representation of the Wedding." Quoted here is only a small exemplary fragment of a quite lengthy, detailed direction. Notice how the figures, arranged in relation to one another, form a complex, wordless configuration of theatrical signs:

The *Curtain* must be let down and soft Musick must play: the *Curtain* being drawn up, discovers a scene of a Temple: the *King* on a throne bowing down to join hands of *Alcippus* and *Ermine* . . . without on the Stage *Philander* with his sword half-drawn held by *Galatea,* who looks ever on *Alcippus: Erminia* still fixing her eyes on *Philander; Pisano* passionately gazing on *Galatea; Aminta* on *Falatio,* and he on her; *Alcander, Issilia, Cleonatis,* in other severall postures, with the rest, all remaining without motion, whilst Musick softly plays; this continues 'till the Curtain falls. . . . [9]

What is significant in this example is that mute, motionless figures serve precisely the function that words or declaimed set-pieces serve within the whole design of the play. The king, bowing down from his throne, equals majesty condescending to heroic glory and beauty; the rightful lover with his sword half-drawn equals heroic love urging toward heroic beauty. His gesture is restrained by a figure, Galatea, that represents heroic honor's curb upon heroic love. The point is that in Behn's earliest play (wherein her practice is indistinguishable from that of her contemporaries of the sixties and early seventies) both characters and the discourse they declaim are figures, positions within a rhetorical design wrought by the discourse of patterning.

We begin, however, to see signs of Behn's desire to break the pattern quite early on in her career, both in her practice and in the comments she addresses to her audience in prefaces and remarks "To the Reader." Throughout her career Behn argued that she was better equipped to write plays than her male contemporaries because she was a woman, her argument being that "We [women] have nobler Souls than you [as] we prove/ By how much more we're sensible of Love" (Epilogue, **Sir Patient Fancy,** 1678) and that "plays have no great room for that which is men's great advantage over women, that is Learning," because plays are "intended for the exercising of man's passions not their understanding" (Preface, **The Dutch Lover,** 1673). Indeed, the male sensibility, hampered as it is by learning and affectation, she argues, is hamstrung by its own discourse: "for affectation hath always a greater share both in the action and discourse of men than truth or judgment have" (Preface, **The Dutch Lover**).

There is nothing remarkable in the notion that drama imitates "the Passions" and in her earliest practice Behn, like her male contemporaries, envisioned imitation of the passions as imitation of ideas, or abstract conceptions, of the passions, as we have seen in the passage from her first play quoted above. Earlier than most and in accordance with the epistemological changes governing her time, however, Behn became aware of the passions as being located not "out there" in the realm of abstract conceptualization but rather within the human psyche; more precisely, she began to see the passions as forces having their origins within the human psyche that are the vehicles by means of which the human connects with the metaphysical realm. Earlier than most, she became impatient with the restrictions that "imitation of idea" and the discourse of patterning required by it imposed upon the playwright. Addressing her male contemporaries, she said:

> Your Way of Writings out of Fashion grown.
> Method, and Rule—you only understand.
> Pursue that way of Fooling and be damn'd.
> Your learned Cant of Action, Time and Place,
> Must all give way to the unlabour'd Farce.
> (Epilogue, *Sir Patient Fancy*)

As early as her second play, *The Amorous Prince* (1671), and throughout her subsequent career as a playwright Behn began to choose as her sources the Spanish tale, the Italian novella, the history, and, finally, the documentary pamphlet. Of her twenty or so plays well over half were taken from romances or novellas, and the source of her last play, *The Widow Ranter,* or *The History of Bacon in Virginia* (produced after her death in 1690) was taken from a news pamphlet, "Strange News from Virginia being a free and true account of the life and Death of Nathaniel Bacon, Esq." (1677).

What is significant for our purposes is that almost from the beginning of her career Aphra Behn was straining against the strictures of dramatic convention and was beginning her search for the novel. Her best known plays—and possibly her worst—*The Rover I* and *II* exhibit what Michael McKeon, in his important book, *The Origins of the English Novel,*[10] calls "generic instability," that dislocation in generic form which, in Bahktinian terms, was the fertile soil in which the novel was born. Both *The Rover I* and *II* were taken from Thomas Killigrew's *Tomaso,* or *The Wanderer,* a strange closet drama written during the Interregnum and never intended for the stage. *Tomaso* is constructed in ten closely consecutive, but structurally loose acts. The action is the serial action of picaresque fiction, and, as Summers said, the work "may better be described as a dramatic romance than a comedy intended for the boards."[11] Behn does two interesting things in these plays. The first, and most important, is that she begins to free discourse from patterning. It would be totally wrong to say that she created character as we understand it today, that is, as the fictional simulation of people having psychology and interiority. It would be equally wrong to suggest that she had yet mastered analytico-referential discourse. Rather, she changes character from figural placement, or position, within a rhetorical design to free-floating type. The consequence is that discourse, while it is still very far from dialogue, becomes disembodied voice. Curiously, in some ways *The Rover* may be understood as a

two-hundred-and-some year foreshadowing of Virginia Woolf's *The Waves.* Rather than placing set rhetorical pieces in relation to other set pieces within a dominant rhetorical design, the discourse of *The Rover I* and *II* consists in typologically determined "voices" that exist in interesting contrapuntal relation to one another.

The second important development in these two plays is Behn's creation of gratuitous character/figures that are designed deliberately to break rhetorical consistency. The courtesans, Angelica Bianca and La Nuche, both of whom are heroines of Herculean "irregular greatness," are designed not only to break accepted moral and social conventions, but, by their extravagance of language (which, in an old-fashioned sixties heroic drama would be perfectly acceptable if placed properly within the confines of a mounting rhetorical design), are extrinsic to the design. Their function, rather, is to dislocate typology from the medley of "voices" upon which the plays depend.

Behn's best play of the seventies, the decade which I have called the great moment in English dramatic satire,[12] is *The Feign'd Courtesans* (1679). In it Behn was striving for the same disjunctive unity in conceptualization toward which the giants of dramatic satire—Dryden, Wycherley, and Etherege—aimed, in which a heightened ideal plays in continuous juxtaposition against a downwardly exaggerated actual. Dryden delineated the opposition most obviously in *Marriage a la Mode,* Wycherley and Etherege more subtly in *The Country Wife* and *The Man of Mode.* What is interesting here is that while her contemporaries render the necessary disjunctive unity of satire structurally, Behn does so dialogically. For example, in playing high (ancient model) against low (immediate actual) where her contemporaries, especially Dryden, interplay planes of action, Behn achieves the effect in a differentiation between the voices:

> *Marcella:* The Evening's soft and calm as
>   happy Lovers thoughts
> And here are Groves where meeting Trees
> Will hide us from the Amorous gazing Crowd
> *Cornelia:* What should we do here, sigh 'till
>   our wandering Breath
> Has rais'd a gentle Gale among the boughs,
> To whose dull melancholy Musick, we
> Laid on a bed of Moss, and new fall'n leaves
> Will read the dismal tale of Eccho's love!
> —No, I can make better use of famous Ovid.
> (act 2. sc. 1)

In the eighties Behn began to transform her dramatic discourse itself, to displace "discursive exchange *within* the [fictional] world" to analytico-referential "practice upon the world"—to use Reiss's terms again. Whereas in *The Feign'd Courtesans* satiric dialectic is contained within the discursive dimensions of the play's rhetorical design, in a play like **The City Heiress** (1682) Behn trains the disjunctive unity, which earlier was contained within a closed literary context, upon the actual circumstances of contemporary life. The satiric disjunction remains the same—that is, the ideal versus the satirically, downwardly exaggerated actual—but the dimensions of disjunctive interplay are secularized and made present. The charming "heroic" vices of "real" Tories (drinking, gambling, and whoring) are contrasted with the mean and despicable vices of "real" Whigs (hypocrisy, greed, and sedition). Character is still concept, but typologically rendered though it is, it is realized in terms of a contemporary situation, in much the way that a modern newspaper cartoonist might exaggerate and typologize the figures and discourse of current political events.

It is in **The Lucky Chance** (1687) that we see clearly for the first time an authorial "I" looking at its world and novelistically describing the problematic condition of it. From her first play, **The Forc'd Marriage,** Behn had been concerned with the evils of forced marriage; but whereas in her first play the idea is elevated to the distant, heroic realm, in 1687 we are made to see the situation not as the occasion for a rhetorical "turn" or two within a dialectical progression but as a contemporary social problem. Character is no longer the delineation of concept or type. Action is no longer subservient to the demands of rhetorical patterning. Rather, a subject which had been fair game for light comic ridicule since Chaucer is presented for serious consideration and, discursively, for sober discussion:

> *Lady Fullbank:* Oh how fatal are forc'd
>   Marriages.
> How many Ruins one such Match pulls on!
> Had I but kept my Sacred Vows to *Gayman*
> How happy had I been—how prosperous he!
> Whilst now I languish in a loath'd embrace
> Pine out my Life with Age—Consumptive
>   Coughs.
>
>   (act 2. sc. 1)

Here is the world of experience—consumptive coughs and all. Here is the present "I"—both writer and reader—looking through the instrument of analytico-referential discourse upon an immediate, familiar "reality." Here is discourse that "practices upon" the world rather than shaping an abstract image of it. The actual circumstances leading to forced marriages are explored; Lucretia is driven to marry Sir Feeble Fainwood by economic necessity. Vows are not broken, as in a play of the early seventies, to set a particular dialectic antithesis between concepts of love and honor. Rather, as in life, persons are forced to break promises by social pressure and economic need.

The Lucky Chance was Behn's "new-modelling" of an old play, Shirley's *The Lady of Pleasure.* In her renovation Behn not only forces us to consider the stock literary situations of an earlier period from a contemporary vantage, and not only transforms discourse from declamation to dialogue, but she uses the specific descriptive techniques of a novelist to bring ideas into what Bahktin calls the "present of still evolving contemporary reality."[13] Over and over again in this play Behn forces us to look behind very old stock comic situations to explore the real circumstances that may underlie them. One such stock situation, prevalent since Jacobean "City Comedy," is that of an aristocratic lover, down on his luck, who is driven to solicit the help of his city landlady. Behn uses the new analytico-referential discourse to make us envision the situation as a novel would do. Lady Fullbank's steward, Bredwell, who has just launched the trick that will finally bring Gayman his reward for having given all for love, reports to Lady Fullbank the conditions under which Gayman lives. So detailed, so novelistic, is the description that it badly strains the limits of dramatic representation:

> *Bred.* . . . at the door [I] encountered the beastly thing he calls a Landlady; who look't as if she had been of her own Husband's making, compos'd of moulded Smith's dust. I ask'd for Mr. Wasteall [Gayman's assumed name] and she began to open—and did so rail at him, that what with her *Billingsgate,* and her Husband's hammers I was both deaf and dumb—at last the hammers ceased and she grew weary, and call'd down Mr. Wasteall, but he not answering—I was sent up a ladder rather than a pair of Stairs. . . .
>
> 'Tis a pretty convenient Tub, Madam, [Gayman's room]. He may lie a long in't, there's just room for an old join'd Stool besides the Bed, which one cannot call a Cabin, about the largeness of a pantry Bin, or a Usurer's Trunk: there had been Dornex Curtains to't in days of Yore; but they were now annihilated, and nothing left to save his Eyes from the Light, but my Landlady's Blue Apron, ty'd by strings before the Window, in which stood a six-penny Looking Glass, that shew'd as many faces as the Scene in *Henry* the Eighth, which cou'd but just stand upright, and then a Combcase fill'd it. (act 1. sc. 3)

The scene is not the ambiguous "A Room in Mrs--House" that we have found in earlier drama; rather, it describes a specific, and visualizable location, such as we are given by a novel. We are made by the description to notice particular details—the sizes, shapes, and colors of objects. We see the ragged apron at the window; we hear the smith's din. Consequently, as in a novel, we are made to enter into and experience the condition of poverty as it actually existed in London in 1687. Here is a discourse that "practices upon" the world, a telescopic instrument by means of which the reader/listener's eye focuses upon a known reality, which, by seeing, he may encompass and possess in consciousness.

At roughly the same time that she wrote *The Lucky Chance* Aphra Behn wrote a prose work, *The Adventure of the Black Lady* (ca. 1685, published 1696), of which George Woodcock says, "The incidents all take place in familiar London surroundings, and the lack of artificiality and elaboration gives the whole piece the air of a little vignette from real life. It is written in an easy, conversational style; which adds to the impression of its authenticity."[14] Of another prose work, written at the same time, *The Wandering Beauty,* Angeline Goreau writes: "This [the narrator's] 'I' was something new not only in literature but in history. It was a very early example of the growing self-consciousness of the individual, which would in the next century and a half develop into a 'given' in the way people thought about themselves. Aphra's focus on individual experience and self-expression was historically avant garde."[15]

This essay has focused on Behn's, the dramatist's, search for the novel. We find the same movement from the discourse of patterning to analytico-referential discourse in the progressive development of Behn's prose fiction. Her first prose work, *Love Letters between a Nobleman and His Sister,* while it is innovative in introducing the epistolary mode, employs the older discourse throughout. In Part 1, composed entirely of letters, it is virtually impossible, without reference to the title heads—"To Philander" or "To Syvia"—to distinguish among the voices of the letter writers. On the other hand, in her late novel, *Oroonoko,* so perfectly has Behn mastered the use of analytico-referential discourse, and so thoroughly aware is she of the operational difference upon a reader between the older and newer discourses, that she skillfully uses interaction between the two styles to create the first tragic novel in English. For example, she uses the older discourse when her aim is to delineate the spiritual essence of her hero: "the Greatness of Soul, those refined Notions of True Honour, that absolute Generosity, and Softness that was capable of the highest Passions of Love and Gallantery" (135). That is to say, she uses the "sacrosanct and traditional" language[16] of heroic romance when her aim is to shape a "Character of Mind" or to figure the Idea of Majesty[17] that Oroonoko the Prince represents. On the other hand, before Behn begins to tell Oroonoko's story, she uses the analytico-referential mode of discourse to create the setting in which his sufferings as Caesar the Slave will take place. The new mode of narrative discourse, full of accurately observed detail and almost scientific description, is used to make the exotic landscape and culture of Surinam familiar, and, more importantly, to make the reader, by virtue of the detailed landscape he has visualized, an inhabitant of the fictional world. The narrative of Coramantien, in which Oroonoko figures Majesty and ideal heroic love, is written wholly in the older discourse. Such is the glistening height from which the tragic hero falls. The narrative of Surinam is written largely in the newer discourse. It realistically pictures the crushing world of experience into which he falls.

Aphra Behn was by no means a great dramatist, but she may be considered the first English novelist, the first literary artist to master the telescope of analytico-referential discourse and to teach us, her readers, how to use that instrument.

Notes

[1] Timothy J. Reiss, *The Discourse of Modernism* (Ithaca: Cornell University Press, 1982), 30.

[2] Paul de Man, "Pascal's Allegory of Persuasion," *Allegory and Representation,* ed. Stephen J. Greenblatt (Baltimore: The Johns Hopkins University Press, 1981), 1.

[3] Reiss, *Modernism,* quoting Gerard Simon, 30.

[4] Rose A. Zimbardo, *A Mirror to Nature: Transformations in Drama and Aesthetics, 1660-1732* (Lexington: University Press of Kentucky, 1986).

[5] *The Works of Aphra Behn,* ed. Montague Summers, 6 vols. (London, 1915; repr., New York: Benjamin Bloom, 1967). All references to Behn's work are to this edition.

[6] Reiss, *Modernism,* 31.

[7] "To the Reader," Preface, *Sir Patient Fancy,* Summers, ed., *Works,* 4:115-16.

[8] Eric Rothstein, *Restoration Tragedy* (Madison: University of Wisconsin Press, 1966), 31.

[9] Summers, ed., *Works,* 3:305.

[10] Michael McKeon, *The Origins of the English Novel* (Baltimore: The Johns Hopkins University Press, 1986), 20.

[11] Summers, ed., *Works,* 1:4.

[12] Zimbardo, *Mirror to Nature,* 9.

[13] M. M. Bahktin, "Epic and Novel," *The Dialogue of Imagination,* trans. C. Emerson and M. Holquist (Austin: University of Texas Press, 1983), 19.

[14] George Woodcock, *The Incomparable Aphra* (London and New York: T. V. Boardman, 1948), 167.

[15] Angeline Goreau, *Reconstructing Aphra: A Social Biography of Aphra Behn* (New York: Dial Press, 1980), 281.

[16] Bahktin, "Epic and Novel," 16.

[17] Zimbardo, *Mirror to Nature,* chap. 2, "Imitation of Nature as Idea."

Catherine Gallagher (essay date 1994)

SOURCE: "The Author-Monarch and the Royal Slave: *Oroonoko* and the Blackness of Representation," in *Nobody's Story: The Vanishing Acts of Women Writers in the Marketplace, 1670-1820*, University of California Press, 1994, pp. 49-87.

[*In the excerpt below, Gallagher discusses the meaning of blackness in relation to European society in* Oroonoko.]

Behn's narrators, to be sure, are not the faceless, third-person, omniscient storytellers invented by later generations of writers. In accordance with the conventions of the seventeenth century, almost all of them intermittently use the first person, especially to explain how they came by their knowledge of the story. In the very process of explaining themselves, however, the narrators often become mysterious. The following passage from *Love-Letters between a Nobleman and His Sister* is typical of these first-person statements: "I have heard her page say, from whom I have had a great part of the truths of her life, that he never saw Sylvia in so pleasant a humour all his life before, nor seemed so well pleased, which gave him, her lover [the page], a jealousy that perplexed him above any thing he had ever felt from love; though he durst not own it."[22] At first glance, the passage seems to reveal the narrator; however, it actually serves to obscure her.[23] Her information comes from servants, who, moreover, like the page mentioned here, long to be actors in the drama they are only allowed to observe. She moves mysteriously below stairs, collecting information like a spy.

Often allied in this way with the frustrated and relatively anonymous instruments of the main characters (Sylvia's page has no name), Behn's narrators are sometimes associated with a marginality that becomes sinister. One such instance is particularly interesting in connection with *Oroonoko.* In "The Unfortunate Bride; or, the Blind Lady a Beauty," the narrator claims that much of her information comes indirectly from a black woman, Mooria, who not only longs to be the object of the hero's love but also steals his letters to his mistress and forges letters to drive the lovers apart. The story makes the lady's blackness a metaphor for her "dark designs" and for her means of accomplishing them: stealing the writings of others and writing "in a disguised hand." The black lady, in other words, is an inky creature who separates people from their written representations and plunges them into obscurity. She is more designing than the narrator and more adept than any other character at achieving her designs by textual misrepresentation.

Although in Behn's stories there are several such designing women, who manipulate the action by disguising their "hands," Mooria is the only one who *embodies* this form of power. The darkness of her skin is associated with invisibility and magical powers of transformation; that is, her black body seems a metaphor for the disembodying potential of writing. The very ink that allows graphic representation, and the consequent dissociation of bodies and language, seems to cover Mooria herself.

Since Mooria's skin becomes an emblem of the disembodying power of writing, for which the blackness of ink is a related sign, her darkness suggests by association the "anonymous hand" par excellence: print, the medium of the story's dissemination. Print intensified anonymity simply by increasing standardization, making the graphemes relatively interchangeable regardless of their origin, and by wide dissemination, which broke the link common in scribal cultures between texts and specific places where they could be read. The more identical copies of a text there were, the less that text seemed to occupy any particular location, and the less it seemed the physical emanation of any body. The figure of the black woman combines the blackness of racial difference, the obscurity of the narrative "I" in this particular story, and the potential erasure of the writer through the "anonymous hand" of publication.[24]

However, since our modern notion of the author is itself a feature of print culture, we must acknowledge that the disembodiment of the writer in the standardized, multiplied, and widely disseminated text was the condition of her appearance as an *author.* As Elizabeth Eisenstein shows, "Until it became possible to distinguish between composing a poem and reciting one, or writing a book and copying one; until books could be classified by something other than incipits;[25] the modern game of books and authors could not be played."[26] The potential anonymity realized in the figure of Mooria, therefore, was merely the underside of that seemingly unmediated and purely mental presence that Behn celebrated in the epistles to the printed edition of her plays. . . .

The relationship of blackness, authorship, textuality, exchange, and transcendence helps explain why Behn's most sustained work on heroic kingship should make black the color of both exchange and sovereignty. In *Oroonoko* Behn breaks the traditional Western metaphoric connection between black bodies and moral degeneracy that she had drawn on in characterizing

Mooria, and blackness takes on unprecedented meanings, including representation itself, kingship, exchange value, and the paradoxes of absolute property.

Oroonoko seems the polar opposite of "The Unfortunate Bride." The narrator not only claims her authorial identity and her personal experience of the events but also gives herself an important role in the story and hence a sustained presence.[33] She identifies herself as Aphra Behn, a writer already known to the public as a playwright, whose established reputation should guarantee her veracity. She even discusses her next play, stressing that, like *Oroonoko,* it is based to some extent on her life experience: "Colonel Martin [was] a man of great gallantry, wit, and goodness, and whom I have celebrated in a character of my new comedy, by his own name, in memory of so brave a man."[34] Clearly, she highlights personal-authorial continuity as a guarantee of the tale's authenticity.

This stress on the work as an expression of the author's identity has a parallel in the metaphoric use of blackness. Whereas in "The Unfortunate Bride" the narrator's anonymity seemed intensified by the "dusky" obscurity of Mooria, the narrative's source, in *Oroonoko* the gleaming blackness of the eponymous hero corresponds to the narrator's heightened presence. If Mooria's color emphasized her invisibility and that of the narrator, Oroonoko's radiates, illuminating the narrator's identity. He is blacker than the black lady—indeed he is blacker than anybody—but that does not make him "dusky." Instead, it makes him brilliant: "His face was not of that brown, rusty black which most of that nation are, but a perfect ebony, or polished jet" (pp. 80-81). He is not a *brown* black, but a black black. Behn's distinction between brown blacks and black blacks departs from the convention of representing sub-Saharan native people, who, according to Winthrop Jordan, were normally all described as absolutely black: "blacke as coles," as one voyager to Guinea put it a century earlier.[35] By making complete blackness a distinguishing characteristic of the noble Oroonoko, Behn attached a positive aesthetic value to the skin color: the brown blacks are dull, but the shiny black black reflects light.[36] Even when he was dressed in slave's clothes, Oroonoko's gleaming blackness "shone through all" (p. 108). The lustrous quality of the hero's blackness, which is "so beyond all report," requires the eyewitness reporting of a known author; Aphra Behn, therefore, must emerge from her obscurity and explain the circumstances of her witnessing. In short, the hero's blackness calls the authorial persona into existence.

As a character, Behn is also clearly paralleled with Oroonoko.[37] Like him, she arrives a stranger in Surinam but is immediately recognized as superior to the local inhabitants; like him, she appears a shining marvel when she travels to the Indian village; and like his

words, hers are always truthful. As narrator, she repeatedly identifies herself as the well-known author Aphra Behn to vouch for the otherwise incredible brightness of Oroonoko. The sustained authorial presence in this book is thus closely connected to the black hero's luster; as the story moves forward, narrator and hero polish each other's fame. Although in the beginning Oroonoko had the misfortune "to fall in an obscure world, that afforded only a female pen to celebrate his fame" (p. 108), by the end the narrator presumes to hope "the reputation of my pen is considerable enough to make his glorious name to survive to all ages" (p. 141).

Hence through an intensification of blackness, hero and narrator emerge into the light. Like Behn's forewords to her plays, this process can be read as a full-blown celebration of the bright, transcendent possibilities inherent in print, possibilities that Mooria only darkly suggested. Oroonoko resembles the mystical body of the text.[38] His blackness is a luminous emanation of the author that gleams forth from multiple inscriptions.

Such an interpretation of this "admirably turned" (p. 80) ebony figure is consonant with one of Oroonoko's most remarked features: he is densely overwritten. Indeed, the narrator seems quite self-consciously to present her hero's story as a layering of narrative conventions. She moves from her de rigueur promise to tell the unadorned truth in the opening paragraph into a brief wonders-of-the-New-World passage whose extreme conventionality has often been noted. Indeed, she notes it herself on the second page when the wonders turn into London's stage spectacles, and the authenticity of her story momentarily depends on its "intertextual" relationship to one of Dryden's plays: "I had a [suit of feathers made by the Indians] presented to me, and I gave them to the King's Theatre; it was the dress of the Indian Queen, infinitely admired by persons of quality; and was inimitable." The momentary uncertainty about which Indian queen is being referred to, a queen of the Indians who owned the dress or Dryden's stage heroine, only emphasizes the lack of distinction between the two possible meanings. As a real Indian artifact transferred to the stage, the dress authenticates both. Readers can be assured of the truth of Behn's claims because their own eyes have seen such things on the stage. The early part of Oroonoko's story is no less dependent on references to the theater and on the self-conscious employment of courtly intrigue conventions to familiarize and authenticate the action. And the brief idyll of the middle section is similarly realized through reference to a literary model; when Oroonoko and his wife, Imoinda, are reunited, Oroonoko's English protector and putative master, looking on, "was infinitely pleased with this novel" (p. 112). One could continue to multiply the evidence, for the last half of Oroonoko's history is particularly thickly encrusted with tragic references and is highly wrought in the histrionic codes of heroic drama.[39]

This dense literary artificiality has exasperated some modern readers of **Oroonoko** and has been the chief evidence in the twentieth century for the story's inauthenticity.[40] The stress on Oroonoko's conformity to literary conventions, however, was probably intended to make him seem believably noble. The narrator proves the hero's greatness by showing how closely he adhered to heroic models. The sense that Oroonoko was made up of myriad literary conventions would have made him familiar and hence credible to contemporary readers, for real heroic action was necessarily imitative.[41] The resolute intertextuality of the narrative was not a failure of imagination but rather a proof that the author deserved fame because she had a legitimately heroic story that was recognizable as such only because it conformed to other such representations.

We can read Oroonoko's gleaming blackness, then, as a celebration of inscription without turning it into a self-reflective modern text. However, a danger lurks in such a reading. If Oroonoko's blackness becomes mainly an allegory of textuality, even with such historical and formal qualifications as have been introduced, we lose sight of the phenomenal wonder that empowers the text in the first place. Unless we acknowledge that Oroonoko's blackness refers most importantly to racial difference and indeed is dependent on a stock response of racial prejudice in the reader, we cannot explain what is so wonderful about him and so meritorious in the author. The reader is frequently invited to marvel that Oroonoko, *although black,* behaves like a conventional European tragic hero. Hence passages such as the following rely for their sense of the marvelous on the very racial prejudice they seem to dispel:

> His nose was rising and Roman, instead of African and flat. His mouth, the finest shaped that could be seen; far from those great turned lips, which are so natural to the rest of the Negroes. The whole proportion and air of his face was so noble, and exactly formed, that, bating his colour, there could be nothing in nature more beautiful, agreeable and handsome. . . . Nor did the perfections of his mind come short of those of his person; for his discourse was admirable upon almost any subject; and whoever had heard him speak, would have been convinced of their errors, that all fine wit is confined to the white men, especially to those of Christendom; and would have confessed that Oroonoko was as capable even of reigning well, and of governing as wisely, had as great a soul, as politic maxims, and was as sensible of power, as any prince civilized in the most refined schools of humanity and learning, or the most illustrious courts. (p. 80)

Oroonoko is a wonder because blackness and heroism are normally thought to be mutually exclusive qualities; indeed, the passage asserts that they normally *are* mutually exclusive. Only in his differences from other Africans does Oroonoko achieve heroism, but in his blackness his heroism partakes of the marvelous. His is a "beauty so transcending all those of his gloomy race, that he struck an awe and reverence, even in those that knew not his quality; as he did in me, who beheld him with surprise and wonder" (p. 79). Thus his color, as a sign of racial difference, itself reminds us that all his features differ from those "which are so natural to the rest of the Negroes."

Oroonoko's blackness must therefore be seen as at once authentically and unnaturally African. It is the exotic trait that makes his story worth writing, the feature that makes him unprecedented as hero, and hence a wonder. However, it is also the feature that necessitates such an energetic marshaling of heroic literary precedents. Both hero and writer must overcome his blackness, which "naturally" threatens to become the condition of his obscurity even though it also makes him worthy of fame. The author packs Oroonoko so densely with heroic reference as to prove him wonderful, making his very blackness shine. Blackness as racial difference at once helps explain why Oroonoko's color gleams with "unnatural" intertextuality and reveals how such gleaming redounds to the glory of the author.

Oroonoko's blackness, a "natural" physical indication of racial difference, even inferiority, is transubstantiated textually into a wonderful sign of heroic distinction. It is thus highly appropriate that descriptions of Oroonoko's and Imoinda's heroic bodies should emphasize their artificiality; they are not so much bodies of flesh and blood as pieces of polished handiwork. "The most famous statuary could not form the figure of a man more admirably turned from head to foot" is the sentence that precedes the description of Oroonoko's color as "not of that brown, rusty black which most of that nation are, but a perfect ebony, or polished jet." Readers are called on here to put the actual African bodies they might have seen (the *brown* black ones) out of mind and substitute for them statues of ebony. Indeed, when Oroonoko alights at Surinam dressed in his "dazzling habits" to be gazed at in his journey to his new home by the whites and the merely "brown" blacks, he resembles nothing so much as the statue of a magus. These common Africans eventually greet him as king and even, in a scene that fuses Christ child and magus, fall to worshiping him as divine when he finally arrives at his destination.

Imoinda's body is also artifactual, but in a slightly different way. At first she is described merely as a female version of Oroonoko; the allusions are appropriately classicized to suggest a female divinity: "To describe her truly, one need say only, she was female to the noble male; the beautiful black Venus, to our young Mars" (p. 81). Her features, like his, are to be imagined as European, and the description of the pair of lovers might well have evoked images of Jonson's *Mask of Blackness,* or of the actors and actresses in black-face and lavish costumes who played the "kings" and "queens" of Africa and India in the lord mayors' pageants.[42] Such figures would have been quite appropriate to the court intrigue section of the novel. However, after Imoinda has been sold into slavery, has had her name changed to Clemene (as Oroonoko has his changed to Caesar), and emerges into our view through the eyes of the white clonists, her body undergoes a fabulous transformation:

> Though from her being carved in fine flowers and birds all over her body, we took her to be of quality before, yet, when we knew Clemene was Imoinda, we could not enough admire her.

> I had forgot to tell you, that those who are nobly born of that country, are so delicately cut and raced all over the fore-part of the trunk of their bodies, that it looks as if it were japanned; the works being raised like high point round the edges of the flowers. (p. 112)

This abrupt scoring of Imoinda's body, so strongly and clumsily marked in the text ("I had forgot to tell you") coincides with the narrator's re-vision of her as at once slave and romantic heroine, "Clemene" and Imoinda. Appropriately, Imoinda's body is not just transformed textually, through metaphor, but is supposed to have been transformed materially into an artificial decorative object of exotic origin; she is "japanned," like a highly varnished and intricate piece of oriental carving. And yet she is not quite statuary in this description because the plasticity and pliancy of actual flesh as well as its susceptibility to wounding, scarring, and discoloration are invoked by the description. Finally, the reference to "high point" makes Imoinda's flesh into its own laced clothing.[43] Her body becomes a fabric for representing other things; it is inscribed.

The descriptions thus stress the exotic artificiality of both Oroonoko and Imoinda, but the decoration of Imoinda suggests that her sublimation, the process of becoming art, is accomplished on her body. That is, the reader's experience of flesh is not altogether banished from Imoinda's description, as it is from Oroonoko's Even more obtrusively than Oroonoko's, Imoinda's is a body of representation. However, we are required, in this revision of her halfway through the story, to imagine her skin as the material out of which the representations are made. Oroonoko, on the one hand, is a completed representation; the African body is useful to his description only as contrast. Imoinda, on the other hand, reminds us that such refinement uses up bodies. Consequently, her image directs us to a consideration of the full relationship between Oroonoko and the commonplace "brown" Africans in the tale.

The overwrought artificiality of Oroonoko, symbolized by the gleaming blackness of his body, not only sets him apart from his countrymen but also suggests the two ways in which he absorbs and represents them: through kingship and commodification. On an abstract level, one could point to a structural homology between Oroonoko's unnatural blackness and kingship as it was conceived from the late Middle Ages through the seventeenth century.[44] Just as Oroonoko can be seen as the mystical body of the text, that which outlives myriad graphic instantiations to become the repository of overlapping forms of heroism; and just as his heroism, like the book's textuality, both depends on and is poised against blackness—the blackness of print, the blackness of racial difference (both, in turn, concepts abstracted from physical objects)—so kingship was perceived as a mystical body standing above and incorporating all bodies in the realm but also outliving them and thus proving the realm's continuity through time.

In Ernst Kantorowicz's well-known account of this concept, the mystical body of the king both depends on physical bodies and is contrasted to them.[45] Since all the realm's bodies are imagined to be incorporated in one, with the king as the head, all are imagined to be, in some sense, the bodies of the king; and yet in no physical body, not even his own, is true kingship completely contained, for the king's physical body, subject to decay and death, merely represents the immortal kingship that temporarily inhabits it. How the king's physical body represented kingship was a subject of some debate, especially in the years preceding and following the regicide, which Parliament justified by claiming in effect that *it* was the mystical body of the king, and Charles I's body was that of an enemy to the "real" sovereign. Such a radical splitting off of the actual and mystical bodies, however, was abnormal, and the explicit ideology of a high Tory like Behn would have held that the king's actual body, as long as it breathed, was the sacred and unique incarnation of the realm's mystical incorporation. Nevertheless, the king's two bodies were conceptually separable, and in **Oroonoko** they emphatically come apart so that the body of kingship itself, like the text, achieves a kind of incorporeality.

The narrator often refers to Oroonoko's kingship as if it were comparable to normal European models. In the initial description quoted earlier, for example, her stress on his heroism culminates in the greatest wonder of all, which her European readers would have found most difficult to believe: "That Oroonoko was as capable even of reigning well, and of governing as wisely . . . as any prince civilized in the most refined schools of humanity and learning, or the most illustrious courts." It is not surprising that such an ideal of princely capability would be figured in a bloodless statue of a body, one contrasted to living bodies and made imperishable through metaphors, for Behn in this figure represents not just a king, but kingship. As a specimen of a mere African king, we are given Oroonoko's grandfather, who is "a man of a hundred and odd years old" (p. 79) but who, far from having any marks of immortality about him, is senile and sexually impotent. Moreover, the actual king's body is indistinguishable from the bodies of his subjects; to get his first glimpse of Imoinda, he dresses himself as the "slave and attendant" of a "man of quality" (p. 84) and is wholly successful in this disguise. This king's body, then, is to be imagined as one of that mass of brown black bodies that Oroonoko's unnatural blackness is defined against.

Even though the king's actual and mystical bodies seem thus separated in Oroonoko's home kingdom, Oroonoko's blackness is nonetheless defined against the mass of African bodies as an abstracted essence of them, as if his blackness were the sum and intensification of their lesser darkness. The mystical body of kingship continues to represent even that against which it is defined, the physical bodies that constitute the realm, and the physical bodies are incorporated into the mystical body. Oroonoko's representation conforms to the imaginative pattern informing centuries of monarchist thought, pageantry, state organization, criminal law, family relations, and so forth; it was the common cultural property of the time.

Such a pattern of thinking, however, does not fully account for the representation of kingship in *Oroonoko,* for it does not explain why the salient physical attribute of the African bodies that is abstracted, refined, and intensified in Oroonoko's body should be their darkness. Of all the attributes of their bodies, why this one? In making her hero darker than his subjects, Behn departed radically from the traditional portrayal of the noble African or Moor,[46] who was usually painted white. Of course, we have already partly answered this question in discussing textuality and racial difference, but neither of those issues comprehends Oroonoko's princeliness, his relationship to his subjects. Why should the sign of his kingship be a body from which everything that is African is explicitly banished except a hue that can only abstractly be described as "black"?

The answer lies in Oroonoko's subjects, who, unlike those of a modern European king, are also his commodities. The narrator painstakingly explains that the word "black" distinguishes the bodies of people who can be bought and sold from those of people who cannot. To a twentieth-century reader the history of slavery makes this linkage obvious, but in the seventeenth century, before racial ideologies of slavery developed fully and as the institution itself was being

racialized, it bore reiterating.[47] The word "blacks" first appears in *Oroonoko* in contrast not to "whites" but to natives of Surinam, who are "a reddish yellow" (p. 76). These last, we are told, are not used as slaves because, through their fishing, hunting, and industry, they supply the colony with such necessities that they must be lived with in "perfect tranquillity, and good understanding" (p. 77).[48] Hence "Negroes, black-slaves altogether," are imported. "Black" here differentiates the body of the African from that of the Native American; it signifies that one has been made a commodity, and the other has not. Because this "blackness" is the mark of commodification, we are then told, everything else about these bodies becomes indistinguishable:

> Those who want slaves, make a bargain with a master, or captain of a ship, and contract to pay him so much apiece, a matter of twenty pound a head. . . . So that when there arrives a ship laden with slaves, they who have so contracted, go aboard, and receive their number by lot; and perhaps in one lot that may be for ten, there may happen to be three or four men; the rest women and children. (p. 78)

The twenty pounds paid, then, is for a "black" body, regardless of any other physical characteristic. Nor will any other color suffice, as the case of the Frenchman, seized along with Oroonoko but turned loose because of his color, makes clear. "Black" is a word that is used to describe a skin tone differing from all others that allows a body to have an abstract exchange value independent of any of its other physical qualities.

"Black," then, is connected to bodies but is also an abstraction from them signifying exchangeable value. It is not so much descriptive of the skin as of the difference between African skin and all other skin that has arbitrarily come to take on the meaning of exchange value per se. Hence the narrator immediately becomes chary of using it as a "literal" term describing bodies. "Coramantien," we are told, is "a country of blacks *so called*" (p. 78, emphasis mine), that is, a country of people one could call black and thus exchange for twenty pounds apiece.[49] But the narrator explicitly rejects this designation "black," as we have already seen, to describe the literal color of the African body, whose physicality is merely brown. "Black" identifies the commodity value of the slave body, its exchangeability for twenty pounds, as opposed to its physicality.

Thus the terrifying condition of slavery—having an African body that could be called "black"—is transfigured in this novel into a gleaming vision of disembodied value in the figure of Oroonoko's kingly blackness. Oroonoko's utterly unnatural body is the only one in which the word signifying exchangeability, "black," and the actual color of the body coincide.

Only in his body is value realized as blackness. The intrinsic, nonnegotiable kingship of Oroonoko is thus paradoxically figured in the same blackness that designates the principle of exchange itself.

The superimposition of kingship and exchange, odd as it might at first appear, was not uncommon. Money, after all, was similarly a representation of exchange value underwritten by the idea of the English state's sovereignty, the mystical body of kingship. Although the relationship between the sovereign power and money was substantially revised in the seventeenth century, and the last decade saw a strong parliamentary attempt to discount the "extrinsic" value that money received from its association with sovereignty, the very agitation of the issue would have given the relationship a pronounced ideological importance.[50] What is odd about *Oroonoko*'s depiction of this relationship is its insistence on the exchangeability of the subjects themselves for money. Exchange value and kingship are both realized in *Oroonoko* at the vanishing point of the African bodies, the moments when the king sells his subjects.

The kingship represented in Oroonoko, then, cannot be explained simply by noting that the king's mystical body underlay commerce; it is, rather, related to developments in the ideology of absolutism that reimagined the king's sovereignty as an absolute *property* right in the bodies of his subjects. It is to this notion of sovereignty that I now turn. . . .

By using the prostitute and the monarch as her most frequent authorial metaphors, Behn views her authorship through Restoration concepts of self-alienation and sovereignty, that is, through the age's self-contradictory notions about property and exchange. Shadowy aspirations of independence from the marketplace are at once raised and renounced in a paradoxical logic of property: ownership of oneself and others, this logic states, entails their commodification or annihilation. Through this reiterated recognition, Behn renders authorship, doomed to the marketplace but struggling for sovereignty, poignant. However, the author-whore and author-king metaphors also point toward ways in which the author, of all traders, seems to escape the direst consequences of the marketplace.

To demonstrate this claim, let us return to the vanishing point of Oroonoko's body, the point at which kingship has achieved a combined dispersion and incorporeality resembling that of the text itself. At that moment, the narrator makes her most striking appropriation in the form of a disclaimer: "Thus died this great man, worthy of a better fate, and a more sublime wit than mine to write his praise. Yet, I hope, the reputation of my pen is considerable enough to make his glorious name to survive to all ages, with that of the brave, the beautiful and the constant Imoinda" (p. 141).

Oroonoko's "worth" demands more sublimity than she can summon, yet her own authorial reputation, itself a mystical body existing in and between texts, will be the support of "his glorious name." Ending the text with the word "Imoinda" reminds us of Behn's special fitness to tell this love story, her femaleness, but the effect of authorship here transcends all such physical accidents even as it takes them into account. If Oroonoko scatters his members to maintain his integrity, Behn performs a similar act of disowning the text (insisting that it is really Oroonoko's and Imoinda's) to open a rhetorical space in which she can remind us of her authorship and the obligation it imposes. In her dedication of the book to Richard Maitland, she similarly effaces herself as the principle of exchange, effecting a transfer of "the nobler part" from one great man, Oroonoko, to another: "'Tis purely the merit of my Slave that must render [the book] worthy of the Honour it begs; and the Author of that of subscribing herself, My Lord, Your Lordship's most oblig'd and obedient Servant, A. Behn."[58]

In this odd mixture of appropriation and disowning ("'Tis purely the merit of *my Slave* that must render" the book worthy of Maitland), the author trades in the "parts" she claims are not exactly hers, and thus she avoids identifying herself with her commodity. Despite the insistent presence of the first-person narrator in *Oroonoko,* then, the phenomenon of authorship per se tends to come into view as the principle of the exchange of representations. Like Sir Cautious Fulbank, the author seems to want to trade in what she does not own, and quite literally she did not own *Oroonoko* by the time the printed book appeared, begging the patronage of Maitland. Or, perhaps more precisely, the authorial effect might be likened to Sir Cautious's reasoning that one may safely trade in "nothing": commodities like Julia's "part," Oroonoko's "nobler part," and finally, his "glorious name." What, after all, is a name? "Why 'tis a word, an empty sound; 'tis breath, 'tis air, 'tis *nothing,*" answers Sir Cautious. Such commodities certainly direct us to the anomalies of ownership in general. However, by insisting on the oddly evanescent materiality of these commodities and by showing that the human body disappears into them, she implies that they are the perfect "nothing" to set against all other commodities. Like authorship itself, they seem endlessly negotiable precisely because they are not really owned, and hence they make their vendor invulnerable.

Little wonder, then, that Aphra Behn seems to us both the victim and the heroine of the literary marketplace. Her two favorite personae invite exploration of the splendors and miseries of authorship as it realized itself on the stage and in print. What is the relationship between these authorial effects and the historical woman Aphra Behn? Throughout the chapter, I have implied that the historical woman was the producer of these effects, that they are therefore not to be confused with her, indeed that "she" warns us against such confusions. Simultaneously, though, I have suggested that Behn had a heightened consciousness of the connection between self-possession and self-alienation because of her experience as a woman in the literary marketplace. Even when she universalizes the paradoxes of property in the oxymoronic "Royal Slave," her insights seem grounded in the specific entanglements between women and commodities in the late seventeenth century. But because these were the entanglements of commodification, they produce an effect of emptiness when we try to reconstruct the historical subjectivity of Aphra Behn. In the first chapter of *Capital*, Marx imagines what commodities would say if they could speak. They would say that their essence is not in their matter; that it is an abstract value seemingly divorced from time and place.[59] To seek to know the interior of the commodity is thus to witness an abstraction from history. My analysis has neither exposed nor exorcised the historical woman, but has rather gained multiple perspectives on her works by composing them around the historically demarcated points where the lady vanishes.

In the chapters that follow, the self-presentations of eighteenth-century women writers will be seen to undergo alterations that are now familiar to students of English literature. The imperceptible change that Sir Walter Scott's great aunt lived through is easy to trace in what might be called the "revirginization" of the woman writer at mid-century. But through this and many other variations, the phenomenon of "Nobodiness" persists, not as an indication of the female author's lack of importance, but as a sign of her success.

Notes

[22] *Love-Letters between a Nobleman and His Sister*, introd. Maureen Duffy (London: Virago, 1987), p. 405.

[23] *Love-Letters* sometimes presents the narrator as masculine, but in the third volume, a feminine persona is consistently used.

[24] As we might also have predicted, the black lady of this story identifies all these aspects of difference with female desire. As in *The Lucky Chance*, the very principle of difference, and hence, paradoxically, of interchangeability, is the "nothing" of female sexuality, whose obscurity is stressed in yet another seventeenth-century slang term for the female sexual part: "the black ace" (Goreau, *Reconstructing Aphra*, p. 232). In *The Lucky Chance*, however, the "nothing" is "but a part" of Julia, whereas the black lady is the black ace writ large. Hence, in the act of identifying her source, the narrator of "The Unfortunate Bride" implies that to appear in print is to reach some apotheosis of femaleness by not appearing at all.

[25] Scribal copies generally did not have title pages; instead they opened with conventional phrases or incipits, a word deriving from the commonplace opening phrase "Incipit Liber" (Here begins the book).

[26] Eisenstein, p. 84. . . .

[33] This presence is not unusual in stories about the wonders of the New World, where narrators routinely felt obliged to claim that they were eyewitnesses of the events they relate. Most of the evidence, though, does point to Behn's presence in Surinam in the early to mid 1660s; see Rogers, "Fact and Fiction in Aphra Behn's *Oroonoko*," pp. 1-3. For discussion of the critical controversy over Behn's eyewitness status, see Chibka, "'Oh! Do Not Fear a Woman's Invention': Truth, Falsehood, and Fiction in Aphra Behn's *Oroonoko*," pp. 510-13.

[34] *Oroonoko; or, the Royal Slave: A True History*, in *Oroonoko, the Rover, and Other Works*, ed. Janet Todd (London: Penguin, 1992), p. 132. Subsequent quotations from this edition are cited parenthetically in the text.

[35] Jordan, *White over Black: American Attitudes toward the Negro, 1550-1800* (Chapel Hill: Univ. of North Carolina Press, 1968), p. 5.

[36] In a footnote Jordan names several later writers who celebrate "the Negro's jet blackness," but Behn's is the earliest instance by over thirty years. Jordan, p. 10 n. 23. Lines 16-20 from Milton's *Il Penseroso*, which Jordan does not cite, might be taken as a precedent:

> Black, but such as in esteme
> Prince Memnon's sister might beseem
> Or that starred Ethiop queen that strove
> To set her beauty's praise above
> The sea nymphs, and their powers
>   offended.

The mythical nature of these beings and their allegorical use as illustrations of the attractiveness of Melancholy's blackness, however, disqualify them as representations of seventeenth-century Africans.

[37] For analyses of the narrator-hero relationship, see Martine Watson Brownley, "The Narrator in *Oroonoko*," *Essays in Literature* 4 (1977): 174-81; Ferguson, "Juggling the Categories of Race, Class and Gender: Aphra Behn's *Oroonoko*," pp. 165-66; Pearson, "Gender and Narrative in the Fiction of Aphra Behn," part 2, pp. 184-90; Spencer, *The Rise of the Woman Novelist*, pp. 47-52; and Starr, "Aphra Behn and the Genealogy of the Man of Feeling," pp. 362-68.

[38] For a fascinating discussion of the parallels between kingship and textuality in the early modern period, see David Lee Miller, *The Poem's Two Bodies: The Poetics of the 1590 Faerie Queene* (Princeton, NJ: Princeton Univ. Press, 1988).

[39] In 1696 Thomas Southerne turned the story into just such a play, which, in various versions, was a staple of the eighteenth-century repertory.

[40] See, for example, Ernest Bernbaum, "Mrs. Behn's *Oroonoko*," in *Anniversary Papers by Colleagues and Pupils of George Lyman Kittredge* (Boston: Ginn and Co., 1913).

[41] On *Oroonoko*'s relation to heroic drama, see Brown, "The Romance of Empire: *Oroonoko* and the Trade in Slaves," pp. 48-51.

[42] For a description of the blackface characters in the lord mayor's pageants, see Anthony Gerard Barthelemy, *Black Face, Maligned Race: The Representation of Blacks in English Drama from Shakespeare to Southerne* (Baton Rouge: Louisiana State Univ. Press, 1987), chapter 3. For other possible references in Imoinda's iconography, see Ferguson, "Juggling the Categories of Race, Class and Gender: Aphra Behn's *Oroonoko*," p. 181 n. 49.

[43] The Reverend Richard Hakluyt, indeed, calls this kind of African body carving a form of "branched damaske" and says that it takes the place of clothing (*Principal Navigations, Voyages, Traffiques and Discoveries of the English Nation,* 12 vols. [Glasgow: James Maclehose and Sons, 1903-05], vol. 4, p. 62). For other discussions of the insistent physicality of Imoinda and its hint of a conflict between the narrator and this black heroine, see Ballaster, "New Hystericism: Aphra Behn's *Oroonoko*," pp. 290-93; and Ferguson, "Juggling the Categories of Race, Class and Gender: Aphra Behn's *Oroonoko*," pp. 170-71.

[44] I am not arguing here that Oroonoko is supposed to be any particular king or all the Stuarts collectively. Rather, Oroonoko, although he may indeed bring to mind certain Stuarts, is the symbol of an entity that is itself symbolic, kingship, and represents a seventeenth-century revision of that entity. For arguments that detect likeness with the Stuart kings, see Guffey, "Aphra Behn's *Oroonoko*: Occasion and Accomplishment," pp. 3-41; and Brown, "The Romance of Empire: *Oroonoko* and the Trade in Slaves," pp. 57-59.

[45] I give in this paragraph a schematic summary of the intricate and complicated arguments described by Kantorowicz in *The King's Two Bodies* (Princeton, NJ: Princeton Univ. Press, 1957).

[46] See Barthelemy's discussion of the contrast between the heroic white Moor and the villainous black Moor in George Peele's *Battle of Alcazar* (1589), pp. 75-81.

[47] For various accounts of why and how Africans came to be the enslaveable race, see Jordan, *White over Black,* esp. pp. 91-101; Barbara Fields, "Ideology and Race in American History," in *Region, Race, and Reconstruction,* ed. J. Morgan Kousser and James M. McPherson (New York: Oxford Univ. Press, 1982); David Brion Davis, *The Problem of Slavery in Western Culture* (Ithaca, NY: Cornell Univ. Press, 1966), p. 178; and William D. Phillips, Jr., *Slavery from Roman Times to the Early Transatlantic Slave Trade* (Minneapolis: Univ. of Minnesota Press, 1985), p. 184.

[48] The narrator is not always consistent on this point. On at least one occasion she speaks of "Indian slaves," but she seems to use that term loosely as a synonym for "lowly servant." She never describes the commodification of Indians.

[49] In fact, Coramantien was not a country at all but a port on the Gold Coast where the English had a trading station. According to Rogers, though, planters in America generally referred to Gold Coast Africans as Coramantiens (Rogers, "Fact and Fiction in Aphra Behn's *Oroonoko*," p. 6).

[50] For the larger political implications of the debate over money at the end of the seventeenth century, see Joyce Oldham Appleby, *Economic Thought and Ideology in Seventeenth-Century England* (Princeton, NJ: Princeton Univ. Press, 1978), pp. 236-41. Appleby argues that "Locke's denial of the extrinsic value of coin carried with it a limitation of government in economic affairs" (p. 237). She also quotes John Briscoe's 1696 attack on the state's power to fix the value of money, an attack phrased in language peculiarly relevant to *Oroonoko*: "[As] it is a mark of slavery, so is it the means of poverty in a State, where the Magistrate assumes a Power to set what price he pleases on the Publick Coin: It is a sign of Slavery, because the Subject in such Case lives merely at the Mercy of the Prince, is Rich, or Poor, has a Competency, or is a Begger, is a Free-Man, or in Fetters at his Pleasure" (p. 237). . . .

[58] "The Epistle Dedicatory to the Right Honourable the Lord Maitland," in *Oroonoko; or, the Royale Slave: A Critical Edition,* ed. and introd. Adelaide P. Amore (Lanham: Univ. Press of Maryland, 1987), p. 3.

[59] *Capital: A Critique of Political Economy* (New York, 1906), p. 95. See also Walter Benjamin: "[T]he commodity attempts to look itself in the face. It celebrates its becoming human in the whore" ("Central Park," *New German Critique* 34 [Winter 1985]: 42).

David E. Hoegberg (essay date 1995)

SOURCE: "Caesar's Toils: Allusion and Rebellion in *Oroonoko*," in *Eighteenth-Century Fiction*, Vol. 7, No. 3, April, 1995, pp. 239-58.

[*In the essay below, Hoegberg explores the idea of power struggle in* Oroonoko, *noting Behn's allusions to Achilles and Julius Caesar.*]

> But those who came prepared for the business enclosed him on every side, with their naked daggers in their hands. Which way soever he turned he met with blows, and saw their swords levelled at his face and eyes, and was encompassed, like a wild beast in the toils, on every side.[1]
>
> Plutarch's "Life of Caesar"

Included in the new sixth edition of the *Norton Anthology of English Literature,* Aphra Behn's **Oroonoko** has passed a literary milestone, raising anew the question of how it fits into and plays against the literary "canon" it is more and more coming to inhabit. While **Oroonoko**'s literary indebtedness has often been noticed, critics have seldom examined how specific literary allusions contribute to the novel's structure and meaning.[2] Citing English heroic drama and French romance as immediate precursors of Behn's work, they view her either as slavishly derivative or as holding a politically conservative ideology.[3] One view produces a picture of Behn as a marginally competent artist following older models, while the other ignores the possibility that Behn's use of convention might be in part subversive. Its subversion does not lie, however, in portraying successful rebellions against those in power—Oroonoko and Imoinda are defeated both at home and abroad—but in revealing the mechanisms by which power operates, including both physical force and subtle forms of mental or psychological control.[4]

Robert Chibka has already done extensive work on the role of deceit by whites in manipulating Oroonoko,[5] but consciously crafted deceit is only one form of mental control. I would like to extend Chibka's work to consider the role of plot in the novel's structures of domination, not only the plot of **Oroonoko** itself, but the way it alludes to and incorporates preexisting classical narrative models, especially those of Achilles and Julius Caesar. At every stage of his life, Oroonoko is dominated by texts that shape his career in ways he cannot control.[6] While his authority to act as an independent being is wrested from him, the authorship of his life story is complicated by literary allusions so that questions of constraint and freedom become wrapped up with questions of literary indebtedness and originality. In **Oroonoko,** the allusions form a supplement to Behn's text that deepens the analysis of power and its problems. If the main plot tells the story of Oroonoko's struggles against the old king, the English captain, and Byam, the allusions—and the processes of mental control they suggest—tell a story of Oroonoko's struggle against less tangible forces of ideology and belief.

To read Behn's allusions as more than literary homage or political nostalgia we must look beyond the standard heroic qualities associated with each character. When considered in a static or synchronic mode, warrior heroes such as Achilles and Caesar, by virtue of their fighting skill and devotion to honour, often become symbols of aristocratic male virtue. The synchronic view, however, may ignore the narratives or plots that place the hero in relation to other characters and in cultural, geographical, and historical contexts that add complexity to the messages or implied ideologies of the story. (In the *Iliad,* for example, Achilles comes to question some aspects of the aristocratic system he represents. Should he not, therefore, be seen as a symbol of radicalism as well as a warrior hero?) The diachronic view acknowledges contextual elements—webs of relations and changes over time—that make characters more than "stock" figures. The potential for complexity is compounded when heroic narratives become the models or scripts for another character's behaviour, since the weaving of one narrative into another increases the number of contextual variables affecting the "meaning" of the allusion.[7] The allusions can thus be seen as sites of ideological struggle and not only as examples of the dominant ideology against which struggle is mounted.[8]

. . . . .

Before I discuss the first heroic allusion in **Oroonoko,** let me illustrate the more general process of mental control that forms one of the novel's central concerns. Oroonoko's native culture in Coramantien instils in him several important values that function like scripts to limit and shape his actions. We learn that Oroonoko and Imoinda are required by custom to inform the king of their intent to marry: "There is a certain Ceremony in these cases to be observ'd . . . 'twas concluded on both sides, that in obedience to him, the Grandfather was to be first made acquainted with the Design: For they pay a most absolute Resignation to the Monarch, especially when he is a Parent also."[9] The respect they are obliged to pay is accompanied by, or encoded in, a "Ceremony" or model for action, while the king's power arises in part from his ability to manipulate such scripts for his own ends. Influenced by his "Court-Flatterers," he decides he wants Imoinda for himself and turns to another cultural custom, the "Royal Veil" or "Ceremony of Invitation," by which any woman he chooses is "secur'd for the King's Use; and 'tis Death to disobey; besides, held a most impious Disobedience" (p. 140).

In these scenes Behn describes the actions of both parties as tied to ritualized narrative or diachronic patterns known within the culture. Furthermore, these patterns have a certain power over the participants that can override their resistance to specific rulers and events.[10] Oroonoko and Imoinda fall automatically into the "ceremony" of obedience to the king, with no thought that this may be against their interests ultimately. The king takes a more consciously manipulative approach, assessing his interests first and then choosing an appropriate "ceremony." A combination of custom and the king's desire—internal belief and external political power—forms the text that ensures Oroonoko's romantic misery. The intangible bonds hold him more securely than physical bonds, as he recognizes when he cries:

> were she in wall'd Cities, or confin'd from me in Fortifications of the greatest Strength; did Inchantments or Monsters detain her from me; I would venture thro' any Hazard to free her; But here, in the Arms of a feeble old Man, my Youth, my violent Love, my Trade in Arms, and all my vast Desire of Glory, avail me nothing. (p. 142)

The old man's strength lies in his political power, which is linked to his symbolic place within the cultural belief system, and against this Oroonoko is restrained by his own virtuous will, which shuns "impious Disobedience." Even the king's death would not free him from the bonds of custom:

> If I would wait tedious Years; till Fate should bow the old King to his Grave, even that would not leave me *Imoinda* free; but still that Custom that makes it so vile a Crime for a Son to marry his Father's Wives or Mistresses, would hinder my Happiness; unless I would either ignobly set an ill Precedent to my Successors, or abandon my Country, and fly with her to some unknown World who never heard our Story. (pp. 142-43)

Oroonoko sees that he can gain Imoinda only by escaping custom through criminal acts, thus becoming a social outsider, or by fleeing to another "World," something he will do, though not by choice.

Despite his inclination towards obedience, Oroonoko rebels against the king by planning to see Imoinda in secret, but his arrangements are neither well designed nor effective. He is caught making love to Imoinda when he might have been wiser to use the time to escape and, although he has the opportunity to bring her away with him when the king's guards retreat, he leaves her to be punished for his crime.

Oroonoko's motives are hard to fathom here. Even when he chooses rebellion, there is something that steers him towards acquiescence to the king's power, and when he breaks laws, he does not go far enough to secure Imoinda for himself. The outcome of his ill-planned rebellion, therefore, is that Imoinda is more than ever lost to him. Could he not have anticipated this result? Why did he not mount a military coup or escape with her when he had the chance? Such questions can be answered by arguing that it is Behn not Oroonoko who is inept: Oroonoko's reasoning is inscrutable because the narrative here is poorly constructed, and it is poorly constructed because the author cares more about setting up the reunion in Surinam than she does about psychological realism.

I prefer to assume that Behn used the long African section of her novel to make some serious points about the nature of political power. Oroonoko's actions become more plausible if we see here the work of a kind of hegemony that keeps his beliefs and choices within the prevailing discourse of power. According to Antonio Gramsci, hegemony is "the 'spontaneous' consent given by the great masses of the population to the general direction imposed on social life by the dominant fundamental group."[11] The word "spontaneous" is in quotation marks because the consent of the masses is not without cause: it is caused by the prestige of the dominant group, that is, by a pervasive belief in the dominant group's superiority and in the superiority of the laws that protect it. Throughout this section of the novel, custom and law work to fulfil the king's desires and to frustrate Oroonoko's, yet Oroonoko acts like one who believes he can achieve no more than an inconsequential and symbolic resistance. Although he may question specific acts of the king, he neither questions nor flees from the system that gives rise to the king's prestige (and his own).

Behn places her allusion to Achilles in the context of Oroonoko's repeated attempts to circumvent the king's authority without assaulting the underlying belief system. The king sells Imoinda into slavery but tells Oroonoko that he has killed her. Oroonoko's response to the news of Imoinda's "death" is to withdraw from warfare and refuse to fight the king's enemies. This departure from the king's script follows a script of its own drawn not from African culture but from European tradition. In a virtual summary of the *Iliad*, the narrator describes how Oroonoko withdraws from battle after his favourite woman is taken by the king. The chiefs of the army beg him to return to the battlefield, "But he made no other Reply to all their Supplications than this, That he had now no more Business for Glory; and for the World, it was a Trifle not worth his Care" (p. 157). Without him, Oroonoko's troops are routed by the enemy, "who pursued 'em to the very tents" (p. 158). At last Oroonoko enters the battle and turns defeat into victory by fighting, like Achilles, "as if he came on Purpose to die" (p. 159).

Oroonoko cannot escape from one script without entering another. Following Achilles' script, he returns to battle, is reconciled with the king, makes a triumphant return from the wars, and is "belov'd like a Deity" (p. 160), but he has lost the person dearest to him. The allusion to Achilles functions on several levels at once. By further defining Oroonoko's character it both ennobles and confines him. Behn increases our appreciation of Oroonoko's military prowess, and at the same time condemns him to live Achilles' painful life. Did she intend to compliment Oroonoko without understanding the full implications of her allusion? Does her use of a tragic pattern indicate a form of racism that will not allow a black hero to succeed? The context of the allusion I have described suggests that Behn, while she may be racist in other ways, is here concerned to show the difficulties inherent in *any* attempt to resist state power. Harming one's enemies may harm one's friends as well, so that both action and inaction are loaded choices. Achilles and Oroonoko, although from different eras, places, and racial backgrounds, face similar obstacles.

They also share a rather ambiguous political position. Achilles is dissatisfied with his treatment by Agamemmon but has the power to question and retaliate only because he is a strong and respected leader who has benefited in the past from the established system of conquests and rewards. Similarly, Oroonoko's ability to court and claim Imoinda arises from his status as prince, general, and member of the courtly inner circle. Both Oroonoko and Achilles, as men, have privileges that effectively limit the scope of any rebellion they might mount. Disputing over women, they are unlikely to challenge the custom that gives them the right to engage in such disputes in the first place, that is, the commodification of women. While part of the heroism of these figures *is* their questioning of authority, neither story allows for full-scale revolution or social reorganization. One effect of Behn's allusion, therefore, is to deepen rather than simplify our sense of the complexities involved in political struggle, for rebellions take place *in* cultural contexts.

There is also the level of Oroonoko's consciousness to be considered. He has been educated in European ways, can converse in French, English, and Spanish, and "knew almost as much as if he had read much" (p. 135). Imitating Achilles may, therefore, be a conscious choice. If so, it is interesting that he chooses a European hero to imitate, as if, having exhausted the options offered by his own culture, he were searching for a new, more effective script. Achilles' script brings him glory. Immersing himself in the male world of camps and battles, he begins to overcome his grief, but he does not gain political or romantic power. Although he tries to act independently, Oroonoko is not in control of his own destiny, but is subjugated by alien texts.

. . . . .

Oroonoko's return and reconciliation with the king coincide with the arrival of the English ship and the beginning of a new phase in his career. Now a colonial power replaces the domestic state power in Oroonoko's life, functioning in a similar way but with more horrifying results. Like the king, the captain uses deceit to maintain power over Oroonoko, and Behn shows that colonial power also has a subtle literary or narrative dimension. At the moment of Oroonoko's capture by the captain, the narrator adds another text to the list of those confining Oroonoko. She writes: "It may be easily guess'd, in what Manner the Prince resented this Indignity, who may be best resembled to a Lion taken in a Toil; so he raged, so he struggled for Liberty, but all in vain" (p. 162). The figure of a lion in toils has a complex literary history that must have been familiar to Behn. It is an allusion to Plutarch's "Life of Julius Caesar," which appeared in a new translation between 1683 and 1686. Describing Caesar's assassination by the senators, Plutarch says that Caesar "was encompassed, like a wild beast in the toils, on every side" (p. 892). Although Oroonoko will not be dubbed "Caesar" by his white owner until he arrives in Surinam, Behn suggests that, from the moment of his capture, he is already caught up in Caesar's script. Plutarch's image of a beast in toils occurs at Caesar's death, but Behn uses the allusion early in her story, thereby suggesting that Oroonoko's end is already written at the time of his capture. For Oroonoko, to be renamed "Caesar" is to have his life symbolically rewritten. Thereafter, try as he might to rebel, he plays the part in a white colonial drama of one who is too strong and dangerous a leader to be trusted, whose popularity with the masses threatens those in power. Like Julius Caesar, Oroonoko will be undone, not only by enemies, but also by those who appear to be his friends and, like Caesar, he will be remembered as a martyr defeated not by honourable battle but by treachery.

This allusion has another source, which provides a colonial parallel to Oroonoko's predicament. In act one, scene two of Dryden's *The Indian Emperour,* Montezuma, King of the Aztecs, observes that he is surrounded by romantic enemies, the result of involvements that he, his two sons, and his daughter have with relatives of his old antagonists in *The Indian Queen,* Zempoalla and Traxalla: "My Lyon-heart is with Loves toyls beset, / Strugling I fall still deeper in the net."[12] No sooner has he spoken than he learns that he is surrounded by military enemies as well. A guard enters and announces that the Spaniards, led by Cortez, have surrounded them. Montezuma and his group are "compast round" (line 196) and "inclos'd" (line 204) by "swarming bands / Of ambush'd men" (lines 193-94). Although Montezuma had used the "toyl" metaphor in the context of love, events on stage show that it is also an accurate description of colonialism, as he is caught simultaneously in the net of love and in the net of Cortez's conquest.

Although Dryden may have had Plutarch in mind when he used this image,[13] there is no other evidence in the play suggesting a parallel between Montezuma and Caesar. It fell to Behn to link these two heroes to Oroonoko by means of an image that could be traced back to both texts. Her explicit use of the name "Caesar" suggests that Plutarch is the more important of the two predecessors, yet Dryden's play may have given Behn ideas about depicting a colonial struggle in literature. Like Oroonoko, Montezuma is a strong leader who resists enslavement and, although he scoffs at the Spaniards' religious rhetoric, always acts honourably towards his enemies. Dryden interweaves gender and colonial conflicts in his play in a way Behn might also have found useful. Finally, Dryden contrives to have the lion-in-toils simile enacted onstage when Montezuma is tied up and tortured by the priest; as we shall see, Behn uses a similar technique at the end of her work.

As if this were not enough, Behn herself had used a similar image in 1677 in a play entitled ***Abdelazer; or, The Moor's Revenge.*** Its titular hero is prince of the north African kingdom of Fez, which has been conquered by Spain, its king having been killed and Abdelazer taken captive to Spain. Although he is treated well by the Spanish king and becomes a general, he nevertheless refers to his captivity as "Slavery"[14] and tries to avenge himself by claiming not only the throne of Fez but also that of Spain. Through a combination of martial prowess and court intrigue he almost succeeds but is captured by the Spaniards and executed. Just before he is stabbed to death, Abdelazer says:

> As humble Huntsmen do the generous Lion;
> Now thou darst see me lash my Sides, and
>   roar,
> And bite my Snare in vain; . . .
> And like that noble Beast, though thus
>   betray'd,
> I've yet an awful Fierceness in my Looks,
> Which makes thee fear t'approach; and 'tis at
>   distance
> That thou dar'st kill me; for come but in my
>   reach,
> And with one Grasp I wou'd confound thy
>   Hopes.
>
> (p. 96)

The similarity to the threats Oroonoko hurls at his hunters before being taken in the woods and to the stabbing of Caesar is obvious.

To say that Behn associates this image with the exercise of colonial power is not to say that she always sympathizes with the colonized: Abdelazer is guilty of several moral outrages that mitigate his claim to justice, and the narrator's ambivalence towards Oroonoko has been well documented.[15] Yet in both these images, and especially in ***Oroonoko,*** Behn is searching for a way to express not only the rage of the colonial victim but also the pervasive nature of the encompassing power, which is represented by the snare or net. By moving the image to the beginning of Oroonoko's captivity, as in Dryden, rather than placing it at the end, as in Plutarch and ***Abdelazer,*** she emphasizes the scripted nature of Oroonoko's slavery, its tendency to follow an existing pattern to a preordained conclusion.

Instead of the word "snare," she employs the less common "toil," used also by Plutarch and Dryden. A look at the etymology of this word may help to explain her choice. The English word "toil" for a hunter's net comes from the Old French *toile* and the Latin *tela,* both meaning a web or net. Other words that come from the same Indo-European root-syllable are "text," from the Latin *texere,* to weave, and "technology," from the Greek *tekhne,* art, craft, or skill.[16] Etymology shows the conceptual links between linguistic or narrative skill (textuality), physical skill (technology), and military aggression (hunting), thereby deepening Behn's allusion. When used as a hunter's tool, the toil ensnares the unsuspecting victim, symbolizing the hunter's power over his prey and his disguise, since toils are always hidden. By analogy, the toil suggests the colonialists' ability to hide their selfish and acquisitive motives behind language that appears benign and selfless, as seen in the captain's actions. It represents also the power of texts or narratives to shape proceedings in a colonial situation—the web of words used to ensnare Oroonoko includes not just the deceit practised by the captain and Byam but also the name "Caesar" and the biography that goes with it. All three aspects of the word may be seen in the captain's capture of Oroonoko.

Caesar's political position, like that of Achilles, is complex. His ambition to become dictator rested upon successful foreign conquests, which gave him the wealth necessary to buy influence and popular support and to make his army intensely loyal. Similarly, Oroonoko's threat to colonial power in Surinam is possible because he has won the loyalty and admiration of the other slaves, who constitute a majority of the population.[17] His symbolic status stems from the power he used to conquer and sell them into slavery in the first place. The ideological contradictions that critics have noticed in the text appear in the allusions as well.[18] That Behn complains about the unjust power used against Oroonoko and Caesar without questioning the colonial power that they also used illustrates a limitation of her critique, but does not entirely undermine it. Her allusions to Achilles and Caesar glorify a certain kind of resistance to unjust rule staged from positions within the aristocracy. At the same time, Oroonoko's ultimate failure—and that of his literary models—indicates Behn's pessimism about the very resistance she praises.

The script of Julius Caesar's life does not account for every detail of Oroonoko's captivity, but it does provide a trajectory for it. He is kept on the trajectory by his enemies and ostensible friends, who do not intend to deceive him, but who are also subject to the hegemony of colonial ideology. Trefry names Oroonoko "Caesar" in homage to Oroonoko's nobility of birth and demeanour and later professes his "Abhorrence" (p. 168) at Oroonoko's capture and promises to free him, but good intentions cannot prevent Caesar's fate from overcoming Oroonoko. Since, as we have seen from the position of the lion-in-toils image, Oroonoko is *already* living Caesar's life, Trefry's homage implies his unwitting consent to the direction imposed by the colonial powers.

The narrator plays a similar role in colonial events, declaring herself Oroonoko's ally yet participating in his subjection. She says she "entertained" Oroonoko and Imoinda "with the Lives of the *Romans,* and great Men, which charmed him to my Company; and her, with teaching her all the pretty Works that I was Mistress of, and telling her Stories of Nuns, and endeavoring to bring her to the Knowledge of the true God" (p. 175). While Oroonoko does not like the narrator's proselytizing, the other entertainments seem pleasant enough to him, yet the word "charmed" here suggests that there is a mechanism at work which he does not see, a kind of narrative magic charm that casts its spell on him. By telling stories about the "Lives of the *Romans,*"[19] the narrator teaches Oroonoko the significance of his new name and of his lines in the white script that will end with his death. Whether the narrator intends it or not, the effect is the same. Although she claims to be on their side, her "entertainment" of Oroonoko and Imoinda gives them clearly circumscribed places in the colonial system. In this respect she is similar to the "Cast-Mistresses" of Coramantien, who assist the king in the education and control of his sexual servants.

A similar point can be made about the narrator's activities as a writer. She excuses the practice of renaming slaves on the grounds that their native names are "likely very barbarous, and hard to pronounce" (p. 169). Trefry's choice of "Caesar" she finds especially appropriate because it

> will live in that Country as long as that (scarce more) glorious one of the great *Roman:* for 'tis most evident he wanted no Part of the personal Courage of that *Caesar,* and acted Things as memorable, had they been done in some Part of the World replenished with People and Historians, that might have given him his Due. (p. 169)

Here the narrator begins to lament that Oroonoko's story will not be as well known as Caesar's. His due, she feels, is to become famous for the martyrdom he has suffered. Unable to save Oroonoko, the narrator wants at least to make his sufferings and accomplishments known. "But his Misfortune was, to fall in an obscure World, that afforded only a Female Pen to celebrate his Fame" (p. 169). The use of a modesty trope indicates that Oroonoko is confined by the text of the novel itself.[20] The narrator hopes to establish Oroonoko as Caesar's equal by writing his "Life," thus liberating him from Plutarch's text and giving him one inscribed with his own name. But she fears that her biography, written by a "mere" female, is doomed to obscurity, censure, or both. There is an uneasy relationship here between racial and gender prejudices: through literary skill the narrator may be able to overcome her readers' prejudice against black protagonists, but her skill cannot change the fact of her own femaleness. Oroonoko, in his literary reincarnation, will thus continue to suffer the neglect and confinement that characterized his life, not because of racism, but because the narrator is confined in a sexist literary power structure.

The narrator's next sentence confirms her declaration of textual impotence. "For the future therefore I must call *Oroonoko Caesar;* since by that Name only he was known in our Western World" (p. 169). She "must" call Oroonoko by the name that entangles him in the white drama, the word "therefore" connecting this necessity causally to the foregoing discussion of female inferiority, as if she, too, were caught in the colonial script and contributed to his sufferings because powerless to do otherwise. Thereafter, Oroonoko's original name does not appear in the text except when he uses it. The narrator's subjection to the narrative convention of naming mirrors her subjection to the political system in Surinam, and henceforth she plays a dual role in the text, as advocate for the downtrodden prince and as participant in the prejudice and distrust that ensure his final defeat. Like Brutus in Plutarch's narrative, she has Oroonoko's "intire Confidence" (p. 177), but she turns out to be part of the conspiracy against him.

The narrator is a key figure in the "Actions and Sports" (p. 176) that the whites use as "Diversions" to turn Oroonoko's mind and energies away from rebellion. These activities serve white colonial interests by making the land safer for colonization. Oroonoko kills a tiger that had stolen a cow and another that had "long infested that Part, and borne away abundance of Sheep and Oxen, and other Things, that were for the Support of those to whom they belong'd" (p. 181). He also catches one of the dreaded "Numb-Eels," which were supposed to render someone unconscious merely by a touch of the bait on his fishing line (pp. 182-83). The shift here from human interaction to combat against monsters suggests the use of another narrative model, Hercules' twelve labours, often taken as civilizing actions to subdue the savage and monstrous elements of the Mediterranean world. The script of Hercules, like that of Achilles, ennobles Oroonoko by endowing him with superhuman strength. It also helps to disarm his otherness by giving it a familiar literary form and by directing his violence away from the monstrosity of slavery itself. Hercules, however, performed his most famous exploits at the command and in the interests of another and, like Oroonoko, he was caught in debasing servitude to an unworthy master.[21] The allusion to Hercules is thus not merely conservative in its ideological thrust; it highlights the exploitation by whites of Oroonoko's labour. The ideological conflict in this allusion centres on Hercules' dual role in relation to acts of exploitation. Each successful labour proves the injustice of his enslavement, but each act also kills or subordinates another being whose right to autonomy is never entertained. Similarly, Oroonoko's Herculean adventures separate him from savage native elements which he tames (including the disgruntled Amerindian villagers) and from other African slaves left behind on plantations, thus proving his right to freedom by showing his "legitimate" superiority over those who will remain enslaved.

. . . . .

The colonial diversion, with its Herculean overtones, is presented as a narrative "Digression" (p. 189), showing once again that Oroonoko cannot leave one script without entering another. The last part of the novel recounts Oroonoko's attempted rebellion against the scripts in which he has become entangled. As in Coramantien, the rebellion has two phases, an overt "criminal" act of defiance that fails, followed by his sullen withdrawal from society. Oroonoko rouses his fellow slaves to mutiny, but, as in Coramantien, there are problems with his plan. Although his rhetoric is high-flown, he does not appreciate the practical obstacles to a successful escape. A slave named Tuscan warns him that the women and children are "unfit for Travel in those unpassable Woods, Mountains and Bogs" that surround them (p. 191). Oroonoko's response is theoretical; he tells them "That Honour [is] the first Principle in Nature" (p. 191) and that "the more Danger the more Glory" (p. 192). Attempting to encourage the slaves, he cites the example of Hannibal, "a great Captain, [who] had cut his Way through Mountains of solid Rocks" (p. 192). Oroonoko has learned well the "Lives of the *Romans,* and great Men" (p. 175) taught him by the narrator, but Hannibal is an inauspicious choice since his efforts, too, were doomed: he crossed the Alps but failed to achieve his goal of conquering Rome.[22] In mentioning Hannibal Oroonoko invokes another script for heroic failure.

The pitiful white militia defeats the slaves not by superior force but by "perplexing" them. Their whips inflict pain but are not deadly. Whips also have a symbolic value, however, which the English augment by crying out *"Yield and Live! Yield, and be Pardon'd!"* as they fight (p. 194). As in Herodotus, where the Scythians resort to whips to put down a slave revolt, the use of whips forces the Africans to "remember they are slaves" and causes them to lose courage.[23] The whites also attack their eyes and faces to demoralize them further (p. 194), a tactic Julius Caesar himself is said to have used successfully against Pompey's cavalry.[24]

In this victory, hegemony is again a factor. Language and symbols are the primary colonial weapons: victory by the whites is complete when Byam makes "use of all his Art of Talking and Dissembling" to obtain Oroonoko's surrender (p. 195). Oroonoko is not at first convinced by Byam's professed deference, but Trefry, himself deceived into "believing the Governor to mean what he said" (p. 196), makes the decisive plea, again becoming an unwitting instrument of the colonialist cause. The narrator's failure to prevent the treacherous whipping of Oroonoko follows a similar pattern. She fears, with other whites, that Oroonoko will come and "cut all our Throats," even though he has specifically promised that he "would act nothing upon the *White* People" (p. 176). She distrusts that promise, she says earlier, because of his "rough and fierce" spirit, a view that now helps to cause her absence at a crucial moment.

Equally prejudicial is the immediate division of the white camp along gender lines: the "Females," accepting their role as weaker beings, "fly down the River, to be secured." While the narrator says that she has "Authority" to preserve Oroonoko, her actions place her firmly within the female stereotype. Her betrayal comes from those deep-seated aspects of culture that are hardest to shed. Oroonoko's suffering may thus be said in a broad way to be caused by the prejudice of European culture against blacks and women. The narrator's "spontaneous" consent to the male-dominated system helps to perpetuate Oroonoko's subjection in the colonial system. The subtle, unconscious workings of hegemony explain why she believes she has "Authority" when, in fact, she does not.

With the failure of his first plan, Oroonoko begins to plot a more radical escape through death. He also plans to "take a dire Revenge" on Byam for subjecting him to the *"contemptible Whip"* instead of merely killing him, proof that the whip's symbolic value is not lost upon Oroonoko: "No, I would not kill myself, even after a Whipping, but will be content to live with that Infamy, and be pointed at by every grinning Slave, till I have completed my Revenge;

and then you shall see, that *Oroonoko* scorns to live with the Indignity that was put on *Caesar*" (p. 199). This is the first time Oroonoko's original name has appeared in the text for some thirty pages and it comes as a bolt of lightning. It shows for the first time that he distinguishes between his two identities of prince and slave. One is a maker of dramas, the other a character in someone else's drama. As Oroonoko begins to compose a script to compete with the powerful white script, he reclaims his former name in a symbolic attempt to summon his princely power. "The Indignity that was put on *Caesar*" is not only the indignity of whipping, it is also the indignity of treacherous assassination. Oroonoko's new script will be a script of suicide to pre-empt the script of assassination already composed for him by the colonists. His ultimate failure to escape Caesar's toils indicates how deeply he is bound in the colonial net.

After Oroonoko reclaims his former name, he begins to re-enact sections of his African life. In addition to imitating other literature, Behn's novel now begins to imitate itself, as if Oroonoko's earlier life as a prince, which has already become the stuff of legends enjoyed by the narrator, Trefry, and others in Surinam, has become a script to be reused. As we might expect, Oroonoko is no more successful now than he was then. After he has killed Imoinda, he wastes himself in grief and remorse:

> He remained in this deplorable Condition for two Days, and never rose from the Ground where he had made her sad Sacrifice. . . . but offering to rise, he found his Strength so decay'd, that he reeled to and fro, like Boughs assailed by contrary Winds; so that he was forced to lie down again, and try to summon all his Courage to his Aid. He found his Brains turned round, and his Eyes were dizzy, and Objects appear'd not the same to him they were wont to do. (pp. 203-4)

His condition here parallels directly the Iliadic episode, mentioned above, in which Oroonoko, believing Imoinda to be dead, languishes "for two Days, without permitting any Sustenance to approach him" (p. 158), yet when he rises to do battle he is able to do "such Things as will not be believed that human Strength could perform" (p. 159). In both cases, Oroonoko is certain his beloved is dead and starves himself, but in the second instance his original strength and determination have been eroded by the ordeal of slavery. Both his body and his "Brains" fail him this time, suggesting that the colonists' linguistic weapons, deceptions, and whipping have affected his mind. In spite of himself, he has internalized the colonists' view of himself as their inferior.[25]

Whereas Oroonoko's Achillean script was partially successful in Coramantien, here it is disastrous. Achilles himself had the favour of gods who could "distil nectar inside his chest, and delicate / ambrosia, so the weakness of hunger [would] not come upon him," but Oroonoko has no such protecting deities. Thetis promises to preserve Patroklos's dead body from decay while Achilles takes his revenge upon Hektor,[26] but Oroonoko's enemies discover him by the "Stink" of Imoinda's decaying body (p. 204).

As the search party surrounds him, he grasps wildly for narrative models, finding three different ones from different parts of his past. The image of a dizzy and weak Oroonoko warning his pursuers to "approach no nearer, if they would be safe" (p. 204) and that *"Fatal will be the Attempt of the first Adventurer"* (p. 205) is a pathetic re-enactment of the scene in which Oroonoko leaps naked from Imoinda's bed, grabs a nearby battleaxe, and promises "the certain Death of him that first enters" (p. 153). This time his attackers are not scared off but merely delayed. Once again the whites rely on language more than on action, entreating Oroonoko to give himself up while they keep a safe distance (p. 205). As he holds off the whites, who approach him like hunters surrounding a lion, he "cut a Piece of Flesh from his own Throat, and threw it at 'em" (p. 205), in imitation of yet another heroic script, this time taken from the culture he observed on his visit to the Indian village.[27] Finally, he imitates the tiger he himself had killed during his "Herculean" adventures, who "feebly wounded him" in the thigh with her claws as she died (p. 180); Oroonoko can only wound Tuscan feebly in the arm before falling completely into the hunters' power (p. 206). His capture in this manner provides a graphic staging of the lion-in-toils simile, itself an echo of Plutarch's description of the death of Caesar, thus re-enacting and completing his subjection to the role of Caesar written for him by his masters.

By killing Oroonoko, the whites ironically give him exactly what he wants. The "Barbaric" Bannister does what all Oroonoko's well-meaning friends are unable to do: he liberates the slave from his hated captivity. Behn suggests that the actions of the whites backfire another way: the "rude and wild . . . Rabble" and the "inhuman . . . Justices" who presided at Oroonoko's execution, she says, "after paid dear enough for their Insolence" (p. 208), implying that some power, perhaps the Lord Governour when he finally arrived, made them atone for their crimes. The passage corresponds to one in Plutarch's "Life of Caesar":

> But the great genius which attended [Caesar] throughout his lifetime even after his death remained as the avenger of his murder, pursuing through every sea and land all those who were concerned in it, and suffering none to escape, but reaching all who in any sort or kind were either actually engaged in the fact, or by their counsels any way promoted it.[28]

By condemning Oroonoko to the fate of Caesar, the whites also condemn themselves to the fate of Caesar's enemies, unconsciously admitting their guilt. While "Caesar" may be subject to their power, they are themselves subject to a divine principle of justice that pursues and finally punishes them. Behn suggests that Caesar's toils return to ensnare the hunters, subjecting them to a part of the text they perhaps did not read carefully enough.

. . . . .

There remain several different levels on which we can read Behn's literary allusions. The allusions are the most striking examples of a process of "scripting" that goes on throughout the novel, in which those in power shape the lives of those they dominate by means other than what Gramsci would call "direct control." Whether the narrative model is a famous story, a ritualized "ceremony," or a new pattern composed by the powerful for a specific situation, some degree of hegemony or "spontaneous" consent appears to be involved on the part of Oroonoko and his friends. In Oroonoko's case this can be seen in those actions he consciously controls: his plan of seeing Imoinda in private, his withdrawal from the battle, and his impractical plan for the slave mutiny are actions where he displays an internal lack of will, judgment, or foresight. In situations beyond Oroonoko's control, such as the whipping, execution, and imposition of Caesar's name and biography upon him, hegemony can be seen most clearly in his allies. When the narrator and Trefry help to keep Oroonoko subdued, they are involved unknowingly in colonial machinery. The failure of acts of resistance is due as much to internal factors as to external force or control. The allusions suggest that it is difficult for people to think and act independently of the cultural biases and patterns that surround them, whether they are natives of the culture in question or displaced aliens. Allusions are a particularly appropriate means of making this point, since they force readers to rely on prior knowledge that is usually acquired from the same education and cultural indoctrination that gave rise to the hegemony.

If hegemony is effective, it may be argued, then Behn's message is essentially conservative. Behn's Toryism and her refusal to criticize slavery have been widely acknowledged, and the evidence discussed here could be used to bolster that view of her. She may evoke our sympathies for Oroonoko, but the failure of his attempted rebellions establishes a pattern that begins to carry the weight of destiny. The pattern of failure could reassure a white, aristocratic audience that such uprisings are always doomed and that, while subjects and slaves may have legitimate complaints, they can never really change the status quo.

To portray the mechanics of power, however, is in some sense to criticize them, even when no solution is offered. The detail with which Behn depicts the multiple and subtle means of control used on Oroonoko and his friends works against the continuing effectiveness of such control, for if hegemony depends upon belief, then it can be upset by changes in belief fostered by literature. The subversive potential in the novel is emphasized if we interpret it not as a modified romance to entertain aristocratic readers but as an extended disquisition on the nature of power both domestic and colonial. I have called for a consideration of Oroonoko's predecessors not as figures but as narratives. All the men are great aristocratic warriors, but all are also caught in complex webs of power and engaged in political struggle. Their stories can therefore be said to have power and rebellion as their main subject. Behn uncovers a tradition of resistance in the midst of the literary tradition, although, as I have suggested, it does not extend to those on the lowest rungs of society.

Furthermore, although none of the heroes can usurp authority for himself, each is the beneficiary of an apotheosis of sorts after death. According to legend, after his death at the hands of Deianira, Hercules was made a god by Zeus. By an act of senate after his death, Julius Caesar was worshipped as a god in Rome. Achilles, though not deified, enjoys a reputation for greater virtue, cunning, and strength than Agamemnon, as a result of Homer's contrasting characterization of the two.[29] Thus in some sense all three heroes triumph over their oppressors. Each story contains a coda in which previously inescapable powers, including death itself, are re-evaluated and shown to be malleable.

As we have seen, Oroonoko's story has a similar coda hinting at the later downfall of his oppressors. In the final paragraph the narrator hopes that Oroonoko's "glorious Name" will, along with Imoinda's, "survive to all Ages" (p. 208). In light of the other narrative models, this plea for lasting fame may be read as a call for a re-evaluation of the power structures that doomed Oroonoko to failure.

Notes

[1] Plutarch, *Lives of the Noble Grecians and Romans* trans. John Dryden, revised by Arthur Hugh Clough (New York: Modern Library, 1932), p. 892.

[2] Exceptions include Adelaide P. Amore on the parallels between Oroonoko and Christ in her introduction to Aphra Behn, *Oroonoko, or, The Royal Slave: A Critical Edition,* ed. Adelaide P. Amore (Lanham, New York, and London: University Press of America, 1987), pp. xxxii-xxxiii; Laura Brown on the links to literature memorializing Charles I in "The Romance of Empire: *Oroonoko* and the Trade in Slaves," *The New Eigh-*

teenth Century, ed. Felicity Nussbaum and Laura Brown (New York and London: Methuen, 1987), pp. 57-59; and Margaret Ferguson on the parallels with Shakespeare's *Othello* in "Juggling the Categories of Race, Class and Gender: Aphra Behn's *Oroonoko,*" *Women's Studies* 19 (1991), 169-73.

[3] See Martine Watson Brownley, "The Narrator in *Oroonoko,*" *Essays in Literature: Western Illinois University* 4 (1977), 174-81; Katherine M. Rogers, "Fact and Fiction in Aphra Behn's *Oroonoko,*" *Studies in the Novel* 20 (Spring 1988), 1-15; William C. Spengemann, "The Earliest American Novel: Aphra Behn's *Oroonoko,*" *Nineteenth-Century Fiction* 38 (1984), 384-414; Rose A. Zimbardo, "Aphra Behn in Search of the Novel," *Studies in Eighteenth-Century Culture* 19 (1989), 277-87.

[4] My distinction here is similar to one between "direct control" and "hegemony" made by Antonio Gramsci, "The Intellectuals," *Selections from the Prison Notebooks,* ed. and trans. Quintin Hoare and Geoffrey Nowell Smith (New York: International Publishers, 1971), p. 12.

[5] Robert L. Chibka, "'Oh! Do Not Fear a Woman's Invention': Truth, Falsehood, and Fiction in Aphra Behn's *Oroonoko,*" *Texas Studies in Literature and Language* 30 (Winter 1988), 510-37.

[6] Sandra M. Gilbert and Susan Gubar discuss the idea that authors are owners and masters of the characters in their texts in *The Madwoman in the Attic: The Woman Writer and the Nineteenth-Century Literary Imagination* (New Haven and London: Yale University Press, 1979), p. 7.

[7] My use of the terms "synchronic" and "diachronic" as well as the idea of well-known myths as "scripts" that can shape social interaction is influenced by the work of Victor Turner, *Dramas, Fields, and Metaphors: Symbolic Action in Human Society* (Ithaca and London: Cornell University Press, 1974), especially pp. 35-36 and p. 123.

[8] I am here taking issue with Laura Brown where she argues that "In Behn's text 'reductive normalizing' is carried out through literary convention, and specifically through that very convention most effectively able to fix and codify the experience of radical alterity, the arbitrary love and honor codes of heroic romance" (p. 49). Mary Louise Pratt's essay, from which the phrase "reductive normalizing" is taken, makes a distinction between "informational" and "experiential" discourses that is similar to the synchronic/diachronic distinction I employ. The typical way of normalizing the colonial native is to reduce him/her to a static list of "manners and customs." Experiential narratives may be equally reductive, Pratt argues, but have a greater potential for

parody, dialogism, and critique because they portray "situated human subjects" (p. 150). See Pratt, "Scratches on the Face of the Country; or, What Mr. Barrow Saw in the Land of the Bushmen," in *"Race," Writing, and Difference,* ed. Henry Louis Gates, Jr. (Chicago: University of Chicago Press, 1986), pp. 138-62.

[9] Aphra Behn, *Oroonoko, The Works of Aphra Behn,* vol. 5, ed. Montague Summers (New York: Benjamin Blom, 1915), p. 139. References are to this edition.

[10] See Turner: "Religious myths—and their episodic components—[can] constitute dramatic or narrative process models which so influence social behavior that it acquires a strange processual inevitability overriding questions of interest, expediency, or even morality" (p. 122).

[11] Gramsci, p. 12.

[12] *The Works of John Dryden,* ed. Edward Niles Hooker and H. T. Swedenberg, Jr. (Berkeley: University of California Press, 1956-), vol. 9 (1966), I.ii.182-83. Further references in the text are to line numbers of this scene.

[13] See James Winn, *John Dryden and His World* (New Haven and London: Yale University Press, 1987), p. 388, for Dryden's contribution to the translation of Plutarch's *Lives.*

[14] Aphra Behn, *Abdelazer; or, The Moor's Revenge,* vol. 2 of *Works,* p. 14. As lines are not numbered in this edition, references are to page numbers. Cf. Margaret Ferguson's article above, which first directed me to this play (p. 179n31).

[15] In addition to Brown, Chibka, and Margaret Ferguson, see for example Moira Ferguson, *Subject to Others: British Women Writers and Colonial Slavery, 1670-1834* (New York: Routledge, 1992), chap. 2; Wylie Sypher, *Guinea's Captive Kings: British Anti-Slavery Literature of the XVIIIth Century* (Chapel Hill: University of North Carolina Press, 1942), pp. 110-13; Michael Echeruo, *The Conditioned Imagination from Shakespeare to Conrad* (New York: Holmes and Meier, 1978), p. 80.

[16] See the *OED,* s.v. "toil" and *The American Heritage Dictionary,* Appendix of Indo-European Roots, s.v. "teks-."

[17] The concern of white colonists over the power of a multitude parallels that of Caesar's adversaries in Plutarch's narrative. At one point, Caesar is elected high priest over Catulus and Isauricus: "When the votes were taken, [Caesar] carried it, and excited among the senate and nobility great alarm lest he might now urge on the people to every kind of insolence" (Plutarch, p. 858).

[18] Margaret Ferguson finds that Oroonoko and the narrator are "both victims and beneficiaries of the international system of the slave trade" (pp. 168-69); Moira Ferguson notes the irony of Oroonoko's "temporary identification with slaves whom he may have originally sold into slavery" (p. 31) and discusses other ways in which the novel is complicated by class distinctions. The point is also discussed in Stephanie Athey and Daniel Cooper Alarcon, "*Oroonoko*'s Gendered Economies of Honor/Horror: Reframing Colonial Discourse Studies in the Americas," *American Literature* 65 (Sept. 1993), 437.

[19] Some editions of *Oroonoko* print "Loves of the *Romans.*" See for example *Oroonoko,* ed. Lore Metzger (London and New York: Norton, 1973), p. 46. Mary Vermillion notes that only "Lives" is consistent with the first edition of *Oroonoko* published in 1688; see "Buried Heroism: Critiques of Female Authorship in Southerne's Adaptation of Behn's *Oroonoko,*" *Restoration: Studies in English Literary Culture, 1660-1700* 16 (1992), 37n13. Although "Loves" indicates a more specific type of story, it does not alter my point.

[20] Behn used this kind of deference ironically, both here and in other works, to assert her superiority; see Larry Carver "Aphra Behn: The Poet's Heart in a Woman's Body," *Papers on Language and Literature* 14 (1978), 414-24; Judith Kegan Gardiner, "Aphra Behn: Sexuality and Self-Respect," *Women's Studies* 7:1/2 (1980), 67-78. Gilbert and Gubar discuss the "bitter irony" of such poses when used by female writers (p. 62).

[21] For an outline of Hercules' story, see Apollodorus, *The Library,* trans. James George Frazer (Cambridge: Harvard University Press, 1921), II.iv-II.vii. Hercules' comment to Odysseus in *Odyssey* 11 is also relevant here: "For I was son of Kronian Zeus, but I had an endless spell of misery. I was made bondman to one who was far worse than I, and he loaded my difficult labors on me"; see *The Odyssey of Homer,* trans. Richmond Lattimore (New York: Harper and Row, 1965), p. 184. For a translation that predates Behn, see that of George Chapman in *Chapman's Homer: The Iliad, the Odyssey, and the Lesser Homerica,* ed. Allardyce Nicoll (New York: Pantheon, 1956). For further discussion of transformations of the Hercules model in the sixteenth and seventeenth centuries, see Eugene M. Waith, *The Herculean Hero in Marlowe, Chapman, Shakespeare, and Dryden* (New York: Columbia University Press, 1962).

[22] On Hannibal see Plutarch, pp. 213-32, 372-88.

[23] Herodotus, *The Histories,* trans. Aubrey de Selincourt (New York: Penguin Books, 1954), book 4, p. 272.

[24] Plutarch, p. 881.

[25] Athey and Alarcon also discuss the parallels between these two scenes, but they focus on the acts of violation that precede the arrival of Oroonoko's pursuers (p. 436).

[26] Homer, *Iliad,* trans. Richmond Lattimore (Chicago: University of Chicago Press, 1951), book 19, pp. 401, 392-93.

[27] Soldiers competing for the "Generalship" in war cut off their own noses, lips, and eyes, says the narrator, "so they slash on 'till one gives out, and many have dy'd in this Debate. And it's by a passive Valour they shew and prove their Activity" (p. 188).

[28] Plutarch, p. 894.

[29] See Apollodorus, II.vii.7; Plutarch, p. 893; and Homer, *Odyssey,* book 24. In book 24 of the *Odyssey* Achilles has a chance to gloat a bit when he says to the soul of Agamemnon that his political status as "lord over numerous people" did not prevent him from suffering an early and inglorious death. Agamemnon then goes on to describe the grand funeral of Achilles, at which both gods and mortals mourned and brought gifts even greater than those normally reserved for a king's funeral (Lattimore translation, pp. 346-47).

FURTHER READING

Baker, Ernest A. "Mrs. Behn and Some English Anti-Romances." In *The History of the English Novel, Volume III: The Later Romances and the Establishment of Realism,* pp. 79-106. New York: Barnes & Noble, 1950.

Provides an overview of Behn's career and argues that *Oroonoko* "has made a ... mark on literary history by virtue of the humanitarian feeling that pervades it."

Ballaster, Ros. "New Hystericism: Aphra Behn's *Oroonoko*: The Body, the Text, and the Feminist Critic." In *New Feminist Discourses: Critical Essays on Theories and Texts,* edited by Isobel Armstrong, pp. 283-95. London and New York: Routledge, 1992.

Argues that the literary criticism of *Oroonoko* has shaped contemporary feminist criticism.

Chikba, Robert L. "'Oh! Do Not Fear a Woman's Invention': Truth, Falsehood, and Fiction in Aphra Behn's *Oroonoko.*" *Texas Studies in Literature and Language* 30, No. 4 (Winter 1988): 510-37.

Argues that the question of validity in *Oroonoko* blurs its significance as fiction depicting ideology.

Duffy, Maureen. "*Oroonoko.*" In *The Passionate Shepherdess: Aphra Behn, 1640-89*, pp. 269-83. London: Methuen, 1989.

Discusses the political context in which *Oroonoko* was written.

Ferguson, Margaret W. "Juggling the Categories of Race, Class, and Gender: Aphra Behn's *Oroonoko.*" *Women's Studies* 19, No. 2 (1991): 159-81.

Discusses the role of gender, race, and class in Behn's depiction of power relations in *Oroonoko*.

Guffey, George. "Aphra Behn's *Oroonoko*: Occasion and Accomplishment." In *Two English Novelists: Aphra Behn and Anthony Trollope, Papers Read at a Clark Library Seminar, May 11, 1974*, edited by George Guffey and Andrew Wright, pp. 3-41. Los Angeles: University of California, Los Angeles, 1975.

Considers the political ramifications of *Oroonoko*.

Hill, Rowland M. "Aphra Behn's Use of Setting." *Modern Language Quarterly* 7, No. 2 (June 1946): 189-203.

Remarks on Behn's attempts to achieve realism in her works through her choice of setting.

MacCarthy, B. G. *Women Writers: Their Contribution to the English Novel 1621-1744*. Oxford: Cork University Press, 1946, 288 p.

Treats Behn in several chapters, examining her contribution to the novel genre and her role among women writers.

Pacheco, Anita. "Royalism and Honor in Aphra Behn's *Oroonoko.*" *Studies in English Literature, 1500-1900* 34, No. 3 (Summer 1994): 491-506.

Argues that the intent of *Oroonoko* is pro-Royalist rather than abolitionist.

Paxman, David. "Oral and Literate Discourse in Aphra Behn's *Oroonoko.*" *Restoration* 18, No. 2 (Fall 1994): 88-103.

Interprets *Oroonoko* as an exposition on power and politics in Restoration England.

Pearson, Jacqueline. "Gender and Narrative in the Fiction of Aphra Behn." *The Review of English Studies* XLII, No. 165 (February 1991): 40-56.

Focuses on the role of the narrator in Behn's works and her treatment of such issues as gender and power.

Ramsaran, J. A. "*Oroonoko*: A Study of the Factual Elements." *Notes and Queries* 7, No. 4 (April 1960): 142-45.

Considers various arguments regarding the factual accuracy of *Oroonoko*.

Reynolds, Myra. "Dramatic Writers." In *The Learned Lady in England*, pp. 127-36. Gloucester, Mass: Peter Smith, 1964.

Considers Behn's importance as a woman writer and the contribution that *Oroonoko* made to the novel genre.

Seeber, Edward D. "Oroonoko and Crusoe's Man Friday." *Modern Language Quarterly* 12, No. 3 (September 1951): 286-91.

Notes parallels between *Oroonoko* and William Defoe's *Robinson Crusoe*. Seeber suggests that Behn's work may have influenced Defoe's choice of setting and his description of Friday.

Spender, Dale. "Aphra Behn." In *Mothers of the Novel: 100 Good Women Writers before Jane Austen*, pp. 47-66. New York: Pandora Press, 1986.

Discusses the major themes of Behn's works and remarks on the difficulties she faced as a woman writer.

Sypher, Wylie. "A Note on the Realism of Mrs. Behn's *Oroonoko.*" *Modern Language Quarterly* 3, No. 3 (September 1942): 401-05.

Argues that Behn's detailed and accurate description of slave conditions in *Oroonoko* suggests that she may indeed have lived in Surinam at some time.

Daniel Defoe: *Robinson Crusoe*

(Also DeFoe and De Foe; born Daniel Foe) English novelist, essayist, poet, journalist, historian, and satirist.

INTRODUCTION

Often credited with the creation of the first English novel, Defoe was one of the most prolific authors in world literature. While the exact number is impossible to determine, scholars attribute as many as 545 works to Defoe, including scores of essays and political pamphlets. Defoe is most famous for his *The Life and Strange Surprising Adventures of Robinson Crusoe, of York, Mariner: Who Lived Eight and Twenty Years All Alone, in an Uninhabited Island on the Coast of America, Near the Mouth of the Great River Oroonoque,* and *The Farther Adventures of Robinson Crusoe: Being the Second and Last Part of His Life; and the Strange Surprising Accounts of His Travels Round Three Parts of the Globe,* both from 1719, and *Serious Reflections during the Life and Surprising Adventures of Robinson Crusoe, with His Vision of the Angelick World,* from 1720. *Robinson Crusoe* gained immediate success which continues to the present. In addition to having been published in hundreds of editions and translations, adapted in many stage and movie versions, and the source for many imitations, including *Gulliver's Travels* and *The Swiss Family Robinson, Robinson Crusoe* has pervaded the culture to such an extent it has been called a modern myth.

Biographical Information

Defoe was born in London to nonconformist, middle-class parents. The noncomformists, or dissenters, were protestant sects that opposed the official state religion of Anglicism and consequently suffered persecution. Despite the oppression of noncomformists during his youth, Defoe enjoyed a relatively secure and religious upbringing. At the age of fourteen his parents sent him to the famous academy at Stoke Newington kept by Charles Morton, where most of the students were dissenters. At this time Defoe was intended for the ministry, but after three years of study he forfeited this ambition and turned to business. Around 1863, he established himself as a hosiery merchant and traveled throughout England and the continent, acquiring an expert knowledge of trade and economics. Defoe speculated in a number of financial ventures, one of which was so ruinous that he

had to file for bankruptcy, with debts mounting to over 17,000 pounds. Though he paid off all but 5000 pounds to his creditors, Defoe was haunted throughout his life by unsatisfied debt collectors. Many critics argue that this fact should always be kept in mind when judging his later political conduct, for he was consistently manipulated by shrewd politicians able to turn him over to his creditors if and when he failed to carry out their programs. After his bankruptcy, Defoe took a position as secretary at a brick factory and gradually improved his position until he became the chief owner of the brickworks. During this time Defoe published his first essays, the most significant being *An Essay upon Projects* (1697). In the 1700s, his spirited defense of the dissenters and staunch support of King William of Orange made Defoe the subject of attack. Arrested and charged with seditious libel, Defoe was found guilty and sentenced to a term in prison, to be served after spending three consecutive days in the pillory. Critics generally believe that the pillory had a lasting effect on Defoe, making him a bitter man and an outcast in his own society. His prison term cut short, Defoe became an instrument of the government, working as a political propagandist and secret agent for the Tories. Defoe began *The Review* in 1704 and continued as its sole writer for ten years. *The Review* served as a vehicle for Tory beliefs, which promoted Anglicanism and resisted religious toleration and foreign entanglements. Upon Queen Anne's death in 1714 and the fall of the Tory government, Defoe was able to devote more time to his imaginative writing. Partly inspired by the true adventures of an ill-disciplined sailor named Alexander Selkirk, *Robinson Crusoe* was extremely popular, particularly with the middle and lower classes for whom Crusoe was an appealing model. After enjoying success with novels and in journalism, Defoe concentrated on travel essays and history. Scholars are uncertain about Defoe's final years. It is known that he left his home at Stoke Newington and disappeared from the public, but the reason has never been determined. Defoe spent his final years alone and died in London near the place of his birth.

Major Works

An Essay upon Projects, which includes Defoe's suggestions for radical reforms, many of them enacted over the next two centuries, show that Defoe was an acute social observer and progressive thinker. *The Shortest Way with the Dissenters; or, Proposals for the Establishment of the Church* (1702) enraged both Dissenters and high churchmen alike who mistook the satire for an honest proposal, and led to Defoe's conviction and sentencing for seditious libel. In 1706 Defoe worked behind the scenes during the secret negotiations for the union of Scotland and England, and knowledge gained during this period found its outlet in *The History of the Union of Great Britain* (1709), a work still valued by historians for its accuracy and scope. *Robinson Crusoe* stands apart and above Defoe's other novels, mainly because its subject and setting lent themselves so well to the author's descriptive talents. The novel has been interpreted as an allegorical presentation of the growth of the British empire, as an attack on economic individualism, as an adaptation of the traditional spiritual autobiography, as an allegory of the author's own life, and—to Defoe's contemporaries—as simply the true story of one man's unusual life. No matter how critics interpret the novel, most agree that it is one of the world's most endearing stories. The story concerns Crusoe who, after abandoning his comfortable middle-class home in England, survives a shipwreck and lives on an island for twenty-eight years, alone for twenty-four of them. Defoe wrote a series of novels in the same mold as *Robinson Crusoe,* including *The Life, Adventures, and Pyracies of the Famous Captain Singleton* (1720); *Memoirs of a Cavalier; or, A Military Journal of the Wars in Germany, and the Wars in England, from the Year 1632 to*

the Year 1648 (1720); *The Fortunes and Misfortunes of the Famous Moll Flanders* (1721); *The History of the Most Remarkable Life and Extraordinary Adventures of the Truly Honourable Colonel Jacque, Vulgarly Called Colonel Jack* (1722); *A Journal of the Plague Year: Being Observations or Memorials of the Most Remarkable Occurences, as Well as Publick as Private, which Happened in London during the Last Great Visitation in 1665* (1722); and *The Fortunate Mistress; or, A History of the Life and Vast Variety of Fortunes of Mademoiselle de Belau, Afterwards Called the Countess de Wintelsheim, in Germany: Being the Person Known by the Name of the Lady Roxana, in the Time of King Charles II* (1724). As with *Robinson Crusoe,* many of Defoe's novels were published as actual biographies with certain well-defined moral messages attached.

Critical Reception

Though always popular with the reading public, Defoe has received ambivalent reactions from many critics and scholars. It was nearly a hundred years after his death before Walter Scott presented the first favorable account of Defoe's merits as a novelist. *Robinson Crusoe* was an instant success with the public but by certain critics was considered un-Christian and attacked for its improbabilities and misconceptions concerning life at sea. Criticism of Defoe's work during the eighteenth century focused on its authenticity and moral implications-two standards poorly suited for an appreciation of Defoe. Twentieth-century critics generally agree that Defoe has been seriously undervalued as an artist. They debate how best to interpret *Robinson Crusoe,* on whether or not—or to what degree—it is allegorical, whether its chief focus should be on its adventure or Puritan themes, and what Defoe's exact message is on moral values, economics, and security. There is also disagreement on whether or not to accept Defoe's own explanation of *Robinson Crusoe* offered in *Serious Reflections during the Life and Surprising Adventures of Robinson Crusoe, with His Vision of the Angelick World,* in which Defoe explains the book as an allegory of his own life.

PRINCIPAL WORKS

An Essay upon Projects (essay) 1697
The True-Born Englishman (poetry) 1701
The Shortest Way with the Dissenters; or, Proposals for the Establishment of the Church (satire) 1702
A Hymn to the Pillory (poetry) 1703
An Essay on the Regulation of the Press (essay) 1704
The Storm; or, A Collection of the Most Remarkable Casualties and Disasters which Happened in the Late

Dreadful Tempest, Both by Sea and Land (history) 1704

A True Relation of the Apparition of One Mrs. Veal, the Next Day After Her Death, to One Mrs. Bargrave, at Canterbury, the 8th of September, 1705 (essay) 1705

Jure Divino (poetry) 1706

The History of the Union of Great Britain (history) 1709

The Family Instructor (handbook) 1715

A Vindication of the Press; or, An Essay on the Usefulness of Writing, On Criticism, and the Qualification of Authors (essay) 1718

The Life and Strange Surprising Adventures of Robinson Crusoe, of York, Mariner: Who Lived Eight and Twenty Years All Alone, in an Uninhabited Island on the Coast of America, Near the Mouth of the Great River Oroonoque (novel) 1719

The Farther Adventures of Robinson Crusoe: Being the Second and Last Part of His Life; and the Strange Surprising Accounts of His Travels Round Three Parts of the Globe (novel) 1719

The History of the Life and Adventures of Mr. Duncan Campbell, a Gentleman (novel) 1720

The Life, Adventures, and Pyracies of the Famous Captain Singleton (novel) 1720

Memoirs of a Cavalier; or, A Military Journal of the Wars in Germany, and the Wars in England, from the Year 1632 to the Year 1648 (novel) 1720

Serious Reflections during the Life and Surprising Adventures of Robinson Crusoe, with His Vision of the Angelick World (novel) 1720

The Fortunes and Misfortunes of the Famous Moll Flanders (novel) 1721

The History of the Most Remarkable Life and Extraordinary Adventures of the Truly Honourable Colonel Jacque, Vulgarly Called Colonel Jack (novel) 1722

A Journal of the Plague Year: Being Observations or Memorials of the Most Remarkable Occurences, as Well as Publick as Private, which Happened in London during the Last Great Visitation in 1665 (fictional history) 1722

A Tour Through the Whole Island of Great Britain. 3 vols. (travel essays and history) 1724-27

The Fortunate Mistress; or, A History of the Life and Vast Variety of Fortunes of Mademoiselle de Belau, Afterwards Called the Countess de Wintelsheim, in Germany: Being the Person Known by the Name of the Lady Roxana, in the Time of King Charles II (novel) 1724

The Political History of the Devil, as Well Antient as Modern (fictional history) 1726

The Compleat English Tradesman. 2 vols. (handbook) 1727

An Essay on the History and Reality of Apparitions (essay) 1727

The Military Memoirs of Captain George Carleton, from the Dutch War, 1672, in which He Served, to the Conclusion of the Peace at Utrecht, 1713 (novel) 1728

A Plan of the English Commerce, Being a Compleat Prospect of the Trade of This Nation, as well as the Home Trade as the Foreign (essay) 1730

Novels and Miscellaneous Works of Daniel Defoe. 7 vols. (novels, history, essays, fictional history, fictional journal, and poetry) 1856-84

**The Compleat English Gentleman: Containing Useful Observations on the General Neglect of the Education of English Gentlemen, with the Reason and Remedies* (handbook) 1890

The Works of Daniel Defoe 16 vols. (novels, history, essays, fictional history, fictional journal, fictional memoirs, and poetry) 1903-04

Defoe's Review: 1704-13. 22 vols. (essays and journalism) 1938

The Letters of Daniel Defoe (letters) 1955

---

*These two works are collectively referred to as *Robinson Crusoe*.
**This work was written in 1729.

CRITICISM

Ian Watt (essay date 1957)

SOURCE: "*Robinson Crusoe*, Individualism and the Novel," in *The Rise of the Novel: Studies in Defoe, Richardson and Fielding*, University of California Press, 1962, pp. 60-92.

[*In the following excerpt, first published in 1957 and reprinted in 1962, Watt discusses the influences of capitalism and Protestantism on the rise of the individual and explores how Robinson Crusoe embodies economic individualism in his quest to better himself through seeking profit.*]

The novel's serious concern with the daily lives of ordinary people seems to depend upon two important general conditions: the society must value every individual highly enough to consider him the proper subject of its serious literature; and there must be enough variety of belief and action among ordinary people for a detailed account of them to be of interest to other ordinary people, the readers of novels. It is probable that neither of these conditions for the existence of the novel obtained very widely until fairly recently, because they both depend on the rise of a society characterised by that vast complex of interdependent factors denoted by the term 'individualism'.

Even the word is recent, dating only from the middle of the nineteenth century. In all ages, no doubt, and in all societies, some people have been 'individualists' in the sense that they were egocentric, unique or conspicuously independent of current opinions and habits; but the concept of individualism involves much more than this. It posits a whole society mainly governed by the idea of every individual's intrinsic independence both from other individuals and from that multifarious allegiance to past modes of thought and action denoted by the word 'tradition'—a force that is always social, not individual. The existence of such a society, in turn, obviously depends on a special type of economic and political organisation and on an appropriate ideology; more specifically, on an economic and political organisation which allows its members a very wide range of choices in their actions, and on an ideology primarily based, not on the tradition of the past, but on the autonomy of the individual, irrespective of his particular social status or personal capacity. It is generally agreed that modern society is uniquely individualist in these respects, and that of the many historical causes for its emergence two are of supreme importance—the rise of modern industrial capitalism and the spread of Protestantism, especially in its Calvinist or Puritan forms.

I

Capitalism brought a great increase of economic specialisation; and this, combined with a less rigid and homogeneous social structure, and a less absolutist and more democratic political system, enormously increased the individual's freedom of choice. For those fully exposed to the new economic order, the effective entity on which social arrangements were now based was no longer the family, nor the church, nor the guild, nor the township, nor any other collective unit, but the individual: he alone was primarily responsible for determining his own economic, social, political and religious roles.

It is very difficult to say when this change of orientation began to affect society as a whole—probably not until the nineteenth century. But the movement certainly began much earlier. In the sixteenth century the Reformation and the rise of national states decisively challenged the substantial social homogeneity of mediaeval Christendom, and, in the famous words of Maitland, 'for the first time, the Absolute State faced the Absolute Individual'. Outside the political and religious sphere, however, change was slow, and it is likely that it was not until the further development of industrial capitalism, especially in England and in the Low Countries, that a mainly individualist social and economic structure came into being and started to affect a considerable part, although by no means a majority, of the total population.

It is, at least, generally agreed that the foundations of the new order were laid in the period immediately following the Glorious Revolution of 1689. The commercial and industrial classes, who were the prime agents in bringing about the individualist social order, had achieved greater political and economic power;

and this power was already being reflected in the domain of literature. The middle classes of the towns, we have seen, were becoming much more important in the reading public; and at the same time literature began to view trade, commerce and industry with favour. This was a rather new development. Earlier writers, Spenser, Shakespeare, Donne, Ben Jonson and Dryden, for example, had tended to support the traditional economic and social order and had attacked many of the symptoms of emergent individualism. By the beginning of the eighteenth century, however, Addison, Steele and Defoe were somewhat ostentatiously setting the seal of literary approval on the heroes of economic individualism.

The new orientation was equally evident in the philosophical domain. The great English empiricists of the seventeenth century were as vigorously individualist in their political and ethical thought as in their epistemology. Bacon hoped to make a really new start in social theory by applying his inductive method to an accumulation of factual data about a great number of particular individuals;[1] Hobbes, also feeling that he was dealing with a subject that had not been properly approached before, based his political and ethical theory on the fundamentally egocentric psychological constitution of the individual;[2] while in his *Two Treatises of Government* (1690) Locke constructed the class system of political thought based on the indefeasibility of individual rights, as against the more traditional ones of Church, Family or King. That these thinkers should have been the political and psychological vanguard of nascent individualism, as well as the pioneers of its theory of knowledge, suggests how closely linked their reorientations were both in themselves and in relation to the innovations of the novel. For, just as there is a basic congruity between the non-realist nature of the literary forms of the Greeks, their intensely social, or civic, moral outlook, and their philosophical preference for the universal, so the modern novel is closely allied on the one hand to the realist epistemology of the modern period, and on the other to the individualism of its social structure. In the literary, the philosophical and the social spheres alike the classical focus on the ideal, the universal and the corporate has shifted completely, and the modern field of vision is mainly occupied by the discrete particular, the directly apprehended sensum, and the autonomous individual.

Defoe, whose philosophical outlook has much in common with that of the English empiricists of the seventeenth century, expressed the diverse elements of individualism more completely than any previous writer, and his work offers a unique demonstration of the connection between individualism in its many forms and the rise of the novel. This connection is shown particularly clearly and comprehensively in his first novel, *Robinson Crusoe.*

II

(a)

Robinson Crusoe has been very appropriately used by many economic theorists as their illustration of *homo economicus*. Just as 'the body politic' was the symbol of the communal way of thought typical of previous societies, so 'economic man' symbolised the new outlook of individualism in its economic aspect. Adam Smith has been charged with the invention; actually, the concept is much older, but it is natural that it should have come to the fore as an abstraction expressing the individualism of the economic system as a whole only when the individualism of that system itself had reached an advanced stage of development.

That Robinson Crusoe, like Defoe's other main characters, Moll Flanders, Roxana, Colonel Jacque and Captain Singleton, is an embodiment of economic individualism hardly needs demonstration. All Defoe's heroes pursue money, which he characteristically called 'the general denominating article in the world';[3] and they pursue it very methodically according to the profit and loss book-keeping which Max Weber considered to be the distinctive technical feature of modern capitalism.[4] Defoe's heroes, we observe, have no need to learn this technique; whatever the circumstances of their birth and education, they have it in their blood, and keep us more fully informed of their present stocks of money and commodities than any other characters in fiction. Crusoe's book-keeping conscience, indeed, has established an effective priority over his other thoughts and emotions; when his Lisbon steward offers him 160 moidores to alleviate his momentary difficulties on return, Crusoe relates: 'I could hardly refrain from tears while he spoke; in short, I took 100 of the moidores, and called for a pen and ink to give him a receipt for them'.[5]

Book-keeping is but one aspect of a central theme in the modern social order. Our civilisation as a whole is based on individual contractual relationships, as opposed to the unwritten, traditional and collective relationships of previous societies; and the idea of contract played an important part in the theoretical development of political individualism. It had featured prominently in the fight against the Stuarts, and it was enshrined in Locke's political system. Locke, indeed, thought that contractual relationships were binding even in the state of nature;[6] Crusoe, we notice, acts like a good Lockean—when others arrive on the island he forces them to accept his dominion with written contracts acknowledging his absolute power (even though we have previously been told that he has run out of ink).[7]

But the primacy of the economic motive, and an innate reverence for book-keeping and the law of contract are by no means the only matters in which Robinson Cru-

soe is a symbol of the processes associated with the rise of economic individualism. The hypostasis of the economic motive logically entails a devaluation of other modes of thought, feeling and action: the various forms of traditional group relationship, the family, the guild, the village, the sense of nationality—all are weakened, and so, too, are the competing claims of non-economic individual achievement and enjoyment, ranging from spiritual salvation to the pleasures of recreation.[8]

This inclusive reordering of the components of human society tends to occur wherever industrial capitalism becomes the dominant force in the economic structure,[9] and it naturally became evident particularly early in England. By the middle of the eighteenth century, indeed, it had already become something of a commonplace. Goldsmith, for instance, thus described the concomitants of England's vaunted freedom in *The Traveller* (1764):

> That independence Britons prize too high,
> Keeps man from man, and breaks the social
> 　tie;
> The self-dependent lordlings stand alone,
> All claims that bind and sweeten life
> 　unknown;
> Here by the bonds of nature feebly held,
> Minds combat minds, repelling and repell'd . . .
> 　Nor this the worst. As nature's ties decay,
> As duty, love, and honour fail to sway,
> Fictitious bonds, the bonds of wealth and law,
> Still gather strength, and force unwilling
> 　awe.[10]

Unlike Goldsmith, Defoe was not a professed enemy of the new order—quite the reverse; nevertheless there is much in ***Robinson Crusoe*** that bears out Goldsmith's picture, as can be seen in Defoe's treatment of such group relationships as the family or the nation.

For the most part, Defoe's heroes either have no family, like Moll Flanders, Colonel Jacque and Captain Singleton, or leave it at an early age never to return, like Roxana and Robinson Crusoe. Not too much importance can be attached to this fact, since adventure stories demand the absence of conventional social ties. Still, in ***Robinson Crusoe*** at least, the hero has a home and family, and leaves them for the classic reason of *homo economicus*—that it is necessary to better his economic condition. 'Something fatal in that propension of nature' calls him to the sea and adventure, and against 'settling to business' in the station to which he is born—'the upper station of low life'; and this despite the panegyric which his father makes of that condition. Later he sees this lack of 'confined desires', this dissatisfaction with 'the state wherein God and Nature has placed' him, as his 'original sin'.[11] At the time, however, the argument between his parents and himself is a debate, not about filial duty or religion, but about whether going or staying is likely to be the most advantageous course materially: both sides accept the economic argument as primary. And, of course, Crusoe actually gains by his 'original sin', and becomes richer than his father was.

Crusoe's 'original sin' is really the dynamic tendency of capitalism itself, whose aim is never merely to maintain the *status quo,* but to transform it incessantly. Leaving home, improving on the lot one was born to, is a vital feature of the individualist pattern of life. It may be regarded as the economic and social embodiment of the 'uneasiness' which Locke had made the centre of his system of motivation,[12] an uneasiness whose existence was, in the very opposite outlook of Pascal, the index of the enduring misery of mortal man. 'All the unhappiness of men arises from one single fact, that they cannot stay quietly in their own room' Pascal had written.[13] Defoe's hero is far from agreeing. Even when he is old, Crusoe tells us how: '. . . nothing else offering, and finding that really stirring about and trading, the profit being so great, and, as I may say, certain, had more pleasure in it, and more satisfaction to the mind, than sitting still, which, to me especially, was the unhappiest part of life'.[14] So, in the *Farther Adventures,* Crusoe sets out on yet another lucrative Odyssey.

The fundamental tendency of economic individualism, then, prevents Crusoe from paying much heed to the ties of family, whether as a son or a husband. This is in direct contradiction to the great stress which Defoe lays on the social and religious importance of the family in his didactic works such as the *Family Instructor;* but his novels reflect not theory but practice, and they accord these ties a very minor, and on the whole obstructive, role.

Rational scrutiny of one's own economic interest may lead one to be as little bound by national as by family ties. Defoe certainly valued individuals and countries alike primarily on their economic merits. Thus one of his most patriotic utterances takes the characteristic form of claiming that his compatriots have a greater productive output per hour than the workmen of any other country.[15] Crusoe, we notice, whom Walter de la Mare has justly called Defoe's Elective Affinity,[16] shows xenophobia mainly where the economic virtues are absent. When they are present—as in the Spanish Governor, a French papist priest, a faithful Portuguese factor—his praise is unstinted. On the other hand, he condemns many Englishmen, such as his English settlers on the island, for their lack of industry. Crusoe, one feels, is not bound to his country by sentimental ties, any more than to his family; he is satisfied by people, whatever their nationality, who are good to do business with; and he feels, like Moll Flanders, that 'with money in the pocket one is at home anywhere'.[17]

What might at first appear to place *Robinson Crusoe* in the somewhat special category of 'Travel and Adventure' does not, then, altogether do so. The plot's reliance on travel does tend to allot *Robinson Crusoe* a somewhat peripheral position in the novel's line of development, since it removes the hero from his usual setting in a stable and cohesive pattern of social relations. But Crusoe is not a mere footloose adventurer, and his travels, like his freedom from social ties, are merely somewhat extreme cases of tendencies that are normal in modern society as a whole, since, by making the pursuit of gain a primary motive, economic individualism has much increased the mobility of the individual. More specifically, Robinson Crusoe's career is based, as modern scholarship has shown,[18] on some of the innumerable volumes which recounted the exploits of those voyagers who had done so much in the sixteenth century to assist the development of capitalism by providing the gold, slaves and tropical products on which trade expansion depended; and who had continued the process in the seventeenth century by developing the colonies and world markets on which the future progress of capitalism depended.

Defoe's plot, then, expresses some of the most important tendencies of the life of his time, and it is this which sets his hero apart from most of the travellers in literature. Robinson Crusoe is not, like Autolycus, a commercial traveller rooted in an extended but still familiar locality; nor is he, like Ulysses, an unwilling voyager trying to get back to his family and his native land: profit is Crusoe's only vocation, and the whole world is his territory.

The primacy of individual economic advantage has tended to diminish the importance of personal as well as group relationships, and especially of those based on sex; for sex, as Weber pointed out,[19] being one of the strongest non-rational factors in human life, is one of the strongest potential menaces to the individual's rational pursuit of economic ends, and it has therefore, as we shall see, been placed under particularly strong controls in the ideology of industrial capitalism.

Romantic love has certainly had no greater antagonist among the novelists than Defoe. Even sexual satisfaction—where he speaks of it—tends to be minimised; he protested in *The Review,* for example, that 'the Trifle called Pleasure in it' was 'not worth the Repentance'.[20] As to marriage, his attitude is complicated by the fact that economic and moral virtue in the male is no guarantee of a profitable matrimonial investment: on his colony 'as it often happens in the world (what the wise ends of God's Providence are in such a disposition of things I cannot say), the two honest fellows had the two worst wives, and the three reprobates, that were scarce worth hanging . . . had three clever, diligent, careful and ingenious wives'[21] His puzzled parenthesis bears eloquent testimony to the seriousness with which he views this flaw in the rationality of Providence.

It is not surprising, therefore, that love plays little part in Crusoe's own life, and that even the temptations of sex are excluded from the scene of his greatest triumphs, the island. When Crusoe does notice the lack of 'society' there, he prays for the solace of company, but we observe that what he desires is a male slave.[22] Then, with Friday, he enjoys an idyll without benefit of woman—a revolutionary departure from the traditional expectations aroused by desert islands from the *Odyssey* to the *New Yorker*.

When eventually Crusoe returns to civilisation, sex is still strictly subordinated to business. Only when his financial position has been fully secured by a further voyage does he marry; and all he tells us of this supreme human adventure is that it was 'not either to my disadvantage or dissatisfaction'. This, the birth of three children, and his wife's death, however, comprise only the early part of a sentence, which ends with plans for a further voyage.[23]

Women have only one important role to play, and that is economic. When Crusoe's colonists draw lots for five women, we are gleefully informed that:

> He that drew to choose first . . . took her that was reckoned the homeliest and eldest of the five, which made mirth enough among the rest . . . but the fellow considered better than any of them, that it was application and business that they were to expect assistance in as much as anything else; and she proved the best wife of all the parcel.[24]

'The best wife of all the parcel.' The language of commerce here reminds us that Dickens once decided on the basis of Defoe's treatment of women that he must have been 'a precious dry and disagreeable article himself'.[25]

The same devaluation of non-economic factors can be seen in Crusoe's other personal relationships. He treats them all in terms of their commodity value. The clearest case is that of Xury, the Moorish boy who helped him to escape from slavery and on another occasion offered to prove his devotion by sacrificing his own life. Crusoe very properly resolves 'to love him ever after' and promises 'to make him a great man'. But when chance leads them to the Portuguese Captain, who offers Crusoe sixty pieces of eight—twice Judas's figure—he cannot resist the bargain, and sells Xury into slavery. He has momentary scruples, it is true, but they are cheaply satisfied by securing a promise from the new owner to 'set him free in ten years if he turn Christian'. Remorse later supervenes, but only when the tasks of his island life make manpower more valuable to him than money.[26]

Crusoe's relations with Man Friday are similarly egocentric. He does not ask him his name, but gives him one. Even in language—the medium whereby human beings may achieve something more than animal relationships with each other, as Crusoe himself wrote in his *Serious Reflections*[27]—Crusoe is a strict utilitarian. 'I likewise taught him to say Yes and No',[28] he tells us; but Friday still speaks pidgin English at the end of their long association, as Defoe's contemporary critic Charles Gildon pointed out.[29]

Yet Crusoe regards the relationship as ideal. He is 'as perfectly and completely happy if any such thing as complete happiness can be found in a sublunary state'.[30] A functional silence, broken only by an occasional 'No, Friday', or an abject 'Yes, Master', is the golden music of Crusoe's *île joyeuse*. It seems that man's social nature, his need for friendship and understanding, is wholly satisfied by the righteous bestowal or grateful receipt, of benevolent but not undemanding patronage. It is true that later, as with Xury, Crusoe promises himself 'to do something considerable' for his servant, 'if he outlive me'. Fortunately, no such sacrifice is called for, as Friday dies at sea, to be rewarded only by a brief word of obituary compassion.[31]

Emotional ties, then, and personal relationships generally, play a very minor part in *Robinson Crusoe,* except when they are focussed on economic matters. For instance, after Crusoe has left, it is only when his faithful old agent in Lisbon reveals that he is now a very rich man that we get any emotional climax: 'I turned pale and grew sick; and had not the old man run and fetched me a cordial, I believe the sudden surprise of joy had overset nature, and I had died upon the spot'.[32] Only money—fortune in its modern sense—is a proper cause of deep feeling; and friendship is accorded only to those who can safely be entrusted with Crusoe's economic interests.

Sitting still, we saw, was 'the unhappiest part of life' to Robinson Crusoe; leisure pursuits are almost as bad. In this he resembles his author, who seems to have made as few concessions to such distractions as anyone. The fewness of Defoe's literary friendships has been commented on, and he is perhaps a unique example of a great writer who was very little interested in literature, and says nothing of interest about it as literature.[33]

In his blindness to aesthetic experience Crusoe is Defoe's peer. We can say of him as Marx said of his archetypal capitalist: 'enjoyment is subordinated to capital, and the individual who enjoys to the individual who capitalises'.[34] Some of the French versions of *Robinson Crusoe* make him address hymns of praise to nature, beginning 'Oh Nature!'[35] Defoe did not. The natural scene on the island appeals not for adoration, but for exploitation; wherever Crusoe looks his acres cry out so loud for improvement that he has no leisure to observe that they also compose a landscape.

Of course, in a wintry way, Crusoe has his pleasures. If he does not, like Selkirk,[36] dance with his goats, he at least plays with them, and with his parrot and his cats; but his deepest satisfactions come from surveying his stock of goods: 'I had everything so ready at my hand,' he says, 'that it was a great pleasure to me to see all my goods in such order, and especially to find my stock of all necessaries so great.'[37]

(b)
If Robinson Crusoe's character depends very largely on the psychological and social orientations of economic individualism, the appeal of his adventures to the reader seems mainly to derive from the effects of another important concomitant of modern capitalism, economic specialisation.

The division of labour has done much to make the novel possible: partly because the more specialised the social and economic structure, the greater the number of significant differences of character, attitude and experience in contemporary life which the novelist can portray, and which are of interest to his readers; partly because, by increasing the amount of leisure, economic specialisation provides the kind of mass audience with which the novel is associated; and partly because this specialisation creates particular needs in that audience which the novel satisfies. Such, at least, was the general view of T. H. Green: 'In the progressive division of labour, while we become more useful as citizens, we seem to lose our completeness as men . . . the perfect organisation of modern society removes the excitement of adventure and the occasion for independent effort. There is less of human interest to touch us within our calling. . . .' 'The alleviation' of this situation, Green concluded, 'is to be found in the newspaper and the novel.'[38]

It is very likely that the lack of variety and stimulation in the daily task as a result of economic specialisation is largely responsible for the unique dependence of the individual in our culture upon the substitute experiences provided by the printing press, particularly in the forms of journalism and the novel. *Robinson Crusoe,* however, is a much more direct illustration of Green's thesis, since much of its appeal obviously depends on the quality of the 'occasions for independent effort' in the economic realm which it offers Defoe's hero, efforts which the reader can share vicariously. The appeal of these efforts is surely a measure of the depth of the deprivations involved by economic specialisation, deprivations whose far-reaching nature is suggested by the way our civilisation has reintroduced some of the basic economic processes as therapeutic recreations: in gardening, home-weaving, pottery, camping, woodwork and keeping pets, we can all partici-

pate in the character-forming satisfactions which circumstances force on Defoe's hero; and like him, demonstrate what we would not otherwise know, that 'by making the most rational judgement of things, every man may be in time master of every mechanic art'.[39]

Defoe was certainly aware of how the increasing economic specialisation which was a feature of the life of his time had made most of the 'mechanic arts' alien to the experience of his readers. When Crusoe makes bread, for instance, he reflects that ''Tis a little wonderful and what I believe few people have thought much upon, viz., the strange multitude of little things necessary in the providing, procuring, curing, dressing, making and finishing this one article of bread'.[40] Defoe's description goes on for seven pages, pages that would have been of little interest to people in mediaeval or Tudor society, who saw this and other basic economic processes going on daily in their own households. But by the early eighteenth century, as Kalm reported, most women did not 'bake, because there is a baker in every parish or village',[41] and Defoe could therefore expect his readers to be interested in the very detailed descriptions of the economic life which comprise such an important and memorable part of his narrative.

Robinson Crusoe, of course, does not deal with the actual economic life of Defoe's own time and place. It would be somewhat contrary to the facts of economic life under the division of labour to show the average individual's manual labour as interesting or inspiring; to take Adam Smith's famous example of the division of labour in *The Wealth of Nations,*[42] the man who performs one of the many separate operations in the manufacture of a pin is unlikely to find his task as absorbing and interesting as Crusoe does. So Defoe sets back the economic clock, and takes his hero to a primitive environment, where labour can be presented as varied and inspiring, and where it has the further significant difference from the pin-maker's at home that there is an absolute equivalence between individual effort and individual reward. This was the final change from contemporary economic conditions which was necessary to enable Defoe to give narrative expression to the ideological counterpart of the Division of Labour, the Dignity of Labour.

The creed of the dignity of labour is not wholly modern: in classical times the Cynics and Stoics had opposed the denigration of manual labour which is a necessary part of a slaveowning society's scale of values; and later, Christianity, originally associated mainly with slaves and the poor, had done much to remove the odium on manual labour. The idea, however, was only fully developed in the modern period, presumably because its compensatory affirmation became the more necessary as the development of economic specialisation made manual labour more stultifying; and the creed itself is closely associated with the advent of Protestantism. Calvinism in particular tended to make its adherents forget the idea that labour was God's punishment for Adam's disobedience, by emphasising the very different idea that untiring stewardship of the material gifts of God was a paramount religious and ethical obligation.[43]

The quality of Crusoe's stewardship cannot be doubted; he allows himself little time for rest, and even the advent of new manpower—Friday's—is a signal, not for relaxation, but for expanded production. Defoe clearly belongs to the tradition of Ascetic Protestantism. He had written much that sounds like the formulations of Weber, Troeltsch and Tawney; in Dickory Cronke's aphorism, for example: 'When you find yourself sleepy in a morning, rouse yourself, and consider that you are born to business, and that in doing good in your generation, you answer your character and act like a man'.[44] He had even—with a certain sophistic obtuseness—propounded the view that the pursuit of economic utility was quite literally an imitation of Christ: 'Usefulness being the great pleasure, and justly deem'd by all good men the truest and noblest end of life, in which men come nearest to the character of our B. Saviour, who went about doing good'.[45]

Defoe's attitude here exhibits a confusion of religious and material values to which the Puritan gospel of the dignity of labour was peculiarly liable: once the highest spiritual values had been attached to the performance of the daily task, the next step was for the autonomous individual to regard his achievements as a quasi-divine mastering of the environment. It is likely that this secularisation of the Calvinist conception of stewardship was of considerable importance for the rise of the novel. *Robinson Crusoe* is certainly the first novel in the sense that it is the first fictional narrative in which an ordinary person's daily activities are the centre of continuous literary attention. These activities, it is true, are not seen in a wholly secular light; but later novelists could continue Defoe's serious concern with man's worldly doings without placing them in a religious framework. It is therefore likely that the Puritan conception of the dignity of labour helped to bring into being the novel's general premise that the individual's daily life is of sufficient importance and interest to be the proper subject of literature.

III

Economic individualism explains much of Crusoe's character; economic specialisation and its associated ideology help to account for the appeal of his adventures; but it is Puritan individualism which controls his spiritual being.

Troeltsch has claimed that 'the really permanent attainment of individualism was due to a religious, and

not a secular movement, to the Reformation and not the Renaissance'.[46] It is neither feasible nor profitable to attempt to establish priorities in such matters, but it is certainly true that if there is one element which all forms of Protestantism have in common it is the replacement of the rule of the Church as the mediator between man and God by another view of religion in which it is the individual who is entrusted with the primary responsibility for his own spiritual direction. Two aspects of this new Protestant emphasis—the tendency to increase consciousness of the self as a spiritual entity, and the tendency to a kind of democratisation of the moral and social outlook—are particularly important both to *Robinson Crusoe* and to the development of the presuppositions on which the formal realism of the novel is based.

The idea of religious self-scrutiny as an important duty for each individual is, of course, much older than Protestantism; it derives from the individualist and subjective emphasis of primitive Christianity, and finds its supreme expression in St. Augustine's *Confessions.* But it is generally agreed that it was Calvin, in the sixteenth century, who re-established and systematised this earlier pattern of purposive spiritual introspection, and made it the supreme religious ritual for the layman as well as for the priest: every good Puritan conducted a continual scrutiny of his inner man for evidence of his own place in the divine plot of election and reprobation.

This 'internalisation of conscience' is everywhere manifested in Calvinism. In New England, it has been said, 'almost every literate Puritan kept some sort of journal';[47] and, in England, *Grace Abounding* is the great monument of a way of life which Bunyan shared with the other members of his sect,[48] the Baptists, who were, with one or two minor additions and subtractions, orthodox Calvinists. In later generations the introspective habit remained even where religious conviction weakened, and there resulted the three greatest autobiographical confessions of the modern period, those of Pepys, Rousseau and Boswell, all of whom were brought up under the Calvinist discipline; their fascination with self-analysis, and indeed their extreme egocentricity, are character traits which they shared both with later Calvinism in general[49] and with Defoe's heroes.

(a)
The importance of this subjective and individualist spiritual pattern to Defoe's work, and to the rise of the novel, is very evident. *Robinson Crusoe* initiates that aspect of the novel's treatment of experience which rivals the confessional autobiography and outdoes other literary forms in bringing us close to the inward moral being of the individual; and it achieves this closeness to the inner life of the protagonist by using as formal basis the autobiographical memoir which was

the most immediate and widespread literary expression of the introspective tendency of Puritanism in general.

Defoe himself, of course, was born and bred a Puritan. His father was a Dissenter, perhaps a Baptist, more probably a Presbyterian, in any case a Calvinist; and he sent his son to a dissenting academy, probably intending him for the ministry. Defoe's own religious beliefs changed a good deal, and he expressed in his writings the whole gamut of doctrines, from intransigent predestinarianism to rational deism, which Puritanism held during its varied course of development; nevertheless, there is no doubt that Defoe remained and was generally considered to be a Dissenter, and that much of the outlook revealed in his novels is distinctively Puritan.

There is nothing to suggest that Robinson Crusoe was intended to be a Dissenter. On the other hand, the note of his religious reflections is often Puritan in character—their tenor has been seen by one theologian as very close to the Presbyterian Shorter Catechism of the 1648 Westminster Assembly.[50] Crusoe certainly exhibits frequent signs of Bibliolatry: he quotes some twenty verses of the Bible in the first part of **Robinson Crusoe** alone, besides making many briefer references; and he sometimes seeks divine guidance by opening the Bible at random. But the most significant aspect of his spiritual life is his tendency to rigorous moral and religious self-examination. Each of his actions is followed by a passage of reflection in which Crusoe ponders over the problem of how it reveals the intentions of divine providence. If the corn sprouts, it is surely a divine miracle 'so directed for my sustenance'; if he has a bout of fever 'a leisurely review of the miseries of death'[51] eventually convinces him that he deserves reprobation for neglecting to show his gratitude for God's mercies to him. The modern reader no doubt tends to pay little attention to these parts of the narrative; but Crusoe and his author showed their point of view very clearly by allotting the spiritual realm as much importance as the practical, both in space and emphasis. It would therefore appear that what are probably the vestigial remnants of the Calvinist introspective discipline helped to provide us for the first time in the history of fiction with a hero whose day-by-day mental and moral life is fully shared by the reader.

This crucial literary advance was not, of course, brought about by the introspective tendency of Puritanism alone. As we have seen, the gospel of work had a similar effect in giving the individual's daily economic task almost as much importance as his daily spiritual self-examination; and the parallel effects of both these tendencies were supplemented by another closely related tendency in Puritanism.

If God had given the individual prime responsibility for his own spiritual destiny, it followed that he must have made this possible by signifying his intentions to the individual in the events of his daily life. The Puritan therefore tended to see every item in his personal experience as potentially rich in moral and spiritual meaning; and Defoe's hero is acting according to this tradition when he tries to interpret so many of the mundane events of the narrative as divine pointers which may help him to find his own place in the eternal scheme of redemption and reprobation.

In that scheme, of course, all souls had equal chances, and it therefore followed that the individual had as full an opportunity of showing his spiritual qualities in the ordinary conduct of life as in its rarer and more dramatic exigencies. This was one reason for the general Puritan tendency towards the democratisation of the moral and social scale, and it was assisted by several other factors. There were, for instance, many social, moral and political reasons why the Puritans should be hostile to the aristocratic scale of values; nor could they fail to disapprove of its literary expression in the traditional heroes of romance, extrovert conquerors whose victories are won, not in the spirit or in the counting-house but on the battlefield and in the boudoir. It is at all events clear that Puritanism brought about a fundamental and in a sense democratic orientation in the social and literary outlook of its adherents, an orientation which was described by Milton's lines in *Paradise Lost:* 'To know / That which before us lies in daily life / Is the prime wisdom',[52] and which evoked one of Defoe's most eloquent pieces of writing, an essay in *Applebee's Journal* (1722) on the funeral of Marlborough. The essay's peroration begins:

> What then is the work of life? What the business of great men, that pass the stage of the world in seeming triumph as these men, we call heroes, have done? Is it to grow great in the mouth of fame, and take up many pages in history? Alas! that is no more than making a tale for the reading of posterity, till it turns into fable and romance. Is it to furnish subject to the poets, and live in their immortal rhymes, as they call them? That is, in short, no more than to be hereafter turned into ballad and song, and be sung by old women to quiet children; or, at the corner of a street, to gather crowds in aid of the pickpocket and the whore. Or is their business rather to add virtue and piety to their glory, which alone will pass them into Eternity, and make them truly immortal? What is glory without virtue? A great man without religion is no more than a great beast without a soul.

Then Defoe modulates into something more like the narrowly ethical evaluation of merit which was to be one of the legacies of Puritanism to the middle-class code: 'What is honour without merit? And what can be called true merit, but that which makes a person a good man, as well as a great man'.[53]

Neither Crusoe, nor indeed any of Defoe's heroes, it must be admitted, are conspicuous by these standards of virtue, religion, merit and goodness; and, of course, Defoe did not intend them to be so. But these standards do represent the moral plane on which Defoe's novels exist, and by which his heroes must be judged: the ethical scale has been so internalised and democratised that, unlike the scale of achievement common in epic or romance, it is relevant to the lives and actions of ordinary people. In this Defoe's heroes are typical of the later characters of the novel: Robinson Crusoe, Moll Flanders and even Colonel Jacque never think of glory or honour; they have their being on the moral plane of day-to-day living more completely than those of previous narratives, and their thoughts and actions only exhibit an ordinary, a democratic goodness and badness. Robinson Crusoe, for instance, is Defoe's most heroic character, but there is nothing unusual about his personality or the way he faces his strange experiences; as Coleridge pointed out, he is essentially 'the universal representative, the person, for whom every reader could substitute himself . . . nothing is done, thought, suffered, or desired, but what every man can imagine himself doing, thinking, feeling, or wishing for'.[54]

Defoe's presentation of Robinson Crusoe as the 'universal representative' is intimately connected with the egalitarian tendency of Puritanism in yet another way. For not only did this tendency make the way the individual faced every problem of everyday life a matter of deep and continuing spiritual concern; it also encouraged a literary outlook which was suited to describing such problems with the most detailed fidelity. . . .

Notes

[1] *Advancement of Learning,* Bk. II, especially ch. 22, sect. xvi and ch. 23, sect. xiv.

[2] *Elements of Law,* Pt. I, ch. 13, sect. iii.

[3] *Review,* III (1706), No. 3.

[4] *The Theory of Social and Economic Organisation,* trans. Henderson and Parsons (New York, 1947), pp. 186-202.

[5] *The Life and Strange Surprising Adventures of Robinson Crusoe,* ed. Aitken (London, 1902), p. 316.

[6] Second treatise, 'Essay concerning . . . Civil Government,' sect. 14.

[7] *Life,* pp. 277, 147.

[8] See Max Weber, *The Protestant Ethic and the Spirit of Capitalism,* trans. Parsons (London, 1930), pp. 59-76; *Social and Economic Organisation,* pp. 341-354.

[9] See, for example, Robert Redfield, *Folk Culture of Yucatan* (Chicago, 1941), pp. 338-369.

[10] ll. 339-352.

[11] *Life,* pp. 2-6, 216.

[12] *Human Understanding,* Bk. II, ch. 21, sects. xxxi-lx.

[13] *Pensées,* No. 139.

[14] *Farther Adventures of Robinson Crusoe,* ed. Aitken (London, 1902), p. 214.

[15] *A Plan of the English Commerce* (Oxford, 1928), pp. 28, 31-32.

[16] *Desert Islands and Robinson Crusoe* (London, 1930), p. 7.

[17] *Moll Flanders,* ed. Aitken (London, 1902), I, 186.

[18] See especially A. W. Secord, *Studies in the Narrative Method of Defoe* (Urbana, 1924).

[19] Weber, *Essays in Sociology,* trans. Gerth and Mills (New York, 1946), p. 350.

[20] I (1705), No. 92.

[21] *Farther Adventures,* p. 78.

[22] *Life,* pp. 208-210, 225.

[23] *Life,* p. 341.

[24] *Farther Adventures,* p. 77.

[25] John Forster, *Life of Charles Dickens,* revised Ley (London, 1928), p. 611 n.

[26] *Life,* pp. 27, 34-36, 164.

[27] *Serious Reflections during the Life and Surprising Adventures of Robinson Crusoe,* ed. Aitken (London, 1902), p. 66.

[28] *Life,* p. 229.

[29] *Robinson Crusoe Examin'd and Criticis'd,* ed. Dottin (London and Paris, 1923), pp. 70, 78, 118.

[30] *Life,* pp. 245-246.

[31] *Farther Adventures,* pp. 133, 177-180.

[32] *Life,* p. 318.

[33] See James R. Sutherland, *Defoe* (London, 1937), p. 25; W. Gückel and E. Günther, 'D. Defoes und J. Swifts Belesenheit und literarische Kritik', *Palaestra,* CIL (1925).

[34] My translation from *Notes on Philosophy and Political Economy,* in *Oeuvres Philosophiqes,* ed. Molitor (Paris, 1937), VI, 69.

[35] See William-Edward Mann, *Robinson Crusoë en France* (Paris, 1916), p. 102.

[36] See Appendix, *Serious Reflections,* ed. Aitken, p. 322.

[37] *Life,* p. 75.

[38] 'Estimate of the Value and Influence of Works of Fiction in Modern Times', *Works,* ed. Nettleship, III, 40.

[39] *Life,* p. 74.

[40] *Life,* p. 130.

[41] *Account of His Visit to England,* p. 326.

[42] Bk. I, ch. 1.

[43] See Ernst Troeltsch, *Social Teaching of the Christian Churches,* trans. Wyon (London, 1931), I, 119; II, 589; Tawney, *Religion and the Rise of Capitalism* (London, 1948), pp. 197-270.

[44] *The Dumb Philosopher* (1719), ed. Scott (London, 1841), p. 21.

[45] *The Case of Protestant Dissenters in Carolina,* 1706, p. 5.

[46] *Social Teaching,* I, 328.

[47] Perry Miller and Thomas H. Johnson, *The Puritans* (New York, 1938), p. 461.

[48] See William York Trindall, *John Bunyan: Mechanick Preacher* (New York, 1934), pp. 23-41.

[49] Troeltsch, *Social Teaching,* II, 590.

[50] James Moffat, 'The Religion of Robinson Crusoe', *Contemporary Review,* CXV (1919), 669.

[51] *Life,* I, 85, 99.

[52] VIII, 192-194.

[53] *Cit.* W. Lee, *Daniel Defoe* (London, 1869), III, 29-30.

[54] *Works,* ed. Potter, p. 419. . . .

J. Paul Hunter (essay date 1966)

SOURCE: "The 'Occasion' of *Robinson Crusoe*," in *The Reluctant Pilgrim: Defoe's Emblematic Method and Quest for Form in "Robinson Crusoe,"* The Johns Hopkins Press, 1966, pp. 1-22.

[*Below, Hunter discredits certain assumptions about what inspired* Robinson Crusoe *as well as the notion that the book falls into the tradition of travel literature; he asserts that* Crusoe *is a Christian work in which geographical facts are introduced primarily for their narrative function.*]

Interpretive problems in eighteenth-century fiction result not so much from a lack of historical interest and knowledge as from a disguised antihistoricism in applying known facts, for it is often tempting to use history rather than surrender to it. Defoe study has, I think, more often settled for the illusion of history than for a full, rigorous, and sensitive examination of the assumed contexts of a particular work. Old generalizations have often seemed more valid than they really are because a façade of fact has obscured a flawed foundation of logic. Such methodology has determined the greater part of *Robinson Crusoe* scholarship, and I wish to examine some of the assumptions of this methodology before arguing another series of contexts which, it seems to me, are more relevant to *Robinson Crusoe* and to the emergence of the novel as a form.

Knowledge of Defoe's political journalism has opened some important windows to his art, but misuse of this knowledge has also led to some serious misconceptions. One such set of misconceptions involves the "occasion" of *Robinson Crusoe,* for Defoe students (working upon assumptions about Defoe's journalistic methods) have reconstructed on the basis of conjecture the events which inspired *Robinson Crusoe* and also those which effected its ultimate form. Alexander Selkirk's four-year sojourn on the desolate island of Juan Fernandez is thus usually considered to be the direct inspiration for *Robinson Crusoe;*[1] and travel books (such as those by Edward Cooke and Woodes Rogers, which give accounts of Selkirk's story) are regarded as formative influences on Defoe's art. This account of Defoe's procedure dates from a generation ago, but because neither its conclusions nor assumptions have been seriously questioned the received opinion is still that articulated by Ernest A. Baker in 1929: "The original incentive to write *Robinson Crusoe* and the central idea of a man left by himself on a desert island . . . came to Defoe from the actual experiences of Alexander Selkirk." The novel must "be considered as [a] fictitious narrative of travel."[2] This account of Defoe's design and procedure is, I think, inadequate and inaccurate; and it seriously misleads us as to the rich and complex traditions which nourish *Robinson Crusoe*—and which influence the form of an emerging genre.

The Selkirk conjecture dates from the middle of the eighteenth century and probably originated from rumors during Defoe's own lifetime.[3] Selkirk's adventure was, of course, well known to Defoe's contemporaries,[4] but Selkirk was only the most recent of several persons who had endured long isolation in remote places. Many other "miraculous preservations" were recorded during the late seventeenth and early eighteenth centuries, and Defoe probably knew as much about some of them as he did about Selkirk. For example, two other men before Selkirk had been stranded at separate times on Juan Fernandez, one of them for five years.[5] Another castaway, Ephraim How, for nearly a year was supposed dead before he was found alone upon a "rocky desolate Island," where he and two companions had been cast in a storm. After his companions died, he had survived by using materials washed ashore from the shipwreck.[6] A fourth castaway, stranded near Scotland in 1616, had become so notable an *exemplum* that eighteenth-century writers still repeated his story.[7] A fifth spent two years alone on an island near the Isle of Providence after nine of his companions perished either on the island or in trying to swim to civilization.[8] A sixth, Anthony Thatcher, stranded with his wife in 1635 after a shipwreck had killed their fellow voyagers, survived by using clothing and debris from the wreck, much as Crusoe does.[9] Many castaways, in fact, underwent hardships much like Crusoe's, reacted to them much as he does, and recounted their experiences in a similarly detailed way.[10]

Any of these castaways might have provided some inspiration for Defoe, but, laying aside for a moment the issue of Defoe's possible indebtedness for facts or incidents, one may question whether any castaway event provided the major impulse for the creation of *Robinson Crusoe*. Selkirk's adventure is closer in time to the publication of *Robinson Crusoe* than are the other adventures I have cited, but almost seven years separate the publication of *Robinson Crusoe* from the publication of accounts of Selkirk. Because the Selkirk conjecture rests primarily on the assumption that Defoe usually "capitalized" on current news events, this seven-year delay would seem crucial. Pope and Horace may have thought a seven-year waiting period advisable, but no journalist would agree.[11]

The assumption that Defoe's writings all stem from current happenings ignores an important distinction about artistic aim. An event often stimulated Defoe to produce a political tract, for his function as a news analyst for the Whigs and/or Tories often demanded that he interpret the current scene so as to influence the English public. But in other kinds of writing Defoe may well have worked differently. In *The Family*

Instructor, for example, and in his other clearly moralistic works, he seems to begin with an ideological aim and to accumulate events (factual or fictional) as examples to support his ideology. The antithetical procedures of the journalist and moralist are only two of many authorial procedures in which Defoe may have engaged, for living by his pen cast him in a variety of roles. And to see what sort of role he assumed in writing *Robinson Crusoe,* one needs to determine what kind of book it is, for his procedures are much more likely to have been dictated by his aim in an individual work than by a standard scheme or method applied indiscriminately to his more than five hundred publications.[12]

The assumptions which, when pursued in one direction, lead to the Selkirk conjecture, when pursued in another, lead to more serious misconceptions about *Robinson Crusoe.* Because it is assumed that Defoe began with factual information (largely from travel literature), wove various facts together, embroidered his by now fictional fabric with a semblance of truth, and, finally, tried to pass off the result as a true account, the conclusion is that Defoe desired to imitate his sources and that he wrote in the tradition of fictionalized travel literature. In "placing" *Robinson Crusoe* on the basis of assumptions about Defoe's method rather than on the basis of the book's text, Defoe students have diverted critical attention from relevant materials in other subliterary traditions and have instead defined a context which does a serious injustice to *Robinson Crusoe,* for while Defoe's novel bears some resemblances to travel literature, it differs from that literature in crucial ways.[13]

Source studies of half a century ago are largely responsible for this definition of context. The search for sources turned rather naturally to travel books, for source hunters were first looking for sources of *information,* and travel books were the atlases and geographical encyclopedias of Defoe's day. But the search never really got beyond travel books, for the searchers never really looked beyond factual information, even though they implied that Defoe's dependence on travel books was almost total and influenced even the structure of books like *Robinson Crusoe.* Then too, they were greatly encouraged in their efforts by a strange and surprising bibliographical discovery of 1895.

Defoe's library had been sold a few months after his death in 1731, and although the *Daily Advertiser* for November 13, 1731, mentioned a sale catalogue, no copy of it had been found before 1895, when George A. Aitken located one in the British Museum.[14] The value of the find was considerably diminished, however, by the fact that Defoe's books were grouped with those of an Anglican clergyman, Philip Farewell, and the catalogue failed to distinguish individual ownership.[15] Announcing his find in the *Athenaeum,* Aitken admitted that because of the catalogue's grouping he was "in some cases . . . unable to say positively that a certain book was Defoe's," but he thought that "we shall not be far wrong if we set on one side certain classes of works as Dr. Farewell's and attribute the remainder to [Defoe]." On this assumption, Aitken proposed a partial list of Defoe's books, setting aside as Dr. Farewell's "the large array of theological and classical literature." He admitted that "in adopting this course we shall, no doubt, pass over not a few works of Defoe's, but this is unavoidable."[16]

Aitken listed more than three dozen travel books and maps as probably belonging to Defoe, and later source students seem to have trusted Aitken's list completely.[17] Although one cannot be certain, it is likely that Defoe did own most of the books on Aitken's list, but his background and interests make it equally probable that he owned many of the theological and devotional books passed over by Aitken. The authority of Aitken's list has never been seriously challenged, however, and its publication lent considerable support to the growing tendency to pass over Defoe's ideas and his intellectual background in favor of a quest for the sources of his facts in travel literature. During the next thirty years source students found enough "parallels" to "establish" the debt that they had anticipated, and since 1924 (when Arthur W. Secord's *Studies in the Narrative Method of Defoe* was published) their conclusions about Defoe's sources, his method of composition, and his aims have been accepted almost without dissent.[18]

The placing of **Robinson Crusoe** itself in the tradition of travel literature is ultimately the most misleading implication of such source studies, but an examination of the premises and procedures of such studies warns us to be wary of accepting even their general conclusions. Secord quotes approvingly the belief of Ernest Bernbaum that "originals will ultimately be found for all of [Defoe's] longer narratives,"[19] and although they do not say so openly, most Defoe source students seem to operate from such a premise. Often a subtle suggestion of Defoe's dishonesty hovers just beneath the surface of their analyses, and they seem anxious to attribute a very different role to Defoe's imagination than to the imagination of most writers. As a result, they often attach far too much importance to parallels which are either coincidental or indicate nothing more than the common knowledge of an age—errors which raise serious questions about generalizations we have come to accept.

Secord emphasizes Defoe's debt to Robert Knox's *An Historical Relation of . . . Ceylon* and William Dampier's *A New Voyage Round the World;* among the sources of **Robinson Crusoe,** he lists these as two of six "certain" ones.[20] Yet his conception of what their contribution was and his method of arguing Defoe's debt to them are most revealing. Knox's *Ceylon,* according

to Secord, provided Defoe with a number of details about resourcefulness in the face of loneliness and hardship, for although Selkirk's adventure provided the inspiration for Defoe, it did not provide sufficient detail for a long story; Defoe therefore turned to Knox, for his *Ceylon* was "less known but more detailed, and more satisfactory to Defoe for both reasons."[21] Secord admits that Knox's external circumstances differ from Crusoe's—"It is true that Knox was a captive on a large and populous island, that he had a dozen or more fellow Englishmen with him so that occasionally they might converse, and that part of their time they were allowed to live together"—but he thinks these "external differences" may have "blinded investigators to the significance of Knox as a prototype of Crusoe. Both were on islands, both were lonely, and both had their existence to maintain under similar handicaps." Secord then notes the stylistic similarities of the two works ("It was now about the year 1673" [Knox]; "It was now the month of December" [Crusoe]), and he next illustrates Defoe's "borrowing" of events. He notes that "the island experiences of each, for instance, begin at about the same time": Knox's ship is disabled on November 19, 1659, and Crusoe is shipwrecked on September 30, 1659. Both have the ague, both wear out their clothes and try to replace them, Knox uses cocoanut oil in his acquired lamp while Crusoe makes a lamp and uses goat's tallow. After several pages of similar "parallels," Secord admits that "many of these similarities are not in themselves very convincing," but because he is sure that Defoe had read Knox he believes the similarities "become of more than superficial importance." "These matters," he concludes, "were known to Defoe and *could not fail* to find some place in Crusoe's endeavors to work out the problem of existence on his island."[22] Even if writers are a part of all that they have met, one may doubt the value of such source study when no specific debt can be discovered.

As he begins to consider Dampier's *Voyages,* Secord indicates his conception of Defoe's imaginative act: "If we think of Selkirk as having suggested to Defoe the idea of writing a story of desert island life, and of Knox as having provided him with a concrete embodiment of that idea, we shall not go far astray. Defoe's next need would be a large storehouse of details of life under unusual circumstances from which he could clothe the skeleton furnished by Selkirk and Knox. Exactly such a storehouse of details is Dampier's '*Voyages.*'"[23] One may doubt the accuracy of this description of creation, but Secord's suggestions about how Defoe used Dampier are even more startling. He does not distinguish clearly between facts and suggestions for episodes, and (as in the Knox argument) his case rests primarily on a long list of inexact parallels and a statement that Defoe must surely have read the book. Defoe might indeed have gotten information about South American geography, climate, and customs from

Dampier, but he might just as well have gotten this information from a number of other sources, for to find such facts in both books hardly proves borrowing. As a political journalist aware of his expanding world, as a man of trade, and as a key figure in the formulation of the South Sea Company, Defoe might well have stored facts like these in his head; if not, the men with whom he conversed daily could have supplied him from memory with the kind of information found in Dampier. If one considers this sort of information as a literary source, there is no end of source study, for the encyclopedia and the dictionary (and how would one decide *which* encyclopedia, *which* dictionary?) would be only the first sources studied in attempts to uncover an author's "materials."[24]

The rage for parallel passages as evidence of borrowing has blurred the one real contribution of source students: evidence that Defoe grounded his story on the geographical and cultural facts and beliefs of his contemporaries, just as he grounded the psychology and religion of his characters on contemporary belief.[25] But by overstating Defoe's debt to contemporary knowledge and by localizing it too exclusively, they have seriously misled us about Defoe's imagination. Once we are aware of the amount and variety of information available to Defoe about shipwrecks, castaways, and primitive life, we are more likely to be impressed by his ability to distinguish the norm in the experiences of island castaways than to be convinced that he wrote with a specific incident in mind. And by generalizing about Defoe's method on the basis of inexact circumstantial evidence and specious logic, source hunters have successfully (but not accurately) promulgated an image of Defoe as a compiler whose art consists in the crafty fusion of unrelated anecdotes.[26] Lately Defoe's imagination and accomplishment have sometimes been viewed differently, but still too typical is the judgment of the Oxford literary historian of Defoe's time: *Robinson Crusoe,* he says, "is not so much invented as compiled from a number of reports."[27]

The artistry of *Robinson Crusoe* is most seriously maligned, however, not by viewing the novel's parts as somehow dependent upon travel books, but by considering its total form to be patterned on the travel tradition. Source hunters did not set out specifically to "place" *Robinson Crusoe* within any literary tradition, but, because they failed to distinguish between what Defoe worked from (sources) and what he worked toward (artistic aims), their conclusions have had the effect of defining *Robinson Crusoe* itself as a fictionalized travel book.[28] Such a definition has serious implications for the structure and meaning of *Robinson Crusoe,* as today's critical commonplaces about the novel clearly demonstrate, for, like the Selkirk conjecture, it suggests that Defoe's art is fact-centered rather than idea-centered. Because questionable assumptions and procedures have led to such a definition, the validity of the conclusion is at least doubtful, but ultimately such a definition has to rest (as Shakespearean studies ought to have taught us) not upon the matter of source materials at all, but upon questions of Defoe's aims and those of the travel writers. Examined on this basis, the categorizing of *Robinson Crusoe* as travel literature is even less valid than other conclusions of Defoe source studies, for (aside from a few surface similarities) *Robinson Crusoe* makes no attempt to follow the conventional pattern of the travel tradition.

Despite their subliterary status, travel books early in the seventeenth century developed a set of distinguishing characteristics almost as rigid as the conventions of a poetic genre: each book tried to answer the same kinds of questions and each was organized in much the same way. Travel books depended for their success on the continued interest of a buying public with specific expectations, and even when their stated purpose was to offer other benefits, travel writers usually fulfilled those expectations.[29] "I know 'tis generally expected," writes Woodes Rogers in his introduction to *A Cruising Voyage Round the World,* "that when far distant Voyages are printed, they should contain new and wonderful Discovries with surprizing Accounts of People and Animals,"[30] and like other voyagers, Rogers condemns this popular taste. But, also like others, he satisfies the very expectations which he rails against.

The expectations satisfied by the travel writers are of various kinds. For the reader interested in adventure and strange occurrence, a story like Selkirk's is often included, and though the story is advertised blatantly, usually on the title page, very sparing and professedly grudging attention is given to it in the book itself.[31] Other general readers, like those referred to by Rogers, sought encyclopedic information about exotic places and peoples. The writers, however, seem (or pretend) to be concerned with readers who expect more technical information, and they usually profess that their only desire is to disseminate knowledge which will benefit country and commerce. In practice, all these expectations are ministered to according to a procedural formula with little variation.

Basically, the formula may be described as chronological in movement from place to place, topical in describing the particulars of each place. Much geographical detail is given about the places and about the natives and their customs, but there is relatively little emphasis on event. When an unusual happening (like the finding of Selkirk) is described, the tone retains the same clam, dispassionate quality that characterizes the rest of the book, for "objectivity" of tone and style characterizes the tradition as a whole.[32] An important aspect of this objectivity is the absence of any informing idea or theme: chronology, replaced by topicality when the narrative is interrupted to describe a particular place, is the only organizing force in the books, thematic considerations being inappropriate to the "pose" or conventions of the form.[33]

Secord notes that Defoe has Crusoe "do a series of things well known in the literature of travel; suffer storm and shipwreck, endure slavery . . . , duplicate the experiences of desert island life, and participate in both commerce and travel," but the resemblances, as Secord's comparison would suggest, are broad ones.[34] Crusoe describes events in chronological order (after a rationale for the first voyage is established) until the "narrator" returns home from his longest, most arduous voyage. The style is matter-of-fact, and the book contains some of the same kinds of "fact" as do the travel books. When Crusoe is at sea, he frequently gives his position, speed, and direction; on land, he describe the animals and the weapons, food, and customs of the natives. About his island he gives full information, detailing its geography, climatic patterns, animal and plant life, and the sailing conditions around it.

But these superficial similarities lose their significance when one notes Defoe's very different emphasis and his considerably different use of similar materials. In *Robinson Crusoe* the facts about various places are never presented as information for its own sake; each fact is introduced because of its function in the narrative situation. Lions and leopards are described in Africa because they represent, in one case, danger to Crusoe and Xury, and, in another, their means of reciprocating the kindness of the natives. The description of the island accumulates gradually as the narrative unfolds; there is no tabular itemizing of descriptive facts. And the island is the only land area which receives anything like a full description. About Brazil the reader learns only a few things pertinent to Crusoe; during the voyage from Sallee, he is given only facts necessary to the narrative. Here, the description serves the narrative; in the travel books, the narrative often merely connects the various descriptions, which are avowedly the most important parts.

Failure to define the rationale and mode of the travel books has led to a general lack of discrimination between various kinds of books concerned with discovery.[35] *Robinson Crusoe* clearly is more like contemporary adventure stories than like the travel books; information is subordinated to event, and the movement is dramatic. Chronology, simple a convenience in the travel books, becomes for Defoe (as for adventure stories) a conscious device to dramatize development.[36] But even more important, *Robinson Crusoe* has a larger coherence than that produced by the narrative sequence—a coherence which ultimately separates *Robinson Crusoe* from both travel literature and adventure stories, for books in both the latter traditions lack an informing idea which gives a meaning to individual events or to the sequence as a whole. These books

seem to lack ideological content, and no thematic meaning can be abstracted from them. Some critics have insisted that *Robinson Crusoe* resembles them in this respect, that it is episodic and lacks fundamental unity. Secord states as a truism that *Robinson Crusoe* "imitates life in its very shapelessness."[37] This view, however, ignores the thematic structure of the novel, a structure set up by the artistic (and ultimately philosophical) rationale for all of Crusoe's wanderings.

Crusoe is never merely an adventurer who goes from place to place, participating in isolated events. Each of his experiences takes on meaning in relation to a pattern set in motion by his "fatal . . . Propension of Nature" (A2)—an irrational inclination to roam. His "rambling Thoughts" (A1) cause him to rebel against parental authority and against his divinely appointed "station"—a rebellion which he interprets as his "Original Sin" (A225). Crusoe views each subsequent tragic event as punishment for his rebellion, and at last concludes that real deliverance from his plight (both physical and spiritual) is only possible when he resigns himself completely to the will of God.

Robinson Crusoe is structured on the basis of a familiar Christian pattern of disobedience-punishment-repentance-deliverance, a pattern set up in the first few pages of the book, Crusoe sees each event of his life in terms of the conflict between man's sinful natural propensity, which leads him into one difficulty after another, and a watchful providence, which ultimately delivers man from himself. Crusoe's continual appraisal of his situation keeps the conflict at the forefront of the action throughout, for his appraisal is not the superficial, unrelated commentary some critics have described, but rather is an integral part of the thematic pattern set up by Crusoe's rebellion and the prophecy of his father that Crusoe "will be the miserablest Wretch that was ever born" (A6). On the first page Crusoe plunges himself, through disobedience by reason of pride, into the universal predicament of fallen man; the remainder of the narrative describes that predicament in detail and dramatizes Crusoe's attempts to confront his world—and his God.

Despite its bias, Charles Gildon's criticism of *Robinson Crusoe* is historically valuable because it suggests how Defoe's contemporaries viewed his aim and accomplishment. Gildon cites several improbabilities and historical inaccuracies, but his main objection is not to Defoe's passing off fiction as fact, but to the book's moral and religious point of view:

> I am far from being an enemy to the Writers of Fables, since I know very well that this Manner of Writing is not only very Ancient, but very useful, I might say sacred, since it has been made use of by the inspired Writers themselves; but then to render any Fable worthy of being received into the Number

of those which are truly valuable, it must naturally produce some useful Moral . . . but this of *Robinson Crusoe* . . . is design'd against . . . publick good.[38]

A Roman Catholic turned deist turned Anglican, Gildon was eager to defend what he now considered the orthodox faith, and his charges are directed primarily against a theological point of view which seems to him unsound and ultimately dangerous.[39] He attacks Defoe's use of the supernatural, and (because he holds a very different, much less orthodox view of God's role in human affairs) he takes issue with almost every religious attitude in the novel. Gildon's motives may have been those of personal jealousy and party animus, but the charges themselves are still revealing, for they suggest that Gildon viewed the book in religious terms and felt that he must attack it ideologically rather than simply expose its fictional nature.

In his statement about *Robinson Crusoe*'s popularity, Gildon suggests that other contemporary readers also saw the book in religious terms. People who buy the book, says Gildon, leave it "as a legacy with the *Pilgrim's Progress,* the *Practice of Piety* and *God's Revenge against Murther.*"[40] The juxtaposition and implied comparison is a sneer at the level of Defoe's readership and suggests (from Gildon's point of view) condemnation by association, for the books he mentions all share a Puritan view of morality and theology. Each of them was well known to Gildon's contemporaries. By 1719, Lewis Bayly's *Practice of Piety* (1613) had reached its fiftieth edition and was probably the best-known Puritan manual of piety and conduct. John Reynolds' *The Triumphs of God's Revenge against Murther* (1621-24) had gone through fewer editions, but it was well known for assigning to providence a particularly active role in human affairs. Bunyan's book, then as now, seemed to epitomize the Puritan view of life.

Ultimately, *Robinson Crusoe* is much closer to *The Pilgrim's Progress* than to the other two books, but it bears a significant relationship to the traditions in which all three of the books belong. In his Author's Preface, Defoe gives two aims of *Robinson Crusoe:* (1) to present *"a religious Application of Events . . . [for] the Instruction of others by this Example,"* and (2) *"to justify and honour the Wisdom of Providence in all the Variety of our Circumstances . . ."* (Avii). These moral and ideological aims have often been regarded as Defoe's afterthoughts or rationalizations; modern scholars have seemed reluctant to take seriously a man who can "lie like truth." But Defoe's Preface, like Gildon's scornful comparison, suggests the connection with Puritan religious traditions; once examined, these traditions illuminate both the theme and structure of *Robinson Crusoe* and, ultimately, the development of the novel as a literary form.

Notes

[1] Arthur W. Secord's assumption is typical: "Selkirk undoubtedly furnished Defoe with the central theme of the story,—a fact upon which too much emphasis cannot be laid and which I shall assume as fundamental" (*Studies in the Narrative Method of Defoe* ["University of Illinois Studies in Language and Literature," IX; Urbana, 1924], p. 31).

[2] *The History of the English Novel* (10 vols.; London, 1929-39), III, 147-48, 150.

[3] Late in the eighteenth century, James Beattie relates, as "the account commonly given," an anecdote about Defoe's taking advantage of Selkirk after hearing Selkirk tell his story personally (*Dissertations Moral and Critical* [London, 1783], p. 565). Another rumor during Defoe's lifetime insisted that *Robinson Crusoe* was really written by the Earl of Oxford.

[4] Accounts of it were published not only in standard travel books but in a periodical (*The Englishman,* December 1-3, 1713) and a separately issued tract (*Providence Displayed* [London, 1712]). But Baker probably exaggerates in calling the incident "*the* great sensation of 1712-1713" (*History,* III, 148; italics mine).

[5] See Woodes Rogers, *A Cruising Voyage Round the World* (London, 1712), pp. 129-30.

[6] See Increase Mather, *An Essay for the Recording of Illustrious Providences* (Boston, 1684), pp. 58-64; and William Turner, *A Compleat History of the Most Remarkable Providences, Both of Judgment and Mercy, Which Have Hapned in This Present Age* (London, 1697), p. 110.

[7] See James Janeway, *Token for Mariners, Containing Many Famous and Wonderful Instances of God's Providence in Sea Dangers and Deliverances, in Mercifully Preserving the Lives of His Poor Creatures, When in Humane Probability, at the Point of Perishing by Shipwreck, Famine, or Other Accidents* (London, 1708), pp. 31-33. Janeway retells the story from Adam Olearius, *The Voyages and Travels of the Ambassadors,* trans. John Davies (London, 1662). For a discussion of Janeway, Mather, Turner, and similar books, see Chapter III below.

[8] See Increase Mather, *Essay,* p. 71, and Turner, *Remarkable Providences,* p. 110.

[9] See Mather, *Essay,* p. 13.

[10] See, for example, Janeway, *Token for Mariners,* Mather, *Essay,* or Turner, *Remarkable Providences.*

[11] John Robert Moore's doubts about the Selkirk conjecture on first glance seem to represent an advance over received opinion, but although his conclusion differs from the usual one, his assumptions have the same weakness. Moore does not think that Selkirk's return to England in 1712 weighed heavily on Defoe's mind in 1719, but he does regard as significant the contemporary economic situation in South America. He points out that England's war with Spain had severed trade relations between South America and England's South Sea Company, and he argues that Defoe's interest in stimulating colonization near the Orinoco led him somehow to write *Robinson Crusoe,* though he is not explicit about how *Robinson Crusoe* delivers Defoe's economic message. Moore argues that "if [Defoe] wrote a novel in 1719, it would likely have something to say of the slave trade, of the jealousy between England and Spain, of pirates and mutineers . . . , and of an island near the mouth of the Orinoco River." He adds that "no one could have foreseen how Defoe would develop his hero's solitary life on the island," and concludes that the development was a "'strange surprise' to Defoe himself" (*Daniel Defoe: Citizen of the Modern World* [Chicago, 1958], pp. 223-24). Another recent critic, Francis Watson, has also been troubled by standard explanations of Defoe's delay in writing the novel; his reading of *Robinson Crusoe* is salutary, but he offers no new insights about the Selkirk conjecture ("Robinson Crusoe: Fact and Fiction," *Listener,* LXII [October 15, 1959], 617-19).

Earlier scholars suggested that a new 1718 edition of Rogers (which contained the Selkirk story) somehow prompted Defoe, but this suggestion does not seem very helpful unless it is meant to indicate that somehow Defoe's memory was jogged. Only briefly has it been suggested that the inspiration is tied to thematic concerns, and these suggestions have been related to biographical conjectures. Moore thinks that Defoe may have felt some concern for having left the calling (the ministry) for which he prepared at Morton's Academy, or that he may have been concerned with the rebellion of his own son, who showed little inclination to obey his father's wishes.

[12] Maximillian Novak has recently suggested that thematic concerns are primary in several of Defoe's works (see *EF*). Received opinion about Defoe is indicated by the response which Professor Novak's suggestion received. See, for example, the review by Michael Shugrue (*JEGP,* LXII [1963], 403-5), in which "Novak's conviction that 'Defoe created his fiction from ideas rather than from incidents'" is regarded as "perhaps the only disturbing note in an otherwise excellent discussion of *Robinson Crusoe*" (p. 404).

[13] At one time, Defoe students recognized that a wider context of traditions nourished *Robinson Crusoe;* they usually mentioned biography, picaresque romance, and moral treatise. But events of the late nineteenth century obscured this contextual richness. The eclipse of Defoe's moral reputation, based on discoveries about his political duplicity, was accompanied by decreasing attention to his ideas, especially moral and religious ones, and emphasis shifted quickly to the adventure-story aspects of his work. At the same time, a new consciousness of the novel as an art form stimulated the desire to evaluate Defoe's contributions to the history of fiction; this desire, combined with the shift of emphasis from ideas to events in Defoe, focused attention on materials from which Defoe could have obtained factual information.

For early discussions of the relationship of Defoe's fiction to other traditions in which he wrote, see George A. Aitken, General Introduction, *Romances and Narratives by Daniel Defoe* (16 vols.; London, 1895), I, xxix ff.; and W. P. Trent, *Daniel Defoe: How To Know Him* (Indianapolis, Ind., 1916), pp. 128, 135, 175. For the rationale behind Defoe source study, see Secord, *Studies,* p. 19.

[14] William Lee had noted the sale and lamented the apparent loss of the catalogue. See his *Daniel Defoe: His Life and Recently Discovered Writings 1716-1729* (3 vols.; London, 1869), I, 470-71.

[15] Besides, some of Defoe's books were apparently not sold through the catalogue. The fact that the Farewell-Defoe sale catalogue contains only a few of Defoe's own writings suggests that part of the library had been dispersed before the catalogue was printed. This possibility casts even further doubt on the reliability of the catalogue as a guide to Defoe's reading habits.

[16] "Defoe's Library," *Athenaeum,* I (1895), 706-7.

[17] Not all scholars who have used Aitken's list have been careful to note the conjecture involved and Aitken's own reservations about the limitations of his list, and their footnotes often cite Aitken's list, not the catalogue itself. Secord and Baker assume the authority of Aitken's judgment. See, for example, Secord, *Studies,* pp. 25, 93, and 104 n.

[18] Since the late nineteen fifties there have been signs of a growing dissatisfaction with received opinion about Defoe (see the Preface to this volume), and, although the conclusions of students of the sources have not been attacked explicitly, the growing awareness of Defoe's artistic complexity has cast some doubt on the generally accepted account of Defoe's imaginative act. But for a recent example of the continuing prominence of source students' procedures, see Gary J. Scrimgeour, "The Problem of Realism in Defoe's *Captain Singleton*" (*HLQ,* XXVII [1963], 21-37).

[19] P. 18. Secord says that Bernbaum offers this conjecture to explain Defoe's large number of publications.

[20] Knox's book was first published in 1681, Dampier's (in two volumes) in 1697 and 1699.

[21] P. 32. Assumptions about Defoe's deviousness seem clear here, as in Secord's statement elsewhere that "Defoe is compelled in the island story to go to . . . [great] lengths to disguise his materials borrowed from published sources so that those borrowings may not appear" (p. 26).

[22] Pp. 32-39. Italics mine.

[23] Pp. 49-50. Secord seems to assume the primacy of printed materials as "sources," apparently believing that an author only makes use of oral information if there is no published word on the subject. Secord also assumes the primacy of English over non-English books, apparently on a similar theory, even though Defoe was conversant with several languages.

[24] The immoderate judgment of source students is suggested by Secord's discussion of two episodes—Crusoe's making of planks and his discovery of a footprint. He finds Crusoe's plank-making to be based either upon Dampier or upon information in the private unpublished journal of Knox, even though both Knox and Dampier describe how two planks are made from a tree and Crusoe is able to make but one. Such a derivation might still be possible if we assume Crusoe's more primitive method to be a part of Defoe's artistic strategy, but to regard these two accounts as the exclusive possibilities seems excessive, especially since the methods are rather obvious and would probably occur to anyone needing a plank.

Secord notes three narratives which contain footprint episodes and attaches much importance to one of them (in Dampier's *Voyages*) because the print evokes fear. Here is his description and interpretation of the incident:

> Dampier and some others, being ashore to kill cattle on the isle of Pines (near Cuba), landed on a sandy bay where they saw "much footing of men and boys; the impressions seemed to be about 8 or 10 days old." "This troubled us a little," said Dampier, who strongly suspected them of being the tracks of Spaniards; "but it being now their Christmas, we concluded that they were gone over to Cuba to keep it there, so we went after our game. . . ." The element of fear is, of course, mild in comparison to that in "Robinson Crusoe," but it is there.

One might, I think, more profitably consider the symbolic overtones of the footprint in *The Pilgrim's Progress,* though not as a "source" in Secord's sense.

[25] I have discussed this subject in my essay, "Friday as a Convert: Defoe and the Accounts of Indian Missionaries" (*RES,* n.s., XIV [1963], 243-48).

[26] The illustrations I have drawn from Secord are, I am afraid, too typical of the evidence and logic of Defoe source study; I choose my examples from Secord not because he is most vulnerable, but because he is the most articulate and detailed of Defoe source students. It now seems almost incredible that Secord's book has been the most influential study of Defoe in the twentieth century; my concern is that these conjectural conclusions have remained unchallenged for so long, have guided a majority of Defoe studies in our time, and have obscured aspects of Defoe's background which bear important implications for the novel as a form.

[27] Bonamy Dobrée, "The Matter-of-Fact Novelist," *Listener,* XLV (1951), 468.

[28] Even Professor Secord fails to make this important distinction, and slips into a "placing" of *Robinson Crusoe* based on sources: "'Robinson Crusoe,' finally, is not so much a fictitious autobiography . . . as it is a fictitious book of travel . . ." (p. 111).

[29] Reader expectation was, of course, largely determined by familiarity with Hakluyt, Purchas, and their seventeenth-century successors. For a good recent account of travel literature, see Percy G. Adams, *Travelers and Travel Liars* (Berkeley and Los Angeles, 1962).

[30] P. xiv.

[31] See the title page of Edward Cooke, *A Voyage to the South Sea, and Round the World* (2 vols.; London, 1712). It is always difficult to tell whether the travel writers are sincere in their protestations or whether they are simply repeating a conventional attitude toward reader expectations.

[32] See, for example, the Hakluyt Society edition of Lionel Wafer's *A New Voyage & Description of the Isthmus of America* (ed. L. E. Elliott Joyce [Oxford, 1934]), in which the contrast between Wafer's "Secret Report" and the published version of his travels suggests the tone and manner expected of a narrator in travel literature.

[33] The typical narrative first states the author's credentials (previous sea experience) and explains the nature and purpose of the current voyage. The ship is described (size, number and type of sails), and often the more important members of the crew are introduced. The log of days at sea is detailed enough for a curious reader to trace the journey; masses of information are given about daily locations, winds, currents, and factors affecting the speed and direction of the voyage.

Unusual events (storms, sighting of other ships, dietary problems, pirate encounters, crew changes) sometimes are given extended treatment, but such anecdotes seldom extend beyond two or three pages. On the other hand, topical descriptions of places and peoples visited are usually lengthy. The amount of detail for each place varies, of course, with the knowledge of the voyager and with the general importance of the particular place, but ordinarily such matters as the kinds of fish inhabiting the coastal waters or native methods of building huts get far more attention than any event. Such information may or may not have sold the books, but travel writers at least pretend to think it did.

[34] Secord, *Studies,* p. 109. The superficiality of the similarities suggests that instead of attempting to imitate the style and format of travel books (which the author of *The Shortest Way with the Dissenters* could surely do, if he tried) Defoe used features like the title page simply to attract a particular kind of reader, one who was perhaps unlikely to be reached by *The Family Instructor.*

[35] Throughout this study, I use the term "travel literature" to refer only to published reports of such explorers as Dampier, Rogers, and Cooke. This kind of literature was the chief type used by source students in their work; Secord, for example, lists ten such books as "certain" or "probable" sources of *Robinson Crusoe* and its two sequels. However, he also includes Defoe's *The Storm* and the anonymous *Providence Displayed* as sources of the same type. Their essentially different aims and forms are discussed in Chapter III below.

The term travel literature is sometimes used in a broader, less precise sense; a recent English Institute program on travel literature contained, for example, a paper on science fiction (as voyages of the mind). Under a broad enough definition of the term, *The Pilgrim's Progress, The Odyssey,* and almost every eighteenth-century novel could fit the category. But it is important to distinguish between different types of publications dealing with travel, and because source students have usually used the term "travel literature" to refer to reports like Dampier's, I have retained their term here. I use it, however, *only* to describe writings like Dampier's, not those with different aims and methods.

[36] Adventure stories often involve travel to far-off places, but travel books seldom involve much adventure. When writers like Dampier or Cooke do describe exciting events, they de-emphasize the action in accordance with their avowal that their only concern is information. Events only explain delays in the voyage or difficulties of exploration: they do not structure a sequential relation. Chronology is less a conscious structure than a convenience. Adventure stories—factual or fictional, episodic or unified—use chronology to suggest movement; they depend upon a world of time, for they are concerned with event, not fact. Even when based on actual happenings, they obviously filter and formulate experience, organizing it in a more or less dramatic manner; travel books, by contrast, pretend to be almost photographic. The difference is that between a story and a report.

[37] P. 232.

[38] *The Life and Strange Surprizing Adventures of Mr. D——— DeF——— of London, Hosier . . .* (London, 1719), p. 2; reprinted in *Robinson Crusoe Examin'd and Criticis'd,* ed. Paul Dottin (London and Paris, 1923), p. 82. Gildon does not accuse Defoe of failing to inculcate a moral, but of not pointing a *useful* moral.

[39] For an account of Gildon's life and a discussion of his various religious positions, see Dottin's "Life of Gildon" in *Crusoe Examin'd and Criticis'd.* Dottin says that Gildon was resolved "to reap the utmost benefit from his conversion" (p. 22).

[40] P. x; in Dottin, p. 72. Because these words are placed in the mouth of "Defoe" in a dialogue, one might suspect that Gildon was simply being facetious—if he did not later attack the book for its theological position on various matters.

In *Tom Jones,* Fielding suggests a similar contemporary classification, even though (like Gildon) he holds very different religious and philosophical positions. Note the kind of books Fielding lists alongside *Robinson Crusoe* in Bk. VIII, chap. v. For a brief discussion of Fielding's different artistic assumptions, see below, Afterword.

Everett Zimmerman (essay date 1975)

SOURCE: "*Robinson Crusoe*: Author and Narrator," in *Defoe and the Novel,* University of California Press, 1975, pp. 20-47.

[*In the following excerpt, Zimmerman explores problems in narrative consistency in* Robinson Crusoe *and contends that* The Farther Adventures *adds psychological aspects to the theological ideas found in the first novel.*]

The Life and Strange Surprizing Adventures of Robinson Crusoe was published in 1719. According to the title page, it was "written by Himself"; the "preface" mentions, in addition, an editor. The work purports to be autobiography, and was lent at least a limited plausibility by the contemporary interest in Alexander Selkirk, a sailor who spent five years alone on an uninhabited island. Defoe's relationship to his book is difficult to define because of his narrative method: he tries to authenticate the account as being entirely Crusoe's. Questions arise: Does Defoe have any discernible attitude toward his character? Or is Defoe perhaps quite literally writing the book that Crusoe would have written? These questions are impelled by the narrative inefficiency of *Robinson Crusoe:* the book is filled with events, but it does not move along easily. It contains many seeming irrelevancies, contradictions, and under-developed suggestions. Are these to be dismissed or interpreted? The manner in which the story is written suggests characteristics of its writer. Are these to be referred to Crusoe or to Defoe? Often the meaning of the narrative seems not to be presented but to be escaping.

Charles Gildon raised the relevant issues in 1719. He imagined a meeting between Defoe and Crusoe:

> D[anie]l. Why, ye airy Fantoms, are you not my Creatures? mayn't I make of you what I please?
>
> Cru[soe]. Why, yes, you may make of us what you please; but when you raise Beings contradictory to common Sense, and destructive of Religion and Morality; they will rise up against you. . . .[1]

Is this "strange whimsical, inconsistent Being,"[2] who writes the book and expounds its morality, Defoe's creature or only his pseudonym? Unfortunately Gildon was interested only in using Crusoe as an example of Defoe's muddles and pretensions—his pamphlet becomes a dreary, though often accurate, catalog of the deficiencies of "Mr. D[aniel] De F[oe], of London, Hosier,"[3] as revealed in his book *Robinson Crusoe.*

Defoe defended himself against Gildon in a collection of moral essays, which he published as *Serious Reflections during the Life and Surprising Adventures of Robinson Crusoe.* His responses to Gildon in this work only complicate the question of his relation to Crusoe. Defoe has Crusoe insist on his own autonomy with an obstinacy that is, at least in retrospect, comic. One may of course dismiss this oddity by citing economic motives: Crusoe's name will help to sell Defoe's old moral essays. But explaining a motive does not necessarily define a performance. Defoe, well known as the author of *Robinson Crusoe,* wrote "Robinson Crusoe's Preface" to a collection of religious essays: "I, Robinson Crusoe, being at this time in perfect and sound mind and memory, thanks be to God therefore, do hereby declare their objection ['that it is all formed and embellished by invention to impose upon the world'] is an invention scandalous in design, and false in fact. . . ."[4] But Crusoe then goes on to hint that the truth about himself is somehow related to the truth about Daniel Defoe: ". . . there is not a circum-

stance in the imaginary story but has its just allusion to a real story" (pp. xi-xii). The introduction to this volume of serious reflections is an entirely transparent equivocation: Crusoe is alive because he is independent of an author, but he is true because he is Defoe.

An author whose actions so bristle with contradictions cannot easily be brought proximate to his creature. One can begin with what author and putative author indubitably share: the language of their common book. "I cannot explain by any possible Energy of Words" is the introduction to a passage about Crusoe's loneliness.[5] In the subsequent account there is no illusion of emotion. We are given this sample of Crusoe's "breaking out": "O that there had been but one or two; nay, or but one Soul sav'd out of this Ship, to have escap'd to me, that I might but have had one Companion, one Fellow-Creature to have spoken to me, and to have convers'd with" (p. 188)! This highly rhetorical passage is addressed to no one except the hypothetical reader. It is followed by an analysis of Crusoe's emotions, which are without fictional reality.

The inadequacies of elevated language are especially apparent in the conversion episodes. Crusoe's undescribed "broken and imperfect Prayer" (p. 94) does not lead to his later ecstatic shout by any progression that we can easily regard as spiritually authentic: *"Jesus, thou Son of David, Jesus, thou exalted, Prince and Saviour, give me Repentance"* (p. 96)! Fever and his loathsome concoctions of tobacco explain Crusoe's rhetoric more plausibly than does repentance. Later Crusoe decides that he cannot recommend his remedies: ". . . I had frequent Convulsions in my Nerves and Limbs for some Time" (p. 97).

The issue is not one of morals: we do not have to decide either that Defoe is being ironic or that he is a hypocrite. He attempts to create, as well as to explain, the emotions that he assumes are Crusoe's. Defoe's attempts to capture emotions are apparent not only in the elevated diction but also in various quantitative increases in the language, such as lists and repetitions. The priest in *The Farther Adventures* speaks in several languages to express his spiritual ecstasy (XIII, 39). But the grandiose speeches that are intended to create emotion only signify its absence.

As words inexorably slide away from their intended signification, Defoe and Crusoe attempt to fix the emotion in gesture:

> I believe it is impossible to express to the Life what the Extasies and Transports of the Soul are, when it is so sav'd. . . . I walk'd about on the Shore, lifting up my Hands, and my whole Being, as I may say, wrapt up in the Contemplation of my Deliverance, making a Thousand Gestures and Motions which I cannot describe (p. 46).

In this book, actions are assumed to have an undeniable reality even if they cannot be definitely described: the more direct and authentic the emotion, the more likely that discursive speech will be suppressed. Recognizing his father, "*Friday* kiss'd him, embrac'd him, hugg'd him, cry'd, laugh'd, hollow'd, jump'd about, danc'd, sung, then cry'd again, wrung his Hands, beat his own Face, and Head, and then sung, and jump'd about again, like a distracted Creature" (p. 238).

Both author and narrator are suspicious of language: it is at times a limitation that they wish to evade. But the psychic reality that appears beyond language is terrifying, and words are also often sought as a defense against fears. Those emotions authenticated by action often produce a state verging on madness. The similes implying a disturbed mind—Friday is "like a distracted Creature," and Crusoe runs about "like a Mad-man" (p. 47)—are literalized in the behavior of the passengers rescued at sea in *The Farther Adventures:* " . . . there were some in Tears, some raging, and tearing themselves, as if they had been in the greatest Agonies of Sorrow, some stark-raving and down-right lunatick, some ran about the Ship stamping with their Feet, others wringing their Hands . . . (XII, 128). . . . for if an Excess of Joy can carry men out to such a Length beyond the Reach of their Reason, what will not the Extravagancies of Anger, Rage, and a provok'd Mind carry us to" (XII, 131)? Intensities of emotion are conceived of as bizarre, uncontrollable, and damaging—a chaos within.

It is not surprising then that one finds a frequent retreat from such manifestations of feeling into language—a journal, lists, elaborate ritualistic bargaining (see p. 256). As much as possible, language itself is concretized. Unnecessary lists are written; though there is nothing with which to write, Crusoe wants the agreement with the Spaniards to be "put in writing" (p. 248); extreme gratitude for the Portuguese captain's kindness inspires a call "for a Pen and Ink to give him a Receipt" (p. 282). If unsatisfying as a simulator of high emotions, words nevertheless produce an order. Language is repressive of the fearsome inner energies and only obliquely expressive.[6]

We have moved from what Defoe and Crusoe share— the language of *Robinson Crusoe*—to what they may perhaps hold opposing notions of—the meaning of the language. Crusoe surveys his life of variety and misfortune with compassion, laughter, and sometimes an exceedingly cold eye. He comments both explicitly and implicitly—and sometimes not at all. But there is little sense of an author judging the narrator. *Robinson Crusoe* is ironic only in the limited sense that the narrator reveals his earlier moral blindness.

Traces of someone who is not a character do, nevertheless, remain; the author tries too blatantly to conceal himself. The twice-mentioned Pocket-Book (XIII, 138, 159), its "leaves rotted," is designed to vouch for the truth of the story and to excuse the omission of place names—but the verisimilitude of the travel book has already been rejected explicitly and repeatedly (XIII, 83, 109). Such declarations too are unnecessary after hundreds of pages have made clear that the narrative is an internal one about the eye *"never satisfied with Seeing"* (XIII, 110).

This sense of an incompletely hidden author appears frequently in the narrative machinery. The action of writing a book exists in the same way as the actions and evaluations of Crusoe—not only as the means for telling Crusoe's story but also as an adjunct to it. For example, when Crusoe flees, unjustly suspected of being a pirate, his letter of outraged innocence is summarized in the text. The letter contains no new information, and Crusoe goes on to note that "we had no Occasion ever to let the Pilot carry this Letter; for he never went back again" (XIII, 137). This is not Crusoe sorting out his life but an act of writing for its own sake, having a meaning independent of the narrative (I am not here arguing that narrative clumsiness is necessarily high art—only that it is not without meaning).

Crusoe uses the material world to obscure and control his destructive impulses. His behavior is not always entirely appropriate to the adventure that he is ostensibly recounting; nor is it always consonant with the moral scheme that he uses to shape his story. There is a blurring of outline, a sense that his actions fulfill psychic requirements neither directly expressed nor entirely moral or utilitarian. These indirections are similar to Defoe's. His writing is not always perfectly adapted to Crusoe: there are mannerisms serving a purpose not exclusively the character's.

Crusoe comments on his fortifications: ". . . as it appear'd afterward, there was no need of all this Caution from the Enemies that I apprehended Danger from" (p. 59). Subsequent events give us more confidence in Crusoe's hindsight than in Defoe's foresight: Defoe eliminates suspense about something to which his narrative persistently returns. Although concealment is essential to Crusoe's defense, fortifications never figure in it. Crusoe fortifies to restore his psychic equilibrium; whenever he has brought his defenses to seeming perfection, he is again disturbed. The many references to the fortified habitation culminate in a lengthy summarizing description (pp. 151-153). Immediately thereafter Crusoe sees the "Print of a Man's naked Foot" (p. 153). In his terror he first proposes to destroy all traces of his presence, but then he finds a better way to relieve his "Burthen of Anxiety" (p. 159): ". . . I resolv'd to draw me a second Fortification, in the same Manner of a Semicircle, at a Distance from my Wall just where I had planted a double Row of Trees about twelve years before, of which I made mention" (p. 161).

Descriptions of this habitation become a set piece in *Robinson Crusoe*—a result of Defoe's amplification as well as of Crusoe's elaboration. Defoe is finally obliged to assert the attractions of Crusoe's not entirely functional construction: he has the captain who rescues Crusoe express amazement at everything in Crusoe's life, "but above all the Captain admir'd my Fortification" (p. 258). In *The Farther Adventures,* the Spaniards explain their changes of it: Crusoe's old habitation has a dignity as a relic of a grander past. As Crusoe's dependents, the Spaniards are held to a more utilitarian standard of behavior than he was: Crusoe immediately inquires, "What put them upon all these Fortifications" (XII, 147)? By this time of course the attacks of savages have provided the justification previously missing.

Years before, the Spaniard had suggested wicker work for defense, but Crusoe "saw no Need of it" (p. 248). Defoe, however, rarely relinquishes a scrap of narrative material. Will Atkins, in many ways resembling the earlier Crusoe, lives in a wicker house that is described in an extended passage reminiscent of the descriptions of Crusoe's old habitation: Crusoe concludes, "Such a Piece of Basketwork, I believe, was never seen in the World, nor House, or Tent, so neatly contriv'd, much less, so built" (XII, 221). The author's unwillingness to give up anything is analogous to an important trait of his central figure. Crusoe attempts to salvage everything from the ship: "I had the biggest Magazin of all Kinds that ever were laid up, I believe, for one Man, but I was not Satisfy'd still; for while the Ship sat upright in that Posture, I thought I ought to get every Thing out of her that I could" (p. 55). Crusoe first attempts to select from the ship that which will be useful; he then takes indiscriminately: " . . . I believe verily, had the calm Weather held, I should have brought away the whole Ship Piece by Piece" (pp. 56-57).

Crusoe's interest in the material world is clearly not merely utilitarian. While escaping from the Moors, he gratuitously shoots an enormous lion and is then "very sorry to lose three Charges of Powder and Shot upon a Creature that was good for nothing" (p. 28). He takes the skin, thinking it may be of some use. It is: he lies on it for a time, and the Portuguese captain later gives him forty ducats for it. But the use that Crusoe so vaguely apprehended is the excuse for the action, not its cause. Here too, Defoe's planning is no more rational than Crusoe's. The episode is not contrived to provide money or a bed for Crusoe: these are afterthoughts. When Crusoe's Moorish adventure is ended, everything is scrupulously transformed into the money needed for the next episode—boat, Xury, lion's skin, leopard's skin, bottles, guns, and beeswax (pp. 33-34). Nothing must be abandoned; Crusoe and Defoe share their attachment to things.

Among the memorable passages of *Robinson Crusoe* is the apostrophe to money: ". . . O Drug! . . . what art thou good for, Thou art not worth to me, no not the taking off of the Ground, one of those Knives is worth all this Heap, I have no Manner of use for thee, e'en remain where thou art, and go to the Bottom as a Creature whose Life is not worth saving" (p. 57). These words are resoundingly false: we are accustomed by this time to see a conflict between Crusoe's abstractions and his actions. Here this conflict is brought sharply to our attention by the contrasting matter-of-fact tone of the immediately succeeding reversal: "However, upon Second thoughts, I took it away, and wrapping all this in a Piece of Canvas, I began to think of making another Raft." But one does not have to conclude that Crusoe's materialism is being derided—only that he has two thoughts, both of which are justified.[7] He plausibly argues that "we enjoy just as much as we can use, and no more" (p. 129). Just as plausibly, he suggests that money might be hidden on the island and recovered if he escapes (p. 193).

Our confidence that he will not leave the money behind results in part from our faith in consistency of character. Crusoe is a collector—and not only of money. His emotions are controlled and defined by many kinds of objects. Surrounded by his booty, he is able to rest "very secure" as the storm breaks up the wreck (p. 57). With "infinite Labour" he carries things to his new habitation (p. 59): ". . . it was a great Pleasure to me to see all my Goods in such Order" (p. 69). He reluctantly thinks of moving when an earthquake threatens to bury him: ". . . but still when I look'd about and saw how every thing was put in order, how pleasantly conceal'd I was, and how safe from Danger, it made me very loath to remove" (p. 82). Having his goods again reduced to a "confus'd Heap" (p. 67) is more distressing than the danger.

Crusoe's dogged collection of the unneeded corresponds to Defoe's cataloging of the irrelevant. Crusoe "got very little . . . that was of any use" (p. 193) from his voyage to the Spanish wreck; nevertheless what he got is listed in several hundreds of words. The enumerating, the organizing of oneself in verbal possessions, is the comfort, perhaps cold, of writer and character: the quantity of material collected by the one has its analogue in the language compiled by the other. The impulse to barricade oneself appears even in metaphor: "I was now come to the Center of my Travels, and had in a little Time all my new discover'd Estate safe about me" (p. 303). This estate is money, his new fortress. Defoe's contradictory claims, in the *Serious Reflections,* for the reality of his book are perhaps relevant here. He insisted on Crusoe's autonomy, on the historical authenticity of the book, but he would not give up the opposing claim that the book reflected his own life. It was his accretion, not Crusoe's.

The most directly expressed of Crusoe's emotions are his fear of being devoured and his hatred of the wild men and beasts who devour. There is for him a fate worse than death—subsequently being eaten up: his body is his last barricade. The cannibals who visit the island produce extravagances of fear and hatred in him—intensities of emotion that are sustained for years. After he first learns of the cannibals, he can think of nothing but how he "might destroy some of these Monsters in their cruel bloody Entertainment, and if possible, save the Victim they should bring hither to destroy" (p. 168; the emphasis of the sentence is significant). He has fantasies and dreams of killing them: ". . . sometimes that I was just going to let fly at them in my Sleep" (p. 169). Both prudential and religious considerations restrain his murderous imagination for a time, but after another visit from the savages he dreams not only of killing them but also of how he "might justify the doing of it" (p. 185). He finally decides that Friday can be used to kill a group of cannibals from another nation because he is in a state of war with them. But seeing a white victim, Crusoe is "enrag'd to the highest Degree" (p. 233). He prepares a balance sheet at the end of the account to record the number of savages killed (p. 237).

As Frank Ellis points out, the parts of the book before and after the island adventure are filled with references to creatures who eat people—the beasts and cannibals of Africa and the bear and wolves of the Pyrenees.[8] But some of these dangers of Africa (and the island) exist only in Crusoe's imagination. He sails southward to escape the Moors: ". . . for who would ha' suppos'd we were sail'd on to the southward to the truly *Barbarian* Coast, where whole Nations of Negroes were sure to surround us with their Canoes, and destroy us; where we could ne'er once go on shoar but we should be devour'd by savage Beasts, or more merciless Savages of human kind" (p. 23). Obviously Crusoe himself regards this as hyperbole, and in fact he encounters little difficulty with savages or animals. Nevertheless the "hideous Cryes and Howlings" of beasts and the fears of Crusoe and Xury are frequently mentioned (pp. 24-25). And early in his island sojourn, Crusoe's principal fear is of dangerous wild beasts, though there is never any evidence of their existence. These fears are finally externalized in the encounter with the wolves of Languedoc: ". . . the Howling of Wolves run much in my Head; and indeed, except the Noise I once heard on the Shore of *Africa* . . . I never heard any thing that filled me with so much Horrour" (p. 297). These are "hellish Creatures" (p. 299), "three hundred Devils . . . roaring and open mouth'd to devour us" (p. 302).

The ubiquitous references to being devoured point to a generalized fear: of being dematerialized—the reversal of the desire to accumulate. It is a fear shared by author and character; "being devoured" is a way of conceiving of diverse fears. Even the language of a passage not directly concerned with cannibals or beasts suggests devouring. Before the shipwreck, Crusoe and the crew expect to be, and are, "swallowed up" (pp. 41, 44); they fear being saved from the sea but devoured by the cannibals (p. 42); the sea is "wild" (p. 43; attention is called to this word, "*Den Wild Zee,* as the *Dutch* call the Sea in a Storm"); the sea pursues Crusoe "as furious as an Enemy" (p. 44); and buries him "deep in its own Body" (p. 45).

The fear represented in the book is finally of the rage within. Knowing his own rage, Crusoe fears the worst of others. When his aggressive impulses are thwarted, he improves his fortress in fear of vicious enemies. When his overimproved habitation affords diminishing opportunities for elaboration, he discovers a cave that is suitable for defense. Frightened by an old goat in the cave, he reassures himself: ". . . I durst to believe there was nothing in this Cave that was more frightful than my self" (p. 177). Although Crusoe has been meditating "a bloody putting twenty or thirty of them to the Sword" (p. 169), he gives no sign of recognizing any ironic meaning in his statement. Crusoe's possessions and fortress, Defoe's lists and amplifications—all serve as self-protective psychic diversions.

Crusoe's expectations of violence are not, however, foundationless; much of **The Farther Adventures** is a documentation of ungovernable passion. The irrational violent impulses of the three mutineers left on the island are brought under control only after several battles with savages. The actions of Crusoe's men at what he calls the "massacre of Madagascar" (XIII, 102) are "Instances of a Rage altogether barbarous, and a Fury, something beyond what was human" (XIII, 96). When suspected of being a pirate, Crusoe will not surrender, even though he can prove his innocence; he agrees with his partner: ". . . we could have expected nothing from them, but what Rage would have dictated, and an ungoverned Passion have executed" (XIII, 122). Crusoe, finally repelled by the continual bloodshed, is pleased when the Cochin-Chinese (who howl like the wolves of Languedoc) are vanquished with the loss of only one life: ". . . for I was sick of killing such poor Savage Wretches, even tho' it was in my own Defence" (XIII, 129).

But his bloodlust is revived. Traveling through China, he indulges in indirect, then direct, insults to the natives. He is clearly bent on mischief even before he finds an idol to provide a focus for his rage. When he learns that a Russian who affronted the idol had been sacrificed, Crusoe "related the Story of our Men at *Madagascar,* and how they burnt and sack'd the Village there, and kill'd Man, Woman, and Child . . . I added, that I thought we ought to do so to this Village" (XIII, 184; Crusoe's previous expressions of abhorrence of this massacre had driven his men to mutiny). Restrained by the information that the sacrifice had occurred at another village, Crusoe organizes an attack on the idol. The subsequent destruction is an exhibition of wild rage exercised against a surrogate human (XIII, 188).

The moral character of this incident is ambiguous in a way that is rare in *Robinson Crusoe.* It is not unusual for an event to be left open to interpretation, but Crusoe usually at least ponders its possible meanings. Rarely is there even a suspicion of Defoe looking with irony on Crusoe's final perceptions. Here the reference to the Madagascar incident quite clearly puts Crusoe in the wrong, but there is no more explicit recognition of guilt. Indeed, Crusoe's behavior is in some ways exemplary: he prevents the others from doing serious harm to the villagers, and justifies his destructive actions as a demonstration of the idol's falseness (the Tartar's angry pursuit of Crusoe and his companions shows that they have not learned the lesson that Crusoe intended). And to vindicate Crusoe, one may also cite "Of the Proportion Between the Christian and Pagan World" from the *Serious Reflections,* where it is argued that the Christian nations ought by force to eradicate the worship of idols (p. 230).

Crusoe's action is explicitly justified and implicitly condemned. The idol's appearance links it with the earlier cannibals and devouring animals: it is a ludicrous conglomeration of the features of various animals, wearing a garment and a hat (XIII, 180). Animals and, on one occasion, a man are sacrificed to it; the priests resemble butchers. Crusoe restrains his earlier rage against the cannibals by religious arguments; here he justifies identical feelings as religious zeal. These moral ambiguities result from contradictory desires of the author: to describe the frenzied mutilation of the idol and also to bring Crusoe (and the book) to a stasis, to a condition in which he is no longer at the mercy of irrational drives.

The pattern for *The Life and Strange Surprizing Adventures of Robinson Crusoe* is that of a fall, repentance, and redemption—both spiritual and secular. A coincidence of dates, among other things, attests to this pattern's providential order (p. 278): Crusoe's spiritual and physical welfare have been brought about by God's interventions. Within this structure are subsidiary narrative cycles (the island episode is the major one) that are interconnected by many cross-references. The ending, however, represents only temporary salvation. Crusoe's fortune is made, but he will continue the rambling that has been symptomatic of his evil. The obvious explanation is that Defoe is touting *The Farther Adventures.*

However, there is an additional reason for his continuing the book. The religious structure has not resolved the psychological problem: Crusoe's story has been organized according to a traditional pattern that does not explain his behavior. The continuation is consistent with the earlier book, but it turns out to be no more conclusive. *The Farther Adventures* sends Crusoe back to the island to tidy up left over narrative matters: the people remaining on the island are organized in a society, and their experiences are shown to be in some ways analogous to Crusoe's. Obsessions from the earlier work are repeated—eating and being eaten, massacres and fortifications. Nevertheless, the only larger order that Defoe finally imposes on the book is a physical one: Crusoe's rambling ceases when he encircles the globe.

In a sense, *The Farther Adventures* reflects Defoe's recognition of disharmonies in the earlier work. It represents the same impulses, but does not so effectively present the structures used to disguise and control them; aggressive impulses build up, are sated, and build up again. Defoe seems powerless to construct any other pattern. The hostility that drives the writer away from a "design" that he himself recognizes is evident in the following laughably overblown sentence—its very prolixity a testimony both to the writer's self-knowledge and his inability to restrain himself:

> . . . and therefore, I must confess, it seem'd strange to me, when I came home, and heard our People say such fine Things of the Power, Riches, Glory, Magnificence, and Trade of the *Chinese;* because I saw, and knew, that they were a contemptible Herd or Crowd of ignorant sorded Slaves, subjected to a Government qualified only to rule such a People; and in a word, for I am now launch'd quite beside my Design, I say, in a word, were not its Distance inconceivably great from *Muscovy,* and was not the *Muscovite* Empire almost as rude, impotent, and ill govern'd a Crowd of Slaves as they, the *Czar* of *Muscovy* might with much Ease drive them all out of their Country, and conquer them in one Campaign; and had the Czar, who I since hear is a growing Prince, and begins to appear formidable in the World, fallen this Way, instead of attacking the Warlike *Swedes,* in which Attempt none of the Powers of *Europe* would have envy'd or interrupted him; he might by this time have been Emperor of China, instead of being beaten by the King of *Sweden at Narva,* when the latter was not One to Six in Number (XIII, 153).

Providence and original sin are the central conceptions that Crusoe uses to explain his earlier life. They are organizing patterns in the book and also essentials of Defoe's faith. But this tells us little about *Robinson Crusoe*—or Defoe. How do these beliefs affect Defoe's imagination? How are they used in *Robinson Crusoe?*

"Of Listening to the Voice of Providence," from the *Serious Reflections,* resolves a few questions. The essay asserts clearly and repeatedly a faith in "the supervising influence and the secret direction of the Creator";

it is man's duty to attempt to understand this secret direction (p. 179). But Defoe recognized enormous difficulties in discerning the dispositions of Providence. His essay is burdened with references to the propensities of men for "tacking the awful name of Providence to every fancy of their own" (p. 196).

In *Robinson Crusoe,* Providence often seems to be a method of interpretation, a theory rather than a force. And on several occasions, events suggest that it may be Crusoe's "fancy." He thinks that his impulse to go to the Spanish wreck "must come from some invisible Direction" (p. 189), but on returning he not only regards his trip as fruitless but also sees that it intensifies his discontent. His subsequent dream of saving a savage, is, he thinks, providential. But it is a response to his desire to have someone to help him escape to the mainland; this desire is "the fruit of a disturb'd Mind, an impatient Temper" (p. 198). When his dream seems to come true, he notes his less than complete reliance on it: ". . . I did not let my Dream come to pass in that Part, *viz.* That he came into my Grove for shelter" (p. 205).

Providence seems to be of two minds about Crusoe's rescue: it prepares him to escape with the aid of the Spaniards, and also sends an English ship. Before rescuing the Spaniard, Crusoe had "Testimonies of the Care of Providence" and an "invincible Impression" that his "Deliverance was at hand" (p. 229). After rescuing the Spaniard, he thinks that he is to be provided with a crew to sail away, a supposition that is supported by the increases in his grain: the supply he is raising for the journey increases tenfold, an allusion to the blessings in the parable of the sower (p. 247). But "a strange and unforseen Accident" occurs—an English ship arrives (p. 249). Crusoe later thinks of this event as evidence of the "secret Hand of Providence governing the World" (p. 273). Although he is not entirely unaware of the difficulties of understanding what he calls the "Checquer-Work" (p. 304) of Providence, this awareness rarely seems to inhibit his speculations.

An inexplicable Providence is of course an aid to Defoe's next book: Crusoe is unexpectedly taken off, the Spaniards and rascally Englishmen are left behind to provide further adventures. But the separation between author and character which is implied by these manipulations is not complete: Crusoe and Defoe continue to respond to forces not explained by their conceptions of Providence or of potboilers. Crusoe's aversion to going from Portugal to England by sea is providentially inspired, as he shows by his account of subsequent shipping disasters (p. 288). Nevertheless, he forgets about Providence after encountering wolves: ". . . I think I would much rather go a thousand Leagues by Sea, though I were sure to meet with a Storm once a Week" (p. 302).

In *The Farther Adventures,* Providence becomes psychological as well as theological. Crusoe has dreams of the evils committed by the Englishmen on his island: they are "never all of them true in Fact" but in general. This, he thinks, suggests the "Converse of Spirits" (XII, 113). Clearly, he feels guilty for deserting the Spaniards, although he previously attributed his leaving the island to Providence. He later acknowledges that even at the time of his rescue he feared what the rascally English mutineers who were left behind would do (XII, 148). The difficulty of applying his conception of Providence to his experience becomes apparent, and he despairs of rational comprehension of the meaning of his life. We are "hurry'd down the Stream of our own Desires" (XIII, 82); although it is our duty to listen to the voice of Providence, it is "impossible to make Mankind wise, but at their own Expence" (XIII, 102).

Original sin too becomes a psychological as well as a theological conception. Crusoe calls his leaving home to ramble his *"Original Sin"* (p. 194); he has no rational object in mind, but is powerless against the compulsion: "But my ill Fate push'd me on now with an Obstinacy that nothing could resist" (p. 14). His repentance subdues this impulse—but only partially and temporarily.

The language of disease and mental illness is used to describe Crusoe's condition at the beginning of *The Farther Adventures*—"chronical Distemper" (XII, 112); "Extasies of Vapours" (XII, 113); he tries to control himself by working on his farm. When his nephew proposes a voyage, Crusoe attributes the suggestion to the Devil (XII, 120), but then gives Providence the blame (XII, 121). Theological language is Crusoe's device for explaining his psychological instability. This time Defoe accepts the consequences of his creature's unregenerate nature and keeps him in motion. In the final sentence, the old and exhausted Crusoe is preparing "a longer Journey than all these" (XIII, 220). The metaphor is retained even in the face of death.

The Farther Adventures embodies Defoe's increased understanding of Crusoe; much that is only implicit in the earlier work is explicit in the later one. In particular, the limitations of Crusoe's repentance are clearly shown in *The Farther Adventures.* But the later book is less interesting than the earlier one. The incongruities between structural device and psychological reality provide an order for the first account. Crusoe's use of religious conceptions to subdue his destructive impulses is both limiting and useful: although his theories do not explain his experience, they enable him to order his responses. In *The Farther Adventures,* Crusoe's disordered impulses result in a distended narrative—obsession without form.

In the earlier work, Crusoe's repentance is narrated in a traditional literary structure—a journal. The awkwardness of Defoe's use of this structure is expressive of the complications of the book. The journal begins ordinarily enough as a day-to-day account of his experiences, but soon Crusoe interprets events from a later point of view. The departure from the journal is frequently unnoted, but when it becomes apparent, variations of the formula "But to return to my Journal" (p. 79) are used to wrench the narrative back to its former structure. Vestiges of the journal remain for some time, but the form is of little narrative use after Crusoe's repentance and recovery.

The traditional use of a journal among the religious was to find and memorialize the spiritual significance of daily existence. One expects this kind of account here because Crusoe begins with events already narrated: what purpose can there be if not to reveal a spiritual dimension? But at first, the journal account is no more spiritual, or even internal, than his previous account: in its compression, it is usually a balder summary of external activity than the first account. It affords in fact the same satisfactions as his earlier frenetic activity: the process of external ordering hides the disorder within. Earlier he briefly described the state of his affairs in writing: " . . . not so much to leave them to any that were to come after me, for I was like to have but few Heirs, as to deliver my Thoughts from daily poring upon them, and afflicting my Mind" (p. 65). Following this exercise, he is able to bring his possessions into order: he exerts a "prodigious deal of Time and Labour" (p. 68) just to make shelving for his goods. By then he has not only attained the stability necessary for keeping a journal but has also acquired a need for this new stabilizing enterprise. The first part of his journal allows the previous ordering process to be enjoyed again.

The providential appearance of the grain is the first substantial departure from the journal form. As Crusoe expatiates on Providence, he moves away from his point of view as a castaway: his consciousness at that time is corrected and expanded until it disappears. Following this, the journal structure is violated extensively: the ill and inactive Crusoe is terror-stricken, and the spiritual significance of his repentance is explained by commentary from a later point of view.

It is not to Crusoe's diminishing supply of ink alone that we must look for an understanding of the exploded journal structure. Defoe could not plausibly have had Crusoe define his own spiritual condition. On the island, Crusoe is characterized by his obsessive actions: he finds pretexts, not explanations, for his behavior. His definitions of his condition must be supplemented by explanation from the vague and distant future. But Defoe's introduction of the journal is expressive as well as awkward. The gap between Crusoe's behavior and his explanations becomes apparent as additional commentary must be inserted to make the narrative assume the shape of a traditional repentance story.

The island experience is another structural device that is effectively exploited by Crusoe and Defoe. Traditional associations are alluded to, but the allegory is discontinuous; the island is interpreted in incompatible ways: it is "my Reign, or my Captivity, which you please" (p. 137). For Crusoe, the island is a way of defining moods; for Defoe, it is a way to shape a story. The *"Island of Despair"* (p. 70) is the wilderness (p. 130) where Crusoe must undergo the suffering that will take him through repentance to the promised land. But he transforms the wilderness into the garden; the island itself becomes his deliverance. The contradictions in his own thoughts are clear to Crusoe: he must subdue his anguish at being cast away, but he should also hope for his deliverance (p. 113). As he explores the island, he becomes increasingly aware that it can be made into a promised land. His habitation becomes "natural" (p. 110).

Defoe mentions many biblical parallels—the prodigal son and Jonah, for example.[9] But any extended interpretation of the story in terms of a single pattern is perilous: patterns obviously alluded to are often just as obviously incongruous. When Crusoe leaves the island, he gives those who remain various seeds "and bad them be sure to sow and encrease them" (p. 277). This incident combines references to two of Christ's parables—that of the sower, often alluded to in *Robinson Crusoe,* and that of the talents, traditionally interpreted as an injunction to prepare for Christ's return. This analogy to divinity, though not strictly suitable to Crusoe, is pursued in *The Farther Adventures.* The Spaniards remain in their original habitation because they expect to "hear from their Governor again, meaning me" (XII, 172). When he returns, they accept his food "as Bread sent from Heaven; and what a reviving Cordial it was to their Spirits to taste it" (XIII, 6). Crusoe soon explains that he did not come to remove them but "to establish them there" (XIII, 7). Their response to this chilling news: ". . . I was a Father to them, and that having such a Correspondent as I was, in so remote a Part of the World, it would make them forget that they were left in a desolate Place" (XIII, 10).

The obvious incongruities resulting from presenting Crusoe as a type of Christ are soon apparent. Crusoe sees how far he is from "understanding the most essential Part of a Christian" (XIII, 23), And in retrospect he comments upon his unkind behavior: ". . . I pleased my self with being the patron of those People I placed there, and doing for them in a kind of haughty majestick Way, like an old Patriarchal Monarch" (XIII,

80). Christ is a role adopted by Crusoe but also sustained by Defoe (Defoe has things external to Crusoe also suggest that he is a savior). The role is soon abandoned, but the attitude is later revived. Speaking to a Russian prince, Crusoe boasts: " . . . never Tyrant, *for such I acknowledged myself to be,* was ever so universally beloved, and yet so horribly feared by his Subjects" (XIII, 200). Christ or tyrant—he can play one as easily as the other.

Robinson Crusoe is highly allusive; yet the references to things outside the book do not lead to expanded meanings: reverberations are quickly muffled. "I might well say, now indeed, That the latter End of *Job* was better than the Beginning" (p. 284), says Crusoe as he recovers his wealth. This comparison at first seems ironical; Job, unlike Crusoe, was a righteous man. Although Defoe understood well the implications of the biblical story, one can find no indications of irony within the text. The reference is used in its limited sense: only Crusoe's ending is expressed in terms of Job's. The broader meanings of both stories are ignored.

Sometimes the allusions are vague, even subliminal. Crusoe fancies himself "like one of the ancient Giants, which are said to live in Caves, and Holes, in the Rocks, where none could come at them" (p. 179). A Polyphemus who is in terror of being himself eaten? (Eric Berne states that "Crusoe's anxieties were based on the principle: 'He who eats shall be eaten.'"[10]) One thinks of Crusoe's often described position on top of his hill looking for cannibals with his perspective glass (monocular). And another example: Crusoe agrees with the Spaniard "about a Signal they should hang out at their Return, by which I should know them again, when they came back, at a Distance, before they came on Shore" (p. 249). The signal is in vain; Crusoe has gone. Has Theseus's father revenged himself? Crusoe has been punished for filial contempt; in this case, he makes his children suffer. Pursuit of these threads does not lead to a precise delimitation of meaning but to the labyrinth where text and author meet. . . .

Notes

[1] "A Dialogue Betwixt D[aniel] F[o]e, Robinson Crusoe and his Man Friday," from *Robinson Crusoe Examin'd and Criticis'd,* ed. Paul Dottin (London: J. M. Dent, 1923), p. 69.

[2] Gildon, p. 70.

[3] Gildon, p. 63.

[4] *Serious Reflections during the Life and Surprising Adventures of Robinson Crusoe,* ed. George Aitken (London: J. M. Dent, 1895), p. ix.

[5] *Robinson Crusoe,* ed. J. Donald Crowley (New York: Oxford University Press, 1972). References to *The Farther Adventures of Robinson Crusoe* are to Volumes XII and XIII of the Shakespeare Head Edition of the Novels and Selected Writings of Daniel Defoe (Oxford, 1927). All subsequent references to *Robinson Crusoe* are in the text.

[6] Benjamin Boyce, "The Question of Emotion in Defoe," *SP* 50 (1953), 50, makes this comment on *Robinson Crusoe:* "Augustan reticence about the horrors has not prevented Defoe's twice giving us plain hints of what 'many dull things'—that is, what shocking, private, and indecorous things—would have gone into a stream-of-consciousness narrative."

[7] This passage has occasioned differences of opinion. Ian Watt, *The Rise of the Novel* (Berkeley and Los Angeles, University of California Press, 1957) p. 119, responds to Coleridge's admiration of the passage by wondering if "the apparent irony [is not] merely the result of the extreme insouciance with which Defoe . . . jerks himself back to his role as novelist, and hastens to tell us what he knows Crusoe, and indeed anyone else, would actually do in the circumstances." William H. Halewood, "Religion and Invention in *Robinson Crusoe,*" *Essays in Criticism* 14 (1964), 350, finds that this passage "concentrates in a little space the central irony of the book and the defining irony of Crusoe's inconsistent character." If "irony" means only the recognition of a discrepancy between conduct and statement, temporarily unnoticed by a character, then this passage is ironic: surely both Defoe and his narrator, Crusoe, must be assumed to be aware of the sharply presented contradictions here. But if in a broader sense, it is meant that Defoe designed a structure to expose the failings of Crusoe's whole mode of behavior—failings never fully recognized by the character himself—then it seems to me that the passage is not ironic.

[8] "Introduction," *Twentieth-Century Interpretations of Robinson Crusoe,* ed. Ellis (Englewood Cliffs, N. J.: Prentice-Hall, 1969), pp. 12-13.

[9] Edwin B. Benjamin, "Symbolic Elements in *Robinson Crusoe,*" *PQ* 30 (1951), 206-211, shows the importance of many of the biblical allusions. J. Paul Hunter, *The Reluctant Pilgrim* (Baltimore: Johns Hopkins Press, 1966) provides information about the conventions of Puritan religious writings, and interprets *Robinson Crusoe* from this perspective. George A. Starr, *Defoe and Spiritual Autobiography* (Princeton: Princeton University Press, 1965) also deals with traditional religious patterns in *Robinson Crusoe.*

[10] "The Psychological Structure of Space with Some Remarks on *Robinson Crusoe,*" *Psychoanalytic Quarterly* 25 (1956), p. 563. . . .

Pat Rogers (essay date 1979)

SOURCE: "Religion and Allegory," in *Robinson Crusoe*, George Allen & Unwin, 1979, pp. 51-72.

[In the following excerpt, Rogers outlines various positions that critics have taken in interpreting Robinson Crusoe *and discusses Defoe's religious background and the novel's treatment of sin.]*

The Puritan Inheritance

The most striking single development in our recent understanding of the novel has lain in the rediscovery of a pervasive spiritual motif. In the nineteenth century *Crusoe* had been treated mainly as an adventure-story, characterised by intense 'realism' of presentation. Robinson himself had been viewed as an upright and manly Englishman, whose Broad Church piety did not get in the way of his real mission—survival and ultimate prosperity. Even as lately as the 1950s it was usual to dismiss Crusoe's religious reflections as not much more than *appliqué* on the surface of the narrative. In the 1860s Karl Marx wrote: 'Of his prayers and the like we take no account, since they are a source of pleasure to him, and he looks upon them as so much recreation.'[1] Almost a hundred years later Ian Watt was inclined to agree:

> Both Marx and Gildon were right in drawing attention to the discontinuity between the religious aspects of the book and its action: but their explanations do Defoe some injustice. His spiritual intentions were probably quite sincere, but they have the weakness of all 'Sunday religion' and manifest themselves in somewhat unconvincing periodical tributes to the transcendental at times when a respite from real action and practical intellectual effort is allowed or enforced.

Watt went on to assert that Defoe's 'religious upbringing forced him from time to time to hand over a brilliant piece of narrative by a star-reporter to a distant colleague on the religious page who could be relied on to supply suitable spiritual commentaries quickly out of stock. Puritanism made the editorial policy unalterable; but it was usually satisfied by a purely formal adherence.'[2]

These sentiments now have an extraordinarily dated look, because of the rapid transformation in our reading habits. Partly this is explicable by reason of a more sympathetic attitude towards the Puritan mind. Watt's book had its intellectual genesis at a time when R. H. Tawney and Max Weber dominated the general response to religious history. They are quoted comparatively infrequently by Watt, but it would not be straining the evidence to detect in his book a subterranean current of ideas deriving from this source. A representative passage in Tawney sums up the outlook:

> The distinctive note of Puritan teaching . . . was individual responsibility, not social obligation. Training its pupils to the mastery of others through the mastery of self, it prized as a crown of glory the qualities which arm the spiritual athlete for his solitary contest with a hostile world, and dismissed concern with the social order as the prop of weaklings and the Capua of the soul.[3]

Subsequent writers have criticised Tawney's general thesis, and have adopted a less jaundiced attitude towards the individualist ethic. It would not now be so readily taken for granted that 'concern with the social order' is always a more desirable or positive element in intellectual life than a concern for private spiritual values.

However, it was the appearance of two critical studies in the 1960s which dramatically reversed the position. Building on other explorations of the Puritan mind, and following up work on Milton and Bunyan in particular, these books set *Crusoe* in a wholly new light. George A. Starr published *Defoe and Spiritual Autobiography* in 1965. He argued that a well-marked cycle of sin and regeneration underlay Crusoe's experiences throughout the novel. There is, indeed, 'a conventional progression in sin' and an equally conventional pattern of redemption. Starr applied the same schemata to other novels (*Moll* and *Roxana*), but *Robinson Crusoe* is granted most space and proves the most amenable to this treatment. Another feature of the reading is the importance given to Crusoe's conversion of Friday, formerly regarded as marginal or even impertinent.[4]

Though the detailed emphases of J. Paul Hunter's *The Reluctant Pilgrim* (1966) are different, the main drift of the argument is remarkably similar. Hunter confines himself to *Crusoe* and examines a number of 'Puritan subliterary traditions' relevant to its making. (Where Starr had tended to stress general religious background, citing Anglican as well as Puritan sources, Hunter prefers to work from the dissenting models.) In his view the external narrative of travel and adventure has been allowed too prominent a place in our assessment of *Crusoe.* Typical of his argument are passages like this:

> What Defoe distills from desert island experience is not an 'agreeable Relation' at all, but rather a rigorous multilevel moral examination of life. . . . Unlike its [adventure-story] analogues, *Robinson Crusoe* derives dramatic power from its understanding of man's struggle against nature as both physical and metaphysical. . . . [It] embodies the Puritan view of man on a most profound level; it . . . portrays, through the struggles of one man, the rebellion and punishment, repentance and

deliverance, of all men, as they sojourn in a hostile world.

Or this:

> Throughout *Robinson Crusoe* physical events reflect Crusoe's spiritual state, for Crusoe is concerned with accommodating himself to his world spiritually and physically at the same time, and his efforts to come to terms with his physical environment parallel his efforts to find a proper relationship with his God. Ultimately, his physical activities become a metaphor for his spiritual aspirations.

What is most important here is the attempt to see *Crusoe* as a *coherent* and formally sophisticated narrative. Hunter, like Starr, divides the plot into clear-cut phases: rebellion and punishment, repentance and deliverance. He, too, pays attention to the 'saving' of Friday. But he goes further than Starr in detecting overall 'emblematic' or allegorical structure, using standard metaphors, parables and symbols to create a moral pilgrimage rather than a bare escape-story. He places particular stress on the biblical and typological allusions, looking for events with a meaning consecrated by their appearance (in identical or closely related terms) in scripture.[5]

Both these approaches show *Crusoe* as dependent on widely known techniques of popular devotional or didactic literature. They make it easier to relate the work to Defoe's vein of pious conduct-books, such as *The Family Instructor*. Moreover, they have in common a desire to emphasise the 'thematic' content of *Crusoe,* as opposed to the fictional rendering of exciting events. It is possible to feel that both critics overstate their case a little, and Hunter in particular is led by his thesis to play down every aspect of the work other than those which fit his case. Nevertheless, these readings have enriched our understanding to a remarkable degree, and in suggesting a new generic context for *Crusoe* they have provided an artistic justification for features and episodes which previously seemed hard to explain. Seen as a Puritan fable of spiritual life, the novel appears not only different but also, in crucial ways, a better book: more deeply imagined and more cunningly wrought.

The major forms lying behind such a version would be these:

(a) *Spiritual autobiography*. The best-known example today is Bunyan's *Grace Abounding* (1666). The keeping of a diary of one's own progress towards salvation was not, as Starr emphasises, confined to dissenting sects, although its most extreme manifestations are found there. The habit inculcated in pious individuals was to scrutinise their own life for signs of advancement or backsliding. In Starr's words, 'Since every man is responsible for the well-being of his own soul, he must mark with care each event or stage in its development. As his own spiritual physician, he must duly note every symptom of progress or relapse.' Another impetus to the composition of spiritual autobiography lay in the belief that 'there are universal and recurrent elements in human affairs, particularly in vicissitudes of the soul. History repeats itself . . . in the spiritual life of individuals.' This in turn connects with the habit of searching the Bible for parallels and portents, to find what were called 'Scripture Similitudes'. Certain biblical images came to have special meanings accredited to them; in this area of moral exegesis Defoe would have the example of innumerable sermons but also formal handbooks such as the *Tropologia* (1681) by a London Baptist preacher, Benjamin Keach (1640-1704), which gathers together many 'express' allegories found in the Bible. Key metaphors included those of pilgrimage, of seafaring, and warfare. Though surrounded in his youth by spiritual autobiographers, Defoe did not attempt the form himself; it is true, however, that his tributes to his family pastor, Dr Annesley (see below, p. 59), and his life of *Daniel Williams* (1718) have been seen as related to the tradition.[6]

Starr, as indicated, discerns a standard 'rhythm' of conversion. From his 'original sin' in running away to sea, through his early wanderings to his shipwreck and gradual restoration on the island, a direct allusion to this pattern can be traced. (For example, the early travels reflect estrangement and alienation from God.) Then on the island come stock episodes such as dreams and earthquakes. God's interposition finally brings Crusoe to a recognition of his errors, and his regeneration reaches a climax in his conversion of Friday—zeal in this direction was a well-understood mark of spiritual advancement. In spiritual biography 'the purposeful pattern of the subject's life is superimposed over the chronological record of events'; Crusoe has first to discover this purpose and then shape his narrative to show its accomplishment.[7]

(b) *The guide tradition*. This is a branch of popular homiletic literature concerned with warning the reader against the perils of moral existence, and designed to offer a ready-to-hand hortatory or consolatory body of instruction. There were many general guides, but also specialised manuals directed towards a group or calling (seamen, tradesmen, farmers, etc.). A major subdivision was that of the guide to young persons, in which Timothy Cruso (see below, p. 60) was a practitioner. Perhaps the best-known of all works in this genre were Arthur Dent's *Plain Mans Pathway to Heaven* (1601) and Lewis Bayly's *Practice of Piety* (1613); the equally popular *Whole Duty of Man* (1658) has its roots in this tradition. Tracts and sermons not specifically organised as a 'guide' drew upon the same habit of advice. Even as late a work as William Law's *A Serious Call to a Devout and Holy Life* (1728) shows some impress; the penultimate chapter, for instance, is set out very much on the 'guide' formula: 'Of evening prayer. Of the nature and necessity of examination. How we are to be particular in the confession of all our sins. How we are to fill our minds with a just horror and of all sin.' Law, of course, was a High Churchman. But Defoe the dissenter would be exposed to many such manuals on practical living, conceived from a religious standpoint. Indeed, his own conduct-books, from *The Family Instructor* through to *The Compleat English Gentleman,* are secularised or dramatised variants of the guide. Hunter is surely justified in saying that *Crusoe* deals 'with the problems which the guide tradition had previously faced'—the nature of a calling, filial obedience, resistance to temptation. As Hunter goes on to remark, '*Robinson Crusoe* ultimately is much more complex than any of the traditions which nourish it, but the complexity should not obscure the ancestry'.[8]

(c) The 'Providence' tradition. This is Hunter's term for a widely employed technique (found in sermons, guides, biographies and elsewhere), showing the intervention of God in the affairs of man. All the forms discussed here were likely to interpret natural phenomena as marks of divine approval or disapproval, as reward for merit or punishment for evil. The specific tradition relates to explicit or extended use of this notion, especially the recital of extraordinary events which are carefully explicated in the light of their providential bearings. A prominent and still highly readable example is the work of an Anglican clergyman, William Turner (1653-1701); it is called *A Compleat History of the Most Remarkable Providences, Both of Judgment and Mercy, Which have Hapned in this Present Age* (1697). Bitty and uneven though it is, this book provides one of the clearest introductions we have to the mental world in which *Robinson Crusoe* came to birth. In a way it is literature of the 'Strange News from . . .' variety; but for contemporaries the overriding interest undoubtedly lay in the interpretations rather than the events themselves—Turner divides his stories into categories, each illustrating particular modes of divine judgement. It should be added that the pamphlet version of Selkirk's story, *Providence Displayed* (see above, p. 49), is in essentials a reworking of Woodes Rogers towards providential ends.[9]

Defoe's awareness of this tradition is quite unmistakable. Even if he had not used as his theme delivery from shipwreck (and, incidentally, escape from Barbary)—standard providential material—and even if he had not stated in his preface (*RC1,* p. 1) that his aim was 'to justify and honour the Wisdom of Providence in all the Variety of our Circumstances', we should still have external evidence. In *RC3* a chapter is devoted to the subject of 'Listening to the Voice of Providence'. In this Defoe offers a definition of Providence ('the operation of the power, wisdom, justice, and

goodness of God by which He influences, governs, and directs not only the means, but the events, of all things which concern us in this world', p. 187). He has Crusoe explain that 'by listening to the voice of Providence, I mean to study its meaning in every circumstance of life'; this should be 'our business and our interest' (p. 189). Crusoe's habit of noting dates, coincidences and significant conjunctions is illuminated by his observation here, 'The concurrence of events is a light to their causes, and the methods of Heaven, in some things, are a happy guide to us to make a judgment in others; he that is deaf to these things shuts his ears to instruction, and, like Solomon's fool, hates knowledge' (p. 195). And at the end of this section:

> To listen to the voice of Providence, is to take strict notice of all the remarkable steps of Providence which relate to us in particular, to observe if there is nothing in them instructing to our conduct, no warning to us for avoiding some danger, no direction for the taking some particular steps for our safety or advantage, no hint to remind of such and such things omitted, no conviction of something committed, no vindictive step, by way of retaliation, marking out the crime in the punishment. (p. 213)

It would be exceedingly rash to assume that this is simply an importunate moral thrust on the self-sufficient narrative, an *ex post facto* signal by Defoe behind the back of his creation Robinson. All the signs are that Defoe, from the very beginning, meant his novel to bear these monitory functions.

A significant clue here lies in a book published fifteen years earlier. All his life Defoe was fascinated by natural disasters, whether volcanic eruptions, earthquakes, fires, or epidemics. One of his most characteristic early works is *The Storm* (1704), assembling reports on the great 'dreadful Tempest' which had struck Britain on 26-27 November 1703. At least 8,000 people are believed to have perished in the savage wind and floods: Eddystone lighthouse was destroyed, men-of-war lost while at anchor, the Bishop of Bath and Wells killed with his wife as they lay in bed. Defoe's compilation is, following the practice of the time, a rambling affair: it moves from Ralph Bohen's theories on the causes of wind through earlier hurricanes to the present storm, with a pastoral elegy sent in by an unnamed contributor. The main part of the book is taken up with eye-witness accounts from all over southern Britain. In his preface Defoe spells out the providential implications, and challenges freethinkers to examine their position: 'I cannot believe any Man so rooted in Atheistical Opinions, as not to find some Cause whether he was not in the Wrong, and a little to apprehend the Possibility of a Supreme Being, when he felt the terrible blasts of this Tempest.' Indeed, Defoe had originally intended to supply an account of 'some unthinking Wretches, who pass'd over this dreadful Judgment with Banter, Scoffing, and Contempt'; but he decided it would be charitable to omit this.[10]

A sceptic might ask whether Defoe would have had one of his early books strongly present in his mind when some 330 items separate this from *Crusoe* in the *Checklist*. But there is separate evidence that *The Storm* had a part to play in the genesis of the novel. As Secord demonstrated at length,[11] the account of the storm off Yarmouth roads (*RC1*, pp. 10-14) has strong affinities with various parts of *The Storm,* besides a connection with a passage on the Norfolk coast published in the *Tour* (1724).[12] The most direct parallel concerns the very last report inserted in *The Storm,* which carries the dateline, '*From on board* the John *and Mary, riding in* Yarmouth *Roads during the great Storm, but now in the River of* Thames'.[13] Secord itemised a number of closely similar features in the two books, showing a correspondence both in the materials of the description and in their ordering. Some aspects of the account in *Crusoe,* however, find their parallels in other reports included in *The Storm.* In addition, Secord briefly indicated a possible link between the Yarmouth narrative of 1704 and Crusoe's final shipwreck, that is, the one in the mouth of the Orinoco which results in his island captivity. There are occasional verbal parallels: 'the Sea went too high for any Boat to live' (*Storm*, pp. 268-9), 'the Sea went so high, that the Boat could not live' (*RC1*, p. 43). In both narratives a boat 'staves' to pieces when dashed against the ship; and other expressions recur ('abate', 'drive', as well as technical terms such as 'cable'). The resemblances are certainly greater than one would expect from two accounts of a storm chosen at random; and, while it would be going too far to list the 1704 description as an immediate 'source' of the 1719 wreck, some imaginative continuity may well be present. We do not know if Defoe himself wrote the relations of 'strange Deliverances' in *The Storm*—he may very easily have done so. In any case, the material stayed in his head for the rest of his life. There are several allusions to this national disaster in his *Tour* (1724-6): it rivals the Plague and the South Sea Bubble as an emblem of catastrophe.

It is probably unnecessary to emphasise here the fact that one of Defoe's later fictions, *A Journal of the Plague Year,* where the narrator refers to the plague as 'a particular Season of Divine Vengeance', is centrally concerned with natural events as a sign of God's wrath. H.F. sees the plague as occurring by 'the Appointment and Direction of Providence';[14] as usual Defoe makes it plain that divine will is expressed through second causes and only exceptionally through direct intervention outside the ordinary processes of nature. *Robinson Crusoe* is shot through with the same inclination to read providential meanings into occurrences both remarkable and humdrum. This proceeds from no ec-

centric or radical enthusiasm; it was a way of interpreting events and a way of telling stories thoroughly acceptable to readers of the day, whatever their particular shade of religious belief.

(*d*) *Other contexts.* Hunter describes a more generalised form, that is, the 'pilgrim' allegory present in Bunyan's masterpiece and sketched less memorably in a thousand sermons or tracts. The abstract scheme is set out by Hunter in these terms:

> A man first sails away from the Home appointed for him (instead of proceeding toward it) and then becomes isolated from God as a result of discontent and selfish pride. Ultimately, however, God intervenes to deliver him from destruction, and the direction of his life is altered to a course pleasing to God and leading at last to the man's ultimate Home. The man, however, still must undergo numerous battles with evil before he can rest content at the end of the journey.

This scenario would also fit many spiritual biographies. The fact that *Crusoe* emerges with much more concrete life and individuality than the scheme allows for does not make the correspondences wholly irrelevant.[15]

In a separate article Hunter draws attention to the many seventeenth-century accounts of missions among the American Indians. The missionaries were largely supported by New England Puritans, like Defoe's early tutor, Charles Morton. In fact a major collection of such accounts, *A Brief Narrative of the Success [of the] Gospel among the Indians in New-England* (1694), was dedicated by its compiler, Matthew Mayhew, to Morton amongst others. Hunter's main purpose on this occasion is to show how the descriptions of native converts square with Defoe's picture of Friday; but his article indicates another kind of work, straddling devotional and 'discovery' themes, which must have lain at the back of the novelist's mind.[16] So, of course, did innumerable sermons and religious tracts; their influence may not be directly felt at any given point in *Crusoe,* but they were abroad in the general imagination as surely as the images of popular television programmes inhabit our consciousness today. In 1719 no living Englishman (or woman) could have escaped the power of the religious word; it was the stuff of his culture.

Education in Dissent

The last comment would apply to any contemporary. But Defoe was marked off by the fact that he had been intended for the nonconformist ministry. His formative years were spent in a highly purposive environment, with a distinct aim in view. He grew up conscious of a special destiny in store and, although he relinquished the calling, he retained the sense of a personal fate.

Whether or not *Crusoe* can be read as an allegory of his private experience, he had a vein of self-pity which commonly expressed itself in laments at the 'afflictions' he was forced to endure. In the nearest he came to an autobiography, *An Appeal to Honour and Justice* (1715), he claimed that he alone had been 'silent under the infinite Clamours and Reproaches, causeless Curses, unusual Threatnings, and the most unjust and injurious Treatment in the World'.[17] Defoe had a profound consciousness of having been cheated somewhere along the line. Whether it was his abandoned career in the ministry, his failed business ventures, his allegiance to fallen ministers, the loss of his royal patron, William III, or a combination of these things—he felt he had not had his deserts. Crusoe and his other highly successful heroes and heroines may involve a compensatory fantasy.

Young Daniel Foe was only 2 years old when the Act of Uniformity passed through Parliament.[18] It meant that ministers were obliged to accept the new Book of Common Prayer, drawn up by a High Church convocation in 1661. In addition they had to submit to episcopal ordination. The vicar of St Giles, Cripplegate (the parish church, one might say, of Grub Street) was Samuel Annesley (?1620-96). He refused the new tests and was duly ejected. He took with him into the Presbyterian Church many parishioners; among these was the tallow-chandler of Fore Street, James Foe, together with his wife Alice and three children. In 1665, during the Plague, the Oxford Parliament passed the so-called Five Mile Act which strengthened the test and drove Annesley farther afield. After the Declaration of Indulgence in 1672 he was licensed to preach again, in Little St Helen's, off the lower end of Bishopsgate, opposite Gresham College. There he remained until his death in 1696, an event prompting Defoe to produce a verse elegy on his character—this stresses Annesley's loyalty to his parents, his piety from childhood on, and his qualities of calm, patience and fortitude in adversity.[19] Another strong link with nonconformity to come was forged by the marriage of his daughter to Samuel Wesley, the father of Charles and John. Moore is justified in saying that, through his association with Annesley, Defoe 'grew up near the center of Presbyterian worship in London'.[20]

Around 1668 Daniel lost his mother, and he was sent to a boarding school for dissenters near Dorking in Surrey. The master, James Fisher, was another ejected minister, although a man of lesser stature than Annesley. He was a Congregationalist, that is, a member of a less tightly organised sect than the Presbyterians. Defoe left school about 1674, and that should have been the end of his formal education. But instead he went on to study under yet another ejected minister, Charles Morton, at the famous Newington Green academy. This indicates that he was by now a candidate for the ministry. Much has been written about Morton

(1627-98) and his possible influence upon Defoe. The basic facts are, first, that he, too, was a Congregationalist; secondly, that he was a widely cultivated man, a graduate of Oxford who had been incorporated at Cambridge and who was ultimately to become Vice-President of Harvard; thirdly, that his special interests were scientific and mathematical (thus reinforcing the bias towards practical subjects which dissenting academies developed in reaction against the obscurantist pedantry—as they saw it—of the universities). Defoe was proud of his association with the man and with the school, and at the end of his life was still propagating the values he had imbibed during this period. It should be added that Morton taught through the medium of English—an act of rebellion in itself—and his own spare prose may possibly have influenced his pupil's style.

A pupil of the academy at just about the same time was a young man some four years senior to Defoe. This was Timothy Cruso (?1656-97), who went on to become a Presbyterian minister and well-known preacher. He wrote some of the popular 'guides', including *God the Guide of Youth* (1695); but he would probably not be associated with Defoe today but for his surname. Since the nineteenth century biographers have speculated on the possibility that this is where the curious name derives. (Other theories would relate it to a Caribbean island, Curaçao, where pirates gathered; or to a Cruso family in King's Lynn; or to German words such as *kreutzen,* 'to cross or cruise', and *Kreutz,* 'a cross'.) Recently Hunter has revived the Timothy Cruso connection, arguing that Defoe employs an allusive mode to alert readers familiar with the career of this dissenting teacher. It is not a matter on which a definitive answer is likely to emerge.[21]

In any case Defoe left the academy about 1679. He made transcripts of sermons delivered by a former Congregationalist, John Collins (?1632-87), who also had Harvard connections. Collins, like Timothy Cruso later, was chosen as Merchant's Lecturer at Pinner's Hall (a major centre of dissent, in Broad Street, halfway between St Giles's and Little St Helen's). Defoe composed at this time some verse meditations which were first published in 1946. They have been described as 'confessional' poetry, but they do not really explain why Defoe should, very soon afterwards, turn his back on the ministry and enter trade. We are left with a long preparation for the role of a pastor; a boyhood and youth spent under the influence of enlightened dissenters like Annesley, Fisher and Morton; and then the sudden *volte-face.* Many 'personal' readings of literature are unconvincing, not least the highly biographic interpretations of *Crusoe* itself. But if it is accepted that Robinson Crusoe is haunted throughout by an early misjudgement, then the possibility that Defoe's switch of career has some deep-level connection with the issue cannot be regarded as implausible.

Crusoe's Original Sin

In the middle of **RC1,** Crusoe reflects on his condition in the period between his discovery of the Spanish wreck and his meeting with Friday—he has spent some twenty-three years on the island:

> I have been in all my Circumstances a *Memento* to those who are touch'd with the general Plague of Mankind, whence, for ought I know, one half of their Miseries flow; I mean, that of not being satisfy'd with the Station wherein God and Nature has plac'd them; for not to look back upon my primitive Condition, and the excellent Advice of my Father, the Opposition to which, was, *as I may call it,* my ORIGINAL SIN; my subsequent Mistakes of the same kind had been the Means of my coming into this miserable Condition; for had that Providence, which so happily had seated me at the *Brasils,* as a Planter, bless'd me with confin'd Desires, and I could have been contented to have gone on gradually, I might have been by this Time; I *mean, in the Time of my being in this Island,* one of the most considerable Planters in the *Brasils.* . . .

Nor do the self-reproaches stop there:

> But as this is ordinarily the Fate of young Heads, so Reflection upon the Folly of it, is as ordinarily the Exercise of more Years, or of the dear bought Experience of Time; and so it was with me now; and yet so deep had the Mistake taken root in my Temper, that I could not satisfy myself in my Station, but was continually poring upon the Means, and Possibility of my Escape from this Place. . . . (pp. 194-5)

What precisely *was* this original sin? As the passage makes clear, it refers to Crusoe's first act of disobedience in leaving home to follow a seafaring life, rather than the legal career marked out for him. But this is only to shift the question back one stage. What kind of error does the 19-year-old Robinson commit? And is the root of his disobedience to be explained in religious, moral or psychological terms? No issue has more exercised recent commentators.

One remarkably clear-cut solution was proposed by Ian Watt. In his view, 'the argument between [Crusoe's] parents and himself is a debate, not about filial duty or religion, but about whether going or staying is likely to be the most advantageous course materially. . . . And, of course, Crusoe actually gains by his "original sin", and becomes richer than his father was.' Consequently, on this showing, 'Crusoe's "original sin" is really the dynamic tendency of capitalism itself, whose aim is never merely to maintain the *status quo,* but to transform it incessantly. Leaving home, improving on the lot one was born to, is a vital feature of the individualist pattern of life'.[22] Watt's verdict has been

repeated by some later critics, including John J. Richetti, who locates Crusoe's urges still more precisely within the 'dangerously dynamic aspect of capitalist ideology which must in the context of the early eighteenth century be denied and suppressed'. Richetti suggests that Crusoe has to do more than merely repudiate his father: 'The destruction of the father . . . seems to be what lies behind Crusoe's desire to go to sea, that is, to become rich above his father's station. To surpass him economically is in a real sense to destroy him.' There is at the start 'a dance among various sorts of explanations—social, moral, and psychoreligious—for Crusoe's desire to roam'. An implied emphasis on 'mysterious internal impulse' is at odds with Crusoe's calculating nature.[23]

A modified and more elaborate version of the economic case was made by Maximillian E. Novak. The central proposition is announced with admirable directness: 'I suggest that Crusoe's sin is his refusal to follow the "calling" chosen for him by his father, and that the rationale for this action may be found in Crusoe's personal characteristics: his lack of economic prudence, his inability to follow a steady profession, his indifference to a calm bourgeois life, and his love of travel.' To buttress this argument Novak brings a variety of evidence. He reviews Crusoe's personal traits, observing that 'When he created the character of Crusoe, Defoe certainly had more empathy with the concept of the colonist than with that of the capitalist'. (Novak has in mind contemporaneous works like the life of Ralegh; see above, p. 27.) Defoe 'admired the merchant, but not the capitalist or even the tradesman who made excessive profits'. An 'excellent sketch' of Crusoe's own character is quoted from **RC2** (p. 216), where the narrator refers to himself as 'a mad rambling Boy'. Crusoe is 'a prototype of Shaw's Bluntschli—the hero raised as a tradesman but with a romantic temperament'. Novak then investigates the concept of 'calling', as evolving from Luther and modified by subsequent Protestant theology. Weber and Tawney again come much into the argument. Perceptively Novak remarks that 'Defoe's hero is not a hermit by nature; he survives his solitude, but he does not enjoy it'—this in itself throws some light on the thesis of Watt and Richetti. The conclusion is that 'Crusoe does not disobey his parents in the name of free enterprise or economic freedom, but for a strangely adventurous, romantic, and unprofitable desire to see foreign lands. If any economic moral can be drawn from Crusoe's narrative, it is a conservative warning that Englishmen about to embark on the economic disaster of the South Sea Bubble should mind their callings and stick to the sure road of trade.'[24]

This reading was quickly challenged by G. A. Starr, who contended that it demanded a 'more individualized portrait than Defoe actually gives us at [the start] of the book'. Starr cites **The Family Instructor** amongst other works to indicate the orthodoxy of Defoe's ideas at this point: 'That man is naturally subject to rebellious impulse is a principle he frequently asserts, and it would appear to provide a sufficient "rationale" for Crusoe's behavior on this occasion. Indeed the episode seems to rest on an orthodox Calvinistic conception of man's innate waywardness and obstinacy.' What we have is simply 'a generalized portrait of the young man'. Starr's counter-suggestion is that 'implicit in Defoe's treatment of the episode is a conventional identification of family, social and divine order, all of which are flouted by Crusoe's deed'. In a sense, Crusoe's act of disobedience 'is merely the first overt expression of a more fundamental source of trouble: the natural waywardness of every unregenerate man'. Its function is to 'initiate a pattern of wrongdoing'. The parallel with the story of Jonah mentioned by Crusoe's shipmate on his first voyage from Hull (*RC1,* p. 15) is seen as a close one: in both episodes the narrative provides 'a kind of "objective correlative" for the hero's turbulent, unruly spirit'. (The story of Jonah, located neither by Starr nor the OEN editor, is found, of course, in the book of Jonah, 1-2; it may be added that Hunter shows it to be a common emblem in providential works.) For Starr, who emphasises the 'special fondness' shown by Providence for the middle station, Crusoe 'like the Prodigal Son before him' displays not just a lack of economic prudence but 'a radical perversity and impiety'.[25]

All these readings have points of interest in them. If Starr seems to me the most convincing overall, this is chiefly on two counts. First, his view of the episode fits more snugly into a general sense of the way the book works: the opening episode contributes to the total pattern without altogether controlling later developments. Secondly, he gives to the phrase 'original sin' the primary acceptation it must have had for most readers, and not only those with a Calvinist background, in Defoe's time. By metaphor the phrase could no doubt be extended to social or economic areas of life, but its prime *theological* cast could never be dispelled. When we find Crusoe making explicit reference to St Luke's parable of the prodigal (*RC1,* pp. 8, 14) as well as to the Jonah story—the standard types of rebellion and disobedience in Puritan homiletics—we are pushed closer to the underlying allegory of the Fall itself, for so long the crucial datum in man's understanding of his own spiritual condition. As Hunter suggests, Crusoe's rejection of his parents 'takes its ultimate mythic dimension' from this source.[26] No interpretation of the opening of **Robinson Crusoe** which ignores this dimension of meaning will disclose the point of this episode in the full trajectory of Crusoe's career.

On the other hand it is possible to make the correspondences too strict and to drown the text in scriptural allusions of doubtful relevance. Robert W. Ayers's typological reading does not altogether avoid this pitfall;

building upon the fundamental analogical identity of Crusoe's father as God and the hero himself as Adam, he discovers emblems of all known temptations within the text. A new etymology for the name 'Crusoe' relates it to *crusader.* Ayers sees a metaphysical overtone in the phrase 'middle State' (*RC1,* p. 4), which makes the father's speech a proleptic hint of Pope's lines in the *Essay on Man:*

> Plac'd on this isthmus of a middle state,
> A being darkly wise, and rudely great.
>   (Epistle II, pp. 3-4)

Ayers finds sacramental symbols thickly strewn about the island (caves, grapes, etc.), and is even able to identify the boy Xury as a Christ figure 'to some degree'.[27] It is not very obvious how one can be Christ to some degree.

But this is at worst an overstatement of genuine elements in the book. Whether we can discern the things detected by Watt and Richetti is a matter of taste and judgement: in general, those who dislike capitalism as a historical phenomenon are the readiest to suppose that Defoe sensed by intuition failings in its effects on the human spirit and that he chose to dramatise these through Crusoe. One of the difficulties in seeing the novel as a work which 'drew attention to the . . . need of building up a network of personal relationships on a new and conscious pattern' is that it neglects a key aspect of the plot: Crusoe achieves salvation, and overcomes his existential isolation, *without* any 'network of personal relationships'—Friday comes late on the scene and is a dependant rather than a friend. This is apart from the awkward fact that Defoe shows Crusoe's 'Island of Despair' as a Godless, not a manless, world; he is reconciled to his condition by solitary devotions (which go on while his capital is accreting), not by healthy interpersonal contacts.[28] True, many modern critics dislike Crusoe even at the end, and find something suspect (if not downright disreputable) in his accumulative habits; but it is far from clear that Defoe meant us to share this disapproval. As for Richetti, he requires us to believe that Crusoe destroys his father, not just symbolically but 'in a real sense'.[29] In that case Defoe badly mismanaged things, for we have no idea how and when the father died. Crusoe simply learns on his return that his parents are dead and almost 'all the Family extinct' (*RC1,* p. 278). I hope it is not being too literal-minded to observe that he has been away from Yorkshire for nearly thirty-six years; his father was described as 'very ancient' when Crusoe was growing up—he had retired even before marrying. In such circumstances the hero's direct responsibility for his parent's demise looks a little blurred.

The fact is that Crusoe is allotted 'something fatal in that Propension of Nature tending directly to the Life of Misery which was to befal me' (*RC1,* p. 3). At the heart of this stands the 'meer wandering Inclination' (p. 4) rightly emphasised by Novak; but it transcends the simple ambition to travel as it does the mere pursuit of monetary gain. He is not deflected by his experiences in the storm off Yarmouth, though the portents are clear enough to him; nor by his captivity at Sallee, though he again recalls his father's 'prophetick Discourse' (p. 19); nor by his early struggles in Brazil, where he sees himself as 'just like a Man cast away upon some desolate Island' (p. 35); nor by his later prosperity there:

> Had I continued in the Station I was now in, I had room for all the happy things to have yet befallen me, for which my Father so earnestly recommended a quiet retired Life, and of which he had so sensibly describ'd the middle Station of Life to be full of; but other things attended me, and I was still to be the wilful Agent of all my own Miseries; and particularly to encrease my Fault and double the Reflections upon my self, which in my future Sorrows I should have leisure to make; all these Miscarriages were procured by my apparent obstinate adhering to my foolish inclination of wandring abroad and pursuing that Inclination, in contradiction to the clearest Views of doing my self good in a fair and plain pursuit of those Prospects and those measures of Life, which Nature and Providence concurred to present me with, and to make my Duty. (p. 38)

Crusoe does indeed have abundant leisure on his island to reflect upon his past mistakes. Filial disobedience was followed by blind obstinacy—a refusal to learn from the past which is not just imprudent but against nature, perverse and, as it were, self-renewing.

Even in **RC2,** after he has grown rich, Crusoe finds the same 'distemper of wandering' (p. 8) overtaking him: he persuades himself 'it would be a kind of resisting Providence' if he were to reject his nephew's offer of a new journey (p. 11). This is not the calculating language of a self-aggrandising manipulator: it has the air of someone possessed by an obscure private fantasy. At the very end of the second part, Crusoe tells us he is finally stifling the demon within:

> And here resolving to harass myself no more, I am preparing for a longer journey than all these, having lived seventy-two years a life of infinite variety, and learnt sufficiently to know the value of retirement, and the blessing of ending our days in peace. (p. 323)

An unconvincing litany to go out upon, some would think; but in my view a truly organic conclusion. The restlessness which drives Crusoe is the very spirit of his being. It will be extirpated not by the end of his actual travels, or by the accomplishment of any economic goal; it is part of man's fallen nature, and will

survive until he achieves salvation in death. Christian was freed of his burden of guilt at the foot of the Cross, although it was not until he crossed the River of Death that he put off his mortal garments.[30] For Crusoe the act of conversion brings insight, joy and a reanimated energy born of self-acceptance; but full release from the innate contradictions of his nature will come only with the 'longer journey' out of mortal existence. . . .

Notes

[1] Quoted in *CH,* pp. 166-7.

[2] Watt, p. 84. The argument that Defoe's secularised Puritanism produced 'the relative impotence of religion' in his novels (pp. 83-5) contains many provocative observations, but it also leaves many handles for rejoinder. For example, the statement that Crusoe must 'make his own way along a path no longer clearly illumined by God's particular providences' seems contradictory in view of Crusoe's own statements after his conversion. See for instance *RC1,* pp. 175-6, on the 'secret Intimations of Providence'. Similarly Crusoe speaks of 'a special Providence' that he was cast away on the side of the island (as he then supposed) where savages did not come (p. 164).

[3] R. H. Tawney, *Religion and the Rise of Capitalism* (London, 1926; Harmondsworth, 1938), p. 212.

[4] Starr, pp. 74-125. For another view of these matters, see Martin J. Grief, 'The conversion of Crusoe', *SEL,* Vol. VI (1966), pp. 551-74. Greif sees the book as 'the record of a notable spiritual pilgrimage across the sea of life, from a lawless course of living to true Christian repentance: a symbolic voyage from sin and folly to the gift of God's grace attained through sincere belief in Jesus Christ' (pp. 551-2). He sets out the 'Protestant scheme of salvation', stressing two primary motives to repentance—love of God and fear of His wrath. Like Hunter, Greif detects a number of 'Christian metaphors pervasively present in homiletic literature' (p. 555), mostly concerned with the sea and storms. He identifies caves as (typologically) the home of thieves and robbers (p. 567) and sheep as symbols of sanctification (p. 574). Less persuasive in detail than Starr or Hunter, Grief presents a sound overall case in harmony with theirs.

[5] Hunter, *passim* (quotations from pp. 126, 189). For the conversion of Friday to Christianity, see pp. 184-6.

[6] Starr, pp. 3-50; Hunter, pp. 76-92.

[7] Starr, pp. 81-125; Hunter, pp. 88, 185.

[8] ibid., pp 23-50.

[9] ibid., pp. 51-75. The Presbyterian minister John Flavell (?1630-91) contributed both to the guide and the Providence traditions, as defined by Hunter; his *Seaman's Companion* is a good example of the guide aimed specifically at mariners.

[10] *The Storm* (London, 1704), sig. A6r, p. 271.

[11] Secord, pp. 78-85.

[12] *Tour,* Vol. I, pp. 69-72.

[13] *The Storm,* pp. 266-70.

[14] See the comments of Louis A. Landa in the OEN edn (London, 1969), p. xxiii.

[15] Hunter, pp. 105-24 (quotation from p. 123).

[16] J. Paul Hunter, 'Friday as a convert', *RES,* Vol. XIV (1963), pp. 243-8.

[17] *Daniel Defoe,* ed. J. T. Boulton (London, 1965), p. 166.

[18] This and the following paragraphs draw on Sutherland, pp. 1-25; *Citizen,* pp. 1-43; and Shinagel, pp. 1-22. See also Lew Girdler, 'Defoe's education at Newington Green', *SP,* Vol. L (1953), pp. 573-91; and J. R. Moore, 'Defoe's religious sect', *RES,* Vol. XVII (1941), pp. 461-7.

[19] *A True Collection of the Writings of the Author of the True Born English-man* (2nd edn, London, 1705), pp. 110-18.

[20] *Citizen,* p. 19.

[21] ibid., pp. 224-5; Hunter, pp. 47-9, 204-7.

[22] Watt, pp. 67-8.

[23] J. J. Richetti, *Defoe's Narratives* (Oxford, 1975), pp. 26-7.

[24] Novak, *Economics,* pp. 32-48. Defoe was certainly deeply affected by the Bubble, as his later works show (it may even be a concealed metaphor in *A Journal of the Plague Year*); but to speak of the nation 'embarking' on the Bubble makes it a strangely purposeful brand of catastrophe.

[25] Starr, pp. 74-81. For the Jonah emblem, see Hunter, p. 68; for a brief consideration of the 'original sin', ibid., pp. 128-33.

[26] See ibid., pp. 133-43.

[27] R. W. Ayers, "*Robinson Crusoe:* 'allusive allegorick history'", *PMLA,* Vol. LXXXII (1967), pp. 399-407.

[28] Watt, p. 96. Watt's reading of Crusoe's experience as one of spiritual alienation, mirroring the isolated state of capitalist man, would ideally require the hero's misery and loneliness to be coterminous with his sojourn by himself on the island. But, as the narrator repeatedly makes clear, his sense of desolation belonged to his Godless rather than his unaccompanied condition.

[29] Richetti, *Defoe's Narratives,* p. 26.

[30] Hunter supplies no direct parallel between *Crusoe* and *The Pilgrim's Progress,* though their comparability lies at the heart of his case. Quite particular links can be discerned, e.g. the pilgrim's imperfect sight of the Celestial City through the shepherd's perspective glass as against Crusoe's vague sight of land to the west of his island (*RC1* p. 108). Both perhaps are variants of the typological Pisgah vision. . . .

A Note on the Texts

There is no complete collected edition of Defoe's works; as yet no volumes have appeared in the series to be published by the Southern Illinois University Press. I have therefore adopted this set of priorities in textual matters:

(1) Where a good modern edition exists, such as the Oxford English Novels volumes, I have used this. *The Life* and *Strange Surprizing Adventures of Robinson Crusoe* is quoted from J. Donald Crowley's edition in that series (1972), which is based on the text of the first edition.

(2) Failing this, I have had recourse to an accessible reprint where the text is not hopelessly corrupt. For the second and third parts of *Robinson Crusoe,* I use *The Works of Daniel Defoe,* ed. G. H. Maynadier (Boston, Mass., 1903-4), Vols II and III. This is a modernised but reasonably accurate text.

(3) If there is no other available source, I quote from the original edition, or in certain cases from a collected edition published in Defoe's lifetime.

This procedure has one unfortunate consequence, in that my quotations present a mosaic of modern- and old-spelling texts. The alternative was to confine myself to largely inaccessible editions, many of them available only in the great libraries of the English-speaking world. I have chosen what seems to me the lesser of two evils.

Abbreviations

The following cue-titles are used for works which are frequently mentioned:

Byrd Max Byrd (ed.), *Daniel Defoe: A Collection of Critical Essays* (Englewood Cliffs, NJ, 1976).

CH P. Rogers (ed.), *Defoe: The Critical Heritage* (London and Boston, Mass., 1972).

Checklist J. R. Moore, *A Checklist of the Writings of Daniel Defoe* (Bloomington, Ind., 1960; rev. edn. 1971).

Citizen J. R. Moore, *Daniel Defoe: Citizen of the Modern World* (Chicago, Ill., 1958).

Earle P. Earle, *The World of Defoe* (London, 1976).

Ellis F. H. Ellis (ed.), *Twentieth Century Interpretations of Robinson Crusoe* (Englewood Cliffs, NJ, 1969).

Gildon Charles Gildon, *The Life and Strange Surprizing Adventures of Mr D——— De F——* (London, 1719).

History of Pyrates *A General History of the Pyrates,* ed. M. Schonhorn (London, 1972).

Hunter J. P. Hunter, *The Reluctant Pilgrim: Defoe's Emblematic Method and Quest for Form in Robinson Crusoe* (Baltimore, Md., 1966).

Hutchins H. C. Hutchins, *Robinson Crusoe and Its Printing 1719-1731* (New York, 1925).

Lee W. Lee, *Daniel Defoe: His Life, and Recently Discovered Writings,* 3 vols. (London, 1869; reprinted Hildesheim, 1968).

Letters *The Letters of Daniel Defoe,* ed. G. H. Healey (Oxford, 1955).

Library *Librorum ex Bibliothecis Philippi Farewell, D.D. et Danielis Defoe, Gen. Catalogus* (1731).

Little B. Little, *Crusoe's Captain* (London, 1960).

Novak, *Economics* M. E. Novak, *Economics and the Fiction of Daniel Defoe* (Berkeley and Los Angeles, Calif., 1962; reprinted New York, 1976).

Novak, *Nature* M. E. Novak, *Defoe and the Nature of Man* (Oxford, 1963).

RC1 *The Life and Strange Surprizing Adventures of Robinson Crusoe* (1719). Text and page references follow the edition by J. Donald Crowley (Oxford English Novels, London, 1972).

RC2 *The Farther Adventures of Robinson Crusoe* (1719). See p. xiii.

RC3 *Serious Reflections . . . of Robinson Crusoe* (1720). See p. xiii.

Review Daniel Defoe, *The Review,* ed. A. W. Secord, 22 vols. (New York, 1938).

Secord A. W. Secord, *Studies in the Narrative Method of Defoe* (Urbana, Ill., 1924; reprinted New York, 1963).

Shinagel M. Shinagel, *Daniel Defoe and Middle-Class Gentility* (Cambridge, Mass., 1968).

Starr G. A. Starr, *Defoe and Spiritual Autobiography* (Princeton, NJ, 1965).

Sutherland J. Sutherland, *Defoe,* 2nd edn. (London, 1950).

Tour Daniel Defoe, *A Tour through the Whole Island of Great Britain,* ed. G. D. H. Cole (London, 1927; reprinted 1968).

Watt I. Watt, *The Rise of the Novel* (London, 1957; paperback, Harmondsworth, 1963).

Other Abbreviations

ECS Eighteenth Century Studies

EIC Essays in Criticism

ELH ELH: A Journal of English Literary History

HLQ Huntington Library Quarterly

JEGP Journal of English and Germanic Philology

MLN Modern Language Notes

MLQ Modern Language Quarterly

MP Modern Philology

N & Q Notes and Queries

OED Oxford English Dictionary

OEN Oxford English Novels

PBSA Papers of the Bibliographical Society of America

PMLA PMLA: Publications of the Modern Language Association of America

PQ Philological Quarterly

RES Review of English Studies

SEL Studies in English Literature 1500-1900

SP Studies in Philology

TLS Times Literary Supplement

Michael Seidel (essay date 1981)

SOURCE: "Crusoe in Exile," in *PMLA*, Vol. 96, No. 3, May, 1981, pp. 363-74.

[In the excerpt below, Seidel discusses the depiction of the exile in literature and the use and function of allegorical history in Robinson Crusoe.*]*

In *Ulysses* Leopold Bloom poses an exile's question to another exile, a figure whom James Joyce calls the English Ulysses: *"O, poor Robinson Crusoe, / How could you possibly do so?"*[1] Bloom's phrasing comes from a popular song that recalls a haunting moment in **Robinson Crusoe** when Defoe's hero, alone at that time for six years, hears the disembodied voice of his previously trained wild parrot, Poll, ask, *"Robin, Robin, Robin Crusoe,* poor *Robin Crusoe,* where are you *Robin Crusoe? Where are you? Where have you been?"*[2] Bloom's "how" and the parrot's "where" are crucial questions for any exile, and the purpose of this essay is to suggest some potential answers to them.

When Crusoe first hears the parrot's words, he has just returned from a reconnaissance mission, or *periplous,* skirting part of his island by foot before returning home to what he by then calls his "perfect Settlement" (p. 111). Poll, having bided its time, chooses the occasion of this insular homecoming to repeat, by imprint, the sounds it has recorded during the early, more trying years of Crusoe's exile. So in the same sense that a loner's experience is rather like talking to other versions of himself, the questions the parrot asks of Crusoe are the same as those asked earlier by Crusoe. The questions themselves possess a double structure, hinting at two times and two places, at the Crusoe who hears them (where *are* you?) and the Crusoe who asked them (where have you *been?*).[3] The exile faces the dilemma that he is, indeed, of two places. Or, to put it another way, where he is displaced becomes his home place. Paradoxically, then, the answers to both the parrot's questions are in a generic sense the same: home. Home is where Crusoe is, and home is where he has been.

It is precisely the doubleness of Crusoe's situation or placement that accounts, in a narrative sense, for the generative and allegorical texture of the narrative. Crusoe refers to his island exile as "my Reign, or my Captivity, which you please" (p. 137). By whatever principle of abundant or redundant locution we *do* please, that place from which the exile is blocked becomes the model for the place in which he resettles his imagination. Crusoe's habit of mind is verbally and metaphorically binary. The very names for his places on the island, for example, key the doubleness implicit in Crusoe's repositioning. In his initial despair, his shelter is but a hovel. With gradual familiarity, his hovel becomes his home. In his full pride of place, his home becomes an estate; his estate, a kingdom. When, and for whatever reasons, his insecurities return, his kingdom shrinks to his cave. When he feels fearfully hostile, his cave becomes his fortification. Experience for the displaced hero is a constant invitation to conversion, not simply a turning or movement from place to place but a transformation—actual, imaginative, and psychological—of one place into another.

The notion of the resituated body and mind in boundary narratives carries with it the figuration of the place of exile as a multifold substitute for, hence an allegory of, home. Exiles suffer from domestic withdrawal, and the trials of separation are, in part, an allegorical reconstruction of the familiar from the strange. Nowhere is this figuration more pronounced than in Crusoe's double entry "Accompt" where he records on the side of exile that *"I am divided from Mankind, a Solitaire, one banish'd from humane Society,"* and on the side of resettling (in every sense) potential, *"But I am not starv'd and perishing on a barren Place, affording no Sustenance"* (p. 66). Crusoe's accounting conforms to his condition as exile: displacement and replacement are something of the same phenomenon.

The archetypal exile in literature, although often by nature a wanderer like Crusoe, is also by habit a homebody.[4] And the memory of home becomes paramount in narratives where home itself is but a memory. In the strongest narrative examples of exile—the biblical Exodus, the *Odyssey,* the *Aeneid,* and even Dante's *Commedia,* where the pilgrim re-creates the substantial spirit of his home city despite the agony, as the poet puts it, of having to climb another man's staircase—"home" is both a previously located territory and a dynamic recollection or promise.[5] The fable of exile derives its power from serving as a commentary not only on the place *to* which one is exiled but also on the place *from* which one is exiled. Such fables render the home place unapproachable or illegitimate, destroyed or taken over by conquerors or false claimants. Without a kingdom (or government) recognized as secure, home itself becomes usurped territory for those still forced to inhabit it. Exiled heroes tend to remain apart from their tainted home until both they and the powers they represent are ready to retake it. In the interim, exiles removed from their land spend their time both trying to replace it and trying, paradoxically, to forget as best they can the trauma that necessitated their original displacement.

The displaced condition or "state" of mind of the exile often results in a decidedly ambiguous relation with the place or places of exile. The murmuring Jews of Exodus, for example, who know little of their promised land before reaching it and who have begun to forget the miseries of their Egyptian past, seem as agonized at the prospect of leaving a temporary home, an oasis like Elim in the Sinai, as Moses, who knows much more, seems agonized at the prospect of staying. At different times in the *Odyssey*, the separate lands of the Lotus Eaters, the Aeolists, and Circe are offered to Odysseus' crew as replacements for the home island, Ithaca; and even after all the crew but Odysseus have perished, the lands of Calypso and the Phaeacians are still proffered to the lone king as new island kingdoms. Most of these landfalls also include substitute queens for a displaced king. The theme of uncertain substitution in exile is even more pronounced in the *Aeneid*, where Aeneas, praying to have done with his trials, attempts to found a new version of Troy on each of the Trojans' marginal landings in the Mediterranean. He acts on the chance that the gods have destined wherever he happens to be as the place where he is supposed to be. The imaginatively conceived boundaries of Rome itself are for Aeneas only another future building site for a dimly remembered Troy.

II

Both new and seasoned readers of *The Life and Strange Surprizing Adventures of Robinson Crusoe* approach Defoe's "moving book," as James Joyce called it, as a narrative of adaptation and endurance, as a study of isolation and fear, and as a fable of the mobile fantasy and transforming imagination. But when Defoe gets around to commenting, seriously or otherwise, on his fictional strategies in *Crusoe,* he inevitably turns toward a wider conception of narrative placement and duplication. However great his urge to substantiate a particular story, Defoe recognizes that any one sequence of action carries with it the pattern for narrative interchangeability or repositioning. Such a pattern even finds its way into the text of *Robinson Crusoe,* and Crusoe himself articulates it on his Brazilian plantation before he has any way of knowing about his subsequent island exile: "I used to say, I liv'd just like a Man cast away upon some desolate Island, that had no body there but himself" (p. 35). Crusoe then points out that those who utter such words may have heaven "oblige them to make the Exchange" (p. 35); and, indeed, heaven and Defoe will do so.

Defoe writes at greater length of narrative interchangeability in his extended commentary on the story of the exiled Crusoe, *Serious Reflections during the Life and Surprizing Adventures of Robinson Crusoe* (1720). His voice is nominally that of Crusoe as a fictional being and actually that of himself as an authorial being: "In a word, there is not a Circumstance in the imaginary story but has its just allusion to a real story, and chimes part for part and step for step with the inimitable Life of Robinson Crusoe."[6] The next paragraph offers an example of what Defoe means, an example chosen not from the original narrative but from a later section of *Serious Reflections:*

> For example, in the latter part of this work called the Vision, I begin thus: "When I was in my island-kingdom I had abundance of strange notions of my seeing apparitions, &c. All these reflections are just history of a state of forced confinement, which in my real history is represented by a confined retreat in an island; and it is as reasonable to represent one kind of imprisonment by another, as it is to represent any thing that really exists by that which exists not."
>
>   (III, xii)

Defoe resists the notion of fiction as a unique imaginative sequence of lies because he sees invention as a way to extend ideas about probable circumstance and imbue fable with entire sets of applicable meaning.[7] In *Serious Reflections,* Defoe makes a claim for what he calls the allegorical historical method of narration while defending himself (in the guise of Crusoe) from those who have charged him with lying:

> I *Robinson Crusoe,* being at this Time in perfect and sound mind and memory, thanks be to God therefor, do hereby declare their objection is an invention scandalous in design, and false in fact; and do affirm that the story, though allegorical, is also historical; and that it is the beautiful representation of a life of unexampled misfortune, and of a variety not to be met with in the world, sincerely adapted to and intended for the common good of mankind, and designed first, *as it is now farther applied,* to the most serious uses possible.
>   (III, ix)

Like most everything else in human experience, fiction gains in value for Defoe when its configurations stimulate, enliven, and expand its uses: "Things seem to appear more lively to the Understanding, and to make a stronger Impression upon the Mind, when they are insinuated under the cover of some Symbol or Allegory, especially when the Moral is good, and the Application easy."[8] In *Robinson Crusoe,* narrative allegorical history in its widest, least circumscribed sense offers Defoe a design for meaningful repetition and allows the adventures to partake of multiple fictional emphases.[9] Allegory always represents one thing *in* another, and this representation is very close to what the word allegory means: a speaking otherwise where difference itself becomes a form of duplication.

For his notion of allusive allegorical history, Defoe draws on various examples, each of which represents in fable something of a more general design: "the historical Parables in the Holy Scripture, such 'The Pilgrim's Progress', and such, in a word, the adventures of your fugitive friend, 'Robinson Crusoe'" (*Serious Reflections,* III, 107). *Robinson Crusoe* takes its position among fables of displacement and reorientation. In exiling Crusoe to an unknown island and resettling him, first as an outcast and only many years later as a returnee to his original, or native, island, Defoe fulfills a traditional narrative pattern of sustained risk, trauma, and return, a pattern of falling away, turning around, and coming home allegorically analogous to patterns in biblical history, various national histories, and spiritual and personal "lives."[10]

Though Crusoe, who possesses a mind of limited range and great suggestibility, comprehends only the merest bits and scraps of the allegorical history he finds himself in, Defoe, the narrative chronicler who masterfully times and double-times events, understands that even the temptation he offers his readers to read allegorically is akin to the narrative frame of extension and return. In *Serious Reflections,* Defoe's signee (R.C.) hedges a bit as to whether the adventures he has experienced happened where he represented them, on an island near the mouth of the Orinoco, or somewhere much closer to home. Defoe poses the possibility of allegorical duplication and wonders if his readers would lose interest "when you are supposing the scene which is placed so far off, had its original so near Home?" (III, xiii). The question comports with Defoe's notion that a unique metaphoric configuration makes a greater impression on the mind than a familiar literal one.

By home here Defoe means, of course, more than the literal home island, England—he alludes metaphorically to any and all familiar mental territory. Still, there is a significant level on which Crusoe's displacement on a remote island allegorizes actual events much nearer England. If there is an interplay in the mind of the narrative chronicler between spatially remote and familiar places, there is also an interplay between the twenty-eight years of Crusoe's island exile and the concurrent years in England: Crusoe is on his island from 1659 to 1686 (actually, he returns to England in 1687), a period virtually overlapping the twenty-eight years of restored Stuart rule before the 1688 Glorious Revolution.[11] This coincidence is not an idle one for Defoe the narrative allegorist, who sees, like his own fugitive hero, "a strange Concurrence of Days, in the various Provinces" of life, a concurrence that he "might have had Reason to have look'd upon with a great deal of Curiosity" (p. 133). In a distinct temporal duplication, Crusoe, without any real political awareness of his own, sustains, like so many exiles, the values of his land during a time when his land seems incapable, at least in Defoe's view, of sustaining them itself. Crusoe begins his exile just before Charles II returns, and he returns just before James II is, in effect, exiled. The invited king, William III, Defoe's hero and later his friend, takes over the home kingdom.

The strategy of Defoe's "allegorick relation" sets the possibility for Crusoe's role as island king away from home representing values that ought to reign *at* home. Defoe establishes in the temporal structure of narrative a way to read historical time in fictional event. The timing of Crusoe's exile in the particular fold of years that envelops the Restoration provides an intriguing variation on the theme of Stuart historiography. Crusoe's experience allegorizes, at least in its temporal dimension, not only the general quality of the fugitive condition but the particular circumstances (historical) that give rise to necessary exodus or hiatus. What happens to Crusoe in the narrative, of course, is either accidental or providential—not of his choosing. But for Defoe, what happens to Crusoe as an embodiment of the English spirit in exile is inevitable. To put the wider temporal structure of the adventures in another way: Crusoe endures an exile that parallels what Defoe saw as a condition of the home island's regressive turn toward more and more oppressive home rule.[12] Crusoe is away from what Defoe saw as an "unsettled" and unsettling nation, and he returns just as his land is about to regain a legitimate status, or return to its senses.

This view of *Robinson Crusoe*'s timing accords with Defoe's practice as a narrative allegorist before and after *Crusoe* and reveals his need to interpret history as a pattern both for the course of a human soul and, more pointedly, for the soul of a nation.[13] For reasons that Defoe never forgot, the Stuart Restoration seemed virtually apostolic to him. He felt that the important gap in the continuity of English history was not the dramatic parliamentary revolution from 1641 to the Protectorate but those lost years from 1660 to 1688, coincidental also with the first twenty-eight years of his own life,[14] when the Stuarts returned to a land whose best interests Defoe was convinced they did not represent. Crusoe's story was, in a sense, possible because the Stuarts had two-timed the home island. On Crusoe's island kingdom, his reign becomes an allegorical version of restored lost years: the powers of fictional invention allow the Stuarts' time to be replaced or absorbed by Crusoe's time.

As a fable of reconstitution in exile and legitimacy on return, *Robinson Crusoe* takes its place alongside exile narratives of traditional stature. But, of course, Crusoe is in a different position from Moses, Odysseus, Aeneas, or even Dante the pilgrim. He may have a general idea about his status as one of Providence's many allegorical projections, but he is never privy to the temporal allegory or "coincidence" of his status as island king. As so many readers have intuited, Crusoe may stand for something central in the English experience; but he is ironically central in the narrative's political vision because, if he represents his nation, he does so while isolated from it and without awareness. His is a provisional or mock reign that figuratively substitutes for an already metaphorical conception, Defoe's sense of national "captivity" at home under the Stuarts.

Georg Luk s and other theorists of narrative have speculated on how irony can complicate, even cancel out, the wholeness of allegory; and Defoe's narrative strategy is not so reductive that it allows absolute reign, so to speak, to the temporal allegory of the adventures at the expense of Crusoe's deep-seated insecurities and the narrative's many other fictional dilemmas. But without inflicting too much damage on the suppleness of the narrative we can still balance out what Defoe projects for Crusoe in historical terms with what Crusoe sometimes tries, pathetically, to figure out for himself. From the beginning of the fable, the questions of separation and exile are thrown into ironic relief. No political reading, for example, can proceed without a double perspective on the initiating event of the action, Crusoe's disobedience to his father's wish that he remain in England and seek the security of the middle state at home: "In a word, that as he would do very kind things for me if I would stay and settle at Home as directed" (p. 5). If Crusoe's spirit during his years of exile is supposed to represent the antithesis of authoritarian home rule, how do we account for his almost continual and unremitting anguish at his original disobedience to his father? One way is to see Crusoe's attitude as ironically faulty, and faulty in more than an allegorical or a political sense. Whatever Crusoe says he feels about his own precipitous withdrawal from England (and he never does quite sort out sin from impulse), his character is better served in the long run by resisting his father's demands than by giving in complacently to them.[15] Some courses of action or inaction cost more in anguish to follow than to resist. And whether the context be literally personal or figuratively political, Crusoe's father's advice has to be tempered by the exclusionary nature of its focus. There are times when the secure and complacent life he recommends is worse than the necessary errantry of a free soul, especially if that freedom seems to conform to a personal necessity. As exile, Crusoe is positioned so that resistance to his home is the prelude to a crisis or series of crises that are themselves steps in a psychic and actual process of self-substantiation. And it almost follows that the measure of Crusoe's hard-won settlement, like the measure of England's greater one at the 1688 Revolution, is the degree to which his impulses force him to avoid too easy a settlement too soon.[16] . . .

IV

It takes Crusoe several years of almost obsessive defensiveness to get used to the notion that what seems to be his opposition might actually be the means by which he can alter his condition as permanent exile. His conversion back to hopes of recivilization makes

positive again what his father, in overstressing security at home, had so many years before envisaged as strictly negative: "I could not satisfy my self in my Station, but was continually poring upon the Means, and Possibility of my Escape from this Place" (p. 195). Once Crusoe's counterturn is set in motion things move, if not as quickly as he would prefer, at least decisively. He readies himself for actual *nostos* by planning a preliminary beach-head on the cannibal mainland.

> All my Calm of Mind in my Resignation to Providence, and waiting the Issue of the Dispositions of Heaven, seem'd to be suspended; and I had, as it were, no Power to turn my Thoughts to any thing, but to the Project of a Voyage to the Main, which came upon me with such Force, and such an Impetuosity of Desire, that it was not to be resisted.
>
> (p. 198)

Crusoe, of course, can give up his scheme to go to the cannibal main because one very useful cannibal comes to him. Friday's companionship during the last few years of Crusoe's island reign provides Crusoe with an actual "other," who becomes a second self in initiating the strength of will toward repatriation. Friday sees his own land from a vantage point on the high side of Crusoe's island: "*O joy!* Says he, *glad! There see my Country, there my Nation*" (p. 223). These stirring words are voiced just after Crusoe anticipates the spatial collapse of the distance between the place of exile and the home island by referring to himself and Friday as "comfort'd restor'd Penitents; we had here the Word of God to read, and no farther off from his Spirit to instruct, than if we had been in *England*" (p. 221).

After Friday's arrival, and without precisely knowing why, Crusoe assumes his deliverance is again providentially opportune: "the great Hopes I had of being effectually, and speedily deliver'd; for I had an invincible Impression upon my Thoughts, that my Deliverance was at hand, and that I should not be another Year in this Place" (p. 229). The scathing tone of Crusoe's reference to "this Place" suggests that he is more than ready to leave, and his "Impression" that the times are ready for him to do so seems as telling in its way as the impression of the footprint years before. Crusoe loses his fear of having his island penetrated when Defoe has him lose the desire to protect that which is no longer allegorically or historically primed for his holding of it.[23]

In the interim between Crusoe's thoughts about redirecting his efforts toward home and his opportunity to make the break, he begins to revise his notions of what sovereignty ought to mean to him. With his intuition of deliverance he turns in his thinking from his sovereignty, his "I-land," to the law of civilized nations.[24] And he does so by readjusting his view of those whose presence on his side of the island had long ago so reduced him to quivering paranoia and unaccountable bloodlust: the cannibals.[25] His unlearning of violent longings in this section of the narrative starts to recivilize him. God has not called on him, Crusoe says, "to take upon me to be a Judge of their Actions, much less an Executioner of his Justice; that whenever he thought fit, he would take the Cause into his own Hands, and by national Vengeance punish them as a People, for nationalist Crimes; but that in the mean time, it was none of my Business" (p. 232). One almost sees in Crusoe's words Defoe's generalized view on political retribution, a view more in keeping with natural law than with the older, heroic code of blood revenge. Any one individual, namely Crusoe, cannot afford to be a scourge on an entire nation, and at the end of his stay, his energies are better employed against those few who have falsely usurped a power that they have no right to hold—the English mutineers who run riot in conspiracy and betrayal.[26]

At the original sighting of the mutineers and their unfortunate captives, matters come to a head. It is curious that when the English party first arrives Crusoe thinks there might be a Dutchman or two with it, a mistaken piece of conjecture for the plot of the actual adventure but perhaps a reminder, in the temporal parallel, of the availability of the Dutch Prince William of Orange for the restitution of Protestant hegemony in England. Crusoe approaches the captives with the mutineers out of earshot and chooses to ally himself with those who face either an exile like his own or, worse, death. That is, he allies himself with legitimacy, with the rightful captain of the English vessel. That captain looks at the bizarre figure of Crusoe coming toward him. Like Odysseus, Crusoe makes his move for legitimacy in clothes unbefitting a civilized island king, and, like Shakespeare's Prospero, he seems possessed of magical powers.[27] Crusoe is a bedraggled version of the mythical stranger-savior figure of legendary tales. He says to the captain:

> But can you put a Stranger in the way how to help you, for you seem to me to be in some great Distress? I saw you when you landed, and when you seem'd to make Applications to the Brutes that came with you, I saw one of them lift up his Sword to kill you.

(p. 254)

The English captain elevates Crusoe beyond or, as Crusoe's father would see it, higher than he merits: *"Am I talking to God or Man! Is it a real Man, or an Angel!"* (p. 254). Crusoe's self-identification is interesting: "I am a Man, an *Englishman,* and dispos'd to assist you" (pp. 254-55). Once an island sovereign, Crusoe now names himself citizen of his native land. The island adventure and the national allegory come together. Again, like Prospero, Crusoe is an island king willing to become a national subject.

Crusoe's actions at the end reveal a homeward turn of mind and a set of principles based on necessity rather than on impulse. His advice about firing on, and possibly killing, the mutineers justifies violence for legal, not tyrannical, ends: "*Necessity* legitimates my Advice" (p. 256). And Crusoe's forces advance in the name of rightful authority: "At the Noise of the Fire, I immediately advanc'd with my whole Army, which was now 8 men, *viz.* my self *Generalissimo, Friday,* my Lieutenant-General, the Captain and his two Men, and the three Prisoners of War, who we had trusted with Arms" (p. 267). Perhaps this force is not so impressive as the advance guard of William III into England, but it wins the day nonetheless.

When the battle for the island and the ship is completed, Crusoe contracts to sail by putting himself under the protection of the rightful English captain. He arrives back in England on 11 June 1687.[28] He comes home truly substantiated, both in status—as returned wanderer, a man of archetypal value[29]—and in funds from his Brazilian plantation, which Defoe totals later at "about a thousand Pounds a Year, as sure as an Estate of Lands in *England*" (p. 285). Defoe's analogy exceeds even the wishes of Crusoe's father: his hero progresses metaphorically as adventurer from the merchant class to the settled landed class. Even though the analogy is comparative and not actual, Crusoe's accumulated property allows him to return, in a sense, properly islanded. Perhaps in a still broader sense, Crusoe's substantial return to his native place allows Defoe to realize the full allegorical potential of a narrative form in which the fictional subject, both abroad and at home, is always king.

Notes

[1] Joyce, *Ulysses* (New York: Random, 1961), p. 109.

[2] Daniel Defoe, *The Life and Strange Surprizing Adventures of Robinson Crusoe,* ed. J. Donald Crowley (London: Oxford Univ. Press, 1972), p. 142. Subsequent citations, given parenthetically in the text by page, are to this edition.

[3] In his essay "The Displaced Self in the Novels of Daniel Defoe," *ELH,* 38 (1971), 562-90, Homer O. Brown makes a similar point about temporal doubling in Crusoe's journal: "The journal is an attempt to define a situation by ordering the present as it becomes the past" (p. 585). The present "becomes" the past in the sense that it will both revert to the past in time and reflect the past's essence.

[4] Crusoe's very name implies a species of wanderer, one for whom an "irresistable Reluctance continu'd to going Home" (p. 16). In his essay "*Robinson Crusoe:* 'Allusive Allegorick History,'" *PMLA,* 82 (1967), 399-407, Robert W. Ayers ponders the original name

of the Crusoe family, Kreutznaer. He suggests various possibilities: *Kreutz* = cross 'to cross, to cruise' (a religious version would be a *Kreutzzug* 'crusade'); *naer* or *naher* = comparative of near; *nahren* 'to journey, to approach.' Crusoe's name, as befits the classical exile, seems to mean both to wander and to come home. For a recent study on the origins of a similar notion, see Douglas Frame, *The Myth of Return in Early Greek Epic* (New Haven: Yale Univ. Press, 1978).

[5] See W. B. Stanford, *The Ulysses Theme: A Study in the Adaptability of a Traditional Hero,* 2nd ed. (Oxford: Oxford Univ. Press, 1963), and a recent study on the poetics of exile, Giuseppe Mazzotta's *Dante, Poet of the Desert* (Princeton: Princeton Univ. Press, 1979).

[6] *Works of Daniel Defoe,* ed. G. H. Maynadier, 16 vols. (New York: Sproul, 1903), III, xi. Subsequent citations are given in the text by volume and page number.

[7] See Maximillian E. Novak, "Defoe's Theory of Fiction," *Studies in Philology,* 61 (1964), 650-68. This seminal essay goes far in addressing the entire matter of fiction, romance, and lying in Defoe's conceptual sense of narrative. Novak maintains, among other things, that Defoe took a traditionally Aristotelian position in valuing invention as an informing pattern of probability (mimesis as history) in fiction. What is probable (though not necessarily actual) is what is useful in extracting the meaning from any fable. Of course Novak knows, as all Defoe's readers should know, that in representing what looks to be probable in fiction Defoe also opens veins of psychological complexity and ambiguity that sustain an interest in his work beyond the theory of usefulness Defoe none too modestly advances for it.

[8] Defoe, *A Collection of Miscellany Letters out of* Mist's *Weekly Journal* (London, 1722-27), IV, 210. Novak cites and discusses this passage and its implications in "Defoe's Theory of Fiction," pp. 662-68.

[9] In *"Robinson Crusoe:* 'Allusive Allegorick History,'" Ayers neatly defines the process as "a story whose literal meaning is augmented by a second meaning which is the construct of allusions in the literal narrative" (p. 400).

[10] These patterns have received considerable attention in J. Paul Hunter's *The Reluctant Pilgrim: Defoe's Emblematic Method and Quest for Form in* Robinson Crusoe (Baltimore: Johns Hopkins Univ. Press, 1966) and in George Starr's *Defoe and Spiritual Autobiography* (Princeton: Princeton Univ. Press, 1965). Everett Zimmerman, "Defoe and Crusoe," *ELH,* 38 (1971), 377-410, sums up the issue: "The pattern for *The Life*

and Strange Surprizing Adventures of Robinson Crusoe is that of a fall, repentance, and redemption—both spiritual and secular" (p. 387).

[11] In many attempts to trace the allegorical import of Crusoe's history, commentators have made scant mention of the historical or national coincidence in its timing. J. Paul Hunter is one of the only critics to notice the parallel: "Crusoe's twenty-eight years of isolation and suffering, for example, parallel the Puritan alienation between the Restoration and the accession of William and Mary; the allusion intensifies the sense of Crusoe's alienation from society and suggests the thematic implications of the Puritan emblematic rendering of events" (*The Reluctant Pilgrim,* p. 204). Douglas Brooks acknowledges Hunter and makes the same point briefly in his *Number and Pattern in the Eighteenth-Century Novel* (London: Routledge and Kegan Paul, 1972), p. 25.

[12] In his *Daniel Defoe and Middle-Class Gentility* (Cambridge: Harvard Univ. Press, 1968), Michael Shinagel hints at the antagonism Defoe, as Dissenter, would have surely felt against the Stuarts: "The persecutions suffered by the Dissenters during the 1660's served to unite rather than disperse them. They found comfort and succor in their shared afflictions. They felt themselves being tested for their religious beliefs, if not also on trial for their souls" (p. 7).

[13] When Defoe first began toying with fictional representation, in his early narrative *The Consolidator* (London, 1705), he called his work an "allegorick Relation" and placed himself in it as a lunar philosopher who acts out the precepts of the 1688 Glorious Revolution on the moon. The narrative is an implicit attack on the less glorious principles of the Stuart kings and on any who would restore those principles in modern times. Significantly, the ascendancy of William III in 1688 marked for Defoe the great chance for a new hero, a hero measuring the value of his nation. In *Essay upon Projects* (London, 1697), Defoe's first full-length work, written in the decade after the Glorious Revolution and a quarter century before *Robinson Crusoe,* we hear of the Crusoe type and symbol, the merchant-adventurer who, in the face of all manner of risk, is still "the most Intelligent Man in the World, and consequently the most capable, when urg'd by Necessity, to Contrive New Ways to live" (p. 8). Defoe repeats the essence of this conception much later in his career, after *Crusoe,* when he refers to the English merchant as a kind of cycle in and of himself, both a personal and a national cycle that conforms to the pattern of risk redemption or ruin recovery: "The English tradesman is a kind of phoenix, who rises out of his own ashes, and makes the ruin of his fortunes be a firm foundation to build his recovery" (*The Compleat English Tradesman* [London, 1726], II, 198-99).

[14] By circumstance or by design Defoe imagined himself to "come alive" after the Restoration. He was born at its outset in 1660; his family suffered under the strict Clarendon Code against Dissenters; he fought in the abortive Monmouth Rebellion of 1685 against James II, barely managing to escape the king's forces in the rain and the subsequent Bloody Assizes of Lord Jeffreys; he rode in the advance guard that welcomed William III, a king Defoe would call his patron and friend, to London. See the early chapters of John Robert Moore's *Daniel Defoe: Citizen of the Modern World* (Chicago: Univ. of Chicago Press, 1958). In his *Life and Adventures of Mr. D— Def—* (London, 1719), Charles Gildon was the first to pick up the allegorical identification of Crusoe's exile with Defoe's life: "You are the true Allegorick Image of thy tender Father D————l" (p. x). And he also sensed that there was a political message in the narrative for which Defoe needed the protection of fiction: "But, honest D————l, I am afraid, with all your Sagaciousness, you do not sufficiently distinguish between the Fear of God, and the Fear of Danger to your own dear Carcass" (p. 18). Defoe's biographer Thomas Wright took another tack and argued that the allegory of *Crusoe* relates to a crisis in Defoe's marital life that resolved itself after his illness in 1714, when he would have been the same age as Crusoe on his return to England (*The Life of Defoe* [London, 1894], pp. 12-13, 24-28). The most detailed account of the personal and public events possibly allegorized in *Robinson Crusoe* is offered by George Parker, "The Allegory of *Robinson Crusoe*," *History*, 10 (1925), 11-25. Parker concentrates on Defoe's entrepreneurial and political career, citing Defoe's comment in his *Appeal to Honour and Justice* (1715): "I have gone through a life of wonders, and am the subject of a vast variety of Providences."

[15] Defoe's notion of obedience in a political context runs counter to the familial disobedience of Crusoe's presumed original sin. Like Locke, Defoe does not confuse patriarchy and monarchy. In fact, passive obedience stands at the center of Defoe's antagonism toward the Stuarts. In his *Jure Divino* (London, 1706), a twelve-book satirical poem on state tyranny, Defoe points out that this "Satyr had never been Publish'd, tho' some of it has been a long time in being, had not the World seem'd to be going mad a second Time with the Error of Passive Obedience and Non-Resistance" (p. i). The first time was in the latter days of an increasingly desperate James II.

[16] For a different development of this notion centering on an economic reading, see Maximillian E. Novak's chapter "Robinson Crusoe's Original Sin," in *Economics and the Fiction of Daniel Defoe* (Berkeley: Univ. of California Press, 1962), pp. 32-48. . . .

[23] The temporal comparison of Crusoe's adventures from the twenty-fifth year of his reign with events at home before and during the hectic last three years of Stuart reign suggests that in both places Providence seems to be readying for something momentous. Invasions, conspiracies, betrayals, cabals, and counter-alliances are unusual, to say the least, on Crusoe's island after his years of isolation, but if they are projected allegorically toward the scramble for power back home they make a certain sense.

[24] The aptness of the sovereign pun on I-land, even if Defoe was unaware of it, was pointed out to me by Richard Braverman of Columbia University. For the wider sets of relations between Crusoe's experience and the law of nations, see Maximillian E. Novak, *Defoe and the Nature of Man* (Oxford: Oxford Univ. Press, 1963).

[25] What Crusoe works out in his response to the cannibals touches on the natural propensity toward tyrannical violence that Defoe saw in mankind. He observes in *Jure Divino*: "Nature has left *this Tincture in the Blood*, / That all Men *would be Tyrants if they cou'd.* / If they forbear their Neighbors to devour, / 'Tis not for want of *Will*, but want of Power" ("Introductory Verses," p. 1). Everett Zimmerman points out that, from Crusoe's early experiences off Africa to the island cannibals to the wolves in the Pyrenees, his fear of being devoured is related to the general fear "of being dematerialized—the reversal of the desire to accumulate. It is a fear shared by author and character" ("Defoe and Crusoe," p. 385).

[26] Defoe may be casting a glance at the illegal cabal of James II in the last days of what Defoe saw as an increasingly illegitimate rule. Charles Gildon assumed that Defoe's hatred of the English in this scene was more general. In his pamphlet attack, Gildon has Defoe remark: "for I always hated the *English,* and took a Pleasure in depreciating and villifying of them" (*Life and Adventures of Mr. D— Def—,* p. xiv). Another possibility is pursued by Defoe's biographer John Robert Moore, who argues that Defoe's representation of the English in the *Crusoe* volumes was repayment in kind for the Englishman's usual xenophobia. At the time, according to Moore, Defoe had an interest in a policy of good will toward Spain in order to keep open or create trade routes off the coast of South America. Most of his English countrymen did not see the matter his way.

[27] If this particular island sequence seems to allude to Shakespeare's *Tempest*, Defoe has a *Winter's Tale* of sorts in mind for Crusoe when, several years later, Crusoe crosses the Pyrenees in winter on the long-way-round trip back from Brazil.

[28] Not only is this date of historical importance to Defoe for personal reasons as the second anniversary of Monmouth's rebellion against James II, in which

Defoe himself took part, but it was precisely at this time in England that leading national figures officially invited the Protestant Dutch prince, William, to mount an invasion and wrest the monarchy from Stuart possession. In a sense, Crusoe's salvation and rearrival home allegorize the English salvation to follow.

²⁹ Homer is careful to make certain that when Odysseus returns to Ithaca he does so with a rich store given him by the Phaeacians. He hides the booty in a cave until he restores his land to *its* true worth. The exile thus brings value back to his home.

Michael M. Boardman (essay date 1983)

SOURCE: "*Robinson Crusoe,*" in *Defoe and the Uses of Narrative*, Rutgers University Press, 1983, pp.25-65.

[*In the excerpt below, Boardman considers some of the differing views of the meaning of* Robinson Crusoe *and argues that Defoe uses a threefold narrative strategy incorporating reportorial, personal, and interactive techniques.*]

Employing a Metaphor, as was his wont, to describe narrative unity, Henry James likens *The Tragic Muse* to "some aromatic bag of gathered herbs of which the string has never been loosed."¹ The question of the final fragrance of the bouquet garni known as ***Robinson Crusoe*** continues to puzzle at least those students of narrative for whom deconstruction has not invalidated the whole enterprise. Clearly, any theory of narrative development concerned with wholes rather than parts, or even with the possibility of making wholes from parts, must consider the question, as well as the additional complication suggested by James's insistence on employing analogy: Is the unity so many have seen in Defoe's first major narrative a critical *ignis fatuus,* the delusive product of our continuing struggle to reduce chaotic stories to ordered patterns? Or is the book with all its admitted but remarkable "Variety," literally unified, every part, like Aesop's belly, "in its dull quiet way . . . doing necesary work for the body"?

The question of coherence floats around other issues that at first perusal do not seem to have much to do with it. For example, what else is at stake in the continuing disagreement about the very subject matter of ***Robinson Crusoe?*** Is it a story about solitary adventure, or religion, or economics, to take only the three top contenders? Does one really get anywhere if one must conclude, as did the most recent critic of the book, that it really is about both religion and economics, indeed that it is two stories? Certainly, two stories could coexist uneasily or somehow become a whole. But how? Allowing the two parts to live together, as

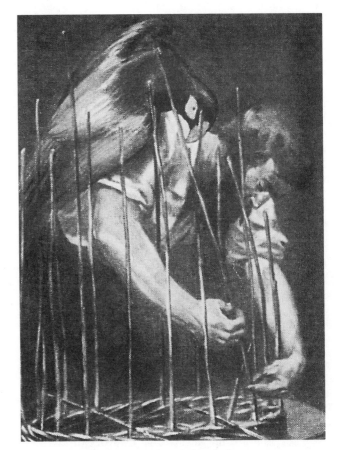

An illustration from Robinson Crusoe.

this critic did, simply does not explain the wedding: unity is a question of the conditions of oneness, by definition.²

Not a few critics have been content to trace unity to Defoe's ideas. Aside from the almost universally held view of literature as a kind of special discourse, a view by no means originating with recent critics of narrative like Todorov,³ there is some warrant for semantic abstraction in Defoe's stated practice. He consistently promulgated, in his prefaces and elsewhere, the neoclassical ideal of uniting "Diversion" and "Instruction" to generate a kind of sweet didacticism. It has therefore been the stated task of many Defoe critics to "show in detail how Defoe unites narration and instruction," a process that entails splitting asunder what Defoe joined. Occasionally a dissenting voice is heard. McKillop argues that "much of the time, of course, we see Crusoe merely following his 'rambling designs.' He does not always live in the presence of Fate or Providence." This is a sane view, but one that creates as many problems as it solves. For one, McKillop's thesis implies a lack of unity, ideological or otherwise, and in the sixties, at least in American criticism, organic criticism was all the rage, no matter how the coherence had to be located, or created. Most of the readings of Defoe's narratives arguing for some kind of semantic coherence come from that decade and are at least in part a reaction to McKillop. The second problem is related to, and actually the cause of, the first: thematic readings, generated as they are by analogically relating literal action to ideology, are *always* successful, at least on their own terms. McKillop's view, then, did not rule out further extraction of meaning but virtually guaranteed that it would take place. So it is that Watt, writing about the same time as McKillop, finds that the economic and not the spiritual dominates. The truths communicated beneath the smooth surface of narrative may differ from critic to critic, but the assumptions about narrative meaning remain fairly constant.[4]

That schemes as diverse as Providence, economic necessity, and "the idea of man's isolation" have arisen to explain the book does not necessarily require one to see *Robinson Crusoe* as fragmented, although that possibility always remains. The procession of competing readings, each somehow claiming authority over the whole, may be enough to cast doubt on Frank Ellis's sanguine statement that reading "the criticism of *Robinson Crusoe* since 1900 is almost enough to restore one's faith in progress."[5] Yet the causes of this plurality of meanings are not self-evident. Is it in the nature of texts, all texts, to mean diversely? Or is it in readers themselves? R. S. Crane, adapting Aristotle's methodological "pluralism," argued that no work of literature yields the same meaning when examined within different frameworks, a theory that seems to locate the problem not in the text but in the tools critics employ to understand it. Any critic can, therefore, select one aspect of *Robinson Crusoe* to subsume others, allusivity reaching, potentially, into all corners of the cosmos—a situation Tristram/Sterne would delight in, but one more than a little disturbing to a critic searching for probable knowledge about texts. This welter of competing readings, taken without logical warrant as evidence of textual treachery, then leads many critics to eschew the search for any sort of common ground in interpretation. In Frank Kermode's recent use of the terms, one must abandon plodding, "carnal" interpretation questing after shared literary experience and seek instead "spiritual" originality, the insight and even elegance of the personal vision.[6] The common assumption, one that is crucial to understanding how recent critics have approached Defoe, of both the unifiers and the deconstructionists, has been that narrativity is but one thing. One can even write a "poetics of prose," as if it really were a single thing (certainly a necessary precondition for Aristotle).[7] The novel, then, exhibits cohesion, or flies apart at the slightest touch, depending on one's prior constitution of what narrative is. Having made a prior commitment either to the order or, more commonly today, to the fragmentation of the world mirrored in narrative, one is prevented from even entertaining another possibility—that some narratives

hold together and some do not. For better or worse, ontology once adopted limits the kinds of questions one can even entertain as significant.

Crane, whose work deserves more attention, actually set up three categories. Some works are unified but relatively barren, either of pleasure or significance (a number of eighteenth-century English tragedies come to mind). Others, also unified, are rich in local texture, abundantly satisfying Coleridge's standard of "the production of as much immediate pleasure in parts as is compatible with the largest sum of pleasure in the whole." Finally, still others "are rich in local virtues but have only a loose or tenuous overall form."[8] It is hardly surprising, since the New Critics in all their guises so assiduously studied their Coleridge, that the second category frequently seemed the only one worth bothering with and that, consequently, they frequently also found unity of some conceptual kind where more literal critics like Crane did not—as for example in the attempts to discover internal coherence in the *Canterbury Tales* or *In Our Time*. The quest for oneness as sole or even primary poetic virtue can mislead, especially if the goal is matter-of-fact, like understanding the development of discrete forms. One may learn more about the generation of new subspecies, within narrative as a whole, if one assumes that early examples have not always sprung forth fully mature and coherent. Early narrative comic development, for example, may be clearer after noting that Goldsmith did not entirely succeed in binding together the two halves of *The Vicar of Wakefield.* One then begins to understand how difficult it must have been in the middle eighteenth century in England to write a first-person comic action, in which moral ambiguities must be clarified by a narrator himself flawed in many ways. Goldsmith's shift to a more direct representation of moral values in the second half makes sense as the uneasy compromise with innovation one might expect from a friend of the man who wrote *Rasselas.*[9] In like manner, if one can accept as a possibility that *Robinson Crusoe* is pleasing because Defoe created a narrator who functions in several ways, one may begin to see how Crusoe can elicit so many responses, how each of his roles exerts its power on one's memory.[10] At times Crusoe is relatively unpersonalized, an "eye," or reporter; at others, he is a developed personage but not a novelistic character; and finally, at times Crusoe seems to interact in novellike sequences with other elements: thought and action. As obvious and unexciting as these functions may be, they hold the key to the mixed form of *Robinson Crusoe*—if "form" is not completely inappropriate, given the context. These roles neither provide a unifying scheme—one must, in fact, resist providing one by analogy in order to see their real importance— nor are they encompassed by something larger. They are not substructures, except in the barest and most critically fruitless sense of taking up space in the same book. Each use of Crusoe provides an isolable kind of narrative experience and a distinct kind of meaning. Each has been pulled out of the fluctuating context and employed as an organizing scheme.

More important for my thesis, the three uses parallel the three lines of development Defoe's narrative career followed. Narrative strategies originate as ways of dealing with remembered or created experience, ways that can vary drastically as the mind works on subject matter and considers effects. As strategies, the reportorial, the personal, and the interactive—to give them arbitrary names—therefore not only entail a number of varying formal relationships within the text, but also betoken significant differences in authorial attitude toward the text and in possibilities for the text as experience or use. For example, the Crusoe who is little more than an observer belongs to a very old tradition of *using* narrators; one does not ordinarily create a fictional narrator and then deprive him of significant traits of personality unless he is to serve a function conceived of as more important than the representation of personality. This Crusoe leads, by clear steps, to the determinate, referential significance of the *Memoirs of a Cavalier* and *A Journal of the Plague Year.* The Crusoe who is a product of Defoe's "keen eye for traits of character and a very vivid idea of persons"[11] becomes Moll, Colonel Jack, and the Roxana of most of her story, refinements of personality and epitomes of the pleasures possible in earlier works, such as real memoirs, that concentrated on the inner lives of diarists or autobiographers. Here is, not novelistic character, but "consciousness," following the sense of John Bayley's distinction. Finally, during brief sequences—Defoe never wrote a coherent traditional novel—Crusoe participates in what Bayley calls "a complex process of rapport between author and ourselves" by which "we know what to think" of him and his story.[12] This last usage of Crusoe is not easy to locate, in part because Defoe does all he can to hide it, destructive as it is of the illusion of factuality. In brief sections, however, Defoe experiments with the kind of control that will culminate in the novelistic conclusion of *Roxana,* not to mention other protonovelistic sequences scattered throughout the other books. Once these separate impulses are discriminated and their importance for the novel articulated, McKillop's contention that Defoe did not advance by "artistic self-discovery" becomes untenable, but for the most literal understanding of "discovery" as being always intellectual and conscious.

Had Defoe written the *Memoirs of a Cavalier* or *A Journal of the Plague Year* before *Robinson Crusoe,* at least one line of his development would long ago have been recognized. Those two later works clearly make virtues of what in the earlier work are minor annoyances, Crusoe's "rambling." The *Memoirs* and the *Journal* are coherent and successful imitations of true stories, and therefore rest securely in a tradition

much older than Defoe. With its alternating intentions intertwined and blended into effects suspended often between potentiality and realization, Crusoe's story seems to mock efforts to specify its teleology. Nor is the problem merely one of subject, the variety Defoe seems to have had in mind as he went about collecting or inventing Crusoe's early "strange surprizing adventures." The process of "communication," as Wolfgang Iser terms it, is also confused.[13] Apart from the few times Crusoe acts in a context that allows the reader to infer specific information—for example, the sequence of fear-longing-action involving the cannibals—one's responses are usually "free" to a large extent. In his reportorial and personal uses, Crusoe remains a potential vehicle for whatever idiosyncratic interpretation individual associations produce. Some degree of significant common response to Crusoe is possible only when Defoe novelistically "pins" Crusoe's developing hopes and fears causally to a situation qualitatively predictable. Crusoe yearns, after years on the island, for the sound of just one voice other than his own; but when visitors finally come, they are the ghastliest of human outcasts, cannibals. He is torn between two powerful impulses of attraction and repulsion, with his desire for contact winning out—it will later be seen how—only after a long period. Just how important this careful "justification" of Crusoe's actions, necessarily involving the taking of life, was to the overall aims of the episode can be seen by the effect it had on many viewers of a public-television version of the book a few years ago. What had required a careful juxtaposition of narrative reasons in order not to seem gratuitous violence now became exactly that: Crusoe attacks because his little kingdom has been threatened by the black savages, and his slaughter of them seemed to be a vicious manifestation of imperialist racism. Crusoe, if not Defoe, may *be* a racist, but the point is that in the midst of this sequence such a judgment has been precluded. Most of the time, however, when Crusoe is just an observer or is vividly but not causally involved in the action sequence, it is impossible to speak of any reader's "appropriate" much less "necessary" reaction to him. And if the text asserts no tyranny, benevolent or otherwise, as the traditional novel does, with all its loose ends, how can the reader determine its meaning? The text itself turns treacherous, as some recent criticism would have it for all narrative.

The problem with Crusoe, however, is not that his story partakes of some special liability to indeterminacy peculiar to narrative in general, but that sometimes Defoe controls with a certain degree of success all the eclectic diversity of the sequence and sometimes he simply refuses to subordinate his materials to a probabilistic pattern. The "Editor" of Crusoe's words tells the reader that this is the "Story" of a "private Man's Adventures," involving "Wonders" that are "scarce capable of greater Variety." Yet "story" is not quite right, since there is no "Appearance of Fiction" in it;

it is rather a "just History of Fact,"[14] an emphatic formulation in light of how much weight "just" carried with all neoclassical critics, including Johnson. Clearly, one is faced here with two orders of probability. The first and least common in ***Robinson Crusoe*** demands that the reader experience Crusoe, at least tacitly, as an artificial construct in a fabricated structure. This view receives confirmation as well as an indeterminate measure of complication from the external knowledge that the whole *is* in fact a fabrication. The second order, introduced and bolstered by title page and preface, requires unambiguously that Crusoe be regarded as a natural person. The distinction is obvious, although it is usually ignored as unimportant, especially since the reader knows the book is a fiction. Yet books do not usually require readers, in effect, to alternate between knowing fully the psyche of a character in order that they may participate in the progression of which he is a subordinated element and, at other times, allowing him the natural opacity, the secrecy, of real people. Indeed, few readers can read the book this way, requiring as it does almost a somatic contradiction, and fewer probably would want to if they could.

The result has been that, appetites honed by expectation of full fictional revelation of character, and the "true story" actually hiding more than it reveals, readers have been forced to construe for themselves, to manufacture, a consistent inner life and ethical being for a Crusoe who does not literally reveal such consistency. This makes *Robinson Crusoe* sound very "modern" in its indeterminacy and capacity for duplicity. The problem is that, with the model of novelistic development I have sketched, this is the opposite direction Defoe should have taken had he wanted to reach the much more determinate significance of the traditional novel. While the formulation may seem both solipsistic and egregiously self-confirming, it is based on literary history. One may, of course, interpret even strong systems such as *Pamela* and *Tom Jones* as freely as one chooses. But to the extent that they are systems, the traditional novel after Richardson was not in the business of mystification but revelation. When readers are confused, about Lovelace or Stephen Dedalus, disclosure is inadequate. Indeed, one definition of the action novel, and one indication of how much its birth owes to the importation of semiological strategies from the drama, would be that it is a system strong enough to mold shared belief, if only for the story's time being. Other works that are recognized as fictions exert no such power, or do so feebly. True stories, or imitated ones, do not do so either, but not by choice: natural people hold close to their motivations and their private chronicles often hide more than they reveal. Still other works, like *Robinson Crusoe,* embody an impossible formal "request," that the reader experience them as both true and fabricated.

This phenomenological problem has its moral side, since Defoe goes on in his preface to suggest that, while this is a true story, with a principle of "Diversion," yet overall rules a didactic intention, "a religious Application of Events to the Uses which wise Men always apply them." Then follows another bifurcation, since the moral consists of Crusoe's negative example, his disobedience, as well as his fate, his final deliverance, intended "to justify and honour the Wisdom of Providence" (p. I). Just as readers' merest instrumental judgments of Crusoe lack moorings at times, their involvement in his moral plight fails of direction and coherence as well when Defoe places his character on the page virtually deprived of a signifying context. Didacticism, certainly of Defoe's plain sort, cannot emerge from such a silence, and events decidedly do not speak for themselves. Yet it would be inaccurate to conclude from this formal and moral liability that Defoe himself has lost touch with the ethical implications of Crusoe's plight. Not only do stories have expectations for readers, they have them for their creators as well, as Sartre reminded us in *What Is Literature?* If the intention to replicate a true story does not require a coherent configuration of subordinated belief, if, in fact, such belief could destroy the illusion, can an author be blamed for not behaving novelistically? The answer is, of course, that he *can,* but should not, be blamed, if only because it is more interesting to see what sorts of semantic blind alleys Defoe leads his reader into than it is to impose some analogical scheme that makes "sense" of the confusion. Crusoe, for example, swears one moment that his companion in escape from slavery, Xury, showed him "so much Affection" that Crusoe had to "love him ever after" (p. 25); ten pages later Crusoe has sold him for sixty pieces of eight, with the eleemosynary stipulation that the boy will gain his freedom in ten years if he turns Christian. The juxtaposition seems inadvert, even unsavory—until one realizes that it literally has no *purpose.* This is not the same as saying it is inadvertent, which would imply a standard of proceeding that would make of such a contradiction an excrescense. When Defoe's mind is on using Crusoe, or any of his narrators, as reporter— as witness of "wonders"—he thinks only of traits of personality as plausible means of transition. He is not "distanced" from Crusoe, as Joyce is from Stephen; he simply does not think of him as a consistent character. How different such a moment is from the cannibal sequence, in its demands on both Defoe and the reader, should be obvious if somewhat unsettling. Defoe's imagination is no more with Crusoe the "reporter" than it was to be with the Cavalier.

The reportorial strategy even requires that the personality Defoe might routinely endow with vividness be muted in order to maintain the illusion of truth. Regardless, whether Crusoe's aimlessness results from Defoe's adherence to an older tradition, from a fixation on the integrity of "the event," or from a desire to replicate quotidian randomness, in the absence of a pervasive and recognizable teleology, Defoe's values remain unknowable unless they are sought outside the fiction—a practice entailing its own hazards. The novel-to-come would utilize value in a radically different way, subordinating it to a strong sequence of action and character having determinate significance. Such, at least, is the novel's intention, even if no novel perfectly achieves it. Having rejected satire—Defoe was not very good at it, although he handled other kinds of irony and invective skillfully[15]—as well as more direct narrative means for conveying beliefs, such as Bunyanesque allegory and the sort of parable or apologue form Johnson used so effectively, Defoe leaves himself little direction to go except toward the novel. Replicating the forms and effects of true stories means relinquishing the possibilities for conveying a moral vision, although one can always simply "insert" beliefs, if care is taken not to appear too systematic. When one merely endows a narrator with a personality, frequently pays it only fitful attention, and avoids the creation of significant interaction with the "and then, and then" of the story, the Horatian ideal falters in practice. Drama, with its commitment to public fictionality and formal structure, proffers its patterned fable unabashedly. But Defoe distrusted drama, although he seems to have liked it well enough.[16] His clinging to the pseudofactual mode seems indeed to be a kind of reaction against the "untruths" of drama so many critics had railed at during Defoe's lifetime. Yet his doing so is ironic in that his seeking a more moral, because truer, genre leads not only to duplicity but to moral ambiguity. True stories often leave meaning to the reader. Interpretation of fictional narrative may be difficult, especially in regard to values. But what standard of meaning resides in narrative propositions that purport merely to be true? "Lee Harvey Oswald killed John F. Kennedy"—a narrative statement, calling not for interpretation but simple verification. Once the "fact" was established, a context for the determination of meaning might be available. But *Robinson Crusoe* begs even this question, since Defoe was careful to distance the story from the real events it vaguely resembles—the Selkirk story.

The novel creates and insists on its own artificial context, which is why, perhaps, in all its variations it seems to some unsuited to modern value chaos. Defoe's approximation to novelistic effects can be tested by comparing most of his works to McKillop's formulation of his practice.

The simplest or minimum form of impersonation consists in providing a reporter or narrator who may appropriately give the details in his own way. This is a natural mode of journalism, and admits of considerable variety of intention. . . . We then proceed in the great fictions to the stage at which the impersonated reporter tells how he was forced to deal with pressing circumstances affecting his own survival or success; the interplay between the impersonated character and the circumstance gets us into a kind of circle, with each giving significance to the other.[17]

It is impossible to dispute at least the partial accuracy of this description of Defoe's practice, although McKillop leaves out a number of steps in the process and it is hard to predict exactly how Defoe's own beliefs would function in the "interplay." But despite my agreement with McKillop, I cannot see much resemblance between the most complex "interplay" and what ordinarily goes on in the novel. Much the commonest case in Defoe, in addition, is for the "circle" to remain firmly closed and resistant to interpretation. A created personage can interact with his or her environment for hundreds of pages through dozens of fascinating episodes, pronouncing all sorts of verdicts on questions of every kind, and one still does not have the novel. The traditional novel attempts to subordinate the interaction among character, event, and belief to something else, a pattern of represented experience that allows the reader continuing knowledge of the qualitative nature of the pattern itself: a novel of this traditional sort includes beliefs, as it includes everything else, to achieve a predictable and satisfying resolution of instability. Such "neatness" may now be distasteful, but the action novel displayed it. Pamela, for example, finally marries her Squire B. and all her troubles seem over. Except the reader knows they are not, and so did Richardson. The novel must go on, because all the issues are not resolved. The issues, of course, are not ideological but experiential. While readers recognize that marriage to the Squire is best for Pamela, given the odious alternatives, they also know that "best" does not mean "ideal" in Richardson's moral world. I can use such terms of cognitive certainty as "know" and "recognized" because the novel in Richardson's hands presents branching alternatives to the characters, each choice charged with ethical implication because of the traits Richardson has called to the forefront in each character. One knows, therefore, not necessarily *what* the outcome of pattern will be, even before the marriage, but that whatever it is, it will involve a shade of moral gray, the ethical ambiguity Sheldon Sacks notes is characteristic of the action-type he calls "serious," as opposed to the comic and tragic.[18] Yet the ambiguity residing in the conclusion of *Pamela* results precisely because we have such a quantity of specifiable knowledge about the deficiencies and strengths of character Squire B. and even dear Pamela have shown us. In the serious action, then, ambiguity can result as a positive consequence of the form. While Pamela's character seemed ambiguous to Fielding, in quite different terms, *that* ambiguity was not a positive, intended consequence of the novel's form.

Such is not the case with most parts of **Robinson Crusoe.** Too often the reader's simplest judgments of better or worse are confused or blocked for lack of evidence and one must, to create the meaning that is not found, yoke traits of personality to events that finally are not mutually illuminating. Causality is a chimera and will remain so until Defoe discovers a narrative structure that makes a positive virtue of represented beliefs.

It might be argued that in my single-minded pursuit of what Defoe does *not* do, I have forgotten that an author's refusals and renunciations are themselves positive evidence of an important sort. We shall see later on that this is the case, that Defoe's consistent refusal to utilize belief positively does imply much about his view of art and the world. But that is not the question now. Only a knowledge of what the novel was to be can allow critics to dispense with the erroneous view of Defoe as one who refused to judge his material—rather than, as I am arguing, an author who refuses to write works that require precise judgment. Nevertheless, **Robinson Crusoe** does contain sequences that tease with their novelistic tendencies. Only by seeing how short they stop can one understand where Defoe's real interest and talent lie, in the creation of personality. The third strategy, the reportorial, actually takes up little space, although Defoe will later isolate and use it almost exclusively in such nonnovels as the **Journal** and the **Memoirs.** Each of the three has its counterpart in later fiction. A Pamela or Pip can "step back" from the flow of events and comment in more or less neutral ways, although the aims of the traditional novel imply the elimination of anything inert. Then, too, narrators can give an impression of being intensely human without their humanity affecting the progress of the fable, at least in any causal fashion. Probably every traditional novel contains at least one character who exists only so that the reader may take pleasure in the portrayal (although one would look long and hard for such an unsubordinated element in most of Jane Austen's novels). This lucid and mutable aura, floating free, characterizes many real memoirs and some twentieth-century lyric novels, such as Virginia Woolf's, that enlist autobiography in the service of fiction. Character implies reintegration; not only the representation of traits must take place, but those traits must lead somewhere qualitatively determined. To suggest that Defoe, much less Virginia Woolf, did not create character may seem absurdly perverse. The terms are not important; I wish only to point out significant differences occurring on both ends of the development of traditional novelistic types.

If one accepts this view of traditional character as an element in a progressive action, then Defoe created few examples of character. In the novel, the "I" reveals himself, or is revealed by a narrator, so that the reader may understand and even anticipate what the

"I" is to become. The world of the novel indeed implies a connection between what one has been and what one will be in the future. Whether the movement is from happiness to misery, the reverse, or some other significant transmutation of status, character, or belief, the fate of a character in an action results as no matter of chance even, in what only masquerades as a paradox, if events fall out from "Fortune." Fielding manages to attain a kind of high and serious decorum with his ludicrous tale of Tom in part because the ordered comic world of *Tom Jones* implies an external world of moral and social chaos.[19] The novel depends on a belief in order. Even Hemingway, whose universe was populated by no gods, benevolent or malign, abided in the clean well-lighted place of art. The novel, then, demands that the people of the book not simply reside as nonpaying guests but contribute their share to the upkeep of the story. It will only be Defoe's discovery of how to reintegrate into the flow of narrative previously revealed information about Roxana that will permit him to approach the threshold of the novel. In **Robinson Cruseo** the three uses of the narrator remain disjoined, as if Defoe contented himself, in this his first effort, with their exemplification. He has created a structure of sorts, but one that makes no systematic use of anything but the moral commonplaces of the age. . . .

Notes

[1] Henry James, Preface to *The Tragic Muse,* p. 81.

[2] See Quentin Kraft, "*Robinson Crusoe* and the Story of the Novel."

[3] See, for example, Todorov, *The Poetics of Prose.*

[4] Starr, *Spiritual Autobiography,* p. 72; McKillop, *Masters,* p. 21; Watt, *Rise,* Chapter 3.

[5] Frank Ellis, Introduction to *Twentieth-Century Views of Robinson Crusoe,* p. 1.

[6] R. S. Crane, *The Languages of Criticism and the Structure of Poetry,* esp. pp. 3-38. For the fullest treatment of the implications of critical pluralism, see Wayne C. Booth, *Critical Understanding: The Powers and Limits of Pluralism.* For Kermode, see *The Genesis of Secrecy,* esp. pp. 1-21.

[7] Todorov's "undertaking" is based on Valéry's remark, "Literature is, and cannot be anything but, a kind of extension and application of certain properties of language" (*Poetics of Prose,* p. 19). For my purposes, it will be useful to consider narrative as just another choice, among many, that authors make to solve the particular problems their own brands of creation present. Defoe, of course, does not initially "choose" narrative—the pseudofactual mode demands it, just as it

does I-narration—but he and later writers discover through experimentation its inherent strengths and liabilities for portraying inner states of being.

[8] Crane, *Languages,* pp. 182-183.

[9] See David H. Richter, *Fable's End,* pp. 171-176.

[10] Paul Alkon argues that "the final shape of memories induced by a text would have to be accepted as one of its formal attributes" (*Defoe and Fictional Time,* p. 11). While responses to a text cannot really be said to be a part of the text itself, it is true that one must boldly commit the affective fallacy to understand Defoe's forms.

[11] *National Review,* in Rogers, *Critical Heritage,* p. 129.

[12] John Bayley, "Character and Consciousness," pp. 225-226.

[13] See Wolfgang Iser, *The Implied Reader.*

[14] Daniel Defoe, *Robinson Crusoe,* p. 1. Subsequent references are in the text.

[15] See Chapter 1, n. 2.

[16] See John Robert Moore, *Daniel Defoe: Citizen of the Modern World,* p. 25.

[17] McKillop, *Masters,* p. 10.

[18] Sacks, *Fiction and the Shape of Belief,* pp. 22-24.

[19] See R. S. Crane, "The Concept of Plot and the Plot of *Tom Jones,*" esp. pp. 637-638; and Sacks, *Fiction and the Shape of Belief,* p. 107.

Works Cited

Bayley, John. "Character and Consciousness." *New Literary History* 5 (1974):225-235. . . .

Crane, R. S. "The Concept of Plot and the Plot of *Tom Jones.*" In *Critics and Criticism, Ancient and Modern.* Chicago: University of Chicago Press, 1952.

————. "Ernest Hemingway: 'The Killers.'" In *The Idea of the Humanities and Other Essays.* 2 vols. Chicago: University of Chicago Press, 1967.

————. *The Languages of Criticism and the Structure of Poetry.* Toronto: University of Toronto Press, 1953. . . .

Defoe, Daniel. *Captain Singleton.* Edited by Shiv K. Kumar. London: Oxford University Press, 1973.

————. *Colonel Jack.* Edited by Samuel Holt Monk. London: Oxford University Press, 1970.

————. *The Farther Adventures of Robinson Crusoe.* In *Romances and Narratives.* Edited by G. A. Aitken. 16 vols. 1895. Reprint. New York: AMS Press, 1974.

————. *A Journal of the Plague Year.* Edited by Louis Landa. London: Oxford University Press, 1969.

————. *Memoirs of a Cavalier.* Edited by James T. Boulton. London: Oxford University Press, 1972.

————. *Moll Flanders.* Edited by George Starr. London: Oxford University Press, 1971.

————. *The Political History of the Devil.* London, 1726.

————. *Robinson Crusoe.* Edited by J. Donald Crowley. London: Oxford University Press, 1972.

————. *Roxana.* Edited by Jane Jack. London: Oxford University Press, 1969. . . .

Ellis, Frank. Introduction to *Twentieth-Century Views of Robinson Crusoe.* Englewood Cliffs, N.J.: Prentice-Hall, 1969. . . .

Goldsmith, Oliver. *The Vicar of Wakefield.* New York: New American Library, 1961. . . .

Iser, Wolfgang. "The Current Situation of Literary Theory: Key Concepts and the Imaginary." *New Literary History* 11 (1979):1-21.

————. *The Implied Reader.* Baltimore: Johns Hopkins University Press, 1974. . . .

James, Henry. "The Art of Fiction." In *Theory of Fiction: Henry James.* Edited by James E. Miller, Jr. Lincoln: University of Nebraska Press, 1972.

————. Preface to *The Tragic Muse.* In *The Art of the Novel.* New York: Scribner's, 1934. . . .

Kermode, Frank. *The Genesis of Secrecy: On the Interpretation of Narrative.* Cambridge and London: Harvard University Press, 1979. . . .

McKillop, Alan D. *The Early Masters of English Fiction.* Lawrence, Kan.: University of Kansas Press, 1956. . . .

Sacks, Sheldon. "*Clarissa* and the Tragic Traditions." In *Irrationalism in the Eighteenth Century.* Edited by Harold E. Pagliaro. Cleveland: Case Western Reserve University Press, 1972.

————. *Fiction and the Shape of Belief.* Berkeley and Los Angeles: University of California Press, 1964. . . .

Todorov, Tzvetan. *The Poetics of Prose.* Translated by Richard Howard. Ithaca, N.Y.: Cornell University Press, 1977. . . .

Watt, Ian. *The Rise of the Novel.* Berkeley and Los Angeles: University of California Press, 1957. . . .

Woolf, Virginia. "Defoe." In *The Common Reader.* New York: Harcourt, Brace and World, 1925.

————. "How It Strikes a Contemporary." In *The Common Reader.* New York: Harcourt, Brace and World, 1925.

————. "Robinson Crusoe." In *The Second Common Reader.* New York: Harcourt, Brace and World, 1932. . . .

Virginia Ogden Birdsall (essay date 1985)

SOURCE: "*Robinson Crusoe*: A Miserable and Almost Hopeless Condition," in *Defoe's Perpetual Seekers: A Study of Major Fiction,* Bucknell University Press, 1985, pp. 24-49.

[*In the following excerpt, Birdsall discusses Crusoe's realization that there can be no wholly successful defense against the human predicament of living in a hostile world.*]

. . . *Robinson Crusoe* is indeed a success story of the sort several recent critics have described. Crusoe becomes master of his fate, bending even God or Providence to his will. He is a victorious rebel against restriction. He controls his circumstances. But in thinking of our actual experience of the adventures of Robinson Crusoe, we must surely acknowledge something a little wrong about all this. For if we take Crusoe's early and continuing defiance of his limitations to have a symbolic suggestiveness, we come abruptly to an inescapable realization about Crusoe's pursuit of absolute power—namely, that it is destined always to remain a pursuit. Defoe repeatedly tells us, in effect, that Crusoe can no more "run away from [his] Master" before he has served his time than can any human being; he cannot escape time or make time his servant. He can neither count on Providence always to save him nor control his own fate by naming it Providence and bowing down before it.

We cannot, if we read Defoe's novel attentively, ignore the fact that neither of the homes Crusoe creates for himself—neither the one in which he serves a higher master nor the one in which he is himself the master—

proves wholly satisfactory. Crusoe at times discovers one to be as uncomfortable as the other.[20] In this regard, then, Crusoe is man as Hobbes and Rochester saw him: feeling powerless and futilely struggling to be or at least to feel all-powerful; experiencing almost constant fearfulness and struggling ineffectually to feel invincible.

Whatever his triumphs and conquests, Crusoe's sense of the precariousness of his existence and his own insufficiency never permanently leaves him from the time he is first thrown up, helpless and naked, on the island shore. He remains the vulnerable child, left all alone in the world without friends or protectors—always in need of father- and mother-figures on whom to rely and always feeling himself in peril of being "swallowed up," whether by the sea, by the earth, by beasts, or by cannibals. The oral fixation that Berne was the first to comment on remains characteristic of Crusoe throughout the novel and tends to undercut fatally any contention that his adventures truly involve a progressive mastery of his environment.

What they do involve are alternating periods of shelter and of exposure, and what Defoe implicitly concedes is that the choice Crusoe seems to have amounts, in reality, to no choice at all. For whether he chooses home or restless wandering, the underlying and inescapable reality is always death. He knows that he must leave the womb if he is to live, and that he is born to die—and that no power, whether human or divine, can change that deadly fact.

The dilemma receives its clearest symbolic expression at the point in Crusoe's island career when, having just constructed a "complete enclosure," he feels the earth shaking beneath him and flees from his cave "for Fear I shou'd be bury'd in it" (p. 80). Here Crusoe confronts the fact that there is no true safety to be found anywhere: "The fear of being swallow'd up alive, made me that I never slept in quiet, and yet the Apprehensions of lying abroad without any Fence was almost equal to it . . ." (p. 82). The scene is, in essence, a recapitulation of Crusoe's earlier experience of leaving home. Again he finds himself driven out of a secure habitation by subterranean rumblings beyond his power to understand or control, and again he discovers the state of things in the outside world to be even more threatening than that he has experienced inside. In the first crisis, he resolves that he will "like a true repenting Prodigal, go Home to my Father" (p. 8); and in the second he does, in fact, return to his cave to find shelter from the "violent Rain." On the whole, he decides, it is safer to be inside than outside: "when I look'd about and saw how every thing was put in order, how pleasantly conceal'd I was, and how safe from Danger, it made me very loath to remove" (p. 82).

Yet along with the comfort and security that Crusoe repeatedly associates with his "Father's House" in particular and with home in general, invariably goes a sense of imprisonment or confinement—of limitation—which Crusoe can never tolerate for long. "I broke loose," he says, in relating his first decision to go to sea (p. 7). It is the perversity of Crusoe—his "fate or fault"—that he is "not very easy and happy" in the "upper Station of *Low Life.*" And indeed Crusoe's father's world, inhabited as it apparently is by models of passive acquiescence, has unmistakable suggestions of entrapment in death and decay.[21] The idyllic way of life that the senior Crusoe describes involves men who go "silently and smoothly thro' the World, and comfortably out of it" (p. 5). His father, in the younger Crusoe's view, has been just such a man: "how easy, how comfortably he had liv'd all his Days," Crusoe reflects, "and never had been expos'd to Tempests at Sea or Troubles on Shore . . ." (p. 8).

What Crusoe already seems to sense, however, and what he is later to learn firsthand, is that any such paradise, any such self-contained existence is actually a lie. In this connection, a modern-day Hobbesian has summed up the human condition in words that might well have been written with Crusoe in mind:

> There is . . . a true and a false way of evaluating the human situation. Of primary importance for the true way is the denudation of the spirit, the stripping away of all subterfuges, comforts, and evasions. Our true condition is one of *exposure:* in reality, we are defenseless, naked to the winds of chance and blind accident. There is an expressive German participle, *geborgen,* which translates into English as "secure" or "safe," but connotes the delightful feeling of protectedness, the comfort of being hidden away or concealed from lurking dangers. The little bird is *geborgen* in the nest, the infant in the womb, the beloved in the arms of a strong and tender lover. By exposure is meant just the opposite of this. Though the desire for protection and security, for *Geborgenheit,* is a characteristic and primary impulse of human creatures, it is also a profound illusion. Spiritually, we are all exposed to the yawning abyss, the primal night which originates all and to which we all return.[22]

In such terms, the action of **Robinson Crusoe** concerns not only the hero's search for a home, but his failure to find one. Clearly, Crusoe's "primary impulse" once he arrives on his island is "for protection and security." And so successful a homemaker does he prove to be that Pat Rogers has actually designated him *homo domesticus.* He points out that Crusoe calls his first night's resting place "my Apartment in the Tree," and he goes on to characterize his subsequent activities as "making a nest." Crusoe bakes bread; he "spends a fair portion of his time cooking and sewing"; he makes butter and cheese; he is the complete household manager—and "a good exemplar of that cherished Renaissance-to-Augustan ideal, the Happy Man."[23]

Yet as Rogers has also noted (though he does not pursue the implications of the fact), Crusoe's two homes turn out to be "easily employed as gaols" in which to incarcerate the mutineers.[24] They are, in other words, as effective as places of confinement for recalcitrant men as they are as fortifications against "wild beasts and men." But the recalcitrant aspect of Crusoe himself soon defies imprisonment and urges him forth to a free-ranging exploration of the island that lies beyond his self-constructed walls. However contented the conservative aspect of his nature may be with the domestic and civilized, the contradictory principle within him—the explorer and aspirer—chafes at the restriction and leads him more than once to refer to his being kept indoors as "this Confinement."

The frequent appearance of circle imagery in association with Crusoe's various efforts at domesticating his environment and thereby protecting himself is instructive. He is constantly preoccupied during his early years on the island either with surrounding (controlling) something or with being surrounded by (protected within) something. After getting two cargoes safely conveyed from ship to shore, for example, he tells of piling "all the empty Chests and Casks up in a Circle round the Tent, to fortify it from any sudden Attempt either from Man or Beast" (p. 59); and when, during the earthquake, the overhanging cave proves too threatening, he thinks of "building me some little Hut in an open Place which I might surround with a Wall as I had done here, and so make my self secure from wild Beasts or Men"—"I would go to work with all Speed to build me a Wall with Piles and Cables, & *c.* in a Circle as before . . ." (p. 82). The country bower that he does eventually devise lies within a "Circle or double Hedge" (p. 104). And he speaks later of the kid "which I had penn'd in within my little Circle" (p. 112).

Crusoe mentions repeatedly bringing projects "to Perfection": he has "brought to Perfection" the cave behind his tent (p. 69); he spends over three months *"working, finishing, and perfecting"* his wall (*"being a half Circle from one Place in the Rock to another Place about eight Yards from it, the Door of the Cave being in the Center behind it"* [p. 76]); he achieves "an unexpected Perfection in [his] Earthen Ware," having devised a wheel with which he can make things "round and shapable" (p. 144).

Yet nothing is, apparently, quite perfect. Crusoe must extend half circles into whole circles; he must surround one half circle of trees with another; and he must, above all, make small circles into bigger circles. So persevering is he in "widening and deepening" his cave that he eventually makes it "spacious enough to accommodate me as a Warehouse or Magazin, a Kitchen, a Dining-room, and a Cellar" (p. 74).

What happens on at least three occasions, however, is that in enlarging or attempting to enlarge the area of his control, he exposes himself to those very fears and outside threats against which he has designed his walls. In speaking of one such occasion, he says, "I began now to think my Cave or Vault finished, when on a Sudden (it seems I had made it too large) a great Quantity of Earth fell down from the Top and one Side, so much, that in short it frighted me . . ." (p. 74). Another time, after he has "work'd daily two or three Hours at enlarging my Cave," he succeeds in fashioning what amounts to a back door to his dwelling. But if his sense of confinement is thus lessened, so also is his peace of mind. "I was not perfectly easy at lying so open," he confesses, "for as I had manag'd my self before, I was in a perfect Enclosure, whereas now I thought I lay expos'd . . ." (p. 103). Most terrifying of all, though, in those early years, is his attempt "to make a Tour round the Island"—"to view the Circumference of my little Kingdom" (p. 137)—an attempt that brings him "a frightful Distance" from the shore and almost proves his undoing.

The world that Crusoe inhabits seems, invariably, either too big or not big enough. Effectually, the pattern of his adventures is one of a circularity involving alternating situations of expansion and contraction, exposure and protection. When, for example, after several months on the island, he makes his first "Journey . . . from Home"—prompted by a desire "to see the whole Island"—he is at first "exceedingly diverted" (pp. 108, 109). But after having lost himself in a valley and having "wandered about very uncomfortably," he finds himself "very impatient to be at Home," and his relief when he is at last back in his cave is plainly heartfelt:

> I cannot express what a Satisfaction it was to me to come into my old Hutch, and lye down in my Hamock-Bed: This little wandring journey, without settled Place of Abode, had been so unpleasant to me, that my own House, as I call'd it to my self, was a perfect Settlement to me, compar'd to that; and it rendred every Thing about me so comfortable, that I resolv'd I would never go a great Way from it again while it should be my Lot to stay on the Island. (P. 117)

Whenever Crusoe ventures far from any home, he encounters an alien world in which he feels at best lost and at worst utterly terrified. Crusoe, we may recall, refers to his years on the island as a "Life of Misery" and at one time names the place itself the "Island of Despaire." Still more to the point, however, the sea on which he suffers shipwreck functions archetypally as both tomb and womb. He emphasizes repeatedly his own helplessness to deliver himself from its grasp: "tho' I swam very well, yet I could not deliver my self from the Waves"; "the Sea, having hurried me along as

before, landed me, or rather dash'd me, against a Piece of Rock, and that with such Force, it left me senseless, and indeed helpless, as to my own Deliverance." But at last the sea, having "buried" Crusoe "20 or 30 Foot deep in its own Body," deposits him on the shore and he is "sav'd . . . out of the very Grave." Yet "sav'd" though he may be, it is, as he says, "a dreadful Deliverance": "I was wet, had no Clothes to shift me, nor any thing either to eat or drink to comfort me, neither did I see any Prospect before me but that of perishing with Hunger, or being devour'd by wild Beasts . . ." (pp. 44-46).

There is no question that Crusoe's effort to tame the wild, to civilize the savage succeeds up to a point.[25] He does seem to become increasingly effective at imposing his will on the world he inhabits. He speaks of having become, in his "twenty third Year of Residence in this Island . . . naturalized to the Place, and to the Manner of Living" (p. 180). In actuality, however, it would be more accurate to say that he has "de-naturalized" his world in order to adapt it to himself and to make it serve him.

He never really succeeds in conquering his own terror, since he can never hide from himself the awareness that outside of himself lies a hostile universe.[26] By his twenty-third year he *seems* to be in control, to have a sense that he is someone to be reckoned with. He has taught three parrots to say "Robin Crusoe," has tamed several sea fowls and "cut their Wings," and keeps three household kids about him (p. 181). But while he has domesticated some of these wild creatures, some of the already domesticated animals who have come with him to the island—namely the cats—multiply so alarmingly that he is "oblig'd to shoot several of them at first, to keep them from devouring me, and all I had," and others have run "wild into the Woods" (p. 180). Moreover, he has discovered, in the process of fencing in his goats, that he "must keep the tame from the wild, or else they would always run wild when they grew up . . ." (p. 146). Crusoe cannot avoid knowing that in the natural world outside himself even the tamed can revert to wildness and become a danger. The awareness rather ironically calls into question his earlier characterization of himself as "Prince and Lord of the whole Island." It proves not to be altogether true that "I had the Lives of all my Subjects at my absolute Command. I could hang, draw, give Liberty, and take it away, and no Rebels among all my Subjects" (p. 148).

Furthermore, although his dog may have proved for sixteen years "a very pleasant and loving Companion" (p. 180), most of the animals he encounters on his adventures are part and parcel of the threatening outside environment in which solitary man walks fearfully and in which he must destroy or be destroyed. Whether Crusoe is confronted with "a dreadful Monster . . . a terrible great Lyon" (p. 27) on the Canaries shore or with "those ravenous Creatures" who, in a pursuit of "great Fury," at last "plung'd themselves into the Sea" (p. 30) near Cape Verde, his experiences never reassure him that the world in which he lives has been made for him. Strive though he may to build defenses, the threat remains. Indeed, in the last major adventure of the novel, as he pursues a seemingly safe overland route home, he faces once again some "ravenous Creatures"—this time a whole pack of them, from whom, after a night of stark terror, he barely escapes with his life. These creatures, he says, "came on like Devils." Still, wild animals play a relatively minor role in the hostile universe into which Crusoe ventures. Far more important to him—and far harder for him to defend himself against—are wind and weather. As he contrives his escape from the *Sallee Rover,* he notes: "The wind blew from the N.NE., which was contrary to my Desire" (p. 22). And the fact is that the winds of the world almost always blow for Crusoe "contrary to [his] Desire." The "dreadful Storm" that strands him on his island is only one of many that he experiences in the course of the novel, and he is never so aware of his own vulnerability as at such times. The rage and fury that he associates with the wild animals of shore and mountain are as nothing compared to the "raging Wave, Mountain-like" that, in the midst of the novel's major storm, "took us with such a Fury, that it overset the Boat at once" (p. 44).

For Crusoe natural forces are frequently "as furious as an Enemy" (p. 44). Even though he has, on the island, constructed his defenses so that "nothing could come at me from without, unless it could first mount my Wall" (p. 79), reasons for terror remain: an alien nature intrudes in the form of an earthquake that cracks the posts in the cave "in a frightful Manner." Crusoe does feel more "safe from Danger" within his cave than outside it, but he continues to pile fortification on fortification.[27] Shelter is always, for him, an overridingly important preoccupation, as it continues to be long after he has left the island. When beset by the wolf pack, he writes, "having nothing to shelter us, or retreat to, I gave myself over for lost . . ." (p. 302).

"Man," Heidegger has written, "shrinks back from losing himself in . . . the nightmarish, demonic frenzy in which nature has unleashed billions of individual organismic appetites of all kinds—not to mention earthquakes, meteors, and hurricanes, which seem to have their own hellish appetites. Each thing, in order to deliciously expand, is forever gobbling up others. Appetites may be innocent because they are naturally given, but any organism caught in the myriad cross-purposes of this planet is a potential victim of this very innocence—and it shrinks away from life lest it lose its own."[28]

Crusoe's dilemma—the human dilemma—is that in shutting himself in to preserve life, he must at the same time shut life out. His responses, while he is on the island, to the sun and the rain are cases in point. Having learned that direct exposure to the rain produces fevers, he finds that he must largely confine himself within his cave during the rainy season. And the sun too is at times an antagonist from which he must retreat: "it is to be considered that the middle of the Day when the Sun was in the Zenith, the Violence of the Heat was too great to stir out . . ." (p. 114).

Corresponding to the "complete Shade" provided by the trees surrounding his country bower ("sufficient to lodge under all the dry Season") are the hat and umbrella (again a piling-up of fortifications) with which Crusoe supplies himself as protection from sun and rain. In enumerating his articles of clothing, Crusoe refers to his umbrella as "the most necessary Thing I had about me, next to my Gun" (p. 150).

That he never ventures abroad without both umbrella and gun strongly indicates that fear remains for him a constant companion all the while he remains on the island. At the time he discovers that deep inner cave in which he stores his weapons, he says, "I fancy'd my self now like one of the ancient Giants, which are said to live in Caves, and Holes, in the Rocks, where none could come at them; for I perswaded my self, while I was here, if five hundred Savages were to hunt me, they could never find me out; or if they did, they would not venture to attack me here." And two paragraphs later he comments about life on the island: "could I have but enjoy'd the Certainty that no Savages would come to the Place to disturb me, I could have been content to have capitulated for spending the rest of my Time there . . ." (p. 180). Hobbes could be describing Crusoe when he writes:

> if one plant, sow, build, or possesse a convenient Seat, others may probably be expected to come prepared with forces united, to dispossesse, and deprive him, not only of the fruit of his labour, but also of his life, or liberty. And the Invader again is in the like danger of another.

> And from this diffidence of one another, there is no way for any man to secure himself, so reasonable, as Anticipation; that is, by force, or wiles, to master the persons of all men he can, so long, till he see no other power great enough to endanger him.

And later in *Leviathan* Hobbes again anticipates Crusoe's behavior in describing a London citizen: "when taking a journey, he arms himself, and seeks to go well accompanied; when going to sleep, he locks his doors; when even in his house he locks his chests; . . . what opinion he has of his fellow-subjects, when he rides armed; of his fellow citizens when he locks his doors; and of his children, and servants, when he locks his chests."[29]

It is not, of course, human beings of flesh and blood who are usually the problem for Crusoe; rather, it is those imaginary figures his own apprehensions conjure up. Humans are, his mind tells him, all either savages or pirates or mutineers. They are attackers who kill and eat one another, prey on one another, or seize power from one another. Crusoe never registers a terror so abject as that he shows upon discovering "the Print of a Man's naked Foot on the Shore" (p. 153). He uses words like *Thunder-struck, perfectly confus'd and out of my self, terrify'd to the last Degree.* He speaks of his *affrighted Imagination,* of *wild Ideas,* of *terror of Mind* (pp. 153, 154). However successful Crusoe may be at defending himself against physical threats, he cannot escape his own mind. Immediately before relating his discovery of the footprint, he has spent two pages describing his plantations, and much of the detail has to do with order and security—keeping his land "duly cultivated and sow'd," keeping his surrounding hedges "in Repair," and so forth (pp. 152, 153). Yet not only is this description followed by the lengthy recording of his apprehensions about the footprint, but it is preceded by his recalling that fear he felt when he found his canoe being carried away from the island: "I had such a Terror upon my Spirits at the Remembrance of the Danger I had been in, that I could not think of it again with any Patience . . ." (p. 151). No matter how seemingly secure he is, he cannot shut out of his mind either the remembrance of dangers past or the anticipation of dangers to come.

To Crusoe's way of thinking, primitive man is as much a part of "wild" nature as any animal. At one point he remarks: "to have fallen into the Hands of any of the Savages had been as bad as to have fallen into the Hands of Lyons and Tygers" (p. 25). Even of Friday, whom he calls a "faithful, loving, sincere Servant," he feels at times a profound mistrust. He arranges matters in his hutch "so that *Friday* could no way come at me in the inside of my innermost Wall, without making so much Noise in getting over, that it must needs waken me . . ." (p. 208). In a way, what he does with Friday is to tame him, as Friday himself suggests he should do for other savages: *"you teach wild Mans be good sober tame Mans . . ."* (p. 226). Yet he has spoken of being "not so easy about my new Man *Friday* as I was before," and although he at once admits to having "wronged the poor honest Creature," he has seriously imagined the possibility of Friday's betraying him and joining with the other members of his nation to "make a Feast upon me" (p. 224).

In fact, Crusoe proves himself in the two later volumes of his life story to be haunted by thoughts of cannibalism, and so does Defoe in his other writings. The subject comes up repeatedly not only in the *Farther Adventures* and the *Serious Reflections,* but in the *Review* and *Applebee's Journal* as well. And it is not, according to Defoe, only savages who experience can-

nibalistic impulses but civilized men, when the threat of starvation makes them desperate enough. Of the incident involving a mother and her son and their maid, whom Crusoe meets early in his *Farther Adventures* on that "unhappy Ship" where all aboard have been brought to "the last Extremity of Hunger," the maid relates: "had my Mistress been dead, as much as I lov'd her, I am certain, I should have eaten a Piece of her Flesh with as much Relish, and as unconcern'd, as ever I did the Flesh of any Creature appointed for Food; and once or twice I was going to bite my own Arm"; and she goes on to tell of drinking her own blood. And when Defoe is telling of the "terrible Famine . . . in Thoulon," he writes: "'Tis said that [the people] . . . have eaten the most loathsome and nauteous Things, such as Dogs, Cats, Rats, Mice, Leather, Starch, Soap, and, in a Word, that they are ready to prey even upon one another."[30]

Crusoe's concluding pages of his *Surprizing Adventures* are tantamount to a concession that neither human fears nor those forces in the universe that inspire such fears by threatening the survival of the self are ever quelled. In speaking of the shipwrecked Spaniards, he says, "I fear'd mostly their Treachery and ill-Usage of me, if I put my Life in their Hands" (p. 244). Moreover, though he has been victorious in his pitched battle with the cannibals, he voices apprehensions about a return engagement wherein he will have to cope with numbers that may prove overwhelming. And Crusoe's battles, as it turns out, are *not* over once he has defeated the savages. He must then face the mutineers, who, like his cats, are once-domesticated creatures now again given over to violence.

What is more, while Crusoe may have brought his tropical island largely under his control, he remains fearful of the sea, and in trying to avoid its perils (which, as he explains, prove again all too real), he finds himself—as he once more makes his way toward the supposed securities of home—facing the rigors of the Pyrenees, whose wintry barrenness has crazed the starving wolves. Crusoe's party have a guide to aid them in circumventing the worst of the snowy mountain terrain, but the guide's knowledge does not enable them to avoid the wolves, and Crusoe is again thrown back on his own resources, called upon again to devise a "stratagem" born of desperation in order to achieve mastery.

Crusoe does at last get home to England, but it is a "home" that represents only a stopping-off and stepping-off place. Remembering what he has told us about his early propensities—"though I had several times loud Calls from my Reason and my more composed Judgment to go Home, yet I had no Power to do it"—we can now see that the words constitute a kind of summary of Defoe's view of the human predicament. It is beyond the power of man truly to "go home." There is no hiding place, and he is fated to remain a restless seeker.

As might be expected, moreover, the circle pattern continues into the second volume of Crusoe's adventures. He speaks several times in the opening pages of the "strong Inclination" he felt "to go Abroad again," and then well along in this continuation of his story he admits, "When I was at Home, I was restless to go abroad; and now I was abroad, I was restless to be at Home." Unlike that Utopian figure the Muscovite prince, who "has got a Victory over his own exorbitant Desires, and has the absolute Dominion over himself, whose Reason entirely governs his Will," Crusoe is unable to remain a "happy Prisoner."[31] He continues to be, as it were, in thrall to the devil, who (as he has taught Friday long before) has "a secret access to our Passions, and to our Affections, to adapt his Snares so to our Inclinations, as to cause us even to be our own Tempters, and to run upon our Destruction by our own Choice" (p. 217).

In the *Farther Adventures* chaos comes again at every level. Crusoe tells, for example, of "a little Quarrel on board our Ship, which I was afraid once would have turned to a second Mutiny"; and on his voyage around the world he again fears mutiny. And earlier, in revisiting the island he discovers an alarming state of disorder to have existed there. Not only does he hear that there has been a new invasion of savages ("now they had, as I may say, a hundred Wolves upon the Island, which would devour every Thing they could come at, yet could very hardly be come at themselves"), but he learns that dissensions among the five Englishmen have led to repeated destruction of settled and ordered habitations.[32]

The destructive passions of men are everywhere in evidence. Perhaps it is no accident that the natural energy most often referred to is fire. Men are burned; a ship is burned; a house is burned; a whole settlement is burned. Again and again Crusoe encounters a world at war; and the "Peace" to whose existence he composes verses and of which he writes wistfully at the end of his *Farther Adventures* remains a future prospect.[33] The storms and tempests of his life have continued to rage within as well as without; the savagery within and without has not been left behind.[34]

Crusoe may have exchanged his goatskins for more civilized garments, but the change is more apparent than real.[35] His physical wanderings do finally end, but in the *Serious Reflections* his mind continues its restless seeking to impose some meaningful order upon the flux of things. And he is still looking over his shoulder. "It is a strange length that some people run in this madness of life," he observes in one passage; and a page later we find him calling himself "your fugitive friend, 'Robinson Crusoe.'"[36]

Even his confidence in an ordering Providence seems here at best a shaky one. "Providence," he affirms, "decrees that events shall attend upon causes in a direct chain, and by an evident necessity, and has doubtless left many powers of good and evil seemingly to ourselves, and as it were, in our hands, as the natural product of such causes and consequences, which we are not to limit and cannot expressly determine about, but which we are accountable for the good or evil application of; otherwise we were in vain exhorted and commanded to do any good thing, or to avoid any wicked one."[37] That is to say, all this *must* be so if the world is to make any sense; yet Crusoe's "seemingly" and "as it were" seriously undercut his "doubtless."

Crusoe-Defoe no more finds it possible to round off his *Surprizing Adventures* satisfactorily than Crusoe as protagonist finds it possible to end his travels and his speculations. Imagination breaks free from the captivity of reason to the extent that the novel concludes in syntactical confusion and leaves us with a sense of incompleteness:

> But all these things, with an Account how 300 Caribbees came and invaded them, and ruin'd their Plantations, and how they fought with that whole Number twice, and were at first defeated, and three of them kill'd; but at last a Storm destroying their Enemies Cannoes, they famish'd or destroy'd almost all the rest, and renew'd and recover'd the Possession of their Plantation, and still liv'd upon the Island.

> All these things, with some very surprizing Incidents in some new Adventures of my own, for ten Years more, I may perhaps give a further Account of hereafter.

We put the book down feeling some bafflement as to the precise nature of the account Crusoe has given of what he tellingly calls his "unaccountable Life" (p. 181). Just what does Crusoe's experience add up to? Is it truly a spiritual autobiography? Or is the form of the spiritual autobiography merely a kind of wishful thinking—a construction within which Crusoe attempts to hide in order to avoid too much exposure?

Repeatedly, in the course of his narrative, Crusoe suggests that he is unable to capture in words the lived reality. "I cannot explain by any possible Energy of Words," he says at one point, "what a strange longing or hankering of Desires I felt in my Soul . . ." (p. 187). Moreover, he gives us three different accounts of his experience immediately following the shipwreck, each of which differs from the others in the details included and some of which actually contradict one another in certain particulars. Which is the true account? Can words capture reality at all, or do they *create* a reality, impose a meaning that does not, in the nature of things, exist?

And who is Robinson Crusoe? Is he all-conquering voyager or believing Christian? Is his name really Crusoe or is that simply what he is "called"?[38] Finally, we cannot as readers avoid some "Confusion of Thoughts"; and we may well end by crying, as Crusoe has taught his parrot to cry, *"Poor Robin Crusoe, Where are you? Where have you been? How come you here?"* (p. 143). We wait in vain for an answer.

Notes

. . .[20] E. A. James points to a number of instances of Defoe's dramatizing his hero's "fluctuating moods and mental states," among which is his referring to himself alternately as a "helpless Prisoner" and "an absolute Monarch." "We are," says James, "given insight into the mentality of a character who is psychologically committed to making the best of things, and often indeed to making things better than they are, but a character who is not always capable of doing so." And among such instances of fluctuation James cites Crusoe's referring to his island dwelling as, on the one hand, "a Room or Cave" and "a Retreat" or "Cell," and on the other, a "Fortress" or "Fortification" or "Castle." *Defoe's Many Voices,* pp. 169-73.

[21] Curt Hartog makes much this same point in his reading of *Robinson Crusoe* as "Defoe's best fictional example of the conflict between individual assertion of drives and the opposed demands of authority. . . . At the beginning of the novel, Crusoe's father describes the middle state in terms that demand not only submission . . . but virtually total passivity. . . . The passivity . . . is a kind of death. . . . to obey his father is to die metaphorically . . . But to disobey is to risk literal death." Aggression, Femininity, and Irony in *Moll Flanders,"* p. 123. On a similar note, Leo Braudy observes: "Part of Defoe's insight about the character in search of security about his identity is his discovery of the similar anxieties of confinement and freedom." "Daniel Defoe and the Anxieties of Autobiography," *Genre* 6 (1973): 82.

[22] J. Glenn Gray, "The Problem of Death in Modern Philosophy," *The Modern Vision of Death,* ed. N. A. Scott (Richmond, VA: John Knox Press, 1968), p. 52.

[23] Rogers, "Crusoe's Home," pp. 380, 384, 386, 390.

[24] Ibid., p. 390.

[25] This is a point on which a number of recent critics have dwelt. J. Paul Hunter, for example, writes of the episode involving the wolves in the Pyrenees: "Crusoe's final victory over bestiality culminates a pattern which had begun early in his life with encounters against a lion, a leopard, and a nameless beast on the coast of Africa." And he adds in a footnote: "The episode of the wolves also climaxes the motif of sav-

agery which runs through the novel." *The Reluctant Pilgrim,* p. 198. John Richetti maintains that "the taming of the goats repeats Crusoe's own story; it is a reenactment of the conversion of his own unruly nature . . . by God, who catches Crusoe on the island and tames him the same way that Crusoe catches goats in a pit and tames them. Crusoe's entire career on the island as a bringer of order is, by extension, a taming of his externalized self." *Defoe's Narratives,* p. 50.

[26] As Maximillian E. Novak says of Crusoe: "he is always afraid, always cautious, and always desirous of abandoning his isolated condition. . . . " And Novak continues, "Fear, Defoe was clearly saying, is the dominant passion of a man in Crusoe's condition. His isolation identifies him with the state of nature which precedes society, a condition in which man could live alone, not because he was godlike, but because he was bestial. . . . Pufendorf described such an existence as being worse than that of a beast. Nothing can be considered secure, and within the soul the passions rule instead of reason. Lacking the aid of his fellow man and forced to meet every enemy alone, the isolated natural man passes his life in continual expectation of destruction." Novak does not, however, seem to me to be justified in going on to maintain that "Crusoe is rescued from this condition by his tools, the symbols of learning, the arts, society, and that civilization which is the reverse of man's natural state." "Robinson Crusoe's Fear and the Search for Natural Man," *Modern Philogy* 58 (1961): 238, 240, 244.

[27] As Zimmerman says, "Although concealment is essential to Crusoe's defense, fortifications never figure in it. Crusoe fortifies to restore his psychic equilibrium; whenever he has brought his defenses to seeming perfection, he is again disturbed." *Defoe and the Novel,* p. 26.

[28] Quoted in Ernest Becker, *The Denial of Death* (New York: The Free Press, 1973), pp. 53-54.

[29] *Leviathan,* pp. 63, 64, 100.

[30] *Father Adventures,* 2:67; *Applebee's Original Weekly Journal,* Saturday, May 20, 1721. *Selected Poetry and Prose of Daniel Defoe,* ed. Michael F. Shugrue (New York: Holt, Rinehart, and Winston, 1968), p. 204.

[31] *Farther Adventures,* 2:112; 3:110, 202, 208.

[32] Ibid., 2:215.

[33] *Serious Reflections,* p. 70:

> Tell us, ye men of notion, tell us why
> You seek for bliss and wild prosperity
> In storms and tempests, feuds and war—

　　Is happiness to be expected there?
　　　Tell us what sort of happiness
　　　Can men in want of peace possess?

・　・　・　・　・

　　Let heav'n, that unknown happiness,
　　Be what it will, 'tis best described by peace.
　　No storms without, or storms within;
　　No fear, no danger there, because no sin:
　　'Tis bright essential happiness,
　　Because He dwells within whose name is
　　　Peace.

[34] David Blewett makes the connection between outer and inner storms explicit: "The storm scenes form part of an accumulating pattern of natural disasters and also dramatize Crusoe's mental state. There is an accompanying 'storm' in Crusoe's mind, a continual struggle between reason and passion, in which his good intentions are repeatedly overpowered by an irrational wilfulness." *Defoe's Art of Fiction: "Robinson Crusoe," "Moll Flanders," "Colonel Jack" and "Roxana"* (Toronto, Buffalo, London: University of Toronto Press, 1979), p. 32. And H. G. Hahn suggests the identification of Crusoe and Friday: "Through Crusoe Friday becomes the modern man, a seething savage beneath a veneer of civilization. He is both cannibal and Christian, a Caliban-Ariel on another Atlantic island. And Crusoe shapes in him what Crusoe really is." "An Approach to Character Development in Defoe's Narrative Prose," *Philological Quarterly* 51 (1972): 856.

[35] William Bysshe Stein also emphasizes Crusoe's island appearance as a reflection of his animality. He calls "Crusoe's beard, the perfect accessory to the animalistic costume" and goes on to point out that "his reference to its Turkish model generates associations with the fabled savagery of these Asiatics." "Robinson Crusoe: The Trickster Tricked," *The Centennial Review* 9 (1965): 283.

[36] *Serious Reflections*, pp. 100-101.

[37] Ibid., p. 182.

[38] Homer O. Brown has explored this whole question of the identity of Defoe's main characters (and of Robinson Crusoe in particular) in his article "The Displaced Self in the Novels of Daniel Defoe," *Journal of English Literary History* 38 (1971): 562-90.

Leopold Damrosch, Jr. (essay date 1985)

SOURCE: "Myth and Fiction in *Robinson Crusoe*," in *God's Plots & Man's Stories: Studies in the Fictional Imagination from Milton to Fielding*, The University of Chicago Press, 1985, pp. 187-212.

[*In the following excerpt, Damrosch considers* Robinson Crusoe*'s "desacralizing" of the world, which in the novel becomes a workplace of men and an equivocal Providence.*]

Mimesis, Allegory, and the Autonomous Self

In 1719, at the age of fifty-nine, the businessman, pamphleteer, and sometime secret agent Daniel Defoe unexpectedly wrote the first English novel. The affinities of *Robinson Crusoe* with the Puritan tradition are unmistakable: it draws on the genres of spiritual autobiography and allegory, and Crusoe's religious conversion is presented as the central event. But this primal novel, in the end, stands as a remarkable instance of a work that gets away from its author, and gives expression to attitudes that seem to lie far from his conscious intention. Defoe sets out to dramatize the conversion of the Puritan self, and he ends by celebrating a solitude that exalts autonomy instead of submission. He undertakes to show the dividedness of a sinner, and ends by projecting a hero so massively self-enclosed that almost nothing of his inner life is revealed. He proposes a naturalistic account of real life in a real world, and ends by creating an immortal triumph of wish-fulfillment. To some extent, of course, Defoe must have been aware of these ambiguities, which are summed up when Crusoe calls the island "my reign, or my captivity, which you please."[1] But it is unlikely that he saw how deep the gulf was that divided the two poles of his story, the Augustinian theme of alienation and the romance theme of gratification. . . .

In a Puritan view the normal course of nature is simply the sum total of an ongoing chain of special providences, for as a modern expositor of Calvin puts it, "Bread is not the natural product of the earth. In order that the earth may provide the wheat from which it is made, God must intervene, ceaselessly and ever anew, in the 'order of nature,' must send the rain and dew, must cause the sun to rise every morning."[6] In the eighteenth century, however, there was an increasing tendency to define providence as the general order of things rather than as a series of specific interventions. Wesley bitterly remarked that "The doctrine of a particular providence is absolutely out of fashion in England—and any but a particular providence is no providence at all."[7] One purpose of *Robinson Crusoe* is to vindicate God's omnipotence by showing the folly of making such a distinction. And Crusoe's isolation (like Ben Gunn's) encourages him to think the matter through. When Moll Flanders, in Defoe's next major novel, is finally arrested and thrown into Newgate, she suddenly perceives her clever career as the condign punishment of "an inevitable and unseen fate." But she admits that she is a poor moralist and unable to retain the lesson for long: "I had no sense of my condition, no thought of heaven or hell at least, that went any farther than a bare flying touch, like the stitch or pain that gives a hint and goes off."[8] Moll sees only at moments of crisis what Crusoe learns to see consistently.

In keeping with this message the narrative contains many scriptural allusions, which are often left tacit for the reader to detect and ponder. The sprouting wheat, for instance, recalls a central doctrine of the Gospels: "Verily, verily I say unto you, Except a corn of wheat fall into the ground and die, it abideth alone; but if it die, it bringeth forth much fruit. He that loveth his life shall lose it, and he that hateth his life in this world shall keep it unto life eternal" (John 12:24-25). Crusoe's life recapitulates that of everyman, a fictional equivalent of what Samuel Clarke recommended in the study of history: "By setting before us what hath been, it premonisheth us of what will be again; sith the self-same fable is acted over again in the world, the persons only are changed that act it."[9] Like other Puritans Crusoe has to grope toward the meaning of the types embodied in his own biography. Defoe often likened himself to persecuted figures in the Bible, but wrote to his political master Harley that his life "has been and yet remains a mystery of providence unexpounded."[10] Translating his experience into the quasi-allegory of *Crusoe* permits him to define typological connections more confidently, from the coincidence of calendar dates to the overarching theme of deliverance (typified in individuals like Jonah, and in the children of Israel released from Egypt).[11] Thus the temporal world, however circumstantially described, can be seen in the Puritan manner as gathered up into eternity. Crusoe's fever is not only a direct warning from God but also, as Alkon shows, a rupture in his careful recording of chronology by which he is "wrenched outside time," an intimation that the various incidents in the story must be subsumed in a single structure.[12] As in other Puritan narratives, separate moments are valued for their significance in revealing God's will, and become elements in an emblematic pattern rather than constituents of a causal sequence.

Nearly all of the essential issues cluster around the crucial theme of solitude. Defoe clearly gives it a positive valuation, and suggests more than once that Crusoe could have lived happily by himself forever if no other human beings had intruded. "I was now in my twenty-third year of residence in this island, and was so naturalized to the place and to the manner of living, that could I have but enjoyed the certainty that no savages would come to the place to disturb me, I could have been content to have capitulated for spending the rest of my time there, even to the last moment, till I had laid me down and died like the old goat in the cave" (p. 180). However obliquely Defoe's *Serious Reflections of Robinson Crusoe* (published in the following year) relates to the novel, it must be significant that it begins with an essay "Of Solitude" which moves at once to the claim that we are solitary even in the midst of society:

Everything revolves in our minds by innumerable circular motions, all centering in ourselves. . . . All reflection is carried home, and our dear self is, in one respect, the end of living. Hence man may be properly said to be alone in the midst of the crowds and hurry of men and business. . . . Our meditations are all solitude in perfection; our passions are all exercised in retirement; we love, we hate, we covet, we enjoy, all in privacy and solitude. All that we communicate of those things to any other is but for their assistance in the pursuit of our desires; the end is at home; the enjoyment, the contemplation, is all solitude and retirement; it is for ourselves we enjoy, and for ourselves we suffer.[13]

Critics have unfairly quoted this disturbing and memorable passage as symptomatic of a peculiar egotism in Defoe. In fact it reflects the logical consequence of Puritan inwardness, also susceptible of course to the charge of egotism—the descent into the interior self that impels Bunyan's Christian to reject his family in order to win eternal life. And it is compatible, as Defoe goes on to make clear, with the traditional view that "Man is a creature so formed for society, that it may not only be said that it is not good for him to be alone, but 'tis really impossible he should be alone" (pp. 11-12). The good man or woman ought to associate with others but seek in meditation that solitude which can be attained anywhere, symbolized in *Robinson Crusoe* by "the life of a man in an island" (p. 2).

In effect Defoe literalizes the metaphor that Descartes (for example) uses: "Among the crowds of a large and active people . . . I have been able to live as solitary and retired as in the remotest desert."[14] But to literalize the metaphor creates profound complications, for it is one thing to live *as if* on a desert island and another to do it in earnest. Jonathan Edwards writes that in his meditations on the Song of Songs, "an inward sweetness . . . would carry me away in my contemplations, . . . and sometimes a kind of vision, or fixed ideas and imaginations, of being alone in the mountains, or some solitary wilderness, far from all mankind, sweetly conversing with Christ, and wrapt and swallowed up in God."[15] This rapture of self-abnegation is very far from Crusoe's experience. The difference is partly explained by the bluff common sense of Crusoe, not to mention of Defoe: Dickens comments, "I have no doubt he was a precious dry disagreeable article himself."[16] But beyond that it is due to the way in which Defoe takes a *topos* of allegory and literalizes it in mimetic narrative. Even though he may believe that the result is still allegorical, he has transformed—to borrow a useful pair of terms from German—*Jenseitigkeit* into *Diesseitigkeit,* collapsing the "other side" of religion into the "this side" of familiar experience. In *The Pilgrim's Progress* everyday images serve as visualizable emblems of an interior experience that belongs to another world. In *Robinson Crusoe* there is no other world.

Another way of saying this is that *Crusoe* reflects the progressive desacralizing of the world that was implicit in Protestantism, and that ended (in Weber's phrase) by disenchanting it altogether. Defoe's God may work through nature, but he does so by "natural" cause and effect (the seeds that sprout), and nature itself is not viewed as sacramental. Rather it is the workplace where man is expected to labor until it is time to go to a heaven too remote and hypothetical to ask questions about. "I come from the City of Destruction," Bunyan's Christian says, "but am going to Mount Sion."[17] In *Crusoe,* as is confirmed by the feeble sequel *The Farther Adventures of Robinson Crusoe* there is no goal at all, at least not in this world. But the world of *The Pilgrim's Progress* was *not* this world: after conversion the believer knew himself to be a stranger in a strange land. Defoe keeps the shape of the allegorical scheme but radically revalues its content.

Defoe is no metaphysician, and his dislocation of the religious schema may seem naive, but in practice if not in theory it subtly images the ambiguity of man's relation to his world, at once a "natural" home and a resistant object to be manipulated. Milton's Adam and Eve fall from the world in which they had been at home, and Bunyan's characters march through the fallen world like soldiers passing through enemy territory. Defoe has it both ways, defining man over against nature and at the same time inventing a fantasy of perfect union with it. As technologist and (halting) thinker Crusoe finds himself in opposition to nature, as when he builds a "periagua" so grotesquely huge that he is unable to drag it to the water, or when he does make a successful canoe but is nearly swept out to sea by unexpected currents. And his concepts function to define his human status in contrast with nature, in keeping with the moral tradition that saw man in a "state of nature" as living in continual fear of death.[18] But as a concord fiction *Robinson Crusoe* still more strongly suggests that man can indeed return to union with nature, so long as other men are not present to disturb him. In important respects the island is an Eden.

This equivocation between punitive doctrine and liberating romance has remarkable consequences in Defoe's treatment of psychology. In effect he carries to its logical conclusion the externalizing of unwanted impulses which we have seen in Bunyan and other Puritan writers. With God generalized into an abstract Providence, Crusoe's universe is peopled by inferior beings, angelic spirits who guide him with mysterious hints and diabolical spirits who seek his ruin. Of these the latter are the more interesting, and Crusoe is scandalized to find that Friday is unaware of any Satan, merely saying "O" to a pleasant but ineffectual deity called Benamuckee who seems not to know how to punish men. Defoe needs the Devil—and this must be his never-articulated answer to Friday's trenchant question, "Why God no kill the Devil?" (p. 218)—because man's unacknowledged impulses have to be explained. Like the older Puritans Defoe externalizes such impulses by calling them tricks of Satan, but he altogether lacks the subtle dialectic by which the Puritans acknowledged man's continued complicity with the hated enslaver. . . .

Defoe makes it absolutely explicit that Crusoe's Eden is an escape from guilt. "I was removed from all the wickedness of the world here. I had neither the *lust of the flesh, the lust of the eye, or the pride of life*" (p. 128; the reference is to a favorite Puritan text, John 2:16). To be alone with God is to be alone with oneself and to find it good:

> Thus I lived mighty comfortably, my mind being entirely composed by resigning to the will of God, and throwing myself wholly upon the disposal of his Providence. This made my life better than sociable, for when I began to regret the want of conversation, I would ask my self whether thus conversing mutually with my own thoughts, and, as I hope I may say, with even God himself by ejaculations, was not better than the utmost enjoyment of human society in the world. (pp. 135-36)

Crusoe has nothing to hide. Whereas Bunyan trembled in the knowledge that God sees "the most secret thoughts of the heart,"[30] Crusoe often applies the word "secret" to emotions of self-satisfaction: "I descended a little on the side of that delicious vale, surveying it with a secret kind of pleasure" (p. 100). This is not the Puritan use of the term, but an ethical and aesthetic ideal that Defoe may have picked up from Addison: "A man of a polite imagination . . . meets with a secret refreshment in a description, and often feels a greater satisfaction in the prospect of fields and meadows than another does in the possession."[31] The solitary Crusoe has no one to keep secrets from: the word "secret" defines his privacy, individuality, possessiveness, and sole claim to pleasure.

Self-congratulation merges with the frequently mentioned "secret hints" of Providence until Crusoe learns to identify Providence with his own desires. When after a time he reflects on his role in saving Friday from paganism, "A secret joy run through every part of my soul" (p. 220). For the older Puritans determinism was a crucial issue, whether one concluded like Milton that man was free to cooperate with God's will in his own way, or like Bunyan that man must learn to make his will conform to the irresistible force of predestination. In strictly theological terms Defoe seems to have followed Baxter in stressing God's desire to welcome all of his children, rather than his power of predestination.[32] But imaginatively Defoe shares with the Puritans a feeling of unfreedom, of being compelled to act by some power beyond himself. In the imaginary world of fiction he can embrace that power instead of resisting it. In its simplest terms this amounts to asserting that Crusoe is an agent of Providence as well as its beneficiary, as he himself indicates after masterminding the defeat of the mutineers:

> "Gentlemen," said I, "do not be surprised at me; perhaps you may have a friend near you when you did not expect it." "He must be sent directly from heaven, then," said one of them very gravely to me, and pulling off his hat at the same time to me, "for our condition is past the help of man." "All help is from heaven, sir," said I. (p. 254)

But beyond this, Defoe's determinism becomes a defense of his own impulses, whereas for Puritans it would have been a confirmation of their sinfulness. Providence is seen as responsible not only for what happens but also for what does not, for what Crusoe is not as well as what he is. "Had Providence . . . blessed me with confined desires" (p. 194) none of the misfortunes—and none of the rewards—would have come about. But Providence did not. Where then does responsibility lie?

The more one ponders this question, the more equivocal the role of Providence becomes, as is vividly apparent when Crusoe reflects on his very first shipwreck.

> Had I now had the sense to have gone back to Hull and have gone home, I had been happy, and my father, an emblem of our blessed Saviour's parable, had even killed the fatted calf for me; for hearing the ship I went away in was cast away in Yarmouth Road, it was a great while before he had any assurance that I was not drowned.

> But my ill fate pushed me on now with an obstinacy that nothing could resist; and though I had several times loud calls from my reason and my more composed judgment to go home, yet I had no power to do it. I know not what to call this, nor will I urge that it is a secret overruling decree that hurries us on to be the instruments of our own destruction, even though it be before us, and that we rush upon it with our eyes open. Certainly nothing but some such decreed unavoidable misery attending, and which it was impossible for me to escape, could have pushed me forward against the calm reasonings and persuasions of my most retired thoughts, and against two such visible instructions as I had met with in my first attempt. (p. 14)

The passage is filled with interesting negatives: (1) Crusoe would have been like the prodigal if he had gone home, but he did *not*; (2) he will *not* say that his fate was compelled by "a secret overruling decree"; (3) yet *nothing but* such a decree can account for it.

One can try to explain these complications in orthodox Christian fashion, as Coleridge does:

> When once the mind, in despite of the remonstrating conscience, has abandoned its free power to a haunting impulse or idea, then whatever tends to give depth and vividness to this idea or indefinite imagination increases its despotism, and in the same proportion renders the reason and free will ineffectual. . . . This is the moral of Shakespeare's *Macbeth,* and the true solution of this paragraph—not any overruling decree of divine wrath, but the tyranny of the sinner's own evil imagination, which he has voluntarily chosen as his master.[33]

Coleridge adds, "Rebelling against his conscience he becomes the slave of his own furious will" (p. 316). But Crusoe does not go so far as this toward accepting the orthodox solution. He shows that he is aware of it, and hence hesitates to ascribe misfortunes to fate or God, but nevertheless the sense of involuntary behavior is so strong that he can only attribute it to "some such decreed unavoidable misery."

An emphasis on God's "decrees," comforting for the elect and dreadful for the reprobate, was fundamental to Calvinism. But Crusoe uses Calvinist language here to suggest that he cannot be morally responsible for actions in which he is moved about like a chess piece. In many places Defoe discusses the kinds of necessity in ordinary life (finding food, self-defense) that may not extenuate crime but impel it so irresistibly that the criminal is simply not free to behave otherwise.[34] A character in *Colonel Jack* says, "I believe my case was what I find is the case of most of the wicked part of the world, *viz.* that to be reduced to necessity is to be wicked; for necessity is not only the temptation, but is such a temptation as human nature is not empowered to resist. How good then is that God which takes from you, sir, the temptation, by taking away the necessity?"[35] Surely the corollary must also hold: the sinner can hardly be blamed if God does *not* remove the temptation by removing the necessity.

Obeying necessity, Crusoe allows himself to ride the current of his secret destiny and is magnificently rewarded. A Puritan reading of *Robinson Crusoe*—such as Defoe himself might have endorsed—would hold that by seeking self-fulfillment and creating a private *nomos,* Crusoe is an abject sinner. But the logic of the story denies this. Starr has shown that Defoe was fascinated with the science of casuistry,[36] which treats necessity as an ethical excuse for behavior instead of—as in Calvinism—a moral condemnation of it. The inverted egotism of Bunyan's "chief of sinners" is turned right-side-up again, as Crusoe's island refuses to remain a metaphor for captivity and quickly develops positive qualities. Since Crusoe is a fictional character and not a real person, what is really involved is Defoe's imaginative conception of the island. And this at bottom is a powerful fantasy of punishment that can be willingly accepted because it ceases to punish. The autonomy of solitude is the happy culmination of those mysterious impulses that first sent Crusoe to sea, and in achieving it he makes his destiny his choice.

The much-discussed economic aspects of *Robinson Crusoe* are suggestive of ambiguities very like the religious ones. On this topic the *locus classicus* is Ian Watt's chapter on *Crusoe* as a myth of capitalism. It is not really relevant to argue, as critics of Watt have done, that Crusoe has little of the rational calculation of the capitalist. For Watt's point is that the book is a myth and not a literal picture, reflecting the dynamic spirit of capitalism rather than its practical application. "Crusoe's 'original sin' is really the dynamic tendency of capitalism itself, whose aim is never merely to maintain the *status quo,* but to transform it incessantly. Leaving home, improving on the lot one was born to, is a vital feature of the individualist pattern of life."[37] The island permits Crusoe (and Defoe) to evade the contradictions in capitalist individualism, and to imagine a Puritan Eden in which work yields gratification instead of vexation and defeat.

The special status of the island makes possible Crusoe's reaction, in a famous passage, when he finds a quantity of coins on board the wrecked ship.

> I smiled to myself at the sight of this money; "O drug!" said I aloud, "What art thou good for? Thou art not worth to me, no not the taking off of the ground, one of those knives is worth all this heap, I have no manner of use for thee, e'en remain where thou art, and go to the bottom as a creature whose life is not worth saving." However, upon second thoughts, I took it away. . . . (p. 57)

Ever since Coleridge, readers have perceived irony in those second thoughts, but the irony is at society's expense rather than Crusoe's. If ever he returns to the world whose lifeblood is money, then this money will be useful if not indispensable. With his usual good sense he therefore saves it. But on the island, as if by enchantment, money is truly valueless, and Crusoe is free of the whole remorseless system whose lubricant it is. His personification of the coins as a "creature" carries its traditional Puritan meaning: all earthly things are "creatures" which the saint is to restrain himself from loving too much. Only on Crusoe's island is it possible to despise money as a useless and indeed harmful drug. . . .

Relating *Robinson Crusoe* to the myth of Mammon, Starr surveys writers who tried to reconcile Christ's injunction "Take no thought for the morrow" with the duty of labor by emphasizing that the labor must be performed in cooperation with Providence.[39] On the island Crusoe need no longer attempt this difficult reconciliation, whereas capitalism, being rational, must always take thought for the morrow. Thus in sociological terms Crusoe escapes the prison of alienated labor, just as in religious terms he escapes the prison of guilt. He inhabits a little world where his tools and products fully embody his desires (or would if he could make ink) and where necessity authenticates his desires instead of punishing them. "The liberty of the individual," Freud says, "is no gift of civilization."[40] It is Defoe's gift to Crusoe.

Yet even in the imagination, this dream of wholeness is at best provisional. The economic system, according to Weber, "is an immense cosmos into which the individual is born, and which presents itself to him, at least as an individual, as an unalterable order of things in which he must live."[41] On the island Crusoe breaks free from that order, but in a deeper sense he has already internalized it, along with the religious order that undergirds it. What is possible finally is only a fantasy of escape, from desire as well as from civilization, that anticipates the poor man's reward in the New Testament.

> I looked now upon the world as a thing remote, which I had nothing to do with, no expectation from, and indeed no desires about: in a word, I had nothing indeed to do with it, nor was ever like to have; so I thought it looked as we may perhaps look upon it hereafter, *viz.* as a place I had lived in, but was come out of it; and well might I say, as Father Abraham to Dives, *Between me and thee is a great gulf fixed.* (p. 128) . . .

If the Puritans believed that they had to study the clues in their lives with fierce attention, they also believed that the ultimate interpretation was reserved for God, not themselves. "In theistic religions," Frye says, "God speaks and man listens."[58] But in *Robinson Crusoe* God himself becomes a kind of fiction, even if an indispensable one, and Crusoe has to do his own interpreting because if he does not, no one else will. *Paradise Lost* and *The Pilgrim's Progress* were texts that depended upon a superior text, the Word of God. *Robinson Crusoe* contains plenty of scriptural allusions, but now they are only allusions. The narrative offers itself as autonomous and freestanding, and in a profound sense it is secular. Here is where the "realism" of Crusoe telling his own story conflicts with the impulse to interpret, and the story tends to roll onward with a momentum of its own rather than successfully embodying the pattern to which it aspires. Crusoe is moved by his father's advice "but alas! a few days wore it all off" (p. 6), and this sets the tone for everything that follows. In a way Defoe participates in the state of continuous starting-over that is characteristic of modern writing, "something whose *beginning* condition, irreducibly, is that *it must always be produced, constantly.*"[59] So in a curious way Defoe's problems lead logically to the solutions of Sterne, who perfectly fulfills Barthes's definition, "Le texte scriptible, c'est *nous en train* d'écrire."[60] But one must not claim too much; ***Robinson Crusoe*** resists any theoretical explanation that sees its meanderings as planned. A recent writer proposes, modestly enough, that "there is a deliberate avoidance of rhetorical or dramatic closure in Defoe's method."[61] The impersonal and passive construction is all too apt: the method itself (not Defoe) does not want to end, and the avoidance of ending is somehow "in" the method.

If Crusoe watches himself writing, Defoe pretends to watch neither Crusoe nor himself, affecting an utterly unsubordinated prose whose heaped up clauses suggest the mind-numbing inconsequentiality of experience. Here is the first half of a typical sentence, with the connective words italicized for emphasis:

> A little after noon I found the sea very calm, *and* the tide ebbed so far out, *that* I could come within a quarter of a mile of the ship; *and* here I found a fresh renewing of my grief, *for* I saw evidently, *that* if we had kept on board, we had all been safe, *that is to say,* we had all got safe on shore, *and* I had not been so miserable *as* to be left entirely destitute of all comfort and company, *as* I now was; *this* forced tears from my eyes again, *but* as there was little relief in that, I resolved, *if* possible, to get to the ship, *so* I pulled off my clothes, *for* the weather was hot to extremity, *and* took the water, *but* when I came to the ship, my difficulty was still greater to know how to get on board, *for* as she lay aground. . . . (p. 48)

In Bunyan the paratactic style suggested the welter of experience that God pulls together into a single shape. In Defoe it just suggests the welter of experience, and the prose keeps toppling forward of its own weight.

Christian faith is well on the way to providing a nostalgic schema rather than an informing principle, even if as Lukács says it has left permanent scars on the landscape: "The river beds, now dry beyond all hope, have marked forever the face of the earth."[62] Defoe's later novels are exceptionally episodic, not only failing to make their inner logic conform to providential plan, but failing to develop an inner logic at all. And the *anomie* that ***Robinson Crusoe*** held at bay returns with a vengeance. The later characters live under aliases while struggling, usually as criminals, to survive in a society that offers no *nomos,* no status that confirms the essential order of things. And guilt is no longer managed by assimilating it to a coherent determinism generated from within. Moll Flanders's rationalizations may be partly shared by the author, but he certainly appreciates the dreadful emptiness (and Pauline urgency) in Roxana's bitter confession: "With my eyes open, and with my conscience, as I may say, awake, I sinned, knowing it to be a sin, but having no power to re-

sist."[63] We cannot know exactly what Defoe thought he was doing in this enigmatic novel, but we do know that it was his last. As one critic puts it, "Defoe stopped when he reached the end."[64]

Meanwhile ***Robinson Crusoe*** survives in all its richness, the starting point of a new genre and yet strangely unfruitful for imitation; it spawned no tradition of its own as *Don Quixote* and *Pamela* did. Later fictions continued to draw upon Christian ideas and to pursue the dream of confirming them, but never again in the naive and direct way that Defoe at first believed possible. ***Robinson Crusoe*** is a remarkable and unrepeatable reconciliation of myth with novel, whose fantasy of isolation without misery and labor without alienation retains all of its remarkable imaginative power. "I am away from home," Kafka wrote to his closest friend, "and must always write home, even if any home of mine has long since floated away into eternity. All this writing is nothing but Robinson Crusoe's flag hoisted at the highest point of the island."[65]

Notes

[1] *The Life and Strange Surprizing Adventures of Robinson Crusoe,* ed. J. Donald Crowley (London, 1972), p. 137. Further references to *Crusoe* are to this edition. . . .

[6] Richard Stauffer, *Dieu, la Création et la Providence dans la Prédication de Calvin* (Berne, 1978), p. 268.

[7] John Wesley, quoted by Keith Thomas, *Religion and the Decline of Magic* (New York, 1971), p. 640; see Thomas's discussion of this point on pp. 639-40.

[8] *Moll Flanders,* ed. G. A. Starr (London, 1976), pp. 274, 279.

[9] *A General Martyrologie* (1677), quoted by J. Paul Hunter, *The Reluctant Pilgrim: Defoe's Emblematic Method and Quest for Form in Robinson Crusoe* (Baltimore, 1966), p. 76.

[10] *The Letters of Daniel Defoe,* ed. G. H. Healey (Oxford, 1969), p. 17. See Paula R. Backscheider, "Personality and Biblical Allusion in Defoe's Letters," *South Atlantic Review* 47 (1982), 1-20.

[11] See Paul J. Korshin, *Typologies in England, 1650-1820* (Princeton, 1982), pp. 218-21.

[12] Paul K. Alkon, *Defoe and Fictional Time* (Athens, Ga., 1979), pp. 61, 146.

[13] *Serious Reflections,* pp. 2-3.

[14] René Descartes, *Discours de la Méthode,* final sentence of Part III.

[15] *Personal Narrative,* in *Jonathan Edwards: Representative Selections,* ed. Clarence H. Faust and Thomas H. Johnson (New York, 1962), p. 60.

[16] From Forster's *Life of Charles Dickens,* reprinted in the Norton Critical Edition of *Robinson Crusoe,* ed. Michael Shinagel (New York, 1975), p. 295.

[17] *The Pilgrim's Progress,* ed. Roger Sharrock (Harmondsworth, 1965), p. 56.

[18] See Maximillian E. Novak, *Defoe and the Nature of Man* (Oxford, 1963), ch. 2. . . .

[30] *Grace Abounding,* ed. Roger Sharrock (Oxford, 1962), p. 76.

[31] *Spectator* 411. There are two similar uses of "secret" in no. 412.

[32] See Martin J. Greif, "The Conversion of Robinson Crusoe," *Studies in English Literature* 6 (1966), 553-55.

[33] Samuel Taylor Coleridge, *Complete Works* (New York, 1884), IV, 312.

[34] See Novak, *Defoe and the Nature of Man,* ch. 3.

[35] *Colonel Jack,* ed. Samuel Holt Monk (London, 1965), p. 161.

[36] *Defoe and Casuistry* (Princeton, 1971).

[37] *The Rise of the Novel: Studies in Defoe, Richardson, and Fielding* (Berkeley, 1957), ch. 3. . . .

[39] G. A. Starr, *Defoe and Spiritual Autobiography* (Princeton, 1965), pp. 185-97.

[40] *Civilization and Its Discontents,* tr. James Strachey (New York, 1962), p. 42.

[41] Max Weber, *The Protestant Ethic and the Spirit of Capitalism,* tr. Talcott Parsons (New York, 1958), p. 54.

[58] Northrop Frye, *The Critical Path: An Essay on the Social Context of Literary Criticism* (Bloomington, Ind., 1973), p. 120.

[59] Edward M. Said, *Beginnings: Intention and Method* (Baltimore, 1975), p. 197.

[60] Roland Barthes, quoted by Said, p. 202 (from (*S/Z*).

[61] Walter R. Reed, *An Exemplary History of the Novel: The Quixotic versus the Picaresque* (Chicago, 1981), p. 111.

[62] Georg Lukács, *The Theory of the Novel,* trans. Anna Bostock (Cambridge, Mass., 1971), p. 38.

[63] *Roxana, The Fortunate Mistress,* ed. Jane Jack (London, 1964), p. 44.

[64] Zimmerman, *Defoe and the Novel,* p. 187.

[65] Letter to Max Brod, 12 July 1922, in Franz Kafka, *Letters to Friends, Family, and Editors,* trans. Richard and Clara Winston (New York, 1977), p. 340.

Michael McKeon (essay date 1987)

SOURCE: "Parables of the Younger Son (I): Defoe and the Naturalization of Desire," in *The Origins of the English Novel, 1600-1740,* The Johns Hopkins University Press, 1987, pp. 315-37.

[*Here, McKeon discusses Crusoe's spiritualization of events and life on the island and explores possible identifications of original sin in the novel.*]

1

Although the second part of **Robinson Crusoe** followed so quickly upon the first that it successfully prevented all spurious continuations, an unauthorized "abridgement" of Part I nevertheless just managed to precede it into print. In the preface to Part II, Defoe condemns that abridgment and complains that its excision of religious and moral reflections precludes the spiritual improvement that had been a principal feature of the original. The narrative "Invention" of Part II, as well, will be legitimated by the ample opportunity that is provided there for "just Application" and "Improvement." *"The Editor"* of Part I *"believes the thing to be a just History of Fact."* The "Editor" of Part II takes a similar stance: in the spirit of the maxim "strange, therefore true," he asserts that it "contains as strange and surprising Incidents" as its predecessor, of which he adds that "all the Endeavours of envious People to reproach it with being a Romance . . . have proved abortive."[1]

Now, amid such claims to historicity, we might expect the argument against abridgment to be based simply on the complaint that it reduced the narrative to a quantitative incompleteness. But as we know, Defoe's commitment to the claim, although real enough, was decidedly complicated in the later years of his career, and in other contexts as well he emphasizes the spiritual "application" and "improvement" of his work by way of justifying its "invention." The impetus for this reevaluation of the claim did not come entirely from within. Already before the year was over, Charles Gildon was attacking Defoe for having invented the protagonist whose biographical memoirs he was purporting to edit.

Gildon is the first in a long line of critics who detect a close relation between the errancy of Robinson Crusoe and the remarkable vicissitudes and duplicities of Daniel Defoe's own career, and he has Defoe tell Crusoe that "I drew thee from the Consideration of my own Mind; I have been all my Life that Rambling, Inconsistent Creature, which I have made thee." "The Fabulous *Proteus* of the Ancient Mythologist," Gildon says of Defoe, "was but a very faint Type of our Hero," and although Defoe would compare his work with *The Pilgrim's Progress,* Gildon's Crusoe sees a much closer resemblance to the "Mob" romances of *Guy of Warwick, Bevis of Southampton,* and *The London Prentice.*[2]

In fact, the dilemma of quantitative completeness arises within the plot of **Robinson Crusoe** itself, as a function of that impulse toward materialistic quantification which is so characteristic of empirical epistemology and which is expressed by Defoe (as by other travel narrators) through a proliferation of times, dates, place names, and nautical terminology. Soon after his arrival on the island and in the spirit both of Puritan teachings and of the Royal Society's instructions to travelers, Robinson undertakes a journal that will begin at the beginning. But since at least the first few weeks of the journal therefore must be a retrospective re-creation of events, they have the ambiguous power both to confirm the historicity of those events by referring back to them, and to undermine their factuality by providing an alternative version of "what happened." Not that Robinson himself is conscious of this ambiguity, since he believes simply that "in it will be told all these Particulars over again" (69). But Defoe was aware of the problem, and in fact many details are omitted from the journal, while others we learn of for the first time there. Even more, the two versions seem occasionally to contradict each other in matters of fact, let alone interpretation. In the narrative, for example, the storm has abated and the weather cleared when Robinson awakes after the first night, whereas in the journal the rain continues for the next few days (47-48, 70-71). And there is a further problem of temporal sequence. Five weeks after the shipwreck, the journal recounts an event (the completion of a chair) we first heard of just prior to the journal's inception, and we may therefore expect all subsequent accounts to be of uncharted territory (68, 72). Yet very soon after this we are told that Robinson is excavating a cave which in the narrative clearly had been made well before the construction of the chair (60, 67, 73). We quickly find, in other words, that the dilemma of quantitative completeness is dwarfed by the apparent problem that the journal violates both the substance and the sequence of the narrative's historicity.[3]

On the other hand, we also begin to be aware, from periodic summarizing and foreshadowing interpolations (e.g., 75, 76), that this is not a strict journal at all, but one that has been subjected to a kind of secondary revision by a larger narrative perspective that resumes for good when Robinson's ink later runs out. Unlike the typical travel journal, which provides rough notes for a later and fuller narrative redaction, Robinson's journal stealthily becomes that redaction even as we read it. Immediately following certain moralizing passages he announces explicitly that now I "return to my Journal" (79, 97)—and at these points the experience is not unlike that of Cervantes' narrative vertigo, in which what we took to be the main thread suddenly is revealed as a digression from it. And yet in the first-person narration of Defoe, the effect is less to throw the historicity of the travels themselves into question than to sensitize us to the personalized veracity of Robinson's experience, which is all the more authentic for having this subjective volatility. Gradually the journal's effort at a temporal ordering of events is subsumed within the larger narrative, and by the time we reach the climactic moment of Robinson's conversion crisis, this formal confusion of "journal" and "narrative" has served as one important guide to the way in which things as usual have come to be suspended on the island.[4]

The peculiar coexistence of historicity and subjectivity in **Robinson Crusoe,** the early dynamic between journal and narrative and the more general one between Character and Narrator—these exemplify the obvious indebtedness of Defoe's work to the formal procedures of spiritual autobiography. The form would of course have been familiar to Defoe, who had been set apart for the nonconformist ministry until his religious crisis at the age of twenty-one. The gap between the sinful young rambler and the repentant convert from whose perspective the story is told is felt very strongly in the first half of **Robinson Crusoe.** "But if I can express at this Distance the Thoughts I had about me at that time," Robinson says at one point, and we are often aware, through retrospective narrative intrusions, of the great divide between this foolish, thoughtless, headstrong, prodigal, sinful youth whose fortunes we attend, and the authoritative, prophetic, but disembodied consciousness that hastens us on into the fateful future (II).[5]

Once on the island, the gap between the two begins to close. The sprouting seeds, the earthquake, his illness and dream, are natural events that we watch Robinson painfully and imperfectly learn to spiritualize, to read as signs of God's presence (78-79, 80-81, 87-91). In order to treat his ague he looks in his seaman's chest for a roll of tobacco, and finds there "a Cure, both for Soul and Body"—not only the roll but a bible as well. Trying "several Experiments" with the tobacco, he listlessly experiments also with bibliomancy for a cure to the spiritual disease of which he is only now, before our eyes, becoming fully conscious (93-94). "Deliverance" is the scriptural word that holds his attention, and he learns to read it in such a way as to release, for the first time, its spiritual application:

Now I began to construe the Words mentioned above, *Call on me, and I will deliver you,* in a different Sense from what I had ever done before; for then I had no Notion of any thing being call'd Deliverance, but my being deliver'd from the Captivity I was in; for tho' I was indeed at large in the Place, yet the Island was certainly a Prison to me, and that in the worst Sense in the World; but now I learn'd to take it in another Sense: . . . [to seek] Deliverance from the Load of Guilt that bore down all my Comfort . . . Deliverance from Sin [is] a much greater Blessing, than Deliverance from Affliction (96-97).

At this point, Robinson's "load," like Christian's, falls from his shoulders because he has learned, like Edward Coxere, to spiritualize his island prison as the prison of the world herebelow. It is the beginning of the movement of narrative "atonement," when Character and Narrator come together, and this can be seen in the ease with which Robinson will shortly distinguish between not aimless past and repentant future but anguished past and contented present: between "Before," when he felt he "was a Prisoner lock'd up with the Eternal Bars and Bolts of the Ocean," and "now," when "I began to exercise my self with new Thoughts" (113). Henceforth he will by no means be immune from backslidings, but they will be ostentatious lapses—his construction of the enormous canoe, his panic over the footprint, his rage against the cannibals—whose rapid moralization will only emphasize how far the Character has internalized the spiritualizing powers of the Narrator.[6]

Thus *Robinson Crusoe* can be seen to be in rather close proximity to the preoccupations of Protestant soteriology in general and of spiritual autobiography in particular. With the spiritualization of "deliverance" Robinson's early urge to "ramble" (3) does not disappear, but it is permanently transvalued for him, as we will see. Physical mobility is reconceived in spiritual terms, as movement both "upward" and "inward": after his dream of the avenging angel he realizes that since leaving home he has had not "one Thought that so much as tended either to looking upwards toward God, or inwards towards a Reflection upon my own Ways" (88). Moreover, the impulse toward introspective veracity that Robinson now evinces is a vital channel for the claim to historicity in spiritual autobiography. But of course the generic status of *Robinson Crusoe* is a good deal more uncertain than this argument would suggest. The dynamic relation between Character and Narrator is, after all, a formal feature of the picaresque as well, and even of that originating strain of picaresque in which the "spiritual" constitution of the protagonist is clearly an "autodidactic" and secular act of self-creation rather than a function of divine creativity. Thus Francis Kirkman, for example, makes more than a gesture toward the language of repentance, confession, and conversion, but we can have

no doubt that the instrumental creativity in this narrative is that of the author and not of the Author—and, indeed, that Francis's physical "rambles" are to be converted to "upward mobility" not in the spiritual but in the social sense of the term. By the same token, we are obliged to recall that the interplay between "journal" and "narrative" with which we began is as central to secular travel narrative as to spiritual autobiography.[7]

These fairly random attempts to "place" *Robinson Crusoe* by associating it with one or another established subgenre recapitulate, in different terms, the most important recent controversy concerning its interpretation. The modern tendency to see Defoe's work as essentially an essay in secular materialism is fairly represented by Ian Watt's view that Robinson's religion is the result of a mechanically Puritan "editorial policy." In reaction to this tendency, the traditions of seventeenth-century Puritan allegory and spiritual autobiography have been reviewed by critics, notably George Starr and Paul Hunter, to the end of assimilating *Robinson Crusoe* to something like an ideal type of Protestant narrative religiosity. Both arguments are made with great skill, but both may appear extreme insofar as they seem unnecessarily obliged to imply a mutual exclusion. As the Weber thesis suggests, in the historically transitional territory of early modern Protestantism, spiritual and secular motives are not only "compatible"; they are inseparable, if ultimately contradictory, parts of a complex intellectual and behavioral system.[8]

If, shortly after his conversion, Robinson demonstrates (as in the preface) his ability to use the terms "application" and "improvement" in their spiritual sense (128, 132), throughout the narrative he is far more inclined to use these words as synonyms for material industry (4, 49, 68, 144, 182, 195, 280). Yet both usages are consistent with the unstable strategies of Protestant casuistry—which in any case is only one sphere of discourse in which the instability of secularization and reform is registered during this period. Defoe's pilgrim is the brother of a wide range of progressive travelers to utopian realms: Edward Coxere, George Pine, Francis Kirkman, Capt. Misson, Sancho Panza. And if we wish to appreciate fully the status of *Robinson Crusoe* as a "Protestant narrative," we will need to attend to its filiations not only with *Grace Abounding* but also with the literal plot of *The Pilgrim's Progress.* Of course, Bunyan's entire plot of "romance" adventure exists in order to be spiritualized. In Defoe the balance between spiritualization and the claim to historicity has been reversed, and it is as though he has—not without the spiraling misgivings of the *Serious Reflections*—taken that perilous next step and, in the name of a "positive" secularization, explicitly sanctioned our resistance to allegorical translation. The result is a literal narrative filled with the mutabilities of religion (providence) and romance (pirates, shipwreck), which do not so much undergo in themselves a transformative specification to the mechanics of social mobility, as engineer the conditions under which that mobility is wonderfully enabled to transpire.

2

One focus of the critical controversy to which I have just referred is the question of what Robinson means when he speaks of his "ORIGINAL SIN" in opposing his father's advice that he stay at home and keep to the "middle Station," or "the upper Station of *Low Life*," to which he was born (194, 4-5). Obviously the term ascribes a religious significance to Robinson's physical mobility; but what sort of social significance does it attribute to it? Should we identify Robinson's "original sin" with capitalist industry; or with an anticapitalist impulse to ramble and to evade his capitalist calling; or with an anti-Puritan motive to evade his Puritan calling; or with a general unregenerate waywardness that really has no special social significance at all?[9] In a certain sense, however, this is to begin at the wrong end. For Robinson's mobility gains its religious overtones only with hindsight, through the retrospective viewpoint of the Narrator. In the present tense of narrative action it is primarily a social *rather* than a religious meaning—even the socially charged meaning of Calvinism—that Robinson's mobility possesses when he first leaves home. His father speaks in a general way about the virtues of "Application and Industry," but this is not really the language of labor discipline and the calling (3-6). His appeal is at least as plausibly to what I have been calling "aristocratic ideology": to a very traditionalistic social stratification and to the advisability of maintaining the station of one's birth. How is it, then, that the young Robinson learns to read the social meaning of his wish to ramble through the religious spectacles of Calvinist discipline? And since the Puritan's pursuit of grace might entail either stasis or pilgrimage, either social stability or change, why should his mobility appear so definitively a sign of his sin rather than a token of his election? When does the language of the calling enter Robinson's vocabulary?

On his first sea voyage, Robinson, in mortal fear, bitterly berates himself for "the Breach of my Duty to God and my Father" (7-8). Before this the narration of his early life has been relatively free of religious injunction. Robinson's father is a merchant who became successful through the sort of travel he now forbids his son. One of the older sons is dead; the other has disappeared. Designed now for the law and a "settled" life, Robinson thinks himself at eighteen too old to be set an attorney's clerk or an apprentice, and he seems momentarily to attribute his wanderlust to the marginality of his status in the family: "Being the third Son of the Family, and not bred to any Trade, my Head

began to be fill'd very early with rambling Thoughts" (3). But whatever the psychological cause of it, Robinson soon finds a more satisfactory explanation for his unsettledness—more satisfactory because empowered with the ascription of sin—in the idea of a "duty" that has been breached. And this idea he seems to hear first from his friend's father, the master of the ship on which he had made his nearly fatal first voyage. Learning that the youth had sailed with him "only for a Trial in order to go farther Abroad," the master tells Robinson *"to take this for a plain and visible Token that you are not to be a Seafaring Man."* "Why, Sir," says Robinson, "will you go to Sea no more?" *"That is another Case,"* said he, *"it is my Calling, and therefore my Duty"* (14-15). This is Robinson's first lesson in casuistry, at least to our knowledge, and it is an important one. Duty is dictated by calling, and to be out of one's calling is certainly to be in sin. But how do you tell your calling if you have no clear intuition of it and have not been definitively bred to one? Parental authority is one guide. Another is the tokens and signs of divine will that can be read in experience, and it does not require a very subtle interpreter to read God's judgment in this particular case.

At this early stage Robinson is quite blind to providential signs. Yet even so, the narrative voice soon lets us know that returning home is not the only way he might at this point have altered his course for the better. For now Robinson begins to ship on a succession of voyages, and because he has "Money in my Pocket, and good Cloaths upon my Back, I would always go on board in the Habit of a Gentleman" rather than that of a common sailor. Like his creator, he is fond of upwardly mobile masquerade, but the result is that he remains idle and forfeits the opportunity to establish his calling at sea: for "as a Sailor . . . I had learn'd the Duty and Office of a Fore-mast Man; and in time might have quallified my self for a Mate or Lieutenant, if not for a Master" (16). Despite this bad choice, Robinson is lucky enough to be befriended by an honest Guinea captain, who teaches him some of the skills of both sailor and merchant (17). But before we can begin to ask if this employment has the potential of being a redemptive discipline, Robinson is captured by pirates and metamorphosed "from a Merchant to a miserable Slave . . . Now the Hand of Heaven had overtaken me, and I was undone without Redemption" (19).

Nor do his spiritual prospects improve when he escapes from Sallee and gains material prosperity as a planter in Brazil. The problem is more general than the fact of his readiness to sell Xury to the Portuguese captain by whom they are "deliver'd" (in any case Defoe seems to exercise some care in formulating the case so as to make it conscientiously acceptable).[10] It is not that Robinson is specifically and spectacularly sacrilegious, but that he is comprehensively devoid of moral and spiritual constraints. The Portuguese captain himself is a man of such exemplary fair dealing that he would seem to epitomize how the merchant is to pursue his calling; and he treats Robinson so "honourably" and "charitably" that the latter's coarse desire to "gr[o]w rich suddenly" can only suffer by comparison (33-34, 37, 89). Rather than follow the rule of charity or regulate his life by the satisfaction of necessities, Robinson simply pursues his self-interest in Brazil. When the captain's good advice leads to his receipt of some valuable goods, Robinson is content to exploit the market for all he can get, selling them "to a very great Advantage; so that I might say, I had more than four times the Value of my first Cargo, and was now infinitely beyond my poor Neighbour." In this way Robinson's overextension and excess are palpably registered by his rapid advancement over others. It is not the fact of being a trader, but his "abus'd Prosperity," his unrationalized exploitation of exchange value, that distinguishes him from those who might be said to pursue their callings (37). The principles of subsistence and consumption are dominated by the unlimited desire to accumulate, a triumph of excess and waste that is also expressed in the irony that now Robinson "was coming into the very Middle Station, or upper Degree of low Life, which my Father advised me to before; and which if I resolved to go on with, I might as well ha' staid at Home" (35).[11]

By the same token, the voice of the Narrator makes it clear that despite past sins, having wandered into this way of life, Robinson might yet have made a decent calling of it. It is not strictly required, in other words, that one remain in the station of one's birth. What Robinson fails in for a second time is the identification of "those Prospects and those measures of Life, which Nature and Providence concurred to present me with, and to make my Duty." Our duty and calling are not objective entities, but conditions in which we find ourselves and which we are able to intuit and interpret into fulfillment. "As I had once done thus in my breaking away from my Parents, so I could not be content now, but I must go and leave the happy View I had of being a rich and thriving Man in my new Plantation, only to pursue a rash and immoderate Desire of rising faster than the Nature of the Thing admitted" (38). An incapacity to limit his desires by sensing the natural and providential limits of his situation is what makes Robinson successively a prodigal son, an unethical trader, and now also an imprudent trader: "Now increasing in Business and in Wealth," says the Narrator, "my Head began to be full of Projects and Undertakings beyond my Reach" (37-38). When he is offered the chance to oversee an illegal and highly profitable shipment of African slaves, he is oblivious to the fact that it would have been "a fair Proposal" only if made to one who did not already possess a "Settlement" in need of looking after. For him to accept the offer is to do "the most preposterous Thing that ever Man in such Circumstances could be guilty of," to

abandon the clear possibility of a settled calling. Nevertheless Robinson enters into an agreement with his fellow planters and goes "on Board in an evil Hour" (39-40).

So the prelude to shipwreck is a chronic incapacity to rationalize worldly activity by the sanctions of a perceived moral duty. The many years on the island overcome this incapacity by obliging Robinson, devoid of human society, to experience the society of God. This experience has two crucial dimensions. First, in a state of solitude the greatest impediments to ethical behavior—other people—suddenly disappear. But second, what then remains is the otherness of divinity itself, the absolute moral standard now so inescapable that its very voice may be heard and internalized within one's own desires. Robinson's long isolation schools him in the psychological discipline needed to transform his activity into his calling. In the following pages I will review the central stages in this schooling.

3

I have already suggested that Robinson's island conversion depends upon a new-found ability to spiritualize his situation, to detect and interpret the signs of God's presence in his life on the island. As he explains it, the pleasures of this presence do not only compensate for the absence of human society. They also alter his understanding of his own desires, of what it is he really wants:

> Thus I liv'd mighty comfortably, my Mind being entirely composed by resigning to the Will of God, and throwing my self wholly upon the Disposal of his Providence. This made my Life better than sociable, for when I began to regret the want of Conversation, I would ask my self whether thus conversing mutually with my own Thoughts, and, as I hope I may say, with even God himself by Ejaculations, was not better than the utmost Enjoyment of humane Society in the World.
>
> I gave humble and hearty Thanks that God had been pleas'd to discover to me, even that it was possible I might be more happy in this Solitary Condition, than I should have been in a Liberty of Society, and in all the Pleasures of the World. That he could fully make up to me, the Deficiencies of my Solitary State, and the want of Humane Society by his Presence, and the Communications of his Grace to my Soul . . . my very Desires alter'd, my Affections chang'd their Gusts, and my Delights were perfectly new . . .
>
> I look'd now upon the World as a Thing remote, which I had nothing to do with, no Expectation from, and indeed no Desires about: . . . I had neither the *Lust of the Flesh, the Lust of the Eye, or the Pride of Life*. I had nothing to covet; for I had all that I was now capable of enjoying. (135-36, 112-13, 128)

At such moments of radiant contentment, Robinson speaks as though he has shed not only all acquisitive appetites but all "wordly" ambition whatsoever, so that even the language of duty, labor discipline, and the calling has become an irrelevance. Yet we know this is not true. It is not only that he tells us that now "I was very seldom idle; but [had] regularly divided my Time, according to the several daily Employments that were before me, such as, *First,* My Duty to God, and the Reading of Scriptures" (114). It is precisely the enterprising and furiously energetic performance of some of those other employments that dominates our permanent impression of this most industrious of narratives. Robinson does not give over vocational ambition; on the contrary, he slowly and steadily makes "all Trades in the World"—farmer, baker, potter, stonecutter, carpenter, tailor, basketmaker—his calling (122). As he remarks, "By making the most rational Judgment of things, every Man may be in time Master of every mechanick Art . . . I improv'd my self in this time in all the mechanick Exercises which my Necessities put me upon applying my self to" (68, 144).

It is therefore not so much that Robinson moderates the immoderate desires that plagued him in his former life, as that their ethical quality has been altered—limited and therefore detoxified—by the alteration in his external circumstance: by the substitution, that is, of the society of God for human society. What this replacement achieves is, first of all, the transformation of exchange value into value in use. After the shipwreck but before his conversion, Robinson still believes that things acquire their value through commodification in the marketplace: although work on the island is discouragingly primitive, "my Time or Labour was little worth, and so it was as well employ'd one way as another" (68). But as we know from his celebrated, King James-version disdain for the found money—"O Drug! Said I aloud, what art thou good for, Thou art not worth to me"—Robinson is not slow to realize that there is no marketplace to be found on the island (57). And after a while he is completely captivated by the distinction between use value and exchange value, which he seizes many opportunities to rehearse. In the following passage he pointedly applies it to his former employment, in which exchange value played such a dominant role:

> I might have rais'd Ship Loadings of Corn; but I had no use for it . . . I had Timber enough to have built a Fleet of Ships. I had Grapes enough to have made Wine, or to have cur'd into Raisins, to have loaded that Fleet, when they had been built. But all I could make use of, was, All that was valuable . . . In a Word, The Nature and Experience of Things dictated to me upon just Reflection, That all the good Things of this World, are no farther good to us, than they are for our Use . . . I possess'd infinitely more than I knew what to do with . . . I had, as I hinted before, a Parcel of Money . . .

> [But] *As it was,* I had not the least Advantage by it, or Benefit from it. (128-29)

Robinson's tone of cautionary sobriety should not obscure for us the liberation of being able to "possess infinitely," to accumulate limitless possessions that cannot entail the risk of becoming commodities in exchange. "*Leaden-hall* Market could not have furnish'd a Table better than I, in Proportion to the Company"; and the differences that are disclosed by this analogy are fully as important to Robinson as are the similarities (109). For here he can lay up great stocks of grain, fully indulging his "Desire of having a good Quantity for Store," without challenging the great end of personal consumption. Indeed, in combining capitalist abstinence with the just belief that "now I work'd for my Bread," Robinson implicitly tempers the danger of attributing an imaginary value to capitalist activity with a labor theory of value, so that all this industry may be confidently sanctified by the biblical conviction "that in time, it wou'd please God to supply me with Bread" (117-18, 123-24).[12]

If the absence of human society prohibits the exchange of goods and the dangerous creation of imaginary value, it also precludes the human register of potentially sinful social advancement and excess. Unlike his sojourn in Brazil, here "there were no Rivals. I had no Competitor, none to dispute Sovereignty or Command with me" (128). Again, this does not prevent Robinson from continuing to behave like a capitalist; it effaces the moral consequences of that behavior. We become aware of this is subtle ways. When he tells us how he first "fenc'd in, and fortify'd," and "enclos'd all my Goods," the voice of the Narrator adds that "there was no need of all this Caution from the Enemies that I apprehended Danger from" (59, 60). But later we see that this is not really so. For once Robinson has again become a farmer in earnest, he finds himself in the position not so much of a Brazilian planter as of an English enclosing landlord. In danger of losing his crop to "Enemies of several Sorts"—goats, hares, and especially birds—he describes his emergency capital improvements in language that is disturbingly evocative of seventeenth- and eighteenth-century agrarian conflicts:[13]

> This I saw no Remedy for, but by making an Enclosure about it with a Hedge, which I did with a great deal of Toil; and the more, because it requir'd Speed. However, as my Arable Land was but small, suited to my Crop, I got it totally well fenc'd, in about three Weeks Time; and shooting some of the Creatures in the Day Time, I set my Dog to guard it in the Night . . . I staid by it to load my Gun, and then coming away I could easily see the Thieves sitting upon all the Trees about me, as if they only waited till I was gone away, and the Event proved it to be so . . . I was so provok'd . . . knowing that every Grain that they eat now, was, *as it might be*

said, a Peck-loaf to me in the Consequence; but coming up to the Hedge, I fir'd again, and kill'd three of them. This was what I wish'd for; so I took them up, and serv'd them as we serve notorious Thieves in *England,* (viz.) Hang'd them in Chains for a Terror to others. (116-17)

But although Robinson gives vent here to the deep and disquieting emotions of the enclosing landlord, these "enemies," with whom he is indeed in mortal competition, are not expropriated peasants but birds and beasts of the field. The equivocal appetite for elevating oneself over one's neighbors has been slaked even as the categories by which such elevation might be registered—the social "stations" so significant to Robinson's father—have been erased. And the obscure but pervasive sense of status inconsistency that has all along been expressed in Robinson's persistent desire to "ramble" is quashed under conditions that paradoxically exclude all reference groups whatsoever. There are only himself and God; and the only criteria by which to experience relative deprivation and reward are those dictated by divine justice and mercy.[14]

But as we have just seen in the image of the thieving wildlife, this is only literally true. All readers of ***Robinson Crusoe*** have been struck by the protagonist's propensity to populate and domesticate his island with figures from home. Unlike many authors of imaginary voyages, Defoe is disinclined to celebrate the reign of use value within the relatively exotic environs of a communist utopia. The passage on the thieving wildlife makes it clear that he is far more attracted by the private property of the landed estate, whose utopian character consists in the "magical extraction," in Raymond Williams's words, of its problematic inhabitants. When Robinson takes his first "Survey of the Island" and comes upon the Edenic valley where he will build the "Bower" that will serve as his "Country-House," he imagines "that this was all my own, that I was King and Lord of all this Country indefeasibly, and had a Right of Possession; and if I could convey it, I might have it in Inheritance, as compleatly as any Lord of a Manor in *England*" (98, 100, 101-2). Later he permits the figure to encompass the entire island: "I was Lord of the whole Mannor; or if I pleas'd, I might call my self King, or Emperor over the whole Country which I had Possession of" (128).[15]

If this fantasy of proprietorship appeals primarily to the impulse toward private ownership and capitalist improvement, there is at least an element here also of contemplative pastoralism and the domestic themes of Horatian retirement. Another way of saying this is that Defoe's island utopia is able to incorporate notions of value that are associated not only with capitalist and laboring industry but also with aristocratic ideology and its location of value in land. Of course, this syncretism can be found in the assimilationist posture of progressive ideology itself. Despite his trenchant attacks on the corruptions of lineage and aristocratic honor, Defoe was obsessed with the illusion of his own gentility, and at various stages in his career he proudly rode in the livery of his merchant's company, outrageously inflated his ancestry, and (going Francis Kirkman one better) employed the medium of print to become armigerous and to aristocratize his name from Foe to De Foe. Marx was certainly right to argue that the utopianism of ***Robinson Crusoe*** is not nostalgically conservative but progressive, that it is not "merely a reaction against over-sophistication and a return to a misunderstood natural life," but "rather, the anticipation of 'civil society'."[16]

What must be added to Marx's view of the function of Defoe's utopia is the crucial and complementary religious element. And Robinson's labor discipline is as successful as it is in confirming his sense of election because the neutralization of its social volatility has been ensured by his utter solitude. This solitude is challenged, of course, when Robinson discovers the print of a man's foot on the shore (an event whose significance I will turn to momentarily). But it is important to recognize the volatility even of Robinson's imaginative figures, which in truth is essential also to the significance of that discovery. As Maximillian Novak has remarked, "If [Robinson's] triumph over the island is mostly an economic conquest, it is an imaginative conquest as well." Like George Pine, Robinson "bestows culture" on his environment, and his creation of mere metaphors for social dominance improves on Pine's procreation of a new population, because it more thoroughly evades the dangers of social ambition and self-aggrandizement. But as we know, Defoe was deeply ambivalent about "the Power of Imagination" and imaginative creativity.[17] Some of its riskiness can be felt in the self-conscious drollery with which Robinson extends the figure of his island lordship: "It would have made a Stoick smile to have seen, me and my little Family sit down to Dinner; there was my Majesty the Prince and Lord of the whole Island; I had the Lives of all my Subjects at my absolute Command. I could hang, draw, give Liberty, and take it away, and no Rebels among all my Subjects" (148). No more than a poignant fiction, of course. But shortly Robinson panics at the thought of being joined by other people, and he is moved not only to reaffirm the old language of social stratification that had been suspended by his utopian solitude but also to remind himself of the *real* sources of absolute sovereignty and creativity: "I consider'd that this was the Station of Life the infinitely wise and good Providence of God had determin'd for me, that . . . I was not to dispute his Sovereignty, who, as I was his Creature, had an undoubted Right by Creation to govern and dispose of me absolutely as he thought fit . . . 'Twas my unquestion'd Duty to resign my self absolutely and entirely to his Will" (157).

Robinson's image of his "little family at dinner" is distracting in part because it suggests the speciousness of a submissive resignation achieved by the brute excision of all opportunities for competitive aggression. Defoe was conscious that his fiction of a desert-island conversion entailed this vulnerability. Still in the voice of Robinson Crusoe he later observed: "It is the Soul's being entangled by outward Objects, that interrupts its Contemplation of divine Objects, which is the Excuse for these Solitudes, and makes the removing the Body from those outward Objects seemingly necessary; but what is there of Religion in all this? . . . a vicious Inclination remov'd from the Object, is still a vicious Inclination." Robinson's imaginative enclosures are more treacherous than his physical ones because they cannot be held accountable to a standard that is clearly distinct from their own. At least part of his island experience, he speculates, was a function of "the brain-sick Fancy, the vapourish Hypochondriack Imagination . . . it was not meer Imagination, but it was the Imagination rais'd up to Disease." Defoe had used similar language— "my brain-begotten faith"—to characterize the nature of his religious doubts during his early crisis over entering the Presbyterian ministry. The Puritan elevation of the private conscience, the saint's injunction to a personal and vigilant spiritualization of all experience, invited simultaneously a rapt sanctification of the world and a nagging uncertainty as to the difference between divine and human spirituality. As we have seen, Robinson's conversion depends on his capacity to look both upward and inward. The lesson of the sprouting seeds, as he tells us pointedly, is not that God works miracles but that he works through us: "For it was really the Work of Providence as to me, that should order or appoint, that 10 or 12 Grains of Corn should remain unspoil'd . . . As also, that I should throw it out in that particular Place" (79). But once the saint has learned to read the presence of God in his own acts and intuitions, he has also become adept at discovering his own intuitions in the world at large. . . .

Notes

1 Daniel Defoe, *The Farther Adventures of Robinson Crusoe* . . . (1719), "Preface," in *Novel and Romance, 1700-1800: A Documentary Record,* ed. Ioan Williams (New York: Barnes and Noble, 1970), 64-65 (hereafter cited as *Farther Adventures*); and idem, *The Life and Strange Surprizing Adventures of Robinson Crusoe* . . . (1719), ed. J. Donald Crowley, Oxford English Novels (London: Oxford University Press, 1972), "Preface," I (hereafter cited as *Robinson Crusoe*). All parenthetical citations in the text are to the Crowley edition. Part II appeared 117 days before Part I. In fact the complaint itself may have been written by Defoe's publisher, William Taylor. Not surprisingly, abridgments of Part I— a dozen or more were published between 1720 and 1830—tended to give priority to the literal events of Robinson's shipwreck and early life on the island; see Pat Rogers, "Classics and Chapbooks," in *Books and Their Readers in Eighteenth-Century England,* ed. Isabel Rivers (New York: St. Martin's, 1982), 30-31. Defoe compares this sort of pirating of printed works to "Robbing on the Highway" (*Farther Adventures,* "Preface," 65). On piracies of Part I see Pat Rogers, *Robinson Crusoe* (London: Allen and Unwin, 1979), 7-8.

2 [Charles Gildon], *The Life and Strange Surprizing Adventures of Mr. D——— De F———* . . . (1719), x, iii. Defoe's own *Serious Reflections During the Life And Surprising Adventures of Robinson Crusoe: with his Vision of the Angelick World* (1720) has played a central role in making the autobiographical interpretation of *Robinson Crusoe* seem plausible and attractive. On the progress of Defoe's commitment to the claim to historicity see above, chap. 3, nn. 63-69.

3 Rogers, *Robinson Crusoe,* 122-23, interestingly discusses a related but more general feature of Defoe's style, which he calls "approximating" and "alternative" figures (e.g., "about a mile," "two or three"). "The effect is often to suggest compulsive mensuration even where accurate counting is not possible." On the interest of Puritans and the Royal Society in keeping autobiographical journals, see above, chap. 3, secs. 1, 3.

4 On Robinson's journal and its destabilization of objective recording and chronology, see Homer O. Brown, "The Displaced Self in the Novels of Daniel Defoe," *ELH,* 38, no. 4 (Dec., 1971), 584-85; and Timothy J. Reiss, *The Discourse of Modernism* (Ithaca: Cornell University Press, 1982), 323-24. J. Paul Hunter, *The Reluctant Pilgrim: Defoe's Emblematic Method and Quest for Form in Robinson Crusoe* (Baltimore: Johns Hopkins University Press, 1966), 144-45, notes that the journal has been edited. On the disruption of temporality in *Robinson Crusoe* see, more generally, Paul Alkon, *Defoe and Fictional Time* (Athens: University of Georgia Press, 1979); and Elizabeth D. Ermarth, *Realism and Consensus in the English Novel* (Princeton: Princeton University Press, 1983), chap. 4. The ambiguous significance of the journal is well conveyed by the fact that its documentary objectivity permits Robinson, "by casting up Times past," to discover the "strange Concurrence of Days" in the typological pattern of his life crises, and its very medium of definitiveness has, through successive dilutions, become so ghostly and "pale it scarce left any Appearance of black upon the Paper" (133). Rather than tax Defoe for discrepancies between narrative and journal, Gildon, 31 (*Adventures of Mr. D——— De F———,* prefers to criticize his lack of inventiveness: "You have been forc'd to give us the same Reflections over and over again, as well as repeat the same Fact afterwards in a Journal, which you had told us before in a plain Narration."

[5] See, e.g., *Robinson Crusoe,* 3, 5-6, 7-8, 9-10, 14-15, 16, 17, 19, 35-36, 38, 40. On Defoe's religious upbringing see Michael Shinagel, *Defoe and Middle-Class Gentility* (Cambridge: Harvard University Press, 1968), chap. I.

[6] See *Robinson Crusoe,* 124-28, 153-57, 168-73. On the conventionality of postconversion lapses in spiritual autobiography, see George A. Starr, *Defoe and Spiritual Autobiography* (Princeton: Princeton University Press, 1965), 160; Hunter, *Reluctant Pilgrim,* 187. On Coxere see above, chap. 6, nn. 41-42. For William Okeley's spiritualization of travel and captivity see above, chap. 3, n. 56.

[7] On the picaresque see above, chap. 3, sec. 2. On Kirkman see above, chap. 6, nn. 35-36.

[8] See Ian Watt, *The Rise of the Novel: Studies in Defoe, Richardson, and Fielding* (Berkeley and Los Angeles: University of California Press, 1957), 81 (but Watt's position is not as extreme as it has sometimes been taken to be; see 82-83); Starr, *Defoe and Spiritual Autobiography;* and Hunter, *Reluctant Pilgrim.* Among more recent critics, John J. Richetti has gone furthest in arguing against this mutual exclusion: see his thoughtful discussions in *Popular Fiction before Richardson: Narrative Patterns, 1700-1739* (Oxford: Clarendon Press, 1969), 13-18, 92-96; and *Defoe's Narratives: Situations and Structures* (Oxford: Clarendon Press, 1975), 23 and chap. 2 passim.

[9] See Watt, *Rise of the Novel,* 65; Starr, *Defoe and Spiritual Autobiography,* 74-81; Hunter, *Reluctant Pilgrim,* 38-39; Shinagel, *Defoe and Middle-Class Gentility,* 126-27 and 268-69n.5; Rogers, *Robinson Crusoe,* 76-77; Maximillian E. Novak, *Economics and the Fiction of Daniel Defoe,* University of California English Studies, no. 24 (Berkeley and Los Angeles: University of California Press, 1962), chap. 2; C. N. Manlove, *Literature and Reality, 1600-1800* (New York: St. Martin's, 1978), chap. 7. Cf. Gildon, *Adventures of Mr. D——— De F———,* 5-6.

[10] See, e.g., Richard Baxter's handling of the question, *"Is it lawful to buy and use men as Slaves?"* in *The Catechizing of Families . . .* (1683), 311.

[11] On the rule of charity and the limiting standard of the satisfaction of necessities, see above, chap. 5, n. 39. On the persistence of a secularized conception of "honor" as "credit" and "trust" in business dealings, see above, chap. 5, nn. 51-53.

[12] On theories of value see above, chap. 5, sec. 4. On capitalist abstinence see, e.g., Eric Roll, *A History of Economic Thought,* 4th ed. rev. (London: Faber and Faber, 1973), 344-46. When Robinson attributes the preservation of the ship-wrecked commodities to prov-

idence, he associates them with the gift of God's grace and achieves a similar sanctification (*Robinson Crusoe,* 130-31). See also Ian Watt's discussion of the mystique of the dignity of labor in relation to *Robinson Crusoe* in "Robinson Crusoe as a Myth," in *Eighteenth-Century English Literature: Modern Essays in Criticism,* ed. James L. Clifford (New York: Oxford University Press, 1959), 163-67. For Robinson's fascination with use and exchange value, see *Robinson Crusoe,* 50, 64, 189, 193, 195, 278.

[13] For useful treatments of several aspects of the subject see Raymond Williams, *The Country and the City* (New York: Oxford University Press, 1973), chap. 10; Douglas Hay, "Poaching and the Game Laws on Cannock Chase," in *Albion's Fatal Tree: Crime and Society in Eighteenth-Century England* (New York: Pantheon, 1975), 189-253. For a discussion that has bearing on mine here, see Richetti, *Popular Fiction before Richardson,* 95-96.

[14] Compare the following passages from *Robinson Crusoe:* "All our Discontents about what we want, appear'd to me, to spring from the Want of Thankfulness for what we have" (130); and "Thus we never see the true State of our Condition, till it is illustrated to us by its Contraries; nor know how to value what we enjoy, but by the want of it" (139).

[15] Defoe was fond of comparing a landowner's absolute possession to a monarch's; see above, chap. 5, n. 4. Later, on his return to the island, Robinson "reserv'd to [him] self the Property of the whole" (*Robinson Crusoe,* 305). For Williams's argument see *Country and City,* 32; his subject is the country-house poems of Jonson and Carew.

[16] Karl Marx, *Grundrisse,* trans. Martin Nicolaus (Harmondsworth: Penguin, 1973), 83. On Defoe's assimilationism see Shinagel, *Defoe and Middle-Class Gentility,* 29-30, 47-48, 73-74, 103-4. On the retirement themes see Pat Rogers, "Crusoe's Home," *Essays in Criticism,* 24 (1974), 375-90.

[17] See above, chap. 3, nn. 63-69; chap. 4, n. 37; chap. 5, n. 52. On Pine see above, chap. 6, n. 40. See Maximillian E. Novak, *Realism, Myth, and History in Defoe's Fiction* (Lincoln: University of Nebraska Press, 1983), 45. On the utility of Robinson's imaginative figures see also Michael Seidel, "Crusoe in Exile," *PMLA,* 96, no. 3 (May, 1981), 363-74. . . .

James O. Foster (essay date 1992)

SOURCE: "*Robinson Crusoe* and the Uses of the Imagination," in *Journal of English and Germanic Philology,* Vol. 91, No. 2, April, 1992, pp. 179-202.

[In the following excerpt, Foster contends that Crusoe exhibits conflicting impulses—one toward submission, the other toward self-assertion—and that Defoe himself enacts the same division throughout Robinson Crusoe.]

. . . In Crusoe's narrative, the allegorical organization of experience is perhaps strongest in the opening pages. Crusoe's single, obsessive trait is his mysterious compulsion to ramble, and this trait possesses him completely. Here we meet character in the root meaning of the term—as distinctive mark or graphic sign. Character in allegory is an elementary sign, a predictable and reliable manifestation of a distinctive disposition or trait. As such, a character has no internal life beyond what Angus Fletcher has termed as "obsessional anxiety": "The typical agent in an allegorical fiction has been seen as a daemon, for whom freedom of active choice hardly exists. This appears to have a major correlate in the theory of compulsive behavior, where it is observed that the mind is suddenly obsessed by an idea over which it has no control, which as it were 'possesses' the mind. The commonest experience of the compulsive neurotic is that his mind is suddenly disturbed by impulses that have no apparent rational meaning, and thence are seen as arbitrary and external 'commands.'"[12]

This monistic and obsessed Crusoe is at first set in opposition to his father, but as the narrative develops, the external and allegorical division between compulsion and authority is gradually internalized into an inner colloquy as Crusoe's father takes on a psychological dimension of the punitive superego manifest in Crusoe's conscience. The first storm at sea catalyzes the first internalized debate in Crusoe when his conscience upbraids him and he resolves to return home (p. 8). Such "wise and sober Thoughts" recur throughout the early part of the narrative, yet Crusoe's commanding sin—the self-assertive impulse which serves as his identity theme and his daemon—always achieves a "compleat . . . Victory over Conscience" (p. 10). Crusoe will eventually have to face this conscience on his island, where submission to the Father's will and resignation to Providence prove to be the only effective (though temporary) ways of channeling and controlling his self-assertive desires. But enough of Crusoe's inner life has been opened to the reader in this early part of the narrative to demonstrate that the allegorical type gives way to a more complex representation of a divided identity in a pattern that will become Defoe's basic technique, in all his prose fictions, of character presentation and development; situations and circumstances serve to specify certain traits in a serial and additive pattern. The result, in *Crusoe,* is the accretive growth of both dissonance and dimension in the main character as Defoe gradually and intuitively devises a series of situations and conflicts that will allow him to project

a character not as an irreducible unit of meaning but as a complex interplay of competing impulses.

The initial division between compulsion and conscience in Crusoe will itself undergo a series of accretive transformations through the rest of the narrative, though the root formulation remains the same; the impulse toward order and submission will be set against the impulse toward self-assertion. This division in impulses is, as I have indicated, in part a product of an inherited theological perspective on the mental life of the individual, and what develops in *Crusoe* is the presentation of a conflict within the will (as controlled by the imagination) which is the most basic conflict in the Puritan *automachia*.[13] Thus, Crusoe gradually introduces a Calvinist idiom and focus into his narrative, particularly in those passages where he tries retrospectively to account for his experience of division and instability. Early in his narrative, he writes: "But my ill Fate push'd me on now with an Obstinacy that nothing could resist; and tho' I had several times loud Calls from my Reason and my more composed Judgement to go home, yet I had no Power to do it. I know not what to call this, nor will I urge, that it is a secret over-ruling Decree that hurries us on to be the Instruments of our own Destruction, even tho' it be before us, and that we rush upon it with our Eyes open" (p. 14). Crusoe here attempts to understand his compulsion by trying to specify its source, but his diction and syntax obscure the point of origin. The phrase "ill Fate" gestures vaguely toward the Satanic springs of sinful behavior in fallen human nature, while "a secret over-ruling Decree" suggests both Providence and predestination. As the adversatives and qualifications pile up in elaborate confusion, we learn only that Crusoe both blames himself for his own errant behavior (and suggests that he can control his compulsions through "Reason" and "composed Judgment") and that this behavior results from a mysterious "Decree" which rules his life. We can only conclude that Crusoe's motivation is beyond his immediate understanding. The operative influence of personal choice remains as ambiguous as the origin of his "ill Fate."[14]

There are at least two reasons for the ambiguity in Crusoe's exposition. The first involves Defoe's own imaginative investment in his character. The official moral voice of the narrative condemns such compulsive behavior while at the same time an unofficial and subversive point of view develops that is fascinated with the transformative power of the unstable self. Defoe, improvising as he invents, becomes increasingly attracted to the creative and destabilizing potential that inheres in his chief character though he cannot logically, or perhaps even consciously, account for this attraction. This divided perspective creates the ambiguity of motive and character. Second, Defoe is intuitively but perhaps to some degree unknowingly exploring the contradictions implicit in his inherited

Puritan view of the self. The retrospective Crusoe suggests that the mind's irrationality is a sign of innate depravity even while he reveals the predicament of a character who is both responsible and not responsible for his actions. One of Defoe's precursors in these matters, John Bunyan, presents the same predicament to his readers at the end of *Grace Abounding* when he paraphrases Paul: "I can do none of those things which God commands me, but my corruptions will thrust in themselves; 'When I would do good, evil is present with me'" ("The Conclusion," par. 6).

Seventeenth-century Puritan theology demanded an introspective analysis of the self in order to control the mental life through the cultivation of reason and the understanding. But introspection led to a confrontation with a jagged, discontinuous interior life full of subconscious compulsions—a threatening other that could not be organized and controlled. In *Grace Abounding,* Bunyan describes the "tumultuous thoughts" of this mysterious inner life as "masterless hellhounds" (par. 174) and emphasizes repeatedly that he can control his compulsions only through the most intense efforts of the will. Even then, control is sporadic. This self which Bunyan describes elsewhere as "full of wickedness and madness" threatens constantly to fragment into a chaos of warring impulses.[15] Yet Bunyan must seek to possess himself rationally and to control his impulses in order to redirect his entire being toward an obliteration of selfhood and an achievement of spiritual unity. And as in *Robinson Crusoe,* throughout Bunyan's autobiography the impulse toward order and the irrational energy of the mind are embodied in conflicting narrative modes. On the one hand Bunyan attempts to render accurately and mimetically his conflictual inner life, while on the other hand he tries to turn his life retrospectively into an extended allegory of the soul's progress toward grace. The constant shifting between conflicting impulses represented in the mimetic mode and the progress inherent in the allegorizing mode counteract and subvert one another. Bunyan's introspective work, like Crusoe's narrative, both embodies and enacts this disjunctive experience of the self. As a result, while the narrative of his island adventures evolves into a series of moral and experiential tests designed to demonstrate the gradual mastery of self and environment, Crusoe takes on more and more of a dimension of psychological ambiguity that will eventually collapse the imposed moral and spiritual frame of the story.

During Crusoe's extended confinement on the island, Defoe attempts to mediate between a superimposed moral framework and the vital, self-assertive impulses of his main character. The mode of accommodation seems simple at first; Crusoe, imprisoned on an island as punishment for his discontent, must learn self-control and must repent and submit passively to God's design. On the most immediate level of critical analysis the island becomes Crusoe's proving ground, and this portion of the narrative presents a series of tests through which Crusoe learns to regulate the physical environment, to construct a stable ego through focusing his will and activity, and to redeem his errant human nature. A pattern of character development is thus imposed through a moralized story line which emphasizes physical, psychological, and spiritual mastery.[16] And the paratactic series of survival projects—the additive "next . . . next . . . next" (pp. 121-23)—demonstrates an evolving self-mastery through an increasingly rational control of energy and will: "So I went to work; and here I must needs observe, that as Reason is the Substance and Original of the Mathematicks, so by stating and squaring every thing by Reason, and by making the most rational Judgement of things, every Man may be in time Master of every mechanick Art" (p. 68). In the accretive pattern of moral and spiritual development, practical reason emerges as an acquired character trait through a series of situations that force Crusoe to overcome his initial brutish state just as faith is acquired gradually through a series of spiritual experiences—Crusoe's dreams and meditations.

Still, an ambivalent presentation and interpretation of both the island experience and Crusoe himself emerge during these early days of isolation. Some time after plundering the ship, Crusoe draws up an "Accompt" of his situation and finds a credit side to counterbalance the physical and psychological debits of complete isolation. The official moral interpretation drawn from this ledger is that a providentially run universe provides as much profit as loss: "Upon the whole, here was an undoubted Testimony, that there was scarce any Condition in the World so miserable, but there was something *Negative* or something *Positive* to be thankful for in it; and let this stand as a Direction from the Experience of the most miserable of all Conditions in this World, that we may always find in it something to comfort our selves from, and to set in the Description of Good and Evil, on the Credit Side of the Accompt" (p. 67). The basic epistemological premise of Crusoe's story is that we learn good only through knowledge of evil, and that our experience must be correctly interpreted in order to derive from it a fundamental knowledge of our spiritual conditions. Thus, even an apparently negative or evil condition can reveal a spiritually positive meaning, if the situation is correctly interpreted. But, since the list projects both a discontented side and a pious side to Crusoe's personality, the ledger also suggests that interpretations are relative to, and controlled by, a flux of moods. It is precisely this built-in doubleness, or duplicity, in interpretation that generates much of the ambiguity of the text as a whole, especially as it informs the conflict between the mimetic and allegorical narrative modes.[17]

The doubleness extends into the presentation and gradual fragmentation of Crusoe's journal as well. The impetus to write a journal is the same as that for drawing up the ledger: "I now began to consider seriously my Condition, and the Circumstance I was reduc'd to, and I drew up the State of my Affairs in Writing, not so much to leave them to any that were to come after me, for I was like to have but few Heirs, as to deliver my Thoughts from daily poring upon them, and afflicting my Mind; and as my Reason began now to master my Despondency, I began to comfort my self as well as I could" (p. 65). The traditional Puritan journal offers a projection of the self into a syntactic order that should ideally produce an orderly and typological interpretation of experience.[18] Writing becomes an attempt at mental therapy for the Puritans, a way of asserting an allegorical pattern and coherence over the apparent chaos and opacity of discontinuous experiences. Crusoe's journal serves as a secular analogue to the spiritually oriented Puritan diary in that Crusoe uses his journal to search out and meditate on a pattern of causality in his experiences. The journal thus provides a means to an increased understanding and control of the self.

But the journal also reveals mimetically the other, unofficial Crusoe. He describes his despondency over his dismal condition, he refers to his island as a "horrid Place" (p. 86), he iterates his fears of being devoured by wild beasts and cannibals and of "being swallow'd up alive" in an earthquake (p. 82). He also notes on several occasions his confused thoughts and his inability, because of his mental agitation, to pray or meditate. Curiously, religion exists in the journal only in its absence; it is the thing which is not. In the journal as written by the younger Crusoe, no explicit references are made to a spiritual condition or to repentance.[19] It is the retrospective narrator who inserts the longer and more meditative passages in order to edit previous experience into a story of repentance. In fact, the journal disappears entirely from the text as the narrator relives his repentance, thus suggesting that the pattern of spiritual development is, in part at least, an imposition on, and an interpretation of, the experiences of the younger Crusoe.

So, like the debit-credit sheet, the journal functions as a narrative accretion which intensifies the division in Crusoe's character. The journal displays an evolving pattern of mastery over the environment, but set against this pattern is the view it offers of a terrified, anxious, and paranoid Crusoe, the victim of a fear-haunted imagination, who builds enclosures around himself. In fact, all through the narrative fear of hostile others has possessed Crusoe. The antagonists have been external and internal: his father, nature, God, Providence, beasts, cannibals, his own conscience, his own imagination. Crusoe's basic desire is to avoid being swallowed—by the sea, the earth, cannibals, madness. There may even

be a suggestion buried within the text that Providence itself seeks to devour the vital and energetic Crusoe by forcing the repression of those compulsions which also constitute a drive toward freedom from restriction.[20] In the journal, then, the mimetically represented Crusoe is the Hobbesian natural man, motivated by fear and by an obsessive need for complete security. So it is that the retrospective narrator becomes an editor who must add material to past events and descriptions, or imaginatively reconstruct them, in order to coerce these passages into a spiritual and rational progress, and who tries to contain the voice of anxiety and discontent through the interpolation of moral platitudes and spiritual reflections.

What the journal suggests is that Crusoe fears the formless, vital self just as he is fascinated by it, and that the moralizing voice wants to control and contain this negative otherness but cannot. So Defoe continues to move his narrative in two directions at once. On the one hand, he overlays his mimetic account of character with a spiritualized narrative that represents an allegiance to prior allegorical and autobiographical patterns of writing. On the other hand, he continues to generate a mimetic presentation of compulsive behavior and conflict. The result is an almost constant tension between the paratactically placed paragraphs and scenes because the platitudinizing and moralizing voice of the older Crusoe never effectively controls the voice of compulsive bitterness and discontent. As a result, the text of the island adventures manifests a rudimentary design—the gradual evolution of self-mastery and spiritual knowledge—and at the same time the randomness and flux of Crusoe's moods, which can shift radically from scene to scene, paragraph to paragraph, even sentence to sentence.

But once Defoe gets his main character onto the island, he begins to evolve as well a more metaphorically expressive pattern of characterization. The island itself becomes a kind of emblem, a means of imaginatively projecting Crusoe's divided nature into an isolated and delimited environment and thus of conferring an overall sense of unity on the text of the island adventures. On one level of narrative presentation, the island is a project of reason and religion as the retrospective narrator charts a development toward mastery and faith. Crusoe's inventive projects result in the creation of an ordered environment and allow Crusoe himself to indulge in "a secret Kind of Pleasure" and in fantasies of kingship (p. 100). The terms he uses—"Country-House" and "Sea-Coast-House" for example (p. 102)—measure his pride in his ability to project his self-assertive nature onto a landscape—in other words, to organize and control rationally his impulses and to mix his labor with the land so that, in a Lockean sense, it becomes his property.[21] Imaginative energy transforms the island, and the island is inextricably linked with a need for order and stability.

On another level, then, the island is a project of the imagination, but here there is no personal change or growth. Rather, as the island is appropriated to the serial projection of character, Defoe explores a view of the self as trapped within a divided and conflictive nature—a self that in its most fundamental features cannot be changed. Here, the island serves as the measure of Crusoe's moods. Set against the descriptions indicating pride in invention, accomplishment, and ownership are passages that measure Crusoe's moments of deepest despair. Crusoe initially terms the island "this dismal unfortunate Island, which I call'd *the Island of Despair*" (p. 70). In "this dreadful Place," where he is "out of the Reach of humane Kind, out of all Hope of Relief, or Prospect of Redemption" (p. 89), Crusoe offers "a melancholy Relation of a Scene of silent life" (p. 63). Again, the interpretations of experience and the valuation of the island are subject to a radical alternation of mood and event, and so the process of characterization moves out of the ledger and journal and into the environment itself.

As the island becomes a measure of mood and a projection of personality, it, like Crusoe, resists reduction to a single meaning. Rather, the metaphoric transformations of the island serve as projections of the deeper pattern of conflict within the main character. As such, there is no necessary development of character, if development implies directional change; but rather, the island experience serves as a catalyst that transforms and deepens the essential conflict in Crusoe from a dialectic of conscience and compulsion into an opposition between imprisonment and desire.

Crusoe recognizes that the island represents both physical imprisonment and spiritual deliverance from an evil life. This pious Crusoe accepts his situation, rejoices in his spiritual deliverance on the island, submits to Providence, and comes almost to thank God for casting him into this prison. But the unofficial Crusoe can never accept comfortably such restrictions. The island, as Crusoe points out, is a prison, but it is a prison of the self, an extension of Crusoe's demoralization: "Before, as I walk'd about, either on my Hunting, or for viewing the Country, the Anguish of my soul at my Condition, would break out upon me on a sudden, and my very Heart would die within me, to think of the Woods, the Mountains, the Desarts I was in; and how I was a Prisoner lock'd up with the Eternal Bars and Bolts of the Ocean, in an uninhabited Wilderness, without Redemption: In the midst of the greatest Composures of my Mind, this would break out upon me like a Storm, and make me wring my Hands and weep like a Child" (p. 113).

Like a host of Puritan writers before him, Crusoe defines himself as a spiritual pilgrim, discontented with the wilderness of this world, imprisoned in the "Desarts" of his soul. But if the island is a place of punishment, purgation, and spiritual deliverance, in passages such as this it comes also to suggest the limitations imposed on the self by a religious and ethical determinism. The soul's anguish, the dying heart, the struggle against "Eternal Bars and Bolts," the passion that disrupts composure—all indicate an energetic, compulsive, desiring Crusoe emerging from beneath the religious and moral surface of the text. It is in such passages that Crusoe's narrative generates deeper resonances—a structure of subversive implications—that Defoe himself could not have been entirely aware of. Yet at the same time, this structure gives the narrative a more complex dimension beyond the simple adventure story, the economic parable, or the spiritual autobiography even as it depends upon these various discourses. What the text implies on this subversive level is that perhaps Crusoe's activities on the island may not necessarily illustrate an economic theory of labor and utility, nor may they be the result of a rational and religious development of the main character, nor may they show an absolute compatibility of secular aims to spiritual ends. Rather, both rationalized and imaginative activity can be seen as a channel for repressed drives and impulses, and as a means of compensatory escape from a debilitating awareness of physical confinement, a psychological constriction within the demands of an internalized and authoritarian conscience, and a spiritual confinement within a deterministic theology. Again, these are not Defoe's conscious formulations; the official text is intended to illustrate a cohesion of secular activity and moral aim, and it has often been so interpreted. But a deep fissure opens up between imaginative projection and moral intention in the narrative, and the island itself, in becoming a product of the transforming energy of Crusoe's imagination, embodies in its various projections different sides of this fissure.[22]

Crusoe's imagination assumes a parallel dialectical function in the narrative. On one side of this dialectic, the imagination is used to support the retrospective narrator's epistemological and moral premises. The narrator notes that pious reflections often quieted his mind while he was on the island so that he could acquiesce "in the Dispositions of Providence" (p. 108). Such passages reinforce the epistemological premise that knowledge comes to us through the "Contraries" of our experience (p. 139). Further, through an imaginative re-creation of his experience, Crusoe can, like the Puritan autobiographer, improve his knowledge of God's ways with the human race. This process begins when Crusoe reviews his life through imaginative recollections and thereby defines his spiritual state as a particular manifestation of God's general covenant with humanity (pp. 128-32). It is precisely in this sense that Crusoe's book becomes, in retrospect, his allegorized re-creation of himself as a *"Memento,"* an emblem of the spiritual pilgrim found as well in the pages of Bunyan and Thomas Shepard.

But if the imagination is a source of invented order, it is also the source of Crusoe's irrational compulsions and of a desire to escape limitations—whether those limitations take the form of the middle station in life, captivity at Sallee, a Brazilian plantation, or a providentially imposed imprisonment on a desert island. In each case, Crusoe imagines himself free, desires that freedom, and plans to set himself free. As the narrative proceeds, Crusoe gradually gathers together discontent, a desire to escape confinement, obsessive mental behavior, and the active influence of the imagination. These traits are set in opposition to those qualities and ideas traditionally said in the seventeenth and early eighteenth centuries to organize the formless energy of the imagination: reason, a sense of moral values, acquiescence to a Providence which seeks to confine desire. In Defoe's text, the serialized accretion of opposed traits occurs in situations, episodes, and actions that then become the means whereby compulsions and conflicts play themselves out. Thus, the limitations imposed on Crusoe by his situation on the island serve to intensify the conflict and to reveal the main character as the victim of the powerfully disruptive force of his imagination.

Crusoe, then, sometimes channels but never completely controls the imagination. So at times this overpowering force can threaten the established order of both island and identity. When Crusoe discovers the footprint, for example, his imagination turns on him and threatens to devour the rational man of faith he thinks he has become. Crusoe describes his immediate reaction to the discovery: "But after innumerable fluttering Thoughts, like a Man perfectly confus'd and out of my self, I came Home to my fortification, not feeling, as we say, the Ground I went on, but terrify'd to the last Degree, looking behind me at every two or three Steps, mistaking every Bush and Tree, and fancying every Stump at a Distance to be a Man; nor is it possible to describe how many various Shapes affrighted Imagination represented Things to me in, how many wild Ideas were found every Moment in my Fancy, and what strange unaccountable Whimsies came into my Thoughts by the Way" (p. 154). Crusoe again loses his self-control and seeks concealment and enclosure. As he does, his imagination—here both the image-making faculty and an uncontrollable and mysterious force—increases his terror by projecting fearsome others into the landscape. As Hobbes had noted, "Without Steddinesse, and Direction to some End, a great Fancy is one kind of madnesse."[23] Reason is occluded as Crusoe becomes again the Hobbesian natural man that he was during his first hours on the island. . . .

Crusoe manages once again to reason himself into a precarious stability and decides that Providence, not obsession, should direct his activity. Yet Providence itself, from this point on in the text, becomes absorbed into the internal functions of the desiring imagination.

In other words, the guiding voice of Providence becomes inseparable from what Crusoe describes as the "secret moving Springs in the Affections, which when they are set a going by some Object in view, or be it some Object, though not in view, yet rendred present to the Mind by the Power of the Imagination, that Motion carries out the Soul by its Impetuosity to such violent eager embracings of the Object, that the Absence of it is insupportable" (p. 188). Crusoe here presents an analysis of the will as it is subject to "the Power of the Imagination." Earlier in the narrative, Crusoe had decided "That whenever I found those secret Hints, or pressings of my Mind, to doing, or not doing any Thing that presented; or to going this Way, or that Way, I never fail'd to obey the secret Dictate" (p. 175). He interprets these promptings as the voice of Providence directing him toward the proper course of action.

Officially, then, Crusoe's narrative demonstrates the internalization of Providence; Crusoe's acquisition of faith issues in an ability to interpret correctly his mental life for signs of providential direction. And certainly, in Defoe's time, the alignment of providential direction and internal impulse was widely accepted. But "secret Hints" seems suspiciously close in phrasing and meaning to the "secret Wishes" that arise from the desiring imagination and that have been opposed by Providence throughout Crusoe's adventures. Further, Defoe's narrative procedure, in which providential hints arise from Crusoe's deepest obsessions and desires, tends to subvert the official interpretation. The discontinuous, accretive mode of character presentation allows the desiring imagination to disrupt the telic pattern which Crusoe's autobiography is meant to enact. So, as it was impossible to discover the origin of Crusoe's compulsion to ramble, it finally becomes difficult, if not impossible, to distinguish between providential direction and the subrational compulsions of a disturbed mind.

Consider in this light what happens when a second ship runs aground near the island. Because of a "Desire after the Society of my Fellow-Creatures," Crusoe becomes obsessed with the desire to visit the wreck. Such is the strength of his desire that "my Hands would clinch together, and my Fingers press the Palms of my Hands, that if I had any soft Thing in my Hand, it wou'd have crusht it involuntarily; and my Teeth in my Head wou'd strike together, and set against one another so strong, that for some time I cou'd not part them again" (p. 188). Crusoe presents himself as a man possessed; his physical reactions are involuntary and uncontrollable. Three paragraphs later, Crusoe decides to visit the wreck: "I thought the Impression was so strong upon my Mind, that it could not be resisted, that it must come from some invisible Direction, and that I should be wanting to my self if I did not go" (p. 189). The reader is meant to respond to such strong impressions as evidence of providential direction because Crusoe has explicitly and officially charted his development as a man of faith who can interpret correctly both external and internal, or mental, events. But in this particular narrative sequence, the notion that the obsession is evidence of the internalization of Providence provides merely a convenient interpretation for what remains a mysterious mental phenomenon. The interpretation itself remains separate from the actual experience, ambiguously hovering over it as a possible explanation but not as a constitutive feature. In fact, the confident internalization of Providence is brought into question by the very nature of the obsession—that is, the uncontrollable desire to find release from a providentially imposed solitude. The conclusion of the episode bears out the spiritual emptiness of the official interpretation, for Crusoe finds the ship to be "a dismal Sight to look at" (p. 191). It contains, besides two corpses, some goods of only marginal value. The entire adventure leaves Crusoe for the next two years "miserable" and with a mind full of decidedly unprovidential designs for escape (p. 194).

If Providence is subsumed by Crusoe's imagination, then what the retrospective narrator unintentionally reveals through the final adventures and the denouement of the story is the collapse of the extended metaphor of spiritual progress. I have argued that the basic conflict in *Crusoe* occurs between a vital, energetic, and imaginative self and the imposed religious framework, a conflict enacted in the discontinuous parataxis of Defoe's narrative technique and in the conflicting modes of mimetic and allegorizing discourse. If Defoe intuitively and imaginatively invests himself in his main character, then he also tries through the retrospective narrator to improvise a moral and theological framework to contain this vital character. The result of these two disjunctive impulses is the eventual collapse of the framework through a merging of theological explanation and psychological compulsion. The ideal conjunction of tenor and vehicle—of religious meaning and personal experience—sought by the retrospective narrator never convincingly takes place because, in a manner of speaking, the tenor of spiritual meaning is absorbed completely by the vehicle of presentation.

The rescue of Friday, for example, officially illustrates, on the dogmatic level of religious meaning, the cohesion of rational activity, self-control, and moral aim. By waiting patiently for signs and hints from Providence, Crusoe is able to align his will with God's determinations. He becomes the instrument of Providence in rescuing Friday, then the Spaniard and Friday's father, and in retaking the English ship from the mutineers. Also, Crusoe converts Friday to Christianity, and Friday's ingenuous questions force Crusoe to examine his own faith more closely. As proof of Crusoe's continuing religious development, Defoe has him explain the designs of Providence to the English cap-

tain, and a connection is forged between spiritual knowledge and Crusoe's "natural" mastery of the situation. Throughout these final scenes on the island, then, Crusoe makes explicit connections among belief, knowledge, mastery, effort, and success.

But Crusoe's character remains much the same in its desires and compulsions. The words "escape" and "deliverance" recur constantly throughout this latter part of the narrative, and the advent of Friday and the English ship allows Crusoe to indulge again in his impulse to escape imposed limitations. Now, however, Providence aids him by appearing to realign itself with those same inclinations which resulted initially in his self-styled original sin, fall, and exile.

First, Crusoe is rewarded. He is allowed to return to society, and in keeping with the Biblical parallels he has on occasion drawn, he compares "the latter End of *Job*" with his almost miraculous acquisition of wealth (p. 284). Crusoe is anxious to suggest a typological pattern and to show that his reward is a result of his penance on the island, his achievement of grace, and his realization of the need for internalized rational and ethical constraints.

But there is a second conclusion to Crusoe's narrative. Though Crusoe may continue to mouth pious sentiments and moral reflections, at the end of his story he quits the middle station of life on a whim and once again sets off on his travels. Thus, he is not only rewarded with wealth and a social position, but he is also granted his complete freedom from providential interference and from the allegorizing pattern which he sought to impose on his earlier adventures. Both G. A. Starr and J. Paul Hunter have argued that Crusoe's earlier sinful independence results in his imprisonment on the island, while his virtuous dependence on God results in his mastery of both self and environment and in his eventual deliverance from his island prison. But there now seems to be another unspoken, even subversive agreement between God and Crusoe; if Crusoe acknowledges his sins, repents, and does penance, then he will be allowed complete independence from the providential system of limitations and interpretations. There may even be a further implication—that Crusoe's initially sinful impulse to ramble is finally approved by God. Nonetheless, the didactic message planted by the retrospective narrator is rooted out, finally, by the imaginative energy of the character. In Defoe's ambiguous creation, Crusoe is rewarded just as much for his conformity and submission as for his active self-assertion and alleged rebellious impulses.

At the conclusion of the first volume of Crusoe's adventures, Defoe is not suggesting that rebellion against God is the surest guarantee of worldly success and salvation. Crusoe has acquired both reason and faith and no longer perceives himself as a "Rebel" against the middle station or against God. Rather, his character has been developed through the retrospective patterning of the autobiographical narrative to reveal a Puritan mediation between the demands of the world and the demands of God. But this mediation shares the ambiguity, the conditional quality, that characterizes the relationships between experiential and spiritualized interpretation as presented in Puritan personal literature. . . .

Defoe's text, in its historical and theological tradition, shares this same ambiguity of interpretation in relation to experience. Throughout the narrative, Defoe has used the voice of the retrospective narrator to improvise a loose series of mediations between the experiential self and a tenor of spiritual meaning. But the result of this improvised process is the collapse of the narrator's didactic intentions. The text ends in a Calvinist fantasy, an imaginative wish-fulfillment dream, in which the central character—still both compulsive and assertive—is rewarded and in which the moral lines drawn between the compulsively sinful and ideal selves are erased. As in Bunyan's autobiography, interpretation is suspended in the conditional; it is "as if" the ideal self were rewarded for its pious and diligent labor in this world on the one hand, while on the other all the possibilities of mediating between the two selves have apparently been exhausted. The providentially based interpretation of Crusoe's life therefore remains just that—an interpretation which attempts to account for all the facts so that the narrator's life makes sense, but which finally fails to account for the troubling paradoxes and contradictions of the text as it presents its account of life in this problematic secular world.

So the ambiguity in *Crusoe* results in part from Defoe's immethodical, paratactic method and in part from his inherited dissenting tradition. *Crusoe* is a work that lacks the teleological interaction between character development and sequences of causally linked events which comes to define the achievement of novelists later in the eighteenth century, just as it lacks the consistent telic pattern that Puritans in the previous century had sought to impose on their own lives. And because of its transitional status as a narrative improvisation on older themes set in a newly commercialized world, *Crusoe*'s status as a novel may remain marginal. Defoe's text lacks the consistency of authorial control and intention that manifests itself in the mid-century works of Richardson and Fielding. Yet the innovative importance of Defoe's first extended fiction in the history of the novel may be said to consist in his intuitive, psychological perception of character in its imaginative and linguistic projection. If Defoe fails to write a thematically and structurally consistent narrative, then he still introduces psychological and interpretive complexity into his fiction. For this reason, then, questions may always remain as to whether *Crusoe,* because of its imaginative vitality, can be dis-

cussed as a novel or as an early prototype manifesting a novelistic potential for the dialectical presentation of a divided identity. But for this reason, too, *Crusoe* will remain a complex and tantalizing work, inviting as well as frustrating interpretive efforts to provide a consistent pattern of meaning for Defoe's improvisations and imaginative inventions.

Notes

. . .[12] Angus Fletcher, *Allegory: The Theory of a Symbolic Mode* (Ithaca: Cornell Univ. Press, 1964), pp. 286-87.

[13] The Puritan automachia, or self-civil-war, is discussed in some detail by Sacvan Bercovitch, *The Puritan Origins of the American Self* (New Haven: Yale Univ. Press, 1979), pp. 19-25. A seventeenth-century discussion can be found in Richard Sibbes, *The Soules Conflict with Itselfe* (London, 1635). The sustained automachia in autobiographical writing is perhaps most powerfully exemplified in the spiritual autobiography of John Bunyan and the journal of Thomas Shepard. See *God's Plot: The Paradoxes of Puritan Piety. Being the Autobiography and Journal of Thomas Shepard,* ed. Michael McGiffert (Amherst: Univ. of Massachusetts Press, 1972).

[14] Leopold Damrosch, Jr., quotes this passage in his *God's Plot and Man's Stories: Studies in the Fictional Imagination from Milton to Fielding* (Chicago: Univ. of Chicago Press, 1985), pp. 199-200. He finds the passage complicated but unambiguous: "Crusoe uses Calvinist language here to suggest that he cannot be morally responsible for actions in which he is moved about like a chess piece" (p. 200). Where Damrosch finds predestination, I see Crusoe trying to understand to what extent he can control his own will in order to affect the outcome of events.

[15] John Bunyan, *"The Doctrine of the Law and Grace Unfolded" and "I Will Pray with the Spirit,"* ed. Richard L. Greaves (Oxford: Clarendon Press, 1976), p. 184.

[16] This pattern is succinctly summarized by G. A. Starr in "Defoe's Prose Style: 1. The Language of Interpretation," *MP,* 71 (1974), 292.

[17] Here I have followed and extended an argument made by Brown, p. 584.

[18] Spacks, among others, assumes that the spiritual autobiography stabilizes—and therefore renders safe—identity (p. 28). Spiritual autobiographies, however, quite often reveal the chaos of subrational compulsions that destabilizes identity and that creates an unbearable anxiety over the state of one's immortal soul. Bunyan's *Grace Abounding* would offer a case in point.

[19] Reiss has also noted that the retrospective narrator adds the religious material to the journal. He analyzes several passages to demonstrate that the retrospective Crusoe is in effect rewriting his story (p. 323). The idea that Crusoe's journal offers superimposed interpretations rather than facts may help to explain the contradictions between the original events and their journalistic redaction that some critics find so troubling.

[20] See Frank H. Ellis's discussion of the recurring imagery of eating and being eaten in his introduction to *Twentieth Century Interpretations of "Robinson Crusoe"* (Englewood Cliffs, N.J.: Prentice-Hall, 1969), pp. 12-13.

[21] See John Locke, *Two Treatises of Government,* ed. Peter Laslett (Cambridge: Cambridge Univ. Press, 1960). In Chapter 5, "Of Property," of *The Second Treatise* (pp. 327-44), Locke argues that when an individual improves and cultivates land and uses its produce then that land becomes the individual's property by right.

[22] In his *Serious Reflections,* Crusoe describes part of his mental experience on the island as the result of a "brain-sick fancy, the vapourish hypochondriac imagination," and equates the function of the imagination with a disease of the mind (Defoe, *Romances and Narratives,* III, 247). The official moral voice condemns the excesses of the imagination in representing to the mind apparitions and spirits, but the passage suggests as well Defoe's dualistic view of the imagination as a force for order and a force for chaos. Defoe may therefore be aware of this deep fissure in the experience and mental life of his main character.

[23] Thomas Hobbes, *Leviathan,* ed. C. B. MacPherson (Harmondsworth: Penguin Books, 1968), p. 136.

Homer Obed Brown (essay date 1997)

SOURCE: "The Displaced Self in the Novels of Daniel Defoe," in *Institutions of the English Novel: From Defoe to Scott,* University of Pennsylvania Press, 1997, pp. 54-60.

[*In the following excerpt, Brown explores the need of Defoe's characters for isolation, concealment, and guarded exposure as defenses against threats of "menacing otherness."*]

> . . . In my youth, I wandered away, too far from your sustaining hand, and created of myself a barren waste.
>
> —Augustine, *Confessions*

Defoe's novels are based on a notion of radical egocentricity. Robinson wonders why his isolation on the island was "any grievance or affliction" since "it seems to me that life in general is, or ought to be, but one universal act of solitude":

> The world, I say, is nothing to us as it is more or less to our relish. All reflection is carried home, and our dear self is, in one respect, the end of living. Hence man may be properly said to be alone in the midst of the crowds and hurry of men and business. All the reflections which he makes are to himself; all that is pleasant he embraces for himself; all that is irksome and grievous is tasted but by his own palate.

> What are the sorrows of other men to us, and what their joy? Something we may be touched indeed with by the power of sympathy, and a secret turn of the affections; but all the solid reflection is directed to ourselves. Our meditations are all solitude in perfection; our passions are all exercised in retirement; we love, we hate, we covet, we enjoy, all in privacy and solitude. All that we communicate of those things to any other is but for their assistance in the pursuit of our desires; the end is at home; the enjoyment, the contemplation, is all solitude and retirement; it is for ourselves we enjoy, and for ourselves we suffer. (*Serious Reflections,* 2-3)

Robinson's thirty years of solitude on a desert island is the metaphor of this selfishness. In fact, his story is based on the etymological metaphor "islanded"—isolated. When Robinson was in Brazil, he "used to say, I lived just like a man cast away upon some desolate island that has nobody there but himself" (VII, 39). The whole book has to do with the progressive materialization of spiritual metaphor for what is implicit in Robinson's condition from the beginning, in the same way that the book itself is a factualization of the metaphors of the whole tradition of spiritual autobiographies.[3]

Selfish, isolated, but is he really alone? Other Defoe narrators are just as solitary in the midst of society. Robinson's island isolation is after all only a metaphor for the solitary selfishness of all men. This seemingly impenetrable selfishness, however, is a Hobbesian "state of nature," transposed into a social world, atomistic, volatile, where the mere existence of another person, for Robinson even the *possibility* of the existence of another person, is a threat to the self. Even Robinson in his wilderness, through all those years of never encountering another human being, is constantly haunted by a sense of menacing otherness. He must always be on guard. He never loses the agonizing sense of being watched. Far from only being a representation of Robinson's egocentric isolation, the book is peopled by signs of the constant presence of the other—Robinson's fear, the footprint of a man, the Hand of God, the constant presence of the older Robinson in the double perspective of the narration, the presence of the spectator-reader before whom Robinson rehearses his solitude. In a sense, no Defoe character, not even Robinson, is ever alone.

The need for secrecy at the moment of narration for most of Defoe's "autobiographers" is no mystery. With the exception of Robinson and H. F., they have committed crimes for which they can be called to justice. Near the beginnings of their stories, however, they also are all bereft of family and protection and are thrown into a harsh and dangerous world of deceptive appearances, whose inhabitants are indifferent, conniving, and menacing. Some, like Robinson or H. F., orphan themselves seemingly by choice. Others, like Colonel Jack and Bob Singleton, are virtually cut off from their origins, and so from their true names. Roxana, even as a young girl, long before she is deserted by her husband and left to protect herself and her family, is removed from France and her childhood, bringing with her nothing "but the Language." The separation from any guardian structure is sharp. Their isolation is complete.

No wonder, then, that Defoe has been said to have discounted the importance of personal relationship in his novels.[4] There is no richly complex conflict between wills more or less equal in strength in his fictional world. The Defoe character has to struggle against all the others, against a harsh necessity.[5] There is no sense of an individualized other consciousness confronting the protagonist as there is in the worlds of Richardson, Austen, or George Eliot. The paradigm is Moll in a crowded London street; her survival depends on her ability to take "the advantages of other people's mistakes" while remaining unseen herself. The value of her story for the reader will be in its warning "to Guard against the like Surprizes, and to have their Eyes about them when they have to do with Strangers of any kind, for 'tis very seldom that some Snare or other is not in their way" (II, 92). Otherness for a Defoe character is generic, anonymous. Individual antagonists like Roxana's landlord or even her Amy, Moll's various men, Robinson's Moorish captor, or Friday can be tricked or subordinated without much apparent difficulty, but a single, anonymous footprint in the sand seizes Crusoe's mind with uncontrollable terror. However easily any Defoe "I" can deal with any individual menace, the unnamed dread remains. Perhaps the most striking example is the London of the plague. The "others" of the *Journal* are anonymous numbers of dead and dying. Any conversation, even the slightest human contact, carries the risk of death.

When Robinson finds himself shipwrecked, almost his first act is to begin to build a wall around himself. He further insulates himself; he creates an island within the island. His action is obsessive. He spends almost three and a half months building the wall—"I thought I should never be perfectly secure 'till this Wall was finish'd" (VII, 87). Although he longs for deliverance from his solitude, he is compelled to hide his presence so "that if any People were to come on Shore there, they would not perceive any Thing like a Habitation" (VII, 87). So in the midst of a threatening and unknown space, Robinson creates for himself an ordered interior, crowded with things that can be listed and enumerated to his satisfaction. He "furnishes" himself "with many things." Like the fallen angels, Robinson sets about to build and secure his own Pandemonium, following the advice of Mammon to "seek / Our own good from ourselves, and from our own / Live to ourselves, though in this vast recess, / Free, and to none accountable" (*Paradise Lost* II, 252-55). But, of course, their self-reliance is a sham, and their Pandemonium is a parody of Heaven, founded upon denial of the divine Other, whose power they can never escape. Like the angels, Robinson's concern with things is a symptom of his fall.

Moll Flanders in disguise in the middle of a crowded London Street, H. F. in his "safe" house surrounded by the plague, Robinson in his fort—the image is a recurrent one. Earlier in Robinson's account, in Brazil he carves out a plantation "among Strangers and Savages in a Wilderness, and at such a Distance, as never to hear from any Part of the World that had the least Knowledge of me" (VII, 30). Still earlier, there is Robinson quavering in the hold of the ship that takes him from home, surrounded by a raging sea.

At the beginning of the book Robinson's father points out to him that his "was the middle State, or what might be called the upper Station of *Low Life, . . .* that this was the State of Life which all other People envied" because

> the middle Station had the fewest Disasters, and was not expos'd to so many Vicissitudes as the higher or lower Part of Mankind . . . that this Way Men went silently and smoothly thro' the World, and comfortably out of it, not embarrass'd with the Labours of the Hands or of the Head, not sold to the Life of Slavery for daily Bread, or harasst with perplx'd Circumstances, which rob the Soul of Peace and the Body of Rest; not enrag'd with the Passion of Envy, or secret burning Lust of Ambition for great things; but in easy Circumstances sliding gently thro' the World, and sensibly tasting the Sweets of living, without the bitter, feeling that they are happy, and learning by every Day's Experience to know it more sensibly. (VII, 2-4)

At the outset, then, Robinson already possesses the kind of security, freedom from exposure, that most other Defoe narrators and later even Robinson himself long for. What is given to Robinson is suddenly taken from other Defoe protagonists by circumstances over which they have no control. Moll Flanders and even H. F. must expose themselves to danger in order to survive. Why does Robinson give up so easily what the others have to struggle so hard to gain? In a sense, this is the question implicit in the beginning of this essay: expressing so strong a desire for concealment, why do they offer their confessions at all? This is as difficult a question as asking why Defoe wrote novels. The desire for concealment could have been easily satisfied by silence, by writing or publishing no books at all.[6] The obvious answer to so manifestly impossible a question—that Defoe wrote books to make money, that is to say, like Moll or H. F., to survive—is less satisfactory than it might at first appear. There were other ways to make money, many of which Defoe tried. Much of the other writing Defoe did involved the need for secrecy or masking.

Defoe's narrators seem obsessed with concealing themselves, but the impulse leading them toward exposure appears equally strong. Complete concealment is impossible, perhaps not even desirable. On the one hand there is the insistence on building a faceless shelter around the self, but on the other a recurring compulsion to move out into the open. This double compulsion can be expressed as a double fear. When an earthquake makes him fear the security of his cave, Robinson writes that "the fear of being swallow'd up alive, made me that I never slept in quiet, and yet the Apprehensions of lying abroad without any Fence was almost equal to it" (VII, 94). These two fears, however—fear of being swallowed up by the earth, fear of lying in the open—are the same at bottom. Why does Robinson fear sleeping without the protection of a wall? He is afraid of ravenous beasts and cannibals. If one is caught abroad with one's guard down, unconscious (sleeping), one risks loss of self. But the dangers are as great, apparently, if one never ventures out. Both fears are basically fears of engulfment: one, the fear of being lost in the recesses of one's own nature (the earth), of solipsism and anonymity; alternately, fear of being captured, "eaten" by the other. Perhaps behind both, Defoe's fear of imprisonment.[7] Fear of forms, equally strong fears of the formless. The fear of being devoured recurs throughout Robinson's narrative. At the beginning, he is afraid of being swallowed alive by the sea. Near the end, he defends himself against the devouring wolves.[8]

Besides fear or biological need, there are other reasons apparently for venturing abroad. Curiosity forces H. F. constantly to risk infection. Moll learns that the others betray moments of unconsciousness from which she can profit: "a Thief being a Creature that Watches the Advantages of other Peoples mistakes" (II, 92). Why does Robinson surrender his initial security? The reasons are intentionally vague to point to the fact that his motivation is beyond his understanding and ambiguously beyond personal choice, for the reasons are generic and at the same time subject to his accountability. His motivation or lack of justifiable motivation,

involving disobedience of the father, is a restlessness of spirit which is simultaneously culpability and its own punishment. He describes the sources of his "meer wandering Inclination" as "something fatal," a "Propension of Nature," symptoms of what he shares with general man, the heritage of the fall. "Design'd" by his father "for the Law," he "would be satisfied with nothing but going to Sea," great symbol of the unformed. The opposition could not be more clear. What is most threatening is also most alluring. Throughout his life, even after his conversion, Robinson will feel the compulsion to leave behind the preformed, the already-given world of law, and face the unknown and undifferentiated, full of menace for the self and simultaneously full of promise. Unable to accept the given definition of himself, the will and legacy of his father, the world of law, Robinson experiences himself as incomplete and searches mistakenly for completion in the world outside. He does not possess himself but is scattered among a world of things. He must externalize himself in the world. He must create a self out of the formless sea of pure possibility, out of the surrounding, anonymous wilderness. The world is for him to make something of his own.

Here is the source of his egocentricity. His feeling of loneliness in Brazil at being "at such a Distance as never to hear from any Part of the World that had the least Knowledge of me" suggests that this distance is an alienation from a part of himself held in thrall by the world outside. This alienation, his longing for companionship through his years of isolation on the "Island of Despair," and his fear of the other all testify to his continuing sense of incompleteness, but also reveal the lie behind the way he has sought fulfillment.

Fear of the other, determining need for concealment; necessity, allurement of the world offering some form of completion to the self, determining the impulse to risk exposure. These oppositions suggest an explanation of the concealment and exposure, or guarded exposure, of Defoe's narrators that is revealed by the play of names. Hiding behind the disguise of Robinson and his factual-seeming narrative, Defoe is doing what Robinson does—constructing and hiding inside a "natural" fortification that cannot be perceived as a "habitation" from the outside. In a sense, this is as close as we can get to an answer to the problem formulated at the beginning. Pursuit of the mystery might, however, give a fuller sense of the implications of this strategy for the development of the novel. . . .

Notes

. . . [3] See G. A. Starr, *Defoe and Spiritual Autobiography* (Princeton, N.J.: Princeton University Press, 1965) and J. Paul Hunter, *The Reluctant Pilgrim* (Baltimore: The Johns Hopkins University Press, 1966).

[4] Ian Watt, *The Rise of the Novel* (Berkeley: University of California Press, 1959), 133.

[5] At least part of the impulse behind Defoe's fiction is the desire to explore human possibilities in the face of a necessity so harsh as to suspend normal laws. The whole question of natural right has been examined in Maximillian E. Novak's *Defoe and the Nature of Man* (Oxford: Oxford University Press, 1963).

[6] The pressures against Defoe's writing these novels seem multiplied when one remembers that Defoe was violating the Puritan ban against realistic fictions. For a discussion of this problem, see Hunter, *The Reluctant Pilgrim,* 114-24. For other accounts of Defoe's ambivalence about "feign'd Histories," see Maximillian Novak, "Defoe's Theory of Fiction," *SP* 61 (1964): 650-68, and the chapter on Defoe in Alan McKillop, *The Early Masters of English Fiction* (Lawrence: University of Kansas Press, 1956). For a discussion of the background of this problem, see William Nelson, "The Boundaries of Fiction in the Renaissance: A Treaty Between Truth and Falsehood," *ELH* 36 (1969): 30-58.

[7] See James Sutherland, *Defoe* (London, 1950), 91.

[8] Frank H. Ellis has revealed in the introduction to his *Twentieth-Century Interpretations of Robinson Crusoe* (Englewood Cliffs, N.J.: Prentice-Hall, 1969), 12ff., the extent to which Defoe organized this book on the basis of images of devouring. . . .

FURTHER READING

Baker, Ernest A. *The History of the English Novel, Vol. III: The Later Romances and the Establishment of Realism,* 1929. Reprint. New York: Barnes and Noble, Inc., 1950, 278 p.

> Volume in acclaimed series examines Defoe's contribution to the establishment of realism in literature.

Bell, Ian A. "*Robinson Crusoe* and Adventure." In *Defoe's Fiction,* pp. 73-114. London: Croom Helm, 1985.

> Argues that *Robinson Crusoe* wavers back and forth between adventure and prudence.

Benjamin, Edwin B. "Symbolic Elements in *Robinson Crusoe.*" *Philological Quarterly* 30, No. 2 (April 1951): 206-11.

> Argues that details in *Robinson Crusoe* should be interpreted symbolically rather than as literally based on specifics in Defoe's life.

Byrd, Max, editor. *Daniel Defoe: A Collection of Critical Essays.* Englewood Cliffs, NJ: Prentice-Hall, Inc., 1976, 177 p.

> Essays by authors including Virginia Woolf, Ian Watt, George A. Starr and others.

Downey, Alan. "*Robinson Crusoe*'s Eighteenth-Century Contexts." In *Robinson Crusoe: Myths and Metamorphoses,* edited by Lieve Spaas and Brian Stimpson, pp. 13-27. Hampshire: Macmillan Press Ltd, 1996.

> Attempts to look at *Robinson Crusoe* from an eighteenth-century perspective, emphasizing its adventure aspects and its Puritanism.

Grief, Martin J. "The Conversion of Robinson Crusoe." *Studies in English Literature* 6, No. 3 (Summer 1966): 551-74.

> Contends that *Robinson Crusoe* is primarily an allegory describing a man's spiritual experiences.

Halewood, William H. "Religion and Invention in *Robinson Crusoe.*" *Essays in Criticism* XIV, No. 4 (October 1964): 339-51.

> Focuses on the spiritual development of Robinson Crusoe and the religious elements in the novel.

James, E. Anthony. *Daniel Defoe's Many Voices: A Rhetorical Study of Prose Style and Literary Method.* Amsterdam: Rodopi, 1972, 269 p.

> Constructs a brief review of Defoe's literary values and their sources, followed by an examination of those values as seen in a selection of his work.

Maddox, James H., Jr. "Interpreter Crusoe." *ELH,* 51, No. 1 (Spring 1984): 33-52.

> Argues that Crusoe changes dramatically from *Robinson Crusoe* to *The Farther Adventures* reflecting the difference between interpreting his own world and having others attempting to impose their views of the world on him.

McKillop, Alan Dugald. "Daniel Defoe." In *The Early Masters of English Fiction,* pp. 1-46. Lawrence: University of Kansas Press, 1967.

> Outlines the development of Defoe's skills as a novelist, beginning with his early conduct-books and political satire and ending with his novels. The development is then related to the growth of the English novel following Defoe, especially the work of Samuel Richardson and Henry Fielding.

Morrissey, Lee. "*Robinson Crusoe* and South Sea Trade, 1710-1720." In *Money: Lure, Lore, and Literature,* edited by John Louis DiGaetani, pp. 209-15. Westport CT: Greenwood Press, 1994.

> Examines Defoe's arguments for trade in the South Seas.

Novak, Maximillian E. "Imaginary Islands and Real Beasts: The Imaginative Genesis of *Robinson Crusoe.*" In *Realism, Myth, and History in Defoe's Fiction,* pp. 23-46. Lincoln: University of Nebraska Press, 1983.

Traces Defoe's journalism and life experiences as inspiration for *Robinson Crusoe*.

Richetti, John J. *Defoe's Narratives: Situations and Structures.* London: Clarendon Press, 1975, 244 p.

Examines Defoe's major novels, paying particular attention to character and fictional technique.

Sill, George M. *Defoe and the Idea of Fiction, 1713-1719.* Newark: University of Delaware Press, 1983, 190 p.

Studies Defoe's activities of this period, his political pamphlets, and his attempts to ground his ideology in history.

Spacks, Patricia Meyer. "The Soul's Imaginings: Daniel Defoe, William Cowper." In *Imagining a Self: Autobiography and Novel in Eighteenth-Century England,* pp. 28-56. Cambridge: Harvard University Press, 1976.

Argues that Crusoe's use of imagination is crucial to his empowerment.

Suerbaum, Ulrich. "'I Repeat and Repeat.' Repetition as Structure in Defoe's *Robinson Crusoe.*" In *Telling Stories: Studies in Honour of Ulrich Broich on the Occasion of His 60th Birthday,* edited by Elmar Lehmann and Bernd Lenz, pp. 69-83. Amsterdam: B. R. Grüner, 1992.

Contends that *Robinson Crusoe*'s unusual structure of duplication was created because Defoe wanted the common reader to understand his messages.

Watt, Ian. "*Robinson Crusoe* as a Myth." *Essays in Criticism* I, No. 2 (April 1951): 95-119.

Argues that society has turned *Robinson Crusoe* into a myth that does not necessarily reflect Defoe's original intentions.

Delarivier Manley

c. 1670-1724

(Also Delariviere) English novelist, political journalist, and playwright.

INTRODUCTION

Delarivier Manley was England's most popular—as well as most controversial—female novelist of the early eighteenth century. She was also that country's first female political journalist, and her partisan writings had a significant impact on public opinion. A lifelong and passionate Tory, Manley infused her fiction with political interests, but from her death until the late twentieth century, this aspect of her work was largely ignored. Her satirical attacks on leading figures of the Whig party, through the agency of her fiction as well as her political pamphlets, made her a reviled figure in some quarters of English society. Modern commentators have demonstrated that her acerbic portraits of prominent Whigs contain at least a modicum of truth, which made her fiction even more sensational and dangerous when it was first published. Manley was attacked for living openly with lovers and trespassing on the male writers' genre of satire. Throughout most of her adult life she defied the social norms that restricted women's personal freedom and set limits on their writing efforts. Manley was an accomplished author and a self-conscious writer. She reworked and subverted established literary conventions, exploiting the French style of amatory fiction and experimenting with narrative voice. Her novels, a blend of realism and romance, feature authentic details of upper-class life, naturalistic dialogue, and candid explorations of the bases of human desire. The *New Atalantis* (1709-10) represents an important contribution to the eighteenth-century development of allegory as a framing device for satirical fiction, and *The Adventures of Rivella* (1714) vividly depicts the challenges facing women writers of the time. Manley's use of imaginary settings and the epistolary form of fiction had an influence on such writers as Defoe, Swift, and Fielding. Dismissed as the author of erotic novels and disparaged by most critics until fairly recently, Manley and her literary reputation are presently the subjects of renewed interest and reappraisal.

Biographical Information

Much of what is known about Manley's life is derived from the stories of her fictional counterparts: Delia, in the *New Atalantis,* and Rivella, the protagonist of Manley's fictionalized autobiography. Her date of birth has not been determined, but it was likely some time between 1667 and 1672. Her father, Sir Roger Manley, was a member of the minor gentry and an army officer; he was lieutenant-governor of the Island of Jersey at the time of her birth. The author of two military histories, he was a well-educated man and a staunch Royalist. His daughter's lifelong Tory sympathies and upper-class identification were family legacies. Manley anticipated becoming an attendant at court, but her opportunities were ruined, first by her father's death in 1687 and then by the Glorious Revolution of 1688—after which Stuart loyalists such as Manley lost all hope of preferment. She was left in the guardianship of her cousin, John Manley, with whom she contracted a bigamous marriage in 1690. Their son was born in 1691, and their relationship ended three years later; her son is not mentioned in any of her writings, and he may have been raised by his father. After the separation, Manley spent six months as a companion to Barbara Villiers, Duchess of Cleveland, a former mistress of Charles II. When the duchess dismissed her, Manley retired to the west of England, and in 1696 returned to London, where she launched her literary career with two plays and her earliest fictional work, *Letters Written by Mrs. Manley.* She had a brief affair with Sir Thomas Skipworth, a wealthy man who underwrote the production of her first play, and from 1696 through 1702 she was the mistress of John Tilly, a lawyer and governor of the Fleet prison. Her first novel appeared in 1705. When the third one was published in 1709, it was immediately suppressed. Manley was held and questioned by the authorities, who demanded that she reveal the names of informants who were supplying her with information for her satirical portraits of Whig leaders. She denied that she had any sources and insisted that her work was entirely imaginative. After spending a week in jail, she was released, and the case against her was discharged four months later. From 1710—when the Tories gained control of the government—through 1714, Manley's literary efforts were focused on political pamphlets and journals. By 1711 she was writing regularly for the *Examiner,* a Tory periodical. She worked closely with its editor, Jonathan Swift, and he passed on the post to her when he resigned it. After the Tory ministry was voted out of office in 1714, there was little opportunity for Manley to continue her political writing. From 1709 until her death on July 11, 1724, Manley lived at the house of John Barber, a printer, alderman, and eventually Lord Mayor of London, reputedly as his mistress. Though her novels were highly successful, they were not a dependable source of revenue for her. She was scorned by her contemporaries and generations of literary commentators for relying on men to support her. Yet recent scholars have pointed out the unfairness of this charge, noting that eighteenth-century social conventions denied Manley—and other women with no money of their own—any ethical means to achieve financial independence.

Major Works

Manley's first attempt at fiction, published as *Letters Written by Mrs. Manley,* is a lively and naturalistic account of a group of travelers as they journey by stagecoach through southwest England. This was issued the same year her first two plays were produced in London. Nearly a decade later, *Queen Zarah* (1705), a so-called secret history modeled along the lines of earlier French and English *romans à clef,* appeared in print. This is generally regarded as Manley's first novel, although some late twentieth-century scholars have questioned whether this is indeed her work. Like the undisputed ones, it is presented as a translation rather than an original work—a device commonly used by authors of this period to forestall charges of libel. The preface to *Queen Zarah* proclaims that historical fiction should have plausible events, naturalistic characters, and a disinterested perspective on what it describes. By contrast, the novel itself features a thinly veiled portrait of Sarah, Duchess of Marlborough—an eminent Whig who was one of Queen Anne's closest confidants. Trading in personal scandal and political invective, it lampoons the duchess, attacking her influence over the queen; the authorial voice shifts back and forth between sophistication and seemingly ingenuous satire. In 1709 the most well-known of Manley's novels was published: the two volumes known as the *New Atalantis.* Its narrative framework is an allegory, in which Astrea, goddess of Justice, visits Earth to learn how a prince should be educated. Her instructor is Intelligence, another allegorical figure, who guides Astrea through English society, alternating between the roles of scandal monger and social or moral commentator. An episodic novel, the *New Atalantis* has frequently been characterized as amatory fiction, yet its initial audience regarded it as political satire as well, for it highlights decades of rumors and innuendoes about political corruption and private depravity allegedly committed by influential Whigs. The most famous episodes in the first volume include a lush boudoir scene, in which a nobleman lures his wife into committing adultery with an alluring young man, and the tale of Charlot, an exemplar of betrayed innocence. The second volume contains the overtly autobiographical story of Delia, a victim of seduction and faithlessness who is tricked into a bigamous marriage. The two-volume *Memoirs of Europe* (1710), which many commentators regard as the third and fourth parts of the *New Atalantis,* portrays a group of eighth-century travelers in eastern Europe gossiping about political and sexual scandals. The *Memoirs* represents an unabashed tribute to two Tory leaders, Robert Haley and Lord Peterborough, and promulgates continuing tales of Whig degeneracy. Modern commentators judge that while some of Manley's anecdotes in this work are based on hearsay and others on fact, much of the narrative is fabricated. Manley's last novel, *The Adventures of Rivella,* is a fictional account of the author's life before and after her bigamous marriage. The narrator is Colonel Lovemore; his auditor is a young French nobleman, the Chevalier d'Aumont. Through Lovemore, Rivella justifies her career as a political writer, defends her amatory novels, and challenges the limitations that male-dominated society places on women. Manley's other fiction includes *The Lady's Pacquet* (1707-08), a collection of imaginative and authentic correspondence, and *The Power of Love* (1720), a reworking of *The Palace of Pleasure,* William Painter's sixteenth-century translation of Italian, French, and classical novellas.

Critical Reception

For more than two hundred years, Manley's literary reputation was circumscribed by commentators who conflated her personal life and her writings—and generally condemned both. Even when critics departed from this tradition and praised some attributes of her novels, they frequently emphasized their erotic content. Malcolm Bosse, for example, alluded to her scenic ability and credited her with a talent for satire, but he focused on her depictions of sensual love. Jerry Beasley allowed her some measure of importance in English letters, suggesting that her use of first-person narrators made readers familiar with this technique and thus helped pave the way for Fielding's novels. Yet most of Beasley's commentary on Manley is devoted to censure: he declared that her characters are stereotypes and her novels little more than scurrilous invective. In 1977 Dolores Palomo charged that previous critics' judgments of Manley's novels were biased by their view of her as a dissolute woman. Palomo further contended that much of Manley's supposedly erotic writing is an intentional parody of conventional romance style. Over the past twenty years, commentators have increasingly focused on Manley's literary technique and defended her mode of writing. Dale Spender, for example, asserted that her contributions to the development of English fiction are authentic and that her novels comprise a genuine protest against the oppression of women. Noting that recent scholarship has demonstrated the factual basis of much of her political satire, Fidelis Morgan proposed that Manley set out to prove that the desire to achieve advancement, money, or power is the principal motivation of sexual liaisons. Janet Spencer argued that while Manley's significance as a Tory propagandist has been overlooked since her death, the author herself is largely responsible for this. In Spencer's view, Manley's self-portrait in *The Adventures of Rivella* created an image of the erotic writer as sensuous woman that persisted through the centuries and affected the reputation of all women writers. By contrast, Janet Todd argued that Manley makes ironic use in *Rivella* of the male equation of woman writer and prostitute, revealing her understanding of the power of language to seduce and gratify. Todd further suggested that the ending of *Rivella* portrays a woman writer who has learned to control and contain desire through the manipulation of words. Similarly, Ros Ballaster contended that despite the narrator's attempt to restrict Rivella within the boundaries he considers appropriate and thus create the ideal woman, the concluding passages of Rivella demonstrate that it is she who conceives him. Ballaster also proposed that if *The Adventures of Rivella* and the story of Delia in the *New Atalantis* are juxtaposed, they illustrate one means of resisting the masculine concept of the "madonna/whore" dichotomy and exposing it as a fiction.

PRINCIPAL WORKS

NOVELS

The Secret History of Queen Zarah, and the Zarazians; Being a Looking-glass for—In the Kingdom of Albigion. 2 vols. 1705
**Secret Memoirs and Manners of Several Persons of Quality, of Both Sexes. From the New Atalantis, an Island in the Mediterranean.* 2 vols. 1709
**Memoirs of Europe, Towards the Close of the Eighth Century.* 2 vols. 1710
The Adventures of Rivella; or, the History of the Author of the Atalantis (fictional autobiography) 1714 (also published as *Mrs Manley's History of her Own Life and Times,* 1725)
The Novels of Mary Delariviere Manley. 2 vols. (facsimiles) 1971

*These four volumes are known collectively as the *New Atalantis.*

OTHER MAJOR WORKS

Letters Written by Mrs. Manley (fictional letters) 1696 (also published as *A Stage Coach Journey to Exeter,* 1725)
The Lost Lover (play) 1696
The Royal Mischief (play) 1696
Almyna (play) 1707
The Duke of M———h's Vindication (political pamphlet) 1711
The Lady's Pacquet of Letters Broke Open (fictional and authentic letters) 1707-08 (also published as

Court Intrigues in a Collection of Original Letters from the Island of the New Atalantis, 1711)
A Learned Comment on Dr. Hare's Sermon (political pamphlet) 1711
A True Narrative of what passed at the Examination of the Marquis de Guiscard (political pamphlet) 1711
A True Relation of the Several Facts and Circumstances of the Intended Riot and Tumult on Queen Elizabeth's Birth-day (political pamphlet) 1711
The Honour and Prerogative of the Queen's Majesty Vindicated (political pamphlet) 1713
A Modest Enquiry into the Reasons of the Joy Expressed by a Certain Sett of People upon the Spreading of a Report of Her Majesty's Death (political pamphlet) 1714
Lucius, the First Christian King of Britain (play) 1717
The Power of Love: in Seven Novels (adaptations) 1720

CRITICISM

Benjamin Boyce (essay date 1952)

SOURCE: Introduction to *Prefaces to Fiction*, William Andres Clark Memorial Library, No. 32, 1952, pp. i-x.

[*In the following excerpt, Boyce contends that Manley's call for realistic action, authentic dialogue, and true-to-life characterization—expressed in the preface to* Queen Zarah—*represents an important development in eighteenth-century prose fiction.*]

The development of the English novel is one of the triumphs of the eighteenth century. Criticism of prose fiction during that period, however, is less impressive, being neither strikingly original nor profound nor usually more than fragmentary. Because the early statements of theory were mostly very brief and are now obscurely buried in rare books, one may come upon the well conceived "program" of *Joseph Andrews* and *Tom Jones* with some surprise. But if one looks in the right places one will realize that mid-eighteenth century notions about prose fiction had a substantial background in earlier writing. And as in the case of other branches of literary theory in the Augustan period, the original expression of the organized doctrine was French. In Georges de Scudery's preface to *Ibrahim* (1641)[1] and in a conversation on the art of inventing a "Fable" in Book VIII (1656) of his sister Madeleine's *Clélie* are to be found the grounds of criticism in prose fiction; practically all the principles are here which eighteenth-century theorists adopted, or seemed to adopt, or from which they developed, often by the simple process of contradiction, their new principles. . . .

The theory of prose fiction offered by the Scudérys was, on the whole, better than their practice. The same remark can be made with even greater assurance of *The Secret History of Queen Zarah, and the Zarazians* (1705) and the other political-scandalous "histories" of Mary De la Riviere Manley. For in spite of the faults of *Queen Zarah,* the preface is one of the most substantial discussions of prose fiction in the century. Boldly and reasonably it repudiates the most characteristic features of the heroic romance—the vastness produced by intercalated stories; the idealized characters, almost "exempted from all the Weakness of Humane Nature;" the marvelous adventures and remote settings; the essay-like conversations; the adulatory attitude; and poetic justice. *Vraisemblance* and *decorum,* we are told, are still obligatory, but the probable character, action, dialogue will now be less prodigious, will be closer to real life as the modern English reader knows it. Thus Mrs. Manley announced a point of view which was, at least in most respects, to dominate the theory and invigorate the practice of prose fiction throughout the century.

A significant phase of Mrs. Manley's discussion is the emphasis upon individual characterization and, in characters, upon not only the "predominant Quality" and ruling passion of each but also upon the elusive and surprising "Turnings and Motions of Humane Understanding." Here one should recognize the influence of historical writing rather than of poetry. As René Rapin had made clear in Chapter XX of his *Instructions for History* (J. Davies's translation, 1680), the historian writes the best portraits who finds the "essential and distinctive lines" of a man's character and the "secret motions and inclinations of [his] Heart." But Mrs. Manley's remarks go beyond Rapin's in implying faith in a sort of scientific psychology, especially of "the passions. . . .'"

Notes

[1] Most scholars attribute the preface to Georges de Scudéry, but it seems impossible to say whether he collaborated with his sister in writing the romance itself or whether the work was written entirely by her.

Cogan's translation of *Ibrahim* and the preface appeared first in 1652.

Malcolm J. Bosse (essay date 1972)

SOURCE: Introduction to *The Adventures of Rivella,* by Mary de la Rivière Manley, Garland Publishing, Inc., 1972, p. 120.

[*In the essay below, Bosse offers a concise appraisal of Manley's autobiographical novel* The Adventures of Rivella, *which he regards as a moving and realistic work.*]

The Adventures of Rivella was hastily written by Mary Manley, according to the publisher Edmund Curll, to offset and possibly forestall the publication of a philippic directed against her by Charles Gildon, which he was apparently composing at Curll's instigation.[1] In her fictionalized autobiography she avoids defending her performance as a political writer and seeks instead to justify her behavior as a woman.

Born the daughter of Sir John Manley, a loyalist who served from 1667 to 1672 as Lieutenant-Governor of Jersey, she never achieved her rightful social status, possibly because early in her life and continuing until her death Mary Manley was involved in a number of illegal liaisons. Among her acknowledged lovers were her cousin, John Manley, with whom she contracted a bigamous "marriage"; Sir Thomas Skipwith, who produced her first play; John Tilly, warden of Fleet Prison; John Barber, publisher and future mayor of London; and John Tidcombe, who may have served as the model for the narrator of *Rivella.*[2] Throughout her life she was a prolific writer whose literary career began with *Letters* in 1696 and in the same year with the production of two plays, a comedy, *The Lost Lover,* and a tragedy, *The Royal Mischief.* Her best known works were scandal chronicles of satiric and political aim in the form of *romans à clef: The Secret History of Queen Zarah* (1705), *The New Atalantis* (1709), and *Memoirs of Europe* (1710). Of this fiction Professor Koster says, "Considered as literature, the novels should have a secure scholarly place, for they show a considerable range of techniques in the development toward the novel."[3]

Rivella begins with a "Translator's Preface," which asserts that the manuscript has been translated from a French original. Although this preface was deleted in the second edition appearing three years later, Mrs. Manley always claimed that her chronicles were translations. Other writers of the period, including Defoe, attempted to achieve some aesthetic distance and verisimilitude by employing the device of a translation of a lost manuscript, but in Mary Manley's case the technique was a means of protecting herself against libel. In an amusing passage she suggests that even such an unconvincing denial of responsibility could keep an author from serious punishment. Questioned by order of the Whig Secretary of State, Charles Sunderland, she pleaded that her characters were imaginary, drawn merely to entertain:

> When this was not believ'd, and the contrary urg'd very home to her by several Circumstances and Likenesses; she said then it must be Inspiration, because knowing her own Innocence she could account for it no other way. (p. 113)

The narrative framework is a dialogue between an amorously inclined young Frenchman, the Chevalier

D'Aumont, and Sir Charles Lovemore, who declares that he has loved Rivella longer and more faithfully than any other man. Mrs. Manley's knowledge of dramatic writing, constantly in evidence throughout her fiction, is put to lively use here, as the two men coolly discuss the physical attributes that women must have to be desirable. The author provides a rather glowing account of her own attractiveness, but ultimately her self-portrait is less a panegyric than a moving confession from a woman whose troubles in life have derived from sensuality, from "the Greatness of her Prepossession" (p. 23).

Although her life story is couched in the form of short romantic episodes, much like those encountered in her novels, what emerges here is a realistic account of female vulnerability to passion and the sad consequences of unfounded optimism. *The Adventures of Rivella,* in spite of stylistic crudities and lack of coherent structure, sets forth with admirable clarity the sources in Mary Manley's life for the themes of her fiction. It is therefore an interesting psychological study of a popular novelist who was also an eighteenth-century woman with insight into the wellsprings of her own creativity.

The Adventures and surprizing Deliverances of James Dubourdieu and his Wife, published in 1719, contains the portrait of a woman markedly unlike Mrs. Manley or her heroines. The first half of the story is narrated by Martha Rattenberg, wife of James Dubourdieu, who together run a Parisian tavern. To a young Englishman who dutifully writes down her account, she explains that she had gone into service after being cheated of an inheritance by a wicked brother. First deceived and then married to a polygamist, she had set out for Barbados to change her fortune.

Her practical approach to life indicates that her central trait of character is strength, and the quiet factual prose augments this impression. After she and other passengers are taken prisoner by pirates, they are shipwrecked on a desert island where some of the women fraternize with the buccaneers. Tartly critical of such immorality, she describes the situation with a touch of sarcastic humor:

> We were indeed all surpriz'd, that a place so adapted for convenient and happy living, should be wholly without inhabitants; and some of us concluded that we were ordain'd to people it; and the young lasses, with whom the pirates had already been familiar, as I told you, seem'd to leave no stone unturn'd to contribute their part towards this work. (p. 44)

Having maintained her own virtue, she is providentially saved from assault by an earthquake which swallows up all the sinners and leaves her with good people, among them a French surgeon, Mr. Dubourdieu,

whom she decides in a typically practical manner to marry. When her husband and a priest fail to return from an exploring expedition, she remains alone for three years on the island. At this juncture in the narrative her husband supplies his own first-person account of what happened to him during their separation, and in so doing shifts the emphasis from adventure to a philosophical discussion of a utopian society. During his exploration of the island he had met and lived with a race of beautiful people whose religion was based on reason and a reverence for life. Finally reunited with his wife, Mr. Dubourdieu returns to civilization thoroughly sobered by his contact with people who call Europeans "the children of wrath" (p. 93). This short narrative, composed of an adventure story and a utopian tale, moves at an admirable pace, and its fanciful content is somewhat offset by a prose style distinguished by clarity and simplicity.

Included with *The Adventures of Mr. Dubourdieu and his Wife* is *The Adventures of Alexander Vendchurch,* a travel story of novella length. In picaresque fashion the narrator runs away from home and becomes the servant of a Spanish master who trades at Panama. Falling in love with a Spanish girl, Alexander Vendchurch is dealt with treacherously by her angry father. In one of those incredible coincidences that haunt eighteenth-century fiction, Alexander Vendchurch is shipwrecked and almost immediately reunited with his beloved Elvira, who, returning to Spain, had been shipwrecked on the same island. "Sea lyons" devour other castaways and Alexander lives idyllically with her until her sudden death, after which he returns to England and a large inheritance. The story moves quickly, but it is too lightly developed to compete with another tale that described life on a desert island—*The Life and Strange Surprizing Adventures of Robinson Crusoe*—published in that same year of 1719.

Notes

[1] See Patricia Koster's comprehensive introduction to *The Novels of Mary Delariviere Manley* (Gainesville, Fla., 1971), I, pp. v-xxviii.

[2] Koster, p. xxi.

[3] Koster, pp. xxi-xxii.

Malcolm J. Bosse (essay date 1972)

SOURCE: Introduction to *Secret Memoirs from the New Atlantis,* by Mary de la Rivière Manley, Garland Publishing, Inc., Vol. I and II, 1972, p. 238.

[*In the essay reprinted below, Bosse emphasizes the unusual mixture of sensuality and high moral tone in the* New Atalantis. *Despite the novel's sensationalism, he argues, it is a skillful satire of early-eighteenth-century political figures.*]

Mary Manley's skill and influence as a Tory propagandist during Queen Anne's reign has been tacitly recognized by the historian Trevelyan, who calls **The New Atalantis,** which first appeared in 1709, "the publication that did most harm to the Ministry that year."[1] Four years earlier Mrs. Manley had attempted in **Queen Zarah** to vilify her Whig enemies, especially the Marlboroughs, by describing their wickedness in terms of lust and avarice. In the new and more ambitious work she extended the range of her targets, and by her own admission in the Dedication to Volume II, she consciously undertook to imitate the bold, belligerent, and often vulgar satirists of classical Rome. The result was satire cast in detachable stories that were moral in tone, polemical in aim, and sensational in execution. She assembled these tales, which in their economy and melodrama are similar to Italian *novelle,* within a narrative framework made popular by European satirists of the period. Marana and Le Sage had achieved at least a partial sense of unity, as well as effects of irony, by introducing into their satire the device of a guided tour, which alien observers take through a society too hypocritical to view its own sinfulness. For Mrs. Manley this constituted an advance in technique beyond that which she had used earlier. **The New Atalantis** begins with the return to earth of Astrea, goddess of Justice, who has come from the moon to study ways of educating a lunar prince. She meets another allegorical figure, Virtue, her mother, who wears symbolic rags, laments the loss of honor through the land, and bitterly declares, "You may indeed preach to him to avoid Vice, but then you must teach him to avoid Mankind" (I, 9). Undaunted by this fierce misanthropy, Astrea persuades Virtue to accompany her. In the familiar tradition of satire, they render themselves invisible as they go forth to study mankind's misuse of justice.

Their journey begins with an account of moral and financial corruption in the British Navy. The following passage illustrates the passionate tone, the fluent if florid style, and the wealth of Juvenalian detail that often informed the prose of Mrs. Manley when she aimed seriously at satiric targets of the age:

> Did only Service and true Merit recommend to Office, were not Bribery, and the Sollicitations of Friends, preferr'd to Duty and Worth; were severe Penalties inflicted upon these Blasphemers (the Commanders themselves first desisting from the use); were Dice, Cards, and an exorbitant Love of Wine, and the hotter Liquors taxed; were faithful Commissioners appointed to inspect the Provision of the Navy; were matter of lawful Complaint made free to the meanest Seaman, provided (upon pain of examplary Punishment) he advance nothing but the Truth; were it made capital to take a Bribe in the Service of their Country: The Regulation might be made easie, if the leading Men and Commanders, gave them but examples of Sobriety, Justice, and Morality; but all is nothing but Oaths, Drunkenness, burning Lust, Riots, Avarice, Cruelty, and Disorder. (I, 17)

After the goddesses meet another allegorical character, Intelligence, who as the symbol of gossip appropriately introduces them to scandals of the day, the emphasis of the book shifts from general criticism of society to a series of sensational vignettes that feature seduction, rape, incest, and homosexuality. Mrs. Manley's libelous account of John Churchill's seduction of Sarah Jennings, which had been the major event described in **Queen Zarah,** is reworked for new effects in **The New Atalantis.** Whereas Sarah Jennings received the brunt of Mrs. Manley's Tory indignation in the early book, John Churchill is the chief target here. He is portrayed as the masculine corrupter of women both innocent and experienced, and his victims include the Duchess of Cleveland, who is depicted rather convincingly as an aging woman easily duped by a handsome young man. Mrs. Manley displays a genuine talent for handling scenes of physical love and for uncovering the psychology of sexual conflict. Her success derives in part from an ability to create a lush setting for erotic action, and her attention to the texture of clothes, the color of flowers, and the symbolism of *objets d'art* set her apart from the majority of eighteenth-century writers who usually failed to provide a properly sensuous atmosphere for stories of love.

To offset her obvious enthusiasm for the erotic tale, Mrs. Manley was careful to castigate those who indulge in unrestrained sexuality or to punish transgressors of the moral code. Charlot, for example, modeled after Stuarta Howard, the ward of the Earl of Portland, acquiesces to her guardian's importunities, and in spite of her deeply felt remorse she receives a stern judgment from Providence:

> The remainder of her Life was one continu'd Scene of Horror, Sorrow, and Repentance: She dy'd a true Landmark: to warn all believing Virgins from shipwracking their Honour upon (that dangerous Coast of Rocks) the Vows and pretended Passion of Mankind. (I, 83)

Her vision of a fantasy world of blighted innocence and glittering corruption doubtlessly accounted for much of Mrs. Manley's contemporary appeal. On the other hand, the libelous nature of her fiction militated against the recognition of her considerable literary skill. Compared to other works of the period, **The New Atalantis** holds up well today. Although the allegorical journey, which was meant to be a scaffolding for the narrative, failed to provide a viable form,

Mrs. Manley drew individual episodes with economy and point. Although her plotting generally overwhelmed her characterizations, in the comic creation of the midwife, Mrs. Nightwork, she realized a character that would become familiar in fiction, the lusty, garrulous servant. Although her moralizing sometimes clogged the flow of the narrative, her blend of realism and romance rarely lost its essentially propulsive force.

Mrs. Manley was a popular novelist who frankly catered to indiscriminating taste, but whose critical eye was that of a genuine satirist. Despite the vulgarity of **The New Atalantis,** Mrs. Manley attempted, like her betters, Swift and Pope, to instill within her readers an abhorrence of greed and lust, those twin aspects of unbridled materialism that she believed the Whigs in politics and the aristocrats in society were forcing upon the god-fearing people of eighteenth-century England.

Notes

[1] G. M. Trevelyan, *England under Queen Anne: The Peace and the Protestant Succession* (London, 1965), iii, 62. Volume I of *The New Atalantis* was published in May 1709; Volume II in October.

Jerry C. Beasley (essay date 1982)

SOURCE: "Fiction as Contemporary History," in *Novels of the 1740s*, University of Georgia Press, 1982, pp. 53-73.

[*In the following excerpt, Beasley points to discrepancies between the literary principles Manley espouses in the preface to* Queen Zarah—*especially realistic characterization—and what he regards as the novel's scurrilous portraits of the Duchess of Marlborough and other leading Whigs of the day.*]

As feigned records of scandal and foolishness in places high and low, the spy fictions of Marana, Montesquieu, Lyttelton, and Mme de Graffigny all belong to the same family of pseudohistories, which also includes a prominent cousin, the secret history, or *chronique scandaleuse*. Secret histories by writers like Delarivière Manley and Eliza Haywood were more controversial than the circumspect spy fictions, although the two kinds of feigned history closely resemble one another. The chief difference between the two is that the secret history usually treats a much more limited range of familiar issues and public characters, for more specialized purposes. Following the example of original French models like Mme d'Aulnoy's *Mémoires de la cour d'Angleterre* (1695), the typical *chronique scandaleuse* is an episodic work purporting to tell the "real truth" about certain thinly disguised figures in contemporary

politics, Court, and fashionable life.[6] Narrower in scope than the more urbane spy story, this type of work trades in personal scandal and political invective. That is, if the work of Marana and Montesquieu functions as a modern adaptation of the Juvenalian attitude, the secret history perverts that attitude. Furthermore, its writers reject conventional standards of taste. Whether motivated by genuine partisan interests or mere lust for success in the marketplace, they deal more in character assassination than in real political or moral discourse, more in licentious gossip than in fruitful satire of the actual manners and machinations of the real people they "expose."

Most secret histories published in the early eighteenth century superimpose upon their real, contemporary subjects the filmy pretext of an ancient or remote civilization. Such a pretext allows them to criticize and scandalize with complete abandon. In this respect they parallel the licentious orientalized political satires of Crébillon *fils*. Some secret histories pretend to deny their contemporary relevance by having the "editor" question the authenticity of the "manuscript," and insist on its antiquity. The preface to part two of Mrs. Manley's **Secret History of Queen Zarah** (1705), one of the earliest, most influential, and most durable English works in this vein (it was revived in editions of 1743, 1745, and 1749), ironically protests against the widely held view that the previously published part one had launched an attack on Sarah Churchill, Duchess of Marlborough. The "whole *Story*," the "editor" suspects, "is a *Fiction*." There is "no such Country" as the Albigion depicted in the tale, "nor any such Person now Living, or ever was, as Zarah, or the other Names Characteriz'd, either in This or the First Part." The "manuscript," therefore, written before there were civilizations or governments, can only be a prophecy of "something yet to come." For it is impossible, the "editor" concludes, that "any Nation under the Moon ever cou'd produce a Creature of so little Use to the rest of the Creation besides herself, as this Wonder of her Sex, Queen *Zarah* is feign'd to be. That alone is sufficient to persuade me this Story is all a Romantick Tale of a Tub."

Although less famous than the same author's much longer **New Atalantis** (1709), **Queen Zarah** provided a kind of immediate native model to which future secret histories were to pay the homage of at least partial emulation.[7] The preface to part one makes a clear distinction between such "little Pieces" as **Queen Zarah** and the extravagant, ill-contrived heroic romances so justly "cry'd down" at present by all "Persons of good Sense." A work like the present one, by contrast to such romances, observes the "Probability of Truth, which consists in saying nothing but what may Morally be believed." In **Queen Zarah,** we are told, nice delineations of character are preserved; and when the characters speak, they do so in the "easie and free

Manner" of everyday discourse and not in the rhetoric of romance. Yet despite Mrs. Manley's ostensible commitment to moral and mimetic ideals, her work is hardly a sober return to real life. On the contrary, it is a scurrilous Tory indictment of the Duchess of Marlborough and the Whig politicians of Queen Anne's reign. Despite the author's insistent claims of moral utility, the logic of the work is that vice is best censured by titillating exposure. The method of **Queen Zarah** is to exhibit very transparent, stereotyped personages— prowling *grandes dames,* lecherous statesmen, wicked libertines preying on imperiled virgins, and so on, all of them copied from a Theophrastian sketchbook— wallowing in scandalous love affairs and indulging in boudoir politics. These characters are the vehicles of partisan invective. Given their polemical function, it is not surprising that except for their ironic treatment, their visible eccentricities, familiar mannerisms, and open eroticism, they are hardly distinguishable from the inflated characters of romance attacked in the preface to the work.

Queen Zarah moves episodically, interrupted by little novellalike tales that pause over the dissolute escapades of readily recognizable figures such as the Earl of Godolphin and the Duke of Marlborough. Many later secret histories, while remaining essentially faithful to the example of **Queen Zarah** and the **New Atalantis,** compressed their bulk into slim volumes or pamphlets. But for Mrs. Manley, the more and juicier the episodes, the better the partisan purpose was served. In such works as hers, as every contemporary reader would have intuitively understood, the only ordering principle lies outside the world of the narrative, in the society that is being reflected in this special manner. The works themselves are only loosely held together by the presence of a presiding narrator. In **Queen Zarah** and the **New Atalantis,** and in their numerous close imitations, a ubiquitous persona moves in and out of salon and court, closet and bedroom, functioning as a kind of invisible spy who details the intrigue, the amorous machinations, the erotic confrontations in which the characters involve themselves. To this end, the separate scene frequently assumes greater importance than the story of which it is a part; this is especially true with Mrs. Manley and later Mrs. Haywood, both of whom were playwrights as well as novelists. The descriptive, judgmental, editorial voice of the narrator, however, always directs the reader's responses. Mrs. Manley's Intelligence, with the help of her mother Virtue and most especially of Astrea, speaks as the final authority on all of the amorous behavior observed at the Court of Atalantis.[8] The first-person narrators of *Joseph Andrews* and *Tom Jones* derive ultimately from a different narrative tradition, but the familiarity of some readers with the methods of Mrs. Manley and others like her would help to prepare them for Fielding's mannerisms. . . .

Notes

[6] Mme d'Aulnoy's work was translated as *Memoirs of the Court of England* in 1707, and it enjoyed a second edition in 1708. The popularity in England of the *Memoirs* and a number of other French works like it seems to have impelled English writers to imitation. The real genesis of this kind of writing, however, was probably in the tradition of anecdotic literature, or *anecdota,* extending all the way back into antiquity and including among its earliest manifestations the *Deipnosophistae* of Athenaeus and the *Lives* of Plutarch.

[7] These would include Eliza Haywood's *Memoirs of a Certain Island Adjacent to the Kingdom of Utopia* (1725-26) and her *Secret History of the . . . Court of Caramania* (1727). Of the most successful among early native secret histories, only *Queen Zarah* was reprinted in the 1740s, and it may have owed its revival to the long-delayed publication (in 1742) of the Duchess of Marlborough's ghost-written *Account of the Conduct of the Dowager Duchess of Marlborough, from her First Coming to Court. . . .* Several other biographical works dealing with the duchess appeared in the early 1740s, including Fielding's *Vindication* (1742).

[8] The name Astrea was borrowed from an earlier purveyor of scandal, Aphra Behn; Mrs. Manley thus assumed the mantle of her predecessor. See P. B. Anderson, "Mistress Delarivière Manley's Biography," *Modern Philology* 33 (1936): 261-62.

Fidelis Morgan (essay date 1986)

SOURCE: Introduction to *A Woman of No Character: An Autobiography of Mrs. Manley,* Faber and Faber, 1986, pp. 17-23.

[*In the essay below, Morgan provides an overview of Manley's autobiographical writings, judging them generally honest and forthright, even though they were all presented in fictional form. The critic also calls attention to Manley's popularity in her own lifetime and the influence of her work on prose writers of the later eighteenth century.*]

I first came upon the autobiographical writings of Mrs Delarivier Manley in my research for *The Female Wits.* So much larger than life do they read that I was unsurprised when dependable reference works dismissed them as pure fiction.

'The testimony of Mrs Manley is of course wholly valueless,' thought a nineteenth-century scholar. This century Winston S. Churchill described her works as 'the lying inventions of a prurient and filthy underworld, served up to those who relish them and paid for by party interest and political malice'. A late professor of English Literature at Stanford University expanded the point: 'It is not only that they are repulsive because of the undisguised licentiousness that everywhere prevails in them; they are occasionally disgusting on account of the large part played by the merely horrible.' Mrs Manley, he believed, stood out 'among the least attractive products of an age of low ideals and scandalous living'. He found her work 'desperately dull and tiresome', despite 'the pornographic horrors of its pages'.[1]

The misogyny implicit in criticism of Mrs Manley comes in various forms. The most common is one about which she complained throughout her life—the double standard. She is criticized for achievements which in a man would have been acceptable and even laudable: *The Cambridge History of English Literature* informs us that Mrs Manley 'achieved an unenviable reputation as a novelist', while *The Oxford Companion to English Literature* boldly states that she 'fell into disreputable courses, and avenged herself on society for an unhappy life by her *New Atalantis*'. 'Her subsequent career was one of highly dubious morality but considerable literary success,' the *Dictionary of Literary Biography* grudgingly admits, while the author of *The Women Novelists* smugly asserts that she 'wrote novels of some vigour, but deservedly forgotten'. A contributor to *Notes and Queries* calls her 'this demirep—to give her a name exactly as much above her deserts as it is below those of an honest woman.'[2]

Winston Churchill, whose judgement was utterly partial (so upset did he feel at Mrs Manley's revelations about his great-great-great-great-great-great-great grandfather), agreed: 'The depths of insult are plumbed by the notorious Mrs Manley . . . [who] was at this time living with the printer of the *Examiner*. She was thus in close touch with Swift . . . who used her to write obscenities and insults beyond the wide limits which he set himself.' (Note how he chose to describe her as Swift's printer's mistress rather than admit she was Swift's partner on the *Examiner*—and had in fact introduced the two men to each other.)[3]

Given this modern critical agreement, my first plans for this book were for an objective biography, backing up the main facts of her life, while exposing an underlying tissue of lies and exaggeration in her autobiography. Surprisingly, the facts proved to be, on the whole, more outrageous than Mrs Manley's fictionalized accounts, and the supporting evidence creates a detective trail which leads right back to her own version. So it seemed more sensible to assemble her autobiographical fragments (which appear in sections varying in length and style in a handful of books which are all unavailable to a wider reading public) in chronological order and write alongside, backing her up and filling in the gaps.

The first obvious question was—who was this woman whose work, though centuries old, drove the British wartime leader to such antipathetic eloquence and language as strong as any he used against Hitler?

What rapidly became clear was that during her own lifetime, and the century following it, political and personal grievances aside, she was widely read and well loved.

The 1699 edition of Langbaine's *Lives and Characters of the English Dramatic Poets* encouraged her early work. 'This lady has very happily distinguished herself from the rest of her sex and gives us a living proof of what we might reasonably expect from womankind if they had the benefit of those artificial improvements of learning the men have, when by mere force of nature they so much excel . . . There is a force and a fire in her tragedy that is the soul that gives it life and for want of which most of our modern tragedies are heavy, languid, unmoving and dull. In her comedy there is an easy freedom of adding [action?] which confesses a conversation in the authoress no less genteel and entertaining.'[4]

The *Poetical Register* of 1719 thought that 'in all her writings . . . there appears a happy sprightliness and an easy turn' and that she herself was 'deservedly esteemed for her affability, wit and loyalty'.[5]

The *Historical Register,* in reporting her death, described her as 'a person of polite genius and uncommon capacity which made her writings naturally delicate and easy and her conversation agreeably entertaining'. And the next year, the unspeakable Curll, bookseller, printer and hack, and not a man to miss any opportunity to exploit a person's frailties, particularly if they could not answer back, wrote this of the 'inimitable author':

> All who had the happiness of her conversation were soon convinced how free she was from the general frailties of her sex; what a nobleness and generosity of temper she possessed; how distant her views from the least appearance of self-interest or mean design. How often have I heard her compassionately regretting the miseries of mankind and never her own, but when they prevented her extensive charity to others.

> Never was she vindictive against the most inveterate enemy; the innate softness of her soul rendered her deportment equally obliging to friends and foes and never did she resent but with the strictest justice.[6]

Swift's most quoted remark about her is that she was 'very homely and very fat'. He also wrote in his *Journal to Stella*, 'Got a set of *Examiners,* and five pamphlets, which I have either written or contributed to, except the best, which is the Vindication of the Duke of Marlborough; and is entirely of the author of the *Atalantis*' and his actions (employing her as an 'understrapper', letting her take over editorship of the *Examiner* and seconding her appeals to the Tories for remuneration for her services) speak louder than his words.[7]

In 1741 she was described as 'a lady of distinguished merit, whose works will be prized whilst eloquence, wit and good sense are in esteem among mankind . . . It seems almost needless to mention the lady's name—not one of the fair sex being at that time so much in vogue for these [qualities] as Mrs Manley.'[8]

Alexander Pope, back in 1712, thought that Mrs Manley's work would be remembered for a very long time. In *The Rape of the Lock* he used the phrase 'As long as *Atalantis* shall be read' as a yardstick for eternity.[9]

It is easy to see the influence Mrs Manley's work had on Swift (particularly *Gulliver's Travels*), Richardson, Sterne, Smollett and many others.

This is not to say that in her own time her work was universally popular. She was a Tory, and therefore not best beloved by the Whigs. Also, like the subjects of William Hickey or Hedda Hopper this century, those who had suffered at the end of her pen squealed very loud.

Delarivier Manley described herself as 'the only person of her sex that knows how to live' and live she certainly did. The daughter of a cavalier, brought up, with her brothers and sisters, in an army camp, she went on to become one of the most feared political satirists—the author of the most sensational bestseller of the eighteenth century, *Secret Memoirs . . . from the New Atalantis,* and by the time of her death had produced at least twenty-one books and six plays, and been editor of and contributor to two thrice-weekly periodicals, the *Female Tatler* and the *Examiner.*

Her work was popular and controversial. her early success inspired a stage lampoon at her expense. Her *Secret Memoirs . . . from the New Atlantis* was read by everyone from lords, ladies and politicians to the lowest country bumpkins. It also provoked satires and insults in response and led to her imprisonment.

Of her four known lovers three were lawyers, two of them were MPs, one of them ran a London prison, one owned two theatres and one was a City alderman who went on to become Lord Mayor of London. All four were unscrupulous. Another questionable relationship was with a multi-titled ex-royal-mistress.

Given all this ready-made subject matter, Mrs Manley did not hesitate to use it. She wrote a full-length autobiographical novel, *The Adventures of Rivella,* under a conveniently male pseudonym, Sir Charles Lovemore. And in her other novels, nestling alongside her fictionalized tales of the rich and famous, she provided us with accounts of incidents in her life not covered in *Rivella.*

It is important to understand that all of Mrs Manley's autobiographical writing was intended to be read as fiction. She made no attempt at either serious factual biography or humorous, anecdotal self-sketches. The incidents she covers are written in a variety of typical eighteenth-century fiction styles: romantic self-pity, urbane dialogues, letters to distant friends, and all the characters within them are given romantic pseudonyms: Hilaria, Vainlove, Don Marcus and Monsieur L'Ingrat.

Delarivier Manley's taste for the romantic and dramatic was well known and frequently satirized, but in her autobiographical sketches (as in her social and political exposés), although she may have embroidered and elevated, she never evaded the truth of her situation, and the personality which bursts through the often high-flown prose is warm, witty, loyal, trusting and mischievously outspoken.

Her sense of humour was of the raised eyebrow variety. She delighted in the foibles, eccentricity and blind stupidity of others and, while exposing folly, generally showed a warm understanding of it.

Her scandals were not the saucy open-air variety of Chaucer, but, rather, the intense hot-house gropings of men and women (not necessarily in heterosexual couplings) whose appetites went further than the desires of the flesh. Mrs Manley enjoyed exposing sexual intrigue for what it really was—the quest for political or social advancement and greed for money or power.

Such greed in the Churchill ancestor, John, Duke of Marlborough, made him one of her favourite targets and, with Swift, she helped to bring about both John's and his wife Sarah's downfalls. The latest scholarship shows that most of her accusations were firmly based on fact. She exposed among other things his need for perpetual war to keep his personal income high, and the very foundation of his rise to power—the financial help and political preferment earned by his services in the bed of Barbara Villiers, Countess of Castlemaine, and mistress at the time to King Charles II.

Although her work frequently described such scenes complete with languishing bodies undergoing ravishment in jasmine-strewn beds, occasionally she stood back to deliver an analysis of her principal subject—Love:

> Of all those passions which may be said to tyrannize over the heart of man, love is not only the most

violent, but the most persuasive. It conducts us through storms, tempests, seas, mountains and precipices with as little terror to the mind and as much ease as though through beautiful gardens and delightful meadows.

> A lover esteems nothing difficult in pursuit of his desires. It is then that fame, honour, chastity and glory have no longer their due estimation, even in the most virtuous breast. When love truly seizes the heart it is like a malignant fever which thence disperses itself through all the sensible parts. The poison preys upon the vitals and is only extinguished by death or, by as fatal a cure, the accomplishment of its own desires.[10]

And the point was not always made with such typically Baroque cynicism. She sometimes dissected love with an almost Jacobean disdain.

> Coquetry may make the fair ridiculous, but love can only make her wretched; that infectious distemper of the heart that poisons all the noble faculties, deludes the sense of glory, degenerates the taste of virtue and by degrees lays the very remembrance of all things but itself into a lethargic slumber.

> Let the tender sex suppress the very first suspicion of inclination that sway 'em to a liking of one more than another: if they stay but till that suspicion be confirmed they stay too long, it will be too late to retreat; neither can all its delights be in the least an equivalent for honour lost.

> The best that can be said of love is that 'tis a fading sweetness, mixed with bitter passions; a lasting misery chequered with a few momentary pleasures! Love gives the thoughts eyes to see to penetrate everywhere, and ears to the heart to listen with anxiety after all things tho' never so minute. 'Tis bred by permitting themselves leave to desire, nursed by a lazy indulgence to delight, weaned (after strong endeavours and much uneasiness) by jealousy, killed by dissembling and buried, never more to rise, by ingratitude![11]

When delivering talks on Mrs Manley and her sister playwrights in *The Female Wits,* I have been accused of dwelling unnecessarily upon their love-lives. Like me, Mrs Manley had an almost obsessive interest in other people's affairs, and often compared people's methods of getting what they wanted in the bedroom with their methods of getting what they wanted in the eighteenth-century version of the boardroom.

She devoted a large part of her biography to her own affairs, and the pattern which stands out is one which is evident in the lives of many people I know (especially women): Solitude—boredom—work—fame—at-tractiveness—love—hiatus in work—loss of attractive-ness—rejection in love and work—solitude—bore-dom—work—etcetera. In her professional life she was fearlessly outspoken and strong; in her home life a warm-hearted vulnerable innocent.

The way that love inspired her work but drained her of the energy to execute it is a timeless problem for creative women.

The authors of *Pamela's Daughters* pointed out that 'Mrs Manley competed creditably with the best of men and won applause from the most vitriolic of them all, Dean Swift himself . . . She had a heart of oak and the skin of a rhinoceros; no vituperation or reprisal could stop her.' She certainly had extraordinary india-rubber qualities and, whatever got her down, whether personal tragedy or public insult, she bounced back with the swashbuckling energy of an eighteenth-century Joan Collins at the centre of the London literary *Dynasty.*[12]

Dolores Duff thought that Swift and Mrs Manley had much in common: 'their minds possessed a coarseness which enabled them to examine and portray the disgusting in a disgusting fashion. Their convictions made them prize honesty and loath hypocrisy; their natural fastidiousness as well as their developed tastes made both almost obsessively concerned with physical cleanliness and decorum.'[13]

Their method of washing other people's dirty linen in public is one still in popular use today. But the exposés of *Private Eye* and the tabloid gossip columns have neither the wit nor literary grace of Mrs Manley's. Even so, they can still be very effective, as a handful of ex-cabinet ministers could tell you.

A delicate genius, a liar, a wit, a pornographer, an unenviable success, a slut, a failure or, as her good friend Dean Swift said, a woman of generous principles with 'a great deal of sense and invention',[14] Mrs Delarivier Manley has always been the subject of passionate opinions, but in her autobiography she is the subject of her own passionate opinion, a far more pleasant arrangement.

Notes

[1] R. Brook Aspland, *Notes and Queries* 46, 2nd series, November 1856; *Marlborough, his Life and Times*, 1938, I, 132; W. H. Hudson, *Idle Hours in a Library*, 1897, pp. 152, 126, 154

[2] *Cambridge History of English Literature*, concise ed., 1970, p. 357; *Oxford Companion to English Literature*, 4th ed., p. 512; *Dictionary of Literary Biography*, 1972, p. 448; R. Brimsley Johnson, *The Women Novelists*, 1918, p. 5; 4 October 1856, ii, 40

[3] Winston S. Churchill, *Marlborough, His Life and Times* IV, p. 367

[4] *The Lives and Characters of the English Dramatic Poets*, p. 90

[5] Giles Jacob, pp. 167, 169

[6] *Historical Register* IX, 1724, p. 35; Introduction to 'A Stagecoach Journey to Exeter', 1725. No page numbers

[7] *Journal to Stella*, Letter XL, 28 January 1712; Letter XXXII, 22 October 1711

[8] *Life and Character of John Barber*, printed T. Cooper, p. 10

[9] *The Rape of the Lock*, canto iii, line 165

[10] *The Power of Love*, 1720, p. 1

[11] *New Atalantis* II, 1709, p. 219

[12] Gwendolyn B. Needham and Utter, *Pamela's Daughters*, 1937, p. 37

[13] 'Materials towards a biography of Mary de la Riviere Manley', dissertation, Indiana 1965, p. 166

[14] *Journal to Stella*, Letter XL, 28 January 1712

Janet Todd (essay date 1989)

SOURCE: "Life after Sex: Delarivier Manley," in *The Sign of Angellica: Women, Writing, and Fiction 1660-1800*, Virago Press, 1989, pp. 84-98.

[*In the following excerpt, Todd examines Manley's treatment of the conventional male linkage of women writers and whores, in her time period. Todd asserts that in* The Adventures of Rivella *the author subverts this identification by depicting a female writer who has learned the social and sexual power of words. She also surveys Manley's other fiction, remarking on her use of alternating narrative voices, her views on the function of literature, and her notions of how women must act in order to survive in a world that is both complex and oppressive.*]

The nastiness of women for male satirists was supremely expressed in the sexual act and its aftermath: male disillusion, impotence and venereal disease. A comfort in this situation was the common narrative of female distress following defloration, a much told tale of madness, disease and death. As the eighteenth century wore on women writers would frequently glorify this female trajectory and give it an immense potency. But it was extremely rare for them to counter the narrative directly and uncover its assumptions, to demystify the sexual act that had taken on such immense proportions. Before the sentimental image of chaste, maternal, subordinate womanhood hardened into a prescription, however, Delarivier Manley was one woman who tried to give the conventional tale a subverting comic turn and provide the sexualised female writing with a cheerful rather than horrific aim.

Manley enters history primarily on the periphery of the lives of her more remembered male colleagues Swift and Steele. Her early years can be glimpsed only through her own creations. In her fictional autobiography *The Adventures of Rivella* (1714) she tells the life of Rivella, a literary character who yet claims to have written Mrs Manley's works: *Rivella* is the *History of the Author of the New Atalantis,* a work which by 1714 everyone knew to have come from the pen of the infamous Mrs Manley.[1]

Rivella was the daughter of a gentleman whose absolute loyalty to Charles I was in due course rewarded by Charles II with the lieutenant-governorship of Jersey. Born unhandsome between two pretty sisters, plump and pockmarked, Rivella nevertheless gained a lifelong admirer who now tells her tale. She had a sheltered upbringing, one of those private virtuous educations that always spell ruin in Manley's novels; in *The New Atalantis* a similar character is infected by an imprudent aunt with French romance and its high notions of female honour and male reverence. On the death of her father, Rivella was easily persuaded into marriage with her older kinsman, now her guardian. The marriage proved bigamous and Rivella was left alone, a fallen woman with an illegitimate son. Recovering her wits if not her reputation, she began writing for the stage, the most obvious outlet at the time for the woman writer.

At this point fiction needs illumination from other sources. Manley lived for a time with the Duchess of Cleveland, Charles II's former mistress, who ejected her guest after some months, suspecting a liaison with her son. Later Manley took her revenge when she created the amorous Duchess de l'Inconstant in *The New Atalantis* out of her onetime friend and benefactor. Amorous entanglements followed, including one with John Tilly, warden of the Fleet Street prison, as well as a sordid effort to gain money from another person's estate, an episode which, when fictionalised in *Rivella,* even the partisan biographer cannot make wholesome. In her later years, Manley had a rather uneasy relationship with John Barber, a printer from the City of London. Despite personal disappointments, difficulties and illnesses, she continued writing until her death in 1724 at Barber's printing house.

Early on in her career she wrote a volume of travel letters and had a modest success with one play. She

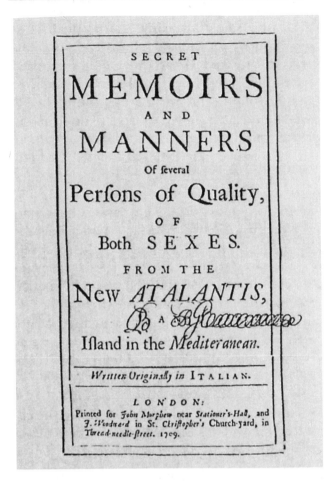

Title page of Secret Memoirs and Manners of
Several Persons of Quality.

then shrewdly turned to the new genre, the scandalous chronicle or secret history, already so successfully used by Aphra Behn, and, more significantly for her purposes, by a Frenchwoman, Marie d'Aulnoy, who, like Behn, had been a spy and who specialised in fictionalised scandal from the more lubricious courts of Europe. For Manley's most famous work in this line, *Secret Memoirs and Manners of Several Persons of Quality, of both sexes. From the New Atalantis* (1709), she was briefly detained by the authorities, an affair made heroic in *Rivella* where she described her spirited admission of guilt to save her publishers and sources. *The New Atalantis* became notorious in later centuries for its erotic depictions, rendered the more unsavoury by the knowledge that they were created by a woman. But, at the time, the work was considered also as political satire, especially aimed at linking Whig public corruption with private indecency.

Steele, who was already promoting the newer, modest and sentimental concept of womanhood in *The Tatler* and *The Spectator,* condemned female political activity on aesthetic grounds, considering that 'there is

nothing so bad for the Face as Party-Zeal'. While she remained immune to this kind of belittling advice, in *Rivella* Manley did appear to succumb to the notion that women should avoid political affairs when she admitted that 'Politicks is not the Business of a Woman'. Considering the date, however—1714, the year that ended Tory influence in government and concluded Stuart rule—she might just as well have written that Tory politics was not good business for anyone. In her choice of genres and subject matter, Manley did indeed make something of being a woman, but she rarely appeared hindered by the notion, expressed by Steele and rapidly gaining ground, that there was a content and mode inappropriate for the female sex.

In her works and the comments of others, Delarivier Manley's life emerged as energetic, disturbed and utterly involved. Without any sentimental views of female friendship and of romantic liaisons, she campaigned as vigorously against erstwhile friends like the Duchess of Cleveland, Richard Steele and the feminist poet Sarah Fyge Egerton—who appears as the applepie toting termagant in *The New Atalantis*—as against established opponents like the hated, immensely powerful Duchess of Marlborough, whose political energy, scandalously transformed into sexual appetite in the satires, Manley seemed covertly to have admired. Often morally dubious in personal, financial and literary dealings, she rarely appeared pathetic, despite the very real difficulties she faced in her life as an unprotected woman making a still unconventional literary living. Much is obviously unknowable about her activities and views, but one thing is sure, that she never achieved the elevated detachment from social and political matters that she attributed to her voyeuristic goddess in *The New Atalantis:* 'I see the World without going into it, and hear so much, that I do not desire to see it'.[2]

More even than Aphra Behn, Delarivier Manley experiments in her fiction with the narrative voice. Points of view shift in a world that is corrupt, trivial, harsh and yet vastly entertaining. In *The New Atalantis* she adopts as connecting device the story of two good but naive goddesses, Virtue and Astrea (Aphra Behn's sobriquet) or Justice, who travel through society in the worldly company of Intelligence, the purveyor of information and gossip about the English upper orders. Anecdote, allegory and social comment mingle as the feminine viewpoints vacillate; sometimes the comment is naive, sometimes condemnatory, sometimes simply cynical or resigned. The goddesses know much and learn more, but they do not and cannot act in the world they perceive; they become fitting examples of the female narrative role of gossip, storyteller, and commentator.

In *The Secret History of Queen Zarah and the Zarazians* (1705), the narrative voice is sometimes close to the voice Behn had used in *Love Letters Between a*

Nobleman and his Sister to allow description but suggest distaste. Sometimes it is closer to the ingenuous voice of satire so skilfully employed by Manley's friend Jonathan Swift: faced with the enormous and preposterous expense to the country of Blenheim Palace, built by the grasping Duchess of Marlborough with public money, it comments, 'There's more in it than a few dull-sighted People are able to see through.' At other times the voice shares sophistication with the reader: 'it is a ticklish Business for a Woman to repent of a Thing that extreamly delights her.'[3] In *The New Atalantis,* Astrea is given the naive view, expecting moral principles and reality to coalesce, and language and the world to run parallel. The naivety of her expectation is heightened when a poetic account expressing pastoral virtue is set beside a prosaic worldly description of the same events in which the absolutes of morality have no place.

Beyond the satiric point in these juxtapositions of different voices, there is in Manley's work a sense of excitement at the power of language. Words can control response and make and unmake a world. Speeches within her tales do not exist in isolation, but are shown manipulating, deceiving, and enlightening their recipients, while responses and reactions are as carefully displayed as the original words themselves.

Manley was much concerned with the craft of writing, with form and genre, and with the relationship of a work to its author and readership. The foreword to *Queen Zarah,* often ascribed to her and certainly illustrating her frequent tendency to justify, excuse and boast all at once, concentrates less on the writer than on the reception of literature, whether it should improve or entertain or illuminate life by copying it. Poetic justice is now praised and now mocked with the opinion that the good are not often the happiest in life and vice need not be obviously punished in literature. Some synthesis comes through the effect on the reader, who must find the vicious worthy of punishment, even if they are not punished by the author.

The problematic relationship of commercial literature to society and its beliefs is caught by the foreword not in extended analysis but simply in the placing together of conflicting views. Distinct unexplored aims of literature and life are juxtaposed, suggesting the equivocal nature of the relationship between moral constructions and experience. At one moment fiction is discerned in strict market terms: it must please, without insisting on onerous judgements or reflections, and it must conclude in aesthetic comfort, must 'satisfie the Disquiets of the Reader'.

The moral mode that would come to dominate fiction during the 1720s and 1730s in the works of, for example, Penelope Aubin, a lay preacher as well as a novelist, and a preacher in both roles, interrupted plots to deliver moral reflections. Writing in a completely antagonistic mode, Manley mocks the habit when, in *The New Atalantis,* she allows the sententious to be interrupted by impatient listeners and when those who speak of moral matters like marriage are cut off with a yawn. A character in *Queen Zarah* begins a long general attack on the practice of duelling, an attack which would be frequently echoed in sentimental literature, but he is silenced by a bored friend who wants to hear of the specific scandal they were enjoying. The habit of making fiction express more morally elevated views than the reader usually holds or could practise in life is often satirised by Manley, who sees it as yet another bizarre construction of a culture that constantly forms ideals it cannot embody.

But at other times the purpose is conventionally moral:

> The chief End of History is to instruct and inspire into Men the Love of Virtue and Abhorrence of Vice, by the Examples propos'd to them; therefore the Conclusions of a Story ought to have some Tract of Morality which may engage Virtue.

Put more succinctly in *The New Atalantis,* fiction should show 'suffering Vertue, crown'd with just Rewards, and Vice beneath the Ax'.[4]

Many of Manley's readers must have chuckled at this statement, for by the time of *The New Atalantis* she was famous for her naughty scenes, however politically motivated and however yielding of morality. She was herself acutely aware of the objections that could be made to her scandalous and sexy subject matter. As many detractors insisted and she could not deny, her main material was gossip about the great, secrets revealed of wicked happenings that people would rather have kept hidden. Inevitably the secrets that she told appealed to the prurient desires of the reader and could titillate the sophisticate and corrupt the innocent. Sometimes she glories in what she is doing and sometimes defangs it by declaring that her revelations are innocuous for the events are all far in the past. But in the preface to the second volume of *The New Atalantis,* after she has had the measure of hostile reaction and enthusiastic consumption, she makes greater claims, setting out grandly to turn her image from a female scandal-monger into a male satirist in the line of Horace, Juvenal and Dryden; satire, she claims, was always personal or it would have had no bite, and the flailing of individual vice signified not a vicious gossip but a 'lofty stedfast Soul'.

Whatever her noble stance, what most struck readers of the time and later was the openness of both the presentation and the discussion of sexuality. In her pages women still suffer for sexual activity far beyond men, but on the whole it is a social suffering and the sexual fall, largely demystified, does not bear the immense religious and moral weight it will achieve in sentimental literature. As she had been in Aphra Behn's work, woman is often here the actual subject of desire, rather than simply the pretty object of male love or lust. Hence such frank descriptions as the following from Part I of *The New Atalantis:*

> the Dutchess softly enter'd that little Chamber of Repose, the Weather violently hot the Umbrelloes were let down from behind the Windows, the Sashes open, and the Jessimine that cover'd 'em blew in with a gentle Fragrancy; Tuberoses set in pretty Gilt and China Posts, were placed advantageously upon Stands, the Curtains of the Bed drawn back to the Canopy, made of yellow Velvet embroider'd with white Bugles, the Panels of the Chamber Looking-Glass, upon the Bed were strow'd with a lavish Profuseness, plenty of Orange and Lemon Flowers, and to compleat the Scene, the young Germanicus in a dress and posture not very decent to describe; it was he that was newly risen from the Bath, and in a lose Gown of Carnation Taffety, stain'd with Indian Figures, his beautiful long, flowing Hair, for then 'twas the Custom to wear their own tied back with a Ribbon of the same Colour, he had thrown himself upon the Bed, pretending to Sleep, with nothing on but his Shirt and Night-Gown, which he had so indecently dispos'd, that slumbring as he appear'd, his whole Person stood confess'd to the Eyes of the Amorous Dutchess, his Limbs were exactly form'd, his Skin shiningly white, and the Pleasure the Ladies graceful entrance gave him, diffus'd Joy and Desire throughout all his Form; his lovely Eyes seem'd to be closed, his Face turn'd on one side . . . was obscur'd by the Lace depending from the Pillows on which he rested . . . with an amorous sign, she gently threw her self on the Bed close to the desiring Youth.[5]

This is a portrait of the Duchess de l'Inconstant, entranced by the charms of a new lover. Much is interchangeable among erotic scenes of Behn, Manley and Haywood but what is unusual for amorous descriptions is that the gaze is female and the languorous artful seductiveness of the body is a man's. Like so many fictional women before and after him, accused of narcissism as they go about their necessarily self-interested business of attracting another, the young man has arranged himself to be seduced. The spontaneity of response is here the woman's; it is engaging to the reader in its frankness and, indeed, in its effectiveness, for the man quickly comes to answer the woman's desire and fulfil the reader's hopes.

It is, however, a kind of dream of equal sexuality. It is made possible partly through Manley's concentration, similar to that in both Behn and Haywood, not on the sexual act itself, but on its prelude and setting. In her stories, stress is on the stimulus to copulation; repeatedly there are details of the heat, flowers and gardens, opened windows, the fragrant smells, the luxurious accessories, and the dishabille of the lovers. The atmospheric details emphasise the inevitability and naturalness of sexual expression for male and female alike, while the social elements, the fashion and luxury, are those associated with women as well as men.

Yet, in the last analysis, there is the sexual act to perform, an act which is absolutely unequal in its physical and social repercussions—in Behn it is often interrupted to the woman's annoyance, in Haywood to the man's, but in Manley it usually takes place without chance or providence to prevent it. Ultimately, the Duchess's spontaneity of response must be ominous, however attractive it might initially seem; it would be so in man or woman in this dangerous, scheming society, but in the latter its result is almost inevitably bound to involve misery. Despite her active, lusty, possessive gaze, when the sexual act occurs, the Duchess becomes simply the object instead of the subject, and she dwindles from active desiring agent into a commodity: 'he got the possession of her Person'. In time her exchange value deteriorates and she sinks from acting as lover of a king to being, like Sylvia, the mistress of servants.

The New Atalantis is a dystopia beside Bacon's utopian *New Atlantis,* replacing the idea of disinterestedness with a reality of self-interest and cupidity. In Manley's works, the driving force of humanity is desire—both for money and sex, which become interchangeable. In the latter women may suffer consequences more than men but the most successful learn to manipulate sexual desire in others and to avoid being, like the Duchess, controlled by it themselves. Although a narrator might condescendingly admire the spontaneous gesture and the authentic emotion, she may also lament, with sophisticated melancholy, that the sincere and transparent are not fitted for a world in which survival means dissimulation and constant devotion to self-interest. Marriages for love may be the ideal, but marriages for financial interest are both common and appropriate, although ritually condemned. Women marry for reputation and maintenance, men marry to clear their mortgages; the success goes to the most manipulative and cunning. When equality is reached, there is an impasse, as happens in Defoe's *Moll Flanders* where the heroine fools and is fooled simultaneously, or in the life of the 'German Princess' who cheats and is cheated by her 'lord'. The answer to the rake, the male predator, who stalks through so much female fiction of this century is not the later, almost compulsory demand for his destruction or for more male protection of women from men, but the recommendation that women achieve more awareness, wit and self-control.

The world of the scandal novels is quite openly sordid and debased, its inhabitants opportunistic and self-aggrandising. Yet it is also energetic and vigorous. Luxury is appalling and attractive. There is much describing of elaborate clothes, coaches and expensive interiors, much detail of gold, lace and costly embroidery. Rich food and drink accompany the intimate bawdy talk on nights that are always oppressively hot, and they augment the sense of intricate social corruption. Sexuality is overwhelming and inevitably isolating through its expression in individual desire, but the sheer number and variety of the sexual scenes Manley describes make physical enslavement a soothingly uniting predicament. As night comes in her tales, the copulations begin and the separate sins become a comfortable communal fall.

To survive in the harsh, complicated society of *Zarah, The New Atalantis* and *Rivella* everyone must wear a mask. Social grace is wanted, not the sentimental virtues of chastity and compassion, so much preached for and to women, decorum not sincerity, good conversation and worldly sense: 'The Knowledge which teaches Men to live among People of civility and Manners'. Yet, although very much a lady as well as a goddess, one of the two onlookers of the scenes in *The New Atalantis* is nevertheless 'Virtue'. Her presence emphasises the apparent need of society to define an ideal of virtue and to try to illustrate it in life—usually, it becomes apparent, at another person's (woman's) expense.

Because of this need, education is especially problematic, although there is general unquestioning acceptance that it should be in virtue, particularly for young girls. Virtue is needed to guard a girl against premature indulgence in sex, and 'virtuous' books must keep out titillating romances that encourage her seemingly natural desire for seduction. Despite a rhetoric of admiration, the purpose of a virtuous education in moral principles, sincerity and chastity seems clearly to be the thwarting of nature, a necessity for existence in a civilised world.

Yet, repeatedly, this education is revealed as socially inept, even dangerous for girls. By suppressing sexual expression, it merely delays and heightens it; as Astrea wearily remarks at the close of yet another story of seduction and betrayal, 'we see the tender Sex, with all their Native Timorousness, Modesty and Shamefac'd Education, when stung by Love, can trample under Foot the consideration of Virtue and Glory'.[6] For the older male seducer, a virtuous education simply renders the young girl a yet more delicious prey; it becomes a seductive attribute to femaleness, sought by men to enhance the charms of the victim and give piquancy to defloration.

As snug havens of domesticity, families do not seem to exist in the cold world of Manley's novels, and the most successful survivors are those who have learned that they are essentially alone. Society is the small group of the court and its hangers-on, and there is no sense of alternative worlds except through rustic exile or foreign escape. Communal activity may give sensation and pleasure but never security, and even associations for political purposes and financial intrigue are temporary and precarious.

There is, however, one striking example of a successful communal venture, the scandalous Cabal of upperclass women described in Book II of *The New Atalantis.* The ladies who form this group have no desire for the high-mindedness and celibacy shown in other fictional female communities, like the learning academy of Mary Astell or the philanthropic institution of Sarah Scott described in *Millenium Hall* (1762); instead they aim at pleasure and they make themselves remarkably comfortable in a country house surrounded by extensive grounds and views, and stocked with good wine. Despite the naive Astrea's initial view, that they are a defensive huddle of women trying to avoid 'that rapacious Sex', they are clearly sexual beings involved in sexual encounters 'beyond what Nature design'd'. Yet, although scandalous, the lesbianism is not especially shocking, and even Astrea, when she comes to understand its existence, opposes it more for social than for moral or religious reasons, seeing it as preventing advantageous marriages and as provoking 'obscene Laughter' in men. And the positive social and psychological side is also stressed, for in the Cabal loving women share property, if only inside relationships: 'In this little Commonwealth is no Property; whatever a Lady possesses is, sans ceremone, at the service, and for the use of her Fair Friend, without the vain nice scruple of being oblig'd.'[7] Here in the Cabal women can play men, taste their power, and reject its usual implications, that 'Woman was only created (with all her Beauty, Softness, Passions and compleat Tenderness) to adorn the Husband's Reign, perfect his Happiness, and propagate the Kind'.[8]

The seemingly feminist tone of this last statement is not a dominant one in Manley's works, although it occurs frequently. Usually, however, it has an ambiguous context that makes it yet another of the many modified tones of the tales. Certainly Manley understands that the cards are stacked against women in the sexual game and that they are therefore at an immense disadvantage in the social one. But individual women, like Aphra Behn's Sylvia in *Love Letters Between a Nobleman and his Sister,* can manipulate others and scheme their way to the top just as well as men. The unremitting pursuit of self-interest, condemned but described with gusto all the same, is a female as well as a male attribute, and this coincidence in activity gives a kind of equality to the fictional society that makes a feminist protest almost irrelevant. All power is socially desirable and morally corrupting and usurped female power is, if anything, marginally more harmful because less expected. The detested Duchess of Marlborough with her enormous power suggests this view to Manley, and Jane Austen illustrates it a century later in her satirical portraits of the haughty Mrs Ferrars and Lady Catherine de Burgh.

Manley expresses the conventional distaste for the use of sexuality by women, and she condemns them for employing their sexual desirability to trap rich men into marriage. Yet she also gives them justification by asserting that the same desire for riches and power animates both sexes; while men have many routes to attain them, women have only their sexual attractiveness.

Because of the different social effects of sexual indulgence on men and women, different narratives are inevitably provided for them. But the difference is not that men may prey on women or guard and save them according to genre, while women must enter the archetypal stories of the virgin or the whore; instead both sexes divide into the naive and the manipulative, and their stories evolve accordingly. Silly innocent women are fooled by men, who are in turn deceived by sophisticated scheming women. The female victim is always pitied at length, but she is given none of the spiritual significance she would acquire in the novels of Samuel Richardson a few years later. She suffers for her sexual activity far beyond men, but on the whole it is a social suffering and the sexual fall, largely demystified, does not bear the immense religious and moral weight it has in sentimental literature.

One sexual narrative is repeated so frequently in Manley's tales that it assumes the status of a myth. It coincides with the developing intertwined stories of virtue in distress and of love betrayed, which will come to dominate literature about women and which is already expressed in the woman-centred tragedies of Otway and Rowe. It is this story that *Rivella* will so naughtily subvert.

A young innocent girl is unprotected by a sensible mother; she finds at puberty that her male guardian or father figure is displaced by or transformed into a lusty and destructive man bent on rape or seduction. The sad account of Charlot from Part I of *The New Atalantis* is typical. In this narrative Manley has ample opportunity to repeat her worldly points about the problematic nature of education and to illustrate the difficulty of constructing a viable self amidst conflicting influences of moral instruction, ambivalent literature, overwhelming personalities and natural sexual but socially destructive drives.

In the tale, the Duke—like Manley's other villains, self-made and acquisitive despite his title—educates his ward Charlot only in virtue, banishing from her environment all novels and poetry that might provoke

lascivious feelings or teach dissimulation. She thus becomes a modest, silent, sincere young woman, a correct product of the education she has experienced. Then literature wickedly intrudes into her chaste scene and all becomes heated and obscure. First Charlot simply reads instructive moral poetry, which reinforces her virtuous inclinations. But her acting-out for her guardian of scenes from the works, her assumption of roles despite her authenticity and innocence, has the effect of inflaming the Duke, whose fatherly love is rapidly transformed into an altogether less proper emotion. Meanwhile he himself is a victim of literature in his assent to the notion of the amoral political author Machiavelli that greatness may be expressed in wickedness; he therefore finds himself lusting after the person whose purity he should guard, uninhibited by any restraint on his inclinations.

Preparing to seduce his ward, the Duke excites her mind with less elevated verse. Charlot has learned to see the father where the Duke is now presenting the lover; consequently his signs of desire assume incestuous overtones for the reader. In due course, his disorder, his trembling and shortness of breath inject Charlot with 'that new and lazy Poison'. Certainly it is the birth of sexuality in her, but it is also the beginning of desire for social power, always a component of sexual feeling in Manley's works. The apparent need to please in women is, according to the author, often less the desire for sexual gratification than a claim to influence; other forms of empire seem 'to be politically deny'd them, because the way to Authority and Glory is stop'd up'.[9] Charlot is excited by a temporary sexual power that gives her social influence but which she does not adequately understand—'ignorant of the Power of Love, that Leveller of Mankind'. So she cannot use this power to promote her own interests.

Under the influence of the seductive Ovid, Petrarch and other licentious reading, 'Books . . . abominable for Virgins . . . such as explain the Mysteries of Nature, the congregated Pleasures of Venus', her moral education melts into 'Precepts of airy Virtue', and she desires and gains sexual fulfilment. The reader becomes the voyeur of the first seduction and is delivered the scene through the eyes both of the amorous Duke and of the naive daughterly girl. But the sexual climax, coming after the expected description of excessive heat, waiting bed and dishabille, is, in literary and social terms, anticlimactic: while yet she was 'doubtful of his designs, he took advantage of her confusion to accomplish 'em . . . Thus was Charlot undone! thus ruin'd by him that ought to have been her Protector!'[10]

Entering the new category of the fallen woman, Charlot finds her virtuous education valueless. Designed to guard virginity for social or moral ends, it has no purpose outside the sexual meaning and no relevance to the fallen woman's need to gain control over herself and her environment. Indeed such an education is now actually harmful, for it simply renders Charlot sincere and without disguise. A worldly-wise countess who 'knew the Management of Mankind, and how to procure herself universal Love and Admiration', a lady who has been bred up in the 'fashionable way of making Love, wherein the Heart has little or no part', gives Charlot new role models from literature of manipulative and powerful women who have understood men and gained power and influence. At the same time she tries to teach the young girl that love must be used by a woman as a tool with which to establish herself in the world. But the good Charlot cannot so quickly learn a new lesson; she fails to fix the Duke in marriage and watches her own passion grow as his declines, not understanding that 'the same unaccountable thing that cools the Swain, more warms the Nymph'. The end is inevitable. Giving up the role of educator, the Countess concentrates on herself and her interest; she sets up the seductive sexual scene, and swiftly catches the Duke in marriage. Charlot is left to 'Horror, Sorrow, and Repentance'. 'She dy'd a true Landmark: to warn all believing Virgins from shipwrecking their Honour upon . . . the Vows and pretended Passion of Mankind.'[11]

But of course the moral is not as clear as this. The repentance has few religious overtones, and the honour and virtue obtain no transcendental meaning. Astrea comments at the end of Charlot's story:

> Men may regain their Reputations, tho' after a Complication of Vices, Cowardice, Robbery, Adultery, Bribery, and Murder, but a Woman once departed from the Road of Virtue, is made incapable of a return; Sorrow and Scorn overtake her, and . . . the World suffers her to perish loath'd, and unlamented.

Vice is translated into sexual activity for a woman, and into murder, robbery and bribery for a man, and both translations are given social not moral significance. Indeed chastity for a woman is not really a virtue at all, but simply good social sense in the absence of consummate ability.

The story of Charlot gains some resonance in Manley's works from its equivocal use of the theme of virtue in distress or love betrayed, and it adds more through the autobiographical content. For a version of the tale of Charlot is so often told that, even without a knowledge of *Rivella*, it would be difficult not to discern that it held some special fascination for the author. Sometimes the story trails off into sorrow and exile, as it did in the narrative of Charlot and the Duke; sometimes it ends in the woman's suicide and the man's unperturbed re-entry into society. But it can also continue in the less dramatic sadness and sordidness of a woman's life outside respectable society. It is into the last narrative that Manley herself most clearly enters.

In *Rivella,* the narrator claims that the story of Delia in *The New Atalantis* is actually the life story of the author of that work. Rivella, the famous writer, becomes the result of the sexual victimisation of Delia, an innocent young orphan; Delia and Rivella unite in Delarivier.

Like so many of her predecessors in Manley's works, Delia is poisoned by romantic tales. She is persuaded into marriage with her guardian, a man twenty-three years her senior. The marriage is simply a variation of seduction, since it proves bigamous. The effect is the usual social isolation of the woman and her realisation at last that virtue is specific to gender. Men may sin and sin and be socially reclaimed, but women, even if only guilty in appearance, are irretrievably lost and cannot be reconciled to society: 'Is it not this Inhospitality that brings so many unhappy Wretches to Distruction? dispairing of Redemption, from one vile degree to another, they plunge themselves down to the lowest ebb of Infamy!'[12]

In its use of the narrative of virtue in distress, the story of Delia highlights many of the difficulties Manley had encountered in the presentation of a public female image. The teller of Delia's story, aiming to rouse as much sympathy as possible in the reader, insists that the young girl is innocent of sexual longing despite her unwise perusal of romance and that she is precipitated into marriage through illness; her guardian cares for her and she is grateful. Such a timely collapse would come to many later heroines who find themselves married or compromised not through sexual desire but through physical weakness. Meanwhile the guardian, like the Duke, is tinged with incest, for he is associated with her father and was present at her birth. Yet, Astrea, goddess of justice, will have none of this special pleading and, in her critical comments, the narrative of virtue in distress becomes a less elevated tale of foolish love betrayed, and the heroine is transformed from a pure child into a silly sexual woman.

The usual narrative ending is withdrawal and death for distressed innocence, and suicide for betrayed passion. But of course Delarivier Manley does not kill herself or pine and die. Instead, she becomes a writer and she uses her infamy to her advantage. The sad story of Delia is continued in the robust *Rivella,* where the reader learns that a woman without reputation and honour may be freed for economic activity. In time she transforms herself from the deceived and confused object of desire into its subject. But, although Rivella is sometimes described as a looker, an amorous gazer on others, far more strikingly she uses herself as a writing subject to create in her inflaming works an elusive and suggestive image of herself as object of male desire. It is, after all, female desirability, not desire itself, that has social currency and gains social power in a patriarchal world.

Manley's view of herself as a young woman in her fictional autobiography, 'Sweet, Clean, Witty, Friendly, Serviceable', is relayed through the medium of a male admirer, whom she created to tell her story. The same useful gentleman is given a quick justification for the older Manley's notorious public life with its sexual irregularities, political scandals and shady legal and financial dealings:

> Her Vertues are her own, her Vices occasion'd by her Misfortunes; and yet as I have often heard her say, If she had been a Man, she had been without Fault: But the Charter of that Sex being much more confin'd than ours, what is not a Crime in Men is scandalous and unpardonable in Woman.[13]

In the work of Manley, as in that of Behn, many signs of woman are hung out. Some follow Behn's fictional narrators in suggesting an older worldly gossip, like Phoebe Crackenthorpe of *The Female Tatler* or Intelligence in **The New Atalantis.** Some, feeding on her reputation as depicter of improper sexual encounters, resemble the signs of Angellica and Mary Carleton and emphasise physical and verbal seductiveness. Others follow the Duchess of Newcastle and the later Aphra Behn in asserting the writer and her fame. Still others merge the two and use the image of the literary lady for a verbal erotic seduction, the prose forming a kind of boudoir into which the reader must expectantly penetrate. As can be discerned, the prude and the ingenu(e) have no place in Mrs Manley's audience.

In **Rivella** the author displays herself for her purchasing male readership and makes a direct link between authorship and seduction, literary consumption and sexual gratification. Her words dissolve her fatness, smooth her pock marks, light up her expressive eyes and give an 'establish'd Reputation' to her neck and breasts. The final scene of the autobiography, echoing the many sexual and scandalous encounters in Manley's books, invites the fictional listener, with the reader, to hear the author's seductive conversation, sit at her well-furnished table, and to repose with her 'during the Heat of the Day' on her bed, 'nicely sheeted and strow'd with Roses, Jessamines or Orange-Flowers . . . her Pillows neatly trim'd with Lace or Muslin, stuck round with Junquils, or other natural Garden Sweets'.[14]

Despite the amorous build-up and the many precedents in her tales, this scene will—just this once—not give way to the narrative of love betrayed, for, even beyond sexual cunning, it hints at a new power of women through their manipulation of literary language. The lady here is a writing woman who has weathered sexual and social disasters and has learned the power of words. No sexual act that might objectify and victimise the female is written into her account, although sexual activity may be implied, and the end is not the rushed retreat of the satisfied man and the sorrow of the abandoned woman. Instead there is a companionable airing in the park or on the water when the heat of the day is gone.

Here in this ending of Manley's fictional autobiography, a mixture of imaginative history and scandalous exposure, desire is controlled and contained, and the reader is made to agree with the listener whom the author has created for herself, that she, a fallen woman who does not die, a maker of wicked romances, is the 'only Person of her sex that knows how to Live'.

Rivella is well aware of the identification of woman writer and whore in male writing and she comically plays with the convention. She uses the image of the literary lady for a verbal erotic seduction brought about through the special female ability of the author to please with scenes of love. In her prose there is a sense of excitement at the power of language, a new social power to set beside or, indeed, to manipulate and direct sexual power. Words can control response and make and unmake desire. They alone can construct the meaning of the sexual act and they alone can create sex without pregnancy, venereal disease or lifelong misery.

In **The New Atalantis,** Manley diffuses the criticism that she is corrupting the mind of the reader with the rather lame excuse that only vicious activity can harm, not the mere hearing of scandal. Yet she does not rest with such simplicity and, in common with the writers throughout the eighteenth century, she is both appalled and excited by the obvious and feared effect of literature on the mind. While declaring that stories of sexual excitement cannot by themselves corrupt and incite to sexual activity, she provides example after example of young girls inflamed into love by the rash perusal of romantic tales. But in **Rivella** she avoids this whole troubling nexus by moving her story into the sophisticated world of the older woman and the always privileged men. Rivella presents an image of herself as consummate mistress of the titillating effect and there need be no pretence that literature does not often and deliciously nudge life: 'After perusing her Inchanting Descriptions, which of us have not gone in Search of Raptures which she every where tells us, as happy Mortals, we are capable of tasting,' remarks the obliging male.[15] Men's often dangerous desire ends, where it ought, in the author herself; female desire need not result in distress but instead it yields delight and money through its representation. The whore becomes storyteller of men's lust and recorder of the comic history of virtue in distress made entertaining and profitable.

Notes

[1] The various fictions are printed together as if they were an actual autobiography by Fidelis Morgan in *A Woman of No Character: An Autobiography of Mrs*

Manley (London: Faber, 1986). Owing possibly to a confusion of sources, it was common until recently to refer to Mrs Manley as 'Mary', although her signed works, private letters, will and tombstone bear the name 'Delarivière' or 'Delarivier'; for a discussion of the matter see Patricia Köster's introduction to *The Novels of Mary Delarivier Manley*, I, pp. v-vi.

[2] Manley, *The Novels*, II, p. 203. See vol. II for a key to *The New Atalantis*.

[3] Manley, *The Novels*, II, pp. 41 and 58-9.

[4] Manley, *The Novels*, II, p. 111.

[5] Manley, *The Novels*, I, pp. 33-4. For a rather different interpretation of the erotic content see John J. Richetti, *Popular Fiction before Richardson: Narrative Patterns, 1700-1739* (Oxford: Clarendon Press, 1969).

[6] Manley, *The Novels*, II, p. 192.

[7] Manley, *The Novels*, II, p. 57.

[8] Manley, *The Novels*, II, pp. 57-8.

[9] Manley, *The Novels*, I, p. 55.

[10] Manley, *The Novels*, I, p. 72.

[11] Manley, *The Novels*, I, p. 88.

[12] Manley, *The Novels*, II, p. 191. (Köster, I, 723).

[13] Manley, *The Novels*, II, 15.

[14] Manley, *The Novels*, II, 16.

[15] Manley, *The Novels*, II, 17.

Catherine Gallagher (essay date 1990)

SOURCE: "Political Crimes and Fictional Alibis: The Case of Delarivier Manley," in *Eighteenth-Century Studies*, Vol. 23, No. 4, Summer, 1990, pp. 502-21.

[*In the essay that follows, Gallagher analyzes the paradoxical relationship between politics, gender, and scandal fiction in Manley's novels. The critic proposes that while Manley, like her contemporaries, used allegory to protect herself from prosecution, she developed this technique further by shaping fictional circumstances into a narrative that could be read for its own enjoyment as well as its slanderous implications.*]

When Delarivier[1] Manley was arrested for seditious libel in 1709, according to her later account of the inquest, fiction was her alibi.[2] She had written *Secret*

Memoirs and Manners of Several Persons of Quality, of Both Sexes. From the New Atalantis, an Island in the Mediterranean (1709), the provocative allegorical satire on sexual and political corruption among the Whigs who then controlled the government of Queen Anne. Like an earlier work that was probably also by Manley, *The Secret History of Queen Zarah and the Zarazians* (1704), *The New Atalantis* was particularly intent upon libeling Sarah Churchill, then Lady Marlborough, and the Whig ministers closest to her. Both books were huge successes; the first went through at least six editions in as many years. *The New Atalantis* was so popular that Sarah Churchill anxiously wrote to Queen Anne complaining that "notwithstanding the prosecution" it was being "sold at every shop."[3]

The prosecution was a partisan affair; the government probably hoped, in questioning Delarivier Manley about her motives, to uncover the active participation of prominent Tories in the composition of *The New Atalantis*.[4] According to her version of the events, written in the third-person, the prosecutors pressed the author to confess her political-economic motivation and admit she had informants in high places. Instead, she pleaded innocent on the grounds that she was merely a fiction writer:

> They used several arguments to make her discover who were the persons in her books, or at least from whom she had received information of some special facts which they thought were above her own intelligence.
>
> Her defence was with much humility and sorrow for having offended, at the same time denying that any persons were concerned with her or that she had a farther design than writing for her own amusement and diversion in the country, without intending particular reflections on characters.
>
> When this was not believed and the contrary urged very home to her by several circumstances and likenesses she said then it must be inspiration, because, knowing her own innocence, she could account for it no other way.
>
> The secretary replied upon her that inspiration used to be upon a good account and her writings were stark naught. She told him, with an air full of patience, that might be true, but it was as true that there were evil angels as well as good, so, nevertheless, what she had wrote might still be by inspiration.[5]

Such a defense, if it were indeed made, was certainly not designed to convince anyone that Manley was an isolated genius or an ignorant but innocent woman merely trying to amuse herself. It was more likely a species of tactical play, calculated to confound and embarrass the prosecution as well as protect Manley's associates.[6] She makes herself liable by claiming full responsibility for the offensive book, but the very terms of her admission simply signal her refusal to cooperate with the prosecution. Insisting on the pure fictionality of the text allowed Manley both to deny her sources and to place the burden of identifying the libeled persons of quality on her interrogators, who were thus tricked into attaching the scandalous stories to the names of Whig ministers, in a sense becoming parties to the libel. Her appeal to "inspiration" was similarly disingenuous, at once evoking and mocking the idea of the isolated literary genius. The alibi of fiction thus had many uses, but deceit was not one of them. It was as transparently untrue (or, since it was not intended to convince, as truly fictional) as the pure fictionality of **The New Atalantis.**

In Delarivier Manley's heroic version of her defense, then, we are given the truth of a political crime opposed by the fictionality of a fictional alibi. Indeed, the transparent fictionality of the alibi indicates the truth of the charge. Delarivier Manley's case is full of paradoxes of this sort, which I will trace to explore an extraordinary moment in the history of English women's writing, a moment when party politics, fiction, the literary marketplace, and feminine sexuality became intricately entangled. I will describe three "knots" of this entanglement: first, the crossing of fiction and politics in legal discourse; second, the conjunction and disjunction of feminine eroticism and politics; and a third crux produced by the dramatization in **The New Atalantis** of a thwarted attempt to undo the first two knots.

An adequate explanation of these entanglements, the sort of explanation I do not have space to develop here, would view them as parts of a process of realignment between politics and commerce in general, and politics and the literary marketplace in particular. Such an explanation might point, for example, to a new discursiveness in English politics, a redefinition of politics as public, indeed, published debate. It would also take into consideration the growth of what J. G. A. Pocock has called "civil humanism," an ideology that conferred a high value on personality traits cultivated both in commerce and in social intercourse between the sexes. It would no doubt also describe the effects of the reciprocal stimulation of the national debt and the growth of speculative finance capital. All of these rearticulations of the connections and boundaries between politics and commerce, one might argue, aggravated anxieties about the possible dependence of reality on language and men on women. Consequently, women writers, who had new opportunities for making themselves useful to both political parties, also found themselves loaded with the collective guilt generated by the new political-commercial-discursive interpenetrations.

"Scandalosissima Scoundrelia," as a contemporary publication dubbed Manley,[7] seems to have carried this guilt by representing the *scandal* of scandal: the affront to propriety offered by the public discrediting of people in authority. Such a figure was especially necessary when almost all political writers were actually scandalmongering, when political discourse had barely entered the process of defining what would be a proper and what an improper accusation, when almost every partisan attack was *ad hominem.* Manley's career, therefore, was conditioned by her genre, which was not "fiction" as she facetiously (and many later critics[8] quite seriously) claimed, but was rather scandalous allegorical narrative. In order to understand her exemplary significance we have to emphasize what recent critics have tended simply to note in passing: that her works were indeed defamatory "reflections" on her contemporaries. Only by moving this fact into the center of our analysis can we give either an adequate formal descripiton of her writings or trace their complicated crossing of politics, fiction, and femininity.

Fiction and Politics: Libelous Crossings

Let me continue to trace the paradox of Delarivier Manley's alibi, the alibi that continually crosses politics with fiction through the economic, political, and legal labyrinth of early eighteenth-century letters. It seems very odd to come up with an alibi that no one is supposed to believe, just as it seems odd to invent allegories and codes that are supposed to be transparent. The normal way of explaining this bizarre feature of Augustan literary life is simply to see it as designed for the use to which Manley put it at her inquest: protection against the libel law. After the Licensing Act lapsed in 1695, and before the new copyright law of 1709 and the Stamp Act of 1712 were passed, the English printing trade was almost entirely unregulated.[9] Because the state found itself without automatic channels of pre-publication censorship, it relied all the more heavily on prosecutions for libel.[10] Almost anything that "reflected" on the government, the crown, the church, the Parliament, the laws, persons of quality, private persons, etc., could be prosecuted.[11] The libelous statements did not need to be false; indeed, they did not even need to be damaging. Merely "reflecting" on the forbidden topics was illegal. Precisely because the law was so broad, prosecutions tended to be highly factional. A Whiggish Secretary, for example, might prosecute High Church Tories for defending the Church against dissenting attacks because such defenses, the prosecutors claimed, might give the people the impression that the Church was in danger and thereby spread alarm. Even zealous patriotism could thus be read as seditious libel. When we add to all this the consideration that during the triumvirate period, the government, itself of no party, was inclined to indict writers of any party, it becomes clear that entering into any controversy on any side could make one vulnerable to prosecution.

Why, then, we might ask, didn't writers just avoid political controversy? This question also has a standard answer. It was all but impossible for a writer to stay out of politics during the period from 1695 (the discontinuance of the Licensing Act) to 1714 (the death of Queen Anne) because political controversy was virtually the only road to making either a name or a living as a writer.[12] The economics of authorship were especially precarious, for although lack of regulation probably swelled the population of Grub Street, it also made authors and printers powerless against pirating.[13] It is extremely difficult to calculate the incomes of the majority of writers, but the conditions of the London printing trade from 1695-1714 suggest that it was probably a period of their unusually harsh exploitation. Predictably, instances of private patronage declined every decade after 1700, although subscription publishing continued throughout the early eighteenth century and was even "democratized" by London syndicates that advertised everywhere for subscribers.[14] But in the period under discussion, patronage remained the dominant and necessary form of literary support, though it tended to flow through partisan political channels. Writers, no longer fully dependent on the Crown or individual aristocrats, found themselves indebted to emergent political institutions that were only beginning to organize and define themselves.

Thus there was an unprecedented politicization of authorship in this period and a new reliance of politics on writing. Writers were central to the process of party formation and to that other enormous change in British politics, the development of ministerial government. The political patrons, the heads of parties, needed writers who could articulate and in numerous instances invent the "principles" on which the patronage depended.[15] The great lords who controlled the political purse-strings, although constantly accused of ingratitude by their writers, in fact did manage to subsidize the production of a large quantity of writing during this period, either by direct payment to writers or by the distribution of pensions, offices, and other places. The nature of both politics and writing, however, was altered in the transaction.

The new public textuality of political controversy was, of course, impossible to restrict to a readership actively involved in running the country. This period famously marks the beginning of a political culture in England, in which the London press, dominated and subsidized by party and ministerial politics, shaped that still-embryonic entity, the reading "public." The vast majority of writers only managed to make their way in the world by engaging in political controversy, that is, by making themselves liable to prosecution for libel. As James Bramston facetiously asked somewhat later in the century,

> Can Statutes keep the British Press in awe
> When that sells best, that's most against the
> law?[16]

Party politics and ministerial government, the very forces that were bringing the libel prosecutions against controversial publications, were also feeding on, stimulating, and subsidizing the marketplace in those very publications.

Hence, like Richard Steele, Joseph Addison, Jonathan Swift, and Susanna Centlivre, Delarivier Manley practiced partisan political writing because: 1) it was the most popular form in the incipient literary marketplace; 2) it held the additional financial advantage of sometimes commanding party patronage; and 3) party loyalty became in the late years of Anne's reign "the new criterion for activity and friendship" in literary London.[17] Although she probably did not receive much for the manuscript of *The New Atalantis,* in 1711 we find her requesting patronage from Robert Harley, Earl of Oxford, and head of the Tory Party: "If your Lordship think I have been any way serviceable, however accidentally, your justice will inspire you to give me your protection; if no, I hope your generosity will incite you to reward my good endeavours, whether by some small pension . . . or some other effect of your bounty, which I humbly leave to your Lordship's choice."[18] Swift also turned over the editorship of *The Examiner,* the Tory organ of abuse, to Manley in 1710, and one of his letters mentions the necessity of "doing something" for Mrs. Manley. She was commissioned to write other Tory pamphlets in the late years of the reign as well. Partisan works were not her only productions, but they were certainly a high percentage of her writings between 1704 and 1714. Delarivier Manley was a phenomenon of the new political culture that kept the Secretary of State so busy issuing warrants.

The relationship between these well-known conditions of authorship and the style of Augustan literature, as I noted earlier, is sometimes said to be quite uncomplicated. Allegories and other stylistic disguises such as ironic inversions and numbered codes, we are told, developed as technicalities through which the penalties of the law might be evaded.[19] Certainly some techniques of the period fit this description, and writers were found of expatiating on both their necessity and their transparency. Swift, for example, would on occasion discuss the disguises of satire as if they were quite extraneous to its substance:

> First, we are careful never to print a man's name out at length; but as I do that of Mr. St—le: So that although every body alive knows who I mean, the plaintiff can have no redress in any court of justice. Secondly, by putting cases [telling recognizable but fictionalized stories] . . . [Lastly,] by nicknames, either commonly known or stamped for the purpose, which every body can tell how to apply.[20]

The literary techniques, in other words, were supposedly mere technicalities for avoiding arrest or hindering successful prosecution. They were legal exigencies imposed from without, not rhetorical strategies developing from within the satirical intent.

We should note that in this view, technique and message, literature and politics, are substantially disengaged; political satire took, for example, the form of allegorical narrative because one could always claim that the story was not meant to reflect on any real, living person or contemporary event. But when one thus sees the stylistic component of the satire simply as a hindrance to prosecution, the literary techniques take on the attributes of mere codes, devices wholly separable from the message, which one extracts by a process of decoding.

Literary historians have sometimes followed this line of reasoning until it yielded an explanation for the appearance of early fiction. The need for legal protection led to increasing diguises, which eventually took on an independent life of their own, leaving behind the context of political controversy (to which the techniques were generally irrelevant anyway) and resulting in the invention of the purely literary. *Gulliver's Travels* has been cited as an example of this development—a satirical allegory that, having thoroughly concealed its topical reflections, remained opaque as "personal" or specific satire and thereby achieved the status of a fictional classic.[21] However, in the above passage by Swift, such a development is not anticipated, for the devices described are imagined to be completely transparent, so transparent that one can hardly call them disguises of political purpose at all. Rather, like Manley's alibi of inspiration, they *indicate,* although in a supposedly arbitrary way, illicit political intentions.

This latter fact, that the techniques indicated rather than concealed libelous statements, leads to a difficulty if one is arguing that the writers were only trying to protect themselves from prosecution by allegorizing, changing names, or altering circumstances. We should note at the outset that these devices did not always protect writers and printers from either arrest or successful prosecution. Of course, we cannot conclude that they were completely ineffective. They multiplied the issues in a libel case to the advantage of the accused, and they introduced legal questions that a jury, rather than the Court alone, could decide.[22] However, one ran an obvious risk in using such artifices, for although they interfered with prosecutions, they also at times alerted prosecutors to the libelous nature of a piece of writing.

Let us look, for example, at the legal status of the "allegorical style" favored by Manley that consisted in telling scandalous stories, placed in distant historical, exotic, or mythical settings, but referring to recognizable real persons. The author of a 1738 book called *State Law: or, The Doctrine of Libels Discussed and*

Examined explains why such fictional allegorizing was by no means a foolproof protection against prosecution: "[W]hat Right has the allegorical Style to escape [the law of libel]? . . . if it be the common Notion, that this Picture represents a certain Person, the Drawer is answerable for the Injury he suffers."[23] Hence the more "every body alive knows who is meant," to paraphrase Swift, the more ineffective the technique as alibi.

This technique, then, could not always be counted on as an effective defense. Quite the contrary, for in many cases such as Manley's it not only indicated but also constituted the crime itself. To explain this, let me continue with the discussion of allegory in *State Law: or, The Doctrine of Libels:*

> If a man draws a picture of another, and paints him in any shameful Posture, or ignominious Manner, 'tho no Name be to it; yet if the Piece be such, that the Person abused is known by it, the Painter is guilty of a Libel; what then should serve in Excuse for the allegorical Libeller? Abusive Allegory in Writing, has a very near Resemblance to this satyrical Kind of Painting: The Man that is painted with Fool's Cap and Horns, is certainly abused; but, says the Painter, he is disguised [by the Fools Cap and Horns], and how can you pretend to know him. This is the very subterfuge of the Allegorist, and ought to have the same Answer.[24]

The answer is that the disguise (fools cap and horns) *is* the libel. The allegories in Manley's works are often precisely of this abusive type. When she "disguises" Godolpohin as "Volpone" or Steele as "M. Ingrat", the fictional names themselves are the guilty "reflections." Swift's "St—le" may be a neutral code and a mere technicality, but "M. Ingrat" conveys the accusation in the very act of changing the name. When Manley portrays Sarah Churchill as the ravenous Queen Zarah, literally usurping the throne from the rightful monarch, such "fictionalizing" of circumstances was itself the criminal message about the Duchess of Marlborough and Queen Anne. To claim the allegorical "disguise" as the grounds of one's defense was thus tantamount to pointing to the most obnoxious aspect of the crime as evidence of one's innocence.[25] The legal status of Manley's style was hence profoundly ambivalent: the style could be viewed in Swift's terms as her alibi or, in the terms of *State Law,* as her crime. If one sees the allegory's function as disguise, it appears to be insurance against political prosecution; but if one sees its function as abuse, the disguise becomes the very thing that would provoke prosecution.

Although both contemporary views of allegory (alibi and crime) inside this legal discourse cross the technique with politics, we should notice that *State Law*'s discussion actually focusses attention on allegory, takes it seriously, in a way that Swift's view does not. When satirical allegory is seen as the crime, the allegorical level, the textual level of technique where the writer invents many of the very circumstances that constitute the defamation, takes on an opacity that Swift's view would deny. It was acknowledged that such techniques marked the controversial text and thereby attracted potential readers. In Swift's description, though, one only looked for such devices in order to look through them, whereas those who recognized the abusive function of allegories such as Manley's perceived the device as the controversial matter and thus bestowed on it an interest of its own. Thus we might conclude that it was the "crime" view of allegory, the view that wholly identified it with political transgression, and not the "alibi" view, the view that tried to make it incidental, that gave greater and greater weight to techniques we now call "fictional" and encouraged their development.

Let us then momentarily hold in abeyance the idea that Manley's technique protected her from prosecution and concentrate instead on how "fictional" allegorical invention furthered her libelous purposes. What Manley gained from the allegorical necessity of altering and therefore inventing circumstances was a representational density that enabled especially effective libel. Manley's talent was for crafting the invented circumstances into what we would now call an intrinsically satisfying narrative, one that is read for its own sake as well as for its scandalous referentiality. At their best, the stories of *The New Atalantis* inspired a partial disregard for veracity that allowed them to develop simultaneously toward a more seemingly specific referentiality and a more independent "fictionality."

For example, in comparing two passages from Manley's works, the first from *Queen Zarah* and the second from *The New Atalantis,* we might say that the first has *only* an allegorical interest and not an independent narrative one. It figures Sarah Churchill as the domineering usurper trying to "tame" a series of ministers:

> Nothing griev'd Zarah like this ungovernable Spirit of the Albigions, who wou'd not bear to think of being rid with a Side-Saddle, having had their Backs gall'd so much before in the Female Reign of Rolando. [Charles II]

> But notwithstanding all these Difficulties, Zarah was resolved to mount on the Stirrup of Hippolito's [Marlborough's] Fame . . . and drive her Beasts forward by the help of Volpone's (Godolphin's) Rod . . . by this Means she got on the Backs of the most Able Pads in the whole Kingdom . . . , some of which she rid to Death, others she jaded, and some she rides still. (I, 110-11)

The episode goes on to satirize a group of noblemen in equestrian language, drawing on the commonplace icon-ographic trope of woman on top[26] to portray the she-favorite. Nothing about it invites the reader to linger on the "literal" level, the invented level of the horse-back-riding "fiction."

The passage from *The New Atalantis* is not allegorical in the same sense. It also gives us the she-favorite on top, but it endeavors to produce its own narrative and erotic interest in doing so. In this often-quoted episode, Hilaria, the fictionalized Duchess of Cleveland (mistress of Charles II) is being tricked by John Churchill into sleeping with his young friend, Henry, Baron Dover. At this point in the story, the Churchill figure, Count Fortunatus, wishes to be free of Hilaria, to whom he had been prostituting himself. Hilaria approaches the bed of Fortunatus, unwilling to perceive that the youth lying before her is not her lover.

> . . . he had thrown himself upon the bed, pretending to sleep, with nothing on but his shirt and night-gown, which he had so indecently disposed that, slumbering as he appeared, his whole person stood confessed to the eyes of the amorous Duchess. His limbs were exactly formed, his skin shiningly white, and the pleasure the lady's graceful entrance gave him diffused joy and desire throughout all his form. His lovely eyes seemed to be closed, his face turned on one side (to favour the deceit) was obscured by the lace depending from the pillows on which he rested.

> The Duchess, who had about her all those desires she expected to employ in the arms of the Count, was so blinded by 'em that at first she did not perceive the mistake, so that giving her eyes time to wander over beauties so inviting and which increased her flame, with an amorous sigh threw herself on the bed beside the desiring youth.

> The ribbon of his shirt-neck not tied, the bosom (adorned with the finest lace) was open, upon which she fixed her charming mouth. Impatient, and finding that he did not awake, she raised her head and laid her lips to that part of his face that was revealed.

> The burning lover thought it was now time to put an end to his pretended sleep. He clasped her in his arms, grasped her to his bosom; her own desires helped the deceit. She shut her eyes with a languishing sweetness, calling him by intervals, 'her dear Count', and 'her only lover', taking and giving a thousand kisses. He got possession of her person with so much transport that she owned all her former enjoyments were imperfect to the pleasure of this. (I, 305-6)

It is easy to see why *The New Atalantis* was a more popular book than *Queen Zarah;* although *Zarah* certainly contains some engaging vignettes,[27] nothing in it approaches the sheer voyeuristic eroticism of the later satire, a voyeurism mirrored in the lascivious gaze of Hilaria herself. The passage is practically a parable about the pleasures of reading *The New Atalantis.* Because the youth on the bed can either be looked at simply as a dazzling surface to be enjoyed, no matter who he is, or as a simulacrum, an allegory, of the Count, complete erotic indulgence is licensed, which makes "all . . . former enjoyments . . . imperfect [compared] to the pleasure of this." If one really wants to enjoy the book, one shouldn't try to sort out the levels of referentiality, but rather, like the Duchess, let one's desire aid the deceit and take one's pleasure both ways at once. This is a text that truly works on two levels: it can be equally enjoyed as mere story, suspending the referential issue, or as defamation. Such doubleness, moreover, makes the defamation all the more pleasurable, effective, and, indeed, *explicit.*

Thus we seem to have exactly reversed the normal way of explaining the dominance of allegorical writing in the eighteenth century and the emergence of densely realized fiction. Instead of maintaining that writers were trying to avoid the law through allegory, we could just as well argue that writers made themselves vulnerable to the law through it. And instead of arguing that purely literary fictions emerged out of evasive actions, out of the search for alibis, we might just as well argue that stories became more elaborate and compelling in themselves, and narrative technique became more "novelistic," because writers became more intent on effective political scandalmongering.

However, instead of holding one of these theses to the exclusion of the other, I am suggesting that it is because Delarivier Manley could vacillate between the poles of alibi and crime in developing her technique that she created a sheer excess of story, which cannot accurately be called "fiction" because it retains the pleasurable and controversial doubleness, the special way of seeming to point "outside," that belongs to allegory. The allegorical style thus met the paradoxical exigencies of her circumstances: it was partisan when viewed from one point of view, neutral when viewed from another, and remunerative when viewed from any. In a sense, then, Delarivier Manley could only win by this crossing of politics and fiction in the discourse of libel.

Politics and Femininity: The Double Cross

It should be apparent from the above passage that *The New Atalantis*'s presentation of female eroticism was at least partly responsible for its irresistible crossing of politics and fiction. To get an adequate understanding of this moment in the history of women's writing, we should briefly note the ways in which the new political culture was simultaneously making use of and redefining femininity.

The simplest way to explain the crossing of partisan politics and female eroticism is to point to the coincidence of the female monarch and the rage for party. A woman on the throne meant that the nobles of the household (Groom of the Stole, Mistress of the Robe, Keeper of the Privy Purse, etc.) would also be women. Since these women controlled access to the Queen, the developing political parties and the increasingly powerful government ministers found themselves relying on and paying court to the ladies of the royal household. Simultaneously, resentment at the power these women were perceived to hold permeated the partisan satires on the Queen's favorites.[28]

The court, however, was more the occasion than the cause of the new emphasis on women in political discourse. J. G. A. Pocock has pointed to a pattern of thought in this period linking changes in the form and concept of property to changes in the ideas of political entitlement and femininity. In making his now well-known distinction between civic and civil humanists, he claims that the former stressed "possession and civic virtue" and the latter "exchange and the civilization of the passions."[29] Moreover, Pocock implies that these different concepts of property were aligned with opposite valuations of female social discourse. The financial revolution of the 1690s, having turned the polity into a network of debtors and creditors, made the state heavily dependent on financial interests, and encouraged new habits of speculation,[30] also inspired both a newly positive assessment of women and new anxieties about them. For the new economic man in the eighteenth-century, according to Pocock, "was seen as on the whole a feminized, even an effeminate being, still wrestling with his own passions and hysterias and with interior and exterior forces let loose by his [stock market-induced] fantasies and appetites."[31]

Pocock thus presents those who rode the crest of that great surge in military and financial growth and who publicized its benefits as buoyed by new representations of the feminine. Civil humanists claimed that the very thing that had liberated the passions—commercial society—would, by providing relations of confidence between men, itself refine the passions. Similarly, a freer and more "rational" intercourse with women in civil society would at once teach women to contain their own passions and allow men to improve that "politeness" which was to be the new support and justification for a commercial civilization. The possibility of rational intercourse with women, therefore, was often promulgated by the same men who were beginning to extol the benefits of exchange, and hence after the 1690s women's public discourse was fastened to the idea of commerce in *positive* as well as negative new ways.

Politically, Manley was aligned with what Pocock calls the civic humanists, those who were most likely to express fears about the new toleration for private interests and women's influence, and her political alliances partly explain the kind of satire she wrote. However, we cannot place Manley squarely inside the Scriblerian milieu we associate with Swift, Pope and Arbuthnot, for the idea of women often functions in their discourse in ways that Manley at once uses and bends to her own self-ironizing purposes.[32] Her authorial presentation, moreover, equally relies on the very civil humanist ideology it mocks.

Manley's own justification for having written *The New Atalantis* displays her complex method of associating and dissociating politics and femininity in her authorial self-portrait. In *The Adventures of Rivella,* the fictionalized, third-person autobiography from which the account of Manley's libel hearing was taken at the opening of this essay, we are given a confession as well as a defense, and the confession helps us to understand the terms in which Manley, as a woman, was constituted a political being:

> She [claimed] she was . . . out of humour with . . . a faction who were busy to enslave their sovereign and overturn the constitution, that she was proud of having more courage than had any of our sex and of throwing the first stone, which might give a hint for other persons of more capacity to examine the defects and vices of some men who took a delight to impose upon the world by the pretence of public good, whilst their true design was only to gratify and advance themselves. (II, 845)

Like most writers of the period, the heroine here dignifies her partisanship as general patriotism.

This passage, however, departs from its own high-mindedness when the author's gender emerges. The woman who is "proud . . . of throwing the first stone" is a figure out of a far less polite political tradition than that of the patriotic martyr. While it is only a rhetorical moment, the phrase nevertheless conjures the common figure of disorder, the woman at the head of the mob, both allegorical and real, who casts the first stone in the riot because her juridical status is ambiguous and she may not be held fully responsible for her action. In the very midst of claiming her political personhood, therefore, Manley raises the specter of the common disorderly woman, politically useful precisely because she cannot be taken seriously as a political agent. An image of the author as the female of the misogynist satirical literature thus intrudes into this high-minded confession, but in doing so she displays both her inappropriateness and her utility.

Moreover, the Biblical echo in the phrase "throw the first stone" reminds us of the sexual nature of Manley's satire; it was directed, especially, against adulterous women. This rhetorical linking of the author with the mob violence of women against women would have had wide resonance in the early eighteenth century, which saw both an enormous growth in London rioting to protest sexual misbehavior and a doubling of the percentage of rioters who were women.[33] Manley thus links herself to an increasingly visible form of female public action against sexual impropriety; the association, however, further feminizes her satire and makes it seem less centrally political.

The fact that women's riots often punished sexual deviance did not erase their own impropriety, moreover. Nor did Manley's many claims to be a satirical scourge keep her from being perceived as a purveyor of licentiousness and a stimulator of the very passions she exposed. In the next paragraph of her confession, indeed, she admits the identity of impropriety between female victim and female accuser in her own works:

> As to exposing those who had never injured her, she said she did no more by others than others had done by her, i.e., tattle of frailties. The Town had never shown her any indulgence but, on the contrary, reported tenfold against her in matters of which she was wholly innocent, whereas she did take up old stories that all the world had long since reported. . . . (II, 845-6)

The heroine is no longer in this passage a decisive individual political subject, full of patriotic fire; instead, she now depicts herself as a slandered woman who is evening a score in an altogether traditionally feminine manner: by "tattling of frailties," and telling "old stories," in short by gossiping. This argument resembles the fiction-alibi of the inquest, for it once again claims the general triviality of Manley's writing; as in her statement to the Secretary of State, she is simply a woman amusing herself with a "few amorous trifles." And, although she is willing to admit in this instance that she didn't completely make them up, she is no longer concerned with their objective truth, only with their prior circulation.

In *Rivella*'s confession, then, as in her alibi, we find ourselves once again moving between political purposes and mere amusement, between high crimes and low excuses, but here the poles are quite clearly gendered. Once again, however, we can also observe a crossing of binary terms, the paradoxical ways in which politics and femininity implicate each other, even when womanhood is constructed within the misogynist assumptions of Augustan satire. Manley presents herself as politically useful because she is a disorderly woman vengefully gossiping about female "secrets" and therefore doing the sort of low and frivolous work considered to be beneath real politicians. Hence, she links her book's peculiar political efficacy to its femininity, which in turn decomposes its political nature.

The confession that presents this paradox is completely exculpatory. As she moves her explanation from patriotic fervor to feminine irresponsibility, she becomes all the more "innocent" in the archaic sense of "unaccountable." As a patriot she was behaving admirably, and as a woman she could not help herself. Although the political and sexual components of the confession work against each other both logically and imagistically, each contributes a kind of innocence, and the passage, by remaining unconscious of its contradictions, tries to add the two kinds of innocence together in order to achieve a complete vindication. We are to see her as both a high-minded stateswoman and a passionate, unruly creature. Her complete innocence is thus based on the juxtaposition/addition of her political and sexual impulses.

We should note, though, that *The New Atalantis*'s female villains are guilty of the same crossing of feminine impulsiveness and politics that supposedly constitutes the author's innocence. Figures representing Lady Marlborough and the Duchess of Cleveland, for example, are exposed as having a dual and contradictory political/sexual nature that makes them doubly corrupt, whereas Manley's made her doubly innocent. We are faced in the text of *The New Atalantis,* as in the confession in *Rivella,* with the undeniable similarity between the satirist and the satirized, which is partly owing, as we've seen, to the concept of womanhood supplied by the Juvenalian tradition, but which also derives from another source: Manley's own dependence on the very civil ideal she seems to be satirizing.

When she exposes the "secret" underside of the new idea of social privacy, the refinement of her victims as mere lechery, their valued personal intercourse as criminal conversation, their cultivation and patronage of the arts as bribery, she invokes not some civic humanist ideal of independent masculine virtue but the very ideas of cultivated exchange, especially between the sexes, that she simultaneously seems to be exposing as hypocritical. Moreover, she betrays her own self-interested reasons for subscribing to those ideas. For example, her allegorical narrator, Lady Intelligence, often makes satirical attacks that conclude with a racy, libertine one-upmanship, as in this criticism of the Duke of Marlborough for not paying his mistresses directly:

> It appears strange to me [says Lady Intelligence], that considering the Count's [Marlborough's] Power and Riches, Daphne [Catherine Trotter] did not make her Fortune by His Fondness. But I think there yet wants an Example of elevated Generosity in him, to any of his Mistresses, tho' the World can't dispute but that he has had many: His ways to pay the Favour, being to desire the lady to study if there is any thing in his Power, by which he may oblige any Relation or Friend of hers; and that he will not fail to grant it. Thus every way a Husband of his

> Money, his Reputation and Grandeur procure him the good Fortune he desires: Tho' were the Ladies with whom he has a mind to converse of my Taste, they would think his own very handsome Person a Reward sufficient for all the Charms they can bestow. (I, 585-6)

The passage cleverly combines charges of stinginess and corrupt influence trading as it comically implies that the Duke's dealings with his mistresses should have been more commercial, indeed that in "preferring" the husband, thus "husbanding" his money (as she puns), the Duke has been less than a perfect gentleman. But then, in order to demonstrate how even the language of fair exchange can and should be translated into that of taste and cultivation, Lady Intelligence announces her own generous and tasteful willingness to make love to Marlborough for nothing. Thus the female satirist imaginatively substitutes herself for Catherine Trotter, a Whig writer of the period and the original object of the satire. The satirized are exposed as lustful and greedy under their politeness, but the satirist playfully converts her lust and ambition into an instance of Taste in Conversation. Lady Intelligence is a figure for the author here, so the passage creates the effect of a satirist endlessly resubscribing to the values of the social interactions she mocks.

Much of the humor of *The New Atalantis* resides in these parallels and resemblances between satirized and satirist,[34] and most of them hinge on either the satirist's erotic desires or her hopes for political patronage. In some instances, the two forms of exchange are explicitly linked, and the impossibility of distinguishing between them, as in the above passage, is the point of the joke. In another sequence, for example, Marlborough is accused of being stingy with both his mistresses and his writers, requiring one poet to leave a receipt for two pieces of silver paid for his panegyric. This report is immediately followed (I, 450-1) by the author's panegyric to the Tory Duke of Beaumond, whom she praises for his patriotism, generosity, and (she emphasizes) irresistible personal attractions.

Politics and femininity are thus interwoven in a series of maneuvers that depend on the terms' normative mutual exclusion. *The New Atalantis* manages to display the available ways of crossing women and politics, and then to make those crossings themselves the object of satire. Hence although femininity, like fiction, can always be opposed to Manley's politics as its excuse, it can also be exposed as the deep truth of political corruption. Femininity has, in short, the same odd potential for exculpation and incrimination that we noted in the concept of fiction. Delarivier Manley, as a Tory scandalmonger impelled by her gender toward the rhetoric of civil humanism, was bound to use it both ways.

Fictional Eroticism and the Challenge to Scandal

So far I have tried to show that, inside the generic assumptions of Manley's scandalous allegories, fiction and femininity had similarly paradoxical relationships to politics. This positional parallel alone, I've been suggesting, created a strong link between them. Finally, however, I would like to note that *The New Atlantis* reflects on this very connection between fictionality and femininity in order to remind us of the crucial differences between the scandalous political text we are reading and women's inconsequential erotic fantasies.

Some of the most sensational episodes of *The New Atlantis* may be read as dramatizations of the tension between the referential political significance of Manley's allegories and the possibility of reading them as merely fictional "amorous trifles." The episodes might be said to reverse the procedure of the hearing by putting the alibi of feminine erotic fictionality on trial, satirizing a drive on the part of certain ladies for forms of feminine eroticism that would be meaningless, "fictional" pleasures that would escape reference, consequence, and, therefore, scandal. The ladies thus practice a kind of sedition against the text they inhabit by attempting to elude the rules of significance and reference proper to scandalous allegories.

In the stories of what Lady Intelligence calls "the New Cabal," we see one such evasive strategy: the attempt by a group of ladies to substitute romantic attachments between women for heterosexual intrigues. The relationships among the women of the New Cabal are designed, we are told, to thwart scandal by substituting an innocent, fictional eroticism for guilty, real (heterosexual) sexuality. Lady Intelligence herself is, ironically, the spokeswoman for the notion that amorous relations between women escape the reach of scandal because they "could only subsist in imagination." By their nature, they are a form of play acting that cannot "wound [a lady's] chastity" (I, 575-6).

But the stories of the New Cabal also continually point out the precariousness of such "pure" fictions that would allow women to indulge themselves erotically without risking their reputations. The pleasures these women seek, the narrator implies, rest on an inherently unstable representational system. Lady Intelligence tells us that they "do not in reality love Men; but doat on the Representations of *Men* in *Women*" (I, 738). The women are not loved as women, neither are they loved as a men, but as cross-dressed representations. A noble widow, for example,

fell in Love with one of the fair *Female Comedians,* when she was acting the Part of a Young *Lover* and

a *Libertine.* The Widow sent for the Girl, and made her very considerable Presents, order'd her Picture, in that Dress, to be taken at length, by one of the best Hands, and carried her to remain with her . . . at her Villa. (I, 739)

At length, however, the actress disappoints the lady by insisting that their play have a meaning:

The Widow . . . assur'd her of her *Tenderness* and *Amity;* she even proceeded to gentle squeezes and *embraces;* nothing cou'd be more innocently indearing than her transports! The *Comedian* was at a loss to know [not] only how to merit so many favours but also the *meaning* of 'em. . . . [She] told the Lady she did not like those hugs and indearments from her own Sex . . . ; did they come from a man, she should be able to guess at his Design, but here she was at a loss—." (I, 740)

The widow's behavior, indeed, has no "meaning" of the sort the actress seeks, and insisting on one only impresses the lack of the significant member on the widow's consciousness, thereby putting the actress further "at a loss." By refusing to be content with representation and play, to suspend her disbelief, the actress spoils the possibility of pleasure, and the widow then appropriately punishes her by symbolically castrating her portrait, the representation of the actress representing a man:

When [the widow] was return'd to her House in Town, to show the lurkings of her malice, tho' but in Effigy, she caus'd the Comedian's Picture to be let down, and with her own Hand cut out the Face; so stamp'd upon and abus'd, sent it back to her whom it represented. . . . (I, 740)

Because she insisted on seeing their fiction as empty, the actress is confronted with her own message; her face cut out of the portrait, she becomes a figure for the blankness of representation.

The widow and the uncooperative actress thus play out what we might see as a conflict between starkly opposed versions of scandal and fiction. The actress, who has not been given an adequate monetary substitute for reality, tries to read the widow's play as if its whole substance resided outside of itself, as if it were supposed to be merely decoded or seen through, as if it were just a screen for some "meaning" on the other side of representation. Hence, she receives, along with the picture of herself as the blankness of representation, the widow's message that the actress, "had . . . made it a Scandal to her House to have such a Picture seen in it." The actress had the chance to indulge innocently in the widow's willed illusion of fiction but instead chose the guilty, penetrating vision of a crude form of allegorical scandal.

Of course, as I have already noted, the actress's insistence on "meaning" differs markedly from the scandalous referentiality of *The New Atalantis,* where the pleasures of the text are often likened to an erotic double-vision in which characters perceive each other as simultaneously disguised and unmasked, where representation and reference try to supplement rather than supplant each other. But the widow's desire to inhabit a completely non-referential fictional world is similarly impermissible within the generic rules of this text. The episode of the widow and the actress reflects not only on the precariousness of "pure" fiction but also on its thinness as an imaginative experience. The widow's insistence on one-dimensional fiction calls forth an equally one-dimensional demand for scandalous referentiality. If the widow had achieved her illusion, it would have been, in *The New Atalantis*'s terms, insignificant. The episode thus suggests that the New Cabal's attempt to escape from the narrative conditions of scandal through feminine fictions threatens to subtract significance from fiction and play from scandal, impoverishing both. By dramatizing the resistance to political scandal, *The New Atalantis* plays out and discredits what it identifies as the feminine impulse toward pure fiction, while at the same time it appropriates fiction as one of its own proper allegorical techniques. The attempted resistance nevertheless stands as a reminder of the tension between fiction and femininity, on the one hand, and politics, on the other. But to say this is merely to repeat what I've been arguing all along, that in Manley's works, femaleness and fictionality strain away from politics in the very process of being filtered through it.

The separation, which Manley had no pressing reason to effect, did finally take place; over the next several decades, the link between fiction and politics slackened as readers became increasingly interested in stories about nobody. Women readers and writers, moreover, were crucially important in thus transforming the cultural significance of fiction.[35] However, in the Queen Anne period, the opposition between politics and women's fictions can only be discerned through the powerful impropriety of their scandalous crossings.

Notes

[1] I am convinced by Patricia Köster's argument that there is no evidence for believing Manley's first name was "Mary." See "Delariviere Manley and the *DNB,*" *Eighteenth Century Life* 3 (1977): 106-111. Furthermore, I follow Fidelis Morgan's lead in spelling Manley's Christian name "Delarivier" because that is the way the author consistently spelled it. See *A Woman of No Character: An Autobiography of Mrs. Manley* (London: Faber & Faber, 1986), p. 14.

[2] Information about Manley's arrest and questioning comes from two sources: Narcissus Luttrell's *A Brief Historical Relation of State Affairs* (London, 1857), pp. 505-8 and 546; and Manley's own fictionalized autobiography, *The Adventures of Rivella; or, The History of the Author of the Atalantis* (London: 1714), pp. 108-16. Excerpts from both accounts are brought together in Fidelis Morgan, pp. 146-51. Manley apparently surrendered herself on October 29, 1709, after a Secretary of State's warrant had been issued against her, and her "publishers and printers" had already been detained. She was questioned in the secretary's office; four days later the publishers and printer were discharged, but Manley remained in custody until November 7th, when she was released on bail. Her trial was heard on February 11, 1710, at the Queen's Bench Court; she was discharged.

[3] Sarah Churchill, Duchess of Marlborough, *Private Correspondence* (London, 1838), p. 237.

[4] I draw this inference from Manley's description of the questioning, quoted below, and from Sarah Churchill's letter to the Queen, which identifies Harley, Peterborough, and Mrs. Masham as Manley's sources of information and financial support: "The woman that has been put upon writing it, and the printer, have been in custody, and are now under prosecution. It has appeared that she kept correspondence with two of her favourite persons in the book, My Lord Peterborough and Mr. Harley, and I think it is to be suspected that she may have had some dealing with Mrs. Masham, who is called Hilaria." Ibid., p. 236.

[5] *The Adventures of Rivella, or The History of the author of Atalantis with secret memoirs and characters of several considerable persons, her contemporaries* (London: 1714); rpt. in *The Novels of Mary Delariviere Manley,* ed. Patricia Köster, vol. II, p. 849. All quotations from Manley's works are taken from this edition. Page numbers are given in the text and refer to Köster's pagination.

[6] For the evidence that Manley did have highly-placed sources, see Gwendolyn B. Needham, "Mary de la Riviere Manley, Tory Defender," *Huntington Library Quarterly* 12 (1949): 253-88.

[7] *General Postscript, being an Extract of all that is most material from the Foreign and English Newspapers, with Remarks upon the 'Observator,' 'Review,' 'Tatlers,' and the Rest of the Scribblers, in a Dialogue between Novel and Scandal* (London: Sept. 27, 1709); quoted in John Wilson Bowyer, *The Celebrated Mrs. Catliver* (Durham, N.C.: 1952), p. 125.

[8] John Richetti's discussion of Manley in *Popular Fiction Before Richardson* (Oxford: Clarendon Press, 1969), pp. 119-53, turned critical attention away from her writings as scandalous histories toward their role in the construction of the myth that female innocence

is constantly besieged by an egotistical and corrupt masculinity. The mythic and the fictional are roughly equivalent concepts for Richetti, and hence Manley's works are fictional despite their contemporary referentiality. Richetti's analysis had the merit of recognizing Manley's importance in developing narrative patterns that would later be incorporated into the novel, but it also somewhat anachronistically imposed the concept of fiction on Manley's work retroactively. More recent discussions tend to follow Richetti's lead in this matter; Jerry Beasley basically repeats the same argument about beleaguered femininity, while noting that Manley exploits the pattern for political purposes. See "Politics and Moral Idealism: The Achievement of Some Early Women Novelists," in *Fetter'd Or Free?,* eds. Mary Anne Schofield and Cecilia Macheski (Athens, Ohio: Ohio University Press, 1986), pp. 223-25. Jane Spencer's *The Rise of the Woman Novelist* (London: Basil Blackwell, 1986), pp. 53-61, 113-16, Michael McKeon's *The Origins of the English Novel, 1660-1740* (Baltimore: Johns Hopkins University Press, 1987), pp. 232-33, and Jacqueline Pearson's *The Prostituted Muse: Images of Women and Women Dramatists 1642-1737* (New York: St. Martin's Press, 1988), pp. 193-95, all attempt to place Manley in various typologies of narrative fiction. Even Delores Palomo, who argues vigorously against Richetti's particular analysis, allows his generic identification to stand. Indeed, she seems almost embarrassed to mention at one point that "Contemporaries recognized the authenticity of this and other stories in her secret histories, and in fact her success resulted partly from the presumption that she told real stories about real people." See "A Woman Writer and the Scholars: A Review of Mary Manley's Reputation," *Women and Literature* 6:1 (Spring, 1978): 44.

9 For accounts of the British printing industry, its modes of regulation, and the general effects of the lapsing of the Licensing Act in 1695, see Marjorie Plant, *The English Book Trade: An Economic History of the Making and Sale of Books* (London: G. Allen Unwin, 1939), especially pp. 115-21; Frank Arthur Mumby, *Publishing and Bookselling. Part One: From the Earliest Times to 1870* (London: Cape, 1974), especially pp. 127-47; and Graham Pollard, "The English Market for Printed Books," *Publishing History* 4 (1978): 7-48.

10 For an overview of seditious libel prosecutions in the early eighteenth century, see Donald Thomas, *A Long Time Burning: The History of Literary Censorship in England* (New York: Routledge & Kegan Paul, 1969), pp. 34-74, and Laurence Hanson, *The Government and the Press, 1695-1763* (Oxford: Clarendon Press, 1936).

11 C. R. Kropf has a very useful summary of the law in his essay "Libel and Satire in the Eighteenth Cen-

tury," *Eighteenth-Century Studies* 8, 2 (1974-5): 153-68. See also Hanson, pp. 7-35.

12 For discussions of this development, see David Harrison Stevens, *Party Politics and English Journalism, 1702-1742* (Madison, Wis.: Banta, 1916); and J. A. Downie, *Robert Harley and the Press: Propaganda and Public Opinion in the Age of Swift and Defoe* (Cambridge Univ. Press, 1979).

13 "In such circumstances," notes A. S. Collins, "the relation of author to publisher existed on a very insecure basis. How could a bookseller pay highly for the rights to a work whose profits another might steal from him by a cheaper edition?" *Authorship in the Days of Johnson: Being a Study of the Relation Between Author, Patron, Publisher and Public 1726-1780* (London: R. Holden & Co. Ltd., 1927), p. 8.

14 Stevens, pp. 1-4. W. A. Speck, however, points out that subscription lists were dominated by the peerage in the early eighteenth century and that subscriptions were often themselves a vehicle for political patronage. See "Politicians, Peers, and Publication by Subscription, 1700-1750," in *Books and Their Readers in Eighteenth-Century England,* ed. Isabel Rivers (New York: St. Martin's 1982), pp. 47-68.

15 See Collins on patronage in this period, pp. 114-18, and pp. 214-21; see also Downie's *Robert Harley* and his *Jonathan Swift: Political Writer* (London: Routledge & Kegan Paul, 1984), passim.

16 *The Man of Taste* (rpt. Los Angeles: Univ. of California Press, 1975), p. 8.

17 Stevens, p. 17.

18 "Mrs. Dela Manley to [the Earl of Oxford]," HMC Portland 5:55.

19 C. R. Kropf's very informative essay views the relationship between satirical technique and libel in these terms.

20 *The Importance of the Guardian Considered,* in *Political Tracts, 1713-1719,* ed. Herbert Davis and Irvin Ehrenpreis (Oxford: Basil Blackwell, 1973), pp. 14-15. See the discussion of this passage in Hanson, p. 25.

21 For example, see Donald Thomas, *A Long Time Burning,* p. 57. See also the more sophisticated reading of Swift that regards his works as purposely elusive mockeries of other authors' allegorizing and the allegory-hunting of the prosecutors in Lennard J. Davis, *Factual Fictions; The Origins of the English Novel* (New York: Columbia Univ. Press, 1983), pp. 149-153. Bertrand A. Goldgar, however, in *Walpole and the Wits:*

The Relation of Politics to Literature, 1722-1742 (Lincoln, Neb.: Univ. of Nebraska Press, 1976), pp. 49-63, demonstrates that parts of *Gulliver's Travels* were immediately received as obvious personal satire.

[22] See Kropf, p. 157-9.

[23] Quoted in Thomas, p. 58.

[24] Ibid. Thomas quotes this passage as the "interpretation [of the law] accepted" when Manley was prosecuted (pp. 58-9), but he does not comment on the passage or note the paradox involved in the concept of *innuendo* to which it draws attention: that in cases of abusive allegory, the same evidence may be cited as either exonerating or incriminating.

[25] It is for this reason that Lennard Davis's very helpful discussion of the news-novel matrix is somewhat too simple. According to Davis, in the early eighteenth century one had to claim that books of "news" were fictional and works of fiction were "true." The very use of the word "fiction," however, could often be a clue to the contemporary reference of the work.

[26] For a discussion of this trope and its functions in early modern Europe see Natalie Zemon Davis, "Women on Top: Symbolic Sexual Inversion and Political Disorder in Early Modern Europe," in *The Reversible World: Symbolic Inversion in Art and Society,* ed. Barbara Babcock (Ithaca: Cornell Univ. Press, 1978), pp. 147-90.

[27] A comparable scene in *Queen Zarah* has Hippolito (John Churchill) encounter the young Zarah (then Sarah Jennings) where he expects to find Clelia (the Duchess of Cleveland), but although the setting is described (actually translated directly from Sebastian de Bremond's earlier *Histoire scandaleuse, Hattige, ou Les Amours du Roy de Tamara* (Paris: 1676), p. 69), the young Zarah is not. Moreover, Hippolito recognizes Zarah immediately, so that the themes of double vision and disguise are absent, whereas they recur frequently in *The New Atalantis.* See, for example, II, 662-65, as well as the passages cited at the end of this essay.

[28] Manley's attacks on Sarah Churchill were matched by equally scandalous Whig satires on Abigail Masham when she became the Queen's favorite. If Churchill was accused of being a whore, Masham was accused of lesbianism. See, for example, John Dunton's *King Abigail: or, the Secret Reign of the She-Favourite, Detected, and Applied: In a Sermon Upon these Words, "And Women rule over them" Isa. 3.12* (London, 1715). For a general discussion of English satires on women and English uses of Juvenalian rhetoric, see Felicity A. Nussbaum, *The Brink of All We Hate: English Satires on Women, 1660-1750* (Lexington: Univ. Press of Kentucky Press, 1984).

[29] "The Mobility of Property," *Virtue, Commerce, and History,* p. 115.

[30] For a detailed description of this process, see John Brewer, *The Sinews of Power: War, Money and the English State, 1688-1783* (New York: Alfred A. Knopf, 1989).

[31] "Mobility of Property," p. 114.

[32] For studies of the functions of "the feminine" in Swift and Pope, see Ellen Pollak, *The Poetics of Sexual Myth: Gender and Ideology in the Verse of Swift and Pope* (Chicago: Univ. of Chicago Press, 1985), passim., and Nussbaum, pp. 94-116 and 137-58.

[33] Robert B. Shoemaker, "The London 'Mob' in the Early Eighteenth Century," *Journal of British Studies* 26 (July 1987): 285.

[34] The irony of *The New Atalantis* has gone largely unremarked since John Richetti directed the attention of critics to the recurrent seduction motif, thereby giving the impression that Manley's narrators vacillate between over-heated prurience and outraged virtue. But in fact Manley structures her book so that the moral pretentions of the two allegorical figures, Virtue and Astrea, are frequently deflated by the interjections of the main narrator, Lady Intelligence, who is a figure for scandal itself, and Intelligence's self-interested motivations are often exposed. Two studies that have noted Manley's irony without concentrating on its self-inclusive quality are Delores Palomo's, op. cit., and Janet Todd's *The Sign of Angelica: Women, Writing, and Fiction, 1660-1800* (London: Columbia Univ. Press, 1989), pp. 84-100.

[35] For arguments detailing the later association between femininity and the discursive practices of fiction, see Patricia Meyer Spacks, "Ev'ry Woman is at Heart a Rake," *Eighteenth-Century Studies* 8 (Fall, 1974): 27-46; and Nancy Armstrong, *Desire and Domestic Fiction: A Political History of the Novel* (Oxford: Oxford Univ. Press, 1987), passim.

FURTHER READING

Anderson, Paul Bunyan. "Delariviere Manley's Prose Fiction." *Philological Quarterly* 13, No. 2 (April 1934): 168-88.

In one of the earliest twentieth-century appraisals of Manley's fictional technique, Anderson looks closely at the *New Atalantis* and *The Lady's Pacquet of Letters* and hails their author as a pioneer of English prose fiction.

————."Mistress Delariviere Manley's Biography." *Modern Philology* XXXIII, No. 3 (February 1936): 261-78.

> More than sixty years after its publication, this is still a highly regarded biographical essay on Manley's life and literary career.

Armistead, Jack M., and Debbie K. Davis. Introduction. In Delariviere Manley, *Lucius, the First Christian King of Britain,* pp. iii-viii. Los Angeles: William Andrews Clark Memorial Library, University of California, 1989.

> Suggests that *Lucius* reveals a different Manley than is generally apparent in her fiction and political writings: a tolerant, conciliatory, and decorous advocate of feminine ideals.

Clark, Constance. "Delarivière Manley." In her *Three Augustan Women Playwrights,* pp. 97-182. New York: Peter Lang, 1986.

> Provides a detailed biography of Manley, extended synopses of her plays, and a critical overview of her work.

Gallagher, Catherine. "Political Crimes and Fictional Alibis: The Case of Delarivier Manley." In her *Nobody's Story: The Vanishing Acts of Women Writers in the Marketplace, 1670-1820,* pp. 88-144. Berkeley: University of California Press, 1994.

> A reworking of Gallagher's earlier essay in *Eighteenth-Century Studies* 23, No. 4 (Summer 1990): 502-21. Here the critic expands her discussion of how Manley's novels reflect the complex implications of scandal in the eighteenth-century literary marketplace and civil society.

Hook, Lucyle. Introduction. In Anonymous, *The Female Wits,* pp. i-xiv. Los Angeles: William Andrews Clark Memorial Library, University of California, 1967.

> Shows how Manley's *The Lost Lover* and *The Royal Mischief* bore the brunt of male critics' increasing attacks against female playwrights in the 1690s. The introduction also provides a vivid account of the London stage at the end of the Restoration period.

Katz, Candace Brook. "The Deserted Mistress Motif in Mrs. Manley's *Lost Lover,* 1696." *Restoration and Eighteenth-Century Theatre Research* 16, No. 1 (May 1977): 17-39

> Describes Manley's distinctive and sympathetic treatment of a conventional figure in Restoration drama: the cast-off mistress.

Köster, Patricia. Introduction. In *The Novels of Mary Delariviere Manley,* ed. Patricia Köster, pp. v-xxviii. Gainesville: Scholars' Facsimiles & Reprints, 1971.

> A comprehensive introduction to Manley's novels that evaluates the degree of truth in her satires, highlights her contribution toward the development of the English novel, and offers in-depth appraisals of *Queen Zarah* and the *New Atalantis.*

————. "Delariviere Manley and the DNB: A Cautionary Tale about Following Black Sheep, with a Challenge to Cataloguers." *Eighteenth-Century Life* 3, No. 4 (June 1977): 106-11.

> Reviews the evidence regarding Manley's first name and points out that there is no authority for continuing the nineteenth-century practice of referring to her as Mary.

MacCarthy, B. G. "From 1689 to 1774." In her *Women Writers: Their Contribution to the English Novel 1621-1744,* pp. 214-62. Cork: University Press, 1946.

> A harsh attack on Manley, accusing her of prurience, maliciousness, and vulgarity. MacCarthy generally disparages the *New Atalantis* as well, though she commends the author's characterization of Charlot.

Needham, Gwendolyn B. "Mary de la Rivière Manley, Tory Defender." *Huntington Library Quarterly* XII, No. 3 (May 1949): 253-88.

> Focuses on Manley as a political writer. Needham declares that Manley's satires contain "a substratum of truth" and that they were instrumental in the Whig party's loss of power in 1710.

————. "Mrs. Manley: An Eighteenth-Century Wife of Bath." *Huntington Library Quarterly* XIV, No. 3 (May 1951): 259-84.

> Praises Manley as an early feminist who challenged conventional standards governing women's role in society and denounced the double standard of morality for men and women.

Richetti, John J. "'As Long as Atalantis Shall be Read': The Scandal Chronicles of Mrs. Manley and Mrs. Haywood." In his *Popular Fiction Before Richardson: Narrative Patterns 1700-1739,* pp. 119-67. Oxford: Clarendon Press, 1969.

> Contends that in her novels Manley exploited a popular social mythology in which the innocent female is inevitably corrupted by the ruthless male. In Richetti's judgment, Manley used this ideological framework to elicit reader sympathy and excite erotic fantasies in her mostly female audience.

Jonathan Swift: *Gulliver's Travels*

English novel.

The following entry presents criticism of Swift's *Gulliver's Travels*. For a discussion of Swift's complete career, see *LC,* Volume 1.

INTRODUCTION

Swift's greatest satire, *Gulliver's Travels*, is considered one of the most important works in the history of world literature. Published as *Travels into Several Remote Nations of the World, in Four Parts; by Lemuel Gulliver* in 1726, *Gulliver's Travels* depicts one man's journeys to several strange and unusual lands. The general theme of *Gulliver's Travels* is a satirical examination of human nature, man's potential for depravity, and the dangers of the misuse of reason. Throughout the volume Swift attacked the baseness of humankind even as he suggested the greatest virtues of the human race; he also attacked the folly of human learning and political systems even as he implied the proper functions of art, science, and government. *Gulliver's Travels*, some scholars believe, had its origins during Swift's years as a Tory polemicist, when he was part of a group of prominent Tory writers known as the Scriblerus Club. The group, which also included Alexander Pope, John Gay, and John Arbuthnot, among others, collaborated on several satires, including *The Scriblerus Papers*. They also planned a satire called *The Memoirs of a Martinus Scriblerus*, which was to include several imaginary voyages. An immediate success, *Gulliver's Travels* was inspired by this work. Swift finished *Gulliver's Travels* was published anonymously, but Swift's authorship was widely suspected. Alternately considered an attack on humanity or a clear-eyed assessment of human strengths and weaknesses, the novel is a complex study of human nature and of the moral, philosophical, and scientific thought of Swift's time which has resisted any single definition of meaning for nearly three centuries.

Plot and Major Characters

Written in the form of a travel journal, *Gulliver's Travels* is the fictional account of four extraordinary voyages made by Lemuel Gulliver, a physician who signs on to serve as a ship's surgeon when he is unable to provide his family with a sufficient income

in London. After being shipwrecked Gulliver first arrives at Lilliput, an island whose inhabitants are just six inches tall and where the pettiness of the political system is mirrored in the diminutive size of its citi-

zens. Gulliver is referred to as the "Man-Mountain" by the Lilliputians and is eventually pressed into service by the King in a nonsensical war with the neighboring island of Blefuscu. Gulliver finally escapes Lilliput and returns briefly to England before a second voyage takes him to Brobdingnag. There he finds himself dwarfed by inhabitants who are sixty feet tall. Gulliver's comparatively tiny size now makes him wholly dependent on the protection and solicitude of others, and he is imperiled by dangerous encounters with huge rats and a curious toddler. Gulliver, however, incurs the disdain of the kindly and virtuous Brobdingnagian rulers when his gunpowder display, intended to impress his hosts as an exemplary product of European civilization, proves disastrous. An address Gulliver delivers to the Brobdingnagians describing English political practices of the day is also met with much scorn. Housed in a miniature box, Gulliver abruptly departs Brobdingnag when a giant eagle flies off with him and drops him in the ocean. He soon embarks on his third voyage to the flying island of Laputa, a mysterious land inhabited by scientists, magicians, and sorcerers who engage in abstract theorizing and conduct ill-advised experiments based on flawed calculations. Here Gulliver also visits Glubbdubdrib where it is possible to summon the dead and to converse with such figures as Aristotle and Julius Caesar. He also travels to Luggnagg, where he encounters the Struldbrugs, a group of people who are given immortality, yet are condemned to live out their eternal existence trapped in feeble and decrepit bodies. Once again Gulliver returns to England before a final journey, to the land of the Houyhnhnms, who are a superior race of intelligent horses. But the region is also home to the Yahoos, a vile and depraved race of ape-like creatures. Gulliver is eventually exiled from Houyhnhnm society when the horses gently insist that Gulliver must return to live among his own kind. After this fourth and final voyage, he returns to England, where he has great difficulty adjusting to everyday life. All people everywhere remind him of the Yahoos.

Major Themes

Each of the four voyages in *Gulliver's Travels* serves as a vehicle for Swift to expose and excoriate some aspect of human folly. The first voyage has been interpreted as an allegorical satire of the political events of the early eighteenth century, a commentary on the moral state of England, a general satire on the pettiness of human desires for wealth and power, and a depiction of the effects of unwarranted pride and self-promotion. The war with the tiny neighboring island of Blefuscu represents England's rivalry with France. In Brobdingnag, Gulliver's diminutive status serves as a reminder of how perspective and viewpoint alter one's condition and claims to power in society. The imperfect, yet highly moral Brobdingnagians represent, according to many critics, Swift's conception of ethical rulers. The voyage to Laputa, the flying island, is a scathing attack upon science in the sixteenth and seventeenth centuries and reveals Swift's thorough acquaintance with the *Philosophical Transactions of the Royal Society*, the leading publication of the scientific community of his day. The third voyage unequivocally manifests Swift's contempt and disdain for abstract theory and ideology that is not of practical service to humans. But it is the voyage to the land of the Houyhnhnms that reveals Swift's ultimate satiric object—man's inability to come to terms with his true nature. In particular, the Houyhnhnms are interpreted as symbols and examples of a human order that, although unattainable, deserves to remain an ideal, while the Yahoos are found to be the representatives of the depths of humanity's potential fall if that ideal is abandoned.

Critical Reception

Gulliver's Travels has always been Swift's most discussed work. Critics have provided a wide variety of interpretations of each of the four voyages, of Swift's satiric targets, and of the narrative voice. But scholars agree that most crucial to an understanding of *Gulliver's Travels* is an understanding of the fourth voyage, to the land of the Houyhnhnms. Merrel D. Clubb has noted that "the longer that one studies Swift, the more obvious it becomes that the interpretations and verdict to be placed on the 'Voyage to the Houyhnhnms' is, after all, the central problem of Swift criticism." Much of the controversy surrounds three possible interpretations of the Houyhnhnms and the Yahoos. One school of thought has traditionally viewed the Yahoos as a satiric representation of debased humanity, while taking the Houyhnhnms as representatives of Swift's ideals of rationality and order. The two races are thus interpreted as symbols of the dual nature of humanity, with Gulliver's misanthropy based on his perception of the flaws of human nature and the failure of humanity to develop its potential for reason, harmony, and order. Another critical position considers both the Houyhnhnms and Yahoos to be the subject of satire, with the Yahoos representing the physical baseness of humans and the Houyhnhnms representing the fatuousness of the idea that humans will ever achieve a rationally-ordered existence. The ultimate satiric intent of the work to critics who accept this interpretation is that the only truly rational or enlightened beings in existence are not humans, but another species altogether. Since the 1950s, however, a variety of critics have tempered these readings by illuminating the complexity of purpose in the fourth voyage. The Houyhnhnms and Yahoos are now most often discussed as both satiric objects and representatives of the duality of human nature. The nature of Gulliver is another much-debated element of the *Travels*. Early critics generally viewed him as the mouthpiece of Swift. Modern critics, who recognize the subtlety of Swift's creation of Gulliver, have discredited that position. The most significant contemporary debate is concerned with Swift's intentions regarding the creation of Gulliver—whether he is meant to be a consistently realized character, a reliable narrator, or a satiric object whose opinions are the object of Swift's ridicule. This debate over the nature of Gulliver is important because critics seek to determine whether Gulliver is intended to be a man with definite character traits who undergoes a transformation, or an allegorical representative of humanity. In general, Gulliver is now considered a flexible persona manipulated by Swift to present a diversity of views or satirical situations and to indicate the complexity, the ultimate indefinability, of human nature. Many scholars have suggested that *Gulliver's Travels* has no ultimate meaning but to demand that readers regard humanity without the prejudices of pessimism or optimism, and accept human beings as a mixture of good and evil. Eighteenth- and nineteenth-century critics of Swift were primarily interested in aspects of his character, although a few did actually discuss the meaning and merits of his work at length.

The eighteenth-century critics were most concerned with depicting Swift's perceived immorality and misanthropy, and they often argued their case with the help of misrepresentations, or deliberate fabrications of facts. Swift's defenders, in attacking these critics, provided the first real criticism of Swift, in particular pointing out the misrepresentations of his life. Twentieth-century critics have been confronted with the task of sifting through the misconceptions to reevaluate Swift's total achievement. There are many psychological examinations of Swift's character; the psychoanalysts, however, have often been criticized for neglecting the literary or intellectual traditions of Swift's age when associating his works with supposed neurotic tendencies. Some commentators believed that psychoanalytic critics also make an obvious mistake when they identify Swift with his characters, assuming, for example, that Gulliver's comments reflect the opinions of his creator. Close textual analysis has demonstrated the complicated elements of Swift's works and proven that they do not always reflect his personal opinions, but are carefully written to reflect the opinions of Swift's created narrators. A master of simple yet vividly descriptive prose and of a style so direct that if often masks the complexity of his irony, Swift is praised for his ability to craft his satires entirely through the eyes of a created persona. He is now regarded as a complex though not mysterious man who created works of art which will permit no single interpretation. The massive amount of criticism devoted to Swift each year reflects his continued literary importance: his work is valuable not for any statement of ultimate meaning, but for its potential for raising questions in the mind of the reader.

CRITICISM

William A. Eddy (essay date 1923)

SOURCE: "Didactic Content of the 'Philosophic Voyage,'" in *Gulliver's Travels: A Critical Study,* Russell & Russell, 1963, pp. 40-50.

[*In the essay below, first published in 1923 and reprinted in 1963, Eddy focuses on Swift's satiric, pessimistic, and misanthropic views in arguing the superiority of* Gulliver's Travels *over other contemporaneous texts employing the "voyage" motif.*]

Turning now from the story form of the *Philosophic Voyage* and from its interest as a romantic tale, let us examine the author's purpose in writing. In its fully developed form the *Philosophic Voyage* was always a vehicle for ideas, never an end in itself. Swift's avowed aim in writing *Gulliver* was "to vex, not to divert, the world"[1]. The survey of the motives, satiric and philosophic, which run through the fore-runners of *Gulliver* must be here very brief. The four *Voyages* of *Gulliver* present so many different criticisms of life that it would be impossible to bring the study to a definite focus as was done with the narrative form. The distinct purpose and satiric method used by Swift in each voyage will be discussed later when the situations are studied in turn.

As has been already suggested, a number of the *Fantastic Voyages,* concerned themselves with fanciful, and wholly impossible, trips of exploration, in the interests of speculative science. Cyrano de Bergerac and his imitators[2] sent their travellers to the moon, the sun, or to the center of the earth, where conversation with the better informed inhabitants disclosed new theories about the constitution of matter, the laws of physics, and the habitation of the planets. In this connexion it is to be noted simply that this motive of scientific speculation is almost wholly absent from Gulliver[3].

Obviously the connection is to be sought, not in abstract philosophy but in satire. No one of the fore-runners is so exclusively a work of satire as is *Gulliver,* and yet satire is usually included; sometimes it is incidental, again it is organic. In quality it ranges from the mild ridicule heaped upon the Lilliputians to the intense misanthropy represented in the picture of the Yahoos. It has been a notable blunder of criticism to suppose that the latter was peculiar to Swift. The satiric method employed by Swift's predecessors was almost invariably that of a contrast between the degenerate state of Western civilization, represented by the traveller, and the ideal life of the people visited. Gulliver's fourth voyage, to the land of the Houyhnhnms, and the latter portion of his second voyage, to Brobdingnag, conform to this type. It is not necessary to seek the elaboration of this method in the pure Utopian literature of Plato's *Republic,* Campanella's *Civitas Solis,* More's *Utopia,* or Bacon's *New Atlantis.* The ideal commonwealth appeared frequently in combination with imaginary adventures as in *Gulliver.* These ideal commonwealths are of two general types. A race, living in a state of innocence, is found to be the product of ideal government, unselfish customs, and benevolent religion, subject to the laws of charity and justice alone. Such are the Lunarians of Cyrano's first romance, *L'Histoire Comique de la Lune,* and the Potuans whom Klimius encounters underground. The satire in *Voyages* of this type is implied in the contrast with European practices, or it is brought out more directly by the surprise with which the natives receive the traveller's account of kings, priests, and lawyers, in his own world. On the whole, however, the stress is placed upon the objective description of the Utopia, in the organization of which there is a wearisome repetition of the formula, charity and justice, which shows the literature to be a phase of the deistic trend of contemporary thought[4].

A variation of this satiric method only a little less popular, is a contrast between European civilization and a superior race of animals, just as in the fourth voyage of Gulliver. Here the accent is shifted from the Utopian quality of the new civilization to a direct satire on mankind. This use of animals is much older than Aesop himself. In general, however, the fable literature, including the cycle of *Reynard the Fox,* presents an allegory in which the vices and foibles of the human race are identified with, or disguised under, the actions of the animals. For the contrast between man and beast, resulting in the humiliation of man, there was plenty of precedent. The tradition of Ulysses and the beasts[5], popularized by Giovanni Gelli in his *Circe*[6] and by Howell in the *Parley of the Beasts*[7], represents the beasts refusing to return to their human shape, and perfectly contented with their animal life. In d'Ablancourt's *Sequel* to Lucian's *True History,* and in Cyrano's second romance, *L'Histoire comique du soleil,* both known to Swift[8], the traveller finds himself despised by a race of animals who refuse to confirm his claim to the status of a reasonable creature. As will appear in my study of the sources, the satire on man in Cyrano is not less brutal than in Gulliver's fourth voyage.

According to Swift, Gulliver does not have to go to the moon, or to the center of the earth to find ideal beings. His travels are confined to this world, in the remote regions of which live the amiable Houyhnhnms and the gentle Brobdingnagians. It is a point very much to the credit of Swift that his ideal races are after all creatures of his imagination, giants and horses, and not natives of India or China. The Utopias of the *Philosophic Voyages,* the voluminous literature of the Oriental Traveller[9], of Montesquieu, DuFresne, Tom Brown, Lyttleton, and Goldsmith, all are marked by cheap sentimentality,—that of the "long distance" illusion. The Australian, Chinaman, Hindoo, or whatnot, is represented as nature's unspoiled child, a sort of Israelite in whom there is no guile, who cannot comprehend the diseases, tyrannies, and vices of the Christian world. The illusion seemed to spring from a theorem that virtue increased as the square of the distance from Europe. It is the sort of sentimentality familiar enough to us today in the writings of H. G. Wells[10] and in the pages of the so-called "liberal" magazines where we find it written that Trotsky of all statesmen is alone sincere, and China, an untainted nation of peaceable villages. It is the illusion which has started a wave of sympathy in favor of the "much abused" Turk, for the wrongs he has suffered at the hand of Christendom, a sympathy never felt by those who have lived under the shadow of the Crescent. From the charge of such nonsense, of which most of his predecessors were more or less guilty, the author of *Gulliver* can be acquitted.

In *Gulliver* another method is followed besides that of contrast between civilizations, and that is the allegorical device of representing the life of the Western world under a disguise. This is the case in Lilliput, Laputa, and the earlier chapters of Brobdingnag[11], where the animal called man is made to appear ridiculous, stupid, or disgusting. While this method of satire seems simple enough, it is exceedingly hard to manage, and was actually very rarely employed[12] in the *Philosophic Voyage* before *Gulliver.* Once made famous by Swift, the idea was copied in a dozen imitations[13], in which Lilliput was England; Blefuscu, Ireland; Flimnap, the prime minister; Nardac, a nobleman; and so forth.

Since *Gulliver's Travels* owed so much of its immediate popularity to this allegorical representation of human society, it will be of interest to notice two examples of it in the *Philosophic Voyage* before Swift. In Baron Holberg's *Journey of Klimius to the World Underground,* a work which Swift in all probability did not know[14], the traveller visits a number of subterranean countries, most of which are contrasted with our world, but two of which are identified with conditions above ground. Lalac is a land inhabited by an idle aristocracy, whose uninterrupted luxury is attended by consequent misery[15]. This is very obviously a picture of court life in Europe. Mascathia is the land of the philosophers. The country is filthy and uncultivated, the philosophers are indistinguishable from pigs. So busy have they been in devising a way to reach the sun and the stars, that they have had no time to improve their own world. To the traveller's practical questions they return absurd and incoherent answers. The author makes it plain that Mascathia is a satire upon academicians, of the same type that we find in Gulliver's voyage to Laputa[16].

Another instance of this satiric method is to be found in an obscure Latin satire by Joseph Hall, *Mundus Alter et Idem*[17], which has never been mentioned in connection with *Gulliver,* even though, as I shall show in the next chapter, it is not unlikely that it was known to Swift. This work, written about the year 1610, is the reverse of the *Utopia.* The author embarks on the good ship Phantasy for a new world located somewhere in Australia, which is conceived of as the duplicate of the Western world, except that the vices and weaknesses of human nature are assigned to separate provinces instead of being spread out over the entire country as in Europe. As the satire has never been translated in full, and is practically unknown, I will give a brief account of it to bring out the unique relation which it bears to the satiric method of Swift in a part of *Gulliver's Travels.*

> The first country to be visited is Crapula, the land of inebriate excess. It is divided into two provinces, Pamphagonia (or Gluttony) and Yvronia (or Drunkenness). In the capital cities, Livona and

Roncara (Snort and Snore), the people sleep continually. The natives are all monks who worship their God, Time, because he eats everything. Adjacent to Crapula is the desert Terra Sancta (Holy Land) which is uninhabited and unexplored. Moronia (Foolsland) is at once the most populous and the most uncultivated of all. There the natives go about naked in winter that the warmth may enter their bodies readily, whereas in mid-summer they wear heavy coats to shut out the heat. Moronia is inhabited by a stupid Philistine class who are subject to the rule of the aristocratic Laverians, or thieves. In Moronia there is an academy of innovators, not unlike the one visited by Gulliver at Lagado, where the single idea is to invent something new, no matter how useless it may be. The innovators have replaced language by a mystical speech, of which several pages of sample vocabulary are given. For example, "ointment," in this language is simplified to "Oppodeltoch;" "spirit" to Nenufarenicaballi;" "health" to "Zeninephidei;" "Mercury" to "Diatessdelton;" etc. The intellectual wizard who invented this Honorificabilitudinitatibus is none other than Bustius Hohenheimus—the headmaster. The treatment is throughout light and witty, and the satire, very obvious. But the method of holding up to ridicule the achievements of the western world is the rare method employed in Gulliver's voyages to Lilliput and Laputa.

So much for the general method and setting for satire in the *Philosophic Voyage.* In regard to the specific objects of satire, there does not seem to be any important development to note. While the choice of subject varies slightly from one author to another, for the most part the range is the same. From Lucian to Swift, the offensive is directed at historians, academicians, lawyers and court procedure, physicians, kings, priests and religion. In *Gulliver* the list is quite as long as in any of the earlier works, but the omission of religion is a conspicuous departure from precedent. The allusion made in passing to the High Church and Low Church parties in Lilliput[19] involves no question of religion, but only a reflection upon the motives of expediency which determined the piety of King George I, and the Prince of Wales. If Swift had followed the tradition of his predecessors he could, like Rabelais[20], have charged Christianity with the guilt of the world's insincerity and disease; and in the manner of the French deists[21] he could have portrayed the sweet and charming piety of the Hindoos or Confucianists as the ideal. That we do not find this in *Gulliver* might be adequately explained by the assumption that Swift knew something about the "gentle" practices of the Hindoos, but this is not necessary. From other of his writings it is clear enough that Swift was not one of those who deny the power of Christianity because they find its obligations inconvenient. In fact, the Christian Gulliver, though bad enough, is ranked by the Houyhnhnms above the Yahoos[22], who unquestionably represent the destiny of a race ruled by instinct and passion alone. Swift is not a Platonist. Man left to his own devices will not

discover the eternal pattern of truth in the stars, for he is loath to look up. At best he may discover its blurred reflection in the mud.

This is perhaps the best place to consider some of the more general features of the satiric style of *Gulliver's Travels,* a style famous for its sustained irony and biting wit, in its relation to its fore-runners. In most of the *Philosophic Voyages* there is no great merit of style and seldom anything that is even consistent. The styles of Lucian, Cyrano and their imitators are for the most part nondescript. One chapter is in the ironic vein, another purely comic, and still another of a straight narrative character. Where there is real art, it is of an eclectic and variable type. Two authors, however, have contributed materially to the method of Swift in *Gulliver.* To an imitation of the works of Rabelais[23], which Swift knew well and quoted from memory, must be assigned the fondness for the filth of the body with its odors, excrements, and pollutions, which appears in *Gulliver*[24]. In Rabelais this element of obscenity is drawn out to burlesque proportions, while in Gulliver it is restrained though not refined. Where Rabelais delights in filth for comical effect, Swift's use of it is always disgusting and never suggestive. The general ideas for Gulliver's method of extinguishing the fire at the palace of Lilliput[25] and for the occupations of some of the professors at Lagado[26], were borrowed from similar situations in Rabelais, as I will show later; but the contrast in diction and tone is the contrast that would exist between a treatise on human physiology and a corresponding anecdote as told in the rear of any saloon.

Swift owes a more considerable debt to the style of his elder contemporary Thomas Brown, a pamphleteer of no mean ability, whose works have been shown to have been assimilated and extensively imitated by Swift[27]. Brown in turn was steeped in the satiric humor of Lucian and Rabelais[28]. His writings carry on the latter's note of obscenity, which appears in combination with sustained irony of the kind found in *Gulliver.* Brown's satire is less grotesque than that of Rabelais, and at the same time not so restrained nor so well proportioned as that of Swift. Rabelais writes with the queer turns of wit peculiar to the drunken man; Brown, with more coherence of thought and with much more consistent drollery, gives the effect of one who has taken a glass too much; but Swift is always sober. The danger is likely to be that Brown's influence be understated, rather than exaggerated. Just as in the Bickerstaff papers Swift continued Brown's joke at the expense of the astrologer Partridge[29], so in *Gulliver,* pages, satirizing physicians, soldiers, and lawyers, are all but verbal counterparts of similar passages in the works of Brown.

In general, the satiric treatment in *Gulliver* can be distinguished in three ways from the style of earlier *Voy-*

ages. It is marked first of all by its pregnancy of thought, condensed to a degree that is frequently epigrammatic. Lucian pounds away at his historians, repeating endlessly that they are all liars, each time as though he were confiding a state secret, until the idea is all surface with no depth. Rabelais runs on and on with his cumulation of incident and synonym without knowing where to stop. The essence of his wit is good, but it could be extracted and bound up into a very thin volume. In *Gulliver* every paragraph is essential. The reader is surprised with satire within satire, with the ingenious wit which turns the subject over and over, always revealing something new. That which sets Swift above not only the other writers of *Philosophic Voyages,* but above all the other Queen Anne wits is the amazing number of his ideas per square inch.

A second distinction of *Gulliver* is the consistent pertinence of its prose style. Tom Brown crowds ideas into condensed space, but it was left for Swift to sort them out. In *Gulliver* there are no excursions into irrelevant fields, the main theme is never forgotten. The narratives of Cyrano are broken by the introduction of tiresome arguments about the nature of a vacuum and the constitution of the atom; and in most of the *Philosophic Voyages* incidents are introduced for their own sake alone. In *Gulliver,* the minutest detail, whether it be the measurements of pygmy life or a humorous incident, is essential. Not only is every idea essential, but the most insignificant details are stated with extreme accuracy. The size of the bed made for Gulliver by the pygmies, as well as his rations, are computed with the most scrupulous regard for the relative proportions assumed[30], in contrast to Rabelais' reckless method of shovelling hundreds of steaks and pies down the throat of his giant, Gargantua[31]. Minimum of digression and the lack of confusion found in *Gulliver's Travels* is the sort of achievement that comes but seldom, and then only with fasting and prayer.

Finally, the style of *Gulliver* is marked by an elevated tone, dignified and grave. Though Swift borrowed some of Robelais' obscene ideas, he avoided the latter's scurilous language. This quality of classical restraint in diction is at once both an hindrance and a help. A certain gaiety and lightness of touch, in dealing with the comic, is lost. On the other hand the solemn treatment of trifles is a very effective device for ridiculing the petty actions of men, clothing them as it does with mock dignity. The net result is satire less spontaneous and comical than in some of the earlier *Voyages,* but infinitely more effective.

In conclusion, what are the achievements of Swift in satire in *Gulliver's Travels,* apart from the characteristics of style just considered? He must be credited with the originality of the idea which runs through the first two voyages, of first reducing and then magnifying the proportions of life to reveal its pettiness and its

ugliness together. Lucian's *Voyage to Heaven* describes an insignificant world as it appears from a great height, but there is much more than this in *Gulliver*[32]. Expanding a bare suggestion in Cyrano, Swift conceives of a relativity in human affairs, in accordance with which false sources of pride can be at once detected when they are viewed in true perspective. This satire of proportion becomes his acid test of true values. He discovers that dominion, rank, feminine beauty, etc., are of relative value, but there is no indication that courage, devotion, or intelligence would change its aspect in Lilliput or Brobdingnag[33]. Gulliver's third Voyage is the most imitative, repeating for the most part borrowed ideas. By common consent of readers it is the least interesting of all[34]. The satire in the fourth *Voyage* has been considered most distinctively Swiftian, though it is less original than the satire in the first two voyages. Contrary to the statements made by Sir Walter Scott, Temple Scott, John Churton Collins and others[35], the complete condemnation of the human race embodied in the contrast between the Houyhnhnms and the Yahoos is not without precedent,—the same satire, no less brutal, is in the second romance of Cyrano, a work that was more carefully read by Swift than it has been by his editors and critics since. There is, however, something original about the satire in this *Voyage,* not its brutality, but something else which a study of the fore-runners of *Gulliver* has made very clear.

In all earlier *Voyages* when man was condemned in the presence of animals, the condemnation was of civilized man. The fault was with his perverted training, his unnatural practices, his abuse of intelligence, and his tyrannous institutions, the state and the church. The philosophical position taken was the plea for a return to nature, as described in the animal kingdoms. All of this appears in Gulliver's fourth voyage with the important difference that the lowest and filthiest lot is reserved for the native Yahoo who is not a product of European civilization at all, but man in a state of nature, "cunning, malicious, libidinous, cowardly and insolent"[36]. Not that Swift takes refuge in civilization, the condemnation of Gulliver is plain enough. But Gulliver is allowed by the Houyhnhnms to be endowed with a spark of intelligence, by so much above the Yahoos; the Governor of the Houyhnhnms even fears that Gulliver may be contaminated by contact with the Yahoos. No hope can be found for the race anywhere, certainly not in letting it run wild according to the notions of the individualist. The conclusion is complete pessimism. The best thing that can be done is to subject the race to some rules imposed from without, thereby curbing the mischief which it fain would accomplish. If it be true, as a study by C. H. Firth[37] has rendered probable, that in the Yahoos, Swift represents especially the degenerate natives of Ireland, then we are only more justified in concluding that the author of Gulliver's fourth voyage was at heart an imperialist, though indeed a very pessimistic one. He would no doubt modify the doctrine of the "White Man's Burden" to make the white man a part of a burden. At any rate Swift makes it very clear that his indictment includes all mankind. The Abbé DesFontaines, who translated *Gulliver* into French, wrote to Swift apologizing for his excision of the more objectionable passages, which he said, with characteristic conceit, were inapplicable to the French, though no doubt they were fair descriptions of the English[38]. To this Swift replied sharply, "The same vices and follies reign everywhere; if I had written of England alone, or of this century alone, so far from meriting translation, my work would not deserve to be read"[39]. The misanthropy increases steadily from the first voyage, where man appears as a strutting Lilliputian to the fourth, where he is a loathsome Yahoo. The pessimism extends, moreover, to all creatures. The peace-loving Brobdingnagians, when examined at close quarters, are ugly and disgusting[40]; the amiable Houyhnhnms, though virtuous and harmless, are at the same time ignorant, stupid, and innocent of any achievement of genius. The world through which Gulliver travels is a very bad world, and man is the worst creature on it.

Notes

[1] Swift to Pope, Sept. 29, 1725. *Correspondence,* III, 276.

[2] Holberg's, *Klimius;* the anonymous *Voyage du Pôle Arctique au Pôle Antarctique,* and *Relation du Monde de Mercure;* Mouhy's *Lamékis;* and Roumier's *Voyages de Céton dans les Sept Planettes.* See Bibliography.

[3] I say "almost" because there is, in the second voyage, a reminiscence of the debate on biology that takes place in Cyrano's *Histoire de la Lune,* in the argument over Gulliver's origin and species. *Gulliver,* 106. See further chapter 7, below.

[4] Atkinson has made a careful and detailed study of the deistic and rationalistic content of the *Realistic Voyages* in French. *op. cit.*

[5] Based on the *Odyssey.* The tradition first took an independent form in Plutarch's dialogue entitled, "That Brute Beasts Make Use of Reason," in which Ulysses vainly argues with Gryllus to reassume his human shape. (*Plutarch's Morals, translated from the Greek by several eminent hands, London, 1704,* V, 203-216.) Plutarch was one of Swift's favorite authors. *Prose Works,* XII, 364.

[6] Translated into English by Tom Brown, 1702, and very likely a part of the latter's works which Swift had "read entire." (See *Prose Works,* XI, 221. *Introduction to "Polite Conversation."*)

[7] 1660. The complete title reads, *The Parley of the Beasts; or Morphandra, Queen of the Enchanted Island. Wherein Men were found, who being transmuted to Beasts, though proffered to be disenchanted, and to become Men again; yet in regard of the crying sins and rebellious humors of the times, they prefer the life of a brute animal before that of a rational creature. Which fancy consists of various philosophical discussions . . . touching the declinings of the world, and late depravation of human nature. With reflexes upon the present state of most countries in Christendom. Divided into XI sections. By Jam. Howell, Esq.* In the preface the author alludes to Gelli as the one who "taught the beasts their grammar."

[8] See further, chapter 4, below.

[9] See Bibliography under these names. Also, M. P. Conant, *op. cit.*

[10] Especially Wells' articles written after his visit to Russia in 1920, in which he contrasts the "sincerity" and "highmindedness" of the Soviet demagogues with the corruption of the Allied statesmen.

[11] The two-fold nature of the satire of the second voyage is discussed in chapter 8 below.

[12] This sort of allegory seems not to have occurred to most of the writers of *Philosophic Voyages.* Their tendency was rather to have the traveller discover something new and different from European custom, hence the predominance of utopian contrast instead of allegory. There were, however, purely allegorical works which do not concern us here directly because of their lack of genuine adventure. So-called *Voyages* were written describing "fake" countries, not located anywhere. See Fontaines' *Pays de Jansénie,* 1664; Tallemant's *Isle d'Amour,* 1663; and other allegories of the Bunyan type, listed together in the Bibliography.

[13] See the list of imitations, appended to Part III, below.

[14] For a more general description of the work, see chapter 1, above. The possibility of its influence upon *Gulliver* is discussed in chapter 4.

[15] *Klimius,* 147-150.

[16] *Ibid,* 167-177.

[17] The only edition I have seen is one dated 1643, 1 vol. in-12, in which the *Mundus* is bound with Bacon's *New Atlantis,* and Campanella's *Civitas Solis,* all in Latin. The first six chapters of the *Mundus* were translated into English by Swift's friend, Dr. William King, sometime before 1711. (See further, chapter 4, below.) This fragmentary translation may be found in Morley's *Ideal Commonwealths,* 1896.

(19) *Gulliver*, 48. (*Lilliput*, chapter 4.)

(20) See synopsis of Rabelais in chapter 1, above.

(21) See Montesquieu, DuFresne, *etc.*, works listed in the Bibliography under "Oriental Traveller."

(22) That Gulliver was a Christian is stated in *Laputa*, chapter XI. *Gulliver*, 226. Gulliver's superiority to the Yahoos is repeatedly stated by the Houyhnhnms, see especially, *Houyhnhnms*, chapter VIII, first paragraph.

(23) See the study of Rabelais as a source in chapter 4, below. Also my article in *Mod. Lang. Notes*, November, 1922.

(24) This is pointed out later in connection with the study of the situations in which it is most marked. See especially chapters 5-7, below.

(25) *Lilliput*, chapter 5.

(26) *Laputa*, chapters 5-6.

(27) See the source study and references in notes 68-71 in chapter 4, below.

(28) Brown's second volume consists of "Letters from the Dead to the Living, together with Dialogues of the Dead, after the manner of Lucian." The influence of Rabelais is evident throughout Brown's works, and he is directly quoted in the following places: I, 86-88; II, 93-96; IV, 57-62. (Edition, 1760.)

(29) See chapter 4, below.

(30) See chapter 5, below.

(31) Rebelais, Book I, chapter 37.

(32) See my study of Lucian as a source, chapter 4, below. Also my article in *Mod. Lang. Notes*, June, 1922.

(33) See further chapter 8, below.

(34) See contemporary opinions of the third voyage quoted in chapter 4, note 24, below.

(35) All of whom depend upon the worthless thesis of Borkowsky in *Anglia*, XV. See Cyrano as a source in chapter 4, below.

(36) *Gulliver*, 277.

(37) *The Political Significance of "Gulliver's Travels,"* C. H. Firth. (*Proceedings of the British Academy*, IX, 1920.)

(38) DesFontaines to Swift, July 4, 1727. *Correspondence*, III, 397-8.

(39) Swift to DesFontaines, July, 1727. *Correspondence*, III, 406-7.

(40) For the double picture of the Brobdingnagians, see chapter 8, below.

Arthur E. Case (essay date 1945)

SOURCE: "The Geography and Chronology of *Gulliver's Travels*," in *Four Essays on "Gulliver's Travels*," Peter Smith, 1958, pp. 50-67.

[*In the following essay, first published in 1945 and reprinted in 1958, Case argues that many of the geographical and chronological inconsistencies in* Gulliver's Travels *are not due to Swift's carelessness, but instead are attributable to engraving and printing errors that remained uncorrected in later editions.*]

Surprisingly little attention has been paid by editors and commentators to the geography and chronology of *Gulliver's Travels*. Sir Henry Craik, in his *Selections from Swift*, found the geography worth a fairly extended passage,[1] Mr. G. R. Dennis, in his edition of *Gulliver*,[2] commented on some of the cruces, and Mr. Harold Williams devoted some space in the introduction of his edition to a discussion of the maps.[3] Mr. Williams also provided his readers with the most satisfactory commentary we possess on the difficulties and inconsistencies of the time-scheme.[4] The conclusions reached by these scholars, and, indeed, by almost all students of Swift who have occupied themselves with the problem, were that Swift worked out for his book a detailed framework in time and space, but that it is (at least as it has come down to us) so imperfect that it is impossible to reconcile it with itself or to be sure, in many instances, of the author's intentions. Recently, however, Professor John R. Moore has suggested that the geography and chronology of the *Travels* are so nonsensical as to indicate intentional confusion: in other words, they are part of a satiric burlesque of travel literature.[5]

Undoubtedly the framework of the *Travels* presents difficulties. Unless some happy chance brings to light more material like the Ford letters we shall have to rely on conjectures with regard to a number of points. Yet it is possible to solve a good deal of the puzzle, and to come much closer to certainty than is usually believed.

Two geographical authorities are spoken of in the *Travels*—Nicolas Sanson and Herman Moll. The only mention of the former is found in the second voyage, where the "little Book" carried by Glumdalclitch is described

(2.2.8) as "not much larger than a *Sanson's Atlas.*" There is nothing to indicate that Swift ever looked inside the covers of this book, which he cites only because it is the largest he can think of. There was, indeed, little reason for using Sanson as an authority. His atlases had all been published in the seventeenth century, and the first quarter of the eighteenth had seen great advances in geographical knowledge, especially in the neighborhood of those regions in which Swift was to place his imaginary countries. Swift's obvious course was to avoid, as far as possible, any gross contradictions of accepted cartography, and he could not have effected this more surely and easily than by following the maps of Moll. This eminent English engraver of Dutch extraction had industriously gathered geographical data from the turn of the century, and by Englishmen, at least, his maps were widely accepted as the standard. As a matter of fact, however, the early eighteenth-century maps were much of a muchness, at least so far as the general physical structure of the world was concerned. Even in the regions of the South Seas (a term which sometimes included the North as well as the South Pacific) the cartographers tended to agree, only venturing to show occasional divergences in minor details, and often attempting to hedge by the use of faintly drawn coast lines which warned the reader not to put too much faith in what was, at best, unverified information.

Swift's remarks about Moll are entirely different in tone from his incidental reference to Sanson. Gulliver ventures (4.11.3) to disagree respectfully with Moll in the matter of the southeastern portion of New Holland, which is, he insists, at least three degrees west of the position it occupies in Moll's maps. This is enough to show that Swift had consulted Moll with attention: it also shows that he felt it safe, in the current state of geographical knowledge, to dispute minor points even with an expert. Whether he relied on any other sources it is impossible to say. No atlas appears in the catalogue of his library as it existed at the time of his death, but he did own numerous books of travel, most of which contained charts of some kind.[6] Among them was Dampier's *New Voyage around the World* (1697) which, it is almost certain, Swift read intensively. This book contains some of Moll's earliest maps, including one of the world, and another of the Netherlands East Indies and the northern part of New Holland or Australia. Some of the place names Swift uses in the ***Travels*** differ in form from those used by Moll: but these Swift may have taken from the mass of travel literature which he read during the period in which the book was composed.[7] In any event, a fairly extensive search among the maps and atlases of the period has brought to light no map which agrees more closely than Moll's with Gulliver's geography, and it will be convenient to use the former's *A New & Correct Map of the Whole World* (1719) as a basis for discussion.[8]

Swift's primary geographical problem was not a difficult one. He had to find, in the unexplored portions of the globe, locations for seven imaginary countries, only two of which were of considerable size. It was desirable that these locations should not be so close to either pole as to be obviously unfit for human habitation, and Swift apparently felt also that they should not be too close to the equator: the climates do not seem to differ much from that of England. It was also necessary to take care that these countries did not lie too close to each other, or to trade routes generally known to Europeans, though, on the other hand, they could not lie too far from these routes, lest it should be difficult to account for Gulliver's arrivals and departures. Accordingly we find that the three smallest countries, Lilliput, Blefuscu, and Houyhnhnmland, are placed not far from Australia, although on different sides, and that Brobdingnag, Balnibarbi, and the islands described in the third voyage are situated in the North Pacific, by far the largest area which remained unexplored by Europeans in 1720.

An examination of Moll's map shows the astuteness of Swift's choices.[9] Most traders with the Orient in the eighteenth century preferred to hug the coast line of Asia, sailing to China through the multitudinous islands which lie between Siam and Australia. Consequently the Malay Archipelago was well known to mariners, save for New Guinea, the eastern and southern coasts of which were in dispute, some cartographers boldly uniting the island with Australia, while others remained noncommittal. The northern and western coasts of Australia had been determined with considerable accuracy, but the eastern and southeastern shores were not even guessed at, although there was a general agreement that it was possible to sail between Australia and New Zealand, the southwestern corner of which appears in Moll's maps. Exploration in the North Pacific had been checked by the disinclination of the Japanese to deal with Europeans: even the Dutch, who had a monopoly of occidental trade with Japan, had for nearly a century been limited to the port of Nagasaki. There was, therefore, almost no knowledge of the geography of northern Japan and of the regions which lay beyond. It was not known how far Iesso (Yezo) extended, whether it was an island or a peninsula, or whether any lands lay to the north or the east of it, although many maps vaguely indicated a territory to the east called "Company's Land"—claimed by the Dutch East India Company on the ground of explorations early in the seventeenth century. This land was separated from Yezo by the "Straits of the Vries," which led to a hypothetical northwest passage to Europe, hope for the discovery of which had not yet been abandoned. The eastward extent of "Company's Land" was frankly a matter of conjecture, some maps indicating only the western tip, others showing (though in faint lines) a coast stretching almost due east to within a short distance of the North American coast, close to the "Straits of Annian." Western North America was perhaps the most mysterious region of all. The cartographers were not even sure whether California was an island or a part of the main continent. Many maps, including Moll's, showed the Gulf of California extending northward until it rejoined the Pacific at the entrance to Puget Sound, north of Cape Blanco. San Francisco Bay was undiscovered, and to the north and west of Puget Sound lay a perfect and absolute blank.

With so much of the globe at his disposal it would seem that Swift should have had no trouble in arranging his hypothetical countries without coming into too violent conflict with accepted geography. And yet a series of misfortunes has led to a very general misunderstanding of his intentions. The chief misfortune was the fact that Swift, because of the secret method employed to publish the *Travels,* was unable to read proof and correct errors of detail. It is impossible to determine to what extent the errors were the fault of the author, the transcriber, and the printer, but that there were errors is undeniable. The second misfortune was that the maker of the maps for the original edition was careless or stupid or both. He was guilty of mistakes for which there can be no excuse—the misspelling of names, the miscalculation of comparative distances, the misplacing of localities with respect to each other when there was no discrepancy in the text from which he worked. But despite all this, and despite the fact that no one believes that Swift approved the maps, certain assumptions which the original engraver made have been accepted by modern scholars without question, with the result that Swift has been charged with errors of which he was not guilty. The engraver's practice seems to have been to read the text until he came to the first description of the location of the land Gulliver was visiting, then to assume that this description was accurate, and that any conflicting supplementary data must be reconciled with it, or ignored, if reconciliation proved to be impossible. It seems never to have occurred to him to assemble all of the geographical data in a given voyage, to try to harmonize the whole and, if conflicts appeared, to seek a solution of the difficulty without giving preference to any statement because it came early in the tale rather than late. And yet such a procedure would have prevented a series of blunders which begins with the first voyage.

The wreck which cast Gulliver upon the shores of Lilliput occurred "Northwest of *Van Diemen's* Land" and "in the Latitude of 30 Degrees 2 Minutes South" (1.1.5). Two areas bear the name "Van Dieman's Land" (or "Dimen's Land") in eighteenth-century maps—northwestern Australia and Tasmania—but as the former lies between ten and twenty degrees south latitude it cannot have been intended here by Swift unless the passage in the *Travels* is hopelessly corrupt. But there are difficulties even if one assumes that the reference is to Tasmania. A glance at a modern map will reveal

what was apparent to the eyes of the engraver of the original maps for the *Travels:* that a point northwest of Tasmania and in latitude 30° 2' S. lies not in the ocean but well inland in Australia. A timid soul might have solved this discrepancy by moving Lilliput a little to the south of Australia, in latitude 32° or 33° S. The engraver was made of bolder stuff. He moved Tasmania some forty-five degrees to the west, and placed Lilliput in the Indian Ocean, due south of the western end of Sumatra. Australia was ruthlessly erased from the map. It is not surprising to find that this was only the beginning of the engraver's liberties. Both Lilliput and Blefuscu are drawn on a scale far too large, as compared with Sumatra, and Mildendo appears as "Mendendo."

Yet after all this manipulation of the facts there are more difficulties to come. When Gulliver left Blefuscu he sailed first north and then northwest (1.8.9). "My Intention," he says, "was to reach, if possible, one of those Islands, which I had reason to believe lay to the North-East of *Van Diemen's* Land." On the third day he was picked up about twenty-four leagues from Blefuscu, in latitude 30° S., by a ship sailing on a southeasterly course in its return from Japan "by the *North* and *South-Seas.*" Either an eighteenth- or a twentieth-century map will show the ridiculousness of this account if we assume that Lilliput lies either south of Sumatra, as Motte's engraver thought, or in the Great Australian Bight, as some later commentators have suggested. It represents Gulliver as attempting to sail entirely around Australia in search of an island on which to land, and it describes the ship's captain as laying a southeasterly course from the neighborhood of Sumatra in order to reach England. If we adopt the theory which seems to be most favored today—that Van Diemen's Land is northwestern Australia, and that the position of Lilliput is about 15° S. and 120° E., similar difficulties arise: they can be solved only by supposing that the island Gulliver was searching for lay northwest of Australia, and that the ship which rescued him was on a southwesterly course—in other words, by changing the text in four places in order to achieve a result which is uncertain and unsatisfactory.

In all the speculation about this crux it does not seem to have occurred to anyone to question the accuracy of the first datum of all. Yet if one supposes that Lilliput lies north*east* of Tasmania, instead of north*west* of it, all difficulties vanish. The position thus indicated lies in the South Pacific about midway between Brisbane and the North Cape of New Zealand. Gulliver's project of sailing northwest from Blefuscu in the hope of reaching an island northeast of Tasmania is seen to be a thoroughly practicable plan, and the ship captain's southeasterly course is recognized as entirely normal, since traveling from the Orient to England by sailing around Australia was an accepted alternative to following the shorter but more difficult route through the

Netherlands East Indies. This solution disposes of all difficulties so simply and completely that there can be little doubt of its correctness.

The geography of Brobdingnag is a much less complicated matter. Even Motte's engraver was right as to its approximate location, though he was characteristically careless in his scale, making the country far too small. Brobdingnag is a peninsula joined to the northern portion of the North American continent (2.4.1). Gulliver's observation (2.4.2) that it is "terminated to the North-east by a Ridge of Mountains" suggests that the main axis of the peninsula runs from southwest to northeast. The dimensions of the country (in which Swift is a little more generous than the map will allow) are "six thousand Miles in Length, and from three to five in Breadth." The most helpful data about the location are given in the last chapter of the voyage. The eagle which captured Gulliver carried him fifty leagues from the coast (presumably the southern coast) of Brobdingnag, and dropped him somewhere near 44° N. 143° E. According to Moll's map this position is just off the coast of Yezo, in the "Straits of the Vries." This would fix one part of the southern coast of Brobdingnag in the vicinity of 45° N. 143° E., though the southernmost tip may lie some distance further to the southeast. A coast line running west-northwest and east-southeast may be extended as far as 20° N. 170° W. without interfering with either Moll's geographical data or the lands described in the third voyage, as their positions are worked out hereafter. From this point the eastern coast line may tentatively be carried north-northeast to 40° N. 140° W., and thence in a still more northerly direction to 70° N. 90° W., from which point the high mountain range which, according to Gulliver, separates Brobdingnag from the rest of North America, may be supposed to run northwest. The coast line, however, must be pure conjecture, since we are given only enough information to locate the points of Gulliver's arrival and departure, which lie very close to each other. The storm at the beginning of the second voyage caught the crew of the *Adventure* just east of the Moluccas, about three degrees north of the equator, and drove them a long distance east-northeast, after which a strong west-southwest wind carried them about five hundred leagues to the east. Such a course could easily have brought them to a position off the southern coast of Brobdingnag if it lay in the region suggested above. No doubt the point at which the landing was made was east of Flanflasnic, which seems to have been close to the southwest tip of the country. Such a location, of course, disposes of the hypothetical "Company's Land," but Swift would have felt no compunction over depriving the Dutch of territory.

It has been remarked that the dimensions of Brobdingnag are too large to be fitted into the map of the world as known to the eighteenth century.[10] The exaggeration was not, after all, very serious. The southern coast, as described above, would have given the country a width of three thousand miles, which might have been increased, farther up the peninsula, to well over four thousand. If the North American shore line above Cape Blanco bent backward to the east, so that the dividing mountain range was on the far side of the pole, a long axis of a good deal more than five thousand miles might be secured. Swift may, of course, have been careless in his calculations: he may even have been deceived as to the area at his disposal because he used a flat map instead of a globe. Most probably, however, he was not so much concerned with precise geography here as he was with providing the Brobdingnagians with a country suitable to their size: note, in the same passage, the mountains thirty miles high. In the first voyage Swift had ignored his scale deliberately for the sake of a picturesque incident—the troop of cavalry exercising on his handkerchief—and this slighter deviation for a more important purpose would probably not have worried him. If this is the case, however, it is pertinent to inquire why he chose just these dimensions as adequate for a country of giants. If one divides them by twelve, in accordance with the scale, they become five hundred miles in length and from two hundred and fifty to four hundred sixteen and two-thirds miles in breadth. The long axis of the British Isles, from Cape Wrath to the Isle of Wight, is about five hundred and sixty miles. The greatest width, taken at right angles to this axis, is from Bray Head, in Ireland, to Scarborough, about four hundred and fifty miles; elsewhere the width is commonly between two and three hundred miles. The figures are at least suggestive.

There is, however, one difficulty about the geography of Brobdingnag which becomes manifest only at the beginning of the third voyage. Here we learn (3.1.8) that Gulliver was boarded by pirates in the neighborhood of "the Latitude of 46 N. and of Longitude 183" (that is, 177° W.). This point, if previous calculations are correct, lies within the boundaries of Brobdingnag. But there are several good reasons for suspecting that the bearings thus given are inaccurate. In the first place, even if this position did lie within the ocean, it would have been an odd spot for eighteenth-century pirates to lurk about in search of prey. In the second place, it is hard to see how Gulliver's sloop could have reached this place by the course he describes. Finally, the bearings are inconsistent with the movements of Gulliver during the remainder of the third voyage. We have once more to do with an initial error which has been accepted without question, and which has consequently darkened counsel.

Motte's engraver outdid himself. He began by placing Balnibarbi (which he makes an island rather than a part of a continent) in latitude 43° N., a few hundred miles due east of Yezo. He was then confronted with the information (3.7.1) that Luggnagg lies northwest of Balnibarbi, and that this island, in turn, lies southeast of Japan. Lest there should be any doubt about this last point, Gulliver gives the exact position of Luggnagg—29° N. 140° E. The engraver compromised: he drew Luggnagg *south*west of Balnibarbi, so that it lay southeast of the northernmost part of Japan, and a good ten degrees east of the position given by Gulliver. His confusion of mind led him to commit the additional errors of attaching the island of Glubbdubdrib to Luggnagg, and placing the port of Maldonada in the latter island as well.

The process of working backward from data given late in the voyage produces, however, a clear and consistent picture. To begin with, the position of Luggnagg is described so circumstantially, and agrees so well with Gulliver's description of his voyage from thence to Japan, that we may feel ourselves on fairly safe ground. Balnibarbi is to the southeast of Luggnagg, and at a considerable distance from it, since Gulliver's voyage between the two countries occupied a month. Still, the length of the voyage was due in part to unfavorable winds, and perhaps we should look for the port of Maldonada in the neighborhood of 24° N. 149° E. This port is situated on the southern or western coast of Balnibarbi, since the island of Glubbdubdrib lies southwest of it. Lagado is about a hundred and fifty miles from Maldonada, and apparently south of it. Now the island from which Gulliver was rescued by the Laputans was ninety leagues (about three hundred and fifty miles) southwest by west of Lagado (3.2.8), and consequently about four hundred and fifty miles southwest by south of Maldonada, if the previous suppositions have been correct. By this reasoning Gulliver was marooned near 20° N. 145° E.—a long way from 46° N. 177° W. Which of these positions agrees more closely with Gulliver's account of his movements before he encountered the pirates?

Three days out of Tongking on a trading voyage, Gulliver's sloop was caught in a storm which drove it for five days, first northeast and then east, after which the weather became fair, but with a strong gale from the west for ten days. It is clear that the only northing the ship made occurred during the first part of the five days' storm. It is equally clear that no storm could drive a sailing vessel twenty-five degrees northward (more than sixteen hundred miles, even if the ship had no eastward motion) in five days. The commonly accepted position for Balnibarbi, east of Yezo, is an impossible one.

Once more, then, it is necessary to follow Gulliver's story with a map before us, in order to discover what Swift really intended. The Gulf of Tongking is a partially enclosed body of water from which Swift desired Gulliver to be carried into the Pacific. The storm which bore the sloop first northeast and then east (3.1.4) was designed to bring it first opposite Hainan Strait

and then eastward through that passage into the open ocean. A ship on such a course would be following the twentieth parallel closely: ten days' progress due east with a strong following gale, partly of storm force, might easily bring it to 144° E. (a run of about thirteen hundred miles), although the precise longitude of the scene of the capture of the sloop may have been a few degrees east or west of this position. That the latitude was not far from 20° N. seems almost certain. How the erroneous "Latitude of 46. N. and of Longitude 183" found its way into the text it is impossible to explain: it may be an overlooked detail surviving from an early draft; it may be a mere error of transcription or a printer's mistake.

The final geographical problem, although it is the simplest of all, has nevertheless led to differences of opinion. In this case the customary geographical details are wanting at the beginning of the voyage, and calculations must be based on a brief passage near the end (4.11.3). From this we learn that Gulliver surmised that Houyhnhnmland lay west of New Holland (Australia), and about 45° S. He therefore decided to sail due east, in the hope of coming either to the southwest coast of Australia, or to some island to the west of that continent. To his surprise, two days' sailing brought him to the south*east* point of Australia. Dennis assumed that this was a mistake for southwest,[11] and in this opinion he has been followed by other commentators. The last part of Gulliver's account, however, confirms the reading of the original text. To begin with, the southwestern point of Australia is approximately 34° S., not 45° S. More important is the fact that if this had been the region intended, the geography would require further revision. After rounding the cape which he had first reached, Gulliver saw the ship which eventually rescued him approaching from the north-north-east (4.11.6)—a patent impossibility by either eighteenth- or twentieth-century maps if Gulliver had been near the southwestern tip of Australia. What Swift really meant was that Gulliver had reached the southern point of Tasmania, which, on Moll's map, lies about 44° S., about half a degree further south than it does in actual fact. Swift, in this passage, commits himself on two points which had not been finally determined by eighteenth-century cartographers: that Tasmania was joined to Australia, and that its southern extremity was "at least three Degrees" west of the location shown on Moll's map. Houyhnhnmland, therefore, lies a short distance due west of the southern tip of Tasmania, at about 44° S. 142° E. Motte's engraver was less at fault than usual in placing it at about 40° S. 125° E.

The foregoing geographical scheme for *Gulliver's Travels* requires only two alternations in the text of the first edition. The time-scheme of the book is more detailed, and cannot be straightened out quite so easily, though the serious difficulties are confined to the third voyage. The second and fourth voyages are extremely simple. There is a slight slip at the beginning of the second. Gulliver returned from Blefuscu on April 13, 1702, and, as he remarked in the last paragraph of the first book, he sailed away again after two months. The actual date of his departure, as we learn from the first paragraph of the voyage to Brobdingnag, was June 20, but in the same paragraph his stay in England is given as ten months. The discrepancy was corrected by Motte in the fourth octavo, though Ford failed to note it in his emendations. The same paragraph contains another minor chronological error. The twenty-day gale which set in on April 19 is said to have ceased before May 2. There is a considerable probability that the former date should read "the 9th of April." Printers habitually read off a fairly long phrase or sentence from a manuscript and set it from memory: if the compositor of the *Travels* worked in this manner it is easy to understand how the similarity of "9th" and "19th" could have brought about the mistake. Another possible example of this kind of slip occurs near the end of the third voyage.

The remainder of the second voyage presents no difficulties. Gulliver landed in Brobdingnag on June 17, 1703, and was taken to the farmhouse on the same day. He began his tour of the country "upon the *17th* of *August,* about two Months after [his] Arrival," (2.2.6) and reached Lorbrulgrud, after ten weeks, on October 26 (2.2.7-8). Here, after a "few Weeks" (2.3.1), he was bought by the Queen. There are no further statements about the times of Gulliver's adventures until the second paragraph of the last chapter of the voyage, where he observes, "I had now been two Years in this Country; and about the beginning of the third, *Glumdalclitch* and I attended the King and Queen in a Progress to the South Coast of the Kingdom." This progress must have taken place during the summer of 1705, and the arrival at Flanflasnic, at the end of the journey (2.8.3), presumably occurred late in the summer. This agrees exactly with the only other pertinent bit of information which Swift gives us. " . . . I never went out of the Ship," Gulliver asserts, "till we came into the Downs, which was on the 3d. Day of *June,* 1706, about nine Months after my Escape."

The chronology of the last voyage is equally simple. Once again there is a minor discrepancy between the dates and the elapsed time of Gulliver's sojourn in England between voyages. He returned from Laputa on April 10, 1710, and sailed from Portsmouth on the second of August following (3.11.7: 4.1.1): this is a little short of four months, instead of five, as the first edition has it. Gulliver was marooned in Houyhnhnmland on May 9, 1711 (4.1.3): after this there are no clues to the calendar until the latter part of the book. The quadrennial assembly which decided upon the exile of Gulliver met at the vernal equinox, that is, about September 21, since the country lay south of the equator (4.8.16), and about three months before Gulliver's

departure (4.9.1). This last is a loose statement: apparently the three months' interval occurred between the assembly and the notice to depart given to Gulliver by his master, which on this supposition should be dated December 21 or thereabouts. Gulliver was allowed two months to build a boat, but completed its construction in a little more than six weeks (4.10.9, 12). The date given for his departure, February 15, 1715 (4.11.1) is consequently in strict accord with his other statements.

Two passages elsewhere in the text have led to some misunderstanding. Gulliver begins the fourth paragraph of the eighth chapter: "Having lived three Years in this Country, the Reader I suppose will expect that I should, like other Travellers, give him some Account of the Manners and Customs of its Inhabitants. . . . " In the seventh paragraph of the twelfth chapter, recounting his capture by the Portuguese sailors, Gulliver says, "I told them, I was born in *England,* from whence I came about five Years ago. . . . " There is no discrepancy between these two statements. Gulliver was speaking in round numbers. His voyage had lasted more than nine months before he was marooned. He dwelt with the Houyhnhnms precisely three years, nine months, and six days; when he was picked up by the Portuguese, on February 20, 1715, he had been absent from England exactly four years, six months, and eighteen days—a little nearer five years than four. The editor of the edition of 1735, not remembering these facts, emended a passage a little later on (4.11.10), in which Gulliver spoke of his three years' residence in Houyhnhnmland, to read "five years' residence." This mistake persists in many modern editions.

The time-scheme of the first voyage falls into two parts, each detailed and coherent in itself, and not inconsistent with the other. Gulliver sailed from Bristol on May 4, 1699 (1.1.4), and on the return from a prosperous voyage to the Pacific Ocean his ship foundered off the coast of Lilliput on November 5. The year is not stated, but subsequent events show that it was 1700. On the morning after the wreck Gulliver found himself in captivity, and on the next day he arrived at Mildendo. About three weeks later (November 28, approximately) he had learned the language of Lilliput sufficiently well to permit him to converse with the Emperor (1.2.6), and to be partially intelligible to the officers who searched his pockets. Their inventory is dated "the fourth Day of the eighty ninth Moon" of the Emperor's reign (1.2.9). The articles by the terms of which Gulliver gained his freedom are dated "the twelfth Day of the Ninety-first moon" (1.3.18). "Moon," presumably, means a lunar month of twenty-eight days, in which case the date of Gulliver's release came at the end of January or the beginning of February, 1701. "About a Fortnight" later Reldresal made a visit to Gulliver to acquaint him with the political state of the kingdom (1.4.4). Here, in the middle of February, the first series of dates comes to an end: there is no clear indication of the length of time spent by Gulliver in maturing his plan for the attack on Blefuscu and carrying it into effect. A second series of dates begins, however, with Gulliver's capture of the Blefuscudian fleet. The plot against Gulliver broke out "less than two Months" after he had refused to help enslave Blefuscu, which he seems to have done immediately after his great exploit (1.5.4, 5). The ambassadors from Blefuscu arrived in Lilliput "about three Weeks" after their naval disaster (1.5.6), but this period seems to have been overlapped by the two-month interval just referred to, and if this is true it may be ignored in the chronology. A "considerable Person at Court" warned Gulliver of the plot just before it was to have been put into execution, and in consequence Gulliver fled to Blefuscu three days later. The exact date of this flight is fixed by the statement (1.6.19) that Gulliver resided in Lilliput for nine months and thirteen days: he departed, therefore, on August 18, 1701. Reckoning backward about two months (the duration of the plot) gives the middle of June as the time of the falling-out of Gulliver and the Emperor. By this calculation the whole affair of the fleet occupied about four months: but this period may have been shorter if it took Gulliver some time to persuade the Emperor to order the inventory, in which case the dates immediately preceding the naval victory should be set somewhat later.

The remainder of the calendar is straightforward. Gulliver discovered a derelict boat on August 21, three days after his arrival in Blefuscu (1.8.1): he spent ten days in making paddles, and brought the boat into the royal port for repairs (1.8.2). He finished these in "about a Month" (1.8.7), and set sail on September 24, 1701 (1.8.9). Two days later he was picked up by an English vessel, which eventually landed him in the Downs on April 13, 1702.

The chronology of the third voyage is by far the most complex and unsatisfactory. The *Hope-well* sailed from England on August 6, 1706, and is said to have reached Fort St. George (Madras) on April 11, 1707: here the ship stayed for three weeks, and then spent an unspecified time in sailing to Tongking (3.1.3). Shortly after the arrival in that port Gulliver set out in a sloop, and eighteen days later he was captured by pirates (3.1.4), who set him adrift. Five days later still he was found by the Laputans and taken up into their flying island (3.1.8-10). He learned the language in "about a Months time" (3.2.18), and spent two months there all told (3.4.2). As the date of his departure is given specifically as February 16 (3.4.6), it is possible by reckoning backward two months and twenty-three days to set November 24 as the approximate time of departure from Tongking. Working still farther backward, we find that the voyage from Madras to Tongking occupied the period from the beginning of May to the middle of November: this is perhaps a little long, but not at all implausible. Going forward from February 16 again,

Gulliver spent "a few days" with Lord Munodi (3.4.16), and one or two more in the Grand Academy of Lagado. Perhaps a week more was spent in the overland journey of a hundred and forty miles to the port of Maldonada (3.7.1). Gulliver then spent ten days on the island of Glubbdubdrib (3.7.6), and another fortnight in Maldonada waiting for his ship, which carried him to Luggnagg in a month. This all adds up to something over two months, which agrees with the date given for the arrival in Luggnagg—April 21 (3.9.1).

At this point difficulties begin. The year should be 1708, but in the first edition it is 1711, which is clearly wrong. The edition of 1735 made the apparently obvious correction to 1708, ignoring the fact that Gulliver, after what is clearly a short stay in Luggnagg (he had not even time to learn the language), departed for Japan in 1709. One easy way out of the maze is to substitute 1708 for 1707 as the year of the arrival in Madras and 1709 for 1711 as that of the landing in Luggnagg. But this gives an abnormally long voyage from England to Madras,[12] and adding a year to the time spent between Madras and Tongking is equally unsatisfactory. For the moment it will be well to adopt 1709 as the year of arrival in Luggnagg and take a fresh start.

The sojourn in Luggnagg, brief as it is, produces its own crux. Gulliver landed on April 21, and left on May 6, 1709 (3.11.4). In the meantime, however, he observes (3.9.7), "I stayed three Months in this Country. . . . " This statement, which is in a passage not primarily concerned with the chronology, and which is some distance from other statements of that kind, may be due to an oversight in revision: there is no possible way of harmonizing it with the text.

Three weeks after Gulliver's departure from Luggnagg he landed in Japan at the mouth of Tokio Bay (3.11.4). He was immediately sent to Yedo (Tokio), about forty miles away, and his audience with the Emperor probably took place on the following day, May 28. He was then convoyed south by a body of troops on the march to Nangasac (Nagasaki), in which city he arrived on June 9, 1709, "after a very long and troublesome Journey." The distance, by Moll's map, is over five hundred miles: in actual fact it is a good deal greater. The average daily distance traveled would therefore have been more than forty miles—a practical impossibility if much of the trip was made overland. But as Yedo and Nagasaki are on different islands, some of the traveling, and perhaps most of it, must have been by sea.

From Nagasaki Gulliver sailed to Amsterdam in the *Amboyna,* and thence to England in a small vessel. According to the first edition, the landing in Amsterdam took place on April 16, 1710, and the arrival in England on April 10 (3.11.6, 7). Some editors have assumed a simple transposition of these dates by the printer: others have preferred to change the second date to April 20. It seems more likely that this is another instance of a compositor's error like that conjectured at the beginning of the second voyage: if so, the true date of the debarkation at Amsterdam was April 6, and the similarity between "sixth" and "sixteenth" led to the confusion in the mind of the typesetter.

The final difficulty with the chronology of this voyage is found in the last paragraph, which stated, in the first edition, that Gulliver's absence from England had been for "Five Years and Six Months compleat." The elapsed time from August 5, 1706, to April 10, 1710, is a little over three years and eight months. The mistake suggests one possible reason which may underlie all the chronological discrepancies of the voyage. It is worth remarking that the other serious errors occur in the ninth and tenth chapters, which are concerned with Luggnagg. If in the original draft the voyage had been intended to occupy over five years, and especially if a visit to another country had intervened between the stay in Balnibarbi and the visit to Luggnagg, then the date "1711" (3.9.1) and the other and lesser discrepancies in these chapters are easily explained as oversights in revision. The explanation is tempting, but it must be admitted that there is no external evidence to support it.

Only one statement remains to be discussed. "Thus, Gentle Reader," says Gulliver at the beginning of the twelfth chapter of the last voyage, "I have given thee a faithful History of my Travels for Sixteen Years, and above Seven Months." Here, at least, Swift was on his guard: the voyage to Lilliput began on May 4, 1699; the final return to England took place on December 5, 1715. This accuracy is more characteristic of Swift's dealing with time in the *Travels* than is the carelessness which is evident in a few places at the end of the third voyage. One possible explanation of the major discrepancies has already been proposed, but of course any or all of these, as well as the trifling mistakes, may have been due to copyists or typesetters. Swift's complaints in the *Letter to Sympson* have a ring of sincerity: "I find likewise, that your Printer hath been so careless as to confound the Times, and mistake the Dates of my several Voyages and Returns; neither assigning the true Year, or the true Month, or Day of the Month: and I hear the original Manuscript is all destroyed, since the Publication of my Book." (Par. 4.) The natural question, of course, is: If this was the case, why did not Ford include the correct dates in his list of emendations, or in his corrected copy of the first edition? To this there can be no positive answer: the most probable is that the errors had already crept into the manuscript, which Ford followed mechanically in his collation, not concerning himself even with the most glaring chronological inconsistencies. There is at least

some evidence for this in the fact that he passed over the date "1711," in 3.9.1, and the obvious contradiction of dates at the end of the third voyage which brought Gulliver home six days before his intermediate sojourn in Amsterdam.

Notes

[1] Craik, Sir Henry, *Selections from Swift,* London, 1893, pp. 441-4.

[2] *Gulliver's Travels* (ed. Dennis), in the notes, *passim.*

[3] *Gulliver's Travels* (ed. Williams), pp. lxxix, lxxx.

[4] *Gulliver's Travels* (ed. Williams), pp. 459-90 *passim.*

[5] "The Geography of *Gulliver's Travels,*" J.E.G.P., 40.214 (1941).

[6] See Williams, Harold, *Dean Swift's Library,* Cambridge, 1932.

[7] *Correspondence,* 3. 134, 137; *The Letters of Swift to Ford,* pp. 36-7.

[8] This map, which is included in various atlases, was apparently the most recent Moll map of the world at the time when Swift began the composition of the *Travels,* though an examination of other Moll maps between 1709 and 1745 indicates that the cartographer made no changes in his data during this period which would have affected Gulliver's geography.

[9] Frederick Bracher has recently published (*Huntington Library Quarterly,* 8.1.59 [1944]) an article entitled "The Maps in *Gulliver's Travels,*" in which he shows that the artist who drew the maps in the first edition used Moll's map of 1719. He agrees with the present author that neither Swift nor any of his friends was in any way responsible for the 1726 maps with their numerous errors, and gives reasons for believing that they were drawn by John Sturt and engraved by Robert Sheppard.

[9] The map of the Gulliverian hemisphere in this volume is based on Moll's map of the world.

[10] Moore, John R., "The Geography of *Gulliver's Travels,*" J.E.G.P., 40.217-20 (1941).

[11] *Gulliver's Travels* (ed. Dennis), p. 295, note.

[12] The late Professor Walter Graham pointed out to me that eight months (as indicated in the first edition) was the normal time for a voyage from England to India, according to the eighteenth-century records of the East India Company.

Roland M. Frye (essay date 1954)

SOURCE: "Swift's *Yahoo* and the Christian Symbols for Sin," in *Journal of the History of Ideas*, Vol. XV, No. 2, April, 1954, pp. 201-17.

[*Below, Frye discusses ways that Swift's characterization of the Yahoos reflects eighteenth-century Protestant dogma equating the misuse and abuse of reason with sin.*]

I

Swift's treatment of the Yahoo in the fourth book of *Gulliver's Travels* has been the center of a prolonged critical controversy. Involving and epitomizing as it does the so-called "misanthropy" of Swift, this controversy has a significance which extends beyond the particular work in question, although that is significant enough in itself. Merrel D. Clubb, who has traced the history of the controversy, writes that "the longer one studies Swift, the more obvious it becomes that the interpretation and verdict to be placed on the 'Voyage to the Houyhnhnms' is, after all, the central problem of Swift criticism."[1]

The Yahoo was, of course, a controversial figure even in the eighteenth century, but Clubb significantly sees the principal deluge of anti-Yahooism as coming between the years 1800 and 1914.[2] For example, he quotes De Quincey as saying that Swift's "own *yahoo* is not a more abominable one-sided degradation of humanity, than is he himself."[3] Again, we have Thackeray's well-known lecture on Swift, in which the post-Romantic attitude is crystallized in its typical form:

As for the moral [of the fourth voyage], I think it horrible, shameful, unmanly, blasphemous. . . . It is Yahoo language: a monster gibbering shrieks, and gnashing imprecations against mankind,—tearing down all shreds of modesty, past all sense of manliness and shame; filthy in word, filthy in thought, furious, raging, obscene.[4]

To the post-Romantic mind, largely divorced as it was from the main stream of Christian realism, and in good part given over to the exaltation of man, Swift's Yahoo as a filthy monster might very well seem "blasphemous."[5]

Much has been made of Swift's misanthropy. He has been accused of having a diseased mind and the Yahoo has been presumed to be a reflection of his mental disorder. It is undeniably true that Swift regarded man's nature as depraved, his unaided conscience as a blind guide, and his carnal reason as an imperfect instrument—witness his sermons "On the Testimony of Conscience" and "On the Trinity." If such views are sufficient to establish misanthropy,

however, then some of the greatest figures of the Christian tradition will keep Dean Swift company on the anthropophile's Index Librorum Prohibitorum. As an effective satirist, Swift was of course writing with overemphasis and with unusual intensity, and this is perhaps one reason his position has seemed more extreme than that of other men of similar views whom we regard as moderate because their mode of expression allowed of moderation. The purpose of this paper, however, is not to add to the present long list another subjective reaction to Swift's view of man, but is rather to explore the relation between one of his imaginative creations, the Yahoo, and that traditional view of human nature which is known as Christian anthropology. By examining the terminology, the symbols, and the typical phraseology of this tradition, as it is found both in the Bible and also in the homiletic and admonitory literature of Christianity, we will be better able to understand both Swift's intention and his rhetoric in creating the Yahoo as a filthy, depraved, and thoroughly repulsive figure.

Gulliver's Travels was published in a period of flux so far as theology and religious symbolism were concerned. In his valuable study, "On the Philosophical Background of *Gulliver's Travels*," T. O. Wedel summarizes the matter as follows: "In theological terms, what was happening of course was the avowed or tacit denial of the doctrine of original sin. Human nature was being absolved of corruption. The ancient Christian faith, in the words of Pascal, had rested on but two things, 'the corruption of nature and the redemption by Jesus Christ.' Half at least of Pascal's formula is seldom spoken of after 1700."[6] When Wedel says that original sin "is seldom spoken of after 1700," he is undoubtedly implying a comparison with the preceding century and a half of English Protestantism. That the doctrine was by no means an unfamiliar one is indicated by the following statement which appeared in *The Tribune* of Dublin in 1719:

The Corruption of Human Nature is a Text that has so long been preached upon, that one might justly conclude the Subject long since exhausted. Yet it continues still to be a darling Theme, not only among some loose and profligate Writers, with a View to dissolve the natural Obligations to Virtue; but likewise by great Numbers of grave and orthodox Divines, who have held it forth as a doctrine of the utmost Importance in Religion, and the Belief of it, absolutely necessary to denominate a Man a good Christian.[7]

Although the conception of original sin was certainly not lost, its popularity had entered upon a decline even in Swift's day, a decline which was to be accelerated with the passage of time. Of equal importance is the fact that even when the idea of natural depravity was retained and emphasized, it gradually lost the symbols traditionally associated with it. In order to understand the Yahoo fully, it is necessary, as we shall see, to keep these symbols in mind.

As a professional clergyman, Swift may rightly be assumed to have had an intimate acquaintance with these symbolic vehicles of orthodox thought. Indeed, it would be illogical to expect him to approach the problem of human nature and human sin in terms of what we currently think of as the lay mind. His training, as well as the daily field of his duties, required serious thinking upon these problems and upon their Biblical base, thinking which might not be encountered to the same degree among his purely literary confrères. That such a personal background, and sincere personal convictions, should have found expression in Swift's satire ought not to surprise us. Thus if we observe the reactions of those for whom these traditional symbols retained vividness and truth, we discover a sympathetic understanding of Swift's intentions in creating the Yahoo. Surely Deane Swift, the biographer of his cousin Jonathan, is well qualified to elucidate this matter, and he declares that the fourth book was conceived in Christian terms. Indeed, he says, the author was fulfilling his duties as "a preacher of righteousness" and "a watchman of the Christian faith" when he described the Yahoo:

> And shall we condemn a preacher of righteousness, for exposing under the character of a nasty unteachable *Yahoo* the deformity, the blackness, the filthiness, and corruption of those hellish, abominable vices, which inflame the wrath of God against the children of disobedience. . . . ?[8]

John Hawkesworth, in his 1755 edition of **Gulliver,** points to the same interpretation:

> Whoever is disgusted with this picture of a *yahoo,* would do well to reflect, that it becomes his own in exact proportion as he deviates from virtue, for virtue is the perfection of reason: the appetites of those abandoned to vice are not less brutal and sordid than that of a *yahoo* for asses flesh, nor is their life a state of less abject servility.[9]

Furthermore, we find that John Wesley in his *Doctrine of Original Sin* (1757) quotes at great length from the "Voyage to the Houyhnhnms" in order to describe man's depravity.[10] In their interpretations, Deane Swift, Hawkesworth and Wesley place the fourth book within its intended frame of reference, having understood its traditional symbolism. My task here is to discover that symbolism, its sources and traditional applications as Jonathan Swift knew it, and to apply it to his picture of the Yahoo. The result of this study will surely not provide the only frame of reference for the fourth book, but I hope that it will indicate an important avenue of approach.

One point should be made at the outset. In a study such as this one, there can be no attempt to delineate

the fully-rounded Christian view of man. It can scarcely be otherwise here, for I am following Swift's treatment of the Yahoo, where the primary concern is with sin and folly. Thus, the "image of God" motif is only incidentally touched upon. Furthermore, the vigorous castigations of the flesh by a number of the theologians whom I quote should not be allowed to stand without some comment, for otherwise an injustice would be done both to these writers and to the tradition of which they are a part. These men were not bigoted, ascetic, or prudish in their attitudes toward man. They were merely using the terms "flesh" and "body" as symbolic vehicles; they were not denying man access to the legitimate outlets for his normal physical drives.

II

Of *Gulliver's Travels,* T. O. Wedel says that when "Swift wrote his own treatise to vex the world, scepticism and the belief in the corruption of human nature, nature had given way to rationalism and an optimistic faith in man."[11] Mr. Louis Landa suggests that, although it cannot be proved, there is justification for thinking that Swift's sermon "On the Testimony of Conscience" is an oblique answer to Shaftesbury, or at least to some similarly flattering view of man's natural benevolence.[12] It would seem reasonable that some such reaction against the growing faith in man's natural goodness lies behind the satiric picture of the Yahoo. Certainly, this is at least implied by Deane Swift when he refers to critics of the Yahoo as "these mighty softners; these kind pretenders to benevolence; these hollow charity-mongers" (p. 220). That Swift regarded theories of natural benevolence as preliminary to moral anarchy, is evidenced by his sermon "On the Testimony of Conscience," as well as by other strains of his work. The result of these theories would be the overthrow of individual honesty and virtue. With this in mind, it would seem quite possible that Swift conceived the "Voyage to the Houyhnhnms" as Christian apologetics, among other things, and that he incorporated into it a sharp satiric attack upon a theologically dangerous doctrine—in this case, upon the conception of man as naturally inclined to goodness. That such an attack would be closely allied with Augustinian theology need not be emphasized. What should be pointed out is that Swift's treatment is thoroughly consistent with certain normative positions of Protestantism in general and of Anglicanism in particular.

Christian symbolism has traditionally used "the flesh" as representative of man's natural propensity towards evil. Bishop Gilbert Burnet, in his *Exposition of the Thirty-Nine Articles* (1699), writes in support of Article IX, "Of Original or Birth Sin," that "it is certain that in Scripture this general corruption of our nature is often mentioned." He then proceeds to quote nine typical passages which emphasize man's natural proclivity for evil, and concludes in this wise: *"The flesh is weak. The flesh lusteth against the spirit. The carnal mind is enmity to the law of God, and is not subject to the law of God, neither indeed can be: and they that are in the flesh cannot please God:* where by *flesh* is meant the natural state of mankind, according to those words, *That which is born of the flesh is flesh, and that which is born of the Spirit is spirit."*[13] Such was the conventional division of man for admonitory purposes, with the spirit as the valuable, redeemable part, and the flesh representing all the natural inclinations to evil which warred against the higher powers.

The most definite and most complete identification of the Yahoo with Gulliver is in terms of the flesh or the body. This is clearly stated when Gulliver is first able to inspect "the beast" at close range. "My Horror and Astonishment are not to be described," he says, "when I observed, in this abominable Animal, a perfect human Figure."[14] Later, Gulliver's master among the Houyhnhnms similarly observes that Gulliver "agreed in every Feature of [his] Body with other *Yahoos*" (pp. 243-44). This perfect correspondence between man and Yahoo in the body is even further emphasized by an elaboration of how they differ. Man differs in having the gift of speech and in having some faculty of reason, even though he does abuse it. There are other minor differences, but throughout the book the reiterated identification is physical. After the episode at the river when he is the object of fleshly desire, Gulliver says "I could no longer deny, that I was a real *Yahoo,* in every Limb and Feature, since the Females had a natural Propensity to me as one of their own Species."[15] The consistent reference is to physical similarities—in short, only one correlation seems valid, that Yahoo is man in "the flesh."

We have seen Bishop Burnet's gloss of this term as indicative of the weakness and evil in man which wars upon the spiritual. Burnet is not alone in this interpretation. Mark Frank (1613-64), who died Master of Pembroke Hall, Cambridge, and chaplain to Archbishop Selden, glosses I Corinthians 9.27 (subjection of the body) in this way: "And by the 'body' here may be understood either the flesh itself, or the fleshliness of it; the body itself, or the sinful passions and affections rising in it."[16] The Rev. John Bradford, a Smithfield martyr of 1555, writes in his "Seventh Meditation" that the body "is to the soul nothing else but a prison, and that most strait, vile, stinking, filthy."[17] Another important Smithfield martyr, John Hooper, Bishop of Gloucester and Worcester, writes in terms strikingly close to those of Swift. Hooper's description of man "as he is, a vile piece of earth with all his pride and pomp,"[18] is similar in thought, though inferior in style, to Swift's "Lump of Deformity, and Diseases both in Body and Mind, smitten with *Pride*" (p. 280), a passage which Wesley quotes verbatim from Gulliver for use in his treatment of original sin. Again, when Bish-

op Hooper,[19] urging the need for self-examination in the light of Scripture, says that whoever *"beholds himself well in that mirror and glass,* will find such a deformity and disgraced physiognomy, that he will abhor his own proportion so horribly disfigured," he is even more misanthropic than Gulliver, who made it a practice *"to behold my Figure often in a Glass,* and thus if possible habituate myself by Time to tolerate the Sight of a human Creature."[20] Bradford speaks of the flesh in the conventional terms when he says: "What a charnel-house of stinking carrion is this body and life of wicked man. . . . "[21]

Jeremie Collier, writing in 1686, treats the same subject in detail. Knowledge, he says, is what sets us "at the greatest distance from the Brutes beneath us," but the mind is hindered in its pursuit of knowledge by "the present constitution of our Bodies."[22] Further, the body subjects us to passions which may prevent our examining "things with that deliberation and indifferency which is necessary to the finding out moral Truth" (p. 18). Like Burnet, Frank, Bradford, Hooper and Wesley, Collier makes much of the biblical pronouncements on the flesh, and in treating Romans 8.6 and 13, he writes: "For the Apostle assures us [that] if we live after the Flesh, and make Provision to fulfill the Lusts thereof, we shall die, for to be carnally or sensually minded is death, and that we cannot expect to live hereafter except we mortify the deeds of the Body" (p. 30). Collier is here speaking in soteriological terms, of course, but the use of the body as a symbol for evil is typical.

Collier points out that man debases himself to the level of the brute beasts if he surrenders to the flesh: " . . . to make the Soul a Slave to the Body; to employ the powers of Reason (the Image of the Glorious God) in providing for the gratification of the Animal Life; is a most degenerous and dangerous abuse of so great a privilege: And when God hath made us little lower than the Angels, ought we not to blush to make our selves less than the Beasts that perish?" (pp. 28-29). A glance through earlier theologians reveals the deep roots of this tradition. Writing to the same effect in 1633, Matthew Griffith expresses the human dichotomy in these terms: "Without this *body* man had bin an *Angell;* and without this *soule* but a *Brute*."[23] Bullinger declares that through sin, men "that were like unto God made themselves brutish," while Hooker speaks to the same effect in his *Ecclesiastical Polity,* and Miles Coverdale translates Erasmus' *Enchiridion* in these words: "If we incline to the flesh, it maketh us beasts."[24]

I suggest that these ideas form part of the intellectual background of the fourth book. The human body was traditionally understood to represent man's natural depravity; it is a logical representation of this tradition, therefore, that the Yahoo has "a perfect *human* figure." According to this view, the Yahoo would then represent those elements in his nature which man must distrust, and which, in Christian terms, he must seek to subdue. The Yahoo is that fleshly element in human nature which cannot be disavowed, which may in fact degrade man to the level of the brute beasts, and which vitiates any argument for the self-redemptive power of human reason and the final efficacy of natural benevolence. As Swift says in his September 29, 1725, letter to Pope: "I have got materials toward a treatise, proving the falsity of that definition *animal rationale,* and to show it would be only *rationis capax.*"

As Swift indicates, this capacity for reason is what distinguishes man from Yahoo. The Houyhnhnm assembly recognizes in Gulliver "some Rudiments of Reason," and Gulliver at last comes to regard his Portuguese rescuer, Don Pedro, as having "some little Portion of Reason." He is never graced with more than "some Glimmerings of Reason," "some Marks of Reason," and the like, but this is an incontrovertible mark of distinction. Yet even this small pittance is degraded by man. At one point Gulliver quotes the master Houyhnhnm as saying that men seem to make no other use of this "small Pittance of *Reason*" than "by its Assistance to aggravate our *natural* Corruptions, and to acquire new ones which Nature had not given us." In the same vein, Gulliver says that his countrymen make "no other Use of Reason, than to improve and multiply those Vices, whereof their Brethren in this Country had only the Share that Nature allotted them."[25]

Such a view of man's use of reason to corrupt himself and to increase even the ills to which his flesh is already heir can be paralleled in a sermon preached on "the scorner" by Richard Fiddes, whom Swift befriended and whose sermons he possessed. The scorner "studies Vice as an Art," says Fiddes, "and his Thoughts are taken up with enquiring how far the Improvement of it may be carry'd. He affects to be thought the Author of some new Discovery in the Theory of Sin, or to do some eminent Service towards promoting the Practice of it."[26] In a striking passage, also cited by Wesley, Gulliver says that although the master Houyhnhnm "hated the *Yahoos* of this Country, yet he no more blamed them for their odious Qualities, than he did a *Gnnayh* (a Bird of Prey) for its Cruelty, or a sharp Stone for cutting his Hoof. But, when a Creature pretending to Reason, could be capable of such Enormities, he dreaded lest the Corruption of that Faculty be worse than Brutality itself" (p. 232). Quite pertinent to this is another passage from Jeremie Collier's sermon. Having just said (as quoted above) that reason is the image of God in man, he proceeds:

> And when God hath made us little lower than the Angels, ought we not to blush to make ourselves less than the Beasts that perish? Now that Sensuality does degrade us in this manner is apparent, it being

unquestionably more scandalous and uncreditable to abuse the use of Reason, than to want it; for the one only argues natural incapacity; which because it could not be prevented, is no just reproach to any Being; but the other besides ingratitude to the Donor implies most egregious folly (p. 29).

Mark Frank, discussing the manner in which we, as "men of reason," debase ourselves, writes that "we must both needs confess that we have done brutishly and unreasonably, and cannot but be ashamed we have so unmanned ourselves, and betrayed the very essence and glory of our nature [*i.e.,* the image of God]: not done like men" (p. 429). The basic ideas in these passages are practically identical: The corruption of reason is far more culpable than the absence of it; by perverting his reason, man becomes far more contemptible than a brute beast. This is the ground-work of the whole satire of Part IV, according to Deane Swift, who elucidates the Yahoo by referring to

> The reasoning of St. Peter throughout his whole second chapter of his second epistle; that creature man, that glorious creature man, is deservedly more contemptible than a brute beast, when he flies in the face of his Creator by enlisting under the banner of the enemy; and perverts that reason, which was designed to have been the glory of his nature, even the directing spirit of his life and demeanor, to the vilest, the most execrable, the most hellish purposes. *And this manifestly appears to be the ground-work of the whole satyre contained in the voyage to the Houyhnhnms* (p. 221, italics mine).

He then observes that "Dr. Swift was not the first preacher, whose writings import this kind of philosophy," a statement which he buttresses by citing biblical uses of bestial symbolism (II Esdras 8.29-30; Isaiah 56.10-12; Philippians 3.2; I Corinthians 15.32; Matthew 3.7; Titus 1.12-13; Revelation 22.14-15; Matthew 7.15 and 10.16).

Thus we may say of the Yahoo that he represents "the flesh," or, as Matthew Griffith, quoted above, says of man without a soul, that "he is but a brute." Whole man, on the contrary, is flesh *plus* reason. Both are joined together in him and interact the one upon the other; such was the traditional conception. Man has a spirit, "the only seat of our understanding and reason," as Bishop Peter Browne (c. 1661-1735) describes it, which should govern the flesh, containing "those bodily appetites which are common to us with brutes."[27] Actually, however, the reverse is too frequently the case, so that the flesh "often drags the spirit with it, to wallow in the mire."[28] Thus it is that man's lower elements are responsible for corrupting his spiritual and rational faculties. Between the two there can be nothing but enmity until "the absolute conquest of the one or the other."[29] In this conflict, the relevance of the

Yahoo to the human dilemma becomes quite apparent.

III

The Yahoo may not only be related to Christian symbolism of the flesh, but may also be seen as embodying many of those elements of filth and deformity which are emblematic of sin throughout the Scriptures, beginning with the Levitical pollutions and carrying on far into the New Testament. Nor did Swift introduce the *literary* employment of dung, deformity and corruption, as is evident if we recall terms used in Milton's descriptions of Sin in *Paradise Lost,* and in Spenser's stripping of Duessa in *The Faerie Queene.*[30] To illustrate the vitality of this tradition in England, let me begin with three examples from the pulpit. I submit that if Swift had been guilty of any one of these statements, it would have been cited innumerable times as proof of his diseased outlook. In one of his Lincoln's Inn sermons, John Donne describes man's condition in this way: "Between that excremental jelly that thy body is made of at first, and that jelly which thy body dissolves to at last; there is not so noisome, so putrid a thing in nature."[31] Such, according to Donne, is man's mortal condition. Writing in 1667, B. Agas describes the godless who professed to be Christians: "As dross among Gold, or as scum upon a pot, such are these, a meer filth among the pure professors. They are the Gospels reproach and Religions shame, equally disgracing both the one and the other, as a dead blasted limb a living Body, or as a loathsome leperous scab a beautiful face."[32] In the same vein, Jeremie Taylor (1613-67) asks in his *Contemplation of the State of Man:* "What is man but a vessel of dung, a stink of corruption, and, by birth, a slave of the devil?"[33] Filth is employed in each of these three passages, in two of which terms for excrement are used. Two also employ a noisome or stinking smell as characteristic of evil, while a third adds the deformity of body and of face.

In Scripture, many passages can be found which reveal this type of terminology for sin. I quote only a few characteristic ones. In Psalms 14.3 we read that "they are all gone aside, they are altogether become filthy: there is none that doeth good, no, not one." Much of the same idea is found in Job 15.16: "How much more abominable and filthy is man, which drinketh inquity like water?" In Ezekiel 24.13, the prophet carries this message to the sinful people of Jerusalem: "In thy filthiness is lewdness." As for the symbolism of deformity, Isaiah 1.6 describes the corrupt Israelites in these terms: "From the sole of the foot even unto the head there is no soundness in it; but wounds, and bruises, and putrefying sores: they have not been closed, neither bound up, neither mollified with ointment." The frequent New Testament admonitions to "cleanse ourselves from all filthiness" of sin need not be enumerated, as they are well enough known to come to the mind merely by suggestion.

These Biblical uses of filth and deformity indicate the importance of the concept. It is in these terms that Donne, Agas, and Taylor must be understood in the passages quoted above. Archbishop Tillotson (1630-94), in the first of a series of sermons entitled *The Shamefulness of Sin,* treats the theme in a somewhat similar fashion: "The natural Ruggedness and Deformity of Sin and Vice render it very shameful. . . . How strangely do we see Men concerned with all their Diligence and Skill, to cover and palliate any Defect or Deformity in their Bodies. . . . Now in regard of our Souls and better part, Sin hath all the monstrousness and deformity in it, which we can imagine in the Body, and much more. . . . "[34] Although he does not use bodily deformity as a direct symbol for sin here, Tillotson does draw his parallel very close.

Writing in 1659 on Job 15.16 ("How much more abominable and filthy is man, which drinketh iniquity like water?"), Anthony Burgess glosses the text in such a way as to illustrate the employment of filth, stench, and the like as symbolic for sin: "The property is twofold, *abominable,* even as a carkass is abominable that hath lost the soul which did animate it, so is man being made carnal and natural, having lost the Spirit of God and his image; *Abhominable* [sic], that denoteth such loathsomeness that we cannot endure to behold or come near the object loathed, that we cannot endure the sight of it. . . . " The last clause is strikingly similar to the view of many readers who see the Yahoo as denoting "such loathsomeness that [they] cannot endure to behold or come near the object loathed, that [they] cannot endure the sight of it." This is surely one of the reactions which Swift wished to elicit—assuming that the reader would go on to make Burgess' connection of loathesomeness with sinfulness:

> Thus man is abominable and loathsome in the eyes of God, and he ought to be so in his own eyes, to his own self, a natural man should not be able to bear or endure himself, because of that loathsome sinfulness that doth adhere to him: how much are *Pelagian*-Doctrines that cry up a purity in man's nature, contrary to this Text? . . . The second property attributed to man is *filthy:* The Hebrew word is only used here, and *Psal.* 14.3 and *Psal.* 53.3. Concerning the root of it, there is no certainty, only it is generally translated that which is *putrid rotten* and *stinking,* and because rotten and putrifying things are unuseful and unprofitable.[35]

William Beveridge (1637-1708), Bishop of St. Asaph, in his outline of a sermon on the admonition of II Corinthians 7.1 to "cleanse ourselves from all filthiness of the flesh and spirit," says that by filthiness St. Paul meant sinfulness, and refers to James 1.21 and to II Peter 2.22 as examples of such symbolism. Again, he says the lust of the flesh brings vengeance upon "the body; witness the stinking breath, loathsome botches, inflamed blood, putrefied flesh. . . . " Further, uncleanness "razeth out the image of God, and stampeth the image of beasts upon us."[36] Matthew Griffith comes even closer to the Yahoo when he says: "Could I character or you but conceive a man in pure naturals, you would not take him for a man but for some monster" (p. 153). It is in this sense, and not in Edward Young's, that Swift has made "a monster . . . of the human face divine."

Peter Browne, Bishop of Corke and Ross, follows the well-established symbolic system in a sermon on the cleansing blood of Christ. He carefully develops the idea that it is impossible for us to understand before the judgment how our *souls* have been polluted or how Christ will purify them, and so we resort to "a form of speaking," and he says that "the holiest person in the world is all over leprous, filthy and abominable in the sight of God, till he is washed in the blood of the lamb," thus expressing the intangible in terms of the concrete.[37] Again, he says that "vice and wickedness have a direct tendency, even in this life to wrest our lineaments." After the resurrection the wicked will be able to see this in themselves and "shall appear in their own eyes the most detestable and loathsome of all beings, terrified with their own deformity."[38]

In the third part of his sermon entitled "The Apples of Sodom," Jeremie Taylor describes the sin of concealing sin in terms of filth, ugliness and disease. Concealment and hypocrisy "are the covers of our shame, like menstrous rags upon a skin of leprosy: but so sometimes we see a decayed beauty besmeared with a lying fucus, and the chinks filled with ceruse."[39] Mark Frank writes that, in view of our sins, " . . . those lips, which we cry up for sweetness, would stink in our conceit with rottenness; the teeth that look white as ivory, we should behold black with calumny and slander, as the soot of the foulest chimneys; . . . the hands that look so white and delicate, would appear filthy, bloody, and unclean" (p. 135).

Another significant treatment of filth and defilement in terms of sin is found in an interesting book by the nonconformists Benjamin Keach and Thomas Delaune, entitled *A Key to Open Scripture Metaphors* (1682). In a section on the metaphorical use of filth we find the following passage:

> Sin is compared to an unclean thing, and Man by reason of Sin is said to be defiled; who can bring a clean thing out of an unclean? . . . Some things are so unclean and filthy, that they defile every thing they touch. Sin is such an Uncleanness; who can touch it, meddle with it, and not be defield by it? . . . Some Uncleanness is so loathsome, that it causes such things to stink, as come near it; Sin

makes the Sinner stink, his Person stink, his Life stink, and his Services and Prayers, and all his best Actions to stink in the Nostrils of God.[40]

In another section, Keach and Delaune write to somewhat the same effect: "By *Mud, Dirt,* and other *Filth* the Members and Apparrel of a man are polluted and contaminated; which contamination is brought frequently to denote the Filthy nature of sin, *Esa.* 64.6; 2 *Cor.* 7.1; *Eph* 5.27; *Tit* 1.15; 2 *Pet.* 2.10, 20 (with ver. 13,22); *Jud.* ver. 23; *Jam.* 1.21; *Rev.* 3.4."[41]

Scripturally, this employment of deformity or filth or both as symbols for sin seems to go back to the ceremonial pollutions which are proscribed in Leviticus. Discussing these in his essay "Of the Guilt and Defilement of Sin" (1740), Isaac Watts writes that God would not allow those to come into His presence

> . . . whose Hearts or Lives are *defiled* (that is) under sinful Disorders. This was typified by the *Levitical* Pollutions of old, when some bodily Defilements excluded the *Israelites* from the Camp, and the Tabernacle where God dwelt . . . to shew that the *disorderly Nature* of Sin made Persons unfit to converse with God. Thus all the ceremonial Pollutions of the *Jews* typify'd one of these two, either the *Guilt* of Sin, or its *Disorder* and Vitiosity.[42]

In the same essay, Watts adds:

> The *Defilement* therefore appears evidently to be nothing but a Figure of Speech borrowed from material things, whereby either the *Guilt* or the *Disorder* of Sin, the relative or real Evil of it are represented (pp. 426-7).

Frank elucidates the symbolism in the same way: "Wheresoever is deformity, or whatsoever is deformed, it is sin that caused it, or sin that is it."[43]

These examples of the use of filth and deformity to symbolize man's sin and imperfection could be multiplied. I have chosen only a few typical ones for my purpose, and I wish now to turn to Swift's use of the same traditional material. First, however, it should be made clear that there is no question of establishing any of the foregoing as sources for any part of **Gulliver's Travels.** The tradition here illustrated, a tradition which employed filth and deformity as symbolic of sin, was part and parcel of the intellectual climate in and before Swift's time, and I suggest that it is within such a frame of reference that we should read Swift's description of the Yahoo.

It is not necessary to debate whether a discharge of excrement upon the head would be regarded as defilement in the Biblical sense. Such, at any rate, is Gulliver's first greeting from the Yahoos. But even before this incident, while he is still more or less unbiased in his outlook, Gulliver remarks that the Yahoo is an "ugly Monster," "singular, and deformed," for whom he immediately conceives a strong antipathy, "full of Contempt and Aversion." They are "detestable Creatures," and he has never seen "any sensitive Being so detestable on all Accounts." The chosen leader of the herd is "more *deformed* in Body and *mischievous*" than any of the rest. The Houyhnhnms describe all evil things in terms of "the Deformities or ill Qualities of the *Yahoos*," who are "the most filthy, noisome and deformed Animal which Nature ever produced." The use of deformity and monstrosity as exemplified in these quotations is spread throughout the book. So, also, is the use of filth. The Yahoo has a "strange Disposition to Nastiness and Dirt; whereas there appears to be a natural Love of Cleanliness in all other Animals." They are "those odious Animals," or "an odious Animal," or "odious Vermin," or "so vile an Animal" with "odious Qualities" and a "most *offensive Smell*."[44] It should not be necessary to expand the list, for it is about such passages as these that the furor of controversy has raged. The point is, that both implicitly and explicitly, such employment of deformity and filth by Swift the artist coincides with the symbolism of natural pravity and actual sin as employed by the theologians. The very words used by Swift in describing the Yahoo are throughout strikingly like—and frequently identical with—those used by the theologians in treating "the flesh" and the sins to which it incites man. Compare with Swift's terms, as summarized above, these words already quoted from the theologians: deformity, brute, beast, animal, monster, excremental, dung, filth, stink, noisome, putrid, vile, loathsome, detestable. Such a close convergence cannot be explained away as fortuitous.

The correspondence, however, can be drawn even closer. The Yahoos may be seen, in almost every aspect of their being, in terms of the laws of pollution in the Old Testament. The food of the Yahoos, with certain exceptions (roots, berries, fish), is definitely polluting. Let us analyze their diet. They eat asses' flesh, battle for the possession of a dead cow, feed upon "the corrupted Flesh of Animals" and other carrion, kill and devour cats and dogs, as well as "Weasels and *Luhimuhs* (a Sort of *wild* Rat)."[45] Each one of these delicacies is proscribed as polluting under the Levitical code. Leviticus 11.3 prohibits the eating of asses' flesh, and in the thirty-ninth and fortieth verses of the same chapter the consumption of any meat from a dead carcass, whether that of a clean or unclean animal, is forbidden. The twenty-seventh verse declares that cats and dogs are unclean. Finally, weasels and rodents are prohibited in the twenty-ninth verse.[46] Thus we see that in diet the Yahoos are guilty of those defilements "whereby either the *Guilt* or the *Disorder* of Sin . . . are represented."

Of further relevance is the fact that the Yahoos are themselves described in such a way as to subject them by their very nature to the Levitical proscription. Leviticus 11.27 declares unclean "whatsoever goeth upon his paws, among all manner of beasts that go on all four, those are unclean to you: whosoever toucheth their carcass shall be unclean until the even." The connection is made much clearer by Bishop Simon Patrick's 1698 commentary on this text: "*Leviticus 11.27. And whatsoever goeth upon his paws, etc.*] Hath feet with fingers like unto a hand; for so it is in the Hebrew, *Whatsoever goeth upon his hands:* Such as the Ape, the Lion, the Bear, Dogs and Cats, etc. whose forefeet resemble hands: These might neither be eaten, nor their carcases touched, without incurring uncleanness until Sunset."[47] Had the Yahoo been created earlier, he might have been included in the bishop's exegetical list. He certainly meets all the qualifications.

What are we to conclude on the basis of the evidence cited here? I certainly would not suggest that the system of symbols and metaphors which I have outlined above is the only frame of reference within which the Yahoo should be studied and interpreted. There are influential thinkers outside the main stream of Christian realism—for example, Montaigne and Charron in France, and Hobbes in England—whose views of the nature of man are in the climate of opinion which influenced Swift. The contributions of those men are well known, and need no development here. Without depreciating the importance of these and other considerations, however, I do suggest that for a full understanding of Swift's intent we must keep in mind the basic and striking similarities between the Yahoo as he is presented in **Gulliver** and the picture of human sin and corruption as painted by the theologians. The Yahoo in his physical resemblance to man suggests the original depravity of man's nature which is called "the flesh," which can degrade man to the level of the brute beasts, and against which all must war. At the same time, the Yahoo suggests through his deformity and filth the breaking forth of that propensity towards sin into the commission of actual sins. I do not argue for exact correspondence so much as for artistic adaptation of theology to Swift's purposes.

Clearly, the correspondence between Swift's descriptions and these symbols of Protestant-Christian theology is too close to have been fortuitous. If Thackeray and others who have been sickened by Swift's imagination had carried their studies back into the expressions of well-known theologians of the sixteenth and seventeenth centuries, they would have avoided a needless misunderstanding both of the Yahoo and of Swift. Certainly, Hawkesworth, Deane Swift, and Wesley understood this important element of the Yahoo's meaning, as we have seen from their remarks on the subject. Indeed, Gulliver states the case when he says: "I had some Rudiments of Reason, added to the natural Pravity of those Animals."[48] What Swift has done is to appropriate ready-made symbols and a Christian rhetoric apt for his purposes, which he has embodied in a fantasy and elevated to the level of great art.

Notes

[1] Merrel D. Clubb, "The Criticism of Gulliver's 'Voyage to the Houyhnhnms,' 1726-1914," *Stanford Studies in Language and Literature* (1941), 206-7.

[2] Ib., 219.

[3] *The Collected Writings of Thomas De Quincey,* ed. David Masson (Edinburgh, 1890), XI, 14. Quoted in Clubb, 223.

[4] W. M. Thackeray, *English Humourists of the Eighteenth Century,* 1st ed. (New York, 1853), 37. Quoted in Clubb, 221.

[5] Thus, in his *Nature and Destiny of Man* (London, 1946), I, 100-1, Reinhold Niebuhr writes that "no cumulation of contradictory evidence seems to disturb modern man's good opinion of himself. He considers himself the victim of corrupting institutions which he is about to destroy or reconstruct, or of the confusions of ignorance which an adequate education is about to overcome. Yet he continues to regard himself as essentially harmless and virtuous."

[6] Wedel, *SP,* XXIII (1926), 441.

[7] *The Tribune,* no. 20 (Dublin, 1719). I am indebted to Mr. Louis Landa for this quotation and also for helpful suggestions and encouragement throughout.

[8] Deane Swift, *An Essay upon the Life, Writings, and Character of Dr. Jonathan Swift* (London, 1755), 219.

[9] John Hawkesworth, ed., *The Works of Jonathan Swift . . .* (London, 1755), I, 217.

[10] John Wesley, *Works* (New York, 1856), V, 510-12. I am indebted to Canon Wedel for this citation.

[11] Wedel, 447.

[12] Louis Landa, ed., *Swift's Irish Tracts and Sermons* (Oxford, 1948), 114.

[13] Gilbert Burnet, *An Exposition of the Thirty-Nine Articles* (London, 1850), 132. Scriptural quotations are from Matt. 26.41; Mark 14.38; Gal. 5.17; Rom. 8.7-8; and John 3.6.

[14] *Gulliver's Travels,* ed. Herbert Davis and Harold Williams (Oxford, 1941), 213-14. All references are to this edition.

[15] *Gulliver's Travels,* 251. For other such physical identifications, see 219, 221, 222, 256, 262.

[16] Mark Frank, *Sermons* (Oxford, 1859), I, 402. See also 411.

[17] John Bradford, *Writings* (Philadelphia: British Reformers Series, n.d.), 412. See also Henry Bullinger, *The Decades* (Cambridge, 1849-51), IV, 386, and Archbishop Edwin Sandys, *Sermons* (Cambridge, 1841), 447.

[18] John Hooper, *Writings* (Philadelphia: British Reformers Series, n.d.), 78.

[19] A discussion such as this necessitates a topical treatment, and it has frequently been impossible for me to cite authorities in a strictly chronological order, as I should have wished to do. Thus we move from Hooper to Wesley and back to Hooper.

[20] Hooper, 76; *Gulliver's Travels,* 279; italics mine.

[21] Hooper, 257-8. See also John Calvin, *The Institute of the Christian Religion,* II, i, 8; Bishop Joseph Hall, *Devotions* (London, 1846), 452; and Richard Fiddes, *Practical Discourses* (London, 1713), I, 97.

[22] Jeremie Collier, *The Difference between the Present and Future State of Our Bodies* (London, 1686), 17.

[23] Matthew Griffith, *Bethel: or, a Frame for Families* (London, 1633), 202.

[24] Bullinger, IV, 351; Richard Hooker, *Works,* ed. John Keble (New York and Phila., 1849), I, 297; Miles Coverdale, *Writings and Translations* (Cambridge, 1844), 505.

[25] *Gulliver's Travels,* 263, 271, 219, 222, 243, and 262. For similar references see 232, 240, 251-2, and 256.

[26] Richard Fiddes, *Practical Discourses* (London, 1713), I, 93.

[27] Peter Browne, *Sermons* (Dublin, 1749), II, 134, 133.

[28] *Ibid.,* II, 142.

[29] Browne, II, 139. See also Frank, I, 404.

[30] *Paradise Lost,* II, 650-66, 795-800; X, 629-37, and *The Faerie Queene,* I, viii, 46-48.

[31] John Donne, *Works* (London, 1839), IV, 231.

[32] B. Agas, *Gospel Conversation, with a short Directory Thereunto* (London, 1667), 47.

[33] Taylor, *The Whole Works* (London, 1880), I, 396.

[34] John Tillotson, *Sermons* (London, 1700), VIII, 151-52.

[35] Anthony Burgess, *The Doctrine of Original Sin* (London, 1659), 439.

[36] William Beveridge, *Thesaurus Theologicus* (Oxford, 1816), II, 86, 198, and 198 resp.

[37] Browne, I, 19-20, and 12.

[38] Browne, II, 214.

[39] Taylor, I, 729. Other uses of the filthy rag symbol may be found in Thomas Becon, *Writings,* 375 and 380, and John Fox, *Writings,* 52 (both Philadelphia: British Reformers Series, n.d.). The Biblical source for the symbol is Isa. 64.6.

[40] Benjamin Keach and Thomas Delaune, *Tropologia: A Key to Open Scripture Metaphors* (London, 1682), Bk. IV, 355.

[41] Keach and Delaune, Bk. I, p. 131. For a similar treatment, see Andrew Symson, ed. of Thomas Wilson's *Complete Christian Dictionarie* (London, 1655), s.v. "filth," "filthy," "filthiness" and "to pollute." Also see Browne, II, 288.

[42] Isaac Watts, *The Ruin and Recovery of Mankind . . . Whereunto are subjoined Three Short Essays* (London, 1740), 422.

[43] Frank, I, 422. In addition to the material already cited, see the following: Becon, 336-7; Hooper, 257-8, 342, 351, 407; Richard Baxter, *The Saints' Everlasting Rest* (New York: American Tract Society, n.d.), 45-6; and summary of attitude, with quotations from Archbishop Ussher and others whom I have not cited, in B. Rajan, *"Paradise Lost" and the Seventeenth Century Reader* (London, 1947), 81-2.

[44] *Gulliver's Travels,* 207-8, 213, 214, 246, 259, 255, 247, 249, 221, 250, 231, 232, and 248. Although I do not maintain that this list is complete, attention is directed to the following passages on characteristic Yahoo traits: Descriptions in terms of filth, stench, odiousness and vileness (in addition to the thirteen references quoted above): 208, 214, 226, 244, 245, 247, 250, 256, 270, 272, 273, and 279; Descriptions in terms of monstrousness, brutishness, and animality: 207, 208, 212, 213, 219, 221, 223, 225, 231, 243, 244, 245, 247, 249, 250, 251, 255, 257, 263, 273, and 280; Descriptions in terms of the deformed, detestable, and contemptible: 207, 208, 213, 214, 220, 221, 222, 226, 227, 244, 245, 246, 255, and 273. Such passages give a coloration to the entire fourth book.

[45] *Gulliver's Travels,* 213, 214, 244, 245, 250, and 255.

[46] Simon Patrick, *Commentary upon Leviticus* (London, 1698), 160, 186, and 179, confirms the currency of these interpretations in the age of Swift.

[47] Patrick, 179.

[48] *Gulliver's Travels,* 263. The implications drawn here will also have relevance for other works of Swift, *e.g.,* the verse and some of the Brobdingnagian descriptions, which have not been discussed in this paper because of the necessity for concentration upon the Yahoos.

David Oakleaf (essay date 1983-84)

SOURCE: "'Trompe l'Oeil': Gulliver and the Distortions of the Observing Eye," in *University of Toronto Quarterly,* Vol. 53, No. 2, Winter 1983/84, pp. 166-80.

[*In the following essay, Oakleaf examines how advancements in the capabilities of visual instruments in the eighteenth century destabilized notions of authoritative fixed points of view, causing philosophers, artists, and writers to reevaluate notions of one's ability to observe as well as the inherent bias of personal perspective.*]

Lemuel Gulliver, the narrator of *Travels into Several Remote Nations of the World,* is obviously an observer. The very title of his narrative appeals to popular interest in observations brought back from voyages of exploration—voyages that represent a geographical conquest of space contemporary with Europe's mathematical conquest of space during the seventeenth-century scientific revolution. Peering through windows and eye glasses and perspective glasses, Gulliver observes both nature and manners. He observes natural curiosities, donating some giant wasp stings to Gresham College. He observes new lands, suggesting alterations to the world's maps. He observes courts and a public execution and a learned society, bringing back the plan of a machine to generate speculative knowledge mechanically. Finally, he publishes his observations, quarrelling with his critics as he does so. No fellow of the Royal Society could do more. Nevertheless, distortion is a more obvious feature of the *Travels* than the transparent record of experience recommended by that Society. Johnson's dismissive comment that 'once you have thought of big men and little men, it is very easy to do all the rest' suggests that the book is based on systematic distortion; this implies that its exploration of science goes beyond its specific satire of the Royal Society and Cartesianism in book III.[1] Surprisingly often, the *Travels* confronts the reader with the act of observation itself, emphasizing not only perspective glasses and empirical scepticism about the evidence of the senses but also, centrally, the dislocations of point of view inherent in observation.

A fairer version of Johnson's dismissal is Marjorie Hope Nicolson's suggestion that the two views through a perspective glass, one magnifying and one diminishing, determine the strategy of the first two voyages of the *Travels.* That perspective glass, however, is untrustworthy because it distorts sense impressions. When Galileo presented the results of his observations, for example, he learned that many men were highly sceptical of the images seen through his strange glass. In the *Anatomy of Melancholy,* Burton expresses this popular distrust of glasses by calling Galileo and earlier investigators of sight deluding magicians who promise 'to do strange miracles by glasses,' much as a modern sceptic announces that stage magicians somehow do it with mirrors. By Swift's day, this distrust has impressive support in philosophical distrust of the faculty of sight itself. Since the ideal observer sees himself as pure mind confronting an objective order but is nevertheless dependent on sense impressions, the eye occupies the ambiguous boundary between mind and matter. The means of investigation consequently becomes an object of investigation for a long list of distinguished observers. Kepler finally discovered how the eye forms images because he was investigating how far the eye and its instruments might introduce errors into his astronomical calculations. Similarly, Descartes, who also wrote on optics, found it natural to begin his *Meditations* by doubting the evidence of his senses, while Locke, in opposition to Descartes, based knowledge on sense impressions but therefore asserted the limitations of human knowledge. Indeed, the empiricist distinction between primary qualities existing in objects themselves and secondary qualities created by the act of perception expresses the ambiguity of the eye's mediation between mind and matter. As the *Travels* often suggests, knowledge of sense impressions can be unreliable even before a glass distorts those impressions.[2]

Gulliver's Houyhnhnm Master, for example, denies man any clear glass of understanding that accurately reflects truth. He suggests instead 'some Quality fitted to increase our natural Vices; as the Reflection from a troubled Stream returns the Image of an ill-shapen Body, not only *larger,* but more *distorted.*'[3] In this view, human reason is as naturally distorting as the human body is 'ill-shapen.' Although Gulliver comes to share this view, for reasons I discuss below, one has, so to speak, nagging doubts about the greater appropriateness of a horse's body to the clear glass of reason the Houyhnhnms seem to possess. Nevertheless, Gulliver's Master is a sound Baconian despite his provincialism, for Bacon too recognized the human idolatry that distorts observations:

... as an uneven mirror distorts the rays of objects according to its own figure and section, so the mind, when it receives impressions of objects through the sense, cannot be trusted to report them truly, but in forming its notions mixes up its own nature with the nature of things.[4]

This echo of St Paul's dark glass is appropriate even in the age of telescopes and microscopes. Newton adopted reflecting telescopes because his work with refraction convinced him of the problems inherent in refracting lenses. Modern research reveals high degrees of spherical aberration—distortion—and chromatic aberration—added colour—in eighteenth-century compound microscopes; that is, they distorted both primary and secondary qualities. Since the eye's instruments are as unreliable as the eye, the imperfect glass still supplies an image of the imperfect understanding.

The observer's dissatisfaction with the eye's weakness and ambiguity is reinforced by his mind's desire to roam more freely than the body permits in search of a more convenient point of view. Since the ambitious observer wants to describe mathematically the configuration of objects with respect to a particular point of view, that convenience is often mathematical. Gulliver's inconvenient description of the motions of the flying island (pp 168-70) reminds us that mathematical convenience is sometimes convenient only to mathematicians, but the tendency to think in terms of their spatial models appears even in unmathematical forms. When Addison describes the delight of experiencing sensations with two senses at once in *Spectator* no. 412, for example, he compares the interplay of sensations to the way 'the different Colours of a Picture, when they are well disposed, set off one another, and receive an additional Beauty from the Advantage of their Situation':[5] he thus translates a complex experience into a purely visual experience of relative positions in space. This suggests that he has assimilated the assumptions of the age of observation, for post-Copernican astronomy similarly but more drastically wrenches the point of view of ordinary experience in order to translate experience into geometrical terms. Although the eye sees the sun go round the earth, we find the equations simpler if we mentally view the solar system from the sun.

Claudio Guillén's study of the history of the notion of point of view relates the conventions of perspective painting not only to the Cartesian split between observer and observed but also to the underlying fiction of a single observing eye located at a fixed point of view. A revealing example of this second notion appears in the *Travels* when Gulliver sees a Brobdingnagian man's eyes magnified by his glasses and compares them to 'the Full-Moon shining into a Chamber at two Windows' (p 96)! Since it is impossible to see the moon through different windows at the same time,

Gulliver's lunatic comparison represents a triumph of theory over observation. Guillén's early examples come from artificial perspective (the linear perspective of painting) rather than natural perspective (optics) or science, but there are many analogies between art and other forms of observation. Like science, art uses glasses to aid observation and uses mathematics to describe the relative positions of objects in space with respect to a particular point of view.[6] Art is important in popularizing the notion of point of view because it can play with the artificiality of its conventions more readily than science can. Exploring Guillén's subject, Ernest B. Gilman demonstrates the impact of linear perspective on seventeenth-century English literature. He suggests especially that curious perspectives supplied the conceptual basis of the literary conceit. (Such perspectives exploited the convention of the single fixed eye by presenting two extreme but complementary points of view in a single painting or engraving; Holbein's *Ambassadors,* in which a second point of view resolves the blur in the foreground into a skull, is perhaps the example most famous today.) Gilman concludes, however, that the eighteenth-century mind was too well balanced to delight in such grotesque games except in the didactic comedy of something like Hogarth's *Method of Perspective*.[7] Johnson's dislike of the conceit, which, like the curious perspective, yoked disparate images by violence together, would seem to support this view, and certainly many eighteenth-century writers yearned for the clear glass of understanding. However, the sceptic might find the interplay of points of view revealing. Writing after the triumph of the scientific revolution based on the perspective glass and the shifting point of view, though, he would have internalized these assumptions, like Addison, and so be less likely to present them as playful novelty. Certainly many of the distortions in the *Travels* suggest the limitations and distortions of the observing eye.

Despite his correct record of the number and orbits of Mars's moons, most of Gulliver's observations exist on the level of commonplace amusement. Brobdingnag is a microscopist's dream come true, for example, but it is hardly novel. Robert Hooke's *Micrographia* published engravings of magnified objects in 1665, and even Hooke later lamented the lack of new discoveries through improved telescopes and complained of the microscope that he could 'hear of none that make any other Use of that Instrument, but for Diversion and Pastime, and that by reason it is become a portable Instrument, and easy to be carried in one's Pocket.' By 1730, even the laziest amateur who purchased a Culpepper microscope received with it a set of four ivory slides of prepared specimens: Gulliver's most memorable images of magnified nature—hair, a bit of human skin, and a louse—appeared together on just one of these slides! When Swift himself contemplated buying Stella a pocket microscope in November 1710, he spoke slightingly of 'the common little ones, to impale a louse (saving your presence) upon a needle's point,' and teased her for her trendy interest by calling her a virtuoso. Gulliver's observations are as banal as his very ordinary background.[8]

His delight in what he sees is partly delight in the distorted—magnified—power conferred by his perspective glass. This appears in his delighted accounts to the King of Brobdingnag and his Houyhnhnm Master of the destructiveness of modern war: the detachment of the distant observer permits his vicarious enjoyment of the power of weapons that act as he looks—from a distance. Similarly, the modern television viewer's detachment permits the disturbing glee evident in many analyses of the success of high-technology weapons in remote conflicts, like that in the Falkland Islands recently. Pat Rogers is surely right to see hypertrophy of the sight in the *Travels'* many glasses: although the moralist can readily find plain reason why man has not a microscopic eye, the ordinary observer asserts with Descartes that 'there is no doubt that the inventions which serve to augment [the eye's] power are among the most useful that there can be.'[9] Since, as Gulliver asserts, 'nothing is great or little otherwise than by Comparison' (p 87), the perspective that magnifies the observed diminishes the observer. In fact, much of the *Travels'* play with proportions is already implicit in the illustrations in Gaspar Schott's seventeenth-century *Magia universalis* that show human observers dwarfed by enormous perspective glasses. S. Bradbury traces the interpretation of these impossible 'giant microscopes' as an engraver's error that substituted a whole man for the still-familiar single eye placed at the aperture of such instruments, commenting that the engravings are at odds with the proportions mentioned in the text (Bradbury, *Evolution,* pp 15-18). What is a 'misreading' from the perspective of a historian of science, however, may, from another perspective, be an interpretation of the new proportion between man and his powerfully augmented sight. Schott treats perspective as one of the magic sciences and devotes a book of his *Magia* to anamorphosis, a term he may have coined (Baltrušaitis, pp 85-6). Imaginative play with the conventions of art is an appropriate context for engravings of the transformations wrought by the magic of optical instruments that dupe the eye. Gulliver is similarly transformed by the same instruments.

At the heart of what a Baconian would call the commerce of Gulliver's mind with the nature of things are his delight in his disproportionate power and his uncritical reliance on distorted sense impressions. That reliance unsettles his point of view, as do scientific models and the conventions of perspective art. Thus Gulliver is disgusted by the skin of a Brobdingnagian woman he sees nursing her baby but then reconsiders his usual point of view:

This made me reflect upon the fair Skins of our *English* Ladies, who appear so beautiful to us, only because they are of our own Size, and their Defects not to be seen but through a magnifying Glass, where we find by Experiment that the smoothest and whitest Skins look rough and coarse, and ill coloured. (Pp 91-2)

Gulliver's 'only' asserts that it is arbitrary to rely on natural rather than artificial perspective, so to speak. The distortion he sees through the glass is more real to him than what he sees unaided, not simply another perspective on it. The observer's reliance on his sense impressions is a more complex criterion of truth than it seems. Since it is not true that skin defects are visible only under magnification, Gulliver is also vindicating his earlier comment on the weakness of his eyes (p 37) at the same time as he celebrates the power conferred by the glass.

The observer, that is, willingly adopts a point of view at odds with his actual place of observation. In Lilliput, his own relative power becomes more real to him when he adopts an external perspective on himself, wondering that the Lilliputians do not tremble 'at the very Sight of so prodigious a Creature *as I must appear to them*' (p 24; my italics). Asserting his power, he prefers the perspective that magnifies him to the equivalent perspective that diminishes his captors. Such self-consciousness seems almost natural to us, but we have become connoisseurs of the chaos imposed by competing points of view. It is more startling in the *Travels,* in Brobdingnag even more than in Lilliput because Gulliver there adopts a Brobdingnagian perspective but refuses to look at himself. He does bring himself to smile when the Queen places him before a mirror that reflects both of them (p 107), but he usually avoids such glasses (p 147). Although he has been a pygmy among giants, he returns from his second voyage seeing his rescuers as 'little contemptible Creatures' (p 147) and looking on his family 'as if they had been Pigmies, and I a Giant' (p 149). Asserting his power, his chosen point of view increasingly blinds him to himself.

Walter Ong speculates that Gulliver's box in Brobdingnag and other images of insulation and confinement in the *Travels* express Swift's interest in the scientific conception of the isolated system.[10] In this context, it especially suggests his interest in isolated visual fields. The eagle that carries Gulliver's box from Brobdingnag and the other eagles that force it to drop the box are *'observed'* (p 145; Swift's italics) by a sailor, but he cannot comment on their size because they are isolated from objects of comparison. A subtler effect of point of view and relative scale appears in Gulliver's glimpse into the palace in Lilliput:

. . . lying down upon my Side, I applied my Face

to the Windows of the middle Stories, which were left open on Purpose, and discovered the most splendid Apartments that can be imagined. There I saw the Empress, and the young Princes in their several Lodgings, with their chief Attendants about them. Her Imperial Majesty was pleased to smile very graciously upon me, and gave me out of the Window her Hand to kiss. (P 47)

Carefully getting close to a tiny passage and peering through small windows, Gulliver presents the commoner's visit to court, complete with splendid apartments, the royal family and their attendants, and a gracious smile from the Queen. Only when the Queen's favour demands putting her hand out of the window does the original discrepancy of scale between observer and observed reassert itself. Although the Queen's point of view is not recorded, it is presumably much like Gulliver's in the parallel scene when a Brobdingnagian monkey suddenly peers into the door and opened windows of Gulliver's cabinet on a scene 'which he seemed to view with great Pleasure and Curiosity' (p 122). The monkey then reaches in its hand to remove a creature little bigger than its finger from the world that gives him an illusion of normal size.

Like magnified images in the *Travels,* these miniature worlds in boxes suggest seventeenth-century popular amusements, especially the perspective box. Viewers looked into peepholes located at strategically selected points of view that gave the small, flat, anamorphically painted scenes on the walls within an illusion of depth and reality. A modern viewer of the perspective box by Samuel de Hoogstraten that is now in the National Gallery, London, reveals the power of the illusion:

A Dutch domestic interior is painted on the sides and bottom of the box in such a way that when viewed through the peep-hole, the visual discrepancy between the size of the box's painted interior and the real world seems to disappear. A complete miniature environment is created, in which the spatial illusion is wholly convincing. 'In a perspective box,' wrote Hoogstraten, 'a figure no larger than a finger appears to be as large as life.'[11]

This *trompe l'oeil* combines the trickery of perspective with a delight in miniature worlds like those literalized in the *Travels.* Hoogstraten's delight in his illusion, however, depends on the observer's awareness that the convincing miniature environment *is* just a clever illusion—that one persuasive point of view is at odds with another. Exactly such a comparison between perspectives explains the microscope's popularity as an instrument of diversion. Similarly, Swift's delight in being taken for a *trompe-l'oeil* artist depends on a superior second perspective. Arbuthnot tells the story of a sailor who said he knew Gulliver, but the anecdote's playfulness reminds us that the joke depends on separating delight in an illusion from gullible acceptance of the illusion as fact.[12]

Much of the comedy of the *Travels* depends on such second perspectives, although the narrator often remains unaware of them in his devotion to his chosen point of view. Queen's hand and monkey's paw mediate between observer and observed. Gulliver emphatically shoves his disproportionate thumb in front of the lens when, in England long after the event, he defends a Lilliputian woman from the charge of an affair with him: his ridiculous pride in being made a Nardac, the Lilliputian equivalent of a Duke, is sufficiently comic, but he could never be as deeply engaged in Lilliputian affairs as this. A second perspective reveals the illusion of the first, as it does more subtly when Gulliver adds a bit of lore about Lilliput's neighbouring kingdom while describing *glimigrim*, the Lilliputian wine that permits his heroism at the palace fire: 'the *Blefuscudians* call it *Flunec*, but ours is esteemed the better Sort' (p 56). That 'ours' presents the transparent recorder as a disproportionate Lilliputian, revealing the absurdity of the perspective he adopts: like the devils in book x of *Paradise Lost*, what he sees he feels himself now changing. Similarly among the Houyhnhnms, Gulliver records his Master's disapproval of purely speculative knowledge, adding that his Master in this 'agreed entirely with the Sentiments of *Socrates*, as *Plato* delivers them; which I mention as the highest Honour I can do that Prince of Philosophers' (p 268). In other words, human knowledge is good, but 'ours' is esteemed the better sort. The observer forgets that he can praise the Houyhnhnms by comparing them to Socrates but cannot convincingly reverse that perspective. Resisting natural constraints, the observer's point of view drifts to a place that flatters his sense of power.

The second perspective that reveals the illusion of the first suggests not only the perspective box but those curious perspectives of self-conscious art that supply two views of a single scene, perspectives in which a second glance comments on something viewed at first from a more conventional point of view. In such art, a second glance could reveal Christ's face in the troubled lake at the centre of a print of the Fall, for example (Baltrušaitis, pp 25-7; Gilman, fig 11). The shift in the physical point of view imitates the shift in theological point of view that reads Genesis from the perspective of the New Testament. Gulliver's 'ours' exploits a shift in grammatical point of view for an analogous effect, while his over-serious defence of a Lilliputian woman's honour forces on the observant reader a second perspective more inclusive than the observing narrator's.

The observer is consequently most averse to those glasses that give him a second perspective on himself. Of the glasses in Brobdingnag that give him 'so despicable a Conceit' (p 147) of himself, Gulliver says that he usually avoided them because 'my Ideas were wholly taken up with what I saw on every Side of me; and I winked at my own Littleness, as People do at their own Faults' (p 148). Indeed, the purpose of telescope and microscope was, as it were, to wink at the littleness of the senses; hence celebration of their power and also Pope's late attempt, in *An Essay on Man,* to celebrate the great chain of being as a corrective to movement up and down the chain by augmented sight. Gulliver finds a double perspective on himself most offensive on his final voyage, where it pulls him down from observing rationality to brute animality:

> When I happened to behold the Reflection of my own Form in a Lake or Fountain, I turned away my Face in Horror and detestation of my self; and could better endure the Sight of a common *Yahoo*, than of my own Person. (P 278)

He rejects the perspective that reveals his 'Person,' his body, because he is not implicated in the sight of a common Yahoo but is implicated in the sight that presents him as, at best, an *un*common Yahoo. That curious perspective yokes by violence together his ugly physical image and his more exalted conception of himself. Although he resists this conceit vigorously, it is inevitable from the moment he looks at a Yahoo and 'observe[s], in this abominable Animal, a perfect human Figure' (p 230). Indeed, this sudden recognition suggests those aggressive anamorphoses directed at the viewer, like the picture of 'We Three' cited by Feste in *Twelfth Night*.[13] A German example of this popular type of picture (Baltrušaitis, pp 26-7) shows a distorted form at once as ass and a fool in cap and bells, the inscription including the viewer as a third. Yahoos are to the Houyhnhnms what asses are to us; in fact, the Houyhnhnms come to lament that reliance on Yahoo labour makes them neglect the more 'comely' race of asses (p 272). Gulliver is also a fool and once compares himself to 'a tame *Jack Daw* with Cap and Stockings' (p 265). His recognition of himself in the Yahoo mirrors the moments when the reader uncritically accepts Gulliver's point of view—includes himself in his 'ours'—before recognizing Gulliver's folly and so his own. Such a reader becomes the third party in the image when Gulliver sees humanity in a Yahoo.

The conflicting perspectives of Gulliver's final voyage suggest confusions of a kind for which Locke found an analogy in anamorphic painting. Locke tactfully describes a typical, safely classical example rather than a specific painting, although anamorphic paintings of Charles I were popular among English Royalists after 1649 (Baltrušaitis, p 28). Describing 'a sort of pictures, usually shown as surprising pieces of art, wherein the colours, as they are laid by the pencil on the table itself, . . . have no discernible order in their position,' Locke argues that the confusion results from the discrepancy between the apparently confused picture and the name attached to it. That name, after all, makes sense only from the second perspective. Lack of symmetry does not make an image confused:

> That which makes it be thought confused is, the applying it to some name to which it does no more discernibly belong than to some other: v.g. when it is said to be the picture of a man, or Caesar, then any one with reason counts it confused; because it is not discernible in that state to belong more to the name man, or Caesar, than to the name baboon, or Pompey: which are supposed to stand for different ideas from those signified by man, or Caesar. But when a cylindrical mirror, placed right, had reduced those irregular lines on the table into their due order and proportion, then the confusion ceases, and the eye presently sees that it is a man, or Caesar; i.e. that it belongs to those names; and that it is sufficiently distinguishable from a baboon, or Pompey; i.e. from the ideas signified by those names. Just thus is it with our ideas, which are as it were the pictures of things. (*Essay,* II.xxix.8)[14]

Locke is more alert than Gulliver to the dangers of perception and the limitations of imposing a conventional point of view on a novel experience. When he elsewhere postulates 'the idea of the shape of an ass with reason,' for example, Locke simply asserts that this idea would be 'different from either that of man or beast, and be a species of animal between, or distinct from both' (*Essay,* IV.iv.13; cf III.vi.29). He thus avoids the extremes of literal-minded reliance on appearance and unstable point of view: he assimilates novelty to his usual point of view without denying its novelty.

When Gulliver asserts that the word '*Houyhnhnm . . .* signifies a *Horse*' despite its more accurate etymological meaning, '*the Perfection of Nature*' (p 235), and when he casually refers to men as Yahoos, his confusions take the form of those for which Locke found an analogy in anamorphosis. Unfortunately for simplicity, Locke's approach to the problem of the rational ass is too glib for the final book of the *Travels.* The Houyhnhnms are, after all, distorted horses and not simply distinct beings; they are horses with a faculty not usually associated with horses—reason, conventionally a human quality—greatly magnified, and animal qualities diminished; so Gulliver, most obviously in the first two books, is a man with one faculty—sight—greatly distorted by perspective glasses. Similarly, Yahoos are men with reason and affection greatly diminished—the observer's body with the observing mind departed for good, as Gulliver would like his mind to do. Observing *as* a Houyhnhnm, Gulliver forgets to observe the Houyhnhnms. The complementary points of view in Swift's curious perspective are so close together that the result seems blurred rather than simply puzzling. Like the ambiguous eye itself, the Houyhnhnms are

borderline creatures, between man and animal, much as the Yahoos, by virtue of their shape, are also at a border between human and animal. Alternatively, these creatures embody diverse perspectives on man, one viewing him (inadequately) as a rational animal and the other (also inadequately) viewing him as a particularly perverse animal, with Gulliver desperately stationed between these perspectives—himself a borderline figure. Both views are sufficiently eccentric, off centre, to cause a distortion very like anamorphosis.

The observer's point of view is the source of this dilemma. Like the resolutely unironic prose espoused by the Royal Society, it asserts a single, 'clear' point of view, a monocular gaze appropriate to the perspective glass or linear perspective. The distortions of the *Travels* resemble those of self-conscious perspective painting because they—and science—share the same assumptions. Gulliver's final confusions demand not a mirror but binocular vision, an ability to see both man and Yahoo, or Houyhnhnm and Yahoo, in the same image. The Yahoos perhaps have the place in the final book that the anamorphic skull has in *The Ambassadors* or that an undistorted skull has at the centre of a mirror anamorphosis of Charles I (Baltrušaitis, p 107). They remind man of his animality much as the more conventional skull reminds him of his mortality. The trick Gulliver seems incapable of, because he is too much an observer, is seeing, juxtaposed, both animal and man. His relentlessly single vision, fostered by his reliance on perspective glasses, views Socrates as a member of a different species and himself as a Houyhnhnm. This is all the stranger as the Houyhnhnms embody recognizable human ideals, notably friendship to one's species. In effect, they represent a more traditional point of view than Gulliver, who is blinded by the sense impressions they share with horses. He abandons his species for theirs, as he thinks, but merely affects a whinny in his speech and a trot in his gait (pp 278-9). When he comes to prefer his groom to other Yahoos because of his smell, we recognize that he has abandoned a stable point of view for the point of view of the stable. Because he cannot stand back from the convincing illusion in the perspective box, he cannot see its ludicrously disproportionate container. The final intensity of his vision is analogous to the startling three-dimensionality of rigorous perspective painting, which distorts objects in the interest of a convincing illusion from a fixed point of view.

The extreme development of this detachment of point of view from place of observation is the mind-body dualism of contemporary thought, which so often finds concrete expression in Swift's poetry and prose. Gulliver hates his family, for example, because they force him to consider that he has become a parent of Yahoos 'by copulating with one of the *Yahoo*-Species'; they consequently fill him with 'the utmost Shame, Confusion and Horror' (p 289). His shame and horror spring from the forced realization of his physical kinship with 'Yahoos' rather than 'Houyhnhnms'; his confusion springs from the discrepancy between the label he would apply to himself and the evidence of the senses that confronts him. The resulting self-loathing, loathing of the self that appears in the glass in contrast to the self that looks through a glass, is the misanthropy resulting from the observer's detachment from his kind. Trying to see as a Houyhnhnm, Gulliver simply worships the idol of a different tribe.

When Gulliver rejects his romantic view of the fair skin of English ladies for the microscope's vision of mottled physicality, he plunges from the ideal into the gross, as he does more complexly when he rejects a human view for a Houyhnhnm view. His fall recalls that in what seems to be one of Swift's favourite stories—that of the philosopher who fell into a ditch while contemplating the stars. That fall, which supplies the witty conclusion to *The Mechanical Operation of the Spirit,* is repeated by Strephon in 'The Lady's Dressing Room.' Strephon's prying gaze displaces an image of the 'Goddess' for one much filthier, but the poet asserts the need for a double perspective, wishing that Strephon could delight to see 'Such Order from Confusion sprung, / Such gaudy Tulips rais'd from Dung.'[15] Even the Houyhnhnms, who are too sexually moderate for either of these extremes, celebrate healthy physicality in their rather Pindaric poetry on the winners of athletic competitions. They also devote poetry to 'exalted notions of Friendship and Benevolence' (p 274), poetry which suggests Swift's tolerant assessment of the Platonism of Charles I's court:

> . . . although we are apt to ridicule the sublime Platonic Nations they had, or personated, in Love and Friendship, I conceive their Refinements were grounded upon Reason, and that a little Grain of the Romance is no ill Ingredient to preserve and exalt the Dignity of human Nature, without which it is apt to degenerate into every Thing that is sordid, vicious and low. (*Writings,* IV, 95)[16]

One need not choose between idealizing romance and Hobbes's state of nature: the rosy perspective of romance complements the filthy perspective of the prying gaze and the magnifying glass. Swift's metaphor for idealism is here the salt that preserves corruptible flesh, a minor theme of the *Travels,*[17] but his 'had, or personated' indicates a saving irony based on complementary visions from extreme points of view, an irony that need not take one point of view too literally. Accepting the value even of illusion, the binocular view can avoid not only extreme eccentricity but also the blinkered gaze of the hack who sees only the middle road and so imitates respectably the dangers of the single point of view.

Such a composite point of view may be superior to a single view, but a mind can readily lose its bearings in the constant, dizzying shift from one point of view to another. That may be why a final glass suggests an appeal to a traditional point of view. One of Gulliver's last exercises is 'to behold [his] Figure often in a Glass, and thus if possible habituate [him] self by Time to tolerate the Sight of a human Creature' (p 295). Gulliver stops short of identifying himself with what he observes in this glass and in doing so recalls a biblical glass:

> For if any be a hearer of the word, and not a doer, he is like unto a man beholding his natural face in a glass: For he beholdeth himself, and goeth his way, and straightway forgetteth what manner of man he was. (James 1:23-4)

This echo appeals beyond Gulliver's eccentric point of view to a shared, Christian point of view, at least for readers who share that point of view. Now a point of view detached from its moorings, Gulliver neglects St James's admonition to remember his natural face in the glass: having heard the word of friendship to his species, he retreats to misanthropy by denying the face that identifies that species. Indeed, given the emphasis of the final voyage on friendship and Gulliver's rejection of it, the *Travels* may recall Bacon's allegorical reading of St James in the essay on friendship (Bacon, pp 80-1), which suggests that a friend is such a glass to correct eccentricity. Thus the *Travels* allows the dizzy reader to appeal beyond his disorientation to a stable point of view.

However, Swift is Hobbesian enough to know very well that social acceptance of a shared point of view depends in part on the vagaries of temporal authority: the shared, Christian point of view is not universally accepted in Swift's form, and even the established church he represents could be displaced by the arbitrary whim of government (*Writings,* II, 74-5). That, presumably, is why he gives the wise King of Brobdingnag his own views on the need to stifle eccentric opinions (p 131; cf *Writings,* IX, 261). His very formulation, however, stresses the existence of other, potentially attractive, points of view into which one can readily slide. There is no intrinsically authoritative or logically necessary point of view to which others can be referred: elsewhere we may see face to face, but here we see through a glass anamorphically. Of course, Swift did have fixed beliefs and so did want to fix things—the English language through an academy, the movements of beggars by issuing badges—but when he expresses these beliefs seriously from a fixed point of view, he risks sounding like the fixed, blinkered narrators he elsewhere satirizes. The alternative to such fixity is a constant shifting of point of view—irony rather than the plain style of the Royal Society. Retreating to a fixed point of view, the reader abandons the experience of the *Travels,* the participation in various points of view that is the source of its unsettling irony. The multiple vision of the *Travels* is a consequence of its central metaphor and satiric target—the observer's point of view, which makes satire possible while demonstrating that there is no escape from differences of point of view and the appearances that trick the eye.

Notes

1 *Boswell's Life of Johnson,* ed G.B. Hill, rev L.F. Powell (Oxford: Clarendon 1934-50), II, 319; however, in 'Vexations and Diversions: Three Problems in *Gulliver's Travels,'* MP, 75 (1978), 351-2, Frank Brady notes the inconsistency of the proportions within books, arguing that Swift called attention to it. On science, see Marjorie Hope Nicolson, *Science and Imagination* (1956; Hamden, Conn: Archon 1976), and David Renaker, 'Swift's Laputians as a Caricature of the Cartesians,' *PMLA,* 94 (1979), 936-44; Nicolson, p 198, relates the perspectives of the *Travels* to the perspective glass. In chapter 2 of *Jonathan Swift: A Critical Introduction* (Cambridge: Cambridge University Press 1969), Denis Donoghue explores the shifting perspectives of the *Travels,* although less literally than I attempt to do here; drawing on *The Gutenberg Galaxy,* he anticipates the more detailed work on anamorphosis and conceit by Ernest B. Gilman (see n 7, below).

2 With Burton—*Anatomy,* ed H. Jackson (London: Dent; New York: Dutton 1932), II, 96—compare V. Ronchi on this initial scepticism in *The Nature of Light,* trans V. Barocas (London: Heinemann 1970), p 95. A.C. Crombie surveys investigations of sight in 'The Mechanist Hypothesis and the Scientific Study of Vision,' in *Historical Aspects of Microscopy,* ed S. Bradbury and G. L'E. Turner (Cambridge: W. Heffer for the Royal Microscopical Society 1967), pp 3-112; see pp 52-3 for Kepler. On scientific optimism about primary qualities and philosophical scepticism about secondary qualities, see Margaret J. Osler, 'Certainty, Skepticism, and Scientific Optimism: The Roots of Eighteenth-Century Attitudes toward Scientific Knowledge,' in *Probability, Time, and Space in Eighteenth-Century Literature,* ed Paula R. Backscheider (New York: AMS 1979), pp 3-28.

3 *The Prose Writings of Jonathan Swift,* ed Herbert Davis and others, 14 vols (Oxford: Blackwell 1939-68), XI, 248; hereafter cited parenthetically as *Writings* with volume and page except that the *Travels* (volume XI) is cited by page only.

4 Francis Bacon, *Essays, Advancement of Learning, New Atlantis, and Other Pieces,* ed R.F. Jones (New York: Odyssey 1937), p 258; on Bacon in the *Travels,* see Dennis Todd, 'Laputa, the Whore of Babylon, and the Idols of Science,' *SP,* 75 (1978), 93-120. S. Bradbury discusses the limitations of period glasses in 'The

Quality of the Image Produced by the Compound Microscope: 1700-1840,' in Bradbury and Turner, pp 151-73, esp fig 5.

5 *The Spectator,* ed Donald F. Bond (Oxford: Clarendon 1965), III, 544; on vision and space, see William M. Ivins, Jr, *On the Rationalization of Sight* (New York: Da Capo Press 1973), pp 7-13.

6 Claudio Guillén, *Literature as System* (Princeton: Princeton University Press 1971), pp 291-3; on artists' glasses, see Arthur K. Wheelock, Jr, *Perspective, Optics, and Delft Artists around 1650* (New York and London: Garland 1977).

7 Ernest B. Gilman, *The Curious Perspective* (New Haven: Yale University Press 1978); his reservation about the eighteenth century appears on pp 235-7. For comment on anamorphosis and, especially, illustrations, I cite the following: Jurgis Baltrušaitis, *Anamorphic Art,* trans W.J. Strachan (New York: Abrams 1977), and Fred Leeman, *Hidden Images* (New York: Abrams 1976).

8 Robert Hooke, *Philosophical Experiments and Observations* (1726; rpt London: Frank Cass 1967), p 261; S. Bradbury, *The Evolution of the Microscope* (Oxford: Pergamon 1967), p 105; and *Journal to Stella,* ed Harold Williams (Oxford: Clarendon 1948), I, 97, with which compare Nicolson, pp 182-93, on the comic tradition of the female virtuoso. On Gulliver's background, see Edward A. Block, 'Lemuel Gulliver: Middle-class Englishman,' *MLN,* 68 (1953), 474-77.

9 Pat Rogers, 'Gulliver's Glasses,' in *The Art of Jonathan Swift,* ed Clive T. Probyn (London: Vision 1978), p 183; René Descartes, *Discourse on Method; Optics; Geometry; and Meteorology,* trans Paul J. Olscamp (Indianapolis, New York and Kansas City: Bobbs-Merrill 1965), p 65.

10 Walter Ong, 'Swift on the Mind: Satire in a Closed Field,' in *Rhetoric, Romance, and Technology* (Ithaca, NY, and London: Cornell University Press 1971), pp 207-8; he sees Swift as a spectator or, in my terms, observer.

11 *Art in Seventeenth Century Holland* (London: National Gallery 1976); I am grateful to Dr Robert Seiler for this reference. See also Leeman, pp 82-3 and pp 67-74.

12 *Correspondence of Jonathan Swift,* ed Harold Williams, III (Oxford: Clarendon 1963), 180.

13 Act II, scene iii; annotated editions gloss the passage and Gilman, pp 129-50, reads the play in terms of perspectives, citing this scene on pp 143-34.

[14] *An Essay Concerning Human Understanding,* ed Alexander Campbell Fraser, 2 vols (1894; New York: Dover 1959); cited by book, chapter, and paragraph as *Essay.*

[15] *Poetical Works,* ed Herbert Davis (London: Oxford University Press 1967), p 480 (lines 141-2).

[16] On Swift and Plato's *Republic,* see John F. Reichert, 'Plato, Swift, and the Houyhnhnms,' *PQ,* 47 (1968), 179-92; for the debate on Swift's relation to ideal societies, especially More's Utopia, see Eugene R. Hammond, 'Nature-Reason-Justice in *Utopia* and *Gulliver's Travels,'* SEL, 22 (1982), 445-68, which fully notes earlier contributions, and Jenny Mezciems, 'Utopia and "the Thing which is not": More, Swift, and Other Lying Idealists,' *UTQ,* 52(1982), 40-62.

[17] See P. Brückmann, 'Gulliver, *Cum Grano Salis,'* *Satire Newsletter,* 1 (1963), 5-11.

Michael McKeon (essay date 1987)

SOURCE: "The Parables of the Younger Son (II): Swift and the Containment of Desire," in *The Origins of the English Novel, 1600-1740,* The Johns Hopkins University Press, 1987, pp. 338-56.

[*In the following essay, McKeon discusses how Gulliver reveals Swift's pessimism concerning one's ability to transcend his or her political and social status because of predetermining cultural forces and inescapable material realities.*]

1

For a brief time fellow servants of the Tory ministry, [Daniel] Defoe and Swift were never on close, or even cordial, terms. The cultural gulf between the two men, evident enough in their educational and religious differences, can be felt most palpably as a matter of social status. Swift's utter disdain—in 1706 he disingenuously referred to Defoe as "the fellow that was *pilloryed,* I have forgot his name"—elicited an exasperated defensiveness that supports the contention that Defoe "lashed out at Swift less as an individual than as the representative of a social class which treated him and his dearest social aspirations with contempt." Yet Swift hardly saw himself as patrician. To Bolingbroke he said that "my Birth although from a Family not undistinguished in its time is many degrees inferior to Yours . . . I a Younger Son of younger Sons, You born to a great Fortune." Swift had no brothers; the stance of the younger son served as a delicate rebuke of the nobleman for assuming that their material hardships were remotely comparable.[1]

In his panegyric to Sir William Temple many years

earlier, Swift had adopted this same stance, complaining that nature unjustly denied to the indifferent poet what she lavished on his esteemed patron:

> Shall I believe a Spirit so divine
>   Was cast in the same Mold with mine?
> Why then does Nature so unjustly share
> Among her Elder Sons the whole Estate?
>   And all her Jewels and her Plate,
> Poor we *Cadets* of Heav'n, not worth her
>   Care,
> Take up at best with Lumber and the Leavings
>   of a Fate . . .

Here the conceit is that Swift by nature is without deserts and yet deserves more than he gets. The posture of the younger son defined for him a condition of extraordinary instability. Swift believed that the delusions of freethinking were most likely to thrive "amongst the worst Part of the Soldiery, made up of Pages, younger Brothers of obscure Families, and others of desperate Fortunes." But he also wistfully imagined that the *"New-men"* whom the crown was periodically obliged to raise to the pinnacles of state service were "sometimes younger Brothers." It is the distressing spectacle of unrecognized merit that most feeds the conservative psychology of the deprived younger son, and Swift was often inclined to see his own career as a series of missed opportunities for advancement—missed not for a lack of talents in the aspirant but for a lack of gratitude and justice in his masters. Inadequately rewarded for his services to the great, Swift learned a cynicism toward them and their favorites that was consonant with his broader reading of recent English history. On occasion he represented this experience of political and social deprivation in terms of aimless mobility and exile. In the ode to Temple he is "to the Muse's Gallies ty'd," perpetually and vainly struggling to reach shore. To his friends he later described himself, torn between countries and employments, as "a vexed unsettled Vagabond." "I may call my self a stranger in a strange land."[2]

The life of Swift's greatest character shares some of these general features. Lemuel Gulliver begins his travel narrative with the following words:

> My Father had a small Estate in *Nottinghamshire;* I was the Third of five Sons. He sent me to *Emanuel-College* in *Cambridge,* at Fourteen Years old, where I resided three Years, and applied my self close to my Studies: But the Charge of maintaining me (although I had a very scanty Allowance) being too great for a narrow Fortune; I was bound Apprentice to Mr. *James Bates,* an eminent Surgeon in *London,* with whom I continued four Years.[3]

Gulliver is one of those younger sons whose "fortunes and employments," in the words of William Sprigge, "are not correspondent to the grandure of their birth and education."[4] Having the foresight to acquire skills "useful in long Voyages," which "I always believed it would be some time or other my Fortune to do," Gulliver studies navigation and physic, and he does make several voyages before resolving "to settle in *London,* to which Mr. *Bates,* my Master, encouraged me" (I, i, 3). So he marries and sets up in practice; but his master soon dies and his business begins to fail. Gulliver goes to sea again, grows "weary" of it, resumes his practice unsuccessfully, and "after three Years Expectation that things would mend," enters employment on the ship that will take him to Lilliput (I, i, 4).

Thus Gulliver's first travels are undertaken in default of a more settled and upward mobility at home. After the voyage to Lilliput, however, the idea of physical travel takes on more of the financial and moral ambiguity it has in other narratives I have discussed, and the change in tone is effected by familiar narrative strategies. The second voyage begins with "my insatiable Desire of seeing foreign Countries," but also "in Hopes to improve my Fortunes." This expectation is not unreasonable, for Gulliver has already "made a considerable Profit by shewing my Cattle to many Persons of Quality" (I, viii, 63-64). But events soon conspire to cast ethical doubts on such "improvements." The tables are turned in Brobdingnag, when the avaricious farmer, "finding how profitable I was like to be, resolved to carry me to the most considerable Cities of the Kingdom" and "to shew me in all the Towns by the Way . . . to any Village or Person of Quality's House where he might expect Custom" (II, ii, 83). The echo is unmistakable: "The more my Master got by me, the more unsatiable he grew" (II, iii, 85). It is no doubt this dangerous connection between physical mobility and the indulgence of unlimited appetite that evokes, as in *Robinson Crusoe,* the retrospective voice of the repentant Narrator. Cornered in the Brobdingnagian cornfield and waiting for the enormous reapers to descend upon him, Gulliver, "wholly overcome by Grief and Despair," "bemoaned my desolate Widow, and Fatherless Children: I lamented my own Folly and Wilfulness in attempting a second Voyage against the Advice of all my Friends and Relations" (II, i, 70). But like Robinson, Gulliver is also able to disown responsibility and to project his desire for a fortune onto Fortune. Part II begins with his "having been condemned by Nature and Fortune to an active and restless Life," and it ends as his "Wife protested I should never go to Sea any more; although my evil Destiny so ordered, that she had not Power to hinder me; as the Reader may know hereafter" (II, i, 67, 133).

The success of the younger son in Defoe's narrative depends on his ability to internalize providence and to naturalize his appetites; less sympathetically, we might say that he learns how to project his desire and then to forget that he has done it. Gulliver never attains that comfort. He undertakes his third voyage because he receives an advantageous proposal, "the Thirst I had of seeing the World, notwithstanding my past Misfortunes, continuing as violent as ever" (III, i, 137-38). His decision to make the fourth interrupts a brief period at home "in a very happy Condition, if I could have learned the Lesson of knowing when I was well" (IV, i, 205). Like Robinson, Gulliver undergoes a decisive island conversion. Inseparable from his conversion experience, however, is the necessity of remaining in the physical presence of the godlike Houyhnhnms and in exile from human society. "But it was decreed by Fortune, my perpetual Enemy, that so great a Felicity should not fall to my Share" (IV, vii, 242). In fact it is a decree of the Grand Council of the Houyhnhnms, "from whence I date all the succeeding Misfortunes of my Life" (IV, ix, 257). Character and Narrator merge at the end, but it is scarcely an act of reconciliation or "atonement." For Gulliver ends radically at odds with himself, violently repudiating his own human nature yet spurned by that other nature with which he has learned to identify so closely. The expectations of the younger son so absolutely and permanently exceed all possibility of reward that status inconsistency becomes a biological condition of existence.

I will return to the land of the Houyhnhnms. For the moment it is enough to see that Swift's narrative both imitates the general movement of the spiritual autobiography and subverts it, by giving us a protagonist whose conviction of depravity issues not in repentance and faith but in the paradoxically prideful mortifications of misanthropy. By the same token, Gulliver's career (and those of several surrogates) both recapitulates that of the progressive, upwardly mobile younger son and parodically negates it in two distinct, and characteristically conservative, trajectories: that of industrious virtue insufficiently rewarded, and that of upstart ambition rewarded beyond all deserts. F. P. Lock is right to compare *Gulliver's Travels* not only to More's *Utopia* but also to Machiavelli's *The Prince,* for Swift's plot is profoundly concerned with questions of state service, and throughout his travels Gulliver repeatedly assumes the role of the "new man," symbolically and unequivocally sundered from any past "inheritance" by his status as a wandering alien who wades ashore willing and eager to serve the reigning prince and receive his due recompense.[5]

The notoriously discontinuous quality of Gulliver's character throughout much of his travels has frequently been cited to confirm the status of *Gulliver's Travels* as a "satire" rather than a "novel." But the retrospective standards by which we judge what is "novelistic" are of problematic relevance to the generically uncertain narratives that are native to the period of the novel's gradual stabilization. It may therefore be more instructive to see the discontinuity of Gulliver's character as a strategy that permits him to reflect satirically upon the serviceable hero of progressive ideology in two very different ways. On the one hand, he is the obsequious sycophant who seems always in the act of "prostrating" himself "at his Majesty's Feet," devoting his "Life to her Majesty's Service," embracing the role of "useful Servant," "most humble Creature and Vassal," and "Favourite," and humbly forbearing to rehearse for us just how honorably he has been treated (I, iii, 28; II, iii, 85-86, 90, iv, 97, viii, 123). Of course, his pride ensures that we will know this very well; a case in point is his vain and insistent allusion to his robe nobility after being honored with the Lilliputian title *Nardac*—"the highest Title of Honour among them"—in reward for the theft of the Blefuscudian fleet (I, v, 37, 39, vi, 49-50). . . .

But in the conservative mentality, the absence of noble blood tends also to persist as a conventional sign, never too closely examined, of the absence of merit. Thus when Gulliver reflects that in Houyhnhmnland, unlike England, "no Scoundrels [are] raised from the Dust upon the Merit of their Vices," he adds: "or Nobility thrown into it on account of their Virtues" (IV, x, 261). We have two instances (albeit less drastic) of such a decline in Lord Munodi and his friend, both of whom are manifestly meritorious, have done great service to the Laputan monarch, and are held in utter contempt for their incapacity for abstraction—and whose virtues, we sense, are due at least in part to their ancient and eminent nobility (III, iv, 157, 159). And when Gulliver depicts the type of upstart found in his native England—"where a little contemptible Varlet, without the least Title to Birth, Person, Wit, or common Sense, shall presume to look with Importance, and put himself upon a Foot with the greatest Persons of the Kingdom"—his list of what is lacking here characteristically gives at least a symbolizing precedence to lineage (II, v, 108). This ghostly insinuation of belief in the justice of a traditional, aristocratic stratification is entirely consistent, I have argued, with conservative ideology. It is a socially useful fiction, a cautiously instrumental faith that germinates in the soil left by the flowers of progressive belief once the conservative critique has, to its own satisfaction, quite deracinated them. This fiction is inseparable from the utopian element in conservative ideology. In *Gulliver's Travels* we fleetingly sense its presence in the "*English* Yeomen of the old Stamp" summoned up at Glubdubdrib (III, viii, 185). We hear it articulated more fully in the account of the militia of Brobdingnag, "which is made up of Tradesmen in the several Cities, and Farmers in the Country, whose Commanders are only the Nobility and Gentry, without Pay or Reward . . . Every Farmer is under the Command of his own Landlord, and every Citizen under that of the principal Men in his own City" (II, vii, 122).[7] In Lord Munodi we see an aristocratic landowner, joined by "some few other Persons of Quality and Gentry," who "was content to go on in the old Forms; to live in the Houses his Ancestors had

built, and act as they did in every Part of Life without Innovation" (III, iv, 161). Munodi's estate combines, more certainly than those other instances, the conservative utopian elements of a status consistency somehow underwritten by tradition and the stable reality of landed property. But the crucial utopian enclave in *Gulliver's Travels* is, of course, Houyhnhnmland.

On first encountering the oddly equable horses, our serviceable hero naturally expects that it is he, the human, who will be "served" by them (IV, i, 211, ii, 213). He is soon disabused of this error, not by any conventional signs of dominion, as in his earlier voyages, but through the gradual and insensible growth of a natural deference toward the Houyhnhnms. He observes first that the household he is engaged with distinguishes itself into "Master" and "Servants," and after speaking to us for a while of "the Master Horse," he offhandedly refers to "my Master (for so I shall henceforth call him)" (IV, ii, 213, 216, iii, 218). Soon it seems natural to call "my Master" "his Honour," and Gulliver sits in long dialogue with his master about the state of European affairs, much as he had once done with the King of Brobdingnag (IV, v, 229). But although he does indeed come to see himself as in "Service" to his master, the nature of the relationship is very different from those he has experienced in the past: "I did not feel the Treachery or Inconstancy of a Friend, nor the Injuries of a secret or open Enemy. I had no Occasion of bribing, flattering or pimping, to procure the Favour of any great Man, or of his Minion" (IV, x, 264, 265, 260).

This negative model of service is still available in Houyhnhnmland, among the Yahoos, for "in most Herds there was a Sort of ruling *Yahoo*" whose fawning and servile "*Favourite* is hated by the whole Herd" and befouled by it when he comes to be replaced in the affections of the ruler (IV, vii, 246-47). But when Gulliver receives favor now, it is "the Favour of being admitted to several *Houyhnhnms,* who came to visit or dine with my Master," and he is happiest in "the Station of an humble Auditor in such Conversations" (IV, x, 261). If we hear an echo of the old obsequiousness in such statements, we must keep in mind (as Gulliver himself knows) that nothing is to be gained by such arts of the courtier. In Houyhnhnmland, service and its rewards appear indistinguishable; they are something like a religious discipline, the contemplation of virtue. Before his banishment Gulliver had resolved "to pass the rest of my Life among these admirable *Houyhnhnms* in the Contemplation and Practice of every Virtue" (IV, vii, 242). And after it his only ambition is "to discover some small Island uninhabited," where he might "reflect with Delight on the Virtues of those inimitable *Houyhnhnms,*" "which I would have thought a greater Happiness than to be first Minister in the politest Court of *Europe;* so horrible was the Idea I conceived of returning to live in the Society and under the Government of *Yahoos*" (IV, xi, 267).

The very terms of the old dynamic of service and reward are altered by the utopian nature of Houyhnhnm culture because the enabling premise of that dynamic, status inconsistency, has vanished. It is not only their morality that is pervaded, in the apt words of C. J. Rawson, by "an absolute standard of congruity or *fittingness*," but also their very existence as natural and social beings. When Gulliver assures the Brobdingnag king of the purity of noble lineages in England, he is acting in bad faith. When the Houyhnhnm master assumes Gulliver's nobility, he is simply and truthfully speaking from his own experience, for "among the *Houyhnhnms*, the *White*, the *Sorrel*, and the *Iron-grey*, were not so exactly shaped as the *Bay*, the *Dapple-grey*, and the *Black;* nor born with equal Talents of Mind, or a Capacity to improve them; and therefore continued always in the Condition of Servants, without ever aspiring to match out of their own Race, which in that Country would be reckoned monstrous and unnatural" (IV, vi, 240). The appetite for upward mobility—through state service, intermarriage, or whatever means—never arises here, because the very conditions of status inconsistency by which it is generated, the very possibility of expectations that are "relative" to anything but one's own race, are absent. We are reminded of the aristocratic ideal—enforced by the futile stratagem of sumptuary legislation—of a correspondence between internals and externals so absolute that even mind and body are in complete accord. But here the romance convention whereby the noble are instantly recognizable through the purity of their complexions or the fineness of their hair has become a social reality.[8]

True, the smooth running of the social order requires more than the unrationalized operation of a purely natural "instinct." But the Houyhnhnms's recourse to "culture" is a good deal more candidly naturalized to the social order than a stealthy, "convenient fiction" like Socrates' myth of autochthonous origins, for it takes the form of a system of eugenics, which is rationally pursued in order "to preserve the Race from degenerating." It is to this end, and neither for love nor for the consolidation of the estate, that marriages are made, and the young couple is pleased to participate in the system because "it is what they see done every Day; and they look upon it as one of the necessary Actions in a reasonable Being" (IV, viii, 252-53). In such policies we see how socially useful conventions are subtly incorporated within Houyhnhnm social practice and obtain the tacit authority of behavior that is at once socialized and natural. The Houyhnhnm institution of marriage is based neither on the progressive fiction of the freedom of choice of the individual, nor on the aristocratic fiction of sacrifice to the greater end of familial lineage, but on their dialectical mediation.[9]

The Houyhnhnm economy is similarly suffused with a principle of congruity or consistency. In the insatiable avarice of the Brobdingnag farmer, we have already seen an ironic reflection of Gulliver's own insatiable desire for profit and mobility after Lilliput. The rest of the narrative does much to argue that these appetites, and the economic base that permits their unlimited growth, are endemic to English culture. The status inconsistency that nourishes the endless round of service and reward is itself fueled, as the Brobdingnag king discerns, by monetary corruption (II, vi, 113-16; III, viii, 185-86). And in Houyhnhnmland, Gulliver describes to his master how the English economy, unlimited by any principle of necessity or subsistence, thrives on the satisfaction of luxurious appetites, all the while creating fanciful new desires that will in turn need slaking. The key to this, Gulliver explains, is the exchange value of money, with which a European Yahoo "was able to purchase whatever he had a mind to . . . Therefore since *Money* alone, was able to perform all these Feats, our *Yahoos* thought, they could never have enough of it to spend or save," and the result is both conspicuous consumption and avaricious accumulation (IV, vi, 235-37). The only example of this sort of behavior in Houyhnhnmland is found, not surprisingly, among the Yahoos. Although Gulliver's master had long known of their fondness for a certain kind of shining stone, "he could never discover the Reason of this unnatural Appetite, or how these *Stones* could be of any Use to a *Yahoo;* but now he believed it might proceed from the same Principle of *Avarice,* which I had ascribed to Mankind." The same could be said of the principle of luxury and uncontrolled consumption, for there is nothing more odious about the Yahoos "than their undistinguishing Appetite to devour every thing that [comes] in their Way" (IV, vii, 244-45).

Among the Houyhnhnms things are, needless to say, very different. Like the Brobdingnag people, they are committed in general to a limiting principle of utility (II, vii, 120; IV, iv, 226, viii, 252). Just as the Houyhnhnm master could not see the use of the Yahoos' stones, so "I was at much Pains to describe to him the Use of *Money*" (IV, vi, 235). For the use of money lies paradoxically in its alienation, in its exchange, and the Houyhnhnms have no use for exchange, because they have no desire for products that are obtainable only through the circulation of commodities (or indeed for the process of circulation itself, the taste for which is one of the most highly developed in capitalist culture). Theirs is not a "free" but a planned economy, whose principle of privileged communism Swift nicely articulates as the "Supposition that all Animals had a Title to their Share in the Productions of the Earth; and especially those who presided over the rest" (IV, vi, 235). In Houyhnhnmland, the manifest reality of social inequality is seen as quite consistent with economic egalitarianism. The closest the Houyhnhnms come to a system of exchange is a mechanism for the redistribution of goods: every four years, "where-ever there is any Want (which is but seldom) it is immediately supplied by unanimous Consent and Contribution" (IV, viii, 254). And despite his deficient preparation for it, Gulliver learns to practice here his "little Oeconomy"—the account both invites and resists comparison with Robinson Crusoe's ostentatiously noncapitalist improvements—so that the very simple wants of his life are fully satisfied by an equally simple productive regimen (IV, x, 260).

3

Thus the conservative utopia of Houyhnhnmland so successfully dispels the imaginary values and unnatural wants of contemporary English civilization that it seems, finally, to establish a "consistency" between nature and culture. And if this is the achievement of Swift's utopia, the analogy of nature and culture, of biological and social existence, is also, of course, the method by which he has entangled his protagonist in adventure all along. In accord with the tradition of the imaginary voyage, Gulliver's travels are an experience of both sociopolitical and physical transformation, and it is clear that Swift would have us understand and ponder the analogical nature of this relationship. When Gulliver recalls the English variety of the "little contemptible Varlet," for example, it is as "the Moral of my own Behaviour" in Brobdingnag, when he acts the diminutive mock-hero in bombastic defense of his honor against his mortal enemy, the palace monkey (II, v, 107-8). And when he tells us soon after that "I was the Favourite of a great King and Queen, and the Delight of the whole Court; but it was upon such a Foot as ill became the Dignity of human Kind," we are obliged to see that he is describing not just the unique status of a pygmy among giants but the typical indignity of a court favorite (II, viii, 123). As we first know him Gulliver is, of course, much more physically than socially conscious. Like Robinson Crusoe, he is a practical man: a student of "Physick," a pragmatic "Projector," and a "Mechanical Genius," "curious enough to dissect" a Brobdingnag louse, "so curious [as] to weigh and measure" a Brobdingnag hailstone, inclined to wander from his shipmates in order "to entertain [his] Curiosity" (I, i, 3, v, 35; II, i, 69, iv, 97, v, 100, vi, 110; III, iv, 162). Entirely devoted to the evidence of the senses, Gulliver is one of those "plain, diligent, and laborious observers" celebrated by Thomas Sprat, who bring their "eyes uncorrupted" to their work, and he is quite preoccupied with an assortment of instruments—spectacles, pocket perspective, pocket compass—with which he hopes artificially to improve upon "the Weakness of [his] Eyes" (I, ii, 21).[10]

In Gulliver we are confronted with the man of science, a naive empiricist whose modernized version of the old sin of *libido sciendi* consists in the reduction of

knowledge to sense impressions. In the problems that plague him in Parts I and II, we first encounter the theme that comes to the center of Swift's narrative in Part III, the critique of scientific empiricism as "the new romance." Already in Brobdingnag we learn that the category of the *"Lusus Naturae"* of "the Modern Philosophy of *Europe*" is, whatever Gulliver believes, no better than "the old Evasion of *occult Causes,* whereby the Followers of *Aristotle* endeavour in vain to disguise their Ignorance" (II, iii, 88). By the time he meets Munodi, Gulliver is content to characterize a projector in terms not of vigorous skepticism but of "much Curiosity and easy Belief," and the Academy of Projectors in Lagado in a monument to the ironic reversal by which the objectivity of scientific projects for reforming the world is shown to entail a stealthy projection of subjective fancy upon it (III, iv, 162; cf. III, v-vi).[11]

But the demystification of objectivity is first enacted in the collisions between Gulliver's quantifying method and the respective standards of Lilliput and Brobdingnag. At the beginning of Part I, Gulliver's careful spatial estimates in leagues, degrees, inches, feet, and miles are soon confounded by phenomena that seem to defy an absolute and unitary measure ("The great Gate . . . about four Foot high"; leg chains "almost as large" as "those that hang to a Lady's Watch in *Europe*"; a prince big enough—"taller by almost the Breadth of my Nail, than any of his Court"—"to strike an Awe into the Beholders") (I, i, 4-5, 11-12, ii, 14). At the outset in Part II, we pass quickly from an account of the ship's movement "by my Computation" to an account of "Trees so lofty that I could make no Computation of their Altitude" (II, i, 68, 69). And now the fact of relativity, the reduction of objective quantification to a completely subjective perception, is impressed upon the bewildered Gulliver with all the force of an ontological theory of relative expectations: "Undoubtedly Philosophers are in the Right when they tell us, that nothing is great or little otherwise than by Comparison: It might have pleased Fortune to let the *Lilliputians* find some Nation, where the People were as diminutive with respect to them, as they were to me. And who knows but that even this prodigious Race of Mortals might be equally overmatched in some distant Part of the World, whereof we have yet no Discovery?" (II, i, 71). But even under these extreme conditions of ontological vertigo, Swift is careful to ensure that physical relativity continues to operate as an analogy for social relativity. Thus Gulliver, although disgusted by the smell of the Brobdingnag "Maids of Honour," through an effort of will concedes that they may be "no more disagreeable to their Lovers . . . than People of the same Quality are with us in *England*" (II, v, 102). But the appalling sight of a nurse's "monstrous Breast, which I cannot tell what to compare with," makes him "reflect upon the fair Skins of our *English* Ladies," and he himself is flatteringly perceived by the Brobdingnags as having "a Complexion fairer than a Nobleman's Daughter of Three Years old" (II, i, 75-76, ii, 80).

The relativizing of physical standards of objectivity is an undeniable accomplishment of the first three voyages, but if we take this to be irreversibly damaging to the equilibrium of the modern empiricist-traveler, we do him an injustice. In fact, Gulliver's fundamental appetite of curiosity—the "insatiable Desire of seeing foreign Countries," that "insatiable Desire I had to see the World in every Period of Antiquity"—is only whetted by the experience of indefinite relativity, for this is after all precisely what he is seeking: the experience of difference. And like all good travelers, he is well equipped for the experience. Despite his disclaimers, he is very adept at comparison, which permits him, at any single moment, to equilibrate difference, and the result is that he is extraordinarily adaptive to change. If "going native" is a cross-cultural version of social assimilation,[12] Gulliver's assimilative powers are so strong that even Brobdingnag is as much an experience of upward as of downward mobility for him. True, when the English ship comes upon his traveling box in the open sea, he imagines it will be an easy matter for one of the crew to slip his finger through its ring and lift it on board (II, viii, 127). But early on, Gulliver also learns to internalize the standards of what he sees around him and to recall with contempt the affectations of "*English* Lords and Ladies": "My Ideas were wholly taken up with what I saw on every Side of me; and I winked at my own Littleness, as People do at their own Faults" (II, iii, 91, viii, 132; cf. iv, 98, viii, 131, 133).

Gulliver's facility for assimilative comparison depends upon his ability to abstract himself from the fact of difference onto a plane of similarity, to manipulate a kind of epistemological exchange value that accommodates qualitatively dissimilar objects to a more general and equalizing standard. For this reason it is not surprising that like the mobile and serviceable seaman Edward Coxere, Gulliver is a master of languages (like language, "money is," in the words of Anthony Ascham, "an invention onely for the more expedite permutation of things"). Gulliver's facility with languages is so great, and his vanity as translator, purveyor of specialized terminologies, and amateur linguist is so well developed, that he appears to aspire in his own being to fulfill the utopian fantasy of seventeenth-century language projectors, the dream of a universal language. And in the Academy of Projectors at Lagado he is greatly taken with the several schemes by which language would be mechanized, materialized, or allegorized by method so as to render it a universal and transparent medium of exchange (III, v, 166-70, vi, 174-76).[13]

But in Houyhnhnmland this complacent dream is shat-

tered. Here Gulliver is put "to the Pains of many Circumlocutions to give my Master a right Idea of what I spoke" (IV, iv, 226). At first it appears that this is the result of the primitive state of the Houyhnhnms' understanding, reflected in their regrettable paucity of words and expressions. But it soon becomes clear that what they lack is rather the superfluity of vicious desires that make language obscure and complicated and that are symbolized in the confusion of the Tower of Babel (IV, iii, 219, iv, 228). Ironically it is Houyhnhnm speech that approximates most closely, in *Gulliver's Travels,* a universal language. It is employed simply "to make us understand one another, and to receive Information of Facts." The Houyhnhnms have no "Occasion to talk of *Lying,* and *false Representation,*" not only because their wills are not infected, but because in their speech there is a perfect correspondence and consistency of word and thing (IV, iv, 224). In Houyhnhnmland, the absence of a highly elaborated language is directly analogous to the absence of a highly elaborated economy. And Gulliver, frustrated in his attempts to translate between English and Houyhnhnm speech—to equalize them on the linguistic market of exchange—humbly acknowledges, with John Bunyan, the persistence and intractability of the old problem of mediation, and strives "to express [him] self by Similitudes" (IV, iv, 227).[14]

4

As in *Robinson Crusoe,* questions of virtue in *Gulliver's Travels* are never widely separated from questions of truth, and at times Swift is willing to juxtapose them quite directly. When the King of Brobdingnag concludes his attack on the inconsistency of status and virtue in England, for example, Gulliver, despite his "extreme Love of Truth," freely admits to having given the king a more favorable account of the matter "than the strictness of Truth would allow" (II, vi-vii, 116-17). And in Glubdubdrib, immediately after telling us of the remarkable "Interruption of Lineages" among royalty and nobility, he narrates how "disgusted" he was "with modern History" and with "how the World had been misled by prostitute Writers" (III, viii, 183). *Gulliver's Travels* is adorned with all the claims to historicity and all the authenticating devices of "modern history" in general, and of travel narrative in particular. The claim itself is made early, late, and with considerable insistence (pp. xxxv-viii; II, i, 78; IV, xii, 275-76). The narrative is interspersed with documents—letters, maps—that attest to its own documentary objecthood (pp. xxxiii-viii, 2, 66, 136, 204), and it makes reference several times to the "Journal Book" on which, in accordance with the Royal Society's instructions, its own historicity is based (I, ii, 21; IV, iii, 218, xii, 276). The prefatory letter added in 1735 alludes to the spurious continuations and keys that have been published since the first printing, thereby buttressing its founding authenticity, but at the same time it complains of some spelling and other errors in that printing, the most serious of which are editorial deletions and insertions that raise the dilemma of quantitative completeness (pp. xxxiii-xxxvi). We encounter familiar hints that the narrative seems strange and therefore true; that "there is an Air of Truth apparent through the whole"; and that the author has chosen "to relate plain matter of Fact in the simplest Manner and Style" (II, iv, 98-99; p. xxxvii; IV, xii, 275). Finally, we are reminded throughout that what we are reading is indeed a book of travels and may be judged accordingly.[15]

The results of such a judgment are not entirely straightforward. *Gulliver's Travels* is, of course, a satire of the travel narrative, and of the naive empiricism with which it is so closely associated. But just as Swift's critique of progressive ideology shares with that ideology a contempt for the fictions of aristocratic honor, so the subversion of the claim to historicity proceeds from a common, if more relentlessly indulged, skeptical impulse. The conventions of imaginary and "real" voyages were the same, and Swift's wide reading in the form bespeaks (as is so characteristic of his interests) an equivocal fascination composed of attraction as well as repulsion.[16] When Gulliver couples his claim to historicity with the aim of moral "Reformation," he is echoing, to be sure, the sort of statement that preceded not only some of Defoe's works but numerous exercises in quasi-spiritual autobiography and travel as well (p. xxxv). But the coexistence of that aim with his disgusted repudiation of "so absurd a Project as that of reforming the *Yahoo* Race in this Kingdom" is entirely typical also of Swift's own lifelong ambivalence about the utility of satiric schemes of reformation (p. xxxvi). By the same token, the Swiftian attack upon the incredibility of "true history" would not be as profound as it is if Swift were not deeply committed to some species of historical truth.[17]

What are the implications of Swift's epistemological double reversal for how he would tell the truth in narrative? Obviously he does not underwrite Gulliver's claim to have related "plain matter of fact." The Houyhnhnms can use language to convey and "receive information of facts," but that is because they are Houyhnhnms. Gulliver's commitment to the factual veracity of his factually vulnerable narrative is thus one clear sign of his error. But he is also committed, however fallibly, to the wisdom of the Houyhnhnms, and in his transmission of their wisdom to us he practices another sort of truth-telling in narrative, which he articulates when he says that "a Traveller's chief Aim should be to make Men wiser and better, and to improve their Minds by the bad, as well as good Example of what they deliver concerning foreign Places" (IV, xii, 275). This formulation of how history teaches truth and virtue by example is in fact rather more traditional than Gulliver's—and Swift's—actual practice would warrant, for the texture of circumstantial and authenticating detail is too dense to be dissolved by our somewhat anxious insistence that it is "all ironic."[18]

The epistemology of *Gulliver's Travels* can be usefully compared with that of the most acute and self-conscious of the spiritual travelers at the end of the previous century, whose plain style and historicity were instruments by which to arrive at a truth that lay through, but not in, the factual.[19] But Swift's parable is noticeably non-Christian, and since we are not asked to acknowledge the Author who lurks behind the author, we are not overly occupied with attributing to an ultimately higher source Swift's creation of the artifice Gulliver has disavowed. As a result, by subverting empirical epistemology, Swift contributes, as fully as Defoe does by sponsoring it, to the growth of modern ideas of realism and the internalized spirituality of the aesthetic. Swift's parabolic pedagogy can tacitly justify its return to an anachronistic attitude toward how to tell the truth in narrative in part because it has, as it were, earned the right to it through a self-conscious evisceration of the more modern alternative, and in part because that modern alternative is learning how to reconcile itself to notions of aesthetic universality through the resuscitation of Aristotelian doctrine. In this respect, as well as in its inevitable dedication to the weapon of perceptual subjectivity, which it employs to attack empirical notions of objectivity, Swift's narrative method is at the forefront of the "modern alternative." The attack would be ineffective if it were based only on the old unsearchability of the divine spirit and its intentions. Yet in substituting for the traditional a modernized critique of materialist sufficiency, Swift participates, as surely as Defoe, in the modern replacement of Spirit by Mind.[20]

But there are also other ways of understanding why *Gulliver's Travels* is non-Christian. In *Robinson Crusoe* Defoe is willing, quasi-metaphorically, to speak of Robinson's "original sin" because in the optimistic spirit of progressive ideology he is willing to conceive that status inconsistency, for which original sin stands as its most irrevocable instance, can be indemnified and overcome. Swift does not speak of original sin because his social vision is too thoroughly infiltrated by a conviction of it, and in the Houyhnhnms he wants to posit a race of mortals—humanoid but necessarily nonhuman—that has no experience of status inconsistency. In Brobdingnag, Gulliver has already shown remarkable powers of resistance to negative socialization. Bestialized at every turn—compared to a weasel, a toad, a spider, a splacknuck, a canary, a frog, a puppy, a diminutive insect, a little odious vermin—it is testimony to his resilience that he is yet able to identify as fully as he does with his enormous human hosts. In Houyhnhnmland the Yahoos confront Gulliver with the similar challenge of an effective theriomorphy, and for a while he fends it off.

When he first encounters the Yahoos they are "Beast[s]," "ugly Monster[s]," deformed "Animals" who bear no relation to the "many Tracks of human Feet" he has earlier observed, a "cursed Brood" that presumably served "the Inhabitants" as "Cattle" (IV, i, 207-8). As the alarming resemblance becomes harder to avoid, he tries to conceal "the Secret of [his] Dress, in order to distinguish [himself] as much as possible" (IV, iii, 220). But at length Gulliver is obliged to acknowledge "that entire Congruity betwixt [himself] and their *Yahoos*," and when a young female, observing him bathe, becomes "inflamed by Desire . . . [he] could no longer deny, that [he] was a real *Yahoo*" (IV, vii, 242, viii, 250-51). Still he entertains some hope that the Houyhnhnms "would condescend to distinguish [him] from the rest of [his] Species," but he is overcome with despair when the General Council exhorts his master "either to employ [him] like the rest of [his] Species, or command [him] to swim back to the Place from whence [he] came" (IV, x, 262, 263).

So Gulliver is obliged against his will to "go native." What is the precise meaning of this assimilation? It is of course in the interest of Gulliver's self-esteem for him to understand himself as the pure form of the species, from whom the "corrupted" Yahoos have "degenerated" (IV, iii, 222, viii, 249). This view receives some support from his master's interpretation of the traditional story of the origins of the Yahoos, "whereof," Gulliver significantly adds, "he had indeed borrowed the Hint from me" (IV, ix, 256).[21] But Gulliver's account of European culture, the impartial observation of the Yahoos, and the wisdom of the Houyhnhnms all point toward the contrary conclusion: that the tincture of reason possessed by the Europeans has aggravated, corrupted, improved, and multiplied the vices and wants that they naturally share with the Yahoos, and made them unquestionably the degenerate and bestial form of the species (IV, v, 232, vii, 243-48, x, 262, xii, 280). The "corruptions" of money, it would appear—its ability to create new and unheard-of desires and vanities—are a subcategory of the "corruptions" of reason. Both are peculiar to that segment of the human race whose vicious appetites have become so unlimited by the constraints of nature and custom as to demand the final and appalling sanction of being, themselves, the standard of what is natural.[22]

One basic argument of the "soft school of interpretation" concerning Part IV of *Gulliver's Travels* is that Swift tacitly and tellingly discredits the Houyhnhnms by making them passionless and cold—an argument which ignores how consistently the containment of the passions operates in Swift's writings as a positive norm. In fact Swift tells us that the language of the Houyhnhnms is well suited to the expression of the passions (IV, i, 210). True, their passions and wants are fewer than ours; but among the appetites they lack is "the Desire of Power and Riches," whereas the detestable

type of the first minister of state in England—possessed of rather fewer passions, apparently, than even the Houyhnhnms—"makes use of no other Passions but a violent Desire of Wealth, Power, and Titles" (IV, iv, 226, 228, vi, 239; see also IV, vi, 236, viii, 253, for passions the Houyhnhnms do not know). It is precisely because the passions of the Houyhnhnms are few, and because they place natural and discretionary limits on them—planned marriages, the practice of abstinence, the selective censorship and eventual banishment of Gulliver—that they have avoided the degenerations and corruptions of the human race (IV, v, 231-32, viii, 252-53, x, 263).[23]

For the wisdom of the Houyhnhnms entails not an invulnerability to corruption but the foresight and will to prevent it. And their wisdom in banishing Gulliver is evident in the fact that his assimilationist vanity is in no way limited by his acceptance of his status as a Yahoo, which instead only whets his appetite to become a Houyhnhnm. In what is surely an extreme case of upwardly mobile ambition, Gulliver aspires to the status of a higher species. And when we call up the image of him trotting and whinnying like a Houyhnhnm, we are struck by the justice with which the materialist sufficiency of this man of science is now expressed in the hopelessly physical mode through which he would imitate moral excellence (IV, x, 262-63).[24] Gulliver's impersonation of a horse is his equivalent of Robinson's figures of absolute dominion and divine providence. Both men are engaged in postconversion projects of "improvement"; but whereas Robinson is permitted by his author to project English society upon his island with impunity and to introject a divinity that sanctions his desires, Gulliver's ethnocentric attempts to find an ideal England abroad are consistently frustrated, and the Houyhnhnms absolutely resist introjection.

Although we might be tempted to draw the easy lesson that only this particular conversion has failed, Swift is really reflecting on all suspect conversions that consist in the psychological process of introjection, conversions that succeed if their subjects are complacent enough to be certain that they have. And so he gives us a protagonist whose utopia cannot be internalized, who cannot "make" himself, whose social mobility manifestly cannot signify spiritual achievement, because try as he might, he cannot become what he is not—a truth that is demonstrated most of all in his very willingness to try. Robinson Crusoe's honest old Portuguese captain serves to reflect back to him his heightened spiritual status, to provide the external accreditation of the community. Gulliver's honest Portuguese captain, Don Pedro de Mendez, exists to provide this same assurance, and the fact that Gulliver barely tolerates him bespeaks a fine doubleness. For it supports both a painful truth—even the best of men are only human (and Gulliver has renounced easy confirmations)—and a painful delusion—Gulliver's distaste for Don Pedro is inseparable from his continuing conviction of his own differentness.

So the inwardly divided Gulliver returns to England, makes a "small Purchase of Land," and retires to cultivate "my little Garden." And by that movement he completes, in the double trajectory with which he began, a characteristically circular conservative plot pattern: the embittered return of the disdained country gentleman to his landed enclave (and the type embraces also the retirement of Munodi and Swift himself); and the comic rustication of the unsuccessful younger son, bloated with pride and incomprehendingly indignant at his failure to make it in town or at court (pp. xxxiv, xxxvi; IV, xii, 279). The power of *Gulliver's Travels* as a narrative explanation of status inconsistency cannot be detached from the force of its will to explain, parabolically, our more general condition of mutability and discord. The ironic theme of historical degeneration and cyclical decay is everywhere: in the testimony of Aristotle at Glubdubdrib when he enunciates the conservative maxim "that new Systems of Nature [are] but new Fashions," and new truths only recapitulate the errors of those they replace; in the case of the Struldbruggs, who seem to Gulliver to promise an "antient Virtue" that may "prevent that continual Degeneracy of human Nature," but who in fact are a terrible emblem of physical and mental decay (III, viii, 182, x, 192, 194).[25]

But the generality of the problems Swift investigates in *Gulliver's Travels* can be overstated. At crucial moments in the critique of ambitious courtiers and ungrateful princes, we are told that our concern is with the modern period and the modern world. The familiar-sounding crises that we hear of in Lilliputian politics began with the present emperor's great-grandfather and continue to very recent times (I, iv, 32-34, vi, 44). The present era of Brobdingang stability dates from the reign of this king's grandfather, who ended a civil war (II, vii, 122). The virtues of the old English yeomen have been prostituted by their corrupted grandchildren, who are even now at large (III, viii, 185-86). The volatile period to which Swift alludes most insistently, in other words, is the previous century. In the last analysis it seems important to recognize that *Gulliver's Travels* intertwines the microplot of Lemuel Gulliver with these allusive invocations of the macroplot of seventeenth-century English history in order to specify, and explain, a species of error and corruption that, to a very important degree, Swift saw as a modern phenomenon.

Notes

[1] Michael Shinagel, *Defoe and Middle-Class Gentility* (Cambridge: Harvard University Press, 1968), 81, 86; Jonathan Swift to Viscount Bolingbroke, Oct. 31, 1729, in *The Correspondence of Jonathan Swift,* ed. Harold Williams (Oxford: Clarendon Press, 1963), III, 354.

[2] Jonathan Swift: "Ode to the Hon[ble] Sir William Temple" (1692), ll. 178-84, in *The Poems of Jonathan Swift,* ed. Harold Williams, 2nd ed. (Oxford: Clarendon Press, 1958), I, 32; (Irish) *Intelligencer,* no. 9 (1728), in *The Prose Works of Jonathan Swift,* vol. 12: *Irish Tracts, 1728-1733,* ed. Herbert Davis (Oxford: Blackwell, 1964), 47; *A Letter to a Young Gentleman, Lately enter'd into Holy Orders . . .* (1721), in *Prose Works,* vol. 9: *Irish Tracts, 1720-1723 and Sermons,* ed. Louis Landa (Oxford: Blackwell, 1948), 78; "Ode to Temple," l. 191, in *Poems,* I, 32; Swift to John Arbuthnot, July 3, 1714, and Swift to Alexander Pope, Aug. 11, 1729, in *Correspondence,* II, 46, and III, 341. On Swift's sense of physical alienation, and on his profound attachment to Ireland, see Carole Fabricant, *Swift's Landscape* (Baltimore: Johns Hopkins University Press, 1983), chap. 6. On the conservative reading of recent English history and the psychology of the younger son, see above, chap. 6, sec. 3.

[3] Jonathan Swift, *Travels into several Remote Nations of the World. In Four Parts. By Lemuel Gulliver . . .* (1726), vol. II of *Prose Works,* ed. Herbert Davis (Oxford: Basil Blackwell, 1941), I, i, 3 (hereafter cited as *Travels*); all parenthetical citations in the text are to this edition, and consist of part, chapter, and page number.

[4] See above chap. 4, n. 62.

[5] F. P. Lock, *The Politics of Gulliver's Travels* (Oxford: Clarendon Press, 1980), 22. Machiavelli was of fundamental importance to both progressive and conservative ideology; for a discussion primarily of the former influence, see above, chap. 5, nn. 16-18.

[6] See above, chap. 5, n. 22. On Castiglione see above, chap. 5, n. 14.

[7] Swift's immediate model here is less the old Cavalier army (see above, chap. 5, n. 19), than the Machiavellian republican tradition.

[8] C. J. Rawson, *Gulliver and the Gentle Reader: Studies in Swift and Our Time* (London: Routledge and Kegan Paul, 1973), 19. On sumptuary legislation see above, chap. 4, nn. 2, 29.

[9] But while status distinctions are thereby reinforced, like many utopian communities, the Houyhnhnms (and the Lilliputians) are opposed to the extreme socialization of sex difference; see *Travels,* I, vi, 46; IV, viii, 253. For other utopian practices in this regard, see above, chap. 6, n. 38. On Socrates see above, chap. 4, nn. 8-9.

[10] See also *Travels,* I, v, 35-36, viii, 62, and, for the utility of the magnifying glass and the looking glass in Brobdingnag, II, i, 76, iii, 88, 91, viii, 131. For Sprat see above, chap. 3, n. 31. Gulliver likes to keep his instruments of sight in his most private and secret pockets, and he tells us of his gratitude when the pirates of Part III and the mutineers of Part IV refrain from a pocket search: *Travels,* III, i, 139; IV, i, 206. Given this empiricist investment in his eyesight, it is particularly disturbing that the punishment with which Gulliver is threatened in Lilliput is blinding: ibid., I, vii, 54, 56. On the potential "corruptions" of the telescope see the comments of Swift's skeptical predecessors in the critique of the new philosophy, Henry Stubbe and Samuel Butler, above, chap. 2, nn. 14-15.

[11] David Renaker has argued that only the science of Lagado represents Newtonianism and the experimental method of the Royal Society, and that the abstracted speculators of Laputa represent Cartesian rationalism: "Swift's Laputians as a Caricature of the Cartesians," *PMLA,* 94, no. 5 (Oct., 1979), 936-44.

[12] See above, chap. 6, n. 37.

[13] Gulliver's facility with languages and translation: *Travels,* I, i, 4, ii, 15, 18-20; II, i, 73; IV, ii, 216. Nautical terminology: ibid., p. xxxv, II, i, 68. Gulliver as a linguist: ibid., II, ii, 79; III, ii, 145-46. On the concern of imaginary voyages with the universal language see above, chap. 6, n. 38. For Ascham see above, chap. 5, n. 50. For Coxere see above, chap. 6, nn. 41-42.

[14] Compare Hosea 12:10: "I have used . . . similitudes," which provides the epigraph for *The Pilgrim's Progress.* In his account of the Brazilian Indians, Michel de Montaigne similarly associates economic with linguistic simplicity: "It is a Nation wherein there is no manner of Traffick . . . no use of Service, Riches or Poverty, no Contracts, no Successions, no Dividents . . . no Agriculture, no Mettal, no use of Corn or Wine, and where so much as the very words that signifie, Lying, Treachery, Dissimulation, Avarice, Envy, Detraction and Pardon, were never heard of" (*Essays of Michael seigneur de Montaigne . . . ,* trans. Charles Cotton [1685], "Of Canniballs," I, 368-69).

[15] See *Travels,* II, i, 78, iv, 98-99, viii, 131; III, xi, 198; IV, ii, 216-17, viii, 251, x, 266, xii, 275-77. Documentation: Part I also contains Gulliver's "Word for Word" translations of several official Lilliputian documents; ibid., I, ii, 18-20, iii, 27-28, vii, 52-53. Gulliver makes clear his intellectual affiliation with the Royal Society by telling us that he has donated several Brobdingnag wasp stings to that institution; ibid., II, iii, 94. Printing errors: The printer has erroneously transformed "Brobdingrag" into "Brobdingnag"; compare Edward Cooke, *A Voyage to the South Sea, and Round the World . . .* (1712), II, vi, where "Selkirk" is corrected to Selcrag." On quantitative completeness see also *Travels,* II, i, 78, vii, 117.

[16] Many narrators of travels, both real and imaginary, made the plausible argument that our doubts concerning the existence of things—lands, peoples, extraordinary animals—we do not know may reflect only our skepticism, not their unreality; e.g., see above, chap. 3, nn. 48-50. John Arbuthnot told Swift of readers who behaved as though *Gulliver's Travels* was authentic; see Arbuthnot to Swift, Nov. 5, 1726, in *Correspondence,* III, 180. On the complexity of Swift's attitude toward travel narratives see also Percy G. Adams, *Travel Literature and the Evolution of the Novel* (Lexington: University Press of Kentucky, 1983), 142-44.

[17] Lock has made an important objection to the common and uncritical assumption that much of the political allegory that has been attributed to *Gulliver's Travels* was intended by Swift. But he is wrong to suggest that reference to particular historical cases was foreign to Swift's aim in that work, and to maintain that "to bury the meanings so deeply that the allegory could neither be recognized nor certainly interpreted if discovered was self-defeating" (*Politics of Gulliver's Travels,* 106). I have earlier argued that the uncertainty of allegorical interpretation provides Swift and his contemporaries with a crucial focus for investigating the problem of mediation, especially as that problem was trivialized and aggravated (for people like Swift) by naive empiricist or enthusiastic beliefs in the possibility of an immediate access to truth. This is nowhere more clear than in *A Tale of a Tub* (1704), where Swift attacks simultaneously the opposed but complementary errors of deep and superficial reading. In the episode of the political allegorizers in *Gulliver's Travels* (III, vi, 175), Swift creates a similar sort of double-bind for his readers by calling them "the Natives called *Langden*" "in the Kingdom of *Tribnia.*" Lock thinks these are "crudely intrusive anagrams that make the satire . . . needlessly specific" (*Politics of Gulliver's Travels,* 82). But the effect of the names is to implicate us inextricably in the problem of interpretation, for by automatically deciphering them as "England" and "Britain," we replicate the behavior of the projectors whom Swift obliges us to scorn. (Another way of saying this is to suggest that Swift here employs a second-order satire whose principal target is not really "the English" at all, but overly elaborate interpretation—like that required to read the currently popular secret histories and *romans à clef* [see above, chap. 1, nn. 99-100].) Here Swift has a little joke at our expense. But the critical problem of interpretive indeterminacy, although it may feel self-defeating, is a serious one that ramifies into many areas of his thought.

[18] See the intelligent discussion of how we are to take Gulliver's claim to historicity in Rawson, *Gulliver and*

the Gentle Reader, 9-10.

[19] E.g., cf. William Okeley, above, chap. 3, n. 56.

[20] On these matters see above, chap. 3, sec. 6.

[21] In the first edition, Gulliver elaborates this interpretation to suggest that the Yahoos are the "very much defaced" descendants of specifically English people; see *Travels,* "Textual Notes," 306.

[22] See above, chap. 5, sec. 4. The idea that human reason works to corrupt rather than to enhance human nature was a familiar one in political and utopian literature; e.g., in [Gabriel de Foigny], *A New Discovery of Terra Incognita Australis . . .* (1693), 75-76, the wise old man tells Sadeur that his countrymen "have some *Sparks of Reason,* but they are so weak, that instead of enlightning them, they only serve to conduct 'em more surely in their Error."

[23] Like other conservative writers, Swift thus implicitly mocks the progressive claim that the indulgence of the avaricious passions may help countervail more destructive ones; see above, chap. 6, nn. 25, 53. On the soft and hard schools of interpretation see James L. Clifford, "Gulliver's Fourth Voyage: Hard and Soft Schools of Interpretation," in *Quick Springs of Sense: Studies in the Eighteenth Century,* ed. Larry S. Champion (Athens: University of Georgia Press, 1974), 33-49.

[24] The amusing silliness of a Houyhnhnm threading a needle, on the other hand, is Swift's mild self-mockery of the inadequacy of his own efforts (a very minor version of his hero's failings) to mediate Houyhnhnm to human nature by way of physical resemblance. But note that even here it is Gulliver who creates the incongruity by lending the mare a needle: *Travels,* IV, ix, 258. With Gulliver's vain ambition compare the desperate and self-censored aspiration of Mary Carleton to be a different sex (above, chap. 6, nn. 32-34). It is easy to sympathize with her ambition, as it is not in the case of Gulliver's, because hers amounts to a just desire to obtain the power she merits rather than a vain emulation of a status that is beyond her internal capacities.

[25] On the circular patterns of conservative plots see above, chap. 6, nn. 21-22.

J. A. Downie (essay date 1989)

SOURCE: "The Political Significance of *Gulliver's Travels,*" in *Swift and His Contexts,* edited by John Irwin Fischer, Herman J. Real and James Woolley, AMS Press, 1989, pp. 1-20.

[*In the following essay, Downie argues that critics have gone too far in making links between real events and people in British history and the contents of* Gulliver's Travels. *He suggests that Swift was writing a more general "parallel history" rather than a decipherable allegorical text intended to serve as an exposé.*]

Seventy years have passed since Sir Charles Firth first made use of the title I have chosen for my essay. "Political allusions abound in the *Travels,*" Firth asserted in his lecture to the British Academy in 1919. In saying this, he was, in one respect, doing little more than endorsing the view which had been taken of Swift's masterpiece ever since its first publication. But Firth wished to codify such general perceptions. "In *Gulliver's Travels* many figures which seem to be imaginary are meant to depict real personages," he claimed, "or at all events are drawn from them."[1] Considering that nearly two centuries had passed since publication, Firth's assurance was breathtaking. It now seems almost incredible that his assertions could have influenced so profoundly the way succeeding generations have approached Swift's book, for Firth wasn't even an expert in eighteenth-century history. "To the politics of Walpole's day he brought only the superficial expertise of a gifted amateur," J. P. Kenyon has observed, "and the literary critics who followed him could contribute little more.[2]

But that was not how it seemed to Firth's immediate successors, and his casual observations were soon being treated as if they had been tablets of stone from Mount Sinai. In 1938, Godfrey Davies claimed that Firth's essay *proved* that Swift often drew upon contemporary events in England for the parts of the book he first wrote," i.e., Parts I and II.[3] Perhaps it was a similar misplaced confidence in Firth's perspicacity which led Arthur E. Case to go one stage further and (among other things) put forward a sustained allegorical interpretation of Gulliver's experiences in Lilliput, centering on British politics between 1708 and 1715 and the fortunes (or misfortunes) of Swift's ministerial friends, Oxford and Bolingbroke, even though, as Kenyon remarks, "a trained historian . . . can casually make mincement of most of Firth's and Case's attributions."[4]

However, Case's views were accepted by the Swift establishment readily enough. Of *Four Essays on "Gulliver's Travels",* Harold Williams wrote that "the third essay, on 'Personal and Political Satire' in the *Travels,* is the best in the book, displaying discernment and balanced thought."[5] For thirty years, the conviction that there was a consistent political allegory running through *Gulliver's Travels* was a critical commonplace. "Professor Case is ordinarily so authoritative," Edward Rosenheim, Jr., wrote in 1970, "that we tend to accept his information without question."[6] It was for that reason that Case's discussion of personal and political satire was reprinted in various collections

Gulliver captured by the Lilliputians.

of essays on Swift,[7] and editions of *Gulliver's Travels* dating from these years—in other words, the ones almost invariably used by students—are inevitably accompanied by notes informing the reader of the import of the alleged political allegory. Even today, critics are to be found who accept Case's views. "To a large extent," Hermann J. Real and Heinz J. Vienken asserted in 1985, "'Gulliver in Lilliput' is a satirical vivisection of the intellectual and moral shortcomings of Whig politics between approximately 1708 and 1715."[8]

But what if, after all, Firth and Case were mistaken in assuming that *Gulliver's Travels* is a political allegory? Phillip Harth was the first to question the validity of the approach of the allegorical critics. In 1976, arguing that "Gulliver in Lilliput" is an "exemplary tale of the ingratitude of princes and the jealousy of ministers," Harth suggested that it was inappropriate to view Gulliver's adventures in Part I as an allegory of political events in early eighteenth-century Britain.[9] Reviewing Harth's essay, Ken Robinson agreed that "he has the support of eighteenth- and nineteenth-century critics for his contention that the first book is simply allusive." Yet Robinson went on to suggest that

Harth's "terms are misleading": "He claims to be abandoning an allegorical reading but is in fact only abandoning a particularized political allegory."[10] For the first time, critics were beginning to argue about the terms used to describe what goes on in *Gulliver's Travels.* This was a significant development, to which I shall return.

The following year, 1977, I tried independently to emphasize the problems facing anyone wishing to argue that there is a consistent political allegory running through the book, or, indeed, any part of it, including "A Voyage to Lilliput."[11] What I did not suggest was that allusions to the politics of early eighteenth-century Britain could not be found. All I did was to question the approach of critics such as Firth and Case. Indeed, I concluded my essay by attempting to direct attention away from Part I and Gulliver's adventures in Lilliput—the traditional hunting ground for political allusions—to Part II and Gulliver's lengthy and meaty conversations with the King of Brobdingnag.[12]

By 1980, however, F. P. Lock was urging us largely to reject not only the specific identifications of Firth and the sustained political allegory of Case but "the accumulated weight of personal and particular allusions that has been read into the book by modern criticism."[13] In order to substantiate his thesis, Lock had to ignore or to reinterpret contemporary evidence bearing on the political significance of *Gulliver's Travels.*[14] Before we can evaluate "those puzzlingly particular annotations that have made generations of readers wonder why Swift clogs his general satire with so many topical references,"[15] therefore, it is necessary to go back to the beginning—that is, to the first publication of the two volumes of *Travels into Several Remote Nations of the World.*

II

"The clandestine comedy with which Swift surrounded the actual publication of *Gulliver* is well known," Lock writes.[16] Nevertheless, it must be rehearsed once more. Benjamin Motte, the publisher, was contacted on 8 August 1726 not by Swift *in propria persona* but by one Richard Sympson, whose covering letter, in the handwriting of John Gay, accompanied a copy of his cousin Mr. Lemuel Gulliver's manuscript. On receiving Motte's reply, Sympson asked for both volumes of Gulliver's account of his travels to "come out together and [to be] published by Christmas at furthest."[17] Two days later Swift left London en route to Ireland. "Motte receiv'd the copy (he tells me) he knew not from whence, nor from whom, dropp'd at his house in the dark, from a Hackney-coach," Pope informed Swift; "by computing the time, I found it was after you left England, so for my part, I suspend my judgment."[18] On 28 October 1726, *Gulliver's Travels* duly appeared.

Why did Swift go to the trouble of covering his tracks? "It was partly due to Swift's desire to preserve his anonymity," Lock suggests, "and partly out of his love of a good joke."[19] "I congratulate you first upon what you call your Couzen's wonderful Book," Pope wrote to Swift on 16 November 1726. "That countenance with which it is received by some statesmen, is delightful," he continued:[20]

> I find no considerable man very angry at the book: some indeed think it rather too bold, and too general a Satire: but none that I hear of accuse it of particular reflections (I mean no persons of consequence, or good judgment; the mob of Criticks, you know, always are desirous to apply Satire to those that they envy for being above them) so that you needed not to have been so secret upon this head.

How should Pope's words be interpreted? He rallied Swift upon what he took to have been the excessive secrecy surrounding Gulliver's appearance. Possibly he was also reassuring Swift about the personal nature of his satire: Pope felt that Swift's precautions were unnecessary in the event because no one "of consequence, or good judgment" had had the discernment (as yet) to apply the satire personally.

The next day, 17 November, Gay endorsed Pope's information:

> The Politicians to a man agree, that it is free from particular reflections. . . . Not but we now and then meet with people of greater perspicuity, who are in search for particular applications in every leaf; and it is highly probable we shall have keys published to give light into Gulliver's design.[21]

Given twentieth-century approaches to *Gulliver's Travels,* Gay's percipience is impressive, even though (presumably) he had failed to keep up with events: a key had already been advertised in the *Whitehall Evening Post* for 8-10 November 1726.[22] My point is this: why should both Pope and Gay take the trouble to assure Swift, in words that are virtually identical, that the consensus was that *Gulliver* is without "particular reflections"?

Significantly, Swift used the same vocabulary in replying to Pope, emphasizing that, in Dublin, if not in London, "the general opinion is, that reflections on particular persons are most to be blamed."[23] Quite clearly, Swift and his friends had at least entertained the possibility that readers would try to find personal satire in *Gulliver's Travels.* The question is whether or not Swift intended that they should find allusions to contemporary events and politicians. Perhaps he had hoped to ruffle the feathers of those in high places, and had simply been trying to avoid any repercussions. When, over a year earlier, he had told Pope about the completion of his "newly Augmented" *Travels,* he had added the rider that they were "intended for the press when the world shall deserve them, or rather when a Printer shall be found brave enough to venture his Eares."[24] This being the case, it is interesting that Swift's letter to Pope of 27 November 1726 concluded:

> Let me add, that if I were Gulliver's friend, I would desire all my acquaintance to give out that his copy was basely mangled, and abused, and added to, and blotted out by the printer; for so to me it seems, in the second volume particularly.[25]

Motte had bravely published *Gulliver's Travels* and had been rewarded by seeing the "whole [first] impression sold in a week."[26] But had he been brave enough?

III

The question of censorship is an important consideration when trying to assess the political significance of *Gulliver's Travels.* On a number of occasions Swift claimed that Motte had cut the manuscript he had been given to print. Pointing out that the first edition "abounds with many gross Errors of the Press," Charles Ford sent Motte a list of corrections on 3 January 1727.[27] It is beyond reasonable doubt that Ford was acting on Swift's instructions. David Woolley suggests that: "It is probable from its substance and phrasing that this letter, though in Ford's autograph, was entirely composed by Swift, and similarly the list."[28] Gay had transcribed "Richard Sympson's" earlier letter to Motte. Clearly Swift was determined to deal, for the time being, through intermediaries. In addition, we have the evidence of letters between Swift and Ford. "Now, you may please to remember how much I complained of Motts suffering some friend of his (I suppose it was M[r] Took a Clergy-man now dead) not onely to blot out some things that he thought might give offence, but to insert a good deal of trash contrary to the Author's manner and Style, and Intention," Swift reminded Ford on 9 October 1733, when George Faulkner was preparing his edition of Swift's *Works*. "I think you had a Gulliver interleaved and set right in those mangled and murdered Pages."[29] Ford's "interleaved" *Gulliver* is preserved in the Forster Collection in the Victoria and Albert Museum.[30]

F P. Lock nonetheless discounts out of hand any suggestion that Motte censored Swift's text. "Certainty is impossible without new evidence, which is unlikely now to come to light," he suggests. "But reading Ford's letter in the light of Swift's love of jests and mystification makes it seem likely that the story of Motte's adulteration of the text of *Gulliver's Travels* was more of a joke than a serious complaint."[31] Fortunately, Michael Treadwell has been able to offer such new evidence. Explaining in detail why Motte would "have been cautious about issuing a work like *Gulliver*, particularly had it contained the manuscript passages preserved in Ford's interleaved copy," Treadwell shows "that the Reverend Andrew Tooke was indeed a specialist in the kind of copy editing Swift accuses him of in the case of *Gulliver's Travels*, that he had the closest possible ties with Benjamin Motte and was, in fact, a sleeping partner in Motte's firm. . . . Such evidence does not, of course, *prove* Swift's claim that Motte and Tooke altered the text of *Gulliver's Travels*," Treadwell concludes, "but I believe that it adds so greatly to the inherent probability of that claim as to make any other explanation impossible to credit."[32]

Therefore it seems we must take Swift seriously when he solemnly told Pope that he had "observe[d] several passages which appear to be patched and altered, and the style of a different sort" in Parts III and IV in particular.[33] In his corrected fourth octavo edition, published on 4 May 1727, Motte made all but three of the corrections listed in Ford's letter. However, even though Ford had also indicated where Swift's style had been tampered with, Motte failed to make any

substantive additions to the text. This angered Swift more than anything else. "Had there been onely omissions, I should not care one farthing," Swift explained to Ford on 20 November 1733, "but change of Style, new things foysted in, that are false facts, and I know not what, is very provoking. . . . Besides, the whole Sting is taken out in severall passages, in order to soften them."[34]

Let us examine in detail one of the passages which, to Swift's annoyance, was allegedly altered in the first edition. Modern readers know that when he visits the Academy of Lagado, Gulliver relates his experiences "in the Kingdom of *Tribnia,* by the Natives called *Langden,*" in which "the Bulk of the People consisted wholly of Discoverers, Witnesses, Informers, Accusers, Prosecutors, Evidences, Swearers; together with their several subservient and subaltern Instruments; all under the Colours, the Conduct, and pay of Ministers and their Deputies."[35] Clearly *Tribnia* is an anagram of "Britain," *Langden* of "England," and it is generally accepted that Swift is referring here to the Atterbury case.[36] But this is the reading of editions of *Gulliver's Travels* published from 1735 onwards. In the first edition, this famous satire on the politics of the 1720s reads rather differently, as Gulliver merely explains what he would do "should [he] happen to live in a Kingdom where Plots, and Conspiracies were either in vogue from the turbulency of the meaner People, or could be turned to the use and service of the higher Rank of them" (p. 311). Not only is the passage narrated in the conditional; the obvious anagrams are not be found.

According to Swift, Motte had deliberately tried to take the sting out of passages such as this, presumably to avoid possible repercussions in high places. Ford told Motte that it "seems to have much of the Author's manner of thinking, but in many places wants his Spirit."[37] F. P. Lock doubts the veracity of such statements. "Although the passages (in both versions) contain several possible references to the Atterbury plot," he argues, "the variants do not seem to be at all influenced by considerations of political caution. Instead, they read like stylistic improvements." Lock regards the version given by Faulkner in 1735 as a revision in which Swift tries unhappily to make his political satire more topical, rather than as a restoration. "Unfortunately," he suggests, "along with the sharpness we are given the crudely intrusive anagrams that make the satire . . . needlessly specific."[38]

But if it was Swift's *intention* all along to make specific allusions to the politics of the 1720s, then it simply won't do to complain that his satire is "needlessly specific." Such an objection is a perfectly proper criticism of *Gulliver's Travels,* of course, but there is the accompanying danger that, in refusing to acknowledge what Swift was doing, Lock may be distorting his meaning. Swift claimed that the sting had been removed from parts of *Gulliver's Travels.* If that were indeed the case, then, presumably, Motte had changed the political significance of his book. We can take such allegations *cum grano salis* if we wish, and present subsequent substantive alterations as revisions. But let us be aware of what we are doing: in reasoning in this way, we are making assumptions about Swift's intentions. Lock's contention that *Gulliver* "was not even primarily intended as a critique of the Whig government then in power"[39] is as much of an assumption as Firth's assertion that allusions to the events of the reigns of Queen Anne and George I "abound in the *Travels*" or Case's insistence on a sustained allegorical interpretation of Gulliver's experiences in Lilliput. The problem merits another look.

IV

Swift claimed that the text of *Gulliver's Travels* was cut because it "may be thought in one or two places to be a little Satyrical."[40] It is worth stressing that Swift's complaints related primarily to Parts III and IV, not to "A Voyage to Lilliput," which is where Firth and Case locate the book's major political significance. Soon after its publication, contemporaries were scrutinizing it not merely for "the Satire on general societies of men" but for "particular reflections." *A Key, Being Observations and Explanatory Notes, upon the Travels of Lemuel Gulliver* considered Part I in November 1726. It pointed out straightaway "that, under the Allegory of a Voyager, Mr. Gulliver gives us an admirable System of modern Politicks."[41] Note that the author of the *Key* (most probably Edmund Curll) is quite specific: the allusions in *Gulliver's Travels* are to *modern* politics, that is, to the politics of the early eighteenth century. Unlike Firth, however, the author makes no attempt at a systematic analysis of Gulliver's adventures in Lilliput. Usually, he contents himself with suggesting resemblances; thus the temple "*polluted some Years* ago *by an unnatural Murder,* bears so near a Resemblance to the *Banquetting-House* at *White-Hall,* before which Structure, King CHARLES I, was Beheaded," "the *Tramecksans,* and the *Slamecksans,* exactly resemble our *Whigs* and *Tories,*" and "the Severities threatned against poor *Lemuel,* some here have resembled to the late Earl of *O—d*'s Sufferings."[42]

It might prove worthwhile to look at these three alleged resemblances once more, because they could be taken as typical of the sort of parallels Swift has been accused of drawing in *Gulliver's Travels.* Ever since the *Key* attempted to "mythologize" the temple in which Gulliver was housed, critics have been prepared to consider the possibility that, for some reason, it was meant to stand for an actual edifice. It is hard to see why such an assumption should be made. There has been no suggestion hitherto in the narrative that features of the Lilliputian landscape should be taken as

allusions to contemporary England. Why, therefore, should we assume that the reference to the temple requires "deciphering"? Where, indeed, are the allegorical pointers in Gulliver's description of the "ancient Temple"? "From the earliest commentaries it has been suggested that this refers to Westminster Hall in which Charles I had been condemned to death, but the real explanation may be," John Chalker sensibly notes, "that Swift had to justify the existence of an empty building large enough to contain Gulliver."[43] As none of the suggestions put forward as a counterpart actually corresponds in any important detail to the description of "an ancient Temple, esteemed to be the largest in the whole Kingdom" (p. 27), narrative exigency rather than allegorical meaning seems a much sounder reason for Swift's reference to "an unnatural Murder."

Instead of proceeding on the assumption that features such as the temple are meant to suggest actual places in contemporary Europe, we should surely ask ourselves two questions. What is there *in the text* to indicate that such an allusion is being made? And what would be the point of the allusion? The author of the *Key* goes about his business in precisely the wrong way when he admits: "I must freely own I cannot find any other Pile in this Kingdom more *à propos* to Mr. *Gulliver*'s Allusion."[44] If he finds it difficult to identify what Swift is allegedly alluding to, then what put it into his head to suspect an allusion in the first place? His casual remark has influenced readers of *Gulliver's Travels* from 1726 to the present day. Had Swift *wished* to suggest the execution of Charles I, why did he mislead by housing Gulliver in a temple and not some more appropriate Lilliputian public building? Nor, seeing the alleged parallel is never developed, is it at all clear why Swift should wish to allude to Charles I's martyrdom in this way.

As far as the Tramecksan and the Slamecksan are concerned, there are no such difficulties. Gulliver reports Reldresal's description of Lilliputian party politics:

> You are to understand, that for above seventy Moons past, there have been two struggling Parties in this Empire, under the Names of *Tramecksan,* and *Slamecksan,* from the high and low Heels on their Shoes, by which they distinguish themselves.

> It is alledged indeed, that the High Heels are most agreeable to our ancient Constitution: But however this be, his Majesty hath determined to make use of only low Heels in the Administration of the Government, and all Offices in the Gift of the Crown; as you cannot but observe; and particularly, that his Majesty's Imperial Heels are lower at least by a *Drurr* than any of his Court. . . . We compute the *Tramecksan,* or High-Heels, to exceed us in Number; but the Power is wholly on our Side. We apprehend his Imperial Highness, the Heir to the Crown, to have some Tendency towards the High-

Heels; at least we can plainly discover one of his Heels higher than the other . . . (p. 48).

In this passage there are not only clear pointers alerting us to a possible parallel between Lilliputian politics and British politics, there are also good reasons why Swift should wish to allude to the state of the nation in this way. In the early eighteenth century, there were indeed "two parties" in the nation. Alternative names for Tories and Whigs were the High Church and the Low Church parties. The preservation of the constitution in Church and State was a fundamental tenet of Tory dogma, yet the government of George I was dominated by Whigs. Despite being nominal head of the Church of England, George I was not an Anglican, and therefore most decidedly not a High Churchman. The Tories were generally thought to comprise the majority of Englishmen. And finally the Prince of Wales, the future George II, was thought in 1726 to favor the Tories to a certain extent.

The author of the *Key* was not the only contemporary to think that "the *Tramecksans,* and the *Slamecksans,* exactly resemble our Whigs and Tories." It did not require much perspicacity to make the connection, which was even being noted in Court circles. Mrs. Howard wrote to Swift in November 1726 to tell him that the Princess of Wales "thinks you can not in Co\d?\mon Deciency appear in heels."[45] Quite clearly, the allusion had been understood. In this instance, we have not only a *general* reflection on political parties, which is at once universal as well as specific, but *particular* reflections on George I and his son, the Prince of Wales. Doubtless, as far as the high heels and the low heels are concerned, I am stating the obvious, but it is worth spelling out that they serve as a perfect example of the way in which *Gulliver's Travels* comments specifically on the politics of early eighteenth-century Britain.

Yet there are problems even here. Presumably, for the comments on the state of political parties to be appropriate, let alone the references to George I and the Prince of Wales, we are to take it that Swift is alluding to the Britain of 1726, even though Gulliver's sojourn in Lilliput and Blefuscu is from 5 November 1699 to 24 September 1701.[46] The dating causes difficulties. Reldresal says that "for above seventy Moons past, there have been two struggling Parties." "If one proceeds, as one surely must, on the assumption that the Voyage to Lilliput is a political allegory in which the events ending the War of the Spanish Succession are adumbrated, Gulliver's fire-extinguishing action stands for the Treaty of Utrecht, signed in April 1713," Vienken and Real contend (following Case). "Counting backwards seventy moons from 1713 lands one in the midst of the bitter party strife of 1707."[47] Once again, we are making assumptions. Why should we set Reldresal's conversation with Gulliver in 1713 when, according to Gulliver, it actually took place some years earlier? Even if we suspect allegorical camouflage, why should we assume that Reldresal's figures are precise? After all, "above seventy Moons past" is scarcely specific.[48] And why, if we believe Swift is using an accurate time-scale, should he wish to locate the origins of political parties in 1707, when the Whigs and Tories had emerged almost thirty years earlier? Finally, how does all this square with the idea that, in the figure of the Emperor of Lilliput, Swift is alluding to George I? 1699-1701 or 1713? Both? Or neither?

The Emperor of Lilliput is "a renowned Patron of Learning" (p. 26) and "an excellent Horseman," "strong and masculine, with an *Austrian* Lip, and arched Nose, his Complexion olive." He is "twenty-eight Years and three Quarters old, of which he had reigned about seven, in great Felicity, and generally victorious" (p. 30). Gulliver refers to him as "a most magnanimous Prince" (p. 36). Now Swift was not in the habit of praising the king, and this does not immediately strike one as a description of George I, who was 66 when *Gulliver's Travels* appeared. No amount of juggling with Swift's figures can make the Emperor of Lilliput's age correspond meaningfully with George I's (nor, indeed, with the age of any of the other candidates that have been put forward as the Emperor's original).[49] It is of course possible to fall back on that old device of the political satirist, irony. As Swift advised in his **"Directions for a Birthday Song:"**

> Thus your Encomiums, to be strong,
> Must be apply'd directly wrong:
> A Tyrant for his Mercy praise,
> And crown a Royal Dunce with Bays:
> A squinting Monkey load with charms;
> And paint a Coward fierce in arms.
> Is he to Avarice inclin'd?
> Extol him for his generous mind. . . . [50]

It is for this reason that Case suggests that "the Emperor was described as being almost the exact antithesis of George [I]."[51]

By 1729, when Swift wrote his "Directions," the Scriblerians had made it their practice, in their onslaught on the Hanoverian Court, to "descant/On Virtues which they know they want."[52] Although Reldresal's description of the state of the parties in Lilliput does not seem appropriate either to the years around 1700 or to those around 1713, it corresponds quite strikingly with the situation in 1726. If the passage I have quoted is meant to allude to contemporary politics, surely the most obvious place to look for its significance is the era in which *Gulliver's Travels* was actually published. To proceed otherwise seems perverse. Unfortunately, when Firth looked at Part I, he wrongly believed it had been written from 1714 onwards, rather than in the early 1720s; therefore he looked for allusions to the earlier period, and, in elaborating his sustained political allegory, Case seems to have followed suit.

Real and Vienken, on the other hand, would appear to want it both ways: in their view, although "'Gulliver in Lilliput' is a satirical vivisection" of the politics of the years "between approximately 1708 and 1715,"[53] they nevertheless refer to "His Imperial Majesty, the Emperor of Lilliput, alias thick, awkward, ungainly George I,"[54] even though, as F.P.Lock has pointed out, such an interpretation "hopelessly conflates the reigns of Anne and George, making Anne (the Empress) George's wife"![55] This would seem to be a crucial consideration: can "Gulliver in Lilliput" be both a sustained allegory of "the joint political fortunes of Oxford and Bolingbroke during the latter half of Queen Anne's reign," as Case and Real and Vienken contend, and, at the same time, a satire of George I?[56] For all this to work, *Gulliver's Travels* would need a double, nay, a *treble* time scheme: in addition to the dates Gulliver supplies for his travels, and the actual date of publication, 1726, we would need, at least in the Lilliputian sequences, a further timescale.

This brings us to the third of the *Key*'s "resemblances":

> The Severities threatned against poor Lemuel, some here have resembled to the late Earl of *O—d*'s Sufferings, and if you will allow any Parallel, then,
>
> *Skyris Bolgolam* High Admiral.
>
> *Flimnap* the High Treasurer.
>
> *Limtoc* the General.
>
> *Lalcon* the Chamberlain.
>
> *Balmuff* the grand Justiciary, and the *Articles* of *Impeachment* by them exhibited, need no other Key than the Posts assigned them.[57]

Quite clearly, in their search for political allusions in *Gulliver's Travels,* contemporaries were prepared to look back to the events of the previous decade. But was that Swift's intention or merely another assumption? The author of the *Key* is much more tentative than Gulliver's twentieth-century commentators: "some here have resembled" virtually denies responsibility for drawing such a parallel.

The terminology he employs is interesting: Gulliver's experience is not described as an allegorical representation of Oxford's impeachment, simply as a possible parallel case. In other words, depending on one's politics, one could, if one was so disposed, see a similarity between Lilliputian ingratitude towards Gulliver and the disgraceful treatment meted out to the man who

had successfully ended the War of the Spanish Succession. For this allusion to work, there is no need for an extended political allegory, no subtle representation of the impeachment of either Oxford or Bolingbroke or both: Swift has simply supplied an analogy to their predicament in 1715. If "you will allow any Parallel, then" the quaintly-named Lilliputian ministers refer to their actual counterparts in 1715. "As to *Limtoc* the General," the author of the *Key* continues, "I heard all his History at *Marlborough* in *Wiltshire.*"

The three last-named Lilliputian ministers—Limtoc, Lalcon, Balmuff—are mentioned on this occasion only. However, the histories of Skyresh Bolgolam, the High Admiral, "a Person well versed in Affairs, but of a morose and sour Complection . . . [who] was pleased, without any Provocation, to be [Gulliver's] mortal Enemy" (p. 42), and Flimnap, the High Treasurer, who could "cut a Caper on the strait Rope, at least an Inch higher than any other Lord in the whole Empire" (p. 38), were developed by Swift at greater length. To what end? The opportunity for political characterization has been too great for ingenious twentieth-century commentators to pass up. Given that Firth suspected that in *Gulliver's Travels* "many figures which seem to be imaginary are meant to depict real personages, or at all events are drawn from them," it is hardly surprising that he tried to identify the counterparts of Skyresh Bolgolam and Flimnap.

According to the *Key,* all that is necessary to interpret the allusion to Skyresh Bolgolam is the reference to his position in the government. He was High Admiral; therefore Swift must be alluding to his British equivalent in 1715, the First Lord of the Admiralty, Edward Russell, Earl of Orford. That was too simple for Firth. He felt Bolgolam was "clearly intended to represent the Earl of Nottingham. The 'morose and sour complexion' attributed to Bolgolam at once suggests the identification."[58] Case also plumps for Nottingham, though for different reasons.[59] But if Swift wished to suggest Nottingham, then why assign the post of High Admiral to him, when, under George I, Nottingham was Lord President of the Council? Once again, one wonders whether narrative exigency rather than political characterization is at the bottom of Swift's description of Skyresh Bolgolam as "morose," rather than an obscure attempt to allude to Nottingham. If Swift wished to allude to Nottingham, why, in describing Bolgolam, did he call him "morose" instead of clinching the point by making use of Nottingham's nickname of "Dismal"? And why did Swift not make Bolgolam chief amongst the Emperor of Lilliput's councillors, rather than High Admiral?

Flimnap also "had always been [Gulliver's] secret Enemy, although he outwardly caressed [him] more than was usual to the Moroseness of his Nature" (p. 64). Once again, Swift draws attention to a Lillirutian's "Moroseness," and if "no other *Key*" is necessary "than the Posts assigned" the Lilliputians, then Flimnap must be identified as Charles Montagu, Earl of Halifax, First Lord of the Treasury in 1715. Yet, as Firth pointed out, Flimnap "was obviously designed to represent Walpole, as all commentators agree."[60] Even the author of the key made the identification, when he ended his account of the rope-dancing thus: "With how much Glee will a T[ownshen]d, or a W[al]p[ol]e read this Pygmaean Account of *Flimnap* and *Reldresal*."[61] What are we to make of it all? Walpole was not Lord Treasurer in 1715: he wasn't even a treasury commissioner! If Gulliver's impeachment is meant to be part of a consistent allegorical representation of the experiences of either Oxford or Bolingbroke or both, then there are serious difficulties over the characters of Skyresh Bolgolam and Flimnap.

When he put forward his thesis, Case admitted that "the burden of proof lies on the shoulders of anyone who argues that the political allegory is consistent," yet he concluded his discussion of "A Voyage to Lilliput" by asserting that the "strongest arguments in favor" of his interpretation were "its consistency and the exactness with which it follows the chronology of the events which it symbolizes."[62] Case's claims have been strongly disputed.[63] Why must we assume that "Gulliver in Lilliput" refers consistently to the latter half of the reign of Queen Anne, when the evidence points in a different direction? If Swift is somehow getting at George I when he describes the conduct of the Emperor of Lilliput, then two basic conclusions can be drawn: first, the Lilliputian characters are not really "drawn from" real personages, even if they are meant to call them to mind; and second, Swift's method of alluding to contemporary politics is not consistent. Once these reservations are conceded, things begin to slot into place. Despite the vast dissimilarities between the Emperor of Lilliput (as described by Gulliver) and George I, the odd detail is supplied to assist the contemporary reader to make the comparison.[64] In the same way, although Walpole was not Lord Treasurer in 1715, most references to Flimnap are meant to satirize Walpole.

After all, this is the basic technique used by the Scriblerians when they made their "particular reflections." When the government prevented *Polly*, the sequel to *The Beggar's Opera*, from being staged, Gay printed it. In a preface, he denied that his play was "fill'd with slander and calumny against particular great persons," much less that "Majesty it-self is endeavour'd to be brought into ridicule and contempt."[65] Notice once again the insistence that this "general" satire of British society is free of "particular reflections." "*Polly*, as it was eventually published," John Fuller suggests, "appears to be no more, indeed perhaps rather less, slanted against Walpole than" *The Beggar's Opera*.[66] However, in drawing attention to the alleged political sig-

nificance of his play in his preface, Gay supervised the way in which it would be read by contemporaries. Whether or not they would otherwise have looked for "slander and calumny against particular great persons" or the "ridicule and contempt" of majesty, in the person of George II, Gay's denial alerted them to the possibility. And of course, in *Polly*, not only are there a number of implicit criticisms of Walpole as the "Great Man," George II's conduct is compared with that of Pohetohee.[67]

Our reading of **Gulliver's Travels** is not supervised in quite this way, but Gay had learned the technique of drawing parallels between actual persons and their fictional counterparts from Swift. The Emperor of Lilliput is not George I in any simple way: he is not, in Firth's terms, "meant to depict" the King of England, nor is he drawn from him. But Swift forces us to compare the two. His method is one of analogy: reasoning from parallel cases. There is no need for him to present a consistent allegory to score his political point. The Scriblerian technique of commenting on topical politics is not a complex one: it consists merely of implying criticism by drawing parallels between the existing situation and what might otherwise obtain. Swift makes this clear in the concluding chapter to **Gulliver,** when he asks us to compare the way the Houyhnhnms run their country with what tends to happen at home: "For, who can read of the Virtues I have mentioned in the glorious *Houyhnhnms,* without being ashamed of his own Vices, when he considers himself as the reasoning, governing Animal of his Country?" (p. 292).

The similarities or "resemblances" that exist between the Tories and Whigs and the High-heels and Low-heels are obvious. The same method can be seen at work when Gulliver describes the dispute between the Bigendians and the Little-endians. I prefer to call what Swift is doing "parallel history" rather than "allegory."[68] The technique is not vastly different from the polemical strategy Swift adopted in his first political work, **A Discourse of the Contests and Dissentions between the Nobles and the Commons in Athens and Rome.**[69] A clear example of this occurs in Part III when Gulliver, in Glubbdubdrib, compares "some *English* Yeomen of the old Stamp" with their grandchildren, to the detriment of the latter (p. 201). This incident might be said to epitomize his method: just as in conclusion he asks you to compare humans with Houyhnhnms as governing animals, so in Glubbdubdrib he holds up two examples for comparison.

In comparing "*English* Yeomen of the old Stamp" with their degenerate successors, Swift is implicitly condemning the Britain of the 1720s. In **Gulliver's Travels,** he is concerned not so much with re-fighting the battles of the previous reign as attacking the system of Walpole. After all, that is the actual historical context of the book: he brought the manuscript to England in

1726 on a visit which was undertaken at least partly in order to confront Walpole personally with what Swift felt to be the deleterious consequences of his administration's policies. The political significance of *Gulliver's Travels,* in Firth's terms,[70] can, I think, be summed up readily enough: Swift comments in a number of ways on the state of the nation in 1726, satirizing the monarchy and the government of Walpole. From time to time he also alludes to the events of earlier years, such as the Atterbury affair of 1722. He even draws parallels with the divisions in religion and politics which by 1726 had been part of English life for so many years. If he alludes to contemporary figures, such allusions assume no more than local allegorical significance: the evidence for a sustained political allegory is strained and raises more questions than it attempts to solve. Many of those "puzzlingly particular annotations" which students find, to their undoubted surprise, in the notes to the various texts of *Gulliver* can be discounted. Swift's allusions to topical politics are rarely that obtrusive: because of the "general" character of much of the satire in *Gulliver's Travels,* it is more profitable, in the later twentieth century, to apply them generally as well.

Notes

[1] C. H. Firth, "The Political Significance of *Gulliver's Travels,*" *Proceedings of the British Academy* (1919-1920), 237-59.

[2] *Times Literary Supplement,* 2 May 1980, p. 494.

[3] Davies, Preface to C. H. Firth, *Essays Historical and Literary* (Oxford, 1938), p. v, emphasis added.

[4] Arthur E. Case, *Four Essays on* Gulliver's Travels (Princeton, 1945), pp. 69-96; *TLS,* 2 May 1980, p. 494.

[5] *Review of English Studies,* 23 (1947), 368.

[6] Edward Rosenheim, Jr., "Swift and the Atterbury Case," in *The Augustan Milieu: Essays Presented to Louis A. Landa,* ed. H. K. Miller, Eric Rothestein, and G. S. Rousseau (Oxford, 1970), p. 194.

[7] See, for example, *Discussions of Jonathan Swift,* ed. John Traugott (Boston, 1962), pp. 105-20; *Jonathan Swift: A Critical Anthology,* ed. Denis Donoghue (Harmondsworth, Mddx., 1971), pp. 317-42.

[8] Hermann J. Real and Heinz J. Vienken, "The Structure of *Gulliver's Travels,*" *Proceedings of the First Münster Symposium on Jonathan Swift,* ed. Hermann J. Real and Heinz J. Vienken (Munich, 1985), p. 203.

[9] Phillip Harth, "The Problem of Political Allegory in *Gulliver's Travels,*" *Modern Philology,* 73 (1976), S40-47.

[10] *The Year's Work in English Studies,* 57 (1976), 223.

[11] J. A. Downie, "Political Characterization in *Gulliver's Travels,*" *Yearbook of English Studies,* 7 (1977), 108-20.

[12] Downie, "Political Characterization," pp. 118-20.

[13] F. P. Lock, *The Politics of* Gulliver's Travels (Oxford, 1980), p. 3.

[14] For instance, Lock refused to consider the question of the "Armagh" *Gulliver,* which is treated magisterially by David Woolley in "Swift's Copy of *Gulliver's Travels:* The Armagh *Gulliver,* Hyde's Edition, and Swift's Earliest Corrections," in *The Art of Jonathan Swift,* ed. Clive T. Probyn (London, 1978), pp. 131-78. "The complexity of the evidence and arguments involved precludes my indicating in detail why I disagree with Woolley's conclusions," Lock claimed, "particularly since they affect my own only indirectly" (p. 75 n). This was a strange assertion to make, seeing that Lock was arguing that the first edition of Swift's book accurately represented his intentions. He returned to the subject in "The Text of *Gulliver's Travels,*" *Modern Language Review,* 76 (1981), 513-33. For a critique of this article, see the *Scriblerian,* 15 (1982-83), 19.

I shall deal with Lock's re-interpretations in the body of my essay.

[15] Lock, *Politics,* p. 3.

[16] Lock, *Politics,* p. 70.

[17] *The Correspondence of Jonathan Swift,* ed. Harold Williams, rev. David Woolley, 5 vols. (Oxford, 1963-72), III, 152-55; hereafter cited as *Corresp.*

[18] *Corresp.,* III, 181.

[19] Lock, *Politics,* p. 70.

[20] *Corresp.,* III, 181.

[21] *Corresp.,* III, 182-23.

[22] *Gulliveriana VI: Critiques of "Gulliver's Travels" and Allusions Thereto: Book One,* intro. Jeanne K. Welcher and George E. Bush, Jr. (Delmar, NY, 1976), p. xiii.

[23] *Corresp.,* III, 189.

[24] *Corresp.,* III, 102.

[25] *Corresp.*, III, 190.

[26] *Corresp.*, III, 182.

[27] *Corresp.*, III, 194-95; cf. Woolley, pp. 161-65.

[28] Woolley, p. 144.

[29] *Corresp.*, IV, 197-98.

[30] Victoria and Albert Museum, Forster Collection, no. 8551.

[31] Lock, *Politics*, p. 78.

[32] Michael Treadwell, "Benjamin Motte, Andrew Tooke and *Gulliver's Travels*," *Proceedings of the First Münster Symposium*, pp. 288-89.

[33] *Corresp.*, III, 189.

[34] *Corresp.*, IV, 211-12.

[35] *Gulliver's Travels*, in [*The Prose Writings of Jonathan Swift*], ed. Herbert Davis et al., XI (rev. ed., 1959; Oxford, 1965), 191. Subsequent references are to this edition, and page numbers are supplied in the body of the text within parentheses.

[36] See Rosenheim, pp. 174-204; cf. Lock, *Politics*, p. 81.

[37] Woolley, p. 164.

[38] Lock, *Politics*, pp. 81-82. More recently, Brean S. Hammond has drawn attention to the same passage to argue that "at least one episode in *Gulliver's Travels* . . . does meet the most rigid conditions demanded by Lock" in order for the claim that political allegory is at work to be valid. Hammond, however, fails to take into account the discrepancy between Motte's edition and Faulkner's edition. See the *Clark Newsletter*, 12 (1987), 2-4.

[39] Lock, *Politics*, p. 2.

[40] *Corresp.*, III, 153.

[41] *A Key, Being Observations and Explanatory Notes, upon the Travels of Lemuel Gulliver. By Signor Corolini, a Noble Venetian Now Residing in London. In a Letter to Dean Swift. Translated from the Italian Original* (London, 1726), p. 5.

[42] *A Key*, pp. 7, 19-20, 26.

[43] Jonathan Swift, *Gulliver's Travels*, ed. Peter Dixon and John Chalker, intro. Michael Foot (Harmondsworth, Mddx., 1967), p. 349.

[44] *A Key*, p. 8.

[45] *Corresp.*, III, 185.

[46] There is confusion over the dating of Gulliver's sojourn in Lilliput. According to his own account, he left Bristol on 4 May 1699, was shipwrecked on 5 November, set sail from Blefuscu on 24 September 1701, and arrived in the Downs on 13 April 1702 (pp. 20, 78-79). Yet he refers to "a Residence of nine Months and thirteen Days" in Lilliput (p. 63). Clearly, there is a discrepancy here, which is perhaps explicable by Gulliver's letter to Sympson: "Your Printer hath been so careless as to confound the Times, and mistake the Dates of my several Voyages and Returns; neither assigning the true Year, or the true Month, or Day of the Month" (p. 7). However, Case (p. 64) suggests that Gulliver arrived in Lilliput on 5 November 1700 (not 1699), although there is nothing in the text to suggest what happened between 4 May 1699 and 5 November 1700. One thing *is* clear: in the light of this initial discrepancy, it would appear to be unwise to construct elaborate allegories using the dates supplied by Gulliver.

[47] Heinz J. Vienken and Hermann J. Real, "*Ex Libris J. S.*: Annotating Swift," *Proceedings of the First Münster Symposium*, p. 316.

[48] It is also ambiguous. Vienken and Real assume that Swift is referring to "a 'moon', or lunar year . . . a period of thirty days" (p. 316), yet one can take the alternative view that, regardless of the "exotic" usage, a "moon" is meant to represent a calendar year. Lilliputian histories go back "six Thousand Moons": is this meant to suggest a period of less than 500 years (if a "moon" is thirty days) or 6,000 years—often cited as the traditional age of the earth? Whichever conclusion we choose to draw, one more thing is clear: unless we can be certain that Swift is talking about lunar years, it would appear to be unwise to "proceed . . . on the assumption" that we are to count backwards from April 1713 for "above seventy" periods of thirty days.

[49] On account of his *"arched Nose,"* William III was first suggested as the original of the Emperor (*A Key*, pp. 8-9). Lock plumps for Louis XIV (*Politics*, p. 116).

[50] *The Poems of Jonathan Swift*, ed. Harold Williams, 2nd ed., 3 vols. (Oxford, 1958), II, 464; hereafter cited as *Poems*.

[51] Case, p. 71.

[52] *Poems*, p. 391.

[53] Real and Vienken, "Structure," p. 203.

[54] Vienken and Real, "*Ex Libris* J. S.," p. 313.

[55] Lock, *Politics,* p. 107.

[56] Case, p. 70.

[57] *A Key,* p. 26.

[58] Firth, p. 242.

[59] Case, p. 72.

[60] Firth, p. 244.

[61] *A Key,* p. 13.

[62] Case, pp. 70, 79.

[63] Downie, "Political Characterization," pp. 109-15; Lock, *Politics,* pp. 106 ff.

[64] Vienken and Real, "*Ex Libris* J. S.," p. 313.

[65] John Gay, *Dramatic Works,* ed. John Fuller, 2 vols. (Oxford, 1983), II, 70.

[66] Gay, I, 53.

[67] On this point, see J. A. Downie, "Gay's Politics," *John Gay and the Scriblerians,* ed. Nigel Wood, forthcoming.

[68] The terminology is important only insofar as it relates to the political significance of *Gulliver's Travels.* The word *allegory* derives from the Greek, and means "speaking otherwise than one seems to speak" (*allos,* other; *-agoria,* speaking). In that many episodes in *Gulliver's Travels* are extended metaphors carrying one or more sets of meanings *in addition* to the apparent and literal ones, in this sense they are perforce allegorical. In *Gulliver's Travels,* as I have argued, Swift alludes to topical politics in a number of ways. However, as there is no extended, particularized political allegory, such allusions are not sufficiently developed to assume more than local allegorical significance. In one sense, therefore, it might be misleading to use the term *allegory.* Hence my preference for the more precise *parallel history,* a phrase which Swift's contemporaries would undoubtedly have comprehended. See, for example, the *London Magazine*'s résumé of an essay appearing in the *Free Briton* no. 124 (13 April 1732): "THE *Craftsman* has lately had Recourse to his ancient Method of defaming by *Parallel History* . . . wherein, as of old in the Tyrant's Bed, all Characters are rack'd and tortur'd, to make them agree to his political Standard." In its own précis of the same article, the *Gentleman's Magazine* also refers to "*Parallel History*" as the *Craftsman*'s "ancient Method."

It is hardly worth pointing out that the early *Craftsman* was largely responsible for drawing attention to the possible political significance of *Gulliver's Travels.*

[69] J. A. Downie, "Swift's *Discourse:* Allegorical Satire or Parallel History?" *Swift Studies,* 2 (1987), 25-32.

[70] In this essay, I have restricted myself to consideration of the political significance of *Gulliver's Travels* in the sense intended by Sir Charles Firth, who was not concerned with the distinction made by hermeneuticians between *Sinn* and *Bedeutung*—terms that have been Englished by E. D. Hirsch, Jr., as "meaning" and "significance" (see *Validity in Interpretation* [New Haven, 1967], pp. 211-12). In that Firth was concerned with Swift's intentions in *Gulliver's Travels,* what he was actually considering was the work's *Sinn* or meaning, and not, in Hirsch's terms, its *Bedeutung* or significance.

It could be argued that any discussion of the political significance of *Gulliver's Travels* should take into account its meaning to us today, either instead of or as well as its meaning to Swift's contemporaries. Perhaps this is what F. P. Lock is primarily concerned with when he writes that "*Gulliver's Travels* remains surprisingly relevant to the politics of the twentieth century" (*Politics,* p. 35).

J. Paul Hunter (essay date 1990)

SOURCE: "*Gulliver's Travels* and the Novel," in *The Genres of "Gulliver's Travels,"* edited by Frederik N. Smith, University of Delaware Press, 1990, pp. 56-74.

[*In the following essay, Hunter discusses the significance of* Gulliver's Travels *as a cutting-edge transitional text that uses satire to parody the subjective, first-person narrative, thus anticipating the rise of the novel as a narrative form.*]

Gulliver's Travels is not a novel in any meaningful sense of that slippery term that I know, yet its generic status would be difficult to establish without having the novel in mind. Swift's masterpiece is, in fact, so conceptually dependent upon the novel that it is almost impossible to imagine the existence of the *Travels* outside the context of the developing novelistic tradition. The relationship of *Gulliver's Travels* to the novel has been obscured, however, by two contextual matters, one historical, the other generic. The historical issue involves the fact that the *Travels* appears when the English novel had barely begun, and it is difficult for us to think of it as involved in the tradition. With only Defoe, among major English novelists, having yet tried the waters, with the issue of definition still two decades away from even being broached, and with the great craze for novel-reading and novel-writing also still well in the future, how can it be meaningful to think of there yet being a *tradition* of the novel even though there are some few discernible examples? Unless one regards the *Travels* as a kind of paradigm—positive or negative—for the tradition, how can one think of it as involved in a tradition-to-be? The second issue, although generic, does not involve the genre of the novel; rather it involves parody and the assumptions we make about its strategy of working from, imitating, and trying to tease or embarrass a particular writer or work. Because of the way we define parody, we do not usually think of Swift as a parodist, and I think we miss something about both Swift and the possibilities of parody by the standard definition. I shall, then, first try to suggest in what sense Swift is a parodist and show how some of his parody works; second, I shall try to suggest how his particular type of parody enables him to associate himself with the developing tradition of the novel; finally, and more briefly, I shall try to suggest how the *Travels* works as a kind of parodic answer to the early novel and as a satire of the novelistic consciousness.

The many faces of Jonathan Swift often remind us of his contemporaries, and there is seldom a moment in his best satires when he is not helping some fool or knave to stand forth and profess a muddled—but nevertheless distinctive and definable—set of values and opinions. Snoop that he is, Swift spends a lot of time in other people's consciousnesses, trying to organize in some memorable way what he finds there. Whether as tale-teller or voyager, modest economist or befuddled Christian apologist, panegyricist of the world and the number three or putative satirist disappointed that all human folly has not been extirpated in six months, Swift is ever the impersonator, borrowing his voice from someone else. We recognize his antagonists clearly—clearly, that is, until we try to be specific, and then we often discover how very little we know about whom he has personated. About some few, everyone can agree: in *A Tale of a Tub,* William Wotton, Richard Bentley, John Dryden, and Sir Roger L'Estrange, for example, or in *Meditation upon a Broomstick,* Robert Boyle. But agreement is possible only because Swift himself names the originals. How good, then, is Swift as a parodist, or (to put the issue more aptly for my argument) is he the kind of parodist through whom one hears the voice of the original: I wish to examine Swift's strategy of personation in a very simplified form, hoping to sort out how his attention to particular writers blends into a broader concern for style and the implication of style. Two of Swift's short minor works offer interesting test cases of Swift's skill and method, for they are "pure" examples of Swift as a parodist in the sense that both the works—*The Last Speech and Dying Words of Ebenezor Elliston* and *A Meditation upon a Broomstick*—pretend to be real works by a real person.

In *The Last Speech and Dying Words,* Swift alludes to a popular subgenre of an important paraliterary form, the "dying confessional" of a criminal about to be executed. Such confessionals, obviously prepared well in advance of the occasion by prison ordinaries, hacks, and booksellers, were hawked about at the execution itself, and their conventional pieties, tearful abjuration of past crimes, and invocation of God's mercy evidently ministered to the audience's need to feel the public usefulness of the occasion. Swift cuts through the easy pieties and has Elliston forego repentance and dispense with the usual rhetoric. Instead, he substitutes a vivid account of knaves driven by baser motives than poverty or ill luck:

> If any Thing in this World be like Hell . . . the truest Picture of it must be in the Back-Room of one of our Alehouses at Midnight; where a Crew of Robbers and their Whores are met together after a Booty, and are beginning to grow drunk; from which Time, until they are past their Senses, is such a continued horrible Noise of Cursing, Blasphemy, Lewdness, Scurrility, and brutish Behaviour; such Roaring and Confusion, such a Clatter of Mugs and Pots at each other's Heads; that *Bedlam,* in Comparison, is a sober and orderly Place: At last they all tumble from their Stools and Benches, . . . and generally the Landlord or his Wife, or some other Whore . . . , picks their Pockets before they wake.[1]

And Swift's Elliston offers a particular incentive to reform, one very different from the high-minded hopes in the usual confessionals.

> Now, as I am a dying Man, something I have done which may be of good Use to the Publick. I have left with an honest Man (and indeed the only honest Man I was ever acquainted with) the Names of all my wicked Brethren, the present Places of their Abode, with a short Account of the chief Crimes they have committed; in many of which I have been their Accomplice, and heard the rest from their own Mouths: I have likewise set down the Names of those we call our Setters, of the wicked Houses we frequent, and of those who receive and buy our stolen Goods. I have solemnly charged this honest Man . . . that whenever he hears of any Rogue to be tryed for robbing, or House-breaking, he will look into his List, and if he finds the Name there of the Thief concerned, to send the whole Paper to the Government. Of this I here give my Companions fair and publick Warning, and hope they will take it. (p. 39)

Prince Posterity has luckily preserved for us the "authentic" last words of Ebenezor Elliston, which, of course, are utterly conventional and predictable. Elliston repents his life of crime, claims he was framed in the fatal instance, and hopes others will learn from his bad example. At least one critic has suggested that

Swift's style is "an almost perfect parody" of Elliston's own.[2] But I find no stylistic resemblance whatever. Unlike the hard, clear syntax that Swift's Elliston uses to express his smug toughness, the real Elliston speaks like this:

> . . . the Roberies which I was concerned in from October 1719 to January 1720 were so many that I cannot give a true account of them all, but leave them aside, and come to acquaint you of my last misfortunes some small time before Christmas last for some reasons best known to my self, not for any Roberies that I committed, I left my House and Familly, and took a private Lodging, in which time there was a Roberey committed on the Gravel Walk on a Captain, which robbery, one Elizabeth Gorden I believe by the perswasions of a Man in power in this City went before the Lord-Mayor and as I am informed swore that I and two or three other Persons in my Company committed the said robbery, which I now declare that Neither they or I had any Hand whatsoever in it, for which Mr. H——s made it his Business to haunt Night and Day for me, and also informed several Persons, that there was Twenty Pounds Reward for any one who would Apprehend me, so that I might be brought to Justice, for which Several People as well as himself made it their Business to look for me, but God knows how Innocent I was at that Time of Committing any Manner of Robbery whatsoever, but to avoid Dangers, I made my Case known to several of my Friends, who advised me to leave this Town, whose advice I took, but Unfortunately I was concerned with another person in taking Counsellor Sweeny's Mare.[3]

It is not really surprising that Swift does not closely imitate Elliston's prose style, for his audience would not have known Ebenezor Elliston's style even if there had been one. We need not suppose he would even have cared to see this particular "real" confession; it was enough for his audience to know what kind of thing it was likely to be. *The Last Speech and Dying Words of Ebenezor Elliston* plainly is not an attack upon an individual person or an individual style but rather upon custom, a particular subspecies of literature that grew out of that custom, and a cheap and self-congratulatory morality that was both a cause and result of such "confessions." There must be some idea in the audience's mind of what the "last speech and dying words" tradition is like, but Elliston himself is irrelevant, ultimately, and so is his flaccid, rambling (and possibly genuine) prose.[4]

We might, on the other hand, expect a close verbal imitation in Swift's *Meditation upon a Broomstick,* for there he personates a writer whose style was distinctive and well known to his audience. Thomas Sheridan's anecdote about the occasion of Swift's *Meditation* is well known.[5] Swift, as a guest of Lord and Lady Berkeley in London, was often asked to attend Lady Berkeley's private devotions, and Lady Berkeley's excessive fondness for Boyle's meditations led her to ask Swift to read repeatedly from them. Swift's careful insertion of his own manuscript imitation in the volume, his solemn reading of it, Lady Berkeley's effusive praise of it first in private and then among company who knew Boyle's meditations well enough to know that there was no such meditation—knowledge of these carefully planned steps of the hoax may add to our appreciation of Swift's finely tuned absurdities:

> This single Stick, which you now behold ingloriously lying in that neglected Corner, I once knew in a flourishing State in a Forest: It was full of Sap, full of Leaves, and full of Boughs: But now, in vain does the busy Art of Man pretend to vye with Nature, by tying that withered Bundle of Twigs to its sapless Trunk: It is now at best but the Reverse of what it was; a Tree turned upside down, the Branches on the Earth, and the Root in the Air: It is now handled by every dirty Wench, condemned to do her Drugery; and by a capricious Kind of Fate, destined to make other things clean and be nasty it self.

> But a *Broom-stick,* perhaps you will say, is an *Emblem* of a Tree standing on its Head; and pray what is Man but a topsy-turvy Creature?[6]

The "parody" is brilliant, but it is hard to say exactly how it works because it is hard to say exactly what is parodied. A quick reading makes Swift's *Meditation* seem quite like Boyle, except for the distortion crucial to parody, but on detailed comparison the similarities become hard to find. No single Boyle meditation has ever been regarded as the model for Swift's parody, and for a very good reason. None of Boyle's meditations is much like Swift's version, either in subject matter or style. The first meditation in Boyle's 1665 volume is perhaps the closest to Swift:

> *Upon his manner of giving meat to his dog.*

> Ignorantly thankful creature, thou beggest in such a way, that by way would appear an antedated gratitude, if it were not a designless action, the manner of thy petitioning before-hand, rewards the grant of thy request; thy addresses and recompence being so made and ordered, that the meat I cast thee may very well feed religion in me. For, but observe this dog, I hold him out meat, and my inviting voice loudly encourages and invites him to take it: it is held indeed higher than he can leap; and yet, if he leap not at it, I do not give it him; but if he do. . . . [7]

But there is not much phraseological or syntactic similarity, and the argument is developed in a very different way. Boyle has favorite words and devices that distinguish him from other meditators (he likes the word "divers" so much, for example, that he once uses it four times in a single paragraph, and many of his meditations are actually dialogues), but Swift pays no attention to these distinctive and easy-to-parody strategies. It is as if he cared not at all for distinctive stylistic devices or even for obvious structural principles. What then makes it a parody of Boyle and not of someone else? The answer, I am afraid, is that one would have a very hard time proving that it *is* a parody of Boyle if it were not for a published subtitle that asserts such a parody and for the fact of Thomas Sheridan's anecdote.[8] If we were to put it beside the meditative effusions of, say John Flavell, we could just as easily think it parodied him. Here is a typical beginning of one of Flavell's meditations in *Husbandry Spiritualized, or The Heavenly Use of Earthly Things* (1669):

Upon the sight of a fair spreading Oak.

> What a lofty flourishing Tree is here? It seems rather to be a little Wood, than a single Tree; every limb thereof having the dimensions and branches of a Tree in it; and yet as great as it is, it was once but a little slip, which one might pull up with two fingers; this vast body was contained virtually, and potentially in a small Acorn. Well, then, I will never despise the day of small things, nor despair of arriving to an eminency of grace, though at present it be but as a bruised reed, and the things that are in me, be ready to dye. As things in nature, so the things of the Spirit, grow up to their fulness and perfection, by slow and insensible degrees. The famous and heroical acts of the most renowned believers, were such as themselves could not once perform, or it may be think they ever should. Great things both in nature and grace, come from small and contemptible beginnings.[9]

There is not much to choose between Boyle and Flavell as meditators, although each has individual stylistic features. That Swift chooses *not* to imitate individual stylistic features suggests that the specifics of style are not his consuming interest. A bright undergraduate with a modestly good ear could come much closer to Boyle than Swift does; unless we judge Swift a thoroughly incompetent personator, we must assume that his interests here lie beyond parody that is individual and personal.

But the objects of laughter in Swift's *Meditation* suggest a cogent and coherent satiric target that would explain Swift's parodic aims and at the same time answer the recurrent charges that it was at least uncharitable, if not downright impious, to attack a man of Boyle's righteousness in the first place. Four things call undue attention to themselves in Swift's version of meditation. First is the strained analogy set up between the broomstick and a human being, based on an inversion of the traditional topos comparing man to a tree. Second is the subtly self-congratulatory, egocentric, even solipsistic, manner in which the analogy is asserted:

> *When I beheld* this, *I sighed,* and said within myself *Surely Mortal Man is a Broomstick. . . .*

Third is the fact that the broomstick is a chance object for meditation. It is simply something at hand—"this broomstick in that neglected corner"—and seems to the speaker as good as any other as a possible object of meditation, rather like Donne's flea or Marvell's dewdrop, which also take their cue from the homiletic tradition of concrete *exempla:* "Mark but this flea . . ." and "This single stick. . . . " The fourth feature is what gives Swift's *Meditation* away as a parody rather than a failed serious effort. The object in question is not a natural object but a man-made one, and this distortion of a meditationist's procedure calls quick attention to the fact that the meditator was stretching the rules, as observed by the likes of Boyle and serious imitators like Flavell, for they had usually concentrated on human activities and observation of objects or patterns in the natural world. Boyle, for example, had meditated "Upon the Sight of some variously-coloured clouds," "Upon the sight of a fair milk-maid singing to her cow," and "Upon one's talking to an echo," and Flavell upon such inspired subjects as "Upon the Sudden Withering of a Rose" or "Upon the Pulling up of a Leek."

But Boyle and Flavell were stretching the rules too; they seriously distort the earlier meditative tradition. The tradition of Christian meditation had regularly devoted itself to biblical events, especially highlights in the life of Christ, or to set contemplations that produced a proper state of serene devotion in the meditator.[10] Meditations were not random, nor did they concentrate on trival objects or observations. The distortion of the new meditators was conscious as well as contrived. Boyle's explanatory perface and a long and tedious introduction to his meditations claim the invention of a new kind of exercise, which Boyle calls "Meleteticks":

> There is scarce any thing, that may not prove the subject of an occasional meditation; . . . natural propensity . . . unperceivably ingages us to pry into the several attributes and relations of the things we consider, to obtain the greater plenty of particulars, for the making up of the more full and compleat parallel betwixt the things whose resemblances we would set forth. By which means a man often comes to discover a multitude of particulars, even in obvious things, which . . . common beholders take no notice of.[11]

Boyle's meletetics is a distinctively "modern"—that is, eighteenth-century modern—version of meditation; its use of material meditative objects, its adaptation to the individual experiences of common men, its emphasis on the power of any individual to interpret adequately, its quiet allegiance to the methods and assumptions of empirical science, its assertion that great truths can be revealed through sense experience: these methods and attitudes and the assumptions that sponsor them seem more crucial to Swift's righteous ire than any particulars of style. Boyle's panegyric on modern writing and his ubiquitous progressivist assumptions might well have irritated or angered Swift, and certainly his confidence in human discovery and interpretative ability seem, when put beside Swift's beliefs, easy and radically optimistic. Here is a taste of Boyle's explanation of why he feels free to depart from classical decorum in language: rules-makers disagree with each other, he says, and

> I see no great reason to confine my self to the magisterial dictates of either ancient or scholastick, writers. For, living in this age, and in this part of the world, where we are not like to have those for readers that died before we were born, I see not why one may not judge of decorum by the examples and practices of those authors of our own times and countries. . . . [12]

Boyle's meletetics, widely influential and limitated, especially among dissenters, carry the every-man-his-own-priest idea to an extreme, and, like many other modern epistemologies and writings attacked by Swift, stressed the validity of individual experience as a means to eternal truth. Boyle and his followers democratized revelation to an incredible degree, turning the Book of Nature into a kind of cosmic book of associations with as many meanings as there are perceivers or even moods. That attitude was not likely to win Swift's approval. Swift does not mention Boyle in his letters (or at least in those that have survived) or elsewhere in his published works, except for a late marginal manuscript note in his copy of Burnet's *History of his own Time* in which he calls him a "a very silly writer."[13] However great a scientist, Boyle was a mannered writer, pedestrian theologian, and sometimes flatulent reasoner, and he had other characteristics likely to infuriate someone of Swift's sensibilities.

He had, for example, made much of his religious conversion at the age of fourteen, and he had repeatedly refused to take holy orders on the grounds that he had not had an inner call. Thus, although a faithful Anglican, Boyle in his personal life as well as in his writing acts more like Swift's dissenting contemporaries than like Swift the High Churchman, and Boyle's lifelong attempts to harmonize religion with empirical science, his fondness for scientific jargon, his scarcely disguised self-praise in *The Christian Virtuoso,* and his founding of the Boyle lectures on physico-theological subjects (Bentley was the first lecturer) all represent commitments that Swift regarded as at best misguided, at worst downright perverse.

We need not wonder, then, why Swift would feel free to attack "so great and pious a man as Mr. Boyle" (it is Sheridan's phrase) or whether his Broomstick hoax had any force of philosophical belief behind it.[14] In fact, the thrust of Swift's hoax aims far more broadly than at the single figure of Boyle. Rather than stylistic parody in the usual sense, *A Meditation upon a Broomstick* is generic or class parody—that is, parody of a kind of writing and the assumptions it is based on, and crucial to its working power is the recognition of the philosophical assumptions that underlie it rather than simple identification of the writer. In *A Tale of a Tub* Swift hints at his characteristic procedure:

> Some of those Passages in this Discourse, which appear most liable to Objection are what they call Parodies, where the Author personates the Style and Manner of other Writers, whom he has a mind to expose. I shall produce one Instance, it is in the 51st page. Dryden, L'Estrange, *and some others I shall not name, are here levelled at, who having spent their Lives in Faction, and Apostacies, and all manner of Vice, pretended to be Sufferers for Loyalty and Religion. So* Dryden *tells us in one of his Prefaces of his Merits and Suffering, thanks God that he possesses his Soul in Patience: In other Places he talks at the same Rate, and L'Estrange often uses the like Style, and I believe the Reader may find more Persons to give that Passage an Application.*[15]

Personating more than one writer at a time is at least as difficult as imitating the individual traits of a single writer, and this kind of class parody—personating writers who share a disagreeable trait of some sort—is rampant in Swift. This is one reason why parody in Swift is so hard to pin down and why so many critics, in despair of being precise, have turned to denial of parody instead. I agree with Edward W. Rosenheim's definition of satire as an attack upon "discernible historic particulars,"[16] but that definition is easy to pervert in studying Swift, for the particular may be a group of writers or a class of thinkers or a category of believers just as easily as an individual. To insist that Swift aims at a single writer in his personations is not only to deprive his prose of much of the larger force that he demonstrably exerts but also to make him more of a lampoonist than thinker. Artist and marksman that he was, Swift could hit several antagonists and their foibles with a single shot, and we need not blame him for our own "either/or" instances, which, if I am right about Swift's *Broomstick,* Swift refused to honor even when it would have been easiest. Swift can, of course, be very particular when he wants to be, and there are times when he singles out a particular knave or fool instead of providing a family portrait. What is surprising is how seldom this occurs as a matter of style, for even in many particularized passages the focus is still on generic or class parody; when, for example, Swift inserts in *Gulliver's Travels* almost verbatim passages in seaman's jargon from Sturmy's *Mariner's Magazine* or when his scientific language is taken directly from the *Transactions* of the Royal Society, his parodic object is the broad and mindless use of these jargons, not Sturmy or the *Transactions* as such.

What I am saying does not mean, of course, that Swift does not invite us to find individuals within the family portraits he concentrates on, and, just as in **Meditation upon a Broomstick** he allows us to think of Boyle while attacking what Boyle stands for, so in many other passages he invites us to think of particular authors that exemplify the qualities embodied in his generic parody. The *Tale of a Tub* passage that I have alluded to, for example, names Dryden and L'Estrange for us and then suggests that we ourselves can find additional examples: "I believe the Reader may find more Persons to give that Passage an Application." Sometimes he gives names that exemplify, and sometimes he provides other clues. We have, I think, hardly begun to find the authors that, in his words, "he has a mind to expose," because we have looked too exclusively for stylistic parody and paid too little attention to other telltale details that can help to identify targets that are not to be identified stylistically.

2

Gulliver's Travels has generally resisted efforts to consider it parodic, and some Swift critics lurch toward apoplexy when the very idea of parody is broached within reaching distance of **Gulliver's Travels.**[17] And yet Swift's consciousness of contemporary writing is nearly as apparent there as in **A Tale of a Tub,** and if passages that specifically echo another writer—such as the plagiarized passage from Sturmy's *Mariner's Magazine*—are rare, a large awareness of contemporary writing habits and the prevailing tastes of readers is visible at nearly every turn. Swift's awareness of contemporary travel writers—William Dampier, for example—has been often remarked, and much of the fun in the book's first appearance had to do with its solemn title page: *Travels into Several Remote Nations of the World,* it advertised, promising something quite other than what is delivered. Swift, in one of his letters, has something of a lark in imagining literal-minded readers who are gulled by such an expectation: he speaks of an Irish bishop who, after reading **Gulliver's Travels,** concluded that it was "full of improbable lies, and for his part, he hardly believed a word of it."[18]

But quite beyond its evocation of travel literature, **Gulliver's Travels** engages a whole tradition of fiction that was then in the process of developing, and Swift saw that this new kind of writing was beginning to codify a "modern," significantly new way of perceiving the world. Contemporary narratives of personal experience—scandalous memoirs and chronicles of personal and public political intrigue, as well as books that charted personal travel to far-off places or new experiences—were increasingly sought by a public that

wanted material, intellectual, and psychological satisfaction in the conquest of space and the accrual of experience. Because of its new popularity, this subjective writing, whether genuine or fictional, seems to offer a personal yet universal key to reality and, like Boyle's *Meditations,* can only deliver on its promise by exaggerated and distorted emblematicism and by verbal sleight-of-hand. The assumptions, values, and forms that seem to be implicitly attacked in **Gulliver's Travels** would be easy enough to defend on their own terms, and in fact in our time most of us find it easier to understand them than we do Swift's objections; but the *Travels* offers us persuasive evidence that Swift perceived the brave new literary world of the 1720s much as Pope did, with the significant difference that Swift merges its personalities and consciousnesses into composite figures who anonymously participate in the creation of a single work that expressed their values and outlook, rather than being named and even individuated by their antagonist.[19] Even in their monotonous sameness, though, some identifiable characteristics emerge, and in the choral voice one can pick out a few distinctive, personalized tones that remind us of a voice insistent on being subjective, authoritative, and modern.

Because Swift's parody works through an accretion and absorption of particulars, it is difficult to illustrate his method without a detailed consideration of the text and its contexts, but here I will be only suggestive through brief attention to one episode and its surrounding circumstances. The suggestive place I want to examine may at first seem a bit unlikely—Lemuel Gulliver's pockets as he empties them for his interrogation in Lilliput. Here is an inventory of what turns up concealed on Gulliver's person:

a handkerchief

a snuffbox

a diary

a comb

a razor

a set of eating utensils

a watch

a set of pistols

a pouch of gunpowder and another pouch of bullets silver and copper money and several pieces of gold

a pair of spectacles

a pocket perspective and "several other little Conveniences."

To appreciate the full effect of this pocketful, we have to remember that Gulliver is supposed to have swum ashore—in dangerous stormy waves—with his pockets jammed like that, and he is also wearing a full set of clothes, a hat, and a large sword.

Because this information is not all presented at once, one might read the *Travels* several times and not notice Gulliver's rich and varied cargo. Gulliver, being Gulliver, does not tell us that his swimming was impeded by his load, nor does he tell us why he hung onto the material things that connect him to his past when, buffeted by waves that threaten to scuttle him, it would have seemed sensible to discharge himself of some of his burdens. The things are, to be sure, useful to Swift in initiating Gulliver's dialogue with the Lilliputians, but they are not necessary, as subsequent voyages show. Swift pretty clearly is having some fun at Gulliver's expense in making him such a dull-witted freighter, and his point seems crucially connected, on the one hand, to a contemporary joke, and, on the other, to Swift's perceptions about first-person narrative and the mind-numbing absurdities it sometimes offered to readers of contemporary narrative.

The joke was seven years old in 1726. It had involved a slip of Defoe's pen in *Robinson Crusoe*—a slip that, when corrected, still exposed a lapse in memory or lack of factual knowledge. When Defoe has Crusoe swim to the shipwreck at one point, he allows him to strip off his clothes to make the journey easier, but a little later we see Crusoe on shipboard stuffing his pockets with biscuits. Defoe later explains that Crusoe had left on his seaman's britches, but as a contemporary, Charles Gildon, pointed out, Defoe didn't thus improve his marks as a purveyor of information about seamen, for seaman's britches usually do not have pockets, and even when they do, the pockets are tiny ones, much too small for biscuits: Defoe's explanation had only pinpointed and elaborated his ignorance. For Gildon, Defoe here makes Crusoe perform unlikely, even absurd actions, and his attack is on the false realism in Defoe, just as in *Gulliver's Travels* the thrust is to demonstrate what the realism and pseudo-factuality of contemporary travel accounts and fictional narratives come to at last.[20] Gildon's joke on Defoe was, by the way, well enough known and remembered in 1725—six years after *Crusoe* and a year before *Gulliver*—that the *London Journal* can speak of the pocket episode as "a most notorious *Blunder*," which had given "Abundances of Pleasure [to] many of his Readers."[21]

Gulliver's pockets, then, work something like this: they remind us of Defoe's mistake and how authors who try to pass off genuine memoirs often are tripped by simple facts. The pockets also remind us of larger points quite beyond the comical allusion—that first-person narrators, in their haste to make a point and glorify

themselves, are hopelessly inaccurate, obtuse, and pretentious; that long lists and particular details do not necessarily add up to some larger truth, and that attempts to read the world and its purpose through the recording of sense impressions and the imparting of symbolic qualities to things and events (as done in *Robinson Crusoe* and in the emblematic tradition represented by meletetic meditators like Robert Boyle) is finally an arrogant, self-serving, even solipsistic way of regarding the world. *Robinson Crusoe* comes up for examination in *Gulliver's Travels* quite often in various ways: in the opening paragraph in which the particulars of Defoe's life (his career as a hosier, his imprisonment as a debtor, his prudent marriage to a woman with a large dowry) are alluded to; in the preparatory events that preface each voyage proper; in the vague motivation for Gulliver's decisions to go repeatedly to sea because of "rambling Thoughts" and an unaccountable sense of destiny; in the habitual phrases that fall from Gulliver's lips and link him repeatedly but not constantly to the consciousness of Crusoe; in the ending in which Swift provides a sharp contrast to Crusoe's homecoming.[22] Defoe, exploring what man can do to achieve salvation and deliverance within a providential pattern, has Crusoe readjust to the company of human beings and society generally with relative ease, giving no hint that lack of conversation, human companionship, sexual relationship, and exile from the familiar for more than a quarter century offer any obtrusive problems in readjustment, and Crusoe returns to find himself remembered, beloved, and provided for by partners and well-wishers who have preserved and improved his property and investments so that he is now a rich plantation owner, soon to be a happy new husband and father. Alexander Selkirk, often said to be the prototype of Crusoe and in any case an island castaway who lived in isolation only a fraction of Crusoe's tenure, found postvoyage life far otherwise, returning to his home a silent misanthrope who avoided all company, living altogether by himself, some say in a cave he himself dug as an emblem of his psychological space. Swift's portrait of Gulliver neighing quietly to himself in his stable, unable to stand the company of his wife and children, his nose stopped with lavender, tobacco, and rue so that he cannot smell human smells, stands in sharp relief to Crusoe's homecoming and tacitly reminds us realistically of historical figures like Selkirk and of civilization and its discontents.

The example of the allusive pockets suggests that *Gulliver's Travels* is, among many other impressive things, an accreting generic or class parody not only of travel narratives per se but also of a larger developing class of first-person fictional narratives that make extraordinary claims for the importance of the contemporary, the knowableness through personal experience of large cosmic patterns, the significance of the individual, and the imperialistic possibilities of the human mind—a class parody, in short, of what we now see as the novel and the assumptions that enable it.

3

Indulge me in a preposterous claim. *A Tale of a Tub* is also, among other things, a parody of the emerging novel. But how can there be a parody of something that does not yet exist? you may well ask, and I admit that I do not want to be taken altogether literally. Still, I am serious about the slight dislocative shock that such an unlikely assertion may provide, and I want to make three quick points about it: one historical, one having to do with Swift's powers of cultural analysis, and one relating back to things I have implied about Swift's tendency to collapse and merge parodic targets, accreting a style and structure that is identifiable as generic or class parody.

First the historical point. Attempts to describe the beginnings of the novel as we know it almost invariably land on a cultural moment and a specific work so that the publication of a particular novel becomes the crucial event; in this view a specific "father" of the novel is usually identified, and a moment of birth can thus be found for the genre, be it 1719, or 1740, or 1749, or whatever—the choice depending ultimately on how one defines the novel and on what sorts of fiction one excludes from the definition. This preoccupation with "firsts" is understandable, given the way an opposite school of literary historians is prone to push origins back, as it were, *ab ovo,* and ultimately end up with Heliodorus or Homer or Ham as the first modern novelist. And the attraction of biological and organic metaphors is certainly appealing to a humanist tradition that wishes to think of literature as an art form to be privileged above mere material existence. I would, however, hate to have to defend a notion of genre that included in it the necessity of firsts, for it seems quite clear that most genres grow out of the shifting and rearranging of conventions, usually in response to some major cultural change, often involving a technological breakthrough that influences the possibilities of existing art without leading immediately to a full-grown, totally defined form that exemplifies and exhausts possibility. I would certainly agree that the modern English novel as we know it comes to exist sometime around the beginning of the eighteenth century, and I would argue that the exploding amount of narrative fiction then, together with distinctive and definable changes in the nature of extended narrative, mean that we can specify the emergence of a genre even if we cannot pin it down to a particular Friday afternoon. But the context of ferment is somewhat broader, even if it does not stretch back to classical times. And I think we need to consider more fully the fiction written in England in the later years of the seventeenth century, which, if not actually describable as novelistic, points clearly to what is going to happen when the

talents of particular writers become more focused on the emerging cultural and technological possibilities. Here, for example, is the kind of self-conscious narrative writing one finds in an extraordinary work of 1691, John Dunton's *A Voyage Round the World, or The Life and Travels of Don Kainophilus:*

> Should I tell you, as the *virtuosi* do, that I was shaped at first like a Todpole, and that I remember very well, when my Tail *Rambled off,* and a pair of little Legs sprung out in the Room on't: Nay, shou'd I protest I pulled out my Note-book, and slapdashed it down the very minute after it happen'd,—let me see,—so many Days, Hours, and Seconds after Conception, yet this Infidel World wou'd hardly believe me. . . . [23]

Dunton has been suggested as a "source" for *A Tale of a Tub,* and many passages from his work—in the *Voyage* and elsewhere—could easily be cited to bloster a claim that Dunton is one of the hacks Swift has in mind as a parodic model for the tubbean author.[24] Dunton's life and works could in fact stand for much of what is under attack, in religion as well as in learning in *A Tale of a Tub,* for Dunton's publishing ventures, religious attitudes and experiences, and his rather volatile personal life make for racy reading that is in many ways symptomatic of the contemporary culture Swift is describing. We are likely to hear more in coming years of Dunton's place in the history of the novel, a place that is far more important than has been recognized.[25] But my point here is that Dunton is one of several writers one might cite—another is Francis Kirkman—to show that novelistic tendencies were already highly developed by 1694 when Swift began work on the *Tale,* even if no full-blown novel of artistic consequence yet existed.

Clearly, Swift saw the handwriting on the wall, a handwriting leading to a new world of print. *A Tale of a Tub* emphasizes the now, the subjective, the rambling recording of the present moment of an individual consciousness, digressiveness from the basic narrative movement, uncertainty of direction, and the portentousness of every word within a framework of fragmentation, lost passages, metaphors run wild, and syntactic madness; what Swift does with these emphases is to provide almost a catalogue of devices appropriate to the attitudes and values inherent in a new conception of writing and artistry then taking shape. Ultimately, it is too much to say that Swift's performance in *A Tale of a Tub* amounts to a parody of the novel, but his parodic representation of modern writing suggests how the wind was blowing, and he isolates a number of features that go on to find their proper home in the new narrative form then in the process of emerging. Swift isolates a number of features that became crucial in the new fiction: narrative interests merging with discursive ones only to be interrupted by the vagaries of individual consciousness; a preoccupation with subjectivity for its own sake; a concentration upon an individual of negligible social importance and an elevation of that individual's claims to significance; an almost boundless faith in the potential of particulars to lead to grand patterns of divine or natural order, empiricism vastly extended. In isolating such features, Swift provides an acute cultural analysis of forces deeply at work in English culture, and if he does not exactly prophesy some of the central features in the writing of Defoe, Richardson, and Sterne, he shows himself already aware of the inevitability that the culture's structure will find its appropriate form at the same time that he distills the implications of what is emerging as modernity by giving it a parodic form even before it has fully defined its own paradigm.

Swift's style in *A Tale of a Tub,* although it bears features of the style of Dunton and Dryden, Roger L'Estrange and Aphra Behn, Wotton, and Bentley and of perhaps scores of other contemporaries, is finally not that of any one hack but instead that of Everyhack. A knowledge of the particulars of writings relevant to the context of the *Tale* can only enhance our appreciation of what Swift does there, not because we are likely to find any one writer or work toward which Swift directs all of his satiric anger but because he collapses them into a chorus made up of individual voices barely distinguishable from one another and, in any case, contributory to what the Augustans soon heard as a universal hum. From hymn to hum, that is the way the Augustans perceived the breakdown of ritual and tradition and the separation from orality, as traditional values and ideas of order slipped into those of novelty. If the novel goes on to provide a different and less gloomy perspective, the vision of Swift is still a perceptive and prophetic one in its articulation of the emerging world's directions and cultural forms.

Like *A Tale of A Tub, Gulliver's Travels* is a vast many things generically, and the novel is only one of the forms that enables Swift's satiric art. Travel books, philosophical voyages, scientific translations, beast fables, children's fantasies, and a host of other formal and informal "kinds" play their part in Swift's act of imagination, and some of them, like the emerging novel, play a prominent role for readers in their ability to receive and perceive the text. Unlike *Don Quixote, Gulliver's Travels* does not contain both type and antitype, both paradigm and parody. But its negative representation of what was and what was to be involves Swift's shrewd (if ultimately doomed) vision of where western thought and western art would go in his own time, and in its response to the directions and assumptions of first-person, fictional narrative, *Gulliver's Travels* is a kind of testimony to a new tradition about to be invented, a form almost formed, a genre nearly generated, as well as a credo, call to arms, a

solvent against solipsism. In a way it transcends its form, its credo, and its values, but it realizes those things too, against a new tradition rigorously engaged if only partly understood.

Notes

[1] In *The Prose Works of Jonathan Swift,* ed. Herbert Davis et al. (Oxford: Basil Blackwell, 1939-68), 9:41. Henceforth referred to as *Prose Works.*

[2] George P. Mayhew, "Jonathan Swift's Hoax of 1722 upon Ebenezor Elliston," *Bulletin of the John Rylands University Library of Manchester* 44 (1962): 366.

[3] "The last Farewell of Ebenezor Ellison to this Transitory World," reprinted as an appendix in *Prose Works,* 9:366.

[4] Most such "confessions" are very much alike, and the conventional wisdom is that someone, often the prison ordinary but sometimes a bookseller's hack, ghostwrote wholesale for the condemned prisoners. Collections of these last words were very popular early in the century; see, for example, *The Wonders of Free Grace: or, a compleat history of all the remarkable penitents that have been executed at Tyburn, and elsewhere . . .* (London, 1690). Elliston's last words are unusually rambling and oral, and it may be that we have here an attempt to transcribe something like what he actually said of himself.

[5] See Herbert Davis's Introduction to vol. 1 of *Prose Works,* pp. xxxiii-xxxiv.

[6] *Prose Works,* 1:239-240.

[7] "Reflection 1," in *Occasional Reflections upon Several Subjects* (1665), reprinted in *Works* (London: 1772), 2: 359-60.

[8] In the *Miscellanies in Prose and Verse,* (London: Benjamin Tooke, 1711), p. 231, Swift said his meditation was "According to the Style and Manner of the Honourable Robert Boyl's Meditations."

[9] *Husbandry Spiritualized: or, The Heavenly Use of Earthly Things* (London: Robert Boulter, 1669), pp. 254-55.

[10] The best description of the meditative tradition is still that of Louis Martz, *The Poetry of Meditation* (New Haven: Yale University Press, 1954).

[11] "A Discourse Touching Occasional Meditations," in *Occasional Reflections,* reprinted in 1772 *Works,* 2:343.

[12] "An Introductory Preface," in *Occasional Reflections,* reprinted in 1772 *Works,* 2:329.

[13] See *Prose Works,* 5:271.

[14] See Thomas Sheridan, *Life of Swift* (London, 1784), p. 42.

[15] "Apology," in *A Tale of a Tub,* ed. A. C. Guthkelch and D. Nichol Smith, 2d ed. (Oxford: Clarendon Press, 1958), p. 7.

[16] See *Swift and the Satirist's Art* (Chicago: University of Chicago Press, 1963), p. 31.

[17] A happy exception is C. J. Rawson. See *Gulliver and the Gentle Reader* (London: Routledge and Kegan Paul, 1973).

[18] Swift to Pope, 27 November 1726, in *Correspondence,* ed. Harold Williams (Oxford: Clarendon Press, 1963) 3:189.

[19] Carole Fabricant, *Swift's Landscape* (Baltimore: Johns Hopkins University Press, 1982), esp. pp. 3-4, usefully reminds us that Swift's and Pope's positions need often to be distinguished from one another, but on this issue they seem to have seen eye to eye. For a good discussion of Swift's distrust of overreading natural phenomena, see Martin Price, *Swift's Rhetorical Art* (New Haven: Yale University Press, 1953), pp. 89-90.

[20] Gildon's attack, published as *The life and strange surprising adventures of Mr. D—DeF—, of London Hosier . . . With remarks serious and comical upon the life of Crusoe,* had two editions in 1719 and another in 1724.

[21] *London Journal,* 4 September 1725, p. 1.

[22] John Robert Moore long ago pointed out that the opening paragraph of *Gulliver's Travels* reviewed satirically the life and career of DeFoe ("A DeFoe Allusion in *Gulliver's Travels,*" *Notes and Queries* 178 (1940): 79-80. The whole issue of Defoe's relationship to Swift needs to be studied afresh, John Ross's study of the subject now being sadly outdated.

[23] *A Voyage Round the World,* 3 vols. (London, 1691), 1:30.

[24] See J. M. Stedmond, "Another Possible Analogue for Swift's *Tale of a Tub,*" *Modern Language Notes* 72 (1957): 13-18. Stedmond, among others, has also studied Sterne's debt to Dunton, but the whole subject needs much more detailed analysis.

[25] I have discussed some aspects of Dunton's importance in "The Insistent I," *Novel* 13 (1979): 19-37. See also Stephen Parks, *John Dunton and the English Book Trade* (New York: Garland, 1976) and Robert Adams Day, "Richard Bentley and John Dunton: Brothers

under the Skin," *Studies in Eighteenth-Century Culture,* ed. O M Brack, Jr. (Madison: University of Wisconsin Press, 1986) 16:125-38.

Christopher Fox (essay date 1992)

SOURCE: "The Myth of Narcissus in Swift's *Travels,*" in *Reader Entrapment in Eighteenth-Century Literature,* edited by Carl R. Kropf, AMS Press, 1992, pp. 89-108.

[*In the following essay, Fox studies Swift's employment of the masturbation motif, (i.e. Gulliver's apprenticeship to "my good Master Bates") as a metaphor for excessive, myopic self-involvement, and as a retelling of the myth of Narcissus.*]

This essay begins with a question posed by the late Frank Brady in 1978 and (more recently) by William Kinsley in 1982. What do we make of Gulliver's apprenticeship, at the opening of the *Travels,* to "my good Master Bates"? Brady noted that it "is easy to find" such "jokes (errors? misstatements?) in *Gulliver;* what is difficult . . . is to determine whether they are (1) accidental, (2) incidental (local, restricted), or (3) significant?"[1]

Let us apply Brady's criteria to the "Master Bates" construct, developed in the opening three paragraphs of the work: in the first readers learn of Gulliver's apprenticeship to "Mr. James Bates" and later "Mr. Bates" who becomes, in the second paragraph, "my good Master Mr. Bates" or "Mr. Bates, my Master" and, in the third, simply "my good Master *Bates.*"[2] To use Brady's first criterion, is this chain of references merely "accidental"? Pointing to Swift's use of "anticipatory variations" here and of "repetition and over-specification with a vengeance," Kinsley finds these elements alone convincing proof that the pun is deliberate,[3] and his contention is sound, though at least one objection remains: was the word "masturbation" even current *in Swift's day?* Milton Voigt, assessing Phyllis Greenacre's attempt to make the pun mean something, argues that it was not; and on the basis of the *OED,* which cites the earliest written use of the word in 1766, he is right. Brady tried to remove this objection by locating an earlier occurrence of the word, in Florio's Montaigne (1603).[4] But there were also some more current uses that (1) suggest the pun is not "accidental" and (2) supply, at the very least, an "incidental" context for the joke.

In *A Modest Defence of Publick Stews (1724),* published two years before the *Travels,* Bernard Mandeville relates that one of the "Ways by which lewd young Men destroy their natural Vigour, and render themselves impotent" is by "Manufriction, *alias* Masturbation." Dr. Mandeville then lists a host of ailments arising from this "lewd Trick" and argues that to "prevent young Men from Laying *violent Hands* upon themselves, we must have recourse to the *Publick Stews.*"[5] In advocating the brothel as a cure for those he calls the youthful *"Onanites,"* Mandeville was not alone. In *The Oeconomy of Love* (1736), another doctor, John Armstrong, counsels young men to "hie / To Bagnio lewd or Tavern, nightly where / Venereal Rites are done" rather than practice that "ungenerous, selfish, solitary Joy."[6] And earlier in the century, in his *Treatise of Venereal Disease* (1709), Dr. John Marten offers vivid case histories which seemingly support such claims. Here, we learn about "a very comely Gentleman . . . whose Case was lost *Erection,* by *Masturbation* in his Youth." Equally unfortunate, Marten adds, was a young student who, "deceiv'd by others, used daily *Masturbation,* as he [later said] lamenting and sorry, and thereby had contracted so great a weakness of his *Seminal Vessels* and *Testicles,* that although he lived afterwards continently, yet he was troubled with a *Gonorrhea* . . . and whereas he was before of a lively colour and strong, afterwards he grew pale, lean, weak, &c."[7] Along with the pre-***Gulliver*** uses of the word "masturbation," the context of such remarks sheds light on the ***Travels*** in 1726. That context is the pervasive early eighteenth-century anti-masturbatory craze sparked, at least in part, by a pamphlet titled ONANIA; OR, THE *Heinous Sin of Self-Pollution,* AND ALL *its Frightful Consequences, in both SEXES, Considered,* WITH *Spiritual and Physical Advice to those, who have already injur'd themselves by this Abominable Practice* (London, c. 1709-1710).

Early in this pamphlet, the author confesses that to "expose a Sin so displeasing to God, so detrimental to the Publick, and so injurious to our selves, requires no Flights of Wit."[8] And the work that ensues—an often tedious compendium of moral and pseudo-medical advice (though not without a certain prurient appeal) —indicates that he is largely correct. In elucidating the frightful consequences of the "SIN OF SELF-POLLUTION" (among them, sterility, blindness, sloth, madness, gonorrhea, death, *"Lying,"* *"Forswearing,"* and even "Murder"), ONANIA raised masturbation to the status of a "collosal bogey."[9] In a 1724 edition of the work, which advertises itself as "The Tenth EDITION Above Fifteen Thousand of the former Editions . . . Sold," we discover that the secret sin has reached contagious proportions in Britain. Indeed, it "has now become almost as frequent amongst Girls, as Masturbation is amongst Boys." It is especially prevalent in the schools, where *"licentious Masturbators"* initiate unsuspecting youths into "that cursed School-Wickedness of Masturbation."[10] P.-G. Boucé notes that ONANIA enjoyed an "amazing success." Judging from the number of editions it ran through and the host of imitations it sparked, ONANIA (as Lawrence Stone adds) "clearly struck some hidden area of anxiety in early eighteenth-century Europe."[11] In the mid-1720s alone, for example, if the

reader did not see ONANIA directly or, say, Mandeville's *Publick Stews,* he could consult *Eronania: On the Misusing of the Marriage-Bed by Er and Onan* (London, 1724). He could then move on, in the same year, to *The Crime of Onan (together with that of his brother Er, punished with sudden death): Or, the hainous Vice of Self defilement* (London, 1724). Four years later, he could read Joseph Cam's *A Practical Treatise on the Consequences of Venereal Disease* (London, 1728), the first part considering that dreaded specter, "onanism."

When Gulliver, in 1726, is apprenticed to "my good Master *Bates*" there are some historical reasons, therefore, for assuming that Swift's chain of references is far from "accidental." But is it only "incidental," that is, in Brady's terms, a "local" or a "restricted" joke? If so, we could end this essay here and simply say that, by introducing this pun—particularly within a larger discussion of Gulliver's schooling—Swift is playfully alluding to a context familiar to his readers.

Another Scriblerian work furnishes additional substance for investigation. In a book Swift contributed to—the ***Memoirs of Scriblerus***—Martinus uses his "sagacity in discovering the distempers of the Mind" to solve the case of a young nobleman, who has cut himself off from others and "converses" with almost "none but *himself.*" Martinus concludes that the young man must be "desperately in love"; and an interview with an aunt confirms the object of this "amorous inclination":

> Whom does he generally talk of? Himself, quoth the Aunt. Whose wit and breeding does he most commend? His own, quoth the Aunt. . . . Whom is he ogling yonder? Himself in his looking-glass . . . . Have you observ'd him to use Familiarities with any body? "With none but himself: he often embraces himself with folded arms, he claps his hand often upon his hip, nay sometimes thrusts it into—his breast."

The prognosis is poor. If the young man's self-love is not cured, we are told, he will be "condemn'd eternally to himself" and perhaps "run to the next pond to get rid of himself, the Fate of most violent Self-lovers."[12]

Important here is a cluster of associations linking masturbation to the "distemper" (i.e. madness) of self-love and to the greatest self-lover of them all. The young man's rejection of others, his fascination and "Familiarities" with his own body, his attempts to embrace himself, the closing evocation of the destructive pond— all suggest the story of Narcissus. Given this Scriblerian context, it is perhaps not surprising that a book which begins with its hero apprenticed to "Master *Bates*" ends with him "condemn'd eternally to himself" and with a vision that also evokes the tale of Narcissus: "When I happened to behold the Reflection of my own Form in a Lake or Fountain," Gulliver tells us near the end of *his* tale, "I turned away my Face in Horror and detestation of my self" (4.10). It is within this larger pattern, suggestive of Gulliver's Narcissistic movement from self-love to self-hatred, that the opening play on "Master *Bates*" becomes—in Brady's third criterion—"significant."

"Narcissism" in Swift's day did not necessarily mean what it means to us—the word itself was probably coined by a German in 1899.[13] It instead meant myth, specifically Ovidian myth,[14] and the traditional interpretations of the mythographers. He is known for the "hard pride" (*dura superbia*) with which he scorns the love of others.[15] He especially dislikes the company of women.[16] Despising all others in comparison with himself, he will not let others love him and tells all who attempt to do so, "embrace me not."[17] He who will not let others love him is doomed to a hopeless love himself; he gazes at the deceptive reflection, mistakes a shadow (*umbra*) for a substance, and blindly falls in love with an idealized vision of himself, a nothingness created by his own imagination: *"quod petis, est nusquam."*[18] As he attempts to grasp the "adored image," it "ever elude[s] his Embraces." Transported "by selfe-love" and wasting away "with that madness," he spends the remainder of his days isolated from the world and attended by a few flatterers who reaffirm his delusion.[19] These traits (among others) were attributed to Narcissus by Ovid's commentators from the late sixteenth through the early eighteenth century. Many of the same characteristics appear, as well, in the Scriblerians' case of the young nobleman in the *Memoirs*—and in Swift's portrayal of Lemuel Gulliver.

We know from "Baucis and Philemon" or "The Fable of Midas" that Swift enjoyed playing with Ovidian types and themes.[20] The similarities between Gulliver and the Narcissus of the Ovidian tradition, and the evocation of the same myth in Book IV of the *Travels,* point to some larger transformations of the tale. Three Ovidian themes in particular, which link Gulliver to the Narcissus figure, shed light on his opening apprenticeship to 'Master *Bates*" and his closing rejection of self and species.

The first theme suggests itself in Gulliver's response to those who love him and his own experience with his beloved Houyhnhnms. This theme, the "frustrated love," had been seen for centuries as a central motif of the Narcissus tale.[21] The story in Ovid is not simply the story of Narcissus, but also of Echo and the others who tried to love him. At a key moment in Ovid's account, Echo sees Narcissus and, "inflamed with love," races up to "throw her arms around" him. He immediately "flees her approach," yelling "Hands off! embrace me not!" (*Metam.*, Bk. 3, line 390). In Book IV of the *Travels,* the same scene is comically re-enacted

in Gulliver's encounter with the Yahoo woman who, "inflamed by Desire," came "running with all Speed" up to him and—his account continues—"embraced me after a most fulsome Manner; I roared as loud as I could . . . whereupon she quitted her Grasp, with the utmost Reluctancy, and leaped upon the opposite Bank, where she stood gazing and howling" (4.8).

This version of the "frustrated love"—with Gulliver playing Narcissus to a Yahoo Echo—is picked up later in a series of embrace scenes that are not as comic. When Gulliver arrives home, he tells us that "my Wife took me in her Arms, and kissed me; at which, having not been used to the Touch of that odious Animal for so many Years, I fell in a Swoon for almost an Hour" (4.11). As in his encounter with the Yahoo Echo, Gulliver's rejection here is explicitly sexual. During his association with "Master *Bates,*" Gulliver had been advised "to alter my Condition" by marrying (1.1). Now, finally returning home, he laments that "by copulating with one of the *Yahoo*-Species, I had become a parent of more; it struck me with the utmost Shame, Confusion, and Horror" (4.11). He does not let this happen in the future and continues to scorn his wife's embraces right up to the time he writes the book; for Gulliver assures us that, in the five years he's been home, he has let no one in his family even "take me by the Hand" (4.11). Gulliver, in other words, commits himself at the end of the work to the Narcissistic isolation evoked at the opening, in his situation with "my good Master *Bates.*" In Ovid's story, Narcissus shows his "hard pride" in rejecting not only Echo, but everyone else who attempts to love him. This theme also appears in another embrace scene in Book IV, this one with Pedro de Mendez, who has treated Gulliver with great humanity. "He took kind Leave of me," Gulliver comments, "and embraced me at parting; which I bore as well as I could" (4.11). In his proud rejection of Pedro de Mendez no less than of his wife, Gulliver's posture is summed up by the boy's words in the tale: "Hands off! embrace me not!"

The "frustrated love" works both ways. As Ovid and his commentators remind us, he who will not let others love him is doomed to a hopeless love himself, and to be tortured by the "unattainability of an idealized self-image."[22] That image in the *Travels* is embodied in Gulliver's "Love and Veneration" (4.7) for the Houyhnhnms, who reject him just as he rejects the others.

Along with the "frustrated love," two other Ovidian motifs are pertinent here. The first is the "reflection" theme, seen in Narcissus's preoccupation with himself in the pond. In their adaptation of the myth in the *Memoirs,* the Scriblerians connect the "reflection" to the young man's masturbation and "Familiarities" with himself, to his absorption in the "looking-glass," and ultimately, to a larger movement from self-love to self-hatred.

All these elements are at work in the *Travels,* where Swift uses the same theme to suggest Gulliver's simultaneous fascination with, and rejection of, his own body—or, one-half of his being. Indeed, the opening play on "Master *Bates*" is only the first in a long series of references to Gulliver's "Familiarities" with himself. Early in Book I, for example, Gulliver reports (1.3) that when "some of the younger Officers" of the Lilliputian army pass under his tattered breeches, they look up not simply with "Laughter" but "Admiration." Elsewhere in the same book, he vividly describes relieving himself and then feels the need to apologize for it: "I would not have dwelt so long upon a Circumstance . . . if I had not thought it necessary to justify my Character in Point of Cleanliness to the World" (1.2). In a parallel passage in Book II, he tells us about relieving himself again and again asks the reader to "excuse me for dwelling on these and the like Particulars; which however insignificant they may appear to grovelling vulgar Minds, yet will certainly help a Philosopher enlarge his Thoughts and Imagination" (2.1). How this is so is unclear. What is clear is that Gulliver dwells "on these and the like Particulars" throughout the entire work. And the particulars he provides—his later defense, for example, of his own smell (2.5) or the "Shame" with which he views his sexual acts (4.11)—reveal a strange preoccupation with, and progressive hatred of, his own body. This same pattern suggests itself in the growing number of references to "mirrors," culminating in Gulliver's stark rejection of his human form in Book IV:

> When I happened to behold the Reflection of my own Form in a Lake or Fountain, I turned away my Face in Horror and detestation of my self; and could better endure the Sight of a common *Yahoo,* than of my own Person (4.10).

In a passage that directly evokes and also modifies the Narcissus myth, Gulliver—here as elsewhere[23]—tells us he hates his "Reflection" in mirrors. A similar modification of the myth appears in the *Fables* of La Fontaine (1621-95), where in "The Man and His Reflection" a Narcissus appears who avoids mirrors:

> Thinking himself one with whom none could compare,
> A man supposed himself the handsomest of mankind
> And found fault with every mirror anywhere,
> So that in time he had become morally blind.
>   . . .
> What could our Narcissus do but stay away,
> In the kind of place in which he would be safe all day
> From any mirror that might catch him unaware?[24]

The reason this Narcissus avoids mirrors is that they show him he looks like everybody else and detract from his idealized self image. Gulliver has similar motivations. Mirrors reflect the human form he has now rejected, a rejection arising, in part, from the Narcissistic fascination with himself adumbrated throughout and in the opening play on masturbation.

Mirrors also detract from Gulliver's idea of what he wants to become. What he wants to become is a rational horse. (As Brady quipped, "Gulliver was not unusual among eighteenth-century squires in preferring his horses to his family, but his reasons for doing so seem unique."[25]) Thus, in the same passage in Book IV, Gulliver immediately turns away from his human "Reflection" to focus on another image—the Houyhnhnms—on which he looks "with Delight" (4.10). When he first found himself "gazing" at that image "for some time" (4.1), he had wondered soon afterwards whether his "Brain was disturbed" and had "rubbed my Eyes often" to see if "I might be in a Dream" (4.2). But the "Truth" of this image—and the possibility of a purely rational life—had since "appeared so amiable" to him that he has "determined upon sacrificing everything to it" (4.7). This is the image evoked again at the end of the *Travels,* where we find Gulliver living "in great Amity" (4.11) with two "Stone-Horses": stallions to most people, but to Gulliver idols of his beloved Houyhnhnms. Gulliver's fixed obsession with this image and his vain attempt to embrace it point to another theme, "illusion," which figures prominently in the Narcissus story.

In Ovid, Narcissus ignorantly (*inprudens*) mistakes an illusion for a reality and worships an insubstantial image that nonetheless "appears" to him "like a statue" (*Metam.*, Bk. 3, line 419). "What you seek is nowhere"—*quod petis, est nusquam*—the narrator laughs (Bk. 3, line 433). Because the illusion has no correspondence in reality, and cannot be attained, the boy is destroyed. Later interpreters link Narcissus's illusion to, among other things, the (a) folly of worshipping an image, to the (b) blindness that arises from pride, and—from the late sixteenth century onward—to a (c) self-pleasing delusion, a mental aberration created by his own imagination. The first two threads are suggested, for instance, in Ben Jonson's *Cynthia's Revels: Or, The Fountain of Self-Love* (1601), where Echo wishes that Narcissus had picked a "truer Mirror" in which to view his real self. "But self-love never yet could look on truth / But with blear'd beams" (i.ii). The third—taking Narcissus's error as a delusion—is prominent in La Fontaine's later Fable, where Narcissus avoids outward mirrors because they interfere with his private vision of himself.

All these strands appear in Gulliver's worship of the Houyhnhnms. At the end of the work, we find Gulliver attempting "to behold my Figure often in a Glass" in order "to Habituate my self by Time to tolerate the

Sight of a human Creature" (4.12). But, like La Fontaine's Narcissus, Gulliver already has an image of himself, a private mirror, he likes better. This is the image he gazes at when he turns away from his human reflection in a lake, or when he enters the stable with his groom to view those two "Stone-Horses." This image pleases him because it allows him to deny that human form he has rejected, and to dream the dream of a purely rational life. Just as important, it enables him to "pretend to some Superiority" over the rest of the human race (4.12). That the Houyhnhnm ideal is a delusion is strongly suggested by the disparity between what Gulliver wants to become and what he is. Attempting to escape his body, he ends up enmeshed in it, enjoying the fumes of his groom while unable to tolerate the smell of his own family. Attempting to live a life of pure reason, he loses it altogether. The references to madness abound. In short, like the boy in the story, Gulliver is deluded by a hopeless love for an unattainable image—in his case, the Houyhnhnms, who become an idealized projection of his own pride.

That Gulliver writes the book to convert *us* to this same image suggests another interpretation of Narcissus's "illusion," taking it as a mental aberration of a specific type. In a popular emblem book reprinted as late as 1784,[26] Andrea Alciati equates Narcissus with the proposer of "new doctrines," one who mistakes his own idea for truth (Figure 1). The image this Narcissus sees is an imaginary construct (*phantasias*) created by his own intellect, a construct he falls in love with and then attempts to impose on the rest of us.[27] Like Alciati's Narcissus, Gulliver has found what he takes to be *the* truth. And being (so he often claims) a lover of truth, he writes the book with the stated intent of teaching us this truth, learned among the Houyhnhnms (4.12). Like the man in the emblem, however, this "truth" is a delusion. Indeed, in his blind love for his delusion and his attempt to get us to embrace it as truth, Gulliver is yet another version of Alciati's Narcissus—and of the "projector" who pervades Swift's works, but with one difference, of course: Gulliver's project is the grandest one of all, no less than the immediate reformation of the entire human race. Whenever someone proposes a new system, Swift tells us in the *Tale of A Tub,* "the first Proselyte he makes, is Himself."[28] In Swift's projector Lemuel Gulliver, as in Alciati's Narcissus, the root of such proselytizing can be found in self-love.

This points to the larger eighteenth-century discussion of self-interest and also, perhaps, to another reason why Gulliver is apprenticed to "my good master *Bates.*" As a Christian and a moralist, Swift inherited a tradition that regarded self-love as a "main cause of psychological distortion," of "prejudice, misperception, misunderstanding, and worse, delusion, in one's thinking about oneself and everything else."[29] In the figure of Lemuel Gulliver, all of these are at work. As a

satirist, Swift—like his favorite La Rochefoucauld or his contemporary, Mandeville—delighted in puncturing inflated claims to purely altruistic acts. As Frederick Keener points out in *The Chain of Becoming,* when Gulliver announces at the opening that he has fled "the corruption of fellow surgeons in London," he becomes one of a number of eighteenth-century heroes who "present themselves as extraordinarily selfless in motivation. . . . " But, Keener adds, "as quickly as these motives" are announced, the reader is set "thinking about the origins of such professions" (79).

Keener's insight can be extended, in Gulliver's case, to the act of writing itself. As we have seen, he consistently claims that he *"strictly adhere[s] to Truth"* (4.12). But the truth he adheres to is a Narcissistic delusion. Gulliver also says that he writes "for the noblest End" and that "my sole Intention was the *PUBLICK GOOD*" (4.12). This can be challenged, too. If Gulliver is so eager to share his truth, why does he wait so long to do it? Given the present mess in Gulliver's stable and the utter impossibility of becoming a rational horse, the reason is obvious: Gulliver has been unable to turn his own immediate world into a Houyhnhnm utopia, or to embrace the ideal himself. In these terms, the book becomes a futile attempt to adjust the outside world to his own private vision.[30] Modern psychologists would call this an exercise (among other things) in fantasy and wish-fulfillment. Augustinian Christians would call it the sin of similitude, evoked most memorably in Milton's allegory of Satan and the creation of Sin and Death. Like Satan—or Narcissus, for that matter—Gulliver is attempting here to replicate an image of himself. Thus, underlying a stated aim to serve the public is Gulliver's unstated desire to serve himself.

If, of course, Gulliver cannot embrace his idea in life, or alter the world to suit his fancy, he does have at least one outlet: to create another world that, while unattainable in life, can be found on the page, in language itself. A modern example of such an activity appears in the "villanelle" scene in Joyce's *Portrait of the Artist,* where Stephen imagines an ideal woman. Because he cannot embrace his ideal, he writes about it, in a process that metaphorically becomes an act of masturbation.

Theorists like Roland Barthes and Maurice Merleau-Ponty have also sensed a connection between *logos* and *eros,* suggesting (in the latter's words) that a "good part of eroticism is on paper."[31] To find writing imaged this way, we don't need to search for modern analogues, however. In Swift's *Mechanical Operation of the Spirit,* for example, the narrator coarsely describes the height (*"Orgasmus"*) of the charismatics' rites, during which the spirit is said "to flag of a sudden" and the group is "forced to hasten to a Conclusion." Soon after this, the narrator himself abruptly ends the work with a sudden announcement—or, should we say, ejaculation: "the Post is just going, which forces me in great Haste to conclude." This conclusion is consistent with the rest of the work, which considers a process for "ejaculating the Soul"—a subject (the narrator boasts) "sparingly handled . . . by any Writer."[32] Swift evokes here what Pope would call "necessary Writing." For "there is hardly any human Creature past Childhood," Pope tells us in *The Art of Sinking* (1728), who hasn't had "some Poetical Evacuation" or enjoyed the "Discharge of the peccant Humour, in exceeding perulent Metre."[33] In these works, masturbation becomes a metaphor for writing that finds its sole basis in self. The same point suggests itself in Gulliver's apprenticeship to "Master *Bates.*" Swift would certainly agree with Glanvill's assertion that "every man is naturally a Narcissus."[34] But he would also argue the need for the writer to go beyond this natural condition, to reach out and embrace the larger orders around him. It is Gulliver's failure to do this, to have intercourse (in any sense of the word) with the world around him, that leads him, in isolation, to fall in love with an idealized image of himself and to write this book.

In his study, *Literary Loneliness,* John Sitter has perceptively noted the gradual isolation, in the mid-eighteenth century, of the writer from his world.[35] Within this larger movement, it is perhaps significant that less than twenty years after the *Travels* Edward Young would invoke Narcissus as a *positive* ideal and compare virtue to

the fabled self-enamour'd boy,
Home-contemplation her supreme delight;
She dreads an interruption from without,
Smit with her own condition; and the more
Intense she gazes, still it charms the more[36]

Swift seems to have foreseen this movement and in the *Travels* worked out some of its less charming implications. Indeed, as a type of Narcissus and a prototype of the Modern author, Lemuel Gulliver is apprenticed, from the very beginning of the work, to "my good Master *Bates.*"

Notes

[1] Frank Brady, "Vexations and Diversions: Three Problems in *Gulliver's Travels," Modern Philology* 75 (1978), 350.

[2] *The Prose Works of Jonathan Swift,* ed. Herbert David (Oxford: Basil Blackwell, 1939-1968), XI, 19-20. All further references are to this edition.

[3] William Kinsley, "Gentle Readings: Recent Work on Swift," *Eighteenth-Century Studies,* 15 (Summer, 1982), 443. Irvin Ehrenpreis has also pointed to Swift's veritable "addiction to word-games." See *Dean Swift,* Vol.

III of *Swift: The Man, His Works, and the Age* (Cambridge: Harvard Univ. Press, 1983), 141.

[4] See Milton Voigt, *Swift and the Twentieth Century* (Detroit: Wayne State Univ. Press, 1964), 158; Phyllis Greenacre, *Swift and Carroll: A Psychoanalytic Study of Two Lives* (New York: International University Presses, 1955), 99-100, 115; and the OED, s.v. "masturbation." The OED, defining "masturbation" as "The practice of self-abuse," cites the earliest written occurrence of the word in *Onanism: Or a Treatise upon the Disorders produced by Masturbation* (1766), forty years after the publication of *Gulliver* in 1726. For the 1603 occurrence, see Brady, 350n.

[5] [Bernard Mandeville,] *A Modest Defence of Publick Stews* (London, 1724; reprint ed., Los Angeles: Augustan Reprint Society, 1973, No. 162), 30-31. The *Defence* also went through a second edition, in 1725.

[6] John Armstrong, *The Oeconomy of Love: A Poetical Essay* (London, 1736), 8-10.

[7] John Marten, *A Treatise of all the Degrees and Symptoms of the Venereal Disease in both Sexes,* 6th ed., corrected and enlarged (London, c. 1709), 398-99. I thank P.-G. Boucé for calling this to my attention. Information on this book, which managed to get Marten prosecuted, is available in David Foxon's *Libertine Literature in England 1660-1745* (New Hyde Park, New York: University Books, 1965), 13.

[8] ONANIA; *Or the Heinous Sin of Self-Pollution and All its Frightful Consequences* (London, 1724; reprint ed., Boston, 1724), 3. The author takes his title from the story of Onan in Genesis (38: 8-10) and is perhaps the first to use the term, "onanism." However, as often pointed out, both the title and the term are based on a probable misreading of the biblical text.

[9] See Edward H. Hare, "Masturbatory Insanity: The History of an Idea," *The Journal of Mental Science,* 108 (1962), 2.

[10] *Onania,* 1724, 16-17. For the same talk of *"licentious Masturbators"* and "that cursed School-Wickedness of Masturbation," also see the London, 1725 edition of ONANIA, 19-20. A 1756 edition of this work, owned by the Kinsey Institute, includes letters written by an "afflicted Onan" in "Dublin, Dec. 31, 1727" (24) who found ONANIA an inspiration; and from a similarly-troubled youth in "London, Dec. 31, 1729" who regrets his past involvement in what he calls "The Sin of Masturbation" (88). The letter from Ireland suggests ONANIA's presence there, as does the copy of the book in the personal library of a longterm Dublin associate of Swift's, John Putland, the stepson of Swift's friend and Dublin physician, Richard Helsham. (See item No. 1490 in Putland's manuscript list of his own library,

Bibliotheca Putlandia, National Library of Ireland, MS 4186). Swift knew Putland well enough to loan him £1500; Putland also apparently ended up with several medical books owned by Swift and left to Helsham. See *The Account Books of Jonathan Swift,* eds. Paul V. Thompson and Dorothy Jay Thompson (Newark: Univ. of Delaware Press, 1984), cxxv, 310, 312, 313; and William LeFanu, *A Catalogue of Books Belonging to Dr. Jonathan Swift* (Cambridge: Cambridge Bibliographical Society, 1988), 2.

[11] See P-G. Boucé, "Aspects of Sexual Tolerance and Intolerance in XVIIIth-Century England," *British Journal of Eighteenth-Century Studies* 3 (1980), 176; and Lawrence Stone, *The Family, Sex and Marriage in England: 1500-1800* (New York: Harper and Row, 1977), 514. For more information, also see Robert H. Mac-Donald, "The Frightful Consequences of Onanism: Notes on the History of a Delusion," *Journal of the History of Ideas,* 28 (1967), 423-31; R. P. Neuman, "Masturbation, Madness, and The Modern Concepts of Childhood and Adolescence," *The Journal of Social History,* 8 (1975), 1-27; J. H. Plumb, "The New World of Children in 18th-Century England," *Past and Present,* 67 (1975), 64-93; Angus McLaren, *Birth Control in Nineteenth-Century England* (New York: Holmes and Meier, 1978), esp. 25-29; M. Foucault, *History of Sexuality,* trans. R. H. Hurley *(London: Penguin, 1978), vol. I., esp. 27-29;* Theodoré Tarczylo, *Sexe et Liberté au Siècle des Lumières* (Paris: Presses de la Renaissance, 1983); G. S. Rousseau's review of this work in *Eighteenth-Century Studies,* 19 (Fall, 1985), 116-20; and H. Tristram Engelhardt, Jr., "The Disease of Masturbation: Values and the Concept of Disease," in *Sickness and Health in America,* eds. Judith Walzer Leavitt and Ronald L. Numbers (Madison: Univ. of Wisconsin Press, 1985), 13-21. Such works are starting to confirm Jean Hagstrum's suspicion that fears of "onanism" and the like "haunted the mind of eighteenth-century man no less than the Victorians" (*Sex and Sensibility* [Chicago: Univ. of Chicago Press, 1980,] 224n.) There are several helpful collections of essays on the subject, including P.-G. Boucé's *Sexuality In Eighteenth-Century Britain* (Manchester: Manchester Univ. Press, 1982).

[12] Jonathan Swift, *et al., Memoirs of the Extraordinary Life, Works, and Discoveries of Martinus Scriblerus,* ed. Charles Kerby-Miller (New Haven: Yale Univ. Press, 1950), 134-36.

[13] Havelock Ellis, "The Conception of Narcissism," in *Studies In The Psychology of Sex* (New York: Random House, 1936), vol. I, 355-56. Though some similarities exist between eighteenth-century views of Narcissus and modern concepts of narcissism, I wish to differentiate the two, as much as possible. For an interesting exploration of Swift and "narcissism," in a modern sense of the term, see Thomas B. Gillmore, "Freud,

Swift, and Narcissism: A Psychological Reading of 'Strephon and Chloe,'" in *Contemporary Studies of Swift's Poetry,* eds. John Irwin Fischer and Donald C. Mell (Newark: Univ. of Delaware Press, 1981), 159-68. On problems of applying modern, psychological terms to eighteenth-century texts, see Christopher Fox, "Defining Eighteenth-Century Psychology: Some Problems and Perspectives," in *Psychology and Literature In the Eighteenth Century,* ed. C. Fox (New York: AMS Studies In the Eighteenth Century, 1987), 1-22.

[14] Though other classical accounts of Narcissus exist, the most influential appears in bk. 3 of Ovid's *Metamorphoses,* lines 339-510. All references are to Vol. I of F. J. Miller's translation (Cambridge: Harvard Univ. Press, 1936).

[15] See Ovid, *Metam.,* bk. 3, line 354 and Natalis Comes, *Mythologiae* (Venice, 1567; reprint ed., New York: Garland Press, 1976), 285-86.

[16] See Henry Reynolds MYTHOMYSTES . . . *To which is annexed the Tale of Narcissus briefly mythologized* (London, 1632): "*Narcissus* is fained to eschew and flye the companie of all women" (107).

[17] See Ovid, *Metam.,* bk. 3, lines 390-91; Marlowe's *Hero and Leander* (First Sest. 75-76), where Leander is compared to Narcissus who "despising many / Died ere he could enjoy the love of any"; and Bacon's *Wisedome of the Ancients* (London, 1619): "*Narcissus* was exceeding faire . . . but wonderful proud and disdainfull; wherefore dispising [sic] all others in respect of himselfe, hee leads a solitary life" (11).

[18] See Ovid, *Metam.,* bk. 3, lines 417, 433-34; George Sandys, *Ovid's Metamorphosis Englished, Mythologized, and Represented in Figures,* eds. K. K. Hulley and S. T. Vandersall (Lincoln: Univ. of Nebraska Press, 1970), 159; and Ben Jonson, *Cynthia's Revels: Or The Fountain of Self-Love, The Works,* ed. W. Gifford (London, 1816), vol. II, 236.

[19] See Richard Steele's *Spectator* No. 238 (Dec. 3, 1711) in *The Spectator,* ed. D. F. Bond (Oxford: Clarendon Press, 1965), vol. II, 427; Sandys, 160; and Bacon's *Wisedome,* where we learn that those afflicted with the disease of Narcissus "leade for the most parte" a "private and obscure life, attended on with a fewe followers, and those such as will . . . like an *Eccho* [sic] flatter them in all their sayings" (12-13).

[20] See *The Poems of Jonathan Swift,* ed. Harold Williams, 2nd. ed. (Oxford: Clarendon Press, 1958), vol. I, 110, 156. Narcissus is not the only Ovidian tale evoked in the *Travels.* For instance, the captain who rescues Gulliver at the end of bk. II compares him to *"Phaeton"*—"although," Gulliver tells us, "I did not much admire the Conceit" (2.8). Why Gulliver didn't

is perhaps suggested by the title alone of an earlier work, by Thomas Hall: *Phaeton's folly, or, the downfal of pride: being a translation of the second book of Ovids Metamorphosis where is lively set forward the danger of pride and rashness (1655)* (1655). (See Douglas Bush, *Mythology and the Renaissance Tradition in English Poetry* [New York: Norton, 1963,] 337).

[21] See Louise Vinge, *The Narcissus Theme in Western European Literature,* trans. R. Dewsnap and L. Grönlund (Lund: Gleerups, 1967), 15.

[22] Frederick Goldin, *The Mirror of Narcissus in The Courtly Love Lyric* (Ithaca: Cornell Univ. Press, 1967), 68.

[23] When, for instance, the Queen of Brobdingnag "used to place" Gulliver "towards a Looking Glass, by which both our Persons appeared before me in full View," he disliked it intensely (2.3). He subsequently tells us that "I could never endure to look in a Glass after mine Eyes had been accustomed to such prodigious Objects; because the Comparison gave me so dispicable a Conceit of my self" (2.8). Mirrors here accentuate the littleness of Gulliver's body and assault his pride. Later, he will reject that body altogether. For other comments on the "mirror" in *Gulliver,* see, especially, W. B. Carnochan, *Lemuel Gulliver's Mirror For Man* (Berkeley: Univ. of California Press, 1968), 139-40, 175-81.

[24] *The Fables of La Fontaine,* trans. Marianne Moore (New York: Viking Press, 1952), 22-23. *The Fables* appear (as No. 502) in the sale catalogue of Swift's books. See A CATALOGUE OF BOOKS, [IN] THE LIBRARY *of . . . Dr.* SWIFT (Dublin, 1745), 13; reprinted in Harold Williams, *Dean Swift's Library* (Cambridge: Cambridge Univ. Press, 1932).

[25] Brady, 360.

[26] For a publication history of Alciati's work, and his influence—both of which are extensive—see Henry Green, *Andrea Alciati and His Books of Emblems: A Biographical and Bibliographical Study* (London: Trübner and Co., 1872); and Vinge, 177-78, 180, 204.

[27] See Andrea Alciatus, *Emblemata . . .* CVM COMMENTARIIS *. . .* PER CLAVDIVM MINOEM (Antwerp, 1581), 261-70; and Figure I. Vinge (141) gives the following translation of Alciati's motto:

> Too much comfort and joy did you find in
> your beauty, Narcissus,
>> Therefore it turned to a flower and
>> stuporous herb.
> Self-love is death and decay of genius, and
> many a scholar
>> Such love brought to his fall; many men it

still destroys;
> Those who, rejecting the ways of their fathers,
> search for new
doctrines—
>> Then have nothing to give but their fanciful
>> whims.

[28] *A Tale of A Tub. To which is added the Battle of the Books, and the Mechanical Operation of the Spirit,* eds. A. C. Guthkelch and David Nichol Smith, 2nd ed., rev. (Oxford: Clarendon Press, 1958), 171.

[29] Frederick M. Keener, *The Chain of Becoming* (New York: Columbia Univ. Press, 1983), 79. Keener's chapter on self-love (55-85) and his analysis of *Gulliver* (89-126) are both relevant to my discussion, as are considerations in A. O. Hirschman, *The Passions and the Interests* (Princeton: Princeton Univ. Press, 1977), 9-66; Anthony Levi, S. J., *French Moralists: The Theory of the Passions* (Oxford: Clarendon Press, 1964), esp. 215-33; Lester Crocker, *The Age of Crisis* (Baltimore: Johns Hopkins Univ. Press, 1959), 202-17, 256-324; and A. O. Lovejoy, *Reflections on Human Nature* (Baltimore: Johns Hopkins Univ. Press, 1961), esp. 217-45.

[30] That Swift is attempting here to evoke a private world may account for one enigma often noticed: that is, the *Travels'* seeming lack of *explicit* allusion. A related point is the connection Swift and others made between pride and madness. In his influential *Two Discourses concerning the Soul of Brutes* (Pordage trans., London, 1683), Thomas Willis, for instance, asserts that "Ambition, Pride, and Emulation, have made some mad" (203). In studying Swift's *Tale,* Michael DePorte has traced the importance of the madness/pride association, and its relation to a corresponding loss of self and assumption of a delusional identity. (See DePorte's "Vehicles of Delusion: Swift, Locke, and the Madhouse Poems of James Carkesse," in *Psychology and Literature In the Eighteenth Century,* ed. C. Fox [New York: AMS Studies In the Eighteenth Century, 1987,] 69-86). A similar case could be made for Gulliver as one who goes mad through pride, and loses his identity while attempting to become something he is not. In discussing the "manner of ravings" of the insane, Willis notes that "Fabulous antiquity scarce ever thought of so many *metamorphoses* of men, which some have not believed really of themselves"; some (Willis adds) have even "believed themselves to be Dogs or Wolves, and have imitated their ways and kind by barking and howling" (*Two Discourses,* 188). Near the end of bk. IV, Gulliver declares that by

> conversing with the *Houyhnhnms,* and looking upon them with Delight, I fell to imitate their Gait and Gesture, which is now grown into a Habit; and my Friends often tell me in a blunt way, that *I trot like*

a Horse; which, however, I take for a great Compliment: Neither shall I disown, that in speaking, I am apt to fall into the Voice and manner of the *Houyhnhnms,* and hear my self ridiculed on that Account (4.10).

When he first saw the Houyhnhnms, Gulliver thought they must be "Magicians" (presumably "men") who had "metamorphosed themselves" into horses (4.1). In Gulliver's subsequent attempt to make the same transformation, to neigh and trot like the horses and imitate "their ways and kind," could we be witnessing yet another "metamorphosis"—in Willis's sense of the term? I have explored this question in a forthcoming essay, "Of Logic and Lycarthropy: Gulliver and the Faculties of the Mind."

[31] Maurice Merleau-Ponty, *Signs,* trans. R. C. McCleary (Evanston: Northwestern Univ. Press, 1964), 310. Also see Roland Barthes, *The Pleasure of the Text,* trans. Richard Miller (New York: Hill and Wang, 1975); and Jacques Derrida, *Of Grammatology,* trans. G. C. Spivak (Baltimore: Johns Hopkins Univ. Press, 1976). Derrida tells us that Rousseau's "masturbation . . . cannot be separated from his activity as a writer" (155). If this statement were applied to the narrator of the *Mechanical Operation,* Swift, I suspect, would agree.

[32] *The Mechanical Operation of the Spirit,* in *A Tale,* 288-89, 267.

[33] Alexander Pope, *The Art of Sinking in Poetry,* ed. Edna L. Steeves (1952; reprint ed., New York: Russell and Russell, 1968), 12-13.

[34] Joseph Glanvill, *The Vanity of Dogmatizing* (London, 1661), 119.

[35] See John Sitter, *Literary Loneliness in Mid-Eighteenth Century England* (Ithaca: Cornell Univ. Press, 1982).

[36] Edward Young, *The Complaint; Or, Night Thoughts,* bk. 8 ("Virtue's Apology") in *The Poetical Works* (London: Aldine, n.d.), vol. I, 210. At about the same time Young was seeing Narcissus as a positive ideal, others, in a related move, were challenging the traditional view of pride, turning the first of the medieval sins into a modern virtue. "[N]othing," said Hume, "is more useful to us in the conduct of life, than a due degree of pride" (*A Treatise of Human Nature,* ed. L. A. Selby-Bigge, rev. P. H. Nidditch, 2nd ed. [Oxford: Clarendon Press, 1978], 596).

Margaret Anne Doody (essay date 1995)

SOURCE: "Swift and Romance," in *Walking Naboth's Vineyard: New Studies of Swift,* edited by Christopher Fox and Brenda Tooley, University of Notre Dame Press, 1995, pp. 98-126.

[*Below, Doody argues that Swift's* Gulliver's Travels, *like all significant Western texts, builds on and is connected to the entire Western literary canon.*]

My topic may seem perverse. After all, in *Gulliver's Travels,* as we remember, the palace at Lilliput is set on fire "by the Carelessness of a Maid of Honour, who fell asleep while she was reading a Romance."[1] We may take this, if we will, as a symptom of Swift's own distrust of novelistic narrative of all kinds; the romance here is associated not only with female waste of time but also with incendiarism.[2] Moreover, this particular romance evidently committed the crowning sin of being boring. It is certainly but a poor compliment to the romance in question, which is not named. Yet perhaps it was too interesting, so the Maid sat up past her bedtime, trying to have some private time. Richardson improves upon Swift's hint in *Clarissa,* where Lovelace, in his elaborately plotted arrangement of the "fire" at Mrs. Sinclair's weaves into his tale the impressively detailed pseudo-fact that the accident was owing "to the carelessness of Mrs. Sinclair's cookmaid, who, having sat up to read the simple *History of Dorastus and Faunia* when she should have been in bed, had set fire to an old pair of callico window-curtains" (4:365).[3] Yet within both of these eighteenth-century works of fiction, the reference to "Romance" may serve not as a means of disposing of an unwanted form but rather as a (comic) admission of the presence of Romance within this romance, and the presence of awkward readers and the insistent absorption of the act of reading—an absorption that makes people careless.

My own project here must inevitably seem perverse, for I want to ignore some or most of the elements in *Gulliver's Travels* which we usually focus upon—and even to ignore temporarily its primary nature as a satire and the questions regarding the historical author's historically satiric intentions. I am going to look at what is often called "background." But we are getting less satisfied with that term. Individual works don't rise like clear blue vases against a background of wallpaper—the "background" proves to be an aspect of the fabric of a work. I believe that all novels are interconnected—at least, I mean in the Western tradition, a tradition which includes influences from Asia and Africa. All novels are connected, and every Western novel is related—in some way, at more or less distance—to every other. Swift's *Gulliver's Travels* is related to the context of Western fiction which is far larger than the developing eighteenth-century English novel. In that full context it looks a little less singular, for the major trends of Western fiction have never been entirely realistic. It is a satiric romance deriving from a host of romances. Let us not forget that the word "Novel" was not the dominant word for the longer prose fiction, and that the word "Romance" could still be used in a positive sense, at least in the first part of the century. In 1715 an English translator of Huet hopes that England will be able to produce romances.[4] Western literature included, as Huet shows, the whole tradition of prose fiction in the West from antiquity. Prose fiction in Greek and Latin had enjoyed a terrific boom in the Renaissance. Works by Heliodorus, Achilles Tatius, Longus, and others were translated and re-translated, as well as the almost omnipresent Latin novel *Asinus Aureus* or *Metamorphoses* by Apuleius. Boccaccio's early novel *Filocolo* shows the influence of Greek romance, well before the age of print, but once the age of print arrived the older fictions as well as new ones had an immensely expanded readership. If you liked reading novels—however much you kept this pastime to appropriately infrequent idle moments—in the seventeenth or eighteenth century, the literature you read included a number of highly popular works, like Heliodorus' *Aithiopika,* which have been occluded in the last two centuries. The anonymous editor of *The Adventures of Theagenes and Chariclia, A Romance* (2 vols., 1717), reproducing yet another English edition of this popular story, says "this book may be styled the *Mother Romance* of the World."[5] The association of Romance with the feminine indicates that prose fiction is considered suspiciously "feminine" as novelists have found, no excusso, quosdam extremi liquoris aspergine, alios putore nidoris faetidi a meis iam quassis scapulis abegisset.

[But the men . . . began to beat me again and would have killed me if my belly, compressed with the pain of the blows and full of an abundance of raw vegetables and weakened by a slimy flux, had not thrown out excrement like water from a pipe, forcing them away from my shattered back, some with the spray of the liquid, others by the putrid stink.] (1:Bk. X, 188)[8]

Much more decorously, it is true, Gulliver forces the Lilliputians away from him, first when he wishes to make water and later too one imagines when he disburthens himself. One pities the unfortunate two servants who must work with wheelbarrows to remove this daily product.

The violence of the ass's pain is picked up again in the description of the suffering dog in Book III of *Gulliver's Travels.* The dog is blown up by the operation of the bellows by the brutal physician—an operation which calls to mind Cervantes' "Prologo" of Part II of *Don Quixote* with its odd anecdote. In Seville, according to Cervantes, there once was a man who was in the habit of seizing any stray dog, thrusting a straw into its fundament and blowing it up as round as a ball. This man would then say to bystanders "and there always were many," ""Perhaps now your worships think that it is little labor to blow up a dog?""[9] In Swift's scene we see that a good deal of work goes into blowing up a dog (*hinchar un perro*) and that the animal suffers in

the infliction of inflation, like Lucius being beaten: "the Animal was ready to burst, and made so violent a Discharge, as was very offensive to me and my Companions" (155). The noxiousness of its discharge does not save this animal as it once saved Apuleius' Lucius, "The Dog died on the Spot. . . . "

Lucius the ass is always greedy (he was saved because of having eaten too many vegetables). Later he is able to indulge his taste for large quantities of food cooked for human beings when he serves the slaves of a pastry-cook and chef:

In the evenings after luxurious dinners . . . my masters used to bring back to their little lodging numerous leftovers: one brought pork, pullets, fish and generous remnants of every kind of meat; the other, breads, crisp biscuits, fritters, hook-shaped pastries, small biscuits and many other honeyed tidbits. When they had locked up and gone to the baths for refreshment, I would stuff myself full with these divine dainties. (2: Bk. X, 240)

Once he is discovered, the slaves and their masters realize there is money to be made out of Lucius' prowess in eating, especially once the master has tested this ass by offering him a feast of spicy food and good wine. "And I, although I was beautifully stuffed, wishing to be agreeable and win his commendation, hungrily fell to on the delicacies exhibited." He proves that he is fit to be instructed, tamed, and shown as a spectacle. "I had made my master famous with my wonderful arts. . . . 'Here' [people] said, 'is the man who possesses as friend and dinner-companion an ass—a wrestling ass, a dancing ass, an ass who understands human voices and can express his own meaning by nods'" (2: Bk. X, 249).

Swift's Gulliver has many of the same propensities—including the ability to save himself (temporarily at least) from extinction or banishment by becoming a spectacle and show. In Lilliput he shows off his eating prowess—very like the Golden Ass:

One day his imperial Majesty being informed of my Way of living, desired that himself, and his Royal Consort, with the young Princes of the Blood of both Sexes, might have the Happiness . . . of dining with me. They came accordingly. . . . *Flimnap* the Lord High Treasurer attended there likewise, with his white Staff; and I observed he often looked on me with a sour Countenance, which I would not seem to regard, but eat more than usual, in Honour to my dear Country, as well as to fill the Court with Admiration. (45)

It is an asinine thing to do, to eat more than usual. Once the pleasure in the wonder at the show has abated, the expense will become more and more noticeable.

Gulliver's odd mixture of pride and greed, like that seen in Lucius, exhibits and emblematizes his asininity. The ass in an older mythology, as Jack Winkler remarks in his commentary on Apuleius, is an emblem or symbol of Seth/Typhon, the enemy of Isis. In *The Golden Ass,* Lucius-as-ass has set himself in opposition to Isis and can be saved only by her.[10] Gulliver, I'd like to suggest—though this speculation isn't necessary to my main argument—likewise sets himself up against the Goddess (comically), illustrated in his urination on the Queen's palace. The Goddess figure reappears in the figure of Glumdalclitch (who treats him like a baby in Book II) in a land which fully illustrates the power of Ceres. In Book IV Gulliver rejects the power of Aphrodite in his rejection of the woman who makes advances to him—yet at the same time, he is comically yoked within a parody of marriage. The "Sorrel Nag" is Gulliver's companion and mate in Houyhnhnmland. Fortuna (Fortune) we may remember in Apuleius' story turns Lucius the ass into the partner of the white horse that he himself owns (or owned):

> Sed quid ego pluribus de Fortunae scaevitate conqueror, quam nec istud puduit me cum meo famulo meoque vectore illo equo factum conservum atque coniugem?

> [But what can I say more in complaint against the savagery of Fortune, than that she was not even ashamed of making me the fellow-slave and yokemate of my own servant and carrier, my own horse?] (2: Bk. VII, 8)

Gulliver boasts that the "Sorrel Nag" is "my Fellow-Servant (for so at this Distance I may presume to call him)" (245), when that horse is ordered by Gulliver's master to follow the talking Yahoo's "instructions." Gulliver asked for this particular helper: "I knew he had a Tenderness for me," Gulliver adds (246). This English traveler is ridiculously proud of what causes shame to Apuleius' hero. Gulliver is a horse's "Fellow-Servant"—an almost literal translation of *"conservum."* As several commentators have noted, Apuleius' word *"coniugem"* normally means "spouse" or "marriage partner," and Lucius is involved in a parodic marriage with his own (male) white horse. In Houyhnhnmland, of course, white is an inferior color, and Gulliver is partnered with a *sorrel* horse. In Gulliver's eyes, at least, this partnership exists—he calls himself a "Fellow Servant" with the Nag because that moves him up in the world. But in the Houyhnhnm's eyes, he cannot be even a servant, or a slave—he is classed with the beasts, the Yahoos. So is Lucius also, like Gulliver—Lucius reclassifies himself and the horse in terms of human beings: *famulus, servus.* As a Yahoo, Gulliver is inferior *even* to the asses. The ass-theme emerges directly in **Gulliver's Travels** towards the end of Book IV, when the Houyhnhnms discuss the matter at their assembly, and decide

That, the Inhabitants taking a Fancy to use the Service of the *Yahoos,* had very imprudently neglected to cultivate the Breed of *Asses,* which were a comely Animal, easily kept, more tame and orderly, without any offensive Smell, strong enough for Labour, although they yield to the other in Agility of Body; and if their Braying be no agreeable Sound, it is far preferable to the horrible Howlings of the *Yahoos.* (237)

The disagreeable sound of the ass's bray was not only proverbial, but enshrined in religious custom, according, for instance, to Plutarch, who tells us "The people of Busiris and Lykopolis do not use trumpets at all because they make a noise like an ass; and they believe the ass to be in general not a pure but a daemonic beast. . . . In the sacrifice to Helios they instruct those who venerate the god not to wear golden objects . . . nor to give food to an ass."[11] We may note that the last taboo is broken by the cook and baker and their master in Apuleius and, metaphorically, by all who give food to Gulliver—as well as literally by Tristram Shandy when he gives the ass a macaroon.[12] Gulliver shouts and hollers and brays—see the account of his rescue from the rocky island at the beginning of Book III, when he sees the flying island: "I called and shouted with the utmost Strength of my Voice" (131). The noises Gulliver makes confirm his Houyhnhnm acquaintance in the opinion that he is a Yahoo, inferior even to an ass in all respects including voice. If Lucius is embarrassed by being able to make only assy noises, Gulliver cannot even rise to that.

Apuleius' novel is only one version of a story perpetually told in novels of all kinds—the story of the hapless self injured, mutilated, transformed, displaced. One of the most common devices used in ancient and early modern fiction to image change and to effect it at the plot level is the shipwreck. Defoe's *Robinson Crusoe,* to which **Gulliver's Travels** is a direct response, is only one strong example of the use of a well-known device or trope of fiction—and *Robinson Crusoe* should itself be seen against the rich background of the fiction of "romance"—or of the story of the Novel of which it is a part. The ancient novelists use the shipwreck with a considerable degree of sophistication and variety. Heliodorus in his *Aithiopika* has caused his characters to encounter the vision of an annoyed Odysseus, condemning them to some accident and delay in requital for the lack of honor they have paid to him—a comic emblem of the Novel's usurping disrespect of the Epic. Achilles Tatius, through incremental repetition of accidents at sea and ghastly events on shipboard, plays with the shipwreck theme, as does Boccaccio in his fourteenth-century adaptation of the Greek novel motifs. The hero of his *Filocolo,* shipwrecked near Parthenope, (Napoli) complains to the gods, asking why they are persecuting him, "I am not Aeneas!"[13] In the Preface to *Ibrahim, ou L'illustre Bassa*, Madeleine de Scudéry (or her brother Georges) comments upon the frequent use of shipwrecks in fiction:

> As for me, I hold, that the more natural adventures are, the more satisfaction they give; and the ordinary Course of the Sun seemes more mervailous to me, than the strange and deadly rayes of Comets; for which reason it is also that I have not caused so many Shipwracks, as there are in some antient Romanzes . . . one might think that *Aeolus* hath given them the Winds inclosed in a bagg, as he gave them to *Vlysses,* soe patly doe they unchain them; they make tempests and shipwrack when they please, they raise them in the Pacifique Sea, they find rocks and shelves where the most expert Pilots have never observed any. . . . Howbeit I pretend not hereby to banish Shipwracks from *Romanzes,* I approve of them in the workes of others, and make use of them in mine; I know likewise that the Sea is the Scene most proper to make great changes in, and that some have named it the Theater of inconstancie. . . . [14]

Swift of course does raise storms (and other accidents) in the literal Pacific Sea (see the beginning of Book II). His well-thoughtout pattern of sea-incidents is based on true accounts like that of Dampier, as others have noted, but it also goes back to the novel tradition that stretches from antiquity. As Scudéry admits, one has to approve of shipwrecks in fiction; "the Sea is the Scene most proper to make great changes in." One catches here something of the late Renaissance sophistication about the emblems and tropes of fiction, and their sense of the depth of metaphorical meaning in fictional incident—a sense that Swift inherited and which enabled him to write fiction (and nonrealistic fiction, "romance," at that).

Both Defoe and Swift could draw on a great body of fiction dealing with transformed states, interracial and intercultural encounters, and sea-changes. Shipwrecked or marooned characters pop up in the pages of fiction. Of course, they still continue to do so—think of George Eliot's *Daniel Deronda* (1876) or Fay Weldon's *The Hearts and Lives of Men* (1987). In Cervantes' last novel, *Persiles y Sigismunda,* there are many surprising characters who have suffered shipwrecks along with other complex accidents. "Whether thou chuse Cervantes' serious air" is a line which can certainly bear reference to *Persiles* as well as to *Don Quixote.*[15] Early in Cervantes' last novel—which was, I believe, a major influence on both Defoe and Swift—we encounter Antonio, a man who has suffered misfortunes. A Spaniard, he was on an English ship leaving Lisbon for England. On the voyage he got into a quarrel with an English sailor and slapped him in the face. This led to a riot—one of the English gentlemen saved Antonio from being killed, but he was cast adrift in the ship's boat, a little dinghy, with some salt fat and hardtack

and two barrels of water. He drifts and rows, is nearly swamped by water, arrives on a rocky shore of a wolf-haunted island and has to flee. Eventually he is tossed upon a wild shore, and laments it, seeing here only the theater of his misfortunes. He sees no people, only mountain goats and small animals. Antonio is soon, however, comforted by the appearance of "a young Barbarian maide, about fifteen yeares of age."[16] He first sees her on the beach, gathering shellfish from the rocks. He takes her in his arms, takes her to his cave and kisses her (but does not rape her). She responds with interest and curiosity, and feeds him with bread not made from wheat; next day she comes to him with more supplies.

Antonio, referred to perpetually as "Spanish barbarian" finds in his "Barbarian maide" Ricla a perfect and providential helpmate. The two marry. His response to her is very visibly the opposite of the response of the terrified Gulliver to the Houyhnhnm girl in Book IV of *Gulliver's Travels.* (Ricla also represents what is so notably missing on Crusoe's island, a lack which Crusoe himself doesn't seem to notice.) The sensations and experiences of Antonio during his marooning-*cum*-shipwreck are very similar to those of Gulliver at the beginning of Book III and to his confused and chaotic travels after leaving Houyhnhnmland, before he is picked up by the Portuguese crew captained by Pedro de Mendez. Some symmetry of reference seems to be involved here. Cervantes' barbarian Antonio is an inhabitant of the Iberian peninsula who embarks *in* Lisbon on an English ship going to England—he is cast adrift by the *English.* In Swift's story (if we keep Cervantes' story in mind) the Portuguese crew are returning good for evil; this crew bound *for* Lisbon rescues an Englishman who is, in their eyes, marooned and adrift—as indeed Gulliver certainly was set adrift by an English crew before he settled among the Houyhnhnms as a Yahoo. In his ill-humor with the crew, Gulliver resembles the young Spanish barbarian who hit a foreign sailor—but Gulliver of course would not wish to touch a human.

In Cervantes' novel we encounter another victim of the sea, another actor in that "Theatre of inconstancie" in Rutilio, the former dancing master of Siena. After some vicissitudes, including his being condemned to death for a seduction and rescued by a witch, and then eluding the power of werewolves, he settled in Norway. He settles with his master and teacher, who is a goldsmith, and on a voyage with that master is wrecked and cast up on a barbarian shore where the first thing he sees is "a Barbarian hanged on a tree":

> having put off my clothes, and buried him in the sand, I put on his attire, which could not chuse but fit mee well, being none other but skinnes unsewed and never cut out by measure but bound onely on the body, as you have seene. The better to dissemble

their language, and not bee knowne for a stranger, I fained my selfe dumbe and deafe: and with this industrie I passed farther into the Isle, skipping & capering in the aire. . . .

. . . with this policie I passed for a Barbarian, and dumbe; and the children to see me leape, fed mee with such victualls as they had. (Bk. I, chap. 9, p. 43)

Rutilio the shipwrecked barbarian represents we might say the state of being shipwrecked in itself—strandedness. In all of these novels, and I am inclined to say in the Novel in general as a genre, coming to a shore is very important. Traversing, changing—coming to a new experience, a new phase of life—all of these are represented by the arrival on a shore. To arrive on a shore is to arrive at an Other Place, to begin to accept becoming Another Self. The traveler to another shore is symbolically naked, unclothed, or inadequately clothed and accoutered—even if like Charlotte Bronte's Lucy Snowe, crossing the Channel in *Villette*, he/she has brought a small trunk along (or has tried to do so). The Novel tends, in its stories and in its metaphors, to dwell on shores, on marshy or sandy margins where earth and water mingle and are not yet separated. Novel characters must always live on an edge, for a while. Gulliver, of course, lives very visibly on an edge several times—ranging from the shallow waters and soft shore of Lilliput to the current-driven edge and hard rocks of the shore of the uncomfortable island to which the castaway takes his canoe in the first chapter of Book III. "I found the Island to be all rocky, only a little intermingled with Tufts of Grass" (129). He lives hard, like Cervantes' Antonio and the "Barbarian maide": "I gathered Plenty of Eggs upon the Rocks, and got a quantity of dry Sea-weed, and parched Grass, which I designed to kindle the next Day, and roast my Eggs as well as I could. . . . My bed was the same dry Grass and Sea-weed which I intended for Fewel [sic]. . . . I considered how impossible it was to preserve my Life, in so desolate a Place" (130).

In another canoe, made of Yahoo skins, Gulliver hides on another shore, hoping to escape the observation of European human beings:

I . . . got into the same Creek from whence I set out in the Morning; choosing rather to trust my self among these *Barbarians* than live with *European Yahoos*. I drew up my Canoo [sic] as close as I could to the Shore, and hid my self behind a Stone by the Little Brook. . . .

Cowering behind a stone at the edge of an island, Gulliver is discovered by the Portuguese seamen:

at last they found me flat on my Face behind the Stone. They gazed a while in Admiration at my

strange uncouth Dress; my Coat made of Skins, my wooden-soaled Shoes, and my furred Stockings; from whence, however, they concluded I was not a Native of the Place, who all go naked. (249-250)

Gulliver is not one of the local tribes, those he termed "Barbarians"—because he is clothed. But his dress proclaims him a Barbarian. Cervantes' Rutilio dressed in skins attracts our attention with a kind of horror—not just because he is wearing uncouth clothing, but because he stole the rough skin garments from a dead man. He is like an executioner, taking the clothes of a hanged man. Rutilio, once a dancing-master (that is, someone who represents and teaches an excess of "civilization") and also formerly a goldsmith (that is, one who dresses people in layers of wealth) undergoes a devolution of civilization. A process of regression seems visibly at work in his fate—interestingly, layers are peeling off, like Peer Gynt's onion. He seems to be unselving in stages. Gulliver's unselving in stages takes longer. We watched him accustom himself to the simplicity demanded by his life in Houyhnhnmland:

When my Cloaths were worn to Rags, I made my self others with the Skins of Rabbets, and of a certain beautiful Animal about the same size, called *Nnuhnoh*, the Skin of which is covered with a fine Down. Of these I likewise made very tolerable Stockings. I soaled [sic] my Shoes with Wood which I cut from a Tree, and fitted to the upper Leather, and when this was worn out, I supplied it with the Skins of *Yahoos*, dried in the Sun. (241)

The Portuguese sailors wonder at Gulliver's clothes, including the wooden-soled shoes; they don't know what the uppers of these shoes are made of—fortunately for them. Rutilio attracts our wonder and horror because he is wearing a dead man's skins: Gulliver, because he is literally dressed in dead men's skins.

The figure of the Man in Skins turns up at odd moments in fiction, throughout the history of fiction. The most benevolent example of the figure is old Philetas in Longus' *Daphnis and Chloe*. He is described when he comes to see the two pubescent lovers; he is

presbyt s sisyran endedymenos, karbatinas hypodedemenos, p ran ex rt menos kai t n p ran palaian.[17]

(an old man wearing a rough outer garment of goatskin, with brogues of undressed leather upon his feet, and his leather wallet—an extremely antiquated leather wallet—hanging down.)

It is this old man who tells Daphnis and Chloe about the appearance of Eros in his garden—thus giving the youths the name of the god they serve and the name of the passion they feel (Love). Philetas can have the vision of Eros, and pass on the identification of Love, because he himself is past it—as indeed we may gather from the description, with the comic emphasis upon the antiquity or obsolence of his bag. The Man in Skins, whenever he appears in fiction, is an outsider, someone outside the central emotions, conduct, and structures known in society. It was the genius of Defoe to take this marginalized supernumery and make him into the central character or consciousness of the novel. But Defoe neither exhausts all the potential meanings nor subsumes all the representations of this figure (that is, men in skins in eighteenth-century fiction do not have to be merely allusions to Robinson in his goatskin garment and moccasins, his *sisyra* and *karbatinai*). Fielding's old Man of the Hill belongs to the whole tradition out of which he arises. He is aged, like Philetas—but unlike Philetas he cannot offer a vision of Eros. His story of his own life and desires is a sour story which has left him soured. Unlike Robinson, but very like Gulliver, he has chosen an antisocial solitude. He is frightening to look at:

> This Person was of the tallest Size, with a long Beard as white as Snow. His Body was cloathed with the Skin of an Ass, made something into the Form of a Coat. He wore likewise Boots on his Legs, and a Cap on his Head, both composed of the Skin of some other Animals. (*Tom Jones*, Bk. VIII, chap. x)[18]

It is because of what we know about Gulliver that Fielding can make us shudder at the phrase "Skin of some other Animals," and because of Gulliver's Yahoos and Apuleius' Lucius, we are not likely to be happy about the "Skin of an Ass."

What Gulliver has in common with all of these—Philetas, Robinson, the Man of the Hill—is a tendency to be both judgmental and prophetic—prophetic in the sense of "telling it like it is" rather than in the sense of foretelling the future. The figure of the Man in Skins, whenever and wherever we encounter him, is always oracular. What a Man in Skins has to say is never the whole truth, for this marginal personage cannot know the whole truth, just as he cannot be integrated into a careless society while remaining poised aside from it. But what the oracular Man in Skins has to say is always *some* truth. One of the later avatars of this figure is James Fenimore Cooper's Natty Bumppo, the deerslayer, Leatherstocking, who appears in all of Cooper's novels as an important figure but not the conventional hero of each story—a role borne by another. Natty, always the Man in Skins, comes to be a Philetas, an old man in skins, when we see him in *The Pioneers* (1823). Tall, thin, sun-tanned, wearing a foxskin cap and a "kind of coat, made of dressed deerskin," he also wears "deer-skin moccasins" and "long leggings of the same material as the moccasins, which, gartering over the knees of his tarnished buck-skin breeches, had obtained for him . . . the nick name of Leatherstocking" (*The Pioneers,* chap. 1).[19] As usual, the figure of the Man in Skins arouses in the reader fascination combined with a certain unease or aversion. The Man in Skins represents some sort of primary state which is a "pre" state, something precedent to a number of other things (such as civilization). Yet that pre-state may also be the post-state to which we tend (after love, marriage, or civilization are done for, or when life itself tends to its end). We fear the advent of the Man in Skins, for he is always a reminder of loss. For Cooper, of course, Bumppo is a reminder of historical loss—the loss of that first phase of individualistic pioneering without need of settlement, the absolute freedom without need of law which it must be the purpose of the other project, the founding of colonies and of the nation of America, to make men relinquish. But the Man in Skins always announces a number of losses, of deprivations. Like John the Baptist, another famous Man in Skins, this figure tells us we must give something up. Daphnis and Chloe, instructed by the mildest and most benign of these figures, must relinquish their childhood state and enter into an adult awareness of heterosexual love. Even such a gain as this means an advent of loss as well as of suffering—closing in the prospect of arriving at old age, and a new deprivation when love becomes impossible once more.

Gulliver is a Man in Skins, external to society, outside the world of marriage and civility. The Portuguese try forcibly to reintroduce him to these things—they strip him of the skins and put European clothing on him. But the captain's shirt smells too human, and inwardly Gulliver remains the Man in Skins comically clinging to his own "barbarism" as a means of informing us about our own. For the truth is that we're all Yahoos—this is the other side of Swift's coin. I am not using the novel's relation to other novels to try to push a view of Swift's story as "soft-boiled" in its moral. Gulliver is bizarre and stupid, with an un-Christian love of barbarism and an un-Platonic love of lurking in caves. These are unworthy and unreasonable tastes which the Portuguese sailors cannot but reprehend—and the more so, perhaps, if they have read Cervantes' *Persiles y Sigismunda.* From their point of view, Gulliver fits in very nicely with the pattern of barbarism in need of further development—the type encountered by the central characters of Cervantes' last novel in their journey towards holiness and fulfillment. But at the very same time, Gulliver's view of human beings holds true—except that he will not recognize that he is to be identified as human and thus must share in the condemnation.

Gulliver in his own progress is both civilized and civilizing hero and crude barbarian. The mixture of elements can be better understood if we consider Swift's story in the light of a work perennially popular from the eighth century A.D. through the Enlightenment, a work (or works) forgotten until very recently. This is the strange book best known as the *Alexander Romance,* though it has many other titles, such as *The Life of Alexander, History of Alexander, The Story of the Battles of Alexander* and so on. In the Middle Ages it existed in several distinct versions, a matter succinctly explained by Richard Stoneman in his preface to *The Greek Alexander Romance* published by Penguin Books (1991). This is a story (in its various versions) which has had an astonishingly wide influence over Western fiction; it can be felt in Dante and Chaucer, we can suspect it in Scudéry and Bunyan. There is a direct reference to it in Behn's *Oroonoko* (1688), or at least to material coming directly from that narrative.[20] It lies, I am convinced, in the background of ***Gulliver's Travels.***

The Story of Alexander might well be entitled "Alexander's Travels," for of course Alexander, conqueror of many lands, travels to many lands, some merely remote and some altogether fabulous. It does not seem to have been appreciated by the classical scholars who have worked on this text that the representation of the Alexander story in this fictional form offers a very sophisticated critique of Alexander's project. The story is told with an apparent simplicity of narrative which hides a deal of cunning in the strategies. Alexander, dauntless, heroic, godlike, is yet psychologically weakened by a dubious parentage which both confirms his claim to be a descendant of the god Ammon and denies him the right of inheritance to Philip's kingdom. Son of a secret liaison between Queen Olympias and an Egyptian priest, Alexander, quasi-Egyptian, is never quite sure what culture he serves, what heritage he has. That which makes him godlike makes him ambiguous. He kills his biological father, but remains in thrall to his mother, Olympias, and throughout his story he has complex relations with women and with the feminine. It is the voices of birds with women's faces (harpies in short) that warn him he can go no further; it is a woman, a black woman, Queen Candace of Ethiopia, who gets the better of him. Part of his response to the strange kingdoms he enters is always terror, which makes him furious. His project is justified in that he encounters both foes and barbarians— barbarians who prove to the Greek forces that they are in the civilizing right of it to come and conquer.

Alexander, like Gulliver, is consumed with curiosity to see new wonders and to make experiments. As he writes to his mother, Olympias, he conducted an experiment in "the country of the Apple-eaters":

> There we saw a huge man with hair all over his body, and we were frightened. I gave orders to capture him. When he was taken, he gazed at us ferociously. I ordered a naked woman to be brought to him; but he grabbed her and ate her. (*The Greek Alexander Romance,* 116)[21]

Not "Apple-eaters," evidently, but raw-flesh-eaters. Alexander's experiment is here carried out at the cost of the female's life, but the hairy man's cannibalism triumphantly proves his inhumanity. (I think this episode is recollected in *Candide,* in the adventure of the Oreillons in South America.)[22] Alexander is Gulliver's prototype not only in his curiosity, but in his activities as a sort of super-projector. He and his men come upon a troop of "animals resembling men": "from their heads to their navels they were like men, but below they were horses" (124). Using trickery, Alexander is able to trap and kill a lot of them with great bloodshed. He doesn't wish to kill them all:

> Alexander wanted to capture some of them and bring them back to our world. He brought about fifty out of the ditch. They survived for twenty-two days, but as he did not know what they fed on, they all died. (125)

The *Alexander Romance* seems satiric and ironic in itself—before Swift, as it were, gets there. Alexander is a careless collector who wants to exhibit the centaurs but forgets to find out what to feed them.

Alexander is, in some of the lights offered by this book, a mad exploiter, forcing upon the world the horrible benefit of his conquest, a hero of what Swift calls "conquests and systems." At one point in the *Alexander Romance* the hero is directly rebuked by a group who set themselves over against him, absolutely. Having conquered India he encounters the "naked philosophers," the gymnosophists, who are not afraid of him, as they have no wealth he can steal, and want nothing from him. Rather, they let him see that they judge him. Their creed is explained in an exchange of questions and answers:

> Alexander asked them some questions. "Do you have no graves?" was the first.
>
> "The ground where we dwell is also our grave," came the reply. "Here we lie down and, as it were, bury ourselves when we sleep. The earth gives us birth, the earth feeds us, and under the earth when we die we spend our eternal sleep."
>
> . . . . .
>
> "Which is the wickedest of all creatures?"
>
> "Man," they replied.
>
> And he, "Why?"
>
> "Learn from yourself the answer to that. You are a wild beast, and see how many other wild beasts you have with you, to help you tear away the lives of other beasts."

Alexander was not angry, but smiled. Then he asked, "What is kingship?"

"Unjust power used to the disadvantage of others; insolence supported by opportunity; a golden burden." (132)

The gymnosophists' answer, that is, is that humans are Yahoo, and Alexander a chief Yahoo. In a way, little needs to be added in Swift's book, save his satire on the idea of the naked philosophers themselves. The Houyhnhnms are the only true naked philosophers, our humanity not being capable of furnishing true gymnosophists. These horse-people truly accept death and dying.

[H]er Husband . . . she said happened that very Morning to *Lhnuwnh*. The Word is strongly expressive in their Language, but not easily rendered into *English;* it signifies, *to retire to his first Mother.* (*Gulliver's Travels,* 240)

The Houyhnhnms do not have tombstones, anymore than the gymnosophists.

The *Alexander Romance* itself could also have been instrumental in suggesting to Swift the employment of horses as the wise race. As we have seen, there are men-horses in the narrative, but the most important horse is Alexander's steed Bucephalus, who has some rational characteristics. Bucephalus, visiting Alexander on the king's deathbed, sheds tears. The Sorrel Nag doesn't go quite that far on bidding farewell to Gulliver, though the last word from Houyhnhnmland is the sound of "the Sorrel Nag (who always loved me) crying out . . . Take care of thy self, gentle *Yahoo*" (248). Bucephalus also possesses the violence that Gulliver himself at length wishes to attribute to the gentle Houyhnhnms. When Bucephalus comes into the presence of the man who has poisoned Alexander, the horse takes revenge for his dying master:

When Bucephalus saw him, he cast off his morose and dejected look, and, just as if he were a rational, even a clever man—I suppose it was done through Providence above—he avenged his master. He ran into the midst of the crowd, seized the slave in his teeth and dragged him to Alexander; he shook him violently and gave a loud whinny to show that he was going to have his revenge. Then he took a great leap into the air, dragging the treacherous and deceitful slave with him, and smashed him against the ground. The slave was torn apart; bits of him flew all over everyone like snow falling off a roof in the wind. (*The Greek Alexander Romance,* 157)

(This event is the less surprising if we remember that Bucephalus was a man-eating and untameable horse until young Alexander tamed him.)

The description of Bucephalus' revenge may remind us of Gulliver's fantasy of the Houyhnhnms' violent resistance to a European conquest:

Their Prudence, Unanimity, Unacquaintedness with Fear, and their Love of their Country would amply supply all Defects in the military Art. Imagine twenty Thousand of them breaking into the Midst of an *European* Army, confounding the Ranks, overturning the Carriages, battering the Warriors faces into Mummy, by terrible Yerks from their hinder Hoofs; For they would well deserve the Character given to *Augustus: Recalcitrat undique tutus.* (257-58)

We may reflect, however, that Gulliver's fantasy may be pious wish, implicitly denied in the *Alexander Romance* where the centaurs, who were unanimous, brave, and patriotic were still miserably defeated because "as beasts they were incapable of understanding the devilment of men" (124). They decide to charge into the Macedonians, despising them for their cowardice, but they tumble into the treacherous grass-covered ditch that has been dug to receive them. Unused to lying, the Houyhnhnms would be outdone by the treacherous Europeans, who, like Alexander's Greeks and Macedonians, do not mind looking cowardly for a time if they can obtain their ends by any means.

Gulliver, then as we have seen thus far, is an Ass, a Victim of Shipwreck, a Man in Skins, and a parodic Alexander. But there are two other aspects of Gulliver which strongly relate him to character types and characteristic events in other fiction. Gulliver is both the Enslaved Person and the Foundling Child—the latter in a special category as Floating Child.

In many novels, central characters undergo a period of enslavement, or at least of imprisonment accompanied by destitution. I believe this experience underlies the plot of the Novel and that metaphorically it can be found in all novels, but novel characters at the most literal level of plot often are forced to enter prisons, vicious schools, insane asylums, etc., in order to fulfill this novelistic fate. In the Greek novels of antiquity the central characters are customarily enslaved for a certain length of time. The slavery involves captivity and customarily bondage. Gulliver is in bondage when tied with strings by the Lilliputians, as Lucian's hero was seized by the sun-people and bound with cobwebs. Even when the slavery is in the most luxurious circumstances, it is nonetheless painful for the person(s) undergoing it. Joseph is the biblical archetype of the wrongfully enslaved free person who becomes servant in a palace. He is the Imprisoned Courtier, whose very virtue in refusing Potiphar's wife lands him in renewed captivity.

In Heliodorus' *Aithiopika,* both hero and heroine

become the captive of the Persians, nominal slaves of Oroondates, the satrap of the Great King, but really the possession of Arsake, his wife, who reigns as queen in her palace at Memphis in Persian splendor. She is much attracted to the hero, Theagenes, who decides to humor her and use his enslaved position with good grace in order to preserve both himself and his beloved Charikleia. Theagenes becomes a special type of the Enslaved Person of fiction—he becomes the Imprisoned Courtier, entering the world of court life with its petty jealousies and jockeyings. In Theagenes' case, he must watch out for his fellow-slave Achaimenes, son of the Queen's nurse Kybele, who wants Charikelia for himself.

> The next day Achiamenes took him to wait at table, as Arsake had commanded. He changed into the sumptuous Persian apparel she had sent him and, with a mixture of delight and disgust, bedecked himself with bangles of gold and collars studded with precious gems. Achaimenes then tried to demonstrate and explain to him something of the art of cup bearing, but Theagenes ran to one of the tripods on which the cups stood, picked up one of the precious vessels, and exclaimed: "I have no need of teachers! I shall use my instinct in serving my mistress. . . . "

He mixes a delicious drink and serves the cup with "exquisite grace" to the charmed Arsake.

> The rage and envy that filled his [Achaimenes'] heart were so obvious that even Arsake noticed him scowling and muttering something under his breath to his companions. (Bk. VII)[23]

Gulliver, we may remember, begins his life in Brobdingnag as a slave—as he tells the Queen:

> She asked, whether I would be content to live at Court. I bowed down to the Board of the Table, and humbly answered, that I was my Master's Slave, but if I were at my own Disposal, I should be proud to devote my Life to her Majesty's Service. (*Gulliver's Travels,* 80)

When the Queen graciously makes the purchase, Gulliver is not slow to pick up the manner of court flattery which the necessity of surviving has evidently taught him. He tells her

> I was out of all fear of being ill treated under the Protection of so great and good an Empress, the Ornament of Nature, the Darling of the World, the Delight of her Subjects, the Phoenix of the Creation. . . . (80-81)

Like Theagenes, he arouses the jealousy of a rival—in his case, the palace Dwarf. Gulliver becomes the pet courtier. Like Theagenes he wears silken garments:

> The Queen likewise ordered the thinnest Silks that could be gotten, to make me Cloaths; not much thicker than an *English* Blanket. . . . They were after the Fashion of the Kingdom, partly resembling the *Persian,* and partly the *Chinese;* and are a very grave decent Habit. (83)

Gulliver does not have to wait at table as a cup-bearer, like those Ganymede figures Theagenes and Joseph—indeed, he could not physically do so. But his life at the Brobdingnagian court is very strongly associated with the table.

> The Queen became so fond of my Company, that she could not dine without me. I had a Table placed upon the same at which her Majesty eat, just at her left Elbow . . . I had an entire set of Silver Dishes and Plates, and other Necessaries. . . . She [the Queen] drank out of a Golden Cup, above a Hogshead at a Draught. (83-84)

Arsake sent her prisoners some food in her own golden dishes (chap. 18); this is "Persian" style. Swift's comedy parodies the oriental splendor.

Of course the palace of Brobdingnag does not have the secret and unwholesome eroticism of the palace of Memphis. Yet there *is* an Oedipal eroticism diffused through the second book of *Gulliver's Travels* which can seem reminiscent of certain elements in the *Aithiopika.* In both cases, imprisoned visitors are subjected perforce to a smothering maternal rule. Kybele, the old nurse, speaks to Arsake as her baby and also treats the imprisoned pair as infants, addressing them as "My children," *"O tekna."* Taking the hint, Theagenes repeatedly addresses her as "Mother" (*O m ter*).[24] Gulliver is perpetually mothered in Brobdingnag, by Glumdalclitch chiefly but also by the Queen. A good case could be made out for Brobdingnag as the land of the Feminine, the abode of Ceres. Ceres is properly worshipped by the King, who forswears fighting and violence, armies and the gift of gunpowder, and celebrates the virtue of making "two Ears of Corn, or two Blades of Grass to grow upon a Spot of Ground where only one grew before" (111). Unlike the realm of the Persian in Heliodorus' story, this feminine place is a good place—the Great Good Place indeed! But Gulliver can partake of its goodness only by becoming like a little child.

This leads me to the last comparison. Gulliver has, as we have seen, in his time played many parts in Romance's repertoire: Curious Traveler, Metamorphosed Man (or Ass), Man in Skins, Enslaved Person, Imprisoned Courtier. The last role I wish to look at may be described as the Foundling, or Rescued Child. More particularly, Gulliver belongs to what may be called a subset of that category, the Precious-Child-in-a-Floating-Box. Moses may be called the most famous as well as the most important representative of that type. But the literary tradition offers numerous other examples in prose fiction.

The most famous case is that of the celebrated Amadis of Gaul. Amadis is illicitly conceived and born illegitimate. His mother, Elisena, long virtuous and known for her great discretion, falls in love with an attractive visitor, King Perion, invited by her father to his castle. The two lovers have ten nights of passion—and Amadis is the result. The Princess bears him secretly, with the help of her maidservant, who also devises the "ark" in which the baby is to be cradled:

> she obtained four boards large enough so that a baby with its swaddling clothes could be contained therein as in an ark, and as long as a sword, and she caused certain materials to be brought for making a pitch with which she might join them together so that water would not enter.[25]

After the birth, the Princess and her faithful Darioleta place the handsome child in the box, along with the sword of King Perion his father, and a letter saying the infant is "Amadis, the Ill-Timed" (*"Amadis sin Tiempo"*).

> This done, she [Darioleta] put the plank on top so well joined and calked that neither water nor anything else could enter there. And taking it in her arms and opening the door, she put it in the river and let it go. And as the water was high and strong it soon passed out to sea, which was not more than half a league away. (Bk. I, 36)

The strange floating object is miraculously saved: a passing ship contains a Scottish knight, Gandales, and his wife, who have just become parents:

> And going at full speed on their way to Scotland, the morning being already clear, they saw the ark floating on the water; and summoning four sailors, he ordered them quickly to cast off a small boat and bring the ark to him, which was speedily done, although the ark had already floated a long distance from the ship. (36)

The Scottish knight and his wife discover the infant; the knight picks the child up, saying "This is from some good place." The wife "put it to the breast of that nurse who was rearing Gandalin, her own son." The baby thus delivered unharmed to its foster parents is called "Child of the Sea" (*el Donzel del Mar*).

Gulliver in Book II is always living in boxes. When Glumdalclitch attends the royal party on a tour of the coast, an accident happens at the seaside; a huge Brobdingnagian bird picks up Gulliver's box and drops it into the sea. Gulliver describes, as baby Amadis could not, the horror of being in the sea and in danger of the waves, as the tight box begins to leak a bit. It is less surprising that Gulliver's box is discovered by a passing ship than that Amadis' container is so discovered, as Gulliver's ark is so huge (a "Swimming House") in the eyes of the English sailors. But, like a baby, Gulliver is "taken into the Ship in a very weak Condition." The Captain is puzzled and "desired I would give him a Relation of my Travels, and by what Accident I came to be set adrift in that monstrous wooden Chest" (II, 118-19).

The Captain thinks of the other alternative, that Gulliver was in that box as a punishment for his crimes. But Gulliver was in the box because of his toylike innocence, the entertaining charm and helpless passivity that he had displayed, babylike in the land of the Big People (which is what children call adults). As a precious child, he has been preserved in his floating box in the sea, according to the best romantic tradition. He does come "from a good place." Unlike Amadis, he loses rather than regains the breast when he is taken aboard. He is a "Child of the Sea"—but once his box is destroyed and he has displayed all the tokens he has with him, he must consent to be adopted into normal English adult life. Unlike the hero of fiction, he will not recover the lost heritage—he can never get back to the feminine comforts and discomforts of Brobdingnag, the babyish pleasure of the company of "my dear little Nurse" (II, 99). Perhaps he is never again as close to the female sexual organs as he was then, in an infancy which placed him perilously close to the holy organs and the monstrous breast. He has lost his Motherland. Unlike Amadis (or Tom Jones, the Foundling) he cannot reclaim anything, or assert a title to something. He tries, at the end of the story, to assert his title to be considered a Horse, but this is not a title he can win by any feats. We can, however, if we wish, call him an Ass—and ourselves too.

Swift had, I believe, a very deep and long-standing knowledge of all kinds of fiction, including long works of prose fiction, or "Romances." One of the reasons *Gulliver's Travels* lasts so very well is that it draws upon the deep traditions of prose fiction in the West and is itself a virtuoso performance within that tradition.

Notes

[1] Jonathan Swift, *Gulliver's Travels,* ed. Robert A. Greenberg (New York and London: W. W. Norton, 1970), 37. All citations refer to this edition.

[2] "Women in (religious or moral) Guides are often advised that their imaginations can become overheated if they read romances (the source of Swift's joke about maids of honor in Lilliput). . . . " J. Paul Hunter, *Before Novels: The Cultural Contexts of Eighteenth-Century Fiction* (New York and London:

W. W. Norton, 1990), 265.

[3] Samuel Richardson, *Clarissa: Or the History of a Young Lady,* rpt. of 3rd edition (1751), 8 volumes, in The Clarissa Project, AMS Press, 1990. The work of fiction alluded to here, usually given as *Dorastus and Fawnia* when not called by its chief title *Pandosto,* is a work of prose fiction by Robert Greene, published in 1588; it supplied the plot for Shakespeare's *The Winter's Tale.*

[4] See the Preface of 1715 to a new translation of Pierre Daniel Huet's *Truité de l'origine des romans,* a work first published as a preface to Mme. De La Fayette's *Zaïde* (1670), then issued in amplified form in French and in Latin. Stephen Lewis, the translator, remarks: "I have no great Reason to fear its being well received in *English:* Especially since *Romance* has of late convey'd it self very far into the Esteem of this Nation, and become the principal Diversion of the Retirement of People of all Conditions.

"And (tho' we have been hitherto, for the most part, supply'd with Translations from the *French*) it is to be hoped, that we *won't* any longer subsist upon *Reverse:* but that some *English Genius* will *dare* to *Naturalize Romance* into our Soil." Preface to *The History of Romance,* "an inquiry into their Original; Instructions for Composing them; an Account of the most Eminent Authors. . . . Written in Latin by Huetius, Made English by Mr. STEPHEN LEWIS" (London: J. Hooke and I. Caldecott, 1715).

[5] "Dedication" to *The Adventures of Theagenes and Chariclia, A Romance. Being the Rise, Progress, Tryals, and happy Success of the HEROIC LOVES of those Two illustrious Persons* (London: W. Taylor, E. Curll, *et al.,* 1717), I, xxvi.

[6] Marjorie Hope Nicolson, *Voyages to the Moon* (New York: Macmillan, 1948).

[7] Lucian of Samosata, "A True History," trans. Lionel Casson in *Selected Satires of Lucian,* ed. and trans. Lionel Casson (New York and London: W. W. Norton, 1962), 13-54. All other references are to this version.

[8] Apuleius, *Metamorphoseon sive Asinus Aureus* (*Metamorphoses,* or *The Golden Ass*) in *The Golden Ass,* Loeb edition, 2 vols., ed. and trans. J. Arthur Hanson (Cambridge, Mass.: Harvard University Press, 1989). Although I have consulted various translations including that in the Loeb, passages are given in my own version.

[9] *Pensarán vuestras mercedes ahora que es poco trabajo hinchar un perro?*—The meaningless performance is, Cervantes indicates, a parallel to writing:—*Pensará vuestra merced ahora que es poco trabajo hacer un libro?*—"Does your worship think now that it is little labor to make a book?"

Miguel de Cervantes, *Don Quijote de la Mancha,* ed. Martin de Riquer (Barcelona; Editorial Juventud, S. A., 1968), 537. All references are to this edition, with my translation unless otherwise indicated.

[10] John J. Winkler, *Auctor & Actor: A Narratological Reading of Apuleius's the Golden Ass* (Berkeley and London: University of California Press, 1985), 313-16.

[11] Plutarch, *de Iside,* as quoted by John J. Winkler, *Auctor & Actor,* 314.

[12] Laurence Sterne, *The Life and Opinions of Tristram Shandy, Gentleman,* ed. Ian Watt (Boston: Houghton Mifflin, 1965), Bk. VII, chap. xxxii, 398-99.

[13] In Giovanni Boccaccio's *Filocolo* (a novel written c. 1336-38), the hero after shipwreck exclaims aggrievedly: "And thou, O highest Aeolus, merciless father of Canace, temper your wrath, unjustly raised against me. Open thine eyes, and know that I am not Aeneas, the great enemy of holy Juno: I am a young man who loves, just as thou hast loved before" (my translation).

[14] *Ibrahim, or the Illustrious Bassa.* An Excellent New Romance. The Whole book. In Five Parts. Written in French by Monsieur de Scudery, and Now Englished by Henry Cogan, Gent. (London: Humphry Moseley, William Bentley & Thomas Heath, 1652). Although Monsieur de Scudéry lent his name to the title pages of the novels, the real author is generally agreed to have been his sister Madeleine de Scudéry. *Ibrahim* (published 1641) was one of her early novels.

[15] Alexander Pope, *The Dunciad Variorum,* I, 1. 19; see *The Poems of Alexander Pope,* ed. John Butt (New Haven: Yale University Press, 1965), 351.

[16] *The History of Persiles and Fayre Sigismunda* (London, 1620), Bk. I, chap. 6, p. 30. All further quotations are taken from this edition. There were later translations of this novel, including *Persiles and Sigismunda: A Celebrated Novel,* published in 2 volumes in 1741, prefaced with an extract from Bayle's "General Historical Dictionary" in praise of the novel, concluding "Briefly, this Performance is of a better Invention, more artificial Contrivance, and of a more sublime Stile than that of *Don Quixote de la Mancha.*"

[17] Longus, *Daphnis and Chloe,* Loeb edition (Cambridge, Mass: Harvard University Press, 1988) [rpt. of 1916 edition], Bk. II, chap. 6, p. 70. My translation is assisted by that supplied in the Loeb (a revision of George Thornley's translation of 1657) and by several other translations, but it is not a reproduction of any of them.

[18] Henry Fielding, *The History of Tom Jones, A Foundling,* as *Tom Jones,* ed. Sheridan Baker (New York: W. W. Norton, 1973), 340.

[19] James Fenimore Cooper, *The Pioneers, or the Sources of the Susquehanna. A Descriptive Tale,* ed. James Franklin Beard (Albany, N.Y.: State University of New York Press, 1980), 23.

[20] See Aphra Behn, *Oroonoko: Or, The Royal Slave.* With an Introduction by Lore Metzger (New York and London: W. W. Norton, 1973): Oroonoko, now named "Caesar," as a slave in South America, according to the female narrator needed activity: "and though all Endeavours were us'd to exercise himself in such Actions and Sports as this World afforded, as . . . Killing *Tygers* of a monstrous size, which this Continent affords in abundance; and wonderful *Snakes,* such as *Alexander* is reported to have encounter'd at the River of *Amazons,* and which *Caesar* took great delight to overcome; yet these were not actions great enough for his large Soul, which was still panting after more renown'd Actions" (47).

This passage recaptures some of the excitements of the adventures and geography of the traditional *Alexander Romance,* and in doing so emphasizes resemblances between Oroonoko and Alexander. Not the least of their resemblances appears to be that both are fictional characters based on factual persons.

[21] *The Greek Alexander Romance,* translated with an Introduction and Notes by Richard Stoneman (Harmondworth, Middlesex: Penguin Books, 1991). All further quotations refer to this edition. This is not, however, the only modern English version available. An Armenian version was translated by A. Wolohojian as *The Romance of Alexander the Great, By Pseudo-Callisthenes* (New York and London: Columbia University Press, 1969). The *Alexander Romance* also appears translated by Ken Dowden in *Collected Ancient Greek Novels,* ed. B. P. Reardon (Berkeley, Los Angeles and London: University of California Press, 1989), 650-735.

[22] See Voltaire, *Candide, ou l'Optimisme* (1759), chap. 16; in *Voltaire: Romans et Contes,* ed. René Pomeau (Paris, Garnier-Flammarion, 1966), 211-14.

[23] Heliodorus, *Aithiopika,* translated by John Morgan as *An Ethiopian Story* in *Collected Ancient Greek Novels,* 349-588; see p. 514.

[24] For the Greek text of Heliodorus' novel I follow the dual-language version *Les Éthiopiques,* 3 vols., ed. R. M. Rattenbury and T. W. Lumb, trans. J. Maillon (Paris: Budé, "Les Belles Lettres," 1960). The passages here referred to are to be found in Bk. VII, chap. 12, chap. 13, chap. 17; see vol. 2: 135, 136, 142.

[25] Garci Rodríguez de Montalvo, *Amadis of Gaul, Books I and II,* translated by Edwin B. Place and Herbert C. Behm (Lexington: University Press of Kentucky, 1974), Bk. I, p. 34. All further quotations are from this translation. Quotations in Spanish are taken from *Amadis de Gaula,* ed. Juan Manuel Cacho Blecua, 2 vols. (Madrid: Catedra Letras Hispanicas, 1987), 1: 246; 253.

Denis Donoghue (essay date 1996)

SOURCE: "The Brainwashing of Lemuel Gulliver," in *The Southern Review,* Vol. 32, No. 1, Winter, 1996, pp. 128-46.

[*Below, Donoghue discusses ways in which Swift challenged Enlightenment thought and mocked Locke's "tabula rasa" conception of human consciousness, and instead viewed men as destined to be "brainwashed" by ineluctable cultural, political, and social forces.*]

On october 28, 1726, the London printer Benjamin Motte issued the first volume of *Travels into Several Remote Nations of the World* by Lemuel Gulliver, "first a surgeon, and then a captain of several ships." A few readers knew that the real author was Jonathan Swift, Dean of St. Patrick's Cathedral—"the cathedral close"—in Dublin. Presumably they took the book as a squib, a throwaway from the Dean's official life or a satire on those in power in London who had banished him to the wilderness of Dublin in 1714. The book was an immediate success: two further editions were required in 1726, two more in 1727. John Gay wrote Swift a few days after the book appeared to report that "from the highest to the lowest it is universally read, from the cabinet-council to the nursery." Some readers enjoyed it as an attack on Whiggery in general and Sir Robert Walpole in particular. Those who brought it into the nursery read it as a yarn populated by big men and little men. Viscount Bolingbroke was evidently the first reader to interpret it as an offensive book, "a design of evil consequence to depreciate human nature." This sense of the book became common twenty-five or thirty years later: that *Gulliver's Travels* is not, as Swift's friend Arbuthnot called it, "a pleasant humorous book," but a libel upon mankind.

It is essential to the character of *Gulliver's Travels* that readers should mistake it for something else that in certain respects it resembles: a serious travel book, a parody travel book, a philosophical allegory like *Candide,* or a vision, like More's, of Utopia. The book is a simulacrum, inserted in the space between whatever at first it may appear to be and what on second thought it may otherwise appear to be. It has lasted for 250 years, mainly because readers can't be certain they know what kind of book they're reading, even if they know that a trick of impersonation is being played on them. The book is as bizarre in its way as, in quite another way, *A Tale of a Tub.* Many readers have read both and decided, like the scholars in Brobdingnag who examine Gulliver, that the object of attention is *relplum scalcath,* or *lusus naturae,* a freak of nature.

The most useful preliminary description of *Gulliver's Travels* I have seen is Northrop Frye's account of the genre it embodies. I refer to his essay "The Four Forms of Prose Fiction," according to which the forms are novel, confession, romance, and anatomy. Most people, Frye says, would call *Gulliver's Travels* fiction but not a novel:

> It must then be another form of fiction, as it certainly has a form, and we feel that we are turning from the novel to this form, whatever it is, when we turn from Rousseau's *Emile* to Voltaire's *Candide,* or from Butler's *The Way of All Flesh* to the Erewhon books, or from Huxley's *Point Counterpoint* to *Brave New World.* The form thus has its own traditions, and, as the examples of Butler and Huxley show, has preserved some integrity even under the ascendancy of the novel. Its existence is easy enough to demonstrate, and no one will challenge the statement that the literary ancestry of *Gulliver's Travels* and *Candide* runs through Rabelais and Erasmus to Lucian.

Gulliver's Travels, then, is an anatomy, as in Robert Burton's *Anatomy of Melancholy,* where anatomy means dissection or analysis. Frye also called it a Menippean satire, a type of fiction that "deals less with people as such than with mental attitudes" (in which respect it differs from the novel). In the anatomy, "pedants, bigots, cranks, parvenus, virtuosi, enthusiasts, rapacious and incompetent men of all kinds are handled in terms of the 'humor' or ruling passion, their occupational approach to life as distinct from their social behavior." It is a feature of the anatomy that characterization is stylized rather than realistic: people are presented as mouthpieces of the ideas or notions they hold. In an anatomy the chief character is often a pedant, a lunatic of one idea. Reading *Gulliver's Travels,* one is bemused to find Gulliver continually doing the same thing, getting himself into the same predicament, like Charlie Chaplin or Buster Keaton. A constant theme in the anatomy, Frye remarks, is ridicule of the *philosophus gloriosus;* Lucian ridicules the Greek philosophers, Rabelais and Erasmus the scholastics, Swift the Cartesians and the Royal Society, Voltaire the Leibnizians, Peacock the Romantics, Samuel Butler the Darwinists, Huxley the behaviorists. The reason for this is that "while the novelist sees evil and folly as social diseases, the Menippean satirist sees them as diseases of the intellect, as a kind of maddened pedantry which the *philosophus gloriosus* at once symbolizes and defines." The anatomy, finally, "presents us with a vision of the world in terms of a single intellectual pattern." It often achieves this pattern by imposing upon its image

of life "a logical and self-consistent shift of perspective, presenting it as Lilliputian or Brobdingnagian," or by telling the story "from the point of view of an ass, a savage, or a drunk." Or else "it will take the form of a 'marvelous journey' and present a caricature of a familiar society as the logical structure of an imaginary one."

My reference to *A Tale of a Tub* allows me to remark that *Gulliver's Travels,* like the *Tale,* exhibits instances of irony stable and unstable, to use Wayne Booth's distinction in *The Rhetoric of Irony.* In stable irony we have only to make one interpretive move and we are back on solid ground. When Gulliver offers to make cannon-guns and explosives for use by the King of Brobdingnag, we have only to make one move to see that Gulliver and the European civilization for which he speaks are being reflected on. But the irony in *Gulliver's Travels* is often unstable: after one interpretive move we find ourselves still on shifting sands, as in the voyage to the Houyhnhnms. In stable irony there is always an imaginary point from which the world can be viewed in its entirety; in unstable irony there is no such point. Instead there is a sequence of equivocation that we bring to an end only arbitrarily, when we have had as much equivocation as we can bear. Nor is the irony Kierkegaardian, that is, propelled by the ironist's desire to feel free, to enjoy the freedom of having no motive other than that enjoyment. We have no such impression of *Gulliver's Travels.* Swift's irony in that book is local, opportunistic, and irregular. You may call it negative if, like F. R. Leavis, you construe the book as sustained by no system of values (unlike, say, Pope's *Dunciad*). If, reading the *Tale,* you are not happy with the serene and peaceful possession of being well deceived, you may choose to be undeceived, with no greater boon of happiness.

It is generally held that the mischief of *Gulliver's Travels* is postponed till the fourth voyage and Gulliver's encounters with the Houyhnhnms and the Yahoos. In fact, the mischief begins with Swift's presentation of Gulliver himself. When writers of fiction establish first-person narration, they usually give their narrators enough capacity to understand their experiences or the events they witness: not necessarily every capacity, but enough to report on events. Some writers, notably Henry James, can't bear to have their stories told by an idiot, a fool, or a villain. James knew that such people exist, and must be acknowledged in fiction, but he didn't think they should have the responsibility of delivering the main issues or of being the chief personages of the fiction. He wondered about Fielding's procedure in *Tom Jones,* and only reluctantly came to think it was acceptable: the gist of his acceptance was that while Tom hasn't a brain in his head, Fielding has enough brains for both of them. But in *Gulliver's Travels,* while Gulliver is neither idiot, fool, nor villain, he is barely qualified to take the force and point of his experience. He is given some competence in navigation and the rudiments of medicine, but he can deal with experience only when it comes in a form he can count or measure. Swift has created in Gulliver one of the most memorable characters in fiction by giving him virtually no character at all, no imagination, no depth of feeling, no resources of inner life beyond the attributes of a hack reporter on a local newspaper. He has no sense of anything beneath the visible surface, no powers of divination, and no inkling of the need for such powers.

We generally assume that each of us sees the world from his or her own point of view. It would be distressing if we found that our sense of the world differed fundamentally from everyone else's. We take it for granted that our perceptions don't differ drastically from those of most other people, and we practice the domestic economy of assuming the world is, by and large, as we see it: we make for ourselves a picture, a rudimentary diagram, and we act upon that. When we say Gulliver has no imagination, we also mean that he doesn't feel the lack or the need of it; he is too busy reporting events as if they had only to be reckoned, weighed, and counted. He thrives—or at least gets along—on the penury of his interests.

So readers must take an unusually active part in constructing the book. We can't take Gulliver's as the true last word on any subject, though as the first word we feel compelled to rely on it. In matters of judgment, discrimination, the relation between one thing and another, readers have to do most of the work for themselves. Gulliver has merely indicated that there is work to be done; he reports the occasions that call for judgment. Again a contrast with James is appropriate. When we read, say, *The Ambassadors,* we find that our main task is to keep up with Lambert Strether, rising to his occasions of perception and divination. We have to think and feel with him up and down and all around the town. In the end we may decide that he's not an impeccable interpreter of the events, and that we are justified in trying to go beyond him or think aside from him. But in *Gulliver's Travels* we start with a conviction that Gulliver's sense of life differs from ours and is palpably inadequate to the reality it negotiates.

Swift sends Gulliver voyaging into several remote nations of the world, and he gives him an absurdly meager supply of qualifications. He is allowed to bring along only the attributes normally found adequate in a settled society—a simple frame of reference, modest expectations, and the disposition of a practical man. We begin to suspect that Gulliver is as he is not because God made him so but because England made him so. If there is an English tradition in politics, education, and morality, it is inscribed in him: it discloses itself in a sense of life that settles comfortably upon its constraints and regards as folly and vanity any interests that range beyond a narrow circle. To put the situation in a phrase: Gulliver has been brainwashed to become what he is. England has made him, written a program beyond which he does not stray. His duty coincides with his inclination: to station himself in front of events and report them in direct prose. Someone else, the reader, must act upon the information that Gulliver supplies. The comedy arises from the fact that a mind programmed to observe nothing more than the ordinary daily events in England is found bringing its limited attributes to bear upon situations inordinate and bizarre. Trained to observe certain constituents of experience, Gulliver's mind has never been instructed in the art of dealing with monsters.

When I say that England made Lemuel Gulliver, I mean to disagree with Terry Eagleton's claim, in *Heathcliff and the Great Hunger,* that **Gulliver's Travels** is about Ireland. According to Eagleton, Gulliver is "an appropriate figure for an Ascendancy which was both colonized and colonialist." I can't read the book that way. Its subject seems to me the susceptibility of the human mind to the experience it happens to undergo; **Gulliver's Travels** denotes the conditions, mostly demeaning, under which the mind somehow manages to persist. Samuel Johnson said of the book: "When once you have thought of big men and little men, it is very easy to do all the rest." It's not at all easy. Or rather: that isn't what's going on. Swift's real achievement is to attract into the orbit of big men and little men a mind somehow capable of surviving experience without understanding it. In the end, Swift darkens the comedy by showing the same mind succumbing to its experience and nearly dying in the event.

In the first three voyages, the humor is fairly simple: it is the comedy of disproportion, which arises from the differences between ends and means, essence and existence, absolutes and relativities, big men and little men, Big Enders and Little Enders, steady states and floating islands. There is little evidence of Gulliver's being brainwashed in Lilliput; for good reason, because he is a giant among these tiny people. It is part of the rhetoric of the book that one is to be impressed by big people and to despise little people. Whenever such words as "little" and "diminutive" appear, they arouse contempt for the people to whom they refer. But in one respect the brainwashing begins in Lilliput: Gulliver adopts the grandiloquent style of address so prevalent there. When he prevents war between Lilliput and Blefuscu by pulling the ships out of the Blefuscu harbor, he addresses the ruler of Lilliput in a loud voice: "Long live the most puissant Emperor of Lilliput!" When he is leaving, and the emperor and his family come out to say good-bye, Gulliver reports that "I lay on the Ground to kiss his Majesty's and the Empress's hand."

But the rhythm of brainwashing gets started in the

second voyage: appropriately, because Gulliver is now the diminutive one. When the King of Brobdingnag has listened for a while to Gulliver's account of life in England, he "observed, how contemptible a Thing was human Grandeur, which could be mimicked by such diminutive Insects as I." Gulliver is inclined to take offense, but on second thought not:

> But, as I was not in a Condition to resent Injuries, so, upon mature Thoughts, I began to doubt whether I were injured or no. For, after having been accustomed several Months to the Sight and Converse of this People, and observed every Object upon which I cast mine Eyes, to be of proportionable Magnitude; the Horror I had first conceived from their Bulk and Aspect was so far worn off, that if I had then beheld a Company of *English* Lords and Ladies in their Finery and Birth-day Cloaths, acting their several Parts in the most courtly Manner of Strutting, and Bowing and Prating; to say the Truth, I should have been strongly tempted to laugh as much at them as this King and his Grandees did at me. Neither indeed could I forbear smiling at my self, when the Queen used to place me upon her Hand towards a Looking-Glass, by which both our Persons appeared before me in full View together; and there could nothing be more ridiculous than the Comparison: So that I really began to imagine my self dwindled many Degrees below my usual Size.

Gulliver is not in a position to resent injuries, so he becomes accustomed to not resenting them. Behaviorism is at work. He starts doubting whether he has cause of resentment. He has begun—as Hermia says in *A Midsummer Night's Dream*—to "choose love by another's eyes." The queen's eyes, for the time being. She keeps a dwarf for her amusement:

> Nothing angred and mortified me so much as the Queen's Dwarf, who being of the lowest Stature that was ever in that Country, (for I verily think he was not full Thirty Foot high) became so insolent at seeing a Creature so much beneath him, that he would always affect to swagger and look big as he passed by me in the Queen's Antichamber, while I was standing on some Table talking with the Lords or Ladies of the Court; and he seldom failed of a smart Word or two upon my Littleness; against which I could only revenge my self by calling him *Brother,* challenging him to wrestle; and such Repartees as are usual in the Mouths of *Court Pages.* One Day at Dinner, this malicious little Cubb was so nettled with something I had said to him, that raising himself upon the Frame of her Majesty's Chair, he took me up by the Middle, as I was sitting down, not thinking any Harm, and let me drop into a large Silver Bowl of Cream; and then ran away as fast as he could.

Here the ironies persist, but virtually every phrase sends them off in a different direction. Choosing derision by

another's eyes, Gulliver affects to despise the dwarf—"of the lowest Stature that was ever in that Country." But the idiom he uses is the "repartee" of court pages: "affect to swagger and look big." Gulliver hardly glances at his own posture—"while I was standing on some Table talking with the Lords or Ladies of the Court"—the word "some" enhancing the sense of inattention. The malice of "this malicious little Cubb" is already prepared for by the force of "dwindled," "diminished," and other such words in earlier passages. The full effect is realized by associating the affected dwarf with the English ladies in their strutting, bowing, and prating.

Forty pages later, when Gulliver has left Brobdingnag and is rescued by the ship, he tells the captain that when he first saw the sailors, he thought them "the most little contemptible Creatures I had ever beheld": "For, indeed, while I was in that Prince's Country, I could never endure to look in a Glass after my Eyes had been accustomed to such prodigious Objects; because the Comparison gave me so despicable a Conceit of my self." In Brobdingnag, Gulliver accepts the local system of values so readily that when he goes to see the chief temple, the tower reckoned "the highest in the Kingdom," he comes back disappointed: it is hardly more than three thousand feet high.

But the most thorough brainwashing takes place in the fourth voyage. Gulliver sees the Yahoos and thinks them hideous brutes; he is still an Englishman. But after a while he comes to see himself as very like a Yahoo, different only because he wears clothes; they run about naked. The apprehension of resemblance makes him loathe the Yahoos even more, presumably because it forces him to see his own nature in a hideous form. When he meets the whinnying horses, he finds them impressively reasonable, and they think him a Yahoo, though notably teachable for such a brute. However, the Houyhnhnms soon decide that while Gulliver's learning ability is good for a Yahoo, and while his personal habits are cleaner than one would expect, in every other respect he is inferior to the rest of his kind.

Gulliver doesn't defend himself against these comparisons: gradually, he is brainwashed enough to find them convincing. Chapter Seven begins:

> The Reader may be disposed to wonder how I could prevail on my self to give so free a Representation of my own Species, among a Race of Mortals who were already too apt to conceive the vilest Opinion of Human Kind, from that entire Congruity betwixt me and their *Yahoos.* But I must freely confess, that the many Virtues of those excellent *Quadrupeds* placed in opposite View to human Corruptions, had so far opened mine Eyes, and enlarged my Understanding, that I began to view the Actions and Passions of Man in a very different Light; and

to think the Honour of my own Kind not worth managing; which, besides, it was impossible for me to do before a Person of so acute a Judgment as my Master, who daily convinced me of a thousand Faults in my self, whereof I had not the least Perception before, and which with us would never be numbered even among human Infirmities. I had likewise learned from his Example an utter Detestation of all Falsehood or Disguise; and *Truth* appeared so amiable to me, that I determined upon sacrificing every thing to it.

Gulliver comes to accept the Houyhnhnm view of things, at whatever cost of his self-esteem. He agrees, for instance, that a being whose eyes are placed directly in front, one on each side of his nose and each directed forward, can't look far on either side without turning his head: a disability from which your true Yahoo is exempt. Gulliver admits the point of these comparisons. A mind already brainwashed by the England that made him is ready to be brainwashed again by his new masters, the Houyhnhnms. Appropriately, the first sign of this process is that Gulliver comes to think the English language "barbarous" by comparison with the language of the Houyhnhnms. The Houyhnhnms don't accept Gulliver as a rational animal; rather, they speak of "those appearances of reason" in him, and decide that instead of being a rational creature he has merely been taught to imitate one:

> He added, how I had endeavoured to persuade him, that in my own and other Countries the *Yahoos* acted as the governing, rational Animal, and held the *Houyhnhnms* in Servitude: That, he observed in me all the Qualities of a *Yahoo,* only a little more civilized by some Tincture of Reason; which however was in a Degree as far inferior to the *Houyhnhnm* Race, as the *Yahoos* of their Country were to me.

When a further comparison arises between Gulliver and the Yahoos, the Houyhnhnms conclude that the comparison works against him. After Gulliver has given his master a full account of human life in England, his master says that "when a Creature pretending to Reason could be capable of such Enormities, he dreaded, lest the Corruption of that Faculty might be worse than Brutality itself." He seemed therefore confident, Gulliver reports, "that instead of Reason, we were only possessed of some Quality fitted to increase our natural Vices." When a young female Yahoo attempts a sexual assault on the naked Gulliver, he has to accept the obvious conclusion: "For now I could no longer deny, that I was a real *Yahoo,* in every Limb and Feature, since the Females had a natural Propensity to me as one of their own Species."

A few pages later Gulliver thinks to himself: "For, supposing I should escape with Life by some strange Adventure, how could I think with Temper, of passing my Days among *Yahoos,* and relapsing into my old Corruptions, for want of Examples to lead and keep me within the Paths of Virtue." Before he has spent a year with the Houyhnhnms, he has contracted, he says, "such a Love and Veneration for the Inhabitants, that I entered on a firm Resolution never to return to human Kind, but to pass the rest of my Life among these admirable *Houyhnhnms* in the Contemplation and Practice of every Virtue; where I could have no Example or Incitement to Vice." After a while, Gulliver comes to think it wonderful that these whinnying horses would condescend to distinguish him from the rest of his species, the Yahoos, and he can't bear to look at the reflection of his body in a lake. He begins to imitate the trotting of the horses and to speak in a whinnying voice. Compelled to leave the country of the Houyhnhnms, he prostrates himself to kiss his master's foot, and thinks it wonderful that his master does him the honour of raising the hoof to his mouth. When it looks as if he will be rescued by a passing ship, Gulliver sails off in another direction, choosing, as he says, to live with barbarians rather than with European Yahoos. When he is befriended by the Portuguese Captain Don Pedro de Mendez, Gulliver concludes that he should descend to treat him "like an Animal which had some little Portion of Reason." Brought to Lisbon, Gulliver can walk the street only if his nose is "well stopped with Rue, or sometimes with Tobacco." When the captain offers to give him his best suit of clothes, Gulliver declines the offer, "abhorring to cover myself with any thing that had been on the Back of a *Yahoo*": "I only desired he would lend me two clean Shirts, which having been washed since he wore them, I believed would not so much defile me. These I changed every second Day, and washed them myself."

Restored to his home, Gulliver finds himself loathing the sight of his family:

> My Wife and Family received me with great Surprize and Joy, because they concluded me certainly dead; but I must freely confess, the Sight of them filled me only with Hatred, Disgust and Contempt; and the more, by reflecting on the near Alliance I had to them. For, although since my unfortunate Exile from the *Houyhnhnm* Country, I had compelled myself to tolerate the Sight of *Yahoos,* and to converse with Don *Pedro de Mendez;* yet my Memory and Imaginations were perpetually filled with the Virtues and Ideas of those exalted *Houyhnhnms.* And when I began to consider, that by copulating with one of the *Yahoo*-Species, I had become a Parent of more, it struck me with the utmost Shame, Confusion and Horror.

As soon as Gulliver entered his home, he reports, "my Wife took me in her Arms, and kissed me; at which, having not been used to the Touch of that odious Animal for so many Years, I fell in a Swoon for almost an Hour." His favorite company in England is that of two horses and their groom, "for I feel my Spirits revived by the Smell he contracts in the Stable." Gradually, the effects wear off: the next phase of brainwashing begins. By the end of the book, Gulliver is becoming an Englishman again, though he will remain for a long time incensed by his countrymen's vanity and pride: "And although it be hard for a Man late in Life to remove old Habits, I am not altogether out of Hopes in some Time to suffer a Neighbour *Yahoo* in my Company, without the Apprehensions I am yet under of his Teeth or his Claws."

There are two overlapping contexts in which brainwashing in *Gulliver's Travels* may be considered. So far as the violence is directed against someone's mind, the first context is epistemological, and the philosophy referred to in all but words is Locke's. I agree with those who hold that Swift had little or no interest in philosophy, and that the third voyage shows how ready he was to make fun of intellectual pursuits. Quite so. But he was interested in religion and in politics, and he liked to think he knew what he was saying in sermons and pamphlets. He needed to have some notion of knowledge: that is all I am concerned to assume. I would be surprised to find him speculating, beyond local need, on the character of a sense-datum.

In the *Essay Concerning Human Understanding,* Locke argues that the mind, to begin with, is a blank page waiting to be written upon, a *tabula rasa.* The first stage in the mind's development is a sensory event: adverting to an external object or action, the mind responds with certain sensations. The only other capacity the mind has is that of reflecting upon those sensations and, finally, upon its own processes. Every word of what I have just said would need to be explicated if I were a professional philosopher, or if Swift were; no such necessity arises now. My few rudimentary sentences indicate that Locke regarded as the basic materials of knowledge, and why in their possession the mind has no choice. "In this Part," Locke writes, "the *understanding* is meerly *passive;* and whether or no, it will have these Beginnings, and as it were materials of Knowledge, is not in its own Power." Against Descartes, Cudworth, and many others, Locke insists that there are no "innate notions," as he calls them in the first book of the *Essay.* He maintains that if there were innate notions, an infant would be born with the idea of God and the conviction that God is to be worshipped. From the child's lack of such an inborn faith, innate ideas do not exist.

Not that Locke's position on that matter was decisive. Leibniz attacked it, for instance, on the ground that it is impossible to construct knowledge from zero—the *tabula rasa*—and the exterior world. Contingent understanding, Leibniz argued, never builds from zero. Locke's "savage," the figure he posited as the zero point of knowledge, is not (in Leibniz's view) a mere

form waiting to be written on, but rather a figure of decadence: savages are not primitives but men who have forgotten the primitive.

I should note, however, that the main reason for Locke's opposition to innate ideas was political or civic rather than epistemological: he saw that those who believed in innate ideas also claimed the right to say what those ideas were and to impose them upon others.

> Nor is it a small power it gives one Man over another, to have the Authority to be the Dictator of Principles, and Teacher of unquestionable Truths; and to make a Man swallow that for an innate Principle, which may serve to his purpose, who teacheth them.

It was for political reasons, therefore, that Locke attacked the assumption that there are innate ideas. Toleration was more important to him than any other consideration. In the *Letter to a Young Clergyman,* some scholars have found Swift criticizing Locke for his stand against inborn principles. The criticism seems to me clearer in the sermon "On the Testimony of Conscience," where Swift defines conscience as "that Knowledge which a Man hath within himself of his own Thoughts and Actions." God, he says, "hath placed Conscience in us to be our Director only in those Actions which Scripture and Reason plainly tell us to be good or evil." Clearly if God placed conscience in us, it is innate. But nothing in Locke's account of sensation and reflection allows for such a moral sense. In Swift's view the denial of conscience as an innate power would undermine religion.

Locke refused to give credence to innate ideas, but he had no hesitation in saying that there are capacities indigenous to humankind: specifically the powers of sensory perception and of reflection. These would assure that you could act in certain ways, but they wouldn't compel you to act in any particular way. Nor would they establish a moral propensity. But Locke recognized an acute problem in the chapter on the "Association of Ideas." His aim was to take the control of our thinking away from passion or any extrinsic authority and to allow us to think for ourselves and take responsibility for our actions. We are to step aside from our spontaneous interests and try to understand our processes of thinking. The mind, according to Locke, has "a power to suspend the execution of any of its desires; and so all, one after another; is at liberty to consider the objects of them, examine them on all sides, and weigh them with others." So Locke included in the power of reflection what we normally call "will." In that respect one's thinking should be a declaration of independence. But in the "Association of Ideas" chapter he meets the difficulty of distinguishing between associations that form customs—which are good—and those that form habits—which are bad. He refers at one point to "the Empire of Habit." Clearly, Locke thinks associations of ideas that set up habits are the very definition of madness; for one thing, they veto the act of reflection by preventing the mind from feeling inclined to it. Hans Aarsleff has noted, in *From Locke to Saussure,* that Locke didn't work out this problem; he left to Condillac's *Essay on the Origin of Human Knowledge* (1746) the development of the premise that the association of ideas was innate, or might be.

My contention, then, is that one of the aims of ***Gulliver's Travels*** is to make dark fun of Locke's epistemology: to show how vulnerable the mind is if it has no capacities but those of sensation and reflection, if its life begins with external events and objects and depends entirely upon them. Gulliver is a parody of Locke's empiricism, an epistemology that assumes the mind is a faculty capable of two and only two acts—perception and reflection. In the extreme version of empiricism called naturalism, the mind is the slave of its contents. That is what Yeats had in view, I assume, when he wrote

> Locke sank into a swoon,
> The garden died,
> God took the spinning jenny
> Out of his side.

The swoon is passivity: the mind, in Locke's account of it, depends upon the contingency of its sensations. Yeats thought that Pound and Joyce capitulated to this wretched assumption. Swift feared that Locke might be right, and he dealt with his fear by parodying it. Assume Locke is right: then if you change the things a mind encounters, you change the mind. This is brainwashing, in effect. Swift is demonstrating in Gulliver what Locke's empire of habit comes to, formed by enforced associations of ideas. Such an imperial force thwarts the act of reflection, upon which Locke's philosophy relies. Swift's position is like the one La Fontaine ironically embodied in the fable of the wolf and the lamb: "The reason of the Stronger is always the best."

The second context also involves Locke, but this time the issue is moral philosophy rather than epistemology. Charles Taylor has outlined the situation very clearly in his *Sources of the Self* (1989), so I will do little more than give the gist of the dispute in his terms. In Swift's time there were two relevant traditions in moral and political philosophy. One was represented by Hobbes and Locke: it expressed a naturalistic transposition of the doctrine of original sin. According to this tradition, God's law is doubly external to us as fallen creatures: first, because we cannot identify the good with the bent of our own natures; and second, because the law of God—if we could discover what it is—runs against the grain of our depraved wills. We cannot,

therefore, deduce a morality from the natural world, so we are well advised to regard nature as neutral. All we can do is be as self-aware as possible and act responsibly under the auspices of tolerance. The other tradition of moral philosophy is represented by the Cambridge Platonists—especially Henry More, Ralph Cudworth, Benjamin Whichcote, and John Smith. They saw human beings as intrinsically attuned to God, and hence spoke freely of our "inward Nature," according to which we are in harmony with the nature of the universe. This philosophy of benevolence was clear enough in Bolingbroke and Pope, but it was most fully articulated by Shaftesbury and by Francis Hutcheson. "I must love whatever happens," Shaftesbury says in his *Philosophic Regimen,* "and see it all as fitted to me and orderly with respect to the whole, even 'the sack of cities and the ruin of mankind.'" Where Locke found the source of morality in the dignity of a disengaged subject confronting a neutral nature, Shaftesbury ascribed it to the benevolent soul participating in the harmony of the universe. His crucial phrase is "natural affection," by which he means the sentiment that prompts us to love the whole world and everyone in it. Taylor refers to Shaftesbury's internalization of a teleological ethic of nature, and to his transformation of the appearances of harmony, order, and equilibrium into an ethic of benevolence. Hutcheson developed this moral philosophy further in his *Inquiry into the Original of Our Ideas of Beauty and Virtue.* Clearly he had Locke in his sights, and he undertook to attack the assumption, common to Hobbes, Locke, and La Rochefoucauld, that the distinction between good and bad is founded upon self-love, self-interest, and nothing else. Hutcheson's first act in this dispute is to posit in each of us a moral sense. "Some actions have to men an immediate goodness," he says, and by *immediate* he means innately delivered, not the result of reflection and training. Taylor notes that this is a risky assumption, especially as Hutcheson acknowledges that God could have given us a wholly different moral sense, or none at all. The fact that God gave us the particular moral sense we have is one of Hutcheson's proofs of His benign providence, but he doesn't see that he has opened the door wide to relativism. It is hard to claim at once that our moral sense is primordially given by God, and that God in His absolute freedom could have made a different choice.

In his *Essay on the Nature and Conduct of the Passions and Affections,* Hutcheson renews his attack on Locke and the skeptical or misanthropic tradition in moral philosophy. Some people, he says, might think the passions "too subtile for common Apprehension, and consequently not necessary for the instruction of Men in *Morals,* which are the common business of Mankind." But in fact certain notions about the passions are already current "to the great Detriment of many a *Natural Temper;* since many have been discourag'd from all Attempts of cultivating *kind gen-*

erous Affections in themselves, by a previous Notion that there are no such Affections in Nature, and that all Pretence to them was only *Dissimulation, Affection,* or at best some *unnatural Enthusiasm.*"

On the question of moral philosophy—but not of epistemology—Swift is of Locke's party, except that he gives far greater allowance to revelation and conscience than Locke did. His general sense of human life in its moral bearing puts him with Hobbes, Mandeville, and La Rochefoucauld in his belief that moral and social life are mainly propelled by self-love. The only mitigations of this dark vision that Swift is willing to concede are religion and the plain decencies of friendship and common sense. His religion was that of the Church of Ireland, unexactingly interpreted; but it was not merely a matter of morals. Faith was crucial, though Swift gave a rather prosaic account of it and cheerfully set aside the hard theological mysteries. "By God's great mercy," he said with evident relief, "those difficult Points [of Divinity] are never of absolute necessity to our salvation." Swift thought the Christianity of Anglicanism a good enough basis for personal and social life, but he was not theologically insistent beyond the basic articles of faith and practice. As for the decencies: his moral philosophy was mostly negative and pessimistic, but he allowed for exceptional instances of merit. Taylor says of Locke that in his philosophy we take our place in the order of nature and society through the exercise of disengaged reason. As I have suggested, Swift thought this a risky position to adopt, because the mind is appallingly susceptible to what it happens to encounter. But I think Swift's relation to the tradition of benevolence, as in Shaftesbury and Hutcheson, was severe if not dismissive: it is clear from his presentation of the Houyhnhnms, who live as if every virtue were innate, a practice that enchants Gulliver, though it hardly adds up to life at all. Was it F. R. Leavis who said that if the Houyhnhnms have all the virtue, the Yahoos have all the life?

I have said that brainwashing embodies the belief that "the reason of the Stronger is always the best." The *Oxford English Dictionary* defines brainwashing as "the systematic and often forcible elimination from a person's mind of all established ideas, especially political ideas, so that another set may take their place." The earliest recorded use of the word dates from 1950, early in the "Cold War," a time we associate with the trial of Cardinal Stepinac and the publication of Richard Condon's novel of brainwashing, *The Manchurian Candidate* (1959). More recently we have seen the case of Patty Hearst, which featured brainwashing (at least in its early stages). The great dictionary also says that brainwashing is "a kind of coercive conversion practised by certain totalitarian states on political dissidents."

But the degree of coercion required in each case depends upon the degree of resistance offered. The U-2 pilot Gary Powers didn't offer as much as Cardinal Stepinac. Gulliver offers little or no resistance. Nothing about him is more revealing than his willingness to have his brain washed by new masters. If the book appeals to our sense of humor and to our sense of discrepancy and disproportion, it touches us also in our sense of imprisonment—not necessarily imprisonment in a concentration camp, but in any imposed system of ideas and values. In those conditions the enforced system becomes our second nature and determines our fate. In his book on Proust, Beckett says that habit has this effect; it becomes our second nature and prevents us from seeing our first.

Any system can become our prison: a tradition we have inherited, a style we have adopted, an official terminology that tells us what to think. These days we often refer to it as ideology, a system of enforced assumptions within which most things go "without saying" by appearing to "stand to reason." *Gulliver's Travels* is only superficially about big men and little men: it is really about entrapment; and the most disturbing episode in the book deals with the struldbruggs, those people in Luggnagg who are immortal in the appalling sense that they get older and older but can't die. That is: they can't leave the system. Nor can Gulliver, until circumstances allow him to escape. As long as he is inside the system, he doesn't bring any irony to bear upon it. Irony is the counterforce to brainwashing: it brings to bear upon a given system values antithetical to those in place; it holds out against the system's blandishments. Gulliver doesn't. That is shown with particular clarity in a passage in the fourth voyage where he describes the certitude of reasoning among the Houyhnhnms:

> As these noble *Houyhnhnms* are endowed by Nature with a general Disposition to all Virtues, and have no Conceptions or Ideas of what is evil in a rational Creature; so their grand Maxim is, to cultivate *Reason,* and to be wholly governed by it. Neither is *Reason* among them a Point problematical as with us, where Men can argue with Plausibility on both Sides of a Question; but strikes you with immediate Conviction; as it must needs do where it is not mingled, obscured, or discoloured by Passion and Interest. I remember it was with extreme Difficulty that I could bring my Master to understand the Meaning of the word *Opinion,* or how a Point could be disputable; because *Reason* taught us to affirm or deny only where we are certain; and beyond our Knowledge we cannot do either. So that Controversies, Wranglings, Disputes, and Positiveness in false or dubious Propositions, are Evils unknown among the *Houyhnhnms.*

It may be said that the irony here is turned upon the Houyhnhnms, who have such a boring life of certitude that there is nothing to be discussed or questioned. But the sentence about "Controversies, Wranglings, Disputes, and Positiveness" doesn't offer a value to be set against the blankness of intellectual and moral life among the Houyhnhnms. Swift's hatred of such faction-fighting is clear. Gulliver can't stand apart from his local experience to the extent of imagining what the proper form of reasoning might be. Swift appears to be saying that if you send the human mind into the world without the benefit of revelation, religious belief, and an innate conscience, it will succumb to every authority it meets.

There is a passage in Andrei Sinyavsky's *A Voice from the Chorus* in which the Russian writer, imprisoned in Lefortovo in 1966, recalls certain books he read as a child, among them *Gulliver's Travels.* Sinyavsky makes the point that Gulliver is well fitted to represent mankind in general, precisely because he has no personality, no permanent qualities: everything depends upon the circumstances in which he is placed. As Sinyavsky has it: "[H]e is short or tall, clean or unclean only by comparison; he is a man by comparison and a non-man by comparison. He is a giant among Lilliputians, a Lilliputian among giants, an animal among the houyhnhnms, a horse among men." Sinyavsky thinks Swift is saying that man is a fiction, a sham. But there is another way of phrasing the conclusion. Man is a function of his environment, trapped in a structure that determines him so long as it holds him there. The only escape is into another structure, where the brainwashing begins all over again, but this time according to a different, though equally arbitrary, set of ideas and principles. The grim comedy of *Gulliver's Travels* arises from the discrepancy between our vaguely acquired sense of what it means to be human and our more pressing fear that "being human" depends—more than we are to realize—upon favorable local circumstances. When circumstances change, being human is the last thing we can be assured of being. *Gulliver's Travels* has become a dauntingly "modern" book again in the past thirty or forty years because it presents as fiction what many people are worried about as fact.

These worries are provided by ideas of mind and society. Marx said that "social existence determines consciousness," but he allowed for a dynamic relation between mind and environment. One of the major axioms of structuralism went far beyond Marx to say that we are determined by the codes we have been given. We don't hear much of structuralism these days, but none of its successors has claimed that the human mind is in any respect autonomous. It is now regularly assumed that reality and knowledge are socially constructed and that sociologists of knowledge are equipped to understand the processes of this construction. In *The Social Construction of Reality* (1966), Peter L. Berger and Thomas Luckmann define "reality" as "a quality appertaining to phenomena that we recognize as having a being independent of our own volition (we cannot 'wish them away')"; and they define "knowledge" as "the certainty that phenomena are real and that they possess specific characteristics." This is old-style positivism translated into sociology: it allows no place for metaphysical, religious, or visionary values. More to the point, it hands over to "society," by which Berger and Luckmann appear to mean the accredited institutions that happen to be in place at this moment, the right to decide what constitutes knowledge in any particular. I don't see how this sociology of knowledge differs from the brainwashing I've been describing in *Gulliver's Travels.*

Gulliver's Travels touches upon another issue, close to the one I've just described but perhaps distinguishable from it because it adverts to the possibility that man may not be the son of God but identical with something he resembles—an artifact, a machine, a gadget made like any other to perform a few simple operations. Hugh Kenner has examined this motif in *The Counterfeiters,* which he subtitles *An Historical Comedy,* presumably because one source of comedy, according to Bergson, is a sense of discrepancy between axioms of life as organism and appearances of life as gadgetry. The optimistic answer to this sense of discrepancy is the assertion that if man is a machine, he is a machine with a difference, and that this difference makes all the difference. We say, for instance, that man is an animal with the further distinguishing power of reason or symbolic action: he can reflect upon his experience and represent it in symbolic terms. If we think the difference exhilarating, we conclude that man's perfection in his kind enables him to transcend his kind: he is not a mere animal at all. This optimism depends upon our emphasizing in man's favor a spiritual dimension, a particular quality or aura, that makes men and women what they are.

Gulliver's Travels incites us to think or to fear that this optimism is false, that the *x*-factor is a delusion, merely yet another manifestation of pride. Hazlitt said that Swift took a new view of human nature, "such as a being of a higher sphere might take of it." Precisely: because it is a matter of perspective. Swift presents in Gulliver a man bereft of spiritual radiance; he is merely the sum of his attributes, and these are few. He is someone to whom certain things happen. This is Swift's main satiric device: to present every ostensibly spiritual quality in a material form, reducing qualities to quantities. And if an optimistic reader declares that man is more than the sum of a few attributes, Swift accepts the challenge. We can almost hear him say, "Prove it."

In the end, Gulliver is restored to himself. But what is the self to which he is restored? Is it that of the true-born Englishman, the ideologically propelled figure projected after the Restoration and the Glorious Revolution by an England desperately anxious to avoid another civil war and the execution of another king? Something like that. Gulliver is an empiricist without memory or the need of it, a man restored to sanity who does not know that he has been mad. He is as close as possible to being "a man without qualities."

FURHER READING

Brown, Laura. "Reading Race and Gender: Jonathan Swift." In *Critical Essays on Jonathan Swift,* edited by Frank Palmeri, pp. 121-40. New York: G.K. Hall, 1993.

Examines the presence of both anti-imperialist and mysogynist, or anti-woman, sentiment in *Gulliver's Travels.*

Carnochan, W. B. "Some Roles of Lemuel Gulliver." *Texas Studies in Literature and Language* V, No. 4 (Winter 1964): 520-29.

Contends that *Gulliver's Travels* cannot be read as a psychological novel of personal transformation, arguing that the character of Gulliver displays change only when he consciously adopts a role and not because he has undergone personal growth.

Crane, Ronald S. "The Houyhnhnms, the Yahoos, and the History of Ideas." In *Reason and the Imagination:Studies in the History of Ideas, 1600-1800,* edited by J. A. Mazzeo, pp. 231-53. New York: Columbia University Press, 1962.

Disputes many critical assessments of the meaning of Gulliver's fourth voyage, suggesting that Swift intended not to confirm but to discount the definition of human beings as rational animals.

Ewald, William Bragg, Jr. "The Character of Lemuel Gulliver." In *The Masks of Jonathan Swift*, pp. 124-41. 1954. Reprint. New York: Russell & Russell, 1967,
203 p.

Examines the character of Gulliver as a vehicle for satire. Ewald contends that Gulliver is a flawed hero who is nevertheless capable of recognizing and striving for high ideals.

Foster, Milton P. *A Casebook on Gulliver among the Houyhnhnms.* New York: Thomas Y. Crowell, 1961, 319 p.

A collection including many seminal essays on the fourth voyage of *Gulliver's Travels.*

Hawes, Clement. "Three Times round the Globe: Gulliver and the Colonial Discourse." *Cultural Critique,* No. 18 (Spring 1991): 187-214.

Analyzes *Gulliver's Travels* as Swift's satiric response to the discourse spurred by Britain's colonial expansion and participation in the slave trade in the seventeenth and eighteenth centuries.

Monk, Samuel H. "The Pride of Lemuel Gulliver." *The Sewannee Review* LXIII, No. 1 (January-March, 1955): 48-71.

Argues that while Swift did not accept the Enlightenment belief in the perfectibility of humankind, he has been wrongly assigned the designation of misanthrope. Monk maintains that critics and biographers have mistakenly attributed to Swift the pessimism of his fictional character Gulliver.

Nicolson, Marjorie. "The Scientific Background of Swift's *Voyage to Laputa.*" In *Science and Imagination,* pp. 110-54. Ithaca, N.Y.: Cornell University Press, 1956.

Examines the third voyage in *Gulliver's Travels* as Swift's critique of the science and mathematics of his time.

Price, Martin. *Swift's Rhetorical Art.* New Haven, Conn.: Yale University Press, 1953, 117 p.

Close study of Swift's use of rhetorical devices to convey satiric intent.

Literature
Criticism from
1400 to 1800

Cumulative Indexes

How to Use This Index

The main references

list all author entries in the following Gale Literary Criticism series:

BLC = Black Literature Criticism
CLC = Contemporary Literary Criticism
CLR = Children's Literature Review
CMLC = Classical and Medieval Literature Criticism
DA = DISCovering Authors
DC = Drama Criticism
HLC = Hispanic Literature Criticism
LC = Literature Criticism from 1400 to 1800
NCLC = Nineteenth-Century Literature Criticism
PC = Poetry Criticism
SSC = Short Story Criticism
TCLC = Twentieth-Century Literary Criticism
WLC = World Literature Criticism, 1500 to the Present

The cross-references

list all author entries in the following Gale biographical and literary sources:

AAYA = Authors & Artists for Young Adults
AITN = Authors in the News
BEST = Bestsellers
BW = Black Writers
CA = Contemporary Authors
CAAS = Contemporary Authors Autobiography Series
CABS = Contemporary Authors Bibliographical Series
CANR = Contemporary Authors New Revision Series
CAP = Contemporary Authors Permanent Series
CDALB = Concise Dictionary of American Literary Biography
CDBLB = Concise Dictionary of British Literary Biography
DLB = Dictionary of Literary Biography
DLBD = Dictionary of Literary Biography Documentary Series
DLBY = Dictionary of Literary Biography Yearbook
HW = Hispanic Writers
JRDA = Junior DISCovering Authors
MAICYA = Major Authors and Illustrators for Children and Young Adults
MTCW = Major 20th-Century Writers
NNAL = Native North American Literature
SAAS = Something about the Author Autobiography Series
SATA = Something about the Author
YABC = Yesterday's Authors of Books for Children

Literary Criticism Series
Cumulative Author Index

DRAM, MST, POET; PC 1; WLC
See also AAYA 18; CA 9-12R; 45-48; CANR 5, 61; CDBLB 1914-1945; DLB 10, 20; MTCW

Audiberti, Jacques 1900-1965CLC 38; DAM DRAM
See also CA 25-28R

Audubon, John James 1785-1851 ..NCLC 47

Auel, Jean M(arie) 1936-CLC 31, 107; DAM POP
See also AAYA 7; BEST 90:4; CA 103; CANR 21, 64; INT CANR-21; SATA 91

Auerbach, Erich 1892-1957 .... TCLC 43
See also CA 118; 155

Augier, Emile 1820-1889 .... NCLC 31
See also DLB 192

August, John
See De Voto, Bernard (Augustine)

Augustine, St. 354-430 .... CMLC 6; DAB

Aurelius
See Bourne, Randolph S(illiman)

Aurobindo, Sri
See Aurobindo Ghose

Aurobindo Ghose 1872-1950 .... TCLC 63
See also CA 163

Austen, Jane 1775-1817 NCLC 1, 13, 19, 33, 51; DA; DAB; DAC; DAM MST, NOV; WLC
See also AAYA 19; CDBLB 1789-1832; DLB 116

Auster, Paul 1947- .... CLC 47
See also CA 69-72; CANR 23, 52

Austin, Frank
See Faust, Frederick (Schiller)

Austin, Mary (Hunter) 1868-1934 . TCLC 25
See also CA 109; DLB 9, 78

Autran Dourado, Waldomiro
See Dourado, (Waldomiro Freitas) Autran

Averroes 1126-1198 .... CMLC 7
See also DLB 115

Avicenna 980-1037 .... CMLC 16
See also DLB 115

Avison, Margaret 1918- CLC 2, 4, 97; DAC; DAM POET
See also CA 17-20R; DLB 53; MTCW

Axton, David
See Koontz, Dean R(ay)

Ayckbourn, Alan 1939- CLC 5, 8, 18, 33, 74; DAB; DAM DRAM
See also CA 21-24R; CANR 31, 59; DLB 13; MTCW

Aydy, Catherine
See Tennant, Emma (Christina)

Ayme, Marcel (Andre) 1902-1967 ... CLC 11
See also CA 89-92; CANR 67; CLR 25; DLB 72; SATA 91

Ayrton, Michael 1921-1975 .... CLC 7
See also CA 5-8R; 61-64; CANR 9, 21

Azorin .... CLC 11
See also Martinez Ruiz, Jose

Azuela, Mariano 1873-1952 . TCLC 3; DAM MULT; HLC
See also CA 104; 131; HW; MTCW

Baastad, Babbis Friis
See Friis-Baastad, Babbis Ellinor

Bab
See Gilbert, W(illiam) S(chwenck)

Babbis, Eleanor
See Friis-Baastad, Babbis Ellinor

Babel, Isaac
See Babel, Isaak (Emmanuilovich)

Babel, Isaak (Emmanuilovich) 1894-1941(?)
TCLC 2, 13; SSC 16

See also CA 104; 155

Babits, Mihaly 1883-1941 .... TCLC 14
See also CA 114

Babur 1483-1530 .... LC 18

Bacchelli, Riccardo 1891-1985 .... CLC 19
See also CA 29-32R; 117

Bach, Richard (David) 1936- CLC 14; DAM NOV, POP
See also AITN 1; BEST 89:2; CA 9-12R; CANR 18; MTCW; SATA 13

Bachman, Richard
See King, Stephen (Edwin)

Bachmann, Ingeborg 1926-1973 .... CLC 69
See also CA 93-96; 45-48; DLB 85

Bacon, Francis 1561-1626 .... LC 18, 32
See also CDBLB Before 1660; DLB 151

Bacon, Roger 1214(?)-1292 .... CMLC 14
See also DLB 115

Bacovia, George .... TCLC 24
See also Vasiliu, Gheorghe

Badanes, Jerome 1937- .... CLC 59

Bagehot, Walter 1826-1877 .... NCLC 10
See also DLB 55

Bagnold, Enid 1889-1981 ...... CLC 25; DAM DRAM
See also CA 5-8R; 103; CANR 5, 40; DLB 13, 160, 191; MAICYA; SATA 1, 25

Bagritsky, Eduard 1895-1934 .... TCLC 60

Bagrjana, Elisaveta
See Belcheva, Elisaveta

Bagryana, Elisaveta ....CLC 10
See also Belcheva, Elisaveta
See also DLB 147

Bailey, Paul 1937-............................... CLC 45
See also CA 21-24R; CANR 16, 62; DLB 14

Baillie, Joanna 1762-1851 .... NCLC 2
See also DLB 93

Bainbridge, Beryl (Margaret) 1933-CLC 4, 5, 8, 10, 14, 18, 22, 62; DAM NOV
See also CA 21-24R; CANR 24, 55; DLB 14; MTCW

Baker, Elliott 1922-............................... CLC 8
See also CA 45-48; CANR 2, 63

Baker, Jean H. .... TCLC 3, 10
See also Russell, George William

Baker, Nicholson 1957-. CLC 61; DAM POP
See also CA 135; CANR 63

Baker, Ray Stannard 1870-1946 ... TCLC 47
See also CA 118

Baker, Russell (Wayne) 1925-........... CLC 31
See also BEST 89:4; CA 57-60; CANR 11, 41, 59; MTCW

Bakhtin, M.
See Bakhtin, Mikhail Mikhailovich

Bakhtin, M. M.
See Bakhtin, Mikhail Mikhailovich

Bakhtin, Mikhail
See Bakhtin, Mikhail Mikhailovich

Bakhtin, Mikhail Mikhailovich 1895-1975
CLC 83
See also CA 128; 113

Bakshi, Ralph 1938(?)- .... CLC 26
See also CA 112; 138

Bakunin, Mikhail (Alexandrovich) 1814-1876
NCLC 25, 58

Baldwin, James (Arthur) 1924-1987CLC 1, 2, 3, 4, 5, 8, 13, 15, 17, 42, 50, 67, 90; BLC; DA; DAB; DAC; DAM MST, MULT, NOV, POP; DC 1; SSC 10; WLC
See also AAYA 4; BW 1; CA 1-4R; 124; CABS 1; CANR 3, 24; CDALB 1941-1968; DLB 2, 7, 33; DLBY 87; MTCW; SATA 9; SATA-Obit 54

Ballard, J(ames) G(raham) 1930- CLC 3, 6, 14, 36; DAM NOV, POP; SSC 1
See also AAYA 3; CA 5-8R; CANR 15, 39, 65; DLB 14; MTCW; SATA 93

Balmont, Konstantin (Dmitriyevich) 1867-1943
TCLC 11
See also CA 109; 155

Balzac, Honore de 1799-1850NCLC 5, 35, 53; DA; DAB; DAC; DAM MST, NOV; SSC 5; WLC
See also DLB 119

Bambara, Toni Cade 1939-1995 CLC 19, 88; BLC; DA; DAC; DAM MST, MULT; WLCS
See also AAYA 5; BW 2; CA 29-32R; 150; CANR 24, 49; DLB 38; MTCW

Bamdad, A.
See Shamlu, Ahmad

Banat, D. R.
See Bradbury, Ray (Douglas)

Bancroft, Laura
See Baum, L(yman) Frank

Banim, John 1798-1842 .... NCLC 13
See also DLB 116, 158, 159

Banim, Michael 1796-1874 .... NCLC 13
See also DLB 158, 159

Banjo, The
See Paterson, A(ndrew) B(arton)

Banks, Iain
See Banks, Iain M(enzies)

Banks, Iain M(enzies) 1954-............. CLC 34
See also CA 123; 128; CANR 61; INT 128

Banks, Lynne Reid .... CLC 23
See also Reid Banks, Lynne
See also AAYA 6

Banks, Russell 1940- .... CLC 37, 72
See also CA 65-68; CAAS 15; CANR 19, 52; DLB 130

Banville, John 1945- .... CLC 46
See also CA 117; 128; DLB 14; INT 128

Banville, Theodore (Faullain) de 1832-1891
NCLC 9

Baraka, Amiri 1934-CLC 1, 2, 3, 5, 10, 14, 33; BLC; DA; DAC; DAM MST, MULT, POET, POP; DC 6; PC 4; WLCS
See also Jones, LeRoi
See also BW 2; CA 21-24R; CABS 3; CANR 27, 38, 61; CDALB 1941-1968; DLB 5, 7, 16, 38; DLBD 8; MTCW

Barbauld, Anna Laetitia 1743-1825NCLC 50
See also DLB 107, 109, 142, 158

Barbellion, W. N. P. .... TCLC 24
See also Cummings, Bruce F(rederick)

Barbera, Jack (Vincent) 1945-......... CLC 44
See also CA 110; CANR 45

Barbey d'Aurevilly, Jules Amedee 1808-1889
NCLC 1; SSC 17
See also DLB 119

Barbusse, Henri 1873-1935 .... TCLC 5
See also CA 105; 154; DLB 65

Barclay, Bill
See Moorcock, Michael (John)

Barclay, William Ewert
See Moorcock, Michael (John)

Barea, Arturo 1897-1957 .... TCLC 14
See also CA 111

Barfoot, Joan 1946-........................... CLC 18
See also CA 105

Baring, Maurice 1874-1945 .... TCLC 8
See also CA 105; DLB 34

Barker, Clive 1952- .... CLC 52; DAM POP
See also AAYA 10; BEST 90:3; CA 121; 129; INT 129; MTCW

MTCW

Bettelheim, Bruno 1903-1990 .... **CLC 79**
See also CA 81-84; 131; CANR 23, 61; MTCW
Betti, Ugo 1892-1953 .... **TCLC 5**
See also CA 104; 155
Betts, Doris (Waugh) 1932- ...... **CLC 3, 6, 28**
See also CA 13-16R; CANR 9, 66; DLBY 82;
INT CANR-9
Bevan, Alistair
See Roberts, Keith (John Kingston)
Bialik, Chaim Nachman 1873-1934**TCLC 25**
Bickerstaff, Isaac
See Swift, Jonathan
Bidart, Frank 1939- .... **CLC 33**
See also CA 140
Bienek, Horst 1930- .... **CLC 7, 11**
See also CA 73-76; DLB 75
Bierce, Ambrose (Gwinett) 1842-1914(?)
**TCLC 1, 7, 44; DA; DAC; DAM MST; SSC
9; WLC**
See also CA 104; 139; CDALB 1865-1917;
DLB 11, 12, 23, 71, 74, 186
Biggers, Earl Derr 1884-1933 .... **TCLC 65**
See also CA 108; 153
Billings, Josh
See Shaw, Henry Wheeler
Billington, (Lady) Rachel (Mary) 1942-**C L C
43**
See also AITN 2; CA 33-36R; CANR 44
Binyon, T(imothy) J(ohn) 1936- ...... **CLC 34**
See also CA 111; CANR 28
Bioy Casares, Adolfo 1914-1984**CLC 4, 8, 13,
88; DAM MULT; HLC; SSC 17**
See also CA 29-32R; CANR 19, 43, 66; DLB
113; HW; MTCW
Bird, Cordwainer
See Ellison, Harlan (Jay)
Bird, Robert Montgomery 1806-1854**NCLC 1**
Birney, (Alfred) Earle 1904-1995**CLC 1, 4, 6,
11; DAC; DAM MST, POET**
See also CA 1-4R; CANR 5, 20; DLB 88;
MTCW
Bishop, Elizabeth 1911-1979 **CLC 1, 4, 9, 13,
15, 32; DA; DAC; DAM MST, POET; PC
3**
See also CA 5-8R; 89-92; CABS 2; CANR 26,
61; CDALB 1968-1988; DLB 5, 169;
MTCW; SATA-Obit 24
Bishop, John 1935- .... **CLC 10**
See also CA 105·
Bissett, Bill 1939- .... **CLC 18; PC 14**
See also CA 69-72; CAAS 19; CANR 15; DLB
53; MTCW
Bitov, Andrei (Georgievich) 1937- .. **CLC 57**
See also CA 142
Biyidi, Alexandre 1932-
See Beti, Mongo
See also BW 1; CA 114; 124; MTCW
Bjarme, Brynjolf
See Ibsen, Henrik (Johan)
Bjornson, Bjornstjerne (Martinius) 1832-1910
TCLC 7, 37
See also CA 104
Black, Robert
See Holdstock, Robert P.
Blackburn, Paul 1926-1971 .... **CLC 9, 43**
See also CA 81-84; 33-36R; CANR 34; DLB
16; DLBY 81
Black Elk 1863-1950**TCLC 33; DAM MULT**
See also CA 144; NNAL
Black Hobart
See Sanders, (James) Ed(ward)
Blacklin, Malcolm

See Chambers, Aidan
Blackmore, R(ichard) D(oddridge) 1825-1900
TCLC 27
See also CA 120; DLB 18
Blackmur, R(ichard) P(almer) 1904-1965
CLC 2, 24
See also CA 11-12; 25-28R; CAP 1; DLB 63
Black Tarantula
See Acker, Kathy
Blackwood, Algernon (Henry) 1869-1951
TCLC 5
See also CA 105; 150; DLB 153, 156, 178
Blackwood, Caroline 1931-1996**CLC 6, 9, 100**
See also CA 85-88; 151; CANR 32, 61, 65;
DLB 14; MTCW
Blade, Alexander
See Hamilton, Edmond; Silverberg, Robert
Blaga, Lucian 1895-1961 .... **CLC 75**
Blair, Eric (Arthur) 1903-1950
See Orwell, George
See also CA 104; 132; DA; DAB; DAC; DAM
MST, NOV; MTCW; SATA 29
Blais, Marie-Claire 1939-**CLC 2, 4, 6, 13, 22;
DAC; DAM MST**
See also CA 21-24R; CAAS 4; CANR 38; DLB
53; MTCW
Blaise, Clark 1940- .... **CLC 29**
See also AITN 2; CA 53-56; CAAS 3; CANR
5, 66; DLB 53
Blake, Fairley
See De Voto, Bernard (Augustine)
Blake, Nicholas
See Day Lewis, C(ecil)
See also DLB 77
Blake, William 1757-1827 **NCLC 13, 37, 57;
DA; DAB; DAC; DAM MST, POET; PC
12; WLC**
See also CDBLB 1789-1832; DLB 93, 163;
MAICYA; SATA 30
Blasco Ibanez, Vicente 1867-1928 **TCLC 12;
DAM NOV**
See also CA 110; 131; HW; MTCW
Blatty, William Peter 1928-**CLC 2; DAM POP**
See also CA 5-8R; CANR 9
Bleeck, Oliver
See Thomas, Ross (Elmore)
Blessing, Lee 1949- .... **CLC 54**
Blish, James (Benjamin) 1921-1975 . **CLC 14**
See also CA 1-4R; 57-60; CANR 3; DLB 8;
MTCW; SATA 66
Bliss, Reginald
See Wells, H(erbert) G(eorge)
Blixen, Karen (Christentze Dinesen) 1885-1962
See Dinesen, Isak
See also CA 25-28; CANR 22, 50; CAP 2;
MTCW; SATA 44
Bloch, Robert (Albert) 1917-1994 .... **CLC 33**
See also CA 5-8R; 146; CAAS 20; CANR 5;
DLB 44; INT CANR-5; SATA 12; SATA-
Obit 82
Blok, Alexander (Alexandrovich) 1880-1921
TCLC 5; PC 21
See also CA 104
Blom, Jan
See Breytenbach, Breyten
Bloom, Harold 1930- .... **CLC 24, 103**
See also CA 13-16R; CANR 39; DLB 67
Bloomfield, Aurelius
See Bourne, Randolph S(illiman)
Blount, Roy (Alton), Jr. 1941- .... **CLC 38**
See also CA 53-56; CANR 10, 28, 61; INT
CANR-28; MTCW
Bloy, Leon 1846-1917 .... **TCLC 22**

See also CA 121; DLB 123
Blume, Judy (Sussman) 1938- ... **CLC 12, 30;
DAM NOV, POP**
See also AAYA 3; CA 29-32R; CANR 13, 37,
66; CLR 2, 15; DLB 52; JRDA; MAICYA;
MTCW; SATA 2, 31, 79
Blunden, Edmund (Charles) 1896-1974 **C L C
2, 56**
See also CA 17-18; 45-48; CANR 54; CAP 2;
DLB 20, 100, 155; MTCW
Bly, Robert (Elwood) 1926-**CLC 1, 2, 5, 10, 15,
38; DAM POET**
See also CA 5-8R; CANR 41; DLB 5; MTCW
Boas, Franz 1858-1942 .... **TCLC 56**
See also CA 115
Bobette
See Simenon, Georges (Jacques Christian)
Boccaccio, Giovanni 1313-1375 .. **CMLC 13;
SSC 10**
Bochco, Steven 1943- .... **CLC 35**
See also AAYA 11; CA 124; 138
Bodenheim, Maxwell 1892-1954 .... **TCLC 44**
See also CA 110; DLB 9, 45
Bodker, Cecil 1927- .... **CLC 21**
See also CA 73-76; CANR 13, 44; CLR 23;
MAICYA; SATA 14
Boell, Heinrich (Theodor) 1917-1985 **CLC 2,
3, 6, 9, 11, 15, 27, 32, 72; DA; DAB; DAC;
DAM MST, NOV; SSC 23; WLC**
See also CA 21-24R; 116; CANR 24; DLB 69;
DLBY 85; MTCW
Boerne, Alfred
See Doeblin, Alfred
Boethius 480(?)-524(?) .... **CMLC 15**
See also DLB 115
Bogan, Louise 1897-1970 . **CLC 4, 39, 46, 93;
DAM POET; PC 12**
See also CA 73-76; 25-28R; CANR 33; DLB
45, 169; MTCW
Bogarde, Dirk .... **CLC 19**
See also Van Den Bogarde, Derek Jules Gaspard
Ulric Niven
See also DLB 14
Bogosian, Eric 1953- .... **CLC 45**
See also CA 138
Bograd, Larry 1953- .... **CLC 35**
See also CA 93-96; CANR 57; SAAS 21; SATA
33, 89
Boiardo, Matteo Maria 1441-1494 .... **LC 6**
Boileau-Despreaux, Nicolas 1636-1711 **LC 3**
Bojer, Johan 1872-1959 .... **TCLC 64**
Boland, Eavan (Aisling) 1944- .. **CLC 40, 67;
DAM POET**
See also CA 143; CANR 61; DLB 40
Bolt, Lee
See Faust, Frederick (Schiller)
Bolt, Robert (Oxton) 1924-1995 ..... **CLC 14;
DAM DRAM**
See also CA 17-20R; 147; CANR 35, 67; DLB
13; MTCW
Bombet, Louis-Alexandre-Cesar
See Stendhal
Bomkauf
See Kaufman, Bob (Garnell)
Bonaventura .... **NCLC 35**
See also DLB 90
Bond, Edward 1934- **CLC 4, 6, 13, 23; DAM
DRAM**
See also CA 25-28R; CANR 38, 67; DLB 13;
MTCW
Bonham, Frank 1914-1989 .... **CLC 12**
See also AAYA 1; CA 9-12R; CANR 4, 36;
JRDA; MAICYA; SAAS 3; SATA 1, 49;

See also Mavor, Osborne Henry
See also DLB 10

Brin, David 1950- .... **CLC 34**
See also AAYA 21; CA 102; CANR 24; INT
CANR-24; SATA 65

Brink, Andre (Philippus) 1935- **CLC 18, 36,**
106
See also CA 104; CANR 39, 62; INT 103;
MTCW

Brinsmead, H(esba) F(ay) 1922- ...... **CLC 21**
See also CA 21-24R; CANR 10; CLR 47;
MAICYA; SAAS 5; SATA 18, 78

Brittain, Vera (Mary) 1893(?)-1970 **CLC 23**
See also CA 13-16; 25-28R; CANR 58; CAP
1; DLB 191; MTCW

Broch, Hermann 1886-1951 .... **TCLC 20**
See also CA 117; DLB 85, 124

Brock, Rose
See Hansen, Joseph

Brodkey, Harold (Roy) 1930-1996 .. **CLC 56**
See also CA 111; 151; DLB 130

Brodsky, Iosif Alexandrovich 1940-1996
See Brodsky, Joseph
See also AITN 1; CA 41-44R; 151; CANR 37;
DAM POET; MTCW

Brodsky, Joseph 1940-1996 **CLC 4, 6, 13, 36,**
100; PC 9
See also Brodsky, Iosif Alexandrovich

Brodsky, Michael (Mark) 1948- ...... **CLC 19**
See also CA 102; CANR 18, 41, 58

Bromell, Henry 1947- .... **CLC 5**
See also CA 53-56; CANR 9

Bromfield, Louis (Brucker) 1896-1956 **T C L C**
11
See also CA 107; 155; DLB 4, 9, 86

Broner, E(sther) M(asserman) 1930- **CLC 19**
See also CA 17-20R; CANR 8, 25; DLB 28

Bronk, William 1918- .... **CLC 10**
See also CA 89-92; CANR 23; DLB 165

Bronstein, Lev Davidovich
See Trotsky, Leon

Bronte, Anne 1820-1849 .... **NCLC 4**
See also DLB 21

Bronte, Charlotte 1816-1855 **NCLC 3, 8, 33,**
58; DA; DAB; DAC; DAM MST, NOV;
WLC
See also AAYA 17; CDBLB 1832-1890; DLB
21, 159

Bronte, Emily (Jane) 1818-1848 **NCLC 16, 35;**
DA; DAB; DAC; DAM MST, NOV, POET;
PC 8; WLC
See also AAYA 17; CDBLB 1832-1890; DLB
21, 32

Brooke, Frances 1724-1789 .... **LC 6**
See also DLB 39, 99

Brooke, Henry 1703(?)-1783 .... **LC 1**
See also DLB 39

Brooke, Rupert (Chawner) 1887-1915 **T C L C**
2, 7; DA; DAB; DAC; DAM MST, POET;
WLC
See also CA 104; 132; CANR 61; CDBLB
1914-1945; DLB 19; MTCW

Brooke-Haven, P.
See Wodehouse, P(elham) G(renville)

Brooke-Rose, Christine 1926(?)- ...... **CLC 40**
See also CA 13-16R; CANR 58; DLB 14

Brookner, Anita 1928- **CLC 32, 34, 51; DAB;**
DAM POP
See also CA 114; 120; CANR 37, 56; DLBY
87; MTCW

Brooks, Cleanth 1906-1994 .... **CLC 24, 86**
See also CA 17-20R; 145; CANR 33, 35; DLB
63; DLBY 94; INT CANR-35; MTCW

Brooks, George
See Baum, L(yman) Frank

Brooks, Gwendolyn 1917- **CLC 1, 2, 4, 5, 15,**
49; BLC; DA; DAC; DAM MST, MULT,
POET; PC 7; WLC
See also AAYA 20; AITN 1; BW 2; CA 1-4R;
CANR 1, 27, 52; CDALB 1941-1968; CLR
27; DLB 5, 76, 165; MTCW; SATA 6

Brooks, Mel .... **CLC 12**
See also Kaminsky, Melvin
See also AAYA 13; DLB 26

Brooks, Peter 1938- .... **CLC 34**
See also CA 45-48; CANR 1

Brooks, Van Wyck 1886-1963 .... **CLC 29**
See also CA 1-4R; CANR 6; DLB 45, 63, 103

Brophy, Brigid (Antonia) 1929-1995 **CLC 6,**
11, 29, 105
See also CA 5-8R; 149; CAAS 4; CANR 25,
53; DLB 14; MTCW

Brosman, Catharine Savage 1934- ..... **CLC 9**
See also CA 61-64; CANR 21, 46

Brother Antoninus
See Everson, William (Oliver)

The Brothers Quay
See Quay, Stephen; Quay, Timothy

Broughton, T(homas) Alan 1936- ..... **CLC 19**
See also CA 45-48; CANR 2, 23, 48

Broumas, Olga 1949- .... **CLC 10, 73**
See also CA 85-88; CANR 20

Brown, Alan 1951- .... **CLC 99**

Brown, Charles Brockden 1771-1810 **N C L C**
22
See also CDALB 1640-1865; DLB 37, 59, 73

Brown, Christy 1932-1981 .... **CLC 63**
See also CA 105; 104; DLB 14

Brown, Claude 1937- .. **CLC 30; BLC; DAM**
MULT
See also AAYA 7; BW 1; CA 73-76

Brown, Dee (Alexander) 1908-.. **CLC 18, 47;**
DAM POP
See also CA 13-16R; CAAS 6; CANR 11, 45,
60; DLBY 80; MTCW; SATA 5

Brown, George
See Wertmueller, Lina

Brown, George Douglas 1869-1902 **TCLC 28**
See also CA 162

Brown, George Mackay 1921-1996 **CLC 5, 48,**
100
See also CA 21-24R; 151; CAAS 6; CANR 12,
37, 62, 67; DLB 14, 27, 139; MTCW; SATA
35

Brown, (William) Larry 1951- .... **CLC 73**
See also CA 130; 134; INT 133

Brown, Moses
See Barrett, William (Christopher)

Brown, Rita Mae 1944- **CLC 18, 43, 79; DAM**
NOV, POP
See also CA 45-48; CANR 2, 11, 35, 62; INT
CANR-11; MTCW

Brown, Roderick (Langmere) Haig-
See Haig-Brown, Roderick (Langmere)

Brown, Rosellen 1939- .... **CLC 32**
See also CA 77-80; CAAS 10; CANR 14, 44

Brown, Sterling Allen 1901-1989 **CLC 1, 23,**
59; BLC; DAM MULT, POET
See also BW 1; CA 85-88; 127; CANR 26; DLB
48, 51, 63; MTCW

Brown, Will
See Ainsworth, William Harrison

Brown, William Wells 1813-1884 .. **NCLC 2;**
BLC; DAM MULT; DC 1
See also DLB 3, 50

Browne, (Clyde) Jackson 1948(?)- .... **CLC 21**

See also CA 120

Browning, Elizabeth Barrett 1806-1861
NCLC 1, 16, 61, 66; DA; DAB; DAC; DAM
MST, POET; PC 6; WLC
See also CDBLB 1832-1890; DLB 32

Browning, Robert 1812-1889 **NCLC 19; DA;**
DAB; DAC; DAM MST, POET; PC 2;
WLCS
See also CDBLB 1832-1890; DLB 32, 163;
YABC 1

Browning, Tod 1882-1962 .... **CLC 16**
See also CA 141; 117

Brownson, Orestes (Augustus) 1803-1876
NCLC 50

Bruccoli, Matthew J(oseph) 1931- ....**CLC 34**
See also CA 9-12R; CANR 7; DLB 103

Bruce, Lenny .... **CLC 21**
See also Schneider, Leonard Alfred

Bruin, John
See Brutus, Dennis

Brulard, Henri
See Stendhal

Brulls, Christian
See Simenon, Georges (Jacques Christian)

Brunner, John (Kilian Houston) 1934-1995
CLC 8, 10; DAM POP
See also CA 1-4R; 149; CAAS 8; CANR 2, 37;
MTCW

Bruno, Giordano 1548-1600 .... **LC 27**

Brutus, Dennis 1924-... **CLC 43; BLC; DAM**
MULT, POET
See also BW 2; CA 49-52; CAAS 14; CANR
2, 27, 42; DLB 117

Bryan, C(ourtlandt) D(ixon) B(arnes) 1936-
CLC 29
See also CA 73-76; CANR 13, 68; DLB 185;
INT CANR-13

Bryan, Michael
See Moore, Brian

Bryant, William Cullen 1794-1878 **NCLC 6,**
46; DA; DAB; DAC; DAM MST, POET;
PC 20
See also CDALB 1640-1865; DLB 3, 43, 59,
189

Bryusov, Valery Yakovlevich 1873-1924
TCLC 10
See also CA 107; 155

Buchan, John 1875-1940 .... **TCLC 41; DAB;**
DAM POP
See also CA 108; 145; DLB 34, 70, 156; YABC
2

Buchanan, George 1506-1582 .... **LC 4**

Buchheim, Lothar-Guenther 1918- ....**CLC 6**
See also CA 85-88

Buchner, (Karl) Georg 1813-1837 . **NCLC 26**

Buchwald, Art(hur) 1925- .... **CLC 33**
See also AITN 1; CA 5-8R; CANR 21, 67;
MTCW; SATA 10

Buck, Pearl S(ydenstricker) 1892-1973 **CLC 7,**
11, 18; DA; DAB; DAC; DAM MST, NOV
See also AITN 1; CA 1-4R; 41-44R; CANR 1,
34; DLB 9, 102; MTCW; SATA 1, 25

Buckler, Ernest 1908-1984 ... **CLC 13; DAC;**
DAM MST
See also CA 11-12; 114; CAP 1; DLB 68;
SATA 47

Buckley, Vincent (Thomas) 1925-1988 **CLC 57**
See also CA 101

Buckley, William F(rank), Jr. 1925- . **CLC 7,**
18, 37; DAM POP
See also AITN 1; CA 1-4R; CANR 1, 24, 53;
DLB 137; DLBY 80; INT CANR-24;
MTCW

See also AAYA 3; BEST 89:2; CA 1-4R; 124; CANR 3, 28, 61; MTCW

Campbell, Maria 1940- .... **CLC 85; DAC**
See also CA 102; CANR 54; NNAL

Campbell, (John) Ramsey 1946-**CLC 42; SSC 19**
See also CA 57-60; CANR 7; INT CANR-7

Campbell, (Ignatius) Roy (Dunnachie) 1901-1957 .... **TCLC 5**
See also CA 104; 155; DLB 20

Campbell, Thomas 1777-1844 .... **NCLC 19**
See also DLB 93; 144

Campbell, Wilfred .... **TCLC 9**
See also Campbell, William

Campbell, William 1858(?)-1918
See Campbell, Wilfred
See also CA 106; DLB 92

Campion, Jane .... **CLC 95**
See also CA 138

Campos, Alvaro de
See Pessoa, Fernando (Antonio Nogueira)

Camus, Albert 1913-1960**CLC 1, 2, 4, 9, 11, 14, 32, 63, 69; DA; DAB; DAC; DAM DRAM, MST, NOV; DC 2; SSC 9; WLC**
See also CA 89-92; DLB 72; MTCW

Canby, Vincent 1924- .... **CLC 13**
See also CA 81-84

Cancale
See Desnos, Robert

Canetti, Elias 1905-1994**CLC 3, 14, 25, 75, 86**
See also CA 21-24R; 146; CANR 23, 61; DLB 85, 124; MTCW

Canin, Ethan 1960- .... **CLC 55**
See also CA 131; 135

Cannon, Curt
See Hunter, Evan

Cape, Judith
See Page, P(atricia) K(athleen)

Capek, Karel 1890-1938 ... **TCLC 6, 37; DA; DAB; DAC; DAM DRAM, MST, NOV; DC 1; WLC**
See also CA 104; 140

Capote, Truman 1924-1984**CLC 1, 3, 8, 13, 19, 34, 38, 58; DA; DAB; DAC; DAM MST, NOV, POP; SSC 2; WLC**
See also CA 5-8R; 113; CANR 18, 62; CDALB 1941-1968; DLB 2, 185; DLBY 80, 84; MTCW; SATA 91

Capra, Frank 1897-1991 .... **CLC 16**
See also CA 61-64; 135

Caputo, Philip 1941- .... **CLC 32**
See also CA 73-76; CANR 40

Caragiale, Ion Luca 1852-1912 ...... **TCLC 76**
See also CA 157

Card, Orson Scott 1951-**CLC 44, 47, 50; DAM POP**
See also AAYA 11; CA 102; CANR 27, 47; INT CANR-27; MTCW; SATA 83

Cardenal, Ernesto 1925- ....**CLC 31; DAM MULT, POET; HLC**
See also CA 49-52; CANR 2, 32, 66; HW; MTCW

Cardozo, Benjamin N(athan) 1870-1938
TCLC 65
See also CA 117; 164

Carducci, Giosue (Alessandro Giuseppe) 1835-1907 .... **TCLC 32**
See also CA 163

Carew, Thomas 1595(?)-1640 .... **LC 13**
See also DLB 126

Carey, Ernestine Gilbreth 1908- ..... **CLC 17**
See also CA 5-8R; SATA 2

Carey, Peter 1943- .... **CLC 40, 55, 96**

See also CA 123; 127; CANR 53; INT 127; MTCW; SATA 94

Carleton, William 1794-1869 .... **NCLC 3**
See also DLB 159

Carlisle, Henry (Coffin) 1926- .... **CLC 33**
See also CA 13-16R; CANR 15

Carlsen, Chris
See Holdstock, Robert P.

Carlson, Ron(ald F.) 1947- .... **CLC 54**
See also CA 105; CANR 27

Carlyle, Thomas 1795-1881 . **NCLC 22; DA; DAB; DAC; DAM MST**
See also CDBLB 1789-1832; DLB 55; 144

Carman, (William) Bliss 1861-1929**TCLC 7; DAC**
See also CA 104; 152; DLB 92

Carnegie, Dale 1888-1955 .... **TCLC 53**

Carossa, Hans 1878-1956 .... **TCLC 48**
See also DLB 66

Carpenter, Don(ald Richard) 1931-1995**CLC 41**
See also CA 45-48; 149; CANR 1

Carpentier (y Valmont), Alejo 1904-1980
CLC 8, 11, 38; DAM MULT; HLC
See also CA 65-68; 97-100; CANR 11; DLB 113; HW

Carr, Caleb 1955(?)- .... **CLC 86**
See also CA 147

Carr, Emily 1871-1945 .... **TCLC 32**
See also CA 159; DLB 68

Carr, John Dickson 1906-1977 .... **CLC 3**
See also Fairbairn, Roger
See also CA 49-52; 69-72; CANR 3, 33, 60; MTCW

Carr, Philippa
See Hibbert, Eleanor Alice Burford

Carr, Virginia Spencer 1929- .... **CLC 34**
See also CA 61-64; DLB 111

Carrere, Emmanuel 1957- .... **CLC 89**

Carrier, Roch 1937-**CLC 13, 78; DAC; DAM MST**
See also CA 130; CANR 61; DLB 53

Carroll, James P. 1943(?)- .... **CLC 38**
See also CA 81-84

Carroll, Jim 1951- .... **CLC 35**
See also AAYA 17; CA 45-48; CANR 42

Carroll, Lewis ...... **NCLC 2, 53; PC 18; WLC**
See also Dodgson, Charles Lutwidge
See also CDBLB 1832-1890; CLR 2, 18; DLB 18, 163, 178; JRDA

Carroll, Paul Vincent 1900-1968 ......**CLC 10**
See also CA 9-12R; 25-28R; DLB 10

Carruth, Hayden 1921- **CLC 4, 7, 10, 18, 84; PC 10**
See also CA 9-12R; CANR 4, 38, 59; DLB 5, 165; INT CANR-4; MTCW; SATA 47

Carson, Rachel Louise 1907-1964 .. **CLC 71; DAM POP**
See also CA 77-80; CANR 35; MTCW; SATA 23

Carter, Angela (Olive) 1940-1992**CLC 5, 41, 76; SSC 13**
See also CA 53-56; 136; CANR 12, 36, 61; DLB 14; MTCW; SATA 66; SATA-Obit 70

Carter, Nick
See Smith, Martin Cruz

Carver, Raymond 1938-1988**CLC 22, 36, 53, 55; DAM NOV; SSC 8**
See also CA 33-36R; 126; CANR 17, 34, 61; DLB 130; DLBY 84, 88; MTCW

Cary, Elizabeth, Lady Falkland 1585-1639
LC 30

Cary, (Arthur) Joyce (Lunel) 1888-1957

TCLC 1, 29
See also CA 104; 164; CDBLB 1914-1945; DLB 15, 100

Casanova de Seingalt, Giovanni Jacopo 1725-1798 .... **LC 13**

Casares, Adolfo Bioy
See Bioy Casares, Adolfo

Casely-Hayford, J(oseph) E(phraim) 1866-1930
TCLC 24; BLC; DAM MULT
See also BW 2; CA 123; 152

Casey, John (Dudley) 1939- .... **CLC 59**
See also BEST 90:2; CA 69-72; CANR 23

Casey, Michael 1947- ....**CLC 2**
See also CA 65-68; DLB 5

Casey, Patrick
See Thurman, Wallace (Henry)

Casey, Warren (Peter) 1935-1988 ....**CLC 12**
See also CA 101; 127; INT 101

Casona, Alejandro ....**CLC 49**
See also Alvarez, Alejandro Rodriguez

Cassavetes, John 1929-1989 ....**CLC 20**
See also CA 85-88; 127

Cassian, Nina 1924- ....**PC 17**

Cassill, R(onald) V(erlin) 1919- ... **CLC 4, 23**
See also CA 9-12R; CAAS 1; CANR 7, 45; DLB 6

Cassirer, Ernst 1874-1945 .... **TCLC 61**
See also CA 157

Cassity, (Allen) Turner 1929- ...... **CLC 6, 42**
See also CA 17-20R; CAAS 8; CANR 11; DLB 105

Castaneda, Carlos 1931(?)- .... **CLC 12**
See also CA 25-28R; CANR 32, 66; HW; MTCW

Castedo, Elena 1937- ....**CLC 65**
See also CA 132

Castedo-Ellerman, Elena
See Castedo, Elena

Castellanos, Rosario 1925-1974**CLC 66; DAM MULT; HLC**
See also CA 131; 53-56; CANR 58; DLB 113; HW

Castelvetro, Lodovico 1505-1571 .... **LC 12**

Castiglione, Baldassare 1478-1529 ..... **LC 12**

Castle, Robert
See Hamilton, Edmond

Castro, Guillen de 1569-1631 .... **LC 19**

Castro, Rosalia de 1837-1885**NCLC 3; DAM MULT**

Cather, Willa
See Cather, Willa Sibert

Cather, Willa Sibert 1873-1947 **TCLC 1, 11, 31; DA; DAB; DAC; DAM MST, NOV; SSC 2; WLC**
See also AAYA 24; CA 104; 128; CDALB 1865-1917; DLB 9, 54, 78; DLBD 1; MTCW; SATA 30

Cato, Marcus Porcius 234B.C.-149B.C.
CMLC 21

Catton, (Charles) Bruce 1899-1978 ..**CLC 35**
See also AITN 1; CA 5-8R; 81-84; CANR 7; DLB 17; SATA 2; SATA-Obit 24

Catullus c. 84B.C.-c. 54B.C. .... **CMLC 18**

Cauldwell, Frank
See King, Francis (Henry)

Caunitz, William J. 1933-1996 ....**CLC 34**
See also BEST 89:3; CA 125; 130; 152; INT 130

Causley, Charles (Stanley) 1917- ....**CLC 7**
See also CA 9-12R; CANR 5, 35; CLR 30; DLB 27; MTCW; SATA 3, 66

Caute, (John) David 1936- ....**CLC 29; DAM NOV**

See also CA 1-4R; CAAS 4; CANR 1, 33, 64;
DLB 14

**Cavafy, C(onstantine) P(eter) 1863-1933
TCLC 2, 7; DAM POET**
See also Kavafis, Konstantinos Petrou
See also CA 148

Cavallo, Evelyn
See Spark, Muriel (Sarah)

Cavanna, Betty .... CLC 12
See also Harrison, Elizabeth Cavanna
See also JRDA; MAICYA; SAAS 4; SATA 1,
30

Cavendish, Margaret Lucas 1623-1673LC 30
See also DLB 131

Caxton, William 1421(?)-1491(?) .... LC 17
See also DLB 170

Cayrol, Jean 1911- .... CLC 11
See also CA 89-92; DLB 83

**Cela, Camilo Jose 1916-CLC 4, 13, 59; DAM
MULT; HLC**
See also BEST 90:2; CA 21-24R; CAAS 10;
CANR 21, 32; DLBY 89; HW; MTCW

Celan, Paul .... CLC 10, 19, 53, 82; PC 10
See also Antschel, Paul
See also DLB 69

**Celine, Louis-FerdinandCLC 1, 3, 4, 7, 9, 15,
47**
See also Destouches, Louis-Ferdinand
See also DLB 72

Cellini, Benvenuto 1500-1571 .... LC 7

Cendrars, Blaise 1887-1961 ..... CLC 18, 106
See also Sauser-Hall, Frederic

**Cernuda (y Bidon), Luis 1902-1963 CLC 54;
DAM POET**
See also CA 131; 89-92; DLB 134; HW

**Cervantes (Saavedra), Miguel de 1547-1616
LC 6, 23; DA; DAB; DAC; DAM MST,
NOV; SSC 12; WLC**

**Cesaire, Aime (Fernand) 1913-. CLC 19, 32;
BLC; DAM MULT, POET**
See also BW 2; CA 65-68; CANR 24, 43;
MTCW

Chabon, Michael 1963- .... CLC 55
See also CA 139; CANR 57

Chabrol, Claude 1930- .... CLC 16
See also CA 110

Challans, Mary 1905-1983
See Renault, Mary
See also CA 81-84; 111; SATA 23; SATA-Obit
36

Challis, George
See Faust, Frederick (Schiller)

Chambers, Aidan 1934- .... CLC 35
See also CA 25-28R; CANR 12, 31, 58; JRDA;
MAICYA; SAAS 12; SATA 1, 69

Chambers, James 1948-
See Cliff, Jimmy
See also CA 124

Chambers, Jessie
See Lawrence, D(avid) H(erbert Richards)

Chambers, Robert W. 1865-1933 .. TCLC 41

**Chandler, Raymond (Thornton) 1888-1959
TCLC 1, 7; SSC 23**
See also CA 104; 129; CANR 60; CDALB
1929-1941; DLBD 6; MTCW

Chang, Eileen 1921- .... SSC 28

Chang, Jung 1952- .... CLC 71
See also CA 142

**Channing, William Ellery 1780-1842 N C L C
17**
See also DLB 1, 59

Chaplin, Charles Spencer 1889-1977CLC 16
See also Chaplin, Charlie

See also CA 81-84; 73-76

Chaplin, Charlie
See Chaplin, Charles Spencer
See also DLB 44

**Chapman, George 1559(?)-1634LC 22; DAM
DRAM**
See also DLB 62, 121

Chapman, Graham 1941-1989 .... CLC 21
See also Monty Python
See also CA 116; 129; CANR 35

Chapman, John Jay 1862-1933 .... TCLC 7
See also CA 104

Chapman, Lee
See Bradley, Marion Zimmer

Chapman, Walker
See Silverberg, Robert

Chappell, Fred (Davis) 1936- ..... CLC 40, 78
See also CA 5-8R; CAAS 4; CANR 8, 33, 67;
DLB 6, 105

**Char, Rene(-Emile) 1907-1988CLC 9, 11, 14,
55; DAM POET**
See also CA 13-16R; 124; CANR 32; MTCW

Charby, Jay
See Ellison, Harlan (Jay)

Chardin, Pierre Teilhard de
See Teilhard de Chardin, (Marie Joseph) Pierre

Charles I 1600-1649 .... LC 13

Charriere, Isabelle de 1740-1805 ..NCLC 66

Charyn, Jerome 1937- .... CLC 5, 8, 18
See also CA 5-8R; CAAS 1; CANR 7, 61;
DLBY 83; MTCW

Chase, Mary (Coyle) 1907-1981 .... DC 1
See also CA 77-80; 105; SATA 17; SATA-Obit
29

Chase, Mary Ellen 1887-1973 .... CLC 2
See also CA 13-16; 41-44R; CAP 1; SATA 10

Chase, Nicholas
See Hyde, Anthony

**Chateaubriand, Francois Rene de 1768-1848
NCLC 3**
See also DLB 119

Chatterje, Sarat Chandra 1876-1936(?)
See Chatterji, Saratchandra
See also CA 109

**Chatterji, Bankim Chandra 1838-1894NCLC
19**

Chatterji, Saratchandra .... TCLC 13
See also Chatterje, Sarat Chandra

**Chatterton, Thomas 1752-1770 . LC 3; DAM
POET**
See also DLB 109

**Chatwin, (Charles) Bruce 1940-1989CLC 28,
57, 59; DAM POP**
See also AAYA 4; BEST 90:1; CA 85-88; 127

Chaucer, Daniel
See Ford, Ford Madox

**Chaucer, Geoffrey 1340(?)-1400 LC 17; DA;
DAB; DAC; DAM MST, POET; PC 19;
WLCS**
See also CDBLB Before 1660; DLB 146

Chaviaras, Strates 1935-
See Haviaras, Stratis
See also CA 105

Chayefsky, Paddy ....CLC 23
See also Chayefsky, Sidney
See also DLB 7, 44; DLBY 81

Chayefsky, Sidney 1923-1981
See Chayefsky, Paddy
See also CA 9-12R; 104; CANR 18; DAM
DRAM

Chedid, Andree 1920- .... CLC 47
See also CA 145

Cheever, John 1912-1982CLC 3, 7, 8, 11, 15,

25, 64; DA; DAB; DAC; DAM MST, NOV,
POP; SSC 1; WLC
See also CA 5-8R; 106; CABS 1; CANR 5, 27;
CDALB 1941-1968; DLB 2, 102; DLBY 80,
82; INT CANR-5; MTCW

Cheever, Susan 1943- .... CLC 18, 48
See also CA 103; CANR 27, 51; DLBY 82; INT
CANR-27

Chekhonte, Antosha
See Chekhov, Anton (Pavlovich)

**Chekhov, Anton (Pavlovich) 1860-1904TCLC
3, 10, 31, 55; DA; DAB; DAC; DAM
DRAM, MST; SSC 2, 28; WLC**
See also CA 104; 124; SATA 90

**Chernyshevsky, Nikolay Gavrilovich 1828-
1889 ....NCLC 1**

Cherry, Carolyn Janice 1942-
See Cherryh, C. J.
See also CA 65-68; CANR 10

Cherryh, C. J. .... CLC 35
See also Cherry, Carolyn Janice
See also AAYA 24; DLBY 80; SATA 93

**Chesnutt, Charles W(addell) 1858-1932
TCLC 5, 39; BLC; DAM MULT; SSC 7**
See also BW 1; CA 106; 125; DLB 12, 50, 78;
MTCW

Chester, Alfred 1929(?)-1971 .... CLC 49
See also CA 33-36R; DLB 130

**Chesterton, G(ilbert) K(eith) 1874-1936
TCLC 1, 6, 64; DAM NOV, POET; SSC 1**
See also CA 104; 132; CDBLB 1914-1945;
DLB 10, 19, 34, 70, 98, 149, 178; MTCW;
SATA 27

Chiang Pin-chin 1904-1986
See Ding Ling
See also CA 118

Ch'ien Chung-shu 1910- .... CLC 22
See also CA 130; MTCW

Child, L. Maria
See Child, Lydia Maria

Child, Lydia Maria 1802-1880 .... NCLC 6
See also DLB 1, 74; SATA 67

Child, Mrs.
See Child, Lydia Maria

Child, Philip 1898-1978 .... CLC 19, 68
See also CA 13-14; CAP 1; SATA 47

**Childers, (Robert) Erskine 1870-1922 T C L C
65**
See also CA 113; 153; DLB 70

**Childress, Alice 1920-1994CLC 12, 15, 86, 96;
BLC; DAM DRAM, MULT, NOV; DC 4**
See also AAYA 8; BW 2; CA 45-48; 146;
CANR 3, 27, 50; CLR 14; DLB 7, 38; JRDA;
MAICYA; MTCW; SATA 7, 48, 81

Chin, Frank (Chew, Jr.) 1940- .... DC 7
See also CA 33-36R; DAM MULT

Chislett, (Margaret) Anne 1943- ..... CLC 34
See also CA 151

Chitty, Thomas Willes 1926-............ CLC 11
See also Hinde, Thomas
See also CA 5-8R

Chivers, Thomas Holley 1809-1858NCLC 49
See also DLB 3

Chomette, Rene Lucien 1898-1981
See Clair, Rene
See also CA 103

**Chopin, Kate TCLC 5, 14; DA; DAB; SSC 8;
WLCS**
See also Chopin, Katherine
See also CDALB 1865-1917; DLB 12, 78

Chopin, Katherine 1851-1904
See Chopin, Kate
See also CA 104; 122; DAC; DAM MST, NOV

Chretien de Troyes c. 12th cent. - . **CMLC 10**
Christie
  See Ichikawa, Kon
Christie, Agatha (Mary Clarissa) 1890-1976
  **CLC 1, 6, 8, 12, 39, 48; DAB; DAC; DAM
  NOV**
    See also AAYA 9; AITN 1, 2; CA 17-20R; 61-
    64; CANR 10, 37; CDBLB 1914-1945; DLB
    13, 77; MTCW; SATA 36
Christie, (Ann) Philippa
  See Pearce, Philippa
  See also CA 5-8R; CANR 4
Christine de Pizan 1365(?)-1431(?) ...... **LC 9**
Chubb, Elmer
  See Masters, Edgar Lee
Chulkov, Mikhail Dmitrievich 1743-1792 **L C
  2**
  See also DLB 150
Churchill, Caryl 1938- ..... **CLC 31, 55; DC 5**
  See also CA 102; CANR 22, 46; DLB 13;
  MTCW
Churchill, Charles 1731-1764 .... **LC 3**
  See also DLB 109
Chute, Carolyn 1947- .... **CLC 39**
  See also CA 123
Ciardi, John (Anthony) 1916-1986 . **CLC 10,
  40, 44; DAM POET**
    See also CA 5-8R; 118; CAAS 2; CANR 5, 33;
    CLR 19; DLB 5; DLBY 86; INT CANR-5;
    MAICYA; MTCW; SAAS 26; SATA 1, 65;
    SATA-Obit 46
Cicero, Marcus Tullius 106B.C.-43B.C.
  CMLC 3
Cimino, Michael 1943- .... **CLC 16**
  See also CA 105
Cioran, E(mil) M. 1911-1995 .... **CLC 64**
  See also CA 25-28R; 149
Cisneros, Sandra 1954-**CLC 69; DAM MULT;
  HLC**
  See also AAYA 9; CA 131; CANR 64; DLB
  122, 152; HW
Cixous, Helene 1937- .... **CLC 92**
  See also CA 126; CANR 55; DLB 83; MTCW
Clair, Rene .... **CLC 20**
  See also Chomette, Rene Lucien
Clampitt, Amy 1920-1994 .... **CLC 32; PC 19**
  See also CA 110; 146; CANR 29; DLB 105
Clancy, Thomas L., Jr. 1947-
  See Clancy, Tom
  See also CA 125; 131; CANR 62; INT 131;
  MTCW
Clancy, Tom .... **CLC 45; DAM NOV, POP**
  See also Clancy, Thomas L., Jr.
  See also AAYA 9; BEST 89:1, 90:1
Clare, John 1793-1864 **NCLC 9; DAB; DAM
  POET**
  See also DLB 55, 96
Clarin
  See Alas (y Urena), Leopoldo (Enrique Garcia)
Clark, Al C.
  See Goines, Donald
Clark, (Robert) Brian 1932- .... **CLC 29**
  See also CA 41-44R; CANR 67
Clark, Curt
  See Westlake, Donald E(dwin)
Clark, Eleanor 1913-1996 .... **CLC 5, 19**
  See also CA 9-12R; 151; CANR 41; DLB 6
Clark, J. P.
  See Clark, John Pepper
  See also DLB 117
Clark, John Pepper 1935- ..... **CLC 38; BLC;
  DAM DRAM, MULT; DC 5**
  See also Clark, J. P.

  See also BW 1; CA 65-68; CANR 16
Clark, M. R.
  See Clark, Mavis Thorpe
Clark, Mavis Thorpe 1909- ....**CLC 12**
  See also CA 57-60; CANR 8, 37; CLR 30;
  MAICYA; SAAS 5; SATA 8, 74
Clark, Walter Van Tilburg 1909-1971**CLC 28**
  See also CA 9-12R; 33-36R; CANR 63; DLB
  9; SATA 8
Clarke, Arthur C(harles) 1917-**CLC 1, 4, 13,
  18, 35; DAM POP; SSC 3**
  See also AAYA 4; CA 1-4R; CANR 2, 28, 55;
  JRDA; MAICYA; MTCW; SATA 13, 70
Clarke, Austin 1896-1974 .... **CLC 6, 9; DAM
  POET**
  See also CA 29-32; 49-52; CAP 2; DLB 10, 20
Clarke, Austin C(hesterfield) 1934-**CLC 8, 53;
  BLC; DAC; DAM MULT**
  See also BW 1; CA 25-28R; CAAS 16; CANR
  14, 32, 68; DLB 53, 125
Clarke, Gillian 1937- ....**CLC 61**
  See also CA 106; DLB 40
Clarke, Marcus (Andrew Hislop) 1846-1881
  NCLC 19
Clarke, Shirley 1925- ....**CLC 16**
Clash, The
  See Headon, (Nicky) Topper; Jones, Mick;
  Simonon, Paul; Strummer, Joe
Claudel, Paul (Louis Charles Marie) 1868-1955
  TCLC 2, 10
  See also CA 104; DLB 192
Clavell, James (duMaresq) 1925-1994**CLC 6,
  25, 87; DAM NOV, POP**
  See also CA 25-28R; 146; CANR 26, 48;
  MTCW
Cleaver, (Leroy) Eldridge 1935- ..... **CLC 30;
  BLC; DAM MULT**
  See also BW 1; CA 21-24R; CANR 16
Cleese, John (Marwood) 1939- .... **CLC 21**
  See also Monty Python
  See also CA 112; 116; CANR 35; MTCW
Cleishbotham, Jebediah
  See Scott, Walter
Cleland, John 1710-1789 .... **LC 2**
  See also DLB 39
Clemens, Samuel Langhorne 1835-1910
  See Twain, Mark
  See also CA 104; 135; CDALB 1865-1917; DA;
  DAB; DAC; DAM MST, NOV; DLB 11, 12,
  23, 64, 74, 186, 189; JRDA; MAICYA;
  YABC 2
Cleophil
  See Congreve, William
Clerihew, E.
  See Bentley, E(dmund) C(lerihew)
Clerk, N. W.
  See Lewis, C(live) S(taples)
Cliff, Jimmy ....**CLC 21**
  See also Chambers, James
Clifton, (Thelma) Lucille 1936- **CLC 19, 66;
  BLC; DAM MULT, POET; PC 17**
  See also BW 2; CA 49-52; CANR 2, 24, 42;
  CLR 5; DLB 5, 41; MAICYA; MTCW;
  SATA 20, 69
Clinton, Dirk
  See Silverberg, Robert
Clough, Arthur Hugh 1819-1861 ...**NCLC 27**
  See also DLB 32
Clutha, Janet Paterson Frame 1924-
  See Frame, Janet
  See also CA 1-4R; CANR 2, 36; MTCW
Clyne, Terence
  See Blatty, William Peter

Cobalt, Martin
  See Mayne, William (James Carter)
Cobb, Irvin S. 1876-1944 .... **TCLC 77**
  See also DLB 11, 25, 86
Cobbett, William 1763-1835 .... **NCLC 49**
  See also DLB 43, 107, 158
Coburn, D(onald) L(ee) 1938- ....**CLC 10**
  See also CA 89-92
Cocteau, Jean (Maurice Eugene Clement)
  1889-1963**CLC 1, 8, 15, 16, 43; DA; DAB;
  DAC; DAM DRAM, MST, NOV; WLC**
  See also CA 25-28; CANR 40; CAP 2; DLB
  65; MTCW
Codrescu, Andrei 1946-**CLC 46; DAM POET**
  See also CA 33-36R; CAAS 19; CANR 13, 34,
  53
Coe, Max
  See Bourne, Randolph S(illiman)
Coe, Tucker
  See Westlake, Donald E(dwin)
Coen, Ethan 1958- .... **CLC 108**
  See also CA 126
Coen, Joel 1955- .... **CLC 108**
  See also CA 126
The Coen Brothers
  See Coen, Ethan; Coen, Joel
Coetzee, J(ohn) M(ichael) 1940- **CLC 23, 33,
  66; DAM NOV**
  See also CA 77-80; CANR 41, 54; MTCW
Coffey, Brian
  See Koontz, Dean R(ay)
Cohan, George M(ichael) 1878-1942**TCLC 60**
  See also CA 157
Cohen, Arthur A(llen) 1928-1986 **CLC 7, 31**
  See also CA 1-4R; 120; CANR 1, 17, 42; DLB
  28
Cohen, Leonard (Norman) 1934- **CLC 3, 38;
  DAC; DAM MST**
  See also CA 21-24R; CANR 14; DLB 53;
  MTCW
Cohen, Matt 1942- .... **CLC 19; DAC**
  See also CA 61-64; CAAS 18; CANR 40; DLB
  53
Cohen-Solal, Annie 19(?)- .... **CLC 50**
Colegate, Isabel 1931- .... **CLC 36**
  See also CA 17-20R; CANR 8, 22; DLB 14;
  INT CANR-22; MTCW
Coleman, Emmett
  See Reed, Ishmael
Coleridge, M. E.
  See Coleridge, Mary E(lizabeth)
Coleridge, Mary E(lizabeth) 1861-1907**TCLC
  73**
  See also CA 116; DLB 19, 98
Coleridge, Samuel Taylor 1772-1834**NCLC 9,
  54; DA; DAB; DAC; DAM MST, POET;
  PC 11; WLC**
  See also CDBLB 1789-1832; DLB 93, 107
Coleridge, Sara 1802-1852 ....**NCLC 31**
Coles, Don 1928- .... **CLC 46**
  See also CA 115; CANR 38
Coles, Robert (Martin) 1929- .... **CLC 108**
  See also CA 45-48; CANR 3, 32, 66; INT
  CANR-32; SATA 23
Colette, (Sidonie-Gabrielle) 1873-1954**T C L C
  1, 5, 16; DAM NOV; SSC 10**
  See also CA 104; 131; DLB 65; MTCW
Collett, (Jacobine) Camilla (Wergeland) 1813-
  1895 ....**NCLC 22**
Collier, Christopher 1930- .... **CLC 30**
  See also AAYA 13; CA 33-36R; CANR 13, 33;
  JRDA; MAICYA; SATA 16, 70
Collier, James L(incoln) 1928-**CLC 30; DAM**

See also AITN 1; CA 17-18; 41-44R; CANR 35; CAP 2; CDBLB 1914-1945; DLB 10; MTCW

Cowley, Malcolm 1898-1989 .... **CLC 39**
See also CA 5-8R; 128; CANR 3, 55; DLB 4, 48; DLBY 81, 89; MTCW

Cowper, William 1731-1800 . **NCLC 8; DAM POET**
See also DLB 104, 109

Cox, William Trevor 1928- ... **CLC 9, 14, 71; DAM NOV**
See also Trevor, William
See also CA 9-12R; CANR 4, 37, 55; DLB 14; INT CANR-37; MTCW

Coyne, P. J.
See Masters, Hilary

Cozzens, James Gould 1903-1978 **CLC 1, 4, 11, 92**
See also CA 9-12R; 81-84; CANR 19; CDALB 1941-1968; DLB 9; DLBD 2; DLBY 84, 97; MTCW

Crabbe, George 1754-1832 .... **NCLC 26**
See also DLB 93

Craddock, Charles Egbert
See Murfree, Mary Noailles

Craig, A. A.
See Anderson, Poul (William)

Craik, Dinah Maria (Mulock) 1826-1887 **NCLC 38**
See also DLB 35, 163; MAICYA; SATA 34

Cram, Ralph Adams 1863-1942 ..... **TCLC 45**
See also CA 160

Crane, (Harold) Hart 1899-1932 **TCLC 2, 5; DA; DAB; DAC; DAM MST, POET; PC 3; WLC**
See also CA 104; 127; CDALB 1917-1929; DLB 4, 48; MTCW

Crane, R(onald) S(almon) 1886-1967 **CLC 27**
See also CA 85-88; DLB 63

Crane, Stephen (Townley) 1871-1900 **TCLC 11, 17, 32; DA; DAB; DAC; DAM MST, NOV, POET; SSC 7; WLC**
See also AAYA 21; CA 109; 140; CDALB 1865-1917; DLB 12, 54, 78; YABC 2

Crase, Douglas 1944- .... **CLC 58**
See also CA 106

Crashaw, Richard 1612(?)-1649 .... **LC 24**
See also DLB 126

Craven, Margaret 1901-1980 . **CLC 17; DAC**
See also CA 103

Crawford, F(rancis) Marion 1854-1909 **TCLC 10**
See also CA 107; DLB 71

Crawford, Isabella Valancy 1850-1887 **NCLC 12**
See also DLB 92

Crayon, Geoffrey
See Irving, Washington

Creasey, John 1908-1973 .... **CLC 11**
See also CA 5-8R; 41-44R; CANR 8, 59; DLB 77; MTCW

Crebillon, Claude Prosper Jolyot de (fils) 1707-1777 .... **LC 28**

Credo
See Creasey, John

Credo, Alvaro J. de
See Prado (Calvo), Pedro

Creeley, Robert (White) 1926- **CLC 1, 2, 4, 8, 11, 15, 36, 78; DAM POET**
See also CA 1-4R; CAAS 10; CANR 23, 43; DLB 5, 16, 169; MTCW

Crews, Harry (Eugene) 1935- **CLC 6, 23, 49**
See also AITN 1; CA 25-28R; CANR 20, 57;

DLB 6, 143, 185; MTCW

Crichton, (John) Michael 1942- **CLC 2, 6, 54, 90; DAM NOV, POP**
See also AAYA 10; AITN 2; CA 25-28R; CANR 13, 40, 54; DLBY 81; INT CANR-13; JRDA; MTCW; SATA 9, 88

Crispin, Edmund .... **CLC 22**
See also Montgomery, (Robert) Bruce
See also DLB 87

Cristofer, Michael 1945(?)- ... **CLC 28; DAM DRAM**
See also CA 110; 152; DLB 7

Croce, Benedetto 1866-1952 .... **TCLC 37**
See also CA 120; 155

Crockett, David 1786-1836 .... **NCLC 8**
See also DLB 3, 11

Crockett, Davy
See Crockett, David

Crofts, Freeman Wills 1879-1957 .. **TCLC 55**
See also CA 115; DLB 77

Croker, John Wilson 1780-1857 .... **NCLC 10**
See also DLB 110

Crommelynck, Fernand 1885-1970 .. **CLC 75**
See also CA 89-92

Cronin, A(rchibald) J(oseph) 1896-1981 **CLC 32**
See also CA 1-4R; 102; CANR 5; DLB 191; SATA 47; SATA-Obit 25

Cross, Amanda
See Heilbrun, Carolyn G(old)

Crothers, Rachel 1878(?)-1958 ...... **TCLC 19**
See also CA 113; DLB 7

Croves, Hal
See Traven, B.

Crow Dog, Mary (Ellen) (?)- .... **CLC 93**
See also Brave Bird, Mary
See also CA 154

Crowfield, Christopher
See Stowe, Harriet (Elizabeth) Beecher

Crowley, Aleister .... **TCLC 7**
See also Crowley, Edward Alexander

Crowley, Edward Alexander 1875-1947
See Crowley, Aleister
See also CA 104

Crowley, John 1942- .... **CLC 57**
See also CA 61-64; CANR 43; DLBY 82; SATA 65

Crud
See Crumb, R(obert)

Crumarums
See Crumb, R(obert)

Crumb, R(obert) 1943- .... **CLC 17**
See also CA 106

Crumbum
See Crumb, R(obert)

Crumski
See Crumb, R(obert)

Crum the Bum
See Crumb, R(obert)

Crunk
See Crumb, R(obert)

Crustt
See Crumb, R(obert)

Cryer, Gretchen (Kiger) 1935- .... **CLC 21**
See also CA 114; 123

Csath, Geza 1887-1919 .... **TCLC 13**
See also CA 111

Cudlip, David 1933- .... **CLC 34**

Cullen, Countee 1903-1946 **TCLC 4, 37; BLC; DA; DAC; DAM MST, MULT, POET; PC 20; WLCS**
See also BW 1; CA 108; 124; CDALB 1917-1929; DLB 4, 48, 51; MTCW; SATA 18

Cum, R.
See Crumb, R(obert)

Cummings, Bruce F(rederick) 1889-1919
See Barbellion, W. N. P.
See also CA 123

Cummings, E(dward) E(stlin) 1894-1962 **CLC 1, 3, 8, 12, 15, 68; DA; DAB; DAC; DAM MST, POET; PC 5; WLC 2**
See also CA 73-76; CANR 31; CDALB 1929-1941; DLB 4, 48; MTCW

Cunha, Euclides (Rodrigues Pimenta) da 1866-1909 .... **TCLC 24**
See also CA 123

Cunningham, E. V.
See Fast, Howard (Melvin)

Cunningham, J(ames) V(incent) 1911-1985 **CLC 3, 31**
See also CA 1-4R; 115; CANR 1; DLB 5

Cunningham, Julia (Woolfolk) 1916- **CLC 12**
See also CA 9-12R; CANR 4, 19, 36; JRDA; MAICYA; SAAS 2; SATA 1, 26

Cunningham, Michael 1952- .... **CLC 34**
See also CA 136

Cunninghame Graham, R(obert) B(ontine) 1852-1936 .... **TCLC 19**
See also Graham, R(obert) B(ontine) Cunninghame
See also CA 119; DLB 98

Currie, Ellen 19(?)- .... **CLC 44**

Curtin, Philip
See Lowndes, Marie Adelaide (Belloc)

Curtis, Price
See Ellison, Harlan (Jay)

Cutrate, Joe
See Spiegelman, Art

Cynewulf c. 770-c. 840 .... **CMLC 23**

Czaczkes, Shmuel Yosef
See Agnon, S(hmuel) Y(osef Halevi)

Dabrowska, Maria (Szumska) 1889-1965 **CLC 15**
See also CA 106

Dabydeen, David 1955- .... **CLC 34**
See also BW 1; CA 125; CANR 56

Dacey, Philip 1939- .... **CLC 51**
See also CA 37-40R; CAAS 17; CANR 14, 32, 64; DLB 105

Dagerman, Stig (Halvard) 1923-1954 **TCLC 17**
See also CA 117; 155

Dahl, Roald 1916-1990 **CLC 1, 6, 18, 79; DAB; DAC; DAM MST, NOV, POP**
See also AAYA 15; CA 1-4R; 133; CANR 6, 32, 37, 62; CLR 1, 7, 41; DLB 139; JRDA; MAICYA; MTCW; SATA 1, 26, 73; SATA-Obit 65

Dahlberg, Edward 1900-1977 .. **CLC 1, 7, 14**
See also CA 9-12R; 69-72; CANR 31, 62; DLB 48; MTCW

Daitch, Susan 1954- .... **CLC 103**
See also CA 161

Dale, Colin .... **TCLC 18**
See also Lawrence, T(homas) E(dward)

Dale, George E.
See Asimov, Isaac

Daly, Elizabeth 1878-1967 .... **CLC 52**
See also CA 23-24; 25-28R; CANR 60; CAP 2

Daly, Maureen 1921- .... **CLC 17**
See also AAYA 5; CANR 37; JRDA; MAICYA; SAAS 1; SATA 2

Damas, Leon-Gontran 1912-1978 .... **CLC 84**
See also BW 1; CA 125; 73-76

Dana, Richard Henry Sr. 1787-1879 **NCLC 53**

Daniel, Samuel 1562(?)-1619 .... **LC 24**

See also DLB 132, 146
Duncan, Dora Angela
  See Duncan, Isadora
Duncan, Isadora 1877(?)-1927 .... **TCLC 68**
  See also CA 118; 149
Duncan, Lois 1934- .... **CLC 26**
  See also AAYA 4; CA 1-4R; CANR 2, 23, 36;
  CLR 29; JRDA; MAICYA; SAAS 2; SATA
  1, 36, 75
Duncan, Robert (Edward) 1919-1988 **CLC 1,
  2, 4, 7, 15, 41, 55; DAM POET; PC 2**
  See also CA 9-12R; 124; CANR 28, 62; DLB
  5, 16, 193; MTCW
Duncan, Sara Jeannette 1861-1922 **TCLC 60**
  See also CA 157; DLB 92
Dunlap, William 1766-1839 .... **NCLC 2**
  See also DLB 30, 37, 59
Dunn, Douglas (Eaglesham) 1942- **CLC 6, 40**
  See also CA 45-48; CANR 2, 33; DLB 40;
  MTCW
Dunn, Katherine (Karen) 1945- .... **CLC 71**
  See also CA 33-36R
Dunn, Stephen 1939- .... **CLC 36**
  See also CA 33-36R; CANR 12, 48, 53; DLB
  105
Dunne, Finley Peter 1867-1936 ...... **TCLC 28**
  See also CA 108; DLB 11, 23
Dunne, John Gregory 1932- .... **CLC 28**
  See also CA 25-28R; CANR 14, 50; DLBY 80
Dunsany, Edward John Moreton Drax Plunkett
  1878-1957
  See Dunsany, Lord
  See also CA 104; 148; DLB 10
Dunsany, Lord .... **TCLC 2, 59**
  See also Dunsany, Edward John Moreton Drax
  Plunkett
  See also DLB 77, 153, 156
du Perry, Jean
  See Simenon, Georges (Jacques Christian)
Durang, Christopher (Ferdinand) 1949- **C L C
  27, 38**
  See also CA 105; CANR 50
Duras, Marguerite 1914-1996 **CLC 3, 6, 11, 20,
  34, 40, 68, 100**
  See also CA 25-28R; 151; CANR 50; DLB 83;
  MTCW
Durban, (Rosa) Pam 1947- .... **CLC 39**
  See also CA 123
Durcan, Paul 1944- **CLC 43, 70; DAM POET**
  See also CA 134
Durkheim, Emile 1858-1917 .... **TCLC 55**
Durrell, Lawrence (George) 1912-1990 **C L C
  1, 4, 6, 8, 13, 27, 41; DAM NOV**
  See also CA 9-12R; 132; CANR 40; CDBLB
  1945-1960; DLB 15, 27; DLBY 90; MTCW
Durrenmatt, Friedrich
  See Duerrenmatt, Friedrich
Dutt, Toru 1856-1877 .... **NCLC 29**
Dwight, Timothy 1752-1817 .... **NCLC 13**
  See also DLB 37
Dworkin, Andrea 1946- .... **CLC 43**
  See also CA 77-80; CAAS 21; CANR 16, 39;
  INT CANR-16; MTCW
Dwyer, Deanna
  See Koontz, Dean R(ay)
Dwyer, K. R.
  See Koontz, Dean R(ay)
Dye, Richard
  See De Voto, Bernard (Augustine)
Dylan, Bob 1941- .... **CLC 3, 4, 6, 12, 77**
  See also CA 41-44R; DLB 16
Eagleton, Terence (Francis) 1943-
  See Eagleton, Terry

See also CA 57-60; CANR 7, 23, 68; MTCW
Eagleton, Terry .... **CLC 63**
  See also Eagleton, Terence (Francis)
Early, Jack
  See Scoppettone, Sandra
East, Michael
  See West, Morris L(anglo)
Eastaway, Edward
  See Thomas, (Philip) Edward
Eastlake, William (Derry) 1917-1997 **CLC 8**
  See also CA 5-8R; 158; CAAS 1; CANR 5, 63;
  DLB 6; INT CANR-5
Eastman, Charles A(lexander) 1858-1939
  TCLC 55; DAM MULT
  See also DLB 175; NNAL; YABC 1
Eberhart, Richard (Ghormley) 1904- **CLC 3,
  11, 19, 56; DAM POET**
  See also CA 1-4R; CANR 2; CDALB 1941-
  1968; DLB 48; MTCW
Eberstadt, Fernanda 1960- .... **CLC 39**
  See also CA 136
Echegaray (y Eizaguirre), Jose (Maria Waldo)
  1832-1916 .... **TCLC 4**
  See also CA 104; CANR 32; HW; MTCW
Echeverria, (Jose) Esteban (Antonino) 1805-
  1851 .... **NCLC 18**
Echo
  See Proust, (Valentin-Louis-George-Eugene-)
  Marcel
Eckert, Allan W. 1931- .... **CLC 17**
  See also AAYA 18; CA 13-16R; CANR 14, 45;
  INT CANR-14; SAAS 21; SATA 29, 91;
  SATA-Brief 27
Eckhart, Meister 1260(?)-1328(?) ... **CMLC 9**
  See also DLB 115
Eckmar, F. R.
  See de Hartog, Jan
Eco, Umberto 1932- **CLC 28, 60; DAM NOV,
  POP**
  See also BEST 90:1; CA 77-80; CANR 12, 33,
  55; MTCW
Eddison, E(ric) R(ucker) 1882-1945 **TCLC 15**
  See also CA 109; 156
Eddy, Mary (Morse) Baker 1821-1910 **T C L C
  71**
  See also CA 113
Edel, (Joseph) Leon 1907-1997 .. **CLC 29, 34**
  See also CA 1-4R; 161; CANR 1, 22; DLB 103;
  INT CANR-22
Eden, Emily 1797-1869 .... **NCLC 10**
Edgar, David 1948- .. **CLC 42; DAM DRAM**
  See also CA 57-60; CANR 12, 61; DLB 13;
  MTCW
Edgerton, Clyde (Carlyle) 1944- ...... **CLC 39**
  See also AAYA 17; CA 118; 134; CANR 64;
  INT 134
Edgeworth, Maria 1768-1849 .... **NCLC 1, 51**
  See also DLB 116, 159, 163; SATA 21
Edmonds, Paul
  See Kuttner, Henry
Edmonds, Walter D(umaux) 1903- .. **CLC 35**
  See also CA 5-8R; CANR 2; DLB 9; MAICYA;
  SAAS 4; SATA 1, 27
Edmondson, Wallace
  See Ellison, Harlan (Jay)
Edson, Russell .... **CLC 13**
  See also CA 33-36R
Edwards, Bronwen Elizabeth
  See Rose, Wendy
Edwards, G(erald) B(asil) 1899-1976 **CLC 25**
  See also CA 110
Edwards, Gus 1939- .... **CLC 43**
  See also CA 108; INT 108

Edwards, Jonathan 1703-1758 ..... **LC 7; DA;
  DAC; DAM MST**
  See also DLB 24
Efron, Marina Ivanovna Tsvetaeva
  See Tsvetaeva (Efron), Marina (Ivanovna)
Ehle, John (Marsden, Jr.) 1925- .... **CLC 27**
  See also CA 9-12R
Ehrenbourg, Ilya (Grigoryevich)
  See Ehrenburg, Ilya (Grigoryevich)
Ehrenburg, Ilya (Grigoryevich) 1891-1967
  CLC 18, 34, 62
  See also CA 102; 25-28R
Ehrenburg, Ilyo (Grigoryevich)
  See Ehrenburg, Ilya (Grigoryevich)
Eich, Guenter 1907-1972 .... **CLC 15**
  See also CA 111; 93-96; DLB 69, 124
Eichendorff, Joseph Freiherr von 1788-1857
  NCLC 8
  See also DLB 90
Eigner, Larry .... **CLC 9**
  See also Eigner, Laurence (Joel)
  See also CAAS 23; DLB 5
Eigner, Laurence (Joel) 1927-1996
  See Eigner, Larry
  See also CA 9-12R; 151; CANR 6; DLB 193
Einstein, Albert 1879-1955 .... **TCLC 65**
  See also CA 121; 133; MTCW
Eiseley, Loren Corey 1907-1977 .... **CLC 7**
  See also AAYA 5; CA 1-4R; 73-76; CANR 6
Eisenstadt, Jill 1963- .... **CLC 50**
  See also CA 140
Eisenstein, Sergei (Mikhailovich) 1898-1948
  TCLC 57
  See also CA 114; 149
Eisner, Simon
  See Kornbluth, C(yril) M.
Ekeloef, (Bengt) Gunnar 1907-1968 **CLC 27;
  DAM POET**
  See also CA 123; 25-28R
Ekelof, (Bengt) Gunnar
  See Ekeloef, (Bengt) Gunnar
Ekelund, Vilhelm 1880-1949 .... **TCLC 75**
Ekwensi, C. O. D.
  See Ekwensi, Cyprian (Odiatu Duaka)
Ekwensi, Cyprian (Odiatu Duaka) 1921- **CLC
  4; BLC; DAM MULT**
  See also BW 2; CA 29-32R; CANR 18, 42;
  DLB 117; MTCW; SATA 66
Elaine .... **TCLC 18**
  See also Leverson, Ada
El Crummo
  See Crumb, R(obert)
Elder, Lonne III 1931-1996 .... **DC 8**
  See also BLC; BW 1; CA 81-84; 152; CANR
  25; DAM MULT; DLB 7, 38, 44
Elia
  See Lamb, Charles
Eliade, Mircea 1907-1986 .... **CLC 19**
  See also CA 65-68; 119; CANR 30, 62; MTCW
Eliot, A. D.
  See Jewett, (Theodora) Sarah Orne
Eliot, Alice
  See Jewett, (Theodora) Sarah Orne
Eliot, Dan
  See Silverberg, Robert
Eliot, George 1819-1880 **NCLC 4, 13, 23, 41,
  49; DA; DAB; DAC; DAM MST, NOV; PC
  20; WLC**
  See also CDBLB 1832-1890; DLB 21, 35, 55
Eliot, John 1604-1690 .... **LC 5**
  See also DLB 24
Eliot, T(homas) S(tearns) 1888-1965 **CLC 1, 2,
  3, 6, 9, 10, 13, 15, 24, 34, 41, 55, 57; DA;**

1882 ....NCLC 17
See also DLB 123
Godard, Jean-Luc 1930- .... CLC 20
See also CA 93-96
Godden, (Margaret) Rumer 1907- .. CLC 53
See also AAYA 6; CA 5-8R; CANR 4, 27, 36, 55; CLR 20; DLB 161; MAICYA; SAAS 12; SATA 3, 36
Godoy Alcayaga, Lucila 1889-1957
See Mistral, Gabriela
See also BW 2; CA 104; 131; DAM MULT; HW; MTCW
Godwin, Gail (Kathleen) 1937- CLC 5, 8, 22, 31, 69; DAM POP
See also CA 29-32R; CANR 15, 43; DLB 6; INT CANR-15; MTCW
Godwin, William 1756-1836 .... NCLC 14
See also CDBLB 1789-1832; DLB 39, 104, 142, 158, 163
Goebbels, Josef
See Goebbels, (Paul) Joseph
Goebbels, (Paul) Joseph 1897-1945 TCLC 68
See also CA 115; 148
Goebbels, Joseph Paul
See Goebbels, (Paul) Joseph
Goethe, Johann Wolfgang von 1749-1832
NCLC 4, 22, 34; DA; DAB; DAC; DAM DRAM, MST, POET; PC 5; WLC 3
See also DLB 94
Gogarty, Oliver St. John 1878-1957 TCLC 15
See also CA 109; 150; DLB 15, 19
Gogol, Nikolai (Vasilyevich) 1809-1852 NCLC 5, 15, 31; DA; DAB; DAC; DAM DRAM, MST; DC 1; SSC 4, 29; WLC
Goines, Donald 1937(?)-1974 CLC 80; BLC; DAM MULT, POP
See also AITN 1; BW 1; CA 124; 114; DLB 33
Gold, Herbert 1924- .... CLC 4, 7, 14, 42
See also CA 9-12R; CANR 17, 45; DLB 2; DLBY 81
Goldbarth, Albert 1948- .... CLC 5, 38
See also CA 53-56; CANR 6, 40; DLB 120
Goldberg, Anatol 1910-1982 .... CLC 34
See also CA 131; 117
Goldemberg, Isaac 1945- .... CLC 52
See also CA 69-72; CAAS 12; CANR 11, 32; HW
Golding, William (Gerald) 1911-1993 CLC 1, 2, 3, 8, 10, 17, 27, 58, 81; DA; DAB; DAC; DAM MST, NOV; WLC
See also AAYA 5; CA 5-8R; 141; CANR 13, 33, 54; CDBLB 1945-1960; DLB 15, 100; MTCW
Goldman, Emma 1869-1940 .... TCLC 13
See also CA 110; 150
Goldman, Francisco 1954- .... CLC 76
See also CA 162
Goldman, William (W.) 1931- ..... CLC 1, 48
See also CA 9-12R; CANR 29; DLB 44
Goldmann, Lucien 1913-1970 .... CLC 24
See also CA 25-28; CAP 2
Goldoni, Carlo 1707-1793 LC 4; DAM DRAM
Goldsberry, Steven 1949- .... CLC 34
See also CA 131
Goldsmith, Oliver 1728-1774 LC 2; DA; DAB; DAC; DAM DRAM, MST, NOV, POET; DC 8; WLC
See also CDBLB 1660-1789; DLB 39, 89, 104, 109, 142; SATA 26
Goldsmith, Peter
See Priestley, J(ohn) B(oynton)
Gombrowicz, Witold 1904-1969 CLC 4, 7, 11, 49; DAM DRAM

See also CA 19-20; 25-28R; CAP 2
Gomez de la Serna, Ramon 1888-1963 CLC 9
See also CA 153; 116; HW
Goncharov, Ivan Alexandrovich 1812-1891
NCLC 1, 63
Goncourt, Edmond (Louis Antoine Huot) de 1822-1896 ....NCLC 7
See also DLB 123
Goncourt, Jules (Alfred Huot) de 1830-1870
NCLC 7
See also DLB 123
Gontier, Fernande 19(?)- .... CLC 50
Gonzalez Martinez, Enrique 1871-1952
TCLC 72
See also HW
Goodman, Paul 1911-1972 ..... CLC 1, 2, 4, 7
See also CA 19-20; 37-40R; CANR 34; CAP 2; DLB 130; MTCW
Gordimer, Nadine 1923- CLC 3, 5, 7, 10, 18, 33, 51, 70; DA; DAB; DAC; DAM MST, NOV; SSC 17; WLCS
See also CA 5-8R; CANR 3, 28, 56; INT CANR-28; MTCW
Gordon, Adam Lindsay 1833-1870 NCLC 21
Gordon, Caroline 1895-1981 CLC 6, 13, 29, 83; SSC 15
See also CA 11-12; 103; CANR 36; CAP 1; DLB 4, 9, 102; DLBY 81; MTCW
Gordon, Charles William 1860-1937
See Connor, Ralph
See also CA 109
Gordon, Mary (Catherine) 1949- CLC 13, 22
See also CA 102; CANR 44; DLB 6; DLBY 81; INT 102; MTCW
Gordon, N. J.
See Bosman, Herman Charles
Gordon, Sol 1923- .... CLC 26
See also CA 53-56; CANR 4; SATA 11
Gordone, Charles 1925-1995 CLC 1, 4; DAM DRAM; DC 8
See also BW 1; CA 93-96; 150; CANR 55; DLB 7; INT 93-96; MTCW
Gore, Catherine 1800-1861 .... NCLC 65
See also DLB 116
Gorenko, Anna Andreevna
See Akhmatova, Anna
Gorky, Maxim 1868-1936 TCLC 8; DAB; SSC 28; WLC
See also Peshkov, Alexei Maximovich
Goryan, Sirak
See Saroyan, William
Gosse, Edmund (William) 1849-1928 TCLC 28
See also CA 117; DLB 57, 144, 184
Gotlieb, Phyllis Fay (Bloom) 1926- .. CLC 18
See also CA 13-16R; CANR 7; DLB 88
Gottesman, S. D.
See Kornbluth, C(yril) M.; Pohl, Frederik
Gottfried von Strassburg fl. c. 1210- . CMLC 10
See also DLB 138
Gould, Lois .... CLC 4, 10
See also CA 77-80; CANR 29; MTCW
Gourmont, Remy (-Marie-Charles) de 1858-1915 ....TCLC 17
See also CA 109; 150
Govier, Katherine 1948- .... CLC 51
See also CA 101; CANR 18, 40
Goyen, (Charles) William 1915-1983 CLC 5, 8, 14, 40
See also AITN 2; CA 5-8R; 110; CANR 6; DLB 2; DLBY 83; INT CANR-6
Goytisolo, Juan 1931- . CLC 5, 10, 23; DAM

MULT; HLC
See also CA 85-88; CANR 32, 61; HW; MTCW
Gozzano, Guido 1883-1916 ....PC 10
See also CA 154; DLB 114
Gozzi, (Conte) Carlo 1720-1806 ....NCLC 23
Grabbe, Christian Dietrich 1801-1836 N C L C 2
See also DLB 133
Grace, Patricia 1937- .... CLC 56
Gracian y Morales, Baltasar 1601-1658 LC 15
Gracq, Julien .... CLC 11, 48
See also Poirier, Louis
See also DLB 83
Grade, Chaim 1910-1982 .... CLC 10
See also CA 93-96; 107
Graduate of Oxford, A
See Ruskin, John
Grafton, Garth
See Duncan, Sara Jeannette
Graham, John
See Phillips, David Graham
Graham, Jorie 1951- .... CLC 48
See also CA 111; CANR 63; DLB 120
Graham, R(obert) B(ontine) Cunninghame
See Cunninghame Graham, R(obert) B(ontine)
See also DLB 98, 135, 174
Graham, Robert
See Haldeman, Joe (William)
Graham, Tom
See Lewis, (Harry) Sinclair
Graham, W(illiam) S(ydney) 1918-1986 C L C 29
See also CA 73-76; 118; DLB 20
Graham, Winston (Mawdsley) 1910- CLC 23
See also CA 49-52; CANR 2, 22, 45, 66; DLB 77
Grahame, Kenneth 1859-1932 TCLC 64; DAB
See also CA 108; 136; CLR 5; DLB 34, 141, 178; MAICYA; YABC 1
Grant, Skeeter
See Spiegelman, Art
Granville-Barker, Harley 1877-1946 TCLC 2; DAM DRAM
See also Barker, Harley Granville
See also CA 104
Grass, Guenter (Wilhelm) 1927- CLC 1, 2, 4, 6, 11, 15, 22, 32, 49, 88; DA; DAB; DAC; DAM MST, NOV; WLC
See also CA 13-16R; CANR 20; DLB 75, 124; MTCW
Gratton, Thomas
See Hulme, T(homas) E(rnest)
Grau, Shirley Ann 1929- .. CLC 4, 9; SSC 15
See also CA 89-92; CANR 22; DLB 2; INT CANR-22; MTCW
Gravel, Fern
See Hall, James Norman
Graver, Elizabeth 1964- .... CLC 70
See also CA 135
Graves, Richard Perceval 1945- .... CLC 44
See also CA 65-68; CANR 9, 26, 51
Graves, Robert (von Ranke) 1895-1985 C L C 1, 2, 6, 11, 39, 44, 45; DAB; DAC; DAM MST, POET; PC 6
See also CA 5-8R; 117; CANR 5, 36; CDBLB 1914-1945; DLB 20, 100, 191; DLBY 85; MTCW; SATA 45
Graves, Valerie
See Bradley, Marion Zimmer
Gray, Alasdair (James) 1934- ....CLC 41
See also CA 126; CANR 47; INT 126; MTCW
Gray, Amlin 1946- ....CLC 29
See also CA 138

Gray, Francine du Plessix 1930- ..... **CLC 22; DAM NOV**
See also BEST 90:3; CA 61-64; CAAS 2; CANR 11, 33; INT CANR-11; MTCW

Gray, John (Henry) 1866-1934 ...... **TCLC 19**
See also CA 119; 162

Gray, Simon (James Holliday) 1936- **CLC 9, 14, 36**
See also AITN 1; CA 21-24R; CAAS 3; CANR 32; DLB 13; MTCW

Gray, Spalding 1941-**CLC 49; DAM POP; DC 7**
See also CA 128

Gray, Thomas 1716-1771**LC 4, 40; DA; DAB; DAC; DAM MST; PC 2; WLC**
See also CDBLB 1660-1789; DLB 109

Grayson, David
See Baker, Ray Stannard

Grayson, Richard (A.) 1951- .... **CLC 38**
See also CA 85-88; CANR 14, 31, 57

Greeley, Andrew M(oran) 1928- .... **CLC 28; DAM POP**
See also CA 5-8R; CAAS 7; CANR 7, 43; MTCW

Green, Anna Katharine 1846-1935 **TCLC 63**
See also CA 112; 159

Green, Brian
See Card, Orson Scott

Green, Hannah
See Greenberg, Joanne (Goldenberg)

Green, Hannah 1927(?)-1996 .... **CLC 3**
See also CA 73-76; CANR 59

Green, Henry 1905-1973 .... **CLC 2, 13, 97**
See also Yorke, Henry Vincent
See also DLB 15

Green, Julian (Hartridge) 1900-
See Green, Julien
See also CA 21-24R; CANR 33; DLB 4, 72; MTCW

Green, Julien .... **CLC 3, 11, 77**
See also Green, Julian (Hartridge)

Green, Paul (Eliot) 1894-1981**CLC 25; DAM DRAM**
See also AITN 1; CA 5-8R; 103; CANR 3; DLB 7, 9; DLBY 81

Greenberg, Ivan 1908-1973
See Rahv, Philip
See also CA 85-88

Greenberg, Joanne (Goldenberg) 1932-**C L C 7, 30**
See also AAYA 12; CA 5-8R; CANR 14, 32; SATA 25

Greenberg, Richard 1959(?)- .... **CLC 57**
See also CA 138

Greene, Bette 1934- .... **CLC 30**
See also AAYA 7; CA 53-56; CANR 4; CLR 2; JRDA; MAICYA; SAAS 16; SATA 8

Greene, Gael ....**CLC 8**
See also CA 13-16R; CANR 10

Greene, Graham (Henry) 1904-1991**CLC 1, 3, 6, 9, 14, 18, 27, 37, 70, 72; DA; DAB; DAC; DAM MST, NOV; SSC 29; WLC**
See also AITN 2; CA 13-16R; 133; CANR 35, 61; CDBLB 1945-1960; DLB 13, 15, 77, 100, 162; DLBY 91; MTCW; SATA 20

Greene, Robert 1558-1592 .... **LC 41**
See also DLB 62, 167

Greer, Richard
See Silverberg, Robert

Gregor, Arthur 1923- ....**CLC 9**
See also CA 25-28R; CAAS 10; CANR 11; SATA 36

Gregor, Lee

See Pohl, Frederik

Gregory, Isabella Augusta (Persse) 1852-1932 **TCLC 1**
See also CA 104; DLB 10

Gregory, J. Dennis
See Williams, John A(lfred)

Grendon, Stephen
See Derleth, August (William)

Grenville, Kate 1950- .... **CLC 61**
See also CA 118; CANR 53

Grenville, Pelham
See Wodehouse, P(elham) G(renville)

Greve, Felix Paul (Berthold Friedrich) 1879-1948
See Grove, Frederick Philip
See also CA 104; 141; DAC; DAM MST

Grey, Zane 1872-1939 .. **TCLC 6; DAM POP**
See also CA 104; 132; DLB 9; MTCW

Grieg, (Johan) Nordahl (Brun) 1902-1943 **TCLC 10**
See also CA 107

Grieve, C(hristopher) M(urray) 1892-1978 **CLC 11, 19; DAM POET**
See also MacDiarmid, Hugh; Pteleon
See also CA 5-8R; 85-88; CANR 33; MTCW

Griffin, Gerald 1803-1840 .... **NCLC 7**
See also DLB 159

Griffin, John Howard 1920-1980 ..... **CLC 68**
See also AITN 1; CA 1-4R; 101; CANR 2

Griffin, Peter 1942- ....**CLC 39**
See also CA 136

Griffith, D(avid Lewelyn) W(ark) 1875(?)-1948 **TCLC 68**
See also CA 119; 150

Griffith, Lawrence
See Griffith, D(avid Lewelyn) W(ark)

Griffiths, Trevor 1935- .... **CLC 13, 52**
See also CA 97-100; CANR 45; DLB 13

Griggs, Sutton Elbert 1872-1930(?)**TCLC 77**
See also CA 123; DLB 50

Grigson, Geoffrey (Edward Harvey) 1905-1985 **CLC 7, 39**
See also CA 25-28R; 118; CANR 20, 33; DLB 27; MTCW

Grillparzer, Franz 1791-1872 .... **NCLC 1**
See also DLB 133

Grimble, Reverend Charles James
See Eliot, T(homas) S(tearns)

Grimke, Charlotte L(ottie) Forten 1837(?)-1914
See Forten, Charlotte L.
See also BW 1; CA 117; 124; DAM MULT, POET

Grimm, Jacob Ludwig Karl 1785-1863**NCLC 3**
See also DLB 90; MAICYA; SATA 22

Grimm, Wilhelm Karl 1786-1859 ... **NCLC 3**
See also DLB 90; MAICYA; SATA 22

Grimmelshausen, Johann Jakob Christoffel von 1621-1676 .... **LC 6**
See also DLB 168

Grindel, Eugene 1895-1952
See Eluard, Paul
See also CA 104

Grisham, John 1955- ..... **CLC 84; DAM POP**
See also AAYA 14; CA 138; CANR 47

Grossman, David 1954- .... **CLC 67**
See also CA 138

Grossman, Vasily (Semenovich) 1905-1964 **CLC 41**
See also CA 124; 130; MTCW

Grove, Frederick Philip .... **TCLC 4**
See also Greve, Felix Paul (Berthold Friedrich)
See also DLB 92

Grubb
See Crumb, R(obert)

Grumbach, Doris (Isaac) 1918-**CLC 13, 22, 64**
See also CA 5-8R; CAAS 2; CANR 9, 42; INT CANR-9

Grundtvig, Nicolai Frederik Severin 1783-1872 **NCLC 1**

Grunge
See Crumb, R(obert)

Grunwald, Lisa 1959- .... **CLC 44**
See also CA 120

Guare, John 1938- .. **CLC 8, 14, 29, 67; DAM DRAM**
See also CA 73-76; CANR 21; DLB 7; MTCW

Gudjonsson, Halldor Kiljan 1902-1998
See Laxness, Halldor
See also CA 103; 164

Guenter, Erich
See Eich, Guenter

Guest, Barbara 1920- .... **CLC 34**
See also CA 25-28R; CANR 11, 44; DLB 5, 193

Guest, Judith (Ann) 1936- .**CLC 8, 30; DAM NOV, POP**
See also AAYA 7; CA 77-80; CANR 15; INT CANR-15; MTCW

Guevara, Che .... **CLC 87; HLC**
See also Guevara (Serna), Ernesto

Guevara (Serna), Ernesto 1928-1967
See Guevara, Che
See also CA 127; 111; CANR 56; DAM MULT; HW

Guild, Nicholas M. 1944- .... **CLC 33**
See also CA 93-96

Guillemin, Jacques
See Sartre, Jean-Paul

Guillen, Jorge 1893-1984 .... **CLC 11; DAM MULT, POET**
See also CA 89-92; 112; DLB 108; HW

Guillen, Nicolas (Cristobal) 1902-1989 . **C L C 48, 79; BLC; DAM MST, MULT, POET; HLC**
See also BW 2; CA 116; 125; 129; HW

Guillevic, (Eugene) 1907- .... **CLC 33**
See also CA 93-96

Guillois
See Desnos, Robert

Guillois, Valentin
See Desnos, Robert

Guiney, Louise Imogen 1861-1920 **TCLC 41**
See also CA 160; DLB 54

Guiraldes, Ricardo (Guillermo) 1886-1927 **TCLC 39**
See also CA 131; HW; MTCW

Gumilev, Nikolai Stepanovich 1886-1921 **TCLC 60**

Gunesekera, Romesh 1954- .... **CLC 91**
See also CA 159

Gunn, Bill ....**CLC 5**
See also Gunn, William Harrison
See also DLB 38

Gunn, Thom(son William) 1929-**CLC 3, 6, 18, 32, 81; DAM POET**
See also CA 17-20R; CANR 9, 33; CDBLB 1960 to Present; DLB 27; INT CANR-33; MTCW

Gunn, William Harrison 1934(?)-1989
See Gunn, Bill
See also AITN 1; BW 1; CA 13-16R; 128; CANR 12, 25

Gunnars, Kristjana 1948- .... **CLC 69**
See also CA 113; DLB 60

Gurdjieff, G(eorgei) I(vanovich) 1877(?)-1949

TCLC 71
See also CA 157
Gurganus, Allan 1947-.. CLC 70; DAM POP
See also BEST 90:1; CA 135
Gurney, A(lbert) R(amsdell), Jr. 1930- C L C 32, 50, 54; DAM DRAM
See also CA 77-80; CANR 32, 64
Gurney, Ivor (Bertie) 1890-1937 ... TCLC 33
Gurney, Peter
See Gurney, A(lbert) R(amsdell), Jr.
Guro, Elena 1877-1913 .... TCLC 56
Gustafson, James M(oody) 1925- .. CLC 100
See also CA 25-28R; CANR 37
Gustafson, Ralph (Barker) 1909- .... CLC 36
See also CA 21-24R; CANR 8, 45; DLB 88
Gut, Gom
See Simenon, Georges (Jacques Christian)
Guterson, David 1956- .... CLC 91
See also CA 132
Guthrie, A(lfred) B(ertram), Jr. 1901-1991 CLC 23
See also CA 57-60; 134; CANR 24; DLB 6; SATA 62; SATA-Obit 67
Guthrie, Isobel
See Grieve, C(hristopher) M(urray)
Guthrie, Woodrow Wilson 1912-1967
See Guthrie, Woody
See also CA 113; 93-96
Guthrie, Woody .... CLC 35
See also Guthrie, Woodrow Wilson
Guy, Rosa (Cuthbert) 1928- .... CLC 26
See also AAYA 4; BW 2; CA 17-20R; CANR 14, 34; CLR 13; DLB 33; JRDA; MAICYA; SATA 14, 62
Gwendolyn
See Bennett, (Enoch) Arnold
H. D. .... CLC 3, 8, 14, 31, 34, 73; PC 5
See also Doolittle, Hilda
H. de V.
See Buchan, John
Haavikko, Paavo Juhani 1931-.. CLC 18, 34
See also CA 106
Habbema, Koos
See Heijermans, Herman
Habermas, Juergen 1929- .... CLC 104
See also CA 109
Habermas, Jurgen
See Habermas, Juergen
Hacker, Marilyn 1942- CLC 5, 9, 23, 72, 91; DAM POET
See also CA 77-80; CANR 68; DLB 120
Haggard, H(enry) Rider 1856-1925TCLC 11
See also CA 108; 148; DLB 70, 156, 174, 178; SATA 16
Hagiosy, L.
See Larbaud, Valery (Nicolas)
Hagiwara Sakutaro 1886-1942TCLC 60; PC 18
Haig, Fenil
See Ford, Ford Madox
Haig-Brown, Roderick (Langmere) 1908-1976 CLC 21
See also CA 5-8R; 69-72; CANR 4, 38; CLR 31; DLB 88; MAICYA; SATA 12
Hailey, Arthur 1920-CLC 5; DAM NOV, POP
See also AITN 2; BEST 90:3; CA 1-4R; CANR 2, 36; DLB 88; DLBY 82; MTCW
Hailey, Elizabeth Forsythe 1938- .... CLC 40
See also CA 93-96; CAAS 1; CANR 15, 48; INT CANR-15
Haines, John (Meade) 1924-............. CLC 58
See also CA 17-20R; CANR 13, 34; DLB 5
Hakluyt, Richard 1552-1616 .... LC 31

Haldeman, Joe (William) 1943-........ CLC 61
See also CA 53-56; CAAS 25; CANR 6; DLB 8; INT CANR-6
Haley, Alex(ander Murray Palmer) 1921-1992 CLC 8, 12, 76; BLC; DA; DAB; DAC; DAM MST, MULT, POP
See also BW 2; CA 77-80; 136; CANR 61; DLB 38; MTCW
Haliburton, Thomas Chandler 1796-1865 NCLC 15
See also DLB 11, 99
Hall, Donald (Andrew, Jr.) 1928- CLC 1, 13, 37, 59; DAM POET
See also CA 5-8R; CAAS 7; CANR 2, 44, 64; DLB 5; SATA 23, 97
Hall, Frederic Sauser
See Sauser-Hall, Frederic
Hall, James
See Kuttner, Henry
Hall, James Norman 1887-1951 .... TCLC 23
See also CA 123; SATA 21
Hall, (Marguerite) Radclyffe 1886-1943 TCLC 12
See also CA 110; 150
Hall, Rodney 1935-........................... CLC 51
See also CA 109
Halleck, Fitz-Greene 1790-1867 .... NCLC 47
See also DLB 3
Halliday, Michael
See Creasey, John
Halpern, Daniel 1945- .... CLC 14
See also CA 33-36R
Hamburger, Michael (Peter Leopold) 1924- CLC 5, 14
See also CA 5-8R; CAAS 4; CANR 2, 47; DLB 27
Hamill, Pete 1935- .... CLC 10
See also CA 25-28R; CANR 18
Hamilton, Alexander 1755(?)-1804 NCLC 49
See also DLB 37
Hamilton, Clive
See Lewis, C(live) S(taples)
Hamilton, Edmond 1904-1977 .... CLC 1
See also CA 1-4R; CANR 3; DLB 8
Hamilton, Eugene (Jacob) Lee
See Lee-Hamilton, Eugene (Jacob)
Hamilton, Franklin
See Silverberg, Robert
Hamilton, Gail
See Corcoran, Barbara
Hamilton, Mollie
See Kaye, M(ary) M(argaret)
Hamilton, (Anthony Walter) Patrick 1904-1962 CLC 51
See also CA 113; DLB 10
Hamilton, Virginia 1936- ...... CLC 26; DAM MULT
See also AAYA 2, 21; BW 2; CA 25-28R; CANR 20, 37; CLR 1, 11, 40; DLB 33, 52; INT CANR-20; JRDA; MAICYA; MTCW; SATA 4, 56, 79
Hammett, (Samuel) Dashiell 1894-1961 C L C 3, 5, 10, 19, 47; SSC 17
See also AITN 1; CA 81-84; CANR 42; CDALB 1929-1941; DLBD 6; DLBY 96; MTCW
Hammon, Jupiter 1711(?)-1800(?) NCLC 5; BLC; DAM MULT, POET; PC 16
See also DLB 31, 50
Hammond, Keith
See Kuttner, Henry
Hamner, Earl (Henry), Jr. 1923- ...... CLC 12
See also AITN 2; CA 73-76; DLB 6

Hampton, Christopher (James) 1946- CLC 4
See also CA 25-28R; DLB 13; MTCW
Hamsun, Knut .... TCLC 2, 14, 49
See also Pedersen, Knut
Handke, Peter 1942-CLC 5, 8, 10, 15, 38; DAM DRAM, NOV
See also CA 77-80; CANR 33; DLB 85, 124; MTCW
Hanley, James 1901-1985 ..... CLC 3, 5, 8, 13
See also CA 73-76; 117; CANR 36; DLB 191; MTCW
Hannah, Barry 1942- .... CLC 23, 38, 90
See also CA 108; 110; CANR 43, 68; DLB 6; INT 110; MTCW
Hannon, Ezra
See Hunter, Evan
Hansberry, Lorraine (Vivian) 1930-1965CLC 17, 62; BLC; DA; DAB; DAC; DAM DRAM, MST, MULT; DC 2
See also BW 1; CA 109; 25-28R; CABS 3; CANR 58; CDALB 1941-1968; DLB 7, 38; MTCW
Hansen, Joseph 1923- .... CLC 38
See also CA 29-32R; CAAS 17; CANR 16, 44, 66; INT CANR-16
Hansen, Martin A. 1909-1955 .... TCLC 32
Hanson, Kenneth O(stlin) 1922- .... CLC 13
See also CA 53-56; CANR 7
Hardwick, Elizabeth 1916-.... CLC 13; DAM NOV
See also CA 5-8R; CANR 3, 32; DLB 6; MTCW
Hardy, Thomas 1840-1928TCLC 4, 10, 18, 32, 48, 53, 72; DA; DAB; DAC; DAM MST, NOV, POET; PC 8; SSC 2; WLC
See also CA 104; 123; CDBLB 1890-1914; DLB 18, 19, 135; MTCW
Hare, David 1947- .... CLC 29, 58
See also CA 97-100; CANR 39; DLB 13; MTCW
Harewood, John
See Van Druten, John (William)
Harford, Henry
See Hudson, W(illiam) H(enry)
Hargrave, Leonie
See Disch, Thomas M(ichael)
Harjo, Joy 1951-........ CLC 83; DAM MULT
See also CA 114; CANR 35, 67; DLB 120, 175; NNAL
Harlan, Louis R(udolph) 1922-......... CLC 34
See also CA 21-24R; CANR 25, 55
Harling, Robert 1951(?)- .... CLC 53
See also CA 147
Harmon, William (Ruth) 1938- .... CLC 38
See also CA 33-36R; CANR 14, 32, 35; SATA 65
Harper, F. E. W.
See Harper, Frances Ellen Watkins
Harper, Frances E. W.
See Harper, Frances Ellen Watkins
Harper, Frances E. Watkins
See Harper, Frances Ellen Watkins
Harper, Frances Ellen
See Harper, Frances Ellen Watkins
Harper, Frances Ellen Watkins 1825-1911 TCLC 14; BLC; DAM MULT, POET; PC 21
See also BW 1; CA 111; 125; DLB 50
Harper, Michael S(teven) 1938- .. CLC 7, 22
See also BW 1; CA 33-36R; CANR 24; DLB 41
Harper, Mrs. F. E. W.
See Harper, Frances Ellen Watkins
Harris, Christie (Lucy) Irwin 1907-. CLC 12

Hemans, Felicia 1793-1835 .... NCLC 29
See also DLB 96

Hemingway, Ernest (Miller) 1899-1961 C L C
1, 3, 6, 8, 10, 13, 19, 30, 34, 39, 41, 44, 50,
61, 80; DA; DAB; DAC; DAM MST, NOV;
SSC 25; WLC
See also AAYA 19; CA 77-80; CANR 34;
CDALB 1917-1929; DLB 4, 9, 102; DLBD
1, 15, 16; DLBY 81, 87, 96; MTCW

Hempel, Amy 1951- .... CLC 39
See also CA 118; 137

Henderson, F. C.
See Mencken, H(enry) L(ouis)

Henderson, Sylvia
See Ashton-Warner, Sylvia (Constance)

Henderson, Zenna (Chlarson) 1917-1983 S S C
29
See also CA 1-4R; 133; CANR 1; DLB 8; SATA
5

Henley, Beth .... CLC 23; DC 6
See also Henley, Elizabeth Becker
See also CABS 3; DLBY 86

Henley, Elizabeth Becker 1952-
See Henley, Beth
See also CA 107; CANR 32; DAM DRAM,
MST; MTCW

Henley, William Ernest 1849-1903 .. TCLC 8
See also CA 105; DLB 19

Hennissart, Martha
See Lathen, Emma
See also CA 85-88; CANR 64

Henry, O. .... TCLC 1, 19; SSC 5; WLC
See also Porter, William Sydney

Henry, Patrick 1736-1799 .... LC 25

Henryson, Robert 1430(?)-1506(?) ..... LC 20
See also DLB 146

Henry VIII 1491-1547 .... LC 10

Henschke, Alfred
See Klabund

Hentoff, Nat(han Irving) 1925- .... CLC 26
See also AAYA 4; CA 1-4R; CAAS 6; CANR
5, 25; CLR 1; INT CANR-25; JRDA;
MAICYA; SATA 42, 69; SATA-Brief 27

Heppenstall, (John) Rayner 1911-1981 C L C
10
See also CA 1-4R; 103; CANR 29

Heraclitus c. 540B.C.-c. 450B.C. .... CMLC 22
See also DLB 176

Herbert, Frank (Patrick) 1920-1986 CLC 12,
23, 35, 44, 85; DAM POP
See also AAYA 21; CA 53-56; 118; CANR 5,
43; DLB 8; INT CANR-5; MTCW; SATA
9, 37; SATA-Obit 47

Herbert, George 1593-1633 ..... LC 24; DAB;
DAM POET; PC 4
See also CDBLB Before 1660; DLB 126

Herbert, Zbigniew 1924- ... CLC 9, 43; DAM
POET
See also CA 89-92; CANR 36; MTCW

Herbst, Josephine (Frey) 1897-1969 CLC 34
See also CA 5-8R; 25-28R; DLB 9

Hergesheimer, Joseph 1880-1954 .. TCLC 11
See also CA 109; DLB 102, 9

Herlihy, James Leo 1927-1993 .... CLC 6
See also CA 1-4R; 143; CANR 2

Hermogenes fl. c. 175- .... CMLC 6

Hernandez, Jose 1834-1886 .... NCLC 17

Herodotus c. 484B.C.-429B.C. ...... CMLC 17
See also DLB 176

Herrick, Robert 1591-1674 LC 13; DA; DAB;
DAC; DAM MST, POP; PC 9
See also DLB 126

Herring, Guilles

See Somerville, Edith

Herriot, James 1916-1995 CLC 12; DAM POP
See also Wight, James Alfred
See also AAYA 1; CA 148; CANR 40; SATA
86

Herrmann, Dorothy 1941- .... CLC 44
See also CA 107

Herrmann, Taffy
See Herrmann, Dorothy

Hersey, John (Richard) 1914-1993 CLC 1, 2, 7,
9, 40, 81, 97; DAM POP
See also CA 17-20R; 140; CANR 33; DLB 6,
185; MTCW; SATA 25; SATA-Obit 76

Herzen, Aleksandr Ivanovich 1812-1870
NCLC 10, 61

Herzl, Theodor 1860-1904 .... TCLC 36

Herzog, Werner 1942- .... CLC 16
See also CA 89-92

Hesiod c. 8th cent. B.C.- .... CMLC 5
See also DLB 176

Hesse, Hermann 1877-1962 CLC 1, 2, 3, 6, 11,
17, 25, 69; DA; DAB; DAC; DAM MST,
NOV; SSC 9; WLC
See also CA 17-18; CAP 2; DLB 66; MTCW;
SATA 50

Hewes, Cady
See De Voto, Bernard (Augustine)

Heyen, William 1940- .... CLC 13, 18
See also CA 33-36R; CAAS 9; DLB 5

Heyerdahl, Thor 1914- .... CLC 26
See also CA 5-8R; CANR 5, 22, 66; MTCW;
SATA 2, 52

Heym, Georg (Theodor Franz Arthur) 1887-
1912 .... TCLC 9
See also CA 106

Heym, Stefan 1913- .... CLC 41
See also CA 9-12R; CANR 4; DLB 69

Heyse, Paul (Johann Ludwig von) 1830-1914
TCLC 8
See also CA 104; DLB 129

Heyward, (Edwin) DuBose 1885-1940 T C L C
59
See also CA 108; 157; DLB 7, 9, 45; SATA 21

Hibbert, Eleanor Alice Burford 1906-1993
CLC 7; DAM POP
See also BEST 90:4; CA 17-20R; 140; CANR
9, 28, 59; SATA 2; SATA-Obit 74

Hichens, Robert (Smythe) 1864-1950 T C L C
64
See also CA 162; DLB 153

Higgins, George V(incent) 1939- CLC 4, 7, 10,
18
See also CA 77-80; CAAS 5; CANR 17, 51;
DLB 2; DLBY 81; INT CANR-17; MTCW

Higginson, Thomas Wentworth 1823-1911
TCLC 36
See also CA 162; DLB 1, 64

Highet, Helen
See MacInnes, Helen (Clark)

Highsmith, (Mary) Patricia 1921-1995 CLC 2,
4, 14, 42, 102; DAM NOV, POP
See also CA 1-4R; 147; CANR 1, 20, 48, 62;
MTCW

Highwater, Jamake (Mamake) 1942(?)- C L C
12
See also AAYA 7; CA 65-68; CAAS 7; CANR
10, 34; CLR 17; DLB 52; DLBY 85; JRDA;
MAICYA; SATA 32, 69; SATA-Brief 30

Highway, Tomson 1951- CLC 92; DAC; DAM
MULT
See also CA 151; NNAL

Higuchi, Ichiyo 1872-1896 .... NCLC 49

Hijuelos, Oscar 1951- CLC 65; DAM MULT,

POP; HLC
See also BEST 90:1; CA 123; CANR 50; DLB
145; HW

Hikmet, Nazim 1902(?)-1963 .... CLC 40
See also CA 141; 93-96

Hildegard von Bingen 1098-1179 . CMLC 20
See also DLB 148

Hildesheimer, Wolfgang 1916-1991 . CLC 49
See also CA 101; 135; DLB 69, 124

Hill, Geoffrey (William) 1932- CLC 5, 8, 18,
45; DAM POET
See also CA 81-84; CANR 21; CDBLB 1960
to Present; DLB 40; MTCW

Hill, George Roy 1921- .... CLC 26
See also CA 110; 122

Hill, John
See Koontz, Dean R(ay)

Hill, Susan (Elizabeth) 1942- . CLC 4; DAB;
DAM MST, NOV
See also CA 33-36R; CANR 29; DLB 14, 139;
MTCW

Hillerman, Tony 1925- .. CLC 62; DAM POP
See also AAYA 6; BEST 89:1; CA 29-32R;
CANR 21, 42, 65; SATA 6

Hillesum, Etty 1914-1943 .... TCLC 49
See also CA 137

Hilliard, Noel (Harvey) 1929- .... CLC 15
See also CA 9-12R; CANR 7

Hillis, Rick 1956- .... CLC 66
See also CA 134

Hilton, James 1900-1954 .... TCLC 21
See also CA 108; DLB 34, 77; SATA 34

Himes, Chester (Bomar) 1909-1984 CLC 2, 4,
7, 18, 58, 108; BLC; DAM MULT
See also BW 2; CA 25-28R; 114; CANR 22;
DLB 2, 76, 143; MTCW

Hinde, Thomas .... CLC 6, 11
See also Chitty, Thomas Willes

Hindin, Nathan
See Bloch, Robert (Albert)

Hine, (William) Daryl 1936- .... CLC 15
See also CA 1-4R; CAAS 15; CANR 1, 20;
DLB 60

Hinkson, Katharine Tynan
See Tynan, Katharine

Hinton, S(usan) E(loise) 1950- CLC 30; DA;
DAB; DAC; DAM MST, NOV
See also AAYA 2; CA 81-84; CANR 32, 62;
CLR 3, 23; JRDA; MAICYA; MTCW;
SATA 19, 58

Hippius, Zinaida .... TCLC 9
See also Gippius, Zinaida (Nikolayevna)

Hiraoka, Kimitake 1925-1970
See Mishima, Yukio
See also CA 97-100; 29-32R; DAM DRAM;
MTCW

Hirsch, E(ric) D(onald), Jr. 1928- .... CLC 79
See also CA 25-28R; CANR 27, 51; DLB 67;
INT CANR-27; MTCW

Hirsch, Edward 1950- .... CLC 31, 50
See also CA 104; CANR 20, 42; DLB 120

Hitchcock, Alfred (Joseph) 1899-1980 CLC 16
See also AAYA 22; CA 159; 97-100; SATA
27; SATA-Obit 24

Hitler, Adolf 1889-1945 .... TCLC 53
See also CA 117; 147

Hoagland, Edward 1932- .... CLC 28
See also CA 1-4R; CANR 2, 31, 57; DLB 6;
SATA 51

Hoban, Russell (Conwell) 1925- .. CLC 7, 25;
DAM NOV
See also CA 5-8R; CANR 23, 37, 66; CLR 3;
DLB 52; MAICYA; MTCW; SATA 1, 40,

See also CA 117; DLB 19
Johnson, Mel
See Malzberg, Barry N(athaniel)
Johnson, Pamela Hansford 1912-1981CLC 1, 7, 27
See also CA 1-4R; 104; CANR 2, 28; DLB 15; MTCW
Johnson, Robert 1911(?)-1938 .... **TCLC 69**
Johnson, Samuel 1709-1784LC 15; DA; DAB; DAC; DAM MST; WLC
See also CDBLB 1660-1789; DLB 39, 95, 104, 142
Johnson, Uwe 1934-1984 .. CLC 5, 10, 15, 40
See also CA 1-4R; 112; CANR 1, 39; DLB 75; MTCW
Johnston, George (Benson) 1913- .... CLC 51
See also CA 1-4R; CANR 5, 20; DLB 88
Johnston, Jennifer 1930- .... CLC 7
See also CA 85-88; DLB 14
Jolley, (Monica) Elizabeth 1923-CLC 46; SSC 19
See also CA 127; CAAS 13; CANR 59
Jones, Arthur Llewellyn 1863-1947
See Machen, Arthur
See also CA 104
Jones, D(ouglas) G(ordon) 1929- ..... CLC 10
See also CA 29-32R; CANR 13; DLB 53
Jones, David (Michael) 1895-1974CLC 2, 4, 7, 13, 42
See also CA 9-12R; 53-56; CANR 28; CDBLB 1945-1960; DLB 20, 100; MTCW
Jones, David Robert 1947-
See Bowie, David
See also CA 103
Jones, Diana Wynne 1934- .... CLC 26
See also AAYA 12; CA 49-52; CANR 4, 26, 56; CLR 23; DLB 161; JRDA; MAICYA; SAAS 7; SATA 9, 70
Jones, Edward P. 1950- .... CLC 76
See also BW 2; CA 142
Jones, Gayl 1949- ...... CLC 6, 9; BLC; DAM MULT
See also BW 2; CA 77-80; CANR 27, 66; DLB 33; MTCW
Jones, James 1921-1977 ...... CLC 1, 3, 10, 39
See also AITN 1, 2; CA 1-4R; 69-72; CANR 6; DLB 2, 143; MTCW
Jones, John J.
See Lovecraft, H(oward) P(hillips)
Jones, LeRoi .... CLC 1, 2, 3, 5, 10, 14
See also Baraka, Amiri
Jones, Louis B. .... CLC 65
See also CA 141
Jones, Madison (Percy, Jr.) 1925- ......CLC 4
See also CA 13-16R; CAAS 11; CANR 7, 54; DLB 152
Jones, Mervyn 1922- .... CLC 10, 52
See also CA 45-48; CAAS 5; CANR 1; MTCW
Jones, Mick 1956(?)- .... CLC 30
Jones, Nettie (Pearl) 1941- .... CLC 34
See also BW 2; CA 137; CAAS 20
Jones, Preston 1936-1979 .... CLC 10
See also CA 73-76; 89-92; DLB 7
Jones, Robert F(rancis) 1934- ....CLC 7
See also CA 49-52; CANR 2, 61
Jones, Rod 1953- .... CLC 50
See also CA 128
Jones, Terence Graham Parry 1942-CLC 21
See also Jones, Terry; Monty Python
See also CA 112; 116; CANR 35; INT 116
Jones, Terry
See Jones, Terence Graham Parry
See also SATA 67; SATA-Brief 51

Jones, Thom 1945(?)- .... CLC 81
See also CA 157
Jong, Erica 1942- CLC 4, 6, 8, 18, 83; DAM NOV, POP
See also AITN 1; BEST 90:2; CA 73-76; CANR 26, 52; DLB 2, 5, 28, 152; INT CANR-26; MTCW
Jonson, Ben(jamin) 1572(?)-1637 .. LC 6, 33; DA; DAB; DAC; DAM DRAM, MST, POET; DC 4; PC 17; WLC
See also CDBLB Before 1660; DLB 62, 121
Jordan, June 1936- ...... CLC 5, 11, 23; DAM MULT, POET
See also AAYA 2; BW 2; CA 33-36R; CANR 25; CLR 10; DLB 38; MAICYA; MTCW; SATA 4
Jordan, Pat(rick M.) 1941- .... CLC 37
See also CA 33-36R
Jorgensen, Ivar
See Ellison, Harlan (Jay)
Jorgenson, Ivar
See Silverberg, Robert
Josephus, Flavius c. 37-100 .... CMLC 13
Josipovici, Gabriel 1940- .... CLC 6, 43
See also CA 37-40R; CAAS 8; CANR 47; DLB 14
Joubert, Joseph 1754-1824 .... NCLC 9
Jouve, Pierre Jean 1887-1976 .... CLC 47
See also CA 65-68
Jovine, Francesco 1902-1950 .... TCLC 79
Joyce, James (Augustine Aloysius) 1882-1941 TCLC 3, 8, 16, 35, 52; DA; DAB; DAC; DAM MST, NOV, POET; SSC 3, 26; WLC
See also CA 104; 126; CDBLB 1914-1945; DLB 10, 19, 36, 162; MTCW
Jozsef, Attila 1905-1937 .... TCLC 22
See also CA 116
Juana Ines de la Cruz 1651(?)-1695 ..... LC 5
Judd, Cyril
See Kornbluth, C(yril) M.; Pohl, Frederik
Julian of Norwich 1342(?)-1416(?) .... LC 6
See also DLB 146
Junger, Sebastian 1962- .... CLC 109
Juniper, Alex
See Hospital, Janette Turner
Junius
See Luxemburg, Rosa
Just, Ward (Swift) 1935- .... CLC 4, 27
See also CA 25-28R; CANR 32; INT CANR-32
Justice, Donald (Rodney) 1925- .. CLC 6, 19, 102; DAM POET
See also CA 5-8R; CANR 26, 54; DLBY 83; INT CANR-26
Juvenal c. 55-c. 127 .... CMLC 8
Juvenis
See Bourne, Randolph S(illiman)
Kacew, Romain 1914-1980
See Gary, Romain
See also CA 108; 102
Kadare, Ismail 1936- ....CLC 52
See also CA 161
Kadohata, Cynthia ....CLC 59
See also CA 140
Kafka, Franz 1883-1924TCLC 2, 6, 13, 29, 47, 53; DA; DAB; DAC; DAM MST, NOV; SSC 5, 29; WLC
See also CA 105; 126; DLB 81; MTCW
Kahanovitsch, Pinkhes
See Der Nister
Kahn, Roger 1927- ....CLC 30
See also CA 25-28R; CANR 44; DLB 171; SATA 37

Kain, Saul
See Sassoon, Siegfried (Lorraine)
Kaiser, Georg 1878-1945 .... TCLC 9
See also CA 106; DLB 124
Kaletski, Alexander 1946- .... CLC 39
See also CA 118; 143
Kalidasa fl. c. 400- .... CMLC 9
Kallman, Chester (Simon) 1921-1975 CLC 2
See also CA 45-48; 53-56; CANR 3
Kaminsky, Melvin 1926-
See Brooks, Mel
See also CA 65-68; CANR 16
Kaminsky, Stuart M(elvin) 1934- ..... CLC 59
See also CA 73-76; CANR 29, 53
Kane, Francis
See Robbins, Harold
Kane, Paul
See Simon, Paul (Frederick)
Kane, Wilson
See Bloch, Robert (Albert)
Kanin, Garson 1912- .... CLC 22
See also AITN 1; CA 5-8R; CANR 7; DLB 7
Kaniuk, Yoram 1930- .... CLC 19
See also CA 134
Kant, Immanuel 1724-1804 ..... NCLC 27, 67
See also DLB 94
Kantor, MacKinlay 1904-1977 ....CLC 7
See also CA 61-64; 73-76; CANR 60, 63; DLB 9, 102
Kaplan, David Michael 1946- .... CLC 50
Kaplan, James 1951- .... CLC 59
See also CA 135
Karageorge, Michael
See Anderson, Poul (William)
Karamzin, Nikolai Mikhailovich 1766-1826 NCLC 3
See also DLB 150
Karapanou, Margarita 1946- ....CLC 13
See also CA 101
Karinthy, Frigyes 1887-1938 .... TCLC 47
Karl, Frederick R(obert) 1927- ....CLC 34
See also CA 5-8R; CANR 3, 44
Kastel, Warren
See Silverberg, Robert
Kataev, Evgeny Petrovich 1903-1942
See Petrov, Evgeny
See also CA 120
Kataphusin
See Ruskin, John
Katz, Steve 1935- ....CLC 47
See also CA 25-28R; CAAS 14, 64; CANR 12; DLBY 83
Kauffman, Janet 1945- .... CLC 42
See also CA 117; CANR 43; DLBY 86
Kaufman, Bob (Garnell) 1925-1986 .CLC 49
See also BW 1; CA 41-44R; 118; CANR 22; DLB 16, 41
Kaufman, George S. 1889-1961CLC 38; DAM DRAM
See also CA 108; 93-96; DLB 7; INT 108
Kaufman, Sue .... CLC 3, 8
See also Barondess, Sue K(aufman)
Kavafis, Konstantinos Petrou 1863-1933
See Cavafy, C(onstantine) P(eter)
See also CA 104
Kavan, Anna 1901-1968 .... CLC 5, 13, 82
See also CA 5-8R; CANR 6, 57; MTCW
Kavanagh, Dan
See Barnes, Julian (Patrick)
Kavanagh, Patrick (Joseph) 1904-1967 C L C 22
See also CA 123; 25-28R; DLB 15, 20; MTCW
Kawabata, Yasunari 1899-1972 CLC 2, 5, 9,

Kinsella, Thomas 1928- .... CLC 4, 19
See also CA 17-20R; CANR 15; DLB 27;
MTCW

Kinsella, W(illiam) P(atrick) 1935- CLC 27,
43; DAC; DAM NOV, POP
See also AAYA 7; CA 97-100; CAAS 7; CANR
21, 35, 66; INT CANR-21; MTCW

Kipling, (Joseph) Rudyard 1865-1936 T C L C
8, 17; DA; DAB; DAC; DAM MST, POET;
PC 3; SSC 5; WLC
See also CA 105; 120; CANR 33; CDBLB
1890-1914; CLR 39; DLB 19, 34, 141, 156;
MAICYA; MTCW; YABC 2

Kirkup, James 1918- .... CLC 1
See also CA 1-4R; CAAS 4; CANR 2; DLB
27; SATA 12

Kirkwood, James 1930(?)-1989 .... CLC 9
See also AITN 2; CA 1-4R; 128; CANR 6, 40

Kirshner, Sidney
See Kingsley, Sidney

Kis, Danilo 1935-1989 .... CLC 57
See also CA 109; 118; 129; CANR 61; DLB
181; MTCW

Kivi, Aleksis 1834-1872 .... NCLC 30

Kizer, Carolyn (Ashley) 1925-CLC 15, 39, 80;
DAM POET
See also CA 65-68; CAAS 5; CANR 24; DLB
5, 169

Klabund 1890-1928 .... TCLC 44
See also CA 162; DLB 66

Klappert, Peter 1942- .... CLC 57
See also CA 33-36R; DLB 5

Klein, A(braham) M(oses) 1909-1972CLC 19;
DAB; DAC; DAM MST
See also CA 101; 37-40R; DLB 68

Klein, Norma 1938-1989 .... CLC 30
See also AAYA 2; CA 41-44R; 128; CANR 15,
37; CLR 2, 19; INT CANR-15; JRDA;
MAICYA; SAAS 1; SATA 7, 57

Klein, T(heodore) E(ibon) D(onald) 1947-
CLC 34
See also CA 119; CANR 44

Kleist, Heinrich von 1777-1811 NCLC 2, 37;
DAM DRAM; SSC 22
See also DLB 90

Klima, Ivan 1931- .... CLC 56; DAM NOV
See also CA 25-28R; CANR 17, 50

Klimentov, Andrei Platonovich 1899-1951
See Platonov, Andrei
See also CA 108

Klinger, Friedrich Maximilian von 1752-1831
NCLC 1
See also DLB 94

Klingsor the Magician
See Hartmann, Sadakichi

Klopstock, Friedrich Gottlieb 1724-1803
NCLC 11
See also DLB 97

Knapp, Caroline 1959- .... CLC 99
See also CA 154

Knebel, Fletcher 1911-1993 .... CLC 14
See also AITN 1; CA 1-4R; 140; CAAS 3;
CANR 1, 36; SATA 36; SATA-Obit 75

Knickerbocker, Diedrich
See Irving, Washington

Knight, Etheridge 1931-1991 CLC 40; BLC;
DAM POET; PC 14
See also BW 1; CA 21-24R; 133; CANR 23;
DLB 41

Knight, Sarah Kemble 1666-1727 .... LC 7
See also DLB 24

Knister, Raymond 1899-1932 .... TCLC 56
See also DLB 68

Knowles, John 1926- ..CLC 1, 4, 10, 26; DA;
DAC; DAM MST, NOV
See also AAYA 10; CA 17-20R; CANR 40;
CDALB 1968-1988; DLB 6; MTCW; SATA
8, 89

Knox, Calvin M.
See Silverberg, Robert

Knox, John c. 1505-1572 .... LC 37
See also DLB 132

Knye, Cassandra
See Disch, Thomas M(ichael)

Koch, C(hristopher) J(ohn) 1932- ....CLC 42
See also CA 127

Koch, Christopher
See Koch, C(hristopher) J(ohn)

Koch, Kenneth 1925- .... CLC 5, 8, 44; DAM
POET
See also CA 1-4R; CANR 6, 36, 57; DLB 5;
INT CANR-36; SATA 65

Kochanowski, Jan 1530-1584 .... LC 10

Kock, Charles Paul de 1794-1871 .NCLC 16

Koda Shigeyuki 1867-1947
See Rohan, Koda
See also CA 121

Koestler, Arthur 1905-1983CLC 1, 3, 6, 8, 15,
33
See also CA 1-4R; 109; CANR 1, 33; CDBLB
1945-1960; DLBY 83; MTCW

Kogawa, Joy Nozomi 1935-.. CLC 78; DAC;
DAM MST, MULT
See also CA 101; CANR 19, 62

Kohout, Pavel 1928- ....CLC 13
See also CA 45-48; CANR 3

Koizumi, Yakumo
See Hearn, (Patricio) Lafcadio (Tessima Carlos)

Kolmar, Gertrud 1894-1943 .... TCLC 40

Komunyakaa, Yusef 1947- .... CLC 86, 94
See also CA 147; DLB 120

Konrad, George
See Konrad, Gyoergy

Konrad, Gyoergy 1933- .... CLC 4, 10, 73
See also CA 85-88

Konwicki, Tadeusz 1926- .... CLC 8, 28, 54
See also CA 101; CAAS 9; CANR 39, 59;
MTCW

Koontz, Dean R(ay) 1945- ..... CLC 78; DAM
NOV, POP
See also AAYA 9; BEST 89:3, 90:2; CA 108;
CANR 19, 36, 52; MTCW; SATA 92

Kopit, Arthur (Lee) 1937-CLC 1, 18, 33; DAM
DRAM
See also AITN 1; CA 81-84; CABS 3; DLB 7;
MTCW

Kops, Bernard 1926- ....CLC 4
See also CA 5-8R; DLB 13

Kornbluth, C(yril) M. 1923-1958 .... TCLC 8
See also CA 105; 160; DLB 8

Korolenko, V. G.
See Korolenko, Vladimir Galaktionovich

Korolenko, Vladimir
See Korolenko, Vladimir Galaktionovich

Korolenko, Vladimir G.
See Korolenko, Vladimir Galaktionovich

Korolenko, Vladimir Galaktionovich 1853-
1921 .... TCLC 22
See also CA 121

Korzybski, Alfred (Habdank Skarbek) 1879-
1950 .... TCLC 61
See also CA 123; 160

Kosinski, Jerzy (Nikodem) 1933-1991CLC 1,
2, 3, 6, 10, 15, 53, 70; DAM NOV
See also CA 17-20R; 134; CANR 9, 46; DLB
2; DLBY 82; MTCW

Kostelanetz, Richard (Cory) 1940- ..CLC 28
See also CA 13-16R; CAAS 8; CANR 38

Kostrowitzki, Wilhelm Apollinaris de 1880-
1918
See Apollinaire, Guillaume
See also CA 104

Kotlowitz, Robert 1924- ....CLC 4
See also CA 33-36R; CANR 36

Kotzebue, August (Friedrich Ferdinand) von
1761-1819 .... NCLC 25
See also DLB 94

Kotzwinkle, William 1938-..... CLC 5, 14, 35
See also CA 45-48; CANR 3, 44; CLR 6; DLB
173; MAICYA; SATA 24, 70

Kowna, Stancy
See Szymborska, Wislawa

Kozol, Jonathan 1936- ....CLC 17
See also CA 61-64; CANR 16, 45

Kozoll, Michael 1940(?)- ....CLC 35

Kramer, Kathryn 19(?)- ....CLC 34

Kramer, Larry 1935-CLC 42; DAM POP; DC
8
See also CA 124; 126; CANR 60

Krasicki, Ignacy 1735-1801 ....NCLC 8

Krasinski, Zygmunt 1812-1859 ....NCLC 4

Kraus, Karl 1874-1936 .... TCLC 5
See also CA 104; DLB 118

Kreve (Mickevicius), Vincas 1882-1954TCLC
27

Kristeva, Julia 1941- ....CLC 77
See also CA 154

Kristofferson, Kris 1936- ....CLC 26
See also CA 104

Krizanc, John 1956- ....CLC 57

Krleza, Miroslav 1893-1981 ....CLC 8
See also CA 97-100; 105; CANR 50; DLB 147

Kroetsch, Robert 1927-CLC 5, 23, 57; DAC;
DAM POET
See also CA 17-20R; CANR 8, 38; DLB 53;
MTCW

Kroetz, Franz
See Kroetz, Franz Xaver

Kroetz, Franz Xaver 1946- ....CLC 41
See also CA 130

Kroker, Arthur (W.) 1945- ....CLC 77
See also CA 161

Kropotkin, Peter (Alexseevich) 1842-1921
TCLC 36
See also CA 119

Krotkov, Yuri 1917- ....CLC 19
See also CA 102

Krumb
See Crumb, R(obert)

Krumgold, Joseph (Quincy) 1908-1980 C L C
12
See also CA 9-12R; 101; CANR 7; MAICYA;
SATA 1, 48; SATA-Obit 23

Krumwitz
See Crumb, R(obert)

Krutch, Joseph Wood 1893-1970 .....CLC 24
See also CA 1-4R; 25-28R; CANR 4; DLB 63

Krutzch, Gus
See Eliot, T(homas) S(tearns)

Krylov, Ivan Andreevich 1768(?)-1844N C L C
1
See also DLB 150

Kubin, Alfred (Leopold Isidor) 1877-1959
TCLC 23
See also CA 112; 149; DLB 81

Kubrick, Stanley 1928- ....CLC 16
See also CA 81-84; CANR 33; DLB 26

Kumin, Maxine (Winokur) 1925- CLC 5, 13,
28; DAM POET; PC 15

14, 21, 35, 44, 60; DA; DAB; DAC; DAM MST, NOV; SSC 5; WLC
See also CA 104; 128; DLB 66; MTCW
Mannheim, Karl 1893-1947 .... **TCLC 65**
Manning, David
See Faust, Frederick (Schiller)
Manning, Frederic 1887(?)-1935 ... **TCLC 25**
See also CA 124
Manning, Olivia 1915-1980 .... **CLC 5, 19**
See also CA 5-8R; 101; CANR 29; MTCW
Mano, D. Keith 1942- .... **CLC 2, 10**
See also CA 25-28R; CAAS 6; CANR 26, 57;
DLB 6
Mansfield, Katherine **TCLC 2, 8, 39; DAB; SSC 9, 23; WLC**
See also Beauchamp, Kathleen Mansfield
See also DLB 162
Manso, Peter 1940- .... **CLC 39**
See also CA 29-32R; CANR 44
Mantecon, Juan Jimenez
See Jimenez (Mantecon), Juan Ramon
Manton, Peter
See Creasey, John
Man Without a Spleen, A
See Chekhov, Anton (Pavlovich)
Manzoni, Alessandro 1785-1873 ....**NCLC 29**
Mapu, Abraham (ben Jekutiel) 1808-1867
NCLC 18
Mara, Sally
See Queneau, Raymond
Marat, Jean Paul 1743-1793 .... **LC 10**
Marcel, Gabriel Honore 1889-1973 **CLC 15**
See also CA 102; 45-48; MTCW
Marchbanks, Samuel
See Davies, (William) Robertson
Marchi, Giacomo
See Bassani, Giorgio
Margulies, Donald .... **CLC 76**
Marie de France c. 12th cent. - .... **CMLC 8**
Marie de l'Incarnation 1599-1672 ...... **LC 10**
Marier, Captain Victor
See Griffith, D(avid Lewelyn) W(ark)
Mariner, Scott
See Pohl, Frederik
Marinetti, Filippo Tommaso 1876-1944
TCLC 10
See also CA 107; DLB 114
Marivaux, Pierre Carlet de Chamblain de
1688-1763 .... **LC 4; DC 7**
Markandaya, Kamala .... **CLC 8, 38**
See also Taylor, Kamala (Purnaiya)
Markfield, Wallace 1926- ....**CLC 8**
See also CA 69-72; CAAS 3; DLB 2, 28
Markham, Edwin 1852-1940 .... **TCLC 47**
See also CA 160; DLB 54, 186
Markham, Robert
See Amis, Kingsley (William)
Marks, J
See Highwater, Jamake (Mamake)
Marks-Highwater, J
See Highwater, Jamake (Mamake)
Markson, David M(errill) 1927- ...... **CLC 67**
See also CA 49-52; CANR 1
Marley, Bob .... **CLC 17**
See also Marley, Robert Nesta
Marley, Robert Nesta 1945-1981
See Marley, Bob
See also CA 107; 103
Marlowe, Christopher 1564-1593 **LC 22; DA; DAB; DAC; DAM DRAM, MST; DC 1; WLC**
See also CDBLB Before 1660; DLB 62
Marlowe, Stephen 1928-

See Queen, Ellery
See also CA 13-16R; CANR 6, 55
Marmontel, Jean-Francois 1723-1799 . **LC 2**
Marquand, John P(hillips) 1893-1960**CLC 2, 10**
See also CA 85-88; DLB 9, 102
Marques, Rene 1919-1979 ..... **CLC 96; DAM MULT; HLC**
See also CA 97-100; 85-88; DLB 113; HW
Marquez, Gabriel (Jose) Garcia
See Garcia Marquez, Gabriel (Jose)
Marquis, Don(ald Robert Perry) 1878-1937
TCLC 7
See also CA 104; DLB 11, 25
Marric, J. J.
See Creasey, John
Marryat, Frederick 1792-1848 .... **NCLC 3**
See also DLB 21, 163
Marsden, James
See Creasey, John
Marsh, (Edith) Ngaio 1899-1982 **CLC 7, 53; DAM POP**
See also CA 9-12R; CANR 6, 58; DLB 77;
MTCW
Marshall, Garry 1934- ....**CLC 17**
See also AAYA 3; CA 111; SATA 60
Marshall, Paule 1929-**CLC 27, 72; BLC; DAM MULT; SSC 3**
See also BW 2; CA 77-80; CANR 25; DLB 157;
MTCW
Marsten, Richard
See Hunter, Evan
Marston, John 1576-1634**LC 33; DAM DRAM**
See also DLB 58, 172
Martha, Henry
See Harris, Mark
Marti, Jose 1853-1895 .... **NCLC 63; DAM MULT; HLC**
Martial c. 40-c. 104 .... **PC 10**
Martin, Ken
See Hubbard, L(afayette) Ron(ald)
Martin, Richard
See Creasey, John
Martin, Steve 1945- .... **CLC 30**
See also CA 97-100; CANR 30; MTCW
Martin, Valerie 1948- ....**CLC 89**
See also BEST 90:2; CA 85-88; CANR 49
Martin, Violet Florence 1862-1915 **TCLC 51**
Martin, Webber
See Silverberg, Robert
Martindale, Patrick Victor
See White, Patrick (Victor Martindale)
Martin du Gard, Roger 1881-1958 **TCLC 24**
See also CA 118; DLB 65
Martineau, Harriet 1802-1876 .... **NCLC 26**
See also DLB 21, 55, 159, 163, 166, 190;
YABC 2
Martines, Julia
See O'Faolain, Julia
Martinez, Enrique Gonzalez
See Gonzalez Martinez, Enrique
Martinez, Jacinto Benavente y
See Benavente (y Martinez), Jacinto
Martinez Ruiz, Jose 1873-1967
See Azorin; Ruiz, Jose Martinez
See also CA 93-96; HW
Martinez Sierra, Gregorio 1881-1947**TCLC 6**
See also CA 115
Martinez Sierra, Maria (de la O'LeJarraga)
1874-1974 .... **TCLC 6**
See also CA 115
Martinsen, Martin
See Follett, Ken(neth Martin)

Martinson, Harry (Edmund) 1904-1978**C L C 14**
See also CA 77-80; CANR 34
Marut, Ret
See Traven, B.
Marut, Robert
See Traven, B.
Marvell, Andrew 1621-1678**LC 4; DA; DAB; DAC; DAM MST, POET; PC 10; WLC**
See also CDBLB 1660-1789; DLB 131
Marx, Karl (Heinrich) 1818-1883 .**NCLC 17**
See also DLB 129
Masaoka Shiki .... **TCLC 18**
See also Masaoka Tsunenori
Masaoka Tsunenori 1867-1902
See Masaoka Shiki
See also CA 117
Masefield, John (Edward) 1878-1967**CLC 11, 47; DAM POET**
See also CA 19-20; 25-28R; CANR 33; CAP 2; CDBLB 1890-1914; DLB 10, 19, 153, 160; MTCW; SATA 19
Maso, Carole 19(?)- .... **CLC 44**
Mason, Bobbie Ann 1940-**CLC 28, 43, 82; SSC 4**
See also AAYA 5; CA 53-56; CANR 11, 31, 58; DLB 173; DLBY 87; INT CANR-31; MTCW
Mason, Ernst
See Pohl, Frederik
Mason, Lee W.
See Malzberg, Barry N(athaniel)
Mason, Nick 1945- ....**CLC 35**
Mason, Tally
See Derleth, August (William)
Mass, William
See Gibson, William
Masters, Edgar Lee 1868-1950 **TCLC 2, 25; DA; DAC; DAM MST, POET; PC 1; WLCS**
See also CA 104; 133; CDALB 1865-1917; DLB 54; MTCW
Masters, Hilary 1928- ....**CLC 48**
See also CA 25-28R; CANR 13, 47
Mastrosimone, William 19(?)- .... **CLC 36**
Mathe, Albert
See Camus, Albert
Mather, Cotton 1663-1728 .... **LC 38**
See also CDALB 1640-1865; DLB 24, 30, 140
Mather, Increase 1639-1723 .... **LC 38**
See also DLB 24
Matheson, Richard Burton 1926- .....**CLC 37**
See also CA 97-100; DLB 8, 44; INT 97-100
Mathews, Harry 1930- .... **CLC 6, 52**
See also CA 21-24R; CAAS 6; CANR 18, 40
Mathews, John Joseph 1894-1979 .. **CLC 84; DAM MULT**
See also CA 19-20; 142; CANR 45; CAP 2; DLB 175; NNAL
Mathias, Roland (Glyn) 1915- .... **CLC 45**
See also CA 97-100; CANR 19, 41; DLB 27
Matsuo Basho 1644-1694 .... **PC 3**
See also DAM POET
Mattheson, Rodney
See Creasey, John
Matthews, Greg 1949- ....**CLC 45**
See also CA 135
Matthews, William (Procter, III) 1942-1997
CLC 40
See also CA 29-32R; 162; CAAS 18; CANR 12, 57; DLB 5
Matthias, John (Edward) 1941- .... **CLC 9**
See also CA 33-36R; CANR 56

Matthiessen, Peter 1927-CLC 5, 7, 11, 32, 64; **DAM NOV**
See also AAYA 6; BEST 90:4; CA 9-12R; CANR 21, 50; DLB 6, 173; MTCW; SATA 27

Maturin, Charles Robert 1780(?)-1824NCLC 6
See also DLB 178

Matute (Ausejo), Ana Maria 1925- . CLC 11
See also CA 89-92; MTCW

Maugham, W. S.
See Maugham, W(illiam) Somerset

Maugham, W(illiam) Somerset 1874-1965
CLC 1, 11, 15, 67, 93; **DA; DAB; DAC; DAM DRAM, MST, NOV; SSC 8; WLC**
See also CA 5-8R; 25-28R; CANR 40; CDBLB 1914-1945; DLB 10, 36, 77, 100, 162; MTCW; SATA 54

Maugham, William Somerset
See Maugham, W(illiam) Somerset

Maupassant, (Henri Rene Albert) Guy de 1850-1893NCLC 1, 42; **DA; DAB; DAC; DAM MST; SSC 1; WLC**
See also DLB 123

Maupin, Armistead 1944-CLC 95; **DAM POP**
See also CA 125; 130; CANR 58; INT 130

Maurhut, Richard
See Traven, B.

Mauriac, Claude 1914-1996 ....CLC 9
See also CA 89-92; 152; DLB 83

Mauriac, Francois (Charles) 1885-1970 C L C 4, 9, 56; **SSC 24**
See also CA 25-28; CAP 2; DLB 65; MTCW

Mavor, Osborne Henry 1888-1951
See Bridie, James
See also CA 104

Maxwell, William (Keepers, Jr.) 1908-.C L C 19
See also CA 93-96; CANR 54; DLBY 80; INT 93-96

May, Elaine 1932- ....CLC 16
See also CA 124; 142; DLB 44

Mayakovski, Vladimir (Vladimirovich) 1893-1930 ....TCLC 4, 18
See also CA 104; 158

Mayhew, Henry 1812-1887 ....NCLC 31
See also DLB 18, 55, 190

Mayle, Peter 1939(?)-.......................CLC 89
See also CA 139; CANR 64

Maynard, Joyce 1953- ....CLC 23
See also CA 111; 129; CANR 64

Mayne, William (James Carter) 1928-CLC 12
See also AAYA 20; CA 9-12R; CANR 37; CLR 25; JRDA; MAICYA; SAAS 11; SATA 6, 68

Mayo, Jim
See L'Amour, Louis (Dearborn)

Maysles, Albert 1926- ....CLC 16
See also CA 29-32R

Maysles, David 1932- ....CLC 16

Mazer, Norma Fox 1931- ....CLC 26
See also AAYA 5; CA 69-72; CANR 12, 32, 66; CLR 23; JRDA; MAICYA; SAAS 1; SATA 24, 67

Mazzini, Guiseppe 1805-1872 ....NCLC 34

McAuley, James Phillip 1917-1976 . CLC 45
See also CA 97-100

McBain, Ed
See Hunter, Evan

McBrien, William Augustine 1930-. CLC 44
See also CA 107

McCaffrey, Anne (Inez) 1926-CLC 17; **DAM NOV, POP**

See also AAYA 6; AITN 2; BEST 89:2; CA 25-28R; CANR 15, 35, 55; CLR 49; DLB 8; JRDA; MAICYA; MTCW; SAAS 11; SATA 8, 70

McCall, Nathan 1955(?)- ....CLC 86
See also CA 146

McCann, Arthur
See Campbell, John W(ood, Jr.)

McCann, Edson
See Pohl, Frederik

McCarthy, Charles, Jr. 1933-
See McCarthy, Cormac
See also CANR 42; DAM POP

McCarthy, Cormac 1933-CLC 4, 57, 59, 101
See also McCarthy, Charles, Jr.
See also DLB 6, 143

McCarthy, Mary (Therese) 1912-1989CLC 1, 3, 5, 14, 24, 39, 59; **SSC 24**
See also CA 5-8R; 129; CANR 16, 50, 64; DLB 2; DLBY 81; INT CANR-16; MTCW

McCartney, (James) Paul 1942- CLC 12, 35
See also CA 146

McCauley, Stephen (D.) 1955- ....CLC 50
See also CA 141

McClure, Michael (Thomas) 1932-CLC 6, 10
See also CA 21-24R; CANR 17, 46; DLB 16

McCorkle, Jill (Collins) 1958- ....CLC 51
See also CA 121; DLBY 87

McCourt, Frank 1930- ....CLC 109
See also CA 157

McCourt, James 1941- ....CLC 5
See also CA 57-60

McCoy, Horace (Stanley) 1897-1955TCLC 28
See also CA 108; 155; DLB 9

McCrae, John 1872-1918...............TCLC 12
See also CA 109; DLB 92

McCreigh, James
See Pohl, Frederik

McCullers, (Lula) Carson (Smith) 1917-1967
CLC 1, 4, 10, 12, 48, 100; **DA; DAB; DAC; DAM MST, NOV; SSC 9, 24; WLC**
See also AAYA 21; CA 5-8R; 25-28R; CABS 1, 3; CANR 18; CDALB 1941-1968; DLB 2, 7, 173; MTCW; SATA 27

McCulloch, John Tyler
See Burroughs, Edgar Rice

McCullough, Colleen 1938(?)- CLC 27, 107; **DAM NOV, POP**
See also CA 81-84; CANR 17, 46, 67; MTCW

McDermott, Alice 1953- ....CLC 90
See also CA 109; CANR 40

McElroy, Joseph 1930- ....CLC 5, 47
See also CA 17-20R

McEwan, Ian (Russell) 1948-.... CLC 13, 66; **DAM NOV**
See also BEST 90:4; CA 61-64; CANR 14, 41; DLB 14; MTCW

McFadden, David 1940- ....CLC 48
See also CA 104; DLB 60; INT 104

McFarland, Dennis 1950- ....CLC 65

McGahern, John 1934-CLC 5, 9, 48; **SSC 17**
See also CA 17-20R; CANR 29; DLB 14; MTCW

McGinley, Patrick (Anthony) 1937-.CLC 41
See also CA 120; 127; CANR 56; INT 127

McGinley, Phyllis 1905-1978 ....CLC 14
See also CA 9-12R; 77-80; CANR 19; DLB 11, 48; SATA 2, 44; SATA-Obit 24

McGinniss, Joe 1942- ....CLC 32
See also AITN 2; BEST 89:2; CA 25-28R; CANR 26; DLB 185; INT CANR-26

McGivern, Maureen Daly
See Daly, Maureen

McGrath, Patrick 1950- ....CLC 55
See also CA 136; CANR 65

McGrath, Thomas (Matthew) 1916-1990CLC 28, 59; **DAM POET**
See also CA 9-12R; 132; CANR 6, 33; MTCW; SATA 41; SATA-Obit 66

McGuane, Thomas (Francis III) 1939-CLC 3, 7, 18, 45
See also AITN 2; CA 49-52; CANR 5, 24, 49; DLB 2; DLBY 80; INT CANR-24; MTCW

McGuckian, Medbh 1950-.....CLC 48; **DAM POET**
See also CA 143; DLB 40

McHale, Tom 1942(?)-1982 .... CLC 3, 5
See also AITN 1; CA 77-80; 106

McIlvanney, William 1936-.............CLC 42
See also CA 25-28R; CANR 61; DLB 14

McIlwraith, Maureen Mollie Hunter
See Hunter, Mollie
See also SATA 2

McInerney, Jay 1955-...CLC 34; **DAM POP**
See also AAYA 18; CA 116; 123; CANR 45; INT 123

McIntyre, Vonda N(eel) 1948- ....CLC 18
See also CA 81-84; CANR 17, 34; MTCW

McKay, ClaudeTCLC 7, 41; **BLC; DAB; PC 2**
See also McKay, Festus Claudius
See also DLB 4, 45, 51, 117

McKay, Festus Claudius 1889-1948
See McKay, Claude
See also BW 1; CA 104; 124; DA; DAC; DAM MST, MULT, NOV, POET; MTCW; WLC

McKuen, Rod 1933- ....CLC 1, 3
See also AITN 1; CA 41-44R; CANR 40

McLoughlin, R. B.
See Mencken, H(enry) L(ouis)

McLuhan, (Herbert) Marshall 1911-1980
CLC 37, 83
See also CA 9-12R; 102; CANR 12, 34, 61; DLB 88; INT CANR-12; MTCW

McMillan, Terry (L.) 1951-CLC 50, 61; **DAM MULT, NOV, POP**
See also AAYA 21; BW 2; CA 140; CANR 60

McMurtry, Larry (Jeff) 1936-CLC 2, 3, 7, 11, 27, 44; **DAM NOV, POP**
See also AAYA 15; AITN 2; BEST 89:2; CA 5-8R; CANR 19, 43, 64; CDALB 1968-1988; DLB 2, 143; DLBY 80, 87; MTCW

McNally, T. M. 1961- ....CLC 82

McNally, Terrence 1939-...CLC 4, 7, 41, 91; **DAM DRAM**
See also CA 45-48; CANR 2, 56; DLB 7

McNamer, Deirdre 1950- ....CLC 70

McNeile, Herman Cyril 1888-1937
See Sapper
See also DLB 77

McNickle, (William) D'Arcy 1904-1977 C L C 89; **DAM MULT**
See also CA 9-12R; 85-88; CANR 5, 45; DLB 175; NNAL; SATA-Obit 22

McPhee, John (Angus) 1931- ....CLC 36
See also BEST 90:1; CA 65-68; CANR 20, 46, 64; DLB 185; MTCW

McPherson, James Alan 1943-... CLC 19, 77
See also BW 1; CA 25-28R; CAAS 17; CANR 24; DLB 38; MTCW

McPherson, William (Alexander) 1933-C L C 34
See also CA 69-72; CANR 28; INT CANR-28

Mead, Margaret 1901-1978 ....CLC 37
See also AITN 1; CA 1-4R; 81-84; CANR 4; MTCW; SATA-Obit 20

Meaker, Marijane (Agnes) 1927-

See Kerr, M. E.
See also CA 107; CANR 37, 63; INT 107;
JRDA; MAICYA; MTCW; SATA 20, 61
Medoff, Mark (Howard) 1940- ... **CLC 6, 23;
DAM DRAM**
See also AITN 1; CA 53-56; CANR 5; DLB 7;
INT CANR-5
Medvedev, P. N.
See Bakhtin, Mikhail Mikhailovich
Meged, Aharon
See Megged, Aharon
Meged, Aron
See Megged, Aharon
Megged, Aharon 1920- .... **CLC 9**
See also CA 49-52; CAAS 13; CANR 1
Mehta, Ved (Parkash) 1934- .... **CLC 37**
See also CA 1-4R; CANR 2, 23; MTCW
Melanter
See Blackmore, R(ichard) D(oddridge)
Melikow, Loris
See Hofmannsthal, Hugo von
Melmoth, Sebastian
See Wilde, Oscar (Fingal O'Flahertie Wills)
Meltzer, Milton 1915- .... **CLC 26**
See also AAYA 8; CA 13-16R; CANR 38; CLR
13; DLB 61; JRDA; MAICYA; SAAS 1;
SATA 1, 50, 80
Melville, Herman 1819-1891**NCLC 3, 12, 29,
45, 49; DA; DAB; DAC; DAM MST, NOV;
SSC 1, 17; WLC**
See also CDALB 1640-1865; DLB 3, 74; SATA
59
Menander c. 342B.C.-c. 292B.C. ... **CMLC 9;
DAM DRAM; DC 3**
See also DLB 176
Mencken, H(enry) L(ouis) 1880-1956 **T C L C
13**
See also CA 105; 125; CDALB 1917-1929;
DLB 11, 29, 63, 137; MTCW
Mendelsohn, Jane 1965(?)- .... **CLC 99**
See also CA 154
Mercer, David 1928-1980 .... **CLC 5; DAM
DRAM**
See also CA 9-12R; 102; CANR 23; DLB 13;
MTCW
Merchant, Paul
See Ellison, Harlan (Jay)
Meredith, George 1828-1909 . **TCLC 17, 43;
DAM POET**
See also CA 117; 153; CDBLB 1832-1890;
DLB 18, 35, 57, 159
Meredith, William (Morris) 1919-**CLC 4, 13,
22, 55; DAM POET**
See also CA 9-12R; CAAS 14; CANR 6, 40;
DLB 5
Merezhkovsky, Dmitry Sergeyevich 1865-1941
TCLC 29
Merimee, Prosper 1803-1870**NCLC 6, 65; SSC
7**
See also DLB 119, 192
Merkin, Daphne 1954- .... **CLC 44**
See also CA 123
Merlin, Arthur
See Blish, James (Benjamin)
Merrill, James (Ingram) 1926-1995**CLC 2, 3,
6, 8, 13, 18, 34, 91; DAM POET**
See also CA 13-16R; 147; CANR 10, 49, 63;
DLB 5, 165; DLBY 85; INT CANR-10;
MTCW
Merriman, Alex
See Silverberg, Robert
Merritt, E. B.
See Waddington, Miriam

Merton, Thomas 1915-1968**CLC 1, 3, 11, 34,
83; PC 10**
See also CA 5-8R; 25-28R; CANR 22, 53; DLB
48; DLBY 81; MTCW
Merwin, W(illiam) S(tanley) 1927- **CLC 1, 2,
3, 5, 8, 13, 18, 45, 88; DAM POET**
See also CA 13-16R; CANR 15, 51; DLB 5,
169; INT CANR-15; MTCW
Metcalf, John 1938-............................**CLC 37**
See also CA 113; DLB 60
Metcalf, Suzanne
See Baum, L(yman) Frank
Mew, Charlotte (Mary) 1870-1928 .. **TCLC 8**
See also CA 105; DLB 19, 135
Mewshaw, Michael 1943- ....**CLC 9**
See also CA 53-56; CANR 7, 47; DLBY 80
Meyer, June
See Jordan, June
Meyer, Lynn
See Slavitt, David R(ytman)
Meyer-Meyrink, Gustav 1868-1932
See Meyrink, Gustav
See also CA 117
Meyers, Jeffrey 1939- ....**CLC 39**
See also CA 73-76; CANR 54; DLB 111
Meynell, Alice (Christina Gertrude Thompson)
1847-1922 .... **TCLC 6**
See also CA 104; DLB 19, 98
Meyrink, Gustav .... **TCLC 21**
See Meyer-Meyrink, Gustav
See also DLB 81
Michaels, Leonard 1933- **CLC 6, 25; SSC 16**
See also CA 61-64; CANR 21, 62; DLB 130;
MTCW
Michaux, Henri 1899-1984 .... **CLC 8, 19**
See also CA 85-88; 114
Micheaux, Oscar 1884-1951 .... **TCLC 76**
See also DLB 50
Michelangelo 1475-1564 .... **LC 12**
Michelet, Jules 1798-1874 ....**NCLC 31**
Michener, James A(lbert) 1907(?)-1997 **C L C
1, 5, 11, 29, 60, 109; DAM NOV, POP**
See also AITN 1; BEST 90:1; CA 5-8R; 161;
CANR 21, 45; DLB 6; MTCW
Mickiewicz, Adam 1798-1855 ....**NCLC 3**
Middleton, Christopher 1926- ....**CLC 13**
See also CA 13-16R; CANR 29, 54; DLB 40
Middleton, Richard (Barham) 1882-1911
TCLC 56
See also DLB 156
Middleton, Stanley 1919-..............**CLC 7, 38**
See also CA 25-28R; CAAS 23; CANR 21, 46;
DLB 14
Middleton, Thomas 1580-1627 **LC 33; DAM
DRAM, MST; DC 5**
See also DLB 58
Migueis, Jose Rodrigues 1901- ....**CLC 10**
Mikszath, Kalman 1847-1910 ....**TCLC 31**
Miles, Jack .... **CLC 100**
Miles, Josephine (Louise) 1911-1985**CLC 1, 2,
14, 34, 39; DAM POET**
See also CA 1-4R; 116; CANR 2, 55; DLB 48
Militant
See Sandburg, Carl (August)
Mill, John Stuart 1806-1873 ... **NCLC 11, 58**
See also CDBLB 1832-1890; DLB 55, 190
Millar, Kenneth 1915-1983 ...**CLC 14; DAM
POP**
See also Macdonald, Ross
See also CA 9-12R; 110; CANR 16, 63; DLB
2; DLBD 6; DLBY 83; MTCW
Millay, E. Vincent
See Millay, Edna St. Vincent

Millay, Edna St. Vincent 1892-1950**TCLC 4,
49; DA; DAB; DAC; DAM MST, POET;
PC 6; WLCS**
See also CA 104; 130; CDALB 1917-1929;
DLB 45; MTCW
Miller, Arthur 1915-**CLC 1, 2, 6, 10, 15, 26, 47,
78; DA; DAB; DAC; DAM DRAM, MST;
DC 1; WLC**
See also AAYA 15; AITN 1; CA 1-4R; CABS
3; CANR 2, 30, 54; CDALB 1941-1968;
DLB 7; MTCW
Miller, Henry (Valentine) 1891-1980**CLC 1, 2,
4, 9, 14, 43, 84; DA; DAB; DAC; DAM
MST, NOV; WLC**
See also CA 9-12R; 97-100; CANR 33, 64;
CDALB 1929-1941; DLB 4, 9; DLBY 80;
MTCW
Miller, Jason 1939(?)- .... **CLC 2**
See also AITN 1; CA 73-76; DLB 7
Miller, Sue 1943- .... **CLC 44; DAM POP**
See also BEST 90:3; CA 139; CANR 59; DLB
143
Miller, Walter M(ichael, Jr.) 1923-**CLC 4, 30**
See also CA 85-88; DLB 8
Millett, Kate 1934- ....**CLC 67**
See also AITN 1; CA 73-76; CANR 32, 53;
MTCW
Millhauser, Steven (Lewis) 1943-**CLC 21, 54,
109**
See also CA 110; 111; CANR 63; DLB 2; INT
111
Millin, Sarah Gertrude 1889-1968 ...**CLC 49**
See also CA 102; 93-96
Milne, A(lan) A(lexander) 1882-1956**TCLC 6;
DAB; DAC; DAM MST**
See also CA 104; 133; CLR 1, 26; DLB 10, 77,
100, 160; MAICYA; MTCW; YABC 1
Milner, Ron(ald) 1938- **CLC 56; BLC; DAM
MULT**
See also AITN 1; BW 1; CA 73-76; CANR 24;
DLB 38; MTCW
Milnes, Richard Monckton 1809-1885**N C L C
61**
See also DLB 32, 184
Milosz, Czeslaw 1911- **CLC 5, 11, 22, 31, 56,
82; DAM MST, POET; PC 8; WLCS**
See also CA 81-84; CANR 23, 51; MTCW
Milton, John 1608-1674 ..... **LC 9; DA; DAB;
DAC; DAM MST, POET; PC 19; WLC**
See also CDBLB 1660-1789; DLB 131, 151
Min, Anchee 1957- ....**CLC 86**
See also CA 146
Minehaha, Cornelius
See Wedekind, (Benjamin) Frank(lin)
Miner, Valerie 1947- ....**CLC 40**
See also CA 97-100; CANR 59
Minimo, Duca
See D'Annunzio, Gabriele
Minot, Susan 1956-............................**CLC 44**
See also CA 134
Minus, Ed 1938-.................................**CLC 39**
Miranda, Javier
See Bioy Casares, Adolfo
Mirbeau, Octave 1848-1917 ....**TCLC 55**
See also DLB 123, 192
Miro (Ferrer), Gabriel (Francisco Victor) 1879-
1930 .... **TCLC 5**
See also CA 104
Mishima, Yukio 1925-1970**CLC 2, 4, 6, 9, 27;
DC 1; SSC 4**
See also Hiraoka, Kimitake
See also DLB 182
Mistral, Frederic 1830-1914 ....**TCLC 51**

CANR 27, 42, 67; CDALB 1968-1988; DLB 6, 33, 143; DLBY 81; MTCW; SATA 57

Morrison, Van 1945- .... **CLC 21**
See also CA 116

Morrissy, Mary 1958- .... **CLC 99**

Mortimer, John (Clifford) 1923-CLC **28, 43; DAM DRAM, POP**
See also CA 13-16R; CANR 21; CDBLB 1960 to Present; DLB 13; INT CANR-21; MTCW

Mortimer, Penelope (Ruth) 1918- ...... **CLC 5**
See also CA 57-60; CANR 45

Morton, Anthony
See Creasey, John

Mosca, Gaetano 1858-1941 .... **TCLC 75**

Mosher, Howard Frank 1943- .... **CLC 62**
See also CA 139; CANR 65

Mosley, Nicholas 1923- .... **CLC 43, 70**
See also CA 69-72; CANR 41, 60; DLB 14

Mosley, Walter 1952-CLC **97; DAM MULT, POP**
See also AAYA 17; BW 2; CA 142; CANR 57

Moss, Howard 1922-1987 CLC **7, 14, 45, 50; DAM POET**
See also CA 1-4R; 123; CANR 1, 44; DLB 5

Mossgiel, Rab
See Burns, Robert

Motion, Andrew (Peter) 1952- .... **CLC 47**
See also CA 146; DLB 40

Motley, Willard (Francis) 1909-1965CLC **18**
See also BW 1; CA 117; 106; DLB 76, 143

Motoori, Norinaga 1730-1801 .... **NCLC 45**

Mott, Michael (Charles Alston) 1930-CLC **15, 34**
See also CA 5-8R; CAAS 7; CANR 7, 29

Mountain Wolf Woman 1884-1960 . CLC **92**
See also CA 144; NNAL

Moure, Erin 1955- .... **CLC 88**
See also CA 113; DLB 60

Mowat, Farley (McGill) 1921-CLC **26; DAC; DAM MST**
See also AAYA 1; CA 1-4R; CANR 4, 24, 42; CLR 20; DLB 68; INT CANAR-24; JRDA; MAICYA; MTCW; SATA 3, 55

Moyers, Bill 1934- .... **CLC 74**
See also AITN 2; CA 61-64; CANR 31, 52

Mphahlele, Es'kia
See Mphahlele, Ezekiel
See also DLB 125

Mphahlele, Ezekiel 1919-1983CLC **25; BLC; DAM MULT**
See also Mphahlele, Es'kia
See also BW 2; CA 81-84; CANR 26

Mqhayi, S(amuel) E(dward) K(rune Loliwe) 1875-1945TCLC **25; BLC; DAM MULT**
See also CA 153

Mrozek, Slawomir 1930- .... **CLC 3, 13**
See also CA 13-16R; CAAS 10; CANR 29; MTCW

Mrs. Belloc-Lowndes
See Lowndes, Marie Adelaide (Belloc)

Mtwa, Percy (?)- .... **CLC 47**

Mueller, Lisel 1924- .... **CLC 13, 51**
See also CA 93-96; DLB 105

Muir, Edwin 1887-1959 .... **TCLC 2**
See also CA 104; DLB 20, 100, 191

Muir, John 1838-1914 .... **TCLC 28**
See also DLB 186

Mujica Lainez, Manuel 1910-1984 .. **CLC 31**
See also Lainez, Manuel Mujica
See also CA 81-84; 112; CANR 32; HW

Mukherjee, Bharati 1940-CLC **53; DAM NOV**
See also BEST 89:2; CA 107; CANR 45; DLB 60; MTCW

Muldoon, Paul 1951-CLC **32, 72; DAM POET**
See also CA 113; 129; CANR 52; DLB 40; INT 129

Mulisch, Harry 1927- .... **CLC 42**
See also CA 9-12R; CANR 6, 26, 56

Mull, Martin 1943- .... **CLC 17**
See also CA 105

Mulock, Dinah Maria
See Craik, Dinah Maria (Mulock)

Munford, Robert 1737(?)-1783 .... **LC 5**
See also DLB 31

Mungo, Raymond 1946- .... **CLC 72**
See also CA 49-52; CANR 2

Munro, Alice 1931- ... CLC **6, 10, 19, 50, 95; DAC; DAM MST, NOV; SSC 3; WLCS**
See also AITN 2; CA 33-36R; CANR 33, 53; DLB 53; MTCW; SATA 29

Munro, H(ector) H(ugh) 1870-1916
See Saki
See also CA 104; 130; CDBLB 1890-1914; DA; DAB; DAC; DAM MST, NOV; DLB 34, 162; MTCW; WLC

Murasaki, Lady .... **CMLC 1**

Murdoch, (Jean) Iris 1919-CLC **1, 2, 3, 4, 6, 8, 11, 15, 22, 31, 51; DAB; DAC; DAM MST, NOV**
See also CA 13-16R; CANR 8, 43; CDBLB 1960 to Present; DLB 14; INT CANR-8; MTCW

Murfree, Mary Noailles 1850-1922 ...SSC **22**
See also CA 122; DLB 12, 74

Murnau, Friedrich Wilhelm
See Plumpe, Friedrich Wilhelm

Murphy, Richard 1927- .... **CLC 41**
See also CA 29-32R; DLB 40

Murphy, Sylvia 1937- .... **CLC 34**
See also CA 121

Murphy, Thomas (Bernard) 1935- ...CLC **51**
See also CA 101

Murray, Albert L. 1916- .... **CLC 73**
See also BW 2; CA 49-52; CANR 26, 52; DLB 38

Murray, Judith Sargent 1751-1820NCLC **63**
See also DLB 37

Murray, Les(lie) A(llan) 1938-CLC **40; DAM POET**
See also CA 21-24R; CANR 11, 27, 56

Murry, J. Middleton
See Murry, John Middleton

Murry, John Middleton 1889-1957 TCLC **16**
See also CA 118; DLB 149

Musgrave, Susan 1951- .... **CLC 13, 54**
See also CA 69-72; CANR 45

Musil, Robert (Edler von) 1880-1942 T C L C **12, 68; SSC 18**
See also CA 109; CANR 55; DLB 81, 124

Muske, Carol 1945- ....CLC **90**
See also Muske-Dukes, Carol (Anne)

Muske-Dukes, Carol (Anne) 1945-
See Muske, Carol
See also CA 65-68; CANR 32

Musset, (Louis Charles) Alfred de 1810-1857 NCLC **7**
See also DLB 192

My Brother's Brother
See Chekhov, Anton (Pavlovich)

Myers, L(eopold) H(amilton) 1881-1944 TCLC **59**
See also CA 157; DLB 15

Myers, Walter Dean 1937- ....CLC **35; BLC; DAM MULT, NOV**
See also AAYA 4, 23; BW 2; CA 33-36R; CANR 20, 42, 67; CLR 4, 16, 35; DLB 33;

INT CANR-20; JRDA; MAICYA; SAAS 2; SATA 41, 71; SATA-Brief 27

Myers, Walter M.
See Myers, Walter Dean

Myles, Symon
See Follett, Ken(neth Martin)

Nabokov, Vladimir (Vladimirovich) 1899-1977 CLC **1, 2, 3, 6, 8, 11, 15, 23, 44, 46, 64; DA; DAB; DAC; DAM MST, NOV; SSC 11; WLC**
See also CA 5-8R; 69-72; CANR 20; CDALB 1941-1968; DLB 2; DLBD 3; DLBY 80, 91; MTCW

Nagai Kafu 1879-1959 .... **TCLC 51**
See also Nagai Sokichi
See also DLB 180

Nagai Sokichi 1879-1959
See Nagai Kafu
See also CA 117

Nagy, Laszlo 1925-1978 .... **CLC 7**
See also CA 129; 112

Naipaul, Shiva(dhar Srinivasa) 1945-1985 CLC **32, 39; DAM NOV**
See also CA 110; 112; 116; CANR 33; DLB 157; DLBY 85; MTCW

Naipaul, V(idiadhar) S(urajprasad) 1932- CLC **4, 7, 9, 13, 18, 37, 105; DAB; DAC; DAM MST, NOV**
See also CA 1-4R; CANR 1, 33, 51; CDBLB 1960 to Present; DLB 125; DLBY 85; MTCW

Nakos, Lilika 1899(?)- .... **CLC 29**

Narayan, R(asipuram) K(rishnaswami) 1906- CLC **7, 28, 47; DAM NOV; SSC 25**
See also CA 81-84; CANR 33, 61; MTCW; SATA 62

Nash, (Frediric) Ogden 1902-1971 . CLC **23; DAM POET; PC 21**
See also CA 13-14; 29-32R; CANR 34, 61; CAP 1; DLB 11; MAICYA; MTCW; SATA 2, 46

Nashe, Thomas 1567-1601(?) .... **LC 41**
See also DLB 167

Nashe, Thomas 1567-1601 .... **LC 41**

Nathan, Daniel
See Dannay, Frederic

Nathan, George Jean 1882-1958 .... **TCLC 18**
See also Hatteras, Owen
See also CA 114; DLB 137

Natsume, Kinnosuke 1867-1916
See Natsume, Soseki
See also CA 104

Natsume, Soseki 1867-1916 .... **TCLC 2, 10**
See also Natsume, Kinnosuke
See also DLB 180

Natti, (Mary) Lee 1919-
See Kingman, Lee
See also CA 5-8R; CANR 2

Naylor, Gloria 1950- CLC **28, 52; BLC; DA; DAC; DAM MST, MULT, NOV, POP; WLCS**
See also AAYA 6; BW 2; CA 107; CANR 27, 51; DLB 173; MTCW

Neihardt, John Gneisenau 1881-1973CLC **32**
See also CA 13-14; CANR 65; CAP 1; DLB 9, 54

Nekrasov, Nikolai Alekseevich 1821-1878 NCLC **11**

Nelligan, Emile 1879-1941 .... **TCLC 14**
See also CA 114; DLB 92

Nelson, Willie 1933- ....CLC **17**
See also CA 107

Nemerov, Howard (Stanley) 1920-1991 C L C

2, 6, 9, 36; DAM POET
See also CA 1-4R; 134; CABS 2; CANR 1, 27, 53; DLB 5, 6; DLBY 83; INT CANR-27; MTCW

Neruda, Pablo 1904-1973CLC 1, 2, 5, 7, 9, 28, 62; DA; DAB; DAC; DAM MST, MULT, POET; HLC; PC 4; WLC
See also CA 19-20; 45-48; CAP 2; HW; MTCW

Nerval, Gerard de 1808-1855NCLC 1, 67; PC 13; SSC 18

Nervo, (Jose) Amado (Ruiz de) 1870-1919 TCLC 11
See also CA 109; 131; HW

Nessi, Pio Baroja y
See Baroja (y Nessi), Pio

Nestroy, Johann 1801-1862 .... NCLC 42
See also DLB 133

Netterville, Luke
See O'Grady, Standish (James)

Neufeld, John (Arthur) 1938- .... CLC 17
See also AAYA 11; CA 25-28R; CANR 11, 37, 56; MAICYA; SAAS 3; SATA 6, 81

Neville, Emily Cheney 1919- .... CLC 12
See also CA 5-8R; CANR 3, 37; JRDA; MAICYA; SAAS 2; SATA 1

Newbound, Bernard Slade 1930-
See Slade, Bernard
See also CA 81-84; CANR 49; DAM DRAM

Newby, P(ercy) H(oward) 1918-1997 CLC 2, 13; DAM NOV
See also CA 5-8R; 161; CANR 32, 67; DLB 15; MTCW

Newlove, Donald 1928- .... CLC 6
See also CA 29-32R; CANR 25

Newlove, John (Herbert) 1938- .... CLC 14
See also CA 21-24R; CANR 9, 25

Newman, Charles 1938- .... CLC 2, 8
See also CA 21-24R

Newman, Edwin (Harold) 1919- ...... CLC 14
See also AITN 1; CA 69-72; CANR 5

Newman, John Henry 1801-1890 ..NCLC 38
See also DLB 18, 32, 55

Newton, Suzanne 1936- .... CLC 35
See also CA 41-44R; CANR 14; JRDA; SATA 5, 77

Nexo, Martin Andersen 1869-1954 TCLC 43

Nezval, Vitezslav 1900-1958 .... TCLC 44
See also CA 123

Ng, Fae Myenne 1957(?)- .... CLC 81
See also CA 146

Ngema, Mbongeni 1955- .... CLC 57
See also BW 2; CA 143

Ngugi, James T(hiong'o) .... CLC 3, 7, 13
See also Ngugi wa Thiong'o

Ngugi wa Thiong'o 1938-CLC 36; BLC; DAM MULT, NOV
See also Ngugi, James T(hiong'o)
See also BW 2; CA 81-84; CANR 27, 58; DLB 125; MTCW

Nichol, B(arrie) P(hillip) 1944-1988 CLC 18
See also CA 53-56; DLB 53; SATA 66

Nichols, John (Treadwell) 1940- ...... CLC 38
See also CA 9-12R; CAAS 2; CANR 6; DLBY 82

Nichols, Leigh
See Koontz, Dean R(ay)

Nichols, Peter (Richard) 1927-CLC 5, 36, 65
See also CA 104; CANR 33; DLB 13; MTCW

Nicolas, F. R. E.
See Freeling, Nicolas

Niedecker, Lorine 1903-1970 .... CLC 10, 42; DAM POET
See also CA 25-28; CAP 2; DLB 48

Nietzsche, Friedrich (Wilhelm) 1844-1900 TCLC 10, 18, 55
See also CA 107; 121; DLB 129

Nievo, Ippolito 1831-1861 .... NCLC 22

Nightingale, Anne Redmon 1943-
See Redmon, Anne
See also CA 103

Nik. T. O.
See Annensky, Innokenty (Fyodorovich)

Nin, Anais 1903-1977CLC 1, 4, 8, 11, 14, 60; DAM NOV, POP; SSC 10
See also AITN 2; CA 13-16R; 69-72; CANR 22, 53; DLB 2, 4, 152; MTCW

Nishiwaki, Junzaburo 1894-1982 .... PC 15
See also CA 107

Nissenson, Hugh 1933- .... CLC 4, 9
See also CA 17-20R; CANR 27; DLB 28

Niven, Larry .... CLC 8
See also Niven, Laurence Van Cott
See also DLB 8

Niven, Laurence Van Cott 1938-
See Niven, Larry
See also CA 21-24R; CAAS 12; CANR 14, 44, 66; DAM POP; MTCW; SATA 95

Nixon, Agnes Eckhardt 1927- .... CLC 21
See also CA 110

Nizan, Paul 1905-1940 .... TCLC 40
See also CA 161; DLB 72

Nkosi, Lewis 1936- ...... CLC 45; BLC; DAM MULT
See also BW 1; CA 65-68; CANR 27; DLB 157

Nodier, (Jean) Charles (Emmanuel) 1780-1844 NCLC 19
See also DLB 119

Nolan, Christopher 1965- .... CLC 58
See also CA 111

Noon, Jeff 1957- .... CLC 91
See also CA 148

Norden, Charles
See Durrell, Lawrence (George)

Nordhoff, Charles (Bernard) 1887-1947 TCLC 23
See also CA 108; DLB 9; SATA 23

Norfolk, Lawrence 1963- .... CLC 76
See also CA 144

Norman, Marsha 1947-CLC 28; DAM DRAM; DC 8
See also CA 105; CABS 3; CANR 41; DLBY 84

Norris, Frank 1870-1902 .... SSC 28
See also Norris, (Benjamin) Frank(lin, Jr.)
See also CDALB 1865-1917; DLB 12, 71, 186

Norris, (Benjamin) Frank(lin, Jr.) 1870-1902 TCLC 24
See also Norris, Frank
See also CA 110; 160

Norris, Leslie 1921- .... CLC 14
See also CA 11-12; CANR 14; CAP 1; DLB 27

North, Andrew
See Norton, Andre

North, Anthony
See Koontz, Dean R(ay)

North, Captain George
See Stevenson, Robert Louis (Balfour)

North, Milou
See Erdrich, Louise

Northrup, B. A.
See Hubbard, L(afayette) Ron(ald)

North Staffs
See Hulme, T(homas) E(rnest)

Norton, Alice Mary
See Norton, Andre
See also MAICYA; SATA 1, 43

Norton, Andre 1912- .... CLC 12
See also Norton, Alice Mary
See also AAYA 14; CA 1-4R; CANR 68; DLB 8, 52; JRDA; MTCW; SATA 91

Norton, Caroline 1808-1877 .... NCLC 47
See also DLB 21, 159

Norway, Nevil Shute 1899-1960
See Shute, Nevil
See also CA 102; 93-96

Norwid, Cyprian Kamil 1821-1883 NCLC 17

Nosille, Nabrah
See Ellison, Harlan (Jay)

Nossack, Hans Erich 1901-1978 .... CLC 6
See also CA 93-96; 85-88; DLB 69

Nostradamus 1503-1566 .... LC 27

Nosu, Chuji
See Ozu, Yasujiro

Notenburg, Eleanora (Genrikhovna) von
See Guro, Elena

Nova, Craig 1945- .... CLC 7, 31
See also CA 45-48; CANR 2, 53

Novak, Joseph
See Kosinski, Jerzy (Nikodem)

Novalis 1772-1801 .... NCLC 13
See also DLB 90

Novis, Emile
See Weil, Simone (Adolphine)

Nowlan, Alden (Albert) 1933-1983 . CLC 15; DAC; DAM MST
See also CA 9-12R; CANR 5; DLB 53

Noyes, Alfred 1880-1958 .... TCLC 7
See also CA 104; DLB 20

Nunn, Kem .... CLC 34
See also CA 159

Nye, Robert 1939-...CLC 13, 42; DAM NOV
See also CA 33-36R; CANR 29, 67; DLB 14; MTCW; SATA 6

Nyro, Laura 1947- .... CLC 17

Oates, Joyce Carol 1938-CLC 1, 2, 3, 6, 9, 11, 15, 19, 33, 52, 108; DA; DAB; DAC; DAM MST, NOV, POP; SSC 6; WLC
See also AAYA 15; AITN 1; BEST 89:2; CA 5-8R; CANR 25, 45; CDALB 1968-1988; DLB 2, 5, 130; DLBY 81; INT CANR-25; MTCW

O'Brien, Darcy 1939- .... CLC 11
See also CA 21-24R; CANR 8, 59

O'Brien, E. G.
See Clarke, Arthur C(harles)

O'Brien, Edna 1936- CLC 3, 5, 8, 13, 36, 65; DAM NOV; SSC 10
See also CA 1-4R; CANR 6, 41, 65; CDBLB 1960 to Present; DLB 14; MTCW

O'Brien, Fitz-James 1828-1862 ..... NCLC 21
See also DLB 74

O'Brien, Flann .... CLC 1, 4, 5, 7, 10, 47
See also O Nuallain, Brian

O'Brien, Richard 1942- .... CLC 17
See also CA 124

O'Brien, (William) Tim(othy) 1946- . CLC 7, 19, 40, 103; DAM POP
See also AAYA 16; CA 85-88; CANR 40, 58; DLB 152; DLBD 9; DLBY 80

Obstfelder, Sigbjoern 1866-1900 ... TCLC 23
See also CA 123

O'Casey, Sean 1880-1964CLC 1, 5, 9, 11, 15, 88; DAB; DAC; DAM DRAM, MST; WLCS
See also CA 89-92; CANR 62; CDBLB 1914-1945; DLB 10; MTCW

O'Cathasaigh, Sean
See O'Casey, Sean

Ochs, Phil 1940-1976 .... CLC 17

DAC; DAM MST; PC 12
See also CA 53-56; CANR 4, 22, 65; DLB 68; MTCW

Page, Thomas Nelson 1853-1922 .... **SSC 23**
See also CA 118; DLB 12, 78; DLBD 13

Pagels, Elaine Hiesey 1943- .... **CLC 104**
See also CA 45-48; CANR 2, 24, 51

Paget, Violet 1856-1935
See Lee, Vernon
See also CA 104

Paget-Lowe, Henry
See Lovecraft, H(oward) P(hillips)

Paglia, Camille (Anna) 1947- .... **CLC 68**
See also CA 140

Paige, Richard
See Koontz, Dean R(ay)

Paine, Thomas 1737-1809 .... **NCLC 62**
See also CDALB 1640-1865; DLB 31, 43, 73, 158

Pakenham, Antonia
See Fraser, (Lady) Antonia (Pakenham)

Palamas, Kostes 1859-1943 .... **TCLC 5**
See also CA 105

Palazzeschi, Aldo 1885-1974 .... **CLC 11**
See also CA 89-92; 53-56; DLB 114

Paley, Grace 1922-CLC **4, 6, 37; DAM POP; SSC 8**
See also CA 25-28R; CANR 13, 46; DLB 28; INT CANR-13; MTCW

Palin, Michael (Edward) 1943- .... **CLC 21**
See also Monty Python
See also CA 107; CANR 35; SATA 67

Palliser, Charles 1947- .... **CLC 65**
See also CA 136

Palma, Ricardo 1833-1919 .... **TCLC 29**

Pancake, Breece Dexter 1952-1979
See Pancake, Breece D'J
See also CA 123; 109

Pancake, Breece D'J .... **CLC 29**
See also Pancake, Breece Dexter
See also DLB 130

Panko, Rudy
See Gogol, Nikolai (Vasilyevich)

Papadiamantis, Alexandros 1851-1911 **TCLC 29**

Papadiamantopoulos, Johannes 1856-1910
See Moreas, Jean
See also CA 117

Papini, Giovanni 1881-1956 .... **TCLC 22**
See also CA 121

Paracelsus 1493-1541 .... **LC 14**
See also DLB 179

Parasol, Peter
See Stevens, Wallace

Pardo Baz<aacute>n, Emilia 1851-1921 **SSC 30**

Pareto, Vilfredo 1848-1923 .... **TCLC 69**

Parfenie, Maria
See Codrescu, Andrei

Parini, Jay (Lee) 1948- .... **CLC 54**
See also CA 97-100; CAAS 16; CANR 32

Park, Jordan
See Kornbluth, C(yril) M.; Pohl, Frederik

Park, Robert E(zra) 1864-1944 ..... **TCLC 73**
See also CA 122

Parker, Bert
See Ellison, Harlan (Jay)

Parker, Dorothy (Rothschild) 1893-1967 **CLC 15, 68; DAM POET; SSC 2**
See also CA 19-20; 25-28R; CAP 2; DLB 11, 45, 86; MTCW

Parker, Robert B(rown) 1932-CLC **27; DAM NOV, POP**

See also BEST 89:4; CA 49-52; CANR 1, 26, 52; INT CANR-26; MTCW

Parkin, Frank 1940- .... **CLC 43**
See also CA 147

Parkman, Francis, Jr. 1823-1893 ..**NCLC 12**
See also DLB 1, 30, 186

Parks, Gordon (Alexander Buchanan) 1912- **CLC 1, 16; BLC; DAM MULT**
See also AITN 2; BW 2; CA 41-44R; CANR 26, 66; DLB 33; SATA 8

Parmenides c. 515B.C.-c. 450B.C. **CMLC 22**
See also DLB 176

Parnell, Thomas 1679-1718 .... **LC 3**
See also DLB 94

Parra, Nicanor 1914- ...... **CLC 2, 102; DAM MULT; HLC**
See also CA 85-88; CANR 32; HW; MTCW

Parrish, Mary Frances
See Fisher, M(ary) F(rances) K(ennedy)

Parson
See Coleridge, Samuel Taylor

Parson Lot
See Kingsley, Charles

Partridge, Anthony
See Oppenheim, E(dward) Phillips

Pascal, Blaise 1623-1662 .... **LC 35**

Pascoli, Giovanni 1855-1912 .... **TCLC 45**

Pasolini, Pier Paolo 1922-1975 . **CLC 20, 37, 106; PC 17**
See also CA 93-96; 61-64; CANR 63; DLB 128, 177; MTCW

Pasquini
See Silone, Ignazio

Pastan, Linda (Olenik) 1932- **CLC 27; DAM POET**
See also CA 61-64; CANR 18, 40, 61; DLB 5

Pasternak, Boris (Leonidovich) 1890-1960 **CLC 7, 10, 18, 63; DA; DAB; DAC; DAM MST, NOV, POET; PC 6; WLC**
See also CA 127; 116; MTCW

Patchen, Kenneth 1911-1972 ... **CLC 1, 2, 18; DAM POET**
See also CA 1-4R; 33-36R; CANR 3, 35; DLB 16, 48; MTCW

Pater, Walter (Horatio) 1839-1894 . **NCLC 7**
See also CDBLB 1832-1890; DLB 57, 156

Paterson, A(ndrew) B(arton) 1864-1941 **TCLC 32**
See also CA 155; SATA 97

Paterson, Katherine (Womeldorf) 1932-**CLC 12, 30**
See also AAYA 1; CA 21-24R; CANR 28, 59; CLR 7; DLB 52; JRDA; MAICYA; MTCW; SATA 13, 53, 92

Patmore, Coventry Kersey Dighton 1823-1896 **NCLC 9**
See also DLB 35, 98

Paton, Alan (Stewart) 1903-1988 **CLC 4, 10, 25, 55, 106; DA; DAB; DAC; DAM MST, NOV; WLC**
See also CA 13-16; 125; CANR 22; CAP 1; MTCW; SATA 11; SATA-Obit 56

Paton Walsh, Gillian 1937-
See Walsh, Jill Paton
See also CANR 38; JRDA; MAICYA; SAAS 3; SATA 4, 72

Patton, George S. 1885-1945 .... **TCLC 79**

Paulding, James Kirke 1778-1860 ... **NCLC 2**
See also DLB 3, 59, 74

Paulin, Thomas Neilson 1949-
See Paulin, Tom
See also CA 123; 128

Paulin, Tom .... **CLC 37**

See also Paulin, Thomas Neilson
See also DLB 40

Paustovsky, Konstantin (Georgievich) 1892-1968 .... **CLC 40**
See also CA 93-96; 25-28R

Pavese, Cesare 1908-1950 ... **TCLC 3; PC 13; SSC 19**
See also CA 104; DLB 128, 177

Pavic, Milorad 1929- .... **CLC 60**
See also CA 136; DLB 181

Payne, Alan
See Jakes, John (William)

Paz, Gil
See Lugones, Leopoldo

Paz, Octavio 1914-CLC **3, 4, 6, 10, 19, 51, 65; DA; DAB; DAC; DAM MST, MULT, POET; HLC; PC 1; WLC**
See also CA 73-76; CANR 32, 65; DLBY 90; HW; MTCW

p'Bitek, Okot 1931-1982**CLC 96; BLC; DAM MULT**
See also BW 2; CA 124; 107; DLB 125; MTCW

Peacock, Molly 1947- .... **CLC 60**
See also CA 103; CAAS 21; CANR 52; DLB 120

Peacock, Thomas Love 1785-1866 **NCLC 22**
See also DLB 96, 116

Peake, Mervyn 1911-1968 .... **CLC 7, 54**
See also CA 5-8R; 25-28R; CANR 3; DLB 15, 160; MTCW; SATA 23

Pearce, Philippa .... **CLC 21**
See also Christie, (Ann) Philippa
See also CLR 9; DLB 161; MAICYA; SATA 1, 67

Pearl, Eric
See Elman, Richard (Martin)

Pearson, T(homas) R(eid) 1956- ...... **CLC 39**
See also CA 120; 130; INT 130

Peck, Dale 1967- .... **CLC 81**
See also CA 146

Peck, John 1941-.................................**CLC 3**
See also CA 49-52; CANR 3

Peck, Richard (Wayne) 1934- .... **CLC 21**
See also AAYA 1, 24; CA 85-88; CANR 19, 38; CLR 15; INT CANR-19; JRDA; MAICYA; SAAS 2; SATA 18, 55, 97

Peck, Robert Newton 1928- ..... **CLC 17; DA; DAC; DAM MST**
See also AAYA 3; CA 81-84; CANR 31, 63; CLR 45; JRDA; MAICYA; SAAS 1; SATA 21, 62

Peckinpah, (David) Sam(uel) 1925-1984**CLC 20**
See also CA 109; 114

Pedersen, Knut 1859-1952
See Hamsun, Knut
See also CA 104; 119; CANR 63; MTCW

Peeslake, Gaffer
See Durrell, Lawrence (George)

Peguy, Charles Pierre 1873-1914 .. **TCLC 10**
See also CA 107

Pena, Ramon del Valle y
See Valle-Inclan, Ramon (Maria) del

Pendennis, Arthur Esquir
See Thackeray, William Makepeace

Penn, William 1644-1718 .... **LC 25**
See also DLB 24

PEPECE
See Prado (Calvo), Pedro

Pepys, Samuel 1633-1703 **LC 11; DA; DAB; DAC; DAM MST; WLC**
See also CDBLB 1660-1789; DLB 101

Percy, Walker 1916-1990**CLC 2, 3, 6, 8, 14, 18,**

47, 65; DAM NOV, POP
See also CA 1-4R; 131; CANR 1, 23, 64; DLB 2; DLBY 80, 90; MTCW

Perec, Georges 1936-1982 .... CLC 56
See also CA 141; DLB 83

Pereda (y Sanchez de Porrua), Jose Maria de 1833-1906 .... TCLC 16
See also CA 117

Pereda y Porrua, Jose Maria de
See Pereda (y Sanchez de Porrua), Jose Maria de

Peregoy, George Weems
See Mencken, H(enry) L(ouis)

Perelman, S(idney) J(oseph) 1904-1979 C L C 3, 5, 9, 15, 23, 44, 49; DAM DRAM
See also AITN 1, 2; CA 73-76; 89-92; CANR 18; DLB 11, 44; MTCW

Peret, Benjamin 1899-1959 .... TCLC 20
See also CA 117

Peretz, Isaac Loeb 1851(?)-1915 .. TCLC 16; SSC 26
See also CA 109

Peretz, Yitzkhok Leibush
See Peretz, Isaac Loeb

Perez Galdos, Benito 1843-1920 .... TCLC 27
See also CA 125; 153; HW

Perrault, Charles 1628-1703 .... LC 2
See also MAICYA; SATA 25

Perry, Brighton
See Sherwood, Robert E(mmet)

Perse, St.-John .... CLC 4, 11, 46
See also Leger, (Marie-Rene Auguste) Alexis Saint-Leger

Perutz, Leo 1882-1957 .... TCLC 60
See also DLB 81

Peseenz, Tulio F.
See Lopez y Fuentes, Gregorio

Pesetsky, Bette 1932- .... CLC 28
See also CA 133; DLB 130

Peshkov, Alexei Maximovich 1868-1936
See Gorky, Maxim
See also CA 105; 141; DA; DAC; DAM DRAM, MST, NOV

Pessoa, Fernando (Antonio Nogueira) 1898-1935 .... TCLC 27; HLC; PC 20
See also CA 125

Peterkin, Julia Mood 1880-1961 ...... CLC 31
See also CA 102; DLB 9

Peters, Joan K(aren) 1945- .... CLC 39
See also CA 158

Peters, Robert L(ouis) 1924- .... CLC 7
See also CA 13-16R; CAAS 8; DLB 105

Petofi, Sandor 1823-1849 .... NCLC 21

Petrakis, Harry Mark 1923- .... CLC 3
See also CA 9-12R; CANR 4, 30

Petrarch 1304-1374 CMLC 20; DAM POET; PC 8

Petrov, Evgeny .... TCLC 21
See also Kataev, Evgeny Petrovich

Petry, Ann (Lane) 1908-1997 ... CLC 1, 7, 18
See also BW 1; CA 5-8R; 157; CAAS 6; CANR 4, 46; CLR 12; DLB 76; JRDA; MAICYA; MTCW; SATA 5; SATA-Obit 94

Petursson, Halligrimur 1614-1674 .... LC 8

Phaedrus 18(?)B.C.-55(?) .... CMLC 25

Philips, Katherine 1632-1664 .... LC 30
See also DLB 131

Philipson, Morris H. 1926- .... CLC 53
See also CA 1-4R; CANR 4

Phillips, Caryl 1958- . CLC 96; DAM MULT
See also BW 2; CA 141; CANR 63; DLB 157

Phillips, David Graham 1867-1911 TCLC 44
See also CA 108; DLB 9, 12

Phillips, Jack
See Sandburg, Carl (August)

Phillips, Jayne Anne 1952-CLC 15, 33; SSC 16
See also CA 101; CANR 24, 50; DLBY 80; INT CANR-24; MTCW

Phillips, Richard
See Dick, Philip K(indred)

Phillips, Robert (Schaeffer) 1938- .... CLC 28
See also CA 17-20R; CAAS 13; CANR 8; DLB 105

Phillips, Ward
See Lovecraft, H(oward) P(hillips)

Piccolo, Lucio 1901-1969 .... CLC 13
See also CA 97-100; DLB 114

Pickthall, Marjorie L(owry) C(hristie) 1883-1922 .... TCLC 21
See also CA 107; DLB 92

Pico della Mirandola, Giovanni 1463-1494LC 15

Piercy, Marge 1936- CLC 3, 6, 14, 18, 27, 62
See also CA 21-24R; CAAS 1; CANR 13, 43, 66; DLB 120; MTCW

Piers, Robert
See Anthony, Piers

Pieyre de Mandiargues, Andre 1909-1991
See Mandiargues, Andre Pieyre de
See also CA 103; 136; CANR 22

Pilnyak, Boris .... TCLC 23
See also Vogau, Boris Andreyevich

Pincherle, Alberto 1907-1990 ... CLC 11, 18; DAM NOV
See also Moravia, Alberto
See also CA 25-28R; 132; CANR 33, 63; MTCW

Pinckney, Darryl 1953- .... CLC 76
See also BW 2; CA 143

Pindar 518B.C.-446B.C. ... CMLC 12; PC 19
See also DLB 176

Pineda, Cecile 1942- .... CLC 39
See also CA 118

Pinero, Arthur Wing 1855-1934 .. TCLC 32; DAM DRAM
See also CA 110; 153; DLB 10

Pinero, Miguel (Antonio Gomez) 1946-1988 CLC 4, 55
See also CA 61-64; 125; CANR 29; HW

Pinget, Robert 1919-1997 .... CLC 7, 13, 37
See also CA 85-88; 160; DLB 83

Pink Floyd
See Barrett, (Roger) Syd; Gilmour, David; Mason, Nick; Waters, Roger; Wright, Rick

Pinkney, Edward 1802-1828 .... NCLC 31

Pinkwater, Daniel Manus 1941- .... CLC 35
See also Pinkwater, Manus
See also AAYA 1; CA 29-32R; CANR 12, 38; CLR 4; JRDA; MAICYA; SAAS 3; SATA 46, 76

Pinkwater, Manus
See Pinkwater, Daniel Manus
See also SATA 8

Pinsky, Robert 1940-CLC 9, 19, 38, 94; DAM POET
See also CA 29-32R; CAAS 4; CANR 58; DLBY 82

Pinta, Harold
See Pinter, Harold

Pinter, Harold 1930-CLC 1, 3, 6, 9, 11, 15, 27, 58, 73; DA; DAB; DAC; DAM DRAM, MST; WLC
See also CA 5-8R; CANR 33, 65; CDBLB 1960 to Present; DLB 13; MTCW

Piozzi, Hester Lynch (Thrale) 1741-1821 NCLC 57

Pirandello, Luigi 1867-1936TCLC 4, 29; DA; DAB; DAC; DAM DRAM, MST; DC 5; SSC 22; WLC
See also CA 104; 153

Pirsig, Robert M(aynard) 1928-CLC 4, 6, 73; DAM POP
See also CA 53-56; CANR 42; MTCW; SATA 39

Pisarev, Dmitry Ivanovich 1840-1868 N C L C 25

Pix, Mary (Griffith) 1666-1709 .... LC 8
See also DLB 80

Pixerecourt, (Rene Charles) Guilbert de 1773-1844 .... NCLC 39
See also DLB 192

Plaatje, Sol(omon) T(shekisho) 1876-1932 TCLC 73
See also BW 2; CA 141

Plaidy, Jean
See Hibbert, Eleanor Alice Burford

Planche, James Robinson 1796-1880NCLC 42

Plant, Robert 1948- .... CLC 12

Plante, David (Robert) 1940- CLC 7, 23, 38; DAM NOV
See also CA 37-40R; CANR 12, 36, 58; DLBY 83; INT CANR-12; MTCW

Plath, Sylvia 1932-1963 CLC 1, 2, 3, 5, 9, 11, 14, 17, 50, 51, 62; DA; DAB; DAC; DAM MST, POET; PC 1; WLC
See also AAYA 13; CA 19-20; CANR 34; CAP 2; CDALB 1941-1968; DLB 5, 6, 152; MTCW; SATA 96

Plato 428(?)B.C.-348(?)B.C. .. CMLC 8; DA; DAB; DAC; DAM MST; WLCS
See also DLB 176

Platonov, Andrei .... TCLC 14
See also Klimentov, Andrei Platonovich

Platt, Kin 1911- .... CLC 26
See also AAYA 11; CA 17-20R; CANR 11; JRDA; SAAS 17; SATA 21, 86

Plautus c. 251B.C.-184B.C.. CMLC 24; DC 6

Plick et Plock
See Simenon, Georges (Jacques Christian)

Plimpton, George (Ames) 1927-........ CLC 36
See also AITN 1; CA 21-24R; CANR 32; DLB 185; MTCW; SATA 10

Pliny the Elder c. 23-79 .... CMLC 23

Plomer, William Charles Franklin 1903-1973 CLC 4, 8
See also CA 21-22; CANR 34; CAP 2; DLB 20, 162, 191; MTCW; SATA 24

Plowman, Piers
See Kavanagh, Patrick (Joseph)

Plum, J.
See Wodehouse, P(elham) G(renville)

Plumly, Stanley (Ross) 1939- .... CLC 33
See also CA 108; 110; DLB 5, 193; INT 110

Plumpe, Friedrich Wilhelm 1888-1931T C L C 53
See also CA 112

Po Chu-i 772-846 .... CMLC 24

Poe, Edgar Allan 1809-1849NCLC 1, 16, 55; DA; DAB; DAC; DAM MST, POET; PC 1; SSC 1, 22; WLC
See also AAYA 14; CDALB 1640-1865; DLB 3, 59, 73, 74; SATA 23

Poet of Titchfield Street, The
See Pound, Ezra (Weston Loomis)

Pohl, Frederik 1919- .... CLC 18; SSC 25
See also AAYA 24; CA 61-64; CAAS 1; CANR 11, 37; DLB 8; INT CANR-11; MTCW; SATA 24

See also CA 65-68; CANR 4, 42, 65; DLB 6; MTCW

Pygge, Edward
See Barnes, Julian (Patrick)

Pyle, Ernest Taylor 1900-1945
See Pyle, Ernie
See also CA 115; 160

Pyle, Ernie 1900-1945 .... **TCLC 75**
See Pyle, Ernest Taylor
See also DLB 29

Pym, Barbara (Mary Crampton) 1913-1980
CLC 13, 19, 37
See also CA 13-14; 97-100; CANR 13, 34; CAP 1; DLB 14; DLBY 87; MTCW

Pynchon, Thomas (Ruggles, Jr.) 1937-CLC 2, 3, 6, 9, 11, 18, 33, 62, 72; DA; DAB; DAC; DAM MST, NOV, POP; SSC 14; WLC
See also BEST 90:2; CA 17-20R; CANR 22, 46; DLB 2, 173; MTCW

Pythagoras c. 570B.C.-c. 500B.C. . . **CMLC 22**
See also DLB 176

Qian Zhongshu
See Ch'ien Chung-shu

Qroll
See Dagerman, Stig (Halvard)

Quarrington, Paul (Lewis) 1953- ..... **CLC 65**
See also CA 129; CANR 62

Quasimodo, Salvatore 1901-1968 .... **CLC 10**
See also CA 13-16; 25-28R; CAP 1; DLB 114; MTCW

Quay, Stephen 1947- .... **CLC 95**
Quay, Timothy 1947- .... **CLC 95**
Queen, Ellery .... **CLC 3, 11**
See also Dannay, Frederic; Davidson, Avram; Lee, Manfred B(ennington); Marlowe, Stephen; Sturgeon, Theodore (Hamilton); Vance, John Holbrook

Queen, Ellery, Jr.
See Dannay, Frederic; Lee, Manfred B(ennington)

Queneau, Raymond 1903-1976 **CLC 2, 5, 10, 42**
See also CA 77-80; 69-72; CANR 32; DLB 72; MTCW

Quevedo, Francisco de 1580-1645 ...... **LC 23**

Quiller-Couch, SirArthur Thomas 1863-1944
TCLC 53
See also CA 118; DLB 135, 153, 190

Quin, Ann (Marie) 1936-1973 .... **CLC 6**
See also CA 9-12R; 45-48; DLB 14

Quinn, Martin
See Smith, Martin Cruz

Quinn, Peter 1947- .... **CLC 91**

Quinn, Simon
See Smith, Martin Cruz

Quiroga, Horacio (Sylvestre) 1878-1937
TCLC 20; DAM MULT; HLC
See also CA 117; 131; HW; MTCW

Quoirez, Francoise 1935- .... **CLC 9**
See also Sagan, Francoise
See also CA 49-52; CANR 6, 39; MTCW

Raabe, Wilhelm 1831-1910 .... **TCLC 45**
See also DLB 129

Rabe, David (William) 1940- .. **CLC 4, 8, 33; DAM DRAM**
See also CA 85-88; CABS 3; CANR 59; DLB 7

Rabelais, Francois 1483-1553**LC 5; DA; DAB; DAC; DAM MST; WLC**

Rabinovitch, Sholem 1859-1916
See Aleichem, Sholom
See also CA 104

Rachilde 1860-1953 .... **TCLC 67**

See also DLB 123, 192

Racine, Jean 1639-1699 . **LC 28; DAB; DAM MST**

Radcliffe, Ann (Ward) 1764-1823**NCLC 6, 55**
See also DLB 39, 178

Radiguet, Raymond 1903-1923 ...... **TCLC 29**
See also CA 162; DLB 65

Radnoti, Miklos 1909-1944 .... **TCLC 16**
See also CA 118

Rado, James 1939- .... **CLC 17**
See also CA 105

Radvanyi, Netty 1900-1983
See Seghers, Anna
See also CA 85-88; 110

Rae, Ben
See Griffiths, Trevor

Raeburn, John (Hay) 1941- .... **CLC 34**
See also CA 57-60

Ragni, Gerome 1942-1991 .... **CLC 17**
See also CA 105; 134

Rahv, Philip 1908-1973 .... **CLC 24**
See also Greenberg, Ivan
See also DLB 137

Raimund, Ferdinand Jakob 1790-1836**NCLC 69**
See also DLB 90

Raine, Craig 1944- .... **CLC 32, 103**
See also CA 108; CANR 29, 51; DLB 40

Raine, Kathleen (Jessie) 1908- ..... **CLC 7, 45**
See also CA 85-88; CANR 46; DLB 20; MTCW

Rainis, Janis 1865-1929 .... **TCLC 29**

Rakosi, Carl 1903- .... **CLC 47**
See also Rawley, Callman
See also CAAS 5; DLB 193

Raleigh, Richard
See Lovecraft, H(oward) P(hillips)

Raleigh, Sir Walter 1554(?)-1618 . **LC 31, 39**
See also CDBLB Before 1660; DLB 172

Rallentando, H. P.
See Sayers, Dorothy L(eigh)

Ramal, Walter
See de la Mare, Walter (John)

Ramon, Juan
See Jimenez (Mantecon), Juan Ramon

Ramos, Graciliano 1892-1953 .... **TCLC 32**

Rampersad, Arnold 1941- .... **CLC 44**
See also BW 2; CA 127; 133; DLB 111; INT 133

Rampling, Anne
See Rice, Anne

Ramsay, Allan 1684(?)-1758 .... **LC 29**
See also DLB 95

Ramuz, Charles-Ferdinand 1878-1947**TCLC 33**

Rand, Ayn 1905-1982**CLC 3, 30, 44, 79; DA; DAC; DAM MST, NOV, POP; WLC**
See also AAYA 10; CA 13-16R; 105; CANR 27; MTCW

Randall, Dudley (Felker) 1914-**CLC 1; BLC; DAM MULT**
See also BW 1; CA 25-28R; CANR 23; DLB 41

Randall, Robert
See Silverberg, Robert

Ranger, Ken
See Creasey, John

Ransom, John Crowe 1888-1974**CLC 2, 4, 5, 11, 24; DAM POET**
See also CA 5-8R; 49-52; CANR 6, 34; DLB 45, 63; MTCW

Rao, Raja 1909- ...... **CLC 25, 56; DAM NOV**
See also CA 73-76; CANR 51; MTCW

Raphael, Frederic (Michael) 1931-**CLC 2, 14**

See also CA 1-4R; CANR 1; DLB 14

Ratcliffe, James P.
See Mencken, H(enry) L(ouis)

Rathbone, Julian 1935- .... **CLC 41**
See also CA 101; CANR 34

Rattigan, Terence (Mervyn) 1911-1977 **C L C 7; DAM DRAM**
See also CA 85-88; 73-76; CDBLB 1945-1960; DLB 13; MTCW

Ratushinskaya, Irina 1954- .... **CLC 54**
See also CA 129

Raven, Simon (Arthur Noel) 1927- ..**CLC 14**
See also CA 81-84

Ravenna, Michael
See Welty, Eudora

Rawley, Callman 1903-
See Rakosi, Carl
See also CA 21-24R; CANR 12, 32

Rawlings, Marjorie Kinnan 1896-1953**TCLC 4**
See also AAYA 20; CA 104; 137; DLB 9, 22, 102; JRDA; MAICYA; YABC 1

Ray, Satyajit 1921-1992 .. **CLC 16, 76; DAM MULT**
See also CA 114; 137

Read, Herbert Edward 1893-1968 ..... **CLC 4**
See also CA 85-88; 25-28R; DLB 20, 149

Read, Piers Paul 1941- .... **CLC 4, 10, 25**
See also CA 21-24R; CANR 38; DLB 14; SATA 21

Reade, Charles 1814-1884 .... **NCLC 2**
See also DLB 21

Reade, Hamish
See Gray, Simon (James Holliday)

Reading, Peter 1946- .... **CLC 47**
See also CA 103; CANR 46; DLB 40

Reaney, James 1926- ... **CLC 13; DAC; DAM MST**
See also CA 41-44R; CAAS 15; CANR 42; DLB 68; SATA 43

Rebreanu, Liviu 1885-1944 .... **TCLC 28**

Rechy, John (Francisco) 1934- **CLC 1, 7, 14, 18, 107; DAM MULT; HLC**
See also CA 5-8R; CAAS 4; CANR 6, 32, 64; DLB 122; DLBY 82; HW; INT CANR-6

Redcam, Tom 1870-1933 .... **TCLC 25**

Reddin, Keith .... **CLC 67**

Redgrove, Peter (William) 1932- . **CLC 6, 41**
See also CA 1-4R; CANR 3, 39; DLB 40

Redmon, Anne .... **CLC 22**
See also Nightingale, Anne Redmon
See also DLBY 86

Reed, Eliot
See Ambler, Eric

Reed, Ishmael 1938-**CLC 2, 3, 5, 6, 13, 32, 60; BLC; DAM MULT**
See also BW 2; CA 21-24R; CANR 25, 48; DLB 2, 5, 33, 169; DLBD 8; MTCW

Reed, John (Silas) 1887-1920 .... **TCLC 9**
See also CA 106

Reed, Lou .... **CLC 21**
See also Firbank, Louis

Reeve, Clara 1729-1807 .... **NCLC 19**
See also DLB 39

Reich, Wilhelm 1897-1957 .... **TCLC 57**

Reid, Christopher (John) 1949- .... **CLC 33**
See also CA 140; DLB 40

Reid, Desmond
See Moorcock, Michael (John)

Reid Banks, Lynne 1929-
See Banks, Lynne Reid
See also CA 1-4R; CANR 6, 22, 38; CLR 24; JRDA; MAICYA; SATA 22, 75

See also CA 9-12R; CANR 23, 66; DLB 83; MTCW

Sarton, (Eleanor) May 1912-1995 **CLC 4, 14, 49, 91; DAM POET**
See also CA 1-4R; 149; CANR 1, 34, 55; DLB 48; DLBY 81; INT CANR-34; MTCW; SATA 36; SATA-Obit 86

Sartre, Jean-Paul 1905-1980 **CLC 1, 4, 7, 9, 13, 18, 24, 44, 50, 52; DA; DAB; DAC; DAM DRAM, MST, NOV; DC 3; WLC**
See also CA 9-12R; 97-100; CANR 21; DLB 72; MTCW

Sassoon, Siegfried (Lorraine) 1886-1967 **CLC 36; DAB; DAM MST, NOV, POET; PC 12**
See also CA 104; 25-28R; CANR 36; DLB 20, 191; MTCW

Satterfield, Charles
See Pohl, Frederik

Saul, John (W. III) 1942- **CLC 46; DAM NOV, POP**
See also AAYA 10; BEST 90:4; CA 81-84; CANR 16, 40; SATA 98

Saunders, Caleb
See Heinlein, Robert A(nson)

Saura (Atares), Carlos 1932- .... **CLC 20**
See also CA 114; 131; HW

Sauser-Hall, Frederic 1887-1961 ..... **CLC 18**
See also Cendrars, Blaise
See also CA 102; 93-96; CANR 36, 62; MTCW

Saussure, Ferdinand de 1857-1913 **TCLC 49**

Savage, Catharine
See Brosman, Catharine Savage

Savage, Thomas 1915- .... **CLC 40**
See also CA 126; 132; CAAS 15; INT 132

Savan, Glenn 19(?)- .... **CLC 50**

Sayers, Dorothy L(eigh) 1893-1957 **TCLC 2, 15; DAM POP**
See also CA 104; 119; CANR 60; CDBLB 1914-1945; DLB 10, 36, 77, 100; MTCW

Sayers, Valerie 1952- .... **CLC 50**
See also CA 134; CANR 61

Sayles, John (Thomas) 1950- . **CLC 7, 10, 14**
See also CA 57-60; CANR 41; DLB 44

Scammell, Michael 1935- .... **CLC 34**
See also CA 156

Scannell, Vernon 1922- .... **CLC 49**
See also CA 5-8R; CANR 8, 24, 57; DLB 27; SATA 59

Scarlett, Susan
See Streatfeild, (Mary) Noel

Schaeffer, Susan Fromberg 1941- **CLC 6, 11, 22**
See also CA 49-52; CANR 18, 65; DLB 28; MTCW; SATA 22

Schary, Jill
See Robinson, Jill

Schell, Jonathan 1943- .... **CLC 35**
See also CA 73-76; CANR 12

Schelling, Friedrich Wilhelm Joseph von 1775-1854 .... **NCLC 30**
See also DLB 90

Schendel, Arthur van 1874-1946 ... **TCLC 56**

Scherer, Jean-Marie Maurice 1920-
See Rohmer, Eric
See also CA 110

Schevill, James (Erwin) 1920- .... **CLC 7**
See also CA 5-8R; CAAS 12

Schiller, Friedrich 1759-1805 **NCLC 39, 69; DAM DRAM**
See also DLB 94

Schisgal, Murray (Joseph) 1926- .... **CLC 6**
See also CA 21-24R; CANR 48

Schlee, Ann 1934- .... **CLC 35**
See also CA 101; CANR 29; SATA 44; SATA-Brief 36

Schlegel, August Wilhelm von 1767-1845 **NCLC 15**
See also DLB 94

Schlegel, Friedrich 1772-1829 .... **NCLC 45**
See also DLB 90

Schlegel, Johann Elias (von) 1719(?)-1749 **LC 5**

Schlesinger, Arthur M(eier), Jr. 1917- **CLC 84**
See also AITN 1; CA 1-4R; CANR 1, 28, 58; DLB 17; INT CANR-28; MTCW; SATA 61

Schmidt, Arno (Otto) 1914-1979 ...... **CLC 56**
See also CA 128; 109; DLB 69

Schmitz, Aron Hector 1861-1928
See Svevo, Italo
See also CA 104; 122; MTCW

Schnackenberg, Gjertrud 1953- .... **CLC 40**
See also CA 116; DLB 120

Schneider, Leonard Alfred 1925-1966
See Bruce, Lenny
See also CA 89-92

Schnitzler, Arthur 1862-1931 **TCLC 4; SSC 15**
See also CA 104; DLB 81, 118

Schoenberg, Arnold 1874-1951 ...... **TCLC 75**
See also CA 109

Schonberg, Arnold
See Schoenberg, Arnold

Schopenhauer, Arthur 1788-1860 . **NCLC 51**
See also DLB 90

Schor, Sandra (M.) 1932(?)-1990 ..... **CLC 65**
See also CA 132

Schorer, Mark 1908-1977 .... **CLC 9**
See also CA 5-8R; 73-76; CANR 7; DLB 103

Schrader, Paul (Joseph) 1946- .... **CLC 26**
See also CA 37-40R; CANR 41; DLB 44

Schreiner, Olive (Emilie Albertina) 1855-1920 **TCLC 9**
See also CA 105; 154; DLB 18, 156, 190

Schulberg, Budd (Wilson) 1914- .. **CLC 7, 48**
See also CA 25-28R; CANR 19; DLB 6, 26, 28; DLBY 81

Schulz, Bruno 1892-1942 **TCLC 5, 51; SSC 13**
See also CA 115; 123

Schulz, Charles M(onroe) 1922- .... **CLC 12**
See also CA 9-12R; CANR 6; INT CANR-6; SATA 10

Schumacher, E(rnst) F(riedrich) 1911-1977 **CLC 80**
See also CA 81-84; 73-76; CANR 34

Schuyler, James Marcus 1923-1991 .. **CLC 5, 23; DAM POET**
See also CA 101; 134; DLB 5, 169; INT 101

Schwartz, Delmore (David) 1913-1966 **CLC 2, 4, 10, 45, 87; PC 8**
See also CA 17-18; 25-28R; CANR 35; CAP 2; DLB 28, 48; MTCW

Schwartz, Ernst
See Ozu, Yasujiro

Schwartz, John Burnham 1965- .... **CLC 59**
See also CA 132

Schwartz, Lynne Sharon 1939- .... **CLC 31**
See also CA 103; CANR 44

Schwartz, Muriel A.
See Eliot, T(homas) S(tearns)

Schwarz-Bart, Andre 1928- .... **CLC 2, 4**
See also CA 89-92

Schwarz-Bart, Simone 1938- .... **CLC 7**
See also BW 2; CA 97-100

Schwob, (Mayer Andre) Marcel 1867-1905 **TCLC 20**
See also CA 117; DLB 123

Sciascia, Leonardo 1921-1989 . **CLC 8, 9, 41**
See also CA 85-88; 130; CANR 35; DLB 177; MTCW

Scoppettone, Sandra 1936- .... **CLC 26**
See also AAYA 11; CA 5-8R; CANR 41; SATA 9, 92

Scorsese, Martin 1942- .... **CLC 20, 89**
See also CA 110; 114; CANR 46

Scotland, Jay
See Jakes, John (William)

Scott, Duncan Campbell 1862-1947 **TCLC 6; DAC**
See also CA 104; 153; DLB 92

Scott, Evelyn 1893-1963 .... **CLC 43**
See also CA 104; 112; CANR 64; DLB 9, 48

Scott, F(rancis) R(eginald) 1899-1985 **CLC 22**
See also CA 101; 114; DLB 88; INT 101

Scott, Frank
See Scott, F(rancis) R(eginald)

Scott, Joanna 1960- .... **CLC 50**
See also CA 126; CANR 53

Scott, Paul (Mark) 1920-1978 ...... **CLC 9, 60**
See also CA 81-84; 77-80; CANR 33; DLB 14; MTCW

Scott, Walter 1771-1832 . **NCLC 15, 69; DA; DAB; DAC; DAM MST, NOV, POET; PC 13; WLC**
See also AAYA 22; CDBLB 1789-1832; DLB 93, 107, 116, 144, 159; YABC 2

Scribe, (Augustin) Eugene 1791-1861 **NCLC 16; DAM DRAM; DC 5**
See also DLB 192

Scrum, R.
See Crumb, R(obert)

Scudery, Madeleine de 1607-1701 .... **LC 2**

Scum
See Crumb, R(obert)

Scumbag, Little Bobby
See Crumb, R(obert)

Seabrook, John
See Hubbard, L(afayette) Ron(ald)

Sealy, I. Allan 1951- .... **CLC 55**

Search, Alexander
See Pessoa, Fernando (Antonio Nogueira)

Sebastian, Lee
See Silverberg, Robert

Sebastian Owl
See Thompson, Hunter S(tockton)

Sebestyen, Ouida 1924- .... **CLC 30**
See also AAYA 8; CA 107; CANR 40; CLR 17; JRDA; MAICYA; SAAS 10; SATA 39

Secundus, H. Scriblerus
See Fielding, Henry

Sedges, John
See Buck, Pearl S(ydenstricker)

Sedgwick, Catharine Maria 1789-1867 **NCLC 19**
See also DLB 1, 74

Seelye, John 1931- .... **CLC 7**

Seferiades, Giorgos Stylianou 1900-1971
See Seferis, George
See also CA 5-8R; 33-36R; CANR 5, 36; MTCW

Seferis, George .... **CLC 5, 11**
See also Seferiades, Giorgos Stylianou

Segal, Erich (Wolf) 1937- .. **CLC 3, 10; DAM POP**
See also BEST 89:1; CA 25-28R; CANR 20, 36, 65; DLBY 86; INT CANR-20; MTCW

Seger, Bob 1945- .... **CLC 35**

Seghers, Anna .... **CLC 7**
See also Radvanyi, Netty
See also DLB 69

See also CA 110; DLB 149; DLBD 10

Strand, Mark 1934- **CLC 6, 18, 41, 71; DAM POET**
See also CA 21-24R; CANR 40, 65; DLB 5; SATA 41

Straub, Peter (Francis) 1943-.. **CLC 28, 107; DAM POP**
See also BEST 89:1; CA 85-88; CANR 28, 65; DLBY 84; MTCW

Strauss, Botho 1944- .... **CLC 22**
See also CA 157; DLB 124

Streatfeild, (Mary) Noel 1895(?)-1986**CLC 21**
See also CA 81-84; 120; CANR 31; CLR 17; DLB 160; MAICYA; SATA 20; SATA-Obit 48

Stribling, T(homas) S(igismund) 1881-1965 **CLC 23**
See also CA 107; DLB 9

Strindberg, (Johan) August 1849-1912**TCLC 1, 8, 21, 47; DA; DAB; DAC; DAM DRAM, MST; WLC**
See also CA 104; 135

Stringer, Arthur 1874-1950 .... **TCLC 37**
See also CA 161; DLB 92

Stringer, David
See Roberts, Keith (John Kingston)

Stroheim, Erich von 1885-1957 ..... **TCLC 71**

Strugatskii, Arkadii (Natanovich) 1925-1991 **CLC 27**
See also CA 106; 135

Strugatskii, Boris (Natanovich) 1933-**CLC 27**
See also CA 106

Strummer, Joe 1953(?)- .... **CLC 30**

Stuart, Don A.
See Campbell, John W(ood, Jr.)

Stuart, Ian
See MacLean, Alistair (Stuart)

Stuart, Jesse (Hilton) 1906-1984**CLC 1, 8, 11, 14, 34**
See also CA 5-8R; 112; CANR 31; DLB 9, 48, 102; DLBY 84; SATA 2; SATA-Obit 36

Sturgeon, Theodore (Hamilton) 1918-1985 **CLC 22, 39**
See Queen, Ellery
See also CA 81-84; 116; CANR 32; DLB 8; DLBY 85; MTCW

Sturges, Preston 1898-1959 .... **TCLC 48**
See also CA 114; 149; DLB 26

Styron, William 1925-**CLC 1, 3, 5, 11, 15, 60; DAM NOV, POP; SSC 25**
See also BEST 90:4; CA 5-8R; CANR 6, 33; CDALB 1968-1988; DLB 2, 143; DLBY 80; INT CANR-6; MTCW

Suarez Lynch, B.
See Bioy Casares, Adolfo; Borges, Jorge Luis

Su Chien 1884-1918
See Su Man-shu
See also CA 123

Suckow, Ruth 1892-1960 .... **SSC 18**
See also CA 113; DLB 9, 102

Sudermann, Hermann 1857-1928 .. **TCLC 15**
See also CA 107; DLB 118

Sue, Eugene 1804-1857 .... **NCLC 1**
See also DLB 119

Sueskind, Patrick 1949- .... **CLC 44**
See also Suskind, Patrick

Sukenick, Ronald 1932- .... **CLC 3, 4, 6, 48**
See also CA 25-28R; CAAS 8; CANR 32; DLB 173; DLBY 81

Suknaski, Andrew 1942- .... **CLC 19**
See also CA 101; DLB 53

Sullivan, Vernon
See Vian, Boris

Sully Prudhomme 1839-1907 .... **TCLC 31**

Su Man-shu .... **TCLC 24**
See also Su Chien

Summerforest, Ivy B.
See Kirkup, James

Summers, Andrew James 1942- .... **CLC 26**

Summers, Andy
See Summers, Andrew James

Summers, Hollis (Spurgeon, Jr.) 1916-. **C L C 10**
See also CA 5-8R; CANR 3; DLB 6

Summers, (Alphonsus Joseph-Mary Augustus) Montague 1880-1948 .... **TCLC 16**
See also CA 118; 163

Sumner, Gordon Matthew 1951- ...... **CLC 26**

Surtees, Robert Smith 1803-1864 ..**NCLC 14**
See also DLB 21

Susann, Jacqueline 1921-1974 .... **CLC 3**
See also AITN 1; CA 65-68; 53-56; MTCW

Su Shih 1036-1101 .... **CMLC 15**

Suskind, Patrick
See Sueskind, Patrick
See also CA 145

Sutcliff, Rosemary 1920-1992**CLC 26; DAB; DAC; DAM MST, POP**
See also AAYA 10; CA 5-8R; 139; CANR 37; CLR 1, 37; JRDA; MAICYA; SATA 6, 44, 78; SATA-Obit 73

Sutro, Alfred 1863-1933 .... **TCLC 6**
See also CA 105; DLB 10

Sutton, Henry
See Slavitt, David R(ytman)

Svevo, Italo 1861-1928 . **TCLC 2, 35; SSC 25**
See also Schmitz, Aron Hector

Swados, Elizabeth (A.) 1951- ....**CLC 12**
See also CA 97-100; CANR 49; INT 97-100

Swados, Harvey 1920-1972 ....**CLC 5**
See also CA 5-8R; 37-40R; CANR 6; DLB 2

Swan, Gladys 1934- ....**CLC 69**
See also CA 101; CANR 17, 39

Swarthout, Glendon (Fred) 1918-1992**CLC 35**
See also CA 1-4R; 139; CANR 1, 47; SATA 26

Sweet, Sarah C.
See Jewett, (Theodora) Sarah Orne

Swenson, May 1919-1989**CLC 4, 14, 61, 106; DA; DAB; DAC; DAM MST, POET; PC 14**
See also CA 5-8R; 130; CANR 36, 61; DLB 5; MTCW; SATA 15

Swift, Augustus
See Lovecraft, H(oward) P(hillips)

Swift, Graham (Colin) 1949- ...... **CLC 41, 88**
See also CA 117; 122; CANR 46

Swift, Jonathan 1667-1745 **LC 1; DA; DAB; DAC; DAM MST, NOV, POET; PC 9; WLC**
See also CDBLB 1660-1789; DLB 39, 95, 101; SATA 19

Swinburne, Algernon Charles 1837-1909 **TCLC 8, 36; DA; DAB; DAC; DAM MST, POET; WLC**
See also CA 105; 140; CDBLB 1832-1890; DLB 35, 57

Swinfen, Ann ....**CLC 34**

Swinnerton, Frank Arthur 1884-1982**CLC 31**
See also CA 108; DLB 34

Swithen, John
See King, Stephen (Edwin)

Sylvia
See Ashton-Warner, Sylvia (Constance)

Symmes, Robert Edward
See Duncan, Robert (Edward)

Symonds, John Addington 1840-1893 **N C L C 34**
See also DLB 57, 144

Symons, Arthur 1865-1945 .... **TCLC 11**
See also CA 107; DLB 19, 57, 149

Symons, Julian (Gustave) 1912-1994 **CLC 2, 14, 32**
See also CA 49-52; 147; CAAS 3; CANR 3, 33, 59; DLB 87, 155; DLBY 92; MTCW

Synge, (Edmund) J(ohn) M(illington) 1871-1909 .. **TCLC 6, 37; DAM DRAM; DC 2**
See also CA 104; 141; CDBLB 1890-1914; DLB 10, 19

Syruc, J.
See Milosz, Czeslaw

Szirtes, George 1948- .... **CLC 46**
See also CA 109; CANR 27, 61

Szymborska, Wislawa 1923- .... **CLC 99**
See also CA 154; DLBY 96

T. O., Nik
See Annensky, Innokenty (Fyodorovich)

Tabori, George 1914- .... **CLC 19**
See also CA 49-52; CANR 4

Tagore, Rabindranath 1861-1941**TCLC 3, 53; DAM DRAM, POET; PC 8**
See also CA 104; 120; MTCW

Taine, Hippolyte Adolphe 1828-1893 . **N C L C 15**

Talese, Gay 1932- .... **CLC 37**
See also AITN 1; CA 1-4R; CANR 9, 58; DLB 185; INT CANR-9; MTCW

Tallent, Elizabeth (Ann) 1954- .... **CLC 45**
See also CA 117; DLB 130

Tally, Ted 1952- .... **CLC 42**
See also CA 120; 124; INT 124

Tamayo y Baus, Manuel 1829-1898 **NCLC 1**

Tammsaare, A(nton) H(ansen) 1878-1940 **TCLC 27**
See also CA 164

Tam'si, Tchicaya U
See Tchicaya, Gerald Felix

Tan, Amy (Ruth) 1952-**CLC 59; DAM MULT, NOV, POP**
See also AAYA 9; BEST 89:3; CA 136; CANR 54; DLB 173; SATA 75

Tandem, Felix
See Spitteler, Carl (Friedrich Georg)

Tanizaki, Jun'ichiro 1886-1965**CLC 8, 14, 28; SSC 21**
See also CA 93-96; 25-28R; DLB 180

Tanner, William
See Amis, Kingsley (William)

Tao Lao
See Storni, Alfonsina

Tarassoff, Lev
See Troyat, Henri

Tarbell, Ida M(inerva) 1857-1944 . **TCLC 40**
See also CA 122; DLB 47

Tarkington, (Newton) Booth 1869-1946 **TCLC 9**
See also CA 110; 143; DLB 9, 102; SATA 17

Tarkovsky, Andrei (Arsenyevich) 1932-1986 **CLC 75**
See also CA 127

Tartt, Donna 1964(?)- .... **CLC 76**
See also CA 142

Tasso, Torquato 1544-1595 .... **LC 5**

Tate, (John Orley) Allen 1899-1979**CLC 2, 4, 6, 9, 11, 14, 24**
See also CA 5-8R; 85-88; CANR 32; DLB 4, 45, 63; MTCW

Tate, Ellalice
See Hibbert, Eleanor Alice Burford

See Tolson, Melvin B(eaunorus)
Tolson, Melvin B(eaunorus) 1898(?)-1966
  CLC **36, 105; BLC; DAM MULT, POET**
  See also BW 1; CA 124; 89-92; DLB 48, 76
Tolstoi, Aleksei Nikolaevich
  See Tolstoy, Alexey Nikolaevich
Tolstoy, Alexey Nikolaevich 1882-1945 TCLC **18**
  See also CA 107; 158
Tolstoy, Count Leo
  See Tolstoy, Leo (Nikolaevich)
Tolstoy, Leo (Nikolaevich) 1828-1910 T C L C **4, 11, 17, 28, 44, 79; DA; DAB; DAC; DAM MST, NOV; SSC 9, 30; WLC**
  See also CA 104; 123; SATA 26
Tomasi di Lampedusa, Giuseppe 1896-1957
  See Lampedusa, Giuseppe (Tomasi) di
  See also CA 111
Tomlin, Lily .... CLC **17**
  See also Tomlin, Mary Jean
Tomlin, Mary Jean 1939(?)-
  See Tomlin, Lily
  See also CA 117
Tomlinson, (Alfred) Charles 1927- CLC **2, 4, 6, 13, 45; DAM POET; PC 17**
  See also CA 5-8R; CANR 33; DLB 40
Tomlinson, H(enry) M(ajor) 1873-1958 TCLC **71**
  See also CA 118; 161; DLB 36, 100
Tonson, Jacob
  See Bennett, (Enoch) Arnold
Toole, John Kennedy 1937-1969 CLC **19, 64**
  See also CA 104; DLBY 81
Toomer, Jean 1894-1967 ... CLC **1, 4, 13, 22; BLC; DAM MULT; PC 7; SSC 1; WLCS**
  See also BW 1; CA 85-88; CDALB 1917-1929; DLB 45, 51; MTCW
Torley, Luke
  See Blish, James (Benjamin)
Tornimparte, Alessandra
  See Ginzburg, Natalia
Torre, Raoul della
  See Mencken, H(enry) L(ouis)
Torrey, E(dwin) Fuller 1937- .... CLC **34**
  See also CA 119
Torsvan, Ben Traven
  See Traven, B.
Torsvan, Benno Traven
  See Traven, B.
Torsvan, Berick Traven
  See Traven, B.
Torsvan, Berwick Traven
  See Traven, B.
Torsvan, Bruno Traven
  See Traven, B.
Torsvan, Traven
  See Traven, B.
Tournier, Michel (Edouard) 1924- CLC **6, 23, 36, 95**
  See also CA 49-52; CANR 3, 36; DLB 83; MTCW; SATA 23
Tournimparte, Alessandra
  See Ginzburg, Natalia
Towers, Ivar
  See Kornbluth, C(yril) M.
Towne, Robert (Burton) 1936(?)- .... CLC **87**
  See also CA 108; DLB 44
Townsend, Sue .... CLC **61**
  See also Townsend, Susan Elaine
  See also SATA 55, 93; SATA-Brief 48
Townsend, Susan Elaine 1946-
  See Townsend, Sue
  See also CA 119; 127; CANR 65; DAB; DAC;

DAM MST
Townshend, Peter (Dennis Blandford) 1945- CLC **17, 42**
  See also CA 107
Tozzi, Federigo 1883-1920 .... TCLC **31**
  See also CA 160
Traill, Catharine Parr 1802-1899 . NCLC **31**
  See also DLB 99
Trakl, Georg 1887-1914 ...... TCLC **5; PC 20**
  See also CA 104
Transtroemer, Tomas (Goesta) 1931- CLC **52, 65; DAM POET**
  See also CA 117; 129; CAAS 17
Transtromer, Tomas Gosta
  See Transtroemer, Tomas (Goesta)
Traven, B. (?)-1969 .... CLC **8, 11**
  See also CA 19-20; 25-28R; CAP 2; DLB 9, 56; MTCW
Treitel, Jonathan 1959- .... CLC **70**
Tremain, Rose 1943- .... CLC **42**
  See also CA 97-100; CANR 44; DLB 14
Tremblay, Michel 1942- CLC **29, 102; DAC; DAM MST**
  See also CA 116; 128; DLB 60; MTCW
Trevanian .... CLC **29**
  See also Whitaker, Rod(ney)
Trevor, Glen
  See Hilton, James
Trevor, William 1928- . CLC **7, 9, 14, 25, 71; SSC 21**
  See also Cox, William Trevor
  See also DLB 14, 139
Trifonov, Yuri (Valentinovich) 1925-1981 CLC **45**
  See also CA 126; 103; MTCW
Trilling, Lionel 1905-1975 ...... CLC **9, 11, 24**
  See also CA 9-12R; 61-64; CANR 10; DLB 28, 63; INT CANR-10; MTCW
Trimball, W. H.
  See Mencken, H(enry) L(ouis)
Tristan
  See Gomez de la Serna, Ramon
Tristram
  See Housman, A(lfred) E(dward)
Trogdon, William (Lewis) 1939-
  See Heat-Moon, William Least
  See also CA 115; 119; CANR 47; INT 119
Trollope, Anthony 1815-1882 .. NCLC **6, 33; DA; DAB; DAC; DAM MST, NOV; SSC 28; WLC**
  See also CDBLB 1832-1890; DLB 21, 57, 159; SATA 22
Trollope, Frances 1779-1863 .... NCLC **30**
  See also DLB 21, 166
Trotsky, Leon 1879-1940 .... TCLC **22**
  See also CA 118
Trotter (Cockburn), Catharine 1679-1749 L C **8**
  See also DLB 84
Trout, Kilgore
  See Farmer, Philip Jose
Trow, George W. S. 1943- .... CLC **52**
  See also CA 126
Troyat, Henri 1911- .... CLC **23**
  See also CA 45-48; CANR 2, 33, 67; MTCW
Trudeau, G(arretson) B(eekman) 1948-
  See Trudeau, Garry B.
  See also CA 81-84; CANR 31; SATA 35
Trudeau, Garry B. .... CLC **12**
  See also Trudeau, G(arretson) B(eekman)
  See also AAYA 10; AITN 2
Truffaut, Francois 1932-1984 .. CLC **20, 101**
  See also CA 81-84; 113; CANR 34

Trumbo, Dalton 1905-1976 .... CLC **19**
  See also CA 21-24R; 69-72; CANR 10; DLB 26
Trumbull, John 1750-1831 .... NCLC **30**
  See also DLB 31
Trundlett, Helen B.
  See Eliot, T(homas) S(tearns)
Tryon, Thomas 1926-1991 CLC **3, 11; DAM POP**
  See also AITN 1; CA 29-32R; 135; CANR 32; MTCW
Tryon, Tom
  See Tryon, Thomas
Ts'ao Hsueh-ch'in 1715(?)-1763 .... LC **1**
Tsushima, Shuji 1909-1948
  See Dazai, Osamu
  See also CA 107
Tsvetaeva (Efron), Marina (Ivanovna) 1892-1941 .... TCLC **7, 35; PC 14**
  See also CA 104; 128; MTCW
Tuck, Lily 1938- .... CLC **70**
  See also CA 139
Tu Fu 712-770 .... PC **9**
  See also DAM MULT
Tunis, John R(oberts) 1889-1975 .... CLC **12**
  See also CA 61-64; CANR 62; DLB 22, 171; JRDA; MAICYA; SATA 37; SATA-Brief 30
Tuohy, Frank .... CLC **37**
  See also Tuohy, John Francis
  See also DLB 14, 139
Tuohy, John Francis 1925-
  See Tuohy, Frank
  See also CA 5-8R; CANR 3, 47
Turco, Lewis (Putnam) 1934- .... CLC **11, 63**
  See also CA 13-16R; CAAS 22; CANR 24, 51; DLBY 84
Turgenev, Ivan 1818-1883 .... NCLC **21; DA; DAB; DAC; DAM MST, NOV; DC 7; SSC 7; WLC**
Turgot, Anne-Robert-Jacques 1727-1781 L C **26**
Turner, Frederick 1943- .... CLC **48**
  See also CA 73-76; CAAS 10; CANR 12, 30, 56; DLB 40
Tutu, Desmond M(pilo) 1931- CLC **80; BLC; DAM MULT**
  See also BW 1; CA 125; CANR 67
Tutuola, Amos 1920-1997 CLC **5, 14, 29; BLC; DAM MULT**
  See also BW 2; CA 9-12R; 159; CANR 27, 66; DLB 125; MTCW
Twain, Mark TCLC **6, 12, 19, 36, 48, 59; SSC 26; WLC**
  See also Clemens, Samuel Langhorne
  See also AAYA 20; DLB 11, 12, 23, 64, 74
Tyler, Anne 1941- . CLC **7, 11, 18, 28, 44, 59, 103; DAM NOV, POP**
  See also AAYA 18; BEST 89:1; CA 9-12R; CANR 11, 33, 53; DLB 6, 143; DLBY 82; MTCW; SATA 7, 90
Tyler, Royall 1757-1826 .... NCLC **3**
  See also DLB 37
Tynan, Katharine 1861-1931 .... TCLC **3**
  See also CA 104; DLB 153
Tyutchev, Fyodor 1803-1873 .... NCLC **34**
Tzara, Tristan 1896-1963 ...... CLC **47; DAM POET**
  See also CA 153; 89-92
Uhry, Alfred 1936- .. CLC **55; DAM DRAM, POP**
  See also CA 127; 133; INT 133
Ulf, Haerved
  See Strindberg, (Johan) August

Literary Criticism Series
Cumulative Topic Index

This index lists all topic entries in Gale's *Classical and Medieval Literature Criticism, Contemporary Literary Criticism, Literature Criticism from 1400 to 1800, Nineteenth-Century Literature Criticism,* and *Twentieth-Century Literary Criticism.*

Topic Index

Topic Index

Topic Index

LC Cumulative Nationality Index

Nationality Index

CUMULATIVE INDEX TO TITLES

Title Index

Title Index

Title Index

Title Index

Title Index

Title Index

Title Index

Title Index

Title Index

Title Index

Title Index

Title Index

Title Index